Lecture Notes in Computer Science 12536

More information about this subseries at http://www.springer.com/series/7412

Adrien Bartoli · Andrea Fusiello (Eds.)

Computer Vision – ECCV 2020 Workshops

Glasgow, UK, August 23–28, 2020
Proceedings, Part II

Springer

Editors
Adrien Bartoli
University of Clermont Auvergne
Clermont Ferrand, France

Andrea Fusiello
Università degli Studi di Udine
Udine, Italy

ISSN 0302-9743 ISSN 1611-3349 (electronic)
Lecture Notes in Computer Science
ISBN 978-3-030-66095-6 ISBN 978-3-030-66096-3 (eBook)
https://doi.org/10.1007/978-3-030-66096-3

LNCS Sublibrary: SL6 – Image Processing, Computer Vision, Pattern Recognition, and Graphics

This Springer imprint is published by the registered company Springer Nature Switzerland AG
The registered company address is: Gewerbestrasse 11, 6330 Cham, Switzerland

Foreword

Hosting the 2020 European Conference on Computer Vision was certainly an exciting journey. From the 2016 plan to hold it at the Edinburgh International Conference Centre (hosting 1,800 delegates) to the 2018 plan to hold it at Glasgow's Scottish Exhibition Centre (up to 6,000 delegates), we finally ended with moving online because of the COVID-19 outbreak. While possibly having fewer delegates than expected because of the online format, ECCV 2020 still had over 3,100 registered participants.

Although online, the conference delivered most of the activities expected at a face-to-face conference: peer-reviewed papers, industrial exhibitors, demonstrations, and messaging between delegates. As well as the main technical sessions, the conference included a strong program of satellite events, including 16 tutorials and 44 workshops.

On the other hand, the online conference format enabled new conference features. Every paper had an associated teaser video and a longer full presentation video. Along with the papers and slides from the videos, all these materials were available the week before the conference. This allowed delegates to become familiar with the paper content and be ready for the live interaction with the authors during the conference week. The 'live' event consisted of brief presentations by the 'oral' and 'spotlight' authors and industrial sponsors. Question and Answer sessions for all papers were timed to occur twice so delegates from around the world had convenient access to the authors.

As with the 2018 ECCV, authors' draft versions of the papers appeared online with open access, now on both the Computer Vision Foundation (CVF) and the European Computer Vision Association (ECVA) websites. An archival publication arrangement was put in place with the cooperation of Springer. SpringerLink hosts the final version of the papers with further improvements, such as activating reference links and supplementary materials. These two approaches benefit all potential readers: a version available freely for all researchers, and an authoritative and citable version with additional benefits for SpringerLink subscribers. We thank Alfred Hofmann and Aliaksandr Birukou from Springer for helping to negotiate this agreement, which we expect will continue for future versions of ECCV.

August 2020

Vittorio Ferrari
Bob Fisher
Cordelia Schmid
Emanuele Trucco

Preface

Welcome to the workshops proceedings of the 16th European Conference on Computer Vision (ECCV 2020), the first edition held online. We are delighted that the main ECCV 2020 was accompanied by 45 workshops, scheduled on August 23, 2020, and August 28, 2020.

We received 101 valid workshop proposals on diverse computer vision topics and had space for 32 full-day slots, so we had to decline many valuable proposals (the workshops were supposed to be either full-day or half-day long, but the distinction faded away when the full ECCV conference went online). We endeavored to balance among topics, established series, and newcomers. Not all the workshops published their proceedings, or had proceedings at all. These volumes collect the edited papers from 28 out of 45 workshops.

We sincerely thank the ECCV general chairs for trusting us with the responsibility for the workshops, the workshop organizers for their involvement in this event of primary importance in our field, and the workshop presenters and authors.

August 2020
Adrien Bartoli
Andrea Fusiello

Organization

General Chairs

Vittorio Ferrari	Google Research, Switzerland
Bob Fisher	The University of Edinburgh, UK
Cordelia Schmid	Google and Inria, France
Emanuele Trucco	The University of Dundee, UK

Program Chairs

Andrea Vedaldi	University of Oxford, UK
Horst Bischof	Graz University of Technology, Austria
Thomas Brox	University of Freiburg, Germany
Jan-Michael Frahm	The University of North Carolina at Chapel Hill, USA

Industrial Liaison Chairs

Jim Ashe	The University of Edinburgh, UK
Helmut Grabner	Zurich University of Applied Sciences, Switzerland
Diane Larlus	NAVER LABS Europe, France
Cristian Novotny	The University of Edinburgh, UK

Local Arrangement Chairs

Yvan Petillot	Heriot-Watt University, UK
Paul Siebert	The University of Glasgow, UK

Academic Demonstration Chair

Thomas Mensink	Google Research and University of Amsterdam, The Netherlands

Poster Chair

Stephen Mckenna	The University of Dundee, UK

Technology Chair

Gerardo Aragon Camarasa	The University of Glasgow, UK

Tutorial Chairs

Carlo Colombo	University of Florence, Italy
Sotirios Tsaftaris	The University of Edinburgh, UK

Publication Chairs

Albert Ali Salah	Utrecht University, The Netherlands
Hamdi Dibeklioglu	Bilkent University, Turkey
Metehan Doyran	Utrecht University, The Netherlands
Henry Howard-Jenkins	University of Oxford, UK
Victor Adrian Prisacariu	University of Oxford, UK
Siyu Tang	ETH Zurich, Switzerland
Gul Varol	University of Oxford, UK

Website Chair

Giovanni Maria Farinella	University of Catania, Italy

Workshops Chairs

Adrien Bartoli	University Clermont Auvergne, France
Andrea Fusiello	University of Udine, Italy

Workshops Organizers

W01 - Adversarial Robustness in the Real World

Adam Kortylewski	Johns Hopkins University, USA
Cihang Xie	Johns Hopkins University, USA
Song Bai	University of Oxford, UK
Zhaowei Cai	UC San Diego, USA
Yingwei Li	Johns Hopkins University, USA
Andrei Barbu	MIT, USA
Wieland Brendel	University of Tübingen, Germany
Nuno Vasconcelos	UC San Diego, USA
Andrea Vedaldi	University of Oxford, UK
Philip H. S. Torr	University of Oxford, UK
Rama Chellappa	University of Maryland, USA
Alan Yuille	Johns Hopkins University, USA

W02 - BioImage Computation

Jan Funke	HHMI Janelia Research Campus, Germany
Dagmar Kainmueller	BIH and MDC Berlin, Germany
Florian Jug	CSBD and MPI-CBG, Germany
Anna Kreshuk	EMBL Heidelberg, Germany

Peter Bajcsy   NIST, USA
Martin Weigert   EPFL, Switzerland
Patrick Bouthemy   Inria, France
Erik Meijering   University New South Wales, Australia

W03 - Egocentric Perception, Interaction and Computing

Michael Wray   University of Bristol, UK
Dima Damen   University of Bristol, UK
Hazel Doughty   University of Bristol, UK
Walterio Mayol-Cuevas   University of Bristol, UK
David Crandall   Indiana University, USA
Kristen Grauman   UT Austin, USA
Giovanni Maria Farinella   University of Catania, Italy
Antonino Furnari   University of Catania, Italy

W04 - Embodied Vision, Actions and Language

Yonatan Bisk   Carnegie Mellon University, USA
Jesse Thomason   University of Washington, USA
Mohit Shridhar   University of Washington, USA
Chris Paxton   NVIDIA, USA
Peter Anderson   Georgia Tech, USA
Roozbeh Mottaghi   Allen Institute for AI, USA
Eric Kolve   Allen Institute for AI, USA

W05 - Eye Gaze in VR, AR, and in the Wild

Hyung Jin Chang   University of Birmingham, UK
Seonwook Park   ETH Zurich, Switzerland
Xucong Zhang   ETH Zurich, Switzerland
Otmar Hilliges   ETH Zurich, Switzerland
Aleš Leonardis   University of Birmingham, UK
Robert Cavin   Facebook Reality Labs, USA
Cristina Palmero   University of Barcelona, Spain
Jixu Chen   Facebook, USA
Alexander Fix   Facebook Reality Labs, USA
Elias Guestrin   Facebook Reality Labs, USA
Oleg Komogortsev   Texas State University, USA
Kapil Krishnakumar   Facebook, USA
Abhishek Sharma   Facebook Reality Labs, USA
Yiru Shen   Facebook Reality Labs, USA
Tarek Hefny   Facebook Reality Labs, USA
Karsten Behrendt   Facebook, USA
Sachin S. Talathi   Facebook Reality Labs, USA

W06 - Holistic Scene Structures for 3D Vision

Zihan Zhou	Penn State University, USA
Yasutaka Furukawa	Simon Fraser University, Canada
Yi Ma	UC Berkeley, USA
Shenghua Gao	ShanghaiTech University, China
Chen Liu	Facebook Reality Labs, USA
Yichao Zhou	UC Berkeley, USA
Linjie Luo	Bytedance Inc., China
Jia Zheng	ShanghaiTech University, China
Junfei Zhang	Kujiale.com, China
Rui Tang	Kujiale.com, China

W07 - Joint COCO and LVIS Recognition Challenge

Alexander Kirillov	Facebook AI Research, USA
Tsung-Yi Lin	Google Research, USA
Yin Cui	Google Research, USA
Matteo Ruggero Ronchi	California Institute of Technology, USA
Agrim Gupta	Stanford University, USA
Ross Girshick	Facebook AI Research, USA
Piotr Dollar	Facebook AI Research, USA

W08 - Object Tracking and Its Many Guises

Achal D. Dave	Carnegie Mellon University, USA
Tarasha Khurana	Carnegie Mellon University, USA
Jonathon Luiten	RWTH Aachen University, Germany
Aljosa Osep	Technical University of Munich, Germany
Pavel Tokmakov	Carnegie Mellon University, USA

W09 - Perception for Autonomous Driving

Li Erran Li	Alexa AI, Amazon, USA
Adrien Gaidon	Toyota Research Institute, USA
Wei-Lun Chao	The Ohio State University, USA
Peter Ondruska	Lyft, UK
Rowan McAllister	UC Berkeley, USA
Larry Jackel	North-C Technologies, USA
Jose M. Alvarez	NVIDIA, USA

W10 - TASK-CV Workshop and VisDA Challenge

Tatiana Tommasi	Politecnico di Torino, Italy
Antonio M. Lopez	CVC and UAB, Spain
David Vazquez	Element AI, Canada
Gabriela Csurka	NAVER LABS Europe, France
Kate Saenko	Boston University, USA
Liang Zheng	The Australian National University, Australia

Xingchao Peng   Boston University, USA
Weijian Deng   The Australian National University, Australia

W11 - Bodily Expressed Emotion Understanding

James Z. Wang   Penn State University, USA
Reginald B. Adams, Jr. Penn State University, USA
Yelin Kim   Amazon Lab126, USA

W12 - Commands 4 Autonomous Vehicles

Thierry Deruyttere   KU Leuven, Belgium
Simon Vandenhende   KU Leuven, Belgium
Luc Van Gool   KU Leuven, Belgium, and ETH Zurich, Switzerland
Matthew Blaschko   KU Leuven, Belgium
Tinne Tuytelaars   KU Leuven, Belgium
Marie-Francine Moens   KU Leuven, Belgium
Yu Liu   KU Leuven, Belgium
Dusan Grujicic   KU Leuven, Belgium

W13 - Computer VISion for ART Analysis

Alessio Del Bue   Istituto Italiano di Tecnologia, Italy
Sebastiano Vascon   Ca' Foscari University and European Centre for Living
                       Technology, Italy
Peter Bell   Friedrich-Alexander University Erlangen-Nürnberg,
                       Germany
Leonardo L. Impett   EPFL, Switzerland
Stuart James   Istituto Italiano di Tecnologia, Italy

W14 - International Challenge on Compositional and Multimodal Perception

Alec Hodgkinson   Panasonic Corporation, Japan
Yusuke Urakami   Panasonic Corporation, Japan
Kazuki Kozuka   Panasonic Corporation, Japan
Ranjay Krishna   Stanford University, USA
Olga Russakovsky   Princeton University, USA
Juan Carlos Niebles   Stanford University, USA
Jingwei Ji   Stanford University, USA
Li Fei-Fei   Stanford University, USA

W15 - Sign Language Recognition, Translation and Production

Necati Cihan Camgoz   University of Surrey, UK
Richard Bowden   University of Surrey, UK
Andrew Zisserman   University of Oxford, UK
Gul Varol   University of Oxford, UK
Samuel Albanie   University of Oxford, UK

| Kearsy Cormier | University College London, UK |
| Neil Fox | University College London, UK |

W16 - Visual Inductive Priors for Data-Efficient Deep Learning

Jan van Gemert	Delft University of Technology, The Netherlands
Robert-Jan Bruintjes	Delft University of Technology, The Netherlands
Attila Lengyel	Delft University of Technology, The Netherlands
Osman Semih Kayhan	Delft University of Technology, The Netherlands
Marcos Baptista-Ríos	Alcalá University, Spain
Anton van den Hengel	The University of Adelaide, Australia

W17 - Women in Computer Vision

Hilde Kuehne	IBM, USA
Amaia Salvador	Amazon, USA
Ananya Gupta	The University of Manchester, UK
Yana Hasson	Inria, France
Anna Kukleva	Max Planck Institute, Germany
Elizabeth Vargas	Heriot-Watt University, UK
Xin Wang	UC Berkeley, USA
Irene Amerini	Sapienza University of Rome, Italy

W18 - 3D Poses in the Wild Challenge

Gerard Pons-Moll	Max Planck Institute for Informatics, Germany
Angjoo Kanazawa	UC Berkeley, USA
Michael Black	Max Planck Institute for Intelligent Systems, Germany
Aymen Mir	Max Planck Institute for Informatics, Germany

W19 - 4D Vision

Anelia Angelova	Google, USA
Vincent Casser	Waymo, USA
Jürgen Sturm	X, USA
Noah Snavely	Google, USA
Rahul Sukthankar	Google, USA

W20 - Map-Based Localization for Autonomous Driving

Patrick Wenzel	Technical University of Munich, Germany
Niclas Zeller	Artisense, Germany
Nan Yang	Technical University of Munich, Germany
Rui Wang	Technical University of Munich, Germany
Daniel Cremers	Technical University of Munich, Germany

W21 - Multimodal Video Analysis Workshop and Moments in Time Challenge

Dhiraj Joshi	IBM Research AI, USA
Rameswar Panda	IBM Research, USA
Kandan Ramakrishnan	IBM, USA
Rogerio Feris	IBM Research AI, MIT-IBM Watson AI Lab, USA
Rami Ben-Ari	IBM-Research, USA
Danny Gutfreund	IBM, USA
Mathew Monfort	MIT, USA
Hang Zhao	MIT, USA
David Harwath	MIT, USA
Aude Oliva	MIT, USA
Zhicheng Yan	Facebook AI, USA

W22 - Recovering 6D Object Pose

Tomas Hodan	Czech Technical University in Prague, Czech Republic
Martin Sundermeyer	German Aerospace Center, Germany
Rigas Kouskouridas	Scape Technologies, UK
Tae-Kyun Kim	Imperial College London, UK
Jiri Matas	Czech Technical University in Prague, Czech Republic
Carsten Rother	Heidelberg University, Germany
Vincent Lepetit	ENPC ParisTech, France
Ales Leonardis	University of Birmingham, UK
Krzysztof Walas	Poznan University of Technology, Poland
Carsten Steger	Technical University of Munich and MVTec Software GmbH, Germany
Eric Brachmann	Heidelberg University, Germany
Bertram Drost	MVTec Software GmbH, Germany
Juil Sock	Imperial College London, UK

W23 - SHApe Recovery from Partial Textured 3D Scans

Djamila Aouada	University of Luxembourg, Luxembourg
Kseniya Cherenkova	Artec3D and University of Luxembourg, Luxembourg
Alexandre Saint	University of Luxembourg, Luxembourg
David Fofi	University Bourgogne Franche-Comté, France
Gleb Gusev	Artec3D, Luxembourg
Bjorn Ottersten	University of Luxembourg, Luxembourg

W24 - Advances in Image Manipulation Workshop and Challenges

Radu Timofte	ETH Zurich, Switzerland
Andrey Ignatov	ETH Zurich, Switzerland
Kai Zhang	ETH Zurich, Switzerland
Dario Fuoli	ETH Zurich, Switzerland
Martin Danelljan	ETH Zurich, Switzerland
Zhiwu Huang	ETH Zurich, Switzerland

Hannan Lu	Harbin Institute of Technology, China
Wangmeng Zuo	Harbin Institute of Technology, China
Shuhang Gu	The University of Sydney, Australia
Ming-Hsuan Yang	UC Merced and Google, USA
Majed El Helou	EPFL, Switzerland
Ruofan Zhou	EPFL, Switzerland
Sabine Süsstrunk	EPFL, Switzerland
Sanghyun Son	Seoul National University, South Korea
Jaerin Lee	Seoul National University, South Korea
Seungjun Nah	Seoul National University, South Korea
Kyoung Mu Lee	Scoul National University, South Korea
Eli Shechtman	Adobe, USA
Evangelos Ntavelis	ETH Zurich and CSEM, Switzerland
Andres Romero	ETH Zurich, Switzerland
Yawei Li	ETH Zurich, Switzerland
Siavash Bigdeli	CSEM, Switzerland
Pengxu Wei	Sun Yat-sen University, China
Liang Lin	Sun Yat-sen University, China
Ming-Yu Liu	NVIDIA, USA
Roey Mechrez	BeyondMinds and Technion, Israel
Luc Van Gool	KU Leuven, Belgium, and ETH Zurich, Switzerland

W25 - Assistive Computer Vision and Robotics

Marco Leo	National Research Council of Italy, Italy
Giovanni Maria Farinella	University of Catania, Italy
Antonino Furnari	University of Catania, Italy
Gerard Medioni	University of Southern California, USA
Trivedi Mohan	UC San Diego, USA

W26 - Computer Vision for UAVs Workshop and Challenge

Dawei Du	Kitware Inc., USA
Heng Fan	Stony Brook University, USA
Toon Goedemé	KU Leuven, Belgium
Qinghua Hu	Tianjin University, China
Haibin Ling	Stony Brook University, USA
Davide Scaramuzza	University of Zurich, Switzerland
Mubarak Shah	University of Central Florida, USA
Tinne Tuytelaars	KU Leuven, Belgium
Kristof Van Beeck	KU Leuven, Belgium
Longyin Wen	JD Digits, USA
Pengfei Zhu	Tianjin University, China

W27 - Embedded Vision

| Tse-Wei Chen | Canon Inc., Japan |
| Nabil Belbachir | NORCE Norwegian Research Centre AS, Norway |

Stephan Weiss   University of Klagenfurt, Austria
Marius Leordeanu   Politehnica University of Bucharest, Romania

W28 - Learning 3D Representations for Shape and Appearance

Leonidas Guibas   Stanford University, USA
Or Litany   Stanford University, USA
Tanner Schmidt   Facebook Reality Labs, USA
Vincent Sitzmann   Stanford University, USA
Srinath Sridhar   Stanford University, USA
Shubham Tulsiani   Facebook AI Research, USA
Gordon Wetzstein   Stanford University, USA

W29 - Real-World Computer Vision from inputs with Limited Quality and Tiny Object Detection Challenge

Yuqian Zhou   University of Illinois, USA
Zhenjun Han   University of the Chinese Academy of Sciences, China
Yifan Jiang   The University of Texas at Austin, USA
Yunchao Wei   University of Technology Sydney, Australia
Jian Zhao   Institute of North Electronic Equipment, Singapore
Zhangyang Wang   The University of Texas at Austin, USA
Qixiang Ye   University of the Chinese Academy of Sciences, China
Jiaying Liu   Peking University, China
Xuehui Yu   University of the Chinese Academy of Sciences, China
Ding Liu   Bytedance, China
Jie Chen   Peking University, China
Humphrey Shi   University of Oregon, USA

W30 - Robust Vision Challenge 2020

Oliver Zendel   Austrian Institute of Technology, Austria
Hassan Abu Alhaija   Interdisciplinary Center for Scientific Computing
                             Heidelberg, Germany
Rodrigo Benenson   Google Research, Switzerland
Marius Cordts   Daimler AG, Germany
Angela Dai   Technical University of Munich, Germany
Andreas Geiger   Max Planck Institute for Intelligent Systems
                             and University of Tübingen, Germany
Niklas Hanselmann   Daimler AG, Germany
Nicolas Jourdan   Daimler AG, Germany
Vladlen Koltun   Intel Labs, USA
Peter Kontschieder   Mapillary Research, Austria
Yubin Kuang   Mapillary AB, Sweden
Alina Kuznetsova   Google Research, Switzerland
Tsung-Yi Lin   Google Brain, USA
Claudio Michaelis   University of Tübingen, Germany
Gerhard Neuhold   Mapillary Research, Austria

Matthias Niessner	Technical University of Munich, Germany
Marc Pollefeys	ETH Zurich and Microsoft, Switzerland
Francesc X. Puig Fernandez	MIT, USA
Rene Ranftl	Intel Labs, USA
Stephan R. Richter	Intel Labs, USA
Carsten Rother	Heidelberg University, Germany
Torsten Sattler	Chalmers University of Technology, Sweden and Czech Technical University in Prague, Czech Republic
Daniel Scharstein	Middlebury College, USA
Hendrik Schilling	rabbitAI, Germany
Nick Schneider	Daimler AG, Germany
Jonas Uhrig	Daimler AG, Germany
Jonas Wulff	Max Planck Institute for Intelligent Systems, Germany
Bolei Zhou	The Chinese University of Hong Kong, China

W31 - The Bright and Dark Sides of Computer Vision: Challenges and Opportunities for Privacy and Security

Mario Fritz	CISPA Helmholtz Center for Information Security, Germany
Apu Kapadia	Indiana University, USA
Jan-Michael Frahm	The University of North Carolina at Chapel Hill, USA
David Crandall	Indiana University, USA
Vitaly Shmatikov	Cornell University, USA

W32 - The Visual Object Tracking Challenge

Matej Kristan	University of Ljubljana, Slovenia
Jiri Matas	Czech Technical University in Prague, Czech Republic
Ales Leonardis	University of Birmingham, UK
Michael Felsberg	Linköping University, Sweden
Roman Pflugfelder	Austrian Institute of Technology, Austria
Joni-Kristian Kamarainen	Tampere University, Finland
Martin Danelljan	ETH Zurich, Switzerland

W33 - Video Turing Test: Toward Human-Level Video Story Understanding

Yu-Jung Heo	Seoul National University, South Korea
Seongho Choi	Seoul National University, South Korea
Kyoung-Woon On	Seoul National University, South Korea
Minsu Lee	Seoul National University, South Korea
Vicente Ordonez	University of Virginia, USA
Leonid Sigal	University of British Columbia, Canada
Chang D. Yoo	KAIST, South Korea
Gunhee Kim	Seoul National University, South Korea
Marcello Pelillo	University of Venice, Italy
Byoung-Tak Zhang	Seoul National University, South Korea

W34 - "Deep Internal Learning": Training with no prior examples

Michal Irani	Weizmann Institute of Science, Israel
Tomer Michaeli	Technion, Israel
Tali Dekel	Google, Israel
Assaf Shocher	Weizmann Institute of Science, Israel
Tamar Rott Shaham	Technion, Israel

W35 - Benchmarking Trajectory Forecasting Models

Alexandre Alahi	EPFL, Switzerland
Lamberto Ballan	University of Padova, Italy
Luigi Palmieri	Bosch, Germany
Andrey Rudenko	Örebro University, Sweden
Pasquale Coscia	University of Padova, Italy

W36 - Beyond mAP: Reassessing the Evaluation of Object Detection

David Hall	Queensland University of Technology, Australia
Niko Suenderhauf	Queensland University of Technology, Australia
Feras Dayoub	Queensland University of Technology, Australia
Gustavo Carneiro	The University of Adelaide, Australia
Chunhua Shen	The University of Adelaide, Australia

W37 - Imbalance Problems in Computer Vision

Sinan Kalkan	Middle East Technical University, Turkey
Emre Akbas	Middle East Technical University, Turkey
Nuno Vasconcelos	UC San Diego, USA
Kemal Oksuz	Middle East Technical University, Turkey
Baris Can Cam	Middle East Technical University, Turkey

W38 - Long-Term Visual Localization under Changing Conditions

Torsten Sattler	Chalmers University of Technology, Sweden, and Czech Technical University in Prague, Czech Republic
Vassileios Balntas	Facebook Reality Labs, USA
Fredrik Kahl	Chalmers University of Technology, Sweden
Krystian Mikolajczyk	Imperial College London, UK
Tomas Pajdla	Czech Technical University in Prague, Czech Republic
Marc Pollefeys	ETH Zurich and Microsoft, Switzerland
Josef Sivic	Inria, France, and Czech Technical University in Prague, Czech Republic
Akihiko Torii	Tokyo Institute of Technology, Japan
Lars Hammarstrand	Chalmers University of Technology, Sweden
Huub Heijnen	Facebook, UK
Maddern Will	Nuro, USA
Johannes L. Schönberger	Microsoft, Switzerland

| Pablo Speciale | ETH Zurich, Switzerland |
| Carl Toft | Chalmers University of Technology, Sweden |

W39 - Sensing, Understanding, and Synthesizing Humans

Ziwei Liu	The Chinese University of Hong Kong, China
Sifei Liu	NVIDIA, USA
Xiaolong Wang	UC San Diego, USA
Hang Zhou	The Chinese University of Hong Kong, China
Wayne Wu	SenseTime, China
Chen Change Loy	Nanyang Technological University, Singapore

W40 - Computer Vision Problems in Plant Phenotyping

Hanno Scharr	Forschungszentrum Jülich, Germany
Tony Pridmore	University of Nottingham, UK
Sotirios Tsaftaris	The University of Edinburgh, UK

W41 - Fair Face Recognition and Analysis

Sergio Escalera	CVC and University of Barcelona, Spain
Rama Chellappa	University of Maryland, USA
Eduard Vazquez	Anyvision, UK
Neil Robertson	Queen's University Belfast, UK
Pau Buch-Cardona	CVC, Spain
Tomas Sixta	Anyvision, UK
Julio C. S. Jacques Junior	Universitat Oberta de Catalunya and CVC, Spain

W42 - GigaVision: When Gigapixel Videography Meets Computer Vision

Lu Fang	Tsinghua University, China
Shengjin Wang	Tsinghua University, China
David J. Brady	Duke University, USA
Feng Yang	Google Research, USA

W43 - Instance-Level Recognition

Andre Araujo	Google, USA
Bingyi Cao	Google, USA
Ondrej Chum	Czech Technical University in Prague, Czech Republic
Bohyung Han	Seoul National University, South Korea
Torsten Sattler	Chalmers University of Technology, Sweden and Czech Technical University in Prague, Czech Republic
Jack Sim	Google, USA
Giorgos Tolias	Czech Technical University in Prague, Czech Republic
Tobias Weyand	Google, USA

Xu Zhang	Columbia University, USA
Cam Askew	Google, USA
Guangxing Han	Columbia University, USA

W44 - Perception Through Structured Generative Models

Adam W. Harley	Carnegie Mellon University, USA
Katerina Fragkiadaki	Carnegie Mellon University, USA
Shubham Tulsiani	Facebook AI Research, USA

W45 - Self Supervised Learning – What is Next?

Christian Rupprecht	University of Oxford, UK
Yuki M. Asano	University of Oxford, UK
Armand Joulin	Facebook AI Research, USA
Andrea Vedaldi	University of Oxford, UK

Contents – Part II

W15 - Sign Language Recognition, Translation and Production

W16 - Visual Inductive Priors for Data-Efficient Deep Learning

W12 - Commands 4 Autonomous Vehicles

W12 - Commands 4 Autonomous Vehicles

Relating visual and linguistic information represents the cornerstone of the human learning process, making the joint understanding of language and vision one of the fundamental challenges in artificial intelligence. Therefore, progress on tasks like visual question answering, image-captioning, object referral provide a stepping stone towards a more seamless interaction between machines and humans, and with it, new products and services. For example, a natural language interface between factory operators and control systems could streamline production processes, resulting in safer and more efficient working environments. In a different vein, being able to express commands in natural language to an autonomous vehicle could eliminate the unsettling feeling of giving up all control. The possible applications are countless. Understandably, this calls for efficient computational models that can address these tasks in a realistic environment. In this workshop, we aim to identify and address the challenges for deploying vision-language models in practical applications.

August 2020

Thierry Deruyttere
Simon Vandenhende
Dusan Grujicic
Yu Liu
Matthew Blaschko
Luc Van Gool
Tinne Tuytelaars
Marie-Francine Moens

Commands 4 Autonomous Vehicles (C4AV) Workshop Summary

Thierry Deruyttere[1(✉)], Simon Vandenhende[2], Dusan Grujicic[2], Yu Liu[2], Luc Van Gool[2], Matthew Blaschko[2], Tinne Tuytelaars[2], and Marie-Francine Moens[1]

[1] Department of Computer Science (CS), KU Leuven, Leuven, Belgium
{thierry.deruyttere,sien.moens}@cs.kuleuven.be
[2] Department of Electrical Engineering (ESAT), KU Leuven, Leuven, Belgium
{simon.vandenhende,dusan.grujicic,yu.liu,
luc.vangool,matthew.blaschko,tinne.tuytelaars}@esat.kuleuven.be

Abstract. The task of visual grounding requires locating the most relevant region or object in an image, given a natural language query. So far, progress on this task was mostly measured on curated datasets, which are not always representative of human spoken language. In this work, we deviate from recent, popular task settings and consider the problem under an autonomous vehicle scenario. In particular, we consider a situation where passengers can give free-form natural language commands to a vehicle which can be associated with an object in the street scene. To stimulate research on this topic, we have organized the *Commands for Autonomous Vehicles* (C4AV) challenge based on the recent *Talk2Car* dataset. This paper presents the results of the challenge. First, we compare the used benchmark against existing datasets for visual grounding. Second, we identify the aspects that render top-performing models successful, and relate them to existing state-of-the-art models for visual grounding, in addition to detecting potential failure cases by evaluating on carefully selected subsets. Finally, we discuss several possibilities for future work.

1 Introduction

The joint understanding of language and vision poses a fundamental challenge for the development of intelligent machines. To address this problem, researchers have studied various related topics such as visual question answering [1,3,17,19,40], image-captioning [49,51], visual grounding [9,34,53], etc. These advancements can provide a stepping stone towards new products and services. For example, a natural language interface between factory operators and control systems could streamline production processes, resulting in safer

---

T. Deruyttere, S. Vandenhende and D. Grujicic—Contributed equally.

Electronic supplementary material The online version of this chapter (https://doi.org/10.1007/978-3-030-66096-3_1) contains supplementary material, which is available to authorized users.

© Springer Nature Switzerland AG 2020
A. Bartoli and A. Fusiello (Eds.): ECCV 2020 Workshops, LNCS 12536, pp. 3–26, 2020.
https://doi.org/10.1007/978-3-030-66096-3_1

and more efficient working environments. In a different vein, providing passengers with the possibility to communicate with their autonomous car could eliminate the unsettling feeling of giving up all control. The possible applications are countless. Understandably, this calls for efficient computational models that can address these tasks in a realistic environment.

In this paper, we focus on the task of visual grounding. Under this setup, the model is tasked with locating the most relevant object or region in an image based on a given natural language query. Several approaches [9,16,20,34,50, 53] tackled the problem using a two-stage pipeline, where region proposals are generated first by an off-the-shelf object detector [31,33], and then matched with an embedding of the sentence. Others [14,18] proposed an end-to-end strategy where the object location is predicted directly from the input image.

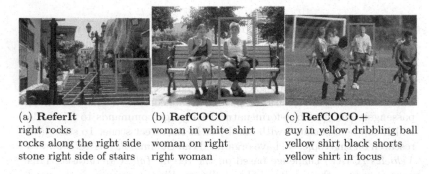

(a) **ReferIt**
right rocks
rocks along the right side
stone right side of stairs

(b) **RefCOCO**
woman in white shirt
woman on right
right woman

(c) **RefCOCO+**
guy in yellow dribbling ball
yellow shirt black shorts
yellow shirt in focus

Fig. 1. Examples from popular benchmarks for visual grounding [21].

In order to quantify progress, several benchmarks were introduced [15,21, 27,54]. From visualizing examples found in existing datasets in Fig. 1, we draw the following conclusions. First, we observe that the language queries are rather artificial, and do not accurately reflect the type of language used by human speakers during their daily routines. For example, in practice, object references are often implicitly defined, complex and long sentences can contain co-referent phrases, etc. Second, existing benchmarks are mostly built on web-based image datasets [13,24,52], where the object of interest is often clearly visible due to its discriminative visual features. From these observations, we conclude that existing benchmarks for visual grounding are not well suited to develop models that need to operate in the wild.

To address these shortcomings, we hosted the *Commands For Autonomous Vehicles Challenge* (C4AV) at the European Conference on Computer Vision (ECCV) 20'. The challenge setting considers a visual grounding task under a self-driving car scenario. More specifically, a passenger gives a natural language command to express an action that needs to be taken by the autonomous vehicle (AV). The model is tasked with visually grounding the object that the command is referring to. The recently proposed *Talk2Car* dataset [10] is used to run the challenge. Some examples are displayed in Fig. 2. An extensive description of the challenge can be found in Sect. 3.

In contrast to existing benchmarks, several additional challenges are encountered on the *Talk2Car* dataset. First, the referred object can be ambiguous (e.g. there are multiple pedestrians in the scene), but can be disambiguated by understanding modifier expressions in language (e.g. the pedestrian wearing the blue shirt). In some cases, the modifier expressions also indicate spatial information. Second, detecting the correct object is challenging both in the language utterance and the urban scene, for example, when dealing with long and complex sentences, and with small objects in the visual scene, respectively. Finally, the model size and the execution time also play an important role under the proposed task setting.

The contributions of our work are as follows:

- We propose the first challenge for grounding commands for self-driving cars in free natural language into the visual context of an urban environment.
- We scrutinize the results obtained by top performing teams. In particular, we compare them against several well-known state-of-the-art models, and further evaluate them on carefully selected subsets that address different key aspects of solving the task at hand, in order to identify potential failure cases.
- Finally, we identify several possibilities for future work under the proposed task setting.

2   Related Work

This section provides an overview of recent work on visual grounding. First, several methods are discussed, including both region proposal and non-region proposal based strategies. Next, we review existing benchmarks for visual grounding.

2.1   Methods

Existing solutions for visual grounding can be subdivided into two main groups of works. In *Region Proposal Based* methods, object proposals are first generated for the image using an off-the-shelf object detector (typically the region proposal network - RPN). Different works have considered how to correctly match the extracted regions with the language query. In *Non-Region Proposal Based* methods, a model reasons over the full image directly, instead of first extracting object proposals. We discuss representative works for both groups next.

Region Proposal Network (RPN) Based Methods. Hu et al. [16] train a model to maximize the likelihood of the referring expression for region proposals that match the object of interest. The global context, spatial configuration and local image features are all taken into account. Rohrbach et al. [34] tackle the problem by learning to attend to regions in the image from which the referring expression can be reconstructed. To this end, they serve a visual representation of the attended regions as input to a text-generating RNN. Wang et al. [50] learn a joint embedding for image regions and expressions by enforcing proximity between corresponding pairs through a maximum-margin ranking loss. More recently, modular approaches have seen an increase in popularity. For example, MAttNet [53] decomposes the referring expression into three distinct components, i.e. subject appearance, location and spatial relationships. The different components are subsequently matched with the visual representations, and combined to get a score for each region in the image. Similarly, MSRR [9] uses separate modules that focus on text, image and spatial location, and ranking of the image regions respectively. Additionally, the predictions of each module are improved in a recursive manner.

Non-region Proposal Based Methods. Hu et al. [15] apply a modular approach directly to the input image. First, they develop a set of modules that each execute a specific task, and return an attention map over image regions. Next, the expression is decomposed into sub-parts using attention. The extracted parts are considered as sub-problems that can be tackled by the smaller modules learned during the first step. Finally, the answers of the different sub-modules are integrated through an attention mechanism. In contrast to region proposal based methods, the image is subdivided into a 2-dimensional grid. The model predicts the grid cell containing the center of the referred object together with the bounding box offset.

Another approach that does not rely on the use of region proposals is the work of Hudson and Manning [18]. Although this method was originally developed for visual question answering, [10] adapted it to tackle the visual grounding task. The model uses a recurrent *MAC cell* to match the natural language command with a global representation of the image. First, the MAC cell decomposes the textual input into a series of reasoning steps. Additionally, the MAC cell uses the decomposed textual input to guide the model to focus on certain parts in the image. Information is passed to the next cell between each of the reasoning steps, allowing the model to represent arbitrarily complex reasoning graphs in a soft sequential manner.

2.2 Datasets

A number of datasets have been proposed to benchmark progress on the visual grounding task. These include both real-world [21,27,54] and synthetic [14] datasets. An overview is provided in Table 1. Some of the most commonly used datasets are *ReferIt* [21], *RefCOCO* [54], *RefCOCO+* [54] and *RefCOCOg* [27]. These datasets were constructed by adding textual annotations on top of the well-known MS COCO dataset [24]. Examples of image-sentence pairs sampled from these datasets can be seen in Fig. 1. Notice that the language utterances are rather artificial, i.e. the queries do not accurately present the language used by human speakers. On the other hand, the examples in Fig. 2 feature expressions that are more representative of everyday language, e.g. object references are often less explicit, and part of longer and more complex sentences. Additionally, the images found in the aforementioned datasets were collected from the web, and as a consequence, the objects of interest are often quite easy to spot. A different situation arises when considering indoor or urban scene environments.

In contrast to prior works, Vasudevan et al. [47] and Deruyttere et al. [10] considered the visual grounding task in a city environment. The main difference between the two works is the use of object descriptions in the former, versus the use of command-like expressions with more implicit object references in the latter. In this work, we use the *Talk2Car* [10] dataset.

Table 1. An overview of public datasets for visual grounding [10].

Dataset	Images	Objects	Expressions	Avg expr length	Video	Lidar	Radar
ReferIt [21]	19,894	96,654	130,525	3.46	✕	✕	✕
RefCOCO [54]	26,711	50,000	142,209	3.61	✕	✕	✕
RefCOCO+ [54]	19,992	49,856	141,564	3.53	✕	✕	✕
RefCOCOg [27]	26,711	54,822	85,474	8.43	✕	✕	✕
CLEVR-Ref [14]	99,992	492,727	998,743	14.50	✕	✕	✕
Cityscapes-Ref [47]	4,818	29,901	30,000	15.59	✓	✕	✕
Talk2Car [10]	9,217	10,519	11,959	11.01	✓	✓	✓

3   Commands for Autonomous Vehicles Challenge

This section describes the 'Commands for Autonomous Vehicles' (C4AV) challenge that was hosted as part of the C4AV workshop at ECCV 20'. First, we introduce the used benchmark. Second, we define three baseline models that were provided at the start of the challenge. Finally, we give an overview of the top performing models at the end of the competition.

3.1   Dataset

The C4AV challenge is based on the *Talk2Car* dataset [10]. The dataset is built on top of the nuScenes [4] dataset which contains 3D object boxes, videos, lidar and radar data obtained by driving a car through Boston and Singapore. Furthermore, the nuScenes dataset covers various weather conditions, different lighting conditions (day and night), and driving directions (left and right). The *Talk2Car* dataset is constructed by adding textual annotations on top of the images sampled from the nuScenes training dataset. More specifically, the text queries consist of commands provided by a passenger to the autonomous vehicle. Each command can be associated with an object visible in the scene. Figure 2 shows text-image pairs from the *Talk2Car* dataset. The challenge required to predict the 2D bounding box coordinates around the object of interest. Additionally,

(a) You can park up ahead behind **the silver car**, next to that lamppost with the orange sign on it

(b) **My friend** is getting out of the car. That means we arrived at our destination! Stop and let me out too!

(c) Yeah that would be **my son** on the stairs next to the bus. Pick him up please

(d) After **that man in the blue top** has passed, turn left

(e) There's **my mum**, on the right! The one walking closest to us. Park near **her**, she might want a lift

(f) Turn around and park in front of **that vehicle in the shade**

Fig. 2. Some examples from the Talk2Car dataset [10]. Each command describes an action that the car has to execute relevant to a referred object found in the scene (here indicated by the red 3D-bounding box). The referred object is indicated in bold in each command. Best seen in color. (Color figure online)

for every image, we provided pre-computed region proposals extracted with a CenterNet [55] model.

The dataset contains 11959 text-image pairs in total. The train, val and test set contain 70%, 10% and 20% of the samples, respectively. Additionally, the test set can be subdivided into four sub-sets of increasing difficulty. One subset was created to study the specific case of objects that are far away from the vehicle. Two sub-sets contain varying command lengths. The fourth subset tests how well the model disambiguates between objects of the same class as the target.

The C4AV challenge was hosted on *AICrowd* prior to ECCV 20'. Every team was allowed a maximum of three submissions per day. The submissions were evaluated on the held-out test set from the *Talk2Car* dataset. The evaluation criterion is described in Sect. 4. Top performing teams were invited to submit a paper to the workshop after undergoing a code verification phase.

3.2 Baselines

The leader board featured three baseline models at the start of the challenge. We describe each of them below. For brevity, we adopt the following notations. Each model takes as input an image I and a natural language expression under the form of a command C. The objective is to localize the referred object o.

Bi-directional Retrieval. Similar to the work from Karpathy et al. [20], a Bi-directional retrieval model is considered. First, a pre-trained object detector [55] is used to generate region proposals from the image I. Second, a pre-trained ResNet-18 model is used to obtain a local feature representation for the extracted regions. Similarly, the command C is encoded by a bi-directional GRU. Finally, we match the command C with the correct region proposal. To this end, we maximize the inner product between the local image features of the correct region and the text encoding, while we minimize the inner product for the other regions. To help participants get started in the challenge, a PyTorch [30] implementation of the Bi-directional retrieval model was made publicly available [44].

MAC. As a second baseline, we consider the MAC model [17], adapted for the visual grounding task by Deruyttere et al. [10]. MAC implements a multi-step reasoning approach, and unlike the Bi-directional retrieval model, does not rely on pre-computed region proposals. First, the image is encoded by a pre-trained ResNet model [12], and the command tokens are encoded by a bidirectional LSTM. Second, the model initiates a multi-step reasoning process by applying attention to the command tokens. In each reasoning step, the model attends to a different word, decomposing the language query into smaller sub-problems. Simultaneously, visual information is extracted from the image through a soft-attention mechanism conditioned on the attended word. The extracted information is stored as a memory vector, and forwarded to the next reasoning step. The final product of the multi-step reasoning process is a 2D bounding box derived from the soft-attention mask applied to the visual features.

MSRR. As a final baseline model, we consider the prior state-of-the-art on the *Talk2Car* dataset. Similar to MAC [17], the MSRR model [9] employs a multi-step reasoning strategy. However, unlike MAC, MSRR obtains its predictions by ranking object region proposals as in Sect. 3.2. First, each region is associated with a separate spatial map for which we indicate the spatial location by assigning ones to the regions, while zeros otherwise. Next, MSRR decomposes the expression C into sub-parts through attention and a region dependent reasoning process. The latter is achieved by (i) multiplying the spatial location of each region and its score with the image features, extracted by a ResNet model, and (ii) applying soft-attention conditioned onto the decomposed sub-expression. The result is combined into a region specific memory vector which can be used to score the region based on the alignment of the newly created memory vector and the command c. Finally, the highest scoring region is returned.

3.3   State-of-the-Art Models

Teams that outperformed all three baselines at the end of the challenge were invited to submit a paper to the workshop detailing their solution. A selection of top performing models is summarized below.

Stacked VLBert. Dai et al. [8] propose a visual-linguistic BERT model named *Stacked VLBert*. The approach relies on region proposals, similarly to the MSRR [9] and the Bi-directional retrieval model [44]. Furthermore, the authors propose a weight stacking method to efficiently train a larger model from a shallow VLBert model. The weight stacking procedure is performed by first training a smaller VLBert variant and then copying its trained weights in a repeated manner into a larger model. They show that by doing this, they can achieve a higher score compared to a larger model initialised with random weights. The Stacked VLBert model is conceptually close to the Bi-directional retrieval model as they first encode the image and object regions with a pre-trained image encoder. They then pass the sentence, the encoded image, and the encoded objects to the VLBert model to find the referred object.

Cross-Modal Representations from Transformers (CMRT). Luo et al. [25] also advocate the use of a region proposal based approach. The commands are fed to the input of a transformer encoder, while the image features are used as the query for the transformer decoder. The image features are refined based on the extracted linguistic features obtained from the encoder, which are used as the key and value input to the multi-head attention layers in the decoder. Unlike the common approaches that leverage the transformer encoder alone to extract visual-linguistic features, CMRT uses the transformer decoder to aggregate features from the two modalities. Additionally, as opposed to extracting local features from the region crops, the features of the whole image are used as the decoder input. This allows to capture long-range dependencies in the image, which is important, since the *Talk2Car* dataset commands also include the surroundings in the description of the objects. After aggregating the feature representations and extracting the feature map at the decoder output, an RoI alignment operation is used to select local image features of interest. The cropped features are fed to a final weight sharing network which is optimized using the same objective function as the Bi-directional retrieval model.

Cosine Meets Softmax: A Tough-to-Beat Baseline for Visual Grounding (CMSVG). Rufus et al. [35] showed that the Bi-directional retrieval approach can outperform more sophisticated approaches such as MSRR [9] and MAC [17] by simply using state-of-the-art object and sentence encoders. They also performed extensive ablation studies to analyse the influence of the used number of region proposals, the used image encoder, and the used text encoder.

Attention Enhanced Single Stage Multi-modal Reasoner (ASSMR). Ou and Zhang [29] also encode the local information of pre-computed region proposals first. Additionally, the position and scale of the region proposals are encoded and supplied as extra information for every region. Note that these properties are often found in the modifier expressions of the commands, and are thus potentially informative of the object location. Next, the local image features are combined with an encoding of the command to compute the weight for every region, emphasizing the ones most relevant for the given command. Afterwards, the weighted region features are augmented with a global image representation, and aggregated with the hidden states of a GRU that was used to encode the command. An attention mechanism is applied to the obtained multi-modal feature representation and the local object features to compute a final score for each region.

AttnGrounder: Talking to Cars with Attention. Mittal [28] proposes a one-stage approach to the visual grounding task. A Darknet-53 [31] backbone is utilized for extracting image features at multiple spatial resolution, while a bidirectional LSTM is used to generate text features. A visual-text attention module that relates every word in the given query with different image regions is used to construct a unique text representation for each region. Additionally, the prediction of a segmentation mask within the bounding box of the referred object is introduced as an auxiliary task, improving the localization performance. The predicted mask serves as an attention map used to weigh the visual features, which are subsequently concatenated with the spatially attended text features and the original visual features along the channel dimension, and fused together by using 1×1 convolutions. Finally, similarly to YOLOv3 [31], the fused features are used to predict the offset from anchor boxes and categorical labels that indicate whether the predicted bounding box corresponds to the ground truth.

4 Evaluation

Every model needs to output a 2D bounding box that indicates the location of the referred object. The challenge submissions were ranked using the evaluation measure from [10]. In particular, we employed the $IoU_{.5}$ metric by thresholding the Intersection over Union (IoU) between the predicted and ground-truth bounding boxes at 0.5. The IoU is defined as follows:

$$IoU = \frac{\text{Area of Overlap of the two boxes}}{\text{Area of Union of the two boxes}}. \tag{1}$$

While the challenge focused on the quality of the predictions, other properties such as model size and inference speed are arguably important as well in our task setting. To draw attention to these problems, for every model, we also report the number of parameters and the inference speed on a Nvidia RTX Titan 2080.

5 Experiments

This section analyses the results obtained by the models described in Sect. 3.2 and 3.3. In particular, Sect. 5.1 draws a comparison between the state-of-the-art on the *Talk2Car* dataset. Section 5.2 evaluates the models on carefully selected subsets to better understand any existing failure cases. Finally, Sect. 5.3 analyses the commonalities and differences between the used models to isolate the elements that render top-performing models successful.

5.1   State-of-the-Art Comparison

Table 2 compares the models from Sect. 3.2 and 3.3 on the *Talk2Car* test set. We compare the models in terms of $IoU_{.5}$, the number of parameters in millions (M) and inference speed in milliseconds (ms). The state-of-the-art prior to the challenge was the MSRR model [9]. Notably, the top-performing models from the challenge [8, 25, 28, 29, 35] show significant gains over the prior state-of-the-art [9] in terms of performance ($IoU_{.5}$). In particular, the Stacked VLBert model establishes a new state-of-the-art, and outperforms prior work by 10.9% $IoU_{.5}$. Furthermore, we find that some of the top-performing models [8, 35] drew a lot of inspiration from the Bi-directional retrieval model [44]. We conclude that when using strong visual and textual feature representations, this simple model can outperform more complex schemes like MAC [17] and MSRR [9].

Extra Test. To verify the validity of the predictions on the leader board, we evaluated the models on an additional hidden test set of 100 commands after the challenge (see $IoU_{.5}$† in Table 2). None of the submissions experiences a significant performance drop compared to the results on the official test set (see $IoU_{.5}$ vs $IoU_{.5}$†). This confirms the validity of the models. The additional test set annotations will be released after the workshop.

Resource Analysis. Although the challenge focuses on the quality of the predictions, the used amount of computational resources needs careful consideration too. We performed a detailed resource analysis in Table 2. Except for ASSMR [29], models that improve over MSRR [9] do this at the cost of increasing the model size (parameters). However, we do see improvement in terms of inference speed. The advantage of using a simple bi-directional retrieval approach over a more complex multi-step reasoning process is clearly visible here.

Table 2. Results on the *Talk2Car* test set. The inference speed was measured on a single Nvidia RTX Titan. † Results on an extra smaller test set that was hidden from the leaderboard.

Model	$IoU_{.5}$	$IoU_{.5}$ †	Params (M)	Inference Speed (ms)
Stacked VLBert [8]	**0.710**	**0.762**	683.80	320.79
CMRT [25]	0.691	0.713	194.97	215.50
CMSVG [35]	0.686	0.733	366.50	164.44
ASSMR [29]	0.660	0.723	**48.91**	126.23
AttnGrounder [28]	0.633	0.613	75.84	**25.50**
MSRR [9]	0.601	0.634	62.25	270.50
MAC [18]	0.505	0.525	41.59	51.23
Bi-Directional retr. [44]	0.441	0.327	15.80	100.24

5.2 Talk2Car Subsets

Section 3.1 described the construction of four carefully selected smaller test sets on the *Talk2Car* benchmark. In this section, we evaluate the models under various challenging conditions using the different subsets. Interestingly, the level of difficulty can be tuned as well. As a concrete example, the first subset is constructed by selecting the top-k examples from the dataset for which the object of interest is furthest away. By reducing the value of k, we effectively test on objects that are harder to spot due to their increased distance from the vehicle. For each subset, we consider four levels of difficulty. Figure 3 shows the results on the subsets. Next, we consider each of the four subsets in detail.

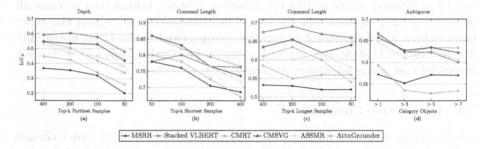

Fig. 3. Results of the state-of-the-art models (Sect. 3.3 on four sub-test sets from the *Talk2Car* dataset. Each plot shows the easy examples on the left, while the difficulty increases as we move to the right along the axis. In plot (a)–(c), we increase the difficulty by choosing the top-k samples under the selected criterion (e.g. depth, expression length). In plot (d), we increase the difficulty by choosing samples for which multiple same-category objects are present in the scene.

Far Away Objects. Figure 3(a) shows the results when focusing on far away objects. All models follow a similar trend, i.e. the performance drops significantly for objects that are further away. This observation follows from the use of the CenterNet [55] region proposals by all models. Notice that far away objects often tend to be small in size. The detection of small objects has been studied by several works, and requires specific dedicated solutions [5, 23].

Short Commands. Figure 3(b) displays the results when increasing the length of the commands. All models tend to score higher on the commands that are shortest in length. Yet, the performance drops significantly when increasing the length of the commands, i.e. going from the top-50 to the top-400 shortest commands. This is surprising since the maximum sentence length only sees a small increase, i.e. from 4 (top-50) to 6 (top-400). We believe that it would be useful to study the reason behind this behavior in future work.

Long Commands. Figure 3(c) measures the performance on the image-sentence pairs with the top-k longest commands. Depending on the used model, the performance is more susceptible to commands of increasing length. In particular,

CMRT [25] shows a decline in performance, while the performance of the other models remains more or less constant (less than 1.5% difference). We hypothesize that the transformer model [25] responsible for aggregating the image and sentence features does not perform well in combination with long sentences.

Ambiguity. Finally, Fig. 3(d) shows the performance when considering scenes with an increasing number of objects of the same category as the referred object. The CMRT [25] model obtains the highest performance when considering scenes with many ambiguous objects (>7). In this case, the object of interest can only be identified through its spatial relationship with other objects in the scene. In this case, the global image representation used by the CMRT model is beneficial. Similarly, the MSRR model [9] handles the ambiguous scenes rather well. This can be attributed to its multi-step reasoning process, taking into account all objects and their spatial relationships. The AttnGrounder [28], on the other hand, experiences a significant performance drop on ambiguous cases, potentially due to the fact that it does not utilize region proposals. Appendix 6 shows a successful case where successive reasoning steps are beneficial.

5.3 Qualitative Comparison

Finally, Table 3 gives a qualitative overview of all the methods under consideration. In particular, we consider the following elements: model performance, visual backbone, language model, word attention, image augmentations, language augmentations, region proposal based vs non-region proposal based and whether a global image representation is used or not. Based on this comparison, we present some additional findings below.

Region Proposal Networks. It is worth noting that all the top-performing models, except for the AttnGrounder [28], are based on pre-computed region proposals. We hypothesize that doing so is particularly interesting under the *Talk2Car* setting since the scenes are often cluttered with information. This is corroborated by the fact that the models that utilize the region proposals perform better on samples with a large number of objects from the target object category (which often implies a large number of objects in general), as can be seen on Fig. 3. However, there is a downside to the use of region proposals as well. For example, the model can not recover when the region proposal network fails to return a bounding box for the object of interest. In this case, relative regression or query-based approaches can be used [7,22].

Backbones and Word Attention. Surprisingly, some of the higher ranked methods use the same visual backbone as their lower ranked competitors. On the other hand, higher ranked models can be associated with more recent, better performing language embeddings. We conclude that the effect of using a deeper or better image encoder is smaller compared to using a better linguistic representation. Furthermore, word attention seems to be an additional important contributing factor in state-of-the-art models, as it allows them to focus on key words.

Augmentations. Remarkably, some models do not use augmentations although it has been shown that these are important for image recognition tasks [38,43]. It is also not surprising that the use of augmentations on the language side has not really been explored, as it is rather difficult. We are interested to see if recent frameworks like [26] can prove helpful in this case.

Global Image Representation. Finally, we consider whether a global image representation is taken into account or not. Note that this is optional in case of region proposal based methods. Apart from the Bi-directional retrieval baseline and CMSVG [35], all models used global context information to make the predictions. This observation confirms that it is beneficial to use global image information. Doing so allows to better capture the spatial relationships between objects. These are likely important to tackle the C4AV challenge.

Table 3. Qualitative comparison of all methods under consideration. A description of every model can be found in Sect. 3.2 and 3.3.

Model	$IoU_{.5}$	Vision Backb.	Language Backb.	Word Att.	Vision Augm.	NLP Augm.	RPN	Global Image repr.
Stacked VLBert [8]	**0.710**	ResNet-101 [12]	VLBERT [39]	Yes	Undisclosed	Undisclosed	Yes	Yes
CMRT [25]	0.691	ResNet-152 [12]	Transformer [48]	Yes	Undisclosed	Undisclosed	Yes	Yes
CMSVG [35]	0.686	EfficientNet [41]	Sent.-Transf. [32]	Yes	No	No	Yes	No
ASSMR [29]	0.660	ResNet-18 [12]	GRU	Yes	HZ Flip Rotation Color Jitter	No	Yes	Yes
AttnGrounder [28]	0.633	Darknet-53	LSTM	Yes	HZ Flip Random Affine Color Jitter	No	No	Yes
MSRR [9]	0.601	ResNet-101 [12]	LSTM	Yes	No	No	Yes	Yes
MAC [18]	0.505	ResNet-101 [12]	LSTM	Yes	No	No	No	Yes
Bi-Dir. retr. [44]	0.441	ResNet-18 [12]	LSTM	No	No	No	Yes	No

6   Conclusion

In this paper, we reviewed the results of the *Commands for Autonomous Vehicles* challenge held at ECCV20'. First, we presented an overview of various strategies to tackle the visual grounding task. For each method, we described its key components, and discussed the commonalities and differences with existing works. Second, we presented an extensive experimental evaluation of the considered methods. We briefly discuss some of the limitations and possibilities for future work.

Dataset. The *Talk2Car* dataset provides a more realistic task setting compared to existing benchmarks [21,27,54], yet we identify several possibilities to extend this work. First, the dataset could be further up-scaled in terms of the number of commands, and the variety of the environments. Second, it would be interesting to add annotations containing novel classes [36] and groups of objects.

Extra Modalities. Surprisingly, the use of other sensor modalities, e.g. depth, LIDAR, maps, etc., remains unexplored. Still, this provides an interesting direction for future research. In particular, leveraging additional data sources as extra input [11] or auxiliary task [45] is expected to boost the performance.

Navigation. The current setup considers the task of visual grounding in isolation. Yet, the agent is also responsible for navigating to the correct destination. Extending the current setup with a navigation task [2,6,37,42,46] would provide a useful addition.

Acknowledgements. This project is sponsored by the MACCHINA project from the KU Leuven with grant number C14/18/065. Additionally, we acknowledge support by the Flemish Government under the Artificial Intelligence (AI) Flanders programme. Finally, we thank Huawei for sponsoring the workshop and AICrowd for hosting our challenge.

Appendix A

A.1 Multi-step Reasoning MSRR

This section discusses the influence of having reasoning steps and showcases an example where the MSRR [9] successfully finds the correct answer for the command by using multiple reasoning steps.

First, we will look at the influence of reasoning steps. Assume we have a MSRR model that uses 10 reasoning steps, Fig. 4 shows in which of these 10 reasoning steps the model makes its final prediction. It is clear that most of the final predictions are made in the very first reasoning step. For instance, if we would only consider the answers in the first step and ignore any change of decision in the following steps, we would achieve $\approx$55% $IoU_{.5}$. Yet, by including more reasoning steps we can further improve this to $\approx$60% $IoU_{.5}$. This shows that having reasoning steps can be beneficial for this kind of task.

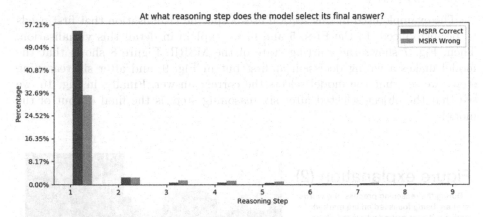

Fig. 4. This plot shows in which step a 10 reasoning step MSRR makes its final decision. We use MSRR Correct (blue) to indicate when the final answer by the model is also the correct answer while MSRR Wrong (orange) is used when the final answer is the wrong answer. (Color figure online)

Figure explanation (1)

- The coloured bounding boxes are the predicted bounding boxes from CenterNet

- The green filled box is the ground truth referred object. The big green arrow also points to the referred object

- Under the image we can find the command

- Under the command we can find the regions (with coloured borders to indicate which bounding box in the image is being used) together with their scores during the reasoning process

- The scores indicated with a green box, are the scores of the correct answer

- The scores indicated in bold represent the region that currently has the highest score. This is also indicated in the image with a bigger border around the object

- Finally, next to each score there is a ↑, ↓ or = to indicate if the score has increased, decreased or remained the same respectively compared to the previous reasoning step

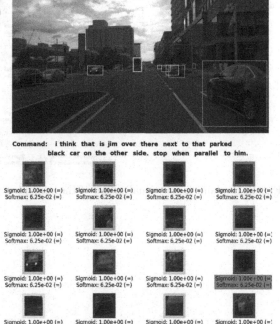

Fig. 5. Explaining the visualisation of the reasoning process (Part 1). Figure from [9].

The example used in this section uses a specific visualisation that first needs to be introduced. In the Figs. 5 and 6, we explain in detail this visualisation. Then, Fig. 7 shows the starting state of the MSRR. Figure 8 shows that the model makes a wrong decision at first but in Fig. 9, and after six reasoning steps, we see that the model selects the correct answer. Finally, in Fig. 10, we see that the object selected after six reasoning step, is the final output of the model.

Figure explanation (2)

- During the reasoning process, the words that are being focussed on are marked with a red background where the alpha channel corresponds with their attention weight. => Bright red background means high attention on that word, light red means low attention

- The object with the highest score will be indicated (i) with an arrow in the image, (ii) the other regions in the image will become less visible and (iii) in the plot under the command, the other regions will also be less visible

Command: i think that is jim over there next to that parked black car on the other side. stop when parallel to him.

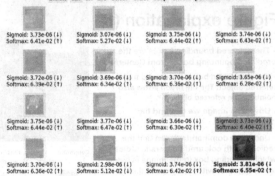

Fig. 6. Explaining the visualisation of the reasoning process (Part 2). Figure from [9].

Command: find me a parking spot near that white car up ahead. not the one on the right.

Sigmoid: 1.00e+00 (=)
Softmax: 6.25e-02 (=)

Sigmoid: 1.00e+00 (=)
Softmax: 6.25e-02 (=)

Sigmoid: 1.00e+00 (=)
Softmax: 6.25e-02 (=)

Sigmoid: 1.00e+00 (=)
Softmax: 6.25e-02 (=)

Sigmoid: 1.00e+00 (=)
Softmax: 6.25e-02 (=)

Sigmoid: 1.00e+00 (=)
Softmax: 6.25e-02 (=)

Sigmoid: 1.00e+00 (=)
Softmax: 6.25e-02 (=)

Sigmoid: 1.00e+00 (=)
Softmax: 6.25e-02 (=)

Sigmoid: 1.00e+00 (=)
Softmax: 6.25e-02 (=)

Sigmoid: 1.00e+00 (=)
Softmax: 6.25e-02 (=)

Sigmoid: 1.00e+00 (=)
Softmax: 6.25e-02 (=)

Sigmoid: 1.00e+00 (=)
Softmax: 6.25e-02 (=)

Sigmoid: 1.00e+00 (=)
Softmax: 6.25e-02 (=)

Sigmoid: 1.00e+00 (=)
Softmax: 6.25e-02 (=)

Sigmoid: 1.00e+00 (=)
Softmax: 6.25e-02 (=)

Sigmoid: 1.00e+00 (=)
Softmax: 6.25e-02 (=)

Fig. 7. Example 3 - The state of the model before the reasoning process starts for the given command, regions and image. Figure from [9].

Command: **find me a parking spot near that white car up ahead. not the one on the right.**

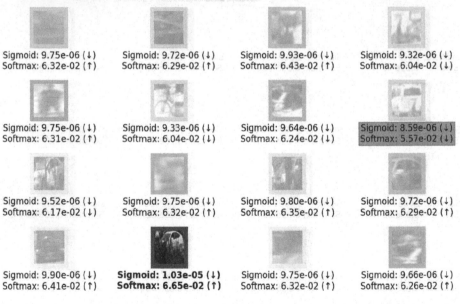

Fig. 8. Example 3 - Visualization of reasoning process. Step 1. Figure from [9].

Command: find me a parking spot near that white car up ahead. not the one on the right.

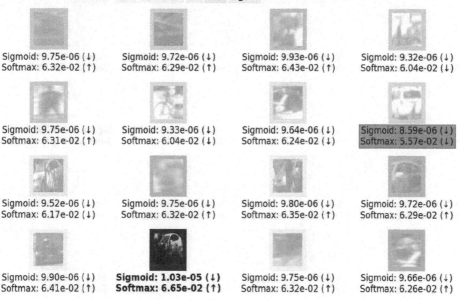

Sigmoid: 9.75e-06 (↓)
Softmax: 6.32e-02 (↑)

Sigmoid: 9.72e-06 (↓)
Softmax: 6.29e-02 (↑)

Sigmoid: 9.93e-06 (↓)
Softmax: 6.43e-02 (↑)

Sigmoid: 9.32e-06 (↓)
Softmax: 6.04e-02 (↓)

Sigmoid: 9.75e-06 (↓)
Softmax: 6.31e-02 (↑)

Sigmoid: 9.33e-06 (↓)
Softmax: 6.04e-02 (↓)

Sigmoid: 9.64e-06 (↓)
Softmax: 6.24e-02 (↓)

Sigmoid: 8.59e-06 (↓)
Softmax: 5.57e-02 (↓)

Sigmoid: 9.52e-06 (↓)
Softmax: 6.17e-02 (↓)

Sigmoid: 9.75e-06 (↓)
Softmax: 6.32e-02 (↑)

Sigmoid: 9.80e-06 (↓)
Softmax: 6.35e-02 (↑)

Sigmoid: 9.72e-06 (↓)
Softmax: 6.29e-02 (↑)

Sigmoid: 9.90e-06 (↓)
Softmax: 6.41e-02 (↑)

Sigmoid: 1.03e-05 (↓)
Softmax: 6.65e-02 (↑)

Sigmoid: 9.75e-06 (↓)
Softmax: 6.32e-02 (↑)

Sigmoid: 9.66e-06 (↓)
Softmax: 6.26e-02 (↑)

Fig. 9. Example 3 - Visualization of reasoning process. Step 6. Figure from [9].

Command: find me a parking spot near that white car up ahead. not the one on the right.

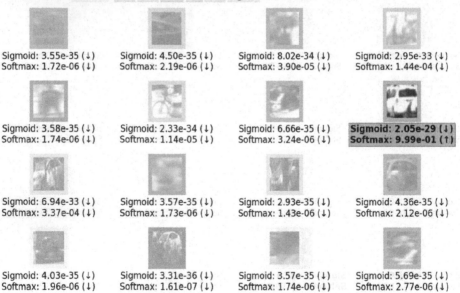

Sigmoid: 3.55e-35 (↓)	Sigmoid: 4.50e-35 (↓)	Sigmoid: 8.02e-34 (↓)	Sigmoid: 2.95e-33 (↓)
Softmax: 1.72e-06 (↓)	Softmax: 2.19e-06 (↓)	Softmax: 3.90e-05 (↓)	Softmax: 1.44e-04 (↓)
Sigmoid: 3.58e-35 (↓)	Sigmoid: 2.33e-34 (↓)	Sigmoid: 6.66e-35 (↓)	**Sigmoid: 2.05e-29 (↓)**
Softmax: 1.74e-06 (↓)	Softmax: 1.14e-05 (↓)	Softmax: 3.24e-06 (↓)	**Softmax: 9.99e-01 (↑)**
Sigmoid: 6.94e-33 (↓)	Sigmoid: 3.57e-35 (↓)	Sigmoid: 2.93e-35 (↓)	Sigmoid: 4.36e-35 (↓)
Softmax: 3.37e-04 (↓)	Softmax: 1.73e-06 (↓)	Softmax: 1.43e-06 (↓)	Softmax: 2.12e-06 (↓)
Sigmoid: 4.03e-35 (↓)	Sigmoid: 3.31e-36 (↓)	Sigmoid: 3.57e-35 (↓)	Sigmoid: 5.69e-35 (↓)
Softmax: 1.96e-06 (↓)	Softmax: 1.61e-07 (↓)	Softmax: 1.74e-06 (↓)	Softmax: 2.77e-06 (↓)

Fig. 10. Example 3 - Visualization of reasoning process. Final step. Figure from [9].

References

1. Anderson, P., et al.: Bottom-up and top-down attention for image captioning and visual question answering. In: Proceedings of the IEEE Conference on Computer Vision and Pattern Recognition, pp. 6077–6086 (2018)
2. Anderson, P., et al.: Vision-and-language navigation: interpreting visually-grounded navigation instructions in real environments. In: Proceedings of the IEEE Conference on Computer Vision and Pattern Recognition, pp. 3674–3683 (2018)
3. Antol, S., et al.: VQA: visual question answering. In: Proceedings of the IEEE International Conference on Computer Vision, pp. 2425–2433 (2015)
4. Caesar, H., et al.: nuScenes: a multimodal dataset for autonomous driving. In: Proceedings of the IEEE/CVF Conference on Computer Vision and Pattern Recognition, pp. 11621–11631 (2020)
5. Chen, C., Liu, M.-Y., Tuzel, O., Xiao, J.: R-CNN for small object detection. In: Lai, S.-H., Lepetit, V., Nishino, K., Sato, Y. (eds.) ACCV 2016. LNCS, vol. 10115, pp. 214–230. Springer, Cham (2017). https://doi.org/10.1007/978-3-319-54193-8_14
6. Chen, H., Suhr, A., Misra, D., Snavely, N., Artzi, Y.: Touchdown: natural language navigation and spatial reasoning in visual street environments. In: Proceedings of the IEEE Conference on Computer Vision and Pattern Recognition, pp. 12538–12547 (2019)
7. Chen, K., Kovvuri, R., Nevatia, R.: Query-guided regression network with context policy for phrase grounding. In: The IEEE International Conference on Computer Vision (ICCV) (2017)
8. Dai, H., Luo, S., Ding, Y., Shao, L.: Commands for autonomous vehicles by progressively stacking visual-linguistic representations. In: Proceedings of the 16th European Conference on Computer Vision, 2020. Commands for Autonomous Vehicles (C4AV) ECCV Workshop (2020)
9. Deruyttere, T., Collell, G., Moens, M.F.: Giving commands to a self-driving car: a multimodal reasoner for visual grounding. In: Reasoning for Complex QA Workshop, AAAI (2020)
10. Deruyttere, T., Vandenhende, S., Grujicic, D., Van Gool, L., Moens, M.F.: Talk2car: taking control of your self-driving car. In: Proceedings of the 2019 Conference on Empirical Methods in Natural Language Processing and the 9th International Joint Conference on Natural Language Processing (EMNLP-IJCNLP), pp. 2088–2098 (2019)
11. Gupta, S., Girshick, R., Arbeláez, P., Malik, J.: Learning rich features from RGB-D images for object detection and segmentation. In: Fleet, D., Pajdla, T., Schiele, B., Tuytelaars, T. (eds.) ECCV 2014. LNCS, vol. 8695, pp. 345–360. Springer, Cham (2014). https://doi.org/10.1007/978-3-319-10584-0_23
12. He, K., Zhang, X., Ren, S., Sun, J.: Deep residual learning for image recognition. CoRR abs/1512.03385 (2015). http://arxiv.org/abs/1512.03385
13. Hodosh, M., Young, P., Hockenmaier, J.: Framing image description as a ranking task: data, models and evaluation metrics. J. Artif. Intell. Res. **47**, 853–899 (2013)
14. Hu, R., Andreas, J., Darrell, T., Saenko, K.: Explainable neural computation via stack neural module networks. CoRR abs/1807.08556 (2018). http://arxiv.org/abs/1807.08556
15. Hu, R., Andreas, J., Darrell, T., Saenko, K.: Explainable neural computation via stack neural module networks. In: Proceedings of the European Conference on Computer Vision (ECCV), pp. 53–69 (2018)

16. Hu, R., Xu, H., Rohrbach, M., Feng, J., Saenko, K., Darrell, T.: Natural language object retrieval. In: Proceedings of the IEEE Conference on Computer Vision and Pattern Recognition, pp. 4555–4564 (2016)
17. Hudson, D.A., Manning, C.D.: Compositional attention networks for machine reasoning. CoRR abs/1803.03067 (2018). http://arxiv.org/abs/1803.03067
18. Hudson, D.A., Manning, C.D.: Compositional attention networks for machine reasoning (2018)
19. Johnson, J., et al.: Inferring and executing programs for visual reasoning. In: Proceedings of the IEEE International Conference on Computer Vision, vol. 2017-October, pp. 3008–3017 (2017)
20. Karpathy, A., Joulin, A., Fei-Fei, L.F.: Deep fragment embeddings for bidirectional image sentence mapping. In: Advances in Neural Information Processing Systems, pp. 1889–1897 (2014)
21. Kazemzadeh, S., Ordonez, V., Matten, M., Berg, T.: Referitgame: referring to objects in photographs of natural scenes. In: Proceedings of the 2014 Conference on Empirical Methods in Natural Language Processing (EMNLP), pp. 787–798 (2014)
22. Kovvuri, R., Nevatia, R.: PIRC net: using proposal indexing, relationships and context for phrase grounding. In: Jawahar, C.V., Li, H., Mori, G., Schindler, K. (eds.) ACCV 2018. LNCS, vol. 11364, pp. 451–467. Springer, Cham (2019). https://doi.org/10.1007/978-3-030-20870-7_28
23. Li, J., Liang, X., Wei, Y., Xu, T., Feng, J., Yan, S.: Perceptual generative adversarial networks for small object detection. In: Proceedings of the IEEE Conference on Computer Vision and Pattern Recognition, pp. 1222–1230 (2017)
24. Lin, T., et al.: Microsoft COCO: common objects in context. CoRR abs/1405.0312 (2014). http://arxiv.org/abs/1405.0312
25. Luo, S., Dai, H., Shao, L., Ding, Y.: Cross-modal representations from transformer. In: Proceedings of the 16th European Conference on Computer Vision, 2020. Commands for Autonomous Vehicles (C4AV) Workshop (2020)
26. Ma, E.: NLP augmentation (2019). https://github.com/makcedward/nlpaug
27. Mao, J., Huang, J., Toshev, A., Camburu, O., Yuille, A.L., Murphy, K.: Generation and comprehension of unambiguous object descriptions. In: Proceedings of the IEEE Conference on Computer Vision and Pattern Recognition, pp. 11–20 (2016)
28. Mittal, V.: Attngrounder: talking to cars with attention. In: Proceedings of the 16th European Conference on Computer Vision, 2020. Commands for Autonomous Vehicles (C4AV) Workshop (2020)
29. Ou, J., Zhang, X.: Attention enhanced single stage multi-modal reasoner. In: Proceedings of the 16th European Conference on Computer Vision, 2020. Commands for Autonomous Vehicles (C4AV) ECCV Workshop (2020)
30. Paszke, A., et al.: Pytorch: an imperative style, high-performance deep learning library. In: Advances in Neural Information Processing Systems, pp. 8026–8037 (2019)
31. Redmon, J., Farhadi, A.: Yolov3: an incremental improvement. arXiv preprint arXiv:1804.02767 (2018)
32. Reimers, N., Gurevych, I.: Sentence-bert: sentence embeddings using siamese bert-networks. In: Proceedings of the 2019 Conference on Empirical Methods in Natural Language Processing. Association for Computational Linguistics (2019). http://arxiv.org/abs/1908.10084
33. Ren, S., He, K., Girshick, R.B., Sun, J.: Faster R-CNN: towards real-time object detection with region proposal networks. CoRR abs/1506.01497 (2015). http://arxiv.org/abs/1506.01497

34. Rohrbach, A., Rohrbach, M., Hu, R., Darrell, T., Schiele, B.: Grounding of textual phrases in images by reconstruction. In: Leibe, B., Matas, J., Sebe, N., Welling, M. (eds.) ECCV 2016. LNCS, vol. 9905, pp. 817–834. Springer, Cham (2016). https://doi.org/10.1007/978-3-319-46448-0_49

35. Rufus, N., Nair, U., Krishnam, M., Gandhi, V.: Cosine meets softmax: a tough-to-beat baseline for visual grounding. In: Proceedings of the 16th European Conference on Computer Vision, 2020. Commands for Autonomous Vehicles (C4AV) Workshop (2020)

36. Sadhu, A., Chen, K., Nevatia, R.: Zero-shot grounding of objects from natural language queries (2019)

37. Savva, M., et al.: Habitat: a platform for embodied AI research. In: Proceedings of the IEEE International Conference on Computer Vision, pp. 9339–9347 (2019)

38. Sohn, K., et al.: Fixmatch: simplifying semi-supervised learning with consistency and confidence (2020)

39. Su, W., et al.: VL-BERT: pre-training of generic visual-linguistic representations. In: International Conference on Learning Representations (2020). https://openreview.net/forum?id=SygXPaEYvH

40. Suarez, J., Johnson, J., Li, F.F.: DDRprog: A CLEVR Differentiable Dynamic Reasoning Programmer (2018). http://arxiv.org/abs/1803.11361

41. Tan, M., Le, Q.V.: Efficientnet: rethinking model scaling for convolutional neural networks. arXiv preprint arXiv:1905.11946 (2019)

42. Thomason, J., Murray, M., Cakmak, M., Zettlemoyer, L.: Vision-and-dialog navigation. In: Conference on Robot Learning, pp. 394–406 (2020)

43. Van Gansbeke, W., Vandenhende, S., Georgoulis, S., Proesmans, M., Van Gool, L.: SCAN: learning to classify images without labels. In: Vedaldi, A., Bischof, H., Brox, T., Frahm, J.-M. (eds.) ECCV 2020. LNCS, vol. 12355, pp. 268–285. Springer, Cham (2020). https://doi.org/10.1007/978-3-030-58607-2_16

44. Vandenhende, S., Deruyttere, T., Grujicic, D.: A baseline for the commands for autonomous vehicles challenge. arXiv preprint arXiv:2004.13822 (2020)

45. Vandenhende, S., Georgoulis, S., Proesmans, M., Dai, D., Van Gool, L.: Revisiting multi-task learning in the deep learning era. arXiv preprint arXiv:2004.13379 (2020)

46. Vasudevan, A.B., Dai, D., Van Gool, L.: Talk2nav: long-range vision-and-language navigation in cities. arXiv preprint arXiv:1910.02029 (2019)

47. Vasudevan, A.B., Dai, D., Van Gool, L., Zurich, E.: Object referring in videos with language and human gaze (2018)

48. Vaswani, A., et al.: Attention is all you need. arXiv 2017. arXiv preprint arXiv:1706.03762 (2017)

49. Vinyals, O., Toshev, A., Bengio, S., Erhan, D.: Show and tell: a neural image caption generator. In: Proceedings of the IEEE Conference on Computer Vision and Pattern Recognition, pp. 3156–3164 (2015)

50. Wang, L., Li, Y., Huang, J., Lazebnik, S.: Learning two-branch neural networks for image-text matching tasks. IEEE Trans. Pattern Anal. Mach. Intell. **41**(2), 394–407 (2018)

51. Xu, K., et al.: Show, attend and tell: neural image caption generation with visual attention. In: International Conference on Machine Learning, pp. 2048–2057 (2015)

52. Young, P., Lai, A., Hodosh, M., Hockenmaier, J.: From image descriptions to visual denotations: new similarity metrics for semantic inference over event descriptions. Trans. Assoc. Comput. Linguist. **2**, 67–78 (2014)

53. Yu, L., et al.: Mattnet: modular attention network for referring expression comprehension. In: Proceedings of the IEEE Conference on Computer Vision and Pattern Recognition, pp. 1307–1315 (2018)
54. Yu, L., Poirson, P., Yang, S., Berg, A.C., Berg, T.L.: Modeling context in referring expressions. In: Leibe, B., Matas, J., Sebe, N., Welling, M. (eds.) ECCV 2016. LNCS, vol. 9906, pp. 69–85. Springer, Cham (2016). https://doi.org/10.1007/978-3-319-46475-6_5
55. Zhou, X., Wang, D., Krähenbühl, P.: Objects as points. arXiv preprint arXiv:1904.07850 (2019)

Commands for Autonomous Vehicles by Progressively Stacking Visual-Linguistic Representations

Hang Dai[1]([✉]), Shujie Luo[3], Yong Ding[3]([✉]), and Ling Shao[1,2]

[1] Mohamed Bin Zayed University of Artificial Intelligence,
Abu Dhabi, United Arab Emirates
hang.dai@mbzuai.ac.ae
[2] Inception Institute of Artificial Intelligence, Abu Dhabi, United Arab Emirates
[3] College of Information Science and Electronic Engineering,
Zhejiang University, Hangzhou, China
dingy@vlsi.zju.edu.cn

Abstract. In this work, we focus on the object referral problem in the autonomous driving setting. We use a stacked visual-linguistic BERT model to learn a generic visual-linguistic representation. Each element of the input is either a word or a region of interest from the input image. To train the deep model efficiently, we use a stacking algorithm to transfer knowledge from a shallow BERT model to a deep BERT model.

1 Introduction

This work aims to tackle the joint understanding of vision and language under a Commands for Autonomous Vehicles (C4AV) setting [5,6,30]. The previous practice is to combine the task-specific networks for image classification [26,34] and natural language processing [24,31], without any generic visual-linguistic representation learning [13,15,25]. However, the task-specific models may suffer from over-fitting when the data for the target task is scarce [14,18,32].

A key goal of various models is to effectively aggregate the multi-modal representations [4,8,20]. The network is expected to integrate both linguistic information from the input command and visual information from the input image by aligning the linguistic meanings with the visual cues [1,17,19,22,29]. Thus, we seek to derive generic representations that can effectively aggregate and align visual and linguistic information using Bidirectional Encoder Representations from Transformers (BERT) [7,21,27,28]. The self-attention of a well-trained BERT model concentrates locally around its position and the starting token in most layers [9]. The weights from a shallow model can be a good warm-start to train a deep model. Motivated by this, we use a stacking algorithm to transfer knowledge from a shallow BERT model to a deep BERT model.

© Springer Nature Switzerland AG 2020
A. Bartoli and A. Fusiello (Eds.): ECCV 2020 Workshops, LNCS 12536, pp. 27–32, 2020.
https://doi.org/10.1007/978-3-030-66096-3_2

2   Method

2.1   Revisit BERT

In BERT [7], the features are transformed in a layer-by-layer manner by aggregating features from the other input elements with adaptive attention weights. The multi-head attention can be defined as:

$$\tilde{h}_i^{l+1} = \sum_{m=1}^{M} W_m^{l+1} \left(\sum_{j=1}^{N} P_{i,j}^m \cdot V_m^{l+1} o_j^l \right) \tag{1}$$

where $P_{i,j}^m \propto \exp\left[\left(Q_m^{l+1} o_i^l\right)^T \left(K_m^{l+1} o_j^l\right) \right]$ indicates the attention weights between the elements i and j in the m_{th} attention head, which is normalized such that $\sum_{j=1}^{N} P_{i,j}^m = 1$. Note that $W_m^{l+1}, Q_m^{l+1}, K_m^{l+1}$ and V_m^{l+1} are learnable weights in the m_{th} attention head. This is followed by a residual learning layer:

$$h_i^{l+1} = \text{LayerNorm}\left(o_i^l + \tilde{h}_i^{l+1} \right) \tag{2}$$

Then a feed-forward layer is used to learn a contextualized meaning of the inputs:

$$\tilde{o}_i^{l+1} = W_2^{l+1} \cdot \text{GELU}\left(W_1^{l+1} h_i^{l+1} + a_1^{l+1} \right) + a_2^{l+1} \tag{3}$$

where W_1^{l+1}, W_2^{l+1} and a_1^{l+1}, a_2^{l+1} are the learnable weights and biases, respectively. Finally, a residual connection is performed to enhance feature extraction:

$$o_i^{l+1} = \text{LayerNorm}\left(h_i^{l+1} + \tilde{o}_i^{l+1} \right) \tag{4}$$

2.2   Visual-Linguistic BERT Model

Figure 1 shows how to adapt VLBERT [27] to C4AV task. VLBERT is an extension of the original BERT model to accommodate the visual inputs. The input

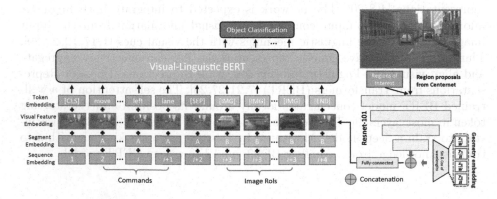

Fig. 1. The adaptation of VLBERT [27] to C4AV task.

is a combination of a classification element [CLS], linguistic information, a separation element [SEP], visual information, and an ending element [END].

There exist four types of embedding: token embedding, visual feature embedding, segment embedding, and sequence embedding. The other three embeddings except the visual feature embedding are the same as the BERT [3,16]. A special token [IMG] is assigned to the visual inputs. The Regions of Interest (RoIs) are obtained from Centernet [33]. The feature map is extracted by applying a Resnet-101 [10] to each RoI. For the non-visual elements, the visual feature maps are learned from the whole input image. The visual geometry embedding is a 4-d vector defined as $\left(\frac{x_1}{W}, \frac{y_1}{H}, \frac{x_2}{W}, \frac{y_2}{H}\right)$, where (x_1, y_1) and (x_2, y_2) indicate the top-left and bottom-right corner, and W, H are the width and height of the input image. The 4-d vector can be projected into a high-dimensional representation by computing sine and cosine functions of different wavelengths [7,11]. We can use two types of segment embedding, A and B, to define two different input sources, visual and linguistic. The segment type A stands for the command words, and B for the RoIs from the input image. A sequence embedding is used to indicate the order in the input sequence [2]. Since no natural order exists among the input visual elements, the sequence embeddings for all the image RoIs are the same.

2.3 Progressively Stacking Algorithm

Figure 2 shows how we employ the progressively stacking algorithm [9] to train a deep VLBERT model. If we have an L-layer trained VLBERT B_0, we can initialize a $2L$-layer VLBERT B_1 by copying the weights in this way: for $i \leq L$, copy the i-th layer of the L-layer trained VLBERT to the i-th and $(i+L)$-th layer of B_1. The weights from a L-layer trained VLBERT is a good warm-start to train the $2L$-layer VLBERT. By stacking, the attention layers focus on both the [CLS] to extract global information and the neighbors to extract local information. An iterative training algorithm can be used to train a very deep VLBERT model.

3 Experiment

In this work, the number of layers in the base VLBERT is set to 24. We use Talk2Car dataset [6] for evaluation. Table 1 illustrates that the proposed method

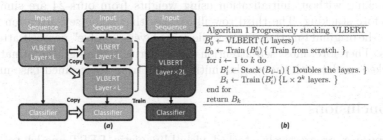

Fig. 2. We employ the stacking algorithm [9] to train a deep VLBERT model.

Table 1. AP50 on the *val* and *test* set, * is the 48-layer VLBERT training without initialization using the weights from ours-24.

Method	C4AV [30]	MAC [12]	MSRR [5]	3rd	2nd [23]	Ours-24	Ours-48*	Ours-48	Ours-96
val	0.435	–	–	–	–	0.662	0.665	**0.682**	0.665
test	0.441	0.505	0.603	0.687	0.691	0.685	0.659	**0.710**	0.685

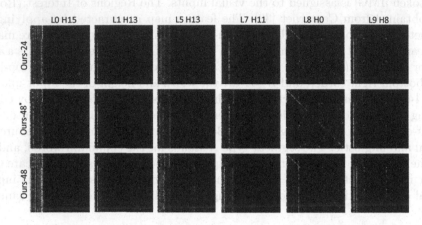

Fig. 3. Attention weights map in terms of layer (L) and attention head (H).

with stacking (k is 1) achieves the best performance when the model is initialized with the weights from the trained 24-layer VLBERT model (ours-24). This implies that the weights initialization from the trained base model is important in training a deep VLBERT model. Training a 48-layer architecture from scratch achieves a substantially worse performance than that with stacking. Furthermore, it performs worse than the 24-layer model. This implies what the stacking achieves is more than doubling the size of the model. When k is 2, ours-96 has worse performance. This lies in the fact that it is very difficult to train a 96-layer BERT model which also easily causes over-fitting. As shown in Table 1, the proposed method with the stacking algorithm (ours-48) is significantly better than the state-of-the-art methods including C4AV [30], MAC [12], and MSRR [5].

As shown in Fig. 3, the stacking preserves some original functionalities from ours-24. The first two rows of the figure show that the attention weights map after stacking without initialization using weights from ours-24 are similar to those before stacking. The third row illustrates that some self-attention layers preserve the original functionalities, while some layers "evolve" new self-attention patterns. Therefore, most self-attention layers derive meaningful information in the stacked model with the weights initialization from the trained base model.

4   Conclusions

We propose a progressively stacked visual-linguistic BERT model to derive generic representations that can effectively aggregate and align visual and linguistic information. The stacking algorithm eases the training of a deeper VLBERT model. Our method ranks the 1st place in the C4AV Challenge.

Acknowledgement. This work was supported in part by the National Key Research and Development Program of China (2018YFE0183900).

References

1. Alberti, C., Ling, J., Collins, M., Reitter, D.: Fusion of detected objects in text for visual question answering. arXiv preprint arXiv:1908.05054 (2019)
2. Carion, N., Massa, F., Synnaeve, G., Usunier, N., Kirillov, A., Zagoruyko, S.: End-to-end object detection with transformers. arXiv preprint arXiv:2005.12872 (2020)
3. Clark, K., Khandelwal, U., Levy, O., Manning, C.D.: What does bert look at? an analysis of bert's attention. arXiv preprint arXiv:1906.04341 (2019)
4. Deng, C., Wu, Q., Wu, Q., Hu, F., Lyu, F., Tan, M.: Visual grounding via accumulated attention. In: Proceedings of the IEEE Conference on Computer Vision and Pattern Recognition, pp. 7746–7755 (2018)
5. Deruyttere, T., Collell, G., Moens, M.F.: Giving commands to a self-driving car: a multimodal reasoner for visual grounding. arXiv preprint arXiv:2003.08717 (2020)
6. Deruyttere, T., Vandenhende, S., Grujicic, D., Van Gool, L., Moens, M.F.: Talk2car: taking control of your self-driving car. arXiv preprint arXiv:1909.10838 (2019)
7. Devlin, J., Chang, M.W., Lee, K., Toutanova, K.: Bert: pre-training of deep bidirectional transformers for language understanding. arXiv preprint arXiv:1810.04805 (2018)
8. Fukui, A., Park, D.H., Yang, D., Rohrbach, A., Darrell, T., Rohrbach, M.: Multimodal compact bilinear pooling for visual question answering and visual grounding. arXiv preprint arXiv:1606.01847 (2016)
9. Gong, L., He, D., Li, Z., Qin, T., Wang, L., Liu, T.: Efficient training of bert by progressively stacking. In: International Conference on Machine Learning, pp. 2337–2346 (2019)
10. He, K., Zhang, X., Ren, S., Sun, J.: Deep residual learning for image recognition. In: Proceedings of the IEEE Conference on Computer Vision and Pattern Recognition, pp. 770–778 (2016)
11. Hu, H., Gu, J., Zhang, Z., Dai, J., Wei, Y.: Relation networks for object detection. In: Proceedings of the IEEE Conference on Computer Vision and Pattern Recognition, pp. 3588–3597 (2018)
12. Hudson, D.A., Manning, C.D.: Compositional attention networks for machine reasoning. arXiv preprint arXiv:1803.03067 (2018)
13. Hudson, D.A., Manning, C.D.: GQA: a new dataset for real-world visual reasoning and compositional question answering. In: Proceedings of the IEEE Conference on Computer Vision and Pattern Recognition, pp. 6700–6709 (2019)
14. Johnson, J., et al: A diagnostic dataset for compositional language and elementary visual reasoning. In: Proceedings of the IEEE Conference on Computer Vision and Pattern Recognition, pp. 2901–2910 (2017)
15. Johnson, J., et al.: Inferring and executing programs for visual reasoning. In: Proceedings of the IEEE International Conference on Computer Vision, pp. 2989–2998 (2017)

16. Lee, J., et al.: Biobert: a pre-trained biomedical language representation model for biomedical text mining. Bioinformatics **36**(4), 1234–1240 (2020)
17. Li, G., Duan, N., Fang, Y., Gong, M., Jiang, D., Zhou, M.: Unicoder-vl: a universal encoder for vision and language by cross-modal pre-training. In: AAAI, pp. 11336–11344 (2020)
18. Li, J., Luo, S., Zhu, Z., Dai, H., Krylov, A.S., Ding, Y., Shao, L.: 3D IOU-net: IOU guided 3D object detector for point clouds. arXiv preprint arXiv:2004.04962 (2020)
19. Li, L.H., Yatskar, M., Yin, D., Hsieh, C.J., Chang, K.W.: Visualbert: a simple and performant baseline for vision and language. arXiv preprint arXiv:1908.03557 (2019)
20. Liu, D., Zhang, H., Wu, F., Zha, Z.J.: Learning to assemble neural module tree networks for visual grounding. In: Proceedings of the IEEE International Conference on Computer Vision, pp. 4673–4682 (2019)
21. Liu, Y., Lapata, M.: Text summarization with pretrained encoders. arXiv preprint arXiv:1908.08345 (2019)
22. Lu, J., Batra, D., Parikh, D., Lee, S.: Vilbert: pretraining task-agnostic visiolinguistic representations for vision-and-language tasks. In: Advances in Neural Information Processing Systems, pp. 13–23 (2019)
23. Luo, S., Dai, H., Shao, L., Ding, Y.: C4av: cross-modal representations from transformer. In: ECCV workshop (2020)
24. Manning, C.D., Surdeanu, M., Bauer, J., Finkel, J.R., Bethard, S., McClosky, D.: The stanford corenlp natural language processing toolkit. In: Proceedings of 52nd Annual Meeting of the Association for Computational Linguistics: System Demonstrations, pp. 55–60 (2014)
25. Perez, E., Strub, F., De Vries, H., Dumoulin, V., Courville, A.: Film: visual reasoning with a general conditioning layer. In: Thirty-Second AAAI Conference on Artificial Intelligence (2018)
26. Simonyan, K., Zisserman, A.: Very deep convolutional networks for large-scale image recognition. arXiv preprint arXiv:1409.1556 (2014)
27. Su, W., et al.: Vl-bert: pre-training of generic visual-linguistic representations. In: International Conference on Learning Representations (2020)
28. Sun, F., et al.: Bert4rec: sequential recommendation with bidirectional encoder representations from transformer. In: Proceedings of the 28th ACM International Conference on Information and Knowledge Management, pp. 1441–1450 (2019)
29. Tan, H., Bansal, M.: Lxmert: learning cross-modality encoder representations from transformers. arXiv preprint arXiv:1908.07490 (2019)
30. Vandenhende, S., Deruyttere, T., Grujicic, D.: A baseline for the commands for autonomous vehicles challenge. arXiv preprint arXiv:2004.13822 (2020)
31. Young, T., Hazarika, D., Poria, S., Cambria, E.: Recent trends in deep learning based natural language processing. IEEE Comput. Intell. Mag. **13**(3), 55–75 (2018)
32. Zhang, Y., Niebles, J.C., Soto, A.: Interpretable visual question answering by visual grounding from attention supervision mining. In: 2019 IEEE Winter Conference on Applications of Computer Vision (WACV), pp. 349–357. IEEE (2019)
33. Zhou, X., Wang, D., Krähenbühl, P.: Objects as points. In: arXiv preprint arXiv:1904.07850 (2019)
34. Zoph, B., Vasudevan, V., Shlens, J., Le, Q.V.: Learning transferable architectures for scalable image recognition. In: Proceedings of the IEEE Conference on Computer Vision and Pattern Recognition, pp. 8697–8710 (2018)

C4AV: Learning Cross-Modal Representations from Transformers

Shujie Luo[1], Hang Dai[2(✉)], Ling Shao[2,3], and Yong Ding[1(✉)]

[1] College of Information Science and Electronic Engineering,
Zhejiang University, Hangzhou, China
dingy@vlsi.zju.edu.cn
[2] Mohamed bin Zayed University of Artificial Intelligence,
Abu Dhabi, United Arab Emirates
hang.dai@mbzuai.ac.ae
[3] Inception Institute of Artificial Intelligence, Abu Dhabi, United Arab Emirates

Abstract. In this paper, we focus on the object referral problem in the autonomous driving setting. We propose a novel framework to learn cross-modal representations from transformers. In order to extract the linguistic feature, we feed the input command to the transformer encoder. Meanwhile, we use a resnet as the backbone for the image feature learning. The image features are flattened and used as the query inputs to the transformer decoder. The image feature and the linguistic feature are aggregated in the transformer decoder. A region-of-interest (RoI) alignment is applied to the feature map output from the transformer decoder to crop the RoI features for region proposals. Finally, a multi-layer classifier is used for object referral from the features of proposal regions.

Keywords: Object referral · Cross-modal representations

1 Introduction

Object referral task, relevant to many real-world scenarios and applications, consists of retrieving the correct object from an image based on a language expression [17,18,22,24]. We focus on the object referral problem in the Command for Autonomous Vehicles (C4AV) setting, where a passenger gives a command which may be associated with an object found in a street scene. For instance, passengers may give instructions that indicate locations that the autonomous car needs to reach, as shown in Fig. 1. This is a challenging task because there are multiple expressions for the same object in a scene and different instructions for the same scene that may correspond to different objects.

Various architectures [1,14,16,29] are explored to address vision-and-language related tasks. These models are pre-trained on tasks for learning general vision-linguistic representations, then fine-tuned for a specific task, including object referral. We propose a novel framework using transformers to learn the cross-modal representations. Instead of just using transformer encoders, which has been a popular approach in many existing solutions, we adopt transformer

© Springer Nature Switzerland AG 2020
A. Bartoli and A. Fusiello (Eds.): ECCV 2020 Workshops, LNCS 12536, pp. 33–38, 2020.
https://doi.org/10.1007/978-3-030-66096-3_3

decoders to aggregate features of different modalities. In order to learn the linguistic feature, we feed the input command to the transformer encoder. A resnet [12] is used as the backbone to extract visual features. The flattened visual and linguistic features are then aggregated in the transformer decoder.

(a) Drive up to the right side of that (b) Park in front of this black SUV.
truck in front of us.

Fig. 1. Examples from the Talk2Car [8] dataset.

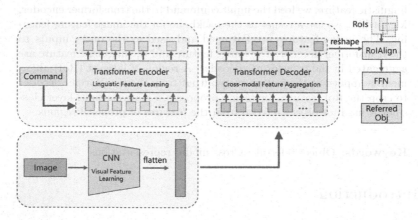

Fig. 2. An overview of the proposed framework.

2   Our Algorithm

In this section, we describe the proposed method, which is composed of three parts: visual feature learning, linguistic feature learning, and cross-modal feature aggregation, as shown in Fig. 2. Region-of-Interest Alignment (RoIAlign) [11] is applied to the feature map output to crop the features of region proposals. We use 32 region proposals for every image which are provided by [26] and obtained by the finetuned CenterNet [30] in the C4AV challenge. Finally, we feed the features to a shared-weights Feed Forward Network (FFN) that predicts whether the region includes the referred object or not.

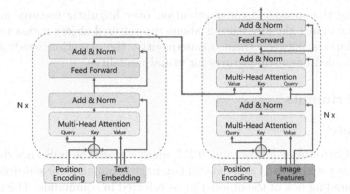

Fig. 3. The architecture of our cross-modal transformers. The model supplements the query and key with a sinusoidal positional encoding in both transformer encoder (left) and transformer decoder (right). N is set to 6 in this work.

Visual Feature Learning. We adopt resnet [12] as the backbone network to extract visual features. The pre-trained model on ImageNet [6] is loaded as the initial weights. The resolution of the output feature map is $H/32 \times W/32$, where H and W are the height and width of the input image.

Linguistic Feature Learning. Transformers are widely used in natural language processing and have achieved great performance in tasks such as machine translation [21,28], question answering [9,23], and language inference [10,25]. In our framework, the transformer encoder is used to extract linguistic features, and the structure is shown in Fig. 3. The model uses sinusoidal positional encoding, which is added to the linguistic features at the query and key input to the multi-head attention module [27]. Then, the residual addition and the layer normalization [2] are performed with the initial linguistic representations. This is followed by an FFN, another residual addition, and layer normalization. Note that the operations above are irrelevant to the order.

Cross-modal Feature Aggregation. The cross-modal feature aggregation is a key component of the framework. The features of the whole image are used as input to the first multi-head attention module in the decoder, in order to learn long-range dependencies between visual feature entries and integrate the global features with features of region proposals. The motivation for this design is the fact that the Talk2Car dataset [8] considers a real autonomous driving street scene where the commands may describe not only the features of the object but also its surrounding environment [15]. Therefore, the characteristics of the environment and the relationship between objects are important for object referral on the Talk2Car dataset. Each decoder layer supplements flattened visual features at the query and key input to the multi-head attention with a sinusoidal positional encoding [4] which contains the x and y coordinates for each pixel, introducing the information about the spatial layout of objects in the image.

By using the encoder-decoder attention over linguistic features and visual features, the model globally reasons about the referred object region using pairwise correlations between them. Consequently, the attention heads learn the attention-pooled linguistic features for visual modality.

3 Experiments

3.1 Dataset

The Talk2Car dataset [8] contains 9,217 images from the nuScenes dataset [3] that are annotated with 11,959 natural language commands for self-driving cars, and the bounding box of the object that is referred in commands. The dataset is officially divided into the train, validation, and test set that contain 70%, 10%, and 20% of the samples, respectively.

3.2 Evaluation

We implement our model with PyTorch [19], and employ SGD with momentum [20] optimizer to train the model on GPU TITAN V100 for 40 epochs. The initial learning rate is set to 0.0008 when batch size is 8 and decayed by a factor 10 at the 20th, 30th epoch. The number of encoder layers and decoder layers are both set to 6.

We compared our method with the state-of-the-art approaches [7,13,26] which are set as the baselines in the C4AV challenge. All methods are evaluated based on the rate at which the IoU between the predicted bounding box and the ground-truth bounding box exceeds 50% (AP50). As illustrated in Table 1, our approach has achieved a significant improvement on the validation and the test set and achieves the best performance of 69.1% AP50 on the test set with a resent-152. In addition, with a resnet-18 as the backbone, our model still achieves a good performance of 67.0% AP50 on the test set. The improvement lies in the fact that the self-attention layers in the transformer decoder enable more efficient information exchange between modalities [5].

Table 1. Performance evaluation on the Talk2Car dataset. CMTR is the abbreviation of the proposed method Cross-Modal TRansformers.

Methods	Backbone	Val Set	Test Set
C4AV [26]	–	43.5	44.1
MAC [13]	–	–	50.5
MSRR [7]	–	–	60.1
CMTR (ours)	resnet-18	68.4	67.0
CMTR (ours)	resnet-101	**68.5**	68.6
CMTR (ours)	resnet-152	68.2	**69.1**

4 Conclusions

We propose a novel framework that uses transformers to learn the cross-modal representations for an object referral task. The proposed model achieves a large performance improvement, which validates the effectiveness of our model in dealing with the object referral task. The proposed method ranks 2nd place in the C4AV Challenge.

Acknowledgement. This work was supported in part by the National Key Research and Development Program of China (2018YFE0183900).

References

1. Alberti, C., Ling, J., Collins, M., Reitter, D.: Fusion of detected objects in text for visual question answering. arXiv preprint arXiv:1908.05054 (2019)
2. Ba, J.L., Kiros, J.R., Hinton, G.E.: Layer normalization. arXiv preprint arXiv:1607.06450 (2016)
3. Caesar, H., et al.: A multimodal dataset for autonomous driving. In: Proceedings of the IEEE/CVF Conference on Computer Vision and Pattern Recognition, pp. 11621–11631 (2020)
4. Carion, N., Massa, F., Synnaeve, G., Usunier, N., Kirillov, A., Zagoruyko, S.: End-to-end object detection with transformers. arXiv preprint arXiv:2005.12872 (2020)
5. Dai, H., Luo, S., Ding, Y., Shao, L.: Commands for autonomous vehicles by progressively stacking visual-linguistic representations. In: ECCV workshop (2020)
6. Deng, J., Dong, W., Socher, R., Li, L.J., Li, K., Fei-Fei, L.: Imagenet: a large-scale hierarchical image database. In: 2009 IEEE Conference on Computer Vision and Pattern Recognition, pp. 248–255. IEEE (2009)
7. Deruyttere, T., Collell, G., Moens, M.F.: Giving commands to a self-driving car: A multimodal reasoner for visual grounding. arXiv preprint arXiv:2003.08717 (2020)
8. Deruyttere, T., Vandenhende, S., Grujicic, D., Van Gool, L., Moens, M.F.: Talk2car: Taking control of your self-driving car. arXiv preprint arXiv:1909.10838 (2019)
9. Fan, A., Grave, E., Joulin, A.: Reducing transformer depth on demand with structured dropout. arXiv preprint arXiv:1909.11556 (2019)
10. Guo, M., Zhang, Y., Liu, T.: Gaussian transformer: a lightweight approach for natural language inference. Proceedings of the AAAI Conference on Artificial Intelligence, vol. 33, pp. 6489–6496 (2019)
11. He, K., Gkioxari, G., Dollár, P., Girshick, R.: Mask r-cnn. In: Proceedings of the IEEE International Conference on Computer Vision, pp. 2961–2969 (2017)
12. He, K., Zhang, X., Ren, S., Sun, J.: Deep residual learning for image recognition. In: Proceedings of the IEEE Conference on Computer Vision and Pattern Recognition, pp. 770–778 (2016)
13. Hudson, D.A., Manning, C.D.: Compositional attention networks for machine reasoning. arXiv preprint arXiv:1803.03067 (2018)
14. Li, G., Duan, N., Fang, Y., Gong, M., Jiang, D., Zhou, M.: Unicoder-vl: a universal encoder for vision and language by cross-modal pre-training. In: AAAI, pp. 11336–11344 (2020)
15. Li, J., et al.: 3D iou-net: Iou guided 3D object detector for point clouds. arXiv preprint arXiv:2004.04962 (2020)

16. Li, L.H., Yatskar, M., Yin, D., Hsieh, C.J., Chang, K.W.: Visualbert: a simple and performant baseline for vision and language. arXiv preprint arXiv:1908.03557 (2019)
17. Lu, J., Batra, D., Parikh, D., Lee, S.: Vilbert: pretraining task-agnostic visiolinguistic representations for vision-and-language tasks. In: Advances in Neural Information Processing Systems, pp. 13–23 (2019)
18. Lu, J., Goswami, V., Rohrbach, M., Parikh, D., Lee, S.: 12-in-1: multi-task vision and language representation learning. In: Proceedings of the IEEE/CVF Conference on Computer Vision and Pattern Recognition, pp. 10437–10446 (2020)
19. Paszke, A., et al.: Pytorch: an imperative style, high-performance deep learning library. In: Advances in Neural Information Processing Systems, pp. 8026–8037 (2019)
20. Qian, N.: On the momentum term in gradient descent learning algorithms. Neural Netw. **12**(1), 145–151 (1999)
21. Raganato, A., et al.: An analysis of encoder representations in transformer-based machine translation. In: Proceedings of the 2018 EMNLP Workshop BlackboxNLP: Analyzing and Interpreting Neural Networks for NLP. The Association for Computational Linguistics (2018)
22. Su, W., et al.: Vl-bert: Pre-training of generic visual-linguistic representations. arXiv preprint arXiv:1908.08530 (2019)
23. Sur, C.: Self-segregating and coordinated-segregating transformer for focused deep multi-modular network for visual question answering. arXiv preprint arXiv:2006.14264 (2020)
24. Tan, H., Bansal, M.: Lxmert: learning cross-modality encoder representations from transformers. arXiv preprint arXiv:1908.07490 (2019)
25. Tsai, Y.H.H., Bai, S., Liang, P.P., Kolter, J.Z., Morency, L.P., Salakhutdinov, R.: Multimodal transformer for unaligned multimodal language sequences. In: Proceedings of the conference. Association for Computational Linguistics. Meeting, vol. 2019, p. 6558. NIH Public Access (2019)
26. Vandenhende, S., Deruyttere, T., Grujicic, D.: A baseline for the commands for autonomous vehicles challenge. arXiv preprint arXiv:2004.13822 (2020)
27. Vaswani, A., et al.: Attention is all you need. Adv. Neural Inf. Process. Syst. **30**, 5998–6008 (2017)
28. Xia, Y., He, T., Tan, X., Tian, F., He, D., Qin, T.: Tied transformers: neural machine translation with shared encoder and decoder. In: Proceedings of the AAAI Conference on Artificial Intelligence, vol. 33, pp. 5466–5473 (2019)
29. Zhou, L., Palangi, H., Zhang, L., Hu, H., Corso, J.J., Gao, J.: Unified vision-language pre-training for image captioning and VQA. In: AAAI, pp. 13041–13049 (2020)
30. Zhou, X., Wang, D., Krähenbühl, P.: Objects as points. arXiv preprint arXiv:1904.07850 (2019)

Cosine Meets Softmax: A Tough-to-beat Baseline for Visual Grounding

Nivedita Rufus[✉], Unni Krishnan R Nair, K. Madhava Krishna, and Vineet Gandhi

International Institute of Information Technology, Hyderabad, India
{nivedita.rufus,unni.krishnan}@research.iiit.ac.in,
{mkrishna,vgandhi}@iiit.ac.in

Abstract. In this paper, we present a simple baseline for visual grounding for autonomous driving which outperforms the state of the art methods, while retaining minimal design choices. Our framework minimizes the cross-entropy loss over the cosine distance between multiple image ROI features with a text embedding (representing the given sentence/phrase). We use pre-trained networks for obtaining the initial embeddings and learn a transformation layer on top of the text embedding. We perform experiments on the Talk2Car dataset and achieve 68.7% AP50 accuracy, improving upon the previous state of the art by 8.6%. Our investigation suggests reconsideration towards more approaches employing sophisticated attention mechanisms or multi-stage reasoning or complex metric learning loss functions by showing promise in simpler alternatives.

Keywords: Autonomous driving · Visual grounding · Deep learning

1 Introduction

The launch of Level 5 autonomous vehicles requires the removal of all human controls. This warrants the need for a better system to direct the self-driving agent to perform maneuvers if the passenger wishes to do so. A convenient way to do so is through language based controls, where you can direct the car using natural language instructions. Sriram et al. [23] were one of the first to address the problem, and they proposed a method to directly guide the car based on language instructions. However, the focus of the paper is on navigation aspect i.e. to employ 3D semantic maps to directly generate waypoints. They used minimal language instructions and their work cannot handle situations where the commands specify maneuvers which are described in rich detail and requires the maneuvers to be spatially constrained around them. We illustrate couple of such richly described examples in Fig. 1.

To perform a requested maneuver the self-driving agent would be required to perform two steps. First, the agent should interpret the given command and ground it to some part of the visual space around it. Secondly, the agent has to devise a plan to perform the maneuver in this visual scene. Our paper focuses

© Springer Nature Switzerland AG 2020
A. Bartoli and A. Fusiello (Eds.): ECCV 2020 Workshops, LNCS 12536, pp. 39–50, 2020.
https://doi.org/10.1007/978-3-030-66096-3_4

"My friend is the guy standing closest to the curb, next to that car in front of us. Pull over so he can get in".   *"Wait for this bus to pass, then turn left here. I mean right sorry".*

Fig. 1. Illustrative examples of the visually grounded bounding boxes for the given commands. The ground truth bounding box is in red and the predicted bounding box is in cyan.

on this former step, or more concretely: given an image I and a command C, the goal is to find the region R in the image I that C is referring to. The task is commonly known as visual grounding or object referral and has been extensively studies in the past [16,19,21]. However, most of the previous studies uses generic datasets and our work focuses on the application of autonomous driving. More specifically, our work employs the recently proposed Talk2Car dataset [7] and our paper comes as an official entry to the Commands 4 Autonomous Vehicles (C4AV) competition 2020. The C4AV challenge reduces the complexity of the object referral task to the case where there is only one targeted object that is referred to in the natural language command. Here, the human occupant is expected to instruct the vehicle with natural language commands to perform actions subjected to predominantly the spatial information from the scene, such as *'Park behind the white car'* or *'Stop next to the pedestrian on the left'*.

There are two common methodologies to tackle the task of visual grounding. The first is to learn a coordinated representation for the image and text, such that matching pairs are highly correlated in the embedded space [10,15,18,27]. Such methods are trained using margin based loss functions (contrastive, triplet etc.). While inference such models compute proposals and select the proposal with maximum correlation for the given text. The major challenge with these methods is difficulty in training due to the requirement of hard negative mining. The other line of approach employs attention modelling [3,21]. In supervised setting, these methods learn a joint embedding space and employ a classification loss to ground the correct proposal [21] or even regress the bounding box refinements around each proposal [3]. Some works employ multiple stages of attention based reasoning [2]. In this work, we align these two streams of thoughts into a single design and employ a classification loss over cosine distance vector of multiple region proposal embeddings over a given sentence embedding. Albeit simple, our experiments show that such a minimal design can outperform state of the art approaches by a significant margin. Formally, our work makes following contributions:

– We propose a novel formulation which combines cross modal metric distances with a proposal level cross entropy loss on a given image.
– We perform experiments on the Talk2Car [7] dataset and achieve 68.7% AP50 accuracy on the test dataset provided by the Commands 4 Autonomous Vehicles (c4av) competition. Our work improves upon the previous state of the art [6] by 8.6%
– We present extensive ablation study to motivate the choice of the base image and language embedding networks. The code for our work is publicly available at: https://github.com/niveditarufus/CMSVG

2   Related Work

Learning coordinated representations has been a common methodology in visual grounding literature. Given the image text feature, the aim here is to find projections of both views into a joint space of common dimensionality in which the correlation between the views is maximized. The correlation is often defined using cosine and euclidean metric. Early efforts rely on linear projections of the views/embeddings and use Canonical Correlation Analysis [19]. More recent efforts employ deep networks on pre trained embeddings to learn a non linear projection [10,26,27]. Most of these approaches employ the idea of region proposals and the goal is to find the best matching proposal in the image for a given phrase. The correlation networks is trained using a contrastive loss or a triplet loss. The requirement of hard negative mining remains a challenging factor in these approaches. A set of interesting proposal based efforts have been made in weakly supervised setting [4,15], which use caption image alignment as the downstream task to guide the process of phrase localization.

Attention modelling is another common methodology to solve the problem of visual phrase grounding. Rohrbach et al. [21] learn a joint embedding and give supervision over the attention to be given to each proposal. They also present an unsupervised formulation, using a proxy task of phrase reconstruction. They hypothesise that the phrase can only be reconstructed correctly if attention happens over correct proposal. Several approaches avoid object proposal and directly learn a spatial attention map instead. Javed et al. [14] uses concept learning as a proxy task. Akbari et al. [1] address visual grounding by learning a multi-level common semantic space shared by the textual and visual modalities.

Our method also relates to the work by Hu et al. [12], which models this problem as a scoring function on candidate boxes for object retrieval, integrating spatial configurations and global scene-level contextual information into the network. Yu et al. [28] address visual grounding using three modular components related to subject appearance, location, and relationship to other objects. Our work, moves away from instance level training to an image level training, where a proposal out of multiple candidates is picked using the cross entropy loss.

Some efforts have been made specific to the autonomous driving scenario. The work by Sriram et al. [23] directly regresses waypoints (the next point for the car to move) for the car based on natural language instructions. However, they work on a limited vocabulary of instructions. The proposal of Talk2Car [7] dataset al.lows a richer exploration for the visual grounding task in autonomous driving scenarios. The work by Deruyttere et al. [6] decomposes a query in a multistep reasoning process while continuously ranking 2D image regions during each step leading to low-scoring regions to be ignored during the reasoning process. This extends the work by Hudson et al. [13] for multistep reasoning. Our work significantly reduces the complexity of the visual grounding architecture while outperforming several baselines and the state of the art model [6].

(a) All region proposals generated by the RPN

(b) The chosen object proposal(cyan) which is referred to by the command

Fig. 2. Textual annotations are added to the nuScenes dataset [2] in the Talk2Car dataset. Each of the textual annotations refers to an object in the scene in the form of a command. The relevant object is selected from the proposals generated by the RPN. (a) shows the different bounding boxes generated by the RPN. The command corresponding to the (b) is *"Park next to the truck"*

3   The Proposed Model

First, an object detector is used to extract region proposals from the input image. In this work, we use the pre-computed proposals provided to us by the competition organizers. These proposals are extracted using CenterNet [9] as the RPN(**R**egion **P**roposal **N**etwork) and are illustrated in Fig. 2. Second, we match the region proposals with the command. In particular, we compute the cosine similarity values between the encodings of the region proposals and the transformed sentence embedding of the command. These similarity values are considered as a score for how well the bounding box fits the command.

Let us assume an object in the image I is referenced by a command C. From the image I we obtain a set of region proposals (each enclosing an object) R_i, $(i = 1, 2, ...P)$,where P is the number of proposals per image, generated by CenterNet [9]. Each of the proposals is passed through an image encoder to obtain the feature vector $\phi_I(R_i)$. The transformation T on sentence encoded feature vector of C is given by $T(\phi_C(C))$, where $\phi_C(C)$ is the feature vector obtained from the sentence encoder. S_i measures the feature similarity i.e. the

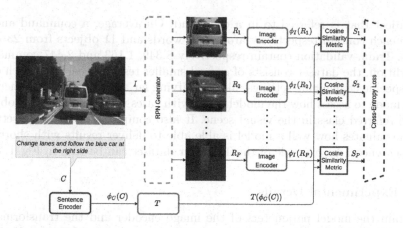

Fig. 3. This figure shows an overview of the proposed method. We compute the cosine similarity between each of the encodings of the region proposals (from the image encoder) and the sentence embedding of the command (from the sentence encoder). The cosine similarity values are then considered as a score for how well the given bounding box fits the command. The criterion used for calculating the loss is a combination of Log-Softmax Loss and Negative Log Likelihood Loss.

cosine similarity between $\phi_I(R_i)$ and $T(\phi_C(C))$ for each proposal R_i, according to (1).

$$S_i = \frac{\phi_I(R_i) \cdot T(\phi_C(C))}{|\phi_I(R_i)||T(\phi_C(C))|}, i = 1, 2, ...P \qquad (1)$$

To estimate the loss L, the criterion we employed that combines Log-Softmax loss and Negative Log Likelihood loss i.e. Cross-Entropy Loss, is given by (2).

$$\alpha = \frac{\exp(S_g)}{\sum_{i=1}^{P} \exp(S_i)} \qquad (2)$$

$$L = -\log(\alpha)$$

where, S_g is the score of the ground-truth proposal. We use pre-trained networks for obtaining the initial embeddings and learn a transformation layer on top of the sentence embedding. These model parameters are tuned using SGD with a small initial learning rate.

4 Experiments and Results

4.1 Dataset

The Talk2Car [7] dataset contains 9,217 images from the nuScenes [2] dataset which have been taken in Sinagpore or Boston in different weather conditions as well as time conditions. They are annotated with natural language commands for self-driving cars, bounding boxes of scene objects, and the bounding box of the object that is referred to in a command. On average, a command and an image each contain respectively around 11 words and 11 objects from 23 categories. Train, validation contain respectively 8,349, 1,163 and 2,447 commands. In addition, the dataset consists of several smaller test sets, each of which evaluate specific challenging settings, like identifying far away objects. Another test set is made to assess how the model copes with cases which has multiple objects of the referred class in the visual scene. It also comprises of test case settings which evaluates how well a model is able able to deliver results with short and long sentences. An example of the Talk2Car dataset can be seen in Fig. 1.

4.2 Experimental Details

We train the model parameters of the image encoder and the transformation block which is a fully-connected layer for 20 epochs using SGD with Nesterov momentum 0.9. The initial learning is set to 0.01 and decayed by a factor 10 every 4 epochs. We use batches of size 8 and a weight decay term 1e–4. The model can be trained in 1 h on four Nvidia 1080ti GPUs. Our best model obtains 68.7% AP50 on the test set.

4.3 Evaluation Metric

We compare our method against some existing baseline approaches and also compare different different design choices for our model. This study was carried out on the Talk2Car [7] dataset. The metric used for the comaparison is their respective AP50 scores on the dataset. AP50 score is defined as the percentage of the predicted bounding boxes that have an Intersection over Union (IoU) with the ground truth bounding boxes of over 0.5.

4.4 Ablation Study

In this section we also show a detailed ablation study of how our model varies with various parameters and design choices. We studied the effect of the no. of proposals chosen has on the AP50 score in Table 1.

Table 1. This table shows the variation of the AP50 scores on the test data with the number of region proposals generated by the RPN being used. The image encoder used is EfficientNet-B2 and the language encoder is STS RoBERTa(large).

No. of proposals	AP50 on the test data
8	62.9
16	66.9
32	68.7
48	67.0
64	65.2

We also observe the trends of ResNet family of image encoders Table 2 and the EfficientNet family of image encoders in Table 3. We also study how the model performance varies with the different language encoders based on BERT [8], RoBERTa [17] and DistilBERT [22] trained on the STS [20] benchmarking.

Table 2. This table shows the variation of the AP50 scores on the test data with various language encoders and the ResNet class of image encoders. Top 32 proposals generated by the RPN were used.

Sentence embedding	AP50 score on the test data				
	resnet-18	resnet-34	resnet-50	resnet-101	resnet-152
STS BERT(base)	65.9	**66.6**	66.2	66.4	64.9
STS BERT(large)	66.5	**67.6**	66.7	64.9	65.1
STS RoBERTa(base)	66.5	65.8	64.4	65.5	**66.8**
STS RoBERTa(large)	66.4	**67.6**	67.0	64.8	65.6
STS DistilBERT(base)	66.1	**66.7**	65.1	66.6	65.8

Table 1 was generated from STS RoBERTa(large) as the language encoder and EfficientNet-B2 as the image encoder (our best performing model). From Table 1 we can infer that having too few proposals result in the object of interest being missed out. On the contrary, having too many proposals not only slows down the network but also decreases the performance. This can be attributed to the presence of multiple similar objects which contribute to the ambiguity in choosing the object that needs to be grounded. To get the best of both worlds, having 32 proposals seems to be a good trade-off.

Table 3. This table shows the variation of the AP50 scores on the test data with various language encoders and the EfficientNet class of image encoders. Top 32 proposals generated by the RPN were used.

Sentence embedding	AP50 score on the test data				
	B0	B1	B2	B3	B4
STS BERT(base)	65.8	**67.4**	67.0	66.3	65.2
STS BERT(large)	67.3	**67.8**	67.3	66.4	65.7
STS RoBERTa(base)	66.9	66.5	**67.6**	66.5	65.8
STS RoBERTa(large)	68.2	67.0	**68.7**	66.1	65.7
STS DistilBERT(base)	**67.8**	66.9	67.1	67.3	65.8

All the results in Table 2 and Table 3 were generated with 32 proposals. Though our best performing model turns out to be a combination of STS RoBERTa(large) as the language encoder and EfficientNet-B2 as the image encoder, STS DistilBERT(base) as the language encoder and EfficientNet-B0

(a) *"Follow the black car that is on your right"*.

(b) *"Do not move too close to this vehicle in front of us"*.

(c) *"Slow down, because there is a man standing in traffic"*.

(d) *"Drop me off behind the red car"*.

Fig. 4. Illustrative examples of when our model predicts the grounded bounding boxes for the given commands correctly. The ground truth bounding box is in red and the predicted bounding box is in cyan.

as the image encoder yields quite close results at a much lower model complexity and higher inference speed. So, this would be the go-to option for real-time implementation. Another observation that can be made is that having deeper networks for the image encoders(both ResNet and EfficientNet) does not really improve the AP50 scores for the images. On the contrary, we get comparable or in some cases worse performance.

4.5 Qualitative Results

Some samples of how well our model performed can be visualized from Fig. 4 and where it fails to deliver good results can be visualized in Fig. 5. In the cases where it fails it can be seen that in Fig. 5b the truck is not visible because of occlusion due to fog, similarly in Fig. 5a the statement is ambiguous since both the cars are on the right and are candidates for an overtake. In Fig. 5c and Fig. 5d there are multiple objects from the same class, people and cars, respectively, so our model is not able to make such fine tuned distinction.

4.6 Comparison with Existing Methods

The improvements we got from the baseline for the competition [25] were majorly due to the embedding from the natural language encoding. Utilizing the embedding which used attention on the important parts of the sentence was a major

(a) *"Accelerate and pass the car on the right, then change into the right lane".*

(b) *"Let the red truck pass while continuing straight. Also use your windshield swipers man I do not see anything anymore".*

(c) *"Do not proceed until this worker has cleared the intersection".*

(d) *"Park next to the 4x4".*

Fig. 5. Illustrative examples of when our model fails to predict the grounded bounding boxes for the given commands correctly. The ground truth bounding box is in red and the predicted bounding box is in cyan.

Table 4. This table shows the comparison of the AP50 scores on the validation data with the existing state-of-the-art methods. The image encoder EfficientNet-B2 and the language encoder STS RoBERTa(large) is used for our model.

S.No.	Name of the method	AP50 on the validation data
1.	MAC	50.51
2.	STACK	33.71
3.	SCRC(top-32)	43.80
4.	A-ATT(top-16)	45.12
5.	MSRR(top-16)	60.04
6	CMSVG(ours)	**68.20**

contributor to the improvement in the performance. This might be because the average sentence length is 11 and there are sentences as big as 30+ words and attention helps the model to learn what is important in such a large command. We compare our model with the existing models in Table 4.

Our best performing model utilized EfficientNet-B2 [24] as the image encoder for the top 32 proposals and RoBERTa [17] pre-trained on STS benchmarking followed by a fully connected layer to calculate the cosine similarity score for the natural language encoding. We use this model to compare with the existing methods on the validation dataset of the Talk2Car [7] dataset such as,

- **MAC:** [13] uses a recurrent MAC cell to match the natural language command represented with a Bi-LSTM model with a global representation of the image. The MAC cell decomposes the textual input into a series of reasoning steps, where the MAC cell selectively attends to certain parts of the textual input to guide the model to look at certain parts of the image.
- **STACK:** The Stack Neural Module Network [11] uses multiple modules that can solve a task by automatically inducing a sub-task decomposition, where each sub-task is addressed by a separate neural module. These modules can be chained together to decompose the natural language command into a reasoning process.
- **SCRC:** [12] A shortcoming of the provided baseline [25] is that the correct region has to be selected based on local information alone. Spatial Context Recurrent ConvNets match both local and global information with an encoding of the command.
- **A-ATT:** [5] Formulates these challenges as three attention problems and propose an accumulated attention (A-ATT) mechanism to reason among them jointly. Their A-ATT mechanism can circularly accumulate the attention for useful information in image, query, and objects, while the noises are ignored gradually.
- **MSRR:** [6] Integrates the regions of a Region Proposal Network (RPN) into a new multi-step reasoning model which we have named a Multimodal Spatial Region Reasoner (MSRR). The introduced model uses the object regions from an RPN as initialization of a 2D spatial memory and then implements a multi-step reasoning process scoring each region according to the query.

5   Conclusion and Future Work

This paper formulates and evaluates a very simple baseline that beats the previous state of the art performance in this specific grounding task.

We used pre-trained networks for obtaining the initial embeddings and learned a transformation layer on the text embedding. We performed experiments on the Talk2Car dataset and achieve 68.7% AP50 accuracy, improving upon the previous state of the art by 8.6%. Our investigation suggests reconsideration towards more simple approaches than employing sophisticated attention mechanisms or multi-stage reasoning, by showing promise in simpler alternatives.

We plan to integrate the depth data with LiDAR-camera calibration for further improvements. We also plan to work on the planning and navigation part and get it working in CARLA for a proof of concept work before integrating it with our in house autonomous driving vehicle SWAHANA.

Acknowledgement. This work was supported in part by Qualcomm Innovation Fellowship (QIF 2020) from Qualcomm Technologies, Inc.

References

1. Akbari, H., Karaman, S., Bhargava, S., Chen, B., Vondrick, C., Chang, S.F.: Multi-level multimodal common semantic space for image-phrase grounding. In: Proceedings of the IEEE Conference on Computer Vision and Pattern Recognition, pp. 12476–12486 (2019)
2. Caesar, H., et al.: Nuscenes: a multimodal dataset for autonomous driving (2019)
3. Chen, K., Kovvuri, R., Nevatia, R.: Query-guided regression network with context policy for phrase grounding. In: Proceedings of the IEEE International Conference on Computer Vision, pp. 824–832 (2017)
4. Datta, S., Sikka, K., Roy, A., Ahuja, K., Parikh, D., Divakaran, A.: Align2ground: weakly supervised phrase grounding guided by image-caption alignment. In: Proceedings of the IEEE International Conference on Computer Vision, pp. 2601–2610 (2019)
5. Deng, C., Wu, Q., Wu, Q., Hu, F., Lyu, F., Tan, M.: Visual grounding via accumulated attention. In: 2018 IEEE/CVF Conference on Computer Vision and Pattern Recognition. pp. 7746–7755 (2018)
6. Deruyttere, T., Collell, G., Moens, M.F.: Giving commands to a self-driving car: a multimodal reasoner for visual grounding (2020)
7. Deruyttere, T., Vandenhende, S., Grujicic, D., Van Gool, L., Moens, M.F.: Talk2car: taking control of your self-driving car. In: Proceedings of the 2019 Conference on Empirical Methods in Natural Language Processing and the 9th International Joint Conference on Natural Language Processing (EMNLP-IJCNLP) (2019). 10.18653/v1/d19-1215, http://dx.doi.org/10.18653/v1/D19-1215
8. Devlin, J., Chang, M.W., Lee, K., Toutanova, K.: Bert: pre-training of deep bidirectional transformers for language understanding (2018)
9. Duan, K., Bai, S., Xie, L., Qi, H., Huang, Q., Tian, Q.: Centernet: keypoint triplets for object detection. In: Proceedings of the IEEE International Conference on Computer Vision (2019)
10. Engilberge, M., Chevallier, L., Pérez, P., Cord, M.: Finding beans in burgers: deep semantic-visual embedding with localization. In: Proceedings of the IEEE Conference on Computer Vision and Pattern Recognition, pp. 3984–3993 (2018)
11. Hu, R., Andreas, J., Darrell, T., Saenko, K.: Explainable neural computation via stack neural module networks. In: Proceedings of the European conference on computer vision (ECCV) (2018)
12. Hu, R., Xu, H., Rohrbach, M., Feng, J., Saenko, K., Darrell, T.: Natural language object retrieval. In: Proceedings of the IEEE Conference on Computer Vision and Pattern Recognition (2016)
13. Hudson, D.A., Manning, C.D.: Compositional attention networks for machine reasoning (2018)
14. Javed, S.A., Saxena, S., Gandhi, V.: Learning unsupervised visual grounding through semantic self-supervision. arXiv preprint arXiv:1803.06506 (2018)
15. Karpathy, A., Joulin, A., Fei-Fei, L.: Deep fragment embeddings for bidirectional image sentence mapping (2014)
16. Kazemzadeh, S., Ordonez, V., Matten, M., Berg, T.: Referitgame: referring to objects in photographs of natural scenes. In: Proceedings of the 2014 Conference on Empirical Methods in Natural Language Processing (EMNLP), pp. 787–798 (2014)
17. Liu, Y., et al.: Roberta: a robustly optimized bert pretraining approach (2019)

18. Musgrave, K., Belongie, S., Lim, S.N.: A metric learning reality check. arXiv preprint arXiv:2003.08505 (2020)
19. Plummer, B.A., Wang, L., Cervantes, C.M., Caicedo, J.C., Hockenmaier, J., Lazebnik, S.: Flickr30k entities: collecting region-to-phrase correspondences for richer image-to-sentence models. In: Proceedings of the IEEE International Conference on Computer Vision, pp. 2641–2649 (2015)
20. Reimers, N., Gurevych, I.: Sentence-bert: sentence embeddings using siamese bert-networks. In: Proceedings of the 2019 Conference on Empirical Methods in Natural Language Processing. Association for Computational Linguistics (2019). http://arxiv.org/abs/1908.10084
21. Rohrbach, A., Rohrbach, M., Hu, R., Darrell, T., Schiele, B.: Grounding of textual phrases in images by reconstruction. In: Leibe, B., Matas, J., Sebe, N., Welling, M. (eds.) ECCV 2016. LNCS, vol. 9905, pp. 817–834. Springer, Cham (2016). https://doi.org/10.1007/978-3-319-46448-0_49
22. Sanh, V., Debut, L., Chaumond, J., Wolf, T.: Distilbert, a distilled version of bert: smaller, faster, cheaper and lighter (2019)
23. Sriram, N.N., Maniar, T., Kalyanasundaram, J., Gandhi, V., Bhowmick, B., Madhava Krishna, K.: Talk to the vehicle: language conditioned autonomous navigation of self driving cars. In: 2019 IEEE/RSJ International Conference on Intelligent Robots and Systems (IROS), pp. 5284–5290 (2019)
24. Tan, M., Le, Q.V.: Efficientnet: rethinking model scaling for convolutional neural networks (2019)
25. Vandenhende, S., Deruyttere, T., Grujicic, D.: A baseline for the commands for autonomous vehicles challenge (2020)
26. Wang, L., Li, Y., Huang, J., Lazebnik, S.: Learning two-branch neural networks for image-text matching tasks. IEEE Trans. Pattern Anal. Mach. Intell. **41**(2), 394–407 (2018)
27. Wang, L., Li, Y., Lazebnik, S.: Learning deep structure-preserving image-text embeddings. In: Proceedings of the IEEE Conference on Computer Vision and Pattern Recognition, pp. 5005–5013 (2016)
28. Yu, L., et al.: Mattnet: modular attention network for referring expression comprehension. In: Proceedings of the IEEE Conference on Computer Vision and Pattern Recognition, pp. 1307–1315 (2018)

Attention Enhanced Single Stage Multimodal Reasoner

Jie Ou and Xinying Zhang[(⊠)]

University of Electronic Science and Technology of China, Chengdu 611731, China
oujieww6@gmail.com, xyzhang676@gmail.com

Abstract. In this paper, we propose an Attention Enhanced Single Stage Multimodal Reasoner (ASSMR) to tackle the object referral task in the self-driving car scenario. We extract features from each modality and establish attention mechanisms to jointly process them. The Key Words Extractor (KWE) is used to extract the attribute and position/scale information of the target in the command, which are used to score the corresponding features through the Position/Scale Attention Module (P/SAM) and the Object Attention Module (OAM). Based on the attention mechanism, the effective part of the position/scale feature, the object attribute feature and the semantic feature of the command is enhanced. Finally, we map different features to a common embedding space to predict the final result. Our method is based on the simplified version of the Talk2Car dataset, and scored on 66.4 AP50 on the test set, while using the official region proposals.

Keywords: Attention · Multimodal · Self-driving

1 Introduction

Visual Grounding (VG) is a very important task in the field of artificial intelligence, involving cutting-edge technologies such as computer vision [16] and natural language processing [9]. Visual Grounding requires the model to parse the textual query and then locate the corresponding object for the query from the image, which is different from the object detection task which only requires the model to detect the regions of interest. Visual Grounding is one of the most challenging tasks of artificial intelligence, as machines need to comprehend both the complicated visual scene and the language [11].

In recent years, with the development of deep learning, there has been a rapid development of many technical fields (computer vision, natural language processing, recommendation algorithms, etc.). The industry is actively seeking commercial value for these fields, especially in automatic/assisted driving, where many scholars and companies have been actively conducting research and development and road testing. VG has very broad prospects and application scenarios in this regard, for instance, when taking a ride in a self-driving car, the passenger might want to instruct the car by giving it a command such as "I need to follow the silver car" (Fig. 1).

© Springer Nature Switzerland AG 2020
A. Bartoli and A. Fusiello (Eds.): ECCV 2020 Workshops, LNCS 12536, pp. 51–61, 2020.
https://doi.org/10.1007/978-3-030-66096-3_5

Fig. 1. Example command for a self-driving car. Command: "I need to follow **the silver car**". The referred object is indicated with the blue bounding box in the image, red boxes is other objects generated by detector.

In this paper, we propose an Attention Enhanced Single Stage Multimodal Reasoner (ASSMR), to deal with the scenarios such as the one described in Fig. 1. We have built a variety of feature extractors for different information: 1) An Easy NLP module for words and linguistic features; 2) A linear transformer for position and scale features; 3) A trainable convolutional neural network for object features; 4) A fixed convolutional neural network for global features. We subsequently establish a variety of attention mechanisms to enhance different types of features: 1) Key Words Extractor (KWE), used to extract the attribute and position/scale information of the target from the command; 2) Position/Scale Attention Module (P/SAM), used to score the position/scale features; 3) Object Attention Module (OAM), used to score the object attribute features; 4) Relationship based Attention Module (RAM), used to refine the textual semantic features by visual and language features. Finally, we map different features to the common embedding space in order to match visual features with language features. We evaluate our method on the Talk2Car dataset [4] which is a referring expression dataset that contains referring commands given to self-driving cars. This dataset consists of multiple modalities (LIDAR, RADAR, Video, ...), however, we only focus on the images and the referring expressions in this paper.

2   Related Work

The Visual Grounding (VG) task involves the localization of image regions relevant to given natural language expressions [13,17]. Karpathy *et al.* [10] used the inner product between the text expression and the representations of detected regions to rank the regions of objects. Yu *et al.* [18] inspired by image captioning task, generated captions for each object, and subsequently compared them with the query. Hu *et al.* [7] employed three LSTMs to process linguistic, local and global information, and output the probability of the query text conditioned on each candidate box as a score for the box. Rohrbach *et al.* [14] trained a visual grounding model by reconstructing the query phrase using the attention mechanism. Liu *et al.* [12] designed a novel cross-modal attention-guided erasing approach to discover complementary textual-visual correspondences with online generation of difficult training samples.

Deng *et al.* [2] proposed an accumulated attention (A-ATT) mechanism to aggregate the attention for useful information in image, query, and objects. The A-ATT, which is a multi-stage method, refines the result according to the predicted results of the previous stage. Hudson *et al.* [8] decomposed the problem into a series of attention-based reasoning steps, each performed by a Memory, Attention, and Composition (MAC) cell. Deruyttere *et al.* [3] built a multi-step Multimodal Spatial Region Reasoner (MSRR) model, where the multi-step reasoning process was employed jointly over the natural language expression and the image with a spatial 2D map for the recognized objects. Although many of the previously mentioned works have demonstrated that a multi-stage reasoning process could achieve better results, these approaches are often computationally intensive. It can be found that the model tends to select the final answer after the first reasoning step, and that the subsequent refinement process consumes more computing resources without bringing much benefit [2]. Furthermore, it has been demonstrated that not all additional stages help improve the result [3]. Therefore, in this paper, we build a single-stage multimodal reasoner with richer attention mechanisms used to strengthen different features compared to the previous works, and establish a Relationship based Attention Module (RAM) to refine the textual semantic features by using visual and language features.

3   Methodology

Our Attention Enhanced Single Stage Multimodal Reasoner (ASSMR) uses the region proposals from the CenterNet [19], included in the Talk2Car dataset [4]. Our pipeline, where we build four information extractors for the textual query, position/scale, global information and objects features, is shown in Fig. 2. We then use a series of different attention mechanisms to strengthen the effective features, after which the different types of features are fused and the result predicted in the common embedding/hidden space.

Easy NLP Module. For a textual query, such as "follow that truck up ahead", we build an Easy NLP module to extract linguistic features. At first, we use the Embedding Layer to transform words into dense vector representations, and then use a bidirectional GRU to obtain the features for each individual word as well as the whole query, $words \in \mathbb{R}^{n \times b \times c}$ and $Qe \in \mathbb{R}^{b \times c}$, where n is the number of words in the command, b is the batch size and c is the channel size, after which we combine outputs for both directions.

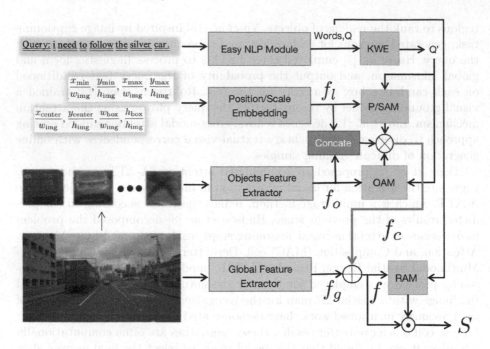

Fig. 2. The pipeline of our method.

Key Words Extractor (KWE). In this module, we aim to extract two types of important information: position/scale and object attribute features, which are very important for locating the target. We use the linear transformation to transform the Qe into the same hidden space as $words$, and then Qe is used as a query to locate the key words. A linear layer is used to predict the similarity score between the transformed query and each word in the sequence. The operation of the KWE module is described by the expressions:

$$words' = W_1(words), \tag{1}$$

$$Q' = Sum(Softmax(W_2(words' \odot Qe)) \odot words), \tag{2}$$

where W_1 and W_2 denote the transformations performed by the linear layers. We use Softmax function to normalize the score for each $word$, and finally we merge them together to get $Q' \in \mathbb{R}^{b \times c}$, which contains the position/scale and attribute linguistic features.

Position/Scale Embbedding. In many commands (e.g. "find a place to park near that big white car on the left."), we come across occurrences of words referring to the scale and position of the target object. This kind of information is very distinguishing and useful, and can therefore be used to effectively filter out certain objects. We use a fixed-length vector to represent each candidate region, which consists of two pieces of information: the spatial and scale information. Following [1,2], we formulate this information for each object candidate as:

$$O_l = \left[\frac{x_{min}}{w_{img}}, \frac{y_{min}}{h_{img}}, \frac{x_{max}}{w_{img}}, \frac{y_{max}}{h_{img}}, \right.$$
$$\left. \frac{x_{center}}{w_{img}}, \frac{y_{center}}{h_{img}}, \frac{w_{box}}{w_{img}}, \frac{h_{box}}{h_{img}} \right], \tag{3}$$

where w and h represent width and height, respectively. The subscript box denotes the bounding box, and subscript img denotes for the image. In contrast to the aforementioned works, we perform an additional transformation in order to extract richer features,

$$f_l = W_3(O_l), \tag{4}$$

where the W_3 donates the linear layer, which transforms the original position/scale information into the embedding/hidden space. The BatchNorm layers are used before and after the linear layer to automatically normalize the features, and ReLU is used as activation.

Position/Scale Attention Module (P/SAM). We establish a linguistic-driven attention mechanism on the position/scale embedding result, as we want to directly use the query and the position/scale information to conduct a pre-scoring process. The query features used in this module are Q', previously generated by the Key Words Extractor (KWE). The operation of the P/SAM module is described by the expression:

$$weight_l = Sigmoid(W_5(W_4(Q') \odot f_l)), \tag{5}$$

where Q' is mapped to the same space as f_l by using a linear transformation, and another linear layer is subsequently used to predict the score for each object directly. As more than one target may meet the corresponding conditions, the sigmoid function is used.

Objects Feature Extractor. This module is used for obtaining the local object features. We crop the patches from the original image based on the bounding box, resize them to 224×224, and use the ResNet18 [5] to extract the feature vector for each patch, f_v. We express this part of the operation as follows:

$$f_o = W_6(f_v). \tag{6}$$

where the W_6 is another linear layer as mentioned above.

Objects Attention Module (OAM). Similarly to the Position/Scale Attention Module (P/SAM), this is another linguistic-driven attention mechanism which attends to the object features based on the linguistic features. We map Q' into the same space as visual features, and compute the weight.

$$weight_o = Sigmoid(W_8(W_7(Q') \odot f_o)), \tag{7}$$

The computational process is very similar to the P/SAM. We subsequently merge the two categories of features, the position/scale features and the object attribute features, and weigh them by the outputs of the P/SAM and OAM modules, as described by the expression:

$$f_c = [f_o, f_l] \odot weight_o + [f_o, f_l] \odot weight_l, \tag{8}$$

where $[,]$ donates the concatination operation, and f_c is the final weighted feature vector.

Global Feature Extractor (GFE). We use ResNet101 to directly perform feature extraction on the whole image. We extract the feature maps from layer3, donate as f_{l3}, and then use linear transformation and global pooling to obtain the feature vector.

$$f_g = pool(W_9(f_{l3})), \tag{9}$$

We then combine the global features with the local object features, extracted from the OAM module:

$$f = f_g + f_c. \tag{10}$$

Thus, each object vector could carry the features of the whole image.

Relationship Based Attention Module (RAM). Sometimes, the command contains descriptions of the relationships between the targets. We aim to extract these relationships through memory and control strategies, and correct the Qe via channel attention. We concatenate the *words* with f, and use a GRU to implement memory and control strategies.

$$Qe' = GRU([words, f]) + Qe, \tag{11}$$

The GRU reviews each semantic word vector and visual vector, using special memory gates and forget gates with transformation to describe the relationship between perceived objects based on semantic relationships, and then uses the relationship between objects to optimize the descriptions of commands. Finally, we perform an element-wise multiplication between Qe' and each object feature vector, and compute the final score S for each object by using a linear layer.

4   Experiments

4.1   Experiment Setup

Dataset. The Commands For Autonomous Vehicles (C4AV) challenge is based on the Talk2Car dataset [4]. Where each sample consists of an image, a command referring to one of the objects in the image and 64 region proposals for each image predicted by finetuning the CenterNet [19]. The dataset is divided into the training set, validation set and test set, consisting of 8349, 1163 and 3610 samples, respectively [15].

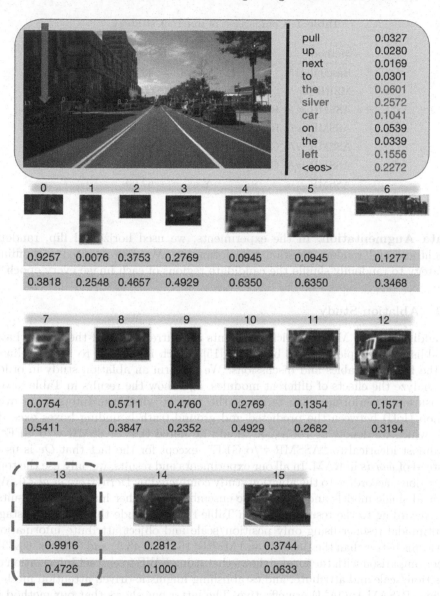

Fig. 3. The visualization of the attention mechanisms. We marked the important words in the command (red) and showed the score of each word. It should be noted that the score does not completely represent the importance of the current word. We show the position/scale attention score (gray) and object attribute attention score (orange) of each candidate region (Color figure online).

Training Detail. We train the model for 22 epochs using SGD with nesterov momentum 0.9. The initial learning is set to 0.01 and decayed by a factor 10 every 4 epochs. We use batch size 18 and a weight decay term 1e–4. The model can be trained in four hours on a single Nvidia 1080ti GPU.

Table 1. Comparison of different strategy

Method	Augment	$IoU_{0.5}(\%)$
Baseline [15]	No	43.5
MSRR [3]	–	60.33
ASSMR w/o RAM,GFE	No	64.4
ASSMR w/o RAM,GFE	Yes	65.58
ASSMR w/o GFE*	Yes	66.61
ASSMR w/o GFE	Yes	67.64
ASSMR	Yes	67.90

Data Augmentation. In the experiments, we used horizontal flip, random brightness and random rotation transformation. We also adopted a shuffling strategy to randomly shuffle the candidate regions of each image every epoch.

4.2 Ablation Study

In addition to the MSRR, which represents the current state-of-the-art, we have established a simple baseline based on [15], which is referred to as "Baseline" in the following tables and discussions. We perform an ablation study in order to analyze the effects of different modules, and show the results in Table 1. We measure the performance in terms of the rate at which the Intersection over Union (IoU) between the predicted and ground-truth bounding boxes exceeds 0.5, which we denote as $IoU_{0.5}$. It should be noted that "ASSMR w/o GFE*" is almost identical to "ASSMR w/o GFE", except for the fact that Qe is used instead of $words$ in RAM. In all our experiments and results, we only use the top-16 regions, according to the ablation study conducted by Deruyttere *et al.* [3]. We trained single models and did not use ensembles to further improve our results.

According to the results shown in Table 1, we conclude that our singe-stage multimodal resoner using only position/scale and object attribute information performs better than the Baseline and MSRR, (64.4 vs. 43.5) and (64.4 vs. 60.33). The comparison with the former shows that using KWE to extract information of position/scale and attribute, and establishing linguistic-driven attention mechanisms (P/SAM & OAM) are effective. The latter one shows that our method is able to obtain better results than a multi stage reasoning approach. Our image augmentation with shuffle strategy further improves $IoU_{0.5}$ by 1.18%. The RAM module improves the final result by a further 1.03% when using Qe, and by 2.06% when using encoded $words$ as input features. This shows that the RAM makes use of mutual relationships between language descriptions and visual objects to disambiguate between different candidate regions. Finally, adding the global information further improves the result, achieving the $IoU_{0.5}$ of 67.90% on the test set. Figure 3 showcases an example that demonstrates the operation of our proposed method.

Table 2. Comparison with the state of the art methods

Method	$IoU_{0.5}$(%)	Inference time (ms)	Params (M)
MAC [8]	50.51	51	41.59
STACK [6]	33.71	52	**35.2**
SCRC (Top-32) [7]	43.80	208	52.47
A-ATT (Top-16) [2]	45.12	180	160.31
MSRR (top-16) [3]	60.04	270.5	62.25
ASSMR (top-16)	**66.4**	**36.02(14.38)**	48.91(21)

4.3 Comparison with the State of the Art Methods

In Table 2, we show a comparison with some of the advanced methods, and one can see that our model reaches 66.4% $IoU_{0.5}$, exceeding the multi-stage method, MAC, A-ATT and MSRR by 15.89%, 21.4% and 6.0%. This proves the effectiveness of our single stage, attention based modular approach.

Additionally, model migration and deployment capabilities, as well as the inference speed, are very important in real-life scenarios. We therefore compare our model in terms of the number of parameters and inference speed, and for a fair comparison, we use the official run-time results with the batch size of 1. We find that our model is very fast, and with the inference time per one image is only 36.02 ms (28 fps), able to run in real-time. Additionally, the model is quite compact, with only 48.91 M parameters.

The value in brackets represents the inference time when the global features (and the Resnet101 used to extract them) are not used, which, as shown in Table 1, can be done at the cost of a very slight performance drop. In this scenario, the inference time per image is as low as 14.38 ms (70 fps) and the number of parameters is reduced to 21 M. This shows that the method we proposed is very fast and effective, and that it could be easily integrated into existing object detection algorithms.

5 Conclusions

This paper has proposed an Attention Enhanced Single-Stage Multimodal Reasoner (ASSMR), which improves the effectiveness and efficiency for Visual Grounding task, especially within the setting of the "Commands 4 Autonomous Vehicles" challenge. A variety of different feature extractors are used to extract different types of information, and linguistic-driven attention mechanisms are used to distinguish the effective and ineffective features. The experimental results show that our method outperforms the current state-of-the-art, achieving 67.9% and 66.4% $IoU_{0.5}$ on validation and test set, respectively. Finally, our model can run in real-time (28 fps), and has a comparatively small number of parameters.

References

1. De Vries, H., Strub, F., Chandar, S., Pietquin, O., Larochelle, H., Courville, A.: Guesswhat?! visual object discovery through multi-modal dialogue. In: Proceedings of the IEEE Conference on Computer Vision and Pattern Recognition, pp. 5503–5512 (2017)
2. Deng, C., Wu, Q., Wu, Q., Hu, F., Lyu, F., Tan, M.: Visual grounding via accumulated attention. In: Proceedings of the IEEE Conference on Computer Vision and Pattern Recognition, pp. 7746–7755 (2018)
3. Deruyttere, T., Collell, G., Moens, M.F.: Giving commands to a self-driving car: a multimodal reasoner for visual grounding. arXiv preprint arXiv:2003.08717 (2020)
4. Deruyttere, T., Vandenhende, S., Grujicic, D., Van Gool, L., Moens, M.F.: Talk2car: Taking control of your self-driving car. arXiv preprint arXiv:1909.10838 (2019)
5. He, K., Zhang, X., Ren, S., Sun, J.: Deep residual learning for image recognition. In: Proceedings of the IEEE Conference on Computer Vision and Pattern Recognition, pp. 770–778 (2016)
6. Hu, R., Andreas, J., Darrell, T., Saenko, K.: Explainable neural computation via stack neural module networks. In: Proceedings of the European Conference on Computer Vision, pp. 53–69 (2018)
7. Hu, R., Xu, H., Rohrbach, M., Feng, J., Saenko, K., Darrell, T.: Natural language object retrieval. In: Proceedings of the IEEE Conference on Computer Vision and Pattern Recognition, pp. 4555–4564 (2016)
8. Hudson, D.A., Manning, C.D.: Compositional attention networks for machine reasoning. arXiv preprint arXiv:1803.03067 (2018)
9. Jones, K.S.: Natural language processing: a historical review. In: Current Issues in Computational Linguistics. In Honour of Don Walker, pp. 3–16. Springer (1994). https://doi.org/10.1007/978-0-585-35958-8_1
10. Karpathy, A., Joulin, A., Fei-Fei, L.F.: Deep fragment embeddings for bidirectional image sentence mapping. In: Advances in Neural Information Processing Systems, pp. 1889–1897 (2014)
11. Krahmer, E., Van Deemter, K.: Computational generation of referring expressions: a survey. Comput. Linguist. $38(1)$, 173–218 (2012)
12. Liu, X., Wang, Z., Shao, J., Wang, X., Li, H.: Improving referring expression grounding with cross-modal attention-guided erasing. In: Proceedings of the IEEE Conference on Computer Vision and Pattern Recognition, pp. 1950–1959 (2019)
13. Mao, J., Huang, J., Toshev, A., Camburu, O., Yuille, A.L., Murphy, K.: Generation and comprehension of unambiguous object descriptions. In: Proceedings of the IEEE Conference on Computer Vision and Pattern Recognition, pp. 11–20 (2016)
14. Rohrbach, A., Rohrbach, M., Hu, R., Darrell, T., Schiele, B.: Grounding of textual phrases in images by reconstruction. In: Leibe, B., Matas, J., Sebe, N., Welling, M. (eds.) ECCV 2016. LNCS, vol. 9905, pp. 817–834. Springer, Cham (2016). https://doi.org/10.1007/978-3-319-46448-0_49
15. Vandenhende, S., Deruyttere, T., Grujicic, D.: A baseline for the commands for autonomous vehicles challenge. arXiv preprint arXiv:2004.13822 (2020)
16. Voulodimos, A., Doulamis, N., Doulamis, A., Protopapadakis, E.: Deep learningfor computer vision: a brief review. Comput. Intell. Neurosci. **2018** (2018)
17. Yu, L., et al.: Mattnet: modular attention network for referring expression comprehension. In: Proceedings of the IEEE Conference on Computer Vision and Pattern Recognition. pp. 1307–1315 (2018)

18. Yu, L., Poirson, P., Yang, S., Berg, A.C., Berg, T.L.: Modeling context in referring expressions. In: Leibe, B., Matas, J., Sebe, N., Welling, M. (eds.) ECCV 2016. LNCS, vol. 9906, pp. 69–85. Springer, Cham (2016). https://doi.org/10.1007/978-3-319-46475-6_5
19. Zhou, X., Wang, D., Krähenbühl, P.: Objects as points. arXiv preprint arXiv:1904.07850 (2019)

AttnGrounder: Talking to Cars with Attention

Vivek Mittal$^{(\boxtimes)}$

Indian Institute of Technology, Mandi, India
b18153@students.iitmandi.ac.in

Abstract. We propose the Attention Grounder (AttnGrounder), a single-stage end-to-end trainable model for the task of visual grounding. Visual grounding aims to localize a specific object in an image based on a given natural language text query. Unlike previous methods that use the same text representation for every image region, we use a visual-text attention module that relates each word in the given query with every region in the corresponding image, constructing a region dependent text representation. Furthermore, to improve the localization ability of our model, we use a visual-text attention module that generates an attention mask around the referred object. The attention mask is trained as an auxiliary task using a rectangular mask generated with the provided ground-truth coordinates. We evaluate the AttnGrounder on the Talk2Car dataset and show an improvement of 3.26% over the existing methods. The code is available at https://github.com/i-m-vivek/AttnGrounder.

Keywords: Object detection · Visual grounding · Attention mechanism

1 Introduction

In recent years, there have been many advances in tasks involving the joint processing of images and text. Researchers are working on various challenging problems like image captioning [1,7,28], visual question answering [1,11,30], text-conditioned image generation [13,31], etc. In this work, we address the task of visual grounding [5,24] in which our goal is to train a model that can localize an image region based on a given natural language text query. The task of visual grounding can be useful in many practical applications. In Fig. 1, we provide an example, in a self-driving car, the passenger can give a command such as *"Do you see that lady walking on the sidewalk, up here on the left. She is the one we need to pick up. Pull over next to her"* to the car. Additional use cases can be found in embodied agents and human-computer interaction. The task of visual grounding is quite challenging as it requires joint reasoning over text and images. Consider the example shown in Fig. 1: in order to correctly identify the women, a model first needs to understand the command properly and then locate the target object in the image.

In this paper, we propose a novel architecture for visual grounding, namely, the AttnGrounder. At a high-level, visual grounding consists of two sub-tasks: object

A. Bartoli and A. Fusiello (Eds.): ECCV 2020 Workshops, LNCS 12536, pp. 62–73, 2020.
https://doi.org/10.1007/978-3-030-66096-3_6

Do you see that lady walking on the sidewalk, up here on the
left. She is the one we need to pick up. Pull over next to her.

Fig. 1. Example of a visual grounding task. Green box indicates the referred object.
(Color figure online)

detection [21,23] and ranking detected objects. In the first task, the model identifies all the objects present in the image, and then it calculates a matching score
between every object and given text query to rank different proposals. These two
tasks are themselves quite challenging to solve, and the object detection task may
become a bottleneck for the performance of the whole system. In contrast to the traditional two-stage [5,29] approaches, our AttnGrounder directly operates on raw
RGB images and text expressions. Our main goal is to combine the image and text
features, and then directly predict bounding boxes from them. To this end, we use
a YOLOv3 [22] backbone to generate visual features (Sect. 3.1) and a Bi-LSTM to
generates text features (Sect. 3.2). In order to jointly reason over visual and text
features, we use two sub-modules: Text Feature Matrix (Sect. 3.3) and Attention
Map (Sect. 3.3). The text feature matrix calculates a text representation for every
image region by selecting important words for that particular region. Predicting a
rough segmentation mask around the referred object can also help in predicting a
bounding box. Thus, we make a rectangular mask around the target object using
the ground truth coordinates, and the goal of our attention map module is to predict that mask. The attention map module is trained jointly with rest of the system
and yields an auxiliary loss which can improve the localization ability of our model.
Finally, we fuse all the features to obtain a multi-modal feature representation with
which we predict the bounding box (Sect. 3.4). In Sect. 2, we give an overview of
the related work. In Sect. 3, we provide a detailed description of our approach. In
Sect. 4, we evaluate our model on the Talk2Car dataset [6]. Finally, we conclude
our paper in Sect. 5.

2   Related Work

In terms of the object detection subtask in visual grounding, there exist two lines
of work in visual grounding: a one-stage approach [3,19,24,27] and a two-stage
approach [5,17,25,26]. In most of the previous work, researchers address the
task of visual grounding with two-stage approaches. In the first stage, several
object proposals are generated using an off-the-shelf object detection algorithm
like Faster-RCNN [23], YOLO [21,22]. In the second stage, the object proposals
are ranked by calculating the matching score with the given text query.

Several works [25,26] explore graph convolutional networks for learning the relationship between objects and text query. The work of [26] focuses on improving the cross-modal relationship between objects and referring expressions by constructing a language-guided visual relation graph. They use a gated graph convolutional network to fuse information from different modalities. In [25], authors also use graph networks for learning the relationship between neighboring objects. NMTree [16] constructs a language parsing tree with which they localize referred object by accumulating grounding confidence per node. MAttNet [29] involves a two-stage modular approach in which they use three modules for processing visual, language, location information, and a relationship module to understand the relationship between the output of these three modules. In [18], the authors use attention to generate difficult examples by discarding the most important information from both text and image. A-ATT [4] constructs three modules to understand the image, objects, and query. They accumulate features from different modalities in a circular manner to guide the reasoning process in multiple steps. MSRR [5] also uses a multi-step reasoning procedure, in which a new matching score is calculated between every object and the language query in each step. After all the reasoning steps, the object that has the highest score is selected as the target object.

In two-stage methods, the offline object detector may become a bottleneck as it may fail to provide good object proposals. For addressing this issue, several recent works explore a one-stage paradigm for visual grounding. One-stage methods fuse image-text features and then directly predict the bounding box for the referred object. Recent works [24,27] fuse visual-text features at every spatial location and predict adjustment in predefined anchor boxes to align the bounding boxes with the referred object. In [3], the authors introduce a guided attention module with which their model also predicts the center coordinates of the referred object along with the referred region. In our AttnGrounder, we predict a mask, rather than the center coordinate, which can help in better localization of image regions. Moreover, previous one-stage methods consider a single text representation for every location, but as we know, different regions correspond to different words, which is why we develop a text feature matrix where every location has its unique text representation. Additionally, one-stage methods are faster than two-stage methods as they do not involve matching between separately encoded image regions and text queries.

3   Methodology

In Fig. 2, we provide an overview of our proposed visual grounding architecture. Our goal is to locate an object in an Image I based on a given text query T. Our proposed model AttnGrounder consists of five sub-modules: image encoder, text encoder, visual attention module, fusion module, and a grounding module. The image encoder uses Darknet-53 [22] with a pyramid structure [14] to extract visual features from the image I in the form of grids $\{G_k\}_{k=0}^{2} \in \mathbb{R}^{C_k \times H_k \times W_k}$ at three different spatial resolutions. To encode text features, we use a Bi-LSTM

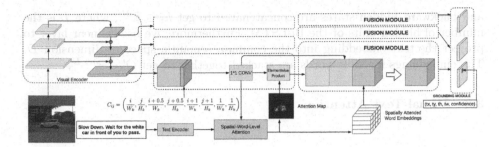

Fig. 2. Overview of AttnGrounder.

that can easily capture the long-range dependencies in the given query. We introduce a visual-text attention mechanism that attends to words w_t in the text query T at every spatial location in the grid G_k. This attention mechanism also generates an attention map M for the referred object. Finally, we fuse the image and text features using 1×1 convolution layers. For training, we use two loss functions: binary cross-entropy loss for training the attention map and the YOLO loss [21] function for complete end-to-end training. For our use, we modify the YOLO loss function by replacing the last sigmiod unit with a softmax unit.

3.1   Image Encoder

We adopted Darknet-53 [22] with a pyramid network [14] structure for encoding visual features. Darknet-53 takes an image I and produces feature grids $\{G_k\}_{k=0}^2 \in \mathbb{R}^{C_k \times H_k \times W_k}$ at three different spatial resolutions, where C_k, H_k and W_k are the number of channels, height and width of the grid at k^{th} resolution. Typically, the referring expressions also contain position information about the referred object (e.g. "park in front of the second vehicle on our *right* side."). Visual features produced by Darknet lack such location information. Similarly to [27], we explicitly add location information by concatenating the vector $C_{ij} \in \mathbb{R}^8$ at every spatial location of the grid G_k, which is computed as:

$$C_{ij} = \left(\frac{i}{W_k}, \frac{j}{H_k}, \frac{i+0.5}{W_k}, \frac{j+0.5}{H_k}, \frac{i+1}{W_k}, \frac{j+1}{H_k}, \frac{1}{W_k}, \frac{1}{H_k} \right)$$

where i, j are row and column in the grid G_k respectively. We then use a 1×1 convolution layer with batch normalization and ReLU unit to map these grid feature to a common semantic dimension D. Now, $G_k \in \mathbb{R}^{H_k \times W_k \times D}$.

3.2   Text Encoder

Our text encoder consists of an embedding layer and a Bi-LSTM layer. The text query T of length n is first converted to its embedding $Q = \{e_i\}_{i=0}^{n-1}$ using the embedding layer. After that, Q is fed as an input to Bi-LSTM that generates two hidden states $[h_i^{right}, h_i^{left}]$ for every word embedding e_i. The forward and backward hidden states are concatenated to get $h_i \in \mathbb{R}^{2L}$, where L is the number of hidden units of the Bi-LSTM. Furthermore, we use a linear layer to project the text embedding into the common semantic space of dimension D. The embeddings for all n words are stacked together to get $Q' \in \mathbb{R}^{n \times D}$.

3.3   Visual-Text Attention

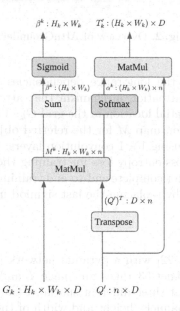

Fig. 3. Visual-Text Attention Module

Every region in an image may correspond to different words in the given query. To better model the dependency between a word and a region, we present a visual-text attention module. Figure 3 illustrates this module. The input consists of the grid G_k from the image encoder and the text embeddings Q' from the text encoder. The grid $G_k \in \mathbb{R}^{H_k \times W_k \times D}$ has $H_k \times W_k$ spatial locations each of dimension D and text embeddings $Q' \in \mathbb{R}^{n \times D}$ have n word features each of dimension D. To measure the matching score between a location $g_i \in \mathbb{R}^D$ and word $w_j \in \mathbb{R}^D$ in the query, we calculate the dot product between them. We multiply G_k with Q', which generates a matrix $M^k = G_k \cdot (Q')^T$, where M_{ij}^k represents the matching score between grid location i and word j. The matrix $M^k \in \mathbb{R}^{(H_k \times W_k) \times n}$, where H_k and W_k are the height and width of the grid at k^{th} resolution generated by our image encoder. This matrix M^k is used in two ways described next.

Text Feature Matrix

For every location in the grid G_k, we can represent its text features by summing up word features from the matrix $Q' \in \mathbb{R}^{n \times D}$. We normalize the matrix M^k using the softmax function to generate a word-level attention matrix $\alpha^k \in \mathbb{R}^{(H_k \times W_k) \times n}$, where α_{ij}^k denotes the correlation between region i in the grid G_k and word j in the text query T.

$$\alpha_{ij}^k = \frac{\exp(M_{ij}^k)}{\sum_{j=0}^{n-1} \exp(M_{ij}^k)} \tag{1}$$

To obtain text features at every location, we multiply α^k and Q', which generates text features matrix $T_k' \in \mathbb{R}^{(H_k \times W_k) \times D}$, denoted as $T_k' = \alpha^k \cdot Q'$. Every row in the matrix T_k' represents text features, which are effectively derived from the word features weighted by the correlation between words and corresponding image region. Thus, every region has its unique text representation.

Attention Map

In visual grounding, a rectangular mask around the referred object can be predicted by using only the provided ground truth bounding boxes. Our attention map module aims to make a rectangular mask around the referred object, which is an auxiliary task that helps improve the overall performance. By learning to generate a mask around the object, the model can indirectly learn to locate objects based on the given query and image. We make use of the matrix $M^k \in \mathbb{R}^{(H_k \times W_k) \times n}$, which already contains the matching score between every image region and every word in the text query. We sum the values in every row of M^k to get a column vector $\beta^k \in \mathbb{R}^{(H_k \times W_k)}$ with entries:

$$\beta_i^k = \sum_{j=0}^{n-1} M_{ij}^k \tag{2}$$

where β_i^k provides the aggregated matching score for an image region i and the given text query T. Now, the image regions matching with the given query will have a high matching score and vice-versa. To create a mask, we feed β^k through a sigmoid unit, which maps the values of β^k to a range between 0 and 1. Therefore, β_i^k can be interpreted as the probability of having the referred object in the region i.

For training, we generate a rectangular mask using the ground truth coordinates. The ground truth mask has the value of 1 inside the rectangular region and 0 elsewhere. Masks are created for all three resolutions and training is done using binary cross-entropy loss (See Fig. 4). At the kth resolution, given the ground truth mask $\beta_{true}^k \in \mathbb{R}^{H_k \times W_k}$ and the predicted mask $\beta^k \in \mathbb{R}^{H_k \times W_k}$; the mask loss is calculated as:

$$L_{mask}^k = -\frac{1}{H_k \times W_k} \sum_{i=0}^{(H_k \times W_k)-1} (\beta_{i,true}^k \log(\beta_i^k) + (1 - \beta_{i,true}^k) \log(1 - \beta_i^k)) \tag{3}$$

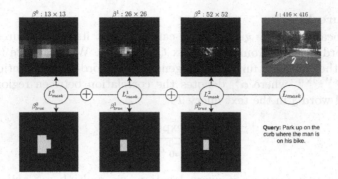

Fig. 4. The mask loss is calculated for every spatial resolution using binary cross-entropy loss and summed to get the final mask loss. First row shows the attention map produced by our AttnGrounder at three different resolutions and the second row shows ground truth mask used for training.

The L_{mask} is obtained by summing up the L_{mask}^k terms calculated for all the three resolutions.

$$L_{mask} = \sum_{k=0}^{2} L_{mask}^k \qquad (4)$$

Using L_{mask} as an auxiliary loss can help in the embedding of visual and text features in the common semantic space D, by encouraging similar visual and text features to be nearby and vice-versa. Furthermore, it can also help discriminate between the referred region and the others.

We also generate attended visual features $V_k \in \mathbb{R}^{H_k \times W_k \times D}$ as an element-wise product between the attention map β^k and grid G_k, $V_k = \beta^k \odot G_k$ ($\odot$ denotes element-wise product). In V_k, every spatial location is scaled by its importance determined by the attention mask β^k. Thus, visual features of regions where the target object may be present are enhanced and the influence of visual features of other regions is diminished.

3.4   Fusion Module

For fusing image and text features, we concatenate the visual feature grid G_k, the text feature matrix T_k' and the attended visual features V_k along the channel dimension. This generates a matrix $F_k \in \mathbb{R}^{H_k \times W_k \times 3D}$. All the features are l_2 normalized before concatenation and the fusion is done for all the three spatial resolutions generated by our image encoder. After that, we use a 1×1 convolution layer to fuse the aforementioned visual and text features. This 1×1 convolution layer maps the concatenated features into a new semantic space of dimension D'. After fusion, we have three feature matrices $\{F_k\}_{k=0}^2 \in \mathbb{R}^{H_k \times W_k \times D'}$.

Fig. 5. Examples of results obtained using our AttnGrounder. The predicted bounding boxes are shown in red and ground truth bounding boxes are shown in green. The second row shows the attention maps generated by our model.

3.5   Grounding Module

The grounding module aims to ground the text query onto an image region. This module takes the fused feature vector F_k as input and generates a bounding box prediction. We follow [27] for designing this module and similar to [27], we replace YOLO [21] output sigmoid layer with the softmax layer.

For every spatial location, YOLOv3 centres three different anchor boxes and for every spatial resolution, YOLOv3 uses different set of anchor boxes. In total, for three different spatial resolutions we have $3 \times 3 = 9$ different predefined anchor boxes. We denote the total number of anchor box predictions made by our model with m, where $m = \sum_{k=0}^{2} H_k \times W_k \times 3$. For every anchor box, YOLOv3 predicts changes in location and size required to fit that particular anchor box around the target object. Specifically, YOLOv3 uses two branches: the first branch predicts the shift in centre, height and width of the predefined anchor box, while the second one uses a sigmoid layer to predict the confidence (on the shifted box) of being the target box. As we only need one bounding box prediction for grounding, we replace the last sigmoid layer with the softmax layer which forces the model to select one box out of the m boxes as prediction. Accordingly, the loss function for confidence is also changed to a cross-entropy loss between the predicted confidence (softmax version) and a one-hot vector with 1 at the entry corresponding to the anchor box that has the highest intersection over union with the ground truth box. We refer the readers to [21,22] for more details and abstract away the YOLO's loss function as L_{yolo}. Thus, the total loss becomes

$$L = L_{yolo} + \lambda L_{mask} \tag{5}$$

where λ is a hyper-parameter which scales the loss L_{mask}.

4   Experiments and Results

In this section, we provide details of our experiments. We evaluate our approach on Talk2Car dataset [6] and compare with five baselines.

Table 1. Comparison with state-of-the-art methods on Talk2Car testset

Method	AP_{50} Score	Time (ms)	Params (M)
STACK [8]	33.71	52	**35.2**
SCRC [9]	43.80	208	52.47
A-ATT [4]	45.12	180	160.31
MAC [10]	50.51	51	41.59
MSRR [5]	60.04	270.5	62.25
AttnGrounder	**63.30**	**25.5**	75.84

4.1 Dataset

The Talk2Car dataset is based on the nuScenes dataset [2] and contains 11,959 referring expressions for 9,217 images. This dataset contains images of a city-like environment traversed by the self-driving car. Talk2Car dataset is a multi-modal dataset that consists of various sensor modalities such as semantic maps, LIDAR, 360-degree RGB images, etc. However, we only use the RGB images for training our AttnGrounder. RGB images contained in the Talk2Car dataset are taken in different weather conditions (sunny, rainy) and time of day (day, night), which makes it even more challenging. Additional challenges that the Talk2Car dataset presents are the ambiguity between the objects belonging to the same class, far away object localization, long text queries, etc. In this dataset, the size of images is 900×1600 and, on average, the referring expressions contain 11 words. The dataset contains 8349, 1163 and 2447 images for training, validation and testing respectively. Figure 1 shows an example of Talk2Car dataset.

4.2 Training Details

Our image encoder backbone i.e. Darknet-53 [22] is pre-trained on the COCO [15] object objection task. We use 300 dimensional GloVe [20] embeddings for initializing word vectors. Words for which the GloVe embeddings were not available were initialized randomly. We resize the images to 416×416 and preserve the original aspect ratio. We resize the longer edge to 416 and pad the shorter edge with the mean pixel value. We also add some data augmentations i.e., horizontal flips, changing saturation and intensity, random affine transformation. The anchors used in our grounding module are (10, 13), (16, 30), (33, 23), (30, 61), (62, 45), (59, 119), (116, 90), (156, 198), (373, 326). We use $\lambda = 0.1$ (defined in Sect. 3.5) for training. We train our model using Adam [12] optimizer with an initial learning rate of 10^{-4} and a polynomial learning rate scheduler with a power of 1. For the Darknet-53 pre-training, we keep maintain the initial learning rate of 10^{-3}. We use a batch size of 14 for training our AttnGrounder.

4.3   Comparison Metrics

We evaluate our approach on three different metrics. The first one is AP_{50} score, which is defined as the percentage of predicted bounding boxes that have an *Intersection Over Union* of more than 0.5 with the ground truth bounding boxes. The second one is *inference time* and the third is the *number of parameters* of the model.

4.4   Results

We compare our AttnGrounder with four baselines and the state-of-the-art MSRR [5] and show the results on the test set of Talk2Car dataset in Table 1. AttnGrounder outperforms all the baselines and improves upon the state-of-the-art by 3.26% in terms of the AP_{50} score. Thanks to our one-stage approach, we also achieve the lowest inference time among all the baseline methods. We provide examples of predictions made by our method in Fig. 5 along with the visualization of the attention map generated by the visual-text attention module (Sect. 3.3).

5   Conclusions

We propose AttnGrounder, a single-stage end-to-end trainable visual grounding model. Our AttnGrounder is fast compared to two-stage approaches as it does not involve matching various region proposals and text queries or multistep reasoning. We combine visual features extracted from YOLOv3 and text features extracted from Bi-LSTM to obtain a multi-modal feature representation with which we directly predict the bounding box for the target object. Our AttnGrounder also generates an attention map that localizes the potential spatial locations where the referred object may be present. This attention map is trained as an auxiliary task which helps improve the overall performance of our model. Finally, we evaluate our proposed method on the Talk2car dataset and show that it outperforms all the baseline methods.

Acknowledgements. The author wants to thank Thierry Deruyttere, Dusan Grujicic, and Monika Jyotiyana for their feedback on an early draft of this paper. The author is grateful to Thierry Deruyttere for his guidance and constant support when writing this paper.

References

1. Anderson, P., et al.: Bottom-up and top-down attention for image captioning and visual question answering. In: Proceedings of the IEEE Conference on Computer Vision and Pattern Recognition, pp. 6077–6086 (2018)
2. Caesar, H., et al.: Nuscenes: a multimodal dataset for autonomous driving. In: Proceedings of the IEEE/CVF Conference on Computer Vision and Pattern Recognition, pp. 11621–11631 (2020)

3. Chen, X., Ma, L., Chen, J., Jie, Z., Liu, W., Luo, J.: Real-time referring expression comprehension by single-stage grounding network. arXiv preprint arXiv:1812.03426 (2018)
4. Deng, C., Wu, Q., Wu, Q., Hu, F., Lyu, F., Tan, M.: Visual grounding via accumulated attention. In: Proceedings of the IEEE Conference on Computer Vision and Pattern Recognition, pp. 7746–7755 (2018)
5. Deruyttere, T., Collell, G., Moens, M.F.: Giving commands to a self-driving car: A multimodal reasoner for visual grounding. arXiv preprint arXiv:2003.08717 (2020)
6. Deruyttere, T., Vandenhende, S., Grujicic, D., Van Gool, L., Moens, M.F.: Talk2car: taking control of your self-driving car. arXiv preprint arXiv:1909.10838 (2019)
7. Feng, Y., Ma, L., Liu, W., Luo, J.: Unsupervised image captioning. In: Proceedings of the IEEE Conference on Computer Vision and Pattern Recognition, pp. 4125–4134 (2019)
8. Hu, R., Andreas, J., Darrell, T., Saenko, K.: Explainable neural computation via stack neural module networks. In: Proceedings of the European Conference on Computer Vision (ECCV), pp. 53–69 (2018)
9. Hu, R., Xu, H., Rohrbach, M., Feng, J., Saenko, K., Darrell, T.: Natural language object retrieval. In: Proceedings of the IEEE Conference on Computer Vision and Pattern Recognition, pp. 4555–4564 (2016)
10. Hudson, D.A., Manning, C.D.: Compositional attention networks for machine reasoning. arXiv preprint arXiv:1803.03067 (2018)
11. Jiang, H., Misra, I., Rohrbach, M., Learned-Miller, E., Chen, X.: In defense of grid features for visual question answering. In: Proceedings of the IEEE/CVF Conference on Computer Vision and Pattern Recognition, pp. 10267–10276 (2020)
12. Kingma, D.P., Ba, J.: Adam: A method for stochastic optimization. arXiv preprint arXiv:1412.6980 (2014)
13. Li, B., Qi, X., Lukasiewicz, T., Torr, P.: Controllable text-to-image generation. In: Advances in Neural Information Processing Systems, pp. 2065–2075 (2019)
14. Lin, T.Y., Dollár, P., Girshick, R., He, K., Hariharan, B., Belongie, S.: Feature pyramid networks for object detection. In: Proceedings of the IEEE Conference on Computer Vision and Pattern Recognition, pp. 2117–2125 (2017)
15. Lin, T.Y., et al.: Microsoft COCO: common objects in context. In: Fleet, D., Pajdla, T., Schiele, B., Tuytelaars, T. (eds.) ECCV 2014. LNCS, vol. 8693, pp. 740–755. Springer, Cham (2014). https://doi.org/10.1007/978-3-319-10602-1_48
16. Liu, D., Zhang, H., Wu, F., Zha, Z.J.: Learning to assemble neural module tree networks for visual grounding. In: Proceedings of the IEEE International Conference on Computer Vision, pp. 4673–4682 (2019)
17. Liu, J., Wang, L., Yang, M.H.: Referring expression generation and comprehension via attributes. In: Proceedings of the IEEE International Conference on Computer Vision, pp. 4856–4864 (2017)
18. Liu, X., Wang, Z., Shao, J., Wang, X., Li, H.: Improving referring expression grounding with cross-modal attention-guided erasing. In: Proceedings of the IEEE Conference on Computer Vision and Pattern Recognition, pp. 1950–1959 (2019)
19. Luo, G., et al.: Multi-task collaborative network for joint referring expression comprehension and segmentation. In: Proceedings of the IEEE/CVF Conference on Computer Vision and Pattern Recognition, pp. 10034–10043 (2020)
20. Pennington, J., Socher, R., Manning, C.D.: Glove: global vectors for word representation. In: Proceedings of the 2014 Conference on Empirical Methods in Natural Language Processing (EMNLP), pp. 1532–1543 (2014)

21. Redmon, J., Divvala, S., Girshick, R., Farhadi, A.: You only look once: unified, real-time object detection. In: Proceedings of the IEEE Conference on Computer Vision and Pattern Recognition, pp. 779–788 (2016)
22. Redmon, J., Farhadi, A.: Yolov3: An incremental improvement. arXiv preprint arXiv:1804.02767 (2018)
23. Ren, S., He, K., Girshick, R., Sun, J.: Faster r-cnn: Towards real-time object detection with region proposal networks. In: Advances in Neural Information Processing Systems, pp. 91–99 (2015)
24. Sadhu, A., Chen, K., Nevatia, R.: Zero-shot grounding of objects from natural language queries. In: Proceedings of the IEEE International Conference on Computer Vision, pp. 4694–4703 (2019)
25. Wang, P., Wu, Q., Cao, J., Shen, C., Gao, L., Hengel, A.V.D.: Neighbourhood watch: referring expression comprehension via language-guided graph attention networks. In: Proceedings of the IEEE Conference on Computer Vision and Pattern Recognition, pp. 1960–1968 (2019)
26. Yang, S., Li, G., Yu, Y.: Cross-modal relationship inference for grounding referring expressions. In: 2019 IEEE/CVF Conference on Computer Vision and Pattern Recognition (CVPR), pp. 4140–4149 (2019)
27. Yang, Z., Gong, B., Wang, L., Huang, W., Yu, D., Luo, J.: A fast and accurate one-stage approach to visual grounding. In: Proceedings of the IEEE International Conference on Computer Vision, pp. 4683–4693 (2019)
28. You, Q., Jin, H., Wang, Z., Fang, C., Luo, J.: Image captioning with semantic attention. In: Proceedings of the IEEE Conference on Computer Vision and Pattern Recognition, pp. 4651–4659 (2016)
29. Yu, L., et al.: Mattnet: modular attention network for referring expression comprehension. In: Proceedings of the IEEE Conference on Computer Vision and Pattern Recognition, pp. 1307–1315 (2018)
30. Yu, Z., Yu, J., Cui, Y., Tao, D., Tian, Q.: Deep modular co-attention networks for visual question answering. In: Proceedings of the IEEE Conference on Computer Vision and Pattern Recognition, pp. 6281–6290 (2019)
31. Zhang, H., et al.: Stackgan: text to photo-realistic image synthesis with stacked generative adversarial networks. In: Proceedings of the IEEE international conference on computer vision, pp. 5907–5915 (2017)

W13 - Computer VISion for ART Analysis

W13 - Computer VISion for ART Analysis

Following the success of the four Workshops on Computer VISion for ART Analysis (VISART) held at the European Conference on Computer Vision (ECCV 2012, 2014, 2016, and 2018), we present the proceedings for the 5th VISART 2020 workshop. Whereas most Computer Vision has to tackle the decoding of images of the outside world, the VISART community deals with images of images (per se, scans of paintings) – in which one can often no longer rely on the physical laws of the outside world. This interdisciplinary field thus greatly benefits Computer Vision research with unique data sources, new problems, and a chance – often – to experiment beyond the typical axioms of Computer Vision research (vision in art can be very far from inverse graphics). It also has a transformative on the study of the history of art and visual culture, that fundamentally change the type of questions it is possible to ask, as well as the scale at which they can be asked.

VISART 2020 brought together leading researchers in the fields of Computer Vision, Machine Learning, and Multimedia Information Retrieval with Art Historians and curators, to discuss research questions at the intersection of computer vision and visual culture. Since the last VISART workshop in 2018, a number of important technical advancements have been made, both in transfer learning across styles and in the analysis of visual patterns. At the same time, the massive digitization efforts and open access strategies in cultural heritage institutions are becoming widespread. The potential uses of Computer Vision for cultural history and cultural analytics has created great interest in the Humanities and Digital Humanities, with research projects on Computer Vision appearing across galleries and museums such as the Getty and MoMA.

A key feature of this workshop is the close institutional, personal, and research collaboration between scholars of computer vision and the arts and humanities, thus both exposing new technical possibilities to the arts and humanities, as well as offering new artistic and humanistic perspectives on computer vision. Our two keynotes brilliantly outlined these two directions of interdisciplinarity. Andreas Maier ("Building Blocks for a Virtual Time Machine," FAU Erlangen-Nuremberg, Germany) outlined the developments in computer vision powering the European Time Machine project, allowing researchers to uncover big data in Europe's past; and Aaron Hertzmann ("Human visual perception of Art as Computation," Adobe Research, USA) introduced a new theoretical, computational model for how visual art works.

September 2020

Alessio Del Bue
Sebastiano Vascon
Leonardo Impett
Peter Bell
Stuart James

Detecting Faces, Visual Medium Types, and Gender in Historical Advertisements, 1950–1995

Melvin Wevers[1]([✉])[iD] and Thomas Smits[2][iD]

[1] DHLab, KNAW Humanities Cluster, Amsterdam, The Netherlands
melvin.wevers@dh.huc.knaw.nl
[2] Utrecht University, Utrecht, The Netherlands
t.p.smits@uu.nl

Abstract. Libraries, museums, and other heritage institutions are digitizing large parts of their archives. Computer vision techniques enable scholars to query, analyze, and enrich the visual sources in these archives. However, it remains unclear how well algorithms trained on modern photographs perform on historical material. This study evaluates and adapts existing algorithms. We show that we can detect faces, visual media types, and gender with high accuracy in historical advertisements. It remains difficult to detect gender when faces are either of low quality or relatively small or large. Further optimization of scaling might solve the latter issue, while the former might be ameliorated using upscaling. We show how computer vision can produce meta-data information, which can enrich historical collections. This information can be used for further analysis of the historical representation of gender.

Keywords: Face detection · Heritage · Historical advertisements · Medium detection · Gender detection

1 Introduction

In 1925, psychologist Alfred Poffenberger encouraged ad makers to "short-circuit the consumer's mind through vivid, pictorial appeals to fundamental emotions"[28]. By tapping into a representational system that produces meaning outside the realm of the advertised product, images could help to sell products [14]. As a result, advertisements have been an important source for historians studying the development of consumerism and consumer society. An important focus in consumer studies is the representation of gender [32,37,42]. How is gender constructed in advertisements? In the late1970 s, sociologist Erving Goffman undertook a systematic investigation of the semiotic content of advertisements printed in contemporary newspapers and glossy magazines. He was particularly interested in what he called Gender Displays [13]. This research interest resulted in his seminal book *Gender Advertisements* 1976].

In this study, Goffman proposed five categories to study the depictions *of* and the relations *between* men, women, and children in advertisements: relative

© Springer Nature Switzerland AG 2020
A. Bartoli and A. Fusiello (Eds.): ECCV 2020 Workshops, LNCS 12536, pp. 77–91, 2020.
https://doi.org/10.1007/978-3-030-66096-3_7

size, feminine touch, function ranking, the ritualization of subordination, and licensed withdrawal. By manually examining advertisements, he reflected how men and women could be placed in these categories, from which he then drew generalizations. Building on this approach, Jonathan Schroeder, contends that in advertisements, men are regularly presented as "the active subject, the business-like, self-assured decision maker, while the female occupies the passive object, the observed sexual/sensual body, eroticized and inactive [36]."

Studies like those by Goffman and Schroeder rely on a qualitative analy-sis, or close-reading, of a limited number of advertisements published in a rela-tively short period. Goffman only examined around 400 different advertisements, which he selected from "newspapers and magazines easy to hand - at least to my hand." As Kang [18] notes, Goffman was often criticized for this method. Instead of relying on a random sample, he purposefully "selected images that mirrored gender differences." To replicate Goffman's findings and demonstrate the validity of his categories with more robust statistical analyses, some studies have used professional annotators to encode small sets of images [4]. They found that individual females were indeed positioned in the top half of adverts more frequently than individual men. At the same time, groups of males dominated the top position compared to groups of women. However, they could not con-firm Goffman's hypothesis that there exists a left-right bias sensitive to gender. Goffman's study has not only been directly replicated [2,18] but also served as the primary theoretical framework for studies of a very similar nature [5,20,24].

In sum: Goffman's work and subsequent replication and follow-up studies have yielded formalizations of visual semiotics, i.e., how the relationship between visual elements of images produces gender displays. These formalizations offer guidelines on what we should look for when studying images. These guidelines also function as a clear starting point for the operationalization of computer vision algorithms. We need to have a clear idea of what we are looking for in images before we can turn to methods that detect specific elements in images.

Moreover, computer vision algorithms and the growing amount of digitized visual material make it possible to study gender displays on larger samples over more extended periods. This approach can add more robustness or offer possible correctives to the claims made by Goffman and existing replication studies.

Before we can proceed with such a replication study, we need to first establish to what extent existing computer vision algorithms and models *work* when they are applied to historical visual material. Therefore, this paper examines the use of computer vision techniques for studying gender in historical advertisements from 1950–1995. This study consists of three main tasks: 1) face detection, 2) detection of visual medium types, and 3) gender detection. We show how these tasks produce information that can be used to enrich historical collections, which can subsequently be used to answer long-standing questions about, for instance, the representation of gender. In simple terms, to be able to detect how males and females are represented in images, we first need to be able to detect them.

2   Related Work

In recent years, bias—systematic underrepresentation of certain groups or traits in data collection and/or statistical analysis—in computer vision models, algorithms, and data sets has become a primary concern for computer scientists. The presence of bias in a computer vision model could be due to certain design choices in an algorithm or the data set, or both. In relation to gender bias, [38] looked at the geo-diversity of the popular ImageNet and Open Images sets and concluded that they exhibited "an observable amerocentric (sic) and eurocentric (sic) representation bias". [8] presented a method to audit the demographics (age and gender) of the 'person' category of ImageNet. In February 2020, Google announced that its popular Cloud Vision service would no longer label persons as either 'male' or 'female', noting that "a person's gender cannot be inferred by appearance" [12]. Some of the founders of ImageNet have taken the almost exact opposite route by arguing that a large-scale annotation of gender, age, and skin color of the person category in their dataset will lead to a more representative dataset and, as a result, fairer algorithms [44]. Our paper builds on this kind of work by pointing to the historical dimension of gender bias in computer vision datasets and models.

While there is a considerable amount of work in the art-historical domain [3,17,27], cultural historians have only recently started to apply computer vision to their large collections of popular images. Advertisements are an excellent source for research that uses computer vision techniques to examine large-scale trends in modern visual culture. Computer vision algorithms have been applied to study how advertising 'works'. Facial expressions and the representations of objects have been analyzed for the visual rhetorics and persuasiveness [40,46]. While these studies offer avenues to explore for historical analysis, the focus in the cited papers is on contemporary advertising, and their primary aim seems to be to better our understanding of the practice of advertising. In contrast, our approach is cultural-historical and our focus is on the historical dimension in advertising. Because gender displays, the way men and women are expected to look, change over time, the accuracy of gender recognition will fluctuate for tasks that have a historical dimension. By evaluating and adapting existing algorithms, this paper sheds light on the extent of this historical side of gender bias.

3   Data

Our data set is SIAMESET, which contains approximately one million advertisements that appeared in the Dutch newspaper *NRC Handelsblad* for the period 1945–1995 (Fig. 1).[1] During the interwar period (1918–1940), advertising changed rapidly in the Netherlands. Technological advances made it cheaper to print images in newspapers. Influenced by developments in the American advertisement industry, Dutch agencies started to use visual material on a large

---

[1] Wevers, M., Lonij, J. (2017) SIAMESET. KB Lab: The Hague. http://lab.kb.nl/dataset/siameset.

scale to increase sales and convey particular brand identities [35]. Throughout
the German occupation of the Netherlands (1940–1945) and in the immediate
post-war years, paper was scarce. However, starting in the early1950 s, the number of advertisements containing visual elements started to increase considerably.
Figure 1 confirms the low number of adverts in the years right after the Second
World War. Because of this, we focus on the post-war period.

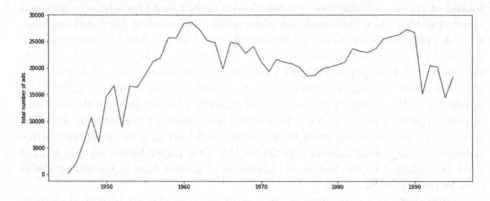

Fig. 1. Total number of advertisements per year in SIAMESET

From SIAMESET, we randomly sampled 1K images per year for the period
1950–1995, resulting in a data set of forty-five thousand advertisements. In these
advertisements, a group of six annotators drew bounding boxes around faces
and annotated their gender. We followed standard protocol by requiring every
bounding box to be as small as possible while including all visible parts of the
face [10,34]. We asked annotators to categorize the faces as either "male" or
"female". Although we are aware that binarization of gender is problematic and
reductionist, advertisers, however, were quite explicit in their representation of
gender. Therefore, there was little ambiguity found in establishing gender for
adults. We also annotated children as "girl" and "boy". Because of the ambiguity
of these annotations, we decided to exclude these from the analysis.

Out of the data set's forty-five thousand advertisements, 8,522 contained at
least one face. In total, the data set contained approximately 10.2 k men and 8.5 k
women. Figure 2 shows the average number of faces in a single ad, containing a
face, either a male or a female. The error bars show the 95% bootstrap confidence
intervals. We see that the average number of male faces has more variance than
that of female faces. In part, this variation is due to pictures with groups of
people, or a sports team, which often-times only included males. In other words,
in cases of pictures with large numbers of faces, these are more often male faces
(see Fig. 3). This finding in itself is already a remarkable result in terms of gender
representations.

Also, Fig. 2 shows that around 1975, the average number of female faces
started to decrease and remained lower than that of males for the next twenty

years. This decreased presence of females in the newspaper might be related to the merger of the *Algemeen Handelsblad* into the *NRC Handelsblad*, a more liberal newspaper. After the merger, the newspaper also set out to target businessmen as its main readership [15]. A comparative analysis with other newspapers would shed more light on these kinds of issues. During annotation, it became clear that the data set contained predominantly white males and females. For this reason, we could not determine how well our algorithms performed on people with an ethnicity other than white [8].

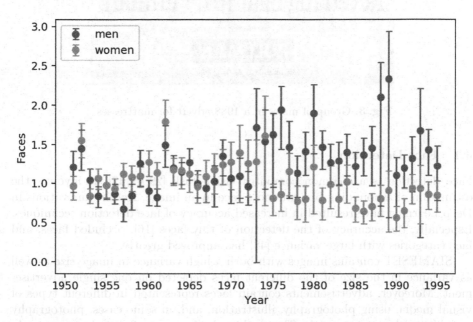

Fig. 2. Average number of male and female faces per advert in SIAMESET

4   Analysis

We divided our analysis of historical advertisements into three tasks. First, we benchmarked face detection algorithms on the annotated collection. Second, we created a classifier to detect the visual medium type in which a face was represented as either an illustration or a photograph. Third, we trained a convolutional neural network to classify the gender of the extracted faces. The following subsections describe these three tasks in more detail.[2]

---

[2] The code can be found here: https://github.com/melvinwevers/detecting_faces-medium-types-gender.

Fig. 3. Group of males in a 1988 advert for mattresses

4.1   Face Detection

Face detection is a common computer vision task [29,41,47]. It involves the estimation of a bounding box around a face in an image. Recent innovations in Deep Learning have resulted in increased accuracy of face detection techniques. Especially, the accuracy of the detection of tiny faces [16], occluded faces, and face categories with large variance [48] has improved greatly.

SIAMESET contains images with both a high variance in image size as well as variance in the size of the different faces depicted on one single advertisement. Moreover, advertisements contain faces represented in different types of visual media, using photography, illustration, and, in some cases, photography and illustration concurrently. Faces, thus, both appear in iconic ways, as in being the central object of the image, and also in non-iconic ways, for example, in adverts where a product is the central object. Since we are working with historical material, the printing techniques used to reproduce the images also varies considerably: from high-definition, full-color, full-page advertisements, to small, smudgy, black-and-white notices. Furthermore, significant differences in quality might arise from the digitization process [11]. Recently, non-iconic views of objects and scenes have been purposefully collected to improve the accuracy of computer vision techniques [23]. Following these efforts, we present a highly heterogeneous annotated set that can be used to test the performance of existing face and gender detection algorithms.[3]

For the evaluation of face detection algorithms, we contrasted the widely-used OpenCV's DNN module with two state-of-the-art models, Dual Shot Face Detection (DSFD) and RetinaFace [7,22]. OpenCV DNN's module uses a Single Shot Detector, which predicts the bounding boxes and the confidence in one

---

[3] The annotated data set and models can be found on Zenodo using the following DOI: 10.5281/zenodo.4008991.

single shot, with ResNet-10 as a backbone. Unfortunately, it is not specified on what data and in what manner the model was trained. DSFD adds a step to a Single Shot Detector that improves its ability to detect tiny faces and occluded faces. Part of this additional step is the use of a Feature Enhance Module that improves discriminability and robustness of features [22]. RetinaFace, which is based on a single-stage design, employs a multi-task learning strategy that predicts a face score, a bounding box, five facial landmarks, and 3D position and correspondence of each facial pixel. The use of facial landmarks improves the algorithm's ability to learn. RetinaFace runs on either a MobileNet or a ResNet-50 backbone. The former is considerably faster and less memory-intensive, while the latter has slightly better results [7].

When applied to the often-used WIDERFACE data set, RetinaFace outperforms DSFD, and is much faster than two-stage methods, such as DSFD (see Table 1). The WIDERFACE data set consists of a total of 32,203 images, containing 393,703 annotated faces with significant variations in scale, pose, and occlusion. Each image is further defined into three levels of difficulty: "Easy", "Medium", "Hard" based on the detection rate of a baseline detector [45].

Table 1. Average precision on WIDER FACE taken from [7, 22]

Method	Easy	Medium	Hard
DSFD	96.6	95.7	90.4
RetinaFace	**96.9**	**96.2**	**91.9**

Results. For OpenCV's DNN, we used the default FaceDetector weights; for the other two algorithms, we relied on weights pre-trained on the WIDER FACE data set. We selected the RetinaFace with ResNet-50 as a backbone rather than MobileNet, the former is slower but has better accuracy on the WIDER FACE data set. For this study, the decreased speed is no issue since we value accuracy above speed. Using these weights, we applied the three algorithms to our annotated data set. We used Average Precision to compare the performance of the algorithms. Average Precision (AP) captures the area under the curve (AUC) of the Precision and Recall curve. We interpolated all data points, following the method of the PASCAL VOC challenge [6]. We employ an IOU (intersection over union) threshold of 0.5 when calculating the AP. This score is calculated by dividing the area of overlap between the predicted bounding box and the ground-truth box by the area of the predicted bounding box and ground-truth bounding box, i.e. the area of union.

DSFD (AP: 71%) and RetinaFace (AP: 68.13%) clearly outperform the Open CV DNN module (AP: 20.54%) (Fig. 4). The slightly better performance by DSFD over RetinaFace can most definitely be explained by the former's ability to detect faces with a large size variance, which is quite common in advertisements. Its default scaling algorithm is more versatile than the one that DSFD offers.

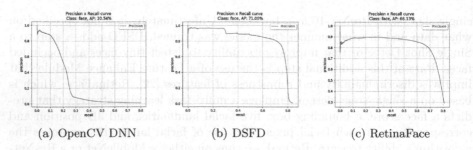

(a) OpenCV DNN   (b) DSFD   (c) RetinaFace

Fig. 4. Precision-Recall Curves

A review of false negatives suggests that relatively large faces are often not detected by the algorithms. In Fig. 5, for example, the large face is not detected. The scaling algorithm probably prohibits drawing a bounding box around objects occupying the majority of the image's area. Further optimization of the scaling algorithms might solve this issue.

Fig. 5. Advertisement with a large face

4.2 Visual Medium Detection

Persons in advertisements can be depicted using different visual media types, ranging from photograph to illustration, or sometimes both in the same advertisement or even the same face. Furthermore, faces can be illustrated using a wide range of different styles, from highly realistic to highly abstract (see Fig. 6). Previous work shows that convolutional neural networks can be used with high accuracy to distinguish between different media types [43, 44]. Because of the co-existence of different visual media and visual styles within a single advertisement, we built a classifier on the level of the face rather than on the level of the full advertisements. Instead of constructing an object detector that detects faces in their specific styles, we combined the face detection with an additional classifier for the visual medium. This two-step approach allowed us to benefit from the ability of existing algorithms, such as RetinaFace, to detect tiny faces and large variance between faces.

Fig. 6. Advertisement containing illustrations and a photograph (1959)

The visual medium classifier was trained on a set of 242 illustrated and 259 photographed faces drawn from the set of forty-five thousand advertisements. We extracted the faces from the advertisements and manually classified them as either illustration or photograph. Next, we applied data augmentation on this image set (resizing, center cropping, horizontal flipping, and random rotation). This augmentation generated new training data from the original set by adding perturbations to the images. In every batch of data, the network is presented with new, slightly different versions of the input data, which forces the network to learn more robust features, making the resulting less prone to overfitting.

Finally, we fed these augmented images into a pre-trained VGG16, a comparatively small network, and extracted the encoded features as a flattened vector from the penultimate Max Pooling layer.[4] We trained a Linear SVC with default settings, using Scikit-learn, on these encoded features.

Results. With ten-fold cross-validation, our classifier reaches a mean accuracy of .91 with a standard deviation of 0.04. In other words, using a relatively small set of training data, our classifier can distinguish between photographs

---

[4] A parameter search found that this layer provided the best results for our classification task.

and illustrations with high accuracy. Closer inspection of the misclassified predictions shows that these are mostly low-quality images or images of which the visual medium is difficult to determine, even for a human annotator. A possible strategy is augmenting the WIDERFACE data set with illustrated faces. Future work will explore whether Deep Adaptation Networks might be leveraged to learn faces across different modalities [25].

4.3 Gender Detection

The detection of gender in images using some form of computer vision has been explored extensively [9,19,30]. Convolutional neural networks can pick up the necessary features to make highly accurate predictions of gender [1,21,33]. The conception of gender used in this kind of research is binary, static, and highly normative. Partly based on Goffman's work, gender studies scholars like Judith Butler have argued that gender is performed. Notions of masculinity and femininity—the way that men and women are expected to look and behave—are not derived from biological sex but from the constant performance of gender in society, for example, in advertisements [39].

These insights are problematic for gender detection techniques because they reveal that annotating faces into binary gender categories is not a clear-cut analytic procedure but a gender performance in itself. The fact that the performance of gender changes over time further complicates the matter. Are we using computer vision to study historical gender displays, or are we superimposing our notion of gender on the historical archive? We will address this question in a forthcoming study.

For the classification of gender in advertised persons, we constructed two data sets. The first set consists of two classes: "male" and "female", excluding images with a width or height smaller than 100 pixels. We separated the data set into a training, validation, and test set according to an 80, 10, 10 division. Table 2 shows the number of images in each set.

Table 2. Training set gender classifier

	Train	Validation	Test	Total
Male	5,068	649	644	6,361
Female	4,489	555	1,204	5,617
Total	9,557	1,204	1,848	11,888

For the second set, we used the visual medium classifier described in Sect. 4.2 to divide the data set into four classes: male photo, female photo, male illustration, and female illustration. This set was also divided according to an 80, 10, 10 division, resulting in the set described in Table 3.

For gender detection, we relied on a VGGFACE, a VGG16 network with weights pre-trained on two large face data sets: Labeled Faces in the Wild and

Table 3. Training set gender classifier divided by style

	Train	Validation	Test	Total
Male photo	2,865	373	374	3,612
Male illustration	2,205	271	272	2,748
Female photo	2,532	293	294	3,119
Female illustration	1,959	280	281	2,520
Total	9,561	1,217	1,221	11,999

the YouTube Faces dataset [31].[5] We compared three optimizers: SGD, ADAM, and ADAbound, and achieved the best performance using the latter. The latter is described to train as fast as ADAM with the performance of SGD [26]. We held out ten percent of the training data as a validation set. Next, we augmented the training data by rotating the images, shifting the width and height, changing the shearing, flipping them horizontally, and applying a random eraser. The latter randomly erases parts of the images and replaces them with random pixels, to make the detection of features more difficult, leading to more robust features [49].

We used a two-step approach to fine-tune the network. As part of the first step, we fine-tuned the head weights. For this, we loaded the VGGFace model with pre-trained weights and left the top layers off. We flattened the last layer and added two fully-connected dense layers with 512 hidden dimensions. Before adding the classification layer with a Sigmoid activation, we added Dropout to reduce overfitting. As part of our training strategy, we used early stopping (patience = 10) and reduced the initial learning rate (0.001) when it did not change for three epochs. For the second step, we unfroze the fully-connected head layers and the final convolution block, allowing them to be fine-tuned as well. Next, we trained the network for a maximum of 20 epochs, or when the learning rate plateaued—this additional step slightly improved accuracy.

Results. We achieved an F_1-score of .91 for females and .92 for males (Table 4). However, when we tried to detect both medium and gender—a more difficult task—the accuracy drops to an average of .84 (Table 5). If the task requires a focus on a particular medium, it might be beneficial to classify the medium and then apply gender detection to those particular media. However, as this result shows, we can estimate gender with a high degree of accuracy, regardless of the medium.

---

[5] We also tried a Resnet-101 architecture, but this approach decreased accuracy.

Table 4. Classification report gender detection

	Prediction	Recall	f1-score	Support
Female	0.91	0.92	0.91	573
Male	0.93	0.91	0.92	644
Weight avg	0.92	0.92	0.92	1,217

Table 5. Classification report gender and style detection

	Prediction	Recall	f1-score	Support
Female drawing	0.90	0.83	0.86	280
Female photo	0.83	0.86	0.84	293
Male drawing	0.81	0.83	0.82	271
Male photo	0.84	0.84	0.84	373
Weight avg	0.84	0.84	0.84	1,217

5   Conclusion

This paper has presented: 1) a heterogenous, non-iconic annotated data set of images—a subset of SIAMESET—which can be used to test the performance of existing face and gender detection algorithms on historical material, 2) our efforts to evaluate and improve the performance of three face detection algorithms (OpenCV, DSFD, RetinaFace) on historical material,; 3) the training of a visual medium classifier to separate photographs from illustrations, and 4) the training of a gender classifier on the extracted faces.

We have shown that we can detect faces, visual media, and gender with a high degree of accuracy in historical advertisements. It remains challenging to detect gender when faces are of low quality, relatively small, or relatively large. Further optimization of scaling and upscaling of the images to improve their resolution might solve these issues. Notwithstanding these concerns, we are confident that we can apply these algorithms and fine-tuned models to enrich other large visual historical collections and use them for a future study, in which we replicate Goffman's formalizations of gender displays using larger data set.

References

1. Antipov, G., Berrani, S.A., Dugelay, J.L.: Minimalistic CNN-based ensemble model for gender prediction from face images. Pattern Recog. Lett. **70**, 59–65 (2016)
2. Belknap, P., Leonard, W.M.: A conceptual replication and and extension of erving Goffman's study of gender advertisements. Sex Roles **25**(3), 103–118 (1991)
3. Bell, P., Schlecht, J., Ommer, B.: Nonverbal communication in medieval illustrations revisited by computer vision and art history. Vis. Res. **29**(1–2), 26–37 (2013). https://doi.org/10.1080/01973762.2013.761111

4. Bell, P., Milic, M.: Goffman's gender advertisements revisited: combining content analysis with semiotic analysis. Vis. Commun. **1**(2), 203–222 (2002). https://doi.org/10.1177/147035720200100205
5. Conley, T.D., Ramsey, L.R.: Killing Us softly? investigating portrayals of women and men in contemporary magazine advertisements. Psychol. Women Q. **35**(3), 469–478 (2011)
6. Davis, J., Goadrich, M.: The relationship between Precision-Recall and ROC curves. In: Proceedings of the 23rd International Conference on Machine Learning - ICML 2006. pp. 233–240. ACM Press, Pittsburgh, Pennsylvania (2006)
7. Deng, J., Guo, J., Zhou, Y., Yu, J., Kotsia, I., Zafeiriou, S.: RetinaFace: Single-stage Dense Face Localisation in the Wild. arXiv:1905.00641 [cs] (May 2019)
8. Dulhanty, C., Wong, A.: Auditing ImageNet: Towards a Model-driven Framework for Annotating Demographic Attributes of Large-Scale Image Datasets. arXiv:1905.01347 (2019), arXiv: 1905.01347
9. Eidinger, E., Enbar, R., Hassner, T.: Age and gender estimation of unfiltered faces. IEEE Trans. Inf. Forensics Secur. **9**(12), 2170–2179 (2014)
10. Everingham, M., Van Gool, L., Williams, C.K.I., Winn, J., Zisserman, A.: The pascal visual object classes (VOC) challenge. Int. J. Comput. Vis. **88**(2), 303–338 (2010)
11. Fyfe, P.: An archaeology of victorian newspapers. Victorian Period. Rev. **49**(4), 546–577 (2016)
12. Ghosh, S.: Google AI will no longer use gender labels like 'woman' or 'man' on images of people to avoid bias Febuary 2020. https://www.businessinsider.com/google-cloud-vision-api-wont-tag-images-by-gender-2020-2
13. Goffman, E.: Gender Advertisements. Harper and Row, New York (1976)
14. Goldman, R.: Reading Ads Socially. Routledge, New York (1992)
15. van der Hoeven, P.: Het succes van een kwaliteitskrant. Prometheus, Soest (2012)
16. Hu, P., Ramanan, D.: Finding Tiny Faces. arXiv:1612.04402 April 2017
17. Impett, L.: Painting by Numbers. Computational Methods and the History of Art. Ph.D. thesis, École Polytechnique Fédérale de Lausanne, Lausanne (2020)
18. Kang, M.E.: The portrayal of women's images in magazine advertisements: Goffman's gender analysis revisited. Sex Roles **37**(11), 979 (1997)
19. Klare, B.F., et al.: Pushing the frontiers of unconstrained face detection and recognition: IARPA Janus Benchmark A. In: 2015 IEEE Conference on Computer Vision and Pattern Recognition (CVPR). pp. 1931–1939 June 2015. iSSN: 1063–6919
20. Kuipers, G., van der Laan, E., Arfini, E.A.G.: Gender models: changing representations and intersecting roles in Dutch and Italian fashion magazines, 1982–2011. J. Gend. Stud. **26**(6), 632–648 (2017)
21. Levi, G., Hassner, T.: Age and gender classification using convolutional neural networks. In: Proceedings of the IEEE Conference on Computer Vision and Pattern Recognition Workshops, pp. 34–42 (2015)
22. Li, J., et al.: DSFD: Dual Shot Face Detector. arXiv:1810.10220 April 2019
23. Lin, T.Y., et al.: Microsoft COCO: Common Objects in Context. arXiv:1405.0312 [cs] (2015). arXiv: 1405.0312
24. Lindner, K.: Images of women in general interest and fashion magazine advertisements from 1955 to 2002. Sex Roles **51**(7), 409–421 (2004)
25. Long, M., Cao, Y., Wang, J., Jordan, M.I.: Learning Transferable Features with Deep Adaptation Networks. arXiv:1502.02791 May 2015
26. Luo, L., Xiong, Y., Liu, Y.: Adaptive gradient methods with dynamic bound of learning rate. In: International Conference on Learning Representations (2019). https://openreview.net/forum?id=Bkg3g2R9FX

27. Madhu, P., Kosti, R., Mührenberg, L., Bell, P., Maier, A., Christlein, V.: Recognizing characters in art history using deep learning. In: Proceedings of the 1st Workshop on Structuring and Understanding of Multimedia heritAge Contents, pp. 15–22. SUMAC '19, Association for Computing Machinery, Nice, France (2019)
28. Marchand, R.: Advertising the American Dream: Making Way for Modernity, 1920–1940. University of California Press, Berkeley (1985)
29. Merler, M., Ratha, N., Feris, R.S., Smith, J.R.: Diversity in Faces. arXiv:1901.10436 April 2019. arXiv: 1901.10436
30. Ng, C.B., Tay, Y.H., Goi, B.-M.: Recognizing human gender in computer vision: a survey. In: Anthony, P., Ishizuka, M., Lukose, D. (eds.) PRICAI 2012. LNCS (LNAI), vol. 7458, pp. 335–346. Springer, Heidelberg (2012). https://doi.org/10.1007/978-3-642-32695-0_31
31. Parkhi, O.M., Vedaldi, A., Zisserman, A.: Deep face recognition. In: Proceedings of the British Machine Vision Conference 2015, pp. 41.1-41.12. British Machine Vision Association, Swansea (2015)
32. Parkin, K.: Food Is Love: Advertising and Gender Roles in Modern America. University of Pennsylvania Press, Philadelphia (2007)
33. Ranjan, R., Patel, V.M., Chellappa, R.: HyperFace: A Deep Multi-task Learning Framework for Face Detection, Landmark Localization, Pose Estimation, and Gender Recognition. arXiv:1603.01249 December 2017
34. Russell, B.C., Torralba, A., Murphy, K.P., Freeman, W.T.: LabelMe: a database and web-based tool for image annotation. Int. J. Comput. Vis. 77(1), 157–173 (2008)
35. Schreurs, W.: Geschiedenis van de Reclame in Nederland. Het Spectrum, Utrecht (2001)
36. Schroeder, J.E., Zwick, D.: Mirrors of masculinity: representation and identity in advertising images. Consumption Mark. Cult. 7(1), 21–52 (2004)
37. Scranton, P.: Beauty and Business: Commerce, Gender, and Culture in Modern America. Routledge, London (2014)
38. Shankar, S., Halpern, Y., Breck, E., Atwood, J., Wilson, J., Sculley, D.: No Classification without Representation: Assessing Geodiversity Issues in Open Data Sets for the Developing World. arXiv:1711.08536 (2017), arXiv: 1711.08536
39. Smith, G.: Reconsidering Gender Advertisements. Performativity, Framing and Display. In: Jacobsen, M. (ed.) The Contemporary Goffman, pp. 165–184. Routledge, New York (2010)
40. Thomas, C., Kovashka, A.: Persuasive faces: Generating faces in advertisements. arXiv preprint arXiv:1807.09882 (2018)
41. Viola, P., Jones, M.J.: Robust real-time face detection. Int. J. Comput. Vis. 57(2), 137–154 (2004)
42. Weinbaum, A.E., Thomas, L., Ramamurthy, P., Poiger, U., Yue Dong, M., Barlow, T. (eds.): The Modern Girl around the World: Consumption, Modernity, and Globalization. Duke University Press, Durham (2008)
43. Wevers, M., Smits, T.: The visual digital turn: using neural networks to study historical images. Digit. Scholar. Hum. 35(1), 194–207 (2020)
44. Yang, K., Qinami, K., Fei-Fei, L., Deng, J., Russakovsky, O.: Towards fairer datasets: filtering and balancing the distribution of the people subtree in the ImageNet hierarchy. In: Proceedings of the 2020 Conference on Fairness, Accountability, and Transparency, pp. 547–558. Association for Computing Machinery, Barcelona, Spain (2020)
45. Yang, S., Luo, P., Loy, C.C., Tang, X.: Wider face: A face detection benchmark. In: IEEE Conference on Computer Vision and Pattern Recognition (CVPR) (2016)

46. Ye, K., Honarvar Nazari, N., Hahn, J., Hussain, Z., Zhang, M., Kovashka, A.: Interpreting the rhetoric of visual advertisements. IEEE Trans. Pattern Anal. Mach. Intell. 1 (2019)
47. Zafeiriou, S., Zhang, C., Zhang, Z.: A survey on face detection in the wild: past, present and future. Comput. Vis. Image Understand. **138**, 1–24 (2015)
48. Zhang, S., Zhu, X., Lei, Z., Shi, H., Wang, X., Li, S.Z.: Sfd: Single Shot Scale-invariant Face Detector. arXiv:1708.05237 November 2017
49. Zhong, Z., Zheng, L., Kang, G., Li, S., Yang, Y.: Random erasing data augmentation. arXiv:1708.04896 (2017)

A Dataset and Baselines for Visual Question Answering on Art

Noa Garcia[1]([✉]), Chentao Ye[2], Zihua Liu[2], Qingtao Hu[2], Mayu Otani[3], Chenhui Chu[1], Yuta Nakashima[1], and Teruko Mitamura[2]

[1] Osaka University, Suita, Japan
noagarcia@ids.osaka-u.ac.jp
[2] Carnegie Mellon University, Pittsburgh, USA
[3] CyberAgent, Inc., Tokyo, Japan

Abstract. Answering questions related to art pieces (paintings) is a difficult task, as it implies the understanding of not only the visual information that is shown in the picture, but also the contextual knowledge that is acquired through the study of the history of art. In this work, we introduce our first attempt towards building a new dataset, coined AQUA (Art QUestion Answering). The question-answer (QA) pairs are automatically generated using state-of-the-art question generation methods based on paintings and comments provided in an existing art understanding dataset. The QA pairs are cleansed by crowdsourcing workers with respect to their grammatical correctness, answerability, and answers' correctness. Our dataset inherently consists of visual (painting-based) and knowledge (comment-based) questions. We also present a two-branch model as baseline, where the visual and knowledge questions are handled independently. We extensively compare our baseline model against the state-of-the-art models for question answering, and we provide a comprehensive study about the challenges and potential future directions for visual question answering on art.

Keywords: Visual question answering · Art dataset · External knowledge

1 Introduction

Providing human-like semantic interpretation of visual information is one of the ultimate goals of technologies around artificial intelligence, computer vision, and natural language processing. Tremendous research efforts have been made towards this goal, including object detection [10], phrase grounding [40], image/video captioning [46], *etc.*. Visual question answering (VQA) is among these works and is now one of the main stream topics [49]. VQA may require high-level comprehension of the image content, as well as questions given as natural language. Recently, various extensions of the VQA task have been proposed, including ones requiring knowledge [50].

The main target of the VQA task has been natural images, which capture real-world objects, scenes, and events. Very few work addresses other types

© Springer Nature Switzerland AG 2020
A. Bartoli and A. Fusiello (Eds.): ECCV 2020 Workshops, LNCS 12536, pp. 92–108, 2020.
https://doi.org/10.1007/978-3-030-66096-3_8

Q: What animal is this?   Q: Who depicts Napoleon in 1814?

A: Horse   **A: Meissonier**

Fig. 1. Examples from the AQUA dataset. There are two different types of QA pairs: generated from paintings (left) and generated from paintings' comments (right).

of visual information, *e.g.*, the abstract image subset of the VQA dataset [2], CLEVR [23], and PororoQA [25]. One of the primary reasons for using non-real-world images is to unburden visual recognition in the VQA pipeline to give more focus on answer prediction.

Meanwhile, artworks, or paintings, are another interesting domain for VQA. Besides their cultural and historical importance, paintings pose extra challenges in VQA: Firstly, paintings may express a subject in different abstraction levels, perhaps being associated to the continuum spanned by naturalism, realism, symbolism, impressionism, cubism, *etc.* Pretrained models for, *e.g.*, object detection, may work well for realism but not necessarily for cubism. Secondly, the interpretation of paintings can be highly dependent on their background, such as the social and the author's personal context, which may not be fully conveyed from the paintings themselves. This implies that external knowledge on the background of paintings may be needed for answering questions.

This paper offers our first attempt to build a benchmark for question answering on artworks by providing the AQUA (**a**rt **qu**estion **a**nswering) dataset, built upon the SemArt dataset [14], together with a baseline model. The QA pairs (see examples in Fig. 1) are automatically generated using multiple state-of-the-art question generation methods, which have been studied in the communities of both natural language processing [8,17,29,55] and computer vision [23,27,36,51]. We use both the paintings themselves and the comments, provided in the SemArt dataset, as the input source for generating QA pairs. In this way, the paintings provide information to generate visual questions (*e.g.* "What animal is this?" in Fig. 1), and the comments are used to generate knowledge-based questions about art (*e.g.* "Who depicts Napoleon in 1814?" in Fig. 1).

To address this new QA task, we propose a baseline model specially designed to leverage knowledge information about art, which comes with modality selection on top of recent VQA and text QA models, which is coined as VIKING (**vi**sual- and **k**nowkedge-branch network for predict**ing** answers). This network handles the dual-modality (visual and external knowledge-based) of the art questions with dedicated branches.

Our contributions can be summarized as follows:

- Firstly, we propose a new task of art question answering, which inherently involves visual understanding of and knowledge on paintings. The latter may be deemed as textual understanding, as such knowledge can be found in books and online documents, *e.g. Wikipedia*. Answering questions that require both visual and textual modalities has not been well explored so far.
- Secondly, we build a preliminary dataset, AQUA, and make it publicly available.[1] The QA pairs are manually cleansed by crowdsourcing workers with respect to each question's answerability and grammatical correctness, as well as the answer's correctness.
- Thirdly, we present a baseline model, named VIKING, for our art QA task. In addition to the question, the baseline model uses the painting and a paragraph retrieved from a knowledge base to predict the answer that is relevant to both the question and the painting.
- Finally, through the results of this study, we can envisage the challenges and possible solutions that future research aiming to address visual question answering on art must consider.

2 Related Work

2.1 Computer Vision for Art

Arts and computer vision have an inevitable link as many artworks have some visual components. One fundamental direction is the digitization of artworks for archiving and restoration (*e.g.* [19]). Several studies have been done for artworks in the computer vision field, including author/style identification [22,42,42], image classification [3,13,18,31,31,44], and image retrieval [3,3–5]. To the best of our knowledge, this is the first work for question answering on paintings.

2.2 Question Generation

Visual Question Generation. Visual question generation (VQG) can be categorized into grounded and open-ended [39]. Grounded VQG generates questions whose answers can be found in the information relevant to the input image [54]. To this end, captions are first generated from the image, and either rule-based [41,57] or neural [54] models are used to further generate questions from the captions. Open-ended VQG are often about abstract concepts such as events and states, which can be inferred by the objects in an image [37]. Diversity is crucial for open-ended VQG, for which variational auto-encoders [20] and generative adversarial network [11] have been used.

---

[1] https://github.com/noagarcia/ArtVQA.

Textual Question Generation. Either rule-based or neural model-based approach has been applied for textual question generation (TQG). Rule-based TQG first constructs question templates either manually [17,35] or via crowdsourcing [28], and then applies the templates to generate questions. [8] pioneers the first neural model for TQG, which apply the sequence-to-sequence model with attention. Neural TQG studies focus on how to encode answers [26,55], generate question words [9,43], and use paragraph-level context [7,55].

2.3 Visual Question Answering

Previous VQA studies are on either natural images or videos. Commonly used techniques for image-based VQA include joint visual and language embeddings, and attention mechanisms that model where to look in an image [49]. One extension of VQA is to answer questions on video. Because of the temporal information in videos, action recognition [21,32,38,53], story understanding [25,45], and temporal coherence [56] have been further incorporated. Another interesting extension is to use external knowledge beyond images and videos. The knowledge can be either general [34,47,50] or dataset specific [12,48].

Because the acquisition of data is not always a trivial task, synthetic datasets have been commonly used by the VQA community. For example, Malinowski and Fritz [33] used automatically generated QA pairs based on some templates. Johnson *et al.* [23] also employed generated QA pairs on synthetic images, mainly for excluding possible biases in standard datasets. Similarly, our AQUA dataset is also synthetic and, as with the datasets in [23,33], we aim that it serves as a proof-of-concept for VQA on the domain of art.

3   AQUA Dataset

We use the SemArt dataset [14], which is originally designed for semantic art understanding, as our source for generating our QA pairs. The SemArt dataset contains paintings and associated comments, where comments are blocks of text, sometimes including the metadata about the painting, such as the author name and created year. They can also have several sentences about the story in the painting and the contextual background when it was created, such as the social and the author's personal situations. These comments serve as knowledge. In order to show the potentials of AI technologies to comprehend paintings, it is important to explore techniques that work not only on the visual content in the painting themselves but also on their surrounding ideas. We therefore generate QA pairs from visual and knowledge modalities with respective question generation methods.

3.1   Question Generation

Visual Question Generation. The inherent necessity of visual understanding makes question generation from the image content a tough problem. A number of methods have been proposed so far [39]. We try two of them to generate a diverse set of visual questions. The first one is iQAN [30] trained on VQA v2.0 [15],[2] which takes an image and an answer word as input and generates a question using a neural network model. We use the object detector provided in Amazon Rekognition[3] to obtain the answer words. The other one uses Pythia[4] to generated a caption for each painting and transforms each generated caption into a QA pair by applying the rule-based TQG technique described below.

Knowledge-Based Question Generation (KQG). For generating questions that involves the knowledge about art, we apply TQG methods, which have been studied by the natural language processing community for the last decades, relying on the natural language knowledge comments available in the SemArt dataset. We tried several TQG approaches, *i.e.*, rule-based and neural ones. The rule-based approach [17] builds a parsing tree from an input sentence and transforms it to QA pairs based on a set of rules. The resulting QA pairs may be filtered by statistical ranking to drop less-likely samples. The neural approach [8] is based on sequence-to-sequence modeling. We found that the rule-based technique yielded more satisfactory QA pairs.

3.2 QA Pair Evaluation and Cleansing

Question Generation Evaluation. We use Amazon Mechanical Turk[5] (AMT) to evaluate the quality of our QA pairs, given a painting as well as its associated comment and question, with the following criteria:

- **Grammatical correctness** measures whether the QA pair is syntactically well-formed, specified by (i) *no grammatical error*, (ii) *minor errors* (there are some errors but the QA pair still makes sense), and (iii) *major errors* (the QA pair does not make any sense).
- **Answer existence** identifies whether the question has a clear answer in the given painting and comment.
- **Answer correctness** measures given the QA pair whether the answer to the question is correct.
- **Necessity of visual information** evaluates whether the visual information in the painting is needed to answer the question.
- **Necessity of textual information** evaluates if the textual information in the comment is needed to answer the question.
- **Question reasonability** judges whether the QA pair looks like human-generated.

We randomly selected 1,000 and 989 QA pairs from both VQG and KQG, respectively, and evaluated them (Table 1). Our VGQ samples have a high grammatical correctness. However, the answer existence and correctness are low. The

---

[2] The code is reproduced by ourselves, and we confirmed a similar performance to that of the original paper.
[3] https://aws.amazon.com/rekognition/.
[4] https://github.com/facebookresearch/pythia.
[5] http://www.mturk.com.

Table 1. Evaluation for question generation by AMT. For grammatical correctness, the proportion of QA pairs with (i) no error and (ii) minor errors are shown, where 0.429 and 0.687 of QA pairs are with no error for VQG and KQG, respectively.

Criterion	VQG	KQG
Grammatical correctness	0.936	0.871
Answer existence	0.504	0.842
Answer correctness	0.337	0.735
Necessity of visual information	0.977	0.514
Necessity of knowledge	0.098	0.935
Question reasonability	0.691	0.690

errors mainly come from two factors: object detection and visual encoding. Our iQAN-based VQG uses an object as input. If the object detector fails, the answer will be incorrect, which will also affect the question generation. As Amazon Rekognition is trained on real-world photos, it sometimes predicts the objects incorrectly in paintings. For the same reason, the visual encoding in iQAN and the image captioning are not as accurate as that for real-world photo datasets. This explains why many questions do not have answers in the associated painting and comment. The necessity of knowledge is low because our models tend to ask relatively simple visual questions. Yet nearly 70% of QA pairs look like human generated.

The result for KQG shows that our generated samples also have a high grammatical quality. A common source of negative responses is pronouns in generated answers (*e.g.*, *it* and *they*) because our rule-based model does not exclude pronouns in grammar trees from the candidate answer list. For 84% of QA pairs, their answers are found in the context, and 74% of answers are correct; a possible reason for these superior results is that the question and answer are generated together from the same grammar tree. Knowledge is required in over 93% of QA pairs as expected because the questions are coming from the comments. Interestingly, crowd workers tend to find visual information is still necessary even for knowledge QA pairs. The question reasonability criterion shows that most QA pairs are likely to be generated by humans.

Dataset Cleansing and Statistics. To exclude QA pairs with major grammatical errors or without (correct) answers, we again use AMT. Unlike the evaluation, this time, we only evaluate grammatical correctness as well as answer existence/correctness but on the entire dataset. Table 2 shows the statistics of our AQUA dataset after cleansing. Due to low answer existence/correctness, the number of visual QA pairs is smaller than that of knowledge QA pairs. The question length comes with an obvious bias because of the difference in the question generation methods.

Table 2. Statistics on the AQUA dataset.

	Train	Val	Test
# QA pairs	69,812	5,124	4,912
# Visual QA pairs	29,568	1,507	1,270
# Knowledge QA pairs	40,244	3,617	3,642
Question length (in word)	8.82	9.21	9.41
For visual QA	6.53	6.50	6.51
For knowledge QA	10.50	10.33	10.43
Answer length	3.13	3.68	3.85
For visual QA	1.00	1.00	1.00
For knowledge QA	4.69	4.79	4.85

3.3 Task Definition

With our AQUA dataset, there can be several possible task definitions. In this paper, we focus on the one in which all the comments that are associated with paintings are available. More specifically, let $C = \{c_i | i = 1, \ldots, N\}$ denote the set of all the comments. The aim of AQUA task is to answer question q given painting v using C, without an explicit association between v and a specific comment in C. In this task, C can be viewed as an external source of knowledge, containing the necessary information to answer the question when the comment associated with q is correctly retrieved.

A more challenging extension of this task is to not use C but other sources of knowledge, *e.g. Wikipedia*. With this extension, the performance also depends on the quality of the sources and their affinity to the original source. We leave the extension as future work.

4   VIKING Model

By construction, the AQUA dataset contains two types of questions. We design our baseline model, coined VIKING, to handle them with dedicated branches. Figure 2 illustrates the overall pipeline. Inspired by the intuition that humans first look into the given question and then try to locate the required information to answer it (in our case, either the associated painting or comment), VIKING consists of three main components: The question and painting are first fed into a *modality selector*, which classifies the question into visual or knowledge-based ones. Questions about the visual content go through the *visual QA branch*. Otherwise, questions are passed to the *knowledge QA branch*, in which an associated comment is retrieved from C. We detail these three components below.

4.1   Modality Selector

Our modality selector S classifies a question q into these two modalities given q and v, so that it can go through the corresponding branch. We use pretrained

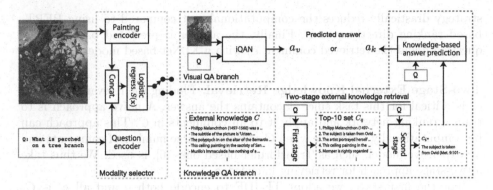

Fig. 2. An overview of our VIKING model for the AQUA dataset.

BERT [6] as the question encoder. More specifically, question q is encoded into a 1,024 dimensional vector $\mathbf{q}$, which is BERT's output corresponding to the special token [CLS]. For our painting encoder, we use pretrained ResNet-152 [16] to encode the painting into a 2,048 dimensional vector $\mathbf{v}$. We concatenate $\mathbf{q}$ and $\mathbf{v}$ into a vector $\mathbf{x}$ and train a logistic regression model

$$S(\mathbf{x}) = \frac{1}{1 + e^{-(\mathbf{w}_s^\top \mathbf{x} - b_s)}},$$

where $\mathbf{w}_s$ and b_s are a trainable vector and scalar. Question q is passed to the visual QA branch when $S(\mathbf{x}) > 0.5$ and to the knowledge QA branch otherwise.

4.2 Visual QA Branch

Visual questions can be answered solely based on the associated painting without any external knowledge. For this question type, the task is reduced to VQA over paintings.

We again use iQAN [30] as our visual QA branch, which is a dual model and can take either a question or an answer as input, then output the counterpart. We separately train the iQAN model over the training split of our AQUA dataset (*i.e.*, we do not use the iQAN model trained for question generation). This branch produces a predicted answer a_v, which is from the answer vocabulary A consisting of the top-5,000 most common words in the training split.

4.3 Knowledge QA Branch

Questions classified as knowledge-based are fed to the knowledge QA branch. We first retrieve the comment in C that is the most relevant to q with a two-stage strategy. In the first stage, we apply TF-IDF to rank all the comments in C with respect to their relevance to q and obtain the subset C_q consisting of the top-10 most relevant comments. In the second stage, comments in C_q are re-ranked using BERT to find the most relevant comment c_q. This two-stage strategy drastically reduces the computational cost compared to using BERT-based ranking directly over C. Finally, the answer is predicted based on the question q and the retrieved comment c_q with a XLNet-based model.

Two-Stage External Knowledge Retrieval. Finding the relevant comment c_q is critical for this task since it contains the answer. A naive approach is to train a ranking network and apply it to all comments in C. This approach can be computationally expensive when C contains a large number of comments and an expensive model, such as Transformer-based ones [6], is used. We thus take a two-stage approach for retrieving knowledge.

For the first stage, we adopt TF-IDF to encode both q and all $c_i \in C$. Letting $\hat{\mathbf{q}}$ and $\hat{\mathbf{c}}_i$ be the respective TF-IDF vectors, we compute the score $s_i = \hat{\mathbf{q}}^\top \hat{\mathbf{c}}_i / (\|\hat{\mathbf{q}}\| \|\hat{\mathbf{c}}_i\|)$. The set C_q consists of c_i's that have the 10 highest s_i's. In order to improve the ranking accuracy, we apply to both q and c_i (i) preprocessing with NLTK[6] for stop word removal and word stemming and (ii) n-gram TF-IDF where $n = 3$.

The second stage further ranks $c_i \in C_q$ to find the comment associated with the question. We cast this into a sentence pair classification problem and use a BERT-based model to predict how likely a given c_i is relevant to q. We concatenate q and each $c_i \in C_q$ with [SEP] and feed it to the pretrained BERT. The output o_i associated with [CLS] is passed to a logistic regression model, given by

$$R(\mathbf{o}_i) = \frac{1}{1 + e^{-(\mathbf{w}_r^\top \mathbf{o}_i - b_r)}},$$

where $\mathbf{w}_r$ and b_r are trainable vector and scalar. The model is trained as a binary classifier that predicts whether q and c_i are relevant or not, but its output $R(\mathbf{o}_i)$ is treated as the score for c_i when inference. We use c_{i^*} where $i^* = \arg\max_i R(\mathbf{o}_i)$ for answering the question.

Knowledge-Based Answer Prediction. We use XLNet[7] [52] for predicting the answer in knowledge-based questions. We concatenate the question q and the c_{i^*} with [SEP], and feed it to XLNet, which predicts the positions of the answer starting and ending in c_{i^*}. We extract the words between the predicted starting and ending position as answer a_k. We use a pre-trained XLNet and fine-tune it over the knowledge QA pairs in our AQUA dataset.

5   Evaluation

In this section, we show the performance of VIKING as well as several more basic baselines and state-of-the-art VQA methods on the AQUA dataset.

---

[6] https://www.nltk.org/.

[7] We used XLNet instead of BERT as XLNet shows better performance on the popular Stanford question answering dataset (SQuAD2.0).

5.1 Evaluation Details

The performance of our task is measured by exact match (EM), *i.e.* the percentage of predictions that match the ground truth answer exactly. This EM-based evaluation enables us to compare baselines, VIKING, and its variants in a single framework. It should be noted that, in the visual QA branch, the answer is the most probable word among the answer vocabulary A (the top 5,000 most common answers in the training split). The upper bound of the accuracy is 0.306 if all QA pairs in the test split would went through the visual QA branch because only 1,505 QA pairs out of 4,912 have the answer in A. In the models that exploit external knowledge, the answer is extracted from the text in C.

5.2 Baselines and VIKING Variants

Our first set of baselines are both blind and ignorant, answering questions without paintings and external knowledge.

- **LSTM.** Each word in a question is converted into word embeddings, which are trained from scratch. The word embeddings are input into a 2-layer LSTM. The hidden state of the last layer is fed into a fully connected layer classifier with the softmax activation over the answer vocabulary A.
- **BERT.** Each question is input into a fine-tuned base and uncased BERT model. The special tokens [CLS] and [SEP] are added at the beginning and at the end of each sentence, respectively. The output from the first token is fed into a fully connected layer classifier followed by softmax to predict the most probable answer in the same way as the LSTM baseline.
- **XLNet.** Instead of the BERT model, XLNet is used to encode questions. The classification is done in the same way as the BERT baseline.

The second set of baselines use paintings but not external knowledge to answer questions.

- **BUTD.** Bottom-up and top-down attention [1] consists of a bottom-up module that generates object proposals from the image, and a top-down module that predicts an attention distribution over those proposals based on the question, encoded with a GRU. The answers are chosen from A.
- **BAN.** Bilinear attention network [24] also extracts a set of region proposals from the image and encodes questions with a GRU. Differently from BUTD, BAN computes attention between all the image proposals and all the words in the question.

For our VIKING model, we have three variants, *i.e.*, VIKING without the knowledge QA branch ($w/o\ K$), without the visual QA branch ($w/o\ P$), and the *full* model. In addition to them, we also evaluate the upper bound performance when the ground truth modality labels are used instead of the modality selector (VIKING w/L).

Table 3. Accuracy for different methods on the AQUA test split. Q, P, K, and L stand for questions, paintings, external knowledge, and labels, which are the information used in the respective models.

Method	Q	P	K	L	EM
LSTM	✓	–	–	–	0.198
BERT	✓	–	–	–	0.194
XLNet	✓	–	–	–	0.193
BUTD	✓	✓	–	–	0.218
BAN	✓	✓	–	–	0.224
VIKING w/o K	✓	✓	–	–	0.204
VIKING w/o P	✓	-	✓	–	0.352
VIKING full	✓	✓	✓	–	0.555
VIKING w/L	✓	✓	✓	✓	0.555

5.3 Results Analysis

Model Comparison. Results are presented in Table 3. As expected, methods relying only on questions to answer perform poorly, showing that the task requires the information from multiple inputs for answering correctly. When the paintings are added into the system, as in BUTD and BAN, performance improves up to 0.224. However, they lag well behind the accuracy obtained with our proposed VIKING that leverages the information from external sources of information. Overall, our proposed model outperforms other methods, including BUTD and BAN, by a huge margin.

VIKING Variants. Our full model improves by more than 0.351 and 0.203 compared to the results of the visual and the knowledge QA branch only models, respectively, showing the benefits of using both the visual information obtained from the paintings and the information obtained from external knowledge. Also, we note that the use of ground truth labels instead of the modality selector hardly affects the overall performance. This implies the modality selector's efficiency.

Qualitative Results. Figure 3 shows example predictions by VIKING *full.* The modalities of all six examples are correctly predicted. The dataset sometimes contains question and answer pairs that are not obvious. The top-right example illustrates this problem, in which it is not clear if there is a wall or any other things next to the fruit. For the bottom-right example, the ground-truth answer is "in the year before his death," while VIKING predicted "before his death." Semantically, the prediction is almost correct, but it is counted as incorrect due to the EM-based evaluation.

5.4 Evaluation of Knowledge-Related Components

Next, we study the performance of the components involving external knowledge.

Question:
what is in the water?

Predicted modality:
Visual

Answer: boat
Ground truth: boat

Question:
what is the green stuff on the ground?

Predicted modality:
Visual

Answer: plant
Ground truth: plant

Question:
what do a pile of fruit sit next to?

Predicted modality:
Visual

Answer: tree
Ground truth: wall

Question:
what had delacroix sold to the french state?

Predicted modality:
Knowledge

Retrieved knowledge:

... It was precisely these effects which, as employed by Constable in the Hay-Wain exhibited at the Paris Salon in 1824, caused a sensation and further exacerbated Delacroix's fashionable Chios to the French State, he set out for London with two English friends, the watercolourists Richard Bonington and Thales Fielding. They visited galleries and the theatre and read English poets. They visited galleries and the theatre ...

Answer:
his picture of the Massacre of Chois
Groupd truth:
his picture of the Massacre of Chois

Question:
what what was painted tapestry?

Predicted modality:
Knowledge

Retrieved knowledge:

With such paintings as painted tapestry, painting within a painting it became possible to use the flat surface of a ceiling vault for narrative depictions. Given a corresponding design of the fictive architecture of a vault structure it became possible to combine an illusory extension of the room upward with an outward extension. Raphael's ingenious idea in the Vatican loggias was applied by Samacchini in Sala Baganza

Answer:
painting within a painting
Groupd truth:
painting within a painting

Question:
when did van gogh live in the asylum of saint-paul-de-mausole

Predicted modality:
Knowledge

Retrieved knowledge:

In the year before his death, Van Gogh lived in the asylum of Saint-Paul-de-Mausole. The present painting reflects an artist determined to heal himself through work. On most mornings between May 1889 and May 1890, the outside world visible to Vincent van Gogh appeared much like it does in this painting: a low stone wall enclosing a wheat field, a few poplars, an old farm house, a ploughman tilling the soil.Catalogue numbers: F 625 JH 1768

Answer:
before his death
Groupd truth:
in the year before his death

Fig. 3. VIKING *full* results for visual (up) and knowledge (down) questions. The rightmost column shows incorrect predictions for both modalities.

Modality Selector. Table 4 shows the confusion matrix of the modality selector on the test split. Since the visual and the knowledge questions are generated using different methods, it is relatively easy for the classifier to distinguish them, getting an accuracy of 0.996. This result supports the fact that there is no gain between VIKING *full* and *w/L*. Most failures in the modality selector (Fig. 4 gives some examples) are reasonable, asking questions that appear to require the other modality.

External Knowledge Retrieval. The performance of the external knowledge retrieval is reported in Table 5, together with its variants. The performance is measured as recall at k (R@k), *i.e.* the percentage of QA pairs whose original

Q: what is the purpose of the white lines?
A: *fog*

Ground truth: Visual
Prediction: Knowledge

Q: what are the flowers surrounded by?
A: *by early Victorian silver, ribbon, and jewelry*

Ground truth: Knowledge
Prediction: Visual

Q: who are the women here?
A: Courbet's sisters

Ground truth: Visual
Prediction: Knowledge

Fig. 4. Failures in modality selector.

Table 4. Confusion matrix of the modality selector.

Label	Prediction	
	Visual	Knowledge
Visual	1,269	1
Knowledge	17	3,625

comment is ranked in the top k positions. Our two-stage external knowledge retrieval achieves the highest performance. Specifically, the full variant (*i.e.*, TF-IDF + PP + n-gram, where PP stands for preprocessing) of the first stage ranked the original comments within top-10 for over 90% of QA pairs, whereas the second stage gains over 5% by the BERT-based ranking.

6   Discussion

This work is presented as a concise first approximation to the task of art-based visual question answering and it aims to set the foundations for incorporating art knowledge in a computer vision system. However, despite the encouraging results obtained in our experimental evaluation, it presents some limitations.

Dataset Limitations: The questions and answers in our proposed AQUA dataset are automatically generated from paintings and their associated comments. This process presents some limitations: 1) questions and their answers are either relate to the visual content or to the background knowledge, but usually not both. It would be interesting to incorporate samples where both are needed, increasing the complexity of the problem; 2) the visual questions are based on the labels extracted by an object detector trained on real-world photos, which introduces noise specially on paintings with non-realistic styles; and 3) because of the automatic generation of answers, the variety of the questions and of the capabilities required to answer them is rather limited, *e.g.*, the answers of visual questions can only be detected objects in the images.

Table 5. External knowledge retrieval performance. PP stands for preprocessing.

First stage	Second stage	R@1	R@5	R@10
TF-IDF	–	0.588	0.775	0.822
TF-IDF + PP	–	0.600	0.803	0.844
TF-IDF + PP + n-gram	–	0.712	0.878	0.907
TF-IDF + PP + n-gram	✓	0.769	0.879	0.907

Baseline Limitation: We introduced VIKING as a baseline model for art-based VQA. VIKING is built on top of state-of-the-art VQA and TQA models. Apart from the specific limitations of those systems, VIKING presents two domain specific limitations: 1) on the visual part, the model is applied equally to all the painting images, without considering the differences on artistic styles. Incorporating style correction techniques would benefit the visual recognition part, specially for object detection; 2) on the knowledge part, VIKING uses the same source of information as in the question generation process (*i.e.*, comments from the SemArt dataset). A more realistic setting would require to query independent sources of external knowledge, such as Wikipedia.

Considering these limitations, we envisage some promising future directions on art-based VQA. On the dataset construction part, it would be interesting to incorporate human expert question-answer pairs that require both visual and knowledge understanding. This would increase the complexity and relevance of the dataset. On the model design part, the addition of specific features related to paintings, differing from the real-world images, would probably improve the model performance. For example, adaptation between the real-world and the painting domain in the object detector, or disentanglement of content and style.

7 Conclusion

This paper proposes a new task of visual question answering on art pieces, and presents our preliminary dataset on this task, coined AQUA, which consists on automatically generated visual and knowledge-based QA pairs. We also present a model called VIKING that serves as a baseline for future exploration on this task. VIKING leverages complementary information in paintings and external knowledge with a two branch model. Our experimental results demonstrated that VIKING outperformed existing models with a large margin, which means that the model is a strong baseline to compare. The task definition in this paper assumes that the external knowledge is strongly tied with the questions (*i.e.*, the comments used for generating the QA pairs are available for the QA module). This may be in a sense viewed as the upper bound of the performance. Using other sources of external knowledge will be our future direction.

Acknowledgment. This work was partly supported by JSPS KAKENHI Nos. 18H03264 and 20K19822, and JST ACT-I.

References

1. Anderson, P., et al.: Bottom-up and top-down attention for image captioning and visual question answering. In: CVPR (2018)
2. Antol, S., et al.: VQA: visual question answering. In: ICCV (2015)
3. Carneiro, G., da Silva, N.P., Del Bue, A., Costeira, J.P.: Artistic image classification: an analysis on the PRINTART database. In: Fitzgibbon, A., Lazebnik, S., Perona, P., Sato, Y., Schmid, C. (eds.) ECCV 2012. LNCS, vol. 7575, pp. 143–157. Springer, Heidelberg (2012). https://doi.org/10.1007/978-3-642-33765-9_11
4. Crowley, E., Zisserman, A.: The state of the art: object retrieval in paintings using discriminative regions. In: BMVC (2014)
5. Crowley, E.J., Parkhi, O.M., Zisserman, A.: Face painting: querying art with photos. In: BMVC (2015)
6. Devlin, J., Chang, M.W., Lee, K., Toutanova, K.: BERT: pre-training of deep bidirectional transformers for language understanding. In: NAACL-HLT (2019)
7. Du, X., Cardie, C.: Harvesting paragraph-level question-answer pairs from Wikipedia. In: ACL (2018)
8. Du, X., Shao, J., Cardie, C.: Learning to ask: neural question generation for reading comprehension. In: ACL (2017)
9. Duan, N., Tang, D., Chen, P., Zhou, M.: Question generation for question answering. In: EMNLP (2017)
10. Everingham, M., Van Gool, L., Williams, C.K.I., Winn, J., Zisserman, A.: The Pascal Visual Object Classes (VOC) challenge. IJCV $88(2)$, 303–338 (2010)
11. Fan, Z., Wei, Z., Wang, S., Liu, Y., Huang, X.: A reinforcement learning framework for natural question generation using bi-discriminators. In: COLING (2018)
12. Garcia, N., Otani, M., Chu, C., Nakashima, Y.: KnowIT VQA: answering knowledge-based questions about videos. In: AAAI (2020)
13. Garcia, N., Renoust, B., Nakashima, Y.: Context-aware embeddings for automatic art analysis. In: ICMR (2019)
14. Garcia, N., Vogiatzis, G.: How to read paintings: semantic art understanding with multi-modal retrieval. In: Leal-Taixé, L., Roth, S. (eds.) ECCV 2018. LNCS, vol. 11130, pp. 676–691. Springer, Cham (2019). https://doi.org/10.1007/978-3-030-11012-3_52
15. Goyal, Y., Khot, T., Summers-Stay, D., Batra, D., Parikh, D.: Making the V in VQA matter: elevating the role of image understanding in visual question answering. In: Proceedings of CVPR (2017)
16. He, K., Zhang, X., Ren, S., Sun, J.: Deep residual learning for image recognition. In: CVPR (2016)
17. Heilman, M., Smith, N.A.: Good question! Statistical ranking for question generation. In: NAACL (2010)
18. Huckle, N., Garcia, N., Vogiatzis, G.: Demographic influences on contemporary art with unsupervised style embeddings. In: ECCV workshops (2020)
19. Ikeuchi, K., et al.: The great Buddha project: digitally archiving restoring, and analyzing cultural heritage objects. IJCV 75, 189–208 (2007)
20. Jain, U., Zhang, Z., Schwing, A.G.: Creativity: generating diverse questions using variational autoencoders. In: CVPR (2017)
21. Jang, Y., Song, Y., Yu, Y., Kim, Y., Kim, G.: TGIF-QA: toward spatio-temporal reasoning in visual question answering. In: Proceedings of CVPR (2017)
22. Johnson, C.R., et al.: Image processing for artist identification. IEEE Signal Process. Mag. $25(4)$, 37–48 (2008)

23. Johnson, J., Hariharan, B., van der Maaten, L., Fei-Fei, L., Zitnick, C.L., Girshick, R.: CLEVR: a diagnostic dataset for compositional language and elementary visual reasoning. In: Proceedings of CVPR (2017)
24. Kim, J.H., Jun, J., Zhang, B.T.: Bilinear attention networks. In: NeurIPS (2018)
25. Kim, K.M., Heo, M.O., Choi, S.H., Zhang, B.T.: DeepStory: video story QA by deep embedded memory networks. In: Proceedings of IJCAI (2017)
26. Kim, Y., Lee, H., Shin, J., Jung, K.: Improving neural question generation using answer separation. In: AAAI (2019)
27. Krishna, R., Bernstein, M., Fei-Fei, L.: Information maximizing visual question generation. In: CVPR (2019)
28. Labutov, I., Basu, S., Vanderwende, L.: Deep questions without deep understanding. In: ACL-IJCNLP (2015)
29. Lewis, M., Fan, A.: Generative question answering: learning to answer the whole question. In: ICLR (2019)
30. Li, Y., et al.: Visual question generation as dual task of visual question answering. In: CVPR (2018)
31. Ma, D., et al.: From part to whole: who is behind the painting? In: ACMMM (2017)
32. Maharaj, T., Ballas, N., Rohrbach, A., Courville, A., Pal, C.: A dataset and exploration of models for understanding video data through fill-in-the-blank question-answering. In: CVPR (2017)
33. Malinowski, M., Fritz, M.: A multi-world approach to question answering about real-world scenes based on uncertain input. In: Proceedings of NIPS (2014)
34. Marino, K., Rastegari, M., Farhadi, A., Mottaghi, R.: OK-VQA: a visual question answering benchmark requiring external knowledge. In: CVPR (2019)
35. Mazidi, K., Nielsen, R.D.: Linguistic considerations in automatic question generation. In: ACL (2014)
36. Misra, I., Girshick, R., Fergus, R., Hebert, M., Gupta, A., van der Maaten, L.: Learning by asking questions. In: CVPR (2018)
37. Mostafazadeh, N., Misra, I., Devlin, J., Mitchell, M., He, X., Vanderwende, L.: Generating natural questions about an image. In: ACL (2016)
38. Mun, J., Hongsuck Seo, P., Jung, I., Han, B.: MarioQA: answering questions by watching gameplay videos. In: Proceedings of ICCV (2017)
39. Pan, L., Lei, W., Chua, T., Kan, M.: Recent advances in neural question generation. CoRR abs/1905.08949 (2019)
40. Plummer, B.A., Wang, L., Cervantes, C.M., Caicedo, J.C., Hockenmaier, J., Lazebnik, S.: Flickr30k Entities: collecting region-to-phrase correspondences for richer image-to-sentence models. In: ICCV (2015)
41. Ren, M., Kiros, R., Zemel, R.S.: Exploring models and data for image question answering. In: NeurIPS (2015)
42. Shamir, L., Macura, T., Orlov, N., Eckley, D.M., Goldberg, I.G.: Impressionism, expressionism, surrealism: automated recognition of painters and schools of art. ACM Trans. Appl. Percept. **7**, 1–17 (2010)
43. Sun, X., Liu, J., Lyu, Y., He, W., Ma, Y., Wang, S.: Answer-focused and position-aware neural question generation. In: EMNLP (2018)
44. Tan, W.R., Chan, C.S., Aguirre, H.E., Tanaka, K.: Ceci n'est pas une pipe: a deep convolutional network for fine-art paintings classification. In: ICIP (2016)
45. Tapaswi, M., Zhu, Y., Stiefelhagen, R., Torralba, A., Urtasun, R., Fidler, S.: MovieQA: understanding stories in movies through question-answering. In: Proceedings of CVPR (2016)

46. Vinyals, O., Toshev, A., Bengio, S., Erhan, D.: Show and tell: a neural image caption generator. In: CVPR (2015)
47. Wang, P., Wu, Q., Shen, C., Dick, A., van den Hengel, A.: FVQA: fact-based visual question answering. TPAMI **40**(10), 2413–2427 (2018)
48. Wang, P., Wu, Q., Shen, C., Dick, A., Van Den Henge, A.: Explicit knowledge-based reasoning for visual question answering. In: IJCAI, pp. 1290–1296 (2017)
49. Wu, Q., Teney, D., Wang, P., Shen, C., Dick, A., van den Hengel, A.: Visual question answering: a survey of methods and datasets. CVIU **163**, 1–20 (2017)
50. Wu, Q., Wang, P., Shen, C., Dick, A., van den Hengel, A.: Ask me anything: free-form visual question answering based on knowledge from external sources. In: CVPR (2016)
51. Yang, J., Lu, J., Lee, S., Dhruv Batra, D.P.: Visual curiosity: learning to ask questions to learn visual recognition. In: CoRL (2018)
52. Yang, Z., Dai, Z., Yang, Y., Carbonell, J., Salakhutdinov, R.R., Le, Q.V.: XLNet: generalized autoregressive pretraining for language understanding. In: NeurIPS (2019)
53. Zellers, R., Bisk, Y., Farhadi, A., Choi, Y.: From recognition to cognition: visual commonsense reasoning. In: Proceedings of CVPR (2019)
54. Zhang, S., Qu, L., You, S., Yang, Z., Zhang, J.: Automatic generation of grounded visual questions. In: IJCAI, pp. 4235–4243 (2017)
55. Zhao, Y., Ni, X., Ding, Y., Ke, Q.: Paragraph-level neural question generation with maxout pointer and gated self-attention networks. In: EMNLP (2018)
56. Zhu, L., Xu, Z., Yang, Y., Hauptmann, A.G.: Uncovering the temporal context for video question answering. IJCV **124**(3), 409–421 (2017)
57. Zhu, Y., Groth, O., Bernstein, M.S., Fei-Fei, L.: Visual7W: grounded question answering in images. In: CVPR (2016)

Understanding Compositional Structures in Art Historical Images Using Pose and Gaze Priors
Towards Scene Understanding in Digital Art History

Prathmesh Madhu[1]([✉]) [iD], Tilman Marquart[1], Ronak Kosti[1] [iD], Peter Bell[2] [iD], Andreas Maier[1] [iD], and Vincent Christlein[1] [iD]

[1] Pattern Recognition Lab, Erlangen, Germany
prathmesh.madhu@fau.de
[2] Institute for Art History, Friedrich-Alexander-Universität Erlangen-Nürnberg, Erlangen, Germany
https://lme.tf.fau.de/, https://www.kunstgeschichte.phil.fau.de/

Abstract. Image compositions as a tool for analysis of artworks is of extreme significance for art historians. These compositions are useful in analyzing the interactions in an image to study artists and their artworks. Max Imdahl in his work called *Ikonik*, along with other prominent art historians of the 20th century, underlined the aesthetic and semantic importance of the structural composition of an image. Understanding underlying compositional structures within images is challenging and a time consuming task. Generating these structures automatically using computer vision techniques (1) can help art historians towards their sophisticated analysis by saving lot of time; providing an overview and access to huge image repositories and (2) also provide an important step towards an understanding of man made imagery by machines. In this work, we attempt to automate this process using the existing state of the art machine learning techniques, without involving any form of training. Our approach, inspired by Max Imdahl's pioneering work, focuses on two central themes of image composition: (a) detection of action regions and action lines of the artwork; and (b) pose-based segmentation of foreground and background. Currently, our approach works for artworks comprising of protagonists (persons) in an image. In order to validate our approach qualitatively and quantitatively, we conduct a user study involving experts and non-experts. The outcome of the study highly correlates with our approach and also demonstrates its domain-agnostic capability. We have open-sourced the code: https://github.com/image-compostion-canvas-group/image-compostion-canvas

Keywords: Compositional structures · Art history · Computer vision

---

P. Madhu and T. Marquart—Equal contribution.

© Springer Nature Switzerland AG 2020
A. Bartoli and A. Fusiello (Eds.): ECCV 2020 Workshops, LNCS 12536, pp. 109–125, 2020.
https://doi.org/10.1007/978-3-030-66096-3_9

1 Introduction

Understanding narratives present in an artwork has always been a challenge and is strongly researched since the late 19th century [29]. A high-level interpretation for the given scene is more ambiguous than a low-level interpretation [3] meaning it is easy to recognize and interpret small objects and characters in the image rather than presenting a high level abstract description of any scene. In the recent times of deep learning, numerous highly successful supervised techniques have been presented for various applications like object detection [11], person identification [22], segmentation [26], retrieval [16] etc. However, these methods have some major drawbacks. First, even though they perform extremely well on the benchmark datasets, they fail to generalize across other real-world datasets. The reason being that it is extremely difficult to capture the real world distribution and it's complexity within a single large dataset. Second, these deep models are very sensitive and error-prone compared to humans who naturally adapt to the visual context as stated in [30].

One solution suggested in the DeepNets [30] paper is the idea of using the compositionality of the images to generate models that can be trained on finite datasets, and then can be generalized across unseen datasets. The assumption is that the structures within an image are composed of various substructures following a grammatical set of rules, which can be learned from a finitely anno- tated datasets. These compositional models can be used to reason and diag- nose the system, extrapolate beyond data and answer varied questions based on learned knowledge structure. On a parallel front, from a theoretical perspective, Bienenstock *et al.* [3] suggested that the hierarchical compositional structure of natural visual scenes can be reduced down to a collection of drastic combinato- rial restrictions; meaning one can break down any scene into 2D projections of objects present in the scene. From this perspective, it can be understood that *composition* is one of the fundamental aspects of human cognition.

Motivated by this understanding of compositional structures within images, in this paper, we investigate the problem of determining and analyzing the com- position of various scenes in art history. Specifically motivating is the work of Max Imdahl called *Ikonik* [12], where he formulates a methodology using an art- work's structure to determine its significance. His work is considered as a model of image analysis, which can be considered as a complement to Panofsky's iconol- ogy [14]. He argues that visual cues or the "visual seeing" overpowers biblical or textural references by giving references to artworks by Giotto, cf.Fig. 1. Giving the examples of *Ascent to Cavalry* and *The kiss of Judas* (Fig. 1a), he explains how the structural relation between foreground and background, the distribu- tion of colors and dynamism between the characters can help in understanding artists and their artworks.

Motivated by his work, we propose an non-supervised computational app- roach to find compositional structures in an image. Our algorithm is driven by the human perception that posture and gaze of the main protagonists help to identify the region of interest (action regions) of any scene (Figs. 1c and 1d). We enable pre-trained OpenPose [4] framework to detect pose-keypoints

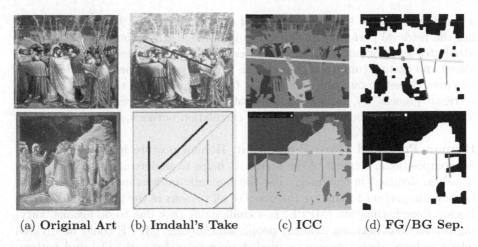

(a) **Original Art** (b) **Imdahl's Take** (c) **ICC** (d) **FG/BG Sep.**

Fig. 1. (a) Giotto's Original Paintings, (top) "The kiss of Judas", (bottom) "Raising of Lazarus"; (b) Imdahl's compositional analysis using structural elements for Giotto's works; (c) Their corresponding Image Composition Canvas (ICC); (d) Binarized ICC to highlight the foreground/background separation.

of protagonists and further exploit them to get a pseudo gaze-estimate without using any existing state of the art gaze detection methods which would have required largely annotated data. We combine all these compositional elements and plot it on an empty canvas which gives an estimate of the representation of the underlying structure and composition within a given scene, which we call *Image Composition Canvas* (ICC). These compositional elements of ICC can later be used as visual features to cross-retrieve images from various datasets. Our method generates *ICCs* that contains two important aspects of image composition: (1) constructing the global action lines and action regions (2) pose-based semantic separation of foreground and background. The detected pose-keypoints [4] not only assist in foreground/background extraction, but also help in generating the global action lines and action regions. The result is a "visual seeing" which concentrates strictly on the compositional structure of an image and is, thereby, complementary to human perception usually driven by the semantics of the narration.

2 Related Work

Semblances in Art History. Max Imdahl showed that discovering similar painting structures or compositional elements is an important aspect in the analysis of artworks [13]. However, detecting the relevant features for the same is a relatively novel task for computer vision. Previous works mainly focus on features for image retrieval, for example, in *SemArt* [10] the paintings are aligned with its attributes such as title, author, type, time and captions by a neural network which learns a common embedding space between them. In another example, these attributes (also called contextual information) are trained jointly in a multi-task manner to achieve a context-aware embedding [9], thereby improving the retrieval performance through a knowledge graph that is created using attributes as prior information. In *Artpedia* [27], the authors are able to align visual and textual content of the artwork without paired supervision. Jenicek *et al.* come closest to our approach in that they link paintings through a two step retrieval process, by finding similarity-of-pose across different motives [2,16]. They also explore the underlying visual correlation between artworks.

Human Pose and Gaze Estimation. Human posture is a strong marker for compositional element of the image. It helps to understand the visual relationships depicted in the image. For the semantic understanding of a scene, it becomes important to analyze the poses of all persons in the given scene. Multi-Person Pose Estimation (MPPE) is a challenging task due to occlusions, varying interactions between different people and objects. MPPE could be divided into *top-down* (detect person $\rightarrow$ predict pose point for each) [24] and *bottom-up* (detect body joints for all persons $\rightarrow$ join the points to detect poses) [4] approaches. The current state-of-art method uses *PoseRefiner* [8] as a post-processing technique to refine the pose estimation to get the best results on the MPII dataset [1]. Empirical tests showed OpenPose [4] performed well on our art-historical dataset, so we use it for all our experiments.

Importance of human gaze is evident in the related work of detecting human gazes for automatic driver analysis and understanding attention spans. Gaze360 [17] works on a diverse set of environments, and it is well suited for video or multi-frame inputs depicting temporal relationship which is absent in our data. Another method, *Where are they looking?* [25], uses head location and the image to predict the gaze direction in the image. This method requires gaze annotations (eye locations and gaze directions), however, since our data is a specialized collection of images chosen to study the compositions in a non-supervised manner, this approach could not be applied for our work. Hence, we derive gaze-bisection-vectors from pose keypoints for gaze priors.

Foreground/Background Separation. Detecting foreground and background has been one of the important pre-processing task for computer vision before the deep learning techniques came into practice. Separating foreground from background helps to focus on where the object/region of interest lies at. For example, in image-reconstruction-guided landmark detection, the algorithms are quite often assisted by fine-grained separation of background and foreground techniques [7,15,21]. Specifically, [7] factorizes the reconstruction task to achieve better landmark-detection for foreground objects by simultaneously improving the background rendering.

Exploiting this prior information about the separation of foreground and background is very useful even for existing state of the art methods. For example, in single stage object detectors the high number of candidate locations ($\approx$100 k) creates huge bias towards background classes [20]. Dynamically weighted focal loss [18] mitigates this imbalance by heavily penalizing the learning model for incorrect foreground objects, thereby forcing the model to attend more to the foreground objects. Our approach inherently uses pose estimates of the protagonists. We use an enhanced k-means clustering with the pose estimates to achieve foreground background separation.

Our algorithm is motivated by how a human understands the composition of scenes in paintings. In brief, our main contributions include: (1) Generation of Image Composition Canvas (ICC) which showcases the global and local action lines and action regions, (2) Semantic separation of foreground/background, (3) Generizability of the approach to images leading a step towards domain-agnostic modeling.

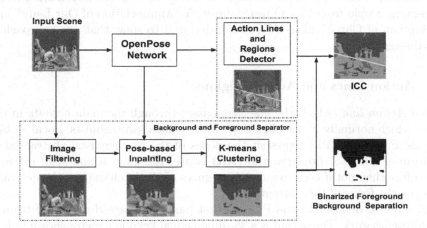

Fig. 2. Generating Image Composition Canvas (*ICC*): Proposed *ICC* pipeline along with foreground/background separation from images. First row details in Fig. 3

3   Methodology

We propose a non-supervised approach to generate *ICC* to assist our understanding of underlying structures in art historical images. Our approach uses a pre-trained OpenPose network [4], image processing techniques and a modified k-means clustering method. The pipeline of the proposed algorithm is shown in Fig. 2 (Fig. 3 shows the visual counterpart). Our method consists of two main branches: (1) a detector for action lines and action regions (Sect. 3.2) and (2) the foreground/background separator (Sect. 3.3). We use the estimated poses to detect pose triangles and propose a simple technique which we call gaze cones to obtain gaze directions estimates without involving any training or fine-tuning. We also use the detected keypoints for foreground/background separation (Sect. 3.3). We combine this information and draw a final ICC that estimates the image composition of the given scene under study (Sect. 3.4). We evaluate the proposed method by performing a user-study where we ask domain experts and non-experts to annotate action lines (global and local) and action regions, details of which are mentioned in Sect. 4.1.

3.1 Data Description

The dataset contains 20 images of fresco paintings from the 13th century. Figures 1a, 4b and 5a show some examples of Giotto's famous fresco paintings. The paintings come from the Scrovegni chapel also known as arena chapel in Padua, Italy and were made by the painter Giotto di Bondone (considered the decisive pioneer of the Italian Renaissance). Most of these images have been analyzed by Max Imdahl in his book *Ikonik Arenafresken* [13]. We also use 10 random images containing people from COCO test dataset, 5 "Annunciation of Our Lady" and 5 "Baptism of Christ" images for evaluation and to show that our approach is domain-agnostic.

3.2 Action Lines and Action Regions

Global *Action line* (AL) is the line that passes through the main *activity* in the scene, which normally is also aligned with the central protagonists. Local *Action Line* or *Pose Line* (PL) represent the poses of the protagonists, abstracted in the form of a line. *Action region*(s) (AR) is(are) the main *region(s) of interest*, more often than not it is the region where gazes of all the characters theoretically meet, or the focus of their attention.

In order to detect ALs and PLs, we first pass the image through pre-trained OpenPose network. The output is a 25-dimensional keypoint vector shown in Fig. 3a. It is easy for OpenPose to detect all the keypoints for a fully visible human body. However, sometimes the full body is not visible, as can be seen for the character in the middle in Fig. 3c. We correct such poses using a pose corrector (Sect. 3.2a). We then detect the gazes of these characters using three major keypoints detected by OpenPose (Sect. 3.2b). The output of the gaze estimator gives us the gaze directions in the form of cones as visualized in Fig. 3d. The intersecting region of all the gaze cones is considered as the region of interest, where the main ARs would be present. Based on the intersection pattern of the cones, there can be multiple ARs. Also, a line representing the direction and intersection of all the views is considered to be the global AL. The slope of this line is calculated by combining all the gaze slopes (Sect. 3.2c).

(a) Pose Correction. For pose estimation, we tried a few SOTA methods, including associative embedding for joint detection and grouping [23], however OpenPose [4] gave the best results. Bottom-up approaches have the overhead of detecting persons in art historical images [22], which is an entirely different problem altogether. Hence, we use OpenPose [4] pre-trained on the Human Foot keypoint dataset [4] in combination with the 2017 version of the COCO [19] dataset. The network takes an entire image as input and returns fully connected body poses for all humans detected in an image as output.

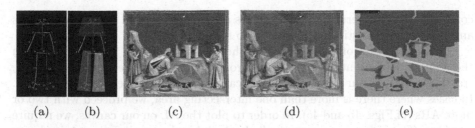

   (a)   (b)   (c)   (d)   (e)

Fig. 3. (a) 25 pose-keypoints used by OpenPose [4]; (b) Pose triangle using groups of keypoints; (c) OpenPose generated keypoints, thicker lines have higher confidence. Generated *Pose Triangles* (Sect. 3.2a) in blue and the final abstracted result in bold green line; (d) Gaze-bisection-vectors (Sect. 3.2c) in bold red, cones in light transparent green, the intersection of all cones in purple; (e) Overlapping intersections in purple (Color figure online)

Often OpenPose would predict incorrect keypoints, which were difficult to interpret, motivating us to come up with the pose-triangles approach which is robust for person interpretation irrespective of the occluded keypoints. With the detected keypoints, we create a pose triangle. For the triangle corners, we split the 25 keypoints into three body regions as shown in Fig. 3b. The region from shoulders towards the head forms the top triangle corner (brown trapezoid). The left (green trapezoid) and the right leg (yellow trapezoid) regions form the left and the right corners of the pose triangle, respectively. The specific keypoints associated with these regions are $top_C \leftarrow$ [0,1,2,5,15,16,17,18], $left_C \leftarrow$ [9–11,22–24], $right_C \leftarrow$ [12–14,19–21]. The key-point from each region with the highest confidence score is chosen to be the representative point from which the pose triangle will be formed. For each of the pose triangles, we create a bisector line called *pose line* (PL) from the top corner of the triangle to the line segment formed by the other two corners (bold green lines as seen in Fig. 3c). The keypoints' splits (3 regions for 3 corners of the pose triangle) are chosen heuristically.

(b) Gaze Estimation + Correction. Our data did not have annotations in order to fine-tune an existing gaze estimation model. Also, our goal was to get a rough estimate of the gazes for all the persons in order to detect the central focus within the image. Looking at the pose keypoints, we can argue that the gaze direction can roughly be estimated from the face and neck keypoints. Here, we exploit this hypothesis and use the pose keypoints $0, 1$ and 8 to generate a bisection vector as the first step (red vector, Fig. 3d). The bisection vector bisects the line segment joining keypoints 0 and 8. In Fig. 3d, we observe that these estimates are few degrees off of the original gaze and hence we also apply a correction to the gaze vector, denoted as correction angle. We skip those cases when one of the three keypoints is missing. Rather than just viewing the exact gaze, we represent gazes using gaze cones with an opening angle of 50 ($25°$ +/− direction) degrees in order to compensate the error estimate (green transparent cones, Fig. 3d). Experiments with various angles however did not affect the ARs and hence, we heuristically chose to keep the value 50^1.

The intersection of these cones are the probable regions where everyone in the scene is looking at. Hence, the centroids of these intersections become the starting points of our global ALs. The cases with no intersection are skipped. In cases where there is more than one intersecting area, we proceed with two or more ARs (cf.Figs. 4b and 4c). In order to plot the AL on our canvas, we require its slope. Therefore, we aggregate all the individual gaze directions in order to find the slope of the global AL.

(c) Combination of All Gaze-bisection-vector Slopes. For calculating the slope of our global ALs, we aggregate all individual gaze directions (average of all the individual gaze slope) and find a common slope, where only the slopes of the gaze-bisection-vectors are considered. The slope value is with respect to the x-axis (Cartesian Coordinates) in the positive horizontal direction. Since the slope remains the same when we rotate the gaze-bisection-vector by 180 degrees, we map all the gaze vectors pointing towards the 2nd and 3rd quadrant to 4th and 1st quadrants respectively (Fig. 4a). We then draw a line in our output canvas through every centroid of the previously calculated intersection areas and use this aggregated slope as the slope of this new line. Figures 3d and 3e show how the aggregated gaze vectors form the global AL.

(a)   (b)   (c)   (d)

Fig. 4. (a) Gaze-Bisection-Vectors (red vectors) that point towards 2nd and 3rd quadrants are mapped to 4th and 1st quadrants (green vectors), respectively. (b), (c) show an example where there are 2 global action lines and 2 action regions detected. (d) is the eye-fixation map [5] of the image. (Color figure online)

3.3   Semantic Foreground/Background Separation

While analyzing human behavior within the semantics of scene understanding, humans present in the scene usually form the foreground. We exploit this property of scene semantics in our approach and consider the humans as our foreground (FG). Additionally, we define the objects near the human poses and

---

[1] Similar results were achieved by using various angles: 10, 20, 60, 80.

the immediate surroundings as part of their foreground and the rest of the image as background (BG). The pipeline for FG and BG separation is shown in Fig. 2. It consists of the following three steps, which are explained in more details below: image filtering, keypoint-based inpainting, and pose- and color-informed k-means clustering.

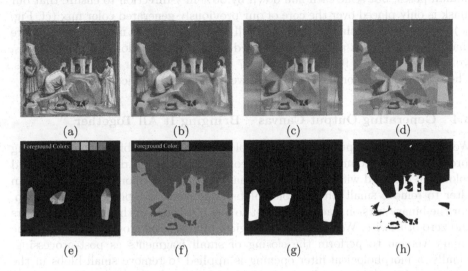

Fig. 5. Visual steps of *ICC*: (a) Original image, (b) Cracks filtered, (c) Bodies and picture frame inpainted, (d) Colors clustered using k-means, (e) Dominant colors under body positions selected as foreground colors, blue colors are below the threshold, (f) Detected foreground colors replaced and output filters applied, (g) Binarization applied to (e), (h) Binarized foreground/background separation. (Color figure online)

(a) Image Filtering. We observe that historical paintings show chipped paint, cracks or weathering, so we first apply a median filter that helps in reducing these artifacts. We apply a bilateral filter to preserve the sharp edges as they are most crucial to separate major objects and protagonists as seen in Fig. 5b.

(b) Keypoint-Based Inpainting. Next, we inpaint all pixels covered by detected human poses. Therefore, we generate the convex hull of all pose keypoints and scale the hull up by 70% in x-direction and 40% in y-direction, to ensure the mask is covering a little more than the human body in the painting. Using this mask, we inpaint the previously filtered image using the fast marching method [28]. Figure 5c shows human bodies being replaced with a color mix marked by the red mask. These colors are considered as the potential foreground colors.

(c) Pose- and Color-Informed K-Means Clustering. The inpainted image is then clustered into a smaller amount of colors using k-means clustering. This creates smaller color clusters (cf. Fig. 5d). The colors near the body postures of the characters are associated with the foreground by virtue of being related to the bodies of the characters. Next, we generate a second mask around the human poses, but scale each hull down by 30% in y-direction to ensure that our mask is only placed over the core of our previously generated color mix (cf. Fig. 5c) using the inpainting (cf. Fig. 5e). All colors under this mask covering more than 6% of the mask are then considered as foreground color. For experiments, we tried k= 3, 5, 7, 9 and found k = 7 to generate better qualitative results. The scaling factors for the convex hull were chosen heuristically.

3.4 Generating Output Canvas – Bringing It All Together

We generate two types of ICC, one colored ICC and a binary one denoting foreground/background pixels. In the colored version, all detected foreground colors are replaced with the most dominant foreground color. We apply median filter to remove small leftover color blobs/fragments as a post-processing step. For the binary version, each pixel is set to one if it is one of the foreground colors and zero otherwise. We apply morphological dilation and erosion filtering on the binary version to perform the closing of small fragments as post-processing. Finally, a morphological filter opening is applied to remove small blobs in the background that are typically due to the k-means results on the clustered cracks. We then gather the ALs, ARs (Sect. 3.2) and overlay it on the canvas with FG/BG separation (Sect. 3.3) to obtain our ICC. We can observe colored canvas in the Fig. 1c; and the binarized canvas in Fig. 1d.

4 Evaluation and Experiments

In this section, we first discuss the user study done for quantitative evaluation and the metrics being used for the same. Then we do a qualitative interpretation of our method, followed by general validity of our method by testing on cross-domain data. In the last part, we give performance evaluation of our method based on the user study.

4.1 User Study – Design and Evaluation Metrics

Design. We evaluate the performance of ICC quantitatively and qualitatively through a user study. A set of 11 images were collected, 6 are Giotto's paintings, an annunciation scene, a baptism scene and 3 are chosen from COCO [19] with people present in them. We asked the annotators to label global action lines (AL), action regions (AR) and pose lines (PL) on these images. For quality control, a demo of the labeling process with an example and associated instructions were continuously available to the annotators while doing the task. This video (https://streamable.com/wk8ol8) describes how the user-study was conducted, including the labeling interface, the definition of each label and instructions to generate them with a sample example. We have 2 set of annotators, domain experts (E) and non-experts (NE). An E has a background in art history or its methodology; NEs are all university graduates. A total of 72 annotators (10 Es and 62 NEs) were presented with this set of images and asked to label the AL, AR and PL in them.

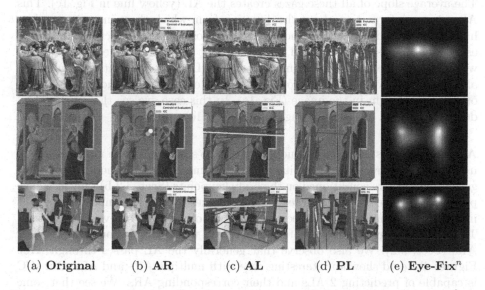

(a) **Original**   (b) **AR**   (c) **AL**   (d) **PL**   (e) **Eye-Fix^n**

Fig. 6. User Study analysis: 1st row shows an example of *The kiss of Judas*, 2nd of *annunciation* and 3rd of *COCO*[19]. (a) column are original images; (b) shows the Action Region (AR) by ICC (cyan), all Evaluators (red) and the centroid (white) of all annotators; (c) and (d) show AL and PL by ICC (yellow, green) and all annotators (red, red) respectively; and (e) highlights the eye-fixation regions [5]

Evaluation Metrics. We evaluate each of AL, AR and PL individually and for all the annotators. We compare the performances between: E *vs.* ICC, NE *vs.* ICC and E *vs.* NE. The standard deviation (SD_{AR}) in the labeling of ARs is a measure of agreement between the annotators, lower SD_{AR} means they agree more where as higher SD_{AR} means they disagree more. For comparison of labeled ARs and predicted ARs, the L_2 distance is considered between E/NE and ICC. For AL and PL, the lines are considered as sets of points in the image. We find the distance between these two sets using Hausdorff Distance (HD) [6]. We also calculate the angular deviation (AD) between the AL of the E/NE and the ICC. Higher angular deviation means higher value of AD.

4.2   Results and Discussion

Action Lines. Each AL represents an important action or geometry in the original painting, however, both differ in their presentation (cf.Max Imdahl's *et al.* manually created analysis in Fig. 1b). It is not easy to quantify such expressions since they are more visually interpretive than quantitatively. In 1st row of Fig. 1a, Giotto's "Kiss of Judas", Judas is hugging Jesus. Many people are directly looking at them. This structure is apparent in other works of Giotto. The average slope of all these gazes creates the AL (yellow line in Fig. 1c). This AL gives us information about the direction from which these important points have been viewed. Sometimes, however, OpenPose fails to detect human poses, especially the poses of Jesus and Judas were not recognized (due to occlusions), which could have had a strong impact on the AL. Giotto's paintings sometimes also have a line of heads, with one head next to each other and most of them on the same height in the image (Fig. 1a). In this case, we see that our method does a very good job of detecting the AL (Fig. 1c).

Action Regions. The gaze structure in Giotto's paintings also motivates us to use their gaze directions in finding the approximate region of action. Since the gaze directions are conditioned on the body keypoints (Sect. 3.2.b) they also have pose context. We use the intersection of all gazes to identify important regions in the picture. In Fig. 1c, we see the locations of the ARs are very interesting. These regions are the center of high activity, which follows our definition of ARs (Sect. 3.2). We also observe that generally the AL passes through ARs. Figures 4b to 4d show an interesting case with multiple ARs and ALs. Our ICC is capable of predicting 2 ALs and their corresponding ARs. We see that some people focus on the 2 central characters accounting for the 1st AL, while the 2 central characters are looking at the sitting character creating the 2nd AL. The corresponding eye-fixation map in Fig. 4d highlights the regions where the 2 ALs are passing through and where the 2 ARs are located.

Semantic Foreground/Background Separation. The main characters usually form the foreground of the image. Additionally, using their poses, we detect which of the areas in the image constitute foreground/ background. We in-paint the image at their body positions. In order to achieve this, K-means clustering is applied with a small k-value (good clustering and a filled, crack-less foreground surface). The small k-value could lead, in some cases, to a completely incorrect separation if the same colors were present in the foreground/background. Giotto's paintings also show the geometry of foreground/ background separation (cf. Fig. 1b) to be an important underlying structuring element. This separation is apparent in Figs. 1c and 3e as the big light brown region covering half of the image and the remaining blue backdrop as the background.

4.3   Cross-Domain Adaptability

The first 2 source (Fig. 7, 1st & 2nd row), images are taken from 2 different iconographies: *Baptism* and *Annunciation*. For the third, (Fig. 7, 3rd row),

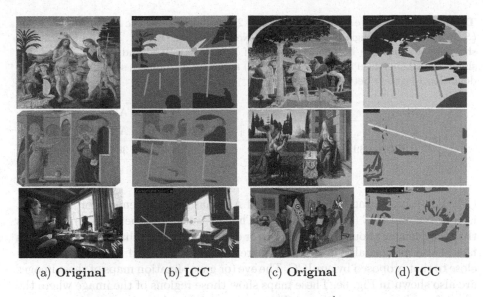

| (a) **Original** | (b) **ICC** | (c) **Original** | (d) **ICC** |

Fig. 7. Cross domain analysis: 1st row depicts *Baptism*, 2nd shows *annunciation*, and the 3rd are images from *COCO* [19]. (a) and (c) columns are original images, (b) and (d) are their corresponding *ICC*.

we use images from COCO – a dataset of images from everyday life. We choose images that contains people doing different activities.

Figures 7a and 7b depict examples where our method is able to locate the AR, AL and PL very effectively. In addition, the foreground/background separation is also clearly visible in the ICC. For example in 2nd row of Fig. 7b, we see that the PLs are correct, the AL passes through the main activity and the AR is localized between the two characters. In 1st row of Fig. 7b, our method is able to detect the presence of 2 ALs: one aligns with the gaze of the female and the waist of the male, and the other aligns through the heads of the males. The AR is also very well localized, with good foreground/background separation.

In Figures 7c and 7d, our method fails either for ALs, or the foreground/ background separation. However, sometimes the ARs are very well localized even in these examples. In 1st row of Fig. 7d, we can observe that the main action region and background-foreground is incorrect, while the AL seems to be acceptable. Similarly, in 2nd and 3rd rows of Fig. 7d, the foreground/background separation is not good and neither is the AL, but the AR is localized very well between the protagonists.

4.4   Quantitative Evaluation of User Study

For comparing action regions (AR) we reduce the image sizes to 1×1. From Table 1, we can see that the Es have more agreement among-st themselves for ARs as compared to NEs. However, the Euclidean distance (L_2) between the centroid of the Es and the ICC (E/ICC) has a similar value to that of the NEs and the ICC

Table 1. Quantitative Evaluation. 1st and 2nd columns show the Standard Deviation (SD_{AR}) for AR amongst Experts (E) and Non-Experts (NE). 3rd, 4th and 5th columns show the L_2 distance between centroids of E/ICC, NE/ICC and E/NE. 6th column shows the HD between all annotators (ALL) and ICC. 7th column shows cosine angular deviation (degrees) between ALL/ICC.

SD_{AR}		L_2			HD	AD
E	NE	E/ICC	NE/ICC	E/NE	ALL/ICC	ALL/ICC
0.054	0.089	0.187	0.180	0.035	664.35	36.57°

(NE/ICC), indicating that the region of ARs has high agreement for all groups, i. e., E, NE and ICC (people *vs. ICC*). The low value of L_2 between E/NE shows that they concur about the ARs (an error of 3.5% for the localization of AR). This fact is also recognizable in Fig. 6b, where the centroids of all annotators lie very close to that proposed by our ICC. The eye (or gaze)-fixation maps of these images are also shown in Fig. 6e. These maps show those regions of the image where the gaze of an observer would focus. These maps are complementary to the compositional elements like ALs and ARs. The structure of these maps follows the slope of ALs and are distributed along the AL and the AR.

HD between all the annotators and ICC (ALL/ICC) is quite low (38%) than the worst HD distance (ALL/Infinity: 1070.2 for the case of end points of the diagonal) showing that the ALs of our ICC has very good correlation to all annotators. We also see that the angular distance (AD) of all ALs with that of our ICC has an average value of 36.57° (ALL/ICC).

We observed that there is a positive correlation (0.2) between the images with low SD_{AR} and their corresponding $L_{2(AR)}$, meaning that when the annotators' agreement for the position of AR was higher, our method predicted AR closer to the labeled ones. Similarly, we observed opposite trend for high SD_{AR} images, with correlation of -0.790, meaning that when there is higher disagreement between the annotators about the location of the AR, our method predicted AR farther away. Similar trend is observed when we correlate SD_{AR} with HD. When annotators agree (low SD_{AR}), the predicted AL is closer to the labeled ones, where as when annotators disagree (high SD_{AR}), the predicted AL is farther to the labeled one.

5   Conclusion and Future Work

With the help of existing machine learning tools, state-of-the-art pose estimation framework and image analysis, we have presented a novel no-training approach to understand underlying structures in art historical scenes. We show that recognizing key elements within a scene, such as ALs, ARs and FG/BG separation, helps in understanding the composition of any scene. Apart from using a pre-trained OpenPose framework, our method does not need any training. This makes our method very light, robust and applicable to any scene for analysis, especially when there is no ground truth available, which is often the case in art historic images. It can be used to pre-compare images for image retrieval and analysis. We also showed that our method works extremely well for images from related domains as well as images from everyday life.

Our method is a complementary approach to the perception of semantics in artworks [10] and iconography in general. It is one of the first attempts at understanding scenes or paintings in art history grounded in compositional elements. Future development could include training OpenPose on art historical data, and including the scene information to explore the role of scene narratives on the underlying compositions. At the same time our algorithm can be applied to various target domains where composition lines and narratives are used.

References

1. Andriluka, M., Pishchulin, L., Gehler, P., Schiele, B.: 2D human pose estimation: new benchmark and state of the art analysis. In: IEEE Conference on Computer Vision and Pattern Recognition, CVPR, June 2014
2. Bell, P., Impett, L.: Ikonographie und Interaktion. Computergestützte Analyse von Posen in Bildern der Heilsgeschichte. Das Mittelalter 24(1), 31–53 (2019). https://doi.org/10.1515/mial-2019-0004. http://www.degruyter.com/view/j/mial.2019.24.issue-1/mial-2019-0004/mial-2019-0004.xml
3. Bienenstock, E., Geman, S., Potter, D.: Compositionality, MDL priors, and object recognition. In: Advances in Neural Information Processing Systems, pp. 838–844 (1997)
4. Cao, Z., Hidalgo, G., Simon, T., Wei, S.E., Sheikh, Y.: OpenPose: realtime multi-person 2D pose estimation using part affinity fields. arXiv:1812.08008 [cs], May 2019
5. Cornia, M., Baraldi, L., Serra, G., Cucchiara, R.: Predicting human eye fixations via an LSTM-based saliency attentive model. IEEE Trans. Image Process. 27(10), 5142–5154 (2018)
6. Dubuisson, M., Jain, A.K.: A modified hausdorff distance for object matching. In: Proceedings of 12th International Conference on Pattern Recognition, vol. 1, pp. 566–568, October 1994. https://doi.org/10.1109/ICPR.1994.576361
7. Dundar, A., Shih, K.J., Garg, A., Pottorf, R., Tao, A., Catanzaro, B.: Unsupervised disentanglement of pose, appearance and background from images and videos. arXiv preprint arXiv:2001.09518 (2020)
8. Fieraru, M., Khoreva, A., Pishchulin, L., Schiele, B.: Learning to refine human pose estimation. In: The IEEE Conference on Computer Vision and Pattern Recognition (CVPR) Workshops, June 2018
9. Garcia, N., Renoust, B., Nakashima, Y.: Context-aware embeddings for automatic art analysis. In: Proceedings of the 2019 on International Conference on Multimedia Retrieval, pp. 25–33 (2019)
10. Garcia, N., Vogiatzis, G.: How to read paintings: semantic art understanding with multi-modal retrieval. In: Proceedings of the European Conference on Computer Vision (ECCV) (2018)
11. Gonthier, N., Gousseau, Y., Ladjal, S., Bonfait, O.: Weakly supervised object detection in artworks. In: Leal-Taixé, L., Roth, S. (eds.) ECCV 2018. LNCS, vol. 11130, pp. 692–709. Springer, Cham (2019). https://doi.org/10.1007/978-3-030-11012-3_53

12. Imdahl, M.: Giotto, Arenafresken: Ikonographie-Ikonologie-Ikonik. Wilhelm Fink, Paderborn (1975)
13. Imdahl, M.: Giotto, Arenafresken: Ikonographie, Ikonologie, Ikonik. W. Fink, München, Paderborn (1980). oCLC: 7627867
14. Ionescu, V.: What do you see? the phenomenological model of image analysis: Fiedler, Husserl, Imdahl. Image Narrative **15**(3), 93–110 (2014)
15. Jakab, T., Gupta, A., Bilen, H., Vedaldi, A.: Unsupervised learning of object landmarks through conditional image generation. In: Advances in Neural Information Processing Systems, pp. 4016–4027 (2018)
16. Jenicek, T., Chum, O.: Linking art through human poses. In: 2019 International Conference on Document Analysis and Recognition (ICDAR), pp. 1338–1345, September 2019. https://doi.org/10.1109/ICDAR.2019.00216
17. Kellnhofer, P., Recasens, A., Stent, S., Matusik, W., Torralba, A.: Gaze360: physically unconstrained gaze estimation in the wild. In: Proceedings of the IEEE International Conference on Computer Vision, pp. 6912–6921 (2019)
18. Lin, T.Y., Goyal, P., Girshick, R., He, K., Dollár, P.: Focal loss for dense object detection. In: Proceedings of the IEEE International Conference on Computer Vision, pp. 2980–2988 (2017)
19. Lin, T.-Y., Maire, M., Belongie, S., Hays, J., Perona, P., Ramanan, D., Dollár, P., Zitnick, C.L.: Microsoft COCO: common objects in context. In: Fleet, D., Pajdla, T., Schiele, B., Tuytelaars, T. (eds.) ECCV 2014. LNCS, vol. 8693, pp. 740–755. Springer, Cham (2014). https://doi.org/10.1007/978-3-319-10602-1_48
20. Liu, W., Anguelov, D., Erhan, D., Szegedy, C., Reed, S., Fu, C.-Y., Berg, A.C.: SSD: single shot MultiBox detector. In: Leibe, B., Matas, J., Sebe, N., Welling, M. (eds.) ECCV 2016. LNCS, vol. 9905, pp. 21–37. Springer, Cham (2016). https://doi.org/10.1007/978-3-319-46448-0_2
21. Lorenz, D., Bereska, L., Milbich, T., Ommer, B.: Unsupervised part-based disentangling of object shape and appearance. In: Proceedings of the IEEE Conference on Computer Vision and Pattern Recognition, pp. 10955–10964 (2019)
22. Madhu, P., Kosti, R., Mührenberg, L., Bell, P., Maier, A., Christlein, V.: Recognizing characters in art history using deep learning. In: Proceedings of the 1st Workshop on Structuring and Understanding of Multimedia HeritAge Contents, SUMAC 2019, New York, NY, USA, pp. 15–22. Association for Computing Machinery (2019). https://doi.org/10.1145/3347317.3357242. https://doi.org/10.1145/3347317.3357242
23. Newell, A., Huang, Z., Deng, J.: Associative embedding: end-to-end learning for joint detection and grouping. In: Advances in Neural Information Processing Systems, pp. 2277–2287 (2017)
24. Papandreou, G., et al.: Towards accurate multi-person pose estimation in the wild. In: Proceedings of the IEEE Conference on Computer Vision and Pattern Recognition, pp. 4903–4911 (2017)
25. Recasens, A., Khosla, A., Vondrick, C., Torralba, A.: Where are they looking? In: Cortes, C., Lawrence, N.D., Lee, D.D., Sugiyama, M., Garnett, R. (eds.) Advances in Neural Information Processing Systems, vol. 28, pp. 199–207. Curran Associates, Inc. (2015)
26. Ronneberger, O., Fischer, P., Brox, T.: U-Net: convolutional networks for biomedical image segmentation. In: Navab, N., Hornegger, J., Wells, W.M., Frangi, A.F. (eds.) MICCAI 2015. LNCS, vol. 9351, pp. 234–241. Springer, Cham (2015). https://doi.org/10.1007/978-3-319-24574-4_28

27. Stefanini, M., Cornia, M., Baraldi, L., Corsini, M., Cucchiara, R.: Artpedia: a new visual-semantic dataset with visual and contextual sentences in the artistic domain. In: Ricci, E., Rota Bulò, S., Snoek, C., Lanz, O., Messelodi, S., Sebe, N. (eds.) Image Analysis and Processing - ICIAP 2019, pp. 729–740. Springer, Cham (2019). https://doi.org/10.1007/978-3-030-30645-8_66
28. Telea, A.: An image inpainting technique based on the fast marching method. J. Graph. Tools **9**(1), 23–34 (2004)
29. Volkenandt, C.: Bildfeld und Feldlinien. Formen des vergleichenden Sehens bei Max Imdahl, Theodor Hetzer und Dagobert Frey, pp. 407–430. Wilhelm Fink, Leiden, The Netherlands (2010). https://www.fink.de/view/book/edcoll/9783846750155/B9783846750155-s021.xml
30. Yuille, A.L., Liu, C.: Deep nets: what have they ever done for vision? arXiv preprint arXiv:1805.04025 (2018)

Demographic Influences on Contemporary Art with Unsupervised Style Embeddings

Nikolai Huckle[1](✉), Noa Garcia[2], and Yuta Nakashima[2]

[1] University of Bamberg, Bamberg, Germany
n.huckle@posteo.de
[2] Osaka University, Suita, Japan
{noagarcia,n-yuta}@ids.osaka-u.ac.jp

Abstract. Computational art analysis has, through its reliance on classification tasks, prioritised historical datasets in which the artworks are already well sorted with the necessary annotations. Art produced today, on the other hand, is numerous and easily accessible, through the internet and social networks that are used by professional and amateur artists alike to display their work. Although this art—yet unsorted in terms of style and genre—is less suited for supervised analysis, the data sources come with novel information that may help frame the visual content in equally novel ways. As a first step in this direction, we present contempArt, a multi-modal dataset of exclusively contemporary artworks. contempArt is a collection of paintings and drawings, a detailed graph network based on social connections on Instagram and additional sociodemographic information; all attached to 442 artists at the beginning of their career. We evaluate three methods suited for generating unsupervised style embeddings of images and correlate them with the remaining data. We find no connections between visual style on the one hand and social proximity, gender, and nationality on the other.

Keywords: Unsupervised analysis · Contemporary art · Social networks

1 Introduction

The methodological melting pot that is the interdisciplinary field of digital art history has, in recent years, been shaped more by exhausting technical novelty than theoretical guidance [2,5]. Alongside proponents of the technological transformation, who see its vast databases as an opportunity to investigate large-scale patterns of various nature [13,23], there has been criticism that its pure empiricism hinders any true discovery [5]. Computer vision (CV), which has also found its way into the field by providing state-of-the-art methods [26] and assembling large multi-modal datasets [4,17,35], has not been exempt from this criticism. Specifically, that only extracting and connecting high-level semantics of paintings ignores the real-world context in which art is being produced and belongs to an outdated form of comparative art history [1,38].

A. Bartoli and A. Fusiello (Eds.): ECCV 2020 Workshops, LNCS 12536, pp. 126–142, 2020.
https://doi.org/10.1007/978-3-030-66096-3_10

Furthermore, recent progress, both visually [25,54] and numerically [4], has not changed the fact that CV's potential to effectively engage the digital humanities is bounded by one recurrent factor: labels. Labels are an obvious necessity for aligning input data with a relevant supervisory signal, in general learning tasks, and a less obvious one in creating image tuples for texture synthesis or generative models. As classification tasks have become omni-present throughout the field, so have labels. At first glance, giving centre stage to typology seems to be in line with it being one of art historians main research interests [24].

However, in supervised learning, the annotations serve as research's means and not its end, rendering the possibility of expanding upon that same annotation impossible. This becomes problematic due to the absence of perfect knowledge in art history, as opposed to more common classification tasks such as object recognition, where the classes are flawless and the image labels non-negotiable [33,51]. Contrary to images of objects, paintings and their historical contextualisation is very much an open-ended and contested subject [23]. By ignoring the uncertainty attached to the labels of art datasets, CV on the one hand handicaps its potential in investigating art in a novel way and, on the other hand perpetuates a misleadingly homogeneous image of the art-historical canon.

Overcoming these limitations and advancing into interdisciplinary depths requires CV to turn away from existing labels and instead embrace two other central research interests in classical art history: a) the visual representation of art and b) the social context of its production [24]. In this work, we present two contributions in line with these two themes:

1. For extracting visual representations in an unsupervised manner, we evaluate and utilise existing techniques from different domains.
2. For studying the social world surrounding art, we introduce contempArt, the first dataset on contemporary painters with images, socio-demographic information and social media data representing social relationships.

Aligning the information on demographics and social relationships with the attained style-embeddings allows us to investigate tangible connections beyond the visual realm. However, we find no evidence that social closeness entails similarity in style or that demographic factors correlate with visual content.

2   Related Work

2.1   Unsupervised Art Analysis

Analysis of Embeddings. Compared to the substantial amount of work on art classification [4,35,37,42,47], only rarely have image representations themselves been at the centre of computational analysis. One of the earliest such works is the seminal paper by [48], in which the fractal dimension of Jackson Pollock's drip paintings is measured and compared over the course of his career. In a similar vein, aggregate image-level statistics based on colour and brightness are used in [28,31,44] to visualise the evolution of artworks. In [15], object recognition features and time annotations are combined to assign creativity scores representing the visual novelty of artworks, at the time of their creation. Due to the success of convolutional neural networks (CNN) in image classification, art analysis has seen handcrafted image representations being replaced by deep feature vectors extracted from these CNNs. Of note is [26], in which deep features from a CNN trained for object recognition outperform older handcrafted features in classifying art styles. [8] also uses features provided by multiple CNNs to investigate connections between artwork and human perception. [6], on the other hand, analyses different variance statistics between the layers of an object-recognition CNN and finds that these values can discern art from non-art.

Analysis of Clusters. Other work is focused on applying complex unsupervised learning techniques on both handcrafted and deep image features [7,21,43,46]. Most notable amongst these clustering studies is [50], in which artistic style is attained by computing statistics at different layers of a pre-trained object recognition CNN, a methodology created for texture synthesis [19], and these features are additionally clustered with archetypal analysis [11].

2.2   Social Context

Expanding art-based deep learning techniques to include information beyond the visual has been premiered in [16], where multi-modal relationships between various artistic metadata are used to increase the performance of image classification and image retrieval. To allow these broader analysis, the Semart dataset [17] was introduced, where images are paired with artistic comments describing them.

An older dataset on deviantArt,[1] one of the largest online social networks for art, initially only contained information on measures of social connections [41] but was later expanded to include large amounts of image data [40]. Although it has been used both for simple social network [40,41] and image analysis [52] never have these data sources been combined in a scientific analysis. [29], exploring a dataset on another creative online community named Behance,[2] does combine artistic images and social network relationships but the visual information is aggregated too coarsely as to have any meaning.

Among the more commonly used art datasets such as Wikiart[3] or Painting91 [27], deviantArt especially stands out, as it is focused exclusively on contemporary art and, more importantly, work that is being produced outside of the commercialised world of galleries, auction houses and museums. The disadvantage being that prospective artists cannot be separated from amateurs, making their joint study more related to cultural analytics than digital art history. As detailed biographical data is never mandatory on online social networks, their user-generated image content can be easily transformed into scientific datasets, but important annotations, characterising and validating the

---

[1] https://www.deviantart.com/.
[2] https://www.behance.net/.
[3] https://www.wikiart.org/.

creators of said content, are lost or never available at the start. With contempArt, we reduce the conventional scope by only including students enrolled at German art schools, thereby guaranteeing detailed socio-demographic information but sacrificing quantity. The result is a unique but narrow snapshot of contemporary painting culture.

(a) Albert Gouthier   (b) Janka Zöller   (c) Soomin Kim   (d) Allistair Walter

(e) Soojie Kang   (f) Olivia Parkes   (g) Rawad Atfeh   (h) Marcel Kimble

(i) Jisub Kim   (j) Yumiko Segawa   (k) Ofra Ohana   (l) Martin Mischner

Fig. 1. contempArt image samples.

3   contempArt Dataset

Data Collection. Due to the manual and time-consuming nature of the data collecting process described in the following text, only art students in Germany were included in the analysis. To create the contempArt dataset, we first gather information on student enrolment in all fine arts programs related to painting or drawing at German art schools. This information is not publicly available until students join a specific painting or drawing class associated with one professor. These painting classes often have an online presence on which the names of current and former students are provided.[4] This data on student names, university and class membership was used to manually locate students individual websites as well as public Instagram[5] accounts, which were subsequently crawled in bulk

---

[4] Example: http://www.klasse-orosz.de/.

[5] https://www.instagram.com.

Table 1. Data sources for contempArt.

ID	Art School	Students	Images
1	Alanus University of Arts and Social Sciences	25	677
2	Weißensee Academy of Art Berlin	8	144
3	Berlin University of the Arts	24	601
4	Braunschweig University of Art	39	1,122
5	University of the Arts Bremen	29	991
6	Dresden Academy of Fine Arts	44	1,743
7	Burg Giebichenstein University of Art and Design	18	777
8	Hochschule für Grafik und Buchkunst Leipzig	68	2,623
9	Mainz Academy of Arts	19	427
10	Academy of Fine Arts München	44	1,227
11	Kunstakademie Münster	33	2,238
12	Academy of Fine Arts Nürnberg	37	555
13	Hochschule für Gestaltung Offenbach am Main	11	191
14	Hochschule der Bildenden Künste Saar	25	553
15	State Academy of Fine Arts Stuttgart	18	690

for image content. If Instagram membership was known, further social media data was collected such as the students Instagram connections or detailed metadata on the images posted on the network. Similarly, if artists webpages were found, self-reported biographical data on nationality and gender was collected. Art students who did not make images of their paintings available were omitted. Furthermore, any images not containing paintings or drawings were manually removed. Aggregate information on included art schools and their students can be seen in Table 1; example images can be seen in Fig. 1.

Dataset Statistics. Less than half of the original list of 1,177 enrolled students had any findable online presence. From the final set of 442 artists, 14,559 images could be collected, with the median number per artists being 20. The data sources were both Instagram accounts and webpages, whereas 37.78% of students only had the former, 17.19% only had the latter, and 45.02% had both. Each data source contributed different metadata to the dataset. Dedicated homepages, the source for 62.37% of all images, generally contain self reported information on the artists nationality and gender. The image data from Instagram, on the other hand, was of lower quality[6] but contained time annotations that allow the

---

[6] Images available on artists dedicated webpages are generally of high resolution and only depict their work. Contrary to Instagram, which limits the image resolution by default to 1080 × 1080 pixels and where the images uploaded by the artists were often noisy; e.g. taken from a larger distance or of artwork surrounded by objects. Cropping away unnecessary content further reduced the image size.

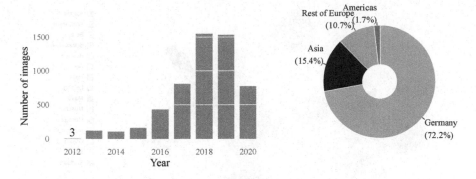

Fig. 2. Metadata distribution for contempArt. Timeframe only available for 5,478 Instagram images. Nationality only available for 234 artists.

estimation of a time range in which the collected artworks were produced. The distribution of images over time and nationality of artists is shown in Fig. 2. Most importantly, the Instagram account metadata provides detailed information on the social media connections between the artists.

Instagram Network Graphs. The sets of Instagram accounts following and being followed by each artist, available for 82.35% of the sample,[7] allow the construction of two directed network graphs capturing information on social relationships. We denote the directed artist network as $\mathfrak{G}^{U} = (O^{U}, D^{U})$, where O^{U} is the set of artists, node $o_i^{U} \in O^{U}$ denotes artist i, and edge $d_{ij}^{U} \in D^{U}$ denotes artist i following artist j. In $\mathfrak{G}^{U}$, the number of nodes is 364, the number of edges 5,614 and the median number of edges per node 27. This network, visualised in Fig. 3, is closely related to art school membership - only 9.73% of edges are between artists of different schools - and to a smaller extent geography, e.g. the proximity of Halle, Leipzig and Berlin. Art schools serve as the primary social hub for most young students and nationwide connections only become common in later stages of their career, so this is to be expected. We denote a second, unconstrained directed network by $\mathfrak{G}^{Y} = (O^{Y}, D^{Y})$, where O^{Y} is the set of all Instagram accounts followed by or following artists. The node $o_k^{Y} \in O^{Y}$ denotes account k, and edge $d_{kl}^{Y} \in D^{Y}$ denotes account k following account l. The number of nodes in $\mathfrak{G}^{Y}$ is 247,087 and the number of edges is 745,144.

4 Unsupervised Style Embeddings

In order to compute image embeddings that are closely related to artistic style, we follow three established, unsupervised approaches that are all based on the VGG network for image classification [45]. Although newer and deeper CNN, such as ResNet [22], have since been proposed that outperform the VGG-network

---

[7] Two Instagram accounts were deleted or renamed during the data collection process so only their image data is available.

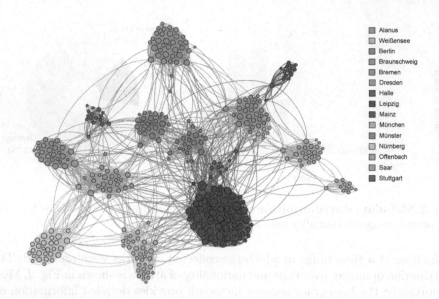

Alanus
Weißensee
Berlin
Braunschweig
Bremen
Dresden
Halle
Leipzig
Mainz
München
Münster
Nürnberg
Offenbach
Saar
Stuttgart

Fig. 3. Visualisation of $\mathfrak{S}^U$ with Gephi [3]. Each node is an artist and the colouring is mapped to art school affiliation. The direction of edges is clockwise and node size represents the number of edges per node.

on its original task, it has become a widely used tool in both art classification tasks [35] and texture synthesis [19,25]. After presenting the different methods, we will examine their visual and numerical connection to labels and images of a commonly used fine art dataset.

Raw VGG Embeddings. We use the deepest network variant of VGG with 19 stacked convolutional layers and three fully connected layers on top. The network is pre-trained on the ImageNet database [12] and the second to last layer fc$_7$ is used as the style embedding $\mathbf{e}_n^V \in \mathbb{R}^{4,096}$ for any image I. Similar deep features [26], that are derived from CNNs trained on ImageNet and not art in particular, have been shown to contain salient information about the latter.

Texture-Based VGG Embeddings. In the seminal work of [19] it has been shown that deep CNNs, and VGG in particular, can be leveraged to perform arbitrary artistic style transfer between images. Specifically, that the correlations inside convolutional feature maps of certain network layers capture positionless information on the texture or rather, the style of images. This, so-called, Gram-based style representation has been widely used in texture synthesis [25] and art classification [10,35]. Contrary to [19], in which this style representation is a part of an optimisation procedure aligning the texture of two images, we utilise it only as a further embedding of style $\mathbf{e}_n^T$. The extraction process is as follows:

Consider the activations at feature map $\mathbf{F}_\ell(I) \in \mathbb{R}^{C_\ell \times (H_\ell W_\ell)}$ of image I at layer ℓ of the VGG network described in the previous subsection. C_ℓ is the number of channels, and W_ℓ and H_ℓ represent the width and height of feature map $\mathbf{F}_\ell(I)$. $\mathbf{F}_\ell(I)[j]$ denotes the column vector in $\mathbb{R}^{C_\ell}$ that holds the feature map activations at pixel position $j \in \{1, \ldots, H_\ell W_\ell\}$. Following the proposed normalisation procedure in [32], the Gram matrix $\mathbf{G}_\ell \in \mathbb{R}^{C_\ell \times C_\ell}$ of the *centered* feature maps at $\ell \in L = \{conv_{1\_1}, conv_{2\_1}, conv_{3\_1}, conv_{4\_1}, conv_{5\_1}\}$, given by

$$\mathbf{G}_\ell = \frac{1}{H_\ell W_\ell} \sum_{j=1}^{H_\ell W_\ell} (\mathbf{F}_\ell(I)[j] - \boldsymbol{\mu}_\ell)(\mathbf{F}_\ell(I)[j] - \boldsymbol{\mu}_\ell)^\top, \tag{1}$$

and the means $\boldsymbol{\mu}_\ell \in \mathbb{R}^{C_\ell}$ themselves, given by

$$\boldsymbol{\mu}_\ell = \frac{1}{H_\ell W_\ell} \sum_{j=1}^{H_\ell W_\ell} \mathbf{F}_\ell(I)[j], \tag{2}$$

are concatenated into a high-dimensional collection $\{\boldsymbol{\mu}'_\ell, \mathbf{G}'_\ell | \ell \in L\}$ with further normalisation by

$$\boldsymbol{\mu}'_\ell = \frac{\boldsymbol{\mu}_\ell}{C_\ell(C_\ell + 1)} \quad \mathbf{G}'_\ell = \frac{\mathbf{G}_\ell}{C_\ell(C_\ell + 1)}, \tag{3}$$

in line with [50]. The Gram matrix $\mathbf{G}_\ell$ is symmetric, so values below the diagonal are omitted. The collection is vectorised to a $S = \sum_\ell C_\ell(C_\ell + 3)/2$-dimensional texture descriptor $\mathbf{v}$, which can be computed for any image I. However, due to $\mathbf{v}$ being very high-dimensional it is common practice to apply a secondary dimensional reduction on the joint N texture descriptors of the present image dataset [18, 36, 50]. To do so, we aggregate $\mathbf{v}_n$ for all images $n = 1, \ldots, N$ in the given dataset and concatenate them into a matrix $\mathbf{V} = [\mathbf{v}_i, \ldots, \mathbf{v}_N] \in \mathbb{R}^{N \times S}$. We apply singular value decomposition to this matrix, extracting 4,096-dimensional features as our second style embedding $\mathbf{e}_n^\top \in \mathbb{R}^{4,096}$ for image I_n.

Archetype Embeddings. Wynen et al. [50] uses the previously described Gramian texture descriptor $\mathbf{e}^\top$ and a classical unsupervised learning method called archetypal analysis [11] to compute and visualise a set of art archetypes.[8] With archetypal analysis, the P K-dimensional samples of an original matrix $\mathbf{X} = [\mathbf{x}_1, \ldots, \mathbf{x}_P]$ are approximately reconstructed as convex mixtures of M archetypes $\mathbf{Z}^\top = [\mathbf{z}_1, \ldots, \mathbf{z}_M] \in \mathbb{R}^{K \times M}$, i.e.,

$$\mathbf{x}_p \approx \mathbf{Z}\boldsymbol{\alpha}_p, \quad \text{with} \quad \sum_{m=1}^{M} \alpha_{pm} = 1, \quad \alpha_{pm} \geq 0 \tag{4}$$

where $\boldsymbol{\alpha}_n \in \mathbb{R}^M$ contain the mixture coefficients, α_{pm}'s, that approximate each $p = 1, \ldots, P$ observations by a combination of archetypes, whereas the

---

[8] Definition of archetype: the original pattern or model of which all things of the same type are representations or copies [39].

$m = 1, \ldots, M$ archetypes are themselves convex mixtures of samples:

$$\mathbf{z}_m = \mathbf{X}\boldsymbol{\beta}_m, \quad \text{with} \quad \sum_{p=1}^{P} \beta_{mp} = 1, \quad \beta_{mp} \geq 0 \tag{5}$$

where $\boldsymbol{\beta}_m \in \mathbb{R}^P$ contain the mixture coefficients, β_{mp}'s, that approximate each archetype with $\mathbf{X}$. For ease of notation, let $\mathbf{A} \in \mathbb{R}^{M \times P}$ and $\mathbf{B} \in \mathbb{R}^{P \times M}$ be matrices that contain $\boldsymbol{\alpha}_p$'s and $\boldsymbol{\beta}_m$'s, respectively. Then, the optimal weights of $\mathbf{A}$ and $\mathbf{B}$ can be found by minimising the residual sum of squares

$$\text{RSS}_M = \| \mathbf{X} - \mathbf{XBA} \|_F^2, \tag{6}$$

subject to the above constraints, with efficient solvers [9]. The number M of archetypes can be predefined, as in [50], or adjusted by visually comparing RSS_M at different M-values as in the original work [11]. We apply archetypal analysis on the matrix of stacked texture descriptors $\mathbf{E}^T = [\mathbf{e}_1^T, \ldots, \mathbf{e}_N^T] \in \mathbb{R}^{N \times 4{,}096}$ for the given dataset containing N images. The estimated archetype-to-image and image-to-archetype mixture weights $\boldsymbol{\alpha}_n$ and $\boldsymbol{\beta}_n^T$ of each image I_n are then concatenated into the final style embedding $\mathbf{e}_n^A \in \mathbb{R}^{2M}$.

5   Comparative Evaluation of Style Embeddings

The unsupervised nature of the described embeddings - subsequently called *VGG*, *Texture* and *Archetype* - requires an evaluation of their connection to artistic style and differences therein. Due to the visual nature of artworks, evaluations of their unsupervised feature spaces often rely only on visual comparisons, as in the case of the archetypal style embeddings [50] or texture synthesis [25,30,53]. In the following, we investigate both the visual differences between the embeddings as well as their relation to existing style labels.

Evaluation Details. We download a balanced subset of Wikiart, sampling 1,000 random images each from the 20 most frequent style labels after excluding non-painting artworks that were classified as photography, architecture, etc.[9] The VGG network is initialised with its pre-trained weights for image classification and this same network is used to generate all three embeddings. Images are scaled down to 512 pixels on their shorter side while maintaining aspect ratio and then center-cropped to 512×512 patches. For the *Archetype* embedding, the number of archetypes was set to $M = 40$ - twice the number of style labels - although further empirical comparisons showed that varying M had only marginal influence on either of the results.

---

[9] Included styles: Abstract Art, Abstract Expressionism, Art Informel, Art Nouveau (Modern), Baroque, Cubism, Early Renaissance, Expressionism, High Renaissance, Impressionism, Naïve Art (Primitivism), Neoclassicism, Northern Renaissance, Post-Impressionism, Realism, Rococo, Romanticism, Surrealism, Symbolism, Ukiyo-e.

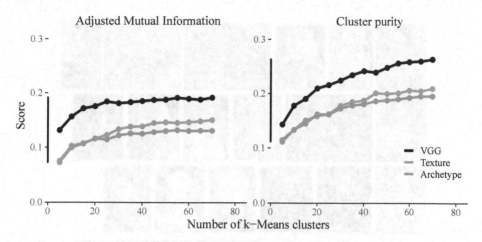

Fig. 4. Evaluation of style embeddings. Similarity between k-Means clustering based on the three unsupervised embeddings and style labels from Wikiart.

Numerical Evaluation. For a range of $k = 5, 10, 15, \ldots, 70$, we partition the three embeddings into k clusters with the k-Means algorithm. The informational overlap between the resulting cluster memberships and the existing style annotations is calculated with the adjusted mutual information (AMI) score [49], a normalised and chance-adjusted metric that quantifies the reduction in class entropy when the cluster labels are known. A value of 1 would represent cluster and class membership matching up perfectly, whereas values around 0 would signify a random clustering. In order to provide a more transparent yet unnormalised evaluation measure, we additionally show the purity score, for which the images in each cluster are assigned to its most frequent style label and the average number of thereby correctly assigned images is calculated. The results in Fig. 4 show that the *VGG* embeddings have the highest AMI and purity score for all values of k. The *Archetype* and *Texture* embeddings have similar results, even though the dimensionality of the former is 50 times less. Even the highest AMI-score of 0.191 can still be considered closer to a random clustering than an informative one, leading to the conclusion that none of the embeddings correspond closely to commonly used labels of artistic style. However, style annotations in fine art datasets are known to be very broad and, in Wikiart's case, noisy [14], allowing for some margin of error and calling for a further, visual inspection of the embeddings.

Visual Evaluation. We visualise a small set of randomly chosen images with their five closest neighbours for each of the style embeddings. Closeness is calculated with the cosine similarity. The comparison in Fig. 5 gives insights into the difference between style annotations and stylistic similarity. The *Archetype* embedding, not being able to cluster the visually unique Ukiyo-e genre as well as failing to align even general colour space, again performs the worst. Archetypal analysis, while allowing a high degree of interpretability and aesthetic

Fig. 5. Visual evaluation of style embeddings. For three images, repeated throughout the first column, the five most similar images in all three style embeddings are shown in descending order from left to right. From top to bottom: *VGG*, *Texture* and *Archetype*. A red border indicates that the chosen image does not share the anchor images style annotation from Wikiart. (Color figure online)

visualisations [9,50] by encoding images as convex mixtures of themselves, has to be evaluated more rigorously to validate its usefulness for art analysis. *VGG* and *Texture* are each able to match up images in terms of a general visual style. However, both are inconsistent in doing the same for labelled style, echoing the results of the numerical evaluation.

The overlap between the evaluated embeddings and regular style annotations was shown to be minimal, but two of the three still contain valid information on artistic visual similarity. Texture, although exceptional in transferring itself, does not capture style in the art historical sense. Conversely, that same style can not be described by visual content alone, validating context-based approaches to art classification tasks as in [16].

Table 2. Local and global style variation with standard deviation.

	σ_c	$\sigma_{c_{\text{global}}}$
VGG	.283 ± .080	.435 ± .101
Texture	.137 ± .049	.211 ± .094
Archetype	.195 ± .121	.323 ± .326

Table 3. Rank correlations of style and network distances.

	$\mathbb{G}^U$	$\mathbb{G}^Y$
VGG	.007	−.032
Texture	.043	−.025
Archetype	.012	−.057

6   Analysis of contempArt

The VGG embeddings of the contempArt images, partially visualised in Fig. 6, exhibit a reasonable connection to visual style by separating broad patterns, such as colourful paintings opposite black and white sketches, as well as smaller ones, such as unique styles of single artists. In order to correlate these embeddings with the collected socio-demographic information we must aggregate them to the artist-level. Consider the set of artists, $A=\{a^l | l = 1, \ldots, N_a\}$ where N_a is the number of artists and each artist a^l has a set of image embeddings $P^l = \{e_i^l | i = 1, \ldots, N^l\}$ where N^l is the number of paintings for the l-th artist. For all further analysis we compute each artists centroid style embedding

$$c^l = \frac{1}{N^l} \sum_i^{N^l} e_i^l. \tag{7}$$

Only few artists have a singular repetitive style, which is especially true for art students for whom experimentation is essential. To be able to judge this variance of style we also compute the average intra-artist style distance to each centroid embedding with cosine distance D_C

$$\sigma_c = \frac{1}{N_a} \sum_j^{N_a} \frac{1}{N^j} \sum_i^{N^j} D_C(c^l, e_i^j) \tag{8}$$

To have a comparable measure of variation we further compute the average centroid distance for all $N = \sum_i^{N_a} N^i$ images in the dataset

$$\sigma_{c_{\text{global}}} = \frac{1}{N} \sum_j^{N_a} \sum_i^{N^j} D_C(\mathbf{c}_N, \mathbf{e}_i^j), \tag{9}$$

where $\mathbf{c}_N$ is the average of all image embeddings. The results are shown in Table 2 for all three style embeddings. The *Texture* embeddings have the smallest amount of variation, both globally and across artists. For the *Archetype* embedding, the number of archetypes was set to $M = 36$ through visual inspection of the reduction in the residual error as in [11].

Fig. 6. Visualisation of contempArt with t-SNE [34].

6.1   Social Networks and Style

We use the node2vec algorithm [20] on both graphs $\mathfrak{S}^U$ and $\mathfrak{S}^Y$ to project their relational data into a low-dimensional feature space. node2vec is a random-walk based graph embedding technique that preserves network neighbourhoods and, contrary to most other methods, structural similarity of nodes. This additional capability is especially useful for the larger network $\mathfrak{S}^Y$, in which the homophily captured by a pure social network such as $\mathfrak{S}^U$ is augmented by detailed and vast information on taste. We compute 128 node2vec features for each of the graphs and use cosine distance to generate a matrix of artist-level social network distances. Similarly, we generate pairwise style distances with the centroid embeddings $\mathbf{c}^l$ for all three embeddings.

Spearmans's rank coefficient is used to compute the correlation between the flattened upper triangular parts of the described distance matrices. The results in Table 3 show that there are only very small correlations between stylistic and social distance. Even though the two graphs share only a minor similarity ($r_{sp} = .166$), neither network contains information that relates to inter-artist differences in style. The clear overlap between school affiliation and the smaller network graph $\mathfrak{G}^U$, as seen in Fig. 3, allows the further conclusion, that art schools too, have no bearing on artistic style.

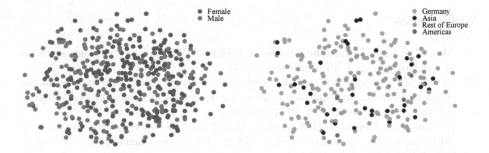

Fig. 7. The independence of artistic style and socio-demographic factors. Visualisation of the centroid VGG embeddings with t-SNE [34].

6.2   Socio-Demographic Factors and Style

We investigate possible connections between the style embeddings and the collected data on the artists by jointly visualising them. Specifically, we extract a two-dimensional feature space from the VGG embeddings with t-SNE [34], both per image and per artist with the previously described aggregation. There were no visible patterns for any of the available variables, including Instagram-specific measures such as likes, comments or the number of followers and general ones such as nationality, gender or art school affiliation. We show two exemplary results in Fig. 7, in which the independence of style from these factors is apparent. This is not a surprising result as the non-visual factors are primarily attached to the individual artist and not their work. Even painting-specific reactions on Instagram depend more on the activity and reach of their creators than the artworks themselves.

7   Conclusion

This work presented the first combined analysis of contemporary fine art and its social context by assembling a unique dataset on German art students and using unsupervised methodologies to extract and correlate artworks with their context. The collected data consisted of images, social network graphs and socio-demographic information on the artists. Three established methods to obtain style embeddings from images of paintings were briefly evaluated, outside of the usual framework of supervision, in their connection to common style annotations and general visual similarity. These embeddings of artistic style were shown to be entirely independent of any non-visual data. Further work will go into increasing dataset size, to reduce the effect of noise induced by the high amount of heterogeneity present in art produced by artists early in their career, and into contrasting the contemporary artworks with historical ones.

Acknowledgement. This work was supported by JSPS KAKENHI No. 20K19822.

References

1. Abe, S., Elsner, J.: Introduction: Some Stakes of Comparison. In: Comparativism in Art History, pp. 1–15. Routledge (2017)
2. Badea, M., Florea, C., Florea, L., Vertan, C.: Can we teach computers to understand art? Domain adaptation for enhancing deep networks capacity to de-abstract art. Image Vis. Comput. **77**, 21–32 (2018)
3. Bastian, M., Heymann, S., Jacomy, M.: Gephi: an open source software for exploring and manipulating networks (2009). http://www.aaai.org/ocs/index.php/ICWSM/09/paper/view/154
4. Bianco, S., Mazzini, D., Napoletano, P., Schettini, R.: Multitask painting categorization by deep multibranch neural network. Expert Syst. Appl. **135**, 90–101 (2019)
5. Bishop, C.: Against digital art history. Int. J. Dig. Art History (3), 122–131 (2018)
6. Brachmann, A., Barth, E., Redies, C.: Using CNN features to better understand what makes visual artworks special. Front. Psychol. **8**, 830 (2017)
7. Castellano, G., Vessio, G.: Deep convolutional embedding for digitized painting clustering. arXiv preprint arXiv:2003.08597 (2020)
8. Cetinic, E., Lipic, T., Grgic, S.: A deep learning perspective on beauty, sentiment, and remembrance of art. IEEE Access **7**, 73694–73710 (2019)
9. Chen, Y., Mairal, J., Harchaoui, Z.: Fast and robust archetypal analysis for representation learning. In: Proceedings of CVPR, pp. 1478–1485 (2014)
10. Chu, W.T., Wu, Y.L.: Image style classification based on learnt deep correlation features. IEEE Trans. Multimedia **20**(9), 2491–2502 (2018)
11. Cutler, A., Breiman, L.: Archetypal analysis. Technometrics **36**(4), 338–347 (1994)
12. Deng, J., Dong, W., Socher, R., Li, L.J., Li, K., Fei-Fei, L.: ImageNet: a large-scale hierarchical image database. In: Proceedings of CVPR, pp. 248–255 (2009)
13. Drucker, J.: Is there a "digital " art history? Vis. Resour. **29**(1–2), 5–13 (2013)
14. Elgammal, A., Liu, B., Kim, D., Elhoseiny, M., Mazzone, M.: The shape of art history in the eyes of the machine. In: Proceedings of AAAI (2018)
15. Elgammal, A., Saleh, B.: Quantifying creativity in art networks. In: Proceedings of ICCC, p. 39 (2015)
16. Garcia, N., Renoust, B., Nakashima, Y.: Context-aware embeddings for automatic art analysis. In: Proceedings of ICMR, pp. 25–33 (2019)

17. Garcia, N., Vogiatzis, G.: How to read paintings: semantic art understanding with multi-modal retrieval. In: Leal-Taixé, L., Roth, S. (eds.) ECCV 2018. LNCS, vol. 11130, pp. 676–691. Springer, Cham (2019). https://doi.org/10.1007/978-3-030-11012-3_52

18. Gatys, L., Ecker, A.S., Bethge, M.: Texture synthesis using convolutional neural networks. In: Proceedings of NeurIPS, pp. 262–270 (2015)

19. Gatys, L.A., Ecker, A.S., Bethge, M.: Image style transfer using convolutional neural networks. In: Proceedings of CVPR, pp. 2414–2423 (2016)

20. Grover, A., Leskovec, J.: node2vec: scalable feature learning for networks. In: Proceedings of SIGKDD, pp. 855–864 (2016)

21. Gultepe, E., Conturo, T.E., Makrehchi, M.: Predicting and grouping digitized paintings by style using unsupervised feature learning. J. Cultur. Heritage **31**, 13–23 (2018)

22. He, K., Zhang, X., Ren, S., Sun, J.: Deep residual learning for image recognition. In: Proceedings of CVPR, pp. 770–778 (2016)

23. Jaskot, P.B.: Digital art history as the social history of art: towards the disciplinary relevance of digital methods. Vis. Resour. **35**(1–2), 21–33 (2019)

24. Jaskot, P.B.: Digital methods and the historiography of art. The Routledge Companion to Digital Humanities and Art History (2020)

25. Jing, Y., Yang, Y., Feng, Z., Ye, J., Yu, Y., Song, M.: Neural style transfer: a review. Trans. Vis. Comput. Graph. **26**, 3365–3385 (2019)

26. Karayev, S., et al.: Recognizing image style. In: Proceedings of BMVC (2013)

27. Khan, F.S., Beigpour, S., Van de Weijer, J., Felsberg, M.: Painting-91: a large scale database for computational painting categorization. Mach. Vis. Appl. **25**(6), 1385–1397 (2014)

28. Kim, D., Son, S.W., Jeong, H.: Large-scale quantitative analysis of painting arts. Sci. Rep. **4**, 7370 (2014)

29. Kim, N.W.: Creative community demystified: a statistical overview of behance. arXiv preprint arXiv:1703.00800 (2017)

30. Kotovenko, D., Sanakoyeu, A., Lang, S., Ommer, B.: Content and style disentanglement for artistic style transfer. In: Proceedings of ICCV, pp. 4422–4431 (2019)

31. Lee, B., Kim, D., Sun, S., Jeong, H., Park, J.: Heterogeneity in chromatic distance in images and characterization of massive painting data set. PloS ONE **13**(9), 1–16 (2018)

32. Li, Y., Fang, C., Yang, J., Wang, Z., Lu, X., Yang, M.H.: Diversified texture synthesis with feed-forward networks. In: Proceedings of CVPR, pp. 3920–3928 (2017)

33. Lin, T.-Y., et al.: Microsoft COCO: common objects in context. In: Fleet, D., Pajdla, T., Schiele, B., Tuytelaars, T. (eds.) ECCV 2014. LNCS, vol. 8693, pp. 740–755. Springer, Cham (2014). https://doi.org/10.1007/978-3-319-10602-1_48

34. Maaten, L.v.d., Hinton, G.: Visualizing data using t-SNE. J. Mach. Learn. Res. **9**(Nov), 2579–2605 (2008)

35. Mao, H., Cheung, M., She, J.: DeepArt: learning joint representations of visual arts. In: Proceedings of ACMMM, pp. 1183–1191 (2017)

36. Matsuo, S., Yanai, K.: CNN-based style vector for style image retrieval. In: Proceedings of ICMR, pp. 309–312 (2016)

37. Mensink, T., Van Gemert, J.: The Rijksmuseum challenge: museum-centered visual recognition. In: Proceedings of ICMR, pp. 451–454 (2014)

38. Mercuriali, G.: Digital art history and the computational imagination. In: International Journal for Digital Art History: Issue 3, 2018: Digital Space and Architecture, vol. 3, p. 141 (2019)

39. Merriam-Webster Online: Merriam-Webster Online Dictionary (2009). http://www.merriam-webster.com
40. Salah, A.A., Manovich, L., Salah, A.A., Chow, J.: Combining cultural analytics and networks analysis: studying a social network site with user-generated content. J. Broadcast. Electron. Med. **57**(3), 409–426 (2013)
41. Salah, A.A., Salah, A.A., Buter, B., Dijkshoorn, N., Modolo, D., Nguyen, Q., van Noort, S., van de Poel, B.: DeviantArt in spotlight: a network of artists. Leonardo **45**(5), 486–487 (2012)
42. Shamir, L., Macura, T., Orlov, N., Eckley, D.M., Goldberg, I.G.: Impressionism, expressionism, surrealism: automated recognition of painters and schools of art. Trans. Appl. Percept. **7**(2), 1–17 (2010)
43. Shamir, L., Tarakhovsky, J.A.: Computer analysis of art. J. Comput. Cultur. Heritag. **5**(2), 1–11 (2012)
44. Sigaki, H.Y., Perc, M., Ribeiro, H.V.: History of art paintings through the lens of entropy and complexity. Proc. Natl. Acad. Sci. **115**(37), E8585–E8594 (2018)
45. Simonyan, K., Zisserman, A.: Very deep convolutional networks for large-scale image recognition. In: Proceedings of ICLR (2015)
46. Spehr, M., Wallraven, C., Fleming, R.W.: Image statistics for clustering paintings according to their visual appearance. In: Eurographics Workshop on Computational Aesthetics in Graphics, Visualization and Imaging, pp. 57–64 (2009)
47. Strezoski, G., Worring, M.: OmniArt: a large-scale artistic benchmark. TOMM **14**(4), 1–21 (2018)
48. Taylor, R.P., Micolich, A.P., Jonas, D.: Fractal analysis of pollock's drip paintings. Nature **399**(6735), 422–422 (1999)
49. Vinh, N.X., Epps, J., Bailey, J.: Information theoretic measures for clusterings comparison: variants, properties, normalization and correction for chance. J. Mach. Learn. Res. **11**, 2837–2854 (2010)
50. Wynen, D., Schmid, C., Mairal, J.: Unsupervised learning of artistic styles with archetypal style analysis. In: Proceedings of NeurIPS, pp. 6584–6593 (2018)
51. Xiao, H., Rasul, K., Vollgraf, R.: Fashion-MNIST: a novel image dataset for benchmarking machine learning algorithms. arXiv preprint arXiv:1708.07747 (2017)
52. Yazdani, M., Chow, J., Manovich, L.: Quantifying the development of user-generated art during 2001–2010. PloS ONE **12**(8), 1–24 (2017)
53. Yeh, M.C., Tang, S., Bhattad, A., Zou, C., Forsyth, D.: Improving style transfer with calibrated metrics. In: Proceedings of WACV, pp. 3160–3168 (2020)
54. Zhu, J.Y., Park, T., Isola, P., Efros, A.A.: Unpaired image-to-image translation using cycle-consistent adversarial networks. In: Proceedings of ICCV, pp. 2223–2232 (2017)

Geolocating Time: Digitisation and Reverse Engineering of a Roman Sundial

Mara Pistellato[1] , Arianna Traviglia[2] , and Filippo Bergamasco[1(✉)]

[1] DAIS - Università Ca'Foscari, Via Torino 155, 30172 Venice, Italy
{mara.pistellato,filippo.bergamasco}@unive.it
[2] Istituto Italiano di Tecnologia (IIT), Center for Cultural Heritage Technology
(CCHT), Via della Libertà 12, 30175 Venice, Italy
arianna.traviglia@iit.it

Abstract. The sundial of Euporus was discovered in 1878 within the ancient Roman city of Aquileia (Italy), in a quite unusual location at the centre of the city's horse race track. Studies have tried to demonstrate that the sundial had been made for a more southern location than the one it was found at, although no specific alternative positions have been suggested. This paper showcases both the workflow designed to fully digitise it in 3D and analyses on the use of the artefact undertaken from it. The final 3D reconstruction achieves accuracies of a few millimetres, thus offering the opportunity to analyse small details of its surface and to perform non-trivial measurements. We also propose a mathematical approach to compute the object's optimal working latitude as well as the gnomon position and orientation. The algorithm is designed as an optimization problem where the sundial's inscriptions and the Sun positions during daytime are considered to obtain the optimal configuration. The complete 3D model of the object is used to get all the geometrical information needed to validate the results of computations.

Keywords: Computational archaeology · 3D reconstruction · Reverse engineering

1 Introduction

Digitisation and archiving play a fundamental role in cultural heritage field [13,22]. Indeed, many technological applications are specifically designed to support such tasks, allowing for fast and precise results which were usually obtained through manual or analogue tools [14,20]. In particular, 3D reconstruction offers a wide range of opportunities in terms of recording artefacts geometry, opening new research directions in terms of conservation, restoration and study [11,15]. The reasons behind such applications are several: digital libraries of high-resolution 3D models bring to the creation of extensive archives, that can be available to a large audience of users, both in research and public communities. Digitisation also allows for restoration and monitoring of artworks which

© Springer Nature Switzerland AG 2020
A. Bartoli and A. Fusiello (Eds.): ECCV 2020 Workshops, LNCS 12536, pp. 143–158, 2020.
https://doi.org/10.1007/978-3-030-66096-3_11

Fig. 1. Left: Inscriptions on the top surface of the Euporus sundial. Right: 3D acquisition of the sundial: on the left the structured light scanner mounted on a tripod.

are often exposed to atmospheric agents. In particular, structured-light scanning techniques have already been employed in some cultural heritage applications, leading to optimal outcomes [1, 2, 21].

In this paper we describe a practical case study showing how structured-light scanning, and particularly phase-shift technique, can be applied in a cultural heritage application. We explore two main aspects regarding the study of an ancient sundial: its digitisation process and the reverse engineering approach determining the gnomon's shape and working latitude.

The object is hosted at the National Archaeological Museum of Aquileia (Italy), and it is known as the *"Sundial of Euporus"*, from the name of its donor, M. Anstitius Euporus, inscribed within the dial. The instrument was likely engraved in the 2nd century AD and was discovered in 1878 in the area of the Roman Circus of Aquileia, in centre of the horse race track [8], probably not in its original position. The object is a rare type of Karst limestone horizontal plane sundial (see Fig. 1), pertaining to the Vitruvian type called *"plinthium sive lacunar"* [10], it is an horizontal slab surrounded by a frame, recalling the form of an overturned coffered ceiling [3]. The top planar surface measures 100×206 cm, and it is surrounded by a $\sim$10 cm frame extending all around its rectangular shape (see Fig. 1, right). A set of inscriptions located on one half of the upper surface reveals its usage as sundial (Fig. 1, left).

The first part of the paper deals with the scanning process and focuses on the methodological aspects of the high-resolution acquisition. For the first time a complete 3D digitisation is attempted on this sundial, opening new possibilities in the analysis of its historical background and providing insights into the level of ancient knowledge of sundial design and construction principles. The complete 3D model enables to perform non-trivial studies without physically accessing the object, like analysing the technique used to chisel the inscriptions or the planarity of the dial surface, which affects the shadows cast by the gnomon.

In the second part of this work we present the reverse engineering technique adopted to recover the original gnomon's shape. This study exploits the 3D model to acquire precise measurements on the sundial's surface and create a

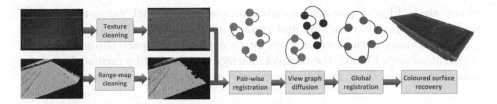

Fig. 2. Schematic representation of the 3D digitisation pipeline (see text for details).

synthetic model of its inscriptions. Then an optimization process is formalised and carried out to simultaneously compute the best gnomon configuration together with the optimal working latitude of the sundial.

2   3D Acquisition Process

The sundial digitisation was accomplished using a custom structured-light scanner formed by a camera and a projector (visible in Fig. 1, right). The 3D reconstruction algorithm employs multi-period phase shift with the unwrapping and correction methods described in [16–18]. Additionally, the signal amplitude is used to get a high-resolution texture of the surface, since it captures the brightness intensity of the object as in a standard grayscale photograph.

Each scanner acquisition generates a *range-map*, that is a surface composed by the 3D triangulated vertices connected by triangles, and the corresponding texture map. Conceptually, the range-map is equivalent to a 3D photograph, capturing both the optical and geometrical properties of the surface.

The digitisation of the whole artefact cannot be performed with a single acquisition; indeed the area recorded by the scanner is not large enough to cover the entire object at a reasonable resolution, and its shape introduces occlusions in the opposite side of each view. For these reasons we acquired several overlapping portions of the surface to collect a set of "3D patches", corresponding to different range-maps. In this way, the entire artefact is recorded with high resolution, especially in the engraved zone. The following section describes the pipeline specifically designed to merge all the views and obtain the final reconstruction.

2.1   Reconstruction Pipeline

Starting from the acquired range-maps and textures, we designed a sequence of operations to reconstruct the complete coloured surface. Figure 2 presents a schematic representation of the tasks involved in the pipeline. They are the following: *pre-cleaning, pairwise matching, view graph diffusion, global registration* and *coloured surface recovery*. Such operations require almost no supervision: the user intervention is limited to the optional configuration of different task-specific parameters.

The most challenging part of the pipeline consists in merging all the individual range-maps: this procedure is referred as *registration* and it has been split in two steps. First, a pair-wise registration operates on each range-map pair to find the best possible rotation and translation that aligns the two. Second, all pairwise transformations are merged into a common 3D space through a global registration step. Finally, the complete surface is recovered by means of an automated algorithm which exploits the registered points and normals.

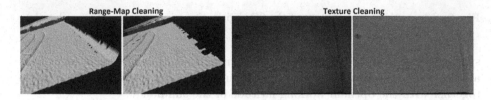

Fig. 3. Pre-cleaning results for range-maps (first and second images) and texture images (third and fourth).

Texture and 3D Pre-cleaning. The first two tasks entail a preliminary cleaning phase, in which range-maps and textures are independently processed to filter out noise and improve the photometric data quality.

Regarding the range-maps cleaning, the process involves (i) the removal of all triangles close to the surface border, (ii) the computation of per-vertex surface normal and (iii) the identification of small connected components that are removed below a certain threshold (we set 1000 vertices). The combination of such steps improves the quality of the range-maps, which are typically prone to exhibit errors near the boundaries of the illuminated area. A visual example of the effect of this cleaning process is shown in Fig. 3.

For what concerns the textures, the goal of the cleaning process is to normalise the uneven illumination exhibited by the intensity images. Indeed, surface areas that are far away from the projector's centre will appear darker than the other ones: the effect is visible in Fig. 3 (third image). To correct this phenomenon, we normalized each texture by means of an high-pass filter designed to remove the low-frequency light variations and thus preserving the high-frequency details of the texture, which are in our interests. This operation was performed with a non-linear top-hat operation using a disc-shaped structuring element of size 51×51. In Fig. 3 (fourth image) we show an example of resulting image texture after the correction. After all the images have been processed, they can be put side by side with no evidence of texture borders or light changes, allowing for a natural range-maps fusion.

Pair-Wise Registration. Given the feature-rich nature of the object surface, the pair-wise registration step was implemented by matching feature points between every couple of views. We exploited well-known SIFT features [12] to provide a set of point-to-point correspondences between each couple of textures.

Each range-map associates a 3D point coordinate to each 2D point on the texture image, therefore the computed feature matching produces two sets of corresponding 3D points in space. Such correspondences are exploited to compute the relative transformation between two views, allowing the registration of the range-maps as described in [6].

Fig. 4. Left: the view graph. Each node represents a range-map and each edge a pairwise transformation (see text for details), the connected components are denoted by different colours. Centre: the yellow component (graph nodes from 41 to 55) forms part of the outer frame. Right: the blue component (nodes from 1 to 25) connects all the range-maps acquired in the engraved area. (Color figure online)

Since some possible matching errors would significantly affect the alignment precision, a RANSAC-based algorithm [4] was adopted to select only the consistent 3D matches and obtain the best transformation between point clouds. The quality of the alignment is measured in terms of inliers, i.e. couples of 3D points for which distance after the transformation is below a threshold (1 mm). This ensures a minimum level of precision for each registration: all the pairwise transformations exhibiting at least 20 inliers were included in the so-called view graph, described in the next paragraph.

View-Graph Diffusion. A view graph is used to group the computed transformations: each node represents an acquired range-map, while each edge denotes the transformation between such views. In other words, when an edge is present, it indicates a valid transformation between two overlapping acquisitions: therefore each connected component represents a group of range-maps that can be merged to obtain a portion of the whole object.

In Fig. 4 (left) the complete view graph is displayed: each connected component is identified by a different colour. Due to small estimation errors, within a connected component different paths between two views would result in two inconsistent transformations. In order to compute a coherent set of transformations within each group of views, a state-of-the-art diffusion technique was applied as described in [24], ensuring the overall error minimisation for each set. After the diffusion, the range-maps belonging to a connected component are

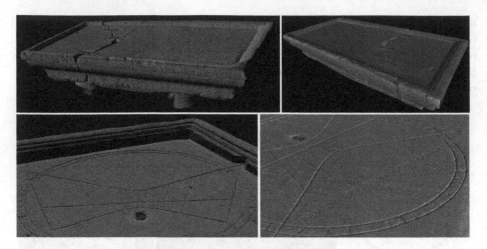

Fig. 5. Some views of the final coloured model after Poisson surface reconstruction. Top: the whole scanned artefact. Bottom: details of the sundial engraving.

merged to form a macro-section of the sundial. In Fig. 4 (centre and right) the merged range-maps coming from the two largest components are shown.

Global Registration and Surface Reconstruction. The global registration step involves the joining of the surfaces obtained from each connected component of the graph. First, a rough registration is performed in a semi-automatic way by manually selecting some correspondence points. Then, to refine the alignment all the components are registered using ICP (Iterative Closest Point) algorithm [25]. Finally, the surface of the sundial was computed applying Screened Poisson Reconstruction method [7]. This algorithm generates closed watertight surface which interpolates all the given points: the output is a set of coloured points and triangles reconstructing the entire object.

2.2   Reconstruction Results

Since the most relevant part of the sundial is the engraved zone, the acquisition process was planned to capture such area with a higher accuracy with respect to the rest. The acquisition was performed in two sessions: first, the scanner was configured to acquire an area of approximately 40×30 cm, at a distance of $\sim$100 cm in order to obtain a high-resolution for the main inscriptions. We acquired 40 range-maps with this configuration: the first 25 were acquired closer to the object, while the rest covered more surface in order to help the global registration of each view. All acquired views were planned so that the overlapping portion of each range-map with its successive was at least $\frac{1}{3}$ of its area. The second session entailed a change of the scanner optics in order to acquire a wider area (approximately 150×200 cm) at a distance of 250 cm. We acquired 45 range-maps all around the whole artefact, capturing both the outer frame

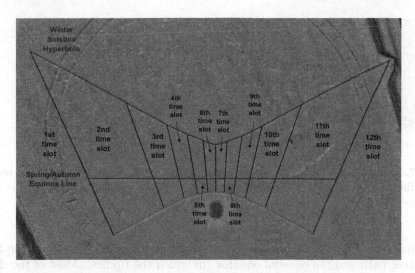

Fig. 6. Time slots displayed by the sundial, each one denotes an equal subdivision of daylight. Solstice hyperbole and equinox line are also highlighted.

and the planar surface. For each range-map, an average of 6.5 million triangles composed from ∼5 million 3D points were acquired. After the global registration, each range-map was resampled to obtain a roughly uniform distribution of the 3D points among all the connected components. The final surface was created using the screened Poisson reconstruction algorithm with a tree depth set to 11 and 3 samples per node. Figure 5 shows the model of the scanned artefact in its entirety (top row) and some details of the sundial engraving (bottom row). The overall resolution is high enough to allow the analysis not only of the whole artefact, but also of the micro-furrows, scratches and unevenness of surface.

3   Gnomon Reverse Engineering

From ancient times, sundials were manufactured with the purpose of measuring time from the apparent position of the sun in the sky. Usually sundials comprise an object casting a shadow (the gnomon) and a surface, where the shadow is casted, in which some marks indicate the time or the current part of the day. Ancient sundials usually divide daylight time (i.e. from sunrise to sunset) into equal parts. For this reason the construction of such objects is easier and longitude correction is not needed, since it does not point the "clock time" as we are used today. Indeed, since daylight has a variable duration depending on day and latitude, each "time slot" does not have the same duration throughout the year.

The line connecting the Sun with the tip of the gnomon describes a cone in a frame which is rotating with the Earth. The shadow of the tip is therefore located on the intersection between that cone and the sundial plane, forming

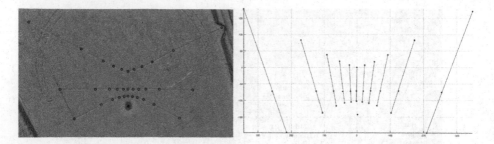

Fig. 7. On the left, the 3D points acquired from the model; on the right, the corresponding 2D points used for optimization. All measures are displayed in mm. (Color figure online)

a conic section depending on the displacement of the plane containing the Sun apparent path and the celestial equator (in which the tip lies). Most of the days the conic section is an hyperbola, more or less curved, becoming a line twice a year during the equinoxes, when light and night times have the same duration.

Figure 6 highlights the salient curves engraved in the studied sundial. Two hyperbole are visible (depicted in blue and yellow), indicating the path traced by the shadow of the gnomon's tip during winter and summer solstices. The horizontal red line is the equinox line, traced by the shadow during two days, in autumn and spring. Finally, the engraved part of the object includes eleven segments used to mark the time during the day (in black).

3.1   Dial Parametrisation

To reverse engineer the Euporus' sundial, we first need to localise all the marks on the sundial's plane. We recovered those points from the 3D reconstruction of the artefact, ensuring a measurement precision of about a millimeter and the computation non-trivial features, such as the object's planarity.

We computed the coordinates of 34 points in three-dimensional space from the intersections between equinox and solstices curves with the 11 time marks. Figure 7 (left) shows a detail of the 3D model and the extracted points: three for each time mark (in red) plus the gnomon's base (in black). Note that the time marks are not perfectly symmetric with respect to the central line (the sixth), that corresponds to the south-north axis. The acquired points were transformed to a convenient reference frame: a plane was fitted to the 34 intersection points to define a *geographical frame* with the y-axis (coinciding with the sundial's main axis) facing north, x-axis faces east and z-axis oriented upward. The applied transformation does not affect the final result since the sundial's axis must be aligned with the North-South axis to work properly.

The measured points are almost coplanar with a maximum distance from the fitted plane of ~ 0.8 mm. Therefore, we can assume the points to lay on the plane (so that their z coordinate is zero) without loss of precision in the following computations. The result of model acquisition is shown in the rightmost part of Fig. 7. After normalization, the point coordinates on the sundial's plane (apart from the gnomon's base) are arranged in a rank 3 tensor $V_{\alpha\beta\gamma}$ with $\alpha \in \{1, 2, 3, 4\}$ denoting respectively spring equinox, summer solstice, autumn equinox and winter solstice, $\beta \in \{1, \ldots, 11\}$ identifying the βth intersection point with the time marks and $\gamma \in \{1, 2\}$ the 2D coordinate of the point. Note that points with $\alpha = 1$ and $\alpha = 3$ are identical since the projection during the two equinoxes must correspond.

3.2   Formalization of Sundial Functioning

In order to introduce the notation that will be used in the following parts, we define the following sets:

- $Y \subset \mathbb{Z}$: set of years (BC negative, AC positive).
- Δ: set of dates s.t. $d \in \Delta$ indicates a day in the format (year, month, day).
- T: set of timestamps. Each element $t \in T$ encodes a date and a time. A timestamp can be interpreted as a sequence of values of the kind (year, month, day, hour, minutes, seconds).
- $L = [-90, 90]$: set of latitudes (in degrees).

Suppose to have a function which returns the Sun's position given a latitude and a timestamp:

$$S(t, l) : T \times L \to \mathbb{S}^2 \tag{1}$$

where $\mathbb{S}^2$ is the set of 3D vectors belonging to the surface of a unitary sphere. The result of such function is a unit vector which points at the Sun's position during timestamp t at latitude l.

As we already discussed, the sundial's marks do not indicate the "clock" time, but the current fraction of light-time, that has been equally split. Therefore, we are only interested in the light time of each day, and not in the real clock time as we were calibrating a clock. In other words, given a date and a place on Earth we just need to compute the 12 time slots, without considering the so-called apparent solar time. For this reason we have no need of longitude corrections, thus our formulation restricts to latitude only, fixing the longitude value in all the computations. Moreover, the geographic area involved in the research is quite narrow in terms of longitude, but it exhibits a wider latitude range. Considering that the optimal working location of the object is extremely sensitive to latitude changes (especially for what concerns the hyperbole curves and equinox line), the longitude can be considered irrelevant for our purposes.

The projection of a generic 3D point on the sundial's plane can be computed considering a projective system in which the Sun is the centre, located at infinity, emitting light rays to be projected on the sundial's plane as a parallel projection [5]. The resulting projection $\mathbf{p}'$ of a 3D point $\mathbf{p}$ on a plane is computed as follows:

$$\mathbf{p}' = \begin{pmatrix} \mathbf{r}_1^T \\ \mathbf{r}_2^T \end{pmatrix} \left(\mathbf{p} + \frac{-\mathbf{p} \cdot \mathbf{n}}{\mathbf{n} \cdot \mathbf{s}} \mathbf{s} \right) \tag{2}$$

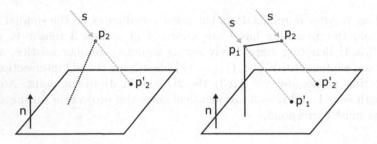

Fig. 8. Left: punctual projection, with unknown gnomon configuration. This setup is sufficient to estimate p_2 coordinates as well as the optimal latitude. Right: presumed gnomon configuration. Points p_1 and p_2 are projected on the plane, forming a segment.

where $\mathbf{s}$ is the vector pointing at Sun's position computed as in (1), and $\mathbf{n}$ is a unitary vector representing the normal direction of the plane (i.e. perpendicular to it) in which the shadow is casted. Finally, $(\mathbf{r}_1 \ \mathbf{r}_2 \ \mathbf{n})^T$ is the rotation matrix transforming the sundial's plane to our geographical plane. Note that we used the first two rows of the matrix so that the final projected point is a 2D point.

We model the gnomon through two junction points, characterizing the shadow's length and slope. The end of the vertical part will be identified as $\mathbf{p}_1$, while the endpoint of the tilted part is $\mathbf{p}_2$. Figure 8 displays a schematic representation of the projection. In particular, points and vectors involved in Eq. 2 are included (the apostrophe denotes the projection of the point).

3.3   Recovery of the Optimal Gnomon's Geometry

Since the sundial works with 12 equally-spaced time slots during daylight, we define a utility function H such that $H(d,l) : \Delta \times L \rightarrow T^{11}$. Given a date d and a latitude l, such function computes the 11 timestamps which should correspond to the marks on sundial's plane. Note that each timestamp marks the transition from one slot to the following one, as sketched in Fig. 6: the first mark denotes the end of the first slot and the beginning of the second, and so on. Our goal is to estimate the parameters so that the gnomon's shadow is projected as close as possible to the corresponding marks at the timestamps returned by function H.

We divided the operation in two independent tasks: (i) the joint optimization of p_2 and the latitude and (ii) the computation of p_1 and thus the inclination of the gnomon. The choice is driven by the following observations: the sundial's working latitude is only affected by the projection of point p_2 during equinoxes and solstices. In fact, the endpoint of the shadow casted by the gnomon must fall exactly on those curves in four specific days in a year. In this terms, we can forget the gnomon's shape and consider only a punctual projection of p_2 onto the plane (see Fig. 8, left). During the four relevant days such projection must overlap with the corresponding curve.

Once the point p_2 is fixed, and hence the latitude is recovered, the shadow's inclination allows to guess a possible shape for the whole gnomon. In particular, we assume a single joint in correspondence of point p_1. This task could be affected by the thickness of the stick, and requires a different criterion to assess the correctness of the projection.

Latitude Optimization. For the sundial to work we need the shadow of the gnomon's tip p_2 to occur in some predefined points during four days every year. Each of these days is associated with a curve and, in turn, each curve is marked with eleven points corresponding to the time slots dividing each day.

Solstices and equinoxes days slightly change each year, thus we define a utility function $\hat{D}(y)$ which returns four dates from Δ corresponding to equinoxes and solstices in year y. These dates are computed as follows: summer and winter solstices are the dates in which the daylight is respectively maximum and minimum (between 20–22 June and 20–23 December), while the two equinoxes are days in which daylight is equal to night time (19–21 March and 21–24 September).

The function $P(y, l, \mathbf{p}_2, \mathbf{n})$ computes a rank 3 tensor, with a structure analogue to V, containing the projections of 3D point $\mathbf{p}_2$ at each of the 11 timestamps of each four dates in $\hat{D}(y)$.

In an ideal configuration the coordinates of the computed projections in P perfectly overlap with the sundial's points in V. In practice the projection can not be perfect, so we aim to minimize the squared distance of all the projections from the corresponding sundial's points. Thus, we formulate the following non-linear least square problem:

$$(l^*, \mathbf{p}_2^*, \mathbf{n}^*) = \underset{l, \mathbf{p}_2, \mathbf{n}}{argmin} \sum_{y \in Y} (\bar{P} - \bar{V})^T (\bar{P} - \bar{V}) \tag{3}$$

where $\bar{V}$ and $\bar{P}$ are the linearized 88-elements row vectors of the tensors $V_{\alpha\beta\gamma}$ and $P(y, l, \mathbf{p}_2, \mathbf{n})$ and the set Y contains a list of years in which solstices and equinoxes dates have been computed. With this formulation we optimize simultaneously the latitude, the gnomon's vertex and the normal of the sundial's plane in such a way that the sum of the distances from the casted shadows to the target points is minimized. Note that the minimization is non-linear due to the function (1) used in P.

Gnomon's Inclination Optimization. In this second step, we keep fixed the coordinates of p_2, the latitude and the plane normal as the optimal values obtained in the previous task, so that the position of p_1 has an impact only on the shadow's shape and inclination. Indeed, in this setup the role of p_1 is simply aesthetic because the oblique part of the gnomon projects a segment which should be aligned with the eleven sundial's marks to ease the time reading.

For this reason the position of p_1 is estimated such that its punctual projection falls as close as possible to the line of the corresponding time mark, determined by the current time slot. Since the original gnomon was supposed to rise vertically from its base, the only parameter we need to optimize is the junction's height. The coordinates of point $\mathbf{p}_1$ are:

$$\mathbf{p}_1 = (x_0, y_0, h)^T \tag{4}$$

where (x_0, y_0) are the coordinates of the gnomon's base (Fig. 7, the black point) and h is the elevation of the junction point.

Similarly to what we did for p_2, we define a function $\mathcal{P}(d, l, \mathbf{p}_1, \mathbf{n})$ returning a rank 2 tensor $\mathcal{P}_{\beta\zeta}$ describing the eleven projections (in homogeneous coordinates, with $\zeta \in \{1 \ldots 3\}$) of point $\mathbf{p}_1$ during day d at latitude l. Such projections are computed in correspondence of the eleven timestamps that split the daylight of d into twelve equal time slots. Note that, unlike the previous function P (computed in four particular days of a year), $\mathcal{P}$ is defined for a single day, since we want the projection of p_1 to be close to the engraved segments during all days and not only during solstices and equinoxes.

We also need to express the parameters of the eleven lines containing the segments of the sundial. In a 2D Euclidean plane, a line can be denoted as $\ell = (a, b, c)$ such that a point (x, y) lies on the line if $\ell \cdot (x, y, 1) = 0$.

We collect these values in a rank 2 tensor $\mathcal{V}_{\beta\zeta}$ such that

$$\mathcal{V}_{ij} = \frac{\ell_i}{\|\ell_i\|} \tag{5}$$

and $\ell_i = (a_i, b_i, c_i)$ are the three parameters of the i-th line lying on the plane. Then, we minimize the squared distance of such projections from the correspondent line engraved on the sundial's surface. Considering $\bar{\mathcal{P}}$ the linearized row-vector of $\mathcal{P}(d, l, \mathbf{p}_1, \mathbf{n})$, the energy function to be minimized is now:

$$h^* = \underset{h}{argmin} \sum_{y \in Y} \sum_{d \in D(y)} (\bar{\mathcal{P}} \cdot \bar{\mathcal{V}})^2. \tag{6}$$

The optimization task is performed selecting a set of years Y and the corresponding sets $D(y)$ containing all the valid dates in y. Unlike the previous energy function, $\mathcal{P}$ is linear since Eq. (1) can be pre-computed for the given dates. Therefore, a global minimum can be found through simple linear least squares.

4   Results

Both the optimization tasks were performed over a set of several years to provide a robust estimation of the gnomon's configuration and latitude. Therefore, we chose a set of years in which the sundial were in use and optimized the configuration for that specific period. To compute the correct Sun's position given a place, time and a date, we used the open-source library Pvlib [23], implementing the Solar Position Algorithm [19]. Such algorithm ensures a precision of ± 0.0003 degrees between the years 2000 BC and 6000 AD.

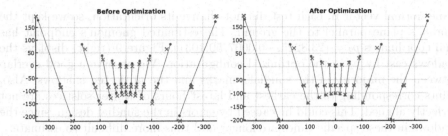

Fig. 9. Projections (red crosses) of point p_2 during equinoxes and solstices before (left) and after (right) optimization of latitude and point p_2. The rightmost configuration exhibits a better overlap between projections and sundial's points. (Color figure online)

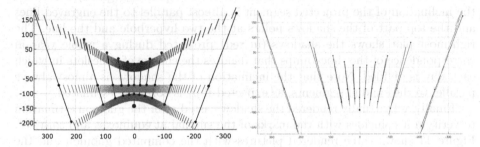

Fig. 10. Final configuration results. Left: shadows projected during daylight time in winter solstice (blue), autumn and spring equinoxes (green) and summer solstice (red). Right: shadows projected during a whole year (every 10 days), in correspondence of the eleven sundial's time marks. (Color figure online)

The joint optimization of the gnomon's tip p_2 and the latitude was performed computing the solstices and equinoxes from 200 AD to 230 AD and minimizing the energy function (3). The Nelder-Mead simplex algorithm for function optimization has been used, as described in [9]. Such method is a numerical algorithm used in multidimensional optimization problems for which derivatives are not known, like in our case where the Sun position function is not derivable.

The initial latitude was set at 45.46° North (Aquileia latitude) and the gnomon's endpoint was positioned in a plausible way such that its shadows fall close to the ideal points lying on the solstices and equinoxes curves. The plane normal was also initialised as $\mathbf{n} = (0, 0, 1)$, that is perfectly parallel with respect to the ground. The initial configuration is displayed in Fig. 9 (left), in which each red cross marks the shadow projected by the gnomon's endpoint p_2 during the selected days of the period.

The optimization took around 250 iterations to converge, setting a maximum tolerance over both the energy values and the optimized value equal to 10^{-5}. Surprisingly, the estimated optimal working latitude of the sundial was 44.019 N (in decimal notation), which is roughly 160 km south of Aquileia. As for the plane normal vector **n**, each test did not change its orientation, so we kept the sundial's plane parallel to the ground. The estimated gnomon's endpoint has final coordinates $p_2 = (23.8225, -0.0007, 50.1031)$. Figure 9 (right) displays the shadows cast by p_2 in the optimized configuration: We observe a good overlap between the majority of the sundial's marks and the projected shadows. Also, points corresponding to the earliest and latest hours of winter solstices are not perfectly aligned. This could be caused by errors in the sundial design, since the shadows in these specific times are longer and thus more difficult to estimate.

Regarding the junction point p_1, we optimized its height over all days of the selected years, resulting in an optimal value $h = 47.97$ mm. Figure 10 displays the results obtained with the complete optimal configuration of the gnomon. The leftmost plot shows the set of shadows projected during the day respectively in: winter solstice (in blue), summer solstice (red) and equinoxes (green). Note that the inclination of the projected segment is almost parallel to the engraved lines and the top part of the shadows points at the two hyperbole and the line. The rightmost plot shows the shadows (in red) projected during a whole year in correspondence of the timestamps that denotes the change of timeslots in which each day is divided. Note that the inclination of the shadows is almost always parallel to the sundial segments, as expected if p_1 is correctly estimated.

Finally, we virtually rendered the shadow casted after the gnomon estimation to verify if it coincides with the marks of the sundial at equinoxes and solstices. Figure 11 shows three rendered pictures with the computed gnomon and the projected shadow for interesting days of the year.

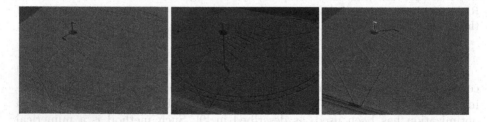

Fig. 11. Digital rendering of the sundial with a simulated gnomon as computed in our optimization process. The Sun position was set according to the optimal latitude. Pictures show the casted shadow during (from left to right): summer solstice, winter solstice and equinox.

5 Conclusions

The scanning of the Euporus sundial is the first step of a more in-depth analysis to be undertaken on the artefact. The reconstruction provides a high quality 3D shape record of the sundial's surface with measurement accuracy to the millimetre level and serve as a fine 3D representation that can be used for documentation, research and conservation purposes.

Moreover, the 3D model supported a further analysis to determine the geographical location for which the sundial was designed and shaped. In particular, a mathematical analysis of the gnomon's projection and the relative optimization process shown that the optimal working latitude for this kind of configuration is indeed a southern location with respect to the place where the object was discovered (lat 44.019 N, while Aquileia latitude is 45.79 N). A plausible hypothesis is that the Euporus sundial inscription was copied from another object designed for more southern latitudes, and perhaps some calculation errors caused its slightly defective functioning in Aquileia area.

References

1. Akca, D., Remondino, F., Novák, D., Hanusch, T., Schrotter, G., Gruen, A.: Recording and modeling of cultural heritage objects with coded structured light projection systems. In: 2nd International Conference on Remote Sensing in Archaeology, pp. 375–382. Institute of Geodesy and Photogrammetry, ETH Zurich (2006)
2. Akça, M.D.: 3D Modeling of Cultural Heritage Objects With a Structured Light System (2012)
3. Auber, P.A.: L'orologio solare orizzontale del circo di aquileia (ii sec. d.c.). il "plintio di euporus". prima parte. Atti dell'Istituto Veneto di Scienze, Lettere ed Arti, Classe di scienze fisiche, matematiche e naturali CLXIII, pp. 231–298 (2004–2005)
4. Fischler, M.A., Bolles, R.C.: Random sample consensus: a paradigm for model fitting with applications to image analysis and automated cartography. Commun. ACM **24**(6), 381–395 (1981)
5. Hartley, R., Zisserman, A.: Multiple View Geometry in Computer Vision. Cambridge University Press, New York (2003)
6. Horn, B.K.: Closed-form solution of absolute orientation using unit quaternions. JOSA A **4**(4), 629–642 (1987)
7. Kazhdan, M., Hoppe, H.: Screened poisson surface reconstruction. ACM Trans. Graph. (ToG) **32**(3), 29 (2013)
8. Kenner, F.: Sonnenuhren aus aquileia, mittheilungen der k.k. central-commission zur erfortschung und erhaltung der kunst und historischen denkmale. VI Jahrgang, Neue Folge, Wien (1880)
9. Lagarias, J.C., Reeds, J.A., Wright, M.H., Wright, P.E.: Convergence properties of the nelder-mead simplex method in low dimensions. SIAM J. Optim. **9**(1), 112–147 (1998)
10. Lancaster, L.C.: Concrete Vaulted Construction in Imperial Rome: Innovations in Context. Cambridge University Press, New York (2005)
11. Li, R., Luo, T., Zha, H.: 3D digitization and its applications in cultural heritage. In: Ioannides, M., Fellner, D., Georgopoulos, A., Hadjimitsis, D.G. (eds.) EuroMed 2010. LNCS, vol. 6436, pp. 381–388. Springer, Heidelberg (2010). https://doi.org/10.1007/978-3-642-16873-4_29
12. Lowe, D.G.: Distinctive image features from scale-invariant keypoints. Int. J. Comput. Vis. **60**(2), 91–110 (2004)
13. Lynch, C.: Digital collections, digital libraries & the digitization of cultural heritage information. Microf. Imag. Rev. **31**(4), 131–145 (2002)
14. Müller, G., Bendels, G.H., Klein, R.: Rapid synchronous acquisition of geometry and appearance of cultural heritage artefacts. In: VAST, pp. 13–20 (2005)

15. Pieraccini, M., Guidi, G., Atzeni, C.: 3D digitizing of cultural heritage. J. Cultur. Heritage **2**(1), 63–70 (2001)
16. Pistellato, M., Bergamasco, F., Albarelli, A., Cosmo, L., Gasparetto, A., Torsello, A.: Robust phase unwrapping by probabilistic consensus. Opt. Lasers Eng. **121**, 428–440 (2019). https://doi.org/10.1016/j.optlaseng.2019.05.006
17. Pistellato, M., Bergamasco, F., Cosmo, L., Gasparetto, A., Ressi, D., Albarelli, A.: Neighborhood-Based Recovery of Phase Unwrapping Faults, vol. 2018-August, pp. 2462–2467 (2018). https://doi.org/10.1109/ICPR.2018.8546052
18. Pistellato, M., Cosmo, L., Bergamasco, F., Gasparetto, A., Albarelli, A.: Adaptive albedo compensation for accurate phase-shift coding, vol. 2018-August, pp. 2450–2455 (2018). https://doi.org/10.1109/ICPR.2018.8545465
19. Reda, I., Andreas, A.: Solar position algorithm for solar radiation applications. Solar Energy **76**(5), 577–589 (2004)
20. Santagati, C., Inzerillo, L., Di Paola, F.: Image-based modeling techniques for architectural heritage 3D digitalization: limits and potentialities. Int. Arch. Photogrammetr. Remote Sens. Spatial Inf. Sci. **5**(w2), 555–560 (2013)
21. Sitnik, R., Krzeslowski, J.F., Maczkowski, G.: Archiving shape and appearance of cultural heritage objects using structured light projection and multispectral imaging. Opt. Eng. **51**(2), 021115 (2012)
22. Stanco, F., Battiato, S., Gallo, G.: Digital Imaging for Cultural Heritage Preservation: Analysis, Restoration, and Reconstruction of Ancient Artworks. CRC Press, Boca Raton (2011)
23. Stein, J.S., Holmgren, W.F., Forbess, J., Hansen, C.W.: PVLIB: open source photovoltaic performance modeling functions for matlab and python. In: 2016 IEEE 43rd Photovoltaic Specialists Conference (PVSC), pp. 3425–3430. IEEE (2016)
24. Torsello, A., Rodola, E., Albarelli, A.: Multiview registration via graph diffusion of dual quaternions. In: CVPR 2011, pp. 2441–2448. IEEE (2011)
25. Zhang, Z.: Iterative point matching for registration of free-form curves and surfaces. Int. J. Comput. Vis. **13**(2), 119–152 (1994)

Object Retrieval and Localization in Large Art Collections Using Deep Multi-style Feature Fusion and Iterative Voting

Nikolai Ufer$^{(\boxtimes)}$, Sabine Lang, and Björn Ommer$^{(\boxtimes)}$

Heidelberg University, HCI/IWR, Heidelberg, Germany
nikolai.ufer@iwr.uni-heidelberg.de, ommer@uni-heidelberg.de

Abstract. The search for specific objects or motifs is essential to art history as both assist in decoding the meaning of artworks. Digitization has produced large art collections, but manual methods prove to be insufficient to analyze them. In the following, we introduce an algorithm that allows users to search for image regions containing specific motifs or objects and find similar regions in an extensive dataset, helping art historians to analyze large digitized art collections. Computer vision has presented efficient methods for visual instance retrieval across photographs. However, applied to art collections, they reveal severe deficiencies because of diverse motifs and massive domain shifts induced by differences in techniques, materials, and styles. In this paper, we present a multi-style feature fusion approach that successfully reduces the domain gap and improves retrieval results without labelled data or curated image collections. Our region-based voting with GPU-accelerated approximate nearest-neighbour search [29] allows us to find and localize even small motifs within an extensive dataset in a few seconds. We obtain state-of-the-art results on the Brueghel dataset [2,52] and demonstrate its generalization to inhomogeneous collections with a large number of distractors.

Keywords: Visual retrieval · Searching art collections · Feature fusion

1 Introduction

For art history, it is crucial to analyze the relationship between artworks to understand individual works, their reception process, and to find connections between them and the artists [22,23,28]. Hereby, the investigation of motifs and objects across different images is of particular importance since it allows more detailed analyses and is essential for iconographic questions. Digitization has produced large image corpora [1,3,4,58], but manual methods are inadequate to analyze them since this would take days or even months. Computer-assisted approaches can dramatically accelerate and simplify this work. However, most

© Springer Nature Switzerland AG 2020
A. Bartoli and A. Fusiello (Eds.): ECCV 2020 Workshops, LNCS 12536, pp. 159–176, 2020.
https://doi.org/10.1007/978-3-030-66096-3_12

of them consist of a simple text search through metadata and are not sufficient since text cannot capture the visual variety, and labels are often either missing, incomplete, or not standardized. Therefore, there is a need for efficient algorithms, capable of searching through visual art collections not only based on textual metadata but also directly through visual queries. In this paper, we present a novel search algorithm that allows users to select image regions containing specific motifs or objects and find similar regions in an extensive image dataset.

While computer vision successfully developed deep learning-based approaches for visual instance retrieval in photographs [42,43], artworks present new challenges. This includes a domain shift from real photos to artworks, unique and unknown search motifs, and a large variation within art collections due to different digitization processes, artistic media, and styles. This strongly highlights the need for specifically tailored algorithms for the arts [50,52]. Solving visual instance retrieval across artworks is difficult and requires local descriptors, which are both highly discriminative to find matching regions and invariant regarding typical variations in art collections. Learning such descriptors in a supervised fashion is extremely time-consuming and requires annotating thousands of corresponding images [51]. Besides, the learned descriptors improve retrieval results only for very similar datasets. Alternative approaches based on self-supervision [52] show promising results. However, they are not stable against images without any repetitions in the dataset, and are very slow in large-scale scenarios since they require a pairwise comparison between all images. We circumvent these issues and present a new multi-style feature fusion, where we utilize generic pre-trained features and current style transfer models to improve their style invariance without any additional supervision. Given a dataset, we stylize all images according to a set of fixed style templates, and by mixing their feature representations, we project them into the same averaged style domain. This massively reduces the domain gap across artworks and improves overall retrieval results.

Contributions. Our main contributions are threefold. (1) We present an unsupervised multi-style feature fusion, which successfully reduces the domain gap and improves overall retrieval results in art collections. (2) The introduced iterative voting in combination with GPU-accelerated nearest-neighbour search [29] enables us to localize and find small regions in large datasets within a few seconds. (3) We demonstrate that the proposed method significantly outperforms current methods in terms of retrieval time and accuracy for object retrieval and localization in art collections.

2   Related Work

In the following, we present the most relevant research related to our work and put our contributions in context.

Computer Vision in the Arts. For quite some time, there has been a mutual exchange between computer vision and the arts. This exchange ranges from the analysis of artworks using computer vision [6,9,18,51] to the development of new methods in collaboration with the art community [48,53,59,64] to generative algorithms that transfer normal photos into artworks [16,21,47] or direct attempts to create art [13,20]. Concerning the analysis of artworks, collaborations are very natural because computer vision and art history are both concerned with the visuality and ask similar questions. In this context, researchers have transformed successful object detection and classification methods for photos to artworks [9,30,48,57]. Some of these works detect gestures, people, or iconographic elements in paintings [17,18,26,48,66,69], recognize object categories occurring in natural images [9,10,67], classify paintings in terms of their style, genre, material, or artist [30,36,45,46,58,60,67], or investigate the aesthetics of paintings [5,12,57]. Some approaches directly try to find visual relationships within art collections automatically [15,51,52] to relieve as much work as possible from art historians. However, these are very time-consuming since they compare all possible image pairs within the dataset. Therefore, they are limited to small collections, which could also be manually analyzed. In this work, we focus on large-scale instance retrieval and localization in the arts. We are convinced, with an efficient search system, art historians can find relevant visual links through several searches faster and more targeted compared to fully automated approaches.

Visual Instance Retrieval. Visual instance retrieval deals with the task of identifying matching regions in other images within a dataset, given a query region or image. This is a well-established research field in computer vision with successful classical [9,24], as well as deep learning-based [38,61,68] approaches. Early methods were based on classical feature point descriptors like SIFT [33] combined with a Bag-of-Words approach [9,24]. Over the years, numerous improvements have been made for different parts of this approach [54]. More recently, Convolutional Neural Networks (CNN) showed remarkable results in many areas of computer vision, including visual instance retrieval [7]. However, the primary retrieval research was always focused on photographs, either of the same place [39,40] or the same object [37]. If researchers dealt with art databases, then often only on an image level without allowing to search for regions [8,35,41,55,59], which is a central requirement to find similar motifs and objects in art collections. Just recently, Shen et al. [52] introduced the first benchmark with annotations for finding and localizing objects and motifs in artworks on a region level, which is also the primary dataset we use for our evaluation. Most closely related to our work is Shen et al. [52] and Seguin et al. [50], which also deal with instance retrieval and finding visual relationships in art collections. In contrast to our work, Seguin et al. [50] use off-the-shelf CNNs that have been fine-tuned in a supervised fashion and thus does not apply to other datasets. The approach of Shen et al. [52] learns dataset-dependent features in a self-supervised manner by mining correspondences between image pairs, similar to [62,63]. However, their approach does not generalize to inhomogeneous collections with many distractors, and their retrieval system is intractable in large-scale scenarios. In contrast, our method improves retrieval results by successfully reducing the domain gap without labelled data or curated image collections and enables us to find even small motifs within an extensive dataset in a few seconds.

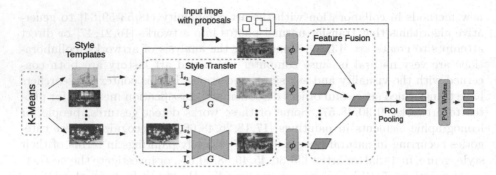

Fig. 1. Overview of our multi-style feature fusion. It consists of three main steps: First, we extract image level features of all dataset images, apply K-means and select the cluster centers as style templates. Given an input image and region proposals, the input image is stylized based on the style templates and features are generated using the pre-trained feature extraction and style transfer network. The image features are fused to create a final image representation, and through ROI pooling, we obtain region descriptors for all proposals with a fixed dimension. Finally, we apply principle-component analysis (PCA) and whitening to reduce the feature dimension.

Method

The following requirements on the image representation and the retrieval system are essential. First, it should be possible to search for any motif in a diverse art collection. This poses particular challenges to the underlying feature descriptors since off-the-shelf models are trained on photographs and are not invariant to colours and artistic styles. We address this problem in the first part of this section and introduce a new multi-style feature fusion, which considerably reduces the domain gap. Second, it should be possible to search for any image region with an arbitrary size across a large dataset, and the search should take only a few seconds and deliver exact retrieval results. These are challenging demands since a single feature descriptor is not capable of capturing multiple objects or motifs in an image accurately, and encoding all regions is not tractable due to memory constraints. We address this problem in the second part of this section. For the query region and all images in the dataset, we extract a moderate number of local descriptors and formulate the search as a voting procedure of local patches within the query region.

Multi-style Feature Fusion

Our multi-style feature fusion is based on the following hypothesis. The dataset contains images or regions that are similar to each other but are depicted in different styles. Generic pre-trained descriptors are capable of finding similar regions if the style differences are small. Based on this assumption, our main idea is to use current style transfer models to project all images into the same averaged style domain to reduce the domain gap and simplify the retrieval task. Therefore, we stylize each image based on multiple fixed style instances and fuse their extracted features to generate a single robust representation. The approach consists of three main steps, which we describe in the following. See Fig. 1 for an overview.

Finding Style Template. To find a diverse set of style templates, we proceed as follows. We denote the collection of images as $\mathcal{I} = \{I_i | 1 \leq i \leq N\}$ and assume that an ImageNet pre-trained CNN, which maps images into an m-dimensional deep feature space, i.e. $\phi\colon \mathcal{X} \to \mathbb{R}^m$, is given. We group all images into k_s clusters according to their pairwise distance in the embedding space using K-means. Since the CNN ϕ is trained on real photos, it is not invariant with respect to styles, and hence different clusters contain different content depicted in different artistic styles. We select k_s images which are closest to the cluster centers in the feature space and obtain a diverse set, which serves as our style templates $\mathcal{S} = \{I_s | 1 \leq s \leq k_s\}$. This selection is sufficient because our style transfer method is independent of the image content, and only the depicted style is important. In our experiments, we set $k_s = 3$ since this has proven to be a good trade-off between performance and computational cost.

Style Transfer. Our style transfer module is a CNN, $G\colon \mathcal{X} \times \mathcal{X} \to \mathcal{X}$, which takes a content image I_c and style image I_s as input to synthesize a new image $G(I_c, I_s)$ with the content from the former and style from the latter. It is based on the network architecture of Li et al. [31] and consists of three main parts: an encoder-decoder, a transformation, and a loss module. The encoder consists of the first layers of the ImageNet pre-trained VGG-19 model [11,56] and the decoder comprises of its symmetrical counterpart. The transformation module consists of two small CNNs which receive the encoded feature maps of the content and style image as input, and provide a transformation matrix as output, respectively. Given a content and style image, the style is transferred by multiplying the encoder's content feature with the two transformation matrices and applying the decoder on the output, which produces the stylized image. Since the network is a pure feed-forward convolution neural network, it allows converting an image into an arbitrary style in milliseconds.

Feature Fusion. Based on the style transfer module G and style templates $\mathcal{S}$, we obtain the multi-style feature representation as follows. Given an input image I and a set of proposals, we stylize the image with respect to all style templates $\mathcal{S}$, and fuse them by taking their mean, i.e.

$$\phi_{ms}(I, \mathcal{S}) = \frac{1}{1 + |\mathcal{S}|} \left(\phi(I) + \sum_{I_s \in \mathcal{S}} \phi(G(I, I_s)) \right). \tag{1}$$

Here we also take the original image feature into account since it contains fine-grained information that can be useful for the retrieval task but are lost during the transformation process. Given the proposals and the new image representation, we apply Precise ROI Pooling [27] to obtain local feature descriptors for all proposals with a fixed feature dimension. Finally, we apply principle-component analysis (PCA) and whitening to reduce their feature dimension.

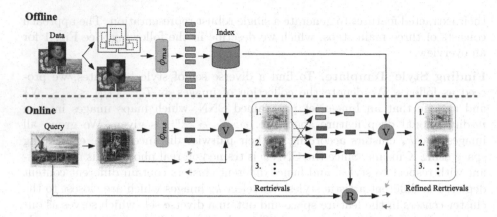

Fig. 2. Overview of our retrieval system. The retrieval system consists of an offline and an online stage. During the offline stage, the search index is initialized before the actual search. For each image, discriminative local patches are determined, and their feature descriptors are extracted, compressed, and stored in the search index. During the online stage, most discriminative local patch descriptors within the marked query region are extracted, and their k-nearest neighbours are determined using the search index. Our voting procedure aggregates these local matches and predicts well-localized retrieval bounding boxes for the whole query. The results are further improved using local query expansion and re-voting.

Retrieval System Using Iterative Voting

To find and localize objects and motifs of arbitrary size in an extensive art collection, we introduce an iterative voting approach based on local patch descriptors. Therefore, we decompose all images into a set of quadratic patches on multiple scales in a sliding-window manner, which are encoded by the multi-style feature extraction network described previously. The actual search consists of finding k-nearest neighbours of local patches within the selected query region across the whole dataset, which are afterwards aggregated to well-localized retrieval bounding boxes. This approach has three main advantages. First, the search is performed on a region level and enables searching for small motifs that cannot be found when images are represented with a single feature descriptor. Second, it allows us to predict well-localized retrieval bounding boxes independent of the local patches we use for the image encoding. Third, we combine several search queries in combination with a spatial verification, which provides better search results.

Our retrieval system consists of an offline and online stage. In the offline stage, the search index is initialized. Therefore, local image descriptors are extracted, compressed, and stored in the index. This step only needs to be done once. In the online stage, most discriminative local feature descriptors within the query region are extracted, and our voting procedure is applied to their k-nearest neighbours to obtain the first search results. Through local query expansion and re-voting, the retrievals results are further improved. In the following, we describe each step in more details. We also provide an overview in Fig. 2.

Image Encoding Using Local Patch Descriptors. In our experiments classic region proposal algorithms [34,65,70] and networks [44] showed insufficient results for artworks. Our strategy for finding suitable regions to extract local patch descriptors consists of two steps. First, we generate a broad set of local patches by dividing the space into quadratic regions on multiple scales in a sliding window manner. Second, we filter them for selecting the most discriminative as follows. We sample a subset of all local patches and assign them into k_e groups using the L_2 distance in the multi-style feature space and K-means. We store the k_e cluster centers, compute the distance of all local patches to these centers, and select those with the highest mean distance. By this, we obtain local patches on different scales that are more discriminative and more suitable for the retrieval task than others. We generate a maximum of 4000 local patches for each image I in this way and extract their multi-style feature descriptors $\mathcal{D}(I)$ as described previously. To keep the search index compact, we reduce the number of extracted proposals per image linearly with the dataset size.

Search Index. We build a search index containing all local patch descriptors of all images $\mathcal{D}$ for fast approximate nearest neighbor search. For the search index, we use the Inverted File Index (IVF) and the Product Quantization (PQ) algorithm from [29]. They provide a high-speed GPU-parallelized variant that allows to search for multiple queries in an extensive database in seconds. The IVF algorithm [25] clusters the feature vectors into groups and calculates their centroids using K-means. Now, given a query vector, the distances to all centroids are determined, and only the feature vectors assigned to the closest centroids are considered for the k-nearest neighbor search, which massively accelerates the search. The actual search uses product quantization. Here the feature vectors are sliced into subvectors, and a codebook for each of these slices is learned. Based on these codebooks, the feature vectors can be stored efficiently using their ids, and a look-up table containing all codebook centroids distances allows a fast approximated nearest neighbor search with a query vector. We calculate the IVF clustering and PQ codebooks for each dataset separately. Therefore, we take all regions from 1000 randomly selected images and train on their multi-style features.

Query Reformulation Using Local Patch Descriptors. In the online stage, the user selects an image and marks a rectangle q as the query region. Besides the selected region itself, we additionally use the most discriminative local patches within the query region for the actual search. We find these local query patches as follows. We extract local patches on multiple scales and select the most discriminative using two criteria. First, we filter all local patches with less than 90% overlap with the query region. Second, we apply non-maximum suppression concerning their feature activation, which we obtain by summing over the feature channel and taking the mean within the proposal region. For the selected patches, we extract their features and store their voting vectors. This set of local query patch descriptors $\mathcal{D}(q)$ for a given query region q are used in the following for our voting strategy.

Voting Based on Local Matches. As described previously, we encode each dataset image $I \in \mathcal{I}$ with a set of local patch descriptors $\mathcal{D}(I)$, where we denote the set of all descriptors in the dataset by $\mathcal{D}$. For a given query rectangle q, we also extract a set of local patch descriptor $\mathcal{D}(q)$. In the following, we do not distinguish between the local patches itself and their feature descriptors, but it should always be clear what is meant from the context. Our voting consist of the following two main steps.

In the first step, we determine the k-nearest neighbours $NN_k(f, \mathcal{D})$ for each local query patch $f \in \mathcal{D}(q)$ using the search index with L_2 distances, where we denote a local query patch with one of its k-nearest neighbours as a local match. Based on the L_2 distances, we define a local matching score via

$$s_f(g) = \exp\left(- \|g - f\|_2^2 / \|\hat{g} - f\|_2^2\right),\tag{2}$$

where $\hat{g} \in NN_k(f, \mathcal{D})$ with a fixed rank and provides a reference distance. For the image ranking, we utilize a majority based voting, where we determine the most promising images. To do this, for a given image I, we look at its local matches and sum their local matching scores, where we consider at most one hit for each local query feature. We select the images with the highest scores and restrict the following voting based on local matches on this subset. Due to this pre-selection, the computational costs of the following steps are independent of the dataset size. However, in contrast to other approaches [49], the pre-selection is conducted on a part, not image level, and hence we do not miss similar small regions in the final search results.

In the second step, we apply our voting scheme on the local matches of the most promising images to predict well-localized retrieval bounding boxes. For the voting, we assume persistent aspect ratios and neglect object rotations to reduce the voting space and accelerate the search. Let us consider a local match (f, g), i.e. $g \in NN_k(f, \mathcal{D}) \cap \mathcal{D}(I)$ for a local query patch $f \in \mathcal{D}(q)$, then this match is voting for a specific location and scale of a rectangle r in image I. If we denote $\mathbf{v}(f) = \mathbf{c}_q - \mathbf{c}_f$ as the vector from the center of the local query patch $\mathbf{c}_f$ to the query rectangle $\mathbf{c}_q$ and d_f, d_g and d_q are the diagonal lengths of f, g and q, respectively. Then this match votes for a rectangle with center $\mathbf{c}_r = \mathbf{c}_g + \mathbf{v}(f) \cdot d_g/d_f$ and diagonal $d_d = d_q \cdot d_g/d_f$. We aggregate these votes and create a voting map in which each point votes for the center of a box at the corresponding position similar to [54]. To keep the voting map compact, we quantize the image space so that the voting map is much smaller than the actual image. Here, we reduce quantization errors by voting for a 5×5 window with a Gaussian kernel for each local match. For the voting score, we use the local matching similarity defined in Eq. 2. To find the correct diagonal lengths for the retrievals, we do not increase the voting space by an additional dimension but average the diagonals of all votes pointing to the same center. This keeps the voting space compact and accelerates the search. For determining the center and diagonal of the best retrieval box in the image I, we take the position of the maximum in the voting map and the corresponding averaged diagonal. This voting approach allows object retrieval and localization at the same time without an exhaustive sliding-window search as a post-processing step, like in [50,52].

Local Query Expansion and Re-voting. After finding our first retrievals across the dataset, we improve our search results using local query expansion and re-voting. Concerning the local query expansion, we consider the first ten nearest neighbours in different images for each local query patch and fuse their feature descriptors by taking their mean and L_2 normalization over the feature channels. By this, we obtain new and more generalized local patch descriptors, containing more diverse information by including multiple instances. The aggregated patches no longer have the same coordinates in the query image because of the combination of local patch descriptors and possible shifts in local matches. Therefore, we also update the voting vectors based on the new patch representations. We do this by determining their nearest neighbours in the query image and measuring the voting vector to the query bounding box center. The generalized local patch queries and updated voting vectors have the same structure as in the first voting stage, and we can apply the previously described voting procedure again, which leads to better search results.

Implementation Details

Concerning the multi-style feature fusion, we use VGG16 with batch normalization [56], pre-trained on ImageNet [11], and truncated after the fourth layers' RELU as backbone architecture. We rescale images to 640 pixels concerning the smallest image side and pad them by 20 pixels on each side. We add a max-pooling layer and hence obtain a ratio of 16 between image and feature space. For the style transfer model, we use the pre-trained model of Li et al. [31], which was trained on the MS-COCO [32] dataset. We also experimented with training on each target dataset separately, but this did not improve the performance and heavily increased the initialization time. We generate the stylized images during the offline stage so they only need to be loaded for the feature extraction.

Concerning the iterative voting, our proposal algorithm uses six different scales with a scaling factor of $2^{-1/2}$. The patch size ranges from $1/12$ up to $1/2$, where we use a stride of $1/50$ regarding the largest image side. For the selection of discriminative patches, we set $k_e = 200$. To keep the search index compact, we linearly decrease the number of proposals per image with increasing dataset size. First, we extract 4000 proposals and reduce the number by 375 for each additional 20k images, starting with a dataset size of 20k images. The OPQ algorithm utilizes 96 sub-quantizers with 8 bits allocated for each sub-quantizer. For the IVF algorithm, we generate 1024 clusters and use 30 for the nearest neighbor search.

Experiments

In this section, we present comparative evaluations on challenging benchmark datasets and diagnostic experiments.

Datasets
To show the efficiency and generalization capability of our system, we evaluate on five different benchmark datasets.

Brueghel. Our main evaluation is based on a collection of Brueghel paintings [2] with annotations from Shen et al. [52]. To the best of our knowledge, no other dataset for instance retrieval and localization in the arts with annotations is available at the moment. The dataset consists of 1,587 paintings, including a variety of different techniques, materials, and depicted scenes. It includes ten annotated motifs with 11 up to 57 instances of each motif, which results in 273 annotations overall. We follow the evaluation protocol of [52], and count retrievals as correct, if the intersection over union (IoU) of predicted with ground-truth bounding boxes is larger than 0.3. For each query, we compute the Average Precision (AP), average these values per class, and report the class level mean Average Precision (mAP).

Brueghel5K and Brueghel101K. We are particularly interested in the large-scale scenario, where the algorithm has to deal with an extensive and inhomogenous image collection. This is a much more common use case for art historians. For this purpose, we introduce the Brueghel5K and Brueghel101K dataset, where we extend the previously described dataset with an additional 3,500 and 100,000 randomly selected images from the Wikiart dataset [4] as distractors, respectively. To avoid false negatives, we used the annotations from Wikiart and excluded all Brueghel paintings from the selection. The evaluation uses the same annotations and evaluation protocol as the Brueghel dataset.

LTLL. We also evaluate our algorithm on the Large Time Lags Location (LTLL) dataset, which was collected by Fernando et al. [14]. It consists of historical and current photos of 25 cities and towns spanning over a range of more than 150 years. The main goal is to recognize the location of an old image using annotated modern photographs, where the old and new images can be considered as belonging to two different domains. In total, the dataset contains 225 historical and 275 modern images. Since our retrieval system assumes that users mark image regions he is interested in, we provide and utilize additional query bounding boxes for our and all baseline models. Analogously to the evaluation protocol [14] we report the accuracy of the first retrieval.

Oxford5K. We also evaluate our approach on the Oxford5K datasets, which was collected by Philbin et al. [39]. It consists of 5,062 photos with 11 different landmarks from Oxford and five different query regions for each location. The occurrence of each landmark ranges from 7 up to 220. We follow the evaluation protocol of [39] and compute the Average Precision (AP) for each query, average them per landmark and report the mean Average Precision (mAP).

Effect of Multi-style Feature Fusion
To validate our multi-style feature fusion, we compare the performance of our algorithm with different feature representations. As baselines, we use VGG16 features truncated after the conv-4 layer, which are either pre-trained on ImageNet

Table 1. Retrieval performance comparison of our multi-style feature fusion (Ours) and features generated from VGG16, which are either pre-trained on ImageNet [11] (ImageNet pre-training) or additionally fine-tuned using [52] (Artminer)

Features	Brueghel	Brueghel5K	Brueghel101K	LTLL	Oxford5K
ImageNet pre-training	79.1	76.7	67.3	88.1	87.9
Artminer [52]	80.6	37.9	34.5	89.0	79.4
Ours	**85.7**	**84.1**	**76.9**	**90.9**	**89.8**

Table 2. Ablation study of our voting approach. We measure the performance for searching only with the selected query region (wo/voting), and for restricting ourselves to the first round of voting (wo/it.voting) and our full system. We also report the performance on the Brueghel dataset for different IoU thresholds

Methods	Brueghel			LTLL	Oxford5K
	IoU@0.3	IoU@0.5	IoU@0.7		
Ours wo/voting	72.3	48.5	5.9	73.2	72.7
Ours wo/it.voting	74.1	54.4	19.1	90.4	87.8
Ours	**85.7**	**63.3**	**21.7**	**90.9**	**89.8**

[11] (ImageNet pre-training) or additionally fined-tuned with the self-supervised approach of Shen et al. [52] (Artminer).

From Table 1 it can be seen that our approach improves the results on all benchmarks. The improvement compared to pre-trained features is especially high for the art datasets since there is a particular large domain gap due to differences in styles between queries and targets. Even for datasets without any domain shift, like Oxford5K, our algorithm improves the search results due to the aggregation of diverse feature representations. We also achieve significantly better results compared to the Artminer [52] fine-tuned variants. Their method has particular problems for image collections containing many distractors as well as on the Oxford5K dataset.

Effect of Iterative Voting

We analyze the impact of our voting procedure on the visual search. For this purpose, we measure the performance of our method for searching only with the selected query region (wo/voting), restricting ourselves to the first round of voting (wo/it.voting) and our full system. To better understand the impact on the localization of retrievals, we also report the performance for different IoU thresholds on the Brueghel dataset.

The results are summarized in Table 2. We see that the first round of voting especially improves the results on the LTLL and the Oxford5K dataset, the performance gain on the Brueghel dataset for the IoU of 0.3 is smaller. The reason is that the query regions for the Brueghel dataset are, on average, much smaller. Therefore, there are fewer voting regions, and the effect of voting

Table 3. Comparison of the retrieval time of our method (Ours) and [52] (Artminer) for different dataset sizes, where we also report the size of our search index (last row)

Method	5K	20K	40K	60K	80K	100K
Artminer [52]	12.9 min	50.4 min	1.7 h	2.8 h	3.8 h	4.6 h
Ours	8.5 s	9.0 s	9.3 s	9.7 s	10.1 s	10.5 s
Ours	1.7 GB	6.8 GB	13.7 GB	20.6 GB	27.4 GB	34.2 GB

Table 4. Retrieval results of our method and state-of-the-art methods on the Brueghel [2,52], Brueghel5K, Brueghel101K, LTLL [14] and Oxford5K [39] dataset. We also report the underlying network architecture (Net), and what dimension the underlying features have (Dim)

Methods	Net	Dim	Brueghel [2,52]	5K	101K	LTLL	Oxford
ImageNet, image level	VGG16	512	24.0	22.5	17.7	47.8	25.6
Radenović et al. [43], wo/ft	VGG16	512	15.5	12.7	5.9	59.3	53.4
Radenović et al. [43]	VGG16	512	15.8	12.8	5.7	76.1	87.8
Artminer [52], wo/ft	ResNet18	256	58.1	56.0	50.2	78.9	84.9
Artminer [52]	ResNet18	256	76.4	46.5	37.4	88.5	85.7
Artminer [52], wo/ft	VGG16	512	54.4	50.5	44.1	81.8	85.0
Artminer [52]	VGG16	512	79.9	39.5	36.4	88.9	81.5
Ours	VGG16	96	85.7	83.9	**76.9**	90.9	**89.9**
Ours	VGG16	128	87.2	85.6	—	90.9	89.8
Ours	VGG16	256	**88.1**	**86.7**	—	**91.3**	89.8

becreases. However, the results for higher IoU thresholds show that the localization is significantly improving. The second round of voting with local query expansion improves the results on all datasets further. This has a particularly strong influence on the retrieval results for the Brueghel dataset.

Computational Cost

We also investigate the search speed of our Python implementation. All measurements are conducted on the same machine with 3 GPUs (Nvidia Quadro P5000). In Table 3, we summarize the results and compare them with [52], where we assumed a perfect implementation of [52] on multiple GPUs by dividing their search times by a factor of 3. Besides the search speed, we also report the index size after storing to disk. It shows that our method is much faster, and its speed depends only moderately on the number of images. The index size mainly determines the size of the image collection that can be searched. Its size primarily depends on the number of proposals extracted per image, which is an important factor in finding small regions. Since the required retrieval accuracy for small regions, available hardware, and dataset size vary from application to application, the number of proposals should be adjusted according to the actual use case.

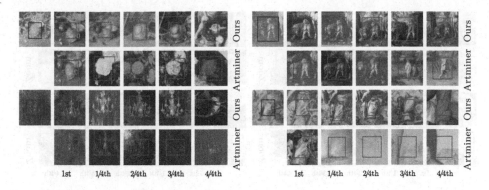

Fig. 3. Qualitative comparison. Retrieval examples of our approach (Ours) and [52] (Artminer) on the Brueghel dataset. We show queries on the left in blue and its nearest-neighbor, as well as four additional retrievals with an equidistant distance given by the number of ground truth annotations for the query divided by four. We draw green bounding boxes if the intersection over union is larger than 0.3 and red otherwise (Color figure online).

Retrieval Performance on Benchmarks

In the following, we give quantitative and qualitative results on the previously introduced benchmark datasets.

Quantitative Evaluation. We compare our results with max-pooled pretrained features on image level (ImageNet, image level) as well as the state-of-the-art results of Shen et al. [52] (Artminer) and Radenović et al. [43] on Brueghel, LTLL, and Oxford5K. For a fair comparison, we select the same backbone architecture for all methods and report also the original numbers from [52] with their fine-tuned ResNet18 model. Our approach utilizes marked query regions within the image. This is not the case for the discovery mode of [52]. According to their publication and our experiments, they obtain the best results using full images as query, which allows their algorithm to utilize more context. The reported numbers refer to their discovery mode.

We summarize all results in Table 4. We outperform all methods on all benchmark datasets without fine-tuning on the retrieval task and with a much smaller feature dimension. The results on the Brueghel datasets with additional distractors show that the self-supervised method of Shen et al. [52] is not stable against images without corresponding regions in the dataset. The main reason is that, the probability of selecting regions without correspondences is very high, which results in few and potentially spurious matches for training. This effect can already be seen for Brueghel5K, where their fine-tuned network leads to worse retrieval results compared to their initial model. In contrast, our method is much more robust against such distractors. Furthermore, it can be seen that we even outperform [43] on the Oxford5K dataset, although, their approach is explicitly designed for geo-localization by fine-tuning on an extensive image collection of various landmarks using ResNet101 [19]. However, since their model is optimized for this task, their search results on art collections are rather weak.

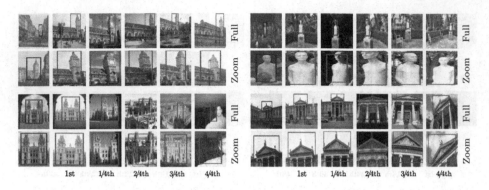

Fig. 4. Retrieval examples. We show examples in rows 1–2 and 3–4 for the LTLL and Oxford5K dataset. The first row shows full images (Full) and the second zoomed-in versions (Zoom). The queries are visualized in blue on the left and its nearest-neighbor, as well as four additional retrievals with an equidistant distance, given by the number of ground truth annotations for the query divided by four on the right. (Color figure online)

Qualitative Evaluation. In Fig. 3, we provide a qualitative comparison with the state-of-the-art of Shen et al. [52] (Artminer). It shows that their method can find first retrievals quite well. However, these become significantly worse for higher ranks, where our approach gives much better results. In Fig. 4, we show some qualitative examples for the other datasets. The retrieval results show that our system is capable of finding similar objects despite differences in colour and style. Furthermore, we see that objects can be precisely located despite changes in perspective and partial occlusions, which is also the case for small regions.

Conclusion

We have presented a novel search algorithm to find and localize motifs or objects in an extensive art collection. This enables art historians to explore large datasets to find visual relationships. Our algorithm is based on a new multi-style feature fusion, which reduces the domain gap and thus improves instance retrieval across artworks. In contrast to previous methods, we require neither object annotations, image labels, nor time-consuming self-supervised training. The presented iterative voting with recent GPU-accelerated approximate nearest-neighbor search [29] enables us to find and localize even small motifs within an extensive database in a few seconds. We have validated the performance of our model on diverse benchmark datasets, including art collections [2,52] and real photos [39]. We have also shown that our method is much more stable against distractors compared to the current state-of-the-art.

Acknowledgement. This work has been funded in part by the German Research Foundation (DFG) - project 421703927.

References

1. Artuk. https://artuk.org. Accessed 31 May 2020
2. "brueghel family: Jan brueghel the elder." the brueghel family database. university of california, berkeley. http://www.janbrueghel.net. Accessed 16 Oct 2018
3. WGA. https://wga.hu. Accessed 31 May 2020
4. Wikiart. https://www.wikiart.org. Accessed 16 Oct 2018
5. Amirshahi, S.A., Hayn-Leichsenring, G.U., Denzler, J., Redies, C.: JenAesthetics subjective dataset: analyzing paintings by subjective scores. In: Agapito, L., Bronstein, M.M., Rother, C. (eds.) ECCV 2014. LNCS, vol. 8925, pp. 3–19. Springer, Cham (2015). https://doi.org/10.1007/978-3-319-16178-5_1
6. Arora, R.S., Elgammal, A.: Towards automated classification of fine-art painting style: a comparative study. In: Proceedings of the 21st International Conference on Pattern Recognition (ICPR2012), pp. 3541–3544. IEEE (2012)
7. Collins, E., Süsstrunk, S.: Deep feature factorization for content-based image retrieval and localization. In: 2019 IEEE International Conference on Image Processing (ICIP), pp. 874–878. IEEE (2019)
8. Crowley, E.J., Parkhi, O.M., Zisserman, A.: Face painting: querying art with photos. In: BMVC (2015)
9. Crowley, E.J., Zisserman, A.: In search of art. In: Agapito, L., Bronstein, M.M., Rother, C. (eds.) ECCV 2014. LNCS, vol. 8925, pp. 54–70. Springer, Cham (2015). https://doi.org/10.1007/978-3-319-16178-5_4
10. Crowley, E.J., Zisserman, A.: The art of detection. In: Hua, G., Jégou, H. (eds.) ECCV 2016. LNCS, vol. 9913, pp. 721–737. Springer, Cham (2016). https://doi.org/10.1007/978-3-319-46604-0_50
11. Deng, J., Dong, W., Socher, R., Li, L.J., Li, K., Fei-Fei, L.: Imagenet: a large-scale hierarchical image database. In: 2009 IEEE Conference on Computer Vision and Pattern Recognition, pp. 248–255. IEEE (2009)
12. Denzler, J., Rodner, E., Simon, M.: Convolutional neural networks as a computational model for the underlying processes of aesthetics perception. In: Hua, G., Jégou, H. (eds.) ECCV 2016. LNCS, vol. 9913, pp. 871–887. Springer, Cham (2016). https://doi.org/10.1007/978-3-319-46604-0_60
13. Elgammal, A., Liu, B., Elhoseiny, M., Mazzone, M.: Can: creative adversarial networks, generating "art" by learning about styles and deviating from style norms. arXiv preprint arXiv:1706.07068 (2017)
14. Fernando, B., Tommasi, T., Tuytelaars, T.: Location recognition over large time lags. Comput. Vis. Image Understanding **139**, 21–28 (2015)
15. Garcia, N., Renoust, B., Nakashima, Y.: Contextnet: representation and exploration for painting classification and retrieval in context. Int. J. Multimedia Inf. Retrieval **9**(1), 17–30 (2020)
16. Gatys, L.A., Ecker, A.S., Bethge, M.: Image style transfer using convolutional neural networks. In: Proceedings of the IEEE Conference on Computer Vision and Pattern Recognition, pp. 2414–2423 (2016)
17. Ginosar, S., Haas, D., Brown, T., Malik, J.: Detecting people in cubist art. In: Agapito, L., Bronstein, M.M., Rother, C. (eds.) ECCV 2014. LNCS, vol. 8925, pp. 101–116. Springer, Cham (2015). https://doi.org/10.1007/978-3-319-16178-5_7
18. Gonthier, N., Gousseau, Y., Ladjal, S., Bonfait, O.: Weakly supervised object detection in artworks. In: Leal-Taixé, L., Roth, S. (eds.) ECCV 2018. LNCS, vol. 11130, pp. 692–709. Springer, Cham (2019). https://doi.org/10.1007/978-3-030-11012-3_53

19. He, K., Zhang, X., Ren, S., Sun, J.: Deep residual learning for image recognition. In: Proceedings of the IEEE Conference on Computer Vision and Pattern Recognition, pp. 770–778 (2016)
20. Hertzmann, A.: Can computers create art? In: Arts, vol. 7, p. 18. Multidisciplinary Digital Publishing Institute (2018)
21. Hertzmann, A., Jacobs, C.E., Oliver, N., Curless, B., Salesin, D.H.: Image analogies. In: Proceedings of the 28th Annual Conference on Computer Graphics and Interactive Techniques, pp. 327–340 (2001)
22. Hristova, S.: Images as data: cultural analytics and aby warburg's mnemosyne. Int. J. Digital Art Histor. (2), 115–133 (2016)
23. Impett, L., Süsstrunk, S.: Pose and pathosformel in Aby Warburg's Bilderatlas. In: Hua, G., Jégou, H. (eds.) ECCV 2016. LNCS, vol. 9913, pp. 888–902. Springer, Cham (2016). https://doi.org/10.1007/978-3-319-46604-0_61
24. Jegou, H., Douze, M., Schmid, C.: Hamming embedding and weak geometric consistency for large scale image search. In: Forsyth, D., Torr, P., Zisserman, A. (eds.) ECCV 2008. LNCS, vol. 5302, pp. 304–317. Springer, Heidelberg (2008). https://doi.org/10.1007/978-3-540-88682-2_24
25. Jegou, H., Douze, M., Schmid, C.: Product quantization for nearest neighbor search. IEEE Trans. Pattern Anal. Mach. Intell. **33**(1), 117–128 (2010)
26. Jenicek, T., Chum, O.: Linking art through human poses. arXiv preprint arXiv:1907.03537 (2019)
27. Jiang, B., Luo, R., Mao, J., Xiao, T., Jiang, Y.: Acquisition of localization confidence for accurate object detection. In: Ferrari, V., Hebert, M., Sminchisescu, C., Weiss, Y. (eds.) Computer Vision – ECCV 2018. LNCS, vol. 11218, pp. 816–832. Springer, Cham (2018). https://doi.org/10.1007/978-3-030-01264-9_48
28. Johnson, C.D.: Memory, Metaphor, and Aby Warburg's Atlas of Images. Cornell University Press, Ithaca (2012)
29. Johnson, J., Douze, M., Jégou, H.: Billion-scale similarity search with gpus. arXiv preprint arXiv:1702.08734 (2017)
30. Karayev, S., et al.: Recognizing image style. arXiv preprint arXiv:1311.3715 (2013)
31. Li, X., Liu, S., Kautz, J., Yang, M.H.: Learning linear transformations for fast arbitrary style transfer. arXiv preprint arXiv:1808.04537 (2018)
32. Lin, T.-Y., et al.: Microsoft COCO: common objects in context. In: Fleet, D., Pajdla, T., Schiele, B., Tuytelaars, T. (eds.) ECCV 2014. LNCS, vol. 8693, pp. 740–755. Springer, Cham (2014). https://doi.org/10.1007/978-3-319-10602-1_48
33. Lowe, D.G.: Distinctive image features from scale-invariant keypoints. Int. J. Comput. Vis. **60**(2), 91–110 (2004)
34. Manen, S., Guillaumin, M., Van Gool, L.: Prime object proposals with randomized prim's algorithm. In: Proceedings of the IEEE International Conference on Computer Vision, pp. 2536–2543 (2013)
35. Mao, H., Cheung, M., She, J.: Deepart: learning joint representations of visual arts. In: Proceedings of the 25th ACM International Conference on Multimedia, pp. 1183–1191 (2017)
36. Mensink, T., Van Gemert, J.: The Rijksmuseum challenge: museum-centered visual recognition. In: Proceedings of International Conference on Multimedia Retrieval, pp. 451–454 (2014)
37. Nister, D., Stewenius, H.: Scalable recognition with a vocabulary tree. In: 2006 IEEE Computer Society Conference on Computer Vision and Pattern Recognition (CVPR 2006), vol. 2, pp. 2161–2168. IEEE (2006)

38. Noh, H., Araujo, A., Sim, J., Weyand, T., Han, B.: Large-scale image retrieval with attentive deep local features. In: Proceedings of the IEEE International Conference on Computer Vision, pp. 3456–3465 (2017)
39. Philbin, J., Chum, O., Isard, M., Sivic, J., Zisserman, A.: Object retrieval with large vocabularies and fast spatial matching. In: 2007 IEEE Conference on Computer Vision and Pattern Recognition, pp. 1–8. IEEE (2007)
40. Philbin, J., Chum, O., Isard, M., Sivic, J., Zisserman, A.: Lost in quantization: improving particular object retrieval in large scale image databases. In: 2008 IEEE Conference on Computer Vision and Pattern Recognition, pp. 1–8. IEEE (2008)
41. Picard, D., Gosselin, P.H., Gaspard, M.C.: Challenges in content-based image indexing of cultural heritage collections. IEEE Signal Process. Mag. **32**(4), 95–102 (2015)
42. Radenović, F., Iscen, A., Tolias, G., Avrithis, Y., Chum, O.: Revisiting Oxford and Paris: large-scale image retrieval benchmarking. arXiv preprint arXiv:1803.11285 (2018)
43. Radenović, F., Tolias, G., Chum, O.: Fine-tuning CNN image retrieval with no human annotation. IEEE Trans. Pattern Anal. Mach. Intell. **41**(7), 1655–1668 (2018)
44. Ren, S., He, K., Girshick, R., Sun, J.: Faster R-CNN: towards real-time object detection with region proposal networks. In: Advances in Neural Information Processing Systems, pp. 91–99 (2015)
45. Saleh, B., Abe, K., Arora, R.S., Elgammal, A.: Toward automated discovery of artistic influence. Multimedia Tools Appl. **75**(7), 3565–3591 (2016)
46. Saleh, B., Elgammal, A.: Large-scale classification of fine-art paintings: learning the right metric on the right feature. arXiv preprint arXiv:1505.00855 (2015)
47. Sanakoyeu, A., Kotovenko, D., Lang, S., Ommer, B.: A style-aware content loss for real-time HD style transfer. In: Ferrari, V., Hebert, M., Sminchisescu, C., Weiss, Y. (eds.) ECCV 2018. LNCS, vol. 11212, pp. 715–731. Springer, Cham (2018). https://doi.org/10.1007/978-3-030-01237-3_43
48. Schlecht, J., Carqué, B., Ommer, B.: Detecting gestures in medieval images. In: 2011 18th IEEE International Conference on Image Processing (ICIP), pp. 1285–1288. IEEE (2011)
49. Seguin, B.: The replica project: Building a visual search engine for art historians. XRDS Crossroads ACM Mag. Students **24**(3), 24–29 (2018)
50. Seguin, B., diLenardo, I., Kaplan, F.: Tracking transmission of details in paintings. In: DH (2017)
51. Seguin, B., Striolo, C., diLenardo, I., Kaplan, F.: Visual link retrieval in a database of paintings. In: Hua, G., Jégou, H. (eds.) ECCV 2016. LNCS, vol. 9913, pp. 753–767. Springer, Cham (2016). https://doi.org/10.1007/978-3-319-46604-0_52
52. Shen, X., Efros, A.A., Aubry, M.: Discovering visual patterns in art collections with spatially-consistent feature learning. In: Proceedings of the IEEE Conference on Computer Vision and Pattern Recognition, pp. 9278–9287 (2019)
53. Shen, X., et al.: Large-scale historical watermark recognition: dataset and a new consistency-based approach. arXiv preprint arXiv:1908.10254 (2019)
54. Shen, X., Lin, Z., Brandt, J., Avidan, S., Wu, Y.: Object retrieval and localization with spatially-constrained similarity measure and K-NN re-ranking. In: 2012 IEEE Conference on Computer Vision and Pattern Recognition, pp. 3013–3020. IEEE (2012)
55. Shrivastava, A., Malisiewicz, T., Gupta, A., Efros, A.A.: Data-driven visual similarity for cross-domain image matching. In: Proceedings of the 2011 SIGGRAPH Asia Conference, pp. 1–10 (2011)

56. Simonyan, K., Zisserman, A.: Very deep convolutional networks for large-scale image recognition. arXiv preprint arXiv:1409.1556 (2014)
57. Spratt, E.L., Elgammal, A.: Computational beauty: aesthetic judgment at the intersection of art and science. In: Agapito, L., Bronstein, M.M., Rother, C. (eds.) ECCV 2014. LNCS, vol. 8925, pp. 35–53. Springer, Cham (2015). https://doi.org/10.1007/978-3-319-16178-5_3
58. Strezoski, G., Worring, M.: Omniart: multi-task deep learning for artistic data analysis. arXiv preprint arXiv:1708.00684 (2017)
59. Takami, M., Bell, P., Ommer, B.: An approach to large scale interactive retrieval of cultural heritage. In: GCH, pp. 87–95 (2014)
60. Tan, W.R., Chan, C.S., Aguirre, H.E., Tanaka, K.: Ceci n'est pas une pipe: a deep convolutional network for fine-art paintings classification. In: 2016 IEEE International Conference on Image Processing (ICIP), pp. 3703–3707. IEEE (2016)
61. Tolias, G., Sicre, R., Jégou, H.: Particular object retrieval with integral max-pooling of cnn activations. arXiv preprint arXiv:1511.05879 (2015)
62. Ufer, N.: Deep semantic feature matching. In: Proceedings of the IEEE Conference on Computer Vision and Pattern Recognition, pp. 6914–6923 (2017). https://doi.org/10.1109/CVPR.2017.628
63. Ufer, N., Lui, K.T., Schwarz, K., Warkentin, P., Ommer, B.: Weakly supervised learning of dense semantic correspondences and segmentation. In: Fink, G.A., Frintrop, S., Jiang, X. (eds.) DAGM GCPR 2019. LNCS, vol. 11824, pp. 456–470. Springer, Cham (2019). https://doi.org/10.1007/978-3-030-33676-9_32
64. Ufer, N., Souiai, M., Cremers, D.: *Wehrli 2.0*: an algorithm for "Tidying up Art". In: Fusiello, A., Murino, V., Cucchiara, R. (eds.) ECCV 2012. LNCS, vol. 7583, pp. 532–541. Springer, Heidelberg (2012). https://doi.org/10.1007/978-3-642-33863-2_55
65. Uijlings, J.R., Van De Sande, K.E., Gevers, T., Smeulders, A.W.: Selective search for object recognition. Int. J. Comput. Vis. **104**(2), 154–171 (2013)
66. Westlake, N., Cai, H., Hall, P.: Detecting people in Artwork with CNNs. In: Hua, G., Jégou, H. (eds.) ECCV 2016. LNCS, vol. 9913, pp. 825–841. Springer, Cham (2016). https://doi.org/10.1007/978-3-319-46604-0_57
67. Wilber, M.J., Fang, C., Jin, H., Hertzmann, A., Collomosse, J., Belongie, S.: Bam! the behance artistic media dataset for recognition beyond photography. In: Proceedings of the IEEE International Conference on Computer Vision, pp. 1202–1211 (2017)
68. Yi, K.M., Trulls, E., Lepetit, V., Fua, P.: LIFT: learned invariant feature transform. In: Leibe, B., Matas, J., Sebe, N., Welling, M. (eds.) ECCV 2016. LNCS, vol. 9910, pp. 467–483. Springer, Cham (2016). https://doi.org/10.1007/978-3-319-46466-4_28
69. Yin, R., Monson, E., Honig, E., Daubechies, I., Maggioni, M.: Object recognition in art drawings: Transfer of a neural network. In: 2016 IEEE International Conference on Acoustics, Speech and Signal Processing (ICASSP), pp. 2299–2303. IEEE (2016)
70. Zitnick, C.L., Dollár, P.: Edge boxes: locating object proposals from edges. In: Fleet, D., Pajdla, T., Schiele, B., Tuytelaars, T. (eds.) ECCV 2014. LNCS, vol. 8693, pp. 391–405. Springer, Cham (2014). https://doi.org/10.1007/978-3-319-10602-1_26

W15 - Sign Language Recognition, Translation and Production

W15 - Sign Language Recognition, Translation and Production

The aim of the Sign Language Recognition, Translation & Production (SLRTP 2020) workshop was to bring together researchers working on the various forms of sign language understanding, using tools from computer vision and linguistics. The workshop sought to promote a greater linguistic and historical understanding of sign languages within the computer vision community, to foster new collaborations, and to identify the most pressing challenges for the field going forward. The workshop was held in conjunction with the European Conference on Computer Vision (ECCV 2020).

We received 25 high-quality submissions, comprising 13 full papers and 12 extended abstracts. Each paper received at least 2 double-blind reviews from 10 reviewers. 18 papers were accepted, of which 10 were full papers and 8 were extended abstracts. All full papers appeared in the proceedings, in addition to the workshop summary paper from the organizers, which was not peer-reviewed. Both full papers and extended abstracts appeared in the workshop webpage.

The program included five keynotes (Bencie Woll, Oscar Koller, Christian Vogler, Matt Huenerfauth, and Lale Akarun). The reviewers nominated five full papers to give five minute presentations, among which one was announced as the best paper of the workshop. The other full papers and extended abstracts had three minute and one minute presentations, respectively. All presentations were recorded and were made available online.

We believe the future versions of SLRTP in computer vision conferences would be a great venue to cultivate collaboration with deaf communities and sign linguists.

We would to thank our sponsors Microsoft (AI for Accessibility Program), Google, and EPSRC project "ExTOL" (EP/R03298X/1). We would also like to thank Ben Saunders, Bencie Woll, Liliane Momeni, Oscar Koller, and Sajida Chaudhary for their help and advice, Robert Adam for ASL and BSL translations, Akbar Sikder and Esther Rose Bevan for BSL Interpretations, Anna Michaels and Brett Best from Arrow Interpreting for ASL Interpretations, and Katy Ryder and Tara Meyer from MyClearText for the live captioning. Last but not least, we want to thank the keynote speakers, the authors, and the participants for being a part of our workshop.

September 2020

Necati Cihan Camgöz
Gül Varol
Samuel Albanie
Neil Fox
Richard Bowden
Andrew Zisserman
Kearsy Cormier

SLRTP 2020: The Sign Language Recognition, Translation & Production Workshop

Necati Cihan Camgöz[1]([⊠]), Gül Varol[2], Samuel Albanie[2], Neil Fox[3],
Richard Bowden[1], Andrew Zisserman[2], and Kearsy Cormier[3]

[1] CVSSP, University of Surrey, Guildford, UK
{n.camgoz,r.bowden}@surrey.ac.uk
[2] Visual Geometry Group, University of Oxford, Oxford, UK
{gul,albanie,az}@robots.ox.ac.uk
[3] Deafness, Cognition and Language Research Centre, University College London,
London, UK
{neil.fox,k.cormier}@ucl.ac.uk
https://www.slrtp.com/

Abstract. The objective of the "Sign Language Recognition, Translation & Production" (SLRTP 2020) Workshop was to bring together researchers who focus on the various aspects of sign language understanding using tools from computer vision and linguistics. The workshop sought to promote a greater linguistic and historical understanding of sign languages within the computer vision community, to foster new collaborations and to identify the most pressing challenges for the field going forwards. The workshop was held in conjunction with the European Conference on Computer Vision (ECCV), 2020.

1 Introduction

In recent years, there has been considerable interest in tasks at the intersection of visual and linguistic modelling, motivated by progress on tasks such as visual dialogue, visual question answering and image captioning. As spatio-temporal linguistic constructs, sign languages represent unique challenges at the intersection of language and vision. For the last three decades, computer vision researchers have been studying sign languages in isolated recognition scenarios. However, large-scale continuous corpora are becoming increasingly available and the focus of the research community is transitioning towards continuous sign language recognition. Sign language translation and production in particular, present themselves as new frontiers that can be approached with modern techniques developed in the context of neural machine translation and generative modelling. In the SLRTP 2020 workshop, we aimed to bring together researchers to discuss the open challenges that lie at the intersection of sign language and computer vision. This report describes the themes covered by the event, statistics associated with workshop submissions and future directions.

© Springer Nature Switzerland AG 2020
A. Bartoli and A. Fusiello (Eds.): ECCV 2020 Workshops, LNCS 12536, pp. 179–185, 2020.
https://doi.org/10.1007/978-3-030-66096-3_13

2   Themes

The workshop covered several core themes through a series of invited keynote talks, which we describe next.

Processing Sign Languages: Linguistic, Technological, and Cultural Challenges. In this invited talk, Prof. Bencie Woll addressed three types of challenge: linguistic, technological and cultural – to researchers working on automated processing of sign languages. The talk offered a brief review of the typological properties of sign language structure, with emphasis on how they exploit the affordances provided by the use of articulators including the hands, upper body and face, and the properties of human visual perception. Technological challenges include the limited availability of tagged and annotated sign language corpora and researchers' lack of sign language awareness and skills. The most crucial challenge, however is cultural. There is little engagement with deaf communities, little attempt to find out whether proposed technology – often described as designed to help deaf people communicate – is what deaf people want and need. True commitment to accessibility involves consideration of all these factors, as well as long-term engagement with creating systemic change. To make progress, better partnerships between sign language linguists and software engineers is required. This includes support for the amount of work required to prepare comprehensive tagging and annotation of corpora, and inclusion within project teams of fluent signers (especially encouraging and supporting members of deaf communities and deaf scholars from diverse backgrounds to develop careers in technology). Most important of all is knowledge exchange with communities during the development of research.

Sign Language Recognition: From Dispersed to Comparable Research. To identify the requirements for future research, a comprehensive survey of the existing state of the art in sign language recognition is necessary. In this invited talk, Oscar Koller gave an overview of the field, focusing on the move from disparate research to the current momentum it has gained. The talk looked into comparable research studies on the available benchmark data sets and analysed the statistics of popular sign language tasks to understand what is needed to continue on the field's accelerated journey to real accessibility [10]. Finally, it concluded with an investigation of how their work [11] helps to deal with the specific challenges present in sign language recognition.

Sign Language Technologies: What are We Hoping to Accomplish? This invited talk by Prof. Christian Vogler discussed elements of the negative perception of sign language recognition technologies in the deaf community and some of the history of how this perception has developed. The talk further provided an analysis of the challenges with the current state of the field [3], and what can be done to improve matters. It highlighted that collaboration with the deaf front and center is key, as is identifying realistic applications that people will want to use, based on inclusive principles that respect the community.

Creating Useful Applications with Imperfect, Sign-Language Technologies. Creating sign-language recognition and synthesis technologies is difficult, and state-of-the-art systems are still imperfect. This limitation presents a challenge for researchers in seeking resources to support dataset creation, user requirements gathering, and other critical infrastructure for the field. This invited talk by Prof. Matt Huenerfauth examined how it is possible to create useful applications in the near-term, to motivate research that would have long-term benefit to the field. Examples of funded projects that integrate imperfect sign-language technologies were discussed, including: providing automatic feedback for students learning American Sign Language (ASL) through analysis of videos of their signing, creating search-by-video interfaces for ASL dictionaries, generating understandable ASL animations to improve information access, and providing ASL content in reading-assistance software. The common thread is that the technologies at the core of each project (i.e. human animation synthesis or recognition of video of human motion) are all imperfect artificial-intelligence systems that occasionally fail in non-human-like ways. The talk discussed investigations of how to adapt these imperfect technologies for new domains, and using human-computer interaction research methods to evaluate alternative system designs. The goal is to enable users to cope with current limitations of these intelligent technologies so that they benefit from applications that employ them.

Turkish Sign Language Recognition at Boğaziçi University. In this invited talk, Prof. Lale Akarun describes work conducted at the Boğaziçi University Sign Language Group, which includes researchers from the domains of computer vision, speech and language processing, and linguistics. In the past, they have carried out projects on applications of sign language recognition, such as automated sign tutoring, and information kiosk for the Deaf in hospitals [5]. These applications involve sign verification and limited vocabulary isolated sign language recognition tasks. They have collected a dataset called BosphorusSign, which is open for researchers [17]. Their current work aims to find better visual embeddings that can generalize across different sign languages. They have shown that the embedding learnt with multitask learning, improves the performance of sign language translation [16]. In their latest work, they investigate unsupervised methodologies for finding hand shapes [23] and for sign unit discovery [19].

3   Programme and Submissions

The SLRTP 2020 workshop received 25 high quality submissions comprising 13 full papers and 12 extended abstracts. Of these, 18 papers were accepted, of which 10 were full papers and 8 were extended abstracts.

The work of Bull *et al.* [4] introduced the problem of automatic segmentation of sign language into *Subtitle-Units* and provided a baseline for this task—such segmentations have direct application for translation and efficient subtitling of sign language content. The modelling of phonologically-meaningful subunits for sign language recognition was investigated by Borg *et al.* [2]: this provides not only a strong basis for recognition with deep learning-based approaches, but also improves the interpretability of the system. Motivated by the important role that facial expressions play in sign languages, da Silva *et al.* [22] develop a system that aims to perform FACS-based [7] action unit classification. Their approach is applied to a collected dataset of Brazilian Sign Language, Libras. An efficient system of sign language detection based on human pose estimation is presented by Moryossef *et al.* [15], who demonstrate its potential for video-conferencing applications. In [18], Parelli *et al.* investigate the use of 3D hand pose estimation, and show that it can be a valuable cue for sign language recognition. A plan for constructing an Auslan communication technologies pipeline encompassing sign recognition, production and natural sign language processing is proposed by Korte *et al.* [12]. Medical applications of automatic recognition are explored by Liang *et al.* [14], who develop a multi-modal toolkit to detect early stages of Dementia among British Sign Language users. The work of Gokce *et al.* [8] investigates multi-cue fusion and shows its effectiveness for improving sign language recognition. Polat *et al.* [19] consider instead the task of unsupervised sign discovery without labels using a k-nearest neighbours approach. The use of hand shape features for improving keyword search performance is investigated by Tamer *et al.* [24].

In addition to the full papers discussed above, the extended abstracts presented at the workshop explored a range of themes related to sign language recognition and production.

Belissen *et al.* [1] investigate the necessity and realizability of recognizing linguistic structures of sign languages, like classifiers, using natural corpora. Yin *et al.* [26] use popular transformer networks to improve the sign language translation performance. Duarte *et al.* [6] give a brief introduction of the newly curated How2Sign dataset, which is an extension of the large scale multi-modal How2 dataset [20]. Using the How2Sign dataset, Ventura *et al.* [25] explore continuous sign language video production conditioned on skeletal pose sequences. Kratimenos *et al.* [13] use state-of-the-art 3D pose estimation techniques to obtain parametric representations of signers and report improved multi-channel sign language recognition performance over using raw RGB images. Wizard-of-Oz experiments are conducted by Hassan *et al.* [9] to investigate the user satisfaction of sign language recognition systems. An iterative visual attention model is proposed by Shi *et al.* for fingerspelling sequence recognition in the wild [21]. Glasser *et al.* investigate sign language user interfaces, identify open questions and challenges including the Deaf and Hard of Hearing communities' interest in such technologies.

4   Practical/Logistical Findings and Recommendations

To meet the workshop objective of bringing sign language researchers from different communities together, we aimed to make the content and workshop discussion accessible to a broad audience. To this end, each submitted paper was accompanied by a short video describing the work, which was then captioned and translated into British Sign Language (BSL) and American Sign Language

(ASL) by overlaid interpreters (or captioned with written English directly from sign language, where appropriate). Similarly, each invited talk was captioned and translated into ASL and BSL, or translated from ASL into written English. All discussions were translated live into both BSL and ASL.

Findings. Due to ongoing global health concerns, the workshop was held virtually via video conferencing software. This presented additional complexity in coordinating interactions, but also provided opportunities to improve accessibility by allowing recruitment of skilled interpreters from a global workforce without geographic constraints. This was particularly beneficial given the highly technical nature of the material covered in live interactions. Video conferencing software also had the additional benefit of allowing attendees to continue conversations with presenters through the chat functionality, even as other presentations continued (typically infeasible in a physical workshop).

Recommendations. Monolingual workshop organisation at computer vision conferences requires a considerable logistical effort: coordinating call-for-papers, submissions, reviews, paper decisions, sponsorship and the running of the workshop day itself. Provision of multi-lingual content requires additional planning: presentations must be sent to interpreters before the workshop to provide them with time to review the material and produce a translation. For live dialogue, interpreters must be sought who can attend the workshop and who feel comfortable with translating technical content. Finally, communication in multiple languages progresses more slowly than in one—the schedule of the workshop itself should be adjusted to reflect this. Our central recommendations are twofold: (1) to start planning as early as possible—several months of work were required to coordinate SLRTP and there was still considerable time pressure at all stages of the process, (2) *dry-runs*—live interpretation through video conferencing adds complexity and the workshop chairs benefited from rehearsals of transitions between presentations, ensuring interpreters are visible at all times to ensure that content remains accessible.

5   Conclusion

The SLRTP 2020 workshop brought together researchers who work on various aspects of sign language understanding spanning techniques from linguistics to computer vision. In addition to providing a platform for a range of technical contributions, there were several key takeaways from the workshop. First, it is crucial that deaf communities and researchers are present at every stage of research projects and workshop/conference organisations about sign languages. Second, the focus of applied sign language research should be realistic applications that people will want to use, rather than those with no practical need. Third, significant further efforts are required in dataset collection if the research community is to benefit from recent advances in neural machine translation.

Acknowledgements. We would like to thank our sponsors Microsoft (AI for Accessibility Program), Google, and EPSRC project "ExTOL" (EP/R03298X/1). We would also like to thank Ben Saunders, Bencie Woll, Liliane Momeni, Oscar Koller, and Sajida Chaudhary for their help and advice, Robert Adam for ASL and BSL translations, Akbar Sikder and Esther Rose Bevan for BSL Interpretations, Anna Michaels and Brett Best from Arrow Interpreting for ASL Interpretations, and Katy Ryder and Tara Meyer from MyClearText for the live captioning.

References

1. Belissen, V., Braffort, A., Gouiffés, M.: Towards continuous recognition of illustrative and spatial structures in sign language. In: Sign Language Recognition, Translation and Production (SLRTP) Workshop - Extended Abstracts (2020)
2. Borg, M., Camilleri, K.P.: Phonologically-meaningful subunits for deep learning-based sign language recognition. In: Bartoli, A., Fusiello, A. (eds.) ECCV 2020 Workshops. LNCS, vol. 12536, pp. 199–217. Springer, Cham (2020)
3. Bragg, D., et al.: Sign language recognition, generation, and translation: an interdisciplinary perspective. In: Proceedings of the International ACM SIGACCESS Conference on Computers and Accessibility (ASSETS) (2019)
4. Bull, H., Gouiffès, M., Braffort, A.: Automatic segmentation of sign language into subtitle-units. In: Bartoli, A., Fusiello, A. (eds.) ECCV 2020 Workshops. LNCS, vol. 12536, pp. 186–198. Springer, Cham (2020)
5. Camgöz, N.C., Kındıroğlu, A.A., Akarun, L.: Sign language recognition for assisting the deaf in hospitals. In: Chetouani, M., Cohn, J., Salah, A.A. (eds.) HBU 2016. LNCS, vol. 9997, pp. 89–101. Springer, Cham (2016). https://doi.org/10.1007/978-3-319-46843-3_6
6. Duarte, A., et al.: How2Sign: a large-scale multimodal dataset for continuous American sign language. In: Sign Language Recognition, Translation and Production (SLRTP) Workshop - Extended Abstracts (2020)
7. Ekman, P., Friesen, W.V.: Manual for The Facial Action Coding System. Consulting Psychologists Press, Palo Alto (1978)
8. Gökçe, c., Özdemir, O., Kındıroğlu, A.A., Akarun, L.: Score-level multi cue fusion for sign language recognition. In: Bartoli, A., Fusiello, A. (eds.) ECCV 2020 Workshops. LNCS, vol. 12536, pp. 294–309. Springer, Cham (2020)
9. Hassan, S., Alonzo, O., Glasser, A., Huenerfauth, M.: Effect of ranking and precision of results on users' satisfaction with search-by-video sign-language dictionaries. In: Sign Language Recognition, Translation and Production (SLRTP) Workshop - Extended Abstracts (2020)
10. Koller, O.: Quantitative survey of the state of the art in sign language recognition. arXiv preprint arXiv:2008.09918 (2020)
11. Koller, O., Camgoz, C., Ney, H., Bowden, R.: Weakly supervised learning with multi-stream CNN-LSTM-HMMs to discover sequential parallelism in sign language videos. IEEE Trans. Pattern Anal. Mach. Intell. **42**, 2306–2320 (2019)
12. Korte, J., Bender, A., Gallasch, G., Wiles, J., Back, A.: A plan for developing an Auslan communication technologies pipeline. In: In: Bartoli, A., Fusiello, A. (eds.) ECCV 2020 Workshops. LNCS, vol. 12536, pp. 264–277. Springer, Cham (2020)
13. Kratimenos, A., Pavlakos, G., Maragos, P.: 3D hands, face and body extraction for sign language recognition. In: Sign Language Recognition, Translation and Production (SLRTP) Workshop - Extended Abstracts (2020)

14. Liang, X., Angelopoulou, A., Kapetanios, E., Woll, B., Al-batat, R., Woolfe, T.: A multi-modal machine learning approach and toolkit to automate recognition of early stages of dementia among British sign language users. In: Bartoli, A., Fusiello, A. (eds.) ECCV 2020 Workshops. LNCS, vol. 12536, pp. 278–293. Springer, Cham (2020)

15. Moryossef, A., Tsochantaridis, I., Aharoni, R., Ebling, S., Narayanan, S.: Real-time sign language detection using human pose estimation. In: Bartoli, A., Fusiello, A. (eds.) ECCV 2020 Workshops. LNCS, vol. 12536, pp. 237–248. Springer, Cham (2020)

16. Orbay, A., Akarun, L.: Neural sign language translation by learning tokenization. arXiv preprint arXiv:2002.00479 (2020)

17. Özdemir, O., Kındıroğlu, A.A., Camgöz, N.C., Akarun, L.: BosphorusSign22k sign language recognition dataset. arXiv preprint arXiv:2004.01283 (2020)

18. Parelli, M., Papadimitriou, K., Potamianos, G., Pavlakos, G., Maragos, P.: Exploiting 3D hand pose estimation in deep learning-based sign language recognition from RGB videos. In: Bartoli, A., Fusiello, A. (eds.) ECCV 2020 Workshops. LNCS, vol. 12536, pp. 249–263. Springer, Cham (2020)

19. Polat, K., Saraçlar, M.: Unsupervised discovery of sign terms by K-nearest neighbours approach. In: Bartoli, A., Fusiello, A. (eds.) ECCV 2020 Workshops. LNCS, vol. 12536, pp. 310–321. Springer, Cham (2020)

20. Sanabria, R., et al.: How2: a large-scale dataset for multimodal language understanding. In: Proceedings of the Workshop on Visually Grounded Interaction and Language (ViGIL). NeurIPS (2018)

21. Shi, B., Del Rio, A.M., Keane, J., Brentari, D., Shakhnarovich, G., Livescu, K.: Fingerspelling recognition in the wild with iterative visual attention. In: Sign Language Recognition, Translation and Production (SLRTP) Workshop - Extended Abstracts (2020)

22. da Silva, E.P., Costa, P.D.P., Kumada, K.M.O., De Martino, J.M., Florentino, G.A.: Recognition of affective and grammatical facial expressions: a study for Brazilian sign language. In: Bartoli, A., Fusiello, A. (eds.) ECCV 2020 Workshops. LNCS, vol. 12536, pp. 218–236. Springer, Cham (2020)

23. Siyli, R.D., Gundogdu, B., Saraclar, M., Akarun, L.: Unsupervised key hand shape discovery of sign language videos with correspondence sparse autoencoders. In: ICASSP 2020–2020 IEEE International Conference on Acoustics, Speech and Signal Processing (ICASSP), pp. 8179–8183. IEEE (2020)

24. Tamer, N.C., Saraçlar, M.: Improving keyword search performance in sign language with hand shape features. In: Bartoli, A., Fusiello, A. (eds.) ECCV 2020 Workshops. LNCS, vol. 12536, pp. 322–333. Springer, Cham (2020)

25. Ventura, L., Duarte, A., Giro-i Nieto, X.: Can everybody sign now? Exploring sign language video generation from 2D poses. In: Sign Language Recognition, Translation and Production (SLRTP) Workshop - Extended Abstracts (2020)

26. Yin, K., Read, J.: Attention is all you sign: sign language translation with transformers. In: Sign Language Recognition, Translation and Production (SLRTP) Workshop - Extended Abstracts (2020)

Automatic Segmentation of Sign Language into Subtitle-Units

Hannah Bull[1,2](✉) , Michèle Gouiffès[1,2] , and Annelies Braffort[1]

[1] LIMSI-CNRS, Campus universitaire 507, Rue du Belvedère, 91405 Orsay, France
{hannah.bull,michele.gouiffes,annelies.braffort}@limsi.fr
[2] University of Paris-Saclay, Route de l'Orme aux Merisiers - RD 128, 91190
Saint-Aubin, France

Abstract. We present baseline results for a new task of automatic segmentation of Sign Language video into sentence-like units. We use a
corpus of natural Sign Language video with accurately aligned subtitles
to train a spatio-temporal graph convolutional network with a BiLSTM
on 2D skeleton data to automatically detect the temporal boundaries of
subtitles. In doing so, we segment Sign Language video into subtitle-units
that can be translated into phrases in a written language. We achieve
a ROC-AUC statistic of 0.87 at the frame level and 92% label accuracy
within a time margin of 0.6s of the true labels.

Keywords: Sign language · Segmentation · Sentence · Subtitle ·
Graph neural network · Skeleton keypoints

1 Introduction

Sign Language (SL) is an essential means of communication for Deaf communities. SLs are visuo-gestual languages with no written form, instead using hands,
body pose and facial expression as the medium of transmission. A natural way of
recording SL is through video. The uniqueness of transmission medium, structure
and grammar of SL requires distinct methodologies.

The treatment of language as a sequence of words from a lexicon is unsuitable
for SLs [10]. The notion of a 'word' in SL is ill-defined, as the beginning or end
of a sign in fluent discourse is unclear. Moreover, signs can occur simultaneously,
further blurring the notion of a 'word' and rendering impossible the modelisation
of SL as a linear sequence of words. The iconicity of SLs means that signs are
strongly modified according to context and meaning, rather than being drawn
largely unmodified from a lexicon.

Classic natural language processing tasks including speech-to-text, word
embeddings and parts-of-speech tagging currently do not have direct counterparts in SL processing. Tasks such as automatic translation between SL and
written language are in a preliminary stage, with translation only possible for
short and rudimentary phrases with limited vocabulary [3].

© Springer Nature Switzerland AG 2020
A. Bartoli and A. Fusiello (Eds.): ECCV 2020 Workshops, LNCS 12536, pp. 186–198, 2020.
https://doi.org/10.1007/978-3-030-66096-3_14

We wish to define a sentence-like unit that can be used to segment SL into short and coherent sequences that can be translated individually. This task of segmentation of SL video is useful for numerous tasks, including software for subtitling assistance, reducing sequence length for continuous SL recognition, or phrase-level alignment between SLs and spoken or written languages. Manual segmentation of SL video into sentence-like units is a fastidious and extremely time consuming task, and so we aim to automatise this problem.

We define a *subtitle-unit* (SU) as a segment of SL video corresponding to the temporal boundaries of a written subtitle in accurately subtitled SL video. The SU is of linguistic relevance, as the person subtitling the SL video purposefully aligns phrases of text with what they consider to be equivalent phrases in SL. Implicitly, the subtitiler labels segments of SL video that can be translated into a phrase in written language.

Our key contribution is to present baseline results of the new task of automatically segmenting SL video at a sentence-like level. Our method is an adaptation of a state-of-the-art graph-based convolutional network for sequences of 2D skeleton data of natural SL. We also study the influence of different sets of articulators (body, face and hands) in this task.

After a short overview on the related work in Sect. 2, Sect. 3 introduces the corpus and Sect. 4 details the proposed methodology. The results are provided in Sect. 5.

2   Related Work

To our knowledge, this paper presents the first attempt of the task of automatic segmentation of SL into sentence-like units. This task has been suggested by Dreuw and Ney [8] as a tool for integration into a SL annotation program.

Despite a large amount of existing work for speech and text segmentation, there is debate surrounding the precise linguistic definition of a sentence in languages such as French or English [7]. Nevertheless, division by punctuation from written language is a good working solution for almost all cases. Automatic punctuation of speech can be achieved either using prosodic cues from audio or directly from a text transcription. On reference datasets, the former method tends to perform worse than the latter, but a combination of prosodic cues and a written transcription can have superior performance than either individually, as shown by Kolář and Lamel [13].

In SLs, purely oral languages, even a working notion of a sentence is unclear. Crasborn [6] proposes the pragmatic solution of identifying sentences in SL by firstly translating them into a written language and then calling a sentence the closest equivalent portion of SL to a sentence in the written language. This solution is somewhat unsatisfactory, as it requires translation to a written language. Nevertheless, Fenlon et al. [9] demonstrate that both native signers and non-signers can reliably segment sentence boundaries in SL using visual cues such as head rotations, nodding, blinks, eye-brow movements, pauses and lowering the hands.

Our definition of a SU requires translation to a written language, but our goal is to learn to segment SL into sentence-like units purely from visual cues without translation into a written language. We note that SUs are not necessarily the same as what are sometimes called clauses, sentences or syntactic units in the linguistic literature on SL. Börstell et al. [2] compare SUs with 'syntactic boundaries' annotated by a Deaf SL researcher. They find that many of the boundaries of the SUs overlap with the syntactic boundaries, but that there are more syntactic boundaries than there are SUs.

We consider SU boundary detection as a continuous SL recognition problem, as we learn visual cues in long sequences of video data. One main approach for continuous SL recognition consists of using RGB SL video as input, and then combining a 3D Convolutional Neural Network (CNN) with a Recursive Neural Network (RNN) to predict a sequence of words in the written language. Koller et al. [14] use a CNN with a bi-directional LSTM (BiLSTM) and Huang et al. [11] use a Hierachical Attention Network (HAN). Both of these articles use corpora in controlled environments with a single signer facing the camera.

Another main approach is to use sequences of skeleton data as input, which is arguably less dependent on the conditions of SL video production. Belissen et al. [1] and Ko et al. [12] use sequences of skeleton keypoints for continuous SL recognition, but concatenate the 2D skeleton keypoints into two vectors rather than exploiting the graph structure of the skeleton keypoints.

Yan et al. [17] propose a Spatio-Temporal Graph Convolution Network (ST-GCN) for action recognition using sequences of skeleton keypoints that achieves state-of-the-art results. This model takes into account the spatio-temporal relationships between body keypoints. Our model is an adaptation of the ST-GCN, as this type of model is appropriate for our 2D skeleton video data. We combine the ST-GCN model with a BiLSTM, as we are predicting sequences not classes. This combination of a convolutional network and a BiLSTM is commonly used in language modelling [15].

3 Corpus

The MEDIAPI-SKEL corpus [4] contains 27h of subtitled French Sign Language (LSF) video in the form of sequences of 2D skeletons (see Fig. 1). This corpus has the unique quality of being both natural SL (produced outside laboratory conditions) and having accurately aligned subtitles. As far as we know, this is the only large existing corpus with these two characteristics.

The subtitles in this corpus are aligned to the SL video such that the video segment corresponds to the subtitle. The original language of almost all the videos is SL, which is then translated into written language for the subtitles.[1] The subtitles have been written by different people and aligned by hand, and so we expect some variation in the length and placement of the SUs.

---

[1] There are rare video segments where a hearing person is interviewed and this interview is translated into SL.

The 2D skeleton data contains 25 body keypoints, 2×21 hand keypoints and 70 facial keypoints for every person at every frame in the 27h hours of video content. Each 2-dimensional coordinate is also associated to a confidence value between 0 and 1.

This corpus contains 2.5 million frames associated to 20k subtitles, where each subtitle has an average length of 4.2 s and 10.9 words. The training data contains 278 videos, the validation data 40 videos, and the test data 50 videos. The average length of a video is 4.5 min. Videos may contain signers at different angles (not necessarily facing the camera) and around one-fifth of the videos contain multiple signers.

Politique : Jean-Marie Le Pen face à la justice.

Fig. 1. MEDIAPI-SKEL corpus [4] with skeleton keypoints of LSF and aligned subtitles in written French. The graph structure connecting body keypoints (blue), face keypoints (red) and hand keypoints (green) is shown (Color figure online)

Since the corpus contains dialogues between multiple people in various environments, it is necessary to clean the data automatically by detecting and tracking the current signer and by removing irrelevant keypoints.

The code for our skeleton data cleaning procedure is available online.[2] The main steps consist in:

- Converting all videos to 25 frames-per-second
- Omitting the legs and feet keypoints, as they are not relevant for SL, leaving us with a total of 125 keypoints
- Tracking each person in each video using a constraint on the distance between body keypoints between consecutive frames
- Omitting people unlikely to be signers, specifically those with hands outside of the video frame, those with hands that hardly move, those that are too small (in the background of the video) or those that appear only for very short time periods (under 10 frames)
- In the case of multiple potential signers, choosing the most likely signer in each second of video based on a criterion involving hand size times variation of wrist movement of the dominant hand
- Imputation of missing skeleton keypoints using past or future frames
- Temporal smoothing with a Savitzky-Golay filter

---

[2] https://github.com/hannahbull/clean_op_data_sl.

Our final input data consist of temporal sequences of variable lengths of 2D skeleton keypoints corresponding to individuals in SL video.

We label a frame of a sequence with 0 if there is no subtitle associated to that frame or if the frame is within a distance of 2 frames from a frame with no associated subtitle. We label all other frames as 1. The padding of the 0-labelled frames partially controls for the fact that the SUs are not precise at the frame-level. Frames labelled 1 are SUs, and frames labelled 0 are SU boundaries.

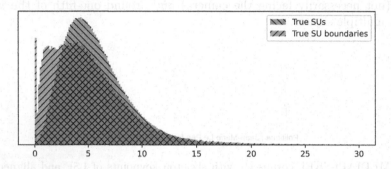

Fig. 2. Density histogram of the average velocity of the 15 upper body keypoints of likely signers in the training set. Units are pixel distance moved per frame with 1080p resolution

Figure 2 shows the distribution of the average velocity of the body keypoints of likely signers in the training set by label. Sequences where there is unlikely to be a signer due to lack of hand visibility or hand movement are omitted using our data cleaning procedure. True SU boundaries tend to have lower average body keypoint velocity compared to true SUs, but velocity is an insufficient indicator to predict SU boundaries in SL discourse.

4   Methodology

4.1   Model

Our model is a spatio-temporal graph convolutional network (ST-GCN) following Yan et al. [17], which we adjoin to a BiLSTM network to capture the sequential nature of the output (Fig. 3). The spatial graph structure of the body keypoints, face keypoints and hand keypoints follows the human joint structure. The temporal graph structure connects body keypoints across time. The edge importance in the graph is learned during training. The convolution operation is across the spatial and temporal edges of the graph.

The ST-GCN architecture is identical to that used by Yan et al. [17], but without temporal pooling. The model is composed of 9 layers of ST-GCN units, where the first 3 layers have 64 output units, the second 3 layers have 128 output units and the final 3 layers have 256 output units. The embedding dimension of

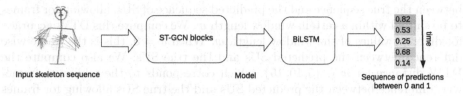

Fig. 3. ST-GCN+BiLSTM model on skeleton sequence for SU detection

the BiLSTM is thus 256 and we also set the hidden dimension of the BiLSTM to be 256.

Each input sequence of skeleton keypoints has a length of 125 frames, but we take every second frame of the video, so this corresponds to a sequence length of 10s. This means that we expect around two or three SUs per sequence, as the average subtitle length is 4.2 s.

Each skeleton sequence is normalised such that the mean and variance of the x-coordinates and y-coordinates of the skeleton over time are equal to 0 and 1. During training, we add random flips to the horizontal dimension of the skeleton keypoints in order to take into account for left-handed and right-handed signers. We also shuffle the order of skeleton sequences at each epoch.

We use SGD optimisation with a learning rate of 0.01, a weight decay of 0.0001, Nesterov momentum of 0.9 and binary cross-entropy loss. The model is trained for 30 epochs. Due to memory constraints, the batch-size is 4.

4.2   Experiments

We train our model on 278 videos and test our model on 50 videos. Our full model uses 15 body keypoints, 70 face keypoints and 2×21 hand keypoints shown respectively in blue, red and green in Fig. 1. In order to understand the contributions of the body, face and hand keypoints, we train the model using only the body keypoints, only the face keypoints and only the hand keypoints, as well as the body + face, the body + hand and the body + face + hand keypoints. We keep the architecture of the model constant.

Moreover, we compare the performance of our model between videos with one signer and videos with multiple signers. The videos with multiple signers often contain dialogues between people not necessarily facing directly at the camera. This is to test the robustness of our model to more diverse scenarios.

4.3   Evaluation Criteria

Our evaluation metrics should take into account that SUs are not annotated by the subtitler at a frame-level accuracy. We propose both frame-wise and unit-wise metrics, allowing for shifts in SUs.

As a flexible frame-wise metric, we propose dynamic time warping (DTW) with a window constraint as an evaluation criteria. This computes the distance between the true sequence and the predicted sequence of SUs, allowing for frames to be shifted within a certain window length w. We compute this DTW accuracy for different values of the window length w. When $w = 0$, this is the frame-wise difference between the predicted SUs and the true SUs. We also compute the DTW distance for $w \in \{5, 10, 15\}$, which corresponds to the minimum frame-wise difference between the predicted SUs and the true SUs allowing for frames to be shifted up to 5, 10 or 15 frames.

Additionally, we compute the ROC-AUC statistic, the frame-wise precision, recall and $F1$-score. The precision is given by the number of frames correctly identified with the label 0 divided by the total number of frames identified with the label 0. The recall is given by the number of frames correctly identified with the label 0 divided by the total number of true frames with the label 0. The $F1$ score is the harmonic mean of precision and recall.

Furthermore, we consider unit-wise evaluation metrics, allowing for 15 frame (0.6s) shifts in SU boundaries. We match each predicted SU boundary to the closest true SU boundary, where the closest true SU boundary is defined as the true SU boundary with the greatest intersection with the predicted SU boundary, or, in the case of no intersection, the closest true SU boundary within 15 frames. Calculating the number of matches divided by the total number of predicted SU boundaries gives us a unit-wise precision metric. In the same way, we can match each true SU boundary to the closest predicted SU boundary. The number of matches divided by the total number of true SU boundaries gives us a unit-wise recall metric. From this precision and recall metric, we can compute a unit-wise $F1$ score.

5   Results and Discussion

Table 1 shows frame-wise evaluation metrics on the test set. Our results are encouraging and we obtain a ROC-AUC statistic of 0.87 for our predictions, with the highest score obtained using the body, face and hand keypoints. Instead of relying on the frame-wise error rate, it is important to account for slight shifts in SUs as those who subtitle the videos do not aim for accuracy at the level of the frame. Allowing for shifts of up to 0.6s (15 frames), we obtain a frame-wise error rate of 8% when using only the body keypoints. Table 2 presents unit-wise evaluation results and shows that 76% of true SU boundaries can be associated to a predicted SU boundary within 15 frames.

When asking native signers to annotate sentence boundaries in SL, Fenlon et al. [9] found inter-participant agreement of sentence boundary annotation within 1 s to be around 63%. Whilst this is not exactly the same task as subtitling SL video, we can expect that there is quite a high degree of variation in the choice of subtitle boundaries. In light of this finding, our error rate seems reasonable.

Part of the accuracy of our model is accounted for by pre-processing the data to label obvious SU boundaries, such as moments where there are no signers in the video. Such frames are correctly identified as having no associated subtitle 78% of the time, as noted in the second last line of Table 1. Errors here seem

Table 1. Frame-wise evaluation metrics on the test set. The full model uses face, body and hand keypoints. The pre-processing version shows an evaluation after annotation of segments without an identified signer as not belonging to SUs. The final line shows the results for a constant prediction. DTW0 is the frame-wise prediction error. DTW5, DTW10 and DTW15 are the DTW errors respectively allowing for a 5, 10 and 15 frame discrepancy in predictions

	DTW0	DTW5	DTW10	DTW15	AUC	Prec.	Recall	F1
Full	0.1660	0.1255	0.1045	0.0927	**0.8723**	0.5023	**0.7510**	0.6019
Face+body	0.1560	0.1172	0.0973	0.0868	0.8708	0.5241	0.7259	0.6087
Body+hands	0.1661	0.1269	0.1064	0.0952	0.8659	0.5023	0.7380	0.5977
Face	0.1858	0.1483	0.1248	0.1100	0.8325	0.4624	0.6830	0.5514
Body	**0.1410**	**0.1055**	**0.0882**	**0.0790**	0.8704	**0.5616**	0.7122	**0.6280**
Hands	0.1821	0.1417	0.1186	0.1053	0.8554	0.4713	0.7360	0.5747
Pre-processing	*0.1406*	*0.1365*	*0.1333*	*0.1309*	*0.6039*	*0.7828*	*0.2201*	*0.3436*
Constant pred.	*0.1672*	*0.1672*	*0.1672*	*0.1672*	*0.5000*	*0.1671*	*1.0000*	*0.2865*

Table 2. Unit-wise evaluation metrics on the test set allowing for 15 frame (0.6s) shifts in SU boundaries. The full model uses face, body and hand keypoints. The pre-processing version shows an evaluation after annotation of segments without an identified signer as not belonging to SUs

	Prec.	Recall	F1
Full	0.6609	**0.7631**	0.7083
Face+body	0.6840	0.7408	**0.7113**
Body+hands	0.6250	0.7492	0.6815
Face	0.6403	0.6909	0.6646
Body	**0.7090**	0.6866	0.6976
Hands	0.6147	0.7619	0.6804
Pre-processing	*0.9341*	*0.0803*	*0.1478*

to be mostly due to subtitles extending beyond scenes containing signers, rather than failure to detect a signer in a scene, however further annotation of signers would be needed to verify this. Our ST-GCN+BiLSTM model makes significant improvements on top of this pre-processing.

From Table 1, we see that the full model has the highest ROC-AUC statistic and the highest recall, suggesting that including the facial and hand keypoints detects the most SU boundaries. However, the body model makes fewer incorrect predictions of SU boundaries and has a higher precision. Our unit-wise metrics in Table 2 reinforce this observation. The full model correctly identifies 76% of the true SU boundaries within 15 frames, but the body model has the highest precision with 71% of the predicted SU boundaries within 15 frames of a true SU boundary. Börstell et al. [2] find that there are more 'syntactic boundaries' than

SUs. Perhaps our full model is good at learning visual cues of such 'syntactic boundaries', which do not always correspond to actual SU boundaries.

Figure 4 shows an example of the predictions and true labels on a video from the test set using the full model. Most of the true SU boundaries are correctly detected, however there is an over-detection of SU boundaries. Figure 7 shows that the predicted lengths of SUs using the full model is shorter than the true lengths of SUs. This difference in length is less pronounced when using the body model. Moreover, predicted SU boundaries tend to be slightly longer than the true SU boundaries. The median difference between predicted SU boundaries and the associated true SU boundaries within 15 frames is around 5–7 frames in all our models. The median absolute difference between predicted SU boundaries and the associated true SU boundaries is 7–9 frames. The problem of over-detection or under-detection of SU boundaries and differences in lengths could be alleviated by assigning length and regularity priors to the SUs. This is similar to applying shape priors in image segmentation [5], [16].

Figure 5 and Fig. 6 show examples of correct and incorrect predictions from Fig. 4. The left of Fig. 5 shows an example of an obvious SU boundary where the signer pauses with their hands folded. This is correctly predicted by our model, albeit our predicted SU boundary is a little longer than the true boundary. The right of Fig. 5 shows a SU boundary with more subtle visual cues, including the head turning towards the camera and a slight deceleration of movement. This is also correctly detected by our model, but with a slight shift of about half of a second.

The left of Fig. 6 shows an SU boundary detected by our model but which is not a true SU boundary. However, this particular example could have been an SU boundary had the subtitles for this video been aligned differently. Some of our incorrectly detected SU boundaries are thus likely to correspond to sentence-like boundaries but which are simply not annotated as such by the subtitler. The right of Fig. 6 shows a SU boundary not detected by our model. This particular SU boundary does not have clear visual cues, and its detection may perhaps require an understanding of the SL sequence.

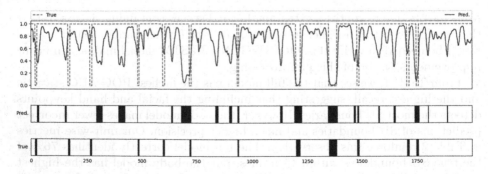

Fig. 4. True and predicted labels for a video sequence using the full (face+body+hands) model

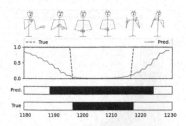 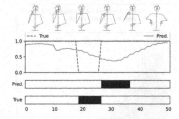

Fig. 5. Correctly detected SU boundaries from Fig. 4

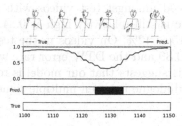 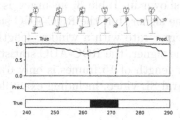

Fig. 6. Incorrectly detected SU boundaries from Fig. 4

Facial visual cues for semantic boundaries in SL can include blinks, eyebrow movements, head nodding or turning the head to stare directly at the camera. Manual cues include specific hand movements and the signer folding their hands together at the waist level. We thus assess whether or not including facial and hand keypoints improves SU detection. We cannot conclude that adding the face and the hand keypoints to the body model makes a significant improvement to SU detection. Nevertheless, the face keypoints or the hand keypoints alone make surprisingly accurate predictions. The face model has a ROC-AUC statistic of 0.83. Subtle facial cues are likely to be picked up by our model. Similarly, the hands alone make relatively accurate predictions.

Table 3. Evaluation metrics for videos with one signer and videos with multiple signers. Models and evaluation metrics are as in Table 1

	DTW0	DTW5	DTW10	DTW15	AUC	Prec.	Recall	F1
Full 1 signer	0.1366	0.0959	0.0776	0.0686	**0.8876**	0.5144	**0.7456**	0.6088
Body 1 s	**0.1204**	**0.0838**	**0.0676**	**0.0601**	0.8854	**0.5611**	0.7140	**0.6284**
Full > 1 s	0.2227	0.1824	0.1562	0.1392	**0.8388**	0.4878	**0.7579**	0.5936
Body > 1 s	**0.1809**	**0.1474**	**0.1278**	**0.1156**	0.8365	**0.5622**	0.7100	**0.6275**

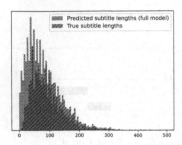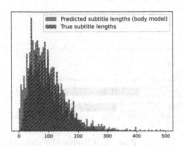

Fig. 7. Length of true SUs compared to predicted SUs

As shown in Table 3, accuracy is reduced amongst test videos with more than one signer, but the ROC-AUC statistic is still relatively high at 0.84. The DTW error rate with a window length of 15 is 12%. On videos in the test set with one signer, the ROC-AUC statistic is 0.89 and the DTW error rate with a window length of 15 frames is only 6%. This suggests that our model is robust to natural SL video, including examples of dialogue between multiple signers.

6   Conclusion

We provide baseline results for automatic segmentation of SL video into sentence-like units. We use natural SL video and allow multiple signers and camera angles. Our results are encouraging, given the variability of identification of semantic boundaries in a SL discourse across different annotators and given the fact that the SU annotations are not accurate at the frame level.

Our full model using face, body and hand keypoints has a high recall statistic but finds more SUs than necessary. We are interested to find out whether or not these additional SU boundaries correspond to semantic boundaries in the SL discourse that are not annotated by the subtitler. Further annotation of our test data would be required in order to see whether or not this is the case.

We would like to improve our model by better controlling the final distribution of the SUs. For example, we would like to be able to set priors on the duration of the SUs in order to control the length of segments and the regularity of the segmentation.

Due to the relative lack of understanding of SL grammar and the lack of a written form of SL, we are constrained to the detection of prosodic cues for this segmentation. In future work, we intend to improve detection of SUs by additionally identifying certain signs.

Acknowledgements. This work has been partially funded by the ROSETTA project, financed by the French Public Investment Bank (Bpifrance). Additionally, we thank *Média-Pi !* for providing the data and for the useful discussions on this idea.

References

1. Belissen, V., Braffort, A., Gouiffès, M.: Dicta-Sign-LSF-v2: remake of a continuous French sign language dialogue corpus and a first baseline for automatic sign language processing. In: Proceedings of the Twelfth International Conference on Language Resources and Evaluation (LREC 2020), pp. 6040–6048. European Language Resource Association (ELRA), Marseille, France, May 2020
2. Börstell, C., Mesch, J., Wallin, L.: Segmenting the Swedish sign language corpus: on the possibilities of using visual cues as a basis for syntactic segmentation. In: Beyond the Manual Channel. Proceedings of the 6th Workshop on the Representation and Processing of Sign Languages, pp. 7–10 (2014)
3. Bragg, D., et al.: Sign language recognition, generation, and translation: an interdisciplinary perspective. In: The 21st International ACM SIGACCESS Conference on Computers and Accessibility, pp. 16–31 (2019)
4. Bull, H., Braffort, A., Gouiffès, M.: MEDIAPI-SKEL - a 2D-skeleton video database of French sign language with aligned French subtitles. In: Proceedings of the Twelfth International Conference on Language Resources and Evaluation (LREC 2020), pp. 6063–6068. European Language Resource Association (ELRA), Marseille, France, May 2020
5. Chan, T., Zhu, W.: Level set based shape prior segmentation. In: 2005 IEEE Computer Society Conference on Computer Vision and Pattern Recognition (CVPR 2005), vol. 2, pp. 1164–1170. IEEE (2005)
6. Crasborn, O.A.: How to recognise a sentence when you see one. Sign Lang. Linguist. 10(2), 103–111 (2007)
7. De Beaugrande, R.: Sentence first, verdict afterwards: on the remarkable career of the "sentence". Word 50(1), 1–31 (1999)
8. Dreuw, P., Ney, H.: Towards automatic sign language annotation for the ELAN tool. In: Proceedings of the Third LREC Workshop on Representation and Processing of Sign Languages, pp. 50–53. European Language Resource Association (ELRA), Marrakech, Morocco, May 2008
9. Fenlon, J., Denmark, T., Campbell, R., Woll, B.: Seeing sentence boundaries. Sign Lang. Linguist. 10(2), 177–200 (2007)
10. Filhol, M., Hadjadj, M.N., Choisier, A.: Non-manual features: the right to indifference. In: 6th Workshop on the Representation and Processing of Sign Languages: Beyond the Manual Channel. Satellite Workshop to the 9th International Conference on Language Resources and Evaluation (LREC 2014), pp. 49–54 (2014)
11. Huang, J., Zhou, W., Zhang, Q., Li, H., Li, W.: Video-based sign language recognition without temporal segmentation. In: Thirty-Second AAAI Conference on Artificial Intelligence (2018)
12. Ko, S.K., Kim, C.J., Jung, H., Cho, C.: Neural sign language translation based on human keypoint estimation. Appl. Sci. 9(13), 2683 (2019)
13. Kolář, J., Lamel, L.: Development and evaluation of automatic punctuation for French and English speech-to-text. In: Thirteenth Annual Conference of the International Speech Communication Association (2012)
14. Koller, O., Zargaran, S., Ney, H.: Re-sign: re-aligned end-to-end sequence modelling with deep recurrent CNN-HMMS. In: 2017 IEEE Conference on Computer Vision and Pattern Recognition (CVPR), pp. 3416–3424, July 2017. https://doi.org/10.1109/CVPR.2017.364
15. Sundermeyer, M., Ney, H., Schlüter, R.: From feedforward to recurrent LSTM neural networks for language modeling. IEEE/ACM Trans. Audio Speech Lang. Process. 23(3), 517–529 (2015)

16. Veksler, O.: Star shape prior for graph-cut image segmentation. In: Forsyth, D., Torr, P., Zisserman, A. (eds.) ECCV 2008. LNCS, vol. 5304, pp. 454–467. Springer, Heidelberg (2008). https://doi.org/10.1007/978-3-540-88690-7_34

17. Yan, S., Xiong, Y., Lin, D.: Spatial temporal graph convolutional networks for skeleton-based action recognition. In: Thirty-second AAAI Conference on Artificial Intelligence (2018)

Phonologically-Meaningful Subunits for Deep Learning-Based Sign Language Recognition

Mark Borg[(✉)] [iD] and Kenneth P. Camilleri[iD]

Department of Systems and Control Engineering, University of Malta, Msida, Malta
{mark.j.borg,kenneth.camilleri}@um.edu.mt

Abstract. The large majority of sign language recognition systems based on deep learning adopt a *word model* approach. Here we present a system that works with subunits, rather than word models. We propose a pipelined approach to deep learning that uses a factorisation algorithm to derive hand motion features, embedded within a low-rank trajectory space. Recurrent neural networks are then trained on these embedded features for subunit recognition, followed by a second-stage neural network for sign recognition. Our evaluation shows that our proposed solution compares well in accuracy against the state of the art, providing added benefits of better interpretability and phonologically-meaningful subunits that can operate across different signers and sign languages.

Keywords: Sign language recognition · Gesture recognition · Deep learning · Assistive technology · Human computer interaction

1 Introduction

It is estimated that over 5% (466 million people) of the global population are deaf. When deaf people are surrounded by hearing people, including their immediate families, with little to no knowledge of sign language, it creates a situation where the deaf struggle to establish effective communication. This creates communication barriers, that can lead to problems in early language acquisition, the development of language skills, and also affecting cognitive development in the long run [49,55].

Automated sign language recognition (ASLR) is one tool, from a set of sign language related technologies [18,28], that can provide some help in 'bridging the gap' between the deaf and the hearing world. ASLR converts a sign language utterance performed by a deaf person, into its textual representation or spoken language equivalent. The current state of the art in the field of ASLR is still limited in terms of accuracy and sign language support [13,15,60]. This is mainly due to the challenging nature of signing, both in terms of vision-based perception, as well as due to the complexities of the sign languages themselves. Compared to speech recognition, the current state of the art in terms of word

© Springer Nature Switzerland AG 2020
A. Bartoli and A. Fusiello (Eds.): ECCV 2020 Workshops, LNCS 12536, pp. 199–217, 2020.
https://doi.org/10.1007/978-3-030-66096-3_15

error rate (WER) for ASLR is ≈26% [34], while for speech, the best WER stands at ≈4% [38] – this equates to roughly 1 in 4 mis-classified signs, versus 1 in 25 words for speech[1]. So having a fully-fledged, robust, and generic sign language-to-text/speech conversion tool, is still at the moment not feasible. Notwithstanding this, advancements in ASLR are progressing at a steady and encouraging pace, especially in recent years with the advent of deep learning (DL) [60].

2   Related Work

From the literature we can identify two broad approaches to performing ASLR. The first approach consists of a traditional pipeline of computer vision components, followed by a sign recognition module. The vision components typically perform body-part detection and tracking, such as the signer's hands and face [1,9,12,44,58]. Depending upon the number and choice of modalities, a set of hand-crafted features are extracted from the video stream, and these are then fed to the recognition module, typically based on hidden Markov models (HMMs) [31,48].

A common trend for these systems is the adoption of a *sub-word model* for sign recognition, in which signs are constructed from a concatenation of subunits (SUs), and recognition models, such as HMMs, trained for each SU [5,6,9,20, 42,47,48,56].

This traditional computer vision approach has seen extensive use in ASLR, with much effort dedicated to investigating different algorithms for body-part tracking, and feature selection and representation. The major challenges faced by systems adopting this approach are: dealing with the visual perception problems, as well as performing sign recognition with all the linguistic complexities that sign languages bring with them.

A more recent approach is that adopted by the DL-based systems, which have made strong inroads into the field of ASLR. DL-based systems are typically trained in an *end-to-end* fashion, with the input consisting of the raw image data [4,10,17,19,25,34,46]. The input is sometimes pre-processed to emphasise particular characteristics of the data (for example, frame differencing to highlight motion), or cropped to focus attention on the hand areas [10,26,30,45]. In these systems, features are extracted automatically by the networks rather than engineered by hand.

DL-based systems tend to outperform traditional computer vision approaches: by working holistically over the entire image, and via automatic feature learning, they are able to capture spatiotemporal context that is too complex to engineer into traditional systems [43,60]. But some drawbacks include the

---

[1] The value for speech is taken from a website which tracks the current state of the art in speech recognition on a number of standard benchmark datasets: http://github.com/syhw/wer_are_we. While the reported value for ASLR is obtained on one of the currently most challenging 'real-life' signing datasets available: http://www-i6.informatik.rwth-aachen.de/~koller/RWTH-PHOENIX/.

lack of interpretability of the model parameters ("black-box" nature of DL systems), as well as their general reliance on a *word model* approach to recognition instead of working with SUs.

A few recent ASLR works [22, 41] have adopted a hybrid DL-based approach: they combine deep neural networks with traditional computer vision or sign recognition elements. These systems do away with an end-to-end architecture in favour of a more pipelined approach. For example DL methods are used to determine the signer's pose in terms of body keypoints (or skeleton models), and then these are used as input 'features' for upstream recognition components (which could consist of DL-based or traditional recognition algorithms) [41]. In this way, DL is leveraged to tackle the perception-related challenges, which is something it excels at, and at the same time, some form of control is maintained on the type of 'features' used by the system rather than relying completely on fully automated feature extraction of end-to-end systems. Only limited work has been done so far using this hybrid approach.

Like Gattupalli et al. [22] and Metaxas et al. [41], we adopt a pipelined DL approach, rather than opt for an end-to-end architecture. But in contrast to these two works, our proposed system can use DL for both the visual perception part and the sign recognition part of the system. A main reason for adopting a pipelined DL approach is to increase the interpretability of the system.

As described earlier, practically all DL-based systems work with word models rather than with SUs. To the best of our knowledge, the only exceptions are the works of Camgöz et al. [10], and Metaxas et al. [41].

Like them, we adopt a SU based approach. But unlike these works, which only generate an implicit set of SUs, our novel SUs are explicitly defined, and we show that they are also phonologically meaningful.

Adopting a SU approach offers a number of advantages: since the set of SUs is much smaller than the number of words, less training data is needed. This is of particular relevance to deep networks that require large training sets, without which they can easily *overfit*. Other advantages include better scaling to larger lexica, more robustness to out-of-vocabulary (OOV) signs, and that more complex sign language understanding (for example, decoding the layered meanings of inflected signs, or handling classifier constructions) would not be possible with word-level DL systems.

In the rest of this paper we describe our contributions: (1) novel use of a structure from motion (SfM) factorisation technique to derive hand motion features for use within our pipelined DL system. When these hand motion features are embedded within a trajectory space, we show that semantic meaning is preserved. (2) a novel choice of SUs for use within our DL-based system. We demonstrate that these SUs are phonologically meaningful.

3   Our Approach

In this section, we describe our proposed ASLR system, which is illustrated in Figs. 1 and 2. We adopt a SU-based approach to recognition, unlike the majority of DL-based systems that work with word models. We also employ a non end-to-end learning approach, and instead utilise hand features embedded within a trajectory space, since we find that this endows our SUs with phonological meaning, making them both data driven as well as semantically meaningful.

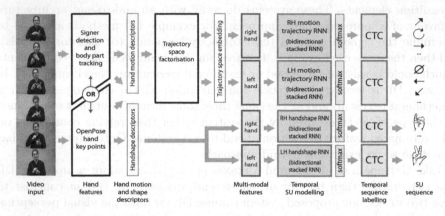

Fig. 1. Our SU RNN-based recognition system. As input, our system can utilise hand features obtained either via a traditional computer vision pipeline, or hand features obtained via a DL-based system. Regardless of the choice of input features, hand motion and handshape descriptors are extracted, and the hand motion descriptors are embedded in a trajectory space via trajectory-space factorisation [3]. These are then fed to the corresponding SU recurrent neural network (RNN). Finally, connectionist temporal classification (CTC) layers provide phonologically-meaningful SU labels.

Figure 1 depicts the four SU networks running in parallel and taking as input the chosen hand features and outputting sequences of SU symbols describing the motions and handshapes of the two hands of the signer. We adopt a parallel approach in order to better handle the multi-modal and concurrent characteristics prevalent in signing activity [21]. Once successfully trained, these four SU networks are then combined together with a second-level network for sign recognition, as shown in Fig. 2.

To the best of our knowledge, the only other DL-based works that focus on SUs are those of Camgöz et al. [10], and Metaxas et al. [41]. Camgöz et al. [10] make use of two SU-based networks, trained in an end-to-end fashion. They use whole image frames and pre-cropped hand patches (fixed-size sub-images centred on the hands) respectively as input to their SU networks: the first network learns an implicit intermediate representation (the 'full frame SUs'), while the second network learns handshape SUs. Once trained, their two SU networks are combined together, and then the resulting system is trained for sign recognition.

Similar to Camgöz et al. [10], our system learns handshape SUs and hand motion hand motion SUs. But unlike their work, we do not perform end-to-end training of the network, instead using hand features embedded within a trajectory space as input. As a result our SUs carry phonological information, while

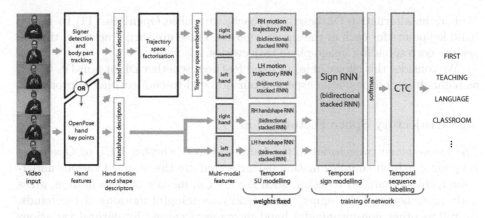

Fig. 2. Extending our SU RNN-based system (of Fig. 1) for sign recognition. The output of the SU RNNs are concatenated together and fed to a second-level RNN for sign recognition.

those of Camgöz et al. [10] are data-driven (video sequence specific), intrinsic, and lack interpretability (particularly for the case of the full-frame network).

Our SUs resemble in principle Metaxas et al.'s [41] choice of linguistically-motivated input features. They estimate the 3D body pose using convolutional pose machines, and from the pose they derive hand-crafted features such as an indicator of whether a sign is 1-handed or 2-handed, as well as 'contact' flags indicating if a hand is visually close to or touching a key body part (e.g. chin, shoulders, etc.). But then unlike our RNN-based system, Metaxas et al. [41] use a classical method for recognition, a conditional random field (CRF), and reserve the DL techniques solely for the extraction of the pose and pose-related features. And a limitation of their approach is that it works only for isolated sign recognition.

3.1 Hand Features

In our ASLR system, the input features can come from either a traditional computer vision pipeline, or from a DL-based system.

For the former case, we employ a face detector [59] for signer localisation and signing space determination. This is followed by hand region detection within the signing space area based on skin colour and motion cues, obtained using an adaptive skin colour model [57] and multi-frame differencing [27] respectively. Kanade-Lucas-Tomasi (KLT) features [50] are then extracted from the hand regions, grouped together based on motion similarity [14], and tracked in time via the use of the multiple hypothesis tracking (MHT) algorithm [7]. The resulting hand features thus consist of two sets of KLT feature points, one set for each hand of the signer, and their corresponding image-plane trajectories as they are tracked in time [8].

For the alternative DL-based approach, we utilise OpenPose [11] to get 20 hand keypoints for each of the signer's hands. These are then tracked in time to get the corresponding image-plane trajectories.

We consider this choice of input hand features, whether DL or non-DL based, as highlighting one versatile aspect of our non end-to-end learning approach.

3.2   Trajectory Space Factorisation

The image-plane trajectories of the hand features (whether KLT or OpenPose keypoints) exhibit complex motion patterns that are the result of various underlying factors entangled together: such factors can include camera motion, gross body movements of the signer, semantically-meaningful motions of the hands, as well as other non-meaningful hand movements caused by natural variations in articulation, inter-signer variations, dialects, disfluencies and noise.

To separate the real hand motions from the camera and whole body movements of the signer, we propose to use a non-rigid structure from motion (NRSfM) technique based on the *factorisation method* [54]. Furthermore, we interpret the motion patterns of the hands themselves during signing as constituting 'deformations' of the visible shape of the signer.

The 2D image plane trajectories of the features of hand h_i, over a temporal window of length Δt, are centred on the signer's torso, and arranged into the matrix $\mathbf{W} \in \mathbb{R}^{2\Delta t \times P}$, where P is the number of hand features. Then a trajectory space factorisation algorithm [3] is used to separate $\mathbf{W}$ into a product of 3 submatrices:

$$\mathbf{W} = \mathbf{R}\mathbf{S} = \mathbf{R}\mathbf{\Theta}\mathbf{A} \tag{1}$$

where matrix $\mathbf{R}$ describes the camera and the signer's whole body movements (rotations), while matrix $\mathbf{S}$ describes the 3D shape of the signer, in this case the varying 3D shape and orientation of the hands with respect to the centroid of the signer's torso over the time window.

As given in Eq. 1, the deformable shape $\mathbf{S}$ can be represented as a weighted linear combination of a trajectory basis in a low-rank trajectory space, with $\mathbf{\Theta}$ being the trajectory basis, while $\mathbf{A}$ contains the weight coefficients. As suggested by Akhter et al. [3], we choose the discrete cosine transform (DCT) basis for $\mathbf{\Theta}$, because it is ideal for representing smooth motions and because of its energy compaction properties. Thus for a single hand feature i, we have:

$$S_i = \sum_j^K a_{j,i}\,\theta_j, \quad \theta_j \in \mathbb{R}^{3\times\Delta t},\ a_{j,i} \in \mathbb{R} \tag{2}$$

where S_i is the 3D trajectory of the ith hand feature, θ_j is the jth DCT basis, K is the rank of the DCT basis, and $a_{j,i}$ is the corresponding weight coefficient of basis θ_j and hand feature i.

Traditionally factorisation algorithms run in batch mode, with matrix $\mathbf{W}$ set to the full duration of a video sequence. We adapt the trajectory space factorisation algorithm of Akhter et al. [3] to run in an online mode. We do this by adopting a sliding window approach and setting the window length Δt to

0.5 s, determined to being roughly the shortest duration for a single sign. For the sliding window at time t, any missing entries in matrix $\mathbf{W}(t)$ (for example, caused by tracking failures, hand occlusion, or missed hand keypoint detection), are filled via the column space fitting (CSF) matrix completion algorithm [53].

And since the shape and motion recovered by the factorisation method are unique up to a scale and a rotation [3], we align matrices $\mathbf{R}(t)$ with $\mathbf{R}(t-1)$ and $\mathbf{S}(t)$ with $\mathbf{S}(t-1)$ for each successive sliding window using the Procrustes superimposition method [2].

3.3   Trajectory Space Embedding of the Hand Motion Descriptors

Given the recovered motion patterns of the hand features of the signer via the factorisation method, we now use their embedding in the trajectory space as a basis for our choice of SUs. The embedding in trajectory space is given by the DCT coefficients $a_{j,i}$ of Eq. 2 (or as grouped together in matrix $\mathbf{A}$ of Eq. 1).

Further analysis of these DCT coefficients across different signers and sign languages reveal that similar motion patterns of the hands exhibit consistent and unique patterns in trajectory space leading us to conclude that this trajectory space embedding of the hand features preserves semantic meaning. This is also corroborated by 2D visualisations of the trajectory space coefficients obtained via the t-distributed stochastic neighbour embedding (t-SNE) algorithm [39], like the one shown in Fig. 3.

We generate five number summary (FNS) statistics for the DCT coefficients of the hand features and use these hand motion descriptors as input vectors to our hand motion trajectory RNNs (see Fig. 1).

3.4   Handshape Descriptors

We derive the 2D handshape descriptors directly from the hand features of Sect. 3.1 on a per-frame basis. The same set of descriptors are used for both the traditional computer vision pipeline as well as for the OpenPose module. These consist of the bounding box, best-fit ellipse, major axis orientation, aspect ratio, circularity, and convexity measures. For the OpenPose module, we also concatenate the normalised hand keypoints themselves to the handshape descriptors, since these represent salient hand features, in contrast to the arbitrariness of the KLT features of the traditional computer vision pipeline.

3.5   Subunit RNNs

The hand motion and handshape descriptors of the previous sections serve as the inputs to our SU-level RNNs. We use separate networks for the hands of the signer, and for the handshape and hand motion SUs.

We select gated RNNs for our networks, and evaluate the use of both long short-term memorys (LSTMs) and gated recurrent units (GRUs) in our experiments. We employ stacked bidirectional versions of these RNNs, combining the

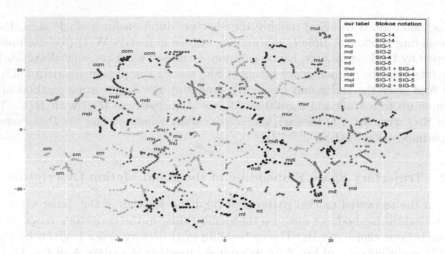

Fig. 3. 2D visualisation (t-SNE) of the trajectory space coefficients and their corresponding SU labels, performed across different signers and sign languages (German sign language (DGS) utterances from the RWTH-Phoenix Weather dataset [35] and Dutch sign language (NGT) utterances from the ECHO NGT dataset [16]). Transitional movements are not labelled. The SU labels follow the Stokoe phonological model [52].

output of the constituent forward and backward layers via vector concatenation. Bidirectional RNNs prove to be better at modelling the temporal nature of our SUs. We use *dropout* within the RNNs, as this is an essential element for preventing overfitting, especially when training the networks with small to medium-sized datasets. We finish off our system by adding a CTC framework [24] for the temporal sequence learning of the SUs, as shown in Fig. 1. And we adopt Stokoe's phonological model [52] for the SU class labels.

3.6   The Connectionist Temporal Classification (CTC) Framework

We add a CTC framework to our system in order to handle the *temporal sequence labelling problem*: while an RNN performs framewise classification, the RNN's output has no clear one-to-one mapping with the target sequence (the SU sequence), the two sequences are often not of the same length, and the mapping itself is often ambiguous in nature [23, §2].

A number of ASLR works use a combination of RNNs and HMMs as an alternative to the CTC framework [34,36,37]: while an RNN provides the framewise class labels, the HMM learns the long-range mappings between the framewise labels and the target labels, since its states can by design "absorb" multiple inputs. But since this method relies on a two-step approach that is iterated several times, it can be sensitive to starting conditions, with accuracy prone to oscillating between iterations.

In contrast, the CTC framework combines the temporal sequence labelling problem directly with the RNN's recognition problem, by defining a CTC loss function that can be incorporated directly within the training mechanism of the RNN, and back-propagated through the network via backpropagation through time (BPTT). In this way, the RNN receives an error for misaligned sequences, even when it predicts the correct labels, and it can learn how to correct for it.

The CTC framework has been used successfully by a number of ASLR works [10,17,46], and we follow their lead and employ CTC within our networks.

3.7 Sign-Level RNN

So far, our proposed ASLR system consists of four separate RNNs, trained to recognise hand motion and handshape SUs. In order to perform sign recognition, we now combine the networks into one system as shown in Fig. 2. This approach is similar in idea to the one employed by Camgöz et al. [10].

We remove the CTC and softmax layers of the trained SU RNNs, freeze their weights, and add a new bidirectional stacked RNN that takes as its input the following feature vector:

$$f_{input} = f_{rh\_motion\_su} \oplus f_{lh\_motion\_su} \oplus f_{rh\_handshape\_su} \oplus f_{lh\_handshape\_su} \quad (3)$$

where $\oplus$ represents the concatenation operation of vectors. This new RNN together with an associated CTC framework is used to perform sign recognition, producing a sequence of sign glosses as output.

3.8 Training Strategy for Our ASLR System

When training our system, we face the challenge that framewise groundtruth labels at SU level is lacking, a common occurrence in the field of ASLR. In the absence of proper groundtruth, we adopt a *weakly supervised* learning strategy for our RNNs, utilising the limited data available to guide the training process.

We utilise simple SU classifiers based on gradient boosting machines (GBMs) [8] that can be trained quickly and with a fraction of the data needed for deep networks. These serve as a source of weakly labelled data, thus providing us with the SU labels and their temporal order. Equipped with such data, weakly supervised training of our networks can proceed via the use of the CTC framework, which allows them to learn to recognise SUs, while at the same time learning to align the input data with the weak labels.

A number of works [17,33,34] employ weakly supervised learning for sign recognition. Of these works, the training method of Cui et al. [17] is the most similar to ours. They adopt a three-stage training strategy for their convolutional neural network (CNN)-LSTM based system: first performing end-to-end training of the whole system using weak labels, followed by fine-tuning of the CNN feature extractor on its own, and finally fine-tuning of the LSTM via CTC. Since Cui et al. [17] have only access to an ordered list of signs as groundtruth, with no alignment information, they initialise their training using a "flat start" approach – the input data is partitioned into equal-sized segments corresponding to the list of groundtruth signs.

We adopt a similar multi-stage training strategy. But in contrast to Cui et al. [17], we do not initialise our training with a "flat start" approach. Since we also have access to "rough" segmentation from the simple SU classifiers, we use this as alignment data to initialise the training.

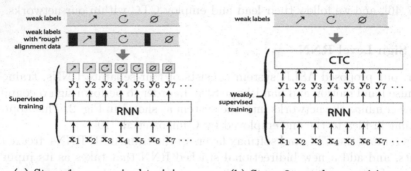

(a) Stage 1 - supervised training   (b) Stage 2 - weak supervision

Fig. 4. Our two-stage training strategy. (A) During the first stage, alignment data is used to train the system in supervised mode. The alignment data is subject to segmentation errors (boundary uncertainty indicated by the broad dashed regions), but framewise labels can still be derived from it. (B) Weakly supervised training is performed in stage 2 to refine the RNN weights.

Figure 4 illustrates our training strategy: we first perform supervised learning of the RNN layers (without the CTC layer), using the weak framewise labels generated by the simple SU classifiers. We use early stopping with a high threshold during this training stage, so that the RNN is close to but does not converge fully. We observe that this stage helps the system to achieve a better initialisation of the layer weights, when compared to a "flat start" approach.

We then add back the CTC layer and continue with weakly supervised training using the SU labels and their temporal order (but with no alignment data). During this stage, the CTC framework helps to fine-tune the weights, improving upon the SU recognition and alignments obtained in the first stage. Training in this stage continues till the network is fully converged.

4 Experiments

We now describe the experiments performed to evaluate our proposed ASLR system. Figure 5 shows the implemented network that we use. The RNN gate type, number of layers, and hidden units are determined via ablation studies, the results of which are not included here due to space limitations. For the CTC part of the network in Fig. 5, the CTC loss and analysis layers are only used during training and evaluation of the validation loss, and ignored otherwise. The CTC decoding layer is configured to use beam search decoding, with the beam width set to 100.

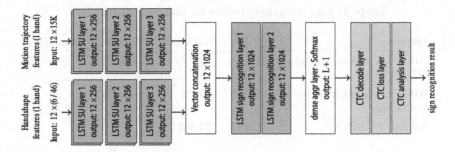

Fig. 5. Implementation of our RNN sign recognition system. In the above figure, K is the number of trajectory bases, while L represents the vocabulary size. The timesteps parameter of the RNNs is set to 12; thus the input to the network is $T \times V = 12 \times V$, where V is the size of the input feature vector.

We initialise the RNN model weights using *He normal* initialisation [29]. Training for both the strongly supervised and weakly supervised stages operate with roughly the same configuration: we use *mini-batch stochastic gradient descent (SGD)* with *Adam* as the optimisation algorithm [32]. For configuring the mini-batch size and the learning rate, we employ a training schedule inspired by the findings and recommendations of Masters and Luschi [40], and Smith et al. [51]. Training of the RNNs proceeds for 500 epochs, with *early stopping* if there is no further improvement in the loss function over 10 consecutive epochs. The loss function employed depends on whether we are doing weakly supervised training (CTC loss is selected), or whether doing strongly supervised training (cross-entropy loss selected).

The datasets available for training the networks at both SU level and sign level, are not balanced in terms of class instances. This is especially true for the handshape SUs and for signs of the RWTH-Phoenix Weather dataset [35]. For example, the ratio of the rarest handshape to the most frequent handshape is of around 0.0007. Because of this strong imbalance, we opted not rely on data augmentation or class re-balancing techniques. Instead, we apply weight corrections to the gradient updates of the SGD algorithm, to compensate for class imbalance – this mechanism adjusts the contribution of each update depending on the how frequent training examples of that particular class are.

5   Results

This section presents the results for the sign recognition experiments, starting with the results of an investigation into the contributions of the hand motion and handshape modalities, for the setup given in Fig. 2. The RWTH-Phoenix Weather dataset [35] is used in these experiments, because its large lexicon provides for a realistic evaluation (1230 unique signs), it is multi-signer (9 signers), and has become a standard benchmarking dataset. WER and word accuracy are used as evaluation metrics.

Table 1. Sign recognition results for different modalities.

Modality	WER ↓	Accuracy ↑	Accuracy difference
RH + LH motion trajectory SU RNNs only	0.446	55.4%	−16.5%
RH + LH handshape SU RNNs only	0.703	29.7%	−42.2%
All four SU RNNs	**0.281**	**71.9%**	–

Table 2. Sign recognition results with different hand features as input.

Input hand features	Ins	Del	Sub	WER ↓	Accuracy ↑
Computer vision pipeline (KLT features)	439	387	1763	0.398	60.2%
DL-based module (OpenPose keypoints)	221	655	953	**0.281**	**71.9%**

Table 1 shows that both hand motion and handshape modalities are important for sign recognition, with the hand motion SU RNNs contributing the most, compared to handshape RNNs – leaving out the hand motion RNNs, results in a reduction of 42.2% in accuracy, while removing the handshape RNNs, reduces accuracy by a smaller margin of 16.5%. While a majority of signs can be discriminated solely based on the gross hand motion trajectory, there are a number of signs (*minimal pairs*) whose appearances differ only by their handshapes. Hence while handshape on its own is a poor discriminator, in conjunction with hand motion, it allows the sign-level RNN to achieve a better recognition rate than with hand motion alone.

Table 2 gives the results when using different types of hand features as input.

Figure 6 presents some qualitative results. Sign alignments are included for illustration purposes only, and are not evaluated since we lack groundtruth – these alignments are extracted directly from the softmax output layer (see Fig. 5). Sign evaluation is performed via the CTC analysis layer and reported in terms of insertions, deletions and substitutions.

Each example of Fig. 6(A) to (E) is performed by a different signer. For example in (C), the sign 'REGEN' is mistaken for a different sign. This is mainly due to sign variations that do not appear within the training set, e.g., hands moving out of sync with each other in this particular case. Figure 7 shows more examples for sign 'REGEN' which are classified correctly, and others which are misclassified. The canonical sign consists of the two hands moving in unison downwards once or multiple times, and exhibiting handshape DEZ-5. Sign variations include: one-handed versions, out-of-sync movements, shortened movements, and varying hand orientations. Despite all these variations, the RNN does a relatively good job at learning the variations, with some exceptions – WER for this sign is 0.85 (25 substitutions, 18 deletions, 0 insertions, out of a total of 290 instances in the test fold).

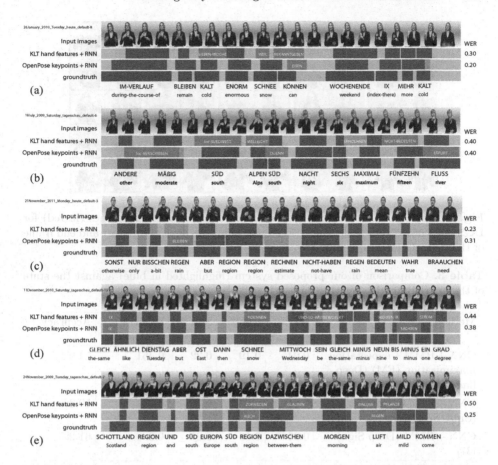

Fig. 6. Qualitative sign recognition results. Groundtruth is depicted in blue, substitution errors in red, insertion errors in orange, and deletions in dark gray. (Color figure online)

We now compare our sign recognition results against the state of the art – this is given in Table 3. The RWTH-Phoenix Weather dataset comes with the training, validation, and test folds pre-defined, thus ensuring a fair comparison.

We can observe that our system outperforms many of the recent DL-based systems, except for the work of Koller et al. [34]. The difference in accuracy between their work and ours is of 1.3%. And the difference between our work and the rest of the systems is of 10.2%.

While Koller et al.'s system [34] does better than ours, it is trained in an end-to-end fashion. It takes the full video frame as input, and uses a CNN for automatic feature extraction. In contrast, our system makes use of trajectory space SUs that are phonologically meaningful, and our RNN-based system is trained on these SUs.

Fig. 7. Examples of correct matches (outlined in green) and mismatches (in red) for DGS sign "REGEN" (English, 'rain'). Each pair of images depicts the start and end frame of the sign. (Color figure online)

Table 3. Comparison of our proposed system (highlighted in blue) against the state of the art (PHOENIX Weather dataset).

Method	Ins %	Del %	Sub %	WER ↓ (test fold)	Accuracy ↑
CNN + HMM + expectation maximisation (EM) (Deep hand) [33]	0.04	0.19	0.22	0.451	54.9%
CNN + LSTM + CTC (SubUNets) [10]	0.04	0.15	0.22	0.407	59.3%
CNN + HMM (Deep Sign) [37]	0.05	0.13	0.21	0.388	61.2%
CNN + LSTM + CTC [17]	0.08	0.12	0.19	0.387	61.3%
Hierarchical attention networks [30]	–	–	–	0.383	61.7%
Our DL-based system	**0.03 (221)** [†]	**0.10 (655)**	**0.15 (953)**	**0.281**	**71.9%**
CNN + RNN method (Re-Sign) [34]	–	–	–	**0.268**	**73.2%**

[†] Numbers in brackets specify the numbers of insertions, deletions, and substitutions. We convert these to percentage values for the purpose of comparison with other works.

We thus argue that our approach provides a number of benefits, including that of better interpretability, albeit at a relatively small cost in accuracy reduction.

6   Conclusions

In this paper we have described a two-stage DL-based ASLR system. Our system takes as input hand features derived from either a traditional computer vision pipeline or a from hand keypoints obtained via OpenPose. A trajectory space factorisation method is then applied to extract the hand motions and these are embedded within a low-rank trajectory space. We demonstrated how this trajectory space embedding preserves semantic meaning, allowing us to base our choice of SUs on descriptors derived from the embedding coefficients. These descriptors are then fed to our SU RNNs for training, utilising a CTC framework to handle the temporal sequence labelling problem. Once the SU RNNs are trained, a second-level RNN is added for sign recognition.

We performed a number of investigations, first to choose between various design options for the RNNs, and then to evaluate the sign recognition accuracy of our system. We compared the results with the state of the art, where we found that our system surpasses ($\geq 10.2\%$) many of the recent works that employ DL in ASLR. Only one recent work performs marginally better (1.3%) than our proposed system. But we argue that our system offers other benefits, such as phonologically-meaningful SUs and better interpretability.

Future work will look at extending the SU RNNs to handle other modalities, including non-manual signals such as facial expressions and mouthings. We will also investigate how our choice of phonologically meaningful SUs operate across different signers and different sign languages.

References

1. von Agris, U., Knorr, M., Kraiss, K.: The significance of facial features for automatic sign language recognition. In: Proceedings of the 8th International Conference on Automatic Face & Gesture Recognition (FG). IEEE (2008)
2. Akhter, I., Sheikh, Y., Khan, S., Kanade, T.: Nonrigid structure from motion in trajectory space. In: Koller, D., et al. (eds.) Advances in Neural Information Processing Systems (NIPS), p. 41. Curran Associates Inc. (2009)
3. Akhter, I., Sheikh, Y., Khan, S., Kanade, T.: Trajectory space: a dual representation for nonrigid structure from motion. IEEE TPAMI **33**(7), 1442–1456 (2011)
4. Avola, D., Bernardi, M., Cinque, L., Foresti, G.L., Massaroni, C.: Exploiting recurrent neural networks and leap motion controller for the recognition of sign language and semaphoric hand gestures. IEEE Trans. Multimedia **21**, 234–245 (2018)
5. Awad, G., Han, J., Sutherland, A.: Novel boosting framework for subunit-based sign language recognition. In: Proceedings of the ICIP, pp. 2729–2732. IEEE (2009)
6. Bauer, B., Karl-Friedrich, K.: Towards an automatic sign language recognition system using subunits. In: Wachsmuth, I., Sowa, T. (eds.) GW 2001. LNCS (LNAI), vol. 2298, pp. 64–75. Springer, Heidelberg (2002). https://doi.org/10.1007/3-540-47873-6_7
7. Blackman, S.S.: Multiple hypothesis tracking for multiple target tracking. IEEE Aero. Electron. Syst. Mag. **19**(1), 5–18 (2004)

8. Borg, M., Camilleri, K.P.: Towards a transcription system of sign language video resources via motion trajectory factorisation. In: Proceedings of the 2017 ACM Symposium on Document Engineering, DocEng 2017, pp. 163–172. ACM, New York (2017). https://doi.org/10.1145/3103010.3103020

9. Bowden, R., Windridge, D., Kadir, T., Zisserman, A., Brady, M.: A linguistic feature vector for the visual interpretation of sign language. In: Pajdla, T., Matas, J. (eds.) ECCV 2004. LNCS, vol. 3021, pp. 390–401. Springer, Heidelberg (2004). https://doi.org/10.1007/978-3-540-24670-1_30

10. Camgöz, N.C., Hadfield, S., Koller, O., Bowden, R.: SubUNets: end-to-end hand shape and continuous sign language recognition. In: Proceedings of the ICCV. IEEE, October 2017

11. Cao, Z., Hidalgo, G., Simon, T., Wei, S.E., Sheikh, Y.: OpenPose: realtime multi-person 2D pose estimation using Part Affinity Fields. In: arXiv preprint 1812.08008 (2018)

12. Charles, J., Pfister, T., Magee, D., Hogg, D., Zisserman, A.: Upper body pose estimation with temporal sequential forests. In: Proceedings of the BMVC (2014)

13. Cheok, M.J., Omar, Z., Hisham Jaward, M.: A review of hand gesture and sign language recognition techniques. Int. J. Mach. Learn. Cybernet. 10 (2017). https://doi.org/10.1007/s13042-017-0705-5

14. Choi, S., Kim, T., Yu, W.: Performance evaluation of RANSAC family. In: Proceedings of the BMVC (2009)

15. Cooper, H., Holt, B., Bowden, R.: Sign language recognition. In: Moeslund, T.B., et al. (eds.) Visual Analysis of Humans - Looking at People, pp. 539–562. Springer, London (2011). https://doi.org/10.1007/978-0-85729-997-0_27. No. 231135

16. Crasborn, O., et al.: ECHO Data Set for Sign Language of the Netherlands (NGT) (2004)

17. Cui, R., Liu, H., Zhang, C.: Recurrent convolutional neural networks for continuous sign language recognition by staged optimization. In: Proceedings of the CVPR, pp. 1610–1618. IEEE, July 2017. https://doi.org/10.1109/CVPR.2017.175

18. Efthimiou, E., et al.: Sign Language technologies and resources of the Dicta-Sign project. In: Proceedings of the International Conference on Language Resources and Evaluation (LREC), RPSL Workshop. ELRA (2012)

19. Fang, B., Co, J., Zhang, M.: DeepASL: enabling ubiquitous and non-intrusive word and sentence-level sign language translation. In: Proceedings of the 15th ACM Conference on Embedded Network Sensor Systems (SenSys). ACM (2017). https://doi.org/10.1145/3131672.3131693

20. Farag, I., Brock, H.: Learning motion disfluencies for automatic sign language segmentation. In: International Conference on Acoustics, Speech and Signal Processing (ICASSP), pp. 7360–7364, May 2019. https://doi.org/10.1109/ICASSP.2019.8683523

21. Fenlon, J., Cormier, K., Brentari, D.: The Phonology of Sign Languages, pp. 453–475. Routledge (2017). https://doi.org/10.4324/9781315675428

22. Gattupalli, S., Ghaderi, A., Athitsos, V.: Evaluation of deep learning based pose estimation for sign language recognition. In: Proceedings of the 9th International Conference on PErvasive Technologies Related to Assistive Environments (PETRA). ACM (2016)

23. Graves, A.: Supervised Sequence Labelling with Recurrent Neural Networks. Studies in Computational Intelligence, vol. 385. Springer, Heidelberg (2012). https://doi.org/10.1007/978-3-642-24797-2

24. Graves, A., Fernández, S., Gomez, F.: Connectionist temporal classification: labelling unsegmented sequence data with recurrent neural networks. In: Proceedings of the International Conference on Machine Learning (ICML), pp. 369–376 (2006)
25. Guo, D., Tang, S., Wang, M.: Connectionist temporal modeling of video and language: a joint model for translation and sign labeling. In: Proceedings of the 28th International Joint Conference on Artificial Intelligence, IJCAI. pp. 751–757 (2019)
26. Guo, D., Zhou, W., Li, H., Wang, M.: Hierarchical LSTM for sign language translation. In: Proceedings of the 32nd AAAI Conference on Artificial Intelligence, pp. 6845–6852 (2018)
27. Guo, J., Wang, J., Bai, R., Zhang, Y., Li, Y.: A new moving object detection method based on frame-difference and background subtraction. IOP Conf. Ser. Mater. Sci. Eng. **242**(1), 012115 (2017)
28. Hanson, V.L.: Computing technologies for deaf and hard of hearing users. In: Sears, A., Jacko, J.A. (eds.) Human-Computer Interaction: Designing for Diverse Users and Domains, chap. 8, pp. 885–893. Taylor & Francis Group (2009). https://doi.org/10.1201/9781420088885
29. He, K., Zhang, X., Ren, S., Sun, J.: Delving deep into rectifiers: surpassing human-level performance on ImageNet classification. In: Proceedings of the ICCV, pp. 1026–1034 (2015). https://doi.org/10.1109/ICCV.2015.123
30. Huang, J., Zhou, W., Zhang, Q., Li, H., Li, W.: Video-based sign language recognition without temporal segmentation. In: 32nd Conference on Artificial Intelligence (AAAI), pp. 2257–2264. AAAI (2018)
31. Kelly, D., McDonald, J., Markham, C.: Recognition of spatiotemporal gestures in sign language using gesture threshold HMMs. In: Wang L., Zhao G., Cheng L., Pietikäinen M. (eds.) Machine Learning for Vision-Based Motion Analysis. Advances in Pattern Recognition, pp. 307–348. Springer, London (2011). https://doi.org/10.1007/978-0-85729-057-1_12
32. Kingma, D.P., Ba, J.: Adam: a method for stochastic optimization. In: ICLR 2015, p. 13 (2015)
33. Koller, O., Ney, H., Bowden, R.: Deep hand: how to train a CNN on 1 million hand images when your data is continuous and weakly labelled. In: Proceedings of the CVPR, pp. 3793–3802. IEEE, June 2016. https://doi.org/10.1109/CVPR.2016.412
34. Koller, O., Zargaran, S., Ney, H.: Re-sign: re-aligned end-to-end sequence modelling with deep recurrent CNN-HMMs. In: Proceedings of the CVPR, pp. 3416–3424. IEEE, July 2017. https://doi.org/10.1109/CVPR.2017.364
35. Koller, O., Forster, J., Ney, H.: Continuous sign language recognition: towards large vocabulary statistical recognition systems handling multiple signers. Comput. Vis. Image Underst. **141**, 108–125 (2015)
36. Koller, O., Zargaran, S., Hermann, N., Bowden, R.: Deep sign: enabling robust statistical continuous sign language recognition via hybrid CNN-HMMs. Int. J. Comput. Vis. **126**(12), 1311–1325 (2018)
37. Koller, O., Zargaran, S., Ney, H., Bowden, R.: Deep sign: hybrid CNN-HMM for continuous sign language recognition. In: Proceedings of the BMVC (2016)
38. Lüscher, C., et al.: RWTH ASR systems for LibriSpeech: hybrid vs attention. In: Proceedings of the Interspeech 2019, pp. 231–235 (2019). https://doi.org/10.21437/Interspeech.2019-1780
39. van der Maaten, L., Hinton, G.: Visualizing high-dimensional data using t-SNE. J. Mach. Learn. Res. **9**, 2579–2605 (2008)

40. Masters, D., Luschi, C.: Revisiting small batch training for deep neural networks. CoRR (2018)
41. Metaxas, D., Dilsizian, M., Neidle, C.: Linguistically-driven framework for computationally efficient and scalable sign recognition. In: Calzolari, N., et al. (eds.) Proceedings of the 11th International Conference on Language Resources and Evaluation (LREC). ELRA (2018)
42. Oszust, M., Wysocki, M.: Modelling and recognition of signed expressions using subunits obtained by data–driven approach. In: Ramsay, A., Agre, G. (eds.) AIMSA 2012. LNCS (LNAI), vol. 7557, pp. 315–324. Springer, Heidelberg (2012). https://doi.org/10.1007/978-3-642-33185-5_35
43. Panzner, M., Cimiano, P.: Comparing hidden Markov models and long short term memory neural networks for learning action representations. In: Pardalos, P.M., Conca, P., Giuffrida, G., Nicosia, G. (eds.) MOD 2016. LNCS, vol. 10122, pp. 94–105. Springer, Cham (2016). https://doi.org/10.1007/978-3-319-51469-7_8
44. Pfister, T., Charles, J., Everingham, M., Zisserman, A.: Automatic and efficient long term arm and hand tracking for continuous sign language TV broadcasts. In: Proceedings of the BMVC (2012)
45. Pigou, L., Herreweghe, M.V., Dambre, J.: Gesture and sign language recognition with temporal residual networks. In: Proceedings of the ICCV Workshops, pp. 3086–3093, October 2017. https://doi.org/10.1109/ICCVW.2017.365
46. Pu, J., Zhou, W., Li, H.: Dilated convolutional network with iterative optimization for continuous sign language recognition. In: Proceedings of the 27th International Joint Conference on Artificial Intelligence (IJCAI 2018), pp. 885–891 (2018)
47. Pu, J., Zhou, W., Zhang, J., Li, H.: Sign language recognition based on trajectory modeling with HMMs. In: Tian, Q., Sebe, N., Qi, G.-J., Huet, B., Hong, R., Liu, X. (eds.) MMM 2016. LNCS, vol. 9516, pp. 686–697. Springer, Cham (2016). https://doi.org/10.1007/978-3-319-27671-7_58
48. Sako, S., Kitamura, T.: Subunit modeling for japanese sign language recognition based on phonetically depend multi-stream hidden Markov models. In: Stephanidis, C., Antona, M. (eds.) UAHCI 2013. LNCS, vol. 8009, pp. 548–555. Springer, Heidelberg (2013). https://doi.org/10.1007/978-3-642-39188-0_59
49. Schirmer, B.R.: Psychological, Social, and Educational Dimensions of Deafness. Allyn & Bacon, Boston (2001)
50. Shi, J., Tomasi, C.: Good features to track. In: Proceedings of the CVPR, pp. 593–600 (1994)
51. Smith, S.L., Kindermans, P.J., Le, Q.V.: Don't decay the learning rate, increase the batch size. In: International Conference on Learning Representations (2018)
52. Stokoe, W.C.: Sign language structure. Ann. Rev. Anthropol. **9**(1), 365–390 (1980). https://doi.org/10.1146/annurev.an.09.100180.002053
53. Sun, Z.L., Fang, Y., Shang, L., Zhu, X.G.: A missing data estimation approach for small size image sequence. In: 5th International Conference on Intelligent Control and Information Processing, pp. 479–481. IEEE, August 2014
54. Tomasi, C., Kanade, T.: Shape and motion from image streams under orthography: a factorization method. Int. J. Comput. Vis. **9**(2), 137–154 (1992)
55. Van Staden, A., Badenhorst, G., Ridge, E.: The benefits of sign language for deaf learners with language challenges. Per Linguam **25**(1), 44–60 (2009)
56. Vogler, C., Goldenstein, S.: Toward computational understanding of sign language. In: Technology and Disability, vol. 20, pp. 109–119. IOS Press (2008)
57. Wimmer, M., Radig, B.: Adaptive skin color classificator. In: Proceedings of the 1st ICGST International Conference on Graphics, Vision and Image Processing (GVIP), pp. 324–327 (2005)

58. Yang, R., Sarkar, S., Loeding, B.: Handling movement epenthesis and hand segmentation ambiguities in continuous sign language recognition using nested dynamic programming. IEEE TPAMI **32**(3), 462–477 (2010)
59. Zhang, K., Zhang, Z., Li, Z., Qiao, Y.: Joint face detection and alignment using multitask cascaded convolutional networks. IEEE Signal Process. Lett. **23**(10), 1499–1503 (2016)
60. Zheng, L., Liang, B., Jiang, A.: Recent advances of deep learning for sign language recognition. In: International Conference on Digital Image Computing: Techniques and Applications (DICTA), November 2017

Recognition of Affective and Grammatical Facial Expressions: A Study for Brazilian Sign Language

Emely Pujólli da Silva[1(✉)], Paula Dornhofer Paro Costa[1],
Kate Mamhy Oliveira Kumada[2], José Mario De Martino[1],
and Gabriela Araújo Florentino[3]

[1] University of Campinas, Campinas, Brazil
emelypujolli@gmail.com, {paulad,martino}@unicamp.br
[2] Federal University of ABC, Santo André, Brazil
[3] Seli Institute, São Paulo, Brazil

Abstract. Individuals with hearing impairment typically face difficulties in communicating with hearing individuals and during the acquisition of reading and writing skills. Widely adopted by the deaf, Sign Language (SL) has a grammatical structure where facial expressions assume grammatical and affective functions, differentiate lexical items, participate in syntactic construction, and contribute to intensification processes. Automatic Sign Language Recognition (ASLR) technology supports the communication between deaf and hearing individuals, translating sign language gestures into written or spoken sentences of a target language. The recognition of facial expressions can improve ASLR accuracy rates. There are cases where the absence of a facial expression can create wrong translations, making them necessary for the understanding of sign language. This paper presents an approach to facial recognition for sign language. Brazilian Sign Language (Libras) is used as a case study. In our approach, we code Libras' facial expression using the Facial Action Coding System (FACS). In the paper, we evaluate two convolutional neural networks, a standard CNN and hybrid CNN+LSTM, for AU recognition. We evaluate the models on a challenging real-world video dataset of facial expressions in Libras. The results obtained were 0.87 f1-score average and indicated the potential of the system to recognize Libras' facial expressions.

Keywords: Facial action unit recognition · Non-manual markers · Libras · Sign language

1 Introduction

Sign Languages (SLs) are visuospatial linguistic systems structured on gestures that are adopted around the world by deaf people to communicate. Analogously to spoken languages, SLs emerged spontaneously, evolved naturally, reflecting the worldwide sociocultural differences and giving origin to a wide range of variations such as the British Sign Language (BSL), the American Sign Language (ASL),

© Springer Nature Switzerland AG 2020
A. Bartoli and A. Fusiello (Eds.): ECCV 2020 Workshops, LNCS 12536, pp. 218–236, 2020.
https://doi.org/10.1007/978-3-030-66096-3_16

the Chinese Sign Language (CSL), the Brazilian Sign Language (Libras), among others.

Being a minority language in most territories, deaf individuals frequently need a sign language interpreter in their access to school and public services. In such scenarios, the absence of interpreters typically results in discouraging experiences, even in educational deficits, preventing the inclusion of deaf individuals in society. In other situations, such as health care, the need for a sign language interpreter can be embarrassing or a risk factor for urgent care.

Aiming to overcome existing obstacles in the communication between hearing and deaf people, in the last decade, many efforts have been dedicated to the development of Automatic Sign Language Recognition (ASLR) technology [40, 43,54,61]. ASLR systems recognize and translate sign language content in video into text. Optionally, the text output can be the input of a Text-To-Speech (TTS) synthesizer, resulting in a translation from source sign language to target spoken language.

Together with hand gestures and other non-manual markers, a key challenge in the development of ASLR technologies is the modeling and classification of facial expressions.

In SLs, more than communicating affective states, facial expressions represent morphemes, that fulfill syntactic and pragmatic functions. For this reason, the problem of recognizing facial expressions in SL context, can be considered more complex than the typical affective computing problem. In fact, facial expressions of emotions represent only a subset of common existing facial expressions in sign languages (Fig. 1). Also, more recently, researchers have argued that the recognition of facial expressions can improve ASLR accuracy rates [1,55].

The present work adopts a deep neural network architecture to recognize SL facial expressions coded as Action Units (AUs) of the Facial Action Coding System (FACS) [9]. Although some works implement AU recognition systems, their application unrelated to emotions is scarce [35]. Taking Brazilian Sign Language (Libras) as our case study, we coded Libras' facial expressions using FACS and we adapted existing network architectures to be more generic in the recognition of action units other than emotional AUs. While state-of-the-art AU classification works only handled eight to twenty AU labels [7,27,48,68], our experiment considers 80 categories, derived from a comprehensive facial expression survey

Fig. 1. Examples of facial expressions in sign language that are not associated to the expression of emotions. The Libras' signs "Motel" and "Skinny" are respectively portrayed in the images [49].

in Libras. Our resulting classification accuracy is competitive with the literature results and with improved generalization ability.

The paper is organized as follows. In Sect. 2, we discuss the state-of-the-art of Facial Expression Recognition (FER), and systems that are based on AU recognition. In Sect. 3, we summarize the role of facial expressions in Libras. Also, their FACS association is introduced. The methodology of our approach is presented in Sect. 4. The experimental results are shown in Sect. 5. We end by considering the implications of our findings in Sect. 6.

2   Related Work

Facial Expression Recognition (FER) has been studied for decades and many approaches have been proposed [10,41]. There are two main approaches to FER. One considers the AUs as the features to be recognized in the face [3]. The second regards a set of prototypical facial expression of emotion defined by Paul Ekman (1993)[8], as the characteristics to be identified.

Due to the availability of facial expression information and data type from the affective perspective, it is more frequently encountered the second FER strand where only emotional labels are considered [34,39,59]. A large number of surveys in Emotional Facial Expression Recognition (EFER) have been published over the years [25,47] and lately, well-design network architectures have achieved better accuracy and exceeded previous results [31,63]. Such architectures are composed with decision tree, naive Bayes, multilayer neural networks and K-nearest neighbours, hidden Markov model (HMM), shallow networks, and deep neural networks [31,62,63].

In SL, there are not enough researches that associated non-manuals markers with FACS. Most of the works that carry a non-manual marker recognition scheme treats the facial expression by creating their classes of facial actions [60]. A comprehensive survey of AU analysis can be found in Martinez *et al.* (2017) [35]. AU recognition can also be applied in intelligent vehicle systems that detect and recognize the facial motion and appearance changes occurring during drowsiness [56]. Moreover, the sensitivity of FACS to subtle expression differences shows its capability and application in the medical field as descriptive of characteristics of painful expressions [30], depression, or to examine evoked and posed facial expressions in schizophrenia patients [16].

Recently, the use of CNN-based representations has been adopted to model facial actions [6]. Walecki *et al.* (2017) [57] proposed a convolutional neural network (CNN) model jointly with a Conditional Random Field structure to ease the inference. In Tran *et al.* (2017)[29], the second layer is conditioned to the latent representation from the first layer, in other words, a two-layer latent space is learned. Although these models are accurate, they have slow performance. Also, like most works, these models generally need a feature extraction step [46]. In Li *et al.* (2017)[26] the Visual Geometry Group (VGG) network is first used with region learning and a fully connected long short-term memory (LSTM) network to obtained features in the task of AU detection, resulting in a complex system. Other recent works have attempted a hybrid approach, by combining AU relations through either generative approaches or discriminative approaches [18]. However, like most works they still try to learn a global representation from the input image [46]. In Chu *et al.* (2019)[7], the presented hybrid network takes advantage of spatial CNNs, temporal LSTMs, and their fusions to achieve multi-label AU detection. The performance over 12 AUs from the BP4D dataset average F1 score of 82.5 with a 10-fold protocol.

The lack of sufficient details (e.g., parameter optimization strategy, preprocessing procedure, training, and testing protocols) makes it difficult to compare some different AU recognition methodologies, even on the same dataset. With the purpose of standardization for a fair comparison, challenges arose. Held for this purpose, FERA (Facial Expression Recognition and Analysis challenge) and EmotioNet challenges evaluated AUs recognition and discrete emotion recognition. The last EmotioNet 2017 challenge involved AUs occurrence detection for 11 AUs. The top algorithm used residual blocks and a sum of binary cross-entropy loss (PingAn-GammaLab) and achieved 94.46% accuracy [68]. The baseline results for the challenge was 80.7% accuracy using Kernel Subclass Discriminant Analysis (KSDA) [3].

The main novelty of our proposed approach resides in the joint region detection of AU and analysis of AU presence. In our framework, we perform a feature extraction stage and a task learning problem. The first architecture builds on a standard CNN. The second one was built upon an ensemble of CNN and LSTM. Differentiated from works where the whole face is used for AU intensity estimation and localization, our approach treats the problem by delimiting face regions in the presence or absence of AU to overcome the greater number of AU available on our sign language application.

3   Facial Expressions in Libras

Most SLs in the world can be considered understudied, meaning that aspects of their grammar and morphology are still undocumented or unknown. Also, compared to spoken languages, there is a lack of annotated SL corpora, a key input for supervised machine learning modeling.

In this scenario, a first contribution of the present work was, with the help of sign language linguists specialists, to conduct a detailed survey of existing facial expressions in Libras, and to code them using FACS.

In Libras, facial expressions that convey an idea of feeling and emotion are called Affective Facial Expressions (AFE). Affective facial expressions may start before a specific sign and end after the sentence has been completed. In other words, AFEs modulate the whole sentence, modifying the full meaning of a sequence of signs. AFEs are adopted, for example, when the signer communicates ideas sarcastically or when he/she is describing a sad event. A visual characteristic of AFEs is that they employ an integrated set of facial muscles.

Grammatical Facial Expressions (GFE) in Libras are expressions that typically occur at specific points of a sentence or are associated to a specific sign execution [14]. Observing the different properties of grammatical facial expressions we categorize them into Grammatical Facial Expression for Sentence (GES), Grammatical Facial Expressions of Intensity (GEI), Grammatical Facial Expressions of Homonymy (GEH) and Grammatical Facial Expressions of Norm (GEN).

GES defines the type of sentence that is being signed [50]. Accordingly with the structure and information of the sentence, it can be classified into: WH-question (WH), Yes/No question (YN), Doubt question (DQ), Topic (T), Negative (N), Affirmative (A), Conditional clause (CC), Focus (F) and Relative clause (RC). In Libras, there are GES markers that are expressed by the face and head movements.

GEI differentiates the meaning of the sign assuming the role of a quantifier. For example, the same sign associated with the word "expensive" can have its meaning attenuated to "little expensive" or "very expensive", depending on the signer's facial expression. In Fig. 2(C), (D) and (G), we show frames of those signs.

Also, without its characteristic GEH a sign is incomplete and cannot be distinguished from other signs with the same manual signal. In other words, GEHs helps to define the meaning of a sign. For example, in the Fig. 2(B) and (F), we have the representation of two signs with different meanings, in which the manual sign is the same, but the facial expression is different.

The facial expressions that are part of the signal by norm and whose function is to complete a manual signal, we define as the GEN. When a GEN sign is performed without the facial expression that defines it, the signal loses its meaning.

It is possible to notice that many of the non-manual articulators found in Libras are also used in other sign languages [11,50]. For example, Yes/No questions in American SL (ASL) are associated with raised eyebrows, head tilted forward and widely-opened eyes, and WH-questions with furrowed eyebrows and head forward. Topics are described by raised eyebrows and head slightly back, and negatives are expressed with a head shake [1,28]. In the German SL (DGS), a change of head pose combined with the lifting of the eyebrows, corresponds to a subjunctive. Lip pattern, tongue, and cheeks that are not related to the articulation of words can provide information redundant to gesturing to support differentiation of similar signs [55]. Thus, these facial expressions function intersections reinforce the ability to generalize an application in Libras to other sign languages.

3.1 Coding Libras' Facial Expressions Using FACS

The lack of pattern in the description of facial expressions in Libras and in SLs in general, becomes a major problem to implement a computational recognition problem. Our approach consisted of coding the Libras' facial expressions using the facial action coding system [9]. FACS describe face muscle variations through 52 action units (AUs), that can occur alone or in combination. Table 1 presents this novel coding of Libras' Facial Expressions using FACS.

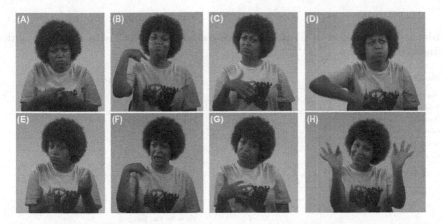

Fig. 2. In the performance of the signs in Libras, we can analyze the variation of the facial expressions by the images (A) and (E), where we have examples of grammatical facial expressions of sentence - GES. In the image (A), the interpreter is signing "why?" and in (E) she is signing "how?". In images (B) and (F), the signs "lawyer" and "crazy" are performed with the same manual gesture. Their difference is only based on the eyes, eyebrows action, and on the mouth open, which is an example of the grammatical expression of distinction - GED. Also, in images (C), (D), and (G), the interpreter performed the sign "expensive", "very expensive", and "little expensive", respectively. The intensity of the sign is displayed by the change in the facial expression, which passed from neutral (C) to frown and inflated cheeks (D), or to frown and crocked mouth down (G). Those are examples of grammatical facial expressions of intensity-GEI. In the last picture (H), the interpreter shows the sign "happy", which is accompanied by a characteristic affective facial expression - AFE.

Due to our limited access to examples of all Libras facial expression, we focus our model on the listed GES class. Likewise, for the AFE class, we adopt the prototypical seven basic emotions: happiness, sadness, surprise, fear, anger, disgust, contempt, as reported in the literature. This assumption is possible since studies show that basic emotions are used and recognized by the Deaf to convey affective states [19,23,42].

Note in Table 1, that the number of AUs that participate in the performance of the basic emotions (16) is at least two times lower than the number of AUs that are found in Libras facial expressions (39). Libras' facial expressions contain and transcend the regular set of AUs attributed to basic emotions.

4   Methodology

Our methodology consisted of, first, building a database of videos of deaf individuals and Libras interpreters. The facial expressions present in the videos were annotated using FACS (Sect. 4.1).

Second, we implemented a feature extraction process, responsible for creating the inputs to the evaluated networks (Sect. 4.2).

Table 1. Classification of libras facial expressions associated with the facial action coding system

Facial Expression in Libras	FACS	Muscular / Action Description
Upper face		
Joined eyebrows	AU1	Inner brow raiser
Raised eyebrows	AU1+AU2	Inner brow raiser and outer brow raiser
Frown	AU4	Brow Lowerer
Wide open eyes	AU5	Upper Lid Raiser
Nose wrinkle	AU9	Nose Wrinkler
Slightly closed eyes	AU41	Lid droop
	AU42	Slit
Closed eyes	AU45	Eyes closed
Left / Right eye closed	AU46	Wink
Direct the eyes	AU61	Eyes to the left
	AU62	Eyes to the right
	AU63	Eyes up
	AU64	Eyes down
Lower face		
Crooked mouth up	AU12	Lip corner puller
Crooked mouth down	AU15+AU17	Lip corner depressor and chin raiser
Projected lips	AU18+AU23	Lip Puckerer and lip tightener
Tongue in lisp position		
Swinging alveolar tongue	AU19	Tongue show
Sibilant tongue		
Tip of the tongue touching the lips		
Contracted lips	AU28	Lip suck
Open mouth	AU25	Lips apart
	AU26	Jaw drop
Inflated cheeks	AU33	Cheek blow
semi-open mouth (blowing)	AU34	Cheek puff
Contracted cheeks	AU35	Cheek suck

(Left margin vertical label: S i m p l e E x p)

Grammatical Facial Expressions of Sentence

WH-Question	AU4+AU53	Brief and upward movement of the head and frown
	AU4+AU18+AU23+AU53	Tilt back, frown and projected lips.
Y/N Question	AU1+AU2+AU53	Brief and upward movement of the head and raised eyebrows
	AU4+AU18+AU23	Tilt to the side, frown and projected lips
	AU4+AU18+AU51+AU52	Balancing sideways, frown and projected lips
Negative	AU15+AU17	Crooked mouth down
	AU4+AU15+AU17+AU54	Quick nod, frown and crooked mouth down
	AU51+AU52	Head balancing sideways
Affirmative	AU53+AU54	Balance back and forth of the head

Affective Facial Expressions

Basic Emotions	AU6+AU12	Happiness
	AU1+AU4+AU15	Sadness
	AU4+AU5+AU7+AU23	Anger
	AU1+AU2+AU5B+AU26	Surprise
	AU1+AU2+AU5+AU20+AU26	Fear
	AU1+AU4+AU5+AU7	
	AU9+AU15+AU16	Disgust
	R12A+R14A	Contempt

(Left margin vertical labels: C o m p o u n d   E x p r e s s i o n s)

Finally, we proposed and evaluated two different deep neural network architectures (Sects. 4.3 and 4.4).

4.1   HM-LIBRAS Database

Our first prototype, the Head Movement in Libras (HM-Libras) database was built using parts of videos from the Internet of deaf individuals and sign language interpreters [51]. We downloaded videos distributed under the Creative Commons license, using different combinations of search keywords: Libras, questions, grammar, answer. Specifically, we target phrases with grammatical facial expressions for sentence. They were not chosen at random, but with the advice of a Libras expert, in such a way that these sentences represent a range of communication elements of the language. The HM-Libras database is composed of 80 FACS labeled videos being: 20 videos with statements, 20 videos with WH-questions, 20 videos with Yes/No questions and 20 videos with negation sentences.

We collected videos where the person starts facing straight to the camera to facilitate face detection. These videos are not always professionally curated and often suffer from perceptual artifacts, varying in illumination, and background. The set of videos has the presence of three women and seven men. In addition, HM-Libras includes a dataset matrix composed of facial points detected using Dlib [21]. The dataset is made available to all interested researchers upon request to the authors.

In summary, HM-Libras was created with the concept of studying head movement in Libras that occurs in the performance of certain types of sentences, where each frame was annotated by a single FACS coder.

4.2   Feature Extraction

We extracted 68 landmarks localized on the face placed alongside the ears, chin, eyes, nose and mouth (Fig. 3A) using DLib [21]. We resized the face images to 96×96 after cropping the face areas. In sign language, one has also to take into consideration the possible partial or total occlusion of the face as a result of the position and the movement of the hands. When that occurs we decide to remove the frames, to keep some continuity. The lost of face tracking happened in 3% of the entire database.

Following these steps, we choose to segment the face into two sets, a lower portion of the face comprehending the chin, mouth, and nose, as well as the upper portion of the face comprehending the forehead, eyebrows, and eyes. This region related approach is adopted to increase the system activity sensitivity.

Given that the displacement of landmarks points is a measurable way to describe facial expression, we argue that the use of geometrical features could improve performance on models designed to learn AU classification. We add the geometric characteristics using the landmarks positions and by calculating some distances. As one can notice, AUs are measured by a change in face configuration. Thereby calculating the distance between the middle point in the lid tightener

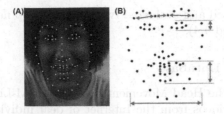

Fig. 3. A prototypical face mask is presented in (A) with white points $p_i = (x_i, y_i)$, $i = 1, \ldots, 68$. In (B) we mark with red line the chosen distances d_2 for measuring configuration of eyebrows, eyes and mouth. Images created for the research itself.

in the eyes can indicate if the eyes are open or closed (Fig. 3B). Likewise, for the mouth, we calculate the distance between the midpoints of the upper and lower lip. Each of these measurements was converted into a single gray pixel. In other words, we compose vectors with the face points p_i, $i = 1, \ldots, 68$ and the distance measures $d_2(p_j, p_k)$ with $(j, k) \in \{(3, 13), (17, 21), (21, 22), (22, 26), (38, 40), (43, 47), (48, 54), (51, 57), (62, 66)\}$, that later were scaled to the range $0 - 1$ and then encoded as gray levels. Finally, these levels are concatenated in the images respectively to the region of the face that belongs (see Fig. 4A).

4.3 CNN Based FACS Classification

Based on Keras implementation [4], a CNN model was built following existing approaches [39,44]. In Pramerdorfer *et al.* (2016)[44] the architectures of a shallow CNN outperform modern deep CNNs. We use the information that a CNN with five hidden layers is already able to learn high-level discriminatory features to design our network. The model consists of a CNN where the image is passed through a stack of three convolutional layers. We use filters with a small kernel field: 2×2 for all convolutional layers, which can be seen as a linear transformation of the input channels followed by non-linearity. The convolution stride is fixed to one; the spatial padding of convolutional layer input is such that the spatial resolution is preserved after convolution, i.e., the filling is one pixel for 2×2 convolutional layers. Spatial pooling is carried out by two Max-Pooling layers, which follow the two first convolutional layers. Max-pooling is performed over a 3×3 window, with stride two. The last of convolutional layers is followed by three fully-connected layers: the first has 4096 channels, the second has 1024 channels and, the third can perform a 30-way AU classification or 50-way AU classification depending on the architecture. In the final layer, we use the softmax layer and thus contains 30 or 50 labels, one for each class whether it is for the upper part of the face or for the lower part of the face, respectively. The activation functions are all set to ReLu (Rectified Linear Functions). The configuration model and other details are shown in Fig. 4B.

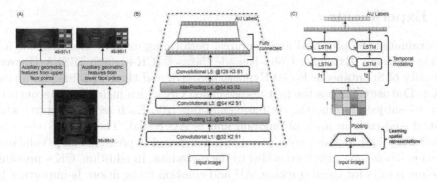

Fig. 4. Input image, CNN architecture and CNN+LSTM architecture. In the image (A), we present the input for our networks. The face image is cropped and later combined with extracted points from the face and their distances. In image (B), we present the architecture of our CNN, consisting of one input layer, three convolution layers, two max pooling layers, and two full connection layer. In image (C), we present the structure of the proposed hybrid network, where the input layer is feed into a convolutional neural network which is followed by a pooling layer that connects to an LSTM. Detailed descriptions are given in the text. Images created for the research itself.

4.4 CNN+LSTM for AUs Classification

Since AUs are an observable event throughout time, learning the recognition of facial expressions can be improved by the knowledge of previous states. Naturally, we extended our system to address temporal context by designing a combination of both CNN and LSTM to fuse static features with temporal cues, inspired by [7, 26, 38].

More specifically, we propose a standard CNN with three convolutional layers alternated by two max-pooling layers. The convolutional layers are composed with a kernel of size three and stride one. The first two convolutional layers have 32 filters and the last one has 64 filters. The max-pooling layers have a stride of size two. All activation functions are set as ReLU. The last layer is the region pooling layer. We model the correlations between spatial and temporal cues by adding a fusion layer. This fusion layer is a concatenation of feature maps, made to get regional features. So, from the CNN we have a pooling layer with 50 filters for the upper part of the face and 30 filters for the lower part of the face. These feature maps, are fed into stacks of LSTMs to fuse temporal dependency. We combine two frames of images as sequence into the LSTM. Then several stacks of LSTMs are used to capture facial actions temporal dependence. Finally, the outputs of LSTMs are aggregated into a dense layer to perform multi-label learning. In Fig. 4C we present a scheme of CNN+LSTM network architecture.

5 Experiments

We evaluated the proposed architectures, performing experiments with the following datasets: Extended Cohn-Kanade dataset (CK+) [32], DISFA (Denver Intensity of Spontaneous Facial Expressions) [37], and the HM-Libras database. **CK+ Dataset** [32] has the first release called CK which includes 486 sequences from 97 subjects posing the six basic emotions [20]. Each sequence starts with neutral and ends in apex of emotion and is AU coded. The second release is called CK+ and includes both posed and non-posed expressions [32]. Validated emotion labels have also been added to the metadata. In addition, CK+ provides baseline results for facial tracking, AU and emotion recognition. Is important to remark that the AU annotations were given at video and not frame wise.

DISFA Dataset. [37] is a spontaneous database composed by videos of 27 subjects that vary in age from 18 to 50 years. The subjects are filmed while reacting to an emotional four-minute video stimuli. Also, it comprehends the manually labeled frame-based annotations of 5-level intensity of twelve FACS, labeled by two FACS coders. The lack of available data for comparing posed and spontaneous expression encouraged the same research group, to construct the Extended DISFA Dataset (DISFA+) [36], which contains the videos and AU annotations of posed and spontaneous facial expressions of 9 participants in the same format as DISFA.

Note that, DISFA and CK+ are standard datasets for AU detection where the AU correspond with the Libras' affective facial expressions class. Also, to the best of our knowledge, HM-Libras is the first Libras database with AU annotations. The combination of such datasets helped in diversifying training samples necessary in the sign language application, despite containing different sets of AUs.

For our first experiment, we choose to separate a percentage of HM-Libras database for testing, and the rest we combine with CK+ and DISFA databases to form the training set. Our train set was composed by 69624 frames and the test set was composed by 7736 frames. To demonstrate the effectiveness of the proposed model to the Libras application, extensive experiments have been conducted on our already described networks using a subject independent and cross databases approach.

Metrics. The performance of AU detection was evaluated on F1 frame-basic metric, the average accuracy, precision, and recall [6,22,65].

Comparative Methods. For a thorough comparison, we selected two popular deep network architectures that were designed and trained on ImageNet, and have been successfully applied to multiple vision problems: AlexNet [24] and VGG-16 [53]. To adapt both networks for our classification model, we modify the input and the output layer. The input layer was adjusted to accommodate images with a size of $60 \times 96 \times 3$. Also, the output layer was arranged to exit 30 labels for the upper part of the face and 50 labels for the lower part of the face. As a baseline, these networks were trained only with the same images, without geometric face information.

Unlike the common practice in AU literature [5,17,27,45,66,67], where only 12 AUs are considered for a single dataset, our research encompass 39 AUs that are descriptive in Libras. The increased number of AUs makes difficult to fairly compare our approach with the state-of-art.

Implementation Details. We train every architecture for up to 300 epochs and a fixed mini-batch size of 500 samples. Both models were initialized with a learning rate of 0.01, optimizing the cross-entropy loss using stochastic gradient descent (SGD) with a momentum of 0.9 and weight decay of 0.001. Simard *et al.* (2003) [52] have shown that if the data is augmented in a reasonable way, the model can perform better. For training data augmentation we use horizontal mirroring, randomly rotations and two types of shift and zoom transformations. These are applied indiscriminately in each epoch creating twice the amount of data.

All experiments are performed on a PC with one NVIDIA GTX 1070 GPU. It took roughly 160 h to train each network until convergence that happened around 250 epochs.

Results and Discussion

Comparison Between Existent Architectures. Table 2 shows the F1 metrics reported on AlexNet, VGG-16, CNN, and CNN+LSTM. Also, "Avg." for the mean score of both face parts. According to the results, both of our networks CNN and CNN+LSTM outperformed AlexNet and VGG-16 when trained with a cross-dataset and subject independence. In addition to the improvement by considering a shallow system, the performance gain of CNN can also be assigned to the usage of geometric features. These observations provide an evidence that the learned representation was transferable even when being tested across subjects and datasets.

CNN+LSTM performs a spatiotemporal fusion which consistently outperformed AlexNet and VGG-16 in all metrics. Our hybrid network uses small time steps window as we want to avoid the suppression of properly detected but short temporal series of AU activation, yet, if the temporal length of AU duration is short, then the CNN+LSTM model could not observe such actions [33]. In general, adding temporal information helped predicting AUs, but a more extensive study in the time steps sizes could be beneficial.

It can be seen that our CNN+LSTM does not bring a lot of gain over our CNN. Surprisingly, for the upper part of the face, we obtain 0.90 of accuracy while in the lower part of the face 0.85 of accuracy in the CNN. The average accuracy for our AU classification using the CNN is 0.88. The value is comparable to other published results [6,15,58,64].

Another way to compare our models' effectiveness is to use an off the shelf AU regressor. OpenFace [2] is an analysis platform capable of face detection and recognize a subset of AUs, specifically: 1, 2, 4, 5, 6, 7, 9, 10, 12, 14, 15, 17, 20, 23, 25, 26, 28, and 45. Setting an experiment where the 80 categories are produced in post prediction and on our test set, the report results are 0.208 avg accuracy and 0.212 for f1-score outcomes considerably lower than the results obtained by our models.

Table 2. Performance comparison of proposed methods with state-of-the-art networks

Architecture	Description	Accuracy	F1	Precision	Recall
AlexNet	Upper face	0.7322	0.7219	0.8565	0.6295
	Lower face	0.6723	0.6639	0.8027	0.5719
	Avg.	0.7022	0.6929	0.8296	0.6007
VGG-16	Upper face	0.6199	0.6199	0.6199	0.6199
	Lower face	0.4800	0.4800	0.4800	0.4800
	Avg.	0.5499	0.5499	0.5499	0.5499
CNN	Upper face	0.9018	0.8900	0.8972	0.8194
	Lower face	0.8585	0.8522	0.8892	0.8091
	Avg.	**0.8805**	**0.8711**	**0.8932**	**0.8142**
CNN+LSTM	Upper face	0.8828	0.8182	0.8714	0.7685
	Lower face	0.8541	0.7047	0.8174	0.6697
	Avg.	0.8684	0.7614	0.8444	0.7191

Moreover, models for AU classification handled typically only eight to twenty AU labels, while our experiment considers 80 categories (including compound expressions), which is much more challenging and realistic compared to many existing methods. Generally, our method explicitly inherits the advantage of information gathered from multiple local regions from complex AU acting as a deep feature ensemble in both architectures, and hence it naturally improves the recognition of simple AUs.

Comparison with Manual Transcription. We compare our CNN AU detection framework with the human transcription of Libras' grammatical syntactic functions and affective facial expressions in Table 3. The human ratings are given by the labeling agreement scores that were obtained by comparing the annotation between two coders. At the same time, the automatic AU detection ratings are collected by comparing the transcription between the CNN framework output and the two coders. The agreement measure chosen was Fleiss' kappa [12], which ranges from −1 to 1. The negative values indicate randomness in labeling or poor agreement; while the values in $0 - 0.2$ indicate slight agreement; between $0.21 - 0.4$, fair agreement; between $0.41 - 0.6$, moderate agreement; between $0.61 - 0.8$, substantial agreement; and, lastly, between $0.81 - 1$, perfect agreement. Kappas coefficients were calculated for five videos from the Sign Language Facial Action (SILFA) corpus [49]. SILFA contains videos of deaf interpreters signing in Libras and is transcribed with facial expressions classes and syntactic functions as defined in Table 1 where the labeling were made by two linguistics Libras experts.

In our approach, we consider the facial occlusion in sign language by annotation, i.e., by the usage of FACS visibility codes. Thereby, when the algorithm cannot detect the face, the output is the visibility code AU74, which means unscorable. However, if the occlusion is due to the hand being in front of the face, and consequentially, occluding the facial expression, the framework output is AU73, which translates to the entire face not visible. The fourth and fifth columns of Table 3 presents the occlusion agreement rates as almost perfect confidence for the human annotation and slight/fair confidence for our framework. Our CNN AU detection framework using geometric and region of interest features outputs obtained fair/moderate confidence when compared to humans. Moreover, when averaging our prediction with the manual annotations, the performance can be further improved. This implies that learning Libras' facial expressions as a function of simple and compound AUs may be a more accurate and systematic way than learning facial expressions from the whole face. Also, in Freitas *et al.* (2017)[13] is presented a model for recognition of grammatical facial expressions of sentence in Libras with shallow structure. Still, it uses only landmarks to predict automatically with a Multi-layer Perceptron, where achieved F-scores over 80% for most of their experiments. By comparison, our CNN AU detection model outperforms Freitas *et al.*(2017)[13], demonstrating the potential of our ensemble detection model if the AU prediction stage is improved.

Table 3. Agreement coefficient for comparison with manual annotation and automatic Libras' AU detection framework

Sentence type	Transcription type		Visibility code	
	Human annotation	Our AU detection framework	Human annotation	Our AU detection framework
WH-Question	0.82	0.33	0.81	0.20
Yes/No Question	0.75	0.30	0.80	0.20
Negation	0.86	0.45	0.82	0.12
Affirmation	0.77	0.29	0.84	0.22
Affective	0.60	0.24	0.78	0.26

6 Conclusions

The first contribution present in this paper is a novel model for recognition of grammatical and affective facial expressions in Brazilian Sign Language. Based on the literature, we construct a CNN and a hybrid CNN LSTM, which consisted of a feature extraction process where we segmented the face into the upper and lower part, creating two resembling networks that were trained in multiple databases. When compared with facial expression recognition works, we found similar results, although our model has capabilities of classification on more AUs labels. Secondly, was the construction of a database with Libras signers' fully annotated with FACS, the HM-Libras database. Also, a detailed survey of existing facial expressions and their syntactic functions in Libras were compiled. To facilitate and support further studies, we establish an association between the Facial Action Coding System and the listed Libras facial expressions. The action unit codification made it possible to observe that the number of facial expressions portrayed in Libras is superior to the prototypical emotion expressions evaluated in the literature.

When discussing our networks' accuracy performance, the interdisciplinary nature, and the amplitude of our study regarding AU recognition should be taken into account. Our built CNN presents an average accuracy of 0.88 by performing facial action unit classification in face images in terms of 80 compound facial actions, suggesting that our model gives some insight into AUs who are not usually included in other studies.

Given this comprehensiveness presented, our model can be generalized to other applications. Also, we can infer that the more significant number of compound AU influenced positively in recognition of simple AUs by analyzing our results. Though it is quite acceptable, the performance of the presented method can be improved in several respects: (1) our proposed method cannot encode the full range of Libras facial behavior; (2) the different characteristics actions between the upper part and the lower part of the face is not contemplate by our network architecture. Further efforts will be required if these limitations are to be addressed. Besides, it will be interesting to test the proposed method with a substantially extensive database.

Acknowledgement. This paper and the research behind was financially supported by the Coordination for the Improvement of Higher Education Personnel (CAPES).

References

1. Antonakos, E., Roussos, A., Zafeiriou, S.: A survey on mouth modeling and analysis for sign language recognition. In: 2015 11th IEEE International Conference and Workshops on Automatic Face and Gesture Recognition (FG), vol. 1, pp. 1–7. IEEE (2015)
2. Baltrusaitis, T., Zadeh, A., Lim, Y.C., Morency, L.P.: Openface 2.0: facial behavior analysis toolkit. In: 2018 13th IEEE International Conference on Automatic Face and Gesture Recognition (FG 2018), pp. 59–66. IEEE (2018)
3. Benitez-Quiroz, C.F., Srinivasan, R., Feng, Q., Wang, Y., Martinez, A.M.: Emotionet challenge: Recognition of facial expressions of emotion in the wild (2017)
4. Chollet, F., et al.: Keras: The python deep learning library. Astrophysics Source Code Library (2018)
5. Chu, W.S., De la Torre, F., Cohn, J.F.: Modeling spatial and temporal cues for multi-label facial action unit detection. arXiv preprint arXiv:1608.00911 (2016)
6. Chu, W.S., De la Torre, F., Cohn, J.F.: Learning spatial and temporal cues for multi-label facial action unit detection. In: 2017 12th IEEE International Conference on Automatic Face and Gesture Recognition (FG 2017), pp. 25–32. IEEE (2017)
7. Chu, W.S., De la Torre, F., Cohn, J.F.: Learning facial action units with spatiotemporal cues and multi-label sampling. Image Vis. Comput. **81**, 1–14 (2019)

8. Ekman, P.: Facial expression and emotion. Am. Psychol. **48**(4), 384 (1993)
9. Ekman, P., Friesen, W.V.: Manual for the facial action coding system. Consulting Psychologists Press (1978)
10. Fasel, B., Luettin, J.: Automatic facial expression analysis: a survey. Pattern Recogn. **36**(1), 259–275 (2003)
11. Felipe, T.A.: The verbalvisual discourse in Brazilian sign language-libras. Bakhtiniana: Revista de Estudos do Discurso, **8**(2) (2013)
12. Fleiss, J.L., Cohen, J.: The equivalence of weighted kappa and the intraclass correlation coefficient as measures of reliability. Educ. Psychol. Meas. **33**(3), 613–619 (1973)
13. Freitas, F.A., Peres, S.M., Lima, C.A., Barbosa, F.V.: Grammatical facial expression recognition in sign language discourse: a study at the syntax level. Inf. Syst. Front. **19**(6), 1243–1259 (2017)
14. Freitas, F.A., Peres, S.M., de Moraes Lima, C.A., Barbosa, F.V.: Grammatical facial expressions recognition with machine learning. In: FLAIRS Conference (2014)
15. Gudi, A., Tasli, H.E., Den Uyl, T.M., Maroulis, A.: Deep learning based facs action unit occurrence and intensity estimation. In: 2015 11th IEEE International Conference and Workshops on Automatic Face and Gesture Recognition (FG), vol. 6, pp. 1–5. IEEE (2015)
16. Hamm, J., Kohler, C.G., Gur, R.C., Verma, R.: Automated facial action coding system for dynamic analysis of facial expressions in neuropsychiatric disorders. J. Neurosci. Methods **200**(2), 237–256 (2011)
17. Han, S., Meng, Z., Li, Z., O'Reilly, J., Cai, J., Wang, X., Tong, Y.: Optimizing filter size in convolutional neural networks for facial action unit recognition. In: Proceedings of the IEEE Conference on Computer Vision and Pattern Recognition, pp. 5070–5078 (2018)
18. Hao, L., Wang, S., Peng, G., Ji, Q.: Facial action unit recognition augmented by their dependencies. In: 2018 13th IEEE International Conference on Automatic Face and Gesture Recognition (FG 2018), pp. 187–194. IEEE (2018)
19. Hosie, J., Gray, C., Russell, P., Scott, C., Hunter, N.: The matching of facial expressions by deaf and hearing children and their production and comprehension of emotion labels. Motiv. Emot. **22**(4), 293–313 (1998)
20. Kanade, T., Tian, Y., Cohn, J.F.: Comprehensive database for facial expression analysis. In: fg, p. 46. IEEE (2000)
21. King, D.E.: Dlib-ml: a machine learning toolkit. J. Mach. Learn. Res. **10**, 1755–1758 (2009)
22. Koelstra, S., Pantic, M., Patras, I.: A dynamic texture-based approach to recognition of facial actions and their temporal models. IEEE Trans. Pattern Analy. Mach. Intell. **32**(11), 1940–1954 (2010)
23. Kolod, E.: How does learning sign language affect perception. Intel Science Talent Search, pp. 1–20 (2004)
24. Krizhevsky, A., Sutskever, I., Hinton, G.E.: Imagenet classification with deep convolutional neural networks. In: Advances in Neural Information Processing Systems, pp. 1097–1105 (2012)
25. Li, S., Deng, W.: Deep facial expression recognition: A survey. arXiv preprint arXiv:1804.08348 (2018)
26. Li, W., Abtahi, F., Zhu, Z.: Action unit detection with region adaptation, multilabeling learning and optimal temporal fusing. In: Proceedings of the IEEE Conference on Computer Vision and Pattern Recognition, pp. 1841–1850 (2017)

27. Li, W., Abtahi, F., Zhu, Z., Yin, L.: Eac-net: A region-based deep enhancing and cropping approach for facial action unit detection. arXiv preprint arXiv:1702.02925 (2017)
28. Liddell, S.K.: American sign language syntax, vol. 52. Mouton De Gruyter (1980)
29. Linh Tran, D., et al.: Deepcoder: Semi-parametric variational autoencoders for automatic facial action coding. In: Proceedings of the IEEE International Conference on Computer Vision, pp. 3190–3199 (2017)
30. Littlewort, G.C., Bartlett, M.S., Lee, K.: Automatic coding of facial expressions displayed during posed and genuine pain. Image Vis. Comput. **27**(12), 1797–1803 (2009)
31. Liu, M., Shan, S., Wang, R., Chen, X.: Learning expressionlets on spatio-temporal manifold for dynamic facial expression recognition. In: Proceedings of the IEEE Conference on Computer Vision and Pattern Recognition, pp. 1749–1756 (2014)
32. Lucey, P., Cohn, J.F., Kanade, T., Saragih, J., Ambadar, Z., Matthews, I.: The extended cohn-kanade dataset (ck+): A complete dataset for action unit and emotion-specified expression. In: 2010 IEEE Computer Society Conference on Computer Vision and Pattern Recognition Workshops (CVPRW), pp. 94–101. IEEE (2010)
33. Ma, C., Chen, L., Yong, J.: Au R-CNN: encoding expert prior knowledge into R-CNN for action unit detection. Neurocomputing **355**, 35–47 (2019)
34. Majumder, A., Behera, L., Subramanian, V.K.: Automatic facial expression recognition system using deep network-based data fusion. IEEE Trans. Cybern. **48**(1), 103–114 (2018)
35. Martinez, B., Valstar, M.F., Jiang, B., Pantic, M.: Automatic analysis of facial actions: a survey. IEEE Trans. Affect. Comput. (2017)
36. Mavadati, M., Sanger, P., Mahoor, M.H.: Extended disfa dataset: investigating posed and spontaneous facial expressions. In: Proceedings of the IEEE Conference on Computer Vision and Pattern Recognition Workshops, pp. 1–8 (2016)
37. Mavadati, S.M., Mahoor, M.H., Bartlett, K., Trinh, P., Cohn, J.F.: Disfa: a spontaneous facial action intensity database. IEEE Trans. Affect. Comput. **4**(2), 151–160 (2013)
38. Mei, C., Jiang, F., Shen, R., Hu, Q.: Region and temporal dependency fusion for multi-label action unit detection. In: 2018 24th International Conference on Pattern Recognition (ICPR), pp. 848–853. IEEE (2018)
39. Mollahosseini, A., Chan, D., Mahoor, M.H.: Going deeper in facial expression recognition using deep neural networks. In: 2016 IEEE Winter Conference on Applications of Computer Vision (WACV), pp. 1–10. IEEE (2016)
40. Ong, S.C., Ranganath, S.: Automatic sign language analysis: a survey and the future beyond lexical meaning. IEEE Trans. Pattern Anal. Mach. Intell. **6**, 873–891 (2005)
41. Pantic, M., Rothkrantz, L.J.M.: Automatic analysis of facial expressions: the state of the art. IEEE Trans. Pattern Anal. Mach. Intell. **22**(12), 1424–1445 (2000)
42. Peterson, C.C., Siegal, M.: Deafness, conversation and theory of mind. J. Child Psychol. Psychiatry **36**(3), 459–474 (1995)
43. Pigou, L., Dieleman, S., Kindermans, P.-J., Schrauwen, B.: Sign language recognition using convolutional neural networks. In: Agapito, L., Bronstein, M.M., Rother, C. (eds.) ECCV 2014. LNCS, vol. 8925, pp. 572–578. Springer, Cham (2015). https://doi.org/10.1007/978-3-319-16178-5_40
44. Pramerdorfer, C., Kampel, M.: Facial expression recognition using convolutional neural networks: state of the art. arXiv preprint arXiv:1612.02903 (2016)

45. Romero, A., León, J., Arbeláez, P.: Multi-view dynamic facial action unit detection. Image Vis. Comput. (2018)
46. Sanchez, E., Tzimiropoulos, G., Valstar, M.: Joint action unit localisation and intensity estimation through heatmap regression. arXiv preprint arXiv:1805.03487 (2018)
47. Sariyanidi, E., Gunes, H., Cavallaro, A.: Automatic analysis of facial affect: a survey of registration, representation, and recognition. IEEE Trans. Pattern Anal. Mach. Intell. **37**(6), 1113–1133 (2015)
48. Savran, A., Sankur, B., Bilge, M.T.: Regression-based intensity estimation of facial action units. Image Vis. Comput. **30**(10), 774–784 (2012)
49. Silva, E., Costa, P., Kumada, K., De Martino, J.M.: Silfa: Sign language facial action database for the development of assistive technologies for the deaf. In: 2020 15th IEEE International Conference on Automatic Face and Gesture Recognition (FG 2020)(FG), pp. 382–386 (2020)
50. Silva, E.P., Costa, P.D.P.: Recognition of non-manual expressions in Brazilian sign language. In: 12th IEEE International Conference on Automatic Face and Gesture Recognition. Doctoral Consortium. IEEE (2017)
51. da Silva, E.P., Costa, P.D.P.: Qlibras: A novel database for grammatical facial expressions in Brazilian sign language. In: X Encontro de Alunos e Docentes do DCA/FEEC/UNICAMP (EADCA) (2017)
52. Simard, P.Y., Steinkraus, D., Platt, J.C.: Best practices for convolutional neural networks applied to visual document analysis. In: Null, p. 958. IEEE (2003)
53. Simonyan, K., Zisserman, A.: Very deep convolutional networks for large-scale image recognition. arXiv preprint arXiv:1409.1556 (2014)
54. Yauri Vidalón, J.E., De Martino, J.M.: Brazilian sign language recognition using kinect. In: Hua, G., Jégou, H. (eds.) ECCV 2016. LNCS, vol. 9914, pp. 391–402. Springer, Cham (2016). https://doi.org/10.1007/978-3-319-48881-3_27
55. Von Agris, U., Knorr, M., Kraiss, K.F.: The significance of facial features for automatic sign language recognition. In: 8th IEEE International Conference on Automatic Face and Gesture Recognition. FG 2008, pp. 1–6. IEEE (2008)
56. Vural, E., Cetin, M., Ercil, A., Littlewort, G., Bartlett, M., Movellan, J.: Drowsy driver detection through facial movement analysis. In: Lew, M., Sebe, N., Huang, T.S., Bakker, E.M. (eds.) HCI 2007. LNCS, vol. 4796, pp. 6–18. Springer, Heidelberg (2007). https://doi.org/10.1007/978-3-540-75773-3_2
57. Walecki, R., Rudovic, O., Pavlovic, V., Schuller, B., Pantic, M.: Deep structured learning for facial action unit intensity estimation. In: 2017 IEEE Conference on Computer Vision and Pattern Recognition (CVPR), pp. 5709–5718. IEEE (2017)
58. Wang, S., Hao, L., Ji, Q.: Facial action unit recognition and intensity estimation enhanced through label dependencies. IEEE Trans. Image Process. (2018)
59. Wu, B.F., Lin, C.H.: Adaptive feature mapping for customizing deep learning based facial expression recognition model. IEEE Access **6**, 12451–12461 (2018)
60. Yabunaka, K., Mori, Y., Toyonaga, M.: Facial expression sequence recognition for a japanese sign language training system. In: 2018 Joint 10th International Conference on Soft Computing and Intelligent Systems (SCIS) and 19th International Symposium on Advanced Intelligent Systems (ISIS), pp. 1348–1353. IEEE (2018)
61. Zafrulla, Z., Brashear, H., Starner, T., Hamilton, H., Presti, P.: American sign language recognition with the kinect. In: Proceedings of the 13th International Conference on Multimodal Interfaces, pp. 279–286. ACM (2011)
62. Zeng, N., Zhang, H., Song, B., Liu, W., Li, Y., Dobaie, A.M.: Facial expression recognition via learning deep sparse autoencoders. Neurocomputing **273**, 643–649 (2018)

63. Zhang, K., Huang, Y., Du, Y., Wang, L.: Facial expression recognition based on deep evolutional spatial-temporal networks. IEEE Trans. Image Process. **26**(9), 4193–4203 (2017)
64. Zhang, Y., Dong, W., Hu, B.G., Ji, Q.: Classifier learning with prior probabilities for facial action unit recognition. In: Proceedings of the IEEE Conference on Computer Vision and Pattern Recognition, pp. 5108–5116 (2018)
65. Zhao, K., Chu, W.S., Martinez, A.M.: Learning facial action units from web images with scalable weakly supervised clustering. In: Proceedings of the IEEE Conference on Computer Vision and Pattern Recognition, pp. 2090–2099 (2018)
66. Zhao, K., Chu, W.S., De la Torre, F., Cohn, J.F., Zhang, H.: Joint patch and multi-label learning for facial action unit detection. In: Proceedings of the IEEE Conference on Computer Vision and Pattern Recognition, pp. 2207–2216 (2015)
67. Zhao, K., Chu, W.S., Zhang, H.: Deep region and multi-label learning for facial action unit detection. In: Proceedings of the IEEE Conference on Computer Vision and Pattern Recognition, pp. 3391–3399 (2016)
68. Zhi, R., Liu, M., Zhang, D.: A comprehensive survey on automatic facial action unit analysis. Vis. Comput., 1–27 (2019)

Real-Time Sign Language Detection
Using Human Pose Estimation

Amit Moryossef[1,2]([⊠]), Ioannis Tsochantaridis[1], Roee Aharoni[1], Sarah Ebling[3],
and Srini Narayanan[1]

[1] Google, Mountain View, USA
ioannis@google.com, roeeaharoni@google.com, srinin@google.com
[2] Bar-Ilan University, Ramat Gan, Israel
amitmoryossef@gmail.com
[3] University of Zurich, Zurich, Switzerland
ebling@cl.uzh.ch

Abstract. We propose a lightweight real-time sign language detection model, as we identify the need for such a case in videoconferencing. We extract optical flow features based on human pose estimation and, using a linear classifier, show these features are meaningful with an accuracy of 80%, evaluated on the Public DGS Corpus. Using a recurrent model directly on the input, we see improvements of up to 91% accuracy, while still working under 4 ms. We describe a demo application to sign language detection in the browser in order to demonstrate its usage possibility in videoconferencing applications.

Keywords: Sign language detection · Sign language processing

1 Introduction

Sign language detection [3] is defined as the binary-classification task for any given frame of a video if a person is using sign-language or not. Unlike sign language recognition [8,9], where the task is to recognize the form and meaning of signs in a video, or sign language identification, where the task is to identify *which* sign language is used, the task of sign language detection is to detect *when* something is being signed.

With the recent rise of videoconferencing platforms, we identify the problem of signers not "getting the floor" when communicating, which either leads to them being ignored or to a cognitive load on other participants, always checking to see if someone starts signing. Hence, we focus on the real-time sign language detection task with uni-directional context to allow for videoconferencing sign language prominence.

We propose a simple human optical-flow representation for videos based on pose estimation (Sect. 3.1), which is fed to a temporally sensitive neural network (Sect. 3.2) to perform a binary classification per frame—is the person signing or

© Springer Nature Switzerland AG 2020
A. Bartoli and A. Fusiello (Eds.): ECCV 2020 Workshops, LNCS 12536, pp. 237–248, 2020.
https://doi.org/10.1007/978-3-030-66096-3_17

not. We compare various possible inputs, such as full-body pose estimation, partial pose estimation, and bounding boxes (Sect. 4), and contrast their acquisition time in light of our targeted real-time application.

We demonstrate our approach on the Public DGS Corpus (German Sign Language) [11], using full-body pose estimation [27] collected through OpenPose [5,28]. We show results of 87%–91% prediction accuracy depending on the input, with per-frame inference time of 350–3500 μs (Sect. 5), and release our training code and models[1].

2   Background

The computational sign language processing (SLP) literature rarely addresses detection [3] and mainly focuses on sign language recognition [8,9,17] and identification [10,19].

2.1   Sign Language Detection

Previous work [3] introduces the classification of frames taken from YouTube videos as either signing or not. They take a spatial and temporal approach based on VGG-16 CNN [29] to encode each frame and use a GRU [7] to encode the sequence of frames, in a window of 20 frames at 5 fps. In addition to the raw frame, they also either encode optical flow history, aggregated motion history, or frame difference. However, for our use case, 5 fps might not be enough, as it introduces an artificial 200 ms delay from when a person starts signing to when they could be detected. Furthermore, this network takes upwards of 3 s to run on CPU per inference.

Most recently, Apple [2] announced sign language detection for group Face-Time calls in iOS 14, iPadOS 14, and macOS Big Sur. They did not share any implementation details of their detection model, which makes it hard to compare their model to the one we propose in this paper. Nonetheless, as FaceTime group calls are encrypted end-to-end, we assume that the detection happens on-device rather than on the server-side.

2.2   Sign Language Recognition

Sign language recognition has been widely studied across different domains and sign languages. As sign language corpora are usually small [4], previous works take one of two approaches to reduce the network's parameters: (1) using pose estimation on the original videos [16,17,32]; or (2) using pre-trained CNNs to get a feature vector per frame [8,9]. While different, both methods can encode adequate features to be used for recognition. Studies of human signers have shown that detailed information like exact descriptions of the hand shape are not always required for humans to interpret sign language [25,31].

---

[1] https://github.com/google-research/google-research/tree/master/sign_language_detection.

Looking at examples of sign videos, we hypothesize that the most challenging part of this task is to identify when a person starts signing, because a signer might initiate hand movement for other purposes, for example, to touch their face. Distinguishing this type of ambient motion from actual linguistic sign movement is not always straightforward. Although not explicitly studied on signers, studies find the average person touches their face between 15.7 and 23 times per hour [18,20]. Further complicating this issue, people in different cultures exhibit different face-touching patterns, including frequency, area, and hand preference [12].

2.3 Sign Language Identification

A study [10] finds that a random-forest classifier can distinguish between British Sign Language (BSL) and Greek Sign Language (ENN) with a 95% F1 score. This finding is further supported by more recent work [19] which manages to differentiate between British Sign Language and French Sign Language (Langue des Signes Française, LSF) with 98% F1 score in videos with static backgrounds, and between American Sign Language and British Sign Language with 70% F1 score for videos mined from popular video sharing sites. The authors attribute their success mainly to the different fingerspelling systems, which is two-handed in the case of BSL and one-handed in the case of ASL and LSF.

3 Model

For a video, for every frame given, we would like to predict whether the person in the video is signing or not.

3.1 Input Representation

As evident by previous work [3], using the raw frames as input is computationally expensive, and noisy. Alternatively, in computer vision, optical flow is one way to calculate the movement of every object in a scene. However, because signing is inherently a human action, we do not care about the flow of every object, but rather only the flow of the human. Optimally, we would like to track the movement of every pixel on the human body from one frame to another, to gauge its movement vector. As a proxy to such data, we opt for full-body human pose estimation, defining a set of points detected in every video frame that marks informative landmarks, like joints and other moving parts (mouth, eyes, eyebrows, and others).

Getting the optical flow F for these predefined points P at time t is then well defined as the L2 norm of the vector resulting from subtracting every two consecutive frames. We normalize the flow by the frame-rate in which the video was captured for the representation to be frame-rate invariant (Eq. 1).

$$F(P)_t = ||P_t - P_{t-1}||_2 * fps \qquad (1)$$

We note that if a point p was not identified in a given frame t, the value of $F(p)_t$ and $F(p)_{t+1}$ automatically equals to 0. This is done to avoid introducing fake movements from a poor pose estimation system or unknown movement from landmarks going out-of-frame.

An additional benefit of using full-body pose estimation is that we can normalize the size of all people, regardless of whether they use a high-/low-resolution camera and the distance at which they are from the camera.

Fig. 1. Optical-flow norm representation of a conversation between two signers. The x-axis is the progression of time, 1,500 frames over 30 s in total. The yellow marks are the gold labels for spans when a signer is signing. (Color figure online)

3.2   Temporal Model

Figure 1 demonstrates our input representation for an example video. It shows, to the naked eye, that this representation is meaningful. The movement, indicated by the bright colors, is well aligned with the gold spans annotation. Thus, we opt to use a shallow sequence tagging model on top of it.

We use a uni-directional LSTM [14] with one layer and 64 hidden units directly on this input, normalized for frame rate, and project the output to a 2-dimensional vector. For training, we use the negative-log-likelihood loss on the predicted classes for every frame. For inference, we take the arg-max of the output vector (Eq. 2).

$$signing(P) = \arg\max LSTM(F(P)) * W \qquad (2)$$

Note that this model allows us to process each frame as we get it, in real-time, by performing a single step of the LSTM and project its output. Unlike autoregressive models, we do not feed the last-frame classification as input for the next frame, as just classifying the new frame with the same tag would almost get 100% accuracy on this task, depending on gold labels to be available. Instead, we rely on the hidden state of the LSTM to hold such information as a probability.

4   Experiments

The Public DGS Corpus [11] includes 301 videos with an average duration of 9 min, of two signers in conversation[2], at 50 fps. Each video includes gloss annotations and spoken language translations (German and English). Using this information, we mark each frame as either "signing" (50.9% of the data) or "not-signing" (49.1% of the data) depending on whether it belongs to a gloss segment. Furthermore, this corpus is enriched with OpenPose [5] full-body pose estimations [27] including 137 points per frame (70 for the face, 25 for the body, and 21 for each hand). In order to disregard video resolution and distance from the camera, we normalize each of these poses such that the mean distance between the shoulders of each person equals 1. We split this dataset into 50:25:25 for training, validation, and test, respectively. For every "part" (face, body, left and right hands), we also calculate its bounding box based on the minimum and maximum value of all of the landmarks.

We experiment with three linear baselines with a fixed context (Linear-1, Linear-25, Linear-50) and four experimental recurrent models with different counts of input features:

1. **Pose-All**—including all of the landmarks from the poses. (Fig. 2a)
2. **Pose-Body**—including only the body landmarks. (Fig. 2b)
3. **Pose-Hands**—including only the left-and right-hand landmarks. (Fig. 2c)
4. **BBOX**—including the bounding boxes of the face, body, and hands. (Fig. 2d)

Finally, we measure the execution time of each model on CPU, using an Intel(R) Xeon(R) CPU E5-2650 v4 @ 2.20 GHz. We measure the execution time per frame given a single frame at a time, using multiple frameworks: Scikit-Learn (sk) [24], TensorFlow (tf) [1] and PyTorch (pt) [23].

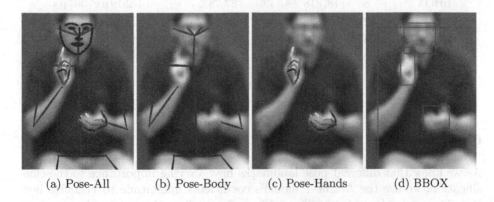

(a) Pose-All   (b) Pose-Body   (c) Pose-Hands   (d) BBOX

Fig. 2. Visualization of our different experiments inputs.

---

[2] There are also monologue story-telling, but both signers are always shown.

5   Results

Table 1 includes the accuracy and inference times for each of our scenarios. Our baseline systems show that using a linear classifier with a fixed number of context frames achieves between 79.9% to 84.3% accuracy on the test set. However, all of the baselines perform worse than our recurrent models, for which we achieve between 87.7% to 91.5% accuracy on the test set. Generally, we see that using more diverse sets of landmarks performs better. Although the hand landmarks are very indicative, using just the hand BBOX almost matches in accuracy, and using the entire body pose, with a single point per hand, performs much better. Furthermore, we see that regardless of the number of landmarks used, our models generally perform faster the fewer landmarks are used. We note that the prediction time varies between the different frameworks, but does not vary much within a particular framework. It is clear, however, that the speed of these models' is sufficient, as even the slowest model, using the slowest framework, runs at 285 frames-per-second on CPU.

We note from manually observing the gold data that sometimes a gloss segment starts before the person actually begins signing, or moving at all. This means that our accuracy ceiling is not 100%. We did not perform a rigorous re-annotation of the dataset to quantify how extensive this problem is.

Table 1. Accuracy and inference-time (∂t) results for the various experiments.

Model	Points	Params	Dev Acc	Test Acc	∂t (sk)	∂t (tf)	∂t (pt)
Linear-1	25	25	79.99%	79.93%	6.49 μs	823 μs	2.75 μs
Linear-25	25	625	84.13%	83.79%	6.78 μs	824 μs	5.10 μs
Linear-50	25	1,250	85.06%	83.39%	6.90 μs	821 μs	7.41 μs
BBOX	8	18,818	87.49%	87.78%	—	3519 μs	367 μs
Pose-Hands	42	27,522	87.65%	88.05%	—	3427 μs	486 μs
Pose-Body	25	23,170	92.17%	90.35%	—	3437 μs	443 μs
Pose-All	137	51,842	92.31%	91.53%	—	3537 μs	588 μs

6   Analysis

As we know that different pose landmarks have varying importance to the classification, we use the *Linear-1* model's coefficients magnitude to visualize how the different landmarks contribute. Figure 3 visualizes the average human pose in the dataset, with the opacity of every landmark being the absolute value of the coefficient.

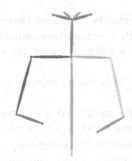

Fig. 3. The average pose in the dataset. The opacity of every landmark is determined by its coefficient in the *Linear-1* model.

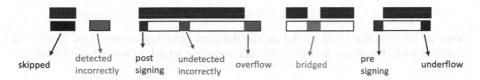

skipped | detected incorrectly | post signing | undetected incorrectly | overflow | bridged | pre signing | underflow

Fig. 4. Visualization of the different types of errors. The first row contains the gold annotations, and the second row contains a model's prediction.

First, we note that the model attributes no importance to any landmark below the waist. This makes sense as they both do not appear in all videos, and bare no meaning in sign language. The eyes and nose seem to carry little weight, while the ears carry more. We do not attribute this to any signing phenomenon.

Additionally, we note hands asymmetry. While both wrists have a high weight, the elbow and shoulder for the right hand carry more weights than their corresponding left counterparts. This could be attributed to the fact that most people are right handed, and that in some sign languages the signer must decide which hand is dominant in a consistent manner. We see this asymmetry as a feature of our model, and note that apps using our models could also include a "dominant hand" selection.

To further understand what situations our models capture, we check multiple properties of them on the test set. We start by generally noting that our data is conversational. 84.87% of the time, only one participant is signing, while 8.5% of the time both participants are signing, and in the remaining 6.63% of the time no one is signing, primarily when the participants are being instructed on the task.

Our test set includes 4,138 *signing* sequences with an average length of 11.35 s, and a standard deviation of 29.82 s. It also includes 4,091 *not-signing* sequences with an average length of 9.95 s, and a standard deviation of 24.18 s.

For each of our models, we compare the following error types (Fig. 4):

- **Bridged**—Cases where the model bridged between two signing sections, still predicting the person to be *signing* while the annotation says they are not.

- **Signing Detected Incorrectly**—Cases where the model predicted a *signing* span fully contained within a *not-signing* annotation.
- **Signing Overflow**—Cases where signing was still predicted after a *signing* section ended.
- **Started Pre-Signing**—Cases where *signing* was predicted before a *signing* section started.
- **Skipped**—Cases where the model did not detect entire *signing* sections.
- **Signing Undetected Incorrectly**—Cases where the model predicted a *not-signing* span fully contained within a *signing* annotation.
- **Started Post-Signing**—Cases where the *signing* section started before it was predicted to start.
- **Signing Underflow**—Cases where the *signing* section was predicted to end prematurely.

Table 2. We evaluate every model on the different error types, and show number of sequences with that error, including average sequence length in seconds and standard deviation.

	linear-1	linear-25	linear-50
Bridged	107 (0.10 ± 0.15)	308 (0.34 ± 0.40)	426 (0.45 ± 0.46)
Signing Detected Incorrectly	132151 (0.04 ± 0.07)	8773 (0.30 ± 0.81)	6594 (0.34 ± 1.06)
Signing Overflow	4094 (0.09 ± 0.15)	3893 (0.32 ± 0.43)	3775 (0.46 ± 1.17)
Started Pre-Signing	873 (0.09 ± 0.13)	345 (0.45 ± 0.68)	257 (0.88 ± 4.27)
Skipped	50 (1.41 ± 1.95)	298 (1.38 ± 1.43)	446 (1.49 ± 1.60)
Signing undetected incorrectly	219531 (0.05 ± 0.10)	26185 (0.27 ± 0.50)	18037 (0.32 ± 0.66)
Started Post-Signing	4199 (0.17 ± 0.23)	3951 (0.48 ± 0.57)	3803 (0.60 ± 0.77)
Signing Underflow	1677 (0.15 ± 0.26)	1092 (0.58 ± 0.91)	827 (0.71 ± 0.96)
	BBOX	Pose-Hands	Pose-Body	Pose-All
Bridged	754 (0.97 ± 1.94)	861 (1.26 ± 2.63)	747 (1.12 ± 2.35)	573 (0.75 ± 1.08)
Signing Detected Incorrectly	5697 (0.64 ± 1.93)	12919 (0.33 ± 1.33)	6286 (0.38 ± 1.29)	11384 (0.25 ± 1.14)
Signing Overflow	3337 (0.95 ± 2.10)	3230 (1.01 ± 2.46)	3344 (0.67 ± 1.29)	3518 (0.48 ± 0.87)
Started Pre-Signing	402 (1.33 ± 2.73)	558 (1.59 ± 5.15)	298 (1.48 ± 3.87)	408 (0.70 ± 1.97)
Skipped	199 (1.31 ± 1.40)	115 (1.45 ± 1.54)	243 (1.31 ± 1.30)	146 (1.41 ± 1.42)
Signing undetected incorrectly	4089 (0.48 ± 0.76)	3526 (0.26 ± 0.51)	4786 (0.32 ± 0.60)	5526 (0.23 ± 0.44)
Started Post-Signing	3939 (0.34 ± 0.44)	4023 (0.24 ± 0.34)	3895 (0.37 ± 0.49)	3992 (0.29 ± 0.36)
Signing Underflow	370 (0.82 ± 1.08)	297 (0.55 ± 0.68)	506 (0.63 ± 0.97)	666 (0.44 ± 0.66)

Table 2 includes the number of sequences, including average length and standard deviation in seconds, for each of the error types. Most notably, we see that the less context the model has, the more sporadic its predictions and thus it will generally completely bridge or skip less sequences. The same locality however introduces many signing detected/undetected incorrectly errors, albeit of short lengths.

In the sequential models, we generally see a lower number of sequences as they can incorporate global features in the classification. As indicated by the accuracy scores, we see fewer errors of most types the more diverse the input points are, with one notable exception for the *Pose-All* model which underperforms *Pose-Body* on all errors except for *Bridged* and *Skipped*.

7   Demo Application

With this publication, we release a demo application working in the browser for computers and mobile devices. Pragmatically, we choose to use the "Pose-Body" model variant, as it performs almost on par with our best model, "Pose-All", and we find it is feasible to acquire the human body poses in real-time with currently available tools.

We use PoseNet [21,22] running in the browser using TensorFlow.js [30]. PoseNet includes two main image encoding variants: MobileNet [15], which is a lightweight model aimed at mobile devices, and ResNet [13], which is a larger model that requires a dedicated GPU. Each model includes many sub-variants with different image resolution and convolutional strides, to further allow for tailoring the network to the user's needs. In our demo, we first tailor a network to the current computation device to run at least at 25 fps. While using a more lightweight network might be faster, it might also introduce pose estimation errors.

The pose estimation we use only returns 17 points compared to the 25 of OpenPose; hence, we map the 17 points to the corresponding indexes for Open-Pose. We then normalize the body pose vector by the mean shoulder width the person had in the past 50 frames in order to disregard camera resolution and distance of the signer from the camera.

Onward, there are two options: either send the pose vector to the videoconferencing server where inference could be done or perform the inference locally. As our method is faster than real-time, we chose the latter and perform inference on the device using TensorFlow.js. For every frame, we get a signing probability, which we then show on the screen.

In a production videoconferencing application, this signing probability should be streamed to the call server, where further processing could be done to show the correct people on screen. We suggest using the signing probability as a normalized "volume", such that further processing is comparable to videoconferencing users using speech.

While this is the recommended way to add sign language detection to a videoconferencing app, as the goal of this work is to empower signers, our demo application can trigger the speaker detection by transmitting audio when the user is signing. Transmitting ultrasonic audio at 20 KHz, which is inaudible for humans, manages to fool Google Meet, Zoom and Slack into thinking the user is speaking, while still being inaudible. One limitation of this method is that videoconferencing app developers can crop the audio to be in the audible human range and thus render this application useless. Another limitation is that using high-frequency audio can sound crackly when compressed, depending on the signer's internet connection strength.

Our model and demo, in their current forms, only allow for the detection of a single signer per video stream. However, if we can detect more than a single person, and track which poses belong to which person in every frame, there is no limitation to run our model independently on each signer.

8   Discussion

8.1   Limitations

We note several limitations to our approach. The first is that it relies on the pose estimation system to run in real-time on any user's device. This proves to be challenging, as even performing state-of-the-art pose estimation on a single frame on a GPU with OpenPose [5,6] can take upwards of 300 ms, which introduces two issues: (1) If in order to get the optical-flow, we need to pose two frames, we create a delay from when a person starts signing to when they could be accurately detected as signing, equal to at least two times the pose processing time. (2) Running this on mobile devices or devices without hardware acceleration like a GPU may be too slow.

As we only look at the input's optical flow norm, our model might not be able to pick up on times when a person is just gesturing rather than signing. However, as this approach is targeted directly at sign language users rather than the general non-signing public, erring on the side of caution and detecting any meaningful movements is preferred.

8.2   Demographic Biases

The data we use for training was collected from various regions of Germany, with equal number of males and females, as well as an equal number of participants from different age groups [26]. Although most of the people in the dataset are European white, we do not attribute any significance between the color of their skin to the performance of the system, as long as the pose estimation system is not biased.

Regardless of age, gender, and race, we do not address general ethnic biases such as different communities of signers outside of Germany signing differently-whether it is the size, volume, speed, or other properties.

9   Conclusions

We propose a simple human optical-flow representation for videos based on pose estimation to perform a binary classification per frame—is the person signing or not. We compare various possible inputs, such as full-body pose estimation, partial pose estimation, and bounding boxes and contrast their acquisition time in light of our targeted real-time videoconferencing sign language detection application.

We demonstrate our approach on the Public DGS Corpus (German Sign Language), and show results of 87%–91% prediction accuracy depending on the input, with per-frame inference time of 350–3500 μs.

References

1. Abadi, M., et al.: TensorFlow: large-scale machine learning on heterogeneous systems (2015). http://tensorflow.org/, software available from tensorflow.org
2. Apple: WWDC (World Wide Developer Conference) (2020). https://developer.apple.com/wwdc20/
3. Borg, M., Camilleri, K.P.: Sign language detection "in the wild" with recurrent neural networks. In: ICASSP 2019-2019 IEEE International Conference on Acoustics, Speech and Signal Processing (ICASSP), pp. 1637–1641. IEEE (2019)
4. Bragg, D., et al.: Sign language recognition, generation, and translation: an interdisciplinary perspective. In: The 21st International ACM SIGACCESS Conference on Computers and Accessibility, pp. 16–31 (2019)
5. Cao, Z., Hidalgo Martinez, G., Simon, T., Wei, S., Sheikh, Y.A.: Openpose: real-time multi-person 2d pose estimation using part affinity fields. IEEE Trans. Pattern Anal. Mach. Intell. (2019)
6. Cao, Z., Simon, T., Wei, S.E., Sheikh, Y.: Realtime multi-person 2D pose estimation using part affinity fields. In: CVPR (2017)
7. Cho, K., et al.: Learning phrase representations using RNN encoder-decoder for statistical machine translation. arXiv preprint arXiv:1406.1078 (2014)
8. Cihan Camgoz, N., Hadfield, S., Koller, O., Ney, H., Bowden, R.: Neural sign language translation. In: Proceedings of the IEEE Conference on Computer Vision and Pattern Recognition, pp. 7784–7793 (2018)
9. Cui, R., Liu, H., Zhang, C.: Recurrent convolutional neural networks for continuous sign language recognition by staged optimization. In: Proceedings of the IEEE Conference on Computer Vision and Pattern Recognition, pp. 7361–7369 (2017)
10. Gebre, B.G., Wittenburg, P., Heskes, T.: Automatic sign language identification. In: 2013 IEEE International Conference on Image Processing, pp. 2626–2630. IEEE (2013)
11. Hanke, T., Schulder, M., Konrad, R., Jahn, E.: Extending the Public DGS Corpus in size and depth. In: Proceedings of the LREC2020 9th Workshop on the Representation and Processing of Sign Languages: Sign Language Resources in the Service of the Language Community, Technological Challenges and Application Perspectives, Marseille, France, pp. 75–82. European Language Resources Association (ELRA), May 2020. https://www.aclweb.org/anthology/2020.signlang-1.12
12. Hatta, T., Dimond, S.J.: Differences in face touching by Japanese and British people. Neuropsychologia 22(4), 531–534 (1984)
13. He, K., Zhang, X., Ren, S., Sun, J.: Deep residual learning for image recognition. In: Proceedings of the IEEE Conference on Computer Vision and Pattern Recognition, pp. 770–778 (2016)
14. Hochreiter, S., Schmidhuber, J.: Long short-term memory. Neural Comput. 9(8), 1735–1780 (1997)
15. Howard, A.G., et al.: Mobilenets: Efficient convolutional neural networks for mobile vision applications. arXiv preprint arXiv:1704.04861 (2017)
16. Isaacs, J., Foo, S.: Hand pose estimation for American sign language recognition. In: Proceedings of the Thirty-Sixth Southeastern Symposium on System Theory, pp. 132–136. IEEE (2004)
17. Konstantinidis, D., Dimitropoulos, K., Daras, P.: Sign language recognition based on hand and body skeletal data. In: 2018–3DTV-Conference: The True Vision-Capture, Transmission and Display of 3D Video (3DTV-CON), pp. 1–4. IEEE (2018)

18. Kwok, Y.L.A., Gralton, J., McLaws, M.L.: Face touching: a frequent habit that has implications for hand hygiene. Am. J. Infect. Control **43**(2), 112–114 (2015)

19. Monteiro, C.D., Mathew, C.M., Gutierrez-Osuna, R., Shipman, F.: Detecting and identifying sign languages through visual features. In: 2016 IEEE International Symposium on Multimedia (ISM), pp. 287–290. IEEE (2016)

20. Nicas, M., Best, D.: A study quantifying the hand-to-face contact rate and its potential application to predicting respiratory tract infection. J. Occup. Environ. Hyg. **5**(6), 347–352 (2008)

21. Papandreou, G., Zhu, T., Chen, L.C., Gidaris, S., Tompson, J., Murphy, K.: Personlab: Person pose estimation and instance segmentation with a bottom-up, part-based, geometric embedding model. In: Proceedings of the European Conference on Computer Vision (ECCV), pp. 269–286 (2018)

22. Papandreou, G., et al.: Towards accurate multi-person pose estimation in the wild. In: Proceedings of the IEEE Conference on Computer Vision and Pattern Recognition, pp. 4903–4911 (2017)

23. Paszke, A., et al.: Pytorch: An imperative style, high-performance deep learning library. In: Wallach, H., et al. (eds.) Advances in Neural Information Processing Systems, vol. 32, pp. 8024–8035. Curran Associates, Inc. (2019). http://papers.neurips.cc/paper/9015-pytorch-an-imperative-style-high-performance-deep-learning-library.pdf

24. Pedregosa, F., et al.: Scikit-learn: machine learning in Python. J. Mach. Learn. Res. **12**, 2825–2830 (2011)

25. Poizner, H., Bellugi, U., Lutes-Driscoll, V.: Perception of American sign language in dynamic point-light displays. J. Exp. Psychol. Hum. Percept. Perform. **7**(2), 430 (1981)

26. Schulder, M., et al.: Data statement for the Public DGS Corpus. Project Note AP06-2020-01, DGS-Korpus project, IDGS, Hamburg University, Hamburg, Germany (2020)

27. Schulder, M., Hanke, T.: OpenPose in the Public DGS Corpus. Project Note AP06-2019-01, DGS-Korpus project, IDGS, Hamburg University, Hamburg, Germany (2019). https://doi.org/10.25592/uhhfdm.842

28. Simon, T., Joo, H., Matthews, I., Sheikh, Y.: Hand keypoint detection in single images using multiview bootstrapping. In: CVPR (2017)

29. Simonyan, K., Zisserman, A.: Very deep convolutional networks for large-scale image recognition. arXiv preprint arXiv:1409.1556 (2014)

30. Smilkov, D., et al.: Tensorflow. js: Machine learning for the web and beyond. arXiv preprint arXiv:1901.05350 (2019)

31. Sperling, G., Landy, M., Cohen, Y., Pavel, M.: Intelligible encoding of ASL image sequences at extremely low information rates. Comput. Vis. Graph. Image Process. **31**(3), 335–391 (1985)

32. Zafrulla, Z., Brashear, H., Starner, T., Hamilton, H., Presti, P.: American sign language recognition with the kinect. In: Proceedings of the 13th International Conference on Multimodal Interfaces, pp. 279–286 (2011)

Exploiting 3D Hand Pose Estimation in Deep Learning-Based Sign Language Recognition from RGB Videos

Maria Parelli[1], Katerina Papadimitriou[2(✉)], Gerasimos Potamianos[2],
Georgios Pavlakos[3], and Petros Maragos[1]

[1] School of ECE, National Technical University of Athens, Athens, Greece
maryparelli@gmail.com, maragos@cs.ntua.gr
[2] ECE Department, University of Thessaly, Volos, Greece
{aipapadimitriou,gpotamianos}@uth.gr
[3] GRASP Laboratory, University of Pennsylvania, Philadelphia, USA
pavlakos@seas.upenn.edu

Abstract. In this paper, we investigate the benefit of 3D hand skeletal information to the task of sign language (SL) recognition from RGB videos, within a state-of-the-art, multiple-stream, deep-learning recognition system. As most SL datasets are available in traditional RGB-only video lacking depth information, we propose to infer 3D coordinates of the hand joints from RGB data via a powerful architecture that has been primarily introduced in the literature for the task of 3D human pose estimation. We then fuse these estimates with additional SL informative streams, namely 2D skeletal data, as well as convolutional neural network-based hand- and mouth-region representations, and employ an attention-based encoder-decoder for recognition. We evaluate our proposed approach on a corpus of isolated signs of Greek SL and a dataset of continuous finger-spelling in American SL, reporting significant gains by the inclusion of 3D hand pose information, while also outperforming the state-of-the-art on both databases. Further, we evaluate the 3D hand pose estimation technique as standalone.

Keywords: Sign language recognition · 3D hand pose · 2D body skeleton · Attention-based encoder-decoder · Convolutional neural network

1 Introduction

Automatic sign language recognition (SLR) from video has been attracting significant interest lately, following recent deep learning advances in the fields of computer vision and human language technologies, as well as the collection of suitable large SL corpora [4,5,34]. However, despite much progress in the field, the problem remains challenging due to the complex nature and multitude of SL articulators (both manual and non-manual), as well as variability in inter-subject signing and in the quality of the available video data.

A significant portion of SLR approaches in the literature utilize hand and/or body skeletal information in their pipelines. Such can be obtained from special data

© Springer Nature Switzerland AG 2020
A. Bartoli and A. Fusiello (Eds.): ECCV 2020 Workshops, LNCS 12536, pp. 249–263, 2020.
https://doi.org/10.1007/978-3-030-66096-3_18

acquisition tools in conjunction with wearable markers or data gloves [26,28], but at the expense of naturalness in the interaction, or provided directly by RGB-D cameras [12,20,40] that also yield a depth information data stream. Specifically, systems utilizing such cameras have been introduced [11,25,35], with most of them relying on hand-crafted feature descriptors extracted from the depth and/or skeleton streams. For example, work in [19] explores the incorporation of 3D skeleton data, leveraging the advancement of depth sensors for SLR. Further, a number of promising works [23,30] are based on 2D body skeletal data inferred from OpenPose [39]. Such representations are often complemented with appearance or optical-flow based motion information [21,24,36].

Since hand-based articulation plays a crucial role in SL and there exist multiple signs with very similar skeletal motion patterns, it is vital to seek schemes that enrich hand motion and structure information. The problem of hand pose estimation in videos is a long-standing one and has given birth to many important applications. Following the emergence of RGB-D sensors, many efforts have been devoted to 3D hand pose estimation through depth sensor and RGB input. However, in the majority of SL corpora and in real-world settings, signs are not recorded with depth sensors and depth information is unavailable. Thus, since RGB cameras are more widely used than depth sensors, recent works focus mostly on 3D hand pose estimation from monocular RGB images. The work in [44] is the first to address the problem with the use of deep learning, adopting a three-stage pipeline that performs hand segmentation, 2D joint generation, and then 3D joint prediction. A similar approach is suggested in [31], where state-of-the-art deep-learning networks are used for 2D hand detection and 2D hand joint localization, and the results are fitted to a generative model formulated as a non-linear least-squares optimization problem. In addition, the work in [29] proposes a cycle-consistent generative adversarial network (CycleGAN) which transforms synthetic 3D annotated hand images into real looking ones, whose statistical distribution matches real-world hand images. The resulting data are trained via a convolutional neural network (CNN) regressor for 2D and 3D hand joint predictions, and the predictions are fitted to a kinematic skeleton model. Finally, one of the most recent advances is the work of [17], which proposes a hand-model regularized graph refinement network for 3D hand pose estimation from a monocular image. It employs an adversarial learning framework and estimations from a parametric hand model as a structure prior, which is then refined via residual graph convolution.

In this paper, we incorporate the depth dimension in the coordinates of the hand joints, in order to enrich model knowledge about the trajectory of hand movement by enabling its observation in 3D. Our motivation is that such enriched information, effectively capturing the relative position between hand joints in the 3D space, will translate to improved SLR performance. To this end, and as detailed in Sect. 2, we extract 3D hand skeletal information exclusively from RGB videos through a powerful architecture [27], originally proposed in the field of 3D human pose estimation. Specifically, after extracting 2D human skeleton data of the body, hands, and face via the OpenPose library [39], we

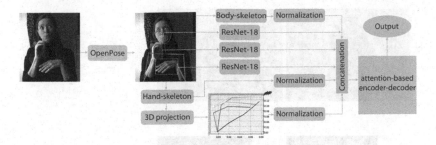

Fig. 1. Architecture of our proposed SLR system operating on RGB videos. Estimated 3D hand pose features are concatenated with additional SL informative feature streams and fed to an attention-based encoder-decoder for SLR.

project 2D hand-joint coordinates to the 3D space via a deep multi-layer neural network [27]. We then utilize an appropriately normalized representation of the 3D hand-joint estimates for SLR, in conjunction with state-of-the-art attention-based encoder-decoder architectures for sequence-to-sequence prediction. Further, we include more SL informative streams in the SLR system, in order to investigate the additional benefit of the 3D hand pose. Specifically, we consider normalized 2D skeletal features, as well as CNN-based representations via the ResNet-18 architecture [16] of the hands and mouth regions-of-interest (ROIs), segmented based on the 2D skeletal information, capturing manual articulation (handshape) and mouthing information, respectively. To our knowledge, this constitutes the first ever investigation of 3D hand pose information within a state-of-the-art, multiple-stream, deep learning-based SLR framework operating on traditional RGB video data.

We conduct SLR evaluations on two suitable multi-signer datasets: (i) a corpus of isolated signs of Greek SL (GSL) [2] and (ii) the ChicagoFSWild database [37], namely a corpus of continuous finger-spelling in the American SL (ASL). On both sets, inclusion of 3D hand pose information is able to benefit SLR on top of all other feature streams combined. Further, our results exceed the current state-of-the-art on both sets. In addition, we report experimental results of the 3D hand pose estimation technique on the Rendered HandPose [44] and the FreiHAND [45] datasets. Details are provided in Sect. 3.

2   The Sign Language Recognition System

We next overview our proposed SLR system, also depicted in Fig. 1, providing details of its feature extraction and sequence-to-sequence prediction modules, as well as its implementation details.

2.1   Feature Extraction

2D Human Skeleton Detection and Features: The system initiates with the extraction of 2D human skeletal data employing the OpenPose human-joint

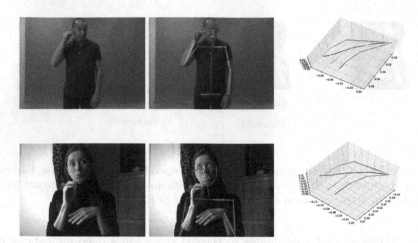

Fig. 2. Examples of extracted human skeleton via OpenPose [39] (middle column) and 3D hand skeleton representation through 3D projection architecture [27] (right column) on original data frames (left column). Images are from the GSL dataset (upper row) and the ChicagoFSWild corpus (lower row).

detector [39], which provides a descriptive motion and structural representation of the human body, employing deep convolutional pose models. Specifically, OpenPose renders in total 137 body skeleton joint descriptors, extracted in the form of image pixel coordinates, namely 25 body pose keypoints, 21 joints for each hand, and 70 face keypoints, as also depicted in the middle column of Fig. 2. Since only upper-body videos are employed in this work, we exploit 57 extracted image coordinates, excluding 10 body joints corresponding to the lower body, as well as the face keypoints. As a result, 114-dimensional (dim) feature vectors are extracted capturing the 2D coordinates of the upper-body skeleton (30-dim) and the two hands (84-dim in total). Note that, to incorporate translation and scale invariance, the estimated 2D human skeletal joints are subjected to normalization by transforming them to a local coordinate system, where the neck joint is assumed to be the origin, whereas further normalization is applied based on the distance between the left and right shoulder keypoints.

2D to 3D Hand Skeleton Projection: Our approach extracts 3D hand-joint keypoints by "lifting" 2D joint locations to the 3D space. Our input is a series of 2D hand-joint keypoints, previously generated by the OpenPose framework, and our output is a series of points in the 3D space. We zero-center both 2D and 3D poses around the wrist joint, so as to ensure that our model learns translation-invariant representations. A noticeable source of error in 3D joint predictions is noise in the input 2D predictions. Since an increase in performance is noticed when smoothing is applied to the input, we use a median filter with radius one to remove noise spikes and eliminate instability in the predictions.

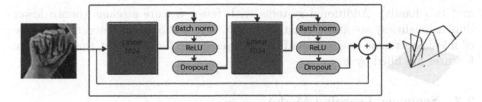

Fig. 3. The building blocks of the architecture that generates 3D hand skeleton joints from 2D hand skeletal data. (figure modified from [27])

Consequently, we implement a simple but powerful architecture, originally proposed in [27] for human pose 3D estimation, also depicted in Fig. 3. Our model is a deep multi-layer neural network with batch normalization, dropout, rectified linear units (ReLU), and residual connections. The latter improve generalization performance, while batch normalization and dropout improve model robustness to noisy 2D detections. Additionally, in order to further stabilize performance, a constraint on the weights of each layer is applied, so that the maximum norm is less than or equal to one. More precisely, the building block of the network is a linear layer followed by batch normalization, dropout, and ReLU activation. This block is repeated twice, and the two blocks share a residual connection. For this task we stack two outer residual blocks, and our model contains approximately 4 million trainable parameters. For network training, we use the Rendered HandPose Dataset [44], a large-scale 3D hand pose dataset based on synthetic hand models (see also Sect. 3.1).

The model yields 21 3D joints for each hand, thus 126-dim feature vectors are extracted. Note that, for translation and scale invariance, the wrist is assumed as the coordinate system origin, and the hand 3D keypoints are further subjected to normalization according to the distance between the shoulder and elbow keypoints of each hand.

Hand and Mouth ROIs Extraction and Appearance Features: Hands contain the most prominent SL information. Additional information also exists in mouthing patterns, being part of non-manual SL articulation. Thus, our system detects the ROIs of the mouth and each hand, exploiting the corresponding 2D human skeleton points returned by OpenPose. To generate appearance feature maps (one for the mouth and one for each hand), each ROI is resized to 224×224 pixels and fed to a ResNet-18 network [16] (using 3×3 convolutional kernels and downsampling with stride 2), pretrained on the ImageNet corpus [9]. This yields 512-dim features for each stream by taking the output of the network fully-connected layer.

Feature Fusion: The extracted feature streams are then fused through simple vector concatenation. Thus, our SLR system employing all aforementioned data streams will have 1776-dim features (114-dim for the 2D human skeleton, 126-dim for the 3D hand joints, and 512-dim for the ROIs of each of the mouth and two hands). Additional systems with fewer feature streams (hence lower dimensionalities) are also evaluated in Sect. 3.4. It should be noted that in case of missing streams due to OpenPose failures or occluded hands, the respective features are filled by zeros.

2.2 Sequence Learning Model

Regarding SLR from videos as a sequence-to-sequence prediction task, we address the SLR problem by a sequence learning approach based on an encoder-decoder module equipped with an attention mechanism. In its general form, the encoder is fed with the latent representations generated by a particular feature learner outputting a hidden states sequence, which is then processed by the decoder producing the predicted output. Further, the attentional models are based on the alignment between input and output accomplished by the likelihood of each portion of source sequence being related to the ongoing output.

Considering the above typical structure, a variety of attention based encoder-decoder schemes have been proposed, with most of them being mainly associated with recurrent neural networks (RNNs). The most dominant RNN encoder-decoder variants are long short-term memory networks (LSTMs) [18] and gated recurrent units (GRUs) [6]. Additionally, various architectures have been introduced relying on bi-directional RNNs [3,42,43]. Recently, the Transformer multi-head attention-based architecture [41] has been proposed that instead of involving CNNs or RNNs, it is complemented with position encoding and layer normalization. Moreover, in [32], a sequence-learning model using multi-step attention-based CNNs (enabling parallelization) is employed for finger-spelling recognition.

In this work, four sequence learning models are considered, namely: an attentional LSTM encoder-decoder [18], an attentional GRU encoder-decoder [6], an attentional CNN encoder-decoder [32], and a Transformer network [41]. Details of their implementation are provided next.

2.3 Implementation Details

All aforementioned deep-learning models are implemented in PyTorch [33], and their training carried out on a GPU. Specifically, the 3D hand skeleton generation network of Sect. 2.1 is trained for 150 epochs using the Adam optimizer [22], a batch size of 64, a starting learning rate of 0.001 and exponential decay. The weights of the linear layers are set using Kaiming He initialization [15].

For the sequence-learning models of Sect. 2.2, we employ a one-layer attentional LSTM encoder-decoder [18] with 128 hidden units and a one-layer GRU encoder-decoder [6] with hidden dimensionality equal to 256. Both RNNs are trained via the Adam optimizer [22] with an initial learning rate of 0.001 decayed by a factor of 0.3 and a dropout rate of 0.3. Beam search is applied during decoding with beam-width 5. The attentional CNN encoder-decoder model has 3 layers with kernel width 5 and 256 hidden units, and its training is based on the Adagrad optimizer [10] with an initial learning rate of 0.003, decreased by a factor of 1.0. Dropout of 0.1 and beam search of width 5 are employed. Finally, the Transformer is a 4-layer one with 8 heads for Transformer self-attention, 2048-dimension hidden Transformer feed-forward, and 512 hidden units. Its training is conducted via the Adam optimizer with an initial learning rate of 0.001 decreased by a factor of 2.0 and dropout 0.4. Parameter initialization is carried out by the Xavier process [14].

3 Experiments

Before proceeding to the SLR experiments that constitute the main focus of this paper, we briefly evaluate our 3D hand pose estimation approach.

3.1 3D Hand Pose Corpora

We conduct experiments on the 3D hand skeleton generation network performance using two corpora: the Rendered HandPose dataset (RHD) [44] and the FreiHand database (FHD) [45]. More details are provided next.

Rendered HandPose Dataset: We use this corpus for network training. It constitutes a large-scale 3D hand pose dataset, based on synthetic hand models [44]. The dataset utilizes 3D human models with corresponding animations from Mixamo 2 [13], and the open-source software Blender 3 [7] is used for image rendering. It consists of 20 different characters performing 39 actions, and for each frame a different camera location is randomly selected. The dataset provides 41,258 images for training and 2,728 images for evaluation with a resolution of 320×320 pixels. Annotations of a 21 keypoint skeleton model of each hand are available, as well as segmentation masks. In our work, we take advantage of the hand keypoints with their coordinates in the image frame and their coordinates in the world frame.

FreiHAND Dataset: The dataset consists of real images and shows samples both with and without object interactions. It is captured with a multi-view setup and contains 33,000 samples. Hand poses are recorded from 32 subjects, and the set of actions include ASL signs, counting and moving fingers to their kinematic limits. 3D annotations for 21 hand keypoints are provided. For this work, we partition the data to 80% for training and 20% for testing.

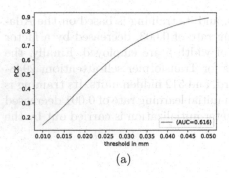
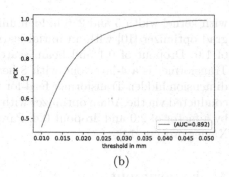

| (a) | (b) |

Fig. 4. Percentage of correct keypoints (PCK) over a certain threshold in mm, evaluated: (a) on RHD-test for model trained on RHD-train; and (b) on FHD-test for model trained on FHD-train.

3.2 3D Hand Pose Estimation Results

In Table 1 and Fig. 4, we evaluate the performance and generalization power of our model on the aforementioned datasets for various training/testing scenarios, reporting average median point error per keypoint of the predicted 3D pose, when given the 2D ground truth pose, as well as the area under the curve (AUC) on the percentage of correct keypoints for different error thresholds. Specifically, in Table 1, among other results, in order to investigate the cross-dataset generalization of our network, we use the model trained on RHD-train and report AUC score and median error per joint on the FHD dataset, after alignment with the ground truth (Procrustes analysis). We also report percentage of correct keypoints (PCK) in Fig. 4, which returns the mean percentage of predicted joints below an Euclidean distance from the correct joint location.

The results show that our method demonstrates good performance on both datasets. The RHD set is characterized as challenging, due to the variations in viewpoints, and as a result we report higher 3D pose error. Since we are mostly interested in the generalization power of our model and its performance "in the wild", we find that our model manages to adapt effectively to unseen data and accurately captures the hand pose.

Table 1. Performance of the 3D hand pose estimation algorithm evaluated by two metrics for different training/testing scenarios.

Metrics ⟹		AUC	Median error
Training	Testing	score	per joint (mm)
RHD-train	RHD-train	0.729	18.1
	RHD-test	0.616	22.6
	FHD-test	0.771	16.2
FHD-train	FHD-test	0.900	11.0

3.3   SL Corpora

As already mentioned, the proposed SLR system is evaluated on two multi-signer SL corpora: (i) The isolated sign GSL dataset [2] and (ii) the continuous ASL fingerspelling ChicagoFSWild database [37]. More details are provided next.

GSL Dataset: This consists of 15 (5 × 3) different dialogues, organized in sets of 5 individual tasks in 3 public services, performed by 7 different signers. The dialogues, between a deaf person and a single service employee, are pre-defined and are performed by each signer 5 consecutive times (5 × 7 × 5 × 3). Signing is captured by an Intel RealSense D435 RGB-D camera at a rate 30 Hz, providing simultaneously RGB and 24-bit depth data streams at the same spatial resolution of 648 × 480 pixels. Additionally, during recording, camera pose adjustments are made, thus offering a desirable variation in the videos. Corpus annotations by GSL linguistic experts are provided at both the signed sentence and signed word levels. The corpus signed vocabulary consists of 310 unique glosses (40,785 gloss instances) and 331 unique sentences (10,290 sentences), with 4.23 glosses per sentence on average. Here, an isolated sign recognition task is built concerning 306 unique words (numerals are discarded) that are expressed between 4 and 10 times by each signer in the dataset, yielding 12,897 clips. The dataset is trained under a multi-signer framework, with all experiments conducted through ten-fold cross-validation, where 80% of each fold is allocated to training, 10% to validation, and 10% to testing.

ChicagoFSWild Database: This corpus includes ASL finger-spelling image frame sequences collected from online videos, providing a natural SL corpus in a real-world setting. The absence of unique signs for several words, such as names, foreign lexical items, and technical terms renders finger-spelling [32,37,38] a meaningful SL variant, basically expressed in a continuous letter signing unscrambling manner. The corpus was annotated through ELAN [1,8] by students that have studied ASL. The data contain 7,304 ASL finger-spelling sequences with frame resolution of 640 × 360 expressed by 160 signers, leading to a 3,553 unique finger-spelled word vocabulary. Here, we employ a small-vocabulary subset concerning 103 unique finger-spelled words, involving 26 English letters with a sufficient number of occurrences among all signers (143 signers) between 10 and 130 times in the corpus. These yield 3,076 video snippets of words obtained by the ELAN annotation time-stamps of the words of interest. Training is conducted under a multi-signer setting, through ten-fold cross-validation with 80% of each fold used for training, 10% for validation, and 10% for testing. For comparison purpose, training is also conducted in a signer-independent (SI) setting, where the dataset is divided into training, validation, and testing sets without signers overlap among the partitions. Applying the same partition as in [37], the training partition corresponds to 5,455 samples, the validation 981 videos, and the testing set 868 clips.

Table 2. Word accuracy (%) on two SL datasets under a multi-signer experimental paradigm, employing various feature stream combinations in conjunction with the attentional multi-step CNN encoder-decoder sequence-learning model of Sect. 2.2.

Feature Streams					Datasets	
Hand CNNs (1024-dim)	Mouth CNN (512-dim)	2D-Hand Skeleton (84-dim)	2D-Body Skeleton (30-dim)	3D-Hand Skeleton (126-dim)	GSL	ChFSWild
✓					88.25	84.71
	✓				29.46	23.57
		✓			40.33	34.20
			✓		33.87	30.07
				✓	78.91	75.29
✓	✓				88.96	86.47
✓	✓	✓			93.17	90.81
✓			✓	✓	90.20	86.33
✓	✓	✓		✓	93.40	91.17
✓	✓			✓	89.13	86.54
✓	✓		✓		89.81	87.65
✓	✓	✓	✓		93.41	91.01
✓	✓		✓	✓	91.23	87.10
			✓	✓	81.22	80.36
		✓	✓	✓	83.42	80.98
✓	✓	✓	✓	✓	**94.56**	**91.38**

3.4   SL Recognition Results

We first evaluate our SLR model for various feature streams using the attentional multi-step CNN encoder-decoder sequence-learning model, showcasing the power of 3D hand skeleton representations in the SLR task. Both datasets are evaluated in terms of word accuracy (%) in a multi-signer setting. As deduced from Table 2, the 3D hand skeleton seems to be a robust representation, achieving the highest accuracies on both datasets when added to 2D skeleton joints (body and hand skeletons) and hand and mouth articulator appearance feature representations, revealing the benefit of using multiple visual features streams that are complementary to each other. Incorporating 3D hand pose information boosts system performance on top of all other streams, obtaining 94.56% accuracy on the GSL dataset and 91.38% on ChicagoFSWild. It can also be viewed that its incorporation as additional hand information performs better when included with the 2D hand skeletal data. As demonstrated, the CNN-based articulator feature representations perform well, while the mouth region is mostly complementary in benefiting other feature streams. Finally, it can be observed that

Table 3. Word accuracy (%) on two SL datasets under a multi-signer experimental paradigm, using various encoder-decoder models with all feature streams concatenated.

Encoder-decoder	GSL corpus	ChFSWild corpus
Attentional LSTM	89.97	86.42
Attentional GRU	89.55	84.50
Attentional CNN	**94.56**	**91.38**
Transformer	88.21	85.63

skeletal features yield lower accuracies when used alone than appearance feature streams, demonstrating the need for their combined used.

Next, in Table 3, we investigate the performance of the various sequence-learning techniques of Sect. 2.2, when employing all feature streams discussed (1776-dim). Again, word accuracy is reported on the two datasets under the multi-signer experimental paradigm. As it can be observed, the best results are obtained by the attentional CNN encoder-decoder, revealing its superiority to the considered alternatives. This is primarily due to the good learning ability of CNNs. It can be readily seen that the worst results for the GSL dataset are obtained by the Transformer encoder-decoder module, while for the ChicagoFS-Wild database by the attentional GRU encoder-decoder.

We also evaluated the performance of the proposed system employing the attentional CNN encoder-decoder under a speaker-independent experimental paradigm in terms of letter accuracy (%) on the ChicagoFSWild dataset, improving over the best reported results of [38] from 45.1% to 47.93%. Additionally, our model outperforms previous reported approaches regarding the GSL dataset [2], yielding word accuracy improvements from 89.74% to 94.56%.

Table 4. Comparative evaluation of model variations of the attentional multi-step CNN encoder-decoder sequence-learning model of Sect. 2.2 in terms of word accuracy (%) in a multi-signer setting, with L being the number of layers, KW the kernel widths, and BW the beam width.

Model details			Datasets	
L	KW	BW	GSL	ChFSWild
1	3	3	84.21	82.74
2	3	3	93.83	87.45
3	3	3	94.33	90.87
1	5	5	87.52	85.48
2	5	5	93.27	91.12
3	5	5	**94.56**	**91.38**

Further, in Table 4, a number of variations of the sequence-learning model (attentional CNN encoder-decoder) are considered, regarding the number of layers, kernel widths, and the beam width employed during decoding. Results demonstrate that deeper architectures enhance model performance.

Finally, it should be noted that our system was evaluated using alternative skeletal joints normalization schemes, namely instead of normalizing 3D hand skeletal data regarding the elbow-shoulder distance, we applied the shoulder-to-shoulder distance, achieving 1.23% less accuracy in the GSL dataset and 2.47% in the ChicagoFSWild dataset. Additionally, employing the Euclidean distance between joints, generating 57 instead of 114 2D skeletal features results in an accuracy decrease for both datasets (6.44% for GSL dataset and 8.91% for the ChicagoFSWild database).

4   Conclusion

In this paper we investigated the benefit of estimated 3D hand skeletal information to the task of SLR from RGB videos, within a state-of-the-art deep-learning recognition system, operating on multiple feature streams. We proposed to infer 3D hand pose from 2D skeletal information obtained from OpenPose, using a deep-learning architecture previously used for 3D human pose estimation. Our results on two multi-signer SL corpora demonstrated that 3D hand pose adds value on top of other feature streams, including 2D skeletal information and CNN-based representations of manual and non-manual articulators. Further, our results outperformed the previously reported state-of-the-art on the two SL corpora considered.

Acknowledgements. The research work was supported by the Hellenic Foundation for Research and Innovation (H.F.R.I.) under the "First Call for H.F.R.I. Research Projects to support Faculty members and Researchers and the procurement of high-cost research equipment grant" (Project Number: 2456).

References

1. ELAN (Version 5.8) [Computer software], Nijmegen: Max Planck Institute for Psycholinguistics, The Language Archive (2019). https://archive.mpi.nl/tla/elan
2. Adaloglou, N., et al.: A comprehensive study on sign language recognition methods. IEEE Trans. Multimedia (2019)
3. Bahdanau, D., Cho, K., Bengio, Y.: Neural machine translation by jointly learning to align and translate. CoRR abs/1409.0473 (2014)
4. Camgoz, N.C., Hadfield, S., Koller, O., Ney, H., Bowden, R.: Neural sign language translation. In: Proceedings of the IEEE Conference on Computer Vision and Pattern Recognition, pp. 7784–7793 (2018)
5. Camgöz, N.C., Koller, O., Hadfield, S., Bowden, R.: Sign language transformers: Joint end-to-end sign language recognition and translation. CoRR abs/2003.13830 (2020)

6. Cho, K., Merrienboer, B.V., Gülçehre, C., Bougares, F., Schwenk, H., Bengio, Y.: Learning phrase representations using RNN encoder-decoder for statistical machine translation. In: Proceedings of the Conference on Empirical Methods in Natural Language Processing, pp. 1724–1734 (2014)

7. Community, B.O.: Blender-a 3D modelling and rendering package. Blender Foundation, Stichting Blender Foundation, Amsterdam (2018). http://www.blender.org

8. Crasborn, O., Sloetjes, H.: Enhanced ELAN functionality for sign language corpora. In: Proceedings of the Workshop on the Representation and Processing of Sign Languages: Construction and Exploitation of Sign Language Corpora, pp. 39–43 (2008)

9. Deng, J., Dong, W., Socher, R., Li, L.J., Li, K., Fei-Fei, L.: ImageNet: a large-scale hierarchical image database. In: Proceedings of the IEEE Conference on Computer Vision and Pattern Recognition, pp. 248–255 (2009)

10. Duchi, J., Hazan, E., Singer, Y.: Adaptive subgradient methods for online learning and stochastic optimization. J. Mach. Learn. Res. **12**, 2121–2159 (2011)

11. Escalera, S., et al.: Chalearn multi-modal gesture recognition 2013: grand challenge and workshop summary. In: Proceedings of the ACM on International Conference on Multimodal Interaction, pp. 365–368 (2013)

12. Fossati, A., Gall, J., Grabner, H., Ren, X., Konolige, K. (eds.): Consumer Depth Cameras for Computer Vision - Research Topics and Applications. Springer, New York (2012)

13. Fuse, M.: Mixamo: Quality 3D Character Animation In Minutes (2015). https://www.mixamo.com

14. Glorot, X., Bengio, Y.: Understanding the difficulty of training deep feedforward neural networks. In: Proceedings of the International Conference on Artificial Intelligence and Statistics, pp. 249–256 (2010)

15. He, K., Zhang, X., Ren, S., Sun, J.: Delving deep into rectifiers: surpassing human-level performance on ImageNet classification. In: Proceedings of the IEEE International Conference on Computer Vision, pp. 1026–1034 (2015)

16. He, K., Zhang, X., Ren, S., Sun, J.: Deep residual learning for image recognition. In: Proceedings of the IEEE Conference on Computer Vision and Pattern Recognition, pp. 770–778 (2016)

17. He, Y., Hu, W., Yang, S.F., Qu, X., Wan, P., Guo, Z.: 3D hand pose estimation in the wild via graph refinement under adversarial learning. In: Proceedings of the IEEE/CVF Conference on Computer Vision and Pattern Recognition (2020)

18. Hochreiter, S., Schmidhuber, J.: Long short-term memory. Neural Comput. **9**, 1735–1780 (1997)

19. Hosain, A.A., Santhalingam, P.S., Pathak, P., Kosecka, J., Rangwala, H.: Sign language recognition analysis using multimodal data. In: Proceedings of the IEEE International Conference on Data Science and Advanced Analytics, pp. 203–210 (2019)

20. Hu, Y., Zhao, H.F., Wang, Z.G.: Sign language fingerspelling recognition using depth information and deep belief networks. Int. J. Pattern Recogn. Artif. Intell. **32**(06) (2018)

21. Kartika, D.R., Sigit, R., Setiawardhana, S.: Sign language interpreter hand using optical-flow. In: Proceedings of the International Seminar on Application for Technology of Information and Communication, pp. 197–201 (2016)

22. Kingma, D.P., Ba, J.: Adam: A method for stochastic optimization. CoRR abs/1412.6980 (2014)

23. Ko, S., Son, J., Jung, H.: Sign language recognition with recurrent neural network using human keypoint detection. In: Proceedings of the Conference on Research in Adaptive and Convergent Systems, pp. 326–328 (2018)
24. Konstantinidis, D., Dimitropoulos, K., Daras, P.: A deep learning approach for analyzing video and skeletal features in sign language recognition. In: Proceedings of the IEEE International Conference on Imaging Systems and Techniques, pp. 1–6 (2018)
25. Kurakin, A., Zhang, Z., Liu, Z.: A real time system for dynamic hand gesture recognition with a depth sensor. In: Proceedings of the European Signal Processing Conference, pp. 1975–1979 (2012)
26. Lee, B.G., Lee, S.M.: Smart wearable hand device for sign language interpretation system with sensors fusion. IEEE Sens. J. **18**(3), 1224–1232 (2018)
27. Martinez, J., Hossain, R., Romero, J., Little, J.J.: A simple yet effective baseline for 3D human pose estimation. In: Proceedings of the IEEE International Conference on Computer Vision, pp. 2659–2668 (2017)
28. Mittal, A., Kumar, P., Roy, P.P., Balasubramanian, R., Chaudhuri, B.B.: A modified LSTM model for continuous sign language recognition using leap motion. IEEE Sens. J. **19**(16), 7056–7063 (2019)
29. Mueller, F., et al.: GANerated hands for real-time 3D hand tracking from monocular RGB. In: Proceedings of the IEEE/CVF Conference on Computer Vision and Pattern Recognition, pp. 49–59 (2018)
30. Nugraha, F., Djamal, E.C.: Video recognition of American sign language using two-stream convolution neural networks. In: Proceedings of the International Conference on Electrical Engineering and Informatics, pp. 400–405 (2019)
31. Panteleris, P., Oikonomidis, I., Argyros, A.A.: Using a single RGB frame for real time 3D hand pose estimation in the wild. In: Proceedings of the IEEE Winter Conference on Applications of Computer Vision, pp. 436–445 (2018)
32. Papadimitriou, K., Potamianos, G.: End-to-end convolutional sequence learning for ASL fingerspelling recognition. In: Proceedings of the Annual Conference of the International Speech Communication Association, pp. 2315–2319 (2019)
33. Paszke, A., et al.: Automatic differentiation in PyTorch. In: Proceedings of the NIPS-W (2017)
34. Pitsikalis, V., Theodorakis, S., Vogler, C., Maragos, P.: Advances in phonetics-based sub-unit modeling for transcription alignment and sign language recognition. In: Proceedings of the IEEE Computer Vision and Pattern Recognition Workshops, pp. 1–6 (2011)
35. Ren, Z., Yuan, J., Zhang, Z.: Robust hand gesture recognition based on finger-earth mover's distance with a commodity depth camera. In: Proceedings of the ACM Multimedia Conference and Co-Located Workshops, pp. 1093–1096 (2011)
36. Roussos, A., Theodorakis, S., Pitsikalis, V., Maragos, P.: Dynamic affine-invariant shape-appearance handshape features and classification in sign language videos. J. Mach. Learn. Res. **14**, 1627–1663 (2013)
37. Shi, B., Rio, A.M.D., Keane, J., Brentari, D., Shakhnarovich, G., Livescu, K.: Fingerspelling recognition in the wild with iterative visual attention. In: Proceedings of the IEEE International Conference on Computer Vision, pp. 5399–5408 (2019)
38. Shi, B., et al.: American sign language fingerspelling recognition in the wild. Proceedings of the IEEE Spoken Language Technology Workshop, pp. 145–152 (2018)
39. Simon, T., Joo, H., Matthews, I., Sheikh, Y.: Hand keypoint detection in single images using multiview bootstrapping. In: Proceedings of the IEEE Conference on Computer Vision and Pattern Recognition, pp. 4645–4653 (2017)

40. Tashev, I.: Kinect development kit: a toolkit for gesture- and speech-based human-machine interaction [best of the web]. IEEE Signal Process. Mag. **30**(5), 129–131 (2013)
41. Vaswani, A., et al.: Attention is all you need. Adv. Neural Inf. Process. Syst. (NeurIPS) **30**, 5998–6008 (2017)
42. Wu, Y., et al.: Google's neural machine translation system: Bridging the gap between human and machine translation. CoRR abs/1609.08144 (2016)
43. Zhou, J., Cao, Y., Wang, X., Li, P., Xu, W.: Deep recurrent models with fast-forward connections for neural machine translation. CoRR abs/1606.04199 (2016)
44. Zimmermann, C., Brox, T.: Learning to estimate 3D hand pose from single RGB images. In: Proceedings of the IEEE International Conference on Computer Vision, pp. 4913–4921 (2017)
45. Zimmermann, C., Ceylan, D., Yang, J., Russell, B., Argus, M., Brox, T.: Frei-HAND: a dataset for markerless capture of hand pose and shape from single RGB images. In: Proceedings of the IEEE International Conference on Computer Vision, pp. 813–822 (2019)

A Plan for Developing an Auslan Communication Technologies Pipeline

Jessica Korte[1]([✉]) [iD], Axel Bender[2], Guy Gallasch[2], Janet Wiles[1] [iD],
and Andrew Back[1] [iD]

[1] The University of Queensland, Brisbane, QLD, Australia
{j.korte,j.wiles,a.back}@uq.edu.au
[2] Defence Science and Technology, Edinburgh, South Australia, Australia
{Axel.Bender,Guy.Gallasch}@dst.defence.gov.au

Abstract. AI techniques for mainstream spoken languages have seen a great deal of progress in recent years, with technologies for transcription, translation and text processing becoming commercially available. However, no such technologies have been developed for sign languages, which, as visual-gestural languages, require multimodal processing approaches. This paper presents a plan to develop an Auslan Communication Technologies Pipeline (Auslan CTP), a prototype AI system enabling Auslan-in, Auslan-out interactions, to demonstrate the feasibility of Auslan-based machine interaction and language processing. Such a system has a range of applications, including gestural human-machine interfaces, educational tools, and translation.

Keywords: Auslan · Australian sign language · Sign language recognition · Sign language production · Sign language processing

1 Introduction

While mainstream spoken languages, with large corpora of written and spoken data, are seeing a surge in the development of AI tools for recognition, translation, production and processing, such tools for sign languages are lacking. From a perspective of equity, sign languages should also have access to such AI tools, to support the access of Deaf and other signers to communication-supporting technologies; and the field is on the cusp of having the technical ability to develop such tools. However, the language processing approaches developed to date are largely not suitable for processing visual-gestural languages with relatively limited datasets, as is the case with many sign languages around the world, including Auslan.

Much of the AI research on sign language recognition to date has been in the field of image or gesture classification. Such automatic gesture classification can provide basic gesture recognition, but experiences problems including robustness, performance under "noisy" real-world conditions, and variability from user to user. We propose a new AI framework for multimodal visual-gestural language

A. Bartoli and A. Fusiello (Eds.): ECCV 2020 Workshops, LNCS 12536, pp. 264–277, 2020.
https://doi.org/10.1007/978-3-030-66096-3_19

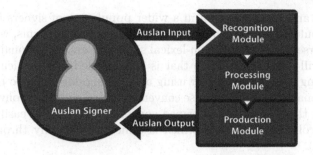

Fig. 1. The proposed Auslan Communication Technologies Pipeline architecture. Each module represents a segment of functionality which requires the development of specific AI approaches: the *Recognition Module*, intended to recognize sign input, requires development of Auslan recognition as a multimodal language; the *Processing Module*, which provides the functionality of the pipeline, requires Natural Sign Language Processing; and the *Production Module*, which will output Auslan signing, requires human-like production of sign output that is acceptable to the Deaf community. Each of these modules will interface with the next module in the Pipeline to deliver a functional application

recognition, incorporating various nuances of lexical signs, visual representation, gestures, body language, and facial expression as sub-language components within the newly developed approach known as entropy-based AI, drawing on both image classification and language processing fields. This project has significant potential for sign language and gesture recognition, and sign language-based human-machine interfaces.

This paper presents a plan for the Auslan Communication Technologies Pipeline (Auslan CTP), a module-based system for recognizing, processing and producing Auslan communication. The modular nature of the system allows for flexibility of purpose, and "plug-and-play" replacement of components as improvements are made to each module. Figure 1 above shows the components of the pipeline.

2   Sign Language Recognition

"Gesture recognition" has been explored in the context of pre-defined non-language gestures [1,27,35] (including military-inspired gesture sets [6,21,29]), and various sign languages (e.g. Auslan [11,18,19]) using techniques including computer vision [5,21,27,28], sensor-based wearables [5,6,18,19,22,29], Markov models [11,22,24,28,31] and neural networks [4,23,25,26]. These approaches require extremely large training sets with multiple examples of a single gesture or sign to learn to recognise input [4]; therefore, the scope of such work has been restricted to date to small vocabularies of strictly lexical signs [5,11,18,19,22,28,31], such as fingerspelling signs [28]. This can result in high accuracies over the known vocabulary and known signers [11,18,19], but lacks real-world applicability, as accuracy decreases due to inter-signer variation [17] in expression and sign formation in a wider population of signers [19], and the limited vocabularies only include lexical signs in standard forms, where natural signed discourse relies on both non-lexical signs [15] and situational use of space [3]. Signers will enact information that is not encoded in a particular sign, e.g. miming looking at a phone [15]; or using areas of signing space to represent referents. Such enactment does not use conventionalised signs but conveys meaning in relation to the context of the signed conversation which is easily intelligible to a human collocutor [15], but which is difficult to classify through machine learning (ML).

There is one Auslan corpus which captures enactment [13], collected and annotated by Johnston and colleagues for linguistic research [14], but it is not fully curated for machine learning, and cannot be made public as it contains sensitive content and signers are identifiable.

We propose that a system for recognising Auslan in real-time must differentiate:

1. Handshape, orientation and location of static signs;
2. Handshape, orientation, location and movement of dynamic signs;
3. Facial expression and body language, and their relevance to a particular sign [16];
4. Fully lexical, semi-lexical and non-lexical signing, and their meanings;
5. Transitions between signs; and
6. Individual variability of sign production.

We are planning to address points 4 and 5 through movement entropy, as this should change between signs or sign components [30,33], allowing for automated segmentation. Entropy-based AI [2] is a new methodology to address points 4 and 6, which in effect, is using entropy as a measure of the characteristics of the signs.

2.1 Entropy-Based AI

While image based recognition of gesture can be performed well in situations when the visibility and related conditions are ideal, in real world situations there can be significant challenges. Hence, one aspect of this work is to consider information theoretic approaches which seek to combine probabilistic information about the signs in order to assist recognition.

For example, a static image or series of images may be insufficient to differentiate signs, especially if visibility is poor; but when aided by movement, then this can make our recognition task considerably easier. While various forms of image recognition approaches have been adopted in the past based on sequential images over time, in this stage, we are aiming to include a measure of how sign movement can assist in recognition.

The basic idea here is to treat sign language as multimodal language rather than an image classification problem. An example of the potential effectiveness of this approach can be understood as follows.

Suppose that instead of treating gesture recognition as a single static image, we now treat it as a short synthetic narrative, where the "words" are each sub-movements within each sign. In the same way that humans can recognise meaning from incomplete or slightly incorrect language input (for example, a signer using the wrong handshape, but correct location and movement; or starting location being obscured), we can now consider a sign in terms of these "synthetic words". For example, suppose we have a set of symbols {A,B,C,D,E,F} - which might correspond to a subset of handshapes and locations - then a given sign might be represented usually by a sequence of [D,A,C,B] with corresponding entropy. For incomplete or obscured input, such as a sequence [D,A,x,B] with corresponding entropy, we can provide an estimate of the most likely sign based on the observed input sequence of synthetic features.

If we compute the probabilistic structure of these "words" for each sign being observed, then in terms of the overall entropy, it is expected that there will be a particular probabilistic structure for each type of sign. Hence, the entropy can be used to assist in identifying signs, and it can also assist in identifying when the movements are "surprising" or "unexpected", thereby indicating that this may be in fact, a different gesture than the sign being recognized by image recognition. This approach is somewhat similar to the use of short-term prediction used in dictionary based systems like predictive text. Here however, we are coupling it with image recognition to provide a richer framework, either confirming the trust in the image, or perhaps, indicating that there is an issue with the observed image. For example, a gesture might appear to be one thing, but the way in which it was formed over the short time it was "constructed", indicates that it cannot be conclusively relied on. We believe that this ability to identify "surprising" or "untrustworthy" input can enable us to identify semi-lexical and non-lexical signs, as well as potentially to differentiate non-linguistic gestures.

Furthermore, the approach suggested here can provide additional insight into improving recognition accuracy under conditions of poor visibility or duress. The image recognition part might indicate that the sign could be one of several possible signs, but when we use the ranking of the entropy-based model, then this could indicate the most likely gesture overall.

This entropy-based AI approach calls for a symbolization of the input space into a "synthetic" entropy-based language. In current work to date, this does not seem to require an optimal process, provided the entire input space is accounted for. The symbolization will segment various sign elements (lexical signs and sign segments, visual representation, handshapes, body language and facial expression) into micro-features, for example, small movements over time. These small features become the basic symbolic building blocks, i.e. "synthetic letters" within our new synthetic language framework. These synthetic letters will then be used to form synthetic words with particular probabilistic structure, for example, adopting a multidimensional N-gram model, and hence it becomes possible to develop this richer approach to not only gesture recognition, but also to introduce a degree of robustness, enabling identification through a multimodal, information theoretic mechanism. This is anticipated to provide more stable communication.

2.2 Open Questions

Treating Auslan as a full, visual-gestural language with meaning encoded in lexical, semi-lexical and non-lexical signing raises the following questions:

1. How can entropy-based AI methods support accuracy and trustworthiness of sign classification, especially considering inter-signer variability?
2. How can entropy-based AI approaches be used to segment sign movements at all levels of lexical?
3. How can time- or sequence-based ML approaches inform Auslan recognition?
4. What are the requirements for a data set of Auslan data for use in machine learning to recognise signs at all levels of lexicality? This includes considerations of:
   (a) file formats, size and resolution;
   (b) approaches to encoding data for machine learning use;
   (c) sourcing data in a post-COVID19 world; and
   (d) transferability of lessons from spoken language ML corpora and/or linguistics corpora.
5. How can an Auslan processing system recognise and respond appropriately to body language communication?
6. How can incremental learning, zero-shot learning, or other similar machine learning paradigms allow for extensibility of Auslan recognition?

2.3 Research Approach

Developing a new framework of trustworthy Auslan recognition requires a comprehensive data set. Hence, the first step is to obtain a sign language dataset. This will be done by collecting Auslan data in video and depth formats from expert and native signers. Deaf signers are as expressive and individual as speakers of any language, and they are experts in the use of visual-gestural communication. Their involvement in the project places them, as sign language experts, in the position of deciding what to communicate, and how to "write" their language into technology, including in terms of determining the approach to encoding. It is expected that data encoding will involve some combination of: handshape; hand orientations; start, end and/or key locations; movements; expressions; mouthing and facial movements; linguistic glosses; Hammocks or Sign Writing encoding; English translation; dialect; signer fluency; and clarity of signing. Once coding has begun, we plan to create machine learning sub-modules to automate some elements of encoding, such as a machine learning model which attempts to identify and recommend handshapes.

Once coded, the dataset will be used to develop the experimental system for evaluating proposed models. In the first instance and for baseline reference purposes, a machine learning model will be implemented for sign language classification. The main aspects of the proposed model will then be developed using the entropy-based AI framework where the first step is as follows:

1. Formulate the sign elements,
2. Determine the entropy characteristics of the sign language,
3. Examine the probabilistic characteristics of Auslan data at all levels of lexicality,
4. Develop the architectural framework of the Entropy-based AI system for sign language and gesture recognition.

A possible machine learning architecture is shown in Fig. 2.

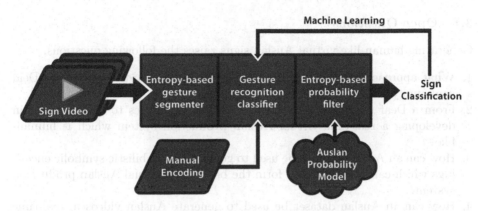

Fig. 2. Possible architecture of entropy-based Auslan recognition machine learning system

3 Virtual Sign Language Production

Virtual production of sign languages is of significant strategic importance as a basis for two-way communication between humans and machine agents. Typically sign production uses one of 3 approaches:

1. encoding of sign representation for automated, usually avatar-based, production e.g. [8,36,38];
2. Pre-rendering video or animation [20] of fixed messages; or
3. AI techniques, e.g. Generative Adversarial Networks [32].

Each approach can have problems in clarity, comprehension and trustworthiness of produced sign. Automated avatar production (approach 1) can lack natural expressions, body movements and non-manual sign aspects [20,38], and is discouraged by the World Federation of the Deaf and the World Association of Sign Language Interpreters for live interpretation [39]. Pre-rendered video or animation (approach 2) is fixed and cannot be altered quickly or inexpensively [12,37,38]. NAG production (approach 3) may resemble a real signer from the dataset [32], which could raise reputation al issues.

This research proposes to develop, in consultation with the Australian Deaf community, a framework for virtual human-like sign and gesture production based on entropy-based AI, which has the potential to provide natural behaviours. It is expected to extend from one or more of the three known approaches, and to include guidance for usage approved by the Deaf community. If all three approaches are found unacceptable by the Deaf community, other avenues such as social robots could be explored; or new approaches could be co-designed with Deaf design partners.

3.1 Open Questions

Generating human-like virtual Auslan signs raises the following questions:

1. What approaches to sign production are acceptable to the Australian Deaf community?
2. From a Deaf user perspective, what are the key issues to be addressed in developing a real-time virtual Auslan production system which is human-like?
3. How can an Auslan dataset be used to generate probabilistic symbolic encodings which can be adapted to form the basis for a virtual Auslan production system?
4. How can an Auslan dataset be used to generate Auslan videos in real-time without co-opting the image of a real signer?
5. How can signs with varying degrees of conventionalisation (lexical, semi-lexical, and non-lexical) be encoded for virtual Auslan sign production?
6. What are the notation requirements for a human-like real-time virtual Auslan production system when used in a human-like framework using entropy-based AI?
7. What probabilistic encoding framework or symbolization can be used for capturing natural expressions, emotions, body movements and other similar features?
8. How can human-like Auslan signing be constructed via the proposed framework?

3.2 Research Approach

To address the questions related to Auslan production, resources for producing or generating Auslan signing will be created. This is intended to allow future systems to be able to output signed communication in the form of human-like Auslan, incorporating elements identified by signers as important, including emotion and naturalistic movement.

Sign production (like speech production), can use a range of techniques, which include direct mapping from sign video to avatar production; generative modelling from sign video; a programmable avatar which generates signs based on sign notation; and a modular database of avatar clips or elements (e.g. signs, sign fragments, handshapes, facial expressions, etc.) which could be concatenated for real-time generation of Auslan sign. Each has advantages and different requirements for effective use: video mapping techniques are directly usable; sign notation provides for generality; and a library of signs could be of general use in Auslan production. Working with Deaf community members, the feasibility and advantages/disadvantages of these approaches will be explored using the Auslan dataset and model (developed in addressing questions of sign language recognition) to inform the design of a sign encoding system.

The Auslan production approach chosen will be used in a prototype system, which should be able to generate signs based on annotations, glosses or videos.

4   Natural Sign Language Processing

Natural language processing (NLP) systems typically rely on symbolised written languages [7]. As Auslan has no native writing, there is a need to consider exactly how symbolisation can be done, in terms of notation systems, grammars and other language constructs. Several sign notations have been created (e.g. HamNoSys [10], SignWriting [34]) but each has limitations, and none are widely used by the Australian Deaf community. HamNoSys receives some use by Auslan linguists [14]. Most sign language processing (SLP) to date has focused on translation, relying on a notation or glossing system (e.g. [9,32]).

4.1   Open Questions

Sign Language Processing raises the following questions:

1. How well can existing NLP approaches be converted to work in SLP?
2. What are the requirements for encodings for an Auslan processing system?
3. Can the use of a video dataset reduce the need for written notation in SLP?
4. How can an Auslan processing system identify and process less conventionalised signed communication, such as enactment?
5. How can sentiment analysis or similar NLP techniques inform the emotional expression and body language of human-like, machine-produced Auslan signs?

4.2   Research Approach

This module is the central processing part of the Auslan Communication Technologies Pipeline, connecting the Auslan Recognition Module with the Auslan Production Module, by developing a method for computational processing of sign language and gesture.

For example, with a question like "How can an Auslan processing system identify and process less conventionalised signed communication, such as enactment?", the research approach would build on prior work around recognising and encoding non-lexical and semi-lexical communication, as well as drawing on existing NLP approaches to draw meaning from context, augmented by entropy-based AI approaches to contextual probability.

The scope and application of the processing system will be determined through consultation with Deaf community members. Options include: an Auslan chatbot, an Auslan digital assistant, an Auslan teaching tool, or a translation system. The choice of application will of course influence the system architecture. A possible chatbot system architecture is shown in Fig. 3.

5   Connection to Communicative Gesture Research for Social and Operational Robotics

The Auslan CTP research, and gestural human-machine interaction more broadly, has significant potential for use in co-operative and social robotics, through explicit gestural interfaces, and robots with human-like implicit awareness of body language and gesture. This research's focus on interaction via lexicalised and non-lexicalised signing as used by diverse individual signers provides a basis for machine recognition and understanding that could underlie human-robot non-verbal communication, as it may result in an approach to encoding multimodal language such that a robot could understand real-time messages communicated robustly in operational environments, with support for inter-signer variability in message production.

For example, the introduction of robotic and autonomous systems in the military domain has resulted in requirements for human-machine interaction that is robust in harsh operational conditions. In such conditions, it is not affordable and often not possible to communicate verbally; lives depend on the accurate interpretation of environmental cues and the effective and efficient communication with team members (whether human or robot). An important argument why Auslan is a good basis for human-robot interaction in the military domain is, firstly, that Auslan is a full visual-gestural language. Different levels of abstraction (symbolic through to semantic) can be communicated in the language and hence represented in the messages between human and robot. This is especially important in situations where context matters – which is the case in most military tactical settings.

Secondly, Auslan varies from individual to individual, in the same way that speakers of every language are individuals; i.e., every signer has preferred vocabulary, expressions and nuances of sign production. Exploring this variability is important for achieving the aim of natural human-robot interaction in a range of contexts, i.e., allowing humans to use individualised language in their interaction with a robot. Current gesture technology has a tendency to require strict and accurate adherence to a known set of gestures, resulting in a non-robust interaction modality or in the need to train the human in the precise execution of gestures. Breaking this paradigm of "changing the human" to get humans and robots to work together is particularly important in demanding contexts such as military operations where the human has to focus on many things concurrently, and may be under high levels of stress or otherwise distracted from executing precise visual-gestural commands.

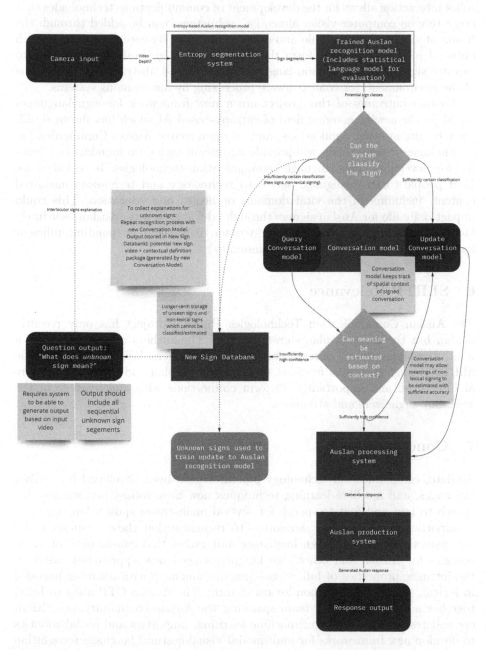

Fig. 3. Possible architecture for a chatbot. Such a system could include capabilities to collect definitions of unknown signs (*dotted arrows on left of diagram*)

Thirdly, use of a multimodal gestural language in social or military human-robot interaction allows for the development of communications technologies that don't rely on computer vision alone, i.e., robustness can be added through the fusion of vision, haptics, audio and other modalities. By extension, the research outlined in this paper may form the basis for more general encoding, able to capture signing, speaking, non-language gestures and abstract representations of the environment, for context-aware processing by autonomous systems.

Further outcomes of this project are a new framework for sign languages based on the newly emerging field of entropy-based AI which has shown significant results in other applications; and an open source Auslan Communication Technologies Pipeline. This will provide significant long term foundational benefits for developing sign language communication technologies. It will increase Deaf people's native-language access to technology and technology-mediated content, including in the vital domains of health and education. This could impact daily life for Auslan signers through educational uses, Auslan user interfaces, and automatic translation of pre-written digital content (pending sufficient levels of accuracy that satisfy the community).

6   SLRTP Relevance

The Auslan Communication Technologies Pipeline project has only recently begun, but the research plan shows promise. The authors of this paper are a multi-disciplinary group of researchers and practitioners. We wish to attend the SLRTP workshop to gain feedback on the research plan and proposed software architectures; and importantly, to form connections with and learn from the workshop organizers and attendees.

7   Conclusions

To date, communication technology pipelines have been developed for spoken languages, and machine learning techniques now have robust performance for speech to text and text to speech for several mainstream spoken languages. It is important for technology developers to recognise that these techniques will not generalise directly to sign languages, but rather that communication technologies for Auslan and other sign languages need new approaches based on the intrinsic properties of full, visual-gestural language with meaning encoded in lexical, semi-lexical and non-lexical signing. The Auslan CTP aims to bring together a multidisciplinary team spanning the Auslan community, practitioners and researchers in design, machine learning, linguistics and social robotics to develop new frameworks for multimodal visual-gestural language recognition and human-like sign production.

Acknowledgements. Many thanks to the project mentors who provided guidance and feedback on this paper: Professor Trevor Johnston, Dr Adam Schembri, Dr Ashfin Rahimi and Associate Professor Marcus Gallagher.

The research for this paper received funding from the Australian Government through the Defence Cooperative Research Centre for Trusted Autonomous Systems. The DCRC-TAS receives funding support from the Queensland Government.

References

1. Amir, A., et al.: DVS128 Gesture Dataset (2017). http://www.research.ibm.com/dvsgesture/
2. Back, A.D., Angus, D., Wiles, J.: Transitive entropy—a rank ordered approach for natural sequences. IEEE J. Sel. Top. Signal Process. **14**(2), 312–321 (2019). https://doi.org/10.1109/JSTSP.2019.2939998
3. Bavelier, D., Corina, D.P., Neville, H.J.: Brain and language: a perspective from sign language. Neuron **21**, 275–278 (1998)
4. Bowden, R., Zisserman, A., Kadir, T., Brady, M.: Vision based interpretation of natural sign languages. In: Proceedings of the 3rd International Conference on Computer Vision Systems (2003). http://info.ee.surrey.ac.uk/Personal/R.Bowden/publications/icvs03/icvs03pap.pdf
5. Brashear, H., Henderson, V., Park, K.H., Hamilton, H., Lee, S., Starner, T.: American sign language recognition in game development for deaf children. In: Proceedings of the 8th International ACM SIGACCESS Conference on Computers and Accessibility-Assets 2006, p. 79 (2006). https://doi.org/10.1145/1168987.1169002, http://portal.acm.org/citation.cfm?doid=1168987.1169002
6. Ceruti, M.G., et al.: Wireless communication glove apparatus for motion tracking, gesture recognition, data transmission, and reception in extreme environments. In: Proceedings of the ACM Symposium on Applied Computing, pp. 172–176 (2009). https://doi.org/10.1145/1529282.1529320
7. da Rocha Costa, A.C., Dimuro, G.P.: SignWriting and SWML: paving the way to sign language processing. In: Traitement Automatique des Langues Naturelles (TALN). Batz-sur-Mer, France (2003)
8. Efthimiou, E., Sapountzaki, G., Karpouzis, K., Fotinea, S.-E.: Developing an e-learning platform for the Greek sign language. In: Miesenberger, Klaus, Klaus, Joachim, Zagler, Wolfgang L., Burger, Dominique (eds.) ICCHP 2004. LNCS, vol. 3118, pp. 1107–1113. Springer, Heidelberg (2004). https://doi.org/10.1007/978-3-540-27817-7_163
9. Elliott, R., Glauert, J.R., Kennaway, J.R., Marshall, I., Safar, E.: Linguistic modelling and language-processing technologies for avatar-based sign language presentation. Univ. Access Inf. Soc. **6**(4), 375–391 (2008). https://doi.org/10.1007/s10209-007-0102-z
10. Hanke, T.: HamNoSys—representing sign language data in language resources and language processing contexts. In: LREC 2004, Workshop Proceedings: Representation and Processing of Sign Languages, pp. 1–6 (2004). http://www.sign-lang.uni-hamburg.de/dgs-korpus/files/inhalt_pdf/HankeLRECSLP2004_05.pdf
11. Holden, E.J., Lee, G., Owens, R.: Australian Sign Language recognition. Mach. Vis. Appl. **16**(5), 312–320 (2005). https://doi.org/10.1007/s00138-005-0003-1
12. Huawei: StorySign: Helping Deaf Children Learn to Read (2018). https://consumer.huawei.com/au/campaign/storysign/

13. Johnston, T.: Auslan Corpus (2008). https://elar.soas.ac.uk/Collection/MPI55247
14. Johnston, T.: Auslan Corpus Annotation Guidelines. Technical Report, Macquarie University & La Trobe University, Sydney and Melbourne Australia (2016). http://media.auslan.org.au/attachments/Johnston_AuslanCorpusAnnotationGuidelines_February2016.pdf
15. Johnston, T.: Wrangling and Structuring a Sign-Language Corpus: The Auslan Dictionary. Presentation at CoEDL Fest (2019)
16. Johnston, T., Schembri, A.: Australian Sign Language (Auslan): An Introduction to Sign Language Linguistics. Cambridge University Press, Cambridge, UK (2007)
17. Johnston, T., Schembri, A.: Variation, lexicalization and grammaticalization in signed languages. Langage et société, 1(131), 19–35 (2010)
18. Kadous, M.W.: Auslan sign recognition using computers and gloves. In: Deaf Studies Research Symposium (1998). https://www.doi.org/10.1.1.51.3816, http://citeseerx.ist.psu.edu/viewdoc/summary?doi=10.1.1.51.3816
19. Kadous, W.: GRASP: Recognition of Australian Sign Language Using Instrumented Gloves. Ph.D. thesis, The University of New South Wales (1995)
20. Kipp, M., Nguyen, Q., Heloir, A., Matthes, S.: Assessing the Deaf user perspective on sign language avatars. In: The Proceedings of the 13th International ACM SIGACCESS Conference on Computers and Accessibility, Dundee, Scotland, UK, pp. 107–114. ACM (2011). https://doi.org/10.1145/2049536.2049557
21. Lebron, J.: Recognizing Military Gestures: Developing a Gesture Recognition Interface. Technical Report, Union College, Schenectady, NY, USA (2013). http://orzo.union.edu/Archives/SeniorProjects/2013/CS.2013/
22. Li, Y., Chen, X., Zhang, X., Wang, K., Wang, Z.J.: A sign-component-based framework for Chinese sign language recognition using accelerometer and sEMG data. IEEE Trans. Biomed. Eng. 59(10), 2695–2704 (2012). https://doi.org/10.1109/TBME.2012.2190734
23. Liao, Y., Xiong, P., Min, W., Min, W., Lu, J.: Dynamic sign language recognition based on video sequence with BLSTM-3D residual networks. IEEE Access,7, 38044–38054 (2019). https://doi.org/10.1109/ACCESS.2019.2904749, https://ieeexplore.ieee.org/document/8667292/
24. Ong, S.C.W., Hsu, D., Lee, W.S., Kurniawati, H.: Partially observable Markov decision process (POMDP) technologies for sign language based human-computer interaction. In: Proceedings of the International Conference on Human-Computer Interaction (2009)
25. Parton, B.S.: Sign language recognition and translation: a multidisciplined approach from the field of artificial intelligence. J. Deaf Stud. Deaf Educ. 11(1), 94–101 (2006). https://doi.org/10.1093/deafed/enj003
26. Pigou, Lionel., Dieleman, Sander., Kindermans, Pieter-Jan, Schrauwen, Benjamin: Sign language recognition using convolutional neural networks. In: Agapito, Lourdes, Bronstein, Michael M., Rother, Carsten (eds.) ECCV 2014. LNCS, vol. 8925, pp. 572–578. Springer, Cham (2015). https://doi.org/10.1007/978-3-319-16178-5_40
27. Pisharady, P.K., Saerbeck, M.: Recent methods and databases in vision-based hand gesture recognition: a review. Comput. Vis. Image Underst. 141(December), 152–165 (2015). https://doi.org/10.1016/j.cviu.2015.08.004
28. Sahoo, A.K., Mishra, G.S., Ravulakollu, K.K.: Sign language recognition: state of the art. ARPN J. Eng. Appl. Sci. 9(2), 116–134 (2014)
29. Sathiyanarayanan, M., Azharuddin, S., Kumar, S., Khan, G.: Gesture controlled robot for military purpose. Int. J. Technol. Res. Eng. 1(11), 2347–4718 (2014). www.ijtre.com

30. So, C.K.F., Baciu, G.: Entropy-based Motion Extraction for Motion Capture Animation, pp. 225–235 (2005). https://www.doi.org/10.1002/cav.107
31. Starner, T., Pentland, A.: Visual Recognition of American Sign Language using Hidden Markov Models. In: Proceedings of the International Workshop on Automatic Face-and Gesture-Recognition, Zurich, Switzerland, pp. 189–194 (1995)
32. Stoll, S., Cihan Camgoz, N., Hadfield, S., Bowden, R.: Text2Sign: towards sign language production using neural machine translation and generative adversarial networks. Int. J. Comput. Vis. (2019). https://doi.org/10.1007/s11263-019-01281-2
33. Suh, I.H., Lee, S.H., Cho, N.J., Kwon, W.Y.: Measuring motion significance and motion complexity. Inf. Sci. **388–389**, 84–98 (2017). https://doi.org/10.1016/j.ins.2017.01.027
34. Sutton, V.: What is SignWriting? https://www.signwriting.org/about/what/what02.html
35. Twenty Billion Neurons GmbH: twentybn (2019). https://20bn.com/datasets/jester/v1
36. University of East Anglia: Virtual Humans Research for Sign Language Animation. http://vh.cmp.uea.ac.uk/index.php/Main_Page
37. University of Hamburg: eSign Overview. https://www.sign-lang.uni-hamburg.de/esign/overview.html
38. Verlinden, M., Zwitserlood, I., Frowein, H.: Multimedia with animated sign language for deaf learners. In: Kommers, P., Richards, G. (eds.) World Conference on Educational Multimedia, Hypermedia and Telecommunications, Montreal, Canada, June 2005. https://www.learntechlib.org/p/20829/
39. World Federation of the Deaf, World Association of Sign Langauge Interpreters: WFD and WASLI Statement on Use of Signing Avatars. Technical Report April, Helsinki, Finland/Melbourne, Australia (2018). https://wfdeaf.org/news/resources/wfd-wasli-statement-use-signing-avatars/

A Multi-modal Machine Learning Approach and Toolkit to Automate Recognition of Early Stages of Dementia Among British Sign Language Users

Xing Liang[1], Anastassia Angelopoulou[2](✉), Epaminondas Kapetanios[2], Bencie Woll[3], Reda Al Batat[2], and Tyron Woolfe[3]

[1] IoT and Security Research Group, University of Greenwich, London, UK
x.liang@greenwich.ac.uk
[2] Cognitive Computing Research Lab, University of Westminster, London, UK
{agelopa,kapetae,r.albatat}@westminster.ac.uk
[3] Deafness Cognition and Language Research Centre, University College London, London, UK
{b.woll,twoolfe}@ucl.ac.uk

Abstract. The ageing population trend is correlated with an increased prevalence of acquired cognitive impairments such as dementia. Although there is no cure for dementia, a timely diagnosis helps in obtaining necessary support and appropriate medication. Researchers are working urgently to develop effective technological tools that can help doctors undertake early identification of cognitive disorder. In particular, screening for dementia in ageing Deaf signers of British Sign Language (BSL) poses additional challenges as the diagnostic process is bound up with conditions such as quality and availability of interpreters, as well as appropriate questionnaires and cognitive tests. On the other hand, deep learning based approaches for image and video analysis and understanding are promising, particularly the adoption of Convolutional Neural Network (CNN), which require large amounts of training data. In this paper, however, we demonstrate novelty in the following way: a) a multi-modal machine learning based automatic recognition toolkit for early stages of dementia among BSL users in that features from several parts of the body contributing to the sign envelope, e.g., hand-arm movements and facial expressions, are combined, b) universality in that it is possible to apply our technique to users of any sign language, since it is language independent, c) given the trade-off between complexity and accuracy of machine learning (ML) prediction models as well as the limited amount of training and testing data being available, we show that our approach is not over-fitted and has the potential to scale up.

Keywords: Hand tracking · Facial analysis · Convolutional neural network · Machine learning · Sign language · Dementia

1 Introduction

British Sign Language (BSL) is a natural human language, which, like other sign languages, uses movements of the hands, body and face for linguistic expression.

A. Bartoli and A. Fusiello (Eds.): ECCV 2020 Workshops, LNCS 12536, pp. 278–293, 2020.
https://doi.org/10.1007/978-3-030-66096-3_20

Recognizing dementia in the signers of BSL, however, is still an open research field, since there is very little information available about dementia in this population. This is also exacerbated by the fact that there are few clinicians with appropriate communication skills and experience working with BSL users. Diagnosis of dementia is subject to the quality of cognitive tests and BSL interpreters alike. Hence, the Deaf community currently receives unequal access to diagnosis and care for acquired neurological impairments, with consequent poorer outcomes and increased care costs [2].

Facing this challenge, we outlined a machine learning based methodological approach and developed a toolkit capable of automatically recognizing early stages of dementia without the need for sign language translation or interpretation. Our approach and tool were inspired by the following two key cross-disciplinary knowledge contributors:

a) Recent clinical observations suggesting that there may be differences between signers with dementia and healthy signers with regards to the envelope of sign space (sign trajectories/depth/speed) and expressions of the face. These clinical observations indicate that signers who have dementia use restricted sign space and limited facial expression compared to healthy deaf controls. In this context, we did not focus only on the hand movements, but also on other features from the BSL user's body, e.g., facial expressions.

b) Recent advances in machine learning based approaches spearheaded by CNN, also known as the *Deep Learning* approach. These, however, cannot be applied without taking into consideration contextual restrictions such as availability of large amounts of training datasets, and lack of real world test data. We introduce a deep learning based sub-network for feature extraction together with the CNN approach for diagnostic classification, which yields better performance and is a good alternative to handle limited data.

In this context, we proposed a multi-featured machine learning methodological approach paving the way to the development of a toolkit. The promising results for its application towards screening for dementia among BSL users lie with using features other than those bound to overt cognitive testing by using language translation and interpretation. Our methodological approach comprises several stages. The first stage of research focuses on analyzing the motion patterns of the sign space envelope in terms of sign trajectory and sign speed by deploying a real-time hand movement trajectory tracking model [17] based on OpenPose[1,2] library. The second stage involves the extraction of the facial expressions of deaf signers by deploying a real-time facial analysis model based on dlib library[3] to identify active and non-active facial expressions. The third stage is to trace elbow joint distribution based on OpenPose library, taken as an additional feature related to the sign space envelope. Based on the differences in patterns obtained from facial and trajectory motion data, the further stage of research implements both VGG16 [25] and ResNet-50 [11] networks using transfer learning from image recognition tasks to incrementally identify and improve

---

[1] https://github.com/CMU-Perceptual-Computing-Lab/openpose.

[2] https://github.com/ildoonet/tf-pose-estimation.

[3] http://dlib.net/.

recognition rates for Mild Cognitive Impairment (MCI) (i.e., pre-dementia). Performance evaluation of the research work is based on datasets available from the Deafness Cognition and Language Research Centre (DCAL) at UCL, which has a range of video recordings of over 500 signers who have volunteered to participate in research. It should be noted that as the deaf BSL-using population is estimated to be around 50,000, the size of this database is equivalent to 1% of the deaf population. Figure 1 shows the pipeline and high-level overview of the network design. The main contributions of this paper are as follows:

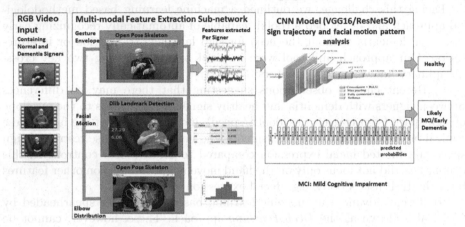

Fig. 1. The Proposed pipeline for dementia screening

1. We outline a methodology for the preliminary identification of early stage dementia among BSL users based on sign language independent features such as:

   - an accurate and robust real-time hand trajectory tracking model, in which both *sign trajectory* to extract sign space envelope and *sign speed* to identify acquired neurological impairment associated with motor symptoms are tracked.
   - a real-time facial analysis model that can identify and differentiate *active* and *non-active facial expressions* of a signer.
   - an elbow distribution model that can identify the *motion characteristics of the elbow joint* during signing.

2. We present an automated screening toolkit for early stage dementia assessment with good test set performance of 87.88% in accuracy, 0.93 in ROC, 0.87 in F1 Score for positive MCI/dementia screening results. As the proposed system uses normal 2D videos without requiring any ICT/medical facilities setup, it is economical, simple, flexible, and adaptable.

The paper is structured as follows: Sect. 2 gives an overview of the related work. Section 3 outlines the methodological approach followed by Sect. 4 with the discussion of experimental design and results. A conclusion provides a summary of the key contributions and results of this paper.

2   Related Work

Recent advances in computer vision and greater availability in medical imaging with improved quality have increased the opportunities to develop deep learning approaches for automated detection and quantification of diseases, such as Alzheimer and dementia [23]. Many of these techniques have been applied to the classification of MR imaging, CT scan imaging, FDG-PET scan imaging or the combined imaging of above, by comparing MCI patients to healthy controls, to distinguish different types or stages of MCI and accelerated features of ageing [12,18,26,28]. Jo et al. in [14] reviewed the deep learning papers on Alzheimer (published between January 2013 and July 2018) with the conclusion that four of the studies used combination of deep learning and traditional machine learning approaches, and twelve used deep learning approaches. Due to currently limited dataset, we also found that ensemble the deep learning approaches for diagnostic classification with the traditional machine learning methods for feature extraction yielded a better performance.

In terms of dementia diagnosis [1], there have been increasing applications of various machine learning approaches, most commonly with imaging data for diagnosis and disease progression [8,13,20] and less frequently in non-imaging studies focused on demographic data, cognitive measures [4], and unobtrusive monitoring of gait patterns over time [9]. In [9], walking speed and its daily variability may be an early marker of the development of MCI. These and other real-time measures of function may offer novel ways of detecting transition phases leading to dementia, which could be another potential research extension to our toolkit, since the real-time hand trajectory tracking sub-model has the potential to track a patient's daily walking pattern and pose recognition as well. AVEID, an interesting method introduced in [22], uses an automatic video system for measuring engagement in dementia, focusing on behaviour on observational scales and emotion detection. AVEID focused on passive engagement on gaze and emotion detection, while our method focuses on sign and facial motion analysis in active signing conversation.

3   Methodology

In this paper, we present a multi-modal feature extraction sub-network inspired by practical clinical needs, together with the experimental findings associated with the sub-network. Each feature extraction model is discussed in greater detail in the following sub-sections and for each method we assume that the subjects are in front of the camera with only the face, upper body, and arms visible. The input to the system is short-term clipped videos. Different extracted motion features will be fed into the CNN network to classify a BSL signer as healthy or atypical. We present the first phase work on automatic assessment of early stage dementia based on real-time hand movement trajectory motion patterns and focusing on performance comparisons between the VGG16 and ResNet-50 networks. Performance evaluation of the research work is based on datasets available from the BSL Corpus[4] at DCAL UCL, a collection of 2D video clips of 250 Deaf signers of BSL from 8 regions of the UK; and two additional datasets: a set of data collected for a previous funded project[5], and a set of signer data collected for the present study.

3.1   Dataset

From the video recordings, we selected 40 case studies of signers (20M, 20F) aged between 60 and 90 years; 21 are signers considered to be healthy cases based on the British Sign Language Cognitive Screen (BSL-CS); 9 are signers identified as having Mild Cognitive Impairment (MCI) on the basis of the BSL-CS; and 10 are signers diagnosed with mild MCI through clinical assessment. We consider those 19 cases as MCI (i.e., early dementia) cases, either identified through the BSL-CS or clinically. Balanced datasets (21 Healthy, 19 MCI) are created in order to decrease the risk of leading to a falsely perceived positive effect of accuracy due to the bias towards one class. While this number may appear small, it represents around 2% of the population of signers likely to have MCI, based on its prevalence in the UK. As the video clip for each case is about 20 min in length, we segmented each into 4–5 short video clips-4 min in length-and fed the segmented short video clip to the multi-modal feature extraction sub-network. The feasibility study and experimental findings discussed in Sect. 4.2 show that the segmented video clips represent the characteristics of individual signers. In this way, we were able to increase the size of the dataset from 40 to 162 clips. Of the 162, 79 have MCI, and 83 are cognitively healthy.

3.2   Real-Time Hand Trajectory Tracking Model

OpenPose, developed by Carnegie Mellon University, is one of the state-of-the-art methods for human pose estimation, processing images through a 2-branch multi-stage CNN [5]. The real-time hand movement trajectory tracking model is developed based on the OpenPose Mobilenet Thin model [21]. A detailed evaluation of tracking performance is discussed in [17]. The inputs to the system are brief clipped videos, and only 14 upper body parts in the image are outputted from the tracking model. These are: eyes, nose, ears, neck, shoulders, elbows, wrists, and hips. The hand movement trajectory is obtained via wrist joint motion trajectories. The curve of the hand movement trajectory is connected by the location of the wrist joint keypoints to track left- and right-hand limb movements across sequential video frames in a rapid and unique way. Figure 2 (top), demonstrates the tracking process for the sign FARM.

---

[4] British Sign Language Corpus Project https://bslcorpusproject.org/.
[5] Overcoming obstacles to the early identification of dementia in the signing Deaf community.

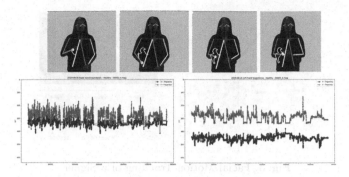

Fig. 2. Real-time hand trajectory tracking (top) and 2D left-and right-hand trajectory (bottom)

Figure 2 (bottom) is the left-and right-hand trajectories obtained from the tracking model plotted by wrist location X and Y coordinates over time in a 2D plot. It shows how hand motion changes over time, which gives a clear indication of hand movement speed (X-axis speed based on 2D coordinate changes, and Y-axis speed based on 2D coordinate changes). A spiky trajectory indicates more changes within a shorter period, thus faster hand movement. Hand movement speed patterns can be easily identified to analyze acquired neurological impairments associated with motor symptoms (i.e., slower movement), as in Parkinson's disease.

3.3   Real-Time Facial Analysis Model

The facial analysis model was implemented based on a facial landmark detector inside the Dlib library, in order to analyse a signer's facial expressions [15]. The face detector uses the classic Histogram of Oriented Gradients (HOG) feature combined with a linear classifier, an image pyramid, and a sliding window detection scheme. The pre-trained facial landmark detector is used to estimate the location of 68 (x, y) coordinates that map to facial features (Fig. 3).

As shown in Fig. 4[6], earlier psychological research [6] identified seven universal common facial expressions: Happiness, Sadness, Fear, Disgust, Anger, Contempt and Surprise. Facial muscle movements for these expressions include lips and brows (Fig. 4). Therefore, the facial analysis model was implemented for the purpose of extract subtle facial muscle movement by calculating the average Euclidean distance differences between the nose and right brow as d1, nose and left brow as d2, and upper and lower lips as d3 for a given signer over a sequence of video frames (Fig. 3). The vector [d1, d2, d3] is an indicator of a signer's facial expression and is used to classify a signer as having an active or non-active facial expression.

---

[6] https://www.eiagroup.com/knowledge/facial-expressions/.

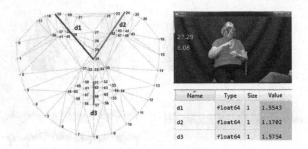

Fig. 3. Facial Motion Tracking of a Signer

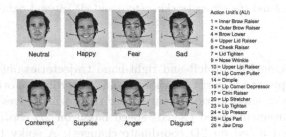

Fig. 4. Common facial expressions

$$d1, d2, d3 = \frac{\sum_{t=1}^{T} |d^{t+1} - d^t|}{T} \tag{1}$$

where T = Total number of frames that facial landmarks are detected.

3.4 Elbow Distribution Model

The elbow distribution model extracts and represents the motion characteristics of elbow joint movement during signing, based on OpenPose upper body keypoints. The Euclidean distance d is calculated between the elbow joint coordinate and a relative midpoint of the body in a given frame. This is illustrated in Fig. 5(a), where the midpoint location on the frame is made up of the x-coordinate of the neck and the y-coordinate of the elbow joint. If $J_{e,n}^t$ represents distances of joints elbow and neck (e,n) at time t, such as $J_{e,n}^t = [X_{e,n}^t, Y_{e,n}^t]$ then d calculates the distance descriptor:

$$d = \sqrt{(X_n^t - X_e^t)^2 + (Y_n^t - Y_e^t)^2} \tag{2}$$

for each frame, resulting in N distances d, where N is the number of frames. In order to get a distribution representation of elbow motion, a virtual coordinate origin is created, which is the mean distance calculated as $d_\mu = \frac{\sum_i^N \mathbf{d}}{N}$, which

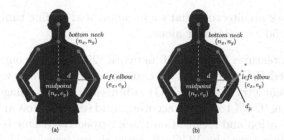

Fig. 5. (a) Elbow tracking distance from the midpoint. (b) Shifted coordinate with mean distance calculated (Color figure online)

can be seen as the resting position of the elbow. Then a relative distance is calculated from this origin d_μ to the elbow joint for each frame, resulting in the many distances shown in Fig. 5(b) as orange dots. If the relative distance is <0 it is closer to the body than the resting distance, and if it is >0, it is further away. This is a much better representation of elbow joint movement as it distinguishes between near and far elbow motion. These points can be represented by a histogram which can then be fed into the CNN model as an additional feature.

3.5   CNN Models

In this section, we summarize the architecture of the VGG16 and ResNet-50 implemented for the early dementia classification, focusing on data pre-processing, architecture overview, and transfer learning in model training.

Data Pre-processing. Prior to classification, we first vertical stack a signer's left-hand trajectory image over the associated right-hand trajectory image obtained from the real-time hand trajectory tracking model, and label the 162 stacked input trajectory images as pairs

$$(X, Y) = \{(X_1, Y_1), ..., (X_i, Y_i), ..., (X_N, Y_N)\} \quad (N = 162) \tag{3}$$

where X_i is the i-th observation (image dimension: $1400 \times 1558 \times 3$) from the MCI and Healthy datasets. The classification has the corresponding class label $Y_i \in \{0, 1\}$, with early MCI (Dementia) as class 0 and Healthy as class 1. The input images are further normalized by subtracting the ImageNet data mean and changed the input shape dimensions to $224 \times 224 \times 3$ to be ready for the Keras deep learning CNN networks.

VGG16 and ResNet-50 Architecture. In our approach, we have used VGG16 and ResNet-50 as the base models with transfer learning to transfer the parameters pre-trained for 1000 object detection task on ImageNet dataset to recognize hand movement trajectory images for early MCI screening. Figure 6 shows the network architecture that we implemented by fine tuning VGG16 and training ResNet-50 as a classifier alone.

1) VGG16 Architecture: The VGG16 network [25] with 13 convolutional and 3 fully connected (FC) layers, i.e. 16 trainable weight layers, were the basis of the Visual Geometry Group (VGG) submission to the ImageNet Challenge 2014, achieving 92.7% top-5 test accuracy, and securing first and second places in the classification and localization track respectively. Due to the very small dataset, we fine tune the VGG 16 network by freezing the Convolutional (Covn) layers and two Fully Connected (FC) layers, and only retrain the last two layers, with 524,674 parameters trainable in total (see Fig. 6). Subsequently, a softmax layer for binary classification is applied to discriminate the two labels: Healthy and MCI, producing two numerical values of which the sum becomes 1.0.

   Several strategies are used to combat overfitting. A dropout layer is implemented after the last FC [27], randomly dropping 40% of the units and their connections during training. An intuitive explanation of its efficacy is that each unit learns to extract useful features on its own with different sets of randomly chosen inputs. As a result, each hidden unit is more robust to random fluctuations and learns a generally useful transformation. Moreover, EarlyStopping is used to halt the training of the network at the right time to avoid overfitting. EarlyStopping callback is configured to monitor the loss on the validation dataset with the patience argument set to 15. The training process is stopped after 15 epochs when there is no improvement on the validation dataset.

2) ResNet-50 Architecture: Residual Networks (ResNets) [11] introduce skip connections to skip blocks of convolutional layers, forming a residual block. These stacked residual blocks greatly improve training efficiency and largely resolve the vanishing gradient problem present in deep networks. This model won the ImageNet challenge in 2015; the top 5 accuracy for ResNet-50 is 93.29%. As complex models with many parameters are more prone to overfitting with a small dataset, we train ResNet-50 as a classifier alone rather than fine tune it (see Fig. 6). Only a softmax layer for binary classification is applied, which introduces 4098 trainable parameters. EarlyStopping callback is also configured to halt the training of the network in order to avoid overfitting.

4 Experiments and Analysis

4.1 Implementation

The networks mentioned above were constructed using Python 3.6.8, OpenCV 3.4.2, and Tensorflow 1.12. VGG16 and ResNet-50 were built with the Keras deep learning library [7], using Tensorflow as backend. We employed a Windows desktop with two Nvidia GeForce GTX 1080Ti adapter cards and 3.3 GHz Intel Core i9-7900X CPU with 16 GB RAM. During training, dropout was deployed in

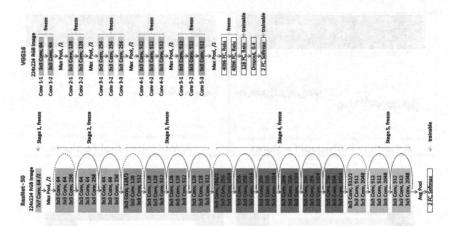

Fig. 6. VGG16 and ResNet-50 Architecture

fully connected layers and EarlyStopping was used to avoid overfitting. To accelerate the training process and avoid local minimums, we used Adam algorithm with its default parameter setting (learning rate = 0.001, beta 1 = 0.9, beta 2 = 0.999) as the training optimizer [16]. Batch size was set to 3 when training VGG16 network and 1 when training ResNet-50 network, as small mini-batch sizes provide more up-to-date gradient calculations and yield more stable and reliable training [3,19]. In training it took several ms per epoch, with ResNet-50 quicker than the other because of less in training parameters. As an ordinary training schedule contains 100 epochs, in most cases, the training loss would converge in 40 epochs for VGG16 and 5 epochs for ResNet-50. During training, the parameters of the networks were saved via Keras callbacks to monitor EarlyStopping to save the best weights. These parameters were used to run the test and validation sets later. During test and validation, accuracies and Receiver Operating Characteristic (ROC) curves of the classification were calculated, and the network with the highest accuracy and area under ROC was chosen as the final classifier.

4.2 Results and Discussion

Experiment Findings. In Fig. 7, feature extraction results show that in a greater number of cases a signer with MCI produces a sign trajectory that resembles a straight line rather than the spiky trajectory characteristic of a healthy signer. In other words, signers with MCI produced more static poses/pauses during signing, with a reduced sign space envelope as indicated by smaller amplitude differences between the top and bottom peaks of the X, Y trajectory lines. At the same time, the Euclidean distance d3 of healthy signers is larger than that of MCI signers, indicating active facial movements by healthy signers. This proves the clinical observation concept of differences between signers with MCI and healthy signers in the envelope of sign space and face movements, with

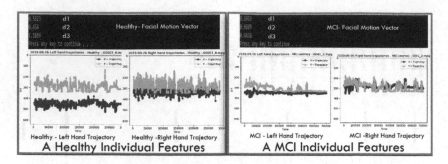

Fig. 7. Experiment finding

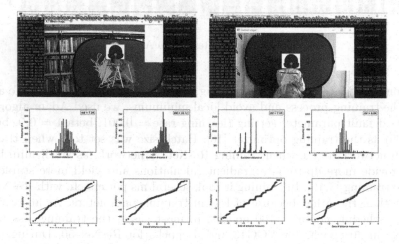

Fig. 8. The top row shows signing space for a healthy (left) and an MCI (right) signer. The bottom row shows the acquired histograms and normal probability plots for both hands. For data protection purposes both faces have been covered.

the former using smaller sign space and limited facial expression. In addition to space and facial expression, the elbow distribution model demonstrates restricted movement around the elbow axis with a lower standard deviation and a skewed distribution for the MCI signer compared to the healthy signer where the distribution is normal (Fig. 8).

Performance Evaluation. In this section, we have performed a comparative study of VGG16 and ResNet-50 networks. Videos of 40 participants have been segmented into short clips with 162 segmented cases in the training processes. Those segmented samples are randomly partitioned into two subsets with splitting into 80% for the training set and 20% for the test set. To validate the model performance, we also kept 6 cases separate (1 MCI and 5 healthy signers) that have not been used in the training process, segmented into 24 cases for performance validation. The validation samples is skewed as a result of limited in

MCI samples but richer in health samples. More MCI samples are kept in the training/test processes than in the validation. Table 1 shows effectiveness results over 46 participants from different networks.

Table 1. Performance Evaluation over VGG16 and RestNet-50 for early MCI screening

Method	40 Participants 21 Healthy, 19 Early MCI			6 Participants 5 Healthy, 1 Early MCI	
	Train Result (129 segmented cases)	Test Result (33 segmented cases)		Validation Result (24 segmented cases)	
	ACC	ACC	ROC	ACC	ROC
VGG 16	87.5969%	**87.8788%**	**0.93**	**87.5%**	**0.96**
ResNet-50	69.7674%	69.6970%	0.72	66.6667%	0.73

The ROC curves are further illustrated in Fig. 9 and Fig. 10 based on test set performance. The best performance metrics are achieved by VGG16 with accuracy of 87.8788%; a micro ROC of 0.93; F1 score for MCI: 0.87, for Healthy: 0.89. Therefore, VGG16 was selected as the baseline classifier and validation was further performed on 24 sub-cases from 6 participants. Table 2 summarises validation performance over the baseline classifier VGG16, and its ROC in Fig. 11. In Table 2, there are two false positive and one false negative based on sub-case prediction, but the model has a correct high confidence prediction rate on most of the sub-cases. If prediction confidence is averaged over all of the sub-cases from a participant, and predict the result, the model achieved 100% accuracy in validation performance.

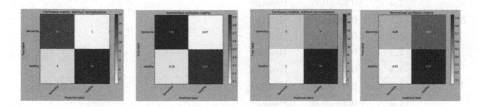

Fig. 9. Test set confusion matrix of VGG16 (left two) and ResNet-50 (right two)

Furthermore, since a deep learning network can easily become over-fitted with relatively small datasets, comparison against simpler approaches such as logistic regression and SVM is also performed. As stated in [10], logistic regression and artificial neural networks are the models of choice in many medical data classification tasks, with one layer of hidden neurons generally sufficient for classifying most datasets. Therefore, we evaluate our datasets on a 2-layer shallow neural network with 80 neurons in hidden layer and logistic sigmoid activation as its output layer.

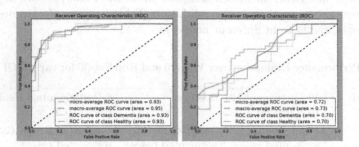

Fig. 10. Test Set ROC of VGG16 (left) and ResNet-50 (right)

Table 2. Validation Performance over Baseline Classifier - VGG16

Participant No	Sub-case	Prediction confidence		Prediction Result based on Sub-case	Prediction Result based on Participant	Ground Truth
		MCI	Health			
1	1_1	0.63	0.37	MCI	Healthy	Healthy
	1_2	0.43	0.57	Healthy		
	1_3	0.39	0.61	Healthy		
	1_4	0.27	0.73	Healthy		
	1_5	0.40	0.60	Healthy		
2	2_1	0.13	0.87	Healthy	Healthy	Healthy
	2_2	0.02	0.98	Healthy		
	2_3	0.56	0.44	MCI		
	2_4	0.23	0.77	Healthy		
3	3_1	0.08	0.92	Healthy	Healthy	Healthy
	3_2	0.02	0.98	Healthy		
	3_3	0.02	0.98	Healthy		
	3_4	0.01	0.99	Healthy		
4	4_1	0.09	0.91	Healthy	Healthy	Healthy
	4_2	0.24	0.76	Healthy		
	4_3	0.16	0.84	Healthy		
	4_4	0.07	0.93	Healthy		
5	5_1	0.01	0.99	Healthy	Healthy	Healthy
	5_2	0.01	0.99	Healthy		
	5_3	0.00	1.00	Healthy		
	5_4	0.07	0.93	Healthy		
6	6_1	0.93	0.07	MCI	MCI	MCI
	6_2	0.29	0.71	Healthy		
	6_3	0.91	0.09	MCI		

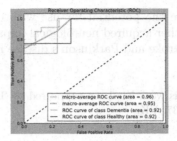

Fig. 11. Validation set ROC on VGG16

Table 3. Comparing deep neural network architecture over shallow networks

	Train accuracy (%)	Test accuracy (%)
VGG16	87.5969	87.8788
Shallow Logistic	86.4865	86.1538
SVM	86.8725	73.8461

Our observations on comparison results in respect with accuracy between shallow (Logistic, SVM) and deep learning CNN prediction models, presented in Table 3, show that, for smaller datasets, shallow models are a considerable alternative to deep learning models, since no significant improvement could be shown. Deep learning models, however, have the potential to perform better in the presence of larger datasets [24]. Since we aspire to train and apply our model with increasingly larger amounts of data made available, our approach is well justified. The comparisons also highlighted that our ML prediction model is not over-fitted despite the fact that small amounts of training and testing data were available.

5   Conclusions

We have outlined a multi-modal machine learning methodological approach and developed a toolkit for an automatic dementia screening system. The toolkit uses VGG16, while focusing on analysing features from various body parts, e.g., facial expressions, comprising the sign space envelope of BSL users recorded in normal 2D videos. As part of our methodology, we report the experimental findings for the multi-modal feature extractor sub-network in terms of hand sign trajectory, facial motion, and elbow distribution, together with performance comparisons between different CNN models in ResNet-50 and VGG16. The experiments show the effectiveness of our machine learning based approach for early stage dementia screening. The results are validated against cognitive assessment scores with a test set performance of 87.88%, and a validation set performance of 87.5% over sub-cases, and 100% over participants. Due to its key features of being economic, simple, flexible, and adaptable, the proposed methodological approach and the implemented toolkit have the potential for use with other sign languages, as well as in screening for other acquired neurological impairments associated with motor changes, such as stroke and Parkinson's disease in both hearing and deaf people.

Acknowledgements. This work has been supported by The Dunhill Medical Trust grant number RPGF1802\37, UK.

References

1. Astell, A., et al.: Technology and dementia: the future is now. Dement. Geriatr. Cogn. Disord. **47**(3), 131–139 (2019). https://doi.org/10.1159/000497800
2. Atkinson, J., Marshall, J., Thacker, A., Woll, B.: When sign language breaks down: deaf people's access to language therapy in the UK. Deaf Worlds **18**, 9–21 (2002)
3. Bengio, Y.: Practical recommendations for gradient-based training of deep architectures. Neural Networks: Tricks of the Trade (2012)
4. Bhagyashree, S., Nagaraj, K., Prince, M., Fall, C., Krishna, M.: Diagnosis of dementia by machine learning methods in epidemiological studies: a pilot exploratory study from south India. Soc. Psychiatry Psychiatr. Epidemiol. **53**(1), 77–86 (2018)
5. Cao, Z., Simon, T., Wei, S., Sheikh, Y.: Realtime multi-person 2D pose estimation using part affinity fields. In: Proceedings of the IEEE Conference on Computer Vision and Pattern Recognition (CVPR), pp. 7291–7299 (2017)
6. Charles, D., Paul, E., Phillip, P.: The Expression of the Emotions in Man and Animals, 3rd edn. Harper Collins, London (1998)
7. Chollet, F., et al.: Keras (2015). https://keras.io
8. Dallora, A., Eivazzadeh, S., Mendes, E., Berglund, J., Anderberg, P.: Machine learning and microsimulation techniques on the prognosis of dementia: a systematic literature review. PLoS One, **12**(6) (2017). https://doi.org/10.1371/journal.pone.0179804
9. Dodge, H., Mattek, N., Austin, D., Hayes, T., Kaye, J.: In-home walking speeds and variability trajectories associated with mild cognitive impairment. Neurology **78**(24), 1946–1952 (2012)
10. Dreiseitl, S., Ohno-Machado, L.: Logistic regression and artificial neural network classification models: a methodology review. J. Biomed. Inf. **35**, 352–359 (2002)
11. He, K., Zhang, X., Ren, S., Sun, J.: Deep residual learning for image recognition. In: Proceedings of Computer Vision and Pattern Recognition (CVPR) (2016)
12. Huang, Y., Xu, J., Zhou, Y., Tong, T., Zhuang, X., ADNI: Diagnosis of alzheimer's disease via multi-modality 3d convolutional neural network. Front Neurosci. **13**(509) (2019). https://doi.org/10.3389/fnins.2019.00509
13. Iizuka, T., Fukasawa, M., Kameyama, M.: Deep-learning-based imaging-classification identified cingulate island sign in dementia with lewy bodies. Sci. Rep. **9**(8944) (2019). https://doi.org/10.1038/s41598-019-45415-5
14. Jo, T., Nho, K., Saykin, A.: Deep learning in alzheimer's disease: Diagnostic classification and prognostic prediction using neuroimaging data. Front Aging Neurosci. **11**(220) (2019). https://doi.org/10.3389/fnagi.2019.00220
15. Kazemi, V., Sullivan, J.: One millisecond face alignment with an ensemble of regression trees. In: Proceedings of IEEE Conference on Computer Vision and Pattern Recognition (CVPR) (2014). https://doi.org/10.1109/CVPR.2014.241

16. Kingma, D., Ba, J.: Adam: a method for stochastic optimization. In: Proceedings of International Conference on Learning Representations (2015)
17. Liang, X., Kapetanios, E., Woll, B., Angelopoulou, A.: Real time hand movement trajectory tracking for enhancing dementia screening in ageing deaf signers of British sign language. In: Holzinger, A., Kieseberg, P., Tjoa, A.M., Weippl, E. (eds.) CD-MAKE 2019. LNCS, vol. 11713, pp. 377–394. Springer, Cham (2019). https://doi.org/10.1007/978-3-030-29726-8_24
18. Lu, D., Popuri, K., Ding, G., Balachandar, R., Beg, M., ADNI: multimodal and multiscale deep neural networks for the early diagnosis of alzheimer's disease using structural MR and FDG-pet images. Sci. Rep. **8**(1), 5697 (2018)
19. Masters, D., Luschi, C.: Revisiting small batch training for deep neural networks. In: Proceedings of International Conference on Learning Representations (2015)
20. Negin, F., et al.: Praxis: Towards automatic cognitive assessment using gesture. Expert Syst. Appl. **106**, 21–35 (2018)
21. OpenPoseTensorFlow. https://github.com/ildoonet/tf-pose-estimation
22. Parekh, V., Foong, P., Zhao, S., Subramanian, R.: Aveid: automatic video system for measuring engagement in dementia. In: Proceedings of the International Conference on Intelligent User Interfaces (IUI 2018), pp. 409–413 (2018)
23. Pellegrini, E., et al.: Machine learning of neuroimaging to diagnose cognitive impairment and dementia: a systematic review and comparative analysis. In: Alzheimer's and Dementia: Diagnosis, Assessment and Disease Monitoring, vol. 10, pp. 519–535 (2018)
24. Schindler, A., Lidy, T., Rauber, A.: Comparing shallow versus deep neural network architectures for automatic music genre classification. In: 9th Forum Media Technology (FMT2016), vol. 1734, pp. 17–21 (2016)
25. Simonyan, K., Zisserman, A.: Very deep convolutional networks for large-scale image recognition. In: Proceedings of International Conference on Learning Representations (2015)
26. Spasova, S., Passamonti, L., Duggento, A., Liò, P., Toschi, N.: ADNI: a parameter-efficient deep learning approach to predict conversion from mild cognitive impairment to alzheimer's disease. NeuroImage **189**, 276–287 (2019)
27. Srivastava, N., Hinton, G., Krizhevsky, A., Sutskever, I., Salakhutdinov, R.: Dropout: a simple way to preventneural networks from overfitting. J. Mach. Learn. Res. **15**, 1929–1958 (2014)
28. Young, A., et al.: The genetic FTD initiative (genfi), the alzheimer's disease neuroimaging initiative (adni): Uncovering the heterogeneity and temporal complexity of neurodegenerative diseases with subtype and stage inference. In: Nature Communications, vol. 9(4273) (2018). https://doi.org/10.1038/s41467-018-05892-0

Score-Level Multi Cue Fusion for Sign Language Recognition

Çağrı Gökçe, Oğulcan Özdemir, Ahmet Alp Kındıroğlu(✉), and Lale Akarun

Computer Engineering Department, Bogaziçi University, Istanbul, Turkey
{cagri.gokce,ogulcan.ozdemir,alp.kindiroglu,akarun}@boun.edu.tr

Abstract. Sign Languages are expressed through hand and upper body gestures as well as facial expressions. Therefore, Sign Language Recognition (SLR) needs to focus on all such cues. Previous work uses hand-crafted mechanisms or network aggregation to extract the different cue features, to increase SLR performance. This is slow and involves complicated architectures. We propose a more straightforward approach that focuses on training separate cue models specializing on the dominant hand, hands, face, and upper body regions. We compare the performance of 3D Convolutional Neural Network (CNN) models specializing in these regions, combine them through score-level fusion, and use the weighted alternative. Our experimental results have shown the effectiveness of mixed convolutional models. Their fusion yields up to 19% accuracy improvement over the baseline using the full upper body. Furthermore, we include a discussion for fusion settings, which can help future work on Sign Language Translation (SLT).

Keywords: Sign language recognition · Turkish sign language (TID) · 3D convolutional neural networks · Score-level fusion

1 Introduction

Sign Language is the means of communication of the Deaf, and each Deaf culture has its own sign language. Sign languages differ from the spoken language of the culture. Communication between the Deaf and the hearing relies mostly on the Deaf individual learning the spoken language and using lipreading and written text to communicate: A huge and unfair burden on the Deaf. The reverse, teaching the general population at least some sign language may be more feasible, and there are available educational courses for such aim. However, gaining expertise in sign language is difficult, and the communication problem is still unsolved. Automatic interpretation of sign languages is a necessary step for not only enabling the human-computer interaction but also facilitating the communication between the Deaf and the hearing individuals.

Automatic Sign Language Recognition (ASLR) refers to a broad field with different tasks, such as recognizing isolated sign glosses and continuous sign sentences.

Electronic supplementary material The online version of this chapter (https://doi.org/10.1007/978-3-030-66096-3_21) contains supplementary material, which is available to authorized users.

The objective of the ASLR system is to infer the meaning of the sign glosses or sentences and translate it to the spoken language. Recently, there has been an increased progress in these efforts: Sign Language Translation (SLT) has become an active research problem for creating interactive sign language interfaces for the deaf [1–3,18]. A number of recent papers on the topic made use of neural network generated features. However, while the quality and representative power of these features in SLT are essential, and it is difficult to evaluate the representative potential of the elements in a pipeline setting where the overall system error is cumulative. For this reason, in this study, we aim to evaluate 3D Residual CNN Based Sign Language embeddings in terms of explanatory power in an Automatic Sign Language Recognition (ASLR) setting where temporal mix-up between signs and co-articulation is minimal. For the general case of Isolated SLR, the system aims to process a sign gloss and assign it to a single sign gloss label. In a limited context of supervised learning set-up, labels are glosses, which are transcription symbols assigned by sign language experts. There may be a single signer or multiple signers in communication; however, the ASLR system should be signer independent.

To convey the meaning of a performed sign gloss, Sign Languages use multiple channels, which are manifested as visual cues. We can classify these visual cues into two categories; (1) cues that are denoted as manual cues including hand shape and movement, and (2) cues that are non-manual features including facial expressions and upper body pose focusing on details without definitive large displacements.

Solving the problem of Isolated SLR requires specialized methods, which can be grouped into two categories. The first category is using handcrafted features, focusing on video trajectories and flow maps [19,27,29]. The second set of methods includes machine learning algorithms and neural networks to improve classification performance [14,19,25]. 3D CNN models have proven successful in various video tasks [23,24]. Li et al. [14] adopted the same architecture in SLR and reported improved performance. However, Ozdemir et al. [19] provided the comparison of 3D CNN models and handcrafted methods but have found that 3D CNNs are inferior to the state-of-the-art handcrafted IDT approach.

The aim of this work is to investigate why 3D CNN models may fail to show similar success in sign language recognition and to observe what modifications improve their performance. We hypothesize that the performance drop occurs because of the common practice of scaling images into smaller size and sampling frames [23,24], due to computational requirements and difficulty of training bigger neural networks. One solution is handling the negative effect of the sampling by increasing the model complexity as in [6,12,30], yet this increases computational requirements. Instead, we firstly apply attentive data selection at the pre-processing phase by determining cues in SLR data. Secondly, we divide the problem into multiple cues and train different expert classifiers on each kind of dense feature. Thirdly, we refine the expert cue network knowledge into one result, by applying score-level fusion.

The paper organization is as follows. Section 2 reviews related work, Sect. 3 explains the presented method, Sect. 4 presents the experimental results, Sect. 5 contains the analysis of experiments and Sect. 6 presents the conclusions.

2   Related Work

Sign Language Recognition (SLR) aims to infer meaning from a performed sign. In the sign classification task, an isolated sign gloss is assigned to a class label. A sign gloss, the written language counterpart of the performed sign, can be used as a mid-level or final stage label for sign language recognition.

SLR is closely connected with video recognition or human action recognition methods, and similar architectures have been used for both. Two popular approaches to sign language representation uses handcrafted features and deep neural network based methods.

Prior to the performance leap achieved by neural networks, hand-crafted features were the best performing approach for representing human actions in a sequential video setting. For a two-frame dynamic flow map estimation, optical flow is used to generate feature-level information. These features perform better representation than RGB image sequences where the motion information is more indicative than appearance [5]. There exist numerous handcrafted feature extraction methods and their application to image sequences such as STIP [15] and spatio-temporal local binary patterns [28]. State of the art performances with constructed features in action recognition and isolated sign language recognition were obtained using Improved Dense Trajectories [19,27], which is an outlier independent trajectory-based motion specialized feature extractor.

Neural Network based methods focus on convolutional architectures for the classification task. Simonyan et al. [21] use a branched CNN architecture that splits the information into spatial and temporal streams, and fuses them to perform video classification. Tran et al. [23] use 3D convolutional kernels to build a 3D CNN variant to process video data in an end-to-end fashion.

One prerequisite for using deep neural networks is the presence of large datasets with ground truth annotations. Recently, big-scale isolated sign language recognition datasets have become publicly available. Isolated SL datasets contain videos of a user performing a single gloss, usually a single word or a phrase. MS-ASL [25] is an American Isolated SL dataset including 200 native performers performing more than a thousand word categories. WL-ASL [14] is a bigger dataset with two thousand word categories performed by one hundred people. For other languages, Chinese [29] and Turkish [19] are among available datasets. Popular human activity recognition datasets [10,11,13,22] are also used as extra data and for finetuning in Isolated SLR. Continuous SL datasets are acquired in a less controlled setting, where a user can perform longer sign sequences [7,8].

SLR methods often use video pre-processing to reduce network bias and variance, and to increase network performance. Random cropping is one of the popular spatial augmentation techniques when training CNNs. Since CNN variants have small input spatial resolution, e.g., 224×224 for the popular ResNet50 network [9], such methods increase the transitive invariance of the models by processing different parts of the image in higher resolution compared to directly downsampling the whole image frame.

Temporal pre-processing techniques operate on the temporal dimension of the video data. The aim is to locate the dense temporal regions which have an increased likelihood of the action flow. In recent work, different approaches are applied for the temporal activity localization, e.g., exploiting both short term and long term samples [26], combining high and low-frequency learners [6], and detecting active window boundaries for the long sequences [17]. Our work differs by applying cue selection before the training phase and combining the classifiers in the feature construction stage.

Combining both pre-processing techniques allows an opportunity to exploit covariance between these spatio-temporal features. Spatio-temporal pre-processing can possibly improve the signal to noise ratio of the processed data when the region of interest is selected from dense regions. This process is shown to be beneficial on other video recognition tasks, e.g., when extracted through handcrafted methods such as optical flow [21], or directly through 3D CNNs [24]. In SLR, due to the nature of the task, SL videos consist of the sparse hand and upper body movements as well as facial expressions. It is possible to use the domain-specific knowledge to exploit spatio-temporal sampling using a guided pre-processing technique. Spatio-temporal multi cue networks [30] exploit spatial regions of interest by firstly using a branch to estimate the region of interest, then training different networks for each unit. However, applying sampling at the training phase becomes more computationally expensive and requires deeper architectures. Our score-level multi cue fusion approach addresses this problem as described in the next section.

3 Method

In this section, we describe our method. We firstly describe the mixed convolutional model, follow up with our multi cue sampling process, and finally discuss the score-level fusion method.

3.1 3D Resnets with Mixed Convolutions

Mixed convolutional networks are 3D Residual CNNs [23], which use 3D convolutional kernels to process video frames in an end-to-end fashion. Tran et al. [24] investigate the success of 3D CNNs and shares two effective variants with strong empirical results. The first is mixed convolutional networks, and the second is residual bottleneck based $2 + 1$ convolutional networks.

The mixed CNN variant builds on the plain 2D residual networks, with the difference that the first layers are replaced with 3D convolutional kernels. While the first layers are capable of processing input video directly with 3D convolutional kernels, later layers efficiently model the semantic knowledge using 2D convolutional kernels. Then, a fully connected layer is employed after the final convolutional layer for the video classification task.

Mixed Convolutional networks are denoted with MCx, where x is the number of 3D convolutional layer blocks. Following the baseline, we empirically experiment with different mixed convolutional variants and employ the MC3 variant of the mixed convolutional network.

3.2   Spatial and Temporal Sampling

The message in a sign gloss is conveyed through manual and non-manual cues. Information is conveyed through the shape and configuration of the hand, body, and face regions. The informative regions and intervals can be sampled with the help of a state-of-the-art pose estimation approach such as OpenPose [4]. Making use of pose estimation allows researchers to filter the entire frame by cropping specific regions according to keypoints, which are hand, face, and upper body keypoints in the case of SLR.

We would like to sample informative body regions to increase efficiency, and to filter out noise. Our approach is two-fold; (1) We design a SLR system by extracting the body, hand, and face regions by cropping the RGB frame spatially (in Fig. 1) using the pose data which was provided in Ozdemir et al. [19], (2) We focus on the temporal dense regions in which we define the active window as the temporal window where the active hand is moving. Then, we filter out the sparse frames and only feed the network with the frames in the active window (in Fig. 2).

Using isolated sign gloss clips guarantees that the temporal sequence is centered on the hand movement. The following steps are used to extract the active window at the center.

1. Use the moving hand detection framework in Sect. 4.2 to detect the active hand(s).
2. Define a selected hand as the active hand. If both hands are active, select the dominant hand.
3. For the selected hand, track hand movements using Euclidean distance. Keep the frame ids of the start of the first-hand movement and end of the last hand-movement.
4. Define two thresholds T_S, T_E. Filter the boundary regions from the start and end frame ids using corresponding thresholds defined earlier, and use extracted frames for the training.

In some videos, the movement is not in the middle of the video. We detect such exception cases by checking the position of the hand relative to the hip. We also filter out segments too short to be a sign.

3.3   Multi Cue Score Fusion

Extracting multiple cues from different settings allows each model to build expertise on each cue. Therefore, there is a need to combine the cues of each model by combining weak expert classifiers. Zhou et al. [30] experiments with distillation

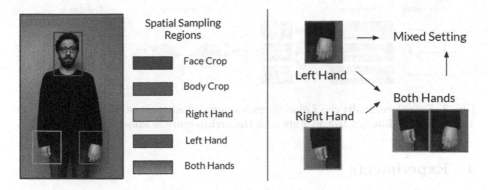

Fig. 1. Spatial Sampling operation is visualized. From left to right; cue regions selected for the process, and hand crop settings

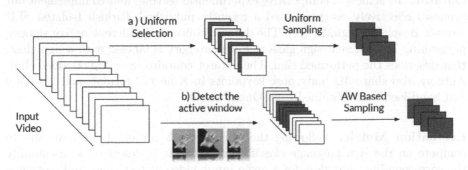

Fig. 2. Different temporal sampling operations are shown in the above figure. Selected frames are shown with color. Two branches represent uniform sampling and the Active Window Based Sampling Process. (Color figure online)

at the training time, by training a big scale model consisting of expert components. This has the drawback of increasing model complexity and training time. Simonyan et al. [21] combines different branches while training, but processes the spatial and temporal branch separately at test time using a score fusion approach. They propose firstly direct score fusion via averaging through the network outputs and secondly, training a meta classifier above the extracted features. We follow the former score fusion approach since it has less model complexity and can achieve better run-time performance.

We experiment with two different multi cue fusion settings. First, we apply the averaging operation to the softmax outputs of each cue network results. Secondly, we apply a weighted fusion, where each cue network is weighted by its validation set performance.

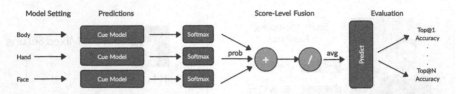

Fig. 3. Score-level multi cue fusion operation applied at the test time. Note that cue networks have different test weights even the architecture is same

4 Experiments

4.1 Experimental Setup

Dataset. To achieve a competitive experimental setting, and to implement our proposal effectively, we have used a recently published Turkish Isolated SLR dataset BosphorusSign22k [19]. The dataset contains 6 different native signers, performing 744 different sign glosses. Each category is labeled with a sign gloss, that describes the performed sign. The dataset contains over 22,000 video clips. Authors also share 3D body pose keypoints in Kinectv2 format, and 2D body and hand keypoints obtained from OpenPose [4].

Evaluation Metric. Following the work of Ozdemir et al. [19], we aim to compete on the sign language classification task. It is described as estimating the corresponding sign gloss for a given input video at test time, and scoring is evaluated in the accuracy of all of the test estimations. Out of all 6 performers, video clips of User 4 is defined as the test set, which is about 1/6 of the total dataset and it includes samples from all of the 744 classes.

Implementation Details. Our experiment setting follows the baseline paper's [19] neural network based experimental setting. We apply the proposed preprocessing pipeline, resize the image into 640 × 360, crop the center square region then resize via bilinear interpolation to achieve 112 × 112 input resolution. Then, we adopt the PyTorch implementation [20] of the mixed convolutional MC3 CNN model which was pretrained on the Kinetics dataset [11]. In our experiments, we only fine-tuned the last 3 residual blocks, and apply uniform frame sampling to input video frames. All experiments has been performed with 32 batch size on a Nvidia 1080TI GPU (with 11GB memory).

Our replicated network resulted in 75.23% accuracy, which is more than 3% lower comparing the reported 78.85% accuracy in Ozdemir et al. [19]. We suspect that the difference is caused by randomized states such as optimizer initialization and different hyperparameter choices such as the learning rate.

Table 1. Hand spatial sampling settings. First table represents hand activity distribution in the BosphorusSign22k dataset. Second table represents test results of the different hand crop settings and resulting accuracy values

Distribution	Relative Frequency (%)	Crop Setting	Accuracy(%)
Both Active	**66.44**	Single Hand	79.13
Only Left Active	33.07	Both Hands	85.81
Only Right Active	0.40	Mixed	**86.25**

4.2 Experimental Results

Spatial Sampling. Spatial sampling operation is applied through two phases. First, the cue region is detected, cropped, and optionally concatenated in a multiple cue setting. Secondly, sampling is applied using bilinear interpolation.

Body Setting. Following the standard SLR pipeline, we crop human body region before training.

Hand Setting. SLR work suggests that the dominant hand, the most used hand, conveys the most information in communication. To detect the dominant hand in the BosphorusSign22k dataset, we employ a hand motion tracking algorithm. The detection process is achieved by the following:

1. Detect the Thumb keypoints on each frame,
2. Define the first thumb keypoint on each hand as two anchors,
3. If the following thumb keypoint on the next frames has greater distance than threshold compared to the anchor, conclude the hand as moving.

To compare keypoints for detecting the dominant hand with threshold values (which is predefined as 150 pixels), we use Euclidean distance. Table 1 provides the detection results on moving hands on BosphorusSign22k dataset. After the detection process, We have seen that signers in the dataset are using their left hands dominantly when performing a sign.

During signing, only one hand may be active, or both hands may be active. We have adopted three different policies; (1) The single cue setting is applied by selecting the dominant hand in which hand crops with 350×350 resolution are obtained around the keypoint #2. (2) Both cue setting is applied by selecting both hands where hand crops with 175×350 resolution are obtained around the Thumb keypoint, and concatenated horizontally. (3) The mixed setting uses the single cue setting when a single hand is active, and uses both cue setting when both hands are active. All three settings are followed by downsampling with bilinear interpolation. Experimental results are provided at the right-hand side of the Table 1.

Face Setting. Signers often have cues with facial expressions or lip movements (mouthings) that can give hints about the sign gloss. For this purpose, we have also experimented on a face setting where we crop the entire face from frames.

Table 2. Classification accuracy results of the sampling and fusion settings. Three different settings are provided in the table. From left to right, (1) Single cue spatial sampling results, (2) Active Window Based Temporal Sampling applied to each crop, and (3) Spatial&Temporal settings are combined in one setting. Note that the bottom two rows include the fusion result of the above three models in each setting.

Setting	Spatial		Temporal		S & T Combined	
	Acc@1	Acc@5	Acc@1	Acc@5	Acc@1	Acc@5
Body	75.73	93.88	81.83	96.02	86.91	98.17
Hand	86.25	97.61	88.70	97.59	91.73	98.72
Face	24.27	44.45	37.00	57.89	39.12	59.33
Fusion	90.63	98.92	93.88	**99.65**	94.47	**99.78**
Weighted Fusion	**92.18**	**99.27**	**94.03**	99.56	**94.94**	99.76

To crop the face, we have used the Nose keypoints which are provided with the Openpose [4] keypoints. After cropping the face, we resize them to 200×200 resolution.

Score-Level Fusion. We follow the insight that the different cue models can capture a different subset of features, which can lead to better results when combined effectively. Standard fusion is applied by averaging softmax outputs as in [21]. In the weighted setting, we have applied weights to each model proportional to their validation accuracy via standard multiplication. Table 2 provides the result of the fusion.

Temporal Sampling. Standard SLR training pipeline involves using the standard uniform frame sampling. We propose the active window based temporal sampling, applied by firstly extracting the dense cue regions before applying the uniform selection. Active window is detected as the part that the active hand is moving and discard the rest of the temporal information.

We used double thresholding for finding the active window. We have found that the start threshold $T_S = 90$, and the end threshold $T_E = 50$ generates competitive empirical results. Using the temporal sampling framework, we have successfully segmented the active window for each video. Then, we applied uniform sampling along with our standard training pipeline. Experimental results can be seen in Table 2.

Spatio-Temporal Sampling. We applied active window based temporal sampling on top of the spatial multi cue regions. Our experiments have shown that the final spatio-temporal sampling framework has improved on both single cue settings. With the addition of score-level fusion, test accuracy reached to 94.94%, which is the best result in all proposed settings as seen in the Table 2.

Our best setting provides 16.09% improvement on our baseline neural network setting [19]. We also managed to improve their previous best hand-crafted

Table 3. Comparison with the baseline approaches IDT and MC3_18 model.

Method	Acc@1	Acc@5
Baseline IDT [19]	88.53	–
Baseline MC3_18 [19]	78.85	94.76
Weighted Fusion - S& T Combined	**94.94**	**99.76**

result with 6.41% accuracy rate. Whereas the previous best method uses more than ten times bigger input spatial resolution (640 × 360), complicated hand-crafted methods [27] and a second stage SVM classifier, our approach only contains a 3D CNN and a sampling pipeline. Comparison with the baseline results is shown in Table 3.

5   Discussion and Analysis

Accuracy lacks informativeness when considering whether the fusion will be beneficial or not. Top-N Accuracy measures how often the Top-N ranks contain the correct class. In our experiments, we also analyze Top-5 Accuracy along with Top-1 Accuracy. Top-N Accuracy results will increase with an increasing N, and are expected to be settled to 1 when N approaches to the maximum class number. Our Top-N accuracy analysis can be seen in Fig. 4.

In the plot on the left-hand side, we report Top-N accuracy of the individual cues. Our analysis shows that hand cue yields the best performance, which is followed by the body cue. In both, there is a sharp increase between ranks 1 and 2. This shows that in a large number of cases, although the correct class fails to be predicted, it is the runner-up. This explains why the fusion is beneficial. Although the Top-N accuracy of the face cue is much lower, it is still beneficial for fusion.

Top-N accuracy of the muti-cue fusion is given in the right-hand side of Fig. 4. We start by the hand model, then include the body model, and finally add the face model to the mix. This analysis allows us to see the cumulative progress over different fusion models. We observe that the Top-2 accuracy of hand alone is higher than Top-1 accuracy of both fusion settings. We believe that this observation is why the weighted fusion outperforms score fusion, and shows that more advanced models can attain higher performance.

5.1   Spatial Ablation Study

To analyze which cue benefits the fusion results the most, we have performed score fusion to all combination pairs of cue settings. According to this ablation study, we were able to observe the effect of each cue to the overall fusion. For example, to find the effect of the face model, we subtract the Body+Hand setting from the Body+Hand+Face setting. Table 4 shows the results of the ablation

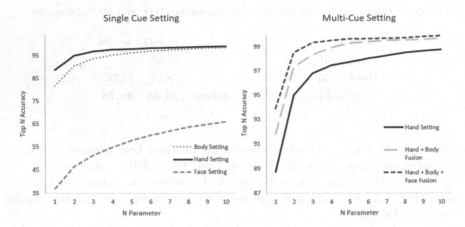

Fig. 4. Comparison of the models in the Top-N accuracy setting. The horizontal axis denotes the increasing N value, and the vertical axis denotes the accuracy value. First plot shows the single cue setting comparison, and second plot shows the multi cue setting additive comparison. Despite the difference in single setting performance, each cue boosts the fusion results.

Table 4. Effects of excluding individual cue units from the final fusion model. Using the different two cue settings and their performance, we infer to the excluded setting and its effect on the final mix.

Setting	Accuracy	Excluded Cue	Effect (%)
Body + Hand	91.80	Face	2.08
Body + Face	**84.66**	Hand	**9.22**
Hands + Face	88.70	Body	5.18

study. In our analysis, we can see that hand cue has the most effect on the fusion by 9.22% which is followed by the body model with 5.18%.

We have provided an analysis of the two most effective cues by comparing the gloss based performance. As a comparison metric, we adopted the F1-score, which should be more representative of false positives and false negatives, thus is more suitable for the gloss based evaluation.

Gloss Based Cue Comparison. We share the top ten sign glosses that the hand cue model has a major advantage compared to the body cue model in Table 5.

In Fig. 5, we provide detailed analysis for the IDENTIFY(v) sign gloss. IDENTIFY(v) sign gloss is performed by using only the left hand, touching the head with the index finger, and the rest of the fingers are on the semi-open position. In this particular example, the body cue model only achieves success in the 5th guess, while the hand cue model has the correct prediction. Additionally, Fig. 5 also shows that misclassifications of the body cue model which are HEAD, EAT, PSYCHOLOGY, and PHONE sign glosses. We inspect each confusion as follows:

Table 5. F1-score comparison for the top ten sign glosses that hand sampling outperforms body sampling. (Sorted in the alphabetical order)

Sign Gloss	Hand	Body	Fusion	Sign Gloss	Hand	Body	Fusion
Aspirin	0.62	0.00	0.67	Internet_2	1.00	0.33	1.00
Deposit(v)_2	0.89	0.25	1.00	Noon	0.91	0.33	1.00
Exchange(v)	0.57	0.00	1.00	Shout(v)_2	0.91	0.33	0.91
Head	0.89	0.29	1.00	Sleep(v)	0.62	0.00	0.67
Identify(v)	0.89	0.00	1.00	Turn(v)	1.00	0.40	0.89

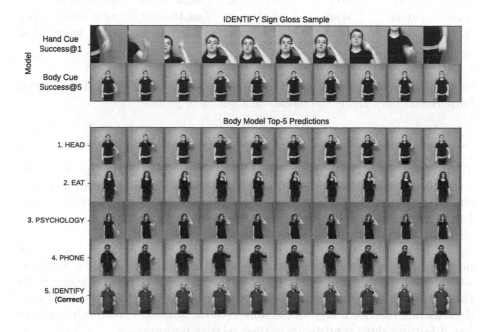

Fig. 5. Class confusions of IDENTIFY(v) sign gloss for the body cue model

- **HEAD** sign differs from IDENTIFY(v) with the close position on all fingers other than the index finger.
- **EAT** sign is performed by moving the left hand close to the mouth and with all fingers are in a closed position.
- **PSYCHOLOGY** and **PHONE** sign glosses are performed with the left hand that and have open and semi-closed hand shapes, respectively.

By evaluating the confused cases, we have concluded that the hand model has an advantage of capturing hand shape information which was possibly due to increased spatial resolution of the hand region.

Effect of the Score-Level Fusion. We share our fusion result of the body and hand cue models in Table 5. Data has shown that the fusion model successfully

Table 6. Analysis of the temporal sampling based recognition approach with respect to signs with certain grammatical sign attributes: one-handed signs, two-handed signs, mono-morphemic signs, compound signs, and signs involving repetitive and circular movements, respectively

	Number of Classes with Selected Attribute								
	234	510	75	669	457	287	375	369	744
	One Handed	Two Handed	Circ.	Not Circ.	Rep.	Not Rep.	Mono	Comp.	All
Body	72.94	86.10	86.43	81.33	80.77	83.55	77.40	86.48	81.83
Hand	83.78	91.07	91.40	88.41	87.54	90.59	85.36	92.24	88.70
Face	45.33	33.01	29.41	37.82	36.39	37.99	33.79	40.52	37.00
Fusion	**91.82**	94.86	**96.15**	93.63	**93.45**	94.57	92.08	95.78	93.88
W.Fusion	90.87	**95.55**	95.70	**93.85**	93.37	**95.09**	**92.21**	**95.96**	**94.03**

captures the hand cue features. We have also seen that the fusion model even outperforms both single cue models in 7 out of 10 glosses.

5.2   Analysis of Method on Types of Gestures Recognized

To further analyze the types of signs which the proposed method performs well and fails, we have labeled the 744 sign glosses in the dataset according to specific sign attributes. The sign classes are grouped into categories such as one-handed signs, two-handed signs, mono-morphemic signs, compound signs, and signs involving repetitive and circular movements of the hands.

Table 6 summarizes the analysis: The experiments are performed using temporal sampling with the best performing mixed convolution approach. Attribute-wise accuracy scores are calculated using the test set samples belonging to the classes containing the selected attributes. Overall, the accuracy scores in Table 6 demonstrate that for nearly all the subsets in the dataset, hand, body, and face-based features show consistency in their relative performance.

Looking at the results for different attributes one by one, we can see that signs involving two moving hands are better recognized than the one-handed sign glosses in the dataset. The performance difference can be explained by the fact that in one-handed signs, the weight of handshape may be more critical than the two-handed signs. The relative positioning and appearance of both hands, which is more apparent, may be easier to represent for the neural network.

Secondly, compound signs have a greater recognition accuracy than mono-morphemic signs (95.96% vs 92.21%). Considering the number of signing hands, the amount of additional information in the form of consecutive morphemes present in an isolated sign makes recognition easier, thus improving the performance system. From this result, we can infer that the method's representation power is higher when a sign is greater in length and contains different hand shape and position combinations.

Looking at repetitive gestures, we see a 1.6% improvement in accuracy when the signs do not contain repetitive hand gestures. The issue with repetitions, which we can attribute to this difference, is that the temporal and spatial forms of repetitions are more prone to differ between performances and users, in comparison to the static hand shape parts of the signs that follow specific rules.

Finally, we take a look at circular signs, which include circular hand and arm movements, which involve at least one entire rotation. These signs are dynamic signs where the hands do not stop while presenting a handshape. As these signs do not conform to the movement-hold phonological model of sign languages [16], representing them by choosing temporal frames is more complicated, reducing the effectiveness of keyframe based approaches [12]. Overall, the method performs well with circular signs, making fusion attempts with methods focusing more on the handshape of signs promising future leads.

6 Conclusion

In this paper, we have proposed a score-level multi cue fusion approach for the Isolated SLR task. Unlike the previous work [12,19], we focused on both spatial and temporal cues. We employed 3D Residual CNNs [24], and trained different models as an expert on the single cue. We distilled the expert knowledge using the weighted and unweighted score-Level fusion. In our experiments, we have seen that our approach has outperformed the baseline results on the Bosphorus-Sign22k Turkish Isolated SL dataset [19].

We have provided the single cue and multi cue Top-N accuracies to demonstrate incremental performance gain with each cue. Our gloss-level study shows that each cue model has specific expertise and provides an indispensable knowledge source to the fusion model. Our analysis of sign gloss attributes hints that the method performs better on temporally more complex signs with two-handed gestures, while performing comparatively worse on mono-morphemic gestures with a single hand. For that reason, the primary approach to improving performance lies in improving hand shape recognition. Possible strategies involve increasing model depth, finding better optimization techniques, or increasing the model input size. We hope that this work will extend the SLR cues into other Sign Language problems, help progress in unresolved SL tasks such as translation, and help uncover language-independent cues. Prob

Acknowledgement. This work has been supported by the TUBITAK Project No. 117E059 and TAM Project No. 2007K120610 under the Turkish Ministry of Development.

References

1. Camgoz, N.C., Hadfield, S., Koller, O., Bowden, R., Ney, H.: Neural sign language translation. In: Proceedings of the IEEE Conference on Computer Vision and Pattern Recognition (CVPR), pp. 7784–7793 (2018)
2. Camgoz, N.C., Koller, O., Hadfield, S., Bowden, R.: Multi-channel transformers for multi-articulatory sign language translation. arXiv preprint arXiv:2009.00299 (2020)

3. Camgoz, N.C., Koller, O., Hadfield, S., Bowden, R.: Sign language transformers: joint end-to-end sign language recognition and translation. In: Proceedings of the IEEE Conference on Computer Vision and Pattern Recognition (CVPR), pp. 10023–10033 (2020)

4. Cao, Z., Hidalgo Martinez, G., Simon, T., Wei, S., Sheikh, Y.A.: Openpose: realtime multi-person 2D pose estimation using part affinity fields. IEEE Trans. Pattern Analy. Mach. Intell. p. 1 (2019)

5. Carreira, J., Zisserman, A.: Quo vadis, action recognition? a new model and the kinetics dataset. In: IEEE Conference on Computer Vision and Pattern Recognition (CVPR), pp. 4724–4733 (2017)

6. Feichtenhofer, C., Fan, H., Malik, J., He, K.: Slowfast networks for video recognition. In: IEEE/CVF International Conference on Computer Vision (ICCV), pp. 6201–6210 (2019)

7. Forster, J., Schmidt, C., Koller, O., Bellgardt, M., Ney, H.: Extensions of the sign language recognition and translation corpus RWTH-PHOENIX-weather. In: Proceedings of the International Conference on Language Resources and Evaluation (LREC), pp. 1911–1916 (2014)

8. Hanke, T., König, L., Wagner, S., Matthes, S.: DGS corpus & dicta-sign: the hamburg studio setup. In: Proceedings of the Representation and Processing of Sign Languages: Corpora and Sign Language Technologies, pp. 106–110 (2010)

9. He, K., Zhang, X., Ren, S., Sun, J.: Deep residual learning for image recognition. In: Proceedings of the IEEE Conference on Computer Vision and Pattern Recognition, pp. 770–778 (2016)

10. Karpathy, A., Toderici, G., Shetty, S., Leung, T., Sukthankar, R., Fei-Fei, L.: Large-scale video classification with convolutional neural networks. In: IEEE Conference on Computer Vision and Pattern Recognition, pp. 1725–1732 (2014)

11. Kay, W., et al.: The kinetics human action video dataset. arXiv:1705.06950 (2017)

12. Kındıroğlu, A.A., Özdemir, O., Akarun, L.: Temporal accumulative features for sign language recognition. In: IEEE/CVF International Conference on Computer Vision Workshop (ICCVW), pp. 1288–1297. IEEE (2019)

13. Kuehne, H., Jhuang, H., Garrote, E., Poggio, T., Serre, T.: Hmdb: a large video database for human motion recognition. In: International Conference on Computer Vision, pp. 2556–2563. IEEE (2011)

14. Li, D., Opazo, C.R., Yu, X., Li, H.: Word-level deep sign language recognition from video: a new large-scale dataset and methods comparison. In: IEEE Winter Conference on Applications of Computer Vision (WACV), pp. 1448–1458 (2020)

15. Li, Y., Xia, R., Huang, Q., Xie, W., Li, X.: Survey of spatio-temporal interest point detection algorithms in video. IEEE Access 5, 10323–10331 (2017)

16. Liddell, S.K., Johnson, R.E.: American sign language: the phonological base. Sign Lang. Stud. 64(1), 195–277 (1989)

17. Lin, T., Liu, X., Li, X., Ding, E., Wen, S.: Bmn: boundary-matching network for temporal action proposal generation. In: IEEE/CVF International Conference on Computer Vision (ICCV), pp. 3888–3897 (2019)

18. Orbay, A., Akarun, L.: Neural sign language translation by learning tokenization. arXiv preprint arXiv:2002.00479 (2020)

19. Özdemir, O., Kındıroğlu, A.A., Camgöz, N.C., Akarun, L.: Bosphorussign22k sign language recognition dataset. arXiv preprint arXiv:2004.01283 (2020)

20. Paszke, A., et al.: Automatic differentiation in PyTorch. In: NIPS Autodiff Workshop (2017)

21. Simonyan, K., Zisserman, A.: Two-stream convolutional networks for action recognition in videos. In Advances in Neural Information Processing Systems, pp. 568–576. MIT (2014)
22. Soomro, K., Zamir, A.R., Shah, M.: Ucf101: a dataset of 101 human actions classes from videos in the wild. arXiv:1212.0402 (2012)
23. Tran, D., Bourdev, L., Fergus, R., Torresani, L., Paluri, M.: Learning spatiotemporal features with 3d convolutional networks. In: Proceedings of the IEEE International Conference on Computer Vision, pp. 4489–4497. IEEE (2015)
24. Tran, D., Wang, H., Torresani, L., Ray, J., LeCun, Y., Paluri, M.: A closer look at spatiotemporal convolutions for action recognition. In: IEEE/CVF Conference on Computer Vision and Pattern Recognition, pp. 6450–6459 (2018)
25. Vaezi Joze, H., Koller, O.: Ms-asl: a large-scale data set and benchmark for understanding american sign language. In: The British Machine Vision Conference (BMVC) (2019)
26. Varol, G., Laptev, I., Schmid, C.: Long-term temporal convolutions for action recognition. IEEE Trans. Pattern Anal. Mach. Intell. **40**(6), 1510–1517 (2017)
27. Wang, H., Schmid, C.: Action recognition with improved trajectories. In: IEEE International Conference on Computer Vision, pp. 3551–3558. IEEE (2013)
28. Wang, Y., See, J., Phan, R.C.W., Oh, Y.H.: Efficient spatio-temporal local binary patterns for spontaneous facial micro-expression recognition. PloS one **10**(5), e0124674 (2015)
29. Zhang, J., Zhou, W., Xie, C., Pu, J., Li, H.: Chinese sign language recognition with adaptive hmm. In: IEEE International Conference on Multimedia and Expo (ICME), pp. 1–6. IEEE (2016)
30. Zhou, H., Zhou, W., Zhou, Y., Li, H.: Spatial-temporal multi-cue network for continuous sign language recognition. In: AAAI, pp. 13009–13016 (2020)

Unsupervised Discovery of Sign Terms by K-Nearest Neighbours Approach

Korhan Polat$^{(\boxtimes)}$ and Murat Saraçlar

Boğaziçi University, Istanbul, Turkey
{korhan.polat,murat.saraclar}@boun.edu.tr

Abstract. In order to utilize the large amount of unlabeled sign language resources, unsupervised learning methods are needed. Motivated by the successful results of unsupervised term discovery (UTD) in spoken languages, here we explore how to apply similar methods for sign terms discovery. Our goal is to find the repeating terms from continuous sign videos without any supervision. Using visual features extracted from RGB videos, we show that a k-nearest neighbours based discovery algorithm designed for speech can also discover sign terms. We also run experiments using a baseline UTD algorithm and comment on their differences.

Keywords: Unsupervised learning · Sign language · Term discovery

1 Introduction

Most of the automatic sign language recognition (ASLR) systems to date require large amounts of training data. Since there does not exist a reliable automatic annotation tool, sign corpora need to be annotated by human experts. Manual annotation being a laborious process, limits the number of available annotated corpora and hinders the development of better ASLR systems. However, there are plenty of sign language resources that can be used if we employ unsupervised learning methods. In this work, we address this issue and investigate how unsupervised term discovery in speech can be adapted to sign languages.

The aim of unsupervised term discovery (UTD) is to discover repeating units in an unknown language, without using any information except the signal itself (zero-resource). In general, UTD systems take feature time series as input and the output is the discovered clusters of segments, where each cluster is hypothesized to be a unit in that language. For spoken languages, the repeating units may correspond to phones, words or common phrases in that language. Usually UTD systems employ three stages. The first one is the matching stage, in which pairs of similar segments are discovered. The second stage involves the clustering of these pairs, so that similar pairs are joined together to form clusters of hypothesized units. The last stage concerns the parsing of the input sequences with discovered word-type IDs. The performance of the clustering and parsing stages depends on

© Springer Nature Switzerland AG 2020
A. Bartoli and A. Fusiello (Eds.): ECCV 2020 Workshops, LNCS 12536, pp. 310–321, 2020.
https://doi.org/10.1007/978-3-030-66096-3_22

the quality of the matching stage. Hence, we narrow our scope to the matching stage only; our aim is to discover pairs of similar sub-sequences from continuous sign language videos, without any additional information.

Unsupervised term discovery has been studied in speech processing for over a decade. The pioneering work [18] in spoken term discovery introduces the segmental variant of dynamic time warping (SDTW) algorithm to search for pairs of similar segments. The input files are processed in pairs and pairwise distance matrices between their time series feature vectors are computed. The idea is to apply DTW in diagonal bands on a distance matrix between two sequences and collect the path fragments with minimal distortions. The discovered diagonal path fragments with high similarities are referred as the matching pairs, which are clustered to form hypothesized word categories. A similar but more efficient algorithm [4] uses locality sensitive hashing to approximate distance matrices. The diagonal fragments with high similarities are searched using efficient image processing techniques. Costly SDTW search is applied only in the vicinity of these candidate fragments, thus reducing runtime significantly. In the following years, Zero Resource speech challenges [3, 25] were held to allow comparison of various zero-resource approaches using standardized metrics. The Bayesian methods [8, 17] that perform full-coverage, require large amounts of data to be trained and assume that tokens of the same types do not show significant variability. We opt to use a simpler discovery method that requires no training, the K-nearest neighbours based algorithm [23]. We show that it can be run for continuous sign videos, by feeding visual features instead of speech features.

Unsupervised learning has been a rather inactive area in sign language recognition. Previous works that focus on lexicon discovery usually rely on weak supervision, in the form of subtitles [19] or text translations [9] that accompany sign videos. Other works that focus on extracting sub-units [22,24,26] do not perform discovery at sign level. A similar work to ours [16] finds common signs among continuous sentences, but uses the information that there is a common sign. These works rely on weak supervision or incorporate linguistic information to the discovery process. Zero resource term discovery for sign language is first explored in [20], in which the SDTW baseline algorithm [4] for speech is used to discover sign terms. Here, we build upon the same idea and show that a KNN based term discovery algorithm [23] can also be adapted for sign language term discovery. We also employ a better cross-validated evaluation scheme and compare our results to SDTW baseline in [20].

In short, our contribution is to show that a KNN based term discovery algorithm [23] can be used for sign languages. We also make a comparison with the SDTW based baseline in [20], while improving the evaluation scheme. In Sect. 2, an overview of the discovery pipeline [23] is given for the sake of completeness. In Sect. 3 the setup for sign language experiments are presented. Results are given and discussed in Sect. 4.

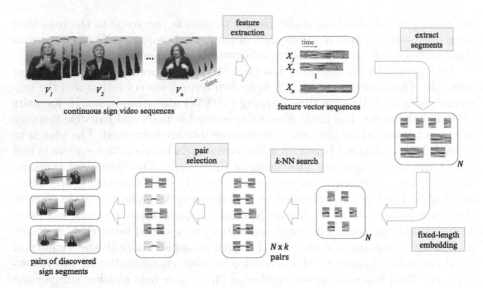

Fig. 1. Flow diagram of the KNN based discovery algorithm

2 K-Nearest Neighbours Based Discovery Algorithm

We adopt the KNN based discovery pipeline in [23], which begins with extracting large number of overlapping segments from the input sequences. These segments, which may have variable lengths, are transformed into fixed dimensional representations using smoothed sampling. Then for each segment representation, k nearest segments are searched so that, each segment is paired with k other segments. From these segment pairs, the ones that overlap and that have lower similarities are discarded. The remaining pairs are the discovered pairs. The flow diagram of this algorithm is displayed in Fig. 1 and details of these steps are explained in the following sections.

2.1 Temporal Segmentation

For an input sequence, the points that are a frames apart are selected as candidate segmentation points. The segments are extracted for all possible combinations of these candidate points. As the parameter a decreases, the chance of finding correct boundaries increases at the expense of more computational cost. The segment lengths are constrained to an interval, which can be adjusted according to the expected term lengths. More formally, for a given d dimensional feature vector time series $X \in \mathbb{R}^{d \times T}$ of length T, a set of segments $\{X_{ij}\}$ are extracted such that

$$i, j \in \{0, a, 2a, \dots, \lfloor T/a \rfloor \cdot a\} \tag{1}$$

$$l_{min} < j - i < l_{max} \tag{2}$$

where l_{min} and l_{max} set the bounds for segment lengths. This procedure considers all possible segments as candidates.

2.2 Fixed-Length Representations

We apply the embedding method described in [23], which simply is the sampling of input vectors, weighted by Gaussian kernels. A segment X_{ij} of L_0 frames is multiplied with a transformation matrix $F \in \mathbb{R}^{L_0 \times L}$ to be mapped to L-frame representation. The lth column of F is the kernel defined as

$$f_l = \mathcal{N}\left(\frac{l \cdot L_0}{L}, \; r \cdot L_0 + s \cdot g_L(l)\right) \tag{3}$$

where $g_L(l)$ is a triangular function such that $g_L(l) = \frac{L}{2} - \left|\frac{L}{2} - l\right|$, r and s are weighting parameters for the kernel's variance. The triangular function makes the frames in the middle more smoothed. This is a very simple method for obtaining fixed dimensional representation and more complex representation learning methods can be incorporated to this step.

2.3 Nearest Neighbour Search

Fixed-length representations are reshaped to 1d vectors so that each segment is represented by one of these vectors. The next step is to collect all of them to a search index, using the FAISS [5] framework, which builds a very efficient search index on GPU and can be scaled up easily. Then for each segment representation, the k nearest segments are found using Euclidean distance. If there are N segments, the search yields $N \times k$ pairs of similar segments.

2.4 Pair Selection

The pairs after the KNN search are mostly redundant because they overlap with each other. Therefore a series of elimination steps are required, so that only non-overlapping high confidence matches remain. The first step is to retrieve and sort all neighbours for an input file, and select only the top δ percent of the pairs. In other words, for an input file i, there are $N_i \times k$ pairs and we select the best $\delta \times N_i \times k$ pairs. The next step is to remove the self-overlapping pairs, whose segments overlap with each other. For a pair $p = (s_1, s_2)$, the self-overlap ratio between the segments s_1, s_2 is computed as the lengths of intersection over union

$$r_{self}(s_1, s_2) = \frac{|s_1 \cap s_2|}{|s_1 \cup s_2|}. \tag{4}$$

The final step removes the remaining overlapping pairs by using non-maximal suppression (NMS). All pairs are sorted by decreasing similarity scores. Beginning from the top, the pairs are compared to worse pairs. Worse pairs are discarded if they overlap with a better pair, where the pair-overlap ratio is computed as

$$r_{pair}(p_i, p_j) = \frac{|s_{i,1} \cap s_{j,1}| \cdot |s_{i,2} \cap s_{j,2}|}{|s_{i,1}| \cdot |s_{i,2}|}. \tag{5}$$

The δ parameter is adjusted to control accuracy-coverage trade-off in the original work [23]. In our implementation, we fix $\delta = 5\%$ and apply another similarity threshold θ at the very end, in order to perform NMS only once and adjust the coverage after all computations are complete.

3   Setup for Sign Language Experiments

We test the term discovery pipeline described in Sect. 2 on sign language videos, by feeding visual features instead of acoustic features, using a similar setup to [20]. The visual features consist of hand shape and pose features which are obtained by running pre-trained models on each video frame. We use the Phoenix Weather 2014 [10] dataset, in which the gloss time boundaries are labelled, enabling us to evaluate the quality of discovered segments. Using the metrics for spoken UTD [15], we compare the KNN based algorithm [23] to the SDTW baseline [4] and comment on their differences.

3.1   Visual Features

Following the feature extraction steps in [20], we obtain two set of features by running pre-trained models on each video frame.

Hand Shapes. We use the DeepHand [11] pre-trained hand shape classifier network. It was originally trained over 1 million right hand images from three different sign corpora [2,10,13], where the hand shape labels were derived according to SignWriting notation [21]. For each video frame, we extract the 61 dimensional final layer activations before the softmax layer. We observed that reducing the dimensions to 40 by applying whitened PCA transformation improved the results in the discovery experiments. We only use the right hand features for all experiments.

Joint Locations. We also use the 2D joint coordinates that are found by running OpenPose [1] estimator on each frame. Concatenating the 8 upper body joints together with 21 keypoints for right and left hand each, we obtain 100 dimensional pose features per frame. The coordinates are normalized by subtracting the neck location and dividing by shoulder length.

3.2   Evaluation Criteria

There are numerous metrics for measuring different aspects of discovery systems. We base our metrics on the ones used in Zero Resource challenges [3,25] which are described in detail by Ludusan et al. [15]. We use the publicly available TDE toolkit[1] designed for spoken UTD. We modify some the metrics for our application.

---

[1] github.com/bootphon/tdev2.

The metrics are computed using the gold transcriptions of discovered segments. In spoken term discovery, the transcriptions are usually at phoneme level and a segment is associated with gold phones if the segment interval overlaps with more than 50% or 30 ms of the phone duration. In our application, we only use the 50% criteria because the gold gloss lengths may vary significantly.

- Coverage: It is the ratio of non-overlapping discovered tokens to the discoverable tokens in all input sequences. In speech, it is computed as discovered phones over all phones; because all phones are assumed to be discoverable since there are usually less then a hundred phones for any spoken language. However, unlike speech, some sign types may appear only once in the whole input. Therefore, to be fair, we divide by the number of discoverable tokens, whose types are seen at least two times.
- Normalized Edit Distance (NED): It measures the quality of pairs, in terms of Levenshtein distance, which simply is the minimum number of modifications (insertion, deletion, substitution) required to make two discrete sequences the same, normalized by the length of the longer sequence. The final NED score is averaged over all pairs.
- Grouping Quality: This set of metrics is computed in terms of precision (P), recall (R) and F-score (harmonic mean of P, R). It is similar to cluster purity and inverse purity. If the pairs within a cluster has the same transcription, then the precision is high. If pairs from separate clusters have the same transcriptions, then the recall is low. For our application we don't expect grouping recall to be high since we don't perform further clustering step and leave them in pairs.

Type/token metrics analyse whether discovered groups of sub-units (phones) correctly represent the units. We don't report type/token metrics because available sign labels are not in the same granularity as phonemes in speech. The gloss labels we have correspond to words in speech. Therefore we report NED and grouping quality metrics, which are still significant even computed with gloss labels instead of sub-units.

3.3 Dataset

The dataset we use is the Phoenix Weather 2014 [10], which consists of German Sign Language interpretations of weather forecast aired in a public TV. This dataset consists of 25 fps, RGB videos that are recorded in similar conditions where all signers face directly into the camera. We use the training set of multi-signer (MS) setup, which contains 5671 sentences that total 10 h of videos. We use this subset because the gloss labels with time boundaries are provided only for this subset. These labels are automatically aligned by HMM-LSTM based model [12] using the sentence level gloss labels, annotated by human experts. The automatic frame level labels also indicate the HMM states of the HMM-LSTM based model [12] but we omit this information and use only the gloss information.

In addition to having time boundaries for labels, this corpus possesses other benefits for our task. The vocabulary is limited to weather related terms; there are only 1081 unique gloss types. Moreover, the signers are professionals which makes the inter-signer variability minimal.

Table 1. Partitions of the Phoenix 2014 MS [10] for cross-validated experiments

Subsets	Signer IDs	# Sentences	Total Size
	4	836	
1	8	704	1705
	9	165	
	1	1475	
2	3	470	1975
	6	30	
	5	1296	
3	7	646	1991
	2	49	

We partition the data into three folds for cross-validation, as shown in Table 1. We aim a partition where the subset sizes in terms of number of sentences are matched. At each fold, 1/3 of the data is used as development set and the remaining is used as unseen test set. Then we switch the development set and re-run the tuning procedure. The results are then reported using the average of test results, weighted by number of sentences. For each experiment, the final score threshold θ is adjusted so that Coverage is about 10%, and NED score is used as decision criterion.

4   Results and Discussion

In this section, we first discuss the KNN based algorithm [23] and then compare it to the SDTW baseline presented in [20].

4.1   KNN Based Discovery

We first explored the effect of different hyper-parameters on discovery performance. The expected term length for the Phoenix dataset [10] is about 10 frames (0.4 s). Using this information, we set the minimum segment length l_{min} as 6 frames and segmentation resolution a to be 3 frames. We observed that setting the maximum segment length l_{max} as 45 frames (1.8 s) allowed discovery of n-grams. With a, l_{min} and l_{max} fixed, we then perform cross-validated grid search to find the best combination of embedding dimension L and smoothing parameters r and s. Even though the optimum values for these parameters vary for

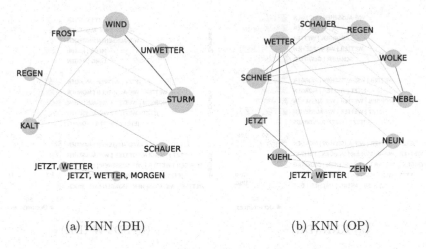

(a) KNN (DH)   (b) KNN (OP)

Fig. 2. Examples of most confused pairs of glosses for hand shape (DH) and pose (OP) features. Darker lines represent more confused pairs and circle radii are proportional to gloss frequencies

each signer and type of feature, we observed that setting $r = 0.1, s = 0.4$ and $L = 6$ frames yield good results in general.

Among the two sets of features (DeepHand and OpenPose [1,11]), the Deep-Hand features yield better results as shown in Table 2. The most confused pairs for each type of feature are given in Fig. 2. Here, we observe that semantically similar signs (e.g. rain-shower, wind-storm etc.) which also have similar forms are easily confused. Interestingly, the clusters of most confused glosses differ according to feature type. This observation leads to the conclusion that in future studies, these two types of features can be fused together to complement each others weaknesses.

4.2   Comparison to SDTW Baseline

The segmental DTW based discovery algorithm [4] is regarded as the baseline for Zero Resource speech challenges [3,25]. It is also the only algorithm previously adapted for sign terms discovery [20]. Therefore we use it as the baseline algorithm to compare our results. We rerun this algorithm in order to obtain the matching pairs without clustering step, so that only matching stages are compared. Since this algorithm is reported to work poorly with pose features [20], we run with the hand shape features only. We apply a similar procedure for removing overlapping pairs, as described in Sect. 2.4.

The biggest difference between the KNN based algorithm [23] and SDTW baseline [4] is the length of discovered segments (see Table 2). The SDTW baseline is able to discover longer segments, often n-grams, therefore less pairs are needed to satisfy 10% Coverage. Correctly discovered n-grams for both algorithms are displayed in Fig. 3. The baseline algorithm uses a sparse approximation of the distance matrix. Then the SDTW search is performed on the diagonal

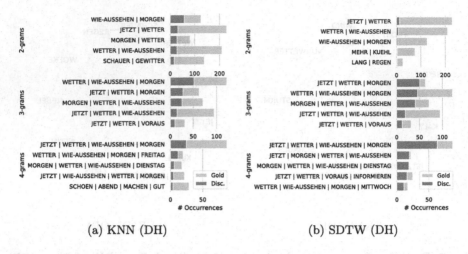

(a) KNN (DH)   (b) SDTW (DH)

Fig. 3. Examples of correctly discovered gloss n-grams (Disc.) for both algorithms, together with the number of occurrences of existing gold n-grams

segments that remain after the median filtering of the sparse matrix. Median filtering allows only long diagonal paths to be searched therefore the segments with this method tend to be longer. Conversely, KNN based algorithm is more receptive to shorter segments, because smoothed embedding method may cause less distortion for shorter segments.

Table 2. Term discovery results of both algorithms at 10% Coverage, averaged for unseen test sets

Experiment	NED	Grouping			Avg. Se.g.	# Discovered
	(%)	P (%)	R (%)	F (%)	Length (sec)	Pairs
SDTW (DH)	**41.0**	18.9	51.8	27.4	2.1	994.9
KNN (OP)	50.7	43.1	39.7	41.0	0.4	1206.4
KNN (DH)	43.4	**50.1**	**52.0**	**51.0**	0.5	1359.2

As shown in Table 2, NED scores for both algorithms are similar. However, grouping precision of the KNN based algorithm is considerably better. This is because the grouping quality metrics are originally designed for evaluating clusters that have more than two segments. Since we don't perform clustering, each cluster has exactly two segments, and therefore the grouping precision gives the ratio of perfect matches over all pairs. As a result, the partial matches between longer segments do not count as positive examples. Another notable difference is that, using pose features does not significantly degrade discovery performance for KNN based algorithm, whereas it was reported to degrade performance in

[20]. It should also be noted that KNN based algorithm runs much faster; pre-computed features for 3 h of video is processed in about one minute using GPU, versus 10 min using the SDTW baseline.

For all setups, nearly 1% of the perfect matches come from different signers, most of the correct matches belong to the same signer. Therefore we can think of these results as the average of signer dependent experiments.

5 Conclusions

In this work, we demonstrate that a KNN based spoken term discovery algorithm [23] can be run for continuous sign language to discover sign terms, by using features extracted from RGB videos only. We compare this algorithm to the baseline SDTW method proposed in [20], using the same dataset [10] and similar metrics. We show that the baseline method is better at discovering longer sequences and KNN method is better for discovering shorter segments. Nonetheless, the KNN based method runs much faster. It is also more flexible in the sense that, more sophisticated segmentation and embedding approaches can be incorporated easily. Henceforth, a future direction is to focus on representation learning methods [14], which may also combine non-manual modalities. Using the discovered pairs, representation learning methods such as frame-wise correspondence autoencoders (CAE) [7] or sequence to sequence CAE [6] can be used. The cross-validated evaluation scheme that we propose may be used in future studies to benchmark other UTD algorithms and representation learning methods.

Acknowledgments. This work is supported in part by the Scientific and Technological Research Council of Turkey (TUBITAK) under Project 117E059.

References

1. Cao, Z., Simon, T., Wei, S.E., Sheikh, Y.: Realtime multi-person 2D pose estimation using part affinity fields. In: Proceeding of IEEE Conference on Computer Vision and Pattern Recognition (CVPR), pp. 1302–1310 (2017)
2. McKee, D., McKee, R., Alexander, S.P., Pivac, L.: The online dictionary of New Zealand sign language (2015). http://nzsl.vuw.ac.nz
3. Dunbar, E., et al.: The zero resource speech challenge 2017. In: Proceeding of IEEE Workshop on Automatic Speech Recognition and Understanding (ASRU), pp. 323–330 (2017)
4. Jansen, A., Durme, B.V.: Efficient spoken term discovery using randomized algorithms. In: Proceeding of IEEE Workshop on Automatic Speech Recognition and Understanding (ASRU), pp. 401–406 (2011)
5. Johnson, J., Douze, M., Jégou, H.: Billion-scale similarity search with GPUS. arXiv preprint arXiv:1702.08734 (2017)
6. Kamper, H.: Truly unsupervised acoustic word embeddings using weak top-down constraints in encoder-decoder models. In: Proceeding of IEEE International Conference on Acoustics, Speech and Signal Processing (ICASSP), pp. 6535–3539 (2019)

7. Kamper, H., Elsner, M., Jansen, A., Goldwater, S.: Unsupervised neural network based feature extraction using weak top-down constraints. In: Proceeding of IEEE International Conference on Acoustics, Speech and Signal Processing (ICASSP), pp. 5818–5822 (2015)

8. Kamper, H., Jansen, A., Goldwater, S.: Unsupervised word segmentation and lexicon discovery using acoustic word embeddings. IEEE/ACM Trans. Audio, Speech, Lang. Process. **24**(4), 669–679 (2016)

9. Kelly, D., Mc Donald, J., Markham, C.: Weakly supervised training of a sign language recognition system using multiple instance learning density matrices. IEEE Trans. Syst. Man, Cybern. Part B (Cybernetics) **41**(2), 526–541 (2011)

10. Koller, O., Forster, J., Ney, H.: Continuous sign language recognition: towards large vocabulary statistical recognition systems handling multiple signers. Comput. Vis. Image Understanding **141**, 108–125 (2015)

11. Koller, O., Ney, H., Bowden, R.: Deep hand: how to train a CNN on 1 million hand images when your data is continuous and weakly labelled. In: Proceeding of IEEE Conference on Computer Vision and Pattern Recognition (CVPR), pp. 3793–3802 (2016)

12. Koller, O., Zargaran, S., Ney, H.: Re-Sign: re-aligned end-to-end sequence modelling with deep recurrent CNN-HMMs. In: Proceeding of IEEE Conference on Computer Vision and Pattern Recognition (CVPR), pp. 3416–3424 (2017)

13. Kristoffersen, J.H., et al.: Ordbog over Dansk Tegnsprog (2008). http://www.tegnsprog.dk

14. Levin, K., Henry, K., Jansen, A., Livescu, K.: Fixed-dimensional acoustic embeddings of variable-length segments in low-resource settings. In: Proceeding of IEEE Workshop on Automatic Speech Recognition and Understanding (ASRU), pp. 410–415 (2013)

15. Ludusan, B., et al.: Bridging the gap between speech technology and natural language processing: an evaluation toolbox for term discovery systems. In: Proceeding of Language Resources and Evaluation Conference (2014)

16. Nayak, S., Duncan, K., Sarkar, S., Loeding, B.L.: Finding recurrent patterns from continuous sign language sentences for automated extraction of signs. J. Mach. Learn. Res. **13**, 2589–2615 (2012)

17. Ondel, L., Burget, L., Černocký, J.: Variational inference for acoustic unit discovery. Procedia Comput. Sci. **81**, 80–86 (2016)

18. Park, A.S., Glass, J.R.: Unsupervised pattern discovery in speech. IEEE Trans. Audio Speech Lang. Process. **16**(1), 186–197 (2008)

19. Pfister, T., Charles, J., Zisserman, A.: Large-scale learning of sign language by watching TV (using co-occurrences). In: Proceedings of the British Machine Vision Conference, pp. 1–11 (2013)

20. Polat, K., Saraçlar, M.: Unsupervised term discovery for continuous sign language. In: Proceedings of the LREC2020 9th Workshop on the Representation and Processing of Sign Languages: Sign Language Resources in the Service of the Language Community, Technological Challenges and Application Perspectives, pp. 189–196. European Language Resources Association (ELRA), Marseille, France (2020)

21. Sutton, V.: Sign writing. Deaf Action Committee (DAC) for Sign Writing (2000)

22. Theodorakis, S., Pitsikalis, V., Maragos, P.: Dynamic-static unsupervised sequentiality, statistical subunits and lexicon for sign language recognition. Image Vis. Comput. **32**, 533–549 (2014)

23. Thual, A., Dancette, C., Karadayi, J., Benjumea, J., Dupoux, E.: A k-nearest neighbours approach to unsupervised spoken term discovery. In: Proceeding of 2018 IEEE Spoken Language Technology Workshop (SLT), pp. 491–497 (2018)

24. Tornay, S., Magimai-Doss, M.: Subunits inference and lexicon development based on pairwise comparison of utterances and signs. Information 10, 298 (2019)
25. Versteegh, M., et al.: The zero resource speech challenge 2015. In: Proceeding of Interspeech, pp. 3169–3173 (2015)
26. Yin, P., Starner, T., Hamilton, H., Essa, I., Rehg, J.M.: Learning the basic units in American sign language using discriminative segmental feature selection. In: IEEE International Conference on Acoustics, Speech and Signal Processing, pp. 4757–4760 (2009)

Improving Keyword Search Performance in Sign Language with Hand Shape Features

Nazif Can Tamer[✉] and Murat Saraçlar

Department of Electrical and Electronic Engineering, Boğaziçi University, Istanbul, Turkey
{can.tamer,murat.saraclar}@boun.edu.tr

Abstract. Handshapes and human pose estimation are among the most used pretrained features in sign language recognition. In this study, we develop a handshape based keyword search (KWS) system for sign language and compare different pose based and handshape based encoders for the task of large vocabulary sign retrieval. We improved KWS performance in sign language by 3.5% mAP score for gloss search and 1.6% for cross-lingual KWS by combining pose and handshape based KWS models in a late fusion approach.

Keywords: Sign language recognition · Keyword search · Handshape recognition

1 Introduction

Sign language is the visual language of the hearing impaired. It has a different lexicon, grammar, and word ordering than spoken language; and the information in sign language is mainly carried through a mixed use of hand movements and facial expressions. To cope with this multimodal nature, recognition studies in sign language have historically divided the problem and focused on these different building blocks separately. Hand shape recognition from RGB hand patches [5,12,14] models common hand shapes, body pose based sign language recognition [1,9] mainly models places of articulation in space or along body, and other studies deal with mouthing [11] and facial expressions [2] which are all important communication channels of continuous sign language. In this paper, we introduce a hand-shape based keyword search (KWS) model for continuous sign language and compare it against KWS with pose key points [17].

Keyword search is a sub-problem of content retrieval which aims to search for a written query inside a large and unlabeled utterance. In spoken language recognition, keyword search is studied as a different problem than other retrieval problems such as keyword spotting and term discovery. Content retrieval from continuous sign language, on the other hand, is generally studied together under the umbrella term sign spotting and encompasses query-by-example search, keyword spotting, keyword search, and weakly supervised term discovery. The general approach in sign spotting requires strong supervision during training/learning.

© Springer Nature Switzerland AG 2020
A. Bartoli and A. Fusiello (Eds.): ECCV 2020 Workshops, LNCS 12536, pp. 322–333, 2020.
https://doi.org/10.1007/978-3-030-66096-3_23

Jantunen et al. [18] used dynamic time warping to search for citation form isolated signs in continuous sign language sentences. Yang et al. [20] used conditional random fields to search for 48 in-vocabulary signs that they learned from isolated examples. Ong et al. used hierarchical random fields to search for 48 the signs inside continuous sign language utterances. Although these approaches can obtain good retrieval performances, their search vocabulary is in the order of tens and their real-world applicability to large vocabulary retrieval systems is limited due to the amount of highly-annotated data they require during training.

Another track in sign spotting research is using weakly labeled continuous sign language in both learning time as well as testing. Most of the available sign language data are in the form of sign language interpreting and translations into the spoken language is the only form of annotation. Since there is no one-to-one relationship between signs and spoken words, several studies in the literature focus on discovering signs under the weak supervision of these translations or subtitles. Cooper and Bowden [7] used mining strategies to learn signs by matching the subtitles from TV shows. Farhadi and Forsyth [8] used HMMs to find sign boundaries assuming the sign sequence and the speech transcripts have the same word ordering. Buehler et al. [3] and Kelly et al. [10] applied multiple instance learning (MIL) based strategies to learn signs from subtitles and Kelly et al. [10] further used the isolated signs they discovered from translations to train a 30-vocabulary sign spotting framework. Being a concept adopted from speech recognition, large vocabulary keyword search methods also use weak labels in both training and test. Tamer and Saraclar [17] used graph convolution on top of skeleton joints for sign language keyword search. In this work, we introduce a hand shape based large vocabulary sign retrieval system and by combining with a pose based KWS model, we increase the recent keyword search performance in sign language by 3.5% mAP for gloss search and 1.6% mAP for cross-lingual KWS in RWTH-PHOENIX-Weather 2014T dataset.

The rest of the paper is organized as follows: In Sect. 2 we briefly summarize our model and in Sect. 3–6 we introduce the details. In Sect. 7, we explain our experimental setting and results. Finally, in Sect. 8 we conclude the paper.

2   Overview

The pipeline of our hand shape based KWS system is summarized in Fig. 1. Our method starts with preprocessing the video to obtain hand shape feature vectors for each frame. Frame-level hand features are then fed into a 4-layer 1D temporal CNN encoder to detect movements. Keyword selection module from [17] represents the keywords in the same embedding space and focuses on relevant parts of the encoded hand shape sequence to detect the keyword.

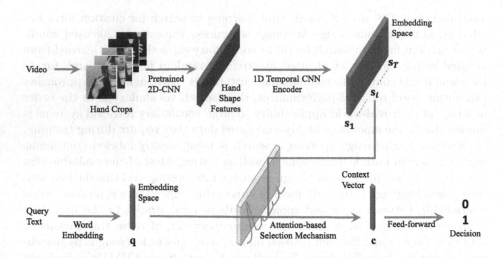

Fig. 1. Sign language KWS with Hand Shape Features. After the hand crops are obtained with the help of openpose, the hand shape features are extracted from frame. Word embeddings, 1D Temporal CNN Encoder, selection mechanism and the final feed-forward layer are trained end-to-end to represent video and text in the same embedding space.

3   Pre-processing

For each frame, the right hand wrist spatial locations are extracted with the help of OpenPose [6] pose estimation toolkit and square hand crops centered around the wrist joint are obtained. By feeding hand crops into one of the two pre-trained 2D CNN options, we represent hand crop with a vectoral feature. The frames are omitted if the OpenPose cannot estimate the location of the wrist joint. For the two 2D CNN options, the resulting one-dimensional hand shape features are 1024-dimensional for DeepHand and 2048-dimensional for MultiTask respectively.

3.1   Deephand Feature Extraction

We used the pre-trained CNN from DeepHand [12] to extract hand shape features. The model takes hand crops and classifies them into 60 pre-defined hand shape classes or a junk class. Their training data consists of two isolated sign language corpora (Danish and New Zealand SL), and continuous Phoenix-2014 Weather dataset. Since the third dataset they used in training is almost identical to our experiment data and the amount of supervision they used in training is more than that of our keyword search models, we believe the pre-trained Deep-Hand model can be viewed as the topline for hand shape encoders in this dataset. In our implementation, we used 1024 dimensional features from the second-last layer of DeepHand CNN.

3.2   Multitask Feature Extraction

Multitask features are introduced as a tokenization layer for sign language translation [14]. The network is trained for hand shape recognition in two datasets: the first one is the Danish and New Zealand SL corpora from DeepHand [12] excluding RWTH-PHOENIX-Weather 2014, and the second one is a framewise labeled and smaller Turkish SL dataset [16]. The network shares parameters at the start, and the final layers are different for matching different hand shape classification tasks. While the first one is 60 hand shapes and a junk class, the target for the smaller dataset al.so includes specific classes for hands showing certain body parts, thus, incorporating background information to some extent. Since the domain data is not used in training of Multitask features, it can be thought of as a real-world scenario for RGB hand shape based KWS. In feature extraction, we used 2048 dimensional vectors from the shared part of the multitask network.

4   1D Temporal CNN Encoder

At the end of pre-processing step, we obtain each frame represented with raw hand shape features. Since duration of a sign is greater than a single frame, however, we cannot learn keyword embeddings with these raw hand shape features and a further sequential modeling step is necessary. To model a 1-second-long temporal sliding window, we used 4-layer 1D convolutional network with kernel size 7 and same padding. We used leaky ReLU as the activation between layers. The first layer has 1024 channels for DeepHand and 2048 for MultiTask features. Then the channel sizes at the end of each layer are 512 for layer 1, 256 for layer 2, 128 for layer 3 and 256 for the last layer, respectively. With the help of same padding during convolution, we kept the encoded sequence length same with raw hand features. Each time step at the encoded sequence has access to 25 time steps of raw hand shape features resulting in a temporal range of 1 s in 25-fps RWTH-PHOENIX-Weather 2014T dataset.

5   Keyword Search Module

The keyword search module follows from [17] and consists of word embeddings, attention-based selection mechanism, and the final feed-forward layer.

5.1   Word Embeddings

A query in the form of text is first converted into an index in the vocabulary, and for all unique queries, a simple linear word embedding $\mathbf{q}$ is learned to match encoded sequence frame $\mathbf{s_i}$ in a mutual embedding space.

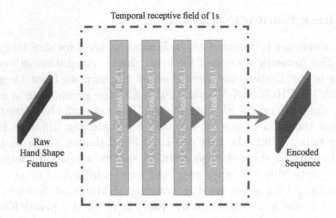

Fig. 2. 1D Temporal CNN Encoder

5.2 Attention-Based Selection Mechanism

Attention is a widely known concept from Neural Machine Translation, where it helps the decoder to focus on relevant parts of the source sentence when predicting the next word in the target sequence [13]. In a similar fashion, we use attention to focus on the most relevant part of the encoded sequence $s_{1:T}$ to the query q. The relevance $score(q, s_i)$ between the ith element of the encoded sequence s_i and the query q is measured by a cosine-similarity-based function with a learnable parameter β:

$$score(q, s_i) = \beta \left[\frac{q \cdot s_i}{\|q\| \cdot \|s_i\|} \right]^2 \tag{1}$$

The context vector c is the weighted average of relevance scores after $softmax$ function is applied:

$$c = \sum_i \left[\frac{\exp(score(q, s_i))}{\sum_{i'} \exp(score(q, s_{i'}))} \right] \cdot s_i \tag{2}$$

Once the context vector c is obtained, it is then fed into a one-layer feed-forward network with sigmoid activation to decide whether the query q is found inside the weakly-labeled sequence $s_{1:T}$.

Although it only has β parameter and the weights of the final feed-forward layer as the learnable parameters, the selection mechanism is the most important layer of the network since it makes the weakly supervised learning of keyword embeddings possible. All the keywords in the vocabulary are searched in tandem in the same sequence. The keywords that appear in the transcription sequence are labeled positive whilst keywords that are not apparent in the transcription are trained to match negative labels.

6 Combining Hand Shape and Pose Based KWS Models

Hand shape and pose keypoints are among the most common pretrained features used in sign language recognition studies. We applied a late fusion approach to test the effectiveness of combining keyword search models trained with hand shapes and pose keypoints.

6.1 Pose Based KWS

The model in [17] is employed for pose based keyword search. OpenPose [6] pose estimation features are extracted from each frame and fed into the Spatial-Temporal Graph Convolution Encoder [19] in 4 different layouts:

Pose1 (UB+RH+LH; x, y, conf): Upper body and right-left hand keypoints with confidence scores alongside (x, y) spatial locations,

Pose2 (UB+RH+LH; x, y): Upper body and right-left hand keypoints with (x, y) spatial locations omitting the OpenPose confidence scores,

Pose3 (UB+RH; x, y, conf): Upper body and right hand keypoints with confidence scores alongside (x, y) spatial locations, and

Pose4 (UB; x, y, conf): Only upper body keypoints with (x, y) spatial locations and OpenPose keypoint prediction confidences.

6.2 Fusion Strategy

In a setting where we search for a single keyword in a single sign language utterance, let $l \in 0,1$ represent the binary label, h the prediction of the hand shape based KWS model, and k the prediction of the pose keypoints based KWS model respectively. The fused prediction p is found as

$$\log p = (1 - \gamma) \cdot \log h + \gamma \cdot \log k \tag{3}$$

The blending ratio γ is the number maximizing the mean average precision (mAP) score in train and development sets and fusion results are reported using this γ-value in the test set.

7 Experiments

7.1 Dataset

RWTH-PHOENIX-Weather 2014T [4] dataset is used for our experiments. This dataset is originally introduced for translation task and includes weather forecasts in German, their sign language interpreting in video format, and gloss sequence corresponding to the signs in the interpreting. The video footage is in 25 fps and in low resolution with heavy amount of blur. There is 9.2 h of training, 37 min of development and 43 min of test partitions in the dataset.

For both the gloss and the cross-lingual keyword search, we used the original dataset labels in the following fashion: We formed our vocabulary from the training set. Each video is weakly labeled with 0 or 1 for every keyword in our vocabulary by looking at whether the keyword is in the label sequence or not. We dropped glosses starting with "_" since they contain on/off tokens and ambiguous signs, and we did not utilize lemmatization for German keywords. At the end, we have 1085 glosses in our gloss vocabulary and 2887 German keywords in cross lingual vocabulary. Since 392 of the glosses and 942 of the German keywords are shared between train and test sets, we report our results on this shared vocabulary. Out-of-vocabulary keyword search is not supported in this implementation.

7.2   Evaluation Metrics

For each keyword, we sorted utterances that give highest prediction scores and used 4 different information retrieval metrics to measure the quality of the keyword search performance. The first three are based on precision values at different ranks and the last one, nDGC, measures the ranking quality.

Mean Average Precision (mAP). is the mean of average precision scores so that all the keywords are equally important no matter how frequent they are in the test set. Average precision (AP) for a keyword q is defined as:

$$AP = \frac{1}{|N|} \sum_{n=1}^{|N|} \text{Precision@}n(q) \tag{4}$$

Precision at 10 (p@10). is the mean of precision scores at first ten retrieved utterances. It is a common metric in information retrieval for historical reasons, however, if the keyword is seen only once in the test set and that utterance is retrieved correctly, we still get p@10 score of 10% for this keyword.

Precision at N (p@N). is the mean of precision scores at first N_{test} retrieved utterances where N_{test}, the number of positive utterances in the test set, is different for each keyword.

Normalized Discounted Cumulative Gain (nDCG). is a measure of ranking quality normalized with the ideal possible ranking. It weights the first retrieved utterances more and the gain gets smaller once we move into higher ranks.

7.3   Effect of Different Encoder Structures on KWS Performance

Keyword search results with various handshape and pose based models are compared in Tables 1 and 2. From the comparison of Pose1 and Pose2 models in both tables, we can see that using confidence scores of OpenPose keypoint estimations increase the retrieval performance in every metric. Both hand shape based gloss search models in Table 1 perform better than Pose4, pose based gloss search with only upper body; but addition of right hand in other pose based models increase the retrieval performance drastically. DeepHand features, which are trained on the domain data, perform universally better than Multitask features in both settings.

The results with the fusion of handshape based and pose based KWS model are also summarized in Tables 1 and 2. We applied a late fusion approach described in Sect. 6.2 with γ values learned from development set. We see that using fusion of handshape based features and Pose1, we can surpass the recent KWS performance in both gloss and cross-lingual KWS. When we compare the fusion models, combining Pose1 with DeepHand is better than combination with the Multitask based one in many of the metrics. However, the Multitask features are trained with only out-of-domain data, and the difference between using Multitask features instead of DeepHand is minimal. Thus, we opted for combining Multitask with Pose1 as our go-to structure.

Table 1. Gloss search results (in %, the higher the better) with different encoder structures. Both Multitask and DeepHand features are extracted from right hand only. UB: upper body, RH: right hand, LH: left hand, and conf refers to the use of OpenPose confidence scores alongside (x, y) spatial locations [17]. In fusion, $\gamma > 0.5$ denotes increasing reliance on the pose model.

Gloss search models	mAP	p@10	p@N	nDCG
Pose1 (UB + RH + LH; x, y, conf)	29.24	26.25	25.84	47.52
Pose2 (UB + RH + LH; x, y)	28.05	24.97	24.38	47.02
Pose3 (UB + RH; x, y, conf)	29.21	26.15	25.94	47.68
Pose4 (UB; x, y, conf)	22.80	21.45	19.95	43.15
Multitask	23.54	23.03	20.71	42.89
Multitask + Pose1, γ=0.54	32.22	27.98	27.66	50.08
DeepHand	24.93	23.65	22.27	43.86
DeepHand + Pose1, γ=0.58	32.78	27.88	28.67	50.02

7.4   Gloss-Specific Comparison of Hand Shape and Pose Based Encoders

In this section, we show that some glosses can be retrieved more easily with handshape features whilst pose based KWS models are better for others. We qualitatively compare the model performances by looking 6 isolated sign samples. Since there is no ground truth labels in RWTH-PHOENIX-Weather 2014T, we use citation form isolated signs taken from SignDict [15] German sign language

Table 2. Cross-lingual search results (in %, the higher the better) with different encoder structures. Both Multitask and DeepHand features are extracted from right hand only. UB: upper body, RH: right hand, LH: left hand, and conf refers to the use of OpenPose confidence scores alongside (x, y) spatial locations [17]. In fusion, $\gamma > 0.5$ denotes increasing reliance on the pose model.

Cross-Lingual KWS Models	mAP	p@10	p@N	nDCG
Pose1 (UB + RH + LH; x, y, conf)	13.14	10.57	10.39	32.54
Pose2 (UB + RH + LH; x, y)	12.61	10.31	10.16	31.79
Pose3 (UB + RH; x, y, conf)	12.92	10.59	10.06	32.52
Pose4 (UB; x, y, conf)	10.79	8.77	8.73	29.99
Multitask	10.44	9.05	8.75	29.30
Multitask + Pose1, $\gamma = 0.68$	14.34	11.52	11.27	33.66
DeepHand	11.11	9.62	9.14	29.85
DeepHand + Pose1, $\gamma = 0.60$	14.75	11.43	11.63	33.97

WENIG   BESSER   ELF   APRIL   GLEICH   NAH

Fig. 3. Hand-picked definitive single frames for the signs in Table 3. Frames are taken from isolated videos in SignDict dictionary [15]. Hand shapes are the most important feature in defining the sign for the first three whilst places of articulation along body are more definitive for the rest.

Table 3. Gloss-specific AP scores for different models. Both MultiTask and DeepHand features are extracted from right hand only. UB: upper body, RH: right hand, LH: left hand. All the pose based KWS models shown in this table are are with (x, y) spatial locations and OpenPose confidence scores.

Gloss search AP (%)	WENIG	BESSER	ELF	APRIL	GLEICH	NAH
Pose1 (UB+RH+LH)	7.47	17.22	19.24	85.24	76.39	50.81
Pose3 (UB+RH)	4.40	3.44	15.53	49.17	48.98	12.31
Pose4 (UB)	2.62	30.20	17.09	50.83	31.68	5.60
Multitask	55.06	100.00	74.34	8.12	1.48	2.40
DeepHand	62.94	81.25	60.51	3.52	13.83	3.32
Multitask + Pose1	43.10	75.00	36.12	67.19	61.48	45.65

dictionary for illustration. When selecting these 6 signs, we simply sorted all gloss queries according to the difference between Multitask and Pose1 models and picked the top 3 that also have a dictionary entry in SignDict for both extremes.

In Table 3, we can see that for the signs WENIG, BESSER, and ELF, both Multitask and DeepHand handshape based KWS models perform better than pose based ones. From the dictionary entries for these signs in Fig. 3, we see that all three of these signs are single-handed and formed of simple hand shapes. The signs APRIL, GLEICH and NAH are the among the signs where Pose based models perform significantly better than handshape based ones. When we do some qualitative analysis, we can see that places of articulation are more important in defining these signs. In Fig. 3, the sign for APRIL includes the thumb touching the nose and for GLEICH and NAH, we see hands interacting with each other. In Table 3, it can be seen that both Multitask and DeepHand handshape based encoders performed poorly compared to Pose1 model that includes upper body and both hands in the graph layout. Lastly, by observing the average performance in all these signs, we conclude that our Multitask + Pose1 fusion model performs reasonably better than relying on either hand shape or pose based models individually.

7.5   Analysis of the Fusion Model

The performance of Multitask + Pose1 model on different gloss vocabulary subsets are shown in Fig. 4. When using weak labels during training, a single utterance is usually not enough to learn which temporal region is relevant for the sign. Thus, we also report our results in smaller vocabulary subsets. For 168

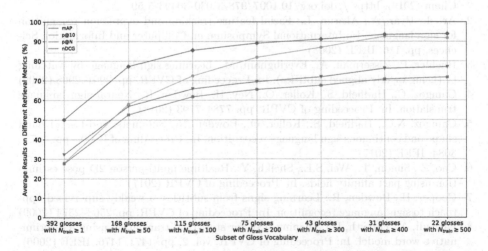

Fig. 4. Gloss search results of the MultiTask+Pose1 fusion model on different vocabulary subsets. N_{train} denotes the number of training utterances labeled with the keyword. In general, the retrieval performance during test time is higher for keywords with more weakly labeled utterances in the training partition.

glosses with number of training samples $N_{train} \geqslant 50$, the mAP score is over 55%. For 115 glosses with $N_{train} \geqslant 100$, more than 7 out of 10 first retrieved utterances are correct. The results in Fig. 4 follows a linear fashion other than the sharp increase in precision@10 scores. It is needed to have at least 10 positive utterances in the test set and this is true for most signs with $N_{train} \geqslant 100$.

8 Conclusion

In this paper, we introduce handshape based keyword search (KWS) models with Multitask [14] and DeepHand [12] pretrained features. We compared the performance of pose and handshape based KWS models in RWTH-PHOENIX-Weather 2014T dataset [4]. We improved the keyword search performance in sign language by applying a late fusion strategy combining pose and handshape based KWS models. Our findings in gloss-specific analysis suggests that handshape and pose based KWS models excel at retrieving different glosses. In future, we aim applying fusion at earlier stages of processing to learn which feature we should rely on for each specific keyword.

Acknowledgements. This study was supported in part by the Scientific and Technological Research Council of Turkey (TUBITAK) under Project 117E059.

References

1. de Amorim, C.C., Macêdo, D., Zanchettin, C.: Spatial-temporal graph convolutional networks for sign language recognition. In: Tetko, I.V., Kůrková, V., Karpov, P., Theis, F. (eds.) ICANN 2019. LNCS, vol. 11731, pp. 646–657. Springer, Cham (2019). https://doi.org/10.1007/978-3-030-30493-5_59
2. Ari, I., Uyar, A., Akarun, L.: Facial feature tracking and expression recognition for sign language. In: International Symposium on Computer and Information Sciences, pp. 1–6. IEEE (2008)
3. Buehler, P., Zisserman, A., Everingham, M.: Learning sign language by watching tv (using weakly aligned subtitles). In: Proceeding of CVPR, pp. 2961–2968 (2009)
4. Camgoz, C., Hadfield, S., Koller, O., Ney, H., Bowden, R.: Neural sign language translation. In: Proceeding of CVPR, pp. 7784–7793 (2018)
5. Camgoz, N.C., Hadfield, S., Koller, O., Bowden, R.: Subunets: end-to-end hand shape and continuous sign language recognition. In: Proceeding of ICCV, pp. 3075–3084. IEEE (2017)
6. Cao, Z., Simon, T., Wei, S.E., Sheikh, Y.: Realtime multi-person 2D pose estimation using part affinity fields. In: Proceeding of CVPR (2017)
7. Cooper, H., Bowden, R.: Learning signs from subtitles: a weakly supervised approach to sign language recognition. In: Proceeding of CVPR, pp. 2568–2574 (2009)
8. Farhadi, A., Forsyth, D.: Aligning ASL for statistical translation using a discriminative word model. In: Proceeding of CVPR, vol. 2, pp. 1471–1476. IEEE (2006)
9. Gattupalli, S., Ghaderi, A., Athitsos, V.: Evaluation of deep learning based pose estimation for sign language recognition. In: Proceedings of the 9th ACM International Conference on Pervasive Technologies Related to Assistive Environments, pp. 1–7 (2016)

10. Kelly, D., Mc Donald, J., Markham, C.: Weakly supervised training of a sign language recognition system using multiple instance learning density matrices. IEEE Trans. Syst. Man Cybern. Part B (Cybernetics) **41**(2), 526–541 (2011)

11. Koller, O., Ney, H., Bowden, R.: Read my lips: continuous signer independent weakly supervised viseme recognition. In: Fleet, D., Pajdla, T., Schiele, B., Tuytelaars, T. (eds.) ECCV 2014. LNCS, vol. 8689, pp. 281–296. Springer, Cham (2014). https://doi.org/10.1007/978-3-319-10590-1_19

12. Koller, O., Ney, H., Bowden, R.: Deep hand: ow to train a CNN on 1 million hand images when your data is continuous and weakly labelled. In: Proceedings of the IEEE conference on computer vision and pattern recognition, pp. 3793–3802 (2016)

13. Luong, T., Pham, H., Manning, C.D.: Effective approaches to attention-based neural machine translation. In: Proceeding of EMNLP, pp. 1412–1421 (2015)

14. Orbay, A., Akarun, L.: Neural sign language translation by learning tokenization. In: 2020 15th IEEE International Conference on Automatic Face and Gesture Recognition (FG 2020), pp. 9–15 (2020)

15. SignDict: Signdict. https://signdict.org/

16. Siyli, R.D.: Hospisign : a framewise annotated turkish sign language dataset. http://dogasiyli.com/hospisign/

17. Tamer, N.C., Saraçlar, M.: Cross-lingual keyword search for sign language. In: Proceeding of LREC2020 9th Workshop on the Representation and Processing of Sign Languages: Sign Language Resources in the Service of the Language Community, Technological Challenges and Application Perspectives, pp. 217–223. European Language Resources Association (ELRA), Marseille, France (2020). https://www.aclweb.org/anthology/2020.signlang-1.35

18. Viitaniemi, V., Jantunen, T., Savolainen, L., Karppa, M., Laaksonen, J.: S-pot-a benchmark in spotting signs within continuous signing. In: Proceeding of Language Resources and Evaluation Conference (LREC) (2014). ISBN 978-2-9517408-8-4

19. Yan, S., Xiong, Y., Lin, D.: Spatial temporal graph convolutional networks for skeleton-based action recognition. In: Thirty-second AAAI conference on artificial intelligence (2018)

20. Yang, H.D., Sclaroff, S., Lee, S.W.: Sign language spotting with a threshold model based on conditional random fields. IEEE Trans. Pattern Anal. Mach. Intell. **31**(7), 1264–1277 (2008)

W16 - Visual Inductive Priors for Data-Efficient Deep Learning

W16 - Visual Inductive Priors
for Data-Efficient Deep Learning

The explosive growth of the amount of available data has lead to many recent breakthroughs in AI and deep learning. However, data is still costly to gather and to annotate, and training on massive datasets has a huge energy consumption adding to our carbon footprint. In addition, there are only a select few deep learning behemoths which have billions of data points and thousands of expensive deep learning hardware GPUs at their disposal. Excellent recent research investigates data efficiency in deep networks by exploiting other data sources such as unsupervised learning, reusing existing datasets, or synthesizing artificial training data. Not enough attention is given to how to overcome the data dependency by adding prior knowledge to deep nets. As a consequence, all knowledge has to be (re-)learned implicitly from data, making deep networks hard to understand black boxes which are susceptible to dataset bias requiring huge data and compute resources. This workshop aims to remedy this gap by investigating how to flexibly pre-wire deep networks with generic visual inductive priors, which allows to incorporate hard won existing knowledge from physics.

There is strong evidence that an innate prior benefits deep nets: adding convolution to deep networks yields a convolutional deep neural network (CNN), which is hugely successful and has permeated the entire field. While convolution was initially applied on images, it is now generalized to graph networks, speech, language, 3D data, video, etc. Convolution models translation invariance in images: an object may occur anywhere in the image, and thus instead of learning parameters at each location in the image, convolution allows to only consider local relations, yet, share parameters over all image locations, and thus saving a huge number of parameters to learn, allowing a strong reduction in the number of examples to learn from. This workshop aims to further the great success of convolution, exploiting innate regularizing structures yielding a significant reduction of training data necessary to learn good machine learning models.

In this First Visual Inductive Priors for Data-Efficient Deep Learning Workshop we had the pleasure to welcome Matthias Bethge, Charles Leek, and Daniel Cremers in a very interesting keynote panel discussion. We received 22 paper submissions, out of which 12 were accepted. In addition, 34 teams participated in our four data deficiency challenge tracks.

We thank all presenters and participants for making this workshop possible.

August 2020

Jan van Gemert
Robert-Jan Bruintjes
Attila Lengyel
Osman Semih Kayhan
Marcos Baptista-Ríos
Anton van den Hengel

Lightweight Action Recognition
in Compressed Videos

Yuqi Huo[1,2], Xiaoli Xu[1,2], Yao Lu[1,2], Yulei Niu[1,2], Mingyu Ding[3],
Zhiwu Lu[1,2(✉)], Tao Xiang[4], and Ji-rong Wen[1,2]

[1] Gaoling School of Artificial Intelligence,
Renmin University of China, Beijing, China
luzhiwu@ruc.edu.cn
[2] Beijing Key Laboratory of Big Data Management and Analysis Methods,
Beijing, China
[3] The University of Hong Kong, Hong Kong, China
[4] University of Surrey, Guildford, UK

Abstract. Most existing action recognition models are large convolutional neural networks that work only with raw RGB frames as input. However, practical applications require lightweight models that directly process compressed videos. In this work, for the first time, such a model is developed, which is lightweight enough to run in real-time on embedded AI devices without sacrifices in recognition accuracy. A new Aligned Temporal Trilinear Pooling (ATTP) module is formulated to fuse three modalities in a compressed video. To remedy the weaker motion vectors (compared to optical flow computed from raw RGB streams) for representing dynamic content, we introduce a temporal fusion method to explicitly induce the temporal context, as well as knowledge distillation from a model trained with optical flows via feature alignment. Compared to existing compressed video action recognition models, it is much more compact and faster thanks to adopting a lightweight CNN backbone.

Keywords: Lightweight action recognition · Compressed videos · Temporal trilinear pooling · Knowledge distillation

1 Introduction

Video analysis has drawn great attention from the computer vision community recently due to an increasing demand for automated video content understanding. In particular, videos account for more than 75% of the global IP traffic everyday [8]. With the advancements of deep learning methods, promising performance has been achieved on a variety of video analysis tasks, including action recognition [1,7,28,33,34], semantic segmentation [5,15], localization [4,23], and detection [3,6].

However, existing convolutional neural network (CNN) based video analysis models still do not meet the requirements of many real-world applications. This is primarily due to two reasons. First, videos such as those on social media sites like YouTube or on smartphones are stored in a compression format to save space. Nevertheless, most existing models work only with uncompressed

© Springer Nature Switzerland AG 2020
A. Bartoli and A. Fusiello (Eds.): ECCV 2020 Workshops, LNCS 12536, pp. 337–352, 2020.
https://doi.org/10.1007/978-3-030-66096-3_24

raw RGB frames. This means that the compressed videos must be decoded first, leading to extra costs on both processing time and storage. Second, most deep video models, based on either two-streams [28] or 3D CNNs [32] are slow (e.g., with high latency for calculating optical flows) and heavy (having a large number of parameters), therefore unsuitable for either processing the vast amount of videos produced everyday, or running on embedded AI devices (e.g., smartphones). There are some recent efforts on lightweight video models [22,41], but they do not work on compressed videos.

Recently, researchers start to address the problem of compressed video action recognition [26,37,39,40]. These models take compressed videos (e.g., MPEG-4) directly as input. Such a video contains only a few key frames and their offsets (i.e., motion vectors and residual errors) for storage reduction. However, none of these models is lightweight, and thus they still incur high latency and cannot run on embedded AI devices for edge computing. Apart from the efficiency limitation, existing models are also ineffective due to the fact that they either ignore B-frames or use them incorrectly for extracting motion vectors and residuals. This is despite the fact that in most video bit-streams, most of the frames (more than 60%) are encoded as B-frames to achieve the best compression rate.

In this paper, for the first time, a challenging video analysis task, called *Lightweight Action Recognition in Compressed Videos*, is tackled to fill a gap in video analysis – to the best of our knowledge, this task has not been studied before. The key challenges of lightweight compressed video action recognition are: 1) how to design a lightweight yet highly effective deep CNN model for action recognition; 2) how to extract meaningful representations from compressed videos that contain far less information than the raw RGB frames.

To address these challenges, we propose a lightweight model for compressed video action recognition. Specifically, we adopt EfficientNet [31] as the backbone network to process the multiple modalities extracted from a compressed video (including RGB I-frames **I**, motion vectors **MV**, and residuals **R**). To fuse these modalities, we propose a novel Aligned Temporal Trilinear Pooling (ATTP) scheme to exploit the complementary information contained in them. To remedy the weaker motion vectors (compared to optical flow computed from raw RGB streams) for representing the dynamic content, we introduce a temporal fusion method to induce the temporal context explicitly. Further, since motion vectors are much coarser than optical flow vectors, we adopt a knowledge distillation strategy via feature alignment between our model and a model trained with optical flow extracted from uncompressed videos. Finally, we overcome a limitation of existing models [26,37,39,40] in that they either ignore the B-frames or utilize them incorrectly. This is because computing motion vectors and residuals from the B-frames is far more challenging than from the alternatives (i.e., P-frames). In this work, by employing correct but more complicated B-frame modeling, our proposed model is applicable to all modern video codecs (e.g., H.264 & HEVC). The result of introducing these new components is a lightweight yet powerful action recognition model: it outperforms the state-of-the-art alternatives in both efficiency and accuracy, as shown in Fig. 1.

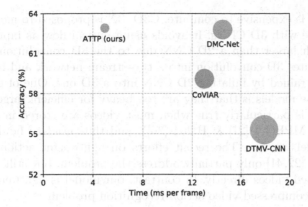

Fig. 1. Efficiency and accuracy comparison among various compressed video action recognition methods on the benchmark dataset HMDB-51 [21] with the same platform (i.e., Dell R730). State-of-the-art baselines include DMC-Net [26], CoViAR [37] and DTMV-CNN [40]. The node size denotes the model size (parameters).

Our contributions are: (1) For the first time, we address the challenging problem of lightweight compressed video action recognition. (2) We propose a trilinear pooling module for fusing the multiple modalities extracted from compressed videos. (3) To work with the weak motion vectors, we propose a temporal fusion method to explicitly induce the temporal context, and also boost the backbone trained with motion vectors by distillation with feature alignment. (4) We are the first to exploit both B-frames and P-frames from compressed videos in the correct manner, making our model more compatible with contemporary video codecs. The efficiency test on a fast embedded AI computing device (i.e., Jetson TX2) indicates that our ATTP model can perform video action recognition at about 40FPS (see Table 1). Moreover, as shown in Fig. 1, our ATTP model achieves the best performance but with significantly fewer parameters, as compared to the state-of-the-art methods. This observation is supported by the extensive results reported on two benchmarks widely used for action recognition (see Table 2). To our best knowledge, the proposed model is *the first end-to-end lightweight one* that can perform real-time action recognition on resource-limited devices without sacrifices in recognition accuracy.

2 Related Work

Conventional Video Action Recognition. Most recent action recognition models [7,17,28,32–35,41] are based on large CNNs [20]. One of the early models is the two-stream network [28], which is proposed to utilize two CNNs to model raw video frames and optical flow, respectively. Various improved versions [28,34], such as the Temporal Segment Network (TSN) [34], are designed to capture the long-range temporal structure, but they still rely on the optical flow stream, which is expensive to compute. C3D [32] is proposed to model the temporal structure with 3D CNNs. It avoids using optical flow as input. However, it is still much larger than a 2D CNN due to the 3D convolution operations. I3D [1] integrates 3D convolution into a two-stream network and benefits from 2D CNN pre-trained by inflating 2D CNN into a 3D one. One of the key limitations of these models is that they are too heavy for efficient large-scale video analysis. This is particularly true when most videos are stored in compression formats (e.g., MPEG-4 [27] & H.264 [36]), and thus need to be decoded first for these models to run. The recent efforts on lightweight action recognition model design [22,41] only partially address the problem, but still cannot work with compressed videos directly. In contrast, our model is lightweight and also addresses the compressed video action recognition problem.

Compressed Video Action Recognition. Due to the limitation of storage space and transfer speed, videos are generally stored and transmitted in a compressed data format. The compression standards, including MPEG-4 [27], H.264/AVC [36], and HEVC [30] (listed in chronological order), commonly use the motion compensation technique that reduces the video data size based on motion estimation from adjacent frames. There are several approaches that leverage useful information from compressed videos for the action recognition task. [16] developed highly efficient video features using motion information based on handcrafted features. DTMC-CNN [39,40] distills the knowledge from optical flows to motion vectors, but the raw video frames are still used for action recognition. CoViAR [37] takes only compressed videos as input, but the whole training process is not end-to-end since multiple modalities are handled separately. Recently, DMC-Net [26] improves CoViAR [37] and achieves state-of-the-art results by adding an optical flow generation network, but both models [26,37] employ the large ResNet-152 [10] as the CNN backbone, which has too many parameters with very high computational cost. Note that both DMC-Net and CoViAR ignore B-frames when extracting motion vectors from compressed videos, while B-frames cover more than 60% of total frames in videos. They need to make transformation into old codecs and thus are not compatible with most recent video codecs. Compared to these models, our proposed model is much more lightweight yet more effective in terms of recognition accuracy. It is also more generally applicable by correctly exploiting both B-frames and P-frames. Note that DTMV-CNN [40] also uses B-frames, but in an incorrect way by treating B-frames as P-frames and only considers forward reference. Further, it needs access to both raw and compressed videos to compute motion vectors. In contrast, using compressed videos alone, our ATTP is clearly superior (see Fig. 1).

Multi-modal Pooling. Pooling methods are required in two-stream networks [28,34] as well as other feature fusion models. [34] utilizes average pooling. [24] proposed bilinear pooling to model local parts of an object: two feature representations are learned separately and then multiplied using the outer product to obtain the holistic representation. However, most of existing pooling models can combine only two features, while in compressed videos, more than two modalities exist. To address such a challenging problem, we propose a novel Aligned

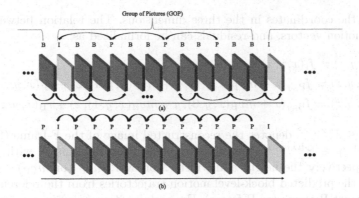

Fig. 2. (a) A modern GOP structure (I-B-B-P-B-B···), which is capable of getting a high amount of data compression. (b) An outdated GOP structure (I-P-P-P-P-P···), which consists of only P-frames and is not used today. Bold arrows denote reference dependencies, and thin arrows denote time flows (from left to right).

Temporal Trilinear Pooling module to exploit the complementary information contained in the three modalities extracted from compressed videos.

Lightweight Neural Networks. Recently, lightweight neural networks including SqeezeNet [14], Xception [2], ShuffleNet [25], MobileNet [12] and Efficient-Net [31] have been proposed, with the number of parameters and computational cost being reduced significantly. Since we focus on lightweight action recognition, they all can be used as the backbone network. In this work, EfficientNet [31] is selected. Note that a lightweight backbone typically leads to performance degradation in action recognition, and hence the temporal fusion and knowledge distillation model designs are introduced in our ATTP model.

3   Methodology

3.1   Modeling Compressed Representation

Modern compression codecs use motion compensation to convert successive raw video frames into several groups of pictures (GOPs), where each GOP contains one I-frame (Intra-coded frame), one or more P-frames (Predicted frames), and one or more B-frames (Bi-directional predicted frames). From Fig. 2 (a), we can see an example GOP frame pattern used by modern compression codecs. I-frame (**I**) is the first frame in the GOP, which is compressed with image compression codecs (e.g., JPEG). P-frames hold the changes in the images w.r.t. the preceding frame and thus save the storage space, while B-frames save even more space by using differences between the current frame and both the preceding and following frames to represent their content. Consequently, images from B-frames and P-frames are stored in a compressed format and are reconstructed using these encoded offsets, namely motion vectors (**MV**) and residuals (**R**). Let x, y, and

z denote the coordinates in the three dimensions. The relation between video frames, motion vectors, and residuals can be formalized as:

$$g_I(x, y, z) = f_I(x, y, z)$$
$$g_P(x, y, z) = f_{P_{ref}}(x + mv_P(x, y, 0), y + mv_P(x, y, 1), z) + r_P(x, y, z) \qquad (1)$$
$$g_B(x, y, z) = f_{B_{ref}}(x + mv_B(x, y, 0), y + mv_B(x, y, 1), z) + r_B(x, y, z),$$

where $g_F \in \mathbb{R}^{h \times w \times 3}$ denotes the reconstructed image of the F-frame (F = I, P, or B) and $f_F \in \mathbb{R}^{h \times w \times 3}$ denotes its counterpart in raw image, with h and w being respectively the height and width. Moreover, mv_P (or mv_B) $\in \mathbb{R}^{h \times w \times 2}$ describes the predicted block-level motion trajectories from the reference frame to the current P-frame (or B-frame). For each position (x, y) in mv, $mv(x, y, 0)$ and $mv(x, y, 1)$ depict the horizontal and vertical movements. In addition, r_P (or r_B) $\in \mathbb{R}^{h \times w \times 3}$ is the RGB-like image describing the residual error between the original P-frame (or B-frame) and its predicted frame. $f_{P_{ref}}$ and $f_{B_{ref}}$ are frames referenced by P-frames and B-frames. $f_{P_{ref}}$ denotes the previous I or P-frame of the current P-frame, and its motion vector contains only backward reference. Note that B-frame has both forward and backward motion information, and different codecs choose different $f_{P_{ref}}$. Since both **MV** and **R** are available in compressed videos, we can readily extract them.

However, since B-frames require a higher computational cost to compress than P-frames, earlier codecs such as MPEG-4 [27] use only P-frames for low-cost applications by default, where P-frames substitute all B-frames since they are capable of getting the highest computational efficiency (see Fig. 2 (b)). Because of the complicated modeling of B-frames, existing compressed video action recognition works [26,37] extract motion vectors and residual representations from only P-frames and thus are only applicable to the outdated MPEG-4 standard, and Zhang et al. [39,40] simply treat B-frames as P-frames. All these methods only consider forward reference, and at least half of the temporal information is thus ignored. When applied to the modern video codecs such as H.264 [36] and HEVC [30], these methods cannot take advantage of both forward and backward motion information induced by B-frames, which thus limits their performance. Note that CoViAR [37] and DMC-Net [26] even need to re-encode the compressed videos using the MPEG-4 codec for avoiding handling B-frames, which leads to extra cost on both processing time and storage.

3.2   Lightweight Video Action Recognition with Multiple Modalities

We now formally define the lightweight video action recognition problem as follows. Given the three modalities (i.e., **I**, **MV**, and **R**) extracted from a compressed video, our goal is to perform high-speed action recognition using a model with fewer parameters. Recent works utilize different CNNs to process the modalities independently. For example, in [37], ResNet-152 [10] is used to process **I**, which is effective but has extremely high computational cost and require large storage space (see Table 1). In this paper, we adopt a lightweight network LiteNet

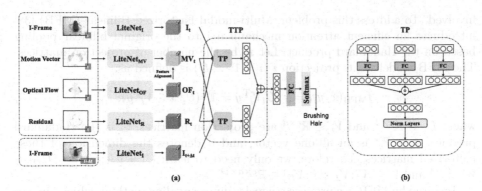

(a)   (b)

Fig. 3. (a) Overview of our Aligned Temporal Trilinear Pooling (ATTP). Note that optical flow is only used at the training phase, but not at the test phase. (b) Complete design of the Trilinear Pooling (TP) module.

instead: LiteNet_I, LiteNet_{MV}, and LiteNet_R take $\mathbf{I}$, $\mathbf{MV}$, and $\mathbf{R}$ as inputs, respectively.

Each of them has the same EfficientNet [31] network architecture. Note that the three modalities are only fused at the test phase in [37], and by doing so, the interactions between different modalities are not fully explored during training for action recognition. More effective multi-modal fusion is thus needed. To that end, we propose our Aligned Temporal Trilinear Pooling (ATTP) framework (see Fig. 3(a)), which is detailed next.

3.3 Trilinear Pooling

We propose a novel trilinear pooling module to model three-factor variations together. This is motivated by bilinear pooling models [24,38], which are initially proposed to model two-factor variations, such as "style" and "content". For lightweight video action recognition, we generalize the bilinear pooling method to fuse the three modalities extracted from compressed videos.

Specifically, a feature vector is denoted as $x \in \mathbb{R}^c$, where c is the dimensions of the feature x. The bilinear combination of two feature vectors with the same dimension $x \in \mathbb{R}^c$ and $y \in \mathbb{R}^c$ is defined as $xy^T \in \mathbb{R}^{c \times c}$ [24]. In general, given two representation matrices $X = [x_1; x_2; \cdots ; x_K] \in \mathbb{R}^{c \times K}$ and $Y = [y_1; y_2; \cdots ; y_K] \in \mathbb{R}^{c \times K}$ for two frames, a pooling layer takes the following bilinear combination:

$$f_{\text{BP}}(X, Y) = \frac{1}{K} \sum_{i=1}^{K} x_i y_i^T = \frac{1}{K} XY^T. \tag{2}$$

It can be seen clearly that the above bilinear pooling allows the outputs (X and Y) of the feature extractor to be conditioned on each other by considering all their pairwise interactions in the form of a quadratic kernel expansion. However, this results in very high-dimensional features with a large number of parameters involved. To address this problem, Multi-modal Factorized Bilinear (MFB) [38] introduces an efficient attention mechanism into the original bilinear pooling based on the Hadamard product. Let D be the number of projection matrices. The MFB model w.r.t. projection i $(i = 1, ..., D)$ is defined as:

$$f_{\mathrm{MFB}}(x, y)_i = x^{\mathrm{T}} U_i V_i^{\mathrm{T}} y = 1^{\mathrm{T}}(U_i^{\mathrm{T}} x \odot V_i^{\mathrm{T}} y), \qquad (3)$$

where $U_i \in \mathbb{R}^{c \times d}$ and $V_i \in \mathbb{R}^{c \times d}$ are projection matrices, $\odot$ is the Hadamard product, $1 \in \mathbb{R}^d$ is an all-one vector, and d denotes the dimension of these factorized matrices. Therefore, we only need to learn $U = [U_1; U_2; \cdots ; U_D] \in \mathbb{R}^{c \times d \times D}$ and $V = [V_1; V_2; \cdots ; V_D] \in \mathbb{R}^{c \times d \times D}$.

Inspired by MFB, we propose a novel trilinear pooling method, which aims to fuse three feature vectors (x, y, and z). Unlike bilinear pooling that can combine only two feature vectors, our Trilinear Pooling method fuse x, y and z using the Hadamard product:

$$f_{\mathrm{TP}}(x, y, z) = 1^{\mathrm{T}}(U^{\mathrm{T}} x \odot V^{\mathrm{T}} y \odot W^{\mathrm{T}} z), \qquad (4)$$

where W is also a projection matrix $W = [W_1; W_2; \cdots ; W_D] \in \mathbb{R}^{c \times d \times D}$, and f_{TP} denotes the output of trilinear pooling. Note that our trilinear pooling becomes MFB if all elements in W and z are fixed as 1. When the inputs are generalized to feature maps (i.e., $X = [x_i], Y = [y_i], Z = [z_i] \in \mathbb{R}^{c \times K}$), every position of these feature maps makes up one group of inputs, and the outputs of them are summed element-wised as follows:

$$f_{\mathrm{TP}}(X, Y, Z) = \sum_{i=1}^{K} f_{\mathrm{TP}}(x_i, y_i, z_i). \qquad (5)$$

We thus utilize trilinear pooling to obtain the multi-modal representation of the t-th GOP by fusing I-frame I_t, motion vector MV_t and residual R_t (see Fig. 3(b)):

$$f_{\mathrm{TP}}(I_t, MV_t, R_t) = \sum_{i=1}^{K} f_{\mathrm{TP}}(I_{t,i}, MV_{t,i}, R_{t,i}), \qquad (6)$$

where I_t, MV_t and R_t are the output feature maps from LiteNet$_I$, LiteNet$_{MV}$ and LiteNet$_R$, respectively. We set LiteNet as EfficientNet. For each GOP t, the I-frame is selected as I_t, while one MV_t and one R_t are randomly selected. As in [19], the trilinear vector is then processed with a signed square root step ($f \leftarrow \mathrm{sign}(f)\sqrt{|f|}$), followed by l_2 normalization ($f \leftarrow f/\|f\|$).

3.4   Temporal Trilinear Pooling

Motion vector is initially introduced to represent the temporal structure as the optical flow does. However, compared to the high-resolution optical flow, motion vector is much coarser: Since it only describes the movement on macroblock-level (e.g., 16 * 16 pixels), all values within the same macroblock are identical.

Although we have proposed to use trilinear pooling to address this drawback, the temporal information still needs to be explicitly explored. We note that, because residuals represent the difference between frames, they are strongly correlated with motion vectors. Therefore, we propose to model the motion vectors and the residuals jointly. Note that the fusion of I_t, MV_t and R_t within only one GOP is not enough to capture the temporal information. We thus further choose to include the adjacent GOP's information. Specifically, in addition to calculating $f_{TP}(I_t, MV_t, R_t)$ by trilinear pooling, we also combine MV_t and R_t with $I_{t+\Delta t}$ (i.e., the I-frame in the adjacent GOP). The output of temporal trilinear pooling (TTP) is defined as (see Fig. 3(a)):

$$f_{TTP}(t) = f_{TP}(t, 0) + f_{TP}(t, \Delta t), \tag{7}$$

where $f_{TP}(t, \Delta t)$ denotes $f_{TP}(I_{t+\Delta t}, MV_t, R_t)$ for notation simplicity. In this paper, we sample the offset Δt from $\{-1, 1\}$ during the training stage. During the test stage, Δt is fixed as 1 for the first GOP and -1 for other GOPs. This temporal fusion method solves the temporal representation drawback without introducing extra parameters, which is efficient and lightweight. The TTP representation is further put into a fully connected layer to calculate the classification scores $s(t) = P^T f_{TTP}(t)$, where $P \in \mathbb{R}^{D \times C}$ is learnable parameters and C is the number of categories.

3.5   Feature Alignment

Since motion vectors can only be regarded as a blurred version of optical flow, we choose to boost them with optical flow by feature alignment based knowledge distillation. Specifically, we employ another lightweight network LiteNet$_{OF}$ which takes optical flow information as input, and align the features generated by LiteNet$_{MV}$ to those by LiteNet$_{OF}$, as illustrated in Fig. 3(a). Different from the original method [11] that transfers knowledge from complex models to simple models, our feature alignment sets LiteNet$_{MV}$ and LiteNet$_{OF}$ to be the same lightweight network. Notably, we find that our feature alignment performs better than conventional knowledge distillation based on classification probability alignment. Moreover, our feature alignment is also much more efficient in the training phase since we do not need a large CNN as a teacher.

Our feature alignment module tries to minimize the difference between features generated by LiteNet$_{MV}$ and those by LiteNet$_{OF}$. Note that Zhang et al. [39, 40] utilized all layers for knowledge distillation from the teacher network to the student network, while we only exploit features before the fully-connected (FC) layer and those after the FC layer for feature alignment (which is more efficient and thus more suitable for lightweight action recognition). Let $f_{MV}^{(3d)}$ (or $f_{OF}^{(3d)}$) be features before the FC layer of LiteNet$_{MV}$ (or LiteNet$_{OF}$) and $f_{MV}^{(fc)}$ (or $f_{OF}^{(fc)}$) as features after the FC layer of LiteNet$_{MV}$ (or LiteNet$_{OF}$). The loss for feature alignment is given by:

$$\mathcal{L}_{Align} = ||f_{MV}^{(3d)} - f_{OF}^{(3d)}||^2 + ||f_{MV}^{(fc)} - f_{OF}^{(fc)}||^2. \tag{8}$$

Given that video action recognition is essentially a multi-class classification problem, we utilize the standard cross-entropy loss for training the TTP module:

$$\mathcal{L}_{TTP}(t) = -\log \text{softmax}(\mathbf{s}_{gt}(t)), \tag{9}$$

where $\mathbf{s}_{gt}(t)$ is the predicted score for t-th GOP with respect to its ground-truth class label. The total loss of our Aligned Temporal Trilinear Pooling (ATTP) model is defined as follows:

$$\mathcal{L}_{ATTP} = \mathcal{L}_{TTP} + \lambda \mathcal{L}_{Align}. \tag{10}$$

where λ is the weight parameter (we empirically set $\lambda = 1$ in this work).

4   Experiments

4.1   Datasets and Settings

In this paper, the main results are reported on two widely-used benchmark datasets, namely **HMDB-51** [21] and **UCF-101** [29], as in [26,34,37] for direct comparison. We employ top-1 accuracy on video-level class predictions as the evaluation metric. As in [13,34,37], we resize frames in all videos to 340×256. In order to implement our proposed model on resource-limited devices, we choose the EfficientNet B1 [31] pre-trained on ImageNet as the core CNN module to extract the representations of I-frames, motion vectors, and residuals. All the parameters of the projection layers are randomly initialized.

4.2   Efficiency Test Results

We firstly demonstrate the per-frame running time and FPS of our model in both limited-resource and sufficient-resource environments. We make comparisons to the state-of-the-art CoViAR [37] and DMC-Net [26] since they also exploit compressed videos for action recognition. Note that CoViAR does not use optical flow, while DMC-Net uses optical flow but only during the training phase like our model. However, both CoViAR and DMC-Net utilize ResNet-152 for I-frames and two ResNet-18 for motion vectors and residuals independently, which means their models are much larger in size and slower to run.

We compare the efficiency of the three models (CoViAR, DMC-Net, and our ATTP model) under precisely the same test setting. On the Dell R730 platform, the preprocessing phase (including loading networks) is mainly run on two Intel Xeon Silver 4110 CPUs, and the CNN forwarding phase (including extracting motion vectors and residuals) is mainly run on one TITAN Xp GPU. As shown in Table 1, our ATTP model runs faster among three models in both preprocessing and CNN phases on the Dell R730 platform. The preprocessing time on contrast is particularly stark. This is due to that both CoViAR and DMC-Net have three large networks with lots of parameters, resulting in massive cost on loading the networks. For the efficiency test on the resource-limited device, the experiments

Table 1. Comparison of per-frame inference efficiency. Following CoViAR [37] and DMC-Net [26], we forward multiple CNNs concurrently. CoViAR and DMC-Net cannot run on Jetson TX2 due to out of memory (OOM).

Method	Platform	Time(ms)		FPS	
		Preprocess	CNN	Preprocess	CNN
ATTP (ours)	Jetson	**12.2**	**24.6**	**82.1**	**40.7**
CoViAR	Jetson	OOM	OOM	OOM	OOM
DMC-Net	Jetson	OOM	OOM	OOM	OOM
ATTP (ours)	R730	**0.6**	**4.3**	**1587.3**	**233.6**
CoViAR	R730	7.8	5.1	127.6	194.9
DMC-Net	R730	7.8	7.0	127.6	142.9

are conducted on the Nvidia Jetson TX2 platform. The preprocessing phase runs on Dual-core Denver 2 64-bit CPU, and the CNN forward phase runs on the GPU. The results in Table 1 demonstrate that CoViAR and DMC-Net are too large to be employable on this device, while our ATTP framework fits well in the embedded environment and runs very fast. These results thus show clearly that our ATTP model outperforms the other two models on efficiency and is the only one that is suitable for embedded AI devices.

4.3 Comparative Results on Accuracy

Now we make a comprehensive comparison between our ATTP method and other state-of-the-art action recognition methods. The compared methods can be divided into two groups: 1) **Raw-Video Based Methods**: Two-stream [28] adopts two-way CNNs to process the optical flow information. ResNet-152 [10], C3D [32], I3D (RGB-only) [1], TSN (RGB-only) [34] employ large CNN models over RGB frames without using other information. ECO [41] and TSM [22] make efforts on lightweight video analysis models, but these models do not work on compressed videos. 2) **Compressed-Video Based Methods**: DTMV-CNN [40] integrates both compressed videos and raw ones into a single two-stream network, while CoViAR [37] and DMC-Net [26] are among the most closely related models that only exploit compressed videos for action recognition. In particular, DMC-Net, DTMV-CNN, and our ATTP model use optical flow during the training phase (but not during the test phase).

The comparative results are shown in Table 2. We have the following observations: (1) Our ATTP model is the most efficient for video action recognition. Specifically, it contains only 23.4 $\times 10^6$ parameters and has only average 3.0 GFLOPs over all frames. (2) Among all compressed video action recognition methods (including CoViAR and DMC-Net), our model performs the best w.r.t. both efficiency and accuracy. (3) As compared to the strongest baseline DMC-Net, although our model only achieves marginal improvement on accuracy, this is obtained with much fewer parameters and only one-tenth of GFLOPS. This

Table 2. Comparative results on the two benchmark datasets for both raw-video based methods and compressed-video based ones. "CV." denotes the usage of compressed videos for action recognition. "OF." denotes the usage of optical flow. ‡ indicates that the model only uses RGB frames.

Model	Setting		Efficiency		Accuracy	
	CV.	OF.	Param.(M)	GFLOPs	HMDB	UCF
Two-Stream [28]	N	Y	46.6	3.3	59.4	88.0
ResNet-152 [10]	N	N	60.2	11.3	48.9	83.4
C3D [32]	N	N	78.4	38.5	51.6	82.3
I3D‡ [1]	N	N	24	108	49.8	84.5
TSN‡ [34]	N	N	28.2	4.3	–	85.7
ECO (4 frames) [41]	N	N	23.8	16	61.7	90.3
TSM (Kinetics) [22]	N	N	24.3	33	**64.7**	**91.7**
DTMV-CNN [40]	Both	Y	181.3	83.4	55.3	87.5
CoViAR [37]	Y	N	83.6	14.9	59.1	90.4
DMC-Net [26]	Y	Y	83.6	15.1	62.8	90.9
ATTP (ours)	Y	Y	**23.4**	**3.0**	62.9	91.1

Table 3. Ablative results (%) for our ATTP model using different modalities on the two benchmarks (each has three splits).

Dataset	HMDB-51				UCF-101			
Splits	S1	S2	S3	Avg	S1	S2	S3	Avg.
I	51.6	51.0	52.0	51.5	84.0	83.0	84.5	83.8
MV	45.2	44.8	44.9	45.0	70.1	70.5	73.2	71.3
R	48.2	45.6	48.5	47.4	81.7	81.1	82.0	81.6
I+MV+R	60.5	57.1	57.9	58.5	86.1	86.3	87.3	86.6
BP	60.9	57.7	58.4	59.0	87.3	87.1	88.4	87.6
TP	61.6	58.5	59.4	59.8	87.7	87.6	89.0	88.1
TTP	62.1	59.0	59.9	60.3	88.3	88.2	89.5	88.7
ATTP	**64.3**	**61.8**	**62.6**	**62.9**	**91.0**	**90.9**	**91.5**	**91.1**

is mainly due to its ability to more effectively fuse multiple modalities using the proposed trilinear pooling module. (4) As compared to CoViAR, our model saves nearly 70% of the storage with a clear advantage on accuracy. To better understand the reason why our lighter model can yield more accurate recognition, in our ablation study (to be presented next), it is noted that "I+MV+R" in Table 3 is essentially CoViAR by using EfficientNet as the core CNN module. Under such a fair comparison setting (same CNN backbone), our model consistently yields accuracy improvements over CoViAR on all dataset splits. (5) Our model achieves even higher (or comparable) accuracies w.r.t. recent raw-video based models (TSM uses the external Kinetics [18] for pre-training), showing its potential for directly analyzing compressed video for action recognition.

4.4   Ablation Study

Ablation Study over Different Modalities. We conduct experiments to show the benefits of using our ATTP model compared with single modality and other fusion options. Specifically, we uniformly use three EfficientNet networks to process the three components (**I**, **MV**, and **R**) extracted from compressed videos and demonstrate all the ablative results on the two benchmarks by training with different parts of our ATTP model. For single-modality based models, "I", "MV" and "R" denote the results obtained by using LiteNet$_I$, LiteNet$_{MV}$ and LiteNet$_R$, respectively. For the late-fusion based model, "I+MV+R" indicates that the output is fused by simply adding the score of the three CNNs together. We also compare our ATTP model with existing bilinear pooling models, which are the simplified version of our Trilinear Pooling. Since existing bilinear pooling methods cannot be directly adapted to the three modalities, we readily apply pairwise combination over them, and sum the three predicted classification scores together like "I+MV+R". Note that conventional bilinear pooling [24] and factorized bilinear pooling [19] have too many parameters to be efficient, we resort to compact bilinear pooling [9] (denoted as "BP") with much fewer parameters. Finally, "TP" denotes our Trilinear Pooling, "TTP" denotes our Temporal Trilinear Pooling, and "ATTP" denotes our Aligned Temporal Trilinear Pooling.

As shown in Table 3, single-modality based models (i.e., I, MV, or R) could not achieve good results without using multi-modal information, indicating that the compressed video needs to be fully explored to obtain high accuracy. I and R yield similar results because they both contain the RGB data: the I-frames contain a small number of informative frames, while the residuals contain a large number of less informative frames. Since the motion vectors only contain the motion information, MV could not perform as well as the other two. Moreover, for multi-modal fusion, all bilinear/trilinear pooling methods outperform I+MV+R, showing the power of pooling methods instead of linearly late fusion. Particularly, our TP method yields %1 gains over BP, validating the effectiveness of our pooling method. In addition, the improvements achieved by TTP over TP (and those achieved by ATTP over TTP) clearly show the importance of boosting motion vectors by inducing temporal context (and feature alignment).

Ablation Study over Different Types of Frames. To show the contribution of each type of frames to action recognition, we make comparison among four versions of the late fusion model: (1) I – only I-frames are used to obtain the single modality **I**; (2) I+P – both I-frames and P-frames are used to extract the three modalities (i.e., **I**, **MV**, and **R**); (3) I+B – both I-frames and B-frames are used to extract the three modalities; (4) I+P+B – all three types of frames are used to extract the three modalities. The ablative results in Fig. 4 (left) show that: (a) The performance of action recognition continuously increases when more types of frames are added, validating the contribution of each type of

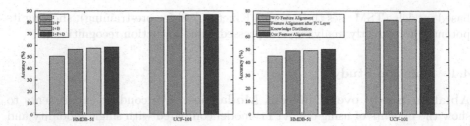

Fig. 4. Left: Ablative results (%) obtained by exploiting different types of frames for late fusion on the two benchmarks. Right: Ablative results (%) for our proposed feature alignment method on the two benchmarks. Only the single modality **MV** is used.

frames. (b) The improvements achieved by I+B over I+P verify that B-frames are more important than P-frames for action recognition.

Ablation Study for Feature Alignment. To conduct the ablation study for our proposed feature alignment method, we make comparisons among four related methods: (1) W/O Feature Alignment – features are directly extracted from motion vectors, without feature alignment; (2) Feature Alignment after FC Layer – our proposed feature alignment method is used, but only the features after the FC layer are aligned; (3) Knowledge Distillation – the knowledge distillation [11] method is used for feature alignment; (4) Our Feature Alignment – our proposed feature alignment method defined in Eq. (8). The ablative results are presented in Fig. 4 (right). It can be seen that: (1) The three feature alignment methods outperform the 'W/O Feature Alignment' method, validating the effectiveness of feature alignment. (2) Our proposed feature alignment method performs the best among the three feature alignment methods. This suggests that aligning the features before and after the FC layer is more effective than feature alignment after the FC Layer and even than knowledge distillation.

5   Conclusion

In this work, we address a key limitation of existing deep neural networks-based video action recognition methods. That is, they either only work with raw RGB video frames instead of the compressed video directly, or heavy in model size and slow to run. We therefore proposed to address a more challenging task, namely lightweight compressed video action recognition. By employing EfficientNet as the backbone, we proposed a novel ATTP model to fuse the multiple modalities for lightweight video action recognition. Importantly, for the first time, our ATTP models the B-frames correctly, therefore being compatible with a wider range of contemporary codecs. The comparative results on three benchmark datasets show that our ATTP model outperforms the state-of-the-art alternatives in both efficiency and accuracy.

Acknowledgements. This work was supported by Beijing Outstanding Young Scientist Program (BJJWZYJH012019100020098), National Natural Science Foundation of China (61976220 and 61832017), and the Outstanding Innovative Talents Cultivation Funded Programs 2018 of Renmin University of China.

References

1. Carreira, J., Zisserman, A.: Quo vadis, action recognition? a new model and the kinetics dataset. In: CVPR, pp. 6299–6308 (2017)
2. Chollet, F.: Xception: deep learning with depthwise separable convolutions. In: CVPR, pp. 1251–1258 (2017)
3. Ding, M., et al.: Learning depth-guided convolutions for monocular 3D object detection. In: CVPR, pp. 4306–4315 (2020)
4. Ding, M., Wang, Z., Sun, J., Shi, J., Luo, P.: Camnet: coarse-to-fine retrieval for camera re-localization. In: ICCV, pp. 2871–2880 (2019)
5. Ding, M., Wang, Z., Zhou, B., Shi, J., Lu, Z., Luo, P.: Every frame counts: joint learning of video segmentation and optical flow. In: AAAI, pp. 10713–10720 (2020)
6. Ding, M., Zhao, A., Lu, Z., Xiang, T., Wen, J.R.: Face-focused cross-stream network for deception detection in videos. In: CVPR, pp. 7802–7811 (2019)
7. Feichtenhofer, C., Fan, H., Malik, J., He, K.: Slowfast networks for video recognition. In: ICCV, pp. 6202–6211 (2019)
8. Forecast, C.V.: Cisco visual networking index: Forecast and trends, 2017–2022. Cisco Public Information, White paper (2019)
9. Gao, Y., Beijbom, O., Zhang, N., Darrell, T.: Compact bilinear pooling. In: CVPR, pp. 317–326 (2016)
10. He, K., Zhang, X., Ren, S., Sun, J.: Deep residual learning for image recognition. In: CVPR, pp. 770–778 (2016)
11. Hinton, G., Vinyals, O., Dean, J.: Distilling the knowledge in a neural network. arXiv preprint arXiv:1503.02531 (2015)
12. Howard, A., et al.: Searching for mobilenetv3. In: ICCV, pp. 1314–1324 (2019)
13. Huo, Y., Xu, X., Lu, Y., Niu, Y., Lu, Z., Wen, J.R.: Mobile video action recognition. arXiv preprint arXiv:1908.10155 (2019)
14. Iandola, F.N., Han, S., Moskewicz, M.W., Ashraf, K., Dally, W.J., Keutzer, K.: Squeezenet: alexnet-level accuracy with 50x fewer parameters and < 0.5 mb model size. arXiv preprint arXiv:1602.07360 (2016)
15. Ji, J., Buch, S., Soto, A., Carlos Niebles, J.: End-to-end joint semantic segmentation of actors and actions in video. In: ECCV, pp. 702–717 (2018)
16. Kantorov, V., Laptev, I.: Efficient feature extraction, encoding and classification for action recognition. In: CVPR, pp. 2593–2600 (2014)
17. Karpathy, A., Toderici, G., Shetty, S., Leung, T., Sukthankar, R., Fei-Fei, L.: Large-scale video classification with convolutional neural networks. In: CVPR, pp. 1725–1732 (2014)
18. Kay, W., et al.: The kinetics human action video dataset. arXiv preprint arXiv:1705.06950 (2017)
19. Kim, J.H., On, K.W., Lim, W., Kim, J., Ha, J.W., Zhang, B.T.: Hadamard product for low-rank bilinear pooling. In: ICLR (2016)
20. Krizhevsky, A., Sutskever, I., Hinton, G.E.: Imagenet classification with deep convolutional neural networks. In: NeurIPS, pp. 1097–1105 (2012)
21. Kuehne, H., Jhuang, H., Garrote, E., Poggio, T., Serre, T.: Hmdb: a large video database for human motion recognition. In: ICCV, pp. 2556–2563. IEEE (2011)

22. Lin, J., Gan, C., Han, S.: Tsm: temporal shift module for efficient video under-standing. In: ICCV, pp. 7083–7093 (2019)
23. Lin, T., Zhao, X., Su, H., Wang, C., Yang, M.: Bsn: boundary sensitive network for temporal action proposal generation. In: ECCV, pp. 3–19 (2018)
24. Lin, T.Y., RoyChowdhury, A., Maji, S.: Bilinear cnn models for fine-grained visual recognition. In: ICCV, pp. 1449–1457 (2015)
25. Ma, N., Zhang, X., Zheng, H.T., Sun, J.: Shufflenet v2: practical guidelines for efficient cnn architecture design. In: ECCV, pp. 116–131 (2018)
26. Shou, Z., et al.: Dmc-net: Generating discriminative motion cues for fast com-pressed video action recognition. In: CVPR, pp. 1268–1277 (2019)
27. Sikora, T.: The mpeg-4 video standard verification model. TCSV **7**(1), 19–31 (1997)
28. Simonyan, K., Zisserman, A.: Two-stream convolutional networks for action recog-nition in videos. In: NeurIPS, pp. 568–576 (2014)
29. Soomro, K., Zamir, A.R., Shah, M.: Ucf101: a dataset of 101 human actions classes from videos in the wild. arXiv preprint arXiv:1212.0402 (2012)
30. Sullivan, G.J., Ohm, J.R., Han, W.J., Wiegand, T.: Overview of the high efficiency video coding (HEVC) standard. TCSV **22**(12), 1649–1668 (2012)
31. Tan, M., Le, Q.V.: Efficientnet: rethinking model scaling for convolutional neural networks. In: ICML, pp. 6105–6114 (2019)
32. Tran, D., Bourdev, L., Fergus, R., Torresani, L., Paluri, M.: Learning spatiotem-poral features with 3D convolutional networks. In: ICCV, pp. 4489–4497 (2015)
33. Tran, D., Wang, H., Torresani, L., Ray, J., LeCun, Y., Paluri, M.: A closer look at spatiotemporal convolutions for action recognition. In: CVPR, pp. 6450–6459 (2018)
34. Wang, L., et al.: Temporal segment networks: towards good practices for deep action recognition. In: Leibe, B., Matas, J., Sebe, N., Welling, M. (eds.) ECCV 2016. LNCS, vol. 9912, pp. 20–36. Springer, Cham (2016). https://doi.org/10.1007/978-3-319-46484-8_2
35. Wang, X., Girshick, R., Gupta, A., He, K.: Non-local neural networks. In: CVPR, pp. 7794–7803 (2018)
36. Wiegand, T., Sullivan, G.J., Bjontegaard, G., Luthra, A.: Overview of the H. 264/AVC video coding standard. TCSV **13**(7), 560–576 (2003)
37. Wu, C.Y., Zaheer, M., Hu, H., Manmatha, R., Smola, A.J., Krähenbühl, P.: Com-pressed video action recognition. In: CVPR, pp. 6026–6035 (2018)
38. Yu, Z., Yu, J., Fan, J., Tao, D.: Multi-modal factorized bilinear pooling with co-attention learning for visual question answering. In: ICCV, pp. 1821–1830 (2017)
39. Zhang, B., Wang, L., Wang, Z., Qiao, Y., Wang, H.: Real-time action recognition with enhanced motion vector CNNs. In: CVPR, pp. 2718–2726 (2016)
40. Zhang, B., Wang, L., Wang, Z., Qiao, Y., Wang, H.: Real-time action recognition with deeply transferred motion vector CNNs. TIP **27**(5), 2326–2339 (2018)
41. Zolfaghari, M., Singh, K., Brox, T.: Eco: efficient convolutional network for online video understanding. In: ECCV, pp. 695–712 (2018)

On Sparse Connectivity, Adversarial Robustness, and a Novel Model of the Artificial Neuron

Sergey Bochkanov$^{(\boxtimes)}$ (iD)

ALGLIB Project, Moscow, Russian Federation
sergey.bochkanov@alglib.net

Abstract. In this paper, we propose two closely connected methods to improve computational efficiency and stability against adversarial perturbations on contour recognition tasks: (a) a novel model of an artificial neuron, a "strong neuron," with inherent robustness against adversarial perturbations and (b) a novel constructive training algorithm that generates sparse networks with $O(1)$ connections per neuron.

We achieved an impressive 10x reduction (compared with other sparsification approaches; 100x when compared with dense networks) in operations count. State-of-the-art stability against adversarial perturbations was achieved without any counteradversarial measures, relying on the robustness of strong neurons alone.

Our network extensively uses unsupervised feature detection, with more than 95% of operations being performed in its unsupervised parts. Less than 10.000 supervised FLOPs per class is required to recognize a contour (digit or traffic sign), which allows us to arrive to the conclusion that contour recognition is much simpler that was previously thought.

Keywords: Sparse neural networks · Unsupervised training · Adversarial robustness

1 Introduction

In recent years, artificial neural networks have achieved impressive results on all computer vision benchmarks. Interestingly, this progress was made using two ideas that are many decades old: (1) an artificial neuron with a linear summator at its core and (2) stochastic gradient descent (SGD) training.

The combination of these ideas was fortuitous, allowing us to fit any decision function, no matter how complex. As a result, neural models surpassed human-level accuracy. However, we believe (and will justify below) that the very properties of summators and SGD impede progress in improving two other important metrics: the sparsity of the neural connections and adversarial stability.

Electronic supplementary material The online version of this chapter (https://doi.org/10.1007/978-3-030-66096-3_25) contains supplementary material, which is available to authorized users.

© Springer Nature Switzerland AG 2020
A. Bartoli and A. Fusiello (Eds.): ECCV 2020 Workshops, LNCS 12536, pp. 353–368, 2020.
https://doi.org/10.1007/978-3-030-66096-3_25

In our work, we propose (1) a novel model of an artificial neuron with inherent robustness against adversarial perturbations and (2) a novel training algorithm that allows us to build extremely sparse networks with $O(1)$ connections per neuron. With these proposals, we achieved state-of-the-art performance and adversarial stability on a number of contour recognition benchmarks.

2   Related Work

Our work touches on several topics: unsupervised feature detection, network sparsification, and adversarial robustness.

Many approaches to unsupervised feature detection have been proposed. Our work follows [4] (learning convolution filters by clustering image patches with k-means). Other notable approaches include autoencoders [1], variational autoencoders [14], noise-as-target [2], learning features invariant under particular transformations [5], and local Hebbian learning [9].

The most popular sparsification strategy is pruning, either via L_0/L_1 penalization [10,18,29] or various explicit pruning strategies [3,12,19]. Usually about 95–97% of weights are pruned [27].

Adversarial robustness is usually addressed via adversarial training [16,20, 25]. One notable approach is to use provable bounds on a network output under attack [15] for training. Another line of thought is to modify the basics of neural architecture in order to make it inherently robust (for instance, [17] proposes to use bounded ReLU).

3   The Novel Artificial Neuron ("Strong Neuron")

3.1   Contour Recognition = Logical AND + Logical OR

Contour recognition is an important subset of computer vision problems. It is deeply connected with properties of our world—we live in a universe full of localized objects with distinctive edges. Many important problems are contour based: handwritten digit recognition, traffic light detection, traffic sign recognition and number plate recognition.

There are also non-contour tasks, however—for example, ones that can only be solved by gathering information from many small cues scattered throughout an image (e.g., distinguishing a food store from an electronics store).

Contour recognition has interesting mathematical properties: (a) it naturally leads to $[0, 1]$-bounded activities; (b) contours are localized and independent from their surrounding (e.g., a crosswalk sign is a crosswalk sign, even in desert or rainforest); (c) complex contours can be decomposed into smaller parts, that are contours too.

Our insight is that contour recognition is essentially a combination of two basic operations on low-level features (see Fig. 1):

- logical AND (detection), which decomposes high-level features as combinations of several low-level ones, placed at different locations. Say, digit "5" can be represented as $AND(5_{TOP}, 5_{BOTTOM})$

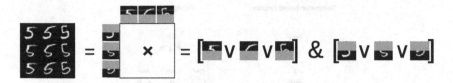

Fig. 1. Contour recognition: AND + OR

- logical OR (generalization), which allows detectors to be activated by more diverse inputs. Say, "5" can be replaced by more general OR(5,5,5)

3.2   What is Wrong with Linear Summators?

First, standalone summator-based neuron is, in some sense, weak. It does not perform detailed evaluation of its inputs—all it sees is just their weighted sum, a position relative to the separating hyperplane. This means that lack of activity in one channel (absence of some critical feature) can be masked by increased activities in other channels. We will need a group of neurons working together in order to make sure that, say, a "face neuron" cannot be activated by many repetitions of just one face part. Our point here is not about computational efficiency, but about the fact that we try to model human intuition about vision by using elements with counterintuitive properties.

Second, summator-based implementation of the AND/OR logic is very brittle, especially in high-dimensional spaces. The neuron can be set to an arbitrarily high value (or, alternatively, zeroed) by feeding it with many small activities in different channels [8].

3.3   Our Proposal

We propose to use $f() = \min(A, B, \dots)$ to implement AND-logic, to use $f() = \max(A, B, \dots)$ to implement OR-logic and to combine both kinds of logic in a novel summator-free artificial neuron—"strong neuron":

$$F_{strong} = \min\left(\max_i(w_{0,i}x_i), \max_i(w_{1,i}x_i), \max_i(w_{2,i}x_i)\right) \qquad (1)$$

The formula above describes a strong neuron with three receptive areas, usually located at different parts of the input image. Here $w_{k,i} \in \{0, 1\}$ are extremely sparse binary weights—just $O(1)$ connections per neuron are generated during training (about 5–10 in most cases). Inputs x_i are either initial low-level features corresponding to small (4×4, 5×5 or 6×6) image patches or medium-level features (computed by the previous layer of strong neurons).

We call our artificial neuron "strong" because it has a much more complex decision boundary than the summator-based neuron. It is not prone to the failure modes described in the previous subsection: (1) nonlinearities introduced by the

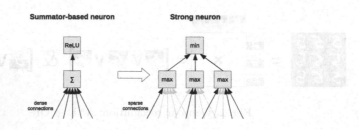

Fig. 2. A summator-based neuron and a strong neuron

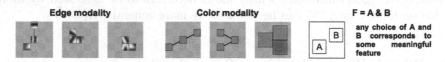

Fig. 3. Strong neurons are interpretable models

min and *max* elements naturally align with human intuitive understanding of the pattern recognition; (2) the neuron is robust with respect to adversarial attacks—an ϵ-bounded perturbation of inputs produces exactly ϵ-bounded perturbation of outputs.

Figure 3 visualizes several strong neurons generated during the solution of the German Traffic Sign Recognition Benchmark. One may see that strong neurons have obvious geometric interpretation. Actually, *any* (even completely random) strong neuron with spatially separate input areas corresponds to some meaningful feature. Some of these features are useful for prediction, most of them are useless—but all of them have obvious geometric meaning. This sharply contrasts with the properties of the convolutional filters—convolution with random coefficients rarely has clear geometric interpretation.

We would like to note here some connection with recent work on adversarial robustness, [28] and [13], which state that there are two kinds of features in images—highly predictive ones that are extremely unstable under unnatural perturbation of input, and less predictive but robust ones. The latter are the ones that are used by human vision; the former are imperceptible by humans but are heavily used by adversarially unstable neural networks. In particular, [28] shows an elegant example of both kinds of features derived from synthetic data. Viewed from this angle, strong neurons are constrained to a realm of geometric inference—and robust feature detectors.

4   The Motivation Behind Our Model

In this section, we will show that our artificial neuron model is motivated by some fundamental considerations, that is, there are some reasonable and intuitive requirements that are satisfied by our model—and are not satisfied by summator-based neurons.

First, we define the L_∞-nonexpansive function as one which in a general N-dimensional case for any N-dimensional input perturbation Δx satisfies

$$|f(x + \Delta x) - f(x)| \leq \max_i |\Delta x_i| = \|\Delta x\|_\infty \tag{2}$$

The L_∞-nonexpansive function has ϵ-bounded perturbation of the output under ϵ-bounded perturbation of its inputs, i.e. it does not accumulate perturbations (compare it with L_1-nonexpansivity that, despite "non" prefix, means that perturbations are summed up).

Human vision—and any artificial vision system that is intended to be robust—has a bounded reaction to bounded perturbations of the input image. The bounding ratio is not always 1:1 because sometimes we want to amplify weak signals. Thus, enforcing L_∞-nonexpansivity on the entire classifier may overconstrain it. However, it makes sense to enforce this constraint at least for some parts of the classifier. One may easily show that both min and max, as well as their superposition, are L_∞-nonexpansive.

The rationale behind our model of the artificial neuron should be obvious by now—making inference as robust as possible. However, we present an even more interesting result—the fact that min and max are the only perfectly stable implementations of AND/OR logic.

One familiar with the history of artificial neural networks may remember the so-called "XOR problem" [21]—a problem of fitting the simple four-point dataset that cannot be separated by the single linear summator. Inspired by its minimalistic beauty, we formulate two similar problems, which address the accumulation of perturbations in multilayer networks:

Theorem 1. L_∞-nonexpansive AND problem. $\exists! \ f(x, y) = min(x, y)$ such that the following holds:

1. $f(x, y)$ is defined for $x, y \in [0, 1]$
2. $f(0, 0) = f(0, 1) = f(1, 0) = 0, \quad f(1, 1) = 1$
3. $a \leq A, \ b \leq B \implies f(a, b) \leq f(A, B)$ (monotonicity)
4. $|f(a + \Delta a, b + \Delta b) - f(a, b)| \leq max(|\Delta a|, |\Delta b|)$

Theorem 2. L_∞-nonexpansive OR problem. $\exists! \ g(x, y) = max(x, y)$ such that the following holds:

1. $g(x, y)$ is defined for $x, y \in [0, 1]$
2. $g(0, 0) = 0, \quad g(0, 1) = g(1, 0) = g(1, 1) = 1$
3. $a \leq A, \ b \leq B \implies g(a, b) \leq g(A, B)$ (monotonicity)
4. $|g(a + \Delta a, b + \Delta b) - g(a, b)| \leq max(|\Delta a|, |\Delta b|)$

Proofs of Theorems 1 and 2 can be found in Appendix A (supplementary materials).

An immediate consequence of these theorems is that it is impossible to implement a robust AND (robust OR) element with just one ReLU neuron—the best that can be achieved is L_1-nonexpansivity, which is not robust. It is possible to 'emulate' robust AND/OR logic by performing tricks with many traditional ReLU neurons ($max(a,b) = a + ReLU(b - a)$, $max(a,b,c) = max(a, max(b,c))$ and so on), but the result will be just another implementation of min and max elements.

5   Contour Engine: Architecture Overview

The key parts of our neural architectures are outlined in Fig. 4.

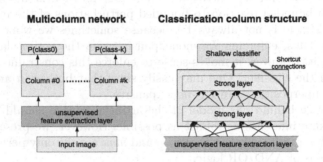

Fig. 4. The Contour Engine network

Strong neurons can perform logical inference on low-level features, but they cannot *produce* these features from raw pixel values. Thus, an initial feature extraction block is essential in order to "prime" the Contour Engine. This part of the network is the one that needs the most FLOPs—about 95% of the floating-point operations are spent in the unsupervised preprocessing.

The next part of our network is organized into many class-specific columns. Each column starts with sparse contour detection layers (one or two is usually enough) that combine low-level features in order to produce medium- and high-level features. Typical column widths are in $[50, 800]$ range. On average, less than 10.000 FLOPs per class are needed to recognize well-centered medium-complexity contour (like a digit, letter or traffic sign).

Finally, a shallow nonlinear classifier on top of each column post-processes the features produced by the robust contour detection stage. In practice, strong neurons are so good at contour detection that we do not need complex nonlinear models at this stage—the basic logistic model is enough.

The training algorithm includes three distinct, sequential stages:

- training unsupervised feature detector.
- training sparse contour detection layers.
- training a shallow classifier.

We train a feature extraction layer using an unsupervised procedure (running k-means over image patches; see [4]). Such an approach makes the input layer independent from label assignment, which allows us to make some interesting conclusions regarding the asymptotic complexity of the image recognition.

Sparse layers are trained by adding layers and neurons one by one, in a greedy fashion, fitting new neurons to the current residual. The second important contribution of our work (in addition to the robust artificial neuron) is the heuristic, which can efficiently fit nonsmooth strong neurons with binarity/sparsity constraints on weights.

Finally, the shallow classifier can be trained by running logistic regression over the activities of the sparse layers.

6 Training Feature Detection Layer

The purpose of our feature extraction layer is to describe the input image using a rich dictionary of visual words. The description includes features such as oriented edges, more complex shapes, colors and gradients, computed at multiple scales and orientations.

The key point of Coates et al. [4] is that one may achieve surprisingly good classification performance by processing images with a single convolutional layer whose filters are trained in an unsupervised manner (k-means on random image patches). Filters as large as 4×4, 5×5 or 6×6 typically give the best results.

We extend their results (see Fig. 5) with:

- separate processing of color-agnostic (shape-sensitive) and color-based features by enforcing constraints on filter coefficients.
- multiple downsampling levels of the layer outputs (2x and 4x max-pooling are used together).
- feature detection at multiple scales.
- capturing positive and negative phases of filters (as recommended in [24]).

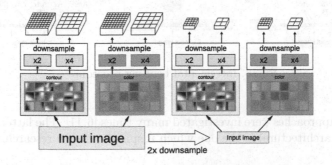

Fig. 5. Multiscale multimodal feature extraction layer

One distinctive trait of our approach to feature detection is high redundancy of the description produced. Neural architectures with dense connectivity try to decrease channels count as much as possible due to quadratic dependency between channels count and coefficients count. However, in our architecture coefficients count scales *linearly* with network width due to the extreme sparsity of subsequent layers ($O(1)$ connections per neuron). Thus, having a wide and redundant feature extraction layer puts much less stress on the computational budget.

7   Training Sparsely Connected Layers

This section discusses the core contribution of our work—the constructive training of sparsely connected strong neurons.

7.1   The Constructive Training Algorithm

Training networks composed of nonconvex and nonsmooth elements is difficult. It is especially difficult with *min*-based activation functions because *min* function is extremely nonconvex and makes training prone to stalling in bad local extrema.

Suppose, however, that *somehow* you can train just one such element to fit some target function of your choice. How can it help you train a network? The answer is to build your model incrementally, training new elements to fit the current residual and adding them one by one (see Fig. 6). Every time you add a neuron to the layer you have to retrain the classifier to obtain new residuals. By feeding new neurons with outputs of the previous ones we can generate multilayer network.

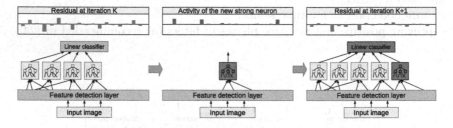

Fig. 6. Incremental training procedure

Similar approaches were investigated many times [6, 11]. The latter (Cascade-Correlation architecture) is the one which inspired our own research.

7.2 Training Strong Neurons

In the subsection above, we reduced the problem of training sparse multilayer networks to training just one neuron with sparse connections:

$$\min_w \sum_i \left(N(w, X_i) - y_i \right)^2 \quad s.t. \quad sparsity \ constraints \tag{3}$$

where w is a weight vector, X_i is an i-th row of the input activities matrix X (activities of the bottom layer at i-th image), $N(w, x)$ is a neuron output and y_i is a target to fit (in our case, the current residual).

For a three-input strong neuron with binary weights, the formulation above becomes:

$$\min_w \sum_i \left[\min \left(\max_j(w_{0,j} \cdot X_{i,j}), \ \max_j(w_{1,j} \cdot X_{i,j}), \ \max_j(w_{2,j} \cdot X_{i,j}) \right) - y_i \right]^2$$
$$w_{0,j}, w_{1,j}, w_{2,j} \in \{0, 1\}$$
$$\|w_0\|_0 \le k \ , \quad \|w_1\|_0 \le k \ , \quad \|w_2\|_0 \le k \tag{4}$$

The problem (4) is a discrete optimization problem. There is likely no other way to solve it except for a brute-force search (no obvious reduction to mixed integer LP/QP). However, we do not need an exact solution—having a good one is sufficient. Our insight is that there is a simple heuristic that can generate good strong neurons in a reasonable time.

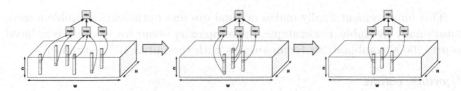

Fig. 7. Progressive simplification of the optimization problem 4

The original discrete optimization problem has no constraints except for sparsity. A max-element can gather information from any element of the input tensor (see Fig. 7, left). As a result, we have to evaluate prohibitively large amount of possible connection structures. For instance, for 15 unit-weight connections to elements with a $32 \times 32 \times 20$ input tensor we have roughly 10^{58} possible geometries.

It is possible to significantly reduce the configuration count by adding some additional restrictions on the inter-layer connections. For example, we may impose two additional constraints: (a) require that max-elements are spatially local (i.e., each element gathers inputs from just one location (x, y) of the input tensor), and (b) require that *max*-elements feeding data into the same *min*-element are located close to each other.

Alternatively—for $1 \times 1 \times D$ input tensors with no spatial component—these restrictions can be reformulated as follows: (a) require that *max*-elements are correlationally local (i.e., each element gathers inputs from strongly correlated channels), and (b) require that *max*-elements feeding data into the same *min*-element are correlated strongly enough.

Having such constraints on the connections of the strong neuron significantly reduces the number of configurations that must be evaluated to solve the problem (Fig. 7, center). In our toy example, the configuration count is reduced from 10^{58} to just 10^{18}.

We can achieve a further reduction in search complexity through a two-step search procedure: (1) evaluate all possible "seed detectors"—strong neurons with single-input *max*-elements (AND without OR), and (2) expand the best seed found—sequentially add connections to its *max*-elements.

As a result of this improvement (see Fig. 7, right), the search complexity for our $32 \times 32 \times 20$ example is reduced from 10^{18} to 10^{9} neural configurations. However, it is still too costly—each of these configurations requires a full pass over the entire dataset in order to evaluate the neuron's performance.

Further improvements can be achieved by assuming the following:

- Good $f_3 = \min(A, B, C)$ can be found by extending good $f_2 = \min(A, B)$ with the best-suited C
- Good $f_2 = \min(A, B)$ can be found by extending good $f_1 = A$ with the best-suited B
- Good $f_1 = A$ can be found by simply evaluating all possible single-input seed detectors

This improvement finally makes original discrete optimization problem computationally tractable. For example, the complexity of our toy example is reduced to just 20000 combinations (compare this with the initial 10^{58} estimate).

Algorithm outline.

1. Setup the initial model (empty with zero output) and a vector of its residuals over the entire dataset. Select a neuron pool size P (a few hundreds works in most cases).
2. Competition phase: generate seed detectors and select the winner from the combined pool:
   - Select a set of P promising input features, "gen-1 seeds," $f_1 = A$. Some form of quick and dirty feature selection is usually enough.
   - Produce P gen-2 seeds by extending gen-1 seeds $f_1 = A$ with such B that $f_2 = \min(A, B)$ produces the best linear fit to the current residual. Only the spatial/correlational neighborhood of f_1 is evaluated.
   - Produce P gen-3 seeds by extending gen-2 seeds $f_2 = \min(A, B)$ with such C that $f_3 = \min(A, B, C)$ produces the best linear fit to the current residual. Only the spatial/correlational neighborhood of f_1 is evaluated.

3. Generalization phase. Having determined a winning seed detector, sequentially extend its inputs with new max-connections:
   - $f = \min(A, B, ...)$
   - $A \to \max(A)$
   - $\max(A) \to \max(A, A_2)$
   - $\max(A, A_2) \to \max(A, A_2, A_3)$ and so on

   Extending is performed in such a way that the extended detector fits the residual better than its previous version. Only the spatial/correlational neighborhood of A is investigated. The procedure stops after the maximum number of connections is formed (good value—5 connections per max-element) or when there is no connection that can improve the fit.
4. Add a detector to the model, and update the classifier and residual vector. Stop after the user-specified amount of detectors is formed. Go to 2 otherwise.

The algorithm above is a batch algorithm—it requires us to keep an entire dataset in memory and make a full pass over it in order to generate new strong neurons. The reason for this is that the algorithm has no way of correcting the neuron structure once it has been added to the model—so, if you train a suboptimal neuron using a subsample of the entire training set, you will be unable to improve it later.

This property raises an old question of the balance between network stability and its plasticity. Networks trained with SGD have high plasticity but zero stability. Plasticity allows us to use SGD—an algorithm that makes only marginal improvements in the network being trained—because these small decrements in the loss function will accumulate over time. At the same time, it impedes cheap nondestructive retraining—once an image is removed from the training set, it is quickly forgotten.

In contrast, our algorithm has zero plasticity—it will not improve the neurons it generated previously—but perfect stability. The drawback of such an approach is that it is necessary to use an entire training set to generate just one strong neuron, and this job has to be done in the best way possible. The upside is that the network never forgets what it learned before. If your task has changed a bit, you can restart training and add a few new neurons without damaging previously learned ones.

8   Training Shallow Classifier Layer

Our proposed strong neurons have a rigid piecewise linear output with a fixed slope, but in order to separate image classes one often needs nonlinearities with steep slopes in some places and flat spots in other parts of the feature space. Hence, a separate classifier layer is needed at the top of the network.

One important point to note is that the shallow classifier layer is the only place in our model where significant adversarial instability is introduced. The initial feature detection layer is a single layer of convolutions with bounded coefficients, and thus it has limited adversarial perturbation growth. The sparsely connected layers of strong neurons do not amplify adversarial perturbations.

As a result, any adversary targeting our model will actually target its last layer. In effect, this means that we reduced the problem of building a robust deep classifier to one of building a robust *shalow* classifier.

Our experimental results show that due to the stability of the bottom layers and computational power of strong neurons a simple logistic model (linear summator + logistic function) on top of the network performs well enough in terms of accuracy and adversarial stability.

9 Experimental Results

9.1 Datasets, Software and Network Architectures

We tested Contour Engine on two popular computer vision benchmarks: German Traffic Sign Recognition Benchmark [26] and Street View House Numbers dataset [22].

Our neural architecture is quite nonstandard, and no present framework can train such models. Thus, we had to write the training and inference code in C++ from scratch. The code—an experimental GPL-licensed machine learning framework with several examples—can be downloaded from the following link: https://www.alglib.net/strongnet/.

We evaluated three versions of the same architecture, listed in Table 1: Contour Engine Micro (ultralightweight version), Contour Engine and Contour Engine 800 (ultrawide contour-only version without color block, intended for SVHN dataset).

We should note that all three architectures have a non-convolutional sparse part (one that is composed of strong neurons). In theory, the constructive training algorithm described in Sect. 7 can be applied to convolutional connection structures (it just needs a bit more coding). However, in this first publication we decided to limit ourselves to the simplest architecture, which achieves interesting enough results.

Table 1. Three Contour Engine versions and their parameters

Name	Unsupervised feature extractor				Classifier columns	
	Contour features	Color features	Multiscale processing	KFLOP	Width per class	KFLOP per class
CE-micro	$10 \times 4 \times 4$	$10 \times 4 \times 4$	16×16	162	50	≈ 1
CE-basic	$50 \times 6 \times 6$	$10 \times 4 \times 4$	32×32, 16×16	5075	200	≈ 7
CE-800	$50 \times 6 \times 6$	—	32×32, 16×16	4590	800	≈ 28

9.2   Results

Table 2 examines Contour Engine performance in two categories: (a) ultra-lightweight networks with sub-megaflop inference cost, and (b) networks with higher computational budget (and higher accuracy requirements).

Reference results for other architectures are cited from [7] (EffNet, ShuffleNet, MobileNet), [3] (Targeted Kernel Networks: TSTN, STN), [12] (pruned VGG) and [3,23] (Capsule Networks).

The *Contour Engine Micro* clearly outperforms other lightweight networks (EffNet, ShuffleNet, MobileNet) by a large margin. It provides superior accuracy while working under smallest computational budget.

Medium-sized Contour Engine also shows impressive results on GTSRB dataset. We have to note, however, that its test set error at SVHN is somewhat larger than that of competing approaches. Visual investigation of misclassified examples shows that it can be attributed to the fact that the SVHN dataset contains large proportion of misaligned (badly centered) images—convolutional models better generalize to such images than the nonconvolutional network which we test here.

Table 2. FLOPs vs Accuracy at GTSRB and SVHN datasets. Results are ordered by FLOP count (ascending)

Network	FLOP	Error	Network	FLOP	Error
GTSRB, lightweight			SVHN, lightweight		
CE-micro	**0.2M**	**6.7%**	**CE-micro**	**0.2M**	**10.1%**
EffNet small	0.3M	8.2%	EffNet small	0.5M	11.5%
ShuffleNet	0.5M	11.0%	ShuffleNet	0.7M	17.3%
MobileNet v1 sml	0.5M	11.9%	MobileNet v1 sml	0.8M	14.4%
MobileNet v2 sml	0.7M	9.3%	MobileNet v2 med	1.2M	13.3%
MobileNet v2 med	1.1M	7.2%	MobileNet v2 big	2.1M	12.8%
GTSRB			SVHN		
CE-basic	**5.3M**	**1.6%**	**CE-800**	**4.8M**	**4.8%**
TSTN	55.7M	1.5%	CapsNet	41.3M	4.3%
STN	145.0M	1.5%	VGG-16 pruned	210.0M	3.9%
VGG-16 pruned	522.9M	1.2%			

Finally, we tested the adversarial stability of the *Contour Engine 800* network trained on the SVHN dataset (with clean test set error equal to 4.8%). We used a powerful PGD attack (iterated FGSM with 20 iterations and backtracking line search) with the perturbation L_∞-norm bounded by $\epsilon = 0.01$, $\epsilon = 0.02$ and $\epsilon = 0.03$.

Table 3. Adversarial stability at SVHN dataset. Results are ordered by attack success rate (ASR).

$\epsilon = 0.01$		$\epsilon = 0.02$		$\epsilon = 0.03$	
Defense	ASR	Defense	ASR	Defense	ASR
no protection	83.4%	no protection	96.4%	no protection	98.6%
Wong	33.7%	Wong	58.9%	IAT	52.8%
CE-800	**18.9%**	ATDA	46.8%	**CE-800**	**46.4%**
		CE-800	**29.7%**		

Table 3 compares the attack success rate with reference values from three independent works ([15] for Wong defense, [25] for Adversarial Training with Domain Adaptation, [16] for Interpolated Adversarial Training).

It can be seen that an unprotected network can be successfully attacked in 83% cases with a perturbation as small as 0.01. Different kinds of adversarial protection (when used on traditional summator-based networks) significantly reduce the attack success rate. However, in all cases Contour Engine outperforms these results without any special counter-adversarial measures.

10   Summary

In this work, we have proposed a novel model of the artificial neuron—the strong neuron—which can separate classes with decision boundaries more complex than hyperplanes and which is resistant to adversarial perturbations of its inputs. We proved that our proposal is a fundamental and well-motivated change and that the constituent elements of our strong neuron, min/max units, are the only robust implementations of the AND/OR logic. We also proposed a novel training algorithm that can generate sparse networks with $O(1)$ connections per strong neuron, a result that far surpasses any present advances in neural network sparsification.

State-of-the-art efficiency (inference cost) is achieved on GTSRB and SVHN benchmarks. We also achieved state-of-the-art results in terms of stability against adversarial attacks on SVHN—without any kind of adversarial training—which surpassed much more sophisticated defenses.

One more interesting result is related to our decision to separate unsupervised feature detection and supervised classification. We found that Contour Engine spends most of the inference time in the unsupervised preprocessor—less than 10.000 FLOP per class is used by the supervised part of the network (one which is composed of strong neurons). This result suggests that contour recognition is much simpler than was previously thought!

Acknowledgements. We would like to thank Anatoly Baksheev (Opencvlabs/Deepseez) for important feedback and suggestions.

References

1. Bengio, Y., Lamblin, P., Popovici, D., Larochelle, H.: Greedy layer-wise training of deep networks. In: IN NIPS. MIT Press (2007)
2. Bojanowski, P., Joulin, A.: Unsupervised learning by predicting noise (2017)
3. Chitta, K.: Targeted kernel networks: faster convolutions with attentive regularization. CoRR abs/1806.00523 (2018). http://arxiv.org/abs/1806.00523
4. Coates, A., Lee, H.: An analysis of single-layer networks in unsupervised feature learning. J. Mach. Learn. Res. - Proc. Track 15, 215–223 (2011)
5. Dosovitskiy, A., Springenberg, J., Riedmiller, M., Brox, T.: Discriminative unsupervised feature learning with exemplar convolutional neural networks. IEEE Trans. Pattern Anal. Mach. Intell. 1, June 2014. https://doi.org/10.1109/TPAMI.2015.2496141
6. Fahlman, S.E., Lebiere, C.: The Cascade-Correlation Learning Architecture, pp. 524–532. Morgan Kaufmann Publishers Inc., San Francisco, CA, USA (1990)
7. Freeman, I., Roese-Koerner, L., Kummert, A.: Effnet: an efficient structure for convolutional neural networks. In: 2018 25th IEEE International Conference on Image Processing (ICIP), pp. 6–10 (2018)
8. Goodfellow, I.J., Shlens, J., Szegedy, C.: Explaining and harnessing adversarial examples. CoRR abs/1412.6572 (2015)
9. Grinberg, L., Hopfield, J.J., Krotov, D.: Local unsupervised learning for image analysis. ArXiv abs/1908.08993 (2019)
10. Han, S., et al.: Eie: efficient inference engine on compressed deep neural network. In: Proceedings of the 43rd International Symposium on Computer Architecture, pp. 243–254. ISCA '2016, IEEE Press (2016). https://doi.org/10.1109/ISCA.2016.30
11. Hettinger, C., Christensen, T., Ehlert, B., Humpherys, J., Jarvis, T., Wade, S.: Forward thinking: building and training neural networks one layer at a time. Arxiv, June 2017
12. Hu, Y., Sun, S., Li, J., Wang, X., Gu, Q.: A novel channel pruning method for deep neural network compression. CoRR abs/1805.11394 (2018). http://arxiv.org/abs/1805.11394
13. Ilyas, A., Santurkar, S., Tsipras, D., Engstrom, L., Tran, B., Madry, A.: Adversarial examples are not bugs, they are features. In: NeurIPS (2019)
14. Kingma, D., Welling, M.: Auto-encoding variational bayes. ICLR, December 2013
15. Kolter, J.Z., Wong, E.: Provable defenses against adversarial examples via the convex outer adversarial polytope. In: ICML (2018)
16. Lamb, A., Verma, V., Kannala, J., Bengio, Y.: Interpolated adversarial training: achieving robust neural networks without sacrificing too much accuracy. In: Proceedings of the 12th ACM Workshop on Artificial Intelligence and Security, p. 95–103. AISec'19, Association for Computing Machinery, New York, NY, USA (2019). https://doi.org/10.1145/3338501.3357369
17. Liew, S.S., Khalil-Hani, M., Bakhteri, R.: Bounded activation functions for enhanced training stability of deep neural networks on visual pattern recognition problems. Neurocomputing 216, 718–734 (2016). https://doi.org/10.1016/j.neucom.2016.08.037
18. Louizos, C., Welling, M., Kingma, D.P.: Learning sparse neural networks through l0 regularization. ArXiv abs/1712.01312 (2018)
19. Ma, X., et al.: Pconv: the missing but desirable sparsity in dnn weight pruning for real-time execution on mobile devices. ArXiv abs/1909.05073 (2020)

20. Madry, A., Makelov, A., Schmidt, L., Tsipras, D., Vladu, A.: Towards deep learning models resistant to adversarial attacks. ArXiv abs/1706.06083 (2017)
21. Minsky, M., Papert, S.: Perceptrons - An Introduction to Computational Geometry. MIT Press, United States (1969)
22. Netzer, Y., Wang, T., Coates, A., Bissacco, A., Wu, B.: Reading digits in natural images with unsupervised feature learning. NIPS, January 2011
23. Sabour, S., Frosst, N., Hinton, G.E.: Dynamic routing between capsules. ArXiv abs/1710.09829 (2017)
24. Shang, W., Sohn, K., Almeida, D., Lee, H.: Understanding and improving convolutional neural networks via concatenated rectified linear units. In: Proceedings of the 33rd International Conference on International Conference on Machine Learning - Volume 48, pp. 2217–2225. ICML'16, JMLR.org (2016)
25. Song, C., He, K., Wang, L., Hopcroft, J.E.: Improving the generalization of adversarial training with domain adaptation. ArXiv abs/1810.00740 (2019)
26. Stallkamp, J., Schlipsing, M., Salmen, J., Igel, C.: Man vs. computer: benchmarking machine learning algorithms for traffic sign recognition. Neural Netw. Official J. Int. Neural Netw. Soc. **32**, 323–32 (2012). https://doi.org/10.1016/j.neunet.2012.02.016
27. Sun, F., Qin, M., Zhang, T., Liu, L., Chen, Y.K., Xie, Y.: Computation on sparse neural networks: an inspiration for future hardware. ArXiv abs/2004.11946 (2020)
28. Tsipras, D., Santurkar, S., Engstrom, L., Turner, A., Madry, A.: Robustness may be at odds with accuracy. arXiv: Machine Learning (2019)
29. Wen, W., Wu, C., Wang, Y., Chen, Y., Li, H.: Learning structured sparsity in deep neural networks. In: Proceedings of the 30th International Conference on Neural Information Processing Systems, pp. 2082–2090. NIPS'2016, Curran Associates Inc., Red Hook, NY, USA (2016)

Injecting Prior Knowledge into Image Caption Generation

Arushi Goel[1]([✉]), Basura Fernando[2], Thanh-Son Nguyen[2], and Hakan Bilen[1]

[1] School of Informatics, University of Edinburgh, Edinburgh, Scotland
goel.arushi@gmail.com
[2] AI3, Institute of High Performance Computing, A*STAR, Singapore, Singapore

Abstract. Automatically generating natural language descriptions from an image is a challenging problem in artificial intelligence that requires a good understanding of the visual and textual signals and the correlations between them. The state-of-the-art methods in image captioning struggles to approach human level performance, especially when data is limited. In this paper, we propose to improve the performance of the state-of-the-art image captioning models by incorporating two sources of prior knowledge: (i) a conditional latent topic attention, that uses a set of latent variables (topics) as an anchor to generate highly probable words and, (ii) a regularization technique that exploits the inductive biases in syntactic and semantic structure of captions and improves the generalization of image captioning models. Our experiments validate that our method produces more human interpretable captions and also leads to significant improvements on the MSCOCO dataset in both the full and low data regimes.

1 Introduction

In recent years there has been a growing interest to develop end-to-end learning algorithms in computer vision tasks. Despite the success in many problems such as image classification [17] and person recognition [21], the state-of-the-art methods struggle to reach human-level performance in solving more challenging tasks such as image captioning within limited time and data which involves understanding the visual scenes and describing them in a natural language. This is in contrast to humans who are effortlessly successful in understanding the scenes which they have never seen before and communicating them in a language. It is likely that this efficiency is due to the strong prior knowledge of structure in the visual world and language [11].

Motivated by this observation, in this paper we ask "How can such prior knowledge be represented and utilized to learn better image captioning models with deep neural networks?". To this end, we look at the state-of-the-art encoder-decoder image captioning methods [3,39,41] where a Convolutional Neural Network (CNN) encoder extracts an embedding from the image, a Recurrent Neural Network (RNN) decoder generates the text based on the embedding.

Electronic supplementary material The online version of this chapter (https://doi.org/10.1007/978-3-030-66096-3_26) contains supplementary material, which is available to authorized users.

© Springer Nature Switzerland AG 2020
A. Bartoli and A. Fusiello (Eds.): ECCV 2020 Workshops, LNCS 12536, pp. 369–385, 2020.
https://doi.org/10.1007/978-3-030-66096-3_26

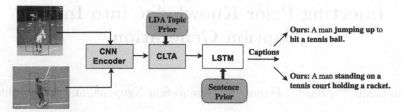

Fig. 1. Our Final Model with Conditional Latent Topic Attention (CLTA) and Sentence Prior (Sentence Auto-Encoder (SAE) regularizer) both rely on prior knowledge to find relevant words and generate non-template like and generalized captions compared to the same Baseline caption for both images - *A man hitting a tennis ball with a racket.*

This framework typically contains two *dynamic* mechanisms to model the sequential output: i) an attention module [4, 41] that identifies the relevant parts of the image embedding based on the previous word and visual features and ii) the RNN decoder that predicts the next words based on the its previous state and attended visual features. While these two components are very powerful to model complex relations between the visual and language cues, we hypothesize that they are also capable of and at the same time prone to overfitting to wrong correlations, thus leading to poor generalization performance when the data is limited. Hence, we propose to regulate these modules with two sources of prior knowledge.

First, we propose an attention mechanism that accurately attends to relevant image regions and better cope with complex associations between words and image regions. For instance, in the example of a "man playing tennis", the input visual attention encoder might only look at the local features (*tennis ball*) leaving out the global visual information (*tennis court*). Hence, it generates a trivial caption as "A man is hitting a tennis ball", which is not the full description of the image in context (as shown in Fig. 1). We solve this ambiguity by incorporating prior knowledge of context via latent topic models [7], which are known to identify semantically meaningful topics [8], into our attention module. In particular we introduce a Conditional Latent Topic Attention (CLTA) module that models relationship between a word and image regions through a latent shared space *i.e.* latent topics to find salient regions in an image. *Tennis ball* steers the model to associate this word with the latent topic, "tennis", which further is responsible for localizing *tennis court* in the image. If a region-word pair has a higher probability with respect to a latent topic and if the same topic has a higher probability with respect to some other regions, then it is also a salient region and will be highly weighted. Therefore, we compute two sets of probabilities conditioned on the current word of the captioning model. We use conditional-marginalized probability where marginalization is done over latent topics to find salient image regions to generate the next word. Our CLTA is modeled as a neural network where marginalized probability is used to weight the image region features to obtain a context vector that is passed to a image captioning decoder to generate the next word.

Second, the complexity in the structure of natural language makes it harder to generate fluent sentences while preserving a higher amount of encoded information (high Bleu-4 scores). Although current image captioning models are able to model this linguistic structure, the generated captions follow a more template-like form, for instance, "A <u>man</u> <u>hitting</u> a <u>tennis ball</u> with a <u>racket</u>." As shown in Fig. 1, visually similar images have template-like captions from the baseline model. This limitation might be due to the challenge of learning an accurate mapping from a high-dimensional input (millions of pixels) to an exponentially large output space (all possible word combinations) with limited data. As the sentences have certain structures, it would be easier to learn the mapping to a lower dimensional output space. Inspired from sequence-to-sequence (seq2seq) machine translation [16,28,35,40], we introduce a new regularization technique for captioning models coined SAE Regularizer. In particular, we design and train an additional seq2seq sentence auto-encoder model ("SAE") that first reads in a whole sentence as input, generates a lower fixed dimensional vector and, then the vector is further used to reconstruct the input sentence. Our SAE is trained to learn the structure of the input (sentence) space in an offline manner by exploiting the regularity of the sentence space.

Specifically, we use SAE-Dec as an auxiliary decoder branch (see Fig. 3). Adding this regularizer forces the representation from the image encoder and language decoder to be more representative of the visual content and less likely to overfit. SAE-Dec is employed along with the original image captioning decoder ("IC-Dec") to output the target sentence during training, however, we do not use SAE regularizer at test time reducing additional computations.

Both of the proposed improvements also help to overcome the problem of training on large image-caption paired data [26,27] by incorporating prior knowledge which is learned from unstructured data in the form of latent topics and SAE. These priors – also known as "inductive biases" – help the models make inferences that go beyond the observed training data. Through an extensive set of experiments, we demonstrate that our proposed CLTA module and SAE-Dec regularizer improves the image captioning performance both in the limited data and full data training regimes on the MSCOCO dataset [26].

2   Related Work

Here, we first discuss related attention mechanisms and then the use of knowledge transfer in image captioning models.

Attention Mechanisms in Image Captioning. The pioneering work in neural machine translation [4,9,29] has shown that attention in encoder-decoder architectures can significantly boost the performance in sequential generation tasks. Visual attention is one of the biggest contributor in image captioning [3,15,19,41]. Soft attention and hard attention variants for image captioning were introduced in [41]. Bottom-Up and Top-Down self attention is effectively used in [3]. Attention on attention is used in recent work [19]. Interestingly, they use attention at both encoder and the decoder step of the captioning process.

Our proposed attention significantly differs in comparison to these attention mechanisms. First, the traditional attention methods, soft-attention [4] and scaled dot product attention [36] aims to find features or regions in an image that highly correlates with a word representation [3,4,34]. In contrast, our *conditional-latent topic attention* uses latent variables *i.e.* topics as anchors to find relationship between word representations and image regions (features). Some image regions and word representations may project to the same set of latent topics more than the others and therefore more likely to co-occur. Our method learns to model these relationships between word-representations and image region features using our latent space. We allow competition among regions and latent topics to compute two sets of probabilities to find salient regions. This competing strategy and our latent topics guided by pre-trained LDA topics [7] allow us to better model relationships between visual features and word representations. Hence, the neural structure and our attention mechanism is quite different from all prior work [3,4,19,41].

Knowledge Transfer in Image Captioning. It is well known that language consists of semantic and syntactic biases [5,30]. We exploit these biases by first training a recurrent caption auto-encoder to capture this useful information using [35]. Our captioning auto-encoder is trained to reconstruct the input sentence and hence, this decoder encapsulates the structural, syntactic and semantic information of input captions. During captioning process we regularize the captioning RNN with this pretrained caption-decoder to exploit biases in the language domain and transfer them to the visual-language domain. To the best of our knowledge, no prior work has attempted such knowledge transfer in image captioning. Zhou *et al.* [46] encode external knowledge in the form of knowledge graphs using Concept-Net [27] to improve image captioning. The closest to ours is the work of [42] where they propose to generate scene graphs from both sentences and images and then encode the scene graphs to a common dictionary before decoding them back to sentences. However, generation of scene graphs from images itself is an extremely challenging task. Finally, we propose to transfer syntactic and semantic information as a regularization technique during the image captioning process as an auxiliary loss. Our experiments suggest that this leads to considerable improvements, specially in more structured measures such as CIDEr [37].

3   Method

In this section, we first review image captioning with attention, introduce our CLTA mechanism, and then our sentence auto-encoder (SAE) regularizer.

3.1   Image Captioning with Attention

Image captioning models are based on encoder-decoder architecture [41] that use a CNN as image encoder and a Long Short-Term Memory (LSTM) [18] as the decoder – see Fig. 1.

The encoder takes an image as input and extracts a feature set $v = \{v_1, \ldots, v_R\}$ corresponding to R regions of the image, where $v_i \in \mathbb{R}^D$ is the D-dimensional feature vector for the ith region. The decoder outputs a caption y by generating one word at each time step. At time step t, the feature set v is combined into a single vector v_a^t by taking weighted sum as follows:

$$v_a^t = \sum_{i=1}^R \alpha_i^t v_i \tag{1}$$

where α_i^t is the CLTA weight for region i at time t, that is explained in the next section. The decoder LSTM ϕ then takes a concatenated vector $[v_a^t | y_{t-1}]$ and the previous hidden state $\mathbf{h_{t-1}}$ as input and generates the next hidden state $\mathbf{h_t}$:

$$\mathbf{h_t} = \phi([v_a^t | E y_{t-1}], \mathbf{h_{t-1}}, \Theta_\phi) \tag{2}$$

where, $|$ denotes concatenation, $y_{t-1} \in \mathbb{R}^K$ is the one-hot vector of the word generated at time $t-1$, K is the vocabulary size, $h^t \in \mathbb{R}^n$ is the hidden state of the LSTM at time t, n is the LSTM dimensionality, and Θ_ϕ are trainable parameters of the LSTM. Finally, the decoder predicts the output word by applying a linear mapping ψ on the hidden state and v_a^t as follows:

$$y_t = \psi([\mathbf{h_t} | v_a^t], \Theta_\psi) \tag{3}$$

where Θ_ψ are trainable parameters. Our LSTM implementation closely follows the formulation in [45]. The word embedding matrix $E \in \mathbb{R}^{m \times K}$ is trained to translate one-hot vectors to word embeddings as in [41], where m is the word embedding dimension. In the next section, we describe our proposed CLTA mechanism.

3.2   CLTA: Conditional Latent Topic Attention

At time step t, our CLTA module takes the previous LSTM hidden state (h^{t-1}) and image features to output the attention weights α^t. Specifically, we use a set of latent topics to model the associations between textual (h^{t-1}) and visual features (v) to compute the attention weights. The attention weight for region i is obtained by taking the conditional-marginalization over the latent topic l as follows:

$$\alpha_i^t = P(\text{region} = i | h^{t-1}, v) = \sum_{l=1}^C P(\text{region} = i | h^{t-1}, v, l) P(l | h^{t-1}, v_i) \tag{4}$$

where l is a topic variable in the C-dimensional latent space. To compute $P(l | h^{t-1}, v_i)$, we first project both textual and visual features to a common C-dimensional shared latent space, and obtain the associations by summing the projected features as follows:

$$q_i^t = W_{sc}v_i + W_{hc}h^{t-1} \tag{5}$$

where $W_{sc} \in \mathbb{R}^{C \times D}$ and $W_{hc} \in \mathbb{R}^{C \times n}$ are the trainable projection matrices for visual and textual features, respectively. Then the latent topic probability is given by:

$$P_L = P(l|h^{t-1}, v_i) = \frac{\exp(q_{il}^t)}{\sum_{k=1}^{C} \exp(q_{ik}^t)} \tag{6}$$

Afterwards, we compute the probability of a region given the textual, vision features and latent topic variable as follows:

$$r_i^t = W_{sr}v_i + W_{hr}h^{t-1} \tag{7}$$

$$P(\text{region} = i|h^{t-1}, v, l) = \frac{\exp(r_{il}^t)}{\sum_{k=1}^{R} \exp(r_{kl}^t)} \tag{8}$$

where $W_{sr} \in \mathbb{R}^{C \times D}$ and $W_{hr} \in \mathbb{R}^{C \times n}$ are the trainable projection matrices for visual and textual features, respectively.

The latent topic posterior in Eq. (6) is pushed to the pre-trained LDA topic prior by adding a KL-divergence term to the image captioning objective. We apply Latent Dirichlet Allocation (LDA) [7] on the caption data. Then, each caption has an inferred topic distribution Q_T from the LDA model which acts as a prior on the latent topic distribution, P_L. For doing this, we take the average of the C-dimensional latent topics at all time steps from $0, \ldots, t-1$ as:

$$P_{L_{avg}} = \frac{1}{t} \sum_{k=0}^{t-1} P(l|h^k, v_i) \tag{9}$$

Hence, the KL-divergence objective is defined as:

$$D_{KL}(P_{L_{avg}} \| Q_T) = \sum_{c \in C} P_{L_{avg}}(c) \times log(\frac{P_{L_{avg}}(c)}{Q_T(c)}) \tag{10}$$

This learnt latent topic distribution captures the semantic relations between the visual and textual features in the form of visual topics, and therefore we also use this latent posterior, P_L as a source of meaningful information during generation of the next hidden state. The modified hidden state $\mathbf{h_t}$ in Eq. (2) is now given by:

$$\mathbf{h_t} = \phi([v_a^t | E y_{t-1} | P_L], \mathbf{h_{t-1}}, \Theta_\phi) \tag{11}$$

We visualize the distribution of latent topics in Fig. 2. While traditional "softmax" attention exploit simple correlation among textual and visual information, we make use of latent topics to model associations between them.

Fig. 2. Image-Caption pairs generated from our CLTA module with 128 dimensions and visualization of Top-20 words from the latent topics.

3.3 SAE Regularizer

Encoder-decoder methods are widely used for translating one language to another [4,10,35]. When the input and target sentences are the same, these models function as auto-encoders by first encoding an entire sentence into a fixed-(low) dimensional vector in a latent space, and then reconstructing it. Autoencoders are commonly employed for unsupervised training in text classification [13] and machine translation [28].

In this paper, our SAE regularizer has two advantages: i) acts as a soft constraint on the image captioning model to regularize the syntactic and semantic space of the captions for better generalization and, ii) encourages the image captioning model to extract more context information for better modelling long-term memory. These two properties of the SAE regularizer generates semantically meaningful captions for an image with syntactic generalizations and prevents generation of naive and template-like captions.

Our SAE model uses network architecture of [35] with Gated Recurrent Units (GRU) [12]. Let us denote the parameter of the decoder GRU by Θ_D. A stochastic variation of the vanilla sentence auto-encoders is de-noising auto-encoders [38] which are trained to "de-noise" corrupted versions of their inputs. To inject such input noise, we drop each word in the input sentence with a probability of 50% to reduce the contribution of a single word on the semantics of a sentence. We train the SAE model in an offline stage on training set of the captioning dataset. After the SAE model is trained, we discard its encoder and integrate only its decoder to regularize the captioning model.

As depicted in Fig. 3, the pretrained SAE decoder takes the last hidden state vector of captioning LSTM h as input and generates an extra caption (denoted as y_{sae}) in addition to the output of the captioning model (denoted as y_{lstm}). We use output of the SAE decoder only in train time to regulate the captioning model ϕ by implicitly transferring the previously learned latent structure with SAE decoder.

Our integrated model is optimized to generate two accurate captions (*i.e.* y_{sae} and y_{lstm}) by minimizing a weighted average of two loss values:

$$\arg\min_{\Omega} \quad \lambda L(y^*, y_{lstm}) + (1 - \lambda) L(y^*, y_{sae}) \tag{12}$$

where L is the cross-entropy loss computed for each caption, word by word against the ground truth caption y^*, λ is the trade-off parameter, and Ω are

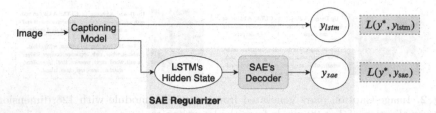

Fig. 3. Illustration of our proposed Sentence Auto-Encoder (SAE) regularizer with the image captioning decoder. The captioning model is trained by adding the SAE decoder as an auxiliary branch and thus acting as a regularizer.

the parameters of our model. We consider two scenarios that we use during our experimentation.

– First, we set the parameters of the SAE decoder Θ_D to be the weights of the pre-trained SAE decoder and freeze them while optimizing Eq. (12) in terms of $\Omega = \{\Theta_\phi, \Theta_\psi, E\}$.
– Second, we initialize Θ_D with the weights of the pre-trained SAE decoder and fine-tune them along with the LSTM parameters, *i.e.* $\Omega = \{\Theta_\phi, \Theta_\psi, E, \Theta_D\}$.

As discussed in Sect. 3.2, we also minimize the KL divergence in Eq. (10) along with the final regularized objective in Eq. (12) as:

$$\arg\min_{\Omega} \quad \lambda L(y^*, y_{\text{lstm}}) + (1 - \lambda)L(y^*, y_{\text{sae}}) + \gamma D_{KL}(P_{L_{avg}}||Q_T) \qquad (13)$$

where, γ is the weight for the KL divergence loss.

Discussion. An alternative way of exploiting the information from the pre-trained SAE model is to bring the representations from the captioning decoder closer to the encodings of the SAE encoder by minimizing the Euclidean distance between the hidden state from the SAE encoder and the hidden state from the captioning decoder at each time-step. However, we found this setting is too restrictive on the learned hidden state of the LSTM.

4   Experiments

Dataset. Our models are evaluated on the standard MSCOCO 2014 image captioning dataset [26]. For fair comparisons, we use the same data splits for training, validation and testing as in [22] which have been used extensively in prior works. This split has 113,287 images for training, 5k images for validation and testing respectively with 5 captions for each image. We perform evaluation on all relevant metrics for generated sentence evaluation - CIDEr [37], Bleu [31], METEOR [14], ROUGE-L [25] and, SPICE [2].

Implementation Details. For training our image captioning model, we compute the image features based on the Bottom-Up architecture proposed by [3], where the model is trained using a Faster-RCNN model [32] on the Visual-Genome Dataset [24] with object and attribute information. These features are extracted from R regions and each region feature has D dimensions, where R and D is 36 and 2048 respectively as proposed in [3]. We use these 36×2048 image features in all our experiments.

4.1 Experimental Setup

LDA Topic Models. The LDA [7] model is learned in an offline manner to generate a C dimensional topic distribution for each caption. Briefly, the LDA model treats the captions as word-documents and group these words to form C topics (cluster of words), learns the word distribution for each topic $(C \times V)$ where V is the vocabulary size and also generates a topic distribution for each input caption, Q_T where each Cth dimension denotes the probability for that topic.

Sentence Auto-encoder. The Sentence Auto-encoder is trained offline on the MSCOCO 2014 captioning dataset [26] with the same splits as discussed above. For the architecture, we have a single layer GRU for both the encoder and the decoder. The word embeddings are learned with the network using an embedding layer and the dimension of both the hidden state and the word embeddings is 1024. During training, the decoder is trained with teacher-forcing [6] with a probability of 0.5. For inference, the decoder decodes till it reaches the end of caption token. The learning rate for this network is $2e-3$ and it is trained using the ADAM [23] optimizer.

Image Captioning Decoder with SAE Regularizer. The architecture of our image captioning decoder is same as the Up-Down model [3] with their "soft-attention" replaced by our CLTA module and trained with the SAE regularizer. We also retrain the AoANet model proposed by Huang *et al.* [19] by incorporating our CLTA module and the SAE regularizer. In the results section, we show improvements over the Up-Down and AoANet models using our proposed approaches. Note, the parameters for training Up-Down and AoANet baselines are same as the original setting. While training the captioning models together with the SAE-decoder, we jointly learn an affine embedding layer (dimension 1024) by combining the embeddings from the image captioning decoder and the SAE-decoder. During inference, we use beam search to generate captions from the captioning decoder using a beam size of 5 for Up-Down and a beam-size of 2 for AoANet. For training the overall objective function as given in Eq. (13), the value of λ is initialized by 0.7 and increased by a rate of 1.1 every 5 epochs until it reaches a value of 0.9 and γ is fixed to 0.1. We use the ADAM optimizer with a learning rate of $2e-4$. Our code is implemented using PyTorch [1] and will be made publicly available.

5   Results and Analysis

First, we study the caption reconstruction performance of vanilla and denoising SAE, then report our model's image captioning performance on MS-COCO dataset with full and limited data, investigate multiple design decisions and analyze our results qualitatively.

5.1   Sentence Auto-encoder Results

An ideal SAE must learn mapping its input to a fixed low dimensional space such that a whole sentence can be summarized and reconstructed accurately. To this end, we experiment with two SAEs, Vanilla-SAE and Denoising-SAE and report their reconstruction performances in terms of Bleu4 and cross-entropy (CE) loss in Fig. 4.

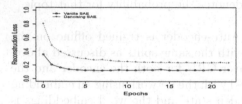

Fig. 4. Error Curve for the Sentence Auto-Encoder on the Karpathy test split. The error starts increasing approximately after 20 epochs.

Table 1. Bleu-4 Evaluation and Reconstruction Cross-Entropy Loss for the Sentence Auto-Encoder on the Karpathy test split of MSCOCO 2014 caption dataset [26].

Models	Bleu-4 ↑	CE-Loss ↓
Vanilla SAE	**96.33**	**0.12**
Denoising SAE	89.79	0.23

The vanilla model, when the inputs words are not corrupted, outperforms the denoising one in both metrics. This is expected as the denoising model is only trained with corrupted input sequences. The loss for both the Vanilla and Denoising SAE start from a relatively high value of approximately 0.8 and 0.4 respectively, and converge to a significantly low error of 0.1 and 0.2. For a better analysis, we also compute the Bleu-4 metrics on our decoded caption against the 5 ground-truth captions. As reported in Fig. 1, both models obtain significantly high Bleu-4 scores. This indicates that an entire caption can be compressed in a low dimensional vector (1024) and can be successfully reconstructed.

5.2   Image Captioning Results

Here we incorporate the proposed CLTA and SAE regularizer to recent image-captioning models including Up-Down [3] and AoANet [19] and report their performance on MS-COCO dataset in multiple metrics (see Table 2). The tables report the original results of these methods from their publications in the top block and the rows in cyan show relative improvement of our models when compared to the baselines.

Table 2. Image captioning performance on the "Karpathy" test split of the MSCOCO 2014 caption dataset [26] from other state-of-the-art methods and our models. Our Conditional Latent Topic Attention with the SAE regularizer significantly improves across all the metrics using both *cross-entropy loss* and *cider optimization*. † denotes our trained models and * indicates the results obtained from the publicly available pre-trained model.

Models	cross-entropy loss						cider optimization					
	B-1	B-4	M	R	C	S	B-1	B-4	M	R	C	S
LSTM-A [44]	75.4	35.2	26.9	55.8	108.8	20.0	78.6	35.5	27.3	56.8	118.3	20.8
RFNet [20]	76.4	35.8	27.4	56.8	112.5	20.5	79.1	36.5	27.7	57.3	121.9	21.2
Up-Down [3]	77.2	36.2	27.0	56.4	113.5	20.3	79.8	36.3	27.7	56.9	120.1	21.4
GCN-LSTM [43]	77.3	36.8	27.9	57.0	116.3	20.9	80.5	38.2	28.5	58.3	127.6	22.0
AoANet [19]	77.4	37.2	28.4	57.5	119.8	21.3	80.2	38.9	29.2	58.8	129.8	22.4
Up-Down†	75.9	36.0	27.3	56.1	113.3	20.1	79.2	36.3	27.7	57.3	120.8	21.2
Up-Down† + CLTA + SAE-Reg	**76.7**	**37.1**	**28.1**	**57.1**	**116.2**	**21.0**	**80.2**	**37.4**	**28.4**	**58.1**	**127.4**	**22.0**
Relative Improvement	+0.8	+1.1	+0.8	+1.0	+2.9	+0.9	+1.0	+1.1	+0.7	+0.8	+6.6	+0.8
AoANet*	77.3	36.9	**28.5**	57.3	118.4	21.6	80.5	39.1	29.0	58.9	128.9	22.7
AoANet† + CLTA + SAE-Reg	**78.1**	**37.9**	28.4	**57.5**	**119.9**	**21.7**	**80.8**	**39.3**	**29.1**	**59.1**	**130.1**	**22.9**
Relative Improvement	+0.8	+1.0	-0.1	+0.2	+1.5	+0.1	+0.3	+0.2	+0.1	+0.2	+1.2	+0.2

The baseline models are trained for two settings - 1) Up-Down†, is the model re-trained on the architecture of Anderson *et al.* [3] and, 2) AoANet†, is the Attention-on-Attention model re-trained as in Huang *et al.* [19]. Note that for both Up-Down and AoANet, we use the original source code to train them in our own hardware. We replace the "soft-attention" module in our Up-Down baseline by CLTA directly. The AoANet model is based on the powerful Transformer [36] architecture with the multi-head dot attention in both encoder and decoder. For AoANet, we replace the dot attention in the decoder of AoANet at each head by the CLTA which results in multi-head CLTA. The SAE-decoder is added as a regularizer on top of these models as also discussed in Sect. 4.1. As discussed later in Sect. 5.5, we train all our models with 128 dimensions for the CLTA and with the Denoising SAE decoder (initialized with h^{last}).

We evaluate our models with the cross-entropy loss training and also by using the CIDEr score oprimization [33] after the cross-entropy pre-training stage (Table 2). For the cross-entropy one, our combined approach consistently improves over the baseline performances across all metrics. It is clear from the results that improvements in CIDEr and Bleu-4 are quite significant which shows that our approach generates more human-like and accurate sentences. It is interesting to note that AoANet with CLTA and SAE-regularizer also gives consistent improvements despite having a strong transformer language model. We show in Sect. 5.4 the differences between our captions and the captions generated from Up-Down and AoANet. Our method is modular and improves on state-of-the-art models despite the architectural differences. Moreover, the SAE decoder is discarded after training and hence it brings no additional computational load during test-time but with significant performance boost. For CIDEr optimization, our

Table 3. Evaluation of our CLTA and SAE-Regularizer methods by training on a subset of the MSCOCO "Karpathy" Training split.

Models	50% data		75% data		100% data	
	Bleu-4	CIDEr	Bleu-4	CIDEr	Bleu-4	CIDEr
Up-Down	35.4	112.0	35.8	112.7	36.0	113.3
Up-Down+CLTA	36.3	113.7	36.3	114.5	36.5	115.0
Up-Down+CLTA+SAE-Reg	**36.6**	**114.8**	**36.8**	**115.6**	**37.1**	**116.2**
AoANet	36.6	116.1	36.8	118.1	36.9	118.4
AoANet+CLTA	36.9	116.7	37.1	118.4	37.4	119.1
AoANet+CLTA+SAE-Reg	**37.2**	**117.5**	**37.6**	**118.9**	**37.9**	**119.9**

models based on Up-Down and AoANet also show significant improvements in all metrics for our proposed approach.

5.3 Learning to Caption with Less Data

Table 3 evaluates the performance of our proposed models for a subset of the training data, where $x\%$ is the percentage of the total data that is used for training. All these subsets of the training samples are chosen randomly. Our CLTA module is trained with 128 dimensions for the latent topics along with the Denoising SAE Regularizer initialized with the last hidden state of the LSTM (Up-Down+CLTA+SAE-Reg). Despite the number of training samples, our average improvement with CLTA and SAE-Regularizer is around 1% in Bleu-4 and 2.9% in CIDEr for the Up-Down model and 0.8% in Bleu-4 and 1.2% in CIDEr for the AoANet model. The significant improvements in Bleu-4 and CIDEr scores with only 50% and 75% of the data compared to the baseline validates our proposed methods as a form of rich prior.

5.4 Qualitative Results

In Fig. 5, we show examples of images and captions generated by the baselines Up-Down and AoANet along with our proposed methods, CLTA and SAE-Regularizer. The baseline models have repetitive words and errors while generating captions (*in front of a mirror, a dog in the rear view mirror*). Our models corrects these mistakes by finding relevant words according to the context and putting them together in a human-like caption format (*a rear view mirror shows a dog* has the same meaning as *a rear view mirror shows a dog in the rear view mirror* which is efficiently corrected by our models by bringing in the correct meaning). From all the examples shown, we can see that our model overcomes the limitation of overfitting in current methods by completing a caption with more semantic and syntactic generalization (*e.g.: different flavoured donuts* and *several trains on the tracks*).

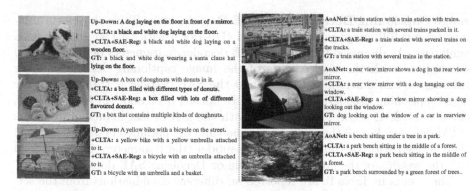

Fig. 5. Example of generated captions from the baseline Up-Down, AoANet, our proposed CLTA and, our final models with both CLTA and SAE Regularizer.

Table 4. Ablative analysis for different settings on our (a) CLTA module and, (b) SAE regularizer training.

Models	Baseline	CLTA		
	Soft-Attention	128	256	512
Bleu-4	36.0	36.5	36.6	**36.7**
CIDEr	113.3	115.0	115.2	**115.3**

(a) Evaluation scores for the Up-Down model with soft-attention and ablations of our CLTA module.

Models	SAE-Decoder	h	Bleu-4	CIDEr
Baseline	No	-	36.0	113.3
CLTA-128	Vanilla	First	36.9	115.8
		Last	36.8	115.3
	Denoising	First	36.8	116.1
		Last	37.1	**116.2**
CLTA-512	Denoising	Last	**37.2**	115.9

(b) Additional quantitative evaluation results from different settings of the SAE decoder when trained with image captioning decoder. h denotes the hidden state.

5.5 Ablation Study

Conditional Latent Topic Attention (CLTA). Table 4a depicts the results for the CLTA module that is described in Sect. 3.2. Soft-attention is used as a baseline and corresponds to the attention mechanism in [41] which is the main attention module in Up-Down image captioning model by Anderson *et al.* [3]. We replace this attention with the CLTA and evaluate its performance for different number of latent dimensions, *i.e.* topics (C). The models trained with latent topic dimensions of 128, 256 and 512 all outperform the baseline significantly. The higher CIDEr and Bleu-4 scores for these latent topics show the model's capability to generate more descriptive and accurate human-like sentences. As we increase the dimensions of latent topics from 128 to 512, we predict more relevant keywords as new topics learnt by the CLTA module with 512 dimensions are useful in encoding more information and hence generating meaningful captions.

Image Captioning Decoder with SAE Regularizer. Table 4b reports ablations for our full image captioning model (Up-Down with CLTA) and the SAE regularizer. As discussed in Sect. 3.3, SAE decoder (parameters defined by Θ_D) is initialized with the hidden state of the image captioning decoder. During training, we test different settings of how the SAE decoder is trained with the image captioning decoder: (1) Vanilla vs Denoising SAE and, (2) h^{first} vs h^{last}, whether the SAE decoder is initialized with the first or last hidden state of the LSTM decoder. For all the settings, we fine-tune the parameters of GRU_D (Θ_D) when trained with the image captioning model (the parameters are initialized with the weights of the pre-trained Vanilla or Denoising SAE decoder).

The results in Table 4b are reported on different combinations from the settings described above, with the CLTA having 128 and 512 dimensions in the image captioning decoder. Adding the auxiliary branch of SAE decoder significantly improves over the baseline model with CLTA and in the best setting, Denoising SAE with h^{last} improves the CIDEr and Bleu-4 scores by 1.2 and 0.6 respectively. As the SAE decoder is trained for the task of reconstruction, fine-tuning it to the task of captioning improves the image captioning decoder.

Initializing the Vanilla SAE decoder with h^{last} does not provide enough gradient during training and quickly converges to a lower error, hence this brings lower generalization capacity to the image captioning decoder. As h^{first} is less representative of an entire caption compared to h^{last}, vanilla SAE with h^{first} is more helpful to improve the captioning decoder training. On the other hand, the Denoising SAE being robust to noisy summary vectors provide enough training signal to improve the image captioning decoder when initialized with either h^{first} or h^{last} but slightly better performance with h^{last} for Bleu-4 and CIDEr as it forces h^{last} to have an accurate lower-dim representation for the SAE and hence better generalization. It is clear from the results in Table 4b, that Denoising SAE with h^{last} helps to generate accurate and generalizable captions. From our experiments, we found that CLTA with 128 topics and Denoising SAE (with h^{last}) has better performance than even it's counterpart with 512 topics. Hence, for all our experiments in Sect. 5.2 and Sect. 5.3 our topic dimension is 128 with Denoising SAE initialized with h^{last}.

6   Conclusion

In this paper, we have introduced two novel methods for image captioning that exploit prior knowledge and hence help to improve state-of-the-art models even when the data is limited. The first method exploits association between visual and textual features by learning latent topics via an LDA topic prior and obtains robust attention weights for each image region. The second one is an SAE regularizer that is pre-trained in an autoencoder framework to learn the structure of the captions and is plugged into the image captioning model to regulate its training. Using these modules, we obtain consistent improvements on two investigate models, bottom-up top-down and the AoANet image captioning model, indicating the usefulness of our two modules as a strong prior. In future work, we plan to further investigate potential use of label space structure learning for other challenging vision tasks with limited data and to improve generalization.

References

1. Pytorch. https://pytorch.org/
2. Anderson, P., Fernando, B., Johnson, M., Gould, S.: SPICE: semantic propositional image caption evaluation. In: Leibe, B., Matas, J., Sebe, N., Welling, M. (eds.) ECCV 2016. LNCS, vol. 9909, pp. 382–398. Springer, Cham (2016). https://doi.org/10.1007/978-3-319-46454-1_24
3. Anderson, P., et al.: Bottom-up and top-down attention for image captioning and visual question answering. In: Proceedings of the IEEE Conference on Computer Vision and Pattern Recognition, pp. 6077–6086 (2018)
4. Bahdanau, D., Cho, K., Bengio, Y.: Neural machine translation by jointly learning to align and translate. arXiv preprint arXiv:1409.0473 (2014)
5. Bao, Y., et al.: Generating sentences from disentangled syntactic and semantic spaces. arXiv preprint arXiv:1907.05789 (2019)
6. Bengio, S., Vinyals, O., Jaitly, N., Shazeer, N.: Scheduled sampling for sequence prediction with recurrent neural networks. In: Advances in Neural Information Processing Systems, pp. 1171–1179 (2015)
7. Blei, D.M., Ng, A.Y., Jordan, M.I.: Latent dirichlet allocation. J. Mach. Learn. Res. 3(Jan), 993–1022 (2003)
8. Chang, J., Gerrish, S., Wang, C., Boyd-Graber, J.L., Blei, D.M.: Reading tea leaves: how humans interpret topic models. In: Advances in Neural Information Processing Systems, pp. 288–296 (2009)
9. Cho, K., van Merrienboer, B., Bahdanau, D., Bengio, Y.: On the properties of neural machine translation: encoder-decoder approaches. In: Proceedings of SSST-8, Eighth Workshop on Syntax, Semantics and Structure in Statistical Translation, pp. 103–111 (2014)
10. Cho, K., et al.: Learning phrase representations using RNN encoder-decoder for statistical machine translation. arXiv preprint arXiv:1406.1078 (2014)
11. Chomsky, N.: Aspects of the Theory of Syntax, vol. 11. MIT press (2014)
12. Chung, J., Gulcehre, C., Cho, K., Bengio, Y.: Empirical evaluation of gated recurrent neural networks on sequence modeling. arXiv preprint arXiv:1412.3555 (2014)
13. Dai, A.M., Le, Q.V.: Semi-supervised sequence learning. In: Advances in Neural Information Processing Systems, pp. 3079–3087 (2015)
14. Denkowski, M., Lavie, A.: Meteor universal: language specific translation evaluation for any target language. In: Proceedings of the Ninth Workshop on Statistical Machine Translation, pp. 376–380 (2014)
15. Fang, H., et al.: From captions to visual concepts and back. In: Proceedings of the IEEE Conference on Computer Vision and Pattern Recognition, pp. 1473–1482 (2015)
16. Gehring, J., Auli, M., Grangier, D., Yarats, D., Dauphin, Y.N.: Convolutional sequence to sequence learning. In: Proceedings of the 34th International Conference on Machine Learning-Volume 70, pp. 1243–1252. JMLR. org (2017)
17. He, K., Zhang, X., Ren, S., Sun, J.: Deep residual learning for image recognition. In: Proceedings of the IEEE Conference on Computer Vision and Pattern Recognition, pp. 770–778 (2016)

18. Hochreiter, S., Schmidhuber, J.: Long short-term memory. Neural Comput. **9**(8), 1735–1780 (1997)
19. Huang, L., Wang, W., Chen, J., Wei, X.Y.: Attention on attention for image captioning. In: The IEEE International Conference on Computer Vision (ICCV), October 2019
20. Jiang, W., Ma, L., Jiang, Y.G., Liu, W., Zhang, T.: Recurrent fusion network for image captioning. In: Proceedings of the European Conference on Computer Vision (ECCV), pp. 499–515 (2018)
21. Joon Oh, S., Benenson, R., Fritz, M., Schiele, B.: Person recognition in personal photo collections. In: Proceedings of the IEEE International Conference on Computer Vision, pp. 3862–3870 (2015)
22. Karpathy, A., Fei-Fei, L.: Deep visual-semantic alignments for generating image descriptions. In: Proceedings of the IEEE Conference on Computer Vision and Pattern Recognition, pp. 3128–3137 (2015)
23. Kingma, D.P., Ba, J.: Adam: method for stochastic optimization. arXiv preprint arXiv:1412.6980 (2014)
24. Krishna, R., et al.: Visual genome: connecting language and vision using crowd-sourced dense image annotations. Int. J. Comput. Vis. **123**(1), 32–73 (2017)
25. Lin, C.Y., Och, F.J.: Automatic evaluation of machine translation quality using longest common subsequence and skip-bigram statistics. In: Proceedings of the 42nd Annual Meeting on Association for Computational Linguistics, p. 605. Association for Computational Linguistics (2004)
26. Lin, T.-Y., et al.: Microsoft COCO: common objects in context. In: Fleet, D., Pajdla, T., Schiele, B., Tuytelaars, T. (eds.) ECCV 2014. LNCS, vol. 8693, pp. 740–755. Springer, Cham (2014). https://doi.org/10.1007/978-3-319-10602-1_48
27. Liu, H., Singh, P.: Conceptnet-a practical commonsense reasoning tool-kit. BT Technol. J. **22**(4), 211–226 (2004)
28. Luong, M.T., Le, Q.V., Sutskever, I., Vinyals, O., Kaiser, L.: Multi-task sequence to sequence learning. arXiv preprint arXiv:1511.06114 (2015)
29. Luong, M.T., Pham, H., Manning, C.D.: Effective approaches to attention-based neural machine translation. arXiv preprint arXiv:1508.04025 (2015)
30. Marcheggiani, D., Bastings, J., Titov, I.: Exploiting semantics in neural machine translation with graph convolutional networks. arXiv preprint arXiv:1804.08313 (2018)
31. Papineni, K., Roukos, S., Ward, T., Zhu, W.J.: Bleu: a method for automatic evaluation of machine translation. In: Proceedings of the 40th Annual Meeting on Association for Computational Linguistics, pp. 311–318. Association for Computational Linguistics (2002)
32. Ren, S., He, K., Girshick, R., Sun, J.: Faster r-cnn: towards real-time object detection with region proposal networks. In: Advances in Neural Information Processing Systems, pp. 91–99 (2015)
33. Rennie, S.J., Marcheret, E., Mroueh, Y., Ross, J., Goel, V.: Self-critical sequence training for image captioning. In: Proceedings of the IEEE Conference on Computer Vision and Pattern Recognition, pp. 7008–7024 (2017)
34. Sharma, P., Ding, N., Goodman, S., Soricut, R.: Conceptual captions: a cleaned, hypernymed, image alt-text dataset for automatic image captioning. In: Proceedings of the 56th Annual Meeting of the Association for Computational Linguistics (Volume 1: Long Papers), pp. 2556–2565 (2018)
35. Sutskever, I., Vinyals, O., Le, Q.V.: Sequence to sequence learning with neural networks. In: Advances in Neural Information Processing Systems, pp. 3104–3112 (2014)

36. Vaswani, A., et al.: Attention is all you need. In: Advances in Neural Information Processing Systems, pp. 5998–6008 (2017)
37. Vedantam, R., Lawrence Zitnick, C., Parikh, D.: Cider: consensus-based image description evaluation. In: Proceedings of the IEEE Conference on Computer Vision and Pattern Recognition, pp. 4566–4575 (2015)
38. Vincent, P., Larochelle, H., Bengio, Y., Manzagol, P.A.: Extracting and composing robust features with denoising autoencoders. In: Proceedings of the 25th International Conference on Machine Learning, pp. 1096–1103. ACM (2008)
39. Vinyals, O., Toshev, A., Bengio, S., Erhan, D.: Show and tell: a neural image caption generator. In: Proceedings of the IEEE Conference on Computer Vision and Pattern Recognition, pp. 3156–3164 (2015)
40. Wiseman, S., Rush, A.M.: Sequence-to-sequence learning as beam-search optimization. arXiv preprint arXiv:1606.02960 (2016)
41. Xu, K., et al.: Show, attend and tell: neural image caption generation with visual attention. In: International Conference on Machine Learning, pp. 2048–2057 (2015)
42. Yang, X., Tang, K., Zhang, H., Cai, J.: Auto-encoding scene graphs for image captioning. In: Proceedings of the IEEE Conference on Computer Vision and Pattern Recognition, pp. 10685–10694 (2019)
43. Yao, T., Pan, Y., Li, Y., Mei, T.: Exploring visual relationship for image captioning. In: Proceedings of the European Conference on Computer Vision (ECCV), pp. 684–699 (2018)
44. Yao, T., Pan, Y., Li, Y., Qiu, Z., Mei, T.: Boosting image captioning with attributes. In: Proceedings of the IEEE International Conference on Computer Vision, pp. 4894–4902 (2017)
45. Zaremba, W., Sutskever, I., Vinyals, O.: Recurrent neural network regularization. arXiv preprint arXiv:1409.2329 (2014)
46. Zhou, Y., Sun, Y., Honavar, V.: Improving image captioning by leveraging knowledge graphs. In: 2019 IEEE Winter Conference on Applications of Computer Vision (WACV), pp. 283–293. IEEE (2019)

Learning Temporally Invariant and Localizable Features via Data Augmentation for Video Recognition

Taeoh Kim[1], Hyeongmin Lee[1], MyeongAh Cho[1], Ho Seong Lee[2],
Dong Heon Cho[2], and Sangyoun Lee[1]($\boxtimes$)

^{1} Yonsei University, Seoul, South Korea
{kto,minimonia,maycho0305,syleee}@yonsei.ac.kr
^{2} Cognex Deep Learning Lab, Seoul, South Korea
{hoseong.lee,david.cho}@cognex.com

Abstract. Deep-Learning-based video recognition has shown promising improvements along with the development of large-scale datasets and spatiotemporal network architectures. In image recognition, learning spatially invariant features is a key factor in improving recognition performance and robustness. Data augmentation based on visual inductive priors, such as cropping, flipping, rotating, or photometric jittering, is a representative approach to achieve these features. Recent state-of-the-art recognition solutions have relied on modern data augmentation strategies that exploit a mixture of augmentation operations. In this study, we extend these strategies to the temporal dimension for videos to learn temporally invariant or temporally localizable features to cover temporal perturbations or complex actions in videos. Based on our novel temporal data augmentation algorithms, video recognition performances are improved using only a limited amount of training data compared to the spatial-only data augmentation algorithms, including the 1st Visual Inductive Priors (VIPriors) for data-efficient action recognition challenge. Furthermore, learned features are temporally localizable that cannot be achieved using spatial augmentation algorithms. Our source code is available at https://github.com/taeoh-kim/temporal_data_augmentation.

1 Introduction

Many augmentation techniques have been proposed to increase the recognition performance and robustness for an environment with limited training data or to prevent overconfidence and overfitting of large-scale data, such as ImageNet [25]. These techniques can be categorized into data-level augmentation [9–11,19,25,30,36,37], data-level mixing [27,28,45,52,53,55], and in-network augmentation [13,14,20,23,40,44,51]. Data augmentation is an important component for recent state-of-the-art self-supervised learning [5,17,34], semi-supervised learning [1,2,38,48], self-learning [49], and generative models [22,54,56,57] because of its ability to learn invariant features.

T. Kim, H. Lee and M. Cho—Equal contribution.

© Springer Nature Switzerland AG 2020
A. Bartoli and A. Fusiello (Eds.): ECCV 2020 Workshops, LNCS 12536, pp. 386–403, 2020.
https://doi.org/10.1007/978-3-030-66096-3_27

The purpose of data augmentation in image recognition is to enhance the generalizability via learning spatially invariant features. Augmentation, such as geometric (cropping, flipping, rotating, *etc.*) and photometric (brightness, contrast, color, *etc.*) transformation, can model uncertain variances in a dataset. Recent algorithms have exhibited state-of-the-art performances in terms of the complexity-accuracy trade-off [10,30] or robustness [18,19]. Some approaches [52,53] learn localizable features that can be used as transferable features for the localization-related tasks, such as object detection and image captioning. They simultaneously learn what to and where to focus for recognition.

Despite evolving through numerous algorithms in image recognition, exploration into data augmentation and regularization in video recognition has rarely been done. In videos, temporal variations and perturbations should be considered. For example, Fig. 1 depicts temporal perturbations across frames in a video. This perturbation can be a geometric perturbation, such as translation, rotation, scale, and so on, or a photometric perturbation, such as brightness, contrast, and so on. To handle perturbation, both well-studied spatial augmentation and temporally varying data augmentation should be considered.

In this paper, we propose several extensions for temporal robustness. More specifically, temporally invariant and localizable features can be modeled via data augmentations. In this paper, we extend upon two recent examples of well-studied spatial augmentation techniques: data-level augmentation and data-level mixing. To the best of our knowledge, this is the first study that deeply analyzes temporal perturbation modeling via data augmentation in video recognition.

The contributions of this paper can summarized as follows:

- We propose an extension of RandAugment [10], called RandAugment-T, to conduct data-level augmentation for video recognition. It can temporally model varying levels of augmentation operations.
- We also propose the temporal extensions of CutOut [11], MixUp [55], and CutMix [53] as examples of deleting, blending, and cut-and-pasting data samples. Considering the temporal dimension improves recognition performance and the temporal localization abilities.
- The recognition results of the proposed extensions on the UCF-101 [39] subset for the 1st Visual Inductive Priors (VIPriors) for data-efficient action recognition challenge, and the HMDB-51 [26] dataset exhibit performance improvements compared to the spatial-only versions in a simple baseline.

2   Related Works

2.1   Data Augmentation

Data-Level Augmentation. First, to enlarge the generalization performance of a dataset and to reduce the overfitting problem of preliminary networks, various data augmentation methods, such as rotate, flip, crop, color jitter [25], and scale jitter [36] have been proposed. CutOut [11] deletes a square-shaped

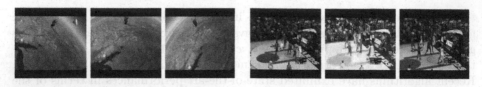

Fig. 1. Example clips of temporal perturbations. *Left*: Geometric perturbation across frames in a sky-diving video due to extreme camera and object movement. *Right*: Photometric perturbation across frames in a basketball stadium due to camera flashes.

box at a random location to encourage the network focus on various properties of images, to avoid relying on the most discriminative regions. Hide-and-Seek [37] is a similar approach, but it deletes multiple regions that are sampled from grid patches.

Recently, the methodology of combining more than one augmentation operation has been proposed. Cubuk *et al.*[9] propose a reinforcement learning-based approach to search for the optimal data augmentation policy in the given dataset. However, because the search space is too large, it requires extensive time to determine the optimal policy. Although an approach to mitigate this problem has been proposed [30], it is difficult hard and time-consuming to determine the optimal augmentation strategy. To solve this, Cubuk *et al.*[10] propose RandAugment, which randomly samples augment operations from the candidate list and cascades them. Similarly, Hendrycks *et al.*[19] propose an approach called Aug-Mix that parallelly blends images that have been augmented by the operations sampled from a set of candidates.

These techniques can model uncertain spatial perturbation, such as the geometric transform, photometric transform, or both. Because studies have focused on static images, applying these approaches to videos is a straightforward extension. For videos, Ji *et al.*[21] propose temporal augmentation operations called time warping and time masking, which randomly adjust or skip temporal frames. In contrast, in this paper, we focus on the temporally varying augmentation.

Data-Level Mixing. Together with data augmentation algorithms, augmentation strategies using multiple samples have been proposed. Zhang *et al.*[55] propose an approach called MixUp to manipulate images with more than one image. This approach makes a new sample by blending two arbitrary images and interpolating their one-hot ground-truth labels. This encourages the model to behave linearly in-between training examples. CutMix [53] combines the concepts of CutOut and MixUp, by taking the best of both worlds. It replaces a square-shaped deleted region in CutOut with a patch from another image. This encourages the model to learn not only what to recognize but also where to recognize it. It can be interpreted as spatially localizable feature learning. Inspired by CutMix, several methods have been proposed. CutBlur [52] propose a CutMix-like approach to solving the restoration problem by cut-and-pasting between low-resolution and high-resolution images. They also proposed Cut-MixUp, which combines MixUp and CutMix. CutMixUp blends the two images inside the one of the masks of CutMix to relax extreme changes in boundary pixels. Attribute Mix [28] uses masks of any shape, not only square-shaped masks. Attentive CutMix [45] also discards the square-shaped masks. It uses multiple patches sampled from the grid and replaces the regions with another image. Smoothmix [27] focuses on the 'strong edge' problem caused by the boundary of the masks.

Although numerous data manipulation methods, including deleting, blending, and cut-and-pasting, have successfully augmented many image datasets, their ability when applied to video recognition to learn temporally invariant and localizable features has not yet been explored.

In-Network Augmentation. Apart from the data-level approaches, several studies have proposed in-network augmentation algorithms. These have usually involved the design of stochastic networks to undergo augmentation at the feature-level to reduce predictive variance and to learn more high-level augmented features rather than to learn features from low-level augmentations. Dropout [40] is the very first approach to regularize the overfitted models. Other approaches, such as DropBlock [14], Stochastic depth [20], Shake-Shake [13], and ShakeDrop [51] regularization, have been proposed. Manifold-MixUp [44] propose a mixing strategy like MixUp but is used instead in the feature space. The most similar approach to this study is a regularization method for video recognition called Random Mean Scaling [23]. It randomly adjusts spatiotemporal features in video networks. In contrast, our approach focuses on data-level manipulation and is extended from spatial-only algorithms into the temporal worlds.

2.2 Video Recognition

For video action recognition, like image recognition, various architectures have been proposed to capture spatiotemporal features from videos. In [42], Tran *et al.* proposed C3D, which extracts features containing objects, scenes, and action information through 3D convolutional layers and then simply passes them through a linear classifier. In [43], a (2+1)D convolution that focuses on layer factorization rather than 3D convolution is proposed. It is composed using a 2D spatial convolution followed by 1D temporal convolution. In addition, the non-local block [47] and GloRe [7] modules have been suggested to capture long-range dependencies via self-attention and graph-based modules. By plugging them into 3D ConvNet, the network can learn long-distance relations in both space and time. Another approach is two-stream architecture [35,41,46]. In [3], a two-stream 3D ConvNet inflated from the deep image classification network and pre-trained features is proposed and achieves state-of-the-art performance by pre-training with the Kinetics dataset, a large-scale action recognition dataset. Based on this architecture, Xie *et al.* [50] combined a top-heavy model design,

```
def randaugment_T(X, N, M1, M2):
"""Generate a set of distortions.

Args:
X: Input video (T x H x W)
N: Number of augmentation transformations to apply sequentially.
M1, M2: Magnitudes for both temporal ends.
"""

ops = np.random.choice(transforms, N)
M = np.linspace(M1, M2, T)
return [[op(X, M[t]) for t in range(T)] for op in ops]
```

Fig. 2. Pseudo-code for RandAugment-T based on Numpy in Python. Template is borrowed from [10]

temporally separable convolution, and spatiotemporal feature-gating blocks to make low-cost and meaningful features. Recently, SlowFast [12] networks that consist of a slow path for semantic information and a fast path for rapidly changing motion information exhibit competitive performance with a different frame rate sampling strategy. In addition, RESOUND [29] proposed a method to reduce the static bias of the dataset, and an Octave convolution [6] is proposed to reduce spatial redundancy by dividing the frequency of features. A debiasing loss function [8] is proposed to mitigate the strong scene bias of networks and focus on the actual action information.

Since the advent of the large-scale Kinetics dataset, most action recognition studies have pre-trained the backbone on Kinetics, which guarantees basic performance. However, based on the results of the study by [16], architectures with numerous parameters are significantly overfitted when learning from scratch on relatively small datasets, such as UCF-101 [39] and HMDB-51 [26]. This indicates that training without a pre-trained backbone is a challenging issue. Compared to existing studies that have been focused on novel dataset and architectures, we focus on regularization techniques, such as data augmentation, to prevent overfitting via learning invariance and robustness in terms of spatiality and temporality.

3   Methods

3.1   Data-Level Temporal Data Augmentations

First, we extend the existing RandAugment [10] method for video recognition. RandAugment has two hyper-parameters for optimization. One is the number of augmentation operations to apply, N, and the other is the magnitude of the operation, M. A grid search of these two parameters in a given dataset produces state-of-the-art performance in image recognition.

For video recognition, RandAugment is directly applicable to every frame of a video; however, this limits temporal perturbation modeling. To cover temporally varying transformations, we propose RandAugment-T, which linearly

(a) Temporally varying geometric augmentations (Top: vertical-down translation, Bottom: clockwise rotation)

(b) Temporally varying photometric augmentations (Top: increasing brightness, Bottom: decreasing contrast)

Fig. 3. Example of temporally varying data augmentation operations for RandAugment-T.

interpolates between two magnitudes from the first frame to the last frame in a video clip. The pseudo-code for RandAugment-T is described in Fig. 2. It receives three hyper-parameters: N, M1, and M2, where N is the number of operations, which is the same as RandAugment, and M1 and M2 indicate the magnitudes for both temporal ends, which can be any combination of levels. The set of augmentation operations (`transforms` in Fig. 2) is identical to RandAugment. However, `rotate`, `shear-x`, `shear-y`, `translate-x`, and `translate-y` can model temporally varying geometric transformation, such as camera or object movements (Fig. 3(a)), and `solarize`, `color`, `posterize`, `contrast`, `brightness`, and `sharpness` can model photometric transformation, such as brightness or contrast changes due to the auto-shot mode in a camera (Fig. 3(b)). The remaining operations (`identity`, `autocontrast`, and `equalize`) have no magnitudes that are applied evenly across frames.

3.2 Data-Level Temporal Deleting, Blending, and Cut-and-pasting

Regularization techniques, which have been proposed for image recognition, such as CutOut [11], MixUp [55], and CutMix [53], can be applied identically across

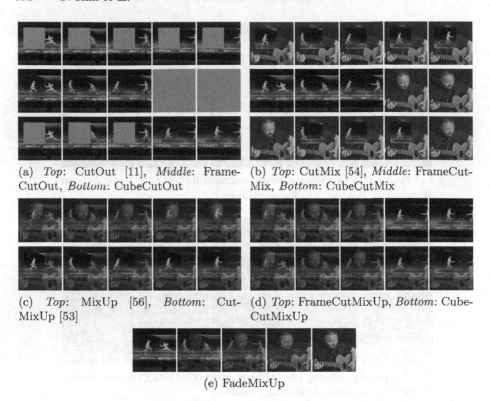

(a) *Top*: CutOut [11], *Middle*: Frame-CutOut, *Bottom*: CubeCutOut

(b) *Top*: CutMix [54], *Middle*: FrameCutMix, *Bottom*: CubeCutMix

(c) *Top*: MixUp [56], *Bottom*: Cut-MixUp [53]

(d) *Top*: FrameCutMixUp, *Bottom*: CubeCutMixUp

(e) FadeMixUp

Fig. 4. Visual comparison of data-level deleting, blending, and cut-and-pasting for videos. Desired ground-truth labels are calculated by the ratio of each class: *Fencing* and *PlayingGuitar*.

frames in a video. CutMixUp is a combination of MixUp and CutMix, which is proposed in [52], can also be used for relaxing the unnatural boundary changes.

In this section, we propose temporal extensions of the above algorithms. FrameCutOut and CubeCutOut are the temporal and spatiotemporal extensions of CutOut (Fig. 4 (a)), respectively. CutOut encourages the network to better use the full context of the images, rather than relying on a small portion of specific spatial regions. Similarly, FrameCutOut encourages the network to better use the full temporal context and the full spatiotemporal context by CubeCutOut.

FrameCutMix and CubeCutMix are extensions of CutMix [53] (Fig. 4 (b)). CutMix is designed for the learning of spatially localizable features. Cut-and-paste mixing between two images encourages the network to learn where to recognize features. Similarly, FrameCutMix and CubeCutMix are designed for the learning of temporally and spatiotemporally localizable features in a video. Like CutMix, the mixing ratio λ is sampled from the beta distribution $Beta(\alpha, \alpha)$, where α is a hyper-parameter, and the locations for random frames or random spatiotemporal cubes are selected based on λ.

Like CutMixUp [52], which is the unified version of MixUp [55] and CutMix [53], FrameCutMixUp and CubeCutMixUp can be designed similarly (Fig. 4 (c) and (d)) to relax extreme boundary changes between two samples. For these blend+cut-and-paste algorithms, MixUp is applied between two data samples by the mixing ratio λ_1, and the other hyper-parameter λ_2 is sampled from $Beta(2,2)$. Based on λ_2, the region mask $\mathbf{M}$ is selected randomly similar to CutMix to cut-and-paste the MixUp-ed sample and one of the two original samples. The final mixed data and desired ground-truth labels are formulated as follows:

$$\tilde{x} = \begin{cases} (\lambda_1 x_A + (1-\lambda_1)x_B) \odot \mathbf{M} + x_A \odot (1 - \mathbf{M}) & \text{if } \lambda_1 < 0.5 \\ (\lambda_1 x_A + (1-\lambda_1)x_B) \odot \mathbf{M} + x_B \odot (1 - \mathbf{M}) & \text{if } \lambda_1 \geq 0.5 \end{cases}$$

$$\tilde{y} = \begin{cases} (\lambda_1 \lambda_2 + (1-\lambda_1))y_A + (1-\lambda_1)\lambda_2 y_B & \text{if } \lambda_1 < 0.5 \\ \lambda_1 \lambda_2 y_A + (1-\lambda_1 \lambda_2)y_B & \text{if } \lambda_1 \geq 0.5 \end{cases}$$

(1)

where $\tilde{x}$, $\tilde{y}$, and $\odot$ indicate the mixed data, modified label, and element-wise multiplication, respectively.

Finally, we propose another extension of MixUp, called FadeMixUp, inspired by the fade-in, fade-out, and dissolve overlap effects in videos. For FadeMixUp, in MixUp, the mixing ratio is smoothly changing along with temporal frames (Fig. 4 (e)). In FadeMixUp, a list of the mixing ratios $\tilde{\lambda}_t$ of a frame t is calculated by linear interpolation between $\lambda - \gamma$ and $\lambda + \gamma$, where λ is the mixing ratio of MixUp, and the γ is sampled from $Uniform(0, min(\lambda, 1-\lambda))$. Because the adjustments in the mixing ratio at both ends are symmetric, the label is the same as MixUp.

$$\tilde{x}_t = \tilde{\lambda}_t X_{A_t} + (1 - \tilde{\lambda}_t)X_{B_t}$$
$$\tilde{y} = \lambda y_A + (1 - \lambda)y_B,$$

(2)

FadeMixUp can be modeled for temporal variations and can learn temporally localizable feature without sharp boundary changes, like other cut-and-pasting algorithms. Because many videos include these overlapping effects at the scene change, FadeMixUp can be applied naturally.

A summary of deleting, blending, and cut-and-pasting data augmentation algorithms is described in Table 1. In the table, a checkmark indicates the elements (pixels) that can be changed along the spatial or temporal axis via augmentation methods. Compared to the existing algorithms [11,52,53,55], our proposed methods are extended temporally and spatiotemporally.

Table 1. Comparison between deleting, blending, and cut-and-pasting frameworks.

Type	Delete			Cut-and-paste			Blend		Blend + Cut-and-paste		
Name	CutOut [11]	Frame CutOut	Cube CutOut	CutMix [53]	Frame CutMix	Cube CutMix	MixUp [55]	Fade MixUp	CutMixUp [52]	Frame CutMixUp	Cube CutMixUp
Axis Spatial	✓		✓	✓		✓			✓		✓
Temporal		✓	✓		✓	✓		✓		✓	✓

4 Experiments

4.1 Experimental Settings

For video action recognition, we train and evaluate the proposed method on the UCF-101 [39] and HMDB-51 [26] datasets. The UCF-101 dataset originally consists of 13,320 videos with 101 classes. The dataset consists of three training/testing splits, but we used the modified split provided by the 1st VIPriors action recognition challenge that consists of 4,795 training videos and 4,742 validation videos. The HMDB-51 dataset consists of 6,766 videos with 51 classes. We use the original three training/testing splits for training and evaluation.

Our experiments are trained and evaluated on a single GTX 1080-ti GPU and are implemented using the PyTorch framework. We use SlowFast-50 [12] as the backbone network with 64 temporal frames because it is more lightweight and faster than other networks such as C3D [42], I3D [3], and S3D [50], without any pre-training and optical-flow. For the baseline, basic data augmentation, such as random crop with a size of 160, random scale jittering between [160, 200] for the short side of a video, and random horizontal flip, are applied. For optimization, the batch size is set to 16, the learning rate is set to 1e-4, and a weight decay of 1e-5 is used. Moreover, we incorporate the learning rate warm-up [15] and cosine learning rate scheduling [32] with the Adam optimizer [24]. We train all models for 150 epochs. For evaluation, we sample 10 clips uniformly along the temporal axis and average softmax predictions. For the challenge, following [12], we sample 30 clips.

4.2 Data-Level Temporal Data Augmentations

Table 2 presents the recognition results on the UCF-101 validation set for the VIPriors challenge. For all result tables, **boldface** indicates the best results, and an underline indicates the second best. RandAugment-spatial indicates an original implementation without temporal variations. In the temporal version, M1 of Fig. 2 is sampled from $Uniform(0.1, M2)$, and M2 is set to M of the spatial RandAugment. For temporal+, M1 and M2 are set to M$-\delta$ and M$+\delta$, respectively, where δ is sampled from $Uniform(0, 0.5 \times M)$. For Mix in Table 2, it randomly chooses the spatial or temporal+ variations. The results reveal that solely applying RandAugment drastically improves recognition performance. Among them, temporally expanded RandAugment-T (temporal+) exhibits the best performance. For all RandAugment results, to produce the best accuracy, a grid search of two hyper-parameters: N $\in [1, 2, 3]$ and M $\in [3, 5, 10]$, is used.

Table 2. Data augmentation results

	Range	Top-1 Acc.	Top-5 Acc.
Baseline		49.37	73.62
RandAugment	Spatial	66.87	88.04
	Temporal	67.33	88.42
	Temporal+	**69.23**	**89.20**
	Mix	68.24	89.25

Table 3. Data deleting results

	Top-1 Acc.	Top-5 Acc.
Baseline	**49.37**	**73.62**
CutOut	46.01	69.80
FrameCutOut	47.60	71.32
CubeCutOut	47.45	72.06

Table 4. Data cut-and-paste results

	Top-1 Acc.	Top-5 Acc.
Baseline	49.37	73.62
CutMix($\alpha = 2$)	50.81	75.62
FrameCutMix($\alpha = 2$)	51.29	74.99
FrameCutMix($\alpha = 5$)	**53.10**	**76.61**
CubeCutMix($\alpha = 2$)	51.86	74.34
CubeCutMix($\alpha = 5$)	51.81	75.16

Table 5. Data blending results

	Top-1 Acc.	Top-5 Acc.
Baseline	49.37	73.62
MixUp	59.60	82.56
FadeMixUp	59.22	82.24
CutMixUp	59.35	81.99
FrameCutMixUp	**60.67**	**83.47**
CubeCutMixUp	59.85	82.20

4.3 Data-Level Temporal Deleting, Cut-and-pasting, and Blending

The results of deleting data (CutOut, FrameCutOut, and CubeCutOut) are described in Table 3. For CutOut, an 80×80 spatial patch is randomly deleted, and for FrameCutOut, 16 frames are randomly deleted. For CubeCutOut, an $80 \times 80 \times 16$ cube is randomly deleted. The results reveal that deleting patches, frames, or spatiotemporal cubes reduces recognition performance in a limited number of training datasets. Among them, CutOut exhibits the worst performance.

For data cut-and-pasting, like that of CutMix [53] and its extensions, the results are described in Table 4. We apply the mixing probability of 0.5 for all methods and employ different hyper-parameters α. Because the object size in the action recognition dataset is smaller than that in ImageNet [25], the mixing ratio should be sampled in a region close to 0.5 by sampling the large α in the beta distribution. The results demonstrate that the temporal and spatiotemporal extensions outperform the spatial-only mixing strategy. Because the probability of object occlusion during temporal mixing is lower than during spatial mixing, the performance of FrameCutMix is the most improved.

Finally, for data blending, compared to MixUp [2] and CutMixUp [52], the temporal and spatiotemporal extensions show slightly superior performance, which is described in Table 5. Compared to deleting and cut-and-pasting augmentations, blending presents the best performances. Because the number of training data is limited, a linear convex combination of samples easily and effectively augments the sample space.

4.4   Results on HMDB-51 Dataset

To determine the generalization to other datasets, we train and evaluate using the HMDB-51 dataset with its original splits. Generally, the recognition performance in HMDB-51 is inferior to the performance of UCF-101 due to its limited number of training samples. We use the same model and hyper-parameters as in UCF-101.

The results in Table 6 indicate that the temporal extensions generally outperforms spatial-only versions, and similar to UCF-101, the RandAugment and blending demonstrate the best accuracy.

Table 6. Temporal Augmentation Results on HMDB51 Dataset

	Split-1		Split-2		Split-3		Average	
	Top-1 Acc	Top-5 Acc	Top-1 Acc	Top-5 Acc	Top-1 Acc	Top-5 Acc	Top-1 Acc	Top-5 Acc
Baseline	36.60	67.25	37.19	65.75	32.88	65.82	35.56	66.27
RandAug	47.45	79.21	47.12	76.86	47.45	77.97	47.34	78.01
RandAug-T	**48.17**	**79.35**	**47.84**	**77.00**	**48.37**	**78.17**	**48.13**	**78.17**
CutOut	**34.71**	**65.49**	**32.35**	63.79	31.76	62.94	**32.94**	**64.07**
FrameCutOut	31.05	61.57	32.16	**65.36**	**31.87**	**64.18**	31.69	63.70
CubeCutOut	33.01	63.99	32.04	64.25	30.59	62.81	31.88	63.68
CutMix	33.95	64.27	33.69	66.84	31.24	63.53	32.96	64.88
FrameCutMix	34.97	**65.56**	34.84	**67.91**	33.27	63.53	34.36	65.67
CubeCutMix	**35.10**	65.10	**35.95**	65.62	**36.54**	**67.97**	**35.86**	**66.23**
MixUp	38.95	68.10	**40.72**	70.92	40.20	71.31	39.96	70.11
CutMixUp	**40.92**	**71.07**	40.16	71.55	39.28	71.48	40.12	71.37
FrameCutMixUp	40.33	70.98	40.52	70.85	39.02	70.65	39.96	70.83
CubeCutMixUp	40.72	70.65	40.70	**72.88**	**40.92**	**71.83**	**40.78**	**71.79**
FadeCutMixUp	39.80	70.39	40.46	71.70	39.61	70.00	39.96	70.70

Table 7. Model Evaluation for VIPriors Challenge

Train Data	Test Data	Augmentation	Regularization	Others	Top-1 Acc	Top-5 Acc
Train	Val				49.37	73.62
Train	Val		FrameCutMixUp		60.67	83.47
Train	Val	RandAug			66.87	88.04
Train	Val	RandAug-T			69.23	89.20
Train	Val	RandAug-T	FadeMixUp		68.73	89.27
Train	Val	RandAug-T	FrameCutMixUp		**69.70**	**89.84**
Train+Val	Test				68.99	-
Train+Val	Test	RandAug-T			81.43	-
Train+Val	Test	RandAug-T	FadeMixUp		82.16	-
Train+Val	Test	RandAug-T	All Methods	Ensemble	**86.04**	-

Table 8. Comparison between Entries of VIPriors Challenge

Entry	Backbone	Two-stream	Ensemble	Top-1 Acc
1st place team	I3D, C3D, 3D-ResNet, R(2+1)D	✓	Across Model	**90.8**
2nd place team [4]	TCDC	✓	Within Model	88.3
3rd place team [33]	SlowFast50, TSM	✓	Across Model	87.6
Ours	SlowFast50			82.2
Ours	SlowFast50		Within Model	86.0

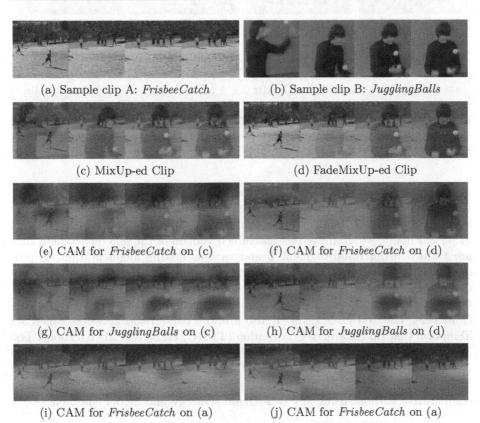

(a) Sample clip A: *FrisbeeCatch* (b) Sample clip B: *JugglingBalls*

(c) MixUp-ed Clip (d) FadeMixUp-ed Clip

(e) CAM for *FrisbeeCatch* on (c) (f) CAM for *FrisbeeCatch* on (d)

(g) CAM for *JugglingBalls* on (c) (h) CAM for *JugglingBalls* on (d)

(i) CAM for *FrisbeeCatch* on (a) (j) CAM for *FrisbeeCatch* on (a)

Fig. 5. Class activation maps. *Left*: MixUp, *Right*: FadeMixUp

4.5 1st VIPriors Action Recognition Challenge

Based on the comprehensive experimental results, we attend the 1st VIPriors action recognition challenge. In this challenge, any pre-training and external datasets are not allowed. The performance of various models is described in Table 7. For validation, applying both RandAugment-T and FrameCutMixUp perform the best. For the test set, 3,783 videos are provided without ground truths. Therefore, we report the results based on the challenge leaderboard.

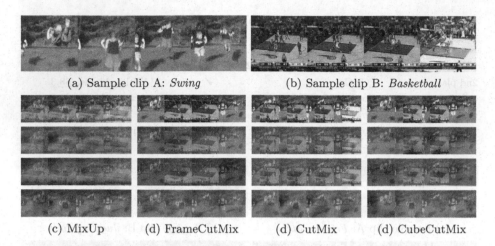

(a) Sample clip A: *Swing*   (b) Sample clip B: *Basketball*

(c) MixUp   (d) FrameCutMix   (d) CutMix   (d) CubeCutMix

Fig. 6. Class actionvation maps. For (c)-(f), from the top to the bottom row: mixed clips, CAMs for *Swing*, CAMs for *Basketball*, and CAMs for *Swing* on pure clip (a), respectively.

A combination of training and validation datasets including 9,537 videos are used to train the final challenge entries. According to the baseline accuracy of 68.99%, adapting RandAugment-T improves the performance by only up to 81.43%. Finally, we submitted an ensembled version of the different models that are trained using RandAugment-T and various mixing augmentation, to produce 86.04% top-1 accuracy. The results including other challenge entries are described in Table 8. The 1st place team proposes two-stream multi-scale spatiotemporal fusion strategy based on hand-craft optical flow and various 3D-ConvNets. The 2nd place team [4] also propose two-stream networks called 3D Temporal Central Difference Convolution (TCDC) based on C3D backbone. The 3rd place team [33] combines SlowFast network and Temporal Shift Module (TSM) [31] with two-stream networks. Compared to these methods, even if our final challenge results are inferior to them, our framework is much simple and comparative without using any two-stream strategy and model ensemble.

4.6   Discussions

Why are the Improvements Not Large? Although temporal extensions generally outperform spatial-only versions in data augmentation algorithms, performance improvements might be not large enough. The possible reasons for this are three-fold. The first reason is the lack of sufficient training data. The second is the lack of temporal perturbation, and the third is that datasets used for experiments consist of trimmed videos. Both UCF-101 and HMDB-51 datasets have little temporal perturbations. Therefore, applying spatial augmentation is sufficient to learn the context. Furthermore, both datasets are trimmed to have few temporal occlusions; therefore, no room is left to learn the ability to localize temporally. Compared to the image dataset, because the action region is relatively small, removing the spatial region can hurt the basic recognition performance for deleting and cut-and-pasting if the volume of training data is not adequate. In contrast, for blending, although it is an unnatural image, as said in [53], the blending can the exploit full region of frames. Therefore, it produces reasonable performance improvements.

Spatiotemporal Class Activation Map Visualization. We visualize the learned features using the class activation map [58] in Fig. 5. In the SlowFast network, we use the features of the last convolutional layer in SlowPath. Figure 5 (a) and (b) present example clips. Figure 5 (c) and (d) are the visualizations of the clips using MixUp-ed and FadeMixUp-ed, respectively. In Fig. 5 (f) and (h) compared to Fig. 5 (e) and (g), the features of FadeMixUp are more localized temporally than those of MixUp. In Fig. 5 (j) compared to Fig. 5 (i), the activations of FadeMixUp are spatiotemporally localized better than those of MixUp in pure Clip A.

Figure 6 compares the spatiotemporal localization abilities of MixUp, Cut-Mix, FrameCutMix, and CubeCutMix. Compared to MixUp, as stated in their paper [53], CutMix can spatially localize a basketball court or a person on a swing. However, compared to CubeCutMix, the activations of CutMix are not well localized temporally. FrameCutMix also cannot localize features like MixUp, but it can separate the weights of activation separately on the temporal axis.

5   Conclusion

In this paper, we proposed several extensions of data-level augmentation and data-level deleting, blending, and cut-and-pasting augmentation algorithms from the spatial (image) domain into the temporal and spatiotemporal (video) domain. Although applying spatial data augmentation increases the recognition performance in a limited amount of training data, extending temporal and spatiotemporal data augmentation boosts performance. Moreover, our models that are trained on temporal augmentation can achieve temporal and spatiotemporal localization ability that cannot be achieved by the model trained only on spatial augmentation. Our next step is an extension to a large-scale dataset, such as Kinetics [3], or untrimmed videos.

Acknowledgments. This research was supported by R&D program for Advanced Integrated-intelligence for Identification (AIID) through the National Research Foundation of KOREA (NRF) funded by Ministry of Science and ICT (NRF-2018M3E3A1057289).

References

1. Berthelot, D., et al.: Remixmatch: semi-supervised learning with distribution matching and augmentation anchoring. In: International Conference on Learning Representations (2019)

2. Berthelot, D., Carlini, N., Goodfellow, I., Papernot, N., Oliver, A., Raffel, C.A.: Mixmatch: a holistic approach to semi-supervised learning. In: Advances in Neural Information Processing Systems, pp. 5049–5059 (2019)

3. Carreira, J., Zisserman, A.: Quo vadis, action recognition? a new model and the kinetics dataset. In: Proceedings of the IEEE Conference on Computer Vision and Pattern Recognition, pp. 6299–6308 (2017)

4. Chen, H., Yu, Z., Liu, X., Peng, W., Lee, Y., Zhao, G.: 2nd place scheme on action recognition track of eccv 2020 vipriors challenges: an efficient optical flow stream guided framework. arXiv preprint arXiv:2008.03996 (2020)

5. Chen, T., Kornblith, S., Norouzi, M., Hinton, G.: A simple framework for contrastive learning of visual representations. arXiv preprint arXiv:2002.05709 (2020)

6. Chen, Y., et al.: Drop an octave: reducing spatial redundancy in convolutional neural networks with octave convolution. In: Proceedings of the IEEE International Conference on Computer Vision, pp. 3435–3444 (2019)

7. Chen, Y., Rohrbach, M., Yan, Z., Shuicheng, Y., Feng, J., Kalantidis, Y.: Graph-based global reasoning networks. In: Proceedings of the IEEE Conference on Computer Vision and Pattern Recognition, pp. 433–442 (2019)

8. Choi, J., Gao, C., Messou, J.C., Huang, J.B.: Why can't i dance in the mall? learning to mitigate scene bias in action recognition. In: Advances in Neural Information Processing Systems, pp. 853–865 (2019)

9. Cubuk, E.D., Zoph, B., Mane, D., Vasudevan, V., Le, Q.V.: Autoaugment: learning augmentation strategies from data. In: Proceedings of the IEEE conference on computer vision and pattern recognition, pp. 113–123 (2019)

10. Cubuk, E.D., Zoph, B., Shlens, J., Le, Q.V.: Randaugment: practical automated data augmentation with a reduced search space. In: Proceedings of the IEEE/CVF Conference on Computer Vision and Pattern Recognition Workshops, pp. 702–703 (2020)

11. DeVries, T., Taylor, G.W.: Improved regularization of convolutional neural networks with cutout. arXiv preprint arXiv:1708.04552 (2017)

12. Feichtenhofer, C., Fan, H., Malik, J., He, K.: Slowfast networks for video recognition. In: Proceedings of the IEEE International Conference on Computer Vision, pp. 6202–6211 (2019)

13. Gastaldi, X.: Shake-shake regularization. arXiv preprint arXiv:1705.07485 (2017)

14. Ghiasi, G., Lin, T.Y., Le, Q.V.: Dropblock: a regularization method for convolutional networks. In: Advances in Neural Information Processing Systems, pp. 10727–10737 (2018)

15. Goyal, P., et al.: Accurate, large minibatch sgd: training imagenet in 1 hour. arXiv preprint arXiv:1706.02677 (2017)

16. Hara, K., Kataoka, H., Satoh, Y.: Can spatiotemporal 3D cnns retrace the history of 2D cnns and imagenet? In: Proceedings of the IEEE Conference on Computer Vision and Pattern Recognition, pp. 6546–6555 (2018)

17. He, K., Fan, H., Wu, Y., Xie, S., Girshick, R.: Momentum contrast for unsupervised visual representation learning. In: Proceedings of the IEEE/CVF Conference on Computer Vision and Pattern Recognition, pp. 9729–9738 (2020)

18. Hendrycks, D., Dietterich, T.: Benchmarking neural network robustness to common corruptions and perturbations. In: Proceedings of the International Conference on Learning Representations (2019)

19. Hendrycks, D., Mu, N., Cubuk, E.D., Zoph, B., Gilmer, J., Lakshminarayanan, B.: Augmix: a simple data processing method to improve robustness and uncertainty. arXiv preprint arXiv:1912.02781 (2019)

20. Huang, G., Sun, Y., Liu, Z., Sedra, D., Weinberger, K.Q.: Deep networks with stochastic depth. In: Leibe, B., Matas, J., Sebe, N., Welling, M. (eds.) ECCV 2016. LNCS, vol. 9908, pp. 646–661. Springer, Cham (2016). https://doi.org/10.1007/978-3-319-46493-0_39
21. Ji, J., Cao, K., Niebles, J.C.: Learning temporal action proposals with fewer labels. In: Proceedings of the IEEE International Conference on Computer Vision, pp. 7073–7082 (2019)
22. Karras, T., Aittala, M., Hellsten, J., Laine, S., Lehtinen, J., Aila, T.: Training generative adversarial networks with limited data. arXiv preprint arXiv:2006.06676 (2020)
23. Kim, J., Cha, S., Wee, D., Bae, S., Kim, J.: Regularization on spatio-temporally smoothed feature for action recognition. In: Proceedings of the IEEE/CVF Conference on Computer Vision and Pattern Recognition, pp. 12103–12112 (2020)
24. Kingma, D.P., Ba, J.: Adam: a method for stochastic optimization. arXiv preprint arXiv:1412.6980 (2014)
25. Krizhevsky, A., Sutskever, I., Hinton, G.E.: Imagenet classification with deep convolutional neural networks. In: Advances in neural information processing systems, pp. 1097–1105 (2012)
26. Kuehne, H., Jhuang, H., Garrote, E., Poggio, T., Serre, T.: Hmdb: a large video database for human motion recognition. In: 2011 International Conference on Computer Vision, pp. 2556–2563. IEEE (2011)
27. Lee, J.H., Zaigham Zaheer, M., Astrid, M., Lee, S.I.: Smoothmix: a simple yet effective data augmentation to train robust classifiers. In: Proceedings of the IEEE/CVF Conference on Computer Vision and Pattern Recognition Workshops, pp. 756–757 (2020)
28. Li, H., Zhang, X., Xiong, H., Tian, Q.: Attribute mix: semantic data augmentation for fine grained recognition. arXiv preprint arXiv:2004.02684 (2020)
29. Li, Y., Li, Y., Vasconcelos, N.: Resound: towards action recognition without representation bias. In: Proceedings of the European Conference on Computer Vision (ECCV), pp. 513–528 (2018)
30. Lim, S., Kim, I., Kim, T., Kim, C., Kim, S.: Fast autoaugment. In: Advances in Neural Information Processing Systems, pp. 6665–6675 (2019)
31. Lin, J., Gan, C., Han, S.: Tsm: temporal shift module for efficient video understanding. In: Proceedings of the IEEE International Conference on Computer Vision, pp. 7083–7093 (2019)
32. Loshchilov, I., Hutter, F.: Sgdr: stochastic gradient descent with warm restarts. arXiv preprint arXiv:1608.03983 (2016)
33. Luo, Z., Xu, D., Zhang, Z.: Challenge report: vipriors action recognition challenge. arXiv preprint arXiv:2007.08180 (2020)
34. Misra, I., Maaten, L.V.D.: Self-supervised learning of pretext-invariant representations. In: Proceedings of the IEEE/CVF Conference on Computer Vision and Pattern Recognition, pp. 6707–6717 (2020)
35. Ryoo, M.S., Piergiovanni, A., Tan, M., Angelova, A.: Assemblenet: searching for multi-stream neural connectivity in video architectures. arXiv preprint arXiv:1905.13209 (2019)
36. Simonyan, K., Zisserman, A.: Very deep convolutional networks for large-scale image recognition. In: International Conference on Learning Representations (2015)
37. Singh, K.K., Lee, Y.J.: Hide-and-seek: forcing a network to be meticulous for weakly-supervised object and action localization. In: 2017 IEEE International Conference on Computer Vision (ICCV), pp. 3544–3553. IEEE (2017)

38. Sohn, K., et al.: Fixmatch: simplifying semi-supervised learning with consistency and confidence. arXiv preprint arXiv:2001.07685 (2020)
39. Soomro, K., Zamir, A.R., Shah, M.: Ucf101: a dataset of 101 human actions classes from videos in the wild. arXiv preprint arXiv:1212.0402 (2012)
40. Srivastava, N., Hinton, G., Krizhevsky, A., Sutskever, I., Salakhutdinov, R.: Dropout: a simple way to prevent neural networks from overfitting. J. Mach. Learn. Res. **15**(1), 1929–1958 (2014)
41. Stroud, J., Ross, D., Sun, C., Deng, J., Sukthankar, R.: D3d: distilled 3D networks for video action recognition. In: The IEEE Winter Conference on Applications of Computer Vision, pp. 625–634 (2020)
42. Tran, D., Bourdev, L., Fergus, R., Torresani, L., Paluri, M.: Learning spatiotemporal features with 3D convolutional networks. In: Proceedings of the IEEE International Conference on Computer Vision, pp. 4489–4497 (2015)
43. Tran, D., Wang, H., Torresani, L., Ray, J., LeCun, Y., Paluri, M.: A closer look at spatiotemporal convolutions for action recognition. In: Proceedings of the IEEE Conference on Computer Vision and Pattern Recognition, pp. 6450–6459 (2018)
44. Verma, V., et al.: Manifold mixup: better representations by interpolating hidden states. In: International Conference on Machine Learning, pp. 6438–6447 (2019)
45. Walawalkar, D., Shen, Z., Liu, Z., Savvides, M.: Attentive cutmix: an enhanced data augmentation approach for deep learning based image classification. In: ICASSP 2020–2020 IEEE International Conference on Acoustics, Speech and Signal Processing (ICASSP), pp. 3642–3646. IEEE (2020)
46. Wang, L., et al.: Temporal segment networks: towards good practices for deep action recognition. In: Leibe, B., Matas, J., Sebe, N., Welling, M. (eds.) ECCV 2016. LNCS, vol. 9912, pp. 20–36. Springer, Cham (2016). https://doi.org/10.1007/978-3-319-46484-8_2
47. Wang, X., Girshick, R., Gupta, A., He, K.: Non-local neural networks. In: Proceedings of the IEEE Conference on Computer Vision and Pattern Recognition, pp. 7794–7803 (2018)
48. Xie, Q., Dai, Z., Hovy, E., Luong, M.T., Le, Q.V.: Unsupervised data augmentation for consistency training. arXiv preprint arXiv:1904.12848 (2019)
49. Xie, Q., Luong, M.T., Hovy, E., Le, Q.V.: Self-training with noisy student improves imagenet classification. In: Proceedings of the IEEE/CVF Conference on Computer Vision and Pattern Recognition, pp. 10687–10698 (2020)
50. Xie, S., Sun, C., Huang, J., Tu, Z., Murphy, K.: Rethinking spatiotemporal feature learning for video understanding. arXiv preprint arXiv:1712.04851 **1**(2), p. 5 (2017)
51. Yamada, Y., Iwamura, M., Akiba, T., Kise, K.: Shakedrop regularization for deep residual learning. IEEE Access **7**, 186126–186136 (2019)
52. Yoo, J., Ahn, N., Sohn, K.A.: Rethinking data augmentation for image superresolution: a comprehensive analysis and a new strategy. In: Proceedings of the IEEE/CVF Conference on Computer Vision and Pattern Recognition, pp. 8375–8384 (2020)
53. Yun, S., Han, D., Oh, S.J., Chun, S., Choe, J., Yoo, Y.: Cutmix: regularization strategy to train strong classifiers with localizable features. In: Proceedings of the IEEE International Conference on Computer Vision, pp. 6023–6032 (2019)
54. Zhang, H., Zhang, Z., Odena, A., Lee, H.: Consistency regularization for generative adversarial networks. In: International Conference on Learning Representations (2019)
55. Zhang, H., Cisse, M., Dauphin, Y.N., Lopez-Paz, D.: mixup: beyond empirical risk minimization. arXiv preprint arXiv:1710.09412 (2017)

56. Zhao, S., Liu, Z., Lin, J., Zhu, J.Y., Han, S.: Differentiable augmentation for data-efficient gan training. arXiv preprint arXiv:2006.10738 (2020)
57. Zhao, Z., Singh, S., Lee, H., Zhang, Z., Odena, A., Zhang, H.: Improved consistency regularization for gans. arXiv preprint arXiv:2002.04724 (2020)
58. Zhou, B., Khosla, A., Lapedriza, A., Oliva, A., Torralba, A.: Learning deep features for discriminative localization. In: Proceedings of the IEEE Conference on Computer Vision and Pattern Recognition, pp. 2921–2929 (2016)

Unsupervised Learning of Video Representations via Dense Trajectory Clustering

Pavel Tokmakov[3(✉)], Martial Hebert[1], and Cordelia Schmid[2]

[1] Carnegie Mellon University, Pittsburgh, USA
[2] Inria, Paris, France
[3] Toyota Research Institute, Los Altos, USA
pavel.tokmakov@tri.global

Abstract. This paper addresses the task of unsupervised learning of representations for action recognition in videos. Previous works proposed to utilize future prediction, or other domain-specific objectives to train a network, but achieved only limited success. In contrast, in the relevant field of image representation learning, simpler, discrimination-based methods have recently bridged the gap to fully-supervised performance. We first propose to adapt two top performing objectives in this class - instance recognition and local aggregation, to the video domain. In particular, the latter approach iterates between clustering the videos in the feature space of a network and updating it to respect the cluster with a non-parametric classification loss. We observe promising performance, but qualitative analysis shows that the learned representations fail to capture motion patterns, grouping the videos based on appearance. To mitigate this issue, we turn to the heuristic-based IDT descriptors, that were manually designed to encode motion patterns in videos. We form the clusters in the IDT space, using these descriptors as a an unsupervised prior in the iterative local aggregation algorithm. Our experiments demonstrates that this approach outperform prior work on UCF101 and HMDB51 action recognition benchmarks. We also qualitatively analyze the learned representations and show that they successfully capture video dynamics.

Keywords: Unsupervised representation learning · Action recognition

1 Introduction

The research on self-supervised learning of image representation has recently experienced a major breakthrough. Early approaches carefully designed objective functions to capture properties that the authors believed would result in learning rich representations [6,11,29,48]. For instance, Doersch et al. [6] proposed to predict relative positions of two patches in an image, and Zhang et al. [48]

Electronic supplementary material The online version of this chapter (https://doi.org/10.1007/978-3-030-66096-3_28) contains supplementary material, which is available to authorized users.

© Springer Nature Switzerland AG 2020
A. Bartoli and A. Fusiello (Eds.): ECCV 2020 Workshops, LNCS 12536, pp. 404–421, 2020.
https://doi.org/10.1007/978-3-030-66096-3_28

trained a network to colorize images. However, they have achieved only limited success. The methods that have brought the performance of self-supervised image representations close to those learned in a fully-supervised way, rely on a different principle instead. They use the standard cross-entropy loss and either treat each image as an individual class [8,30,46], or switch between clustering images in the feature space of the network, and updating the model to classify them into clusters [1,49]. The resulting representations effectively capture discriminative image cues without having to manually separate images into categories.

Self-supervised feature learning for videos has so far mostly relied on manually designed objective functions. While some works adopted their objectives directly from the image-based methods, such as predicting video rotation [19], or relative position of space-time patches [20], others utilize video-specific cues, such as predicting feature representations of video patches in future frames [13]. Very recently, Sun et al. [35], have proposed a variant of the instance classification objective for videos.

In this work we first investigating whether the recent, classification-based objectives proposed for image representation learning can be applied to videos. We introduce a video variant of the non-parametric Instance Recognition approach of Wu et al., [46] (Video IR). It simply treats each video as its own class and trains a 3D ConvNet [14,36] to discriminate between the videos. We observe that this naive approach is already competitive with prior work in the video domain.

To further improve the results, we capitalize on the observation of Zhuang et al. [49] that embedding semantically similar instances close to each other in feature space is equally important to being able to discriminate between any two of them. We adapt their Local Aggregation approach to videos (Video LA). As shown in the top part of Fig. 1, this method first encodes a video using a 3D ConvNet, and the resulting embeddings are clustered with K-means. A non-parametric clustering loss proposed in [49] is then used to update the network and the algorithm is iterated in an Expectation-Maximization framework. This approach results in an improvement over Video IR, but the gap between the two objectives remains smaller than in the image domain.

We identify the reasons behind this phenomenon, by examining the video clusters discovered by the algorithm. Our analysis shows that they mainly capture appearance cues, such as scene category, and tend to ignore the temporal information, which is crucial for the downstream task of action recognition. For instance, as shown in the top right corner of Fig. 1, videos with similar background, but different activities are embedded closer than examples of the same action. This is not surprising, since appearance cues are both dominant in the data itself, and are better reflected in the 3D ConvNet architecture.

To mitigate this issue, we turn to the heuristic-based video representations of the past. Improved Dense Trajectories (IDT) [42] were the state-of-the-art approach for action recognition in the pre-deep learning era, and remained competitive on some datasets until very recently. The idea behind IDT is to manually encode the cues in videos that help to discriminate between human actions. To this end, individual pixels are first tracked with optical flow, and heuristics-based descriptors [4,5,41] are aggregated along the trajectories to encode both appearance and motion cues.

In this work, we propose to transfer the notion of similarity between videos encoded in IDTs to 3D ConvNets via non-parametric clustering. To this end, we first compute IDT descriptors for a collection of unlabeled videos. We then cluster these videos in the resulting features space and use the non-parametric classification objective of [49] to train a 3D ConvNet to respect the discovered clusters (bottom part of Fig. 1). The network is first trained until convergence using the fixed IDT clusters, and then finetuned in the joint IDT and 3D ConvNet space with the iterative Video LA approach. The resulting representation outperforms the baselines described above by a significant margin. We also qualitatively analyze the clusters and find that they effectively capture motion information.

Following prior work [13,19,35], we use the large-scale Kinetics [2] dataset for self-supervised pretraining, ignoring the labels. The learned representations are evaluated by finetuing on UCF101 [33] and HMDB51 [23] action recognition benchmarks. To gain a better insight into the properties of the representations, we additionally provide an in-depth qualitative and quantitative analysis of the proposed approach.

2 Related Work

In this section, we first briefly review previous work on image-based unsupervised representation learning. We then discuss various approaches to video modeling, and conclude by presenting relevant video representation learning methods.

Image representation learning from unlabeled data is a well explored topic. Due to space limitations, we will only review the most relevant approaches here. The earliest methods were built around auto-encoder architectures: one network is trained to compress an image into a vector in such a way, that another network is able to reconstruct the original image from the encoding [7,12,18,21,24]. In practice, however, the success of generative methods in discriminative representation learning has been limited.

Until very recently, manually designing self-supervised objectives has been the dominant paradigm. For example, Doersch et al. [6] and Noroozi and Favaro [29] predict relative positions of patches in an image, Zhang et al. [48] learn to colorize images, and Gidaris et al. [11] learn to recognize image rotations. While these methods have shown some performance improvements compared to random network initialization, they remain significantly below a fully-supervised baseline. The most recent methods, instead of designing specialized objective functions, propose to use the standard cross-entropy loss and either treat every image as its own class [8,30,46], or switch between clustering the examples in the feature space of the network and updating the network with a classification loss to respect the clusters [1,49]. These methods exploit the structural similarity between semantically similar images, to automatically learn a semantic image embedding. In this paper we adapt the methods of Wu et al. [46] and Zhuang et al. [49] to the video domain, but demonstrate that they do not perform as well due to the structural priors being less strong in videos. We then introduce explicit prior in the form of IDT descriptors and show this indeed improves performance.

Video modeling has traditionally been approached with heuristics-based methods. Most notably, Dense Trajectories (DT) [41] sample points in frames and track them with optical flow. Then appearance and motion descriptors are extracted along each track and encoded into a single vector. The discriminative ability of DT descriptors was later improved in [42] by suppressing camera motion with the help of a human detector, and removing trajectories that fall into background regions. The resulting representation focuses on relevant regions in videos (humans and objects in motion) and encodes both their appearance and motion patterns.

More recently, the success of end-to-end trainable CNN representation has been extended to the video domain. Simonyan et al. [32] proposed to directly train 2D CNNs for action recognition, fusing several frames at the first layer of the network. Their approach, however, had a very limited capacity for modeling temporal information. This issue was later addressed in [36] by extending the 2D convolution operation in time. Introduction of the large scale Kinetcis dataset for action recognition [2] was a major step forward for 3D CNNs. Pretrained on this dataset, they were finally able to outperform the traditional, heuristic-based representations. Several variants of 3D ConvNet architectures have been proposed since, to improve performance and efficiency [2,14,47]. In this work, we demonstrate how the IDT descriptors can be used to improve unsupervised learning of 3D ConvNet representations.

Video representation learning from unlabeled data is a less explored topic. This is largely because the community has only recently converged upon the 3D ConvNets as thr standard architecture. Early methods used recurrent networks, or 2D CNNs, and relied on future-prediction [34], as well as various manually designed objectives [9,10,25,27,28]. In particular, several works utilized temporal consistency between consecutive frames as a learning signal [25,27,28], whereas Gan et al. [10] used geometric cues, and Fernando et al. [9] proposed the odd-one-out objective function.

With 3D ConvNets, generative architectures [20,38], as well as some self-supervised objectives have been explored [19,20,43]. For example, Jing et al. [19] train a model to predict video rotation, Kim et al. [20] use relative spatio-temporal patch location prediction as an objective, and Wang et al. [43] regress motion and appearance statistics. In another line of work, future frame colorization was explored as a self-supervision signal [39]. Recently, Han et al. [13] proposed to predict feature representations of video patches in future frames. Most similarly, Sun et al. [35] use a variant of the instance discrimination loss. In this work, we demonstrate that simply adapting instance discrimination [46] and local aggregation [49] objectives from the image to the video domain already achieves competitive results, and augmenting local aggregation with IDT priors further improves the results, outperforming the state-of-the-art.

3   Method

Our goal is to learn an embedding function f_θ that maps videos $V = \{v_1, v_2, ..., v_N\}$ into compact descriptors $f_\theta(v_i) = d_i$ in such a way, that they can be discriminated based on human actions, using unlabeled videos. For instance, as shown in Fig. 1, we want the two videos of people to doing handstands to be close to each other in the embedding space, and well separated from the video of a person training a dog. Below, we first introduce the two objective functions used in our work - instance recognition [46] and local aggregation [49], and then describe our approach of using IDT [42] descriptors as unsupervised priors in non-parametric clustering.

3.1   Video Instance Recognition

This objective is based on the intuition that the best way to learn a discriminative representation is to use a discriminative loss. And, in the absence of supervised class labels, treating each instance as a distinct class of its own is a natural surrogate.

Using the standard softmax classification criterion, the probability of every video v with the feature d belonging to its own class i is expressed as:

$$P(i|d) = \frac{\exp(w_i^T d)}{\sum_{j=1}^{N} \exp(w_j^T d)}, \tag{1}$$

where w_j is the weight vector of the j'th classifier. In this case, however, every class contains only a single example, thus w_j can be directly replaced with d_j. The authors of [46] then propose the following formulation of the class probability:

$$P(i|d) = \frac{\exp(d_i^T d/\tau)}{\sum_{j=1}^{N} \exp(d_j^T d/\tau)}, \tag{2}$$

where τ is a temperature parameter that controls the concentration level of the distribution, and helps convergence [17,40]. The final learning objective is the standard negative log likelihood over the training set. Recall that training is done in batches, thus a memory bank of encodings $D = \{d_1, d_2, ..., d_N\}$ has to be maintained to compute Eq. 2.

3.2   Video Local Aggregation

While being able to separate any two instances is a key property for an image or video embedding space, another, complementary and equally desirable property is minimizing the distance between semantically similar instances. To this end, Zhuang et al. [49] proposed to use clusters of instances instead of individual examples as class surrogates. We adapt their approach to the video domain, and briefly describe it below.

Firstly, the video embedding vectors $d_1, d_2, ..., d_N$ are grouped into K clusters $G = \{G_1, G_2, .., G_K\}$ using K-means. The embedding function f_θ is then updated to respect the cluster, using the non-parametric clustering objective proposed in [49], and the two steps are iterated in an EM-framework. In particular, for every instance v_i together with its embedding d_i, two sets of neighbours are

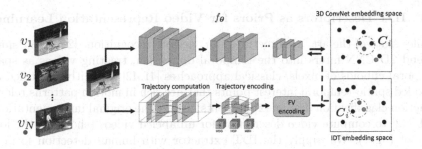

Fig. 1. Our approach for unsupervised representation learning from videos. Directly applying a non-parametric clustering objective results in a representation that groups videos based on appearance (top right corner). To mitigate this issue, we first cluster videos in the space of IDT descriptors (bottom right corner). We then apply the non-parametric clustering loss to transfer properties of this embedding to a 3D ConvNet.

identified: close neighbours C_i (shown with a dashed circle in Fig. 1) and background neighbours B_i. Intuitively, close neighbours are those examples that fall into the same cluster as v_i and background neighbors are simply those that have a small distance to d_i in the feature space (they include both close neighbors and hard negative examples). Please see [49] for more details on how C_i and B_i are constructed.

The objective is then to minimize the distance between d_i and its close neighbours (instances in the same cluster), while maximizing the distance to those background neighbors that are not in C_i (hard negatives). The authors formulate this objective in a probabilistic way as minimizing the negative log likelihood of d_i being recognized as a close neighbor, given that it is recognized as a background neighbor:

$$L(\boldsymbol{C}_i, \boldsymbol{B}_i | \boldsymbol{d}_i, \boldsymbol{\theta}) = -\log \frac{P(\boldsymbol{C}_i \cap \boldsymbol{B}_i | \boldsymbol{d}_i)}{P(\boldsymbol{B}_i | \boldsymbol{d}_i)}, \tag{3}$$

where the probability of d being a member of a set A is defined as $P(\boldsymbol{A}|\boldsymbol{d}) = \sum_{i \in \boldsymbol{A}} P(i|\boldsymbol{d})$, and the definition of $P(i|\boldsymbol{d})$ is adapted from Eq. 2. Despite the involved formulation, one can see that this objective does exactly what it is intended to do - minimizes the distance between examples inside a cluster and maximize it between those belonging to different clusters in a non-parametric way.

Intuitively, the Local Aggregation objective relies on the structural similarity between semantically similar images, together with deep image prior in CNN architectures [37], to form meaningful clusters in the embedding space. In videos, however, both structural and architectural priors are less strong. Indeed, pixels that are close to each other in the spatio-temporal volume of a video are not always strongly correlated due to the presence of object and camera and motion. On the architecture side, 3D ConvNets are also worse at capturing spatio-temoral patterns, compared to CNNs at capturing spatial patterns. To mitigate this lack of implicit priors, we propose to introduce an explicit one in the form of IDT descriptors.

3.3   IDT Descriptors as Priors for Video Representation Learning

While state-of-the-art architectures for action recognition [2,14,36] simply extend 2D CNN filters into the temporal dimension, treating videos as spatio-temporal cuboids of pixels, classical approaches [41,42] explicitly identified and encoded spatio-temporal interest points that are rich in motion patterns relevant to action classification. In our experiments, we use the original implementation of IDT [42] to compute video descriptors for unlabeled videos (shown in the lower part of Fig. 1). We supply the IDT extractor with human detection form the state-of-the-art Mask-RCNN [16] model trained on MS COCO [26] for improved camera stabilization (see [42] for details).

This method, however, produces thousands of descriptors $x \in \mathcal{X}$ per video. To encode them into a compact vector we follow prior work [42,44] and first apply PCA to reduce the dimensionality of each individual trajectory descriptor x_i. We then utilize Fisher vector coding [31], which is based on a Gaussian Mixture Model (GMM) with K components $G(w_k, \mu_k, \sigma_k)$, parameterized by mixing probability, mean, and diagonal standard deviation. The encoding for a trajectory descriptor x is then computed by stacking the derivatives of each components of the GMM with respect to mean and variance:

$$\phi_k^*(x) = \frac{p(\mu_k|x)}{\sqrt{w_k}} [\phi_k(x), \frac{\phi_k'(x)}{\sqrt{2}}], \tag{4}$$

where the first- and second-order features $\phi_k, \phi_k' \in R^D$ are defined as:

$$\phi_k(x) = \frac{(x - \mu_k)}{\sigma_k}, \phi_k'(x) = \phi_k(x)^2 - 1, \tag{5}$$

thus, the resulting Fisher vector encoding $\phi(x) = [\phi_1^*(x), \phi_2^*(x), ..., \phi_k^*(x)]$ is of dimensionality $2KD$. To obtain the video-level descriptor ψ, individual trajectory encodings are averaged $\psi = avg_{x \in \mathcal{X}}\phi(x)$, and power- [22] and l2-normalization are applied. Finally, to further reduce dimensionality, count sketching [45] is used: $p(\psi) = P\psi$, where P is the sketch projection matrix (see [45] for details).

The resulting encoding $p(\psi)$ is a 2000-dimensional vector, providing a compact representation of a video, which captures discriminative motion and appearance information. Importantly, it is completely unsupervised. Both the PCA projection and the parameters of the Gaussian mixture model are estimated using a random sample of trajectory encodings, and matrix P is selected at random as well.

To transfer the cues encoded in IDTs descriptors to a 3D ConvNet, we first cluster the videos in the $p(\psi)$ space with K-means, to obtain the clusters G. We then use G to compute the sets of neighborhoods (C_i, B_i) for each video v_i in an unlabeled collection (shown in the bottom right corner on Fig. 1), and apply the objective in Eq. 3 to train the network. This forces the learned representation to capture the motion patterns that dominate the IDT space (note that IDTs encode appearance cues as well in the form of HOG descriptors).

Finally, we construct a joint space of IDT and 3D ConvNet representations by concatenating the vectors d and $p(\psi)$ for each video. We further finetune the network in this joint space for a few epochs by concatenating the respective feature representations before clustering. This step allows the model to capitalize on appearance cues encoded by the expressive 3D ConvNet architecture. We analyze the resulting model quantitatively and qualitatively, and find that it both outperforms the state-of-the-art, and is better at capturing motion information.

4 Experiments

4.1 Datasets and Evaluation

We use the Kinetics [2] dataset for unsupervised representation learning and evaluate the learned models on UCF101 [33] and HMDB51 [23] in a fully-supervised regime. Below, we describe each dataset in more detail.

Kinetics is a large-scale, action classification dataset collected by querying videos on YouTube. We use the training set of Kinetics-400, which contains 235 000 videos, for most of the experiments in the paper, but additionally report results using fewer as well as more videos in Sect. 4.6. Note that we do not use any annotations provided in Kinetics.

UCF101 is a classic dataset for human action recognition, which consists of 13,320 videos, covering 101 action classes. It is much smaller than Kinetics, and 3D ConvNets fail to outperform heuristic-based methods on it without fully-supervised pretraining on larger datasets. Following prior work [13,19], we use UCF101 to evaluate the quality of representations learned on Kinetics in an unsupervised way via transfer learning. In addition to using the full training set of UCF101, we report few-shot learning results to gain more insight into the learned representations in the supplementary material. We use the first split of the dataset for ablation analysis, and report results averaged over all splits when comparing to prior work.

HMDB51 is another benchmark for action recognition, which consists of 6,770 videos, collected from movies, and split into 51 categories. Due to the small size of the training set, it, poses an even larger challenge for learning-based methods. As with UCF101, we report ablation results on the first split, and use the results averaged over all splits for comparison to prior work.

Following standard protocol, we report classification accuracy as the main evaluation criteria on UCF101 and HMDB51. However, this makes direct comparison between different approaches difficult, due to the differences in network architectures. Thus, whenever possible, we additionally report the fraction of the fully-supervised performance for the same architecture.

4.2   Implementation Details

Self-supervised Objectives. We study three self-supervised objective functions: Video Instance Recognition (Video IR), Video Local Aggregation (Video LA) and Video Local Aggregation with IDT prior. For Video IR we follow the setting of [46] and set τ in Eq. 2 to 0.07. We use 4096 negative samples for approximating the denominator of Eq. 2.

Table 1. Comparison between variants of unsupervised learning objective using classification accuracy and fraction of fully supervised performance on the first split of UCF101 and HMDB51. All models use a 3D ResNet18 backbone, and take 16 frames with resolution of 112×112 as input. Video LA with IDT prior consistently outperforms other objectives, with improvements on HMDB51 being especially significant.

Method	UCF101		HMDB51	
	Accuracy	% sup.	Accuracy	% sup.
Scratch [14]	42.4	50.2	17.1	30.3
Video IR	70.0	82.9	39.9	70.7
Video LA	71.4	84.6	41.7	73.9
Video LA + IDT prior	**72.8**	**86.3**	**44.0**	**78.0**
Supervised [14]	84.4	100	56.4	100

In addition to the parameters described above, Local Aggregation requires choosing the number of clusters K, as well as the number of runs of K-means that are combined for robustness. The authors of [49] do not provide clear guidelines on selecting these hyperparameters, so we choose to take the values used in their ImageNet experiments and decrease them proportionally to the size of Kinetics. As a result, we set K to 6000 and the number of clusterings to 3. We validate the importance of this choice and provide the implementation details for the IDT computation in the supplementary material.

Network Architecture and Optimization. Following most of the prior work, we use a 3D ResNet18 architecture [14] in all the experiments, but also report results with deeper variants in the supplementary material. The embedding dimension for self-supervised objectives is set to 128, as in [49]. We use SGD with momentum to train the networks, and apply multi-scale, random spatio-temporal cropping for data augmentation, with exactly the same setting as in [14]. We also perform the standard mean subtraction. All the models are trained on 16 frames clips of spatial resolution of 112×112, unless stated otherwise.

During self-supervised learning we follow the setting of [49] and set the learning rate to 0.03, and momentum to 0.9, with batch size of 256. All the models are trained for 200 epoch, and the learning rate is dropped by a factor 0.1 at epochs 160 and 190. As in [49], we initialize the LA models with 40 epoch of IR pretraining.

4.3   Analysis of Self-supervised Objectives

We begin by comparing different variants of self-supervised objectives described in Sect. 3. They are used to learn a representation on Kinetics-400 in a self-supervised way, and the resulting models are transferred to UCF101 and HMDB51. We additionally evaluate two baselines - Supervised, which is pre-trained on Kinetics using ground-truth labels, and Scratch, which is initialized with random weights. The results are reported in Table 1.

Firstly, we observe that supervised pretraining is indeed crucial for achieving top performance on both datasets, with the variant trained from scratch reaching only 50.2% and 30.3% of the accuracy of the fully supervised model on UCF101 and HMDB51 respectively. The gap is especially large on HMDB51, due to the small size of the dataset. Using the video variant of the Instance Recognition objective (Video IR in the table), however, results in a 27.6% accuracy improvement on UCF101 and 22.8% HMDB51, reaching 82.9% and 70.7% of the supervised accuracy respectively. Notice that this simple method already outperforms some of the approaches proposed in prior works [13,19,20].

Next, we can see that the Local Aggregation objective (Video LA in the table) further improves the results, reaching 84.6% and 73.9% of the fully-supervised performance on UCF101 and HMDB51 respectively. This shows that despite the higher-dimensionality of the video data, this method is still able to discover meaningful clusters in an unsupervised way. However, the gap to the IR objective is smaller than in the image domain [49].

Finally, our full method, which uses IDT descriptors as an unsupervised prior when clustering the videos (Video LA + IDT prior in the table), is indeed able to further boost the performance, reaching 86.3% and 78.0% of fully supervised performance on the two datasets. The improvement over Video LA is especially significant on HMDB51. We explain this by the fact that categories in UCF101 are largely explainable by appearance, thus the benefits of better modeling the temporal information are limited on this dataset. In contrast, on HMDB51 capturing scene dynamics is crucial for accurate classification.

4.4   Qualitative Analysis of the Representations

To gain further insight into the effect of our IDT prior on representation learning, we now visualize some of the clusters discovered by the vanilla LA, and the variant with the prior in Figs. 2 and 3 respectively. Firstly, we observe that, in the absence of external constraints LA defaults to using appearance, and primarily scene information to cluster the videos. For instance, the first cluster (top left corner) corresponds to swimming pools, the one on the top right seems to focus on grass, and the two clusters in the bottom row capture vehicles and backyards, irrespective of the actual scene dynamics. This is not surprising, since appearance cues are both more dominant in the data itself, and are better reflected by the 3D ConvNet architecture.

Fig. 2. Visualization of the clusters discovered by the Video LA objective without IDT prior. This variant groups videos in the space of a 3D ConvNet. As a results, the clusters are primarily defined by the appearance, grouping swimming pools, grass fields, vehicles, and backyards. The activity happening in the videos does not seem to play a significant role.

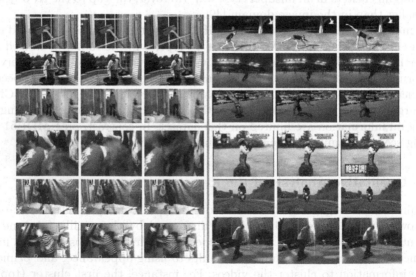

Fig. 3. Visualization of the clusters discovered by variant of Video LA objective that uses IDT prior. In contrast to the examples above, the videos are mainly grouped by motion properties, such as forward-backward hand motion, person rotation, fast person motion, and 'riding' action.

Table 2. Evaluation of the effect of clip length on various objectives on the first split of UCF101 and HMDB51 using classification accuracy. All models use a 3D ResNet18 backbone, and take frames with resolution of 112×112 as input. Both self-supervised and fully-supervised variants benefit from longer sequences, but the model trained from scratch is not able to capitalize on more information.

Method	UCF101			HMDB51		
	16-fr	32-fr	64-fr	16-fr	32-fr	64-fr
Scratch	42.4	44.9	45.3	17.1	18.0	17.4
Video LA	71.4	75.0	79.4	41.7	43.1	48.9
Video LA + IDT prior	**72.8**	**76.3**	**81.5**	**44.0**	**44.7**	**49.6**
Supervised	84.4	87.0	91.2	56.4	63.1	67.5

In contrast, the model learned with IDT prior is better at capturing motion cues. For example, the cluster in the top left corner of Fig. 3 is characterized by forward-backward hand motion, such as observed during cleaning or barbecuing. The cluster in the top-right captures humans spinning or rotating. The bottom left cluster mostly contains videos with very fast actor motion, and the one in the bottom right closely corresponds to the action 'riding'.

Importantly, neither set of clusters is perfectly aligned with the definition of actions in popular computer vision dataset. For instance, despite having a clear motion-based interpretation, the top left cluster in Fig. 3 combines Kinetics categories 'cleaning window', 'cleaning floor', and 'barbecuing'. Indeed, the actions vocabulary used in the literature is defined by a complex combination of actor's motion and scene appearance, making automatic discovery of well-aligned clusters challenging, and partially explaining the remaining gap between clustering-based methods and fully-supervised pretraining.

4.5   Learning Long-Term Temporal Dependencies

Next, we experiment with applying our Video LA objective with IDT prior over longer clips. Recall that this approach attempts to capture the notion of similarity between the videos encoded in the IDT descriptors that are computed over the whole video. The model reported so far, however, only takes 16-frame clips as input, which makes the objective highly ambiguous. In Table 2 we evaluate networks trained using 32- and 64-frame long clips instead, reporting results on UCF101 and HMDB51.

We observe that, as expected, performance of our approach ('Video LA + IDT' in the table) increases with more temporal information, but the improvement is non-linear, and our model is indeed able to better capture long-term motion cues when trained using longer clips. Similar improvements are observed for the plain Video LA objective, but our approach still shows top performance. Supervised model is also able to capitalize on longer videos, but on UCF101 the improvements are lower than seen by our approach (6.8% for the supervised model, compared to 8.7% for ours). Interestingly, the model trained from scratch does not benefit from longer videos as much as self-supervised or supervised variants. In particular, on HMDB51 its performance improves by about 1–2% with 32 frames, but actually decreases with 64. We attribute this to the fact that using longer clips lowers the diversity of the training set. These results further demonstrate the importance of model pretraining for video understanding.

4.6 Effect of the Number of Videos

So far, we have reported all the results using 235 000 videos from Kinetics-400 [2]. We now train the model with our final objective (Video LA with IDT prior) using a varying number of videos to study the effect of the dataset size on the quality of representations. In particular, we subsample the training set to 185 000 and 135 000 examples at random to see whether smaller datasets can be used for representation learning. We also add the videos from Kinetics-600 to see if our method scales to larger video collections. We use the 3D ResNet18 architecture with 16-frames long clips and input resolution of 112 × 112 in all experiments, and report results on the first split of UCF101 and HMDB51 in Fig. 4.

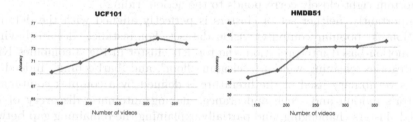

Fig. 4. Varying the number of Kinetics videos when training a 3D ConvNet with the 'Video LA with IDT prior' objective. Using more data for unsupervised pretraining results in better representations, as evident form transfer learning results on the first split of UCF101 and HMDB51 (reported using classification accuracy).

Firstly, we observe that useful representations can be learned with as few 135 000 videos. However, using more data results in improved performance on both datasets. On UCF101 the improvements are mostly linear, but accuracy drops somewhat for the largest training set (370 000 videos). We attribute this to the randomness in training and hypothesize that further improvements can be achieved with more data. On HMDB51 accuracy seems to plateau after 235 000 videos, but improves with 370 000. We will use the model trained on the largest available dataset for comparison to the state-of-the-art in the next section.

4.7 Comparison to the State-of-the-Art

Finally, we compare our approach (Video LA with IDT prior) to the state-of-the-art in Table 3. To fairly compare results achieved by methods with different

Table 3. Comparison to the state-of-the-art using accuracy and fraction of the fully supervised performance on UCF101 and HMDB51, averaged over 3 splits. 'Ours': Video LA with IDT prior. DPC uses a non-standard version of 3D ResNet, and does not report fully-supervised performance for it. Our method shows top accuracy among the models using the same network architecture.

Method	Network	Frame size	#Frames	UCF101		HMDB51	
				Acc.	% sup.	Acc.	% sup.
PMAS [43]	C3D	112 × 112	16	61.2	74.3	33.4	-
3D-Puzzle [20]	3D ResNet18	224 × 224	16	65.8	78.0	33.7	59.8
DPC [13]	3D ResNet18	112 × 112	40	68.2	-	34.5	-
Ours	3D ResNet18	112 × 112	16	73.0	86.5	41.6	73.8
3D-RotNet [19]	3D ResNet18	112 × 112	64	66.0	72.1	37.1	55.5
Ours	3D ResNet18	112 × 112	64	**83.0**	**90.7**	**50.4**	**75.6**
DPC [13]	3D ResNet34	224 × 224	40	75.7	-	35.7	-
CBT [35]	S3D	112 × 112	16	79.5	82.1	44.6	58.8
IDT [42]	-	Full	All	85.9	-	57.2	-

network architectures, we use the fraction of fully supervised performance as an additional metric, whenever this information is available. To make the table size manageable, we only report approaches that use 3D ConvNets pretrained on Kinetics. These, however, cover all the top performing methods in the literature.

Firstly, we observe that our principled approach is indeed a lot more effective that manually designed objectives used in PMAS [43], or 3D-Puzzle [19], confirming the effectiveness of clustering-based training. The improvements are especially large on HMDB, which is, as we have shown previously, can be attributed to the IDT prior helping to better model the temporal information. Our approach also outperforms DPC [13], when the network depth is the same for both methods, even though DPC uses much longer sequences (40 frames with a stride 2, so the effective length is 120). Notably, on HMDB our approach even outperforms a variant of DPC with a deeper network, and bigger frame size by a large margin. When trained with longer temporal sequences, our method also outperforms the deeper variant of DPC on UCF by 7.3%. On HMDB we are 14.7% ahead.

The very recent approach of Sun et al. [35] ('CBT' in the table), reports high accuracy on both datasets. However, we show that this is due to the authors of [35] using a much deeper network than other methods in the literature. In terms of the fraction of fully-supervised performance, the 16-frame variant of our method outperforms CBT by 4.4% on UCF and by 15.0% on HMDB. Moreover, the 64-frame variant also outperforms CBT in raw accuracy on both datasets.

Finally, we report the performance of Fisher vector encoded IDT descriptors ('IDT' in the table, the numbers are taken from [32]). Please note that these descriptors are computed on the full length of the video, using the original resolution. Despite this, our 64-frame model comes close to the IDT performance.

5 Conclusions

This paper introduced a novel approach for unsupervised video representation learning. Our method transfers the heuristic-based IDT descriptors, that are effective at capturing motion information, to 3D ConvNets via non-parametric clustering. We quantitatively evaluated the learned representations on UCF101 and HMDB51, and demonstrated that they outperform prior work. We also qualitatively analyzed the discovered video clusters, showing that they successfully capture video dynamics, in addition to appearance. This analysis highlighted that the clusters do not perfectly match with the human-defined action classes, partially explaining the remaining gap to the fully-supervised performance.

References

1. Caron, M., Bojanowski, P., Joulin, A., Douze, M.: Deep clustering for unsupervised learning of visual features. In: Proceedings of the European Conference on Computer Vision (ECCV), pp. 132–149 (2018)
2. Carreira, J., Zisserman, A.: Quo vadis, action recognition? a new model and the kinetics dataset. In: Proceedings of the IEEE Conference on Computer Vision and Pattern Recognition, pp. 6299–6308 (2017)
3. Chen, W.Y., Liu, Y.C., Kira, Z., Wang, Y.C.F., Huang, J.B.: A closer look at few-shot classification. In: ICLR (2019)
4. Dalal, N., Triggs, B.: Histograms of oriented gradients for human detection. In: IEEE Computer Society Conference on Computer Vision and Pattern Recognition (CVPR 2005), Vol. 1, pp. 886–893. IEEE (2005)
5. Dalal, N., Triggs, B., Schmid, C.: Human detection using oriented histograms of flow and appearance. In: Leonardis, A., Bischof, H., Pinz, A. (eds.) ECCV 2006. LNCS, vol. 3952, pp. 428–441. Springer, Heidelberg (2006). https://doi.org/10. 1007/11744047_33
6. Doersch, C., Gupta, A., Efros, A.A.: Unsupervised visual representation learning by context prediction. In: Proceedings of the IEEE International Conference on Computer Vision, pp. 1422–1430 (2015)
7. Donahue, J., Krähenbühl, P., Darrell, T.: Adversarial feature learning. In: ICLR (2016)
8. Dosovitskiy, A., Springenberg, J.T., Riedmiller, M., Brox, T.: Discriminative unsupervised feature learning with convolutional neural networks. In: Advances in Neural Information Processing Systems, pp. 766–774 (2014)
9. Fernando, B., Bilen, H., Gavves, E., Gould, S.: Self-supervised video representation learning with odd-one-out networks. In: Proceedings of the IEEE conference on computer vision and pattern recognition, pp. 3636–3645 (2017)
10. Gan, C., Gong, B., Liu, K., Su, H., Guibas, L.J.: Geometry guided convolutional neural networks for self-supervised video representation learning. In: Proceedings of the IEEE Conference on Computer Vision and Pattern Recognition, pp. 5589–5597 (2018)
11. Gidaris, S., Singh, P., Komodakis, N.: Unsupervised representation learning by predicting image rotations. In: ICLR (2018)
12. Goodfellow, I., et al.: Generative adversarial nets. In: Advances in Neural Information Processing Systems, pp. 2672–2680 (2014)

13. Han, T., Xie, W., Zisserman, A.: Video representation learning by dense predictive coding. In: Proceedings of the IEEE International Conference on Computer Vision Workshops (2019)
14. Hara, K., Kataoka, H., Satoh, Y.: Can spatiotemporal 3D CNNs retrace the history of 2D CNNs and ImageNet? In: Proceedings of the IEEE Conference on Computer Vision and Pattern Recognition, pp. 6546–6555 (2018)
15. He, K., Girshick, R., Dollár, P.: Rethinking imageNet pre-training. In: Proceedings of the IEEE International Conference on Computer Vision, pp. 4918–4927 (2019)
16. He, K., Gkioxari, G., Dollár, P., Girshick, R.: Mask R-CNN. In: Proceedings of the IEEE International Conference on Computer Vision, pp. 2961–2969 (2017)
17. Hinton, G., Vinyals, O., Dean, J.: Distilling the knowledge in a neural network. arXiv preprint arXiv:1503.02531 (2015)
18. Hinton, G.E., Osindero, S., Teh, Y.W.: A fast learning algorithm for deep belief nets. Neural Comput. 18(7), 1527–1554 (2006)
19. Jing, L., Yang, X., Liu, J., Tian, Y.: Self-supervised spatiotemporal feature learning via video rotation prediction. arXiv preprint arXiv:1811.11387 (2018)
20. Kim, D., Cho, D., Kweon, I.S.: Self-supervised video representation learning with space-time cubic puzzles. In: Proceedings of the AAAI Conference on Artificial Intelligence, Vol. 33, pp. 8545–8552 (2019)
21. Kingma, D.P., Welling, M.: Auto-encoding variational bayes. In: ICLR (2014)
22. Koniusz, P., Zhang, H., Porikli, F.: A deeper look at power normalizations. In: Proceedings of the IEEE Conference on Computer Vision and Pattern Recognition, pp. 5774–5783 (2018)
23. Kuehne, H., Jhuang, H., Garrote, E., Poggio, T., Serre, T.: HMDB: a large video database for human motion recognition. In: International Conference on Computer Vision, pp. 2556–2563. IEEE (2011)
24. Lee, H., Grosse, R., Ranganath, R., Ng, A.Y.: Convolutional deep belief networks for scalable unsupervised learning of hierarchical representations. In: Proceedings of the 26th Annual International Conference on Machine Learning, pp. 609–616 (2009)
25. Lee, H.Y., Huang, J.B., Singh, M., Yang, M.H.: Unsupervised representation learning by sorting sequences. In: Proceedings of the IEEE International Conference on Computer Vision, pp. 667–676 (2017)
26. Lin, T.-Y., et al.: Microsoft COCO: common objects in context. In: Fleet, D., Pajdla, T., Schiele, B., Tuytelaars, T. (eds.) ECCV 2014. LNCS, vol. 8693, pp. 740–755. Springer, Cham (2014). https://doi.org/10.1007/978-3-319-10602-1_48
27. Misra, I., Zitnick, C.L., Hebert, M.: Shuffle and learn: unsupervised learning using temporal order verification. In: Leibe, B., Matas, J., Sebe, N., Welling, M. (eds.) ECCV 2016. LNCS, vol. 9905, pp. 527–544. Springer, Cham (2016). https://doi.org/10.1007/978-3-319-46448-0_32
28. Mobahi, H., Collobert, R., Weston, J.: Deep learning from temporal coherence in video. In: Proceedings of the 26th Annual International Conference on Machine Learning, pp. 737–744 (2009)
29. Noroozi, M., Favaro, P.: Unsupervised learning of visual representations by solving jigsaw puzzles. In: Leibe, B., Matas, J., Sebe, N., Welling, M. (eds.) ECCV 2016. LNCS, vol. 9910, pp. 69–84. Springer, Cham (2016). https://doi.org/10.1007/978-3-319-46466-4_5
30. Oord, A.v.d., Li, Y., Vinyals, O.: Representation learning with contrastive predictive coding. arXiv preprint arXiv:1807.03748 (2018)

31. Perronnin, F., Sánchez, J., Mensink, T.: Improving the fisher kernel for large-scale image classification. In: Daniilidis, K., Maragos, P., Paragios, N. (eds.) ECCV 2010. LNCS, vol. 6314, pp. 143–156. Springer, Heidelberg (2010). https://doi.org/10.1007/978-3-642-15561-1_11

32. Simonyan, K., Zisserman, A.: Two-stream convolutional networks for action recognition in videos. In: Advances in Neural Information Processing Systems, pp. 568–576 (2014)

33. Soomro, K., Zamir, A.R., Shah, M.: UCF101: a dataset of 101 human actions classes from videos in the wild. arXiv preprint arXiv:1212.0402 (2012)

34. Srivastava, N., Mansimov, E., Salakhudinov, R.: Unsupervised learning of video representations using LSTMs. In: International Conference on Machine Learning, pp. 843–852 (2015)

35. Sun, C., Baradel, F., Murphy, K., Schmid, C.: Contrastive bidirectional transformer for temporal representation learning. arXiv preprint arXiv:1906.05743 (2019)

36. Tran, D., Bourdev, L., Fergus, R., Torresani, L., Paluri, M.: Learning spatiotemporal features with 3D convolutional networks. In: Proceedings of the IEEE International Conference on Computer Vision, pp. 4489–4497 (2015)

37. Ulyanov, D., Vedaldi, A., Lempitsky, V.: Deep image prior. In: Proceedings of the IEEE Conference on Computer Vision and Pattern Recognition, pp. 9446–9454 (2018)

38. Vondrick, C., Pirsiavash, H., Torralba, A.: Generating videos with scene dynamics. In: Advances in Neural Information Processing Systems, pp. 613–621 (2016)

39. Vondrick, C., Shrivastava, A., Fathi, A., Guadarrama, S., Murphy, K.: Tracking emerges by colorizing videos. In: Proceedings of the European Conference on Computer Vision (ECCV), pp. 391–408 (2018)

40. Wang, F., Xiang, X., Cheng, J., Yuille, A.L.: Normface: L2 hypersphere embedding for face verification. In: Proceedings of the 25th ACM International Conference on Multimedia, pp. 1041–1049 (2017)

41. Wang, H., Kläser, A., Schmid, C., Liu, C.L.: Dense trajectories and motion boundary descriptors for action recognition. Int. J. Comput. Vision 103(1), 60–79 (2013)

42. Wang, H., Schmid, C.: Action recognition with improved trajectories. In: Proceedings of the IEEE International Conference on Computer Vision, pp. 3551–3558 (2013)

43. Wang, J., Jiao, J., Bao, L., He, S., Liu, Y., Liu, W.: Self-supervised spatio-temporal representation learning for videos by predicting motion and appearance statistics. In: Proceedings of the IEEE Conference on Computer Vision and Pattern Recognition, pp. 4006–4015 (2019)

44. Wang, L., Koniusz, P., Huynh, D.Q.: Hallucinating IDT descriptors and I3D optical flow features for action recognition with CNNs. In: Proceedings of the IEEE International Conference on Computer Vision, pp. 8698–8708 (2019)

45. Weinberger, K., Dasgupta, A., Langford, J., Smola, A., Attenberg, J.: Feature hashing for large scale multitask learning. In: Proceedings of the 26th Annual International Conference on Machine Learning, pp. 1113–1120 (2009)

46. Wu, Z., Xiong, Y., Yu, S.X., Lin, D.: Unsupervised feature learning via nonparametric instance discrimination. In: Proceedings of the IEEE Conference on Computer Vision and Pattern Recognition, pp. 3733–3742 (2018)

47. Xie, S., Sun, C., Huang, J., Tu, Z., Murphy, K.: Rethinking spatiotemporal feature learning for video understanding. In: ECCV (2018)

48. Zhang, R., Isola, P., Efros, A.A.: Colorful image colorization. In: Leibe, B., Matas, J., Sebe, N., Welling, M. (eds.) ECCV 2016. LNCS, vol. 9907, pp. 649–666. Springer, Cham (2016). https://doi.org/10.1007/978-3-319-46487-9_40
49. Zhuang, C., Zhai, A.L., Yamins, D.: Local aggregation for unsupervised learning of visual embeddings. In: Proceedings of the IEEE International Conference on Computer Vision, pp. 6002–6012 (2019)

Distilling Visual Priors from Self-Supervised Learning

Bingchen Zhao[1,2(✉)] and Xin Wen[1]

[1] Tongji University, Shanghai, China
[2] Megvii Research Nanjing, Nanjing, China
zhaobc.gm@gmail.com, wx99@tongji.edu.cn

Abstract. Convolutional Neural Networks (CNNs) are prone to overfit small training datasets. We present a novel two-phase pipeline that leverages self-supervised learning and knowledge distillation to improve the generalization ability of CNN models for image classification under the data-deficient setting. The first phase is to learn a teacher model which possesses rich and generalizable visual representations via self-supervised learning, and the second phase is to distill the representations into a student model in a self-distillation manner, and meanwhile fine-tune the student model for the image classification task. We also propose a novel margin loss for the self-supervised contrastive learning proxy task to better learn the representation under the data-deficient scenario. Together with other tricks, we achieve competitive performance in the VIPriors image classification challenge.

Keywords: Self-supervised learning · Knowledge-distillation

1 Introduction

Convolutional Neural Networks (CNNs) have achieved breakthroughs in image classification [8] via supervised training on large-scale datasets, e.g., ImageNet [4]. However, when the dataset is small, the over-parametrized CNNs tend to simply memorize the dataset and can not generalize well to unseen data [21]. To alleviate this over-fitting problem, several regularization techniques have been proposed, such as Dropout [15], BatchNorm [11]. In addition, some works seek to combat with over-fitting by re-designing the CNN building blocks to endow the model with some encouraging properties (e.g., translation invariance [12] and shift-invariance [22]).

Recently, self-supervised learning has shown a great potential of learning useful representation from data without external label information. In particular, the contrastive learning methods [1,7] have demonstrated advantages over other self-supervised learning methods in learning better transferable representations for downstream tasks. Compared to supervised learning, representations learned by self-supervised learning are unbiased to image labels, which can effectively prevent the model from over-fitting the patterns of any object category. Furthermore, the data augmentation in modern contrastive learning [1] typically

A. Bartoli and A. Fusiello (Eds.): ECCV 2020 Workshops, LNCS 12536, pp. 422–429, 2020.
https://doi.org/10.1007/978-3-030-66096-3_29

involves diverse transformation strategies, which significantly differ from those used by supervised learning. This may also suggest that contrastive learning can better capture the diversity of the data than supervised learning.

In this paper, we go one step further by exploring the capability of contrastive learning under the data-deficient setting. Our key motivation lies in the realization that the label-unbiased and highly expressive representations learned by self-supervised learning can largely prevent the model from over-fitting the small training dataset. Specifically, we design a new two-phase pipeline for data-deficient image classification. The first phase is to utilize self-supervised contrastive learning as a proxy task for learning useful representations, which we regard as visual priors before using the image labels to train a model in a supervised manner. The second phase is use the weight obtained from the first phase as the start point, and leverage the label information to further fine-tune the model to perform classification.

In principle, self-supervised pre-training is an intuitive approach for preventing over-fitting when the labeled data are scarce, yet constructing the pre-training and fine-tuning pipeline properly is critical for good results. Specifically, there are two problems to be solved. First, the common practice in self-supervised learning is to obtain a memory bank for negative sampling. While MoCo [7] has demonstrated accuracy gains with increased bank size, the maximum bank size, however, is limited in the data-deficient setting. To address this issue, we propose a margin loss that can reduce the bank size while maintaining the same performance. We hope that this method can be helpful for fast experiments and evaluation. Second, directly fine-tuning the model on a small dataset still faces the risk of over-fitting, based on the observation that fine-tuning a linear classifier on top of the pre-train representation can yield a good result. We proposed to utilize a recent published feature distillation method [9] to perform self-distillation between the pre-trained teacher model and a student model. This self-distillation module plays a role of regularizing the model from forgetting the visual priors learned from the contrastive learning phase, and thus can further prevent the model from over-fitting on the small dataset.

2   Related Works

Self-supervised learning focus on how to obtain good representations of data from heuristically designed proxy tasks, such as image colorization [23], tracking objects in videos [17], de-noising auto-encoders [16] and predicting image rotations [6]. Recent works using contrastive learning objectives [18] have achieved remarkable performance, among which MoCo [2,7] is the first self-supervised method that outperforms supervised pre-training methods on multiple downstream tasks. In SimCLR [1], the authors show that the augmentation policy used by self-supervised method is quite different from the supervised methods, and is often harder. This phenomenon suggests that the self-supervised learned representations can be more rich and diverse than the supervised variants.

Knowledge distillation aims to distill useful knowledge or representation from a teacher model to a student model [10]. Original knowledge distillation uses the predicted logits to transfer knowledge from teacher to student [10]. Then, some works found that transferring the knowledge conveyed by the feature map from the teacher to student can lead to better performance [14,20]. Heo *et al.*[9] provided a overhaul study of how to effectively distill knowledge from the feature map, which also inspires our design for knowledge distillation. Self-distillation uses the same model for both teacher and student [5], which has been shown to improve the performance of the model. We utilize the self-distillation method as a regulation term to prevent our model from over-fitting.

3   Method

Our method contains two phases, the first phase is to use the recently published MoCo v2 [2] to pre-train the model on the given dataset to obtain good representations. The learned representations can be considered as visual priors before using the label information. The second phase is to initialize both the teacher and student model used in the self-distillation process with the pre-trained weight. The weight of the teacher is frozen, and the student is updated using a combination of the classification loss and the overhaul-feature-distillation (OFD) [9] loss from the teacher. As a result, the student model is regularized by the representation from the teacher when performing the classification task. The two phases are visualized in Fig. 1.

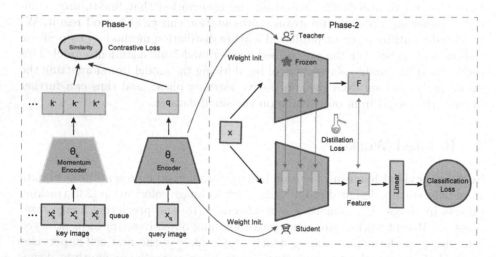

Fig. 1. The two phases of our proposed method. The first phase is to construct a useful visual prior with self-supervised contrastive learning, and the second phase is to perform self-distillation on the pre-trained checkpoint. The student model is fine-tuned with a distillation loss and a classification loss, while the teacher model is frozen.

3.1   Phase-1: Pre-Train with Self-Supervised Learning

The original loss used by MoCo is as follows:

$$\mathcal{L}_{moco} = -\log \left[\frac{\exp\left(\mathbf{q} \cdot \mathbf{k}^+ / \tau\right)}{\exp\left(\mathbf{q} \cdot \mathbf{k}^+ / \tau\right) + \sum_{\mathbf{k}^-} \exp\left(\mathbf{q} \cdot \mathbf{k}^- / \tau\right)} \right], \quad (1)$$

where $\mathbf{q}$ and $\mathbf{k}^+$ is a positive pair (different views of the same image) sampled from the given dataset $\mathcal{D}$, and $\mathbf{k}^-$ are negative examples (different images). As shown in Fig. 1, MoCo uses a momentum encoder θ_k to encode all the $\mathbf{k}$ and put them in a queue for negative sampling, the momentum encoder is a momentum average of the encoder θ_q:

$$\theta_k \leftarrow \eta\theta_k + (1 - \eta)\theta_q. \quad (2)$$

As shown in MoCo [7], the size of the negative sampling queue is crucial to the performance of the learned representation. In a data-deficient dataset, the maximum size of the queue is limited, we propose to add a margin to the original loss function to help the model obtain a larger margin between data samples thus help the model obtain a similar result with fewer negative examples.

$$\mathcal{L}_{margin} = -\log \left[\frac{\exp\left(\left(\mathbf{q} \cdot \mathbf{k}^+ - m\right) / \tau\right)}{\exp\left(\left(\mathbf{q} \cdot \mathbf{k}^+ - m\right) / \tau\right) + \sum_{\mathbf{k}^-} \exp\left(\mathbf{q} \cdot \mathbf{k}^- / \tau\right)} \right]. \quad (3)$$

3.2   Phase-2: Self-Distill on Labeled Dataset

The self-supervised trained checkpoint from phase-1 is then used to initialize the teacher and student for fine-tuning on the whole dataset with labels. We choose to use OFD [9] to distill the visual priors from teacher to student. The distillation process can be seen as a regulation to prevent the student from over-fitting the small train dataset and give the student a more diversed representation for classification.

The distillation loss can be formulated as follows:

$$\mathcal{L}_{distill} = \sum_{\mathbf{F}} d_p \left(\text{StopGrad}\left(\mathbf{F}_t\right), r(\mathbf{F}_s)\right), \quad (4)$$

where $\mathbf{F}_t$ and $\mathbf{F}_s$ stands for the feature map of the teacher and student model respectively, the StopGrad means the weight of the teacher will not be updated by gradient descent, the d_p stands for a distance metric, r is a connector function to transform the feature from the student to the teacher.

Along with a cross-entropy loss for classification:

$$\mathcal{L}_{ce} = -\log p(y = i | \mathbf{x}), \quad (5)$$

the final loss function for the student model is:

$$\mathcal{L}_{stu} = \mathcal{L}_{ce} + \lambda \mathcal{L}_{distill}. \quad (6)$$

The student model is then used for evaluation.

4   Experiments

Dataset. Only the subset of the ImageNet [4] dataset given by the VIPrior challenge is used for our experiments, no external data or pre-trained checkpoint is used. The VIPrior challenge dataset contains 1,000 classes which is the same with the original ImageNet [4], and is split into train, val and test splits, each of the splits has 50 images for each class, resulting in a total of 150,000 images. For comparison, we use the train split to train the model and test the model on the validation split.

Implementation Details. For phase-1, we set the momentum η as 0.999 in all the experiments as it yields better performance, and the size of the queue is set to 4,096. The margin m in our proposed margin loss is set to be 0.4. We train the model for 800 epochs in phase-1, the initial learning rate is set to 0.03 and the learning rate is dropped by 10x at epoch 120 and epoch 160. Other hyperparameter is set to be the same with MoCo v2 [2],

For phase-2, the λ in Eq. 6 is set to 10^{-4}. We also choose to use ℓ_2 distance as the distance metric d_p in Eq. 4. We train the model for 100 epochs in phase-2, the initial learning rate is set to 0.1 and is dropped by 10x every 30 epochs.

Ablation Results. We first present the overall performance of our proposed two phase pipeline, then show some ablation results.

As shown in Table 1, supervised training of ResNet50 [8] would lead to over-fitting on the train split, thus the validation top-1 accuracy is low. By first pre-training the model with the phase-1 of our pipeline, and fine-tuning a linear classifier on top of the obtained feature representation [18], we can reach a 6.6 performance gain in top-1 accuracy. This indicates that the feature learned from self-supervised learning contain more information and can generalize well on the validation set. We also show that fine-tuning the full model from phase-1 can reach better performance compared to only fine-tuning a linear classifier, which indicates that the weight from phase-1 can also serve as a good initialization, but the supervised training process may still cause the model to suffer from over-fitting. Finally, by combining phase-1 and phase-2 together, our proposed pipeline achieves 16.7 performance gain in top-1 accuracy over the supervised baseline.

The Effect of Our Margin Loss. Table 2 shows that effect of the number negative samples in contrastive learning loss, the original loss function used by MoCo v2 [7] is sensitive to the number of negatives, the fewer negative, the lower the linear classification result is. Our modified margin loss can help alleviate the issue with a margin to help the model learn a larger margin between data points. Thus leading to a more discriminative feature space. The experiments show that our margin loss is less sensitive to the number negatives and can be used in a data-deficient setting.

Table 1. Training and Pre-training the model on the train split and evaluate the performance on the validation split on the given dataset. 'finetune fc' stands for train a linear classifier on top of the pretrained representation, 'finetune' stands for train the weight of the whole model. Our proposed pipeline (Phase-1 + Phase-2) can have 16.7 performance gain in top-1 validation accuracy.

ResNet50	#Pretrain Epoch	#Finetune Epoch	Val Acc
Supervised Training	-	100	27.9
Phase-1 + finetune fc	800	100	34.5
Phase-1 + finetune	800	100	39.4
Phase-1 + Phase-2 (Ours)	800	100	44.6

Table 2. The Val Acc means the linear classification accuracy obtained by fine-tune a linear classifier on top of the learned representation. The original MoCo v2 is sensitive to the number of negative, the performance drops drastically when number negatives is small. Our modified margin loss is less sensitive to the number negatives, as shown in the table, even has 16x less negatives the performance only drops 0.9.

	#Neg	Margin	Val Acc
MoCo v2 [7]	4096	-	34.5
	1024	-	32.1
	256	-	29.1
Margin loss	4096	0.4	34.6
	1024	0.4	34.2
	256	0.4	33.7

Table 3. The tricks used in the competition, our final accuracy is 68.8 which is a competitive result in the challenge. Our code will be made public. Results in this table are obtain by train the model on the combination of train and validation splits.

	#Pretrain Epoch	#Finetune Epoch	Test Acc
Phase-1 + Phase-2	800	100	47.2
+Input Resolution 448	800	100	54.8
+ResNeXt101 [19]	800	100	62.3
+Label-Smooth [13]	800	100	64.2
+Auto-Aug [3]	800	100	65.7
+TenCrop	800	100	66.2
+Ensemble two models	800	100	68.8

Competition Tricks. For better performance in the competition, we combine the train and val split to train the model that generate the submission. Several other tricks and stronger backbone models are used for better performance, such as Auto-Augment [3], ResNeXt [19], label-smooth [13], TenCrop and model ensemble. Detailed tricks are listed in Table 3.

5 Conclusion

This paper proposes a novel two-phase pipeline for image classification using CNNs under the data-deficient setting. The first phase is to learn a teacher model which obtains a rich visual representation from the dataset using self-supervised learning. The second phase is transfer this representation into a student model in a self-distillation manner, meanwhile the student is fine-tuned for downstream classification task. Experiments shows the effectiveness of our proposed method, Combined with additional tricks, our method achieves a competitive result in the VIPrior Image Classification Challenge.

References

1. Chen, T., Kornblith, S., Norouzi, M., Hinton, G.: A simple framework for contrastive learning of visual representations. arXiv preprint arXiv:2002.05709 (2020)
2. Chen, X., Fan, H., Girshick, R., He, K.: Improved baselines with momentum contrastive learning. arXiv preprint arXiv:2003.04297 (2020)
3. Cubuk, E.D., Zoph, B., Mané, D., Vasudevan, V., Le, Q.V.: Autoaugment: learning augmentation strategies from data. In: IEEE/CVF Conference on Computer Vision and Pattern Recognition, pp. 113–123. IEEE (2019)
4. Deng, J., Dong, W., Socher, R., Li, L.J., Li, K., Fei-Fei, L.: Imagenet: a large-scale hierarchical image database. In: IEEE Conference on Computer Vision and Pattern Recognition, pp. 248–255. IEEE (2009)
5. Furlanello, T., Lipton, Z., Tschannen, M., Itti, L., Anandkumar, A.: Born again neural networks. In: International Conference on Machine Learning, pp. 1607–1616 (2018)
6. Gidaris, S., Singh, P., Komodakis, N.: Unsupervised representation learning by predicting image rotations. In: International Conference on Learning Representations (2018)
7. He, K., Fan, H., Wu, Y., Xie, S., Girshick, R.: Momentum contrast for unsupervised visual representation learning. In: IEEE/CVF Conference on Computer Vision and Pattern Recognition, pp. 9729–9738 (2020)
8. He, K., Zhang, X., Ren, S., Sun, J.: Deep residual learning for image recognition. In: IEEE Conference on Computer Vision and Pattern Recognition, pp. 770–778 (2016)
9. Heo, B., Kim, J., Yun, S., Park, H., Kwak, N., Choi, J.Y.: A comprehensive overhaul of feature distillation. In: IEEE/CVF International Conference on Computer Vision, pp. 1921–1930 (2019)
10. Hinton, G., Vinyals, O., Dean, J.: Distilling the knowledge in a neural network. In: NIPS Deep Learning and Representation Learning Workshop (2015). http://arxiv.org/abs/1503.02531
11. Ioffe, S., Szegedy, C.: Batch normalization: accelerating deep network training by reducing internal covariate shift. In: International Conference on Machine Learning, pp. 448–456 (2015)
12. Kayhan, O.S., Gemert, J.C.V.: On translation invariance in cnns: Convolutional layers can exploit absolute spatial location. In: 2020 IEEE/CVF Conference on Computer Vision and Pattern Recognition. pp. 14274–14285 (2020)
13. Müller, R., Kornblith, S., Hinton, G.E.: When does label smoothing help? In: Advances in Neural Information Processing Systems, pp. 4694–4703 (2019)

14. Romero, A., Ballas, N., Kahou, S.E., Chassang, A., Gatta, C., Bengio, Y.: Fitnets: hints for thin deep nets. In: International Conference on Learning Representations (2014)

15. Srivastava, N., Hinton, G., Krizhevsky, A., Sutskever, I., Salakhutdinov, R.: Dropout: a simple way to prevent neural networks from overfitting. J. Mach. Learn. Res. **15**(56), 1929–1958 (2014). http://jmlr.org/papers/v15/srivastava14a.html

16. Vincent, P., Larochelle, H., Bengio, Y., Manzagol, P.A.: Extracting and composing robust features with denoising autoencoders. In: International Conference on Machine Learning, pp. 1096–1103 (2008)

17. Wang, X., Gupta, A.: Unsupervised learning of visual representations using videos. In: IEEE International Conference on Computer Vision, pp. 2794–2802 (2015)

18. Wu, Z., Xiong, Y., Yu, S.X., Lin, D.: Unsupervised feature learning via non-parametric instance discrimination. In: IEEE/CVF Conference on Computer Vision and Pattern Recognition, pp. 3733–3742 (2018)

19. Xie, S., Girshick, R., Dollár, P., Tu, Z., He, K.: Aggregated residual transformations for deep neural networks. In: IEEE/CVF Conference on Computer Vision and Pattern Recognition, pp. 1492–1500 (2017)

20. Zagoruyko, S., Komodakis, N.: Paying more attention to attention: Improving the performance of convolutional neural networks via attention transfer. In: 2017 International Conference on Learning Representations (2016)

21. Zhang, C., Bengio, S., Hardt, M., Recht, B., Vinyals, O.: Understanding deep learning requires rethinking generalization. arXiv preprint arXiv:1611.03530 (2017)

22. Zhang, R.: Making convolutional networks shift-invariant again. In: International Conference on Machine Learning (2019)

23. Zhang, R., Isola, P., Efros, A.A.: Colorful image colorization. In: Leibe, B., Matas, J., Sebe, N., Welling, M. (eds.) ECCV 2016. LNCS, vol. 9907, pp. 649–666. Springer, Cham (2016). https://doi.org/10.1007/978-3-319-46487-9_40

Unsupervised Image Classification
for Deep Representation Learning

Weijie Chen[1]([✉]), Shiliang Pu[1]([✉]), Di Xie[1], Shicai Yang[1], Yilu Guo[1],
and Luojun Lin[2]

[1] Hikvision Research Institute, Hangzhou, China
{chenweijie5,pushiliang.hri,xiedi,yangshicai,guoyilu5}@hikvision.com
[2] School of Electronic and Information Engineering,
South China University of Technology, Guangzhou, China
linluojun2009@126.com

Abstract. Deep clustering against self-supervised learning (SSL) is a
very important and promising direction for unsupervised visual representation learning since it requires little domain knowledge to design
pretext tasks. However, the key component, embedding clustering, limits
its extension to the extremely large-scale dataset due to its prerequisite
to save the global latent embedding of the entire dataset. In this work,
we aim to make this framework more simple and elegant without performance decline. We propose an unsupervised image classification framework without using embedding clustering, which is very similar to standard supervised training manner. For detailed interpretation, we further
analyze its relation with deep clustering and contrastive learning. Extensive experiments on ImageNet dataset have been conducted to prove the
effectiveness of our method. Furthermore, the experiments on transfer
learning benchmarks have verified its generalization to other downstream
tasks, including multi-label image classification, object detection, semantic segmentation and few-shot image classification.

Keywords: Unsupervised learning · Representation learning

1 Introduction

Convolutional neural networks (CNN) [5,16,19] had been applied to many computer vision applications [14,25,26] due to their powerful representational capacity. The normal working flow is to pretrain the networks on a very large-scale
dataset with annotations like ImageNet [31] and then transfer to a small dataset
via fine-tuning. However, the dataset collection with manually labelling for pre-
training is strongly resource-consuming, which draws lots of researchers' attention to develop unsupervised representation learning approaches.

Among the existing unsupervised learning methods, self-supervision is highly
sound since it can directly generate supervisory signal from the input images, like
image inpainting [8,30] and jigsaw puzzle solving [28]. However, it requires rich

© Springer Nature Switzerland AG 2020
A. Bartoli and A. Fusiello (Eds.): ECCV 2020 Workshops, LNCS 12536, pp. 430–446, 2020.
https://doi.org/10.1007/978-3-030-66096-3_30

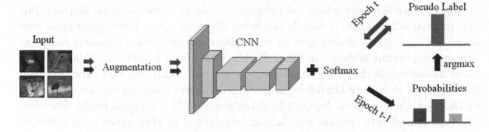

Fig. 1. The pipeline of unsupervised image classification learning. The black and red arrows separately denote the processes of pseudo-label generation and representation learning. These two processes are alternated iteratively. For efficient implementation, the pseudo labels in current epoch are updated by the forward results from the previous epoch which means our training framework is twice faster than DeepCluster.

empirical domain knowledge to design pretext tasks and is not well-transferred to downsteam tasks. Compared with this kind of self-supervised approaches, Deep-Cluster is a simple yet effective method which involves litter domain knowledge. It simply adopts embedding clustering to generate pseudo labels by capturing the manifold and mining the relation of all data points in the dataset. This process is iteratively alternated with an end-to-end representation learning which is exactly the same with supervised one. However, along with the advantage brought by embedding clustering, an obvious defect naturally appears that the latent embedding of each data point in the dataset should be saved before clustering, which leads to extra memory consumption linearly growing with the dataset size. It makes it difficult to scale to the very large-scale datasets. Actually, this problem also happens in the work of DeeperCluster [3], which uses distributed k-means to ease the problem. However, it still did not solve the problem in essence. Also, the data points in most of datasets are usually independently identically distributed ($i.i.d$). Therefore, building a framework analogous to DeepCluster, we wonder if we can directly generate pseudo class ID for each image without explicitly seeing other images and take it as an image classification task for representation learning.

The answer is excitedly YES! We integrate both the processes of pseudo label generation and representation learning into an unified framework of image classification. Briefly speaking, during the pseudo label generation, we directly feed each input image into the classification model with softmax output and pick the class ID with highest softmax score as pseudo label. It is very similar to the inference phase in supervised image classification. After pseudo class IDs are generated, the representation learning period is exactly the same with supervised training manner. These two periods are iteratively alternated until convergence. A strong concern is that if such unsupervised training method will be easily trapped into a local optima and if it can be well-generalized to other downstream tasks. In supervised training, this problem is usually solved by data augmentation which can also be applied to our proposed framework. It is worth noting that we not only adopt data augmentation in representation learning but also in pseudo label generation. It can bring disturbance to label assignment and make the task more challenging to learn data augmentation agnostic features. The entire pipeline is shown in Fig. 1. To the best of our knowledge, this unsupervised framework is the closest to the supervised one compared with other existing works. Since it is very similar to supervised image classification, we name our method as *Unsupervised Image Classification* (UIC) correspondingly. For simplicity, without any specific instruction, *clustering* in this paper only refers to embedding clustering via k-mean, and *classification* refers to CNN-based classification model with cross-entropy loss function.

To further explain why UIC works, we analyze its hidden relation with both deep clustering and contrastive learning. We point out that UIC can be considered as a special variant of them. We hope our work can bring a deeper understanding of deep clustering series work to the self-supervision community.

We empirically validate the effectiveness of UIC by extensive experiments on ImageNet. The visualization of classification results shows that UIC can act as clustering although lacking explicit clustering. We also validate its generalization ability by the experiments on transfer learning benchmarks. All these experiments indicate that UIC can work comparable with deep clustering. To summarize, our main contributions are listed as follows:

- A simple yet effective unsupervised image classification framework is proposed for visual representation learning, which can be taken as a strong prototype to develop more advanced unsupervised learning methods.
- Our framework simplifies DeepCluster by discarding embedding clustering while keeping no performance degradation and surpassing most of other self-supervised learning methods. We demonstrate that embedding clustering is not the main reason why DeepCluster works.
- Our training framework is twice faster than DeepCluster since we do not need an extra forward pass to generate pseudo labels.

2   Related Work

2.1   Self-supervised Learning

Self-supervised learning is a major form of unsupervised learning, which defines pretext tasks to train the neural networks without human-annotation, including image inpainting [8,30], automatic colorization [23,39], rotation prediction [13], cross-channel prediction [40], image patch order prediction [28], and so on. These pretext tasks are designed by directly generating supervisory signals from the raw images without manually labeling, and aim to learn well-pretrained representations for downstream tasks, like image classification, object detection, and semantic segmentation. Recently, contrastive learning [15,18,29,33] is developed to improve the performance of self-supervised learning. Its corresponding pretext task is that the features encoded from multi-views of the same image are similar to each others. The core insight behind these methods is to learn multi-views invariant representations. This is also the essence of our proposed method.

2.2 Clustering-Based Methods

Clustering-based methods are mostly related to our proposed method. Coates et al. [7] is the first to pretrain CNNs via clustering in a layer-by-layer manner. The following works [2,24,36,37] are also motivated to jointly cluster images and learn visual features. Among them, DeepCluster [2] is one of the most representative methods in recent years, which applies k-means clustering to the encoded features of all data points and generates pseudo labels to drive an end-to-end training of the target neural networks. The embedding clustering and representation learning are iterated by turns and contributed to each other along with training. Compared with other SSL methods with fixed pseudo labels, this kind of works not only learn good features but also learn meaningful pseudo labels. However, as a prerequisite for embedding clustering, it has to save the latent features of each sample in the entire dataset to depict the global data relation, which leads to excessive memory consumption and constrains its extension to the very large-scale datasets. Although another work DeeperCluster [3] proposes distributed k-means to ease this problem, it is still not efficient and elegant enough. Another work SelfLabel [1] treats clustering as a complicated optimal transport problem. It proposes label optimization as a regularized term to the entire dataset to simulate clustering with the hypothesis that the generated pseudo labels should partition the dataset equally. However, it is hypothesized and not an $i.i.d$ solution. Interestingly, we find that our method can naturally divide the dataset into nearly equal partitions without using label optimization.

3 Methods

3.1 Preliminary: Deep Clustering

We first review deep clustering to illustrate the process of pseudo label generation and representation learning, from which we analyze the disadvantages of embedding clustering and dig out more room for further improvement.

Pseudo Label Generation. Most self-supervised learning approaches focus on how to generate pseudo labels to drive unsupervised training. In deep clustering, this is achieved via k-means clustering on the embedding of all provided training images $X = x_1, x_2, ..., x_N$. In this way, the images with similar embedding representations can be assigned to the same label.

Commonly, the clustering problem can be defined as to optimize cluster centroids and cluster assignments for all samples, which can be formulated as:

$$\min_{C \in \mathbb{R}^{d \times k}} \frac{1}{N} \sum_{n=1}^{N} \min_{y_n \in \{0,1\}^k \ s.t. y_n^T 1_k = 1} \| C_{y_n} - f_\theta(x_n) \| \tag{1}$$

where $f_\theta(\cdot)$ denotes the embedding mapping, and θ is the trainable weights of the given neural network. C and y_n separately denote cluster centroid matrix with shape $d \times k$ and label assignment to n_{th} image in the dataset, where d, k and N separately denote the embedding dimension, cluster number and dataset size. For simplicity in the following description, y_n is presented as an one-hot vector, where the non-zero entry denotes its corresponding cluster assignment.

Representation Learning. After pseudo label generation, the representation learning process is exactly the same with supervised manner. To this end, a trainable linear classifier W is stacked on the top of main network and optimized with θ together, which can be formulated as:

$$\min_{\theta, W} \frac{1}{N} \sum_{n=1}^{N} l(y_n, W f_\theta(x_n)) \tag{2}$$

where l is the loss function.

Certainly, a correct label assignment is beneficial for representation learning, even approaching the supervised one. Likewise, a disentangled embedding representation will boost the clustering performance. These two steps are iteratively alternated and contribute positively to each other during optimization.

Analysis. Actually, clustering is to capture the global data relation, which requires to save the global latent embedding matrix $E \in \mathbb{R}^{d \times N}$ of the given dataset. Taking k-means as an example, it uses E to iteratively compute the cluster centroids C. Here naturally comes a problem. It is difficult to scale to the extremely large datasets especially for those with millions or even billions of images since the memory of E is linearly related to the dataset size. Thus, an existing question is, how can we group the images into several clusters without explicitly using global relation? Also, another slight problem is, the classifier W has to reinitialize after each clustering and train from scratch, since the cluster IDs are changeable all the time, which makes the loss curve fluctuated all the time even at the end of training.

3.2   Unsupervised Image Classification

From the above section, we can find that the two steps in deep clustering (Eq. 1 and Eq. 2) actually illustrate two different manners for images grouping, namely clustering and classification. The former one groups images into clusters relying on the similarities among them, which is usually used in unsupervised learning. While the latter one learns a classification model and then directly classifies them into one of pre-defined classes without seeing other images, which is usually used in supervised learning. For the considerations discussed in the above section, we can't help to ask, why not directly use classification model to generate pseudo labels to avoid clustering? In this way, it can integrate these two steps pseudo label generation and representation learning into a more unified framework. Here pseudo label generation is formulated as:

$$\min_{y_n} \frac{1}{N} \sum_{n=1}^{N} l(y_n, f_{\theta'}^{'}(x_n)) \ \ s.t. \ \ y_n \in \{0,1\}^k, y_n^T \mathbf{1}_k = 1 \tag{3}$$

where $f_{\theta'}^{'}(\cdot)$ is the network composed by $f_\theta(\cdot)$ and W. Since cross-entropy with softmax output is the most commonly-used loss function for image classification, Eq. 3 can be rewritten as:

$$y_n = p(f_{\theta'}^{'}(x_n)) \tag{4}$$

where $p(\cdot)$ is an arg max function indicating the non-zero entry for y_n. Iteratively alternating Eq. 4 and Eq. 2 for pseudo label generation and representation learning, can it really learn a disentangled representation? Apparently, it will easily fall in a local optima and learn less-representative features. The breaking point is data augmentation which is the core of many supervised and unsupervised learning algorithms. Normally, data augmentation is only adopted in representation learning process. However, this is not enough, which can not make this task challenging. Here data augmentation is also adopted in pseudo label generation. It brings disturbance for pseudo label, and make the task challenging enough to learn more robust features. Hence, Eq. 4 and Eq. 2 are rewritten as:

$$y_n = p(f_{\theta'}^{'}(t_1(x_n))) \tag{5}$$

$$\min_{\theta'} \frac{1}{N} \sum_{n=1}^{N} l(y_n, f_{\theta'}^{'}(t_2(x_n))) \tag{6}$$

where $t_1(\cdot)$ and $t_2(\cdot)$ denote two different random transformations. For efficiency, the forward pass of label generation can reuse the forward results of representation learning in the previous epoch. The entire pipeline of our proposed framework is illustrated in Fig. 1. Since our proposed method is very similar to the supervised image classification in format. Correspondingly, we name our method as unsupervised image classification.

Compared with deep clustering, our method is more simple and elegant. It can be easily scaled to large datasets, since it does not need global latent embedding of the entire dataset for image grouping. Further, the classifier W is optimized with the backbone network simultaneously instead of reinitializing after each clustering. Our method makes it a real end-to-end training framework.

3.3 Interpretation

The Relation with Embedding Clustering. Embedding clustering is the key component in deep clustering, which mainly focuses on three aspects: 1) sample embedding generation, 2) distance metric, 3) grouping manner (or cluster centroid generation). Actually, from these aspects, using image classification to generate pseudo labels can be taken as a special variant of embedding clustering, as visualized in Fig. 2. Compared with embedding clustering, the embedding in classification is the output of softmax layer and its dimension is exactly the class

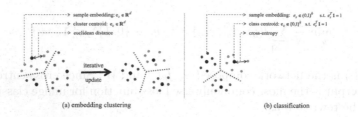

Fig. 2. The difference and relation between embedding clustering and classification.

number. Usually, we call it the probability assigned to each class. As for distance metric, compared with the euclidean distance used in embedding clustering, cross-entropy can also be considered as an distance metric used in classification. The most significant point is the grouping manner. In k-means clustering, the cluster centroids are dynamically determined and iteratively updated to reduce the intra-classes distance and enlarge the inter-classes distance. Conversely, the class centroids for classification are predefined and fixed as k orthonormal one-hot vectors, which helps directly classify images via cross-entropy.

Briefly speaking, *the key difference between embedding clustering and classification is whether the class centroids are dynamicly determined or not.* In Deep-Cluster [2], 20-iterations k-means clustering is operated, while in DeeperCluster [3], 10-iterations k-means clustering is enough. It means that clustering actually is not that important. Our method actually can be taken as an 1-iteration variant with fixed class centroids. Considering the representations are still not well-learnt at the beginning of training, both clustering and classification cannot correctly partition the images into groups with the same semantic information. During training, we claim that it is redundant to tune both the embedding features and class centroids meanwhile. It is enough to fix the class centroids as orthonormal vectors and only tune the embedding features. Along with representation learning drived by learning data augmentation invariance, the images with the same semantic information will get closer to the same class centroid. What's more, compared with deep clustering, the class centroids in UIC are consistent in between pseudo label generation and representation learning.

The Relation with Contrastive Learning. Contrastive learning has become a popular method for unsupervised learning recently. Implicitly, unsupervised image classification can also be connected to contrastive learning to explain why it works. Although Eq. 5 for pseudo label generation and Eq. 6 for representation learning are operated by turns, we can merge Eq. 5 into Eq. 6 and get:

$$\min_{\theta'} \frac{1}{N} \sum_{n=1}^{N} l(p(f_{\theta'}(t_1(x_n))), f_{\theta'}(t_2(x_n))) \tag{7}$$

which is optimized to maximize the mutual information between the representations from different transformations of the same image and learn data augmentation agnostic features. This is a basic formula used in many contrastive learning methods. More concretely, our method use a random view of the images to select their nearest class centroid, namely positive class, in a manner of taking the argmax of the softmax scores. During optimization, we push the representation of another random view of the images to get closer to their corresponding positive class. Implicitly, the remaining orthonormal k-1 classes will automatically turn into negative classes. Since we use cross-entropy with softmax as the loss function, they will get farther to the negative classes during optimization. Intuitively, this may be a more proper way to generate negative samples. In normal contrastive learning methods, given an image I in a (large) minibatch , they treat the other images in the minibatch as the negative samples. But there exist the risk that the negative samples may share the same semantic information with I.

4   Experimental Results

4.1   Dataset Benchmarks and Network Architectures

We mainly apply our proposed unsupervised image classification to ImageNet dataset [31] without annotations, which is designed for 1000-categories image classification consisting of 1.28 millions images. As for network architectures, we select the most representative one in unsupervised representation learning, AlexNet [22], as our baseline model for performance analysis and comparison. It is composed by five convolutional layers for features extraction and three fully-connected layers for classification. Note that the Local Response Normalization layers are replaced by batch normalization layers. After unsupervised training, the performance is mainly evaluated by

- linear probes;
- transfer learning on downstream tasks.

Linear probes [40] had been a standard metric followed by lots of related works. It quantitatively evaluates the representation generated by different convolutional layers through separately freezing the convolutional layers (and Batch Normalization layers) from shallow layers to higher layers and training a linear classifier on top of them using annotated labels. For evaluation by linear probing, we conduct experiments on ImageNet datasets with annotated labels. Linear probes is a direct approach to evaluate the features learnt by unsupervised learning through fixing the feature extractors. Compared with this approach, transfer learning on downsteam tasks is closer to practical scenarios. Following the existing works, we transfer the unsupervised pretrained model on ImageNet to PASCAL VOC dataset [11] for multi-label image classification, object detection and semantic segmentation via fine-tuning. To avoid the performance gap brought by hyperparameter difference during fine-tuning, we further evaluate the representations by metric-based few-shot classification on *mini*ImageNet [34] without fine-tuning.

Table 1. Ablation study on class number. We also report NMI t/labels, denoting the NMI between pseudo labels and annotated labels. FFT means further fine-tuning with fixed label assignments.

Methods	Top1 Accuracy			NMI t/labels
	Conv3	Conv4	Conv5	
UIC 3k	41.2	41.0	38.1	38.5
UIC 5k	40.6	40.9	38.2	40.8
UIC 10k	40.6	40.8	37.9	42.6
UIC 3k (FFT)	41.6	41.5	39.0	–

Table 2. Ablation study on whether data augmentation is adopted in pseudo label generation.

Methods	Aug	Top1 Accuracy		
		Conv3	Conv4	Conv5
UIC 3k	×	39.5	39.9	37.9
UIC 3k	√	41.6	41.5	39.0

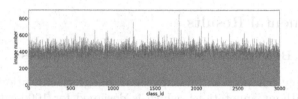

Fig. 3. Nearly uniform distribution of image number assigned to each class.

4.2   Unsupervised Image Classification

Implementation Details. Similar to DeepCluster, two important implementation details during unsupervised image classification have to be highlighted: 1) Avoid empty classes, 2) Class balance sampling. At the beginning of training, due to randomly initialization for network parameters, some classes are unavoidable to assign zero samples. To avoid trivial solution, we should avoid empty classes. When we catch one class with zero samples, we split the class with maximum samples into two equal partitions and assign one to the empty class. We observe that this situation of empty classes only happens at the beginning of training. As for class balance sampling, this technique is also used in supervised training to avoid the solution biasing to those classes with maximum samples.

Optimization Settings. We optimize AlexNet for 500 epochs through SGD optimizer with 256 batch size, 0.9 momentum, 1e-4 weight decay, 0.5 drop-out ratio and 0.1 learning rate decaying linearly. Analogous to DeepCluster, we apply Sobel filter to the input images to remove color information. During pseudo label generation and representation learning, we both adopt randomly resized cropping and horizontally flipping to augment input data. Compared with standard supervised training, the optimization settings are exactly the same except one extra hyperparameter, class number. Since over-clustering had been a consensus for clustering-based methods, here we only conduct ablation study about class number from 3k, 5k to 10k.

Fig. 4. Visualization of the classification results with low entropy.

Evaluation via Normalized Mutual Information. Normalized mutual information (NMI) is the main metric to evaluate the classification results, which ranges in the interval between 0 and 1. If NMI is approaching 1, it means two label assignments are strongly coherent. The annotated labels are unknown in practical scenarios, so we did not use them to tune the hyperparameters. But if the annotated labels are given, we can also use the NMI of label assignment against annotated one (NMI t/labels) to evaluate the classification results after training. As shown in the fifth column in Table 1, when the class number is 10k, the NMI t/labels is comparable with DeepCluster (refer to Fig. 2(a) in the paper [2]), which means the performance of our proposed unsupervised image classification is approaching to DeepCluster even without explicitly embedding clustering. However, the more class number will be easily to get higher NMI t/labels. So we cannot directly use it to compare the performance among different class number.

Evaluation via Visualization. At the end of training, we take a census for the image number assigned to each class. As shown in Fig. 3, our classification model nearly divides the images in the dataset into equal partitions. This is a interesting finding. In the work of [1], this result is achieved via label optimization solved by *sinkhorn-Knopp algorithm*. However, our method can achieve the same result without label optimization. We infer that class balance sampling training manner can implicitly bias to uniform distribution. Furthermore, we also visualize the classification results in Fig. 4. Our method can classify the images with similar semantic information into one class.

4.3   Linear Classification on Activations

Optimization Settings. We use linear probes for more quantitative evaluation. Following [40], we use max-pooling to separately reduce the activation dimensions to 9600, 9216, 9600, 9600 and 9216 (conv1-conv5). Freezing the feature extractors, we only train the inserted linear layers. We train the linear layers for

Table 3. Linear probing evaluation on ImageNet. We mainly compare the performance of our method with DeepCluster. For reference, we also list the results of other methods.

Methods	ImageNet				
	Conv1	Conv2	Conv3	Conv4	Conv5
ImageNet labels	19.3	36.3	44.2	48.3	50.5
Random	11.6	17.1	16.9	16.3	14.1
DeepCluster [2]	13.4	32.3	41.0	39.6	38.2
SelfLabel $3k \times 1$ [1]	–	–	43.0	44.7	40.9
SelfLabel $3k \times 10$ [1]	22.5	37.4	44.7	47.1	44.1
Ours	**12.8**	**34.3**	**41.6**	**41.5**	**39.0**
Take a look at other self-supervised learning methods					
Contenxt [8]	16.2	23.3	30.2	31.7	29.6
BiGan [9]	17.7	24.5	31.0	29.9	28.0
Split-brain [40]	17.7	29.3	35.4	35.2	32.8
Jigsaw puzzle [28]	18.2	28.8	34.0	33.9	27.1
RotNet [13]	18.8	31.7	38.7	38.2	36.5
AND [20]	15.6	27.0	35.9	39.7	37.9
AET [38]	19.3	35.4	44.0	43.6	42.4
RotNet+retrieval [12]	22.2	38.2	45.7	48.7	48.3

32 epochs with zero weight decay and 0.1 learning rate divided by ten at epochs 10, 20 and 30. The shorter size of the images in the dataset are resized to 256 pixels. And then we use 224×224 random crop as well as horizontal flipping to train the linear layer. After training, the accuracy is determined with 10-crops (center crop and four-corners crop as well as horizontal flipping).

Ablation Study on Class Number Selection. We conduct ablation study on class number as shown in Table 1. Different from DeepCluster, the performance 3k is slightly better than 5k and 10k, which is also confirmed by [1].

Further Fine-Tuning. During training, the label assignment is changed every epoch. We fix the label assignment at last epoch with center crop inference in pseudo label generation, and further fine-tune the network with 30 epochs. As shown in Table 1, the performance can be further improved.

Ablation Study on Data Augmentation. Data augmentation plays an important role in clustering-based self-supervised learning since the pseudo labels are almost wrong at the beginning of training since the features are still not well-learnt and the representation learning is mainly driven by learning data augmentation invariance at the beginning of training. In this paper, we also

Table 4. Transfer the pretrained model to downstream tasks on PASCAL VOC.

Methods	Classification (%mAP)		Detection (%mAP)	Segmentation (%mIU)
	FC6-8	ALL	ALL	ALL
ImageNet Labels	78.9	79.9	56.8	48.0
Random-RGB	33.2	57.0	44.5	30.1
Random-Sobel	29.0	61.9	47.9	32.0
DeepCluster [2]	72.0	73.7	55.4	45.1
SelfLabeling $3k \times 10$ [1]	–	75.3	55.9	43.7
Ours	76.2	75.9	54.9	45.9
Take a look at other kinds of self-supervised methods				
BiGan [9]	52.5	60.3	46.9	35.2
Contenxt [8]	55.1	63.1	51.1	–
Split-brain [40]	63.0	67.1	46.7	36.0
Jigsaw puzzle [28]	–	67.6	53.2	37.6
RotNet [13]	70.87	72.97	54.4	39.1
RotNet+retrieval [12]	–	74.7	58.0	45.9

use data augmentation in pseudo label generation. As shown in Table 2, it can improve the performance. In this paper, we simply adopt randomly resized crop to augment data in pseudo label generation and representation learning.

Comparison with Other State-of-The-Art Methods. Since our method aims at simplifying DeepCluster by discarding clustering, we mainly compare our results with DeepCluster. As shown in Fig. 3, our performance is comparable with DeepCluster, which validates that the clustering operation can be replaced by more challenging data augmentation. Note that it is also validated by the NMI t/labels mentioned above. SelfLabel [$3k \times 1$] simulates clustering via label optimization which classifies datas into equal partitions. However, as discussed above in Fig. 3, our proposed framework also divides the dataset into nearly equal partitions without the complicated label optimization term. Therefore, theoretically, our framework can also achieve comparable results with Self-Label [$3k \times 1$], and we impute the performance gap to their extra augmentation. With strong augmentation, our can still surpass SelfLabel as shown in Table 6. Compared with other self-supervised learning methods, our method can surpass most of them which only use a single type of supervisory signal. We believe our proposed framework can be taken as strong baseline model for self-supervised learning and make a further performance boost when combined with other supervisory signals, which will be validated in our future work.

Table 5. Evaluation via few-shot classification on the test set of *mini*ImageNet. Note that 224 resolution is center-cropped from 256 which is upsampled from 84 low-resolutional images. It can be regarded as inserting a upsampling layer at the bottom of the network while the input is still 84×84. MP is short for max-pooling. For reference, the 5way-5shot accuracy of prototypical networks [32] via supervised manner is 68.2%.

Methods	resolution	5way-5shot accuracy			
		Conv3	Conv4	Conv5	Conv5+MP
UIC 3k	224×224	48.79	53.03	62.46	65.05
DeepCluster	224×224	51.33	54.42	60.32	65.04
UIC 3k	84×84	52.43	54.76	54.40	52.85
DeepCluster	84×84	53.46	54.87	49.81	50.18

4.4 Transfer to Downstream Tasks

Evaluation via Fine-Tuning: Multi-label Image Classification, Object Detection, Semantic Segmentation on Pascal-VOC. In practical scenarios, self-supervised learning is usually used to provide a good pretrained model to boost the representations for downstream tasks. Following other works, the representation learnt by our proposed method is also evaluated by fine-tuning the models on PASCAL VOC datasets. Specifically, we run the object detection task using fast-rcnn [14] framework and run the semantic segmentation task using FCN [26] framework. As shown in Table 4, our performance is comparable with other clustering-based methods and surpass most of other SSL methods.

Evaluation Without Fine-Tuning: Metric-Based Few-Shot Image Classification on *mini*ImageNet. Few-shot classification [32,34] is naturally a protocol for representation evaluation, since it can directly use unsupervised pretrained models for feature extraction and use metric-based methods for few-shot classification without any finetuning. It can avoid the performance gap brought by fine-tuning tricks. In this paper, we use Prototypical Networks [32] for representation evaluation on the test set of *mini*ImageNet. As shown in Table 5, our method is comparable with DeepCluster overall. Specifically, our performances in highest layers are better than DeepCluster.

5   More Experiments

In the above sections, we try to keep training settings the same with DeepCluster for fair comparison. Although achieving SOTA results is not the main starting point of this work, we would not mind to further improve our results through combining the training tricks proposed by other methods.

Table 6. More experimental results with more data augmentations.

Methods	Arch	ImageNet			
		Conv3	Conv4	Conv5	NMI t/labels
DeepCluster [2]	AlexNet	41.0	39.6	38.2	–
SelfLabel $3k \times 1$ [1]	AlexNet	43.0	44.7	40.9	–
SelfLabel $3k \times 10$ [1]	AlexNet+10heads	44.7	47.1	44.1	–
UIC (Ours)	AlexNet	41.6	41.5	39.0	38.5
UIC + strong aug (Ours)	AlexNet	43.5	45.6	44.3	40.0

Table 7. More experimental results with more network architectures.

Methods	Arch	Top-1	NMI t/labels
Jigsaw [21]	Res50	38.4	–
Rotation [21]	Res50	43.8	–
InstDisc [35]	Res50	54.0	–
BigBiGAN [10]	Res50	56.6	–
Local Agg. [41]	Res50	60.2	–
Moco [15]	Res50	60.6	–
PIRL [27]	Res50	63.6	–
CPCv2 [17]	Res50	63.8	–
SimCLR [4]	Res50 + MLP-head	69.3	–
Mocov2 [6]	Res50 + MLP-head	71.1	–
SelfLabel $3k \times 10$ [1]	Res50+10heads	61.5	–
UIC + strong aug (Ours)	VGG16	57.7	46.9
UIC + strong aug (Ours)	Res50	62.7	50.6
UIC + strong aug (Ours)	Res50 + MLP-head	64.4	53.3

5.1   More Data Augmentations

As discussed above, data augmentation used in the process of pseudo label generation and network training plays a very important role for representation learning. Recently, SimCLR [4] consumes lots of computational resources to do a thorough ablation study about data augmentation. They used a strong color jittering and random Gaussian blur to boost their performance. We find such strong augmentation can also benefit our method as shown in Table 6. Our result in conv5 with a strong augmentation surpasses DeepCluster and SelfLabel by a large margin and is comparable with SelfLabel with 10 heads. Note that the results in this section do not use further fine-tuning.

5.2   More Network Architectures

To further convince the readers, we supplement the experiments of ResNet50 (500epochs) with the strong data augmentation and an extra MLP-head proposed by SimCLR [4] (we fix and do not discard MLP-head when linear probing). As shown in Table 7, our method surpasses SelfLabel and achieves SOTA results when compared with non-contrastive-learning methods. Although our method still has a performance gap with SimCLR and MoCov2 (>>500epochs), our method is the simplest one among them. We believe it can bring more improvement by applying more useful tricks.

6   Conclusions

We always believe that the greatest truths are the simplest. Our method validates that the embedding clustering is not the main reason why DeepCluster works. Our method makes training a SSL model as easy as training a supervised image classification model, which can be adopted as a strong prototype to further develop more advanced unsupervised learning approaches. We make SSL more accessible to the community which is very friendly to the academic development.

References

1. Asano, Y.M., Rupprecht, C., Vedaldi, A.: Self-labelling via simultaneous clustering and representation learning. arXiv preprint arXiv:1911.05371 (2020)
2. Caron, M., Bojanowski, P., Joulin, A., Douze, M.: Deep clustering for unsupervised learning of visual features. In: Proceedings of the European Conference on Computer Vision (ECCV), pp. 132–149 (2018)
3. Caron, M., Bojanowski, P., Mairal, J., Joulin, A.: Unsupervised pre-training of image features on non-curated data. In: Proceedings of the IEEE International Conference on Computer Vision, pp. 2959–2968 (2019)
4. Chen, T., Kornblith, S., Norouzi, M., Hinton, G.E.: A simple framework for contrastive learning of visual representations. arXiv: Learning (2020)
5. Chen, W., Xie, D., Zhang, Y., Pu, S.: All you need is a few shifts: designing efficient convolutional neural networks for image classification. In: Proceedings of the IEEE Conference on Computer Vision and Pattern Recognition, pp. 7241–7250 (2019)
6. Chen, X., Fan, H., Girshick, R., He, K.: Improved baselines with momentum contrastive learning. arXiv preprint arXiv:2003.04297 (2020)
7. Coates, A., Ng, A.Y.: Learning feature representations with K-means. In: Montavon, G., Orr, G.B., Müller, K.-R. (eds.) Neural Networks: Tricks of the Trade. LNCS, vol. 7700, pp. 561–580. Springer, Heidelberg (2012). https://doi.org/10.1007/978-3-642-35289-8_30
8. Doersch, C., Gupta, A., Efros, A.A.: Unsupervised visual representation learning by context prediction. In: Proceedings of the IEEE International Conference on Computer Vision, pp. 1422–1430 (2015)
9. Donahue, J., Krähenbühl, P., Darrell, T.: Adversarial feature learning. arXiv preprint arXiv:1605.09782 (2017)
10. Donahue, J., Simonyan, K.: Large scale adversarial representation learning. In: Advances in Neural Information Processing Systems, pp. 10541–10551 (2019)
11. Everingham, M., Eslami, S.M.A., Van Gool, L., Williams, C.K.I., Winn, J., Zisserman, A.: The PASCAL visual object classes challenge: a retrospective. Int. J. Comput. Vis. 111(1), 98–136 (2014). https://doi.org/10.1007/s11263-014-0733-5

12. Feng, Z., Xu, C., Tao, D.: Self-supervised representation learning by rotation feature decoupling. In: Proceedings of the IEEE Conference on Computer Vision and Pattern Recognition, pp. 10364–10374 (2019)

13. Gidaris, S., Singh, P., Komodakis, N.: Unsupervised representation learning by predicting image rotations. arXiv preprint arXiv:1803.07728 (2018)

14. Girshick, R.: Fast r-cnn. In: Proceedings of the IEEE International Conference on Computer Vision, pp. 1440–1448 (2015)

15. He, K., Fan, H., Wu, Y., Xie, S., Girshick, R.: Momentum contrast for unsupervised visual representation learning. arXiv preprint arXiv:1911.05722 (2019)

16. He, K., Zhang, X., Ren, S., Sun, J.: Deep residual learning for image recognition. In: Proceedings of the IEEE Conference on Computer Vision and Pattern Recognition, pp. 770–778 (2016)

17. Henaff, O.J., et al.: Data-efficient image recognition with contrastive predictive coding. In: International Conference on Machine Learning, pp. 4182–4192. PMLR (2019)

18. Hjelm, R.D., et al.: Learning deep representations by mutual information estimation and maximization. arXiv preprint arXiv:1808.06670 (2019)

19. Huang, G., Liu, Z., Van Der Maaten, L., Weinberger, K.Q.: Densely connected convolutional networks. In: Proceedings of the IEEE Conference on Computer Vision and Pattern Recognition, pp. 4700–4708 (2017)

20. Huang, J., Dong, Q., Gong, S., Zhu, X.: Unsupervised deep learning by neighbourhood discovery. arXiv preprint arXiv:1904.11567 (2019)

21. Kolesnikov, A., Zhai, X., Beyer, L.: Revisiting self-supervised visual representation learning. In: Proceedings of the IEEE conference on Computer Vision and Pattern Recognition, pp. 1920–1929 (2019)

22. Krizhevsky, A., Sutskever, I., Hinton, G.E.: Imagenet classification with deep convolutional neural networks. Commun. ACM **60**(6), 84–90 (2012)

23. Larsson, G., Maire, M., Shakhnarovich, G.: Learning representations for automatic colorization. In: Leibe, B., Matas, J., Sebe, N., Welling, M. (eds.) ECCV 2016. LNCS, vol. 9908, pp. 577–593. Springer, Cham (2016). https://doi.org/10.1007/978-3-319-46493-0_35

24. Liao, R., Schwing, A., Zemel, R., Urtasun, R.: Learning deep parsimonious representations. In: Advances in Neural Information Processing Systems, pp. 5076–5084 (2016)

25. Lin, L., Liang, L., Jin, L., Chen, W.: Attribute-aware convolutional neural networks for facial beauty prediction. In: IJCAI, pp. 847–853 (2019)

26. Long, J., Shelhamer, E., Darrell, T.: Fully convolutional networks for semantic segmentation. In: Proceedings of the IEEE Conference on Computer Vision and Pattern Recognition, pp. 3431–3440 (2015)

27. Misra, I., Der Maaten, L.V.: Self-supervised learning of pretext-invariant representations. arXiv: Computer Vision and Pattern Recognition (2019)

28. Noroozi, M., Favaro, P.: Unsupervised learning of visual representations by solving jigsaw puzzles. In: Leibe, B., Matas, J., Sebe, N., Welling, M. (eds.) ECCV 2016. LNCS, vol. 9910, pp. 69–84. Springer, Cham (2016). https://doi.org/10.1007/978-3-319-46466-4_5

29. Oord, A.v.d., Li, Y., Vinyals, O.: Representation learning with contrastive predictive coding. arXiv preprint arXiv:1807.03748 (2018)

30. Pathak, D., Krahenbuhl, P., Donahue, J., Darrell, T., Efros, A.A.: Context encoders: feature learning by inpainting. In: Proceedings of the IEEE Conference on Computer Vision and Pattern Recognition, pp. 2536–2544 (2016)

31. Russakovsky, O., et al.: ImageNet large scale visual recognition challenge. Int. J. Comput. Vis. **115**(3), 211–252 (2015). https://doi.org/10.1007/s11263-015-0816-y
32. Snell, J., Swersky, K., Zemel, R.S.: Prototypical networks for few-shot learning. In: Advances in Neural Information Processing Systems, pp. 4077–4087 (2017)
33. Tian, Y., Krishnan, D., Isola, P.: Contrastive multiview coding. arXiv preprint arXiv:1906.05849 (2019)
34. Vinyals, O., Blundell, C., Lillicrap, T., Kavukcuoglu, K., Wierstra, D.: Matching networks for one shot learning. In: Advances in Neural Information Processing Systems, pp. 3630–3638 (2016)
35. Wu, Z., Xiong, Y., Yu, S.X., Lin, D.: Unsupervised feature learning via non-parametric instance discrimination. In: Proceedings of the IEEE Conference on Computer Vision and Pattern Recognition, pp. 3733–3742 (2018)
36. Xie, J., Girshick, R., Farhadi, A.: Unsupervised deep embedding for clustering analysis. In: International Conference on Machine Learning, pp. 478–487 (2016)
37. Yang, J., Parikh, D., Batra, D.: Joint unsupervised learning of deep representations and image clusters. In: Proceedings of the IEEE Conference on Computer Vision and Pattern Recognition, pp. 5147–5156 (2016)
38. Zhang, L., Qi, G.J., Wang, L., Luo, J.: Aet vs. aed: unsupervised representation learning by auto-encoding transformations rather than data. In: Proceedings of the IEEE Conference on Computer Vision and Pattern Recognition, pp. 2547–2555 (2019)
39. Zhang, R., Isola, P., Efros, A.A.: Colorful image colorization. In: Leibe, B., Matas, J., Sebe, N., Welling, M. (eds.) ECCV 2016. LNCS, vol. 9907, pp. 649–666. Springer, Cham (2016). https://doi.org/10.1007/978-3-319-46487-9_40
40. Zhang, R., Isola, P., Efros, A.A.: Split-brain autoencoders: unsupervised learning by cross-channel prediction. In: Proceedings of the IEEE Conference on Computer Vision and Pattern Recognition, pp. 1058–1067 (2017)
41. Zhuang, C., Zhai, A.L., Yamins, D.: Local aggregation for unsupervised learning of visual embeddings. In: Proceedings of the IEEE International Conference on Computer Vision, pp. 6002–6012 (2019)

TDMPNet: Prototype Network with Recurrent Top-Down Modulation for Robust Object Classification Under Partial Occlusion

Mingqing Xiao[1]($\boxtimes$), Adam Kortylewski[2], Ruihai Wu[1], Siyuan Qiao[2], Wei Shen[2], and Alan Yuille[2]

[1] Peking University, Beijing, China
{mingqing_xiao,wuruihai}@pku.edu.cn
[2] Johns Hopkins University, Baltimore, MD, USA
{akortyl1,siyuan.qiao,wshen10}@jhu.edu, alan.l.yuille@gmail.com

Abstract. Despite deep convolutional neural networks' great success in object classification, recent work has shown that they suffer from a severe generalization performance drop under occlusion conditions that do not appear in the training data. Due to the large variability of occluders in terms of shape and appearance, training data can hardly cover all possible occlusion conditions. However, in practice we expect models to reliably generalize to various novel occlusion conditions, rather than being limited to the training conditions. In this work, we integrate inductive priors including prototypes, partial matching and top-down modulation into deep neural networks to realize robust object classification under novel occlusion conditions, with limited occlusion in training data. We first introduce prototype learning as its regularization encourages compact data clusters for better generalization ability. Then, a visibility map at the intermediate layer based on feature dictionary and activation scale is estimated for partial matching, whose prior sifts irrelevant information out when comparing features with prototypes. Further, inspired by the important role of feedback connection in neuroscience for object recognition under occlusion, a structural prior, i.e. top-down modulation, is introduced into convolution layers, purposefully reducing the contamination by occlusion during feature extraction. Experiment results on partially occluded MNIST, vehicles from the PASCAL3D+ dataset, and vehicles from the cropped COCO dataset demonstrate the improvement under both simulated and real-world novel occlusion conditions, as well as under the transfer of datasets.

M. Xiao and R. Wu—Work done at Johns Hopkins University.

Electronic supplementary material The online version of this chapter (https://doi.org/10.1007/978-3-030-66096-3_31) contains supplementary material, which is available to authorized users.

A. Bartoli and A. Fusiello (Eds.): ECCV 2020 Workshops, LNCS 12536, pp. 447–463, 2020.
https://doi.org/10.1007/978-3-030-66096-3_31

1 Introduction

In recent years, deep convolutional neural networks (DCNNs) have achieved great success in computer vision tasks, like image classification [6,19,22] and object detection [17,18]. However, widely used deep learning models are not robust under occlusion conditions, especially when ldocclusion does not appear in the training data [3,8,25,31]. While occlusion conditions in accordance with the training data may be solved by e.g. multi-label classification, it is impossible to collect data covering all possible occlusion conditions, and novel occlusion conditions are much tougher to tackle. Over-fitting on the limited training conditions results in failure of generalization to novel occlusion conditions, which can cause fatal consequences in real applications as shown in accidents of driver-assistant systems [2]. In the real world, unexpected occlusion such as a flying tissue in front of objects, which would look like a white box patch on the captured image, always exists. Deep networks can be misguided when they have not seen such a scene in the training data. Humans, on the other hand, are still able to recognize objects under extreme occlusions by unexpected occluders [32]. Therefore, a reliable computer vision model must be robust to novel occlusion other than training conditions. In the following, occlusion refers to **novel occlusion conditions that do not appear in the training data**.

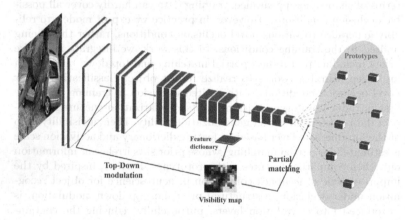

Fig. 1. Overall architecture of TDMPNet. We use the convolution layers of VGG-16 as our feature extractor and conduct prototype matching on the features. We estimate a visibility map from the pool-4 layer to focus on target object parts. The visibility map is first used for top-down feedback modulation, reducing the contamination of occlusion during feature extraction, and then for partial matching, sifting irrelevant information out when comparing features and prototypes.

A distribution inconsistency between training and testing data in terms of occlusion causes failures of traditional DCNNs at image classification. Because occlusion patterns are highly variable in terms of appearance and shape, including all possible patterns in the training data is impossible, while biased occlusion patterns do not improve the generalization performance in unbiased conditions [8].

Hence, the inconsistency cannot be avoided and data efficiency regarding occlusion should be considered. Therefore, our work focuses on training a model on limited occlusions while being able to generalize to novel occlusion conditions without assumptions on the occlusion patterns.

There are two main challenges. The first is the over-fitting on the training data, which reduces the generalization ability under novel occlusion conditions. The second is that occluders will contaminate surrounding features during feature extraction. We introduce partial prototype matching to deal with the first problem, and a top-down feedback modulation to tackle the second problem.

In cognitive science, prototype-matching is a popular theory for object recognition. From mathematical perspective, prototypes can be viewed as cluster centers of points from the same class in an embedding space, and distance performs as the matching function. Prototype learning after feature extraction is able to deal with over-fitting [20], as it imposes regularization with a nearest neighbor inductive bias to encourage compact data clusters. Furthermore, different prototypes in one class are able to account for large changes in spatial patterns, such as different viewpoints for 3D objects [8]. Prototypes have been introduced and integrated into deep network structure in few-shot learning task [20] and for rejection and class-incremental learning [27]. However, their distances are simply euclidean distances, which cannot be used directly in occlusion conditions due to the distortion of features in the occluded regions.

To tackle the problem of prototype matching under occlusion conditions, we introduce partial matching with a visibility map to focus on target object parts as illustrated in Fig. 1. Wang et al. [24] first discovered that semantic part representations for objects can be found from the internal states of trained DCNNs, based on which Wang et al. [25] and Zhang et al. [31] developed semantic part detection methods. Besides, larger activation scales of internal states are also correlated with objects [30]. Inspired by these works, we employ a filter with a visibility map on possible target object parts based on internal DCNN states and a dictionary to sift out irrelevant information. Experiments show the effective functioning of partial matching according to the filter.

In addition, we propose a top-down feedback modulation with the estimated visibility map (the feedback connection shown in Fig. 1) as a structural prior because occluders also contaminate surrounding features during the feature extraction stage. The feedback modulation helps the bottom layers to filter occlusion-induced distortions in the feature activations with high-level information, so that areas around the occluders become less distorted. Our experiments in Sect. 4 demonstrate the effective contamination reduction. Our top-down modulation is related with some neuroscience conjectures. There are several neuroscience evidence show that recurrent and feedback connections play an important role in object recognition when stimuli are partially occluded [5,15,16,21]. The main conjectures include that the recurrence fills missing data and that it sharpens certain representations by attention refinement [14]. Here we assume that top-down connection could be a neural modulation to filter occlusion-caused anomalous activations.

There are also other techniques that implicitly encourage robustness under occlusion, like cutout regularization [1]. Our model does not conflict with them and can be further combined with these techniques to improve the robustness under novel occlusion conditions.

In summary, this paper makes the following contributions:

- We introduce partial prototype matching with a visibility map based on a feature dictionary into deep neural networks for robust object classification under novel occlusion, with limited occlusion in training data. The prototypes and the visibility map are integrated into a neural network and can be trained end-to-end.
- We further propose a top-down feedback modulation in convolution layers. It imitates the neurological modulation from higher cortex to lower cortex and serves as a structural inductive prior. Experiments show that the feedback effectively reduce the contamination of occlusion during feature extraction.
- Extensive experiments on PASCAL3D+, MNIST, and COCO demonstrate that the proposed model significantly improves the robustness of DCNNs under both simulated and real novel occlusion conditions, as well as under the transfer of datasets. Furthermore, our model can be combined with regularization methods for occlusion-robustness to improve the performance.

2   Related Work

Object classification under partial occlusion. Fawzi and Frossard [3] have shown that DCNNs are not robust to partial occlusion when inputs are masked out by patches. Devries and Taylor [1] and Yun et al. [29] proposed regularization methods, e.g. cutout, by masking out patches from the images during training, which can improve robustness under occlusion to some extent. Kortylewski et al. [8] proposed dictionary-based Compositional Model. Their model is composed of a traditional DCNN and a compositional model based on the features extracted by DCNN. At runtime, the input is first classified by the DCNN, and will turn to compositional model only when the prediction uncertainty exceeds a threshold, because compositional models are less discriminative than DCNNs. Their model is not end-to-end, does not consider contamination of occlusion during feature extraction and requires a model of occluders. Kortylewski et al. [7] further extended this model to be end-to-end. Differently, our proposed model follows the deep network architecture, reduces influence of occlusions both during and after feature extraction, and is generalizable to novel occlusion conditions.

Prototype learning in deep networks. Prototype learning is a classical method in pattern recognition. After the rise of deep neural networks, Yang et al. [27] replace the traditional hand-designed features with features extracted by convolutional neural networks in prototype learning and integrate it into deep networks for both high accuracy and robust pattern classification. Prototypes are also introduced in few-shot and zero-shot learning as part of metric learning [20,23]. Nevertheless, all these works use basic measures like euclidean or cosine distance in prototype matching, which is not suitable for occlusion conditions. We introduce a filter focusing on target object parts to extend prototype matching to occlusion conditions.

Object part representation inside DCNNs. Wang et al. [24] found that by clustering feature vectors at different positions from the intermediate layer of a pre-trained deep neural network, e.g. pool-4 layer in VGG, the patterns of some cluster centers are able to reflect specific object parts. Wang et al. [25] and Zhang et al. [31] use it for semantic part detection, and Kortylewski et al. [8] use it to obtain part components in the compositional model. Related works also include [11], which added a regularizer to encourage the feature representations of DCNNs to cluster during learning, trying to obtain part representations. From another perspective, Zhang et al. [30] tried to encourage each filter to be a part detector by restricting the activations of each filter to be independent, and they estimated the part position by the activation scale. These works demonstrate that object part representation is available inside DCNNs, and activation scale contains information. Based on these ideas, we obtain a filter with a visibility map for partial prototype matching under occlusion by finding possible target object parts with their representations and activation scales, and sifting out other irrelevant information.

Feedback connections in deep networks. Despite top-down feedback connection is an ubiquitous structure in biological vision systems, it is not used in typical feed-forward DCNNs. Nayebi et al. [14] has summarized the function conjectures of recurrence in the visual systems and explored possible recurrence structures in CNNs to improve classification performance through architecture search. As for classification task under occlusion, Spoerer et al. [21] explored top-down and lateral connections for digit recognition under occlusion, but their connections are simply convolutional layers without explicit functioning. As for top-down feedback information, Fu et al. [4] learned to focus on smaller areas in the image and Li et al. [10] designed a feedback layer and an emphasis layer. But all of their feedback layers are composed of fully connected layers, which is not interpretable. Some DCNN architectures also borrow the top-down feedback idea, like CliqueNet [28]. Different from these works, our top-down feedback modulation is composed of explainable visibility map focusing on target object parts and is purposefully for reduction in contamination of occlusion.

3   Method

Our model is composed of three main parts. The first is prototype learning after feature extraction. Following it is partial matching based on a filter focusing on target object parts to extend prototype matching under occlusion. Finally, top-down modulation is introduced to reduce the contamination of occlusion.

3.1   Prototype Learning

We conduct prototype learning after feature extraction by DCNNs. Let $x \in \mathbb{R}^{H_0 \times W_0 \times 3}$ denote the input image, our feature extractor is $f_\theta : \mathbb{R}^{H_0 \times W_0 \times 3} \rightarrow$

$\mathbb{R}^{H \times W \times C}$, which is composed of convolution layer blocks in typical DCNNs. In contrast to related works [20,27], our feature is a tensor $f_\theta(x) \in \mathbb{R}^{H \times W \times C}$ rather than a vector, in order to maintain spatial information for partial matching in the next section. Suppose there are N classes for classification, we set M prototypes for each class to account for differences in spatial activation patterns. Therefore prototypes are a set of tensors $p_{i,j} \in \mathbb{R}^{H \times W \times C}$, where $i \in \{1, 2, ..., N\}$ denotes the class of the prototype, and $j \in \{1, 2, ..., M\}$ represents the index in its class.

For feedforward prediction, the image is classified to the class of its nearest prototype according to a distance function $d : \mathbb{R}^{H \times W \times C} \times \mathbb{R}^{H \times W \times C} \to [0, +\infty)$:

$$Pred(x) = \arg\min_i\{\min_j d(f_\theta(x), p_{i,j})\}. \tag{1}$$

The distance function d can simply be euclidean distance, but experiments in Sect. 4.2 show that it improves networks slightly due to the contamination of occlusion. A distance for partial matching will be introduced next section.

For backward update of parameters, we use cross entropy loss based on the distances. To be specific, distances between the feature $f_\theta(x)$ and prototypes $p_{i,j}$ produce a probability distribution over classes:

$$Pr(y = k|x) = \frac{\exp(-\gamma d_k)}{\sum_{i=1}^{N} \exp(-\gamma d_i)}, \tag{2}$$

where $d_k = \min_j d(f_\theta(x), p_{k,j})$, and γ is a parameter that control the hardness of probability assignment. We set γ to be learned by network automatically. Then based on the probability, cross entropy loss is defined:

$$L_{ce}((x, k); \theta, \{p_{i,j}\}) = -\log Pr(y = k|x). \tag{3}$$

Further, a prototype loss is added as the regularization of prototype learning:

$$L_p((x, k); \theta, \{p_{i,j}\}) = \min_{i,j} d(f_\theta(x), p_{i,j}). \tag{4}$$

Different from [27], we only consider the nearest prototype when computing distances and probabilities, because our M prototypes in the same class are designed to represent different states of objects, such as different viewpoints, which may vary a lot in spatial distribution.

We initialize the prototypes by clustering the features of a sub dataset using k-means algorithm [13]. It prevents the degeneration of multiple prototypes to a single prototype.

3.2 Partial Matching Under Occlusion

The core problem for extending prototype learning directly to occlusion conditions is the matching function. Since occlusion will contaminate the object feature representation, simple distance between the feature and prototypes won't be valid enough to do classification. Experiments in Sect. 4.2 show that pure

(a)   (b)   (c)   (d)

Fig. 2. Visualization of activation scale in the pool-4 layer. It shows that the activation scale at parts informative for classification, e.g. object parts, is larger than other areas.

prototype matching improves deep neural networks slightly. Focusing on valid parts in features is required.

We employ a filter with a visibility map based on feature dictionary and activation scale to focus on valid unoccluded parts in features, which enables partial matching. We learn a feature dictionary in the intermediate layer by clustering feature vectors over the whole dataset on the feature map, which can represent specific activation patterns of parts in the images. Specifically, feature dictionary is obtained by clustering all normalized vector $v_{k,i,j} \in \mathbb{R}^{1 \times 1 \times C^l}$ at position (i,j) of the feature map $f_\theta^l(x_k) \in \mathbb{R}^{H^l \times W^l \times C^l}$ at the intermediate layer l over the dataset $\{x_k\}$. Related works [8,24] show that cluster centers are mostly activated by similar parts in the images, most of which are object parts. More detailed visualization refer to related works [8,24,25]. Based on the feature dictionary $\{D_k\}$, we compare the similarity between the vectors $f_\theta^l(x)_{i,j}$ of the feature at layer l and each component D_k: $S(f_\theta^l(x)_{i,j}, D_k) = \frac{f_\theta^l(x)_{i,j}}{\left\| f_\theta^l(x)_{i,j} \right\|_2} \cdot D_k$. The higher the maximum similarity over $\{D_k\}$ is, the more likely is the area a target object part. Therefore, we can sift occlusion out by its low similarity.

However, there are also a few background activation patterns irrelevant to classification in the dictionary. We use the relative scale of activations to filter them out. As shown in the Fig. 2, the scales of activations in a trained network for most irrelevant background are much lower than objects. It is probably because deep networks could learn to focus on image parts that contribute to discrimination most. Considering activation scales is helpful to filter irrelevant background and maintain most informative signals.

Combining the similarity with the feature dictionary and the activation scale enables us to estimate a visibility map that focuses on unoccluded target object parts. The formulation for focusing attention at position (i,j) in layer l is:

$$a_{i,j}^l = ReLU(\max_k f_\theta(x)_{i,j}^l \cdot D_k). \tag{5}$$

Since the scale of the activation after the ReLU function could be large, we normalize $a_{i,j}^l$. We use the following linear function with clipping since it preserves proper relative relationship among activation scales:

$$A_{i,j}^l = \frac{\min(\max(a_{i,j}^l, a_l), a_u)}{a_u}, \tag{6}$$

where a_l and a_u are lower and upper thresholds that can be dynamically determined according to $\{a_{i,j}^l\}$.

Subsequently, the visibility map is down-sampled to the same spatial scale of $f_\theta(x)_{i,j}$ for partial matching. We let $\{A_{i,j}\}$ denote it. Based on $\{A_{i,j}\}$, partial matching between the feature and prototypes is enabled. Let $f_\theta(x) \odot A$ denote the application of the filter by scaling vectors $f_\theta(x)_{i,j}$ with $A_{i,j}$. A distance for partial matching under occlusion used for Eq.(1), (2) and (4) is defined as:

$$d(f_\theta(x), p_{i,j}) = \frac{1}{2} \left\| f_\theta(x) \odot A - p_{i,j} \odot A \right\|_2^2 \tag{7}$$

In this way, we only compare unoccluded target object parts based on the estimated visibility map. Due to the high-dimension of $f_\theta(x)$ and $p_{i,j}$, we normalize them on a unit sphere at first and compute the euclidean distance after applying the filter, in order to obtain a valid distance.

We learn the feature dictionary $\{D_k\}$ through clustering. So similar to prototype learning, we initialize it with clustering result on the pre-trained neural network, and add the clustering loss in the whole loss function during training:

$$L_D = \sum_{i,j} \min_k \frac{1}{2} \left\| \frac{f_\theta(x)_{i,j}}{\|f_\theta(x)_{i,j}\|_2} - D_k \right\|_2^2 \tag{8}$$

Note that we simply add a normalization layer in the network to normalize d_k and ignore the notation in the formula.

3.3 Top-Down Feedback Modulation

Our proposed partial matching only sifts out irrelevant feature vectors when comparing features and prototypes. However, occluders may also contaminate its nearby feature vectors. We propose to filter the occlusion-caused anomalous activitions in the lower layers to reduce such contamination and thus obtain cleaner features around the occluder.

Based on the estimated visibility map at a higher layer, a top-down feedback connection is introduced to reduce the contamination of occlusion in lower layers. Formally, let $\{A_{i,j}^b\}$ denote the up-sampling filter result of $\{A_{i,j}^l\}$ to the same spatial size as the bottom layer b, such as pool-1 layer, and f_θ^b as the function from input to layer b. A new activation pattern at layer b can be obtained by applying the filter to the old activation:

$$f_\theta^b(x)_{new} = f_\theta^b(x) \odot A^b \tag{9}$$

The new activation is again feed-forwarded, as a recurrent procedure. The recurrence can be carried out for multiple times, gradually refining features to reduce the contamination of occlusion. The upper threshold in Eq.(6) prevents degeneration of the filter attention to only one point, and the lower threshold in Eq.(6) prevents mistaken filtration due to the possible contamination of occlusion from the bottom layer to top layers.

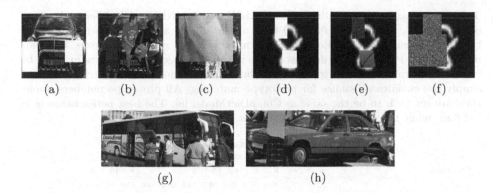

(a)   (b)   (c)   (d)   (e)   (f)

(g)   (h)

Fig. 3. Examples of synthetic occlusion and real-world occlusion. (a), (b), (c) correspond to level 1–3 on PASCAL3D+; (d), (e), (f) correspond to level 1–3 on MNIST. Different types of occlusion appearances are: white boxes (a&d), random noise (f), textures (c&e), and natural objects (b). (g) and (h) are real-world occlusion conditions from the COCO dataset.

In summary, the overall architecture with our three components is shown in Fig. 1. Our overall loss function for training is:

$$L = L_{ce}((x, k); \theta, \{p_{i,j}\}) + \lambda_1 L_p((x, k); \theta, \{p_{i,j}\}) + \lambda_2 L_D \qquad (10)$$

4   Experiments

4.1   Dataset and Settings

We evaluate our model for object classification on partially occluded MNIST digits [9], vehicles from the PASCAL3D+ dataset [26], and vehicles from the COCO dataset [12]. For PASCAL3D+ and MNIST, we simulate novel occlusion, while for COCO, we split non-occlusion images and occlusion images, and test both direct generalization from PASCAL3D+ to novel occlusion in COCO and performance under training on non-occlusion COCO images.

First, to test the generalization ability to novel occlusion conditions in MNIST and PASCAL3D+, we train our model on original images and test under simulation of partial occlusion by masking out patches in the images and filling them with white boxes, random noise or textures following [8], to imitate unexpected occlusion in front of objects like flying tissues. In addition, we also use the images provided in the VehicleSemanticPart dataset [25] for the PASCAL3D+ vehicles, where occlusion was simulated by superimposing segmented objects over the target object. Different occlusion levels are also defined corresponding to the percentage of occlusion over objects based on the object segmentation masks provided in the PASCAL3D+ and threshold segmentation of the MNIST digits. Examples refer to Fig. 3. We use the standard splits for the train and test data. For the PASCAL3D+ dataset, we follow the setup in [24] and [8], that is

Table 1. Classification results for PASCAL3D+ and MNIST with different levels of occlusion (0%, 20–40%, 40–60%, 60–80% of the object are occluded) and different types of occlusion (w = white boxes, n = noise boxes, t = textured boxes, o = natural objects). PrototypeNet denotes only replacing fully-connected layers in VGG by prototype learning, without top-down modulation. Without partial matching denotes simply use euclidean distance for prototype matching. All prototype numbers in one class are set to 4, to be the same as CompDictModel [8]. The best performance is in red font, while the second best is in blue font.

PASCAL3D+ Classification under Occlusion

Occ. Area	0%	Level-1: 20-40%				Level-2: 40-60%				Level-3: 60-80%				Mean
Occ. Type	-	w	n	t	o	w	n	t	o	w	n	t	o	-
VGG	99.4	97.5	97.5	97.3	92.1	91.7	90.6	90.2	73.0	65.0	60.7	56.4	52.2	81.8
CompDictModel [8]	98.3	96.8	95.9	96.2	94.4	91.2	91.8	91.3	91.4	71.6	80.7	77.3	87.2	89.5
PrototypeNet without partial matching	99.2	97.1	97.6	97.2	95.3	91.2	93.0	91.3	81.3	61.9	60.9	57.9	61.5	83.5
PrototypeNet with partial matching	99.3	98.4	98.9	98.5	97.3	96.4	97.1	96.2	89.2	84.0	87.4	79.7	74.5	92.1
TDMPNet with 1 recurrence	99.3	98.4	98.9	98.7	97.2	96.1	97.4	96.4	90.2	81.1	87.6	81.2	76.8	92.3
TDMPNet with 2 recurrence	99.2	98.5	98.8	98.5	97.3	96.2	97.4	96.6	90.2	81.5	87.7	81.9	77.1	92.4
TDMPNet with 3 recurrence	99.3	98.4	98.9	98.5	97.4	96.1	97.5	96.6	91.6	82.1	88.1	82.7	79.8	92.8
TDMPNet with 4 recurrence	99.3	98.4	98.9	98.4	97.2	96.0	97.5	96.5	91.4	81.5	87.7	82.4	79.3	92.7
VGG + cutout [1]	99.4	98.1	97.9	98.2	93.8	94.8	92.3	92.4	81.3	75.4	67.7	66.3	64.8	86.3
TDMPNet + cutout	99.3	98.8	98.9	98.8	97.5	97.7	97.9	97.2	91.9	88.2	90.2	84.7	80.5	94.0
Human [8]	100.0	100.0				100.0				98.3				99.5

MNIST Classification under Occlusion

Occ. Area	0%	Level-1: 20-40%			Level-2: 40-60%			Level-3: 60-80%			Mean
Occ. Type	-	w	n	t	w	n	t	w	n	t	-
VGG	99.4	76.8	63.1	71.4	51.1	41.9	43.2	24.9	25.7	23.5	52.1
CompDictModel [8]	99.1	85.2	82.3	83.4	72.4	71.0	72.8	45.3	41.2	43.0	69.4
PrototypeNet without partial matching	99.3	81.0	71.8	77.4	53.4	44.4	50.4	27.4	28.3	29.9	56.3
PrototypeNet with partial matching	99.4	86.3	78.8	82.9	67.3	56.1	59.7	43.6	36.8	37.6	64.9
TDMPNet with 1 recurrence	99.4	87.6	81.4	85.3	69.3	57.9	64.0	46.1	36.8	42.1	67.0
TDMPNet with 2 recurrence	99.4	88.2	82.2	85.5	70.6	59.8	64.9	47.0	38.8	42.8	67.9
TDMPNet with 3 recurrence	99.4	88.7	82.9	85.7	71.4	60.2	65.2	47.8	38.7	42.8	68.3
TDMPNet with 4 recurrence	99.5	88.3	84.2	86.3	72.7	61.6	66.3	49.3	40.0	44.0	69.3
VGG + cutout [1]	99.4	91.5	75.8	82.0	78.8	59.0	60.4	50.4	40.6	37.0	67.5
TDMPNet + cutout	99.4	92.2	95.4	93.5	79.7	84.1	78.5	57.7	59.0	51.4	79.1
Human [8]	100.0	92.7			91.3			64			84.4

the task is to discriminate between 12 objects during training, while at test time the 6 vehicle categories are tested.

Then, we crop the COCO dataset with the bounding box ground truth and divide the occluded and unoccluded images manually, whose categories accord with the setup of PASCAL3D+ above. We first directly employ the model trained on PASCAL3D+ on the occluded images from COCO (occluders do not appear in PASCAL3D+), to evaluate the generalization ability under real novel occlusion and transferred datasets. Then, we train our model on non-occlusion images from COCO and test on occluded images. We enrich the training data with PASCAL3D+ due to the insufficiency of images. The occlusion examples are shown in Fig. 3.

We utilize convolution layers in a VGG-16 pre-trained on the ImageNet dataset as the feature extraction part. Prototype learning is conducted on the pool-5 layer. The visibility map is estimated from the pool-4 layer, and the top-down modulation is imposed on pool-1 layer. We set feature dictionary components to be 512 for all datasets and use von Mises-Fisher clustering result [8] as the initialization. Other training details refer to the Supplementary Material. We compare our model with VGG-16 finetuned on the datasets, dictionary-based Compositional Model [8], and human baseline. We also compare cutout regularization [1] in VGG and our model, which is similar to adding occlusion in the training data as it masks out patches. The hole number and the length of cutout is set to be 1 and 48. Other training settings follow the previous settings. The recurrence number of TDMPNet is three if unspecified.

4.2   Results on Simulated Novel Occlusion

Results for classification at different occlusion levels are shown in Table 1. They show that DCNNs do not generalize well under synthetic novel occlusion. TDMP-Net significantly outperforms VGG in every occlusion conditions and remains about the same accuracy when there's no occlusion. Further augmented by cutout regularization, our model achieves significantly best results.

Pure prototype learning improves DCNNs slightly. As shown in the results, direct prototype learning with simple distance function has little improvement. Though it outperforms VGG in some conditions, the improvements are low compared with follow-up results.

Partial matching plays a crucial role. As illustrated by the results, partial matching significantly improves the performance. For the mean accuracy over all conditions, it improves 10.3 % on PASCAL3D+ and 14.5 % on MNIST compared with VGG. In the low occlusion level on PASCAL3D+, partial matching achieves the best results even without top-down modulation.

Top-Down modulation works well for severe occlusions. Top-down recurrence could effectively improve the performance in relatively hard tasks that even human performance drops. As recurrence times goes up, the features are more pure and therefore performance increases. A more detailed analysis is in the following section. With top-down modulation, the finial mean accuracy outperforms VGG 11 % on PASCAL3D+ and 17.2 % on MNIST, reflecting its robustness under partial occlusion.

Combination with other techniques can further improve the performance greatly. As shown in Table 1, cutout regularization can significantly boost both VGG and TDMPNet. It shows that TDMPNet does not conflict with other occlusion-robust techniques, and their combination can lead to better results. TDMPNet with cutout regularization achieves the best result for robustness under synthetic novel occlusion, with a boost of 7.7 % on PASCAL3D+ and 11.6 % on MNIST compared with VGG with cutout regularization.

Table 2. Classification results for cropped COCO. Transfer Accuracy is the direct transfer generalization performance from PASCAL3D+ to cropped COCO. Accuracy is the performance when trained on non-occlusion images of COCO with supplementary images from PASCAL3D+, and tested on occlusion images of COCO.

Model	Transfer Accuracy	Accuracy
VGG	86.66	87.27
VGG + cutout	86.22	88.58
TDMPNet	86.92	89.45
TDMPNet + cutout	87.88	90.32

Comparison between TDMPNet and CompDictModel. Dictionary-based Compositional Model [8] is a model that uses both VGG and a compositional model for classification under partial occlusion. Details refer to Related Work and the original paper. Results show that TDMPNet outperforms CompDictModel in most conditions except Level-3 'o' condition in PASCAL3D+. A possible reason is that CompDictModel requires a complex model of occlusion. Differently, our model aims at generalization to novel occlusion conditions and makes no assumptions on occlusion. Another reason is that CompDictModel learn compositional models from the pool-4 layer, which may benefit certain conditions. Detailed analysis refer to the Supplementary Material. In addition, our model is end-to-end, with fewer parameters and is simpler in computation compared with CompDictModel.

4.3   Results on Real-World Novel Occlusion

Table 2 are the results of transfer generalization from PASCAL3D+ to novel occlusion in cropped COCO dataset, and the results of training on non-occlusion images from COCO with supplements. It shows actual improvement of TDMP-Net under real-world novel occlusion, even under the transfer of datasets. As shown in Table 2, under the transfer generalization, TDMPNet outperforms VGG by 0.26 % and TDMPNet with cutout demonstrate a more considerable improvement with 1.22 % accuracy boost, while VGG with cutout do not improve the performance. When trained on unoccluded images from COCO, TDMPNet still demonstrate its superiority over VGG, with a boost of 2.18 % both without cutout and 1.74 % both with cutout. Note that VGG with cutout regularization does not generalize its improvement to transferred datasets, while TDMPNet maintains the superiority. It demonstrates the better generalization ability of TDMPNet under novel real-world occlusion conditions and transferred datasets.

4.4   Comparison of Prototype Number

In the previous experiments, we set prototype number as 4 to compare with CompDictModel. We further compare different prototype numbers and visualize images that are assigned to the same prototype.

Table 3. Comparison of different prototype numbers for TDAPNet on PASCAL3D+. The best performance is in red font, while the second best is in blue font.

PASCAL3D+ Classification under Occlusion

Occ. Area	0%	Level-1: 20-40%				Level-2: 40-60%				Level-3: 60-80%				Mean
Occ. Type	-	w	n	t	o	w	n	t	o	w	n	t	o	-
1 prototype, 1 recurrence	99.2	97.9	98.5	97.9	96.4	95.1	96.5	95.2	88.6	79.1	84.8	77.9	75.1	90.9
1 prototype, 2 recurrence	99.2	97.9	98.3	97.9	96.3	95.1	96.6	95.0	89.1	78.9	85.2	78.2	75.5	91.0
1 prototype, 3 recurrence	99.0	98.0	98.3	97.8	96.5	94.7	96.3	95.3	89.5	79.7	85.2	79.0	76.9	91.2
4 prototype, 1 recurrence	99.3	98.4	98.9	98.7	97.2	96.1	97.4	96.4	90.2	81.1	87.6	81.2	76.8	92.3
4 prototype, 2 recurrence	99.2	98.5	98.8	98.5	97.3	96.2	97.4	96.6	90.2	81.5	87.7	81.9	77.1	92.4
4 prototype, 3 recurrence	99.3	98.4	98.9	98.5	97.4	96.1	97.5	96.6	91.6	82.1	88.1	82.7	79.8	92.8
8 prototype, 1 recurrence	99.3	98.7	98.9	98.7	97.5	96.4	97.5	96.7	89.6	81.1	87.6	80.9	74.7	92.1
8 prototype, 2 recurrence	99.4	98.7	99.0	98.6	97.7	96.1	97.5	96.8	90.8	82.5	88.7	82.5	78.6	92.8
8 prototype, 3 recurrence	99.3	98.6	99.1	98.6	97.6	96.2	97.5	96.7	91.4	82.4	88.2	83.0	78.6	92.9

Multiple prototypes improve the performance. As shown in Table 3, 4 prototypes outperform 1 prototype, while 8 prototypes are about the same as 4 prototypes. It implies that modeling different spatial patterns enables prototypes to be more inclusive, and 4 prototypes are enough to account for the spatial variance in the PASCAL3D+ dataset.

Multiple prototypes maintain spatial structures. As shown in the Supplementary Material, the four prototypes in our model mainly correspond to different viewpoints with certain spatial structure. When there is only one prototype for each class, network simply learns a metric to push all possible activation patterns at a position close with each other, to ensure that the prototype is the closest to all entities. This may lose spatial structure of objects. Multiple prototypes are able to tackle such problem effectively.

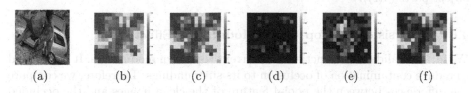

(a)   (b)   (c)   (d)   (e)   (f)

Fig. 4. Visualization of visibility maps. Lighter areas represent more focusing attention and darker areas are likely to be filtered. (a) is the occluded image. (b) is the visibility map only based on activation scale. (c) is the visibility map based on feature dictionary and activation scale in the first feed-forward procedure. (d) is the visibility map where feature dictionary enhance attention compared with (b). (e) is the visibility map where feature dictionary reduce attention compared with (b). (f) is the final visibility map after one top-down recurrence.

Table 4. Contamination reduction percentage by top-down modulation on PAS-CAL3D+. Larger number reflects better results.

Occ. Area	Level-1: 20–40%				Level-2: 40–60%				Level-3: 60–80%			
Occ. Type	w	n	t	o	w	n	t	o	w	n	t	o
TDMPNet with 1 recurrence	14.1%	15.2%	15.7%	12.5%	9.5%	9.2%	10.1%	11.7%	11.1%	11.1%	12.9%	10.9%
TDMPNet with 2 recurrence	16.7%	17.9%	18.6%	13.9%	10.3%	10.0%	10.9%	13.1%	13.0%	13.1%	15.3%	12.1%
TDMPNet with 3 recurrence	19.8%	21.1%	21.9%	16.0%	10.9%	10.7%	11.6%	15.3%	15.3%	15.5%	17.8%	14.1%
TDMPNet with 4 recurrence	19.9%	21.4%	22.2%	15.8%	10.6%	10.4%	11.4%	15.3%	15.6%	15.8%	18.2%	14.2%

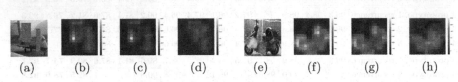

(a)   (b)   (c)   (d)   (e)   (f)   (g)   (h)

Fig. 5. Visualization of difference reduction after one top-down recurrence at pool-4 layer. (a)&(e) are the occluded images. (b)&(f) are the activation difference between clean and occluded images before top-down recurrence, while (c)&(g) are the activation difference after top-down recurrence. Lighter areas represent more difference. (d)&(h) are the difference reduction. Lighter areas represent more difference reduction.

4.5 Analysis of the Filter Functioning

The classification results demonstrate the importance of the filter with visibility maps for partial matching. We illustrate how the two components in the filter contribute to focusing on informative parts through visualization of visibility maps. As shown in the Fig. 4, the activation scale (4(b)) increases the filtering to the background in 4(a). Based on it the feature dictionary further increases the filtering on the occluding parrots (4(e)) and enhance attention on several positions (4(d)), resulting in visibility map 4(c). After a top-down recurrence, the filter further sifts irrelevant information out and mainly focuses on target object parts (4(f)).

4.6 Analysis of the Top-Down Modulation Effect

We further validate the function of recurrent top-down modulation. It is designed to reduce contamination of occlusion to its surroundings. Therefore, we compare the differences between the pool-4 feature of the clean images and the occluded images before and after top-down recurrence. Specifically, let f_c^0, f_c^r, f_o^0, f_o^r denote the pool-4 feature of the clean image before and after recurrence and the occluded image before and after recurrence respectively, and let m_o denote the mask of occlusion area obtained by average down-sampling of the occlusion ground truth. We compute $R_c = 1 - \frac{sum(|f_o^r \odot m_o - f_c^r \odot m_o|)}{sum(|f_o^1 \odot m_o - f_c^1 \odot m_o|)}$ as the contamination reduction percentage. Results in Table 4 clearly show that top-down recurrence is capable of reducing contamination in the bottom layer based on the information from the top layer, and nearly the more the recurrence, the more the reduction. Further, the visualization of difference reduction is in Fig. 5, showing the reduction of occlusion-caused difference in features surrounding the occluders.

5   Conclusion

In this work, we integrate inductive priors including prototypes, partial matching, and top-down modulation into deep neural networks for robust object classification under novel occlusion conditions, with limited occlusion in training data. The filter in partial matching extends prototype matching to occlusion conditions, and the top-down modulation deals with the contamination of occlusion during feature extraction. Our model significantly improves current deep networks, and its combination with other regularization methods leads to better results. Experiments demonstrate the superiority under both simulated and real novel occlusion conditions and under the transfer of datasets.

Acknowledgements. This work was partly supported by ONR N00014-18-1-2119.

References

1. DeVries, T., Taylor, G.W.: Improved regularization of convolutional neural networks with cutout. arXiv preprint arXiv:1708.04552 (2017)
2. Economist, T.: Why uber's self-driving car killed a pedestrian (2017)
3. Fawzi, A., Frossard, P.: Measuring the effect of nuisance variables on classifiers. In: Proceedings of the British Machine Vision Conference (BMVC), pp. 137.1-137.12. BMVA (2016). https://doi.org/10.5244/C.30.137
4. Fu, J., Zheng, H., Mei, T.: Look closer to see better: recurrent attention convolutional neural network for fine-grained image recognition. In: Proceedings of the IEEE Conference on Computer Vision and Pattern Recognition, pp. 4438–4446 (2017)
5. Gilbert, C.D., Li, W.: Top-down influences on visual processing. Nat. Rev. Neurosci. **14**(5), 350 (2013)
6. He, K., Zhang, X., Ren, S., Sun, J.: Deep residual learning for image recognition. In: Proceedings of the IEEE Conference on Computer Vision and Pattern Recognition, pp. 770–778 (2016)
7. Kortylewski, A., He, J., Liu, Q., Yuille, A.L.: Compositional convolutional neural networks: A deep architecture with innate robustness to partial occlusion. In: Proceedings of the IEEE/CVF Conference on Computer Vision and Pattern Recognition, pp. 8940–8949 (2020)
8. Kortylewski, A., Liu, Q., Wang, H., Zhang, Z., Yuille, A.: Combining compositional models and deep networks for robust object classification under occlusion. In: The IEEE Winter Conference on Applications of Computer Vision, pp. 1333–1341 (2020)
9. LeCun, Y.: The mnist database of handwritten digits. http://yann.lecun.com/exdb/mnist/ (1998)
10. Li, X., Jie, Z., Feng, J., Liu, C., Yan, S.: Learning with rethinking: recurrently improving convolutional neural networks through feedback. Pattern Recognit. **79**, 183–194 (2018)
11. Liao, R., Schwing, A., Zemel, R., Urtasun, R.: Learning deep parsimonious representations. In: Advances in Neural Information Processing Systems, pp. 5076–5084 (2016)

12. Lin, T.-Y., et al.: Microsoft COCO: common objects in context. In: Fleet, D., Pajdla, T., Schiele, B., Tuytelaars, T. (eds.) ECCV 2014. LNCS, vol. 8693, pp. 740–755. Springer, Cham (2014). https://doi.org/10.1007/978-3-319-10602-1_48
13. Lloyd, S.: Least squares quantization in PCM. IEEE Trans. Inf. Theory **28**(2), 129–137 (1982)
14. Nayebi, A., et al.: Task-driven convolutional recurrent models of the visual system. In: Advances in Neural Information Processing Systems, pp. 5290–5301 (2018)
15. O'Reilly, R.C., Wyatte, D., Herd, S., Mingus, B., Jilk, D.J.: Recurrent processing during object recognition. Front. Psychol. **4**, 124 (2013)
16. Rajaei, K., Mohsenzadeh, Y., Ebrahimpour, R., Khaligh-Razavi, S.M.: Beyond core object recognition: recurrent processes account for object recognition under occlusion. PLoS Comput. Biol. **15**(5), e1007001 (2019)
17. Redmon, J., Divvala, S., Girshick, R., Farhadi, A.: You only look once: unified, real-time object detection. In: Proceedings of the IEEE Conference on Computer Vision and Pattern Recognition, pp. 779–788 (2016)
18. Ren, S., He, K., Girshick, R., Sun, J.: Faster r-cnn: towards real-time object detection with region proposal networks. In: Advances in Neural Information Processing Systems, pp. 91–99 (2015)
19. Simonyan, K., Zisserman, A.: Very deep convolutional networks for large-scale image recognition. arXiv preprint arXiv:1409.1556 (2014)
20. Snell, J., Swersky, K., Zemel, R.: Prototypical networks for few-shot learning. In: Advances in Neural Information Processing Systems, pp. 4077–4087 (2017)
21. Spoerer, C.J., McClure, P., Kriegeskorte, N.: Recurrent convolutional neural networks: a better model of biological object recognition. Front. Psychol. **8**, 1551 (2017)
22. Sutskever, I., Hinton, G.E., Krizhevsky, A.: Imagenet classification with deep convolutional neural networks. In: Advances in Neural Information Processing Systems, pp. 1097–1105 (2012)
23. Vinyals, O., et al.: Matching networks for one shot learning. In: Advances in Neural Information Processing Systems, pp. 3630–3638 (2016)
24. Wang, J., Zhang, Z., Xie, C., Premachandran, V., Yuille, A.: Unsupervised learning of object semantic parts from internal states of cnns by population encoding. arXiv preprint arXiv:1511.06855 (2015)
25. Wang, J., et al.: Visual concepts and compositional voting. arXiv preprint arXiv:1711.04451 (2017)
26. Xiang, Y., Mottaghi, R., Savarese, S.: Beyond pascal: a benchmark for 3D object detection in the wild. In: IEEE Winter Conference on Applications of Computer Vision, pp. 75–82. IEEE (2014)
27. Yang, H.M., Zhang, X.Y., Yin, F., Liu, C.L.: Robust classification with convolutional prototype learning. In: Proceedings of the IEEE Conference on Computer Vision and Pattern Recognition, pp. 3474–3482 (2018)
28. Yang, Y., Zhong, Z., Shen, T., Lin, Z.: Convolutional neural networks with alternately updated clique. In: Proceedings of the IEEE Conference on Computer Vision and Pattern Recognition, pp. 2413–2422 (2018)
29. Yun, S., Han, D., Oh, S.J., Chun, S., Choe, J., Yoo, Y.: Cutmix: regularization strategy to train strong classifiers with localizable features. arXiv preprint arXiv:1905.04899 (2019)
30. Zhang, Q., Nian Wu, Y., Zhu, S.C.: Interpretable convolutional neural networks. In: Proceedings of the IEEE Conference on Computer Vision and Pattern Recognition, pp. 8827–8836 (2018)

31. Zhang, Z., Xie, C., Wang, J., Xie, L., Yuille, A.L.: Deepvoting: a robust and explainable deep network for semantic part detection under partial occlusion. In: Proceedings of the IEEE Conference on Computer Vision and Pattern Recognition, pp. 1372–1380 (2018)

32. Zhu, H., Tang, P., Yuille, A.: Robustness of object recognition under extreme occlusion in humans and computational models. arXiv preprint arXiv:1905.04598 (2019)

What Leads to Generalization of Object Proposals?

Rui Wang$^{(\boxtimes)}$, Dhruv Mahajan, and Vignesh Ramanathan

Facebook AI, Menlo Park, USA
{ruiw,dhruvm,vigneshr}@fb.com

Abstract. Object proposal generation is often the first step in many detection models. It is lucrative to train a good proposal model, that generalizes to unseen classes. Motivated by this, we study how a detection model trained on a small set of source classes can provide proposals that *generalize* to unseen classes. We systematically study the properties of the dataset – visual diversity and label space granularity – required for good generalization. We show the trade-off between using fine-grained labels and coarse labels. We introduce the idea of prototypical classes: a set of sufficient and necessary classes required to train a detection model to obtain generalized proposals in a more data-efficient way. On the Open Images V4 dataset, we show that only 25% of the classes can be selected to form such a prototypical set. The resulting proposals from a model trained with these classes is only 4.3% worse than using all the classes, in terms of average recall (AR). We also demonstrate that Faster R-CNN model leads to better generalization of proposals compared to a single-stage network like RetinaNet.

Keywords: Object proposals · Object detection · Generalization

1 Introduction

Object detection systems have shown considerable improvements for fully [3, 18,20,25,26] and weakly supervised settings [1,7,31] that only use image-level labels. Both approaches typically consider detection as a combination of two tasks: (a) localization of the objects using proposals and (b) classification of the proposals into correct classes. A generalized proposal model that localizes all classes can help in scaling object detection. This could lead to the use of fewer or no bounding box annotations to only solve the classification task and development of more sophisticated classifiers, as explored in works like [29,34].

Many detection models [18,26] have been developed in recent years, which can be used to obtain high quality object proposals. However, an equally important aspect that determines the generalization ability of proposals is *the dataset* used

Electronic supplementary material The online version of this chapter (https://doi.org/10.1007/978-3-030-66096-3_32) contains supplementary material, which is available to authorized users.

to train these models. In particular, the extent to which object localization depends on the categories used to train the model has not been well quantified and studied in detail. Towards this end, we define "generalization" as the ability of a model to localize (not classify) objects not annotated in the training dataset. In our work, we answer several questions about *dataset properties* and *modeling choices* required for generalized proposals:

- **What are the properties of object classes to ensure generalization of proposals from a model?** First, we show that it is crucial to have visual diversity to obtain generalized proposals. We need examples of different vehicles like "car" and "boats", even if the examples are only labelled as "vehicle". Further, we hypothesize the existence of *prototypical classes* as a subset of leaf classes in a semantic hierarchy that are sufficient and necessary to construct a dataset to train a generalized proposal model. We define new quantitative metrics to measure these properties for any set of classes and show that it is possible to construct a small prototypical set of object classes. This has positive implications for large taxonomies, since it is sufficient to annotate examples only for the prototypical classes.
- **Does the label-granularity of the dataset affect generalization? If so, what is the coarsest granularity that can be used?** Coarse-grained labels ("vehicles" instead of "taxis") are significantly less tedious to annotate and more accurate than fine-grained labels. Past works like RFCNN-3000 [29] argued that a single super class might be sufficient to obtain good proposals. However, we show that there is a trade-off between using very few coarse classes and large-number of fine-grained classes, and a middle-ground approach leads to best generalization.
- **What are the *modeling* choices that are critical for leveraging state-of-the-art detectors to obtain generalized proposals?** We show that: (a) detections from two-stage networks like Faster R-CNN are better for obtaining generalized proposals than a single-stage network like RetinaNet, (b) while class-specific bounding box regression is typically used in Faster R-CNN, it is beneficial only when considering larger number of proposals (average recall AR@1000) and class-agnostic regression is better when considering fewer proposals (AR@100) and (c) choice of NMS threshold is dependent on the number of proposals being considered (AR@100 or AR@1000).

On OIV4 [16], we show that compared to training with all the object classes, using a prototypical subset of 25% of the object classes only leads to a drop of 4.3% in average recall (AR@100), while training with 50% of such classes leads to a negligible drop of 0.9%. We also show how the detections from Faster R-CNN can be fused to obtain high quality proposals that have 10% absolute gain in AR@100 compared to the class-agnostic proposals of the RPN from the same network and 3.5% better than RetinaNet. To stress the practical importance of generalized proposals, we also show that generalization ability is directly correlated with the performance of weakly supervised detection models.

2 Related Work

Generalizing Localization Across Multiple Classes: The idea of different object classes sharing the same structure has been exploited in building detection models for a long time [5, 21, 22, 28, 33]. More recently, [3, 26] also have a dedicated proposal network for object localization. However these works do not measure the transferability of proposals trained on one set of classes to another.

Uijlings *et al.* [34] tried to transfer information from coarse source classes to fine-grained target classes that share similar localization properties. They showed that this can help weakly supervised detection for the target classes. LSDA [11] transformed classifiers into detectors by sharing knowledge between classes. Multiple works [9, 12, 27, 32] showed the benefit of sharing localization information between similar classes to improve semi supervised and weakly supervised detection. Yang *et al.* [36] trained a large-scale detection model following similar principles. Singh *et al.* [29] showed that even a detector trained with one class can localize objects of different classes sufficiently well due to commonality between classes. We generalize this idea further. There has also been work on learning models [6, 25, 36] with a combination of bounding boxes for certain classes and only class labels for others. They inherently leverage the idea that localization can generalize across multiple classes. We provide systematic ways to quantify and measure this property for proposal models.

Object Proposal Generation Models: There have been many seminal works on generating class-agnostic object proposals [14, 24, 35, 37]. A comprehensive study of different methods can be found in [13] and a study of proposal evaluation metrics can be found in [2]. Proposal models have also been trained with dedicated architectures and objectives in [15, 23, 30]. In our work, we leverage standard models like Faster R-CNN and focus on the dataset properties required to achieve generalization with this model.

3 Approach

We study two important aspects involved in obtaining generalized proposals:

(1) **Data Properties** such as the granularity of the label space (shown in Fig. 1a), and the visual diversity of object classes under each label, required for generalization of proposals. The idea of label granularity and visual diversity is shown in Fig. 1b. We investigate how a smaller subset of "prototypical" object classes in a dataset which is representative of all other classes can be identified.

(2) **Modeling Choice** for leveraging a detector trained on a dataset with seen classes to obtain proposals that generalize to unseen classes.

3.1 Dataset Properties

The choice of labels and data used to train the model is crucial for generalization. To study these properties, we assume: (a) classes are organized in a semantic tree and (b) internal nodes do not have any data of their own, that are not categorized into one of its child nodes.

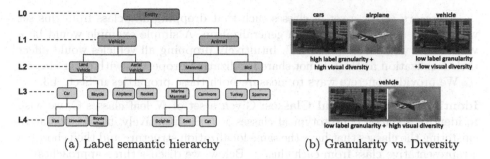

(a) Label semantic hierarchy   (b) Granularity vs. Diversity

Fig. 1. We study two important dataset properties needed to train a proposal model: label granularity and visual diversity. (a) Label granularity can be represented by different levels in a semantic hierarchy as shown. (b) The difference between label granularity and visual diversity is illustrated. At the same granularity, we can either have high or low visual diversity as shown

Label Space Granularity. As we noted through some examples earlier, it is intuitive that we might not need fine-grained labels to train a good localization model. To quantitatively study the effect of granularity, we construct different datasets with the same set of images and object bounding boxes, but consider classes at different levels of semantic hierarchy (Fig. 1a). We then train a model with these datasets and evaluate the generalization ability as a function of label granularity. For instance, for the coarsest root level, we assign all the bounding boxes the same "object" label. For an intermediate level, we collapse all leaf-labels to their corresponding parent labels at that level to train the model. While a fine-grained label space provides more information, a model trained at this level also attempts to distinguish object classes with similar structure and this could affect generalization. We quantify this trade-off in Sect. 4.3.

Prototypical Classes to Capture Visual Diversity. Note that in Sect. 3.1, we wanted to study if a small set of coarse labels are sufficient to train a generalized proposal model. However, this does not answer anything about the visual diversity of objects within each sub-category that is required for generalization. As an example (shown in Fig. 1), in order to localize different types of vehicles like "car" or "airplane" it might be sufficient to collapse the label for all these objects into a single label named "vehicle", however dropping all instances of airplane during training will lead to a drop in performance for this class.

To quantitatively study this effect, we introduce the notion of "prototypical" classes. Given a large set of leaf classes, these are the smallest subset such that a model trained only with instances from them is sufficient to localize objects from the remaining classes. We identify the two properties that are required to quantify the prototypicality of a set of classes:

Sufficient set: is a set of classes such that training a model only with examples from them should be sufficient to localize objects from all other classes. The most superfluous sufficient set would be the entire set of leaf classes themselves.

Necessary set: is a set of classes such that dropping any class from this set will lead to a significant drop in generalization. A simple example would be a very coarse vertical like "vehicle". Intuitively dropping all vehicles would affect their localization as they do not share localization properties with other classes.

We provide concrete ways to measure both these properties in Sect. 4.3.

Identifying Prototypical Classes: Given a set of N leaf classes $\mathbb{C}$, we wish to identify a set of P prototypical classes $\mathbb{P} \subset \mathbb{C}$. Intuitively, this is similar to clustering the classes that have the same localization structure and then choosing a representative class from each cluster. Below, we discuss three approaches:

(a) **Oracle visual clustering:** To get an upper bound for choosing the best P prototypical classes, we assume that bounding box annotations for all the N leaf classes are available. We then use these bounding boxes to compute visual similarity between classes. We note that this is not a practical approach, but is crucial to evaluate the effectiveness of proxies we introduce later.

We first train a detection model using the annotations of all the leaf classes. We then measure the visual similarity between two classes i, j as

$$S_{ij} = \max \left(\frac{\mathrm{AP}^i(j)}{\mathrm{AP}^j(j)}, \frac{\mathrm{AP}^j(i)}{\mathrm{AP}^i(i)} \right), \tag{1}$$

where $AP^i(j)$ is the detection average precision (AP) for the jth class when we use the detections corresponding to the ith class as detections of class j. S_{ij} is a measure of how well one class can replace another class in localizing it. We then use the resulting similarity measure to hierarchically cluster the classes into P clusters using agglomerative clustering. We then pick the class with the highest number of examples in each cluster to construct the set of prototypical classes. For practical reasons, we use frequency to choose the representative class, since this results in the construction of the largest dataset.

(b) **Semantic clustering based on frequency:** Semantic similarity is often viewed as a good proxy for visual similarity as shown through datasets like Imagenet [4] and OIV4. Hence, we use the semantic tree to cluster the classes in an hierarchical fashion starting from the leaves. At any given step, we cluster together two leaf classes that share a common parent if they jointly have the lowest number of examples. The algorithm stops when P clusters are left. We then select the most frequent class from each cluster as a prototypical class.

(c) **Most frequent prototypical subset:** For this baseline, we choose the top P most frequently occurring classes in the dataset as the prototypical classes. Note that unlike the previous approaches, this does not require any knowledge of the semantic hierarchy.

3.2   Modeling Choice

Once the dataset is fixed, the next step is to train a detection model. In our work, we explore the use of two popular models: Faster R-CNN and RetinaNet.

In the case of a single-stage network, the detections from a model trained on a source dataset with seen classes can directly be treated as proposals. Their ability to localize novel classes in a target dataset can be evaluated to test generalization. However, for a two-stage network, another natural choice would be to use the Region Proposal Network (RPN) of the model, since it is trained in a class-agnostic fashion and aims to localize all objects in the image. However, as noted by He et al. [10], the detection part of the model is better at localizing the object due to more fine-tuned bounding box regression and better background classification. We study this more rigorously, by comparing the generalization of proposals obtained from the detection head as well as RPN.

4   Experiments

We evaluate the ability of the object proposal obtained from detection models learned with different settings in Sect. 3.2 to generalize to new unseen classes. We also explore the effects of label-space granularity and the need for semantic and visual diversity. Finally, we show that a small set of prototypical classes could be used to train an effective proposal model for all classes in the dataset.

4.1   Experimental Setup

Source and Target Splits: We split each dataset into two parts: (a) *Source dataset* consisting of a set of seen classes called *source classes* and (b) *Target dataset* consisting of a set of unseen classes called *target classes*. *Target dataset* is used to evaluate the generalization of proposal models trained with the *Source dataset*. Since an image can contain both source and target classes, we ensure that such images are not present in the source class dataset. However, there may be a small number of images in the target dataset that contain source classes. We use the following two datasets for our experiments:

(1) *Open Images V4 (OIV4)* [16] consists of 600 classes. We retain only object classes which have more than 100 training images. This results in a total of 482 leaf classes. We randomly split all the leaf classes into 432 source (OIV4-source dataset) and 50 target (OIV4-target dataset) classes. There are also annotations associated only with internal nodes (for example, "animal") and without a specific leaf label (like the type of animal). We remove such annotations and all associated images, since such images cannot be unambiguously assigned to a source or target split. This leaves us with $1.2M$ images with $7.96M$ boxes in the train split and $73k$ images with $361K$ boxes in the test split. For training proposal models, we always use the train split and for evaluation we use the test split. Wherever needed, we explicitly suffix the dataset with "train" and "test" (for example, OIV4-source-train and OIV4-source-test).

(2) *COCO* [19]: We use the 2017 version of the COCO dataset and randomly split the classes in to 70 source (COCO-source dataset) and 10 target (COCO-target dataset) classes. For training, we use the train split and for evaluation, we use the 5000 images from the validation set. Wherever needed, we explicitly suffix the dataset with "train" and "test".

Target classes list is provided in the supplementary.

Evaluation Metrics: We report the standard average recall (AR@k) [13] metric to evaluate the quality of proposals. One of the main motivations for building a generalized proposal model is to use the resulting proposals to train detection models for unseen classes with limited or no bounding box annotation. Hence, we implement a weakly supervised detector with the approach used in YOLO9000 [25][1]. We report the detection AP (averaged over IoU thresholds ranging from 0.5 to 0.95) on the test set of the target dataset. Please see the supplementary material for more details.

Implementation Details: We fix Imagenet pre-trained ResNet-50 with Feature Pyramid Networks [17] as the backbone for all models. We use the Detectron codebase [8]. For COCO, we train the models for $90k$ iterations with an initial learning rate and the decay suggested in [26]. For OIV4, we train the models for $800k$ iterations with an initial learning rate of 0.01 and cosine decay.

4.2 Modeling Choices

We first identify the best detection model and setting to extract proposals that generalize to new unseen classes. We then analyze generalization ability under different settings from this model. We reiterate that in order to test generalization, evaluation is done on target classes that have no intersection with the source classes used during training.

Choice of Detection Model: We compare the generalization ability of a two-stage network (Faster R-CNN) and a single-stage network (RetinaNet) in Fig. 2a. Since, in a two-stage model like Faster R-CNN, the output from the RPN is class-agnostic and can be used as proposals too, we compare the performance of the RPN as well. The models are trained on COCO-source-train dataset. We report AR@100 on seen classes in the COCO-source-test dataset, as well as unseen classes in the COCO-target-test. The difference in performance between seen and unseen classes reflects the generalization gap. We also show an upper-bound performance on COCO-target-test obtained by models trained on the full training dataset containing both COCO-source-train and COCO-target-train.

We notice that on seen classes, RetinaNet achieves a lower performance compared to Faster R-CNN (drop of 2.4%). However, the drop is larger for unseen target classes (3.5%), indicating a larger generalization gap for RetinaNet. One reason for this is that RetinaNet is more sensitive to missing bounding boxes corresponding to unlabelled unseen classes in the source dataset. Proposals corresponding to unseen object classes that are not annotated in the training data are treated as hard-negatives, due to the use of focal-loss. Hence, the model heavily penalizes proposals corresponding to unannotated bounding boxes, leading to overall drop in AR. Since some seen classes share visual similarity with unseen classes, this affects AR for seen classes too.

---

[1] We chose [25] due to its simplicity. In practice, we can use other weakly supervised approaches too.

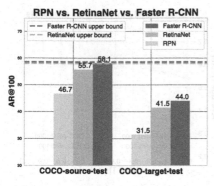

(a) Comparison of detection models

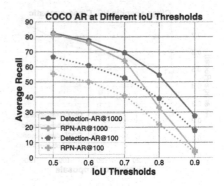

(b) RPN vs. detection head

Fig. 2. (a) AR@100 corresponding to different models trained on COCO-source-train and evaluated on different test splits. Upper-bound corresponds to model trained on full COCO dataset and evaluated on COCO-target-test. (b) Average recall of RPN and detection head at different IoU thresholds, for model trained on COCO-source-train and evaluated on COCO-target-test

We also notice that the detection head of Faster R-CNN provides better overall performance *without* sacrificing generalization compared to RPN. This can be attributed to better bounding box regression from the detection head. To investigate this effect, we measure AR at different IoU thresholds for both sets of proposals for the model trained on COCO-source and evaluated on COCO-target in Fig. 2b. We see that the difference in AR@1000 increases drastically at higher values of IoU threshold, and is negligible at a threshold of 0.5. This implies that the boxes from the detection head are more fine-tuned to exactly localize objects, unlike the RPN.

Choice of Faster R-CNN Settings: The results so far were obtained using class-specific bounding box regression (which is the standard setting in Faster R-CNN) for the detection head. Since we want the bounding boxes to generalize to unseen classes, class agnostic regression could be a valid choice too. We study this in Fig. 3 for OIV4 and COCO. We see that class agnostic regression is better for small number of proposals as seen by AR@10,20,50. However, when we consider more proposals (AR@1000), class specific regression provides a significant gain (4.5% for OIV4 and 7.5% for COCO).

Previously, we fixed the NMS threshold to 0.5. We study the effect of this threshold in Fig. 4. We train on OIV4-source, COCO-source and test on OIV4-target, COCO-target respectively. Intuitively, a low threshold can improve spatial coverage of objects by ensuring proposals are spatially well spread out. When considering a larger number of proposals, there are sufficient boxes to ensure spatial coverage, and having some redundancy is helpful. This is witnessed by the steeper drop in AR@1000 at low NMS thresholds, unlike AR@100.

Based on these observations, we use class-specific bounding box regression with an NMS threshold of 0.5 for rest of the experiments.

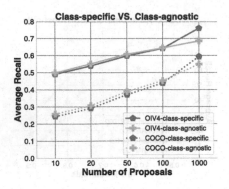
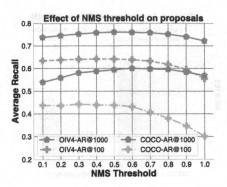

Fig. 3. Effect of class agnostic regression vs. class specific regression

Fig. 4. Effect of NMS threshold on performance of proposals

Weakly Supervised Detection: An important practical use case for generalized proposals is where no box annotations is available. Hence, we measure the effect of better generalized proposals on the performance of a weakly supervised detection model, trained without bounding box annotations. We show results corresponding to the RPN head and detection head of Faster R-CNN in Table 1. The weakly supervised model is trained on OIV4-target-train and evaluated on OIV4-target-test. We also show results for proposals obtained from training with OIV4-source as well as OIV4-all (upper-bound). We see that the performance of the weakly supervised detector is directly correlated with the quality of the proposals being used, showing the need for good generalized proposals.

Table 1. Comparing performance of proposals generated by RPN head and detection head for weakly supervised detection. We also show the AR@100 numbers which are seen to be correlated with detection AP

Target dataset - OIV4-target	Source: OIV4-source		Source: OIV4-all	
	Det. AP	AR@100	Det. AP	AR@100
Faster R-CNN RPN	8.7	55.0	9.6	60.4
Faster R-CNN detection	**24.0**	**69.4**	**30.8**	**76.9**

4.3   Dataset Properties

Effect of Label Space Granularity: OIV4 organizes object classes in a semantic hierarchy with 5 levels. We directly leverage this hierarchy to measure the effect of label granularity (Fig. 1a). We construct a dataset at each level L_i (OIV4-source-L_i) by retaining all the images in OIV4-source, but relabeling bounding boxes corresponding to leaf labels with their ancestor at L_i. We construct 5 datasets, one for each level with the same set of images and bounding boxes.

We report the performance of these models on OIV4-target in Table 2. Along with AR@100/1000, we also report the detection AP of the weakly supervised detection models trained with the proposals obtained from the corresponding levels. The weakly supervised models are trained on OIV4-target-train and evaluated on OIV4-target-test.

Some past works like [29] postulated that one super-class (similar to L_0) could be sufficient. However, we observe that both AR@100 and AR@1000 increase as we move from L_0 to L_1 along with a significant gain (3.1%) in AP. This indicates that training with just a binary label yields lower quality proposals compared to training with at least a coarse set of labels at L_1. While both AP and AR@100 increase as the granularity increases from L_1 to L_3, the difference is fairly small for both metrics (<2% change). However, annotating bounding boxes with labels at L_1 (86 labels) is significantly cheaper than L_3 (398 labels). Hence, L_1 can be seen as a good trade-off in terms of labelling cost, and training a good model.

Table 2. Effect of different label space granularities on the quality of proposal for OIV4 dataset. The number of classes at each level is shown in brackets. Evaluation is done on OIV4-target-eval dataset. Both AR and weakly supervised detection AP are reported

Source dataset	AR@100	AR@1000	AP (weak)
OIV4-source-L_0(1)	61.7	72.0	19.5
OIV4-source-L_1(86)	63.4	73.0	22.6
OIV4-source-L_2(270)	63.7	75.2	23.1
OIV4-source-L_3(398)	65.2	77.2	24.3
OIV4-source-L_4(432)	64.2	76.1	24.0

Need for Visual and Semantic Diversity: We noticed that training with coarse labels can yield good proposals. It would be interesting to observe if all or only some of these coarse classes are crucial to build a good proposal model. To study this, we conduct ablation experiments where we train a model with OIV4-source-train after dropping all images having a specific L_1 label and evaluate the proposals on the OIV4-source-test images belonging to this label in Fig. 5a. We repeat this experiment for a few fine-grained classes at L_4 in Fig. 5b.

We notice that certain coarse classes (like "clothing" and "vehicle") experience a huge drop in performance. On the other hand, "animal" and "food" are less affected. This can be explained from the fact that, there are many toy-animal images within the coarse label "toy", similarly "containers" is a coarse class in OIV4 which is often depicted with food in it. These classes can act as proxies for "animal" and "food" respectively. However, "clothing" and "vehicle" do not have good proxies. More interestingly, we make a similar observation for finer classes at L_4 like airplanes and helicopters. This suggests that there is a smaller set of objects that have unique localization properties in OIV4.

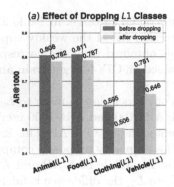 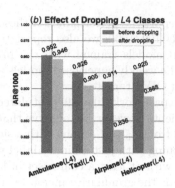

Fig. 5. Effect of Semantic Diversity, measured by dropping an object class during training and measuring the resulting change in AR for that class: (a) dropping L1 classes and (b) dropping L4 classes

Prototypical Classes: Some object classes are similar to others in terms of localization, while there are classes that are unique and need to be included in training. Motivated by this observation, we try to identify a small set of classes called "prototypical" classes which are both necessary and sufficient to train a generalizable proposal model. We use the OIV4-source dataset as before with 432 leaf classes.

We introduce two ways to measure *sufficiency* and *necessity*. From the 432 classes, once we pick a subset of P prototypical classes, we train a proposal model and evaluate the resulting model on the 50 target classes in OIV4-target, to measure *sufficiency* and *necessity*.

Dataset Construction for Fair Comparison. We ensure that the total number of images as well as bounding box annotations are kept fixed when we construct datasets for different prototypical subsets to ensure that proposals trained with different subsets are comparable. Details are shown in supplementary document.

Training with Prototypical Subsets. For a set of prototypical classes and the corresponding dataset, we train a Faster R-CNN with those classes as labels. We combine the detections as described in Sect. 3.2 to obtain proposals.

Measuring Sufficiency of Prototypical Classes. A subset of classes are sufficient, if a proposal model trained with them generalizes as well as a model trained with all classes. We follow this notion and evaluate the proposals obtained from the models trained with different prototypical subsets on OIV4-target and report the average recall (AR@100) in Fig. 6a. Similar trends are observed with AR@1000 as well (shown in supplementary).

Looking at the proposals obtained from oracle visual clustering, training with less than 25% of the classes (100) leads to only a drop of 4.8% in AR@100, compared to training with images belonging to all object classes. This gap reduces to 0.4% if we train with 50% (200) of all the classes. This provides an empirical proof for the existence of a significantly smaller number of object classes that are sufficient to train a generalizable proposal model.

Next, we look at the prototypical classes obtained from a more practical approach: semantic clustering. We notice that the proposal model trained with these prototypical classes always outperform other approaches such as choosing a random set of classes or the most frequent set of classes. Further, the performance of this method is only lower by a margin of 3% compared to oracle visual clustering for different value of P. Selecting most frequent set of classes as the prototypical subset performs slightly worse than semantic clustering. This shows that semantic clustering can serve as a good way to identify prototypical classes for large taxonomies when the semantic hierarchy is available for the dataset, else the most frequent subset is a weaker alternative.

Measuring Necessity of Prototypical Classes. A set of classes are considered necessary, if there is no redundancy among the classes in terms of localization properties. For a given class in the set, there should be no equivalent class which can provide similar bounding boxes. We measure this property for a prototypical subset by evaluating the corresponding proposal model on OIV4-target dataset using the following method. For every target class in OIV4-target, we measure the relative change in AR@100 and AR@1000 by removing proposals corresponding to the most similar class in the prototypical subset (similarity measured by Eq. 1). The change in AR would be minimal if there is another

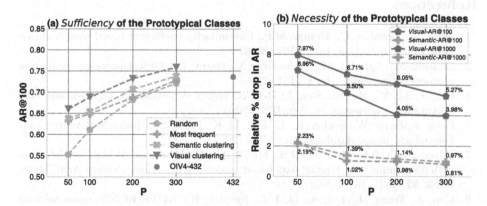

Fig. 6. (a) Average recall AR@100 for proposals obtained from models trained with varying number of prototypical classes chosen by different methods. We show the average recall on the OIV4-target dataset with 50 unseen classes. P denotes the number of prototypical classes. Higher value indicates higher sufficiency. (b) The relative change in AR for target classes by dropping proposals corresponding to the most similar class in the prototypical subset. Higher value indicates lower redundancy in prototypical subset and higher necessity

class in the prototypical subset which can localize the target class. This measure, averaged over all target classes provides a good estimate of necessity. A high value symbolizes a high degree of necessity, while a low value corresponds to redundancy among the prototypical classes. We plot this for different number of prototypical classes for oracle visual clustering and semantic clustering in Fig. 6b.

We notice that at any given number of prototypical classes, the change in average recall is higher for oracle visual clustering compared to semantic clustering. This demonstrates that visual clustering leads to prototypical classes which are less redundant (and more necessary). As expected, we see the necessity drops with increasing number of prototypical classes since redundancy between classes increases with more number of classes. For oracle visual clustering as we move from 200 to 300 classes, sufficiency changes by a small amount from 73.2 to 75.9 (Fig. 6a), while the necessity drops steeply in Fig. 6b. This suggests that the ideal number of prototypical classes for OIV4 could be around 200.

5   Conclusion

We quantitatively measured the importance of visual diversity and showed that using a very fine-grained or very coarse label-space can both affect generalization. We introduced the idea of prototypical classes that are sufficient and necessary to obtain generalized proposals. We showed that Faster R-CNN can be used to obtain better proposals for unseen classes than RetinaNet, and studied the effect of class-agnostic bounding box regression and NMS threshold.

References

1. Arun, A., Jawahar, C., Kumar, M.P.: Dissimilarity coefficient based weakly supervised object detection. In: CVPR (2019)
2. Chavali, N., Agrawal, H., Mahendru, A., Batra, D.: Object-proposal evaluation protocol is 'gameable'. In: CVPR (2016)
3. Dai, J., Li, Y., He, K., Sun, J.: R-FCN: object detection via region-based fully convolutional networks. In: NeurIPS (2016)
4. Deng, J., Dong, W., Socher, R., Li, L.J., Li, K., Fei-Fei, L.: ImageNet: a large-scale hierarchical image database. In: CVPR (2009)
5. Felzenszwalb, P.F., Girshick, R.B., McAllester, D., Ramanan, D.: Object detection with discriminatively trained part-based models. IEEE Trans. Pattern Anal. Mach. Intell. **32**, 1627–1645 (2009)
6. Gao, J., Wang, J., Dai, S., Li, L.J., Nevatia, R.: NOTE-RCNN: noise tolerant ensemble RCNN for semi-supervised object detection. In: ICCV (2019)
7. Gao, Y., et al.: C-MIDN: coupled multiple instance detection network with segmentation guidance for weakly supervised object detection. In: ICCV (2019)
8. Girshick, R., Radosavovic, I., Gkioxari, G., Dollár, P., He, K.: Detectron (2018)
9. Guillaumin, M., Ferrari, V.: Large-scale knowledge transfer for object localization in ImageNet. In: CVPR (2012)
10. He, K., Gkioxari, G., Dollár, P., Girshick, R.: Mask R-CNN. In: ICCV (2017)

11. Hoffman, J., et al.: LSDA: large scale detection through adaptation. In: NeurIPS (2014)
12. Hoffman, J., et al.: Large scale visual recognition through adaptation using joint representation and multiple instance learning. J. Mach. Learn. Res. **17**, 4954–4984 (2016)
13. Hosang, J., Benenson, R., Dollár, P., Schiele, B.: What makes for effective detection proposals? IEEE Trans. Pattern Anal. Mach. Intell. **38**, 814–830 (2015)
14. Krähenbühl, P., Koltun, V.: Geodesic object proposals. In: Fleet, D., Pajdla, T., Schiele, B., Tuytelaars, T. (eds.) ECCV 2014. LNCS, vol. 8693, pp. 725–739. Springer, Cham (2014). https://doi.org/10.1007/978-3-319-10602-1_47
15. Kuo, W., Hariharan, B., Malik, J.: DeepBox: learning objectness with convolutional networks. In: ICCV (2015)
16. Kuznetsova, A., et al.: The open images dataset v4: unified image classification, object detection, and visual relationship detection at scale. arXiv preprint arXiv:1811.00982 (2018)
17. Lin, T.Y., Dollár, P., Girshick, R., He, K., Hariharan, B., Belongie, S.: Feature pyramid networks for object detection. In: CVPR (2017)
18. Lin, T.Y., Goyal, P., Girshick, R., He, K., Dollár, P.: Focal loss for dense object detection. In: ICCV (2017)
19. Lin, T.-Y., et al.: Microsoft COCO: common objects in context. In: Fleet, D., Pajdla, T., Schiele, B., Tuytelaars, T. (eds.) ECCV 2014. LNCS, vol. 8693, pp. 740–755. Springer, Cham (2014). https://doi.org/10.1007/978-3-319-10602-1_48
20. Liu, W., et al.: SSD: single shot MultiBox detector. In: Leibe, B., Matas, J., Sebe, N., Welling, M. (eds.) ECCV 2016. LNCS, vol. 9905, pp. 21–37. Springer, Cham (2016). https://doi.org/10.1007/978-3-319-46448-0_2
21. Novotny, D., Larlus, D., Vedaldi, A.: I have seen enough: transferring parts across categories. In: BMVC (2016)
22. Ott, P., Everingham, M.: Shared parts for deformable part-based models. In: CVPR (2011)
23. Pinheiro, P.O., Collobert, R., Dollár, P.: Learning to segment object candidates. In: NeurIPS (2015)
24. Pont-Tuset, J., Arbelaez, P., Barron, J.T., Marques, F., Malik, J.: Multiscale combinatorial grouping for image segmentation and object proposal generation. IEEE Trans. Pattern Anal. Mach. Intell. **39**, 128–140 (2016)
25. Redmon, J., Farhadi, A.: YOLO9000: better, faster, stronger. In: CVPR (2017)
26. Ren, S., He, K., Girshick, R., Sun, J.: Faster R-CNN: towards real-time object detection with region proposal networks. In: NeurIPS (2015)
27. Rochan, M., Wang, Y.: Weakly supervised localization of novel objects using appearance transfer. In: CVPR (2015)
28. Salakhutdinov, R., Torralba, A., Tenenbaum, J.: Learning to share visual appearance for multiclass object detection. In: CVPR (2011)
29. Singh, B., Li, H., Sharma, A., Davis, L.S.: R-FCN-3000 at 30fps: decoupling detection and classification. In: CVPR (2018)
30. Szegedy, C., Reed, S., Erhan, D., Anguelov, D., Ioffe, S.: Scalable, high-quality object detection. arXiv preprint arXiv:1412.1441 (2014)
31. Tang, P., et al.: PCL: proposal cluster learning for weakly supervised object detection. IEEE Trans. Pattern Anal. Mach. Intell. **42**, 176–191 (2018)
32. Tang, Y., Wang, J., Gao, B., Dellandréa, E., Gaizauskas, R., Chen, L.: Large scale semi-supervised object detection using visual and semantic knowledge transfer. In: CVPR (2016)

33. Torralba, A., Murphy, K.P., Freeman, W.T., et al.: Sharing features: efficient boosting procedures for multiclass object detection. In: CVPR (2004)
34. Uijlings, J., Popov, S., Ferrari, V.: Revisiting knowledge transfer for training object class detectors. In: CVPR (2018)
35. Uijlings, J.R., Van De Sande, K.E., Gevers, T., Smeulders, A.W.: Selective search for object recognition. Int. J. Comput. Vis. **104**, 154–171 (2013)
36. Yang, H., Wu, H., Chen, H.: Detecting 11K classes: large scale object detection without fine-grained bounding boxes. arXiv preprint arXiv:1908.05217 (2019)
37. Zitnick, C.L., Dollár, P.: Edge boxes: locating object proposals from edges. In: Fleet, D., Pajdla, T., Schiele, B., Tuytelaars, T. (eds.) ECCV 2014. LNCS, vol. 8693, pp. 391–405. Springer, Cham (2014). https://doi.org/10.1007/978-3-319-10602-1_26

A Self-supervised Framework for Human Instance Segmentation

Yalong Jiang[1]([✉]), Wenrui Ding[1], Hongguang Li[1], Hua Yang[2], and Xu Wang[2]

[1] Unmanned System Research Institute, Beihang University, Beijing, China
AllenYLJiang@outlook.com
[2] HeyIntelligence Technology, Beijing, China

Abstract. Existing approaches for human-centered tasks such as human instance segmentation are focused on improving the architectures of models, leveraging weak supervision or transforming supervision among related tasks. Nonetheless, the structures are highly specific and the weak supervision is limited by available priors or number of related tasks. In this paper, we present a novel self-supervised framework for human instance segmentation. The framework includes one module which iteratively conducts mutual refinement between segmentation and optical flow estimation, and the other module which iteratively refines pose estimations by exploring the prior knowledge about the consistency in human graph structures from consecutive frames. The results of the proposed framework are employed for fine-tuning segmentation networks in a feedback fashion. Experimental results on the OCHuman and COCOPersons datasets demonstrate that the self-supervised framework achieves current state-of-the-art performance against existing models on the challenging datasets without requiring additional labels. Unlabeled video data is utilized together with prior knowledge to significantly improve performance and reduce the reliance on annotations. Code released at: https://github.com/AllenYLJiang/SSINS.

Keywords: Human instance segmentation · Prior knowledge · Self-supervised

1 Introduction

In recent years, the computer vision community has devoted great efforts in understanding human from images. Typical applications include human instance segmentation which predicts human masks [14,37], pose estimation [2,10,16,23, 28,32,34] and human parsing [8,15,20,22,36]. The three lines of research play a crucial role in surveillance systems. This study concentrates on human instance segmentation and leverages prior knowledge to reduce the need for annotations while improving generalization.

Existing research have explored either new model structures [5] or feature propagation methods [13]. However, the generalization capability of models cannot be greatly improved due to the domain discrepancy between training data

© Springer Nature Switzerland AG 2020
A. Bartoli and A. Fusiello (Eds.): ECCV 2020 Workshops, LNCS 12536, pp. 479–495, 2020.
https://doi.org/10.1007/978-3-030-66096-3_33

and real-world test data. For intance, the identities in input images are with a limited set of poses, a model cannot detect a human with the pose that does not appear in training data. Moreover, model architectures are also limited by the available data, a typical example is the NAS-based model Auto-Deeplab [25] which was built by searching over the network space and maximizing the accuracy on training data. Nonetheless, the optimal architecture on training data leads to suboptimal performance on test set. Even if some weakly supervised methods [13] augmented supervision by exploiting the relations between different tasks, they suffer from the upper limit on the number of related tasks. The performance cannot be further improved because the approach for training with unlabelled data is under-explored.

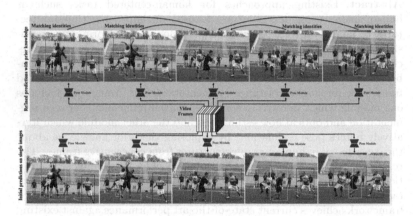

Fig. 1. The rationale behind the proposed approach. All the images are without any annotations. The training data of Pose Module covers limited poses and does not include the special cases in test images. For instance, the person which is occluded by another one in red bounding box in the middle image from the bottom row cannot be detected because this scenario with severe partial occlusion is not included in training data. However, if we refer to the predictions from neighboring frames, the occluded person can be recovered. The scenarios in adjacent frames are more similar to those in training data and the same person can be detected in those frames. The trajectories estimated from consecutive frames facilitate the recovery. In this way, the mistakes in the bottom middle image from test set can be fixed by the prior knowledge about motion consistency in videos. By fine-tuning on the recovered predictions, the Pose Module can generalize to the cases in test set which are not included in training data.

Existing solutions to improve generalization include employing more generalizable backbones [3,17] which were pre-trained on larger classification datasets, revising loss functions and resorting to prior knowledge [9,15,20]. However, the above-mentioned methods cannot resolve the challenging cases and the priors can only function as weak constraints. To significantly improve generalization by leveraging prior knowledge, we present a novel self-supervised framework for instance-segmentation. The framework is able to be trained on real-world unlabelled video sequences and achieves improvement on test set. The rationale behind the proposed framework is shown in Fig. 1.

The human-centered images can be regarded as vectors in a high-dimensional manifold. Different from common distances such as Wasserstein metrics which consider the intensities on all pixels, we measure the distances between images by using the similarities in human structures (poses) and human appearances. As is shown in the bottom row in Fig. 1, the model cannot detect all identities in the middle image because the patterns of poses did not appear in training images. However, the missed identity can be detected in adjacent frames. By recovering the missed detections with the consistency in temporal movements and fine-tuning the Pose Module with the recovered predictions, the Pose Module can generalize from familiar cases to previously unfamiliar cases.

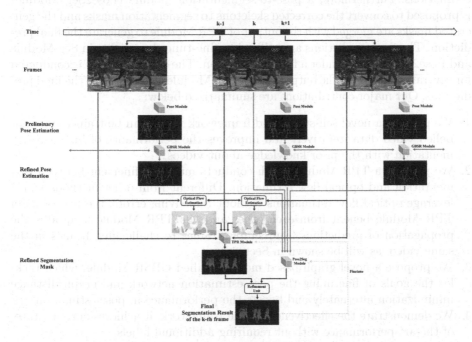

Fig. 2. The proposed framework for human instance segmentation. It is composed of a temporal parsing refinement module (TPR Module) for mutually refining segmentation masks and optical flow estimations, a graph-based skeleton refinement module (GBSR Module) for iteratively conducting graph distances minimization and poes estimation. The refined pose estimations are then converted to parsing results using pose-to-segmentation module (Pose2Seg Module) whose outputs are combined with those from TPR Module to produce final predictions. The final results are leveraged to fine-tune segmentation networks. The full details of GBSR Module and TPR Module are demonstrated in Fig. 3 and Fig. 5(a), respectively.

As is shown in Fig. 2, the proposed framework is composed of a GBSR Module, a TPR Module and a Pose2Seg Module. The unlabelled videos are collected online resources which include [1] and other online videos. In the self-supervised training phase, the Seg Module in TPR Module and Pose Module in GBSR Module firstly conduct inference on each frame. Optical flow estimation is also conducted [18] in this phase. Then segmentation refinement and optical flow refinement are alternately conducted and mutually benefit each other. In this way, the TPR Module iteratively tackles two coherent goals: minimizing cross-entropy loss [3] for segmentation and minimizing matching error for optical flow estimations, as will be introduced in Sect. 3.3.

In pose estimation, the GBSR Module builds a graph for each detected human, the attributes of each node in a graph include both the appearance of the semantic part and its connections with other nodes. The distances between corresponding graphs in adjacent frames are minimized with the aim of refining pose estimations. Furthermore, a pose-to-segmentation module (Pose2Seg Module) is proposed to convert the corrected skeletons to segmentation masks and the generated masks are merged with the output of TPR Module to generate the final prediction. The final predictions are utilized to fine-tune the weights in Seg Module and Pose2Seg Module under a feedback fashion. The overall process is conducted for several rounds until the outputs of the Seg Module approximates the final predictions. Our major contributions are summarized below:

1. We propose a novel self-supervised framework which can be trained on unlabelled video data iteratively and improves the performance of instance segmentation with the prior knowledge about videos.
2. We propose a TPR Module which conducts mutual refinement between segmentation and optical flow estimation. Different from other methods which leverage optical flow estimations without remedying errors, the two tasks in TPR Module benefit from each other and the TPR Module facilitates the propagation of predictions from simple frames to challenging frames in the same video, as will be shown in Sect. 3.3.
3. We propose a novel graph based module, called GBSR Module, which tackles the goals of finetuning the pose estimation network and graph distance minimization alternately and boosts the performance in pose estimation.
4. We demonstrate the effectiveness of the framework, it achieves current state-of-the-art performance without requiring additional labels.

2   Related Work

Instance Segmentation. In this task, a single mask is assigned for each object in an image. Existing deep learning methods for instance segmentation are divided into two categories. The first type of methods are composed of more than one stage [7,11,16,35]. The second type of models jointly conduct detection and segmentation in one pass [19,26]. For instance, [26] grouped the detected line segments into connected components before figuring out object boundaries. [14] unified semantic segmentation and instance-aware edge detection in an end-to-end pass. A typical shortcome of the two-stage methods lies in their failure in detection when nearby bounding boxes are highly overlapped. Besides, different stages are trained using independent targets and their predictions are inconsistent. Even if the second type of methods do not rely on bounding boxes, some of them are composed of several sub-networks [14]. As a result, the great number of learnable parameters easily leads to over-fitting. The OCHuman and COCOPersons datasets [24] are introduced by [35]. In this paper, we introduce a self-supervised framework for instance segmentation and human parsing, unlabelled images from real-world scenarios contribute to generalization. Besides, the proposed framework is not built on detection modules.

Human Pose Estimation. The large datasets such as COCO Key-points Challenge have contributed to the remarkable progress in human pose estimation [3,4,15,21,22,27,30,31,33,37]. Existing approaches can be divided into top-down [30] and bottom-up methods [28]. The former localize bounding boxes before estimating the poses inside boxes. However, challenging cases with occlusion, complex lightening conditions or entanglement usually lead to the failures of detectors. The missed detections cannot be recovered by pose estimating models. Even when parts of occluded humans are detected, the accuracy of predictions is unsatisfactory and the precision of pose estimation also drops significantly. The efficiency of top-down approaches is also inferior to bottom-up methods because their inference time is proportional to the number of people in images. Bottom-up methods predict the locations of body joints before organizing them into human structures. However, the limbs belonging to different humans are easy to be mixed because adjacent identities are highly entangled. Additionally, the variations in scales and poses lead to the failures in organizing joints into people. To improve the robustness to occlusions and entanglement while improving generalization, we propose a GBSR Module which leverages the consistency between human poses in adjacent frames as a constraint, and refines pose predictions to meet the constraint.

3   Self-supervised Framework

3.1   The Structure of the Framework

The framework is composed of a GBSR Module, a TPR Module and a Pose2Seg Module. The GBSR Module and the TPR Module are introduced in Sect. 3.2 and Sect. 3.3, respectively. The method for integrating the modules are introduced in Sect. 3.4 The deeplabv3+ model [5] is incorporated in TPR Module as the Seg Module while the model proposed in [28] is incorporated in GBSR Module as the Pose Module. The Pose2Seg Module has the same structure as the Seg Module.

The available training data for pose estimation is significantly larger than that for segmentation. As a result, the Pose Module has a better generalization capacity and thus its predictions are leveraged to improve the segmentation performance after the post-processing of Pose2Seg Module.

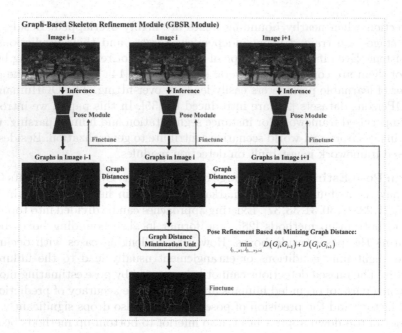

Fig. 3. The structure of the proposed GBSR Module.

3.2   Graph-Based Skeleton Refinement Module (GBSR Module)

The GBSR Module is introduced in Fig. 3. In the inference on single RGB images, some body joints cannot be detected due to occlusions, motion blurs or complex lightening conditions. However, the influences change from frame to frame and the same keypoint is unlikely to be missing in consecutive frames. The GBSR Module builds one graph for each human and enforces the consistency between corresponding graphs in consecutive frames by minimizing graph distances. The minimization serves the purpose of refining pose estimations. Each node in a human graph corresponds to one keypoint (body joint) and the attributes of a node involve both the appearances of the joint and its structural information such as the connections between the node and other nodes. Figure 3 demonstrates the workflow of the GBSR Module and Fig. 4 shows human part graphs, the cells in the right table are marked in black if corresponding nodes are connected.

Suppose that G_i and G_{i+1} are the two graphs describing the same person in the i-th and $(i + 1)$-th frames. Each graph is composed of $N = 17$ nodes if without occlusion. The 17 nodes are nose, left and right eyes, left and right ears, left and right shoulders, left and right elbows, left and right wrists, left and right hips, left and right knees, left and right ankles. The distance between two graphs is the sum of two parts

$$D(G_i, G_{i+1}) = (1 - \alpha) * L_1(G_i, G_{i+1}) + \alpha * L_2(C_i, C_{i+1}) \tag{1}$$

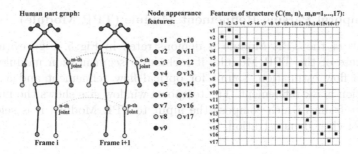

Fig. 4. The structure of a human graph where the representations of both appearances and structures are involved.

The first term $L_1(G_i, G_{i+1})$ measures the similarity in appearances:

$$L_1(G_i, G_{i+1}) = \sum_{m,o} v_{m,o} d(f_i(l_{m,i}), f_{i+1}(l_{o,i+1})) \tag{2}$$

where $l_{m,i}$ and $l_{o,i+1}$ denote the predicted locations of the m-th and o-th body joints in the i-th and $(i+1)$-th frames, respectively. A feature extraction stage consisting of 14 convolutional layers is employed to obtain the featuremaps of both frames f_i and f_{i+1}. $f_i(l_{n,i})$ and $f_{i+1}(l_{n,i+1})$ are obtained by cropping a bounding box with an appropriate side length (twice the distance between neck and nose) from the predicted locations on feature maps and input images. $f_i(l_{n,i})$ and $f_{i+1}(l_{n,i+1})$ include both low-level and high-level contextual cues. The second term $L_2(C_i, C_{i+1})$ measures the similarity in graph structures. The structure of each graph is described by a matrix which is shown by the right column in Fig. 4. C_i and C_{i+1} are two $N - by - N$ matrices and $C_i(m, n) = 1$ if there is connection between the m-th and the n-th body joints, $m, n, o, p = 1, ..., N$, the arrangements of indices are shown in the left part of Fig. 4. $L_2(C_i, C_{i+1})$ is computed by

$$L_2(C_i, C_{i+1}) = \sum_{m,o} v_{m,o} \sum_{n,p} v_{n,p} d(C_i(m, n) - C_{i+1}(o, p)) \tag{3}$$

$d()$ is implemented using 1-norm, $v_{m,n}$ and $v_{o,p}$ denote the visibility scores of different body joints and ranges from 0 to 1. For instance, m and n denote the joints with same semantic meaning in two frames, $v_{m,n}$ is higher only when both of them are visible. As people in consecutive frames have quite similar poses, the Graph Distance Minimization Unit minimizes the distances with respect to visibility scores:

$$\min_{v_{m,o}, v_{n,p}, m,n,o,p \in 1, ..., N} D(G_i, G_{i-1}) + D(G_i, G_{i+1}) \tag{4}$$

Visibility scores are obtained in this way and are used to adjust the side lengths of boxes for cropping regions around body joints. For instance, the size of a box decreases if its visibility score is lower. The regions cropped with new sizes are leveraged in the matching of joints for a second time. Then the matching results are used to refine body joint predictions.

3.3   Temporal Parsing Refinement Module (TPR Module)

The details of the TPR Module is demonstrated in Fig. 5. Figure 5(a) shows the structure of the TPR Module, it includes a segmentation module, a unit for optical flow estimation, a unit for optical flow refinement and a unit for segmentation mask refinement. The temporal window size shows the number of consecutive frames which compose the input to TPR Module, it is selected to be three for clear demonstration.

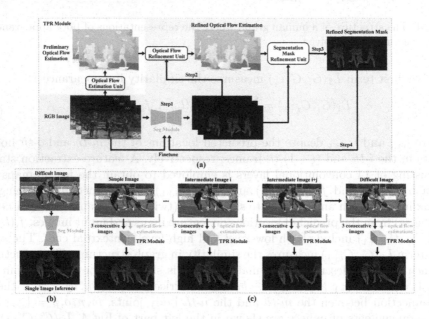

Fig. 5. Introduction to the proposed TPR Module. (a) Structure of the TPR Module. The shaded area denotes the iteration steps. (b) Applying the Seg Module on a single challenging frame. (c) The application of TPR Module in a video sequence where the last frame is the same as the input of (b), the consistency among consecutive frames is improved by refinement and the performance on that frame is significantly improved.

Firstly, optical flow estimation is conducted and the segmentation module predicts three consecutive masks. The optical flow vectors which are inconsistent with the predicted masks are regarded as unreliable vectors and are fed into the Optical Flow Refinement Unit which re-conducts a search over surrounding regions and minimizes pixel-level matching error. For the first frame and the last frame, the activations before softmax layer are warped to the middle frame based on refined flow vectors, then the element-wise sum of activations from three consecutive frames are fed to the Softmax layer (5) to produce the output. Finally the refined segmentation mask is leveraged to finetune the segmentation module. The 4 steps in the shaded area in Fig. 5(a) are conducted iteratively.

The size of temporal window can be revised to adjust the dependency among consecutive predictions, as will be shown in experiments.

$$Softmax_i = Softmax(a_t(x_i, y_i) + a_{t+1}(x_i + u_{t+1}(x_i, y_i), y_i + v_{t+1}(x_i, y_i)) \\ + a_{t-1}(x_i - u_t(x_i, y_i), y_i - v_t(x_i, y_i))) \tag{5}$$

where $Softmax_i$ denotes the i-th pixel on the output of softmax layer, a_t and a_{t+1} denote the activations before softmax layers in the t-th and $(t+1)$-th frames. The corrected optical flow vectors on the i-th pixel are $(u_t(x_i, y_i), v_t(x_i, y_i))$ and $(u_{t+1}(x_i, y_i), v_{t+1}(x_i, y_i))$. The rationality behind applying iterations in Fig. 5(a) is the fact that optical flow estimations are quite noisy and many estimated motion vectors are incorrect. The input in Fig. 5(b) is the same as the last input in Fig. 5(c). The improvements demonstrate the merits of mutual refinement which improves the consistency among consecutive predictions.

Suppose that image A is easy to conduct segmentation on while image B is challenging. A and B belong to the same video sequence. The refined optical flow estimations in Fig. 5(a) implicitly facilitate the propagation of predictions from A to B and obtain better results on B. The propagation can be expressed in the following form

$$I_A(x, y) = I_B(x + u(x, y), y + v(x, y)), x \in [1, H], y \in [1, W] \tag{6}$$

where I_A and I_B denote the segmentation masks of RGB images A and B with width W and height H. $I_A(x, y)$ shows the color intensity at location (x, y) in image A. The pixel (x, y) belongs to a certain semantic part and the pixel moves to a different location $(x + u(x, y), y + v(x, y))$ in image B. The transformation of human poses from A to B is divided into many intermediate steps each of which corresponds to the refined optical flow estimations in one frame. $u(x, y)$ and $v(x, y)$ are achieved by integrating the refined vectors from all intermediate steps:

$$u(x, y) = \sum_{t=1}^{T} u_t(x, y) \tag{7}$$

$$v(x, y) = \sum_{t=1}^{T} v_t(x, y) \tag{8}$$

A series of intermediate refined segmentation masks between A and B are obtained, such as $I_{A+1}(x, y)$, ..., $I_{A+T-1}(x, y)$ which satisfy

$$I_{A+t}(x, y) = I_{A+t+1}(x + u_{t+1}(x, y), y + v_{t+1}(x, y)), t = 1, ..., T - 1 \tag{9}$$

where the motion vectors $u_{t+1}(x, y)$ and $v_{t+1}(x, y)$ are the refined vectors in the $(t+1)$-th step. The refined mask I_B contributes to improvements in Fig. 5(c).

3.4   The Method for Combining TPR Module with GBSR Module

Even if the TPR Module proposed in Sect. 3.3 contributes to improving segmentation performance. There are still some limbs which cannot be detected. On the

Algorithm 1. The pipeline of the proposed approach.

Input: The number of rounds $N_{TPR} = 5$ for mutual refinement in TPR Module, the number of rounds $N_{GBSR} = 1$ in GBSR Module for alternate between finetuning Pose Module and conducting graph distance minimization (pose refinement). The Temporal Window Size $Win_{temporal} = 3$ in both modules.

Output: Predictions on the test sets of benchmark data.

1: Select $Win_{temporal} = 3$ consecutive frames as one group. Apply the Seg Module to generate initial segmentation predictions. Also apply the Optical Flow Estimation Unit to obtain initial optical flow estimations.
2: Obtain refined segmentation masks by alternately conducting optical flow refinement with segmentation predictions and fine-tuning Seg Module using refined segmentation masks.
3: alternately conduct minimization on graph distances by refining pose estimations and re-training Pose Module.
4: Apply Pose2seg Module to generate segmentation masks using the output from Step 3. Combine the outputs from TPR Module and Pose2Seg Module using (10).
5: If the output of Step 4 and that of the Pose Module are similar enough (intersection over union above 0.95), apply the current set of learnable parameters in Seg Module to make predictions on test set and go to Step 6. Else go back to Step 1.
6: **return** Predictions on test set.

---

other hand, The available data for training GBSR Module [24] is different from that for training TPR Module [14] and both modules are better at handling different cases. As a result, it is necessary to combine the predictions from GBSR Module and TPR Module due to their complementary nature.

A pose-to-seg module (Pose2seg Module) is trained in this phase, it has the same structure as the Seg Module except for the input layer which takes in the concatenation of RGB images and skeleton predictions. The activations before the softmax layer in Pose2Seg Module and those before the softmax layer in TPR Module are combined according to (10) to obtain the final predictions.

$$Softmax_i = Softmax(a_{TPR}(x_i, y_i) + a_{Pose2Seg}(x_i, y_i)) \qquad (10)$$

The final predictions obtained by (10) are used to re-train the learnable parameters in the TPR Module and those in the Pose2Seg Module. the pipeline of the proposed approach is presented in Algorithm 1.

4   Experiments

The proposed framework is evaluated on two tasks: instance segmentation and human parsing.

In instance segmentation, the framework is evaluated on two datasets: (1) COCOPersons is a subset of the MSCOCO dataset [24] and contains 64,115 images with 273,469 labelled humans. (2) OCHuman dataset which is proposed in [35] includes 4,731 images with 8,110 labelled humans. The humans in the dataset are heavily occluded and the dataset is challenging. The two datasets are among the largest ones with annotations on both human instance segmentation and pose estimation. The criterion for evaluating segmentation performance is Average Precision (AP). The MSCOCO dataset is split into three subsets: images with small objects, images with medium objects and those with large objects. The corresponding metrics are AP_S, AP_M and AP_L. The OCHuman dataset is divided into two subsets: OCHuman-Moderate and OCHuman-Hard, the first subset contains instances with MaxIoU in the range of 0.5 and 0.75 while the second contains instances with MaxIoU larger than 0.75, the second is more challenging. The metrics are AP_M and AP_H, respectively.

The online collected videos include a comprehensive set of poses and actions, such as sport events, daily exercises and so on. The annotations are automatically generated with the proposed modules. Over 1,100 high-quality videos are collected in this way and will be released after publication.

4.1 Implementation Details

The Seg Module in TPR Module is with Deeplab-V3+ [5] structure and xception-71 [6] backbone. Firstly the Seg Module is trained on the benchmark datasets for 30 epochs with initial learning rate 1e−2 and a polynomial learning rate policy. In each round of mutual refinement, fine-tuning is conducted for 10 epoches. The Pose Module is directly inherited from [28] and it is trained on the COCOPersons dataset [24]. The initial learning rate is 2e−4. The learning rate is decayed by 0.1 after 33 epoches and ends after 40 epoches for instance segmentation.

Our performance of instance segmentation is compared with that of the Mask-RCNN model [16] and the model proposed in [35]. The Mask-RCNN model is trained with the configurations provided by the official website [12]. Resnet-50 [17] is the backbone of Mask-RCNN and the initial learning rate is 2e−2. We have also re-implemented the model proposed in [35] with official settings. The refinements are conducted until convergence, according to Algorithm 1. The training data in each round consists of the combination of the benchmark datasets and the refined segmentation results on the video dataset.

4.2 Performance Comparison on the Heavily Occluded Human Data for Instance Segmentation

In this experiment, we compare the performance of the proposed framework with that of existing methods on the OCHuman dataset with occlusion cases. In this section we fix the number of rounds in mutual refinement and the temporal window size in TPR Module to be both 3, the number of refinements in GBSR Module is fixed to be 1. More choices will be discussed in Sect. 4.5. From Table 1 it can be seen that the performance measured in AP is improved by over 4% over existing methods on the validation and test set. Some subjective results are shown in Fig. 6.

Besides segmentation, our proposed GBSR Module can also improve the performance of keypoint localization over the Pose Module. The Pose Module achieves 0.285/0.303 AP on the val/test set of the OCHuman dataset, the refinement introduced in GBSR Module improves the performance to 0.299 and 0.318, respectively.

Additionally, the α in (1) is selected to be 0.5 because other values including 0.1, 0.2, 0.3, 0.4, 0.6, 0.7, 0.8 and 0.9 all produce lower AP than 0.5.

Table 1. Performance comparison on the validation and test set of the OCHuman dataset [35].

Methods	Backbone	AP val	AP_M val	AP_H val	Methods	Backbone	AP test	AP_M test	AP_H test
Mask-RCNN [16]	Resnet50	0.163	0.194	0.113	Mask-RCNN [16]	Resnet50	0.169	0.189	0.128
Pose to Seg [35]	Resnet50	0.222	0.261	0.150	Pose to Seg [35]	Resnet50	0.238	0.266	0.175
Ours	Resnet50	0.267	0.310	0.181	Ours	Resnet50	0.272	0.305	0.194

Fig. 6. Subject results on the OCHuman dataset [35] with occluded humans. On the top row are the predictions from the current state-of-the-art model [35]. The results of the proposed framework are shown in the bottom row. It can be seen that occlusions are better handled and background interferences are eliminated.

4.3 Performance Comparison on General Human Data for Instance Segmentation

The COCOPersons dataset [24] is the existing largest dataset for human instance segmentation and includes all types of scenarios. The comparison is conducted on the whole dataset, the subset with medium objects and the subset with large objects. Table 2 demonstrates the results. Training is conducted on the training split and the model is evaluated on the validation set.

Table 2. Performance comparison on the COCOPersons dataset [35].

Methods	Backbone	AP	AP_M	AP_L
Mask-RCNN [16]	Resnet50	0.532	0.433	0.648
PersonLab [29]	Resnet101	–	0.476	0.592
PersonLab [29]	Resnet101	–	0.492	0.621
PersonLab [29]	Resnet152	–	0.483	0.595
PersonLab [29]	Resnet152	–	0.497	0.621
Pose to Seg [35]	Resnet50	0.555	0.498	0.670
Ours	Resnet50	0.626	0.565	0.714

Table 3. Performance comparison on the validation/test set of the OCHuman dataset [35] over the numbers of iterations N_{TPR} and N_{GBSR} in TPR Module and GBSR Module.

N_{TPR}	N_{GBSR}	Split	AP	AP_M	AP_H	N_{TPR}	N_{GBSR}	Split	AP	AP_M	AP_H
1	1	val	0.250	0.291	0.169	1	2	val	0.250	0.291	0.169
3	1	val	0.262	0.305	0.177	3	2	val	0.262	0.305	0.177
5	1	val	0.267	0.310	0.181	5	2	val	0.267	0.310	0.181
1	1	test	0.260	0.291	0.187	1	2	test	0.260	0.291	0.187
3	1	test	0.269	0.302	0.192	3	2	test	0.269	0.302	0.192
5	1	test	0.272	0.305	0.194	5	2	test	0.272	0.305	0.194

4.4   Ablation Study

4.4.1   The Number of Rounds for Fine-Tuning

As is introduced in Sect. 4.2, the pipelines of TPR Module and GBSR Module consist of iterations. In this section, we evaluate the influence of the number of iterations on performance. Table 3 shows the results on the OCHuman dataset and Table 4 shows the results on the COCOPersons dataset.

Table 4. Performance comparison on the COCOPersons dataset [24] over the number of iterations N_{TPR} and N_{GBSR}.

N_{TPR}	N_{GBSR}	AP	AP_M	AP_L	N_{TPA}	N_{GBSA}	AP	AP_M	AP_L
1	1	0.598	0.539	0.696	1	2	0.598	0.539	0.696
3	1	0.618	0.558	0.709	3	2	0.618	0.558	0.709
5	1	0.626	0.565	0.714	5	2	0.626	0.565	0.714

From Table 3 and Table 4 it can be inferred that the increase in the round number contributes to improving performance. Besides, the advantage of more rounds in TPR Module demonstrates that the optical flow estimations are also improved during the mutual refinement process.

4.4.2 The Improvements Brought by TPR Module and GBSR Module

The framework is composed of TPR Module and GBSR Module. To demonstrate the merits of both modules, we compare the performance of using neither of them (only using Seg Module and Pose Module), using TPR Module together with Pose Module and using TPR Module together with GBSR Module. According to the discussion section in 4.4.1, $N_{TPR} = 5$ and $N_{GBSA} = 1$. Table 5 shows the results on the OCHuman dataset while Table 6 shows the results on the COCOPersons dataset. Using Seg Module or Pose Module means only using the Seg Module in Fig. 5 or the Pose Module in Fig. 3 without other components and do not introduce iterations. It can be seen that both TPR Module and GBSR Module contribute to improvements on performance. The complementary nature of pose estimation and segmentation has already been demonstrated in [35] and it is necessary to integrate GBSR Module in the framework.

Table 5. Influence on the validation/test set of the OCHuman dataset [35] brought by TPR Module and GBSR Module.

Configuration	Split	AP	AP_M	AP_H
Seg Module and Pose Module	val	0.223	0.262	0.150
TPR Module and Pose Module	val	0.237	0.277	0.163
TPR Module and GBSR Module	val	0.267	0.310	0.181
Seg Module and Pose Module	test	0.239	0.268	0.175
TPR Module and Pose Module	test	0.253	0.285	0.186
TPR Module and GBSR Module	test	0.272	0.305	0.194

Table 6. Influence on the COCOPersons dataset [24] brought by TPR Module and GBSR Module.

Configuration	AP	AP_M	AP_H
Seg Module and Pose Module	0.555	0.498	0.670
TPR Module and Pose Module	0.576	0.519	0.682
TPR Module and GBSR Module	0.626	0.565	0.714

4.4.3 The Influence of Temporal Window Size

In Fig. 3 and Fig. 5, three consecutive images are fed into TPR and GBSR once at a time. Experiments are conducted to evaluate the influence of temporal window size. $N_{TPA} = 5$ and $N_{GBSA} = 1$ are fixed. If the window size is 2, the AP on the validation set and test set of OCHuman dataset [35] drop to 0.264 and 0.268, respectively. The AP on the COCOPersons dataset [24] drops to 0.612. Due to limitations in computational resources, the temporal window size is not further enlarged.

5 Conclusions

The paper presents a novel framework for instance segmentation. The proposed TPR Module conducts mutual refinement between segmentation and optical flow estimation while the GBSR Module refines pose estimations by enforcing the consistency among human graph structures from consecutive frames. Different coherent modules are unified in a framework and produce the final segmentation results. Experimental results on the OCHuman dataset [35] and the COCOPersons dataset [24] have shown that the proposed framework outperforms existing methods on the task by leveraging unlabelled data together with prior knowledge. The self-supervised learning process benefits from the prior knowledge about video data.

References

1. Andriluka, M., et al.: PoseTrack: a benchmark for human pose estimation and tracking. In: CVPR (2018)
2. Cao, Z., Simon, T., Wei, S.E., Sheikh, Y.: Realtime multi-person 2d pose estimation using part affinity fields. In: CVPR (2017)
3. Chen, L.C., Papandreou, G., Kokkinos, I., Murphy, K., Yuille, A.L.: DeepLab: semantic image segmentation with deep convolutional nets, atrous convolution, and fully connected CRFs. arXiv preprint arXiv:1606.00915 (2016)
4. Chen, L.C., Yang, Y., Wang, J., Xu, W., Yuille, A.L.: Attention to scale: scale-aware semantic image segmentation. In: CVPR (2016)
5. Chen, L.-C., Zhu, Y., Papandreou, G., Schroff, F., Adam, H.: Encoder-decoder with atrous separable convolution for semantic image segmentation. In: Ferrari, V., Hebert, M., Sminchisescu, C., Weiss, Y. (eds.) ECCV 2018. LNCS, vol. 11211, pp. 833–851. Springer, Cham (2018). https://doi.org/10.1007/978-3-030-01234-2_49
6. Chollet, F.: Xception: deep learning with depthwise separable convolutions. arXiv Preprint arXiv:1610.02357 (2016)
7. Dai, J., He, K., Sun, J.: Convolutional feature masking for joint object and stuff segmentation. In: CVPR (2015)
8. Dai, J., He, K., Sun, J.: Instance-aware semantic segmentation via multi-task network cascades. In: CVPR (2016)
9. Fang, H.S., Lu, G., Fang, X., Xie, J., Tai, Y.W., Lu., C.: Weakly and semi supervised human body part parsing via pose-guided knowledge transfer. In: CVPR (2018)
10. Fang, H.S., Xie, S., Tai, Y.W., Lu, C.: RMPE: regional multi-person pose estimation. In: CVPR, pp. 2334–2343 (2017)
11. Girshick, R., Iandola, F., Darrell, T., Malik, J.: Deformable part models are convolutional neural networks. In: CVPR (2015)

12. Girshick, R., Radosavovic, I., Gkioxari, G., Dollar, P., He, K.: Detectron (2018). https://github.com/facebookresearch/detectron/
13. Gong, K., Gao, Y., Liang, X., Shen, X., Wang, M., Lin, L.: Graphonomy: universal human parsing via graph transfer learning. In: CVPR (2019)
14. Gong, K., Liang, X., Li, Y., Chen, Y., Yang, M., Lin, L.: Instance-level human parsing via part grouping network. In: Ferrari, V., Hebert, M., Sminchisescu, C., Weiss, Y. (eds.) ECCV 2018. LNCS, vol. 11208, pp. 805–822. Springer, Cham (2018). https://doi.org/10.1007/978-3-030-01225-0_47
15. Gong, K., Liang, X., Zhang, D., Shen, X., Lin, L.: Look into person: self-supervised structure sensitive learning and a new benchmark for human parsing. In: CVPR (2017)
16. He, K., Gkioxari, G., Dollar, P., Girshick, R.: Mask R-CNN. arXiv Preprint arXiv:1703.06870v3 (2018)
17. He, K., Zhang, X., Ren, S., Sun, J.: Identity mappings in deep residual networks. arXiv preprint arXiv:1603.05027 (2016)
18. Ilg, E., Mayer, N., Saikia, T., Keuper, M., Dosovitskiy, A., Brox, T.: FlowNet 2.0: evolution of optical flow estimation with deep networks. In: IEEE Conference on Computer Vision and Pattern Recognition (CVPR), July 2017. http://lmb.informatik.uni-freiburg.de//Publications/2017/IMKDB17
19. Li, Y., Qi, H., Dai, J., Ji, X., Wei, Y.: Fully convolutional instance-aware semantic segmentation. In: CVPR (2017)
20. Liang, X., et al.: Deep human parsing with active template regression. TPAMI **37**, 2402–2414 (2015)
21. Liang, X., Shen, X., Xiang, D., Feng, J., Lin, L., Yan, S.: Semantic object parsing with local-global long short term memory. In: CVPR (2016)
22. Liang, X., et al.: Human parsing with contextualized convolutional neural network. In: ICCV (2015)
23. Lifkooee, M.Z., Liu, C., Liang, Y., Zhu, Y., Li, X.: Real-time avatar pose transfer and motion generation using locally encoded Laplacian offsets. JCST **34**, 256–271 (2019)
24. Lin, T.-Y., et al.: Microsoft COCO: common objects in context. In: Fleet, D., Pajdla, T., Schiele, B., Tuytelaars, T. (eds.) ECCV 2014. LNCS, vol. 8693, pp. 740–755. Springer, Cham (2014). https://doi.org/10.1007/978-3-319-10602-1_48
25. Liu, C., et al.: Auto-DeepLab: hierarchical neural architecture search for semantic image segmentation. arXiv preprint arXiv 1901.02985 (2018)
26. Liu, S., Jia, J., Fidler, S., Urtasun., R.: SGN: sequential grouping networks for instance segmentation. In: ICCV (2017)
27. Liu, S., et al.: Matching-CNN meets KNN: Quasi-parametric human parsing. In: CVPR (2015)
28. Newell, A., Huang, Z., Deng, J.: Associative embedding: end-to-end learning for joint detection and grouping. In: NIPS (2017)
29. Papandreou, G., Zhu, T., Chen, L.C., Gidaris, S., Tompson, J., Murphy, K.: PersonLab: person pose estimation and instance segmentation with a bottom-up, part-based, geometric embedding model. arXiv Preprint arXiv:1803.08225 (2018)
30. Sun, K., Xiao, B., Liu, D., Wang, J.: Deep high-resolution representation learning for human pose estimation. In: CVPR (2019)
31. Xia, F., Wang, P., Chen, L.C., Yuille, A.L.: Zoom better to see clearer: human part segmentation with auto zoom net. In: ECCV (2016)
32. Xia, S., Gao, L., Lai, Y.K., Yuan, M.Z., Chai, J.: A survey on human performance capture and animation. JCST **32**, 536–554 (2017)

33. Yang, L., Song, Q., Wang, Z., Jiang, M.: Parsing R-CNN for instance-level human analysis. In: CVPR (2019)
34. Chen, Y., Wang, Z., Peng, Y., Zhang, Z., Yu, G., Sun, J.: Cascaded pyramid network for multi-person pose estimation. In: CVPR (2018)
35. Zhang, S.H., et al.: Pose2Seg: detection free human instance segmentation. In: CVPR (2019)
36. Zhao, J., et al.: Understanding humans in crowded scenes: deep nested adversarial learning and a new benchmark for multi-human parsing. arXiv preprint arXiv 1804.03287 (2018)
37. Zhou, Q., Liang, X., Gong, K., Lin, L.: Adaptive temporal encoding network for video instance-level human parsing. In: ACM MM (2018)

Multiple Interaction Learning with Question-Type Prior Knowledge for Constraining Answer Search Space in Visual Question Answering

Tuong Do[1](✉), Binh X. Nguyen[1], Huy Tran[1], Erman Tjiputra[1], Quang D. Tran[1], and Thanh-Toan Do[2]

[1] AIOZ, Singapore, Singapore
{tuong.khanh-long.do,binh.xuan.nguyen,huy.tran,
erman.tjiputra,quang.tran}@aioz.io
[2] University of Liverpool, Liverpool, UK
thanh-toan.do@liverpool.ac.uk

Abstract. Different approaches have been proposed to Visual Question Answering (VQA). However, few works are aware of the behaviors of varying joint modality methods over question type prior knowledge extracted from data in constraining answer search space, of which information gives a reliable cue to reason about answers for questions asked in input images. In this paper, we propose a novel VQA model that utilizes the question-type prior information to improve VQA by leveraging the multiple interactions between different joint modality methods based on their behaviors in answering questions from different types. The solid experiments on two benchmark datasets, i.e., VQA 2.0 and TDIUC, indicate that the proposed method yields the best performance with the most competitive approaches.

Keywords: Visual Question Answering · Multiple interaction learning

1 Introduction

The task of Visual Question Answering (VQA) is to provide a correct answer to a given question such that the answer is consistent with the visual content of a given image. The VQA research raises a rich set of challenges because it is an intersection of different research fields including computer vision, natural language processing, and reasoning. Thanks to its wide applications, the VQA has attracted great attention in recent years [2,3,11,20,23,24]. This also leads to the presence of large scale datasets [3,7,10] and evaluation protocols [3,10].

There are works that consider types of question as the side information which gives a strong cue to reason about the answer [1,9,20]. However, the relation between question types and answers from training data have not been investigated yet. Figure 1 shows the correlation between question types and some answers in the VQA 2.0 dataset [7]. It suggests that a question regarding the quantity should

© Springer Nature Switzerland AG 2020
A. Bartoli and A. Fusiello (Eds.): ECCV 2020 Workshops, LNCS 12536, pp. 496–510, 2020.
https://doi.org/10.1007/978-3-030-66096-3_34

be answered by a number, not a color. The observation indicated that the prior information got from the correlations between question types and answers open an answer search space constrain for the VQA model. The search space constrain is useful for VQA model to give out final prediction and thus, improve the overall performance. The Fig. 1 is consistent with our observation, e.g., it clearly suggests that a question regarding the quantity should be answered by a number, not a color.

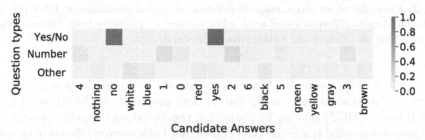

Fig. 1. The distribution of candidate answers in each question type in VQA 2.0.

In current state-of-the-art VQA systems, the joint modality component plays an important role since it would learn meaningful joint representations between linguistic and visual inputs [2,11,15,21,23,24]. Although different joint modality methods or attention mechanisms have been proposed, we hypothesize that each method may capture different aspects of the input. That means different attentions may provide different answers for questions belonged to different question types. Figure 2 shows examples in which the attention models (BAN [11] and SAN [24]) attend on different regions of input images when dealing with questions from different types. Unfortunately, most of recent VQA systems are based on single attention models [2,6,11,20,23,24]. From the above observation, it is necessary to develop a VQA system which leverages the power of different attention models to deal with questions from different question types.

In this paper, we propose a multiple interaction learning with question-type prior knowledge (MILQT) which extracts the question-type prior knowledge from questions to constrain the answer search space and leverage different behaviors of multiple attentions in dealing with questions from different types.

Our contributions are summarized as follows. (i) We propose a novel VQA model that leverages the question-type information to augment the VQA loss. (ii) We identified that different attentions shows different performance in dealing with questions from different types and then leveraged this characteristic to rise performance through our designed model. (iii) The extensive experiments show that the proposed model yields the best performance with the most competitive approaches in the widely used VQA 2.0 [7] and TDIUC [10] datasets.

2   Related Work

Visual Question Answering. In recent years, VQA has attracted a large attention from both computer vision and natural language processing

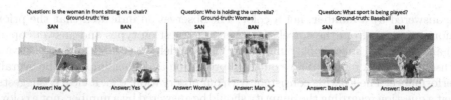

Fig. 2. Examples of attention maps of different attention mechanisms. BAN [11] and SAN [24] identify different visual areas when answering questions from different types. ✓ and ✗ indicate correct and wrong answers, respectively.

communities. The recent VQA researches mainly focus on the development of different attention models. In [6], the authors proposed the Multimodal Compact Bilinear (MCB) pooling by projecting the visual and linguistic features to a higher dimensional space and then convolving both vectors efficiently by using element-wise product in Fast Fourier Transform space. In [24], the authors proposed Stacked Attention Networks (SAN) which locate, via multi-step reasoning, image regions that are relevant to the question for answer prediction. In [2,22], the authors employed the top-down attention that learns an attention weight for each image region by applying non-linear transformations on the combination of image features and linguistic features. In [15], the authors proposed a dense, symmetric attention model that allows each question word attends on image regions and each image region attends on question words. In [11] the authors proposed Bilinear Attention Networks (BAN) that find bilinear attention distributions to utilize given visual-linguistics information seamlessly. Recently, in [21] the authors introduced Cross Modality Encoder Representations (LXMERT) to learn the alignment/relationships between visual concepts and language semantics.

Regarding the question type, previous works have considered question-type information to improve VQA results. Agrawal et al. [1] trained a separated question-type classifier to classify input questions into two categories, i.e., Yes-No and non Yes-No. Each category will be subsequently processed in different ways. In the other words, the question type information is only used for selecting suitable sub-sequence processing. Shi et al. [20] also trained a question-type classifier to predict the question type. The predicted one-hot question type is only used to weight the importance of different visual features. Kafle et al. [9] also used question type to improve the performance of VQA prediction. Similar to [1], the authors separately trained a classifier to predict the type of the input question. The predicted question type is then used to improve VQA prediction through a Bayesian inference model.

In our work, different from [1, 20] and [9], question types work as the prior knowledge, which constrain answer search space through loss function. Additionally, we can further identify the performance of different joint modality methods over questions from different types. Besides, through the multiple interaction learning, the behaviors of the joint modality methods are utilized on giving out the final answer which further improve VQA performance.

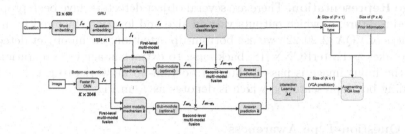

Fig. 3. The proposed MILQT for VQA.

3   Methodology

The proposed multiple interaction learning with question-type prior knowledge (MILQT) is illustrated in Fig. 3. Similar to the most of the VQA systems [2,11,24], multiple interaction learning with question-type prior knowledge (MILQT) consists of the joint learning solution for input questions and images, followed by a multi-class classification over a set of predefined candidate answers. However, MILQT allows to leverage multiple joint modality methods under the guiding of question-types to output better answers.

As in Fig. 3, MILQT consists of two modules: Question-type awareness $\mathcal{A}$, and Multi-hypothesis interaction learning $\mathcal{M}$. The first module aims to learn the question-type representation, which is further used to enhance the joint visual-question embedding features and to constrain answer search space through prior knowledge extracted from data. Based on the question-type information, the second module aims to identify the behaviors of multiple joint learning methods and then justify adjust contributions to giving out final predictions.

In the following, we describe the representation of input questions and images in Sect. 3.1. Section 3.2 presents the Question-type awareness module $\mathcal{A}$. Section 3.3 presents the Multi-hypothesis interaction learning module $\mathcal{M}$. Section 3.4 presents the multi-task loss for entire model training.

3.1   Input Representation

Question Representation. Given an input question, follow the recent state-of-the-art [2,11], we trim the question to a maximum of 12 words. The questions that are shorter than 12 words are zero-padded. Each word is then represented by a 600-D vector that is a concatenation of the 300-D GloVe word embedding [17] and the augmenting embedding from training data as [11]. This step results in a sequence of word embeddings with size of 12×600 and is denoted as f_w in Fig. 3. In order to obtain the intent of question, the f_w is passed through a Gated Recurrent Unit (GRU) [4] which results in a 1024-D vector representation f_q for the input question.

Image Representation. There are several object detectors have been proposed in the literature, of which outputs vary in size and location. Inspired by recent advances of VQA [2,20,22], we use bottom-up attention, i.e. an object detection which takes as FasterRCNN [18] backbone, to extract image representation. At first, the input image is passed through bottom-up networks to get $K \times 2048$ bounding box representation which is denotes as f_v in Fig. 3.

3.2 Question-Type Awareness

Question-Type Classification. This component in module $\mathcal{A}$ aims to learn the question-type representation. Specifically, aforementioned component takes the question embedding f_q as input, which is then passed through several fully-connected (FC) layers and is ended by a softmax layer which produces a probability distribution h over P question types, where P depends on the dataset, i.e., P equals 3 for VQA 2.0 [7] and equals 12 for TDIUC [10]. The question type embedding f_{qt} extracted from question-type classification component will be combined with the attention features to enhance the joint semantic representation between the input image and question, while the predicted question type will be used to augment the VQA loss.

Multi-level Multi-modal Fusion. Unlike the previous works that perform only one level of fusion between linguistic and visual features that may limit the capacity of these models to learn a good joint semantic space. In our work, a multi-level multi-modal fusion that encourages the model to learn a better joint semantic space is introduced which takes the question-type representation got from question-type classification component as one of inputs.

First Level Multi-modal Fusion: The first level fusion is similar to previous works [2,11,24]. Given visual features f_v, question features f_q, and any joint modality mechanism (e.g., bilinear attention [11], stacked attention [24], bottom-up [2] etc.), we combines visual features with question features and learn attention weights to weight for visual and/or linguistic features. Different attention mechanisms have different ways for learning the joint semantic space. The detail of each attention mechanism can be found in the corresponding studies [2,11,24]. The output of first level multi-modal fusion is denoted as f_{att} in the Fig. 3.

Second Level Multi-modal Fusion: In order to enhance the joint semantic space, the output of the first level multi-modal fusion f_{att} is combined with the question-type feature f_{qt}, which is the output of the last FC layer of the

"Question-type classification" component. We try two simple but effective operators, i.e. *element-wise multiplication—EWM* or *element-wise addition—EWA*, to combine f_{att} and f_{qt}. The output of the second level multi-modal fusion, which is denoted as f_{att-qt} in Fig. 3, can be seen as an attention representation that is aware of the question-type information.

Given an attention mechanism, the f_{att-qt} will be used as the input for a classifier that predicts an answer for the corresponding question. This is shown at the "Answer prediction" boxes in the Fig. 3.

Augmented VQA Loss. The introduced loss function takes model predicted question types and prior knowledge question types from data to identify the answer search space constraints when the model outputs predicted answers.

Prior Computation. In order to make the VQA classifier pay more attention on the answers corresponding to the question type of the input question, we use the statistical information from training data to identify the relation between the question type and the answer. The Algorithm 1 presents the calculation of the prior information between the question types and the answers. To calculate the prior, we firstly make statistics of the frequency of different question types in each VQA candidate answer. This results in a matrix m_{qt-ans} (lines 2 to 4). We then column-wise normalize the matrix m_{qt-ans} by dividing elements in a column by the sum of the column (lines 5 to 7).

Algorithm 1: Question type - answer relational prior computation

Input : Q: number of questions in training set.

$\quad\quad$ P: number of question types.

$\quad\quad$ A: number of candidate answers.

$\quad\quad$ $qtLabels \in \{1, ..., P\}^{Q \times 1}$: type labels of questions in training set.

$\quad\quad$ $ansLabels \in \{1, ..., A\}^{Q \times 1}$: answer labels of questions in training set.

Output: $m_{qt-ans} \in \mathbb{R}^{P \times A}$: relational prior of question types and answers.

1 $\quad m_{qt-ans} = zeros(P, A)$ /* init m_{qt-ans} with all zero values */

2 $\quad$ **for** $q = 1 \rightarrow Q$ **do**

3 $\quad\quad |\quad m_{qt-ans}[qtLabels[q], ansLabels[q]] \mathrel{+}= 1$

4 $\quad$ **end**

5 $\quad$ **for** $a = 1 \rightarrow A$ **do**

6 $\quad\quad |\quad m_{qt-ans}[:, a] = normalize(m_{qt-ans}[:, a])$

7 $\quad$ **end**

Augmented VQA Loss Function Design l_{vqa}. Let $y_i \in \mathbb{R}^{A \times 1}$, $g_i \in \mathbb{R}^{A \times 1}$, $h_i \in \mathbb{R}^{P \times 1}$ be the VQA groundtruth answer, VQA answer prediction, and the question-type prediction of the ith input question-image, respectively. Given the question, our target is to increase the chances of possible answers corresponding to the question type of the question. To this end, we first define the weighting (question-type) awareness matrix m_{awn} by combining the predicted question-type h_i and the prior information m_{qt-ans} as follows:

$$m_{awn} = h_i{}^T m_{qt-ans} \tag{1}$$

This weighting matrix is used to weight the VQA groundtruth y_i and VQA answer prediction g_i to as follows:

$$\hat{y}_i = m_{awn}^T \odot y_i \tag{2}$$

$$\hat{g}_i = m_{awn}^T \odot g_i \tag{3}$$

where $\odot$ is the element-wise product. As a result, this weighting increases the chances of possible answers corresponding to the question type of the question. Finally, the VQA loss l_{vqa} is computed as follows:

$$l_{vqa} = -\frac{1}{QA} \sum_{i=1}^{Q} \sum_{j=1}^{A} \hat{y}_{ij} \log(\sigma(\hat{g}_{ij})) + (1 - \hat{y}_{ij}) \log(1 - \sigma(\hat{g}_{ij})) \tag{4}$$

where Q and A are the number of training questions and candidate answers; σ is the element-wise sigmoid function. (4) is a *soft* cross entropy loss and has been shown to be more effective than softmax in VQA problem [22].

It is worth noting that when computing the weighting matrix a_{awn} in (1), instead of using the predicted question type h_i, we can also use the groundtruth question type. However, we found that there are some inconsistency between the groundtruth question types and the groundtruth answers. For example, in VQA 2.0 dataset, most of questions started by "how many" are classified with the question type "number", and the answers to these questions are numeric numbers. However, there are also some exceptions. For example, the question *"How many stripes are there on the zebra?"* is annotated with the groundtruth question-type "number" but its annotated groundtruth answer is "many", which is not a numeric number. By using groundtruth question type to augment the loss, the answer to that question is likely a numeric number, which is an incorrect answer compared to the groundtruth answer. In order to make the model robust to these exceptions, we use the predicted question type to augment the VQA loss. Using the predicted question type can be seen as a self-adaptation mechanism that allows the system to adapt to exceptions. In particular, for the above example, the predicted question type may not be necessary "number" and it can be "other".

3.3 Multi-hypothesis Interaction Learning

As presented in Fig. 3, MILQT allows to utilize multiple hypotheses (i.e., joint modality mechanisms). Specifically, we propose a multi-hypothesis interaction learning design $\mathcal{M}$ that takes answer predictions produced by different joint modality mechanisms and interactively learn to combine them. Let $g \in \mathbb{R}^{A \times J}$

be the matrix of predicted probability distributions over A answers from the J joint modality mechanisms. $\mathcal{M}$ outputs the distribution $\rho \in \mathbb{R}^A$, which is calculated from g through Eq. (5).

$$\rho = \mathcal{M}\left(g, w_{mil}\right) = \sum_j \left(m_{qt-ans}^T w_{mil} \odot g\right) \tag{5}$$

$w_{mil} \in \mathbb{R}^{P \times J}$ is the learnable weight which control the contributions of J considered joint modality mechanisms on predicting answer based on the guiding of P question types; $\odot$ denotes Hardamard product.

3.4 Multi-task Loss

In order to train the proposed MILQT, we define a multi-task loss to jointly optimize the question-type classification, the answer prediction of each individual attention mechanism, and the VQA loss (4). Formally, our multi-task loss is defined as follows:

$$l = \alpha_1 \sum_{j=1}^{k} l_{H_j} + \alpha_2 l_{vqa} + \alpha_3 l_{qt} \tag{6}$$

where $\alpha_1, \alpha_2, \alpha_3$ are parameters controlling the importance of each loss; l_{qt} is the question-type classification loss; l_{H_j} is the answer prediction loss of jth mechanism over J joint modality methods; l_{vqa} is the introduced VQA loss augmented by the predicted question type and the prior information defined by (4).

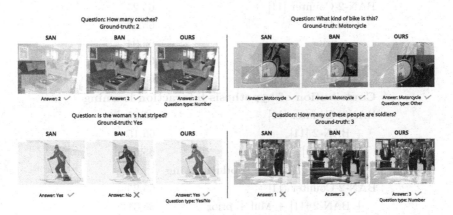

Fig. 4. Example results of SAN [24], BAN [11], and our method on the validation set of VQA 2.0. In all cases, the proposed method produces better attention maps. It also produce more accurate answers than compared methods (second row).

4   Experiments

4.1   Dataset and Implementation Detail

Dataset. We conduct the experiments on two benchmark VQA datasets that are VQA 2.0 [7] and TDIUC [10]. The VQA 2.0 dataset is the most popular and is widely used in VQA problem. In VQA 2.0 dataset, questions are divided into three question types, i.e., "Yes-No", "Number" and "Other" while the TDIUC dataset has 12 different question types.

As standardly done in the literature, we use the standard VQA accuracy metric [3] when evaluating on VQA 2.0 dataset and Arithmetric MPT as well as Harmonic MPT proposed in [10] when evaluating on TDIUC[1].

Implementation Detail. Our proposed MILQT is implemented using PyTorch [16]. The experiments are conducted on a single NVIDIA Titan V with 12 GB RAM.

In all experiments, the learning rate is set to 10^{-3} (or 7×10^{-4} if using Visual Genome [13] as augmenting data) and batch size is set to 256. The number of detected bounding boxes is set to 50 when extracting visual features. The GRU [4] for question embedding has one layer with 1024-D hidden state and processes words in forward order. During training, except image representations f_v, other components are trained end-to-end with the multi-task loss (6). AdaMax optimizer [12] is used to train our model.

Table 1. Contributions of the proposed components and the whole model on the VQA 2.0 validation set.

Models	VQA score
Contribution of question type awareness	
BAN-2-Counter [11]	65.25
+ add	65.68
+ prior	66.04
+ mul	65.80
+ prior	66.13
Contribution of hypothesis interaction learning	
BAN-2-Counter [11]	65.25
+ BAN-2 [11]	66.15
+ SAN [24]	65.64
Whole model testing	
BAN-2-Counter [11]	65.25
+ BAN-2 [11] + Mul + prior	66.31
+ SAN [24] + Mul + prior	66.48

---

[1] In [10], the authors show that using Arithmetric MPT and Harmonic MPT is more suitable than the standard VQA accuracy metric [3] when evaluating on TDIUC.

Table 2. Performance on VQA 2.0 validation set where BAN2 [11] and BAN-2-Counter [11] are ensembled using averaging ensembling and the proposed interacting learning.

Models	BAN-2	BAN-2-Counter	Averaging Ens.	Interaction learning
Accuracy	65.36	65.25	65.61	66.15

4.2 Ablation Study

To evaluate the contribution of question-type awareness $\mathcal{A}$ module and multi-hypothesis interaction learning $\mathcal{M}$ in our method, we conduct ablation studies when training on the train set and testing on the validation set of VQA 2.0 [7].

Starting with the BAN glimpse 2 with counter sub-module (BAN-2-Counter) [11] as the baseline, we show the effectiveness of proposed modules when they are integrated into the baseline. The counter sub-module [25] is used in the baseline to prove the extendability of proposed model on supporting "Number" question. However, any sub-modules can also be applied, e.g., relational reasoning sub-module [19] to support for "Yes/No" and "Other" questions. It is worth noting that in order to make a fair comparison, we use the same visual features and question embedding features for both BAN-2-Counter baseline and our model.

Table 3. The correlation scores extracted from w_{mil} of MILQT. The extracted information got from model trained in VQA 2.0 train set.

Question types	Correlation scores		
	BAN-Counter	BAN	SAN
Yes/No	0.40	0.55	0.05
Numbers	0.55	0.23	0.22
Others	0.35	0.38	0.27

The Effectiveness of Question-Type Awareness and Prior Information Proposed in Sect. 3.2. The first section in Table 1 shows that by having second level multi-modal fusion (Sect. 3.2) which uses element-wise multiplication ($+mul$) to combine the question-type feature f_{qt} and the attention feature f_{att}, the overall performance increases from 65.25% (baseline) to 65.80%. By further using the predicted question type and the prior information ($+prior$) to augment the VQA loss, the performance increases to 66.13% which is +0.88% improvement over the baseline. The results in the first section in Table 1 confirm that combining question-type features with attention features helps to learn a better joint semantic space, which leads to the performance boost over the baseline. These results also confirm that using the predicted question type and the prior provides a further boost in the performance. We also find out that using EWM provides better accuracy than EWA at the second level fusion.

Table 4. Comparison to the state of the arts on the test-dev and test-standard of VQA 2.0. For fair comparison, in all setup except LXMERT which uses BERT [5] as question embedding, Glove embedding and GRU are leveraged for question embedding and Bottom-up features are used to extract visual information. CMP, i.e. Cross-Modality with Pooling, is the LXMERT with the aforementioned setup.

Models	VQA - test-dev				VQA - test-std			
	Overall	Yes/No	Nums	Other	Overall	Yes/No	Nums	Other
SAN [24]	64.80	79.63	43.21	57.09	65.21	80.06	43.57	57.24
Up-Down [2]	65.32	81.82	44.21	56.05	65.67	82.20	43.90	56.26
CMP [21]	68.7	84.91	50.15	59.11	69.23	85.48	49.53	59.6
Pythia [8]	70.01	86.12	48.97	61.06	70.24	86.37	48.46	61.18
BAN [11]	70.04	85.42	54.04	60.52	70.35	85.82	53.71	60.69
LXMERT [21]	**72.4**	88.3	54.2	62.9	**72.5**	88.0	56.7	65.2
MILQT	70.62	86.47	54.24	60.79	70.93	86.80	53.79	61.03

The Effectiveness of Multi-hypothesis Interaction Learning Proposed in Sect. 3.3. The second section in Table 1 shows the effectiveness when leveraging different joint modality mechanisms by using multi-hypothesis interaction learning. By using BAN-2-Counter [11] and BAN-2 [11] (BAN-2-Counter + BAN-2), the overall performance is 66.15% which is +0.9% improvement over the BAN-2-Counter baseline.

Table 3 illustrates the correlation between different joint modality mechanisms and question types. This information is extracted from w_{mil} which identify the contributions of each mechanism in giving final VQA results guiding by the question type information.

The results in Table 4 indicate that some joint modality methods achieve better performance in some specific question types, e.g., joint modality method BAN outperform other methods in Number question type by a large margin. The correlation in Table 3 and performance in Table 4 also indicates that the MILQT model tends to leverage the contribution of joint methods proportional to their performance in each specific question type. Besides, the results in Table 2 indicate that under the guiding of question type, $\mathcal{M}$ module produce better performance when comparing with none-use solution or the weighted sum method [14] in which the predictions of different joint modality mechanisms are summed up and the answer with highest score are considered as the final answer.

The Effectiveness of the Entire Proposed Model. The third section in Table 1 presents results when all components (except the visual feature extractor) are combined in a unified model and are trained end-to-end. To verify the effectiveness of the proposed framework, we conduct two configurations. In the first configuration, we use two joint modality mechanisms BAN-2-Counter and BAN-2, the EWM in the second level multi-modal fusion, and the predicted question type together with the prior information to augment the loss.

The second configuration is similar to the first configuration, except that we use BAN-2-Counter and SAN in interaction learning. The third section on Table 1 shows that both configurations give the performance boost over the baseline. The second configuration achieves better performance, i.e., 66.48% accuracy, which outperforms over the baseline BAN-2-Counter +1.23%. Table 1 also show that using "question-type awareness" gives further boost over using interaction learning only, i.e., the performance of "BAN-2-Counter + SAN + Mul + prior" (66.48) outperforms the performance of "BAN-2-Counter + SAN" (65.64). Figure 4 presents some visualization results of our second configuration and other methods on the VQA 2.0 validation set.

Question-Type Classification Analysis. The proposed MILQT is a model which allows joint training between question-type classification and VQA answer classification. The effectiveness of multi-task learning helps to improve performance in both tasks. To further analyze the effectiveness of MILQT in the question-type classification, we provide in this section the question type classification on TDIUC dataset. We follow QTA [20] to calculate the accuracy, i.e., the overall accuracy is the number of correct predictions over the number of testing questions, across all categories.

The results are presented in Table 5. Our MILQT uses BAN-2 [11], BAN-2-Counter [11], and SAN [24] in the interaction learning, element-wise multiplication in the second level of multi-modal fusion, and the predicted question type with prior information to augment the VQA loss. Compare to the state-of-the-art QTA [20], our MILQT outperforms QTA for most of question types. In overall, we achieve state-of-the-art performance on question-type classification task on TDIUC dataset with 96.45% accuracy.

It is worth noting that for the "Utility and Affordances" category, the question type classification accuracy is 0% for both QTA and MILQT. It is because the imbalanced data problem in TDIUC dataset. The "Utility and Affordances" category has only ≈0.03% samples in the dataset. Hence this category is strongly dominated by other categories when learning the question type classifier. Note that, there are cases in which questions belonging to the "Utility and Affordances" category have similar answers with questions belonging to other categories. Thus, the data becomes less bias w.r.t. answers (in comparing to question categories). This explains why although both MILQT and QTA have 0% accuracy for the "Utility and Affordances" on the question category classification, both of them achieve some accuracy on the VQA classification (see Table 5).

4.3   Comparison to the State of the Art

Experiments on VQA 2.0 Test-dev and Test-Standard. We evaluate MILQT on the test-dev and test-standard of VQA 2.0 dataset [7]. To train the model, similar to previous works [8,11,22,24], we use both training set and validation set of VQA 2.0. We also use the Visual Genome [13] as additional training data.

MILQT consists of three joint modality mechanisms, i.e., BAN-2, BAN-2-Counter, and SAN accompanied with the EWM for the multi-modal fusion, and

Table 5. The comparative question-type classification results between MILQT and state-of-the-art QTA [20] on the TDIUC validation set.

Question-type accuracy	Reference models	
	QTA [20]	MILQT
Scene Recognition	99.40	**99.84**
Sport Recognition	73.08	**85.81**
Color Attributes	86.10	**89.60**
Other Attributes	77.76	**85.03**
Activity Recognition	13.18	**16.43**
Positional Recognition	89.52	**89.55**
Sub-Object Recognition	98.96	**99.42**
Absurd	**95.46**	95.12
Utility and Affordances	00.00	00.00
Object Presence	**100.00**	**100.00**
Counting	99.90	**99.99**
Sentiment Understanding	60.51	**67.82**
Overall	95.66	**96.45**

the predicted question type together with the prior information to augment the VQA loss. Table 4 presents the results of different methods on test-dev and test-std of VQA 2.0. The results show that our MILQT yields the good performance with the most competitive approaches.

Experiments on TDIUC. In order to prove the stability of MILQT, we evaluate MILQT on TDIUC dataset [10]. The results in Table 6 show that the proposed model establishes the state-of-the-art results on both evaluation metrics Arithmetic MPT and Harmonic MPT [10]. Specifically, our model significantly outperforms the recent QTA [20], i.e., on the overall, we improve over QTA 6.1% and 11.1% with Arithemic MPT and Harmonic MPT metrics, respectively. It is worth noting that the results of QTA [20] in Table 6, which are cited from [20], are achieved when [20] used the one-hot *predicted question type* of testing question to weight visual features. When using *the groundtruth question type* to weight visual features, [20] reported 69.11% and 60.08% for Arithemic MPT and Harmonic MPT metrics, respectively. Our model also outperforms these performances a large margin, i.e., the improvements are 3.9% and 6.8% for Arithemic MPT and Harmonic MPT metrics, respectively.

We also note that for the question type "Absurd", we get lower performance than QTA [20]. For this question type, the question is irrelevant with the image content. Consequently, this question type does not help to learn a joint meaningful embedding between the input question and image. This explains for our lower performance on this question type.

Table 6. The comparative results between the proposed model and other models on the validation set of TDIUC.

Score	Reference models			
	QTA-M [20]	MCB-A [10]	RAU [10]	MILQT
Scene Recognition	93.74	93.06	93.96	**94.74**
Sport Recognition	94.80	92.77	93.47	**96.47**
Color Attributes	57.62	68.54	66.86	**75.23**
Other Attributes	52.05	56.72	56.49	**61.93**
Activity Recognition	53.13	52.35	51.60	**65.03**
Positional Recognition	33.90	35.40	35.26	**42.31**
Sub-Object Recognition	86.89	85.54	86.11	**89.63**
Absurd	**98.57**	84.82	96.08	88.95
Utility and Affordances	24.07	35.09	31.58	**38.60**
Object Presence	94.57	93.64	94.38	**96.21**
Counting	53.59	51.01	48.43	**62.41**
Sentiment Understanding	60.06	**66.25**	60.09	64.98
Arithmetic MPT	66.92	67.90	67.81	**73.04**
Harmonic MPT	55.77	60.47	59.00	**66.86**

5   Conclusion

We present a multiple interaction learning with question-type prior knowledge for constraining answer search space—MILQT that takes into account the question-type information to improve the VQA performance at different stages. The system also allows to utilize and learn different attentions under a unified model in an interacting manner. The extensive experimental results show that all proposed components improve the VQA performance. We yields the best performance with the most competitive approaches on VQA 2.0 and TDIUC dataset.

References

1. Agrawal, A., Dhruv Batra, D.P., Kembhavi, A.: Don't just assume; look and answer: overcoming priors for visual question answering. In: CVPR (2018)
2. Anderson, P., et al.: Bottom-up and top-down attention for image captioning and VQA. In: CVPR (2018)
3. Antol, S., et al.: VQA: visual question answering. In: ICCV (2015)
4. Cho, K., et al.: Learning phrase representations using RNN encoder-decoder for statistical machine translation. In: EMNLP (2014)
5. Devlin, J., Chang, M.W., Lee, K., Toutanova, K.: BERT: pre-training of deep bidirectional transformers for language understanding. In: NAACL-HLT (2019)
6. Fukui, A., Park, D.H., Yang, D., Rohrbach, A., Darrell, T., Rohrbach, M.: Multi-modal compact bilinear pooling for visual question answering and visual grounding. In: EMNLP (2016)

7. Goyal, Y., Khot, T., Summers-Stay, D., Batra, D., Parikh, D.: Making the V in VQA matter: elevating the role of image understanding in visual question answering. In: CVPR (2017)
8. Jiang, Y., Natarajan, V., Chen, X., Rohrbach, M., Batra, D., Parikh, D.: Pythia v0.1: the winning entry to the VQA challenge 2018. CoRR (2018)
9. Kafle, K., Kanan, C.: Answer-type prediction for visual question answering. In: CVPR (2016)
10. Kafle, K., Kanan, C.: An analysis of visual question answering algorithms. In: ICCV (2017)
11. Kim, J.H., Jun, J., Zhang, B.T.: Bilinear attention networks. In: NIPS (2018)
12. Kingma, D.P., Ba, J.: Adam: a method for stochastic optimization. In: ICLR (2015)
13. Krishna, R., et al.: Visual genome: connecting language and vision using crowd-sourced dense image annotations. IJCV **123**, 32–73 (2016)
14. Li, L., Gan, Z., Cheng, Y., Liu, J.: Relation-aware graph attention network for visual question answering. In: ICCV (2019)
15. Nguyen, D.K., Okatani, T.: Improved fusion of visual and language representations by dense symmetric co-attention for visual question answering. In: CVPR (2018)
16. Paszke, A., et al.: Automatic differentiation in PyTorch. In: NIPS 2017 Workshop (2017)
17. Pennington, J., Socher, R., Manning, C.D.: GloVe: global vectors for word representation. In: EMNLP (2014)
18. Ren, S., He, K., Girshick, R., Sun, J.: Faster R-CNN: towards real-time object detection with region proposal networks. In: NIPS (2015)
19. Santoro, A., et al.: A simple neural network module for relational reasoning. In: NIPS (2017)
20. Shi, Y., Furlanello, T., Zha, S., Anandkumar, A.: Question type guided attention in visual question answering. In: Ferrari, V., Hebert, M., Sminchisescu, C., Weiss, Y. (eds.) ECCV 2018. LNCS, vol. 11208, pp. 158–175. Springer, Cham (2018). https://doi.org/10.1007/978-3-030-01225-0_10
21. Tan, H., Bansal, M.: LXMERT: learning cross-modality encoder representations from transformers. In: Proceedings of the 2019 Conference on Empirical Methods in Natural Language Processing and the 9th International Joint Conference on Natural Language Processing (EMNLP-IJCNLP) (2019)
22. Teney, D., Anderson, P., He, X., van den Hengel, A.: Tips and tricks for visual question answering: learnings from the 2017 challenge. In: CVPR (2018)
23. Xu, H., Saenko, K.: Ask, attend and answer: exploring question-guided spatial attention for visual question answering. In: Leibe, B., Matas, J., Sebe, N., Welling, M. (eds.) ECCV 2016. LNCS, vol. 9911, pp. 451–466. Springer, Cham (2016). https://doi.org/10.1007/978-3-319-46478-7_28
24. Yang, Z., He, X., Gao, J., Deng, L., Smola, A.J.: Stacked attention networks for image question answering. In: CVPR (2016)
25. Zhang, Y., Hare, J.S., Prügel-Bennett, A.: Learning to count objects in natural images for visual question answering. In: ICLR (2018)

A Visual Inductive Priors Framework for Data-Efficient Image Classification

Pengfei Sun$^{(\boxtimes)}$ (iD), Xuan Jin, Wei Su, Yuan He, Hui Xue, and Quan Lu

Alibaba Group, Hangzhou, China
{yeqing.spf,jinxuan.jx,junyu.sw,heyuan.hy,
hui.xueh,luquan.lq}@alibaba-inc.com

Abstract. State-of-the-art classifiers rely heavily on large-scale datasets, such as ImageNet, JFT-300M, MSCOCO, Open Images, etc. Besides, the performance may decrease significantly because of insufficient learning on a handful of samples. We present Visual Inductive Priors Framework (VIPF), a framework that can learn classifiers from scratch. VIPF can maximize the effectiveness of limited data. In this work, we propose a novel neural network architecture: DSK-net, which is very effective in training from small data sets. With more discriminative feature extracted from DSK-net, overfitting of network is alleviated. Furthermore, a loss function based on positive class as well as an induced hierarchy are also applied to further improve the VIPF's capability of learning from scratch. Finally, we won the **1st Place** in VIPriors image classification competition.

Keywords: Learn from scratch · Classification · Visual inductive priors · DSK-net · Induced hierarchy

1 Introduction

Convolutional Neural Networks (CNNs) have achieved state-of-the-art performance in image classification, object detection, semantic segmentation, etc. With the appearance of AlexNet [14], VGG [18], Inception [12,19–21], ResNet [9], EfficientNet [22], ResNeSt [29], etc., the top-1 accuracy on ImageNet has been increased from 62.5% (AlexNet) to 84.5% (ResNeSt-269). Besides different network backbones, there are also many plug-and-play modules which can significantly improve accuracy, such as SE (Squeeze-and-Excitation) [11], CBAM (Convolutional Block Attention Module) [26], ECA (Efficient Channel Attention) [24], etc.

However, due to the limitation of label data, the performance of CNN is greatly limited. Pre-trained models are the most common solution that can get a fine result because of the prior knowledge. But there are only a few pre-trained models which are fixed architectures and proposed like Inception, ResNet, EfficientNet, etc. For training from scratch on VIPriors classification dataset which has only 50 training samples per class, the effectiveness of learning plays an

A. Bartoli and A. Fusiello (Eds.): ECCV 2020 Workshops, LNCS 12536, pp. 511–520, 2020.
https://doi.org/10.1007/978-3-030-66096-3_35

important role. Effective and sufficient augment strategies are necessary, such as rand erasing [32], Mixup [30], CutMix [28], Cutout [7], AutoAugment [5], RandAugment [6], etc. On the other hand, models would overfit easily with little training data, so it is crucial to lighten the overfitting with appropriate regularization.

In this work, a novel network architecture Dual Selective Kernel network (DSK-net) is proposed to improve the effectiveness on small scale datasets. For more data-efficient learning, positive class classification loss and intra-class compactness loss are applied to enhance discriminative power of the deeply learned features. An induced hierarchy is used which is easier for models to learn from scratch. Methods are evaluated on VIPriors Image Classification dataset. The dataset is derived from ImageNet and contains 50 images per class for training and testing. Experimental results show that our methods achieve the best performance on VIPriors classification dataset.

2 Related Works

2.1 Data Augmentation

Augmentation is an effective way to improve CNNs' performance especially in the case of insufficient data. Mixup [30] trains a model on convex combinations of pairs of examples and their labels together. Cutout [7] randomly erases square regions on input images during training. CutMix [28] cuts and pastes patches among training images where the training labels are also mixed proportionally to the area of patches. It can efficiently make use of training pixels and retain the regularization effect of regional dropout. GridMask [3] drops pixels on the input images with multiple squares and different ratios. Recently, with the emergence of AutoML, network learning strategies also can be searched from data. Auto-Augmentation [5] is a series of augmentation operation strategies searched on ImageNet which needs a huge space for searching. Hence RandAugmentation [6] proposes a simplified search space which has less computational expense.

2.2 Translation Invariance in CNNs

It is generally known that CNNs are not shift-invariant. A small shift or translation of input will result in quite different output. To reduce the influence of translation, several augmentation operations are often used such as scaling, rotation and reflection [2,4,8,17,27]. [31] integrates low-pass filtering to anti-alias which is a common signal processing module. [13] proposes a full convolution architecture by removing spatial location as feature which improves equivariance and invariance of the inductive convolutional prior.

2.3 Important Feature Learning

For image classification, locating and recognizing the discriminative feature is the key to a better performance. And most of discriminative feature extraction modules are based on attention mechanisms which is inspired by human brain neural units. SE (Squeeze-and-Excitation) [11] and ECA [24] are channel attention architectures. Channel and spatial attention modules are applied in CBAM [26]. Inspired by adaptive field sizes of neurons, [15] proposes Selective Kernel (SK) convolution which is based on soft-attention manner to improve feature extraction efficiency. Except attention architecture, loss function can also help model learn more discriminative feature. Center loss [25] is implemented by increasing inter-class dispersion and intra-class compactness. It learns centers form deep features of each class, and then penalizes the distances between deep features and their corresponding class centers.

3 Proposed Method

To be more data-efficient, firstly, a 3-branched network called Dual Selective Kernel (DSK) network is proposed in Fig. 1. DSK has the advantages of discriminative feature extraction, translation invariant and regularization. Secondly, a composite loss function is designed to improve feature discrimination. It helps models not only classify correctly but also increase the diversity of different classes.

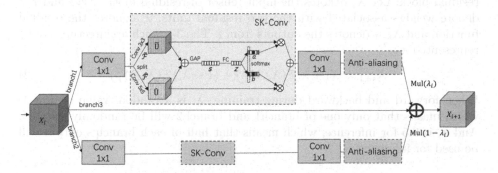

Fig. 1. Dual selective kernel residual block.

3.1 Dual Selective Kernel Network

Discriminative Feature Extraction. To adjust the receptive fields of neurons automatically, selective kernel convolution [15] is added into residual block. For any given feature map $X_i \in \mathbb{R}^{H \times W \times C}$, X_i is respectively conducted by convolutions of kernel size 3 and 5. Then two transforms are conducted: $\widehat{\mathcal{F}}:X_i \rightarrow \widehat{\mathcal{U}} \in \mathbb{R}^{H \times W \times C}$ and $\widetilde{\mathcal{F}}:X_i \rightarrow \widetilde{\mathcal{U}} \in \mathbb{R}^{H \times W \times C}$. Both $\widehat{\mathcal{F}}$ and $\widetilde{\mathcal{F}}$ are composed with depthwise convolution, Batch Normalization and ReLU. Feature $\mathcal{U}$ is a element-wise sum of $\widehat{\mathcal{U}}$ and $\widetilde{\mathcal{U}}$. For $\mathcal{U}$, global average pooling is used for information embedding. Further, a compact feature $s \in \mathbb{R}^C$ is created by passing feature embedding to fully connected layer for squeeze. Then Batch Normalization, ReLU and another two fully connected layers are applied for different kernel excitation. Finally, a soft attention is conducted to select information in different spatial scales. The weights $\widehat{\omega}$ and $\widetilde{\omega}$ for attention is calculated by a channel-wise softmax operation of per channel between a and b. The final feature map is obtained by applying attention weights to feature $\widehat{\mathcal{U}}$ and $\widetilde{\mathcal{U}}$:

$$\mathcal{V} = \widehat{\omega} \cdot \widehat{\mathcal{U}} + \widetilde{\omega} \cdot \widetilde{\mathcal{U}} \tag{1}$$

Translation Invariant. The reducing spatial resolution operations in CNNs including max pooling, average pooling and strided convolution are harmful to shift-equivariance. Blur pool [31] is an anti-aliased architecture which is compatible with above architectures components. For example, max pooling with stride $= 2$ in CNNs will be split into max pooling with stride $= 1$ and blur pool with stride $= 2$. Strided convolution with activation function will be split into convolution with stride $= 1$, activation function and blur pool. As for blur pool kernel, it has several anti-aliasing filters from size 2×2 to 5×5 with increasing smoothing. In DSK, 3×3 filter is applied in max pooling and strided convolution.

Regularization. Like data augmentation techniques applied to input data, it is reasonable to apply corresponding techniques to representation branch in residual block. Let X_i denotes the input tensor of residual block i. $\mathcal{W}_i^1$ and $\mathcal{W}_i^2$ denote weights associated with the two residual units. $\mathcal{F}$ denotes the residual function and X_{i+1} denotes the outputs from i. The 3-branch architecture can be represented as:

$$X_{i+1} = X_i + \lambda_i \mathcal{F}(X_i, \mathcal{W}_i^1) + (1 - \lambda_i)\mathcal{F}(X_i, \mathcal{W}_i^2) \tag{2}$$

When forward and backward during training, λ_i is a random value of 0 or 1, which means that only one of branch1 and branch2 will be randomly selected. And λ_i is 0.5 for inference, which means that half of each branch's output will be used for inference.

3.2 Loss Function

Categorical cross-entropy (CE) loss after softmax is widely used in multi-class classification. But for VIPriors classification dataset, CE is suboptimal. Because it forces models to only focus on training image and ignore the compactness of intra-class. In this section, several loss functions will be discussed and a combined loss is proposed as Eq. 3 for a better performance.

$$L = \alpha L_{PCL} + \beta L_{CL} + \gamma L_{TSL} \tag{3}$$

Positive Class Loss. CE loss is showed in Eq. 4. Let p represents the output of a model and l represents one-hot labels. CE not only directs model to classify the ground truth class correctly but also forces the prediction of other classes as low as possible.

$$L_{CE} = -\frac{1}{N} \sum (l * log(p) + (1 - l) * log(1 - p)) \tag{4}$$

But is it suitable to use a loss on a small dataset in which the number of classes is far greater than the number of samples per class? Additionally, [16] proves that there are many label errors in ImageNet including actual multi-label images but only labeled with singe class label. We have reasons to believe that there is the same question on VIProirs classification dataset. Based on the above, making models only focus on ground truth label may be more beneficial during learning. Consequently, the positive class loss (PCL) is proposed as:

$$L_{PCL} = \frac{1}{N} \sum (-l * log(p) + (1 - cos(l, p)))$$ (5)

PCL has two parts: the former is from CE, the latter is cosine loss [1].

Center Loss. Although PCL can direct model for a better learning, it is easily overfitting with less data. Therefore, center loss (CL) [25] in Eq. 6 is used for more discriminative feature extraction. Let $x_i \in \mathbb{R}_d$ denote the ith deep feature belonging to the y_ith class. The y_ith class center of deep features $c_{y_i} \in \mathbb{R}_d$ is computed by averaging y_ith class features of the corresponding classes in each iteration.

$$L_{CL} = \frac{1}{2} \sum_i ||x_i - c_{y_i}||_2^2$$ (6)

Tree Supervision Loss. The semantic relations of classes in VIPriors can be induced as a hierarchical tree. Child nodes of the tree represent 1000 classes in the dataset and parent nodes represent superclasses such as animal, vehicle and etc. For every parent node, its child nodes often have some commonalities which is helpful for classification. Inspired by Neural-Backed Decision Trees (NBDT) [23], a hierarchical architecture is defined according to the semantic relationship based on 1000 classes. Tree supervision loss (TSL) is used for model training. Let $x \in \mathbb{R}_d$ denotes featurized sample, $w_{r \to i}$ denotes weights of the path from root nodes r to leaf node n_i. TSL can be represented as:

$$L_{TSL} = L_{CE}([\prod x * w_{r \to n_1}, \prod x * w_{r \to n_2}, ...], l)$$ (7)

4   Experiments

4.1   Implementation Details

Following data augmentation methods are used in our models: random resize and crop, random horizontal flip and CutMix (with a probability of 0.5). All models are trained with 16 GPUs and 64 samples per CPU. In the training stage, warm up with initial lr of 0.0001 in 5 epochs, cosine learning rate [10] with initial lr of 0.1, dropout with probability of 0.2, weight decay of 0.0001 and label smooth are used for learning. For coefficients in Eq. 6, α, γ and β are set to 1, 0.0005 and 1. In early time of the competition, we trained model on training set for methods attempt and verification. And in the final stage, we trained models on both training set and most of validation set. Only a little samples in validation set were reserved for validation. For final prediction, Test Time Augmentation (TTA) with 10-crop was used. Additionally, experimental results prove that increasing training epochs from 90 to 360 improve model accuracy by 5.3%.

4.2 Results

Table 1 shows the results for ResneXt, D-ResNeXt, SK-ResNeXt, DSK-ResNeXt, PSL and CL on validation set. Models are trained with 360 epochs.

Table 1. Performance of DSK-net, PSL and CL on validation set.

	top-1 acc. (%)
ResNeXt50_32x4d	52.01
D-ResNeXt50_32x4d	54.45
SK-ResNeXt50_32x4d without anti-aliasing	54.06
SK-ResNeXt50_32x4d	54.37
DSK-ResNeXt50_32x4d	55.97
DSK-ResNeXt50_32x4d+PSL	56.48
DSK-ResNeXt50_32x4d+PSL+CL	**57.51**

Table 2 shows results of TSL for EfficientNet and ResNeSt in the final stage. Models are trained with 720 epochs and tested on partial validation set.

Table 2. The experiment results of TSL.

	top-1 acc. (%)
EfficientNet-b3	62.42
EfficientNet-b3+TSL	63.15
EfficientNet-b5	65.43
EfficientNet-b5+TSL	65.85
EfficientNet-b6	65.67
EfficientNet-b6+TSL	66.26
ResNeSt-101(320x320)	65.96
ResNeSt-101(320x320)+TSL	67.15
ResNeSt-200(320x320)	67.40
ResNeSt-200(320x320)+TSL	**67.81**

Table 3 shows the results of DSK-net in the final stage. Models are trained with 540 epochs and tested on partial validation set. 69.59% is the best single model performance we achieved.

Table 3. The experiment results of DSK-net.

	top-1 acc. (%)
DSK-ResNeXt50_32x4d(224x224)	67.35
DSK-ResNeXt50_32x4d(320x320)	69.20
DSK-ResNeXt101_32x4d(224x224)	68.02
DSK-ResNeXt101_32x4d(320x320)	**69.59**

4.3 Other Tricks

Results for CutMix showed in Table 4 indicate that the global semantic information and local area feature are equally import.

Table 4. The experiment results on validation set for CutMix. Input size is 320×320, training epoch is 90.

	top-1 acc. (%)
ResNeXt50_32x4d	45.23
ResNeXt50_32x4d+CutMix with prob = 0.3	45.73
ResNeXt50_32x4d+CutMix with prob = 0.5	**46.25**
ResNeXt50_32x4d+CutMix with prob = 0.7	45.85
ResNeXt50_32x4d+CutMix with prob = 1.0	44.35

Results of label smooth, dropout and dual pool are showed in Table 5:

Table 5. The experiment results of label smooth, dropout and dual pool on validation set. Models are trained with 360 epochs.

	top-1 acc. (%)
ResNeXt50_32x4d	50.56
ResNeXt50_32x4d+dual pool	50.87
ResNeXt50_32x4d+label smooth	50.70
ResNeXt50_32x4d+dropout with prob=0.2	50.90
ResNeXt50_32x4d+dropout with prob=0.4	50.84
ResNeXt50_32x4d+dual pool+label smooth+dropout with prob=0.2	**51.82**

4.4 Ensembling

For a better performance, we ensembled predictions of above methods in total 16 models including EfficientNet-b5, EfficientNet-b6, ResNeSt-101, ResNest-200, DSK-ResNeXt50, DSK-ResNeXt101. Finally, a weighted score average method was used that the weight of higher performance models was 3, the rest was 1. Finally, we got the score of 73.08% on test set.

Figure 2 shows an overview of methods and appearances. No external image/video data or pre-trained models were used throughout the competition.

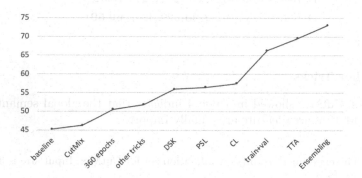

Fig. 2. Performance overview.

5 Conclusions

In this paper, we discuss and explore data-efficient learning, visual inductive priors and training from scratch. In VIPF, we propose a novel architecture called DSK-net, which is robust to translation. Sufficient experiment results fully proved that DSK-net learns efficiently from insufficient data and outperformed EfficientNet, ResNeSt on VIPriors classification dataset. Then a loss based on positive class is applied for model constraint. An induced hierarchy is used which can direct models to learn discriminatively and easily. Experimental results show that VIPF we proposed is effective. Finally we won the 1st place in VIPriors image classification competition.

References

1. Barz, B., Denzler, J.: Deep learning on small datasets without pre-training using cosine loss. In: The IEEE Winter Conference on Applications of Computer Vision, pp. 1371–1380 (2020)
2. Bruna, J., Mallat, S.: Invariant scattering convolution networks. IEEE Trans. Pattern Anal. Mach. Intell. **35**(8), 1872–1886 (2013)
3. Chen, P.: Gridmask data augmentation. arXiv preprint arXiv:2001.04086 (2020)

4. Cohen, T., Welling, M.: Group equivariant convolutional networks. In: International Conference on Machine Learning, pp. 2990–2999 (2016)
5. Cubuk, E.D., Zoph, B., Mane, D., Vasudevan, V., Le, Q.V.: AutoAugment: learning augmentation policies from data. arXiv preprint arXiv:1805.09501 (2018)
6. Cubuk, E.D., Zoph, B., Shlens, J., Le, Q.V.: RandAugment: practical automated data augmentation with a reduced search space. In: Proceedings of the IEEE/CVF Conference on Computer Vision and Pattern Recognition Workshops, pp. 702–703 (2020)
7. DeVries, T., Taylor, G.W.: Improved regularization of convolutional neural networks with cutout. arXiv preprint arXiv:1708.04552 (2017)
8. Esteves, C., Allen-Blanchette, C., Zhou, X., Daniilidis, K.: Polar transformer networks. arXiv preprint arXiv:1709.01889 (2017)
9. He, K., Zhang, X., Ren, S., Sun, J.: Deep residual learning for image recognition. In: Proceedings of the IEEE Conference on Computer Vision and Pattern Recognition, pp. 770–778 (2016)
10. He, T., Zhang, Z., Zhang, H., Zhang, Z., Xie, J., Li, M.: Bag of tricks for image classification with convolutional neural networks. In: Proceedings of the IEEE Conference on Computer Vision and Pattern Recognition, pp. 558–567 (2019)
11. Hu, J., Shen, L., Sun, G.: Squeeze-and-excitation networks. In: Proceedings of the IEEE Conference on Computer Vision and Pattern Recognition, pp. 7132–7141 (2018)
12. Ioffe, S., Szegedy, C.: Batch normalization: accelerating deep network training by reducing internal covariate shift. arXiv preprint arXiv:1502.03167 (2015)
13. Kayhan, O.S., Gemert, J.C.v.: On translation invariance in CNNs: convolutional layers can exploit absolute spatial location. In: Proceedings of the IEEE/CVF Conference on Computer Vision and Pattern Recognition, pp. 14274–14285 (2020)
14. Krizhevsky, A., Sutskever, I., Hinton, G.E.: ImageNet classification with deep convolutional neural networks. In: Advances in Neural Information Processing Systems, pp. 1097–1105 (2012)
15. Li, X., Wang, W., Hu, X., Yang, J.: Selective kernel networks. In: Proceedings of the IEEE Conference on Computer Vision and Pattern Recognition, pp. 510–519 (2019)
16. Northcutt, C.G., Jiang, L., Chuang, I.L.: Confident learning: estimating uncertainty in dataset labels. arXiv preprint arXiv:1911.00068 (2019)
17. Sifre, L., Mallat, S.: Rotation, scaling and deformation invariant scattering for texture discrimination. In: Proceedings of the IEEE Conference on Computer Vision and Pattern Recognition, pp. 1233–1240 (2013)
18. Simonyan, K., Zisserman, A.: Very deep convolutional networks for large-scale image recognition. arXiv preprint arXiv:1409.1556 (2014)
19. Szegedy, C., Ioffe, S., Vanhoucke, V., Alemi, A.A.: Inception-v4, inception-resnet and the impact of residual connections on learning. In: Thirty-First AAAI Conference on Artificial Intelligence (2017)
20. Szegedy, C., et al.: Going deeper with convolutions. In: Proceedings of the IEEE Conference on Computer Vision and Pattern Recognition, pp. 1–9 (2015)
21. Szegedy, C., Vanhoucke, V., Ioffe, S., Shlens, J., Wojna, Z.: Rethinking the inception architecture for computer vision. In: Proceedings of the IEEE Conference on Computer Vision and Pattern Recognition, pp. 2818–2826 (2016)
22. Tan, M., Le, Q.V.: EfficientNet: rethinking model scaling for convolutional neural networks. arXiv preprint arXiv:1905.11946 (2019)
23. Wan, A., et al.: NBDT: neural-backed decision trees. arXiv preprint arXiv:2004.00221 (2020)

24. Wang, Q., Wu, B., Zhu, P., Li, P., Zuo, W., Hu, Q.: ECA-Net: efficient channel attention for deep convolutional neural networks. In: Proceedings of the IEEE/CVF Conference on Computer Vision and Pattern Recognition, pp. 11534–11542 (2020)

25. Wen, Y., Zhang, K., Li, Z., Qiao, Yu.: A discriminative feature learning approach for deep face recognition. In: Leibe, B., Matas, J., Sebe, N., Welling, M. (eds.) ECCV 2016. LNCS, vol. 9911, pp. 499–515. Springer, Cham (2016). https://doi.org/10.1007/978-3-319-46478-7_31

26. Woo, S., Park, J., Lee, J.-Y., Kweon, I.S.: CBAM: convolutional block attention module. In: Ferrari, V., Hebert, M., Sminchisescu, C., Weiss, Y. (eds.) ECCV 2018. LNCS, vol. 11211, pp. 3–19. Springer, Cham (2018). https://doi.org/10.1007/978-3-030-01234-2_1

27. Worrall, D.E., Garbin, S.J., Turmukhambetov, D., Brostow, G.J.: Harmonic networks: deep translation and rotation equivariance. In: Proceedings of the IEEE Conference on Computer Vision and Pattern Recognition, pp. 5028–5037 (2017)

28. Yun, S., Han, D., Oh, S.J., Chun, S., Choe, J., Yoo, Y.: CutMix: regularization strategy to train strong classifiers with localizable features. In: Proceedings of the IEEE International Conference on Computer Vision, pp. 6023–6032 (2019)

29. Zhang, H., et al.: ResNeSt: split-attention networks. arXiv preprint arXiv:2004.08955 (2020)

30. Zhang, H., Cisse, M., Dauphin, Y.N., Lopez-Paz, D.: mixup: beyond empirical risk minimization. arXiv preprint arXiv:1710.09412 (2017)

31. Zhang, R.: Making convolutional networks shift-invariant again. arXiv preprint arXiv:1904.11486 (2019)

32. Zhong, Z., Zheng, L., Kang, G., Li, S., Yang, Y.: Random erasing data augmentation. In: AAAI, pp. 13001–13008 (2020)

W18 - 3D Poses In the Wild Challenge

W18 - 3D Poses In the Wild Challenge

The First 3D Poses in the Wild Challenge, held in conjunction with the European Conference on Computer Vision (ECCV 2020), brought together researchers and practitioners in the field of 3D Computer Vision. The workshop, held virtually on the first day of ECCV 2020, consisted of a series of excellent talks given by the invited speakers, challenge winners, and stimulating discussions throughout the virtual zoom session.

The primary motivation for organizing the challenge was to standardize protocols and metrics, so that researchers compare their methods in a consistent manner in future publications, ultimately to advance the state of the art in 3D human pose estimation in the wild. Most research papers on 3D pose estimation demonstrate performance qualitatively on "in the wild" images as all annotated datasets are limited to indoor environments such as H3.6M or Human-Eva, or to a restricted recording volume like MuPoTs-3D or MPI-INF-3DHP.

This changed with 3DPW, which constitutes the only dataset with accurate reference 3D poses in natural scenes (e.g., people shopping in the city). Up till now, different papers have used different protocols for evaluating their method on 3DPW. As part of our effort to standardize evaluation protocols, we started an evaluation server accessible to all researchers. We define two separate evaluation tracks: A "known association" track where the association between ground truth 3D and all 2D poses in the image is assumed and another "unknown association" track which involves simultaneous pose estimation and tracking. We received 15 submissions before the workshop and plan to keep the evaluation server open so that it serves as a benchmark for 3D pose estimation.

The virtual workshop started off with an exciting talk about the next generation of virtual humans from Tony Tung. Tony described the recent work done at the Facebook reality Labs on reconstructing virtual avatars from single and multi-view images. Next, Yu Sun presented the method that finished as the runner-up in the Challenge. Dushyant Mehta delivered a talk on the limitations of metrics used for evaluating 3D pose estimation algorithms and discussed the limits of monocular pose estimation. Georgios Pavalakos then talked about using weakly annotated data for 3D pose estimation and the inferring details more expressive than body pose from a single image. The workshop continued with a talk by Istavan Sarandi – the winner of the challenge. Next, Jitendra Malik highlighted the progress in motion prediction and scene aware pose estimation. The workshop concluded with a talk from Gul Varol on the use of 3D human body models for action recognition. The workshop was a great success, allowing researchers in the field to exchange ideas, to take a step back to evaluate progress made in recent years and to ascertain what problems remain unresolved.

August 2020

Gerard Pons-Moll
Angjoo Kanazwa
Michael Black
Aymen Mir

Predicting Camera Viewpoint Improves Cross-Dataset Generalization for 3D Human Pose Estimation

Zhe Wang$^{(\boxtimes)}$, Daeyun Shin, and Charless C. Fowlkes

University of California, Irvine, USA
{zwang15,daeyuns,fowlkes}@ics.uci.edu
http://wangzheallen.github.io/cross-dataset-generalization

Abstract. Monocular estimation of 3d human pose has attracted increased attention with the availability of large ground-truth motion capture datasets. However, the diversity of training data available is limited and it is not clear to what extent methods generalize outside the specific datasets they are trained on. In this work we carry out a systematic study of the diversity and biases present in specific datasets and its effect on cross-dataset generalization across a compendium of 5 pose datasets. We specifically focus on systematic differences in the distribution of camera viewpoints relative to a body-centered coordinate frame. Based on this observation, we propose an auxiliary task of predicting the camera viewpoint in addition to pose. We find that models trained to jointly predict viewpoint and pose systematically show significantly improved cross-dataset generalization.

Keywords: Monocular 3d human pose estimation · Cross dataset evaluation · Dataset bias

1 Introduction

A large swath of computer vision research increasingly operates in playing field which is swayed by the quantity and quality of annotated training data available for a particular task. How well do you know your data? Figure 1 presents a sampling images from 5 popular datasets used for training models for 3d human pose estimation (Human3.6M [9], GPA [46], SURREAL [43], 3DPW [18] , 3DHP [22]). We ask the reader to consider the game of "Name That Dataset" in homage to Torralba et al. [36]. Can you guess which dataset each image belongs to? More importantly, if we train a model on the Human3.6M dataset (at Fig. 1 left) how well would you expect it to perform on each of the images depicted?

Each of these datasets were collected using different mocap systems (VICON, The Capture, IMU), different cameras (Kinect, commercial synchronized cameras, phone), and collected in different environments (controlled lab environment, marker-less in the wild environment, or synthetic images) with varying camera viewpoint and pose distributions (see Fig. 3). These datasets contain further

© Springer Nature Switzerland AG 2020
A. Bartoli and A. Fusiello (Eds.): ECCV 2020 Workshops, LNCS 12536, pp. 523–540, 2020.
https://doi.org/10.1007/978-3-030-66096-3_36

variations in body sizes, camera intrinsic and extrinsic parameters, body and background appearance. Despite the obvious presence of such systematic differences, these variables and their subsequent effect on performance have yet to be carefully analyzed.

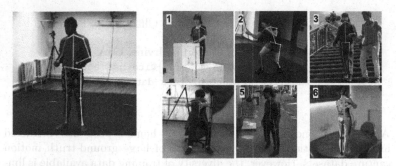

| Training on H36M | Goal: Generalization to Diverse Poses and Scenes |

Fig. 1. In this paper we consider the problem of dataset bias and cross-dataset generalization. Can you guess which human pose dataset each image on the right comes from? If we train a model on H36M data (left) can you predict which image has the lowest/highest 3D pose prediction error? (answer key below)(Answer key: Metric: MPJPE, the lower the better. 1) GPA: 69.7 mm 2) H36M: 29.2 mm, 3) 3DPW, 71.2 mm, 4) 3DHP 107.7 mm, 5) 3DPW 66.2 mm, 6) SURREAL 83.4 mm, H36M image performs best while 3DHP image performs worst.)

In this paper, we study the generalization of 3d pose models across multiple datasets and propose an auxiliary prediction task: estimating the relative rotation between camera viewing direction and a body-centered coordinate system defined by the orientation of the torso. This task serves to significantly improve cross-dataset generalization. Ground-truth for our proposed camera viewpoint task can be derived for existing 3D pose datasets without requiring additional labels. We train off-the shelf models [24,55] which estimate the camera-relative 3d pose, augmented with a viewpoint prediction branch. In our experiments, we show our approach outperforms the state-of-the-art PoseNet [24] and [55] baseline by a large margin across 5 different 3d pose datasets. Perhaps even more startling is that the addition of this auxiliary task results in significant improvement in cross-dataset test performance. This simple approach increases robustness of the model and, to our knowledge, is the first work that systematically confronts the problem of dataset bias in 3d human pose estimation.

To summarize, our main contributions are:

- We analyze the differences among contemporary 3d human pose estimation datasets and characterize the distribution and diversity of viewpoint and body-centered pose.

- We propose the novel use of camera viewpoint prediction as an auxiliary task that systematically improves model generalization by limiting overfitting to common viewpoints and can be directly calculated from commonly available joint coordinate ground-truth.
- We experimentally demonstrate the effectiveness of the viewpoint prediction branch in improving cross-dataset 3d human pose estimation over two popular baseline and achieve state-of-the-art performance on five datasets.

2   Related Work

Cross-Dataset Generalization and Evaluation. 3d human pose estimation from monocular imagery has attracted significant attention due to its potential utility in applications such as motion retargeting [44], gaming, sports analysis, and health care [19]. Recent methods are typically based on deep neural network architectures [3,14,15,20,24,26,27,33,47,48,55] trained on one of a few large scale, publicly available datasets. Among these are [20,26,33] evaluated on H36M, [22,55] work on both H36M [9] and 3DHP [18,22,37] work on TOTAL-CAPTURE [37] and 3DPW[18,46] work on the GPA dataset [46]. [43] works on both SURREAL [43] and H36M [9] dataset.

Given the powerful capabilities of CNNs to overfit to specific data, we are inspired to revisit the work of [36], which presented a comparative study of popular object recognition datasets with the goals of improving dataset collection and evaluation protocols. Recently, [16] observed characteristic biases present in commonly used depth estimation datasets and proposed scale invariant training objectives to enable mixing multiple, otherwise incompatible datasets. [57] introduced the first large-scale, multi-view unbiased hand pose dataset as training set to improve performance when testing on other dataset. Instead of proposing yet another dataset or resorting to domain adaptation approaches (see e.g., [45]), we focus on identifying systematic biases in existing data and identifying generic methods to prevent overfitting in 3d pose estimation.

Coordinate Frames for 3D Human Pose. In typical datasets, gold-standard 3d pose is collected with motion capture systems [9,32,37,46] and used to define ground-truth 3D pose relative one or more calibrated RGB camera coordinate systems [9,18,22,43,46]. To generate regression targets for use in training and evaluation, it is typical to predict the *relative* 3d pose and express the joint positions relative to a specified root joint such as the pelvis (see e.g., [24,33]). We argue that camera viewpoint is an important component of the experimental design which is often overlooked and explore using a body-centered coordinate system which is rotated relative to the camera frame.

This notion of view-point invariant prediction has been explored in the context of 3D object shape estimation [4,5,23,29,31,34,39,51] where many works have predicted shape in either an object-centered or camera-centered coordinate frame [31,35,54]. Closer to our task is the 3d hand pose estimator of [56] which separately estimated the viewpoint and pose (in canonical hand-centered coordinates similar to ours) and then combine the two to yield the final pose in the camera coordinate frame. However, we note that predicting canonical pose directly from image features is difficult for highly articulated objects (indeed subsequent work on hand pose, e.g. [41], abandoned the canonical frame approach). Our use of body-centered coordinate frames differs in that we only use them as a auxiliary training task that improves prediction of camera-centered pose.

3D Human Pose Estimation. With the recent development of deep neural networks (CNNs), there are significant improvements on 3D human pose estimation [6,20,26,49]. Many of them try to tackle in-the-wild images. [55] proposes to add bone length constraint to generalize their methods to in the wild image. [30] seeks to pose anchors as classification template and refine the prediction with further regression loss. [6] propose a new disentangled hidden space encoding of explicit 2D and 3D features for monocular 3D human pose estimation that shows high accuracy and generalizes well to in-the-wild scenes, however, they do not evaluate its capacity on indoor cross-dataset generalization. To the best of our knowledge, our work is the first to exploit cross-dataset task not only towards in-the-wild generalization but also across different indoor datasets.

Multi-task Training. There have has been a wide variety of work in training deep CNNs to perform multiple tasks, for example: joint detection, classification, and segmentation [7], joint surface normal, depth, and semantic segmentation [13], joint face detection, keypoint, head orientation and attributes [28]. Such work typically focuses on the benefits (accuracy and computation) of jointly training a single model for two or more related tasks. For example, predicting face viewpoint has been shown to improve face recognition [52]. Our approach to improving generalization differs in that we train models to perform two tasks (viewpoint and body pose) but discard viewpoint predictions at test time and only utilize pose. In this sense our model is more closely related to work on "deeply-supervised" nets [17,50] which trains using losses associated with auxiliary branches that are not used at test time.

3   Variation in 3D Human Pose Datasets

We begin with a systematic study of the differences and biases across 3d pose datasets. We selected three well established datasets Human3.6m (H36M), MPI-inf-3dhp (3DHP), SURREAL, as well as two more recent datasets 3DPW and GPA for analysis. These are large-scale datasets with a wide variety of characteristics in terms of capture technology, appearance (in-the-wild,in-the-lab,synthetic) and content (range of body sizes, poses, viewpoints, clothing, occlusion and human-scene interaction). In this paper, we focus on characterizing variation in geometric quantities (pose and viewpoint) which can be readily quantified (compared to, e.g., lighting and clothing).

We list some essential statistics from 5 datasets in Table 1. For these datasets, gold-standard 3d pose is collected with motion capture systems [9,32,37,46] and

Table 1. Comparison of existing datasets commonly used for training and evaluating 3D human pose estimation methods. We calculate the mean and std of camera distance, camera height, focal length, bone length from training set. Focal length is in mm while the others are in unit meters. 3DHP has two kinds of cameras and the training set provide 28 joints annotation while test set provide 17 joints annotation.

Dataset	H36M	GPA	SURREAL	3DPW	3DHP
Year	2014	2019	2017	2018	2017
Imaging Space	1000 × 1002	1920 × 1080	320 × 240	1920 × 1080	2048 × 2048 or 1920 × 1080
Camera Distance	5.2 ± 0.8	5.1 ± 1.2	8.0 ± 1.0	3.5 ± 0.7	3.8 ± 0.8
Camera Height	1.6 ± 0.05	1.0 ± 0.3	0.9 ± 0.1	0.6 ± 0.8	0.8 ± 0.4
Focal Length	1146.8 ± 2.0	1172.4 ± 121.3	600 ± 0	1962.2 ± 1.5	1497.88 ± 2.8
No. of Joints	38	34	24	24	28 or 17
No. of Cameras	4	5	1	1	14
No. of Subjects	11	13	145	18	8
Bone Length	3.9 ± 0.1	3.7 ± 0.2	3.7 ± 0.2	3.7 ± 0.1	3.7 ± 0.1
GT source	VICON	VICON	Rendering	SMPL	The Captury
No. Train Images	311,951	222,514	867,140	22,375	366,997
No. Test Images	109,764	82,378	507	35,515	2,875

used to define ground-truth 3D pose relative one or more calibrated RGB camera coordinate systems [9,18,22,43,46]. To generate regression targets for use in training and evaluation, it is typical to predict the *relative* 3d pose (see e.g., [24, 33]) and express the joint positions relative to a specified root joint (typically the pelvis) and crop/scale the input image accordingly. This pre-processing serves to largely "normalize away" dataset differences in camera intrinsic parameters and camera distance shown in Table 1. However, it does not address camera orientation.

To characterize the remaining variability, we factor the camera-relative pose into camera viewpoint (the position of the camera relative to a canonical body-centered coordinate frame defined by the orientation of the person's torso) and the pose relative to this body-centered coordinate frame.

Computing Body-Centered Coordinate Frames. To define a viewpoint-independent pose, we need to specify a canonical body-centered coordinate frame. As shown in Fig. 5a, we take the origin to be the camera-centered coordinates of root joint (pelvis) $p_p = (x_p, y_p, z_p)$ and the orientation is defined

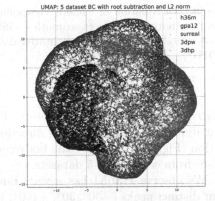

Fig. 2. Distribution of view-independent body-centered pose, visualized as a 2D embedding produced with UMAP [21]

by the plane spanned by p_p, the left shoulder p_l and the right shoulder p_r. Given these joint positions, we can compute an orthogonal frame consisting of the front direction f, up direction u and right direction r are defined as:

$$u = (p_l + p_r)/2 - p_p$$
$$f = (p_l - p_p) \times (p_r - p_p)$$
$$r = f \times u$$

The rotation between the body-centered frame and the camera frame is then given by the matrix $R = -[r, u, f]$. We find it useful to represent rotations using unit quaternions (as have others, e.g. [38,44]). The corresponding unit quaternion representing R has components:

$$q = \frac{1}{4q_0}[4q_0^2, u_2 - f_1, f_0 - r_2, r_1 - u_0], \qquad q_0 = \sqrt{(1 - r_0 - u_1 - f_2)} \qquad (1)$$

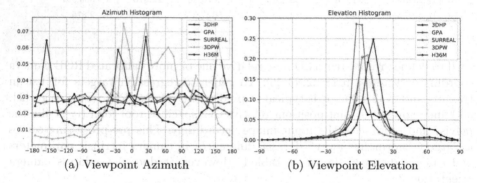

(a) Viewpoint Azimuth   (b) Viewpoint Elevation

Fig. 3. Distribution of camera viewpoints relative to the human subject. We show the distribution of camera azimuth $(-180°, 180°)$ and elevation $(-90°, 90°)$ for 50k poses sampled from each representative dataset (**H36M**, **GPA**, **SURREAL**, 3DPW, **3DHP**).

Distribution of Camera Viewpoints. Figure 3 shows histograms capturing the distribution of camera viewing direction in terms of azimuth (Fig. 3a) and elevation (Fig. 3b) relative to the body-centered coordinate system for 50k sample poses from each of the 5 datasets.

We observe **H36M** has a wide range of view direction over azimuth with four distinct peaks $(-30°, 30°, -160°, 160°)$, it shows during the capture session subjects are always facing towards or facing away the control center while the four RGB cameras captured from four corners. H36M has a clear bias towards elevation above 0; **GPA** is more spread over azimuth compared with H36M, most of the views range from −60° to 90°; **SURREAL** synthetically sampled camera positions with a uniform distribution over azimuth, and also have a uniform distribution over elevation. The viewpoint bias for **3DPW** arises naturally from filming people in-the-wild from a handheld or tripod mounted camera roughly the same height as the subject. Of the non-synthetic datasets, **3DHP** is the most uniform spread over azimuth and includes a wider range of positive elevations, a result of utilizing cameras mounted at multiple heights including the ceiling.

These differences are further highlighted in Fig. 5 which shows the joint distribution of camera views and reveals the source of non-uniformity of the azmuthal distribution for 3DHP and H36M due to subjects tending to face a canonical direction while performing some actions. For example, in H36M in Fig. 5b, actions in which the subject lean over or lie down (extreme elevations) only happen at particular azimuths. Similarly, in 3DHP (Fig. 5f), the 14 camera locations are visible as dense clusters at specific azimuths indicating a significant subset of the data in which the subject was facing in a canonical direction relative to the camera constellation.

Distribution of Pose. To characterize the remaining variability in pose after the viewpoint is factored out, we used the coordinates of 14 joints common to all datasets expressed in the body-centered coordinate frame. We also scaled the body-centered joint locations to a common skeleton size (removing variation in bone length shown in Table 1). To visualize the resulting high-dimensional data distribution, we utilized UMAP [21] to perform a non-linear embedding into 2D. Figure 2 shows the resulting distributions which show a substantial degree of overlap. For comparison, please see the Appendix which show embeddings of the same data when bone length and/or viewpoint are not factored out.

We also trained a multi-layer perceptron to predict which dataset a given body-relative pose came from. It had an average test accuracy of 20% providing further evidence of relatively little bias in the distribution of poses across datasets once viewpoint and body size are factored out.

4   Learning Pose and Viewpoint Prediction

To overcome biases in viewpoint across datasets, we propose to use viewpoint prediction as an auxiliary task to regularize the training of standard camera-centered pose estimation models.

4.1   Baseline Architecture

Our baseline model [24,55] consists of two parts: the first ResNet [8] backbone which takes in images patches cropped around the human; followed by the second part which takes the resulting feature map and upsamples it using three consecutive deconvolutional layers with batch normalization and ReLU. A 1-by-1 convolution is applied to the upsampled feature map to produce the 3D heatmaps for each joint location. The soft-argmax [33] operation is used to extract the 2D image coordinates $(\hat{x}_j, \hat{y}_j)$ of each joint j within the crop, and the root-relative depth $\hat{y}_j$. At test time, we can convert this prediction into into a 3d metric joint location $p_j = (x_j, y_j, z_j)$ using the crop bounding box, an estimate of the root joint depth or skeleton size, and the camera intrinsic parameters (Fig. 4).

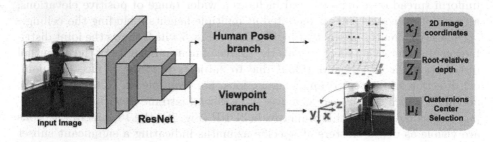

Fig. 4. Flowchart of our model. We augment a model which predicts camera-centered 3d pose using the **human pose branch** with an additional **viewpoint branch** that selections among a set of quantized camera view directions.

The loss function of the coordinate branch is the $L1$ distance between the estimated and groud-truth coordinates.

$$\mathcal{L}_{pose} = \frac{1}{J} \sum_{j=1}^{J} ||p_j - p_j^*||_1$$

4.2 Predicting the Camera Viewpoint

To predict the camera viewpoint relative to the body-centered coordinate frame we considered three approaches: (i) direct regression of q, (ii) quantizing the space or rotations and performing k-way classification, and (iii) a combined approach of first predicting a quantized rotation followed by regressing the residual from the cluster center. In our experiments, we found that the classification-based loss yields less accurate coordinate frame predictions but yielded the largest improvements in the pose prediction branch (see Table 4).

To quantize the space of rotations, we use k-means to cluster the quaternions into $k = 100$ clusters. The clusters are computed from training data of a single dataset (local clusters) or from all five datasets (global clusters). We visualize the global cluster centers in azimuth and elevation space in Fig. 5 b-f, as well as randomly sampled quaternions from H36M, GPA, SURREAL, 3DPW and 3DHP datasets.

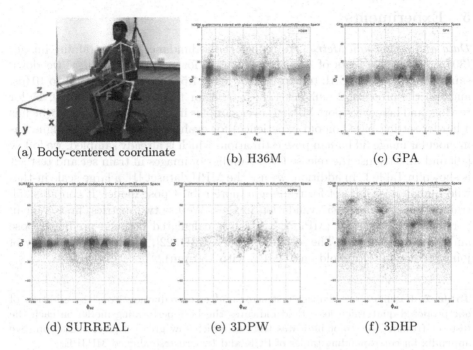

(a) Body-centered coordinate   (b) H36M   (c) GPA

(d) SURREAL   (e) 3DPW   (f) 3DHP

Fig. 5. a: Illustration of our body-centered coordinate frame (up vector, right vector and front vector) relative to a camera-centered coordinate frame. **b-f:** Camera viewpoint distribution of the 5 datasets color by quaternion cluster index. Quaternions (rotation between body-centered and camera frame) are sampled from training sets and clustered using k-means. They are also visualized in azimuth/elevation space following Fig. 3. (Color figure online)

To regress the quaternion q we simply add a branch to our base pose prediction model consisting of a 1×1 convolutional layer to reduce the feature dimension to 4 followed by global average pooling and normalization to yield a unit 4-vector. We train this variant using a standard squared-Euclidan loss on target q^*. For classification, we use the same prediction q but compute the probability it belongs to the correct cluster using a softmax to get a distribution over cluster assignments:

$$p(c|q) = \frac{\exp(-\mu_c^T q)}{\sum_{i=1}^{k} \exp(-\mu_i^T q)}$$

where $\{\mu_1, \mu_2, \ldots, \mu_k\}$ are the quaternions corresponding to cluster centers computed by k-means. We use the negative log-likelihood as the training loss,

$$\mathcal{L}_q = -log(p(c^*|q))$$

where c^* is the viewpoint bin that the training example was assigned during clustering. Our final loss consists of both quaternion and pose terms: $\mathcal{L} = \lambda \mathcal{L}_q + \mathcal{L}_{pose}$.

5   Experiments

Data and Evaluation Metric. To reduce the redundancy of the training images (30 fps video gives lots of duplicated images for network training), we down sample 3DHP, SURREAL to 5 fps. Following [24,55], we sample H36M to 10 fps, and use the protocol 2 (subject 1, 3, 5, 7, 8 for training and subject 9, 11 for testing, and here we report MPJPE over samples instead of over classes, which is a harder setting based on our experience) for evaluation. As GPA is designed as monocular image 3d human pose estimation, which is already sampled, we follow [46] and directly use the released set. Number of images in train set and test set is shown in Table 1. In addition, we use the MPII dataset [1], a large scale in-the-wild human pose dataset for training a more robust pose model. It contains 25k training images and 2,957 validation images. We use two metrics, first is mean per joint position error (MPJPE), which is calculated between predicted pose and ground truth pose. The second one is PCK3D [22], which is the accuracy of joint prediction (threshold on MPJPE with 150 mm).

Table 2. Baseline cross-dataset test error and error reduction from the addition of our proposed quaternion loss. Bold indicates the best performing model on each the test set (rows). Blue color indicates test set which saw greatest error reduction. See appendix for corresponding tables of PCK and Procrustese aligned MPJPE.

		MPJPE (in mm, lower is better)				
	Testing \ Training	H36M	GPA	SURREAL	3DPW	3DHP
Baseline	H36M	**53.2**	110.5	107.1	125.1	108.4
	GPA	105.2	**53.9**	86.8	111.7	90.5
	SURREAL	118.6	103.2	**37.2**	120.8	108.2
	3DPW	108.7	116.4	114.2	**100.6**	113.3
	3DHP	111.8	123.9	120.3	139.7	**91.9**
Our Method	H36M	**52.0**	102.5	103.3	124.2	95.6
	GPA	98.3	**53.3**	85.6	110.2	91.3
	SURREAL	114.0	101.2	**37.1**	113.8	107.2
	3DPW	109.5	112.0	112.2	**89.7**	105.9
	3DHP	111.9	119.7	118.2	136.0	**90.3**
Same-Dataset Error Reduction ↓		1.2	0.6	0.1	10.9	1.5
Cross-Dataset Error Reduction ↓		10.6	18.6	9.1	13.1	20.4

Implementation Details. As different datasets have diverse joint configuration, we select a subset of 14 joints that all datasets share to eliminate the bias introduced by different number of joints during training. We normalize the z value from $(-z_{max}, +z_{max})$ to $(0, 63)$ for integral regression. z_{max} is 2400 mm based all 5 set. We use PyTorch to implement our network. The ResNet-50 [8] backbone is initialized using the pre-trained weights on the ImageNet dataset. We use the Adam [12] optimizer with a mini-batch size of 128. The initial learning rate is set to 1×10^{-3} and reduced by a factor of 10 at the 17th epoch, we train 25 epochs for each of the dataset. We use 256×256 as the size of the input image of our network. We perform data augmentation including rotation, horizontal flip, color jittering and synthetic occlusion following [24]. We set λ to 0.5 for the quaternion loss which is validated on 3DPW validation set.

5.1   Cross-Dataset Evaluation

We list the cross-dataset baseline and our improved results in Table 2. The bold numbers indicate the best performing model on the test set. As expected, the best performance occurs when the model is trained and evaluated on the same set. The numbers marked with blue color indicate the test set where the error reduction is most significant, using our proposed quaternion loss.

Training on H36M. Adding the quaternion loss reduces total cross-dataset error by 10.6 mm (MPJPE), while the same-dataset error reduction is 1.2 mm (MPJPE). This may be explained by the error on H36M already being low. The largest error reduction is on GPA (6.9 mm) which we attribute to de-biasing the azimuth distribution difference as shown in Fig. 3a.

Training on GPA. The total cross-dataset error reduction is 18.6 mm (MPJPE), and the same data error reduction is 0.6 mm (MPJPE). We attribute this to the bias during capture [46]: the coverage of camera viewing directions is centered in the range of −60 to 90° azimuth (as in Fig. 3a). The largest cross-data set error reduction occurs for H36M, with 8.0 mm. This further demonstrates that the view direction distribution is largely different from H36M.

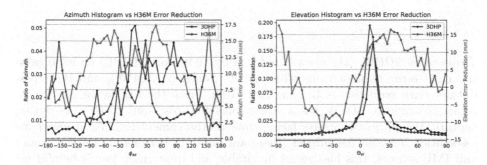

Fig. 6. We visualize viewpoint distributions for train (3DHP) and test (H36M) overlayed with the reduction in pose prediction error relative to baseline

Training on SURREAL. Adding the quaternion loss reduces the cross-dataset error by 9.1 mm (MPJPE), while the same-dataset error reduction is 0.1 mm (MPJPE). We attribute this to the fact that viewpoint distribution on SURREAL itself is already uniform as in Fig. 3a. We can see distribution over azimuths is quite uniform. Thus adding more supervision in the form of quaternion loss helps little. The most error reduction (2.0 mm) is observed on 3DPW. We attribute this to the fact that 3DPW is strongly biased dataset in terms of view direction, and the quaternion loss helps reduce the view difference between SURREAL and 3DPW.

Table 3. Retraining the model of Zhou *et al.* [55] using our viewpoint prediction loss yields also shows significant decrease in prediction error, demonstrating the generality of our finding. See appendix for full table of numerical results.

Metric \ Training Set	MPJPE (in mm, lower is better)				
	H36M	GPA	SURREAL	3DPW	3DHP
Same-Dataset Error Reduction ↓	0.6	4.2	0.2	7.6	1.2
Cross-Dataset Error Reduction ↓	2.4	12.3	1.9	10.1	9.3

Table 4. Ablation analysis: we compare the performance of our proposed camera viewpoint loss using classification (C), regression (R), using both (C+R); using per-dataset clusterings (local) rather than the global clustering; and adding a third branch which also predicts pose in canonical body-centered coordinates.

Datasets	Baseline	C	R	C+R	C+local cluster	C+cannonical pose
3DPW (MPJPE (mm))	100.6	89.7	94.0	93.2	93.1	100.3

Training on 3DPW. The error is reduced by 10.9 mm (MPJPE) on itself (also the most error reduction one with model trained on 3DPW), and the cross-dataset error reduction is 13.1 mm (MPJPE). From the Fig. 3a we can see, in terms of azimuth, 3DPW has a strong bias towards $-30°$ to $60°$. As during capture, the subject is always facing towards the camera to make it easier for association between the subject (there are multiply persons in crowded scene) and IMU sensors, this bias seems inevitable and quaternion loss is helpful for this kind of in the wild dataset to reduce view direction bias. It is also verified in 3DHP, where half of the test set is in the wild, and have view direction bias.

Training on 3DHP. Adding the quaternion loss reduces the total cross-dataset error by 20.4 mm, while the same-dataset error reduction is 1.5 mm (MPJPE). During the capture, 3DHP capture images from a wide range of viewpoints.

We can see from the Fig. 3 that the azimuth of 3DHP is the most uniformly distributed of the real datasets. Thus treating it as training set will enable the network to be robust to view direction. We also calculate error reduction conditioned on azimuth and elevation on the H36M test set (Fig. 6). The blue/black line is azimuth and elevation histogram distribution for H36M/3DHP training sets while the red line shows relative error reduction for H36M. We can see the error is reduced more where H36M has fewer views relative to 3DHP.

5.2 Effect of Model Architecture and Loss Functions

To demonstrate the generalization of our approach to other models, we also added a viewpoint prediction branch to the model of [55] which utilizes a different model architecture. We observe similar results in terms of improved generalization (see Table 3 and appendix). We note that while our primary baseline model [24] uses camera intrinsic parameters to back-project, [55] utilizes an average bone-length estimate from the training set which results in higher prediction errors across datasets.

Table 5. Comparison to state-of-the-art performance. There are many missing entries, indicating how infrequent it is to perform multi-dataset evaluation. Our model provides a new state-of-the art baseline across all 5 datasets and can serve as a reference for future work. * denotes training using extra data or annotations (e.g. segmentation). Underline denotes the second best results.

	MPJPE↓: lower is better					PCK3D↑: higher is better				
	H36M	GPA	SURREAL	3DPW	3DHP	H36M	GPA	SURREAL	3DPW	3DHP
Mehta [22]	72.9	–	–	–	–	–	–	–	–	64.7
Zhou [55]	64.9	96.5	–	–	–	–	82.9	–	–	72.5
Arnab[2]	77.8	–	–	–	–	–	–	–	–	–
Kanazawa [10]	88.0	–	–	–	124.2	–	–	–	–	72.9
Kanazawa [11]	–	–	–	127.1	–	–	–	–	86.4*	–
Moon [24]	54.3	–	–	–	–	–	–	–	–	–
Kolotouros [25]	78.0	–	–	–	–	–	–	–	–	–
Tung[40]	98.4	-	64.4*	–	–	–	–	–	–	–
Varol[42]	51.6*	–	49.1	–	–	–	–	–	–	–
Habibie [6]	65.7	–	–	–	91.0	–	–	–	–	82.0
Yu [53]	59.1	–	–	–	–	–	–	–	–	–
Ours	52.0	53.3	37.1	89.7	90.3	96.0	96.8	97.3	84.6	84.3

Ablation Study. To explore whether our methods are robust to different k-means initialization, we repeat k-means 4 times and report performance on 3DPW. We find the range of the MPJPE is within 90 ± 0.4 ([89.9, 89.6, 90.2, 89.7]) mm. We also vary the number of clusters to select the best $k \in \{10, 24, 50, 100, 200, 500\}$, with corresponding errors [93.0, 95.2, 92.3, 89.7, 93.0, 93.2]. We find k = 100 is the best number with at most 6 mm reduction compared to k = 24. In Table 4, the error of global clusters is 3.4 mm error less than local, per-dataset clusters,

Fig. 7. Predictiosn on 5 datasets from model trained on Human3.6M. The 2d joints are overlaid with the original image, while the 3d prediction (red) is overlaid with 3d ground truth (blue). 3D prediction is **visualized in body-centered coordinate** rotated by the relative rotation between ground truth camera-centered coordinate and body-centered coordinate. From top to bottom are H36M, GPA, SURREAL, 3DPW and 3DHP datasets. We rank the images from left to right in order of increasing MPJPE. (Color figure online)

demonstrating training on global clusters is better than local clusters which are biased towards the training set view distribution. In terms of choice for quaternion regression, k-way classification reduced error by 4.3 mm compared to regression. While utilizing both classification and regression losses gives error than regression only.

Finally, we also consider adding a third branch and loss function to the model which also predicts the 3D pose in the body-centered coordinate system. This is related to the hand pose model of [56], although we don't use this prediction of canonical pose at test time. This variant performs global pooling on the ResNet feature map after upsampling followed by a two layer MLP that predicts the viewpoint q and canonical pose. When training with this additional branch we find the camera-centered pose predictions show no improvement over baseline (Table 4). We also observe that the canonical pose predictions have higher error than the camera-centered predictions which is natural since the the model can't directly exploit the direct correspondence between the 2D keypoint locations and the 3D joint locations.

5.3 Comparison with State-of-the-Art Performance

Table 5 compares the proposed approach with the state-of-the-art performance on all 5 datasets. Note that our method is the first to evaluate 3d human pose estimation on the five representative datasets reporting both MPJPE and PCK3D, which fills in some blanks and serves as a useful baseline for future work. As can be seen, our method achieves state-of-the-art performance on H36M/GPA/SURREAL/3DPW/3DHP datasets in terms of MPJPE. While [11] uses additional data (both H36M and 3DHP, and LSP together with MPII) to train, they have slightly better performance on 3DHP in terms of PCK3D.

Qualitative Results: We visualize the prediction on the 5 datasets with model trained on H36M using our proposed method in Fig 7. The 2d joint prediction is overlaid with cropped images while the 3d joint prediction is visualized in our proposed body-centered coordinates. From top to bottom are H36M, GPA, SURREAL, 3DPW and 3DHP datasets. We display the images from left to right in ascending order by MPJPE.

6   Conclusions

In this paper, we observe strong dataset-specific biases present in the distribution of cameras relative to the human body and propose the use of body-centered coordinate frames. Utilizing the relative rotation between body-centered coordinates and camera-centered coordinates as an additional supervisory signal, we significantly reduce the 3d joint prediction error and improve generalization in cross-dataset 3d human pose evaluation.

References

1. Andriluka, M., Pishchulin, L., Gehler, P., Schiele, B.: 2D human pose estimation: new benchmark and state of the art analysis. In: CVPR (2014)
2. Arnab, A., Doersch, C., Zisserman, A.: Exploiting temporal context for 3D human pose estimation in the wild. In: CVPR (2019)
3. Chen, Y., et al.: Nonparametric structure regularization machine for 2D hand pose estimation. In: WACV (2020)
4. Choy, C.B., Xu, D., Gwak, J.Y., Chen, K., Savarese, S.: 3D-R2N2: a unified approach for single and multi-view 3D object reconstruction. In: Leibe, B., Matas, J., Sebe, N., Welling, M. (eds.) ECCV 2016. LNCS, vol. 9912, pp. 628–644. Springer, Cham (2016). https://doi.org/10.1007/978-3-319-46484-8_38
5. Groueix, T., Fisher, M., Kim, V.G., Russell, B., Aubry, M.: AtlasNet: a Papier-Mâché approach to learning 3D surface generation. In: Proceedings IEEE Conference on Computer Vision and Pattern Recognition (CVPR) (2018)
6. Habibie, K., Xu, W., Mehta, D., Pons-Moll, G., Theobalt, C.: In the wild human pose estimation using explicit 2D features and intermediate 3D representations. In: CVPR (2019)
7. He, K., Gkioxari, G., Dollár, P., Girshick, R.: Mask R-CNN. In: CVPR (2017)

8. He, K., Zhang, X., Ren, S., Sun, J.: Deep residual learning for image recognition. In: CVPR (2016)
9. Ionescu, C., Papava, D., Olaru, V., Sminchisescu, C.: Human3.6m: large scale datasets and predictive methods for 3D human sensing in natural environments. In: PAMI (2014)
10. Kanazawa, A., Black, M.J., Jacobs, D.W., Malik, J.: End-to-end recovery of human shape and pose. In: CVPR (2018)
11. Kanazawa, A., Zhang, J.Y., Felsen, P., Malik, J.: Learning 3D human dynamics from video. In: CVPR (2019)
12. Kingma, D.P., Ba, J.: Adam: a method for stochastic optimization. In: ICLR (2015)
13. Kokkinos, I.: Ubernet: training a 'universal' convolutional neural network for low-, mid-, and high-level vision using diverse datasets and limited memory. Arxiv (2016)
14. Kong, D., Chen, Y., Ma, H., Yan, X., Xie, X.: Adaptive graphical model network for 2D handpose estimation. In: BMVC (2019)
15. Kong, D., Ma, H., Chen, Y., Xie, X.: Rotation-invariant mixed graphical model network for 2d hand pose estimation. In: WACV (2020)
16. Lasinger, K., Ranftl, R., Schindler, K., Koltun, V.: Towards robust monocular depth estimation: Mixing datasets for zero-shot cross-dataset transfer. Arxiv (2019)
17. Lee, C.Y., Xie, S., Gallagher, P., Zhang, Z., Tu, Z.: Deeply-supervised nets. In: AISTATS (2015)
18. von Marcard, T., Henschel, R., Black, M.J., Rosenhahn, B., Pons-Moll, G.: Recovering accurate 3D human pose in the wild using IMUs and a moving camera. In: Ferrari, V., Hebert, M., Sminchisescu, C., Weiss, Y. (eds.) ECCV 2018. LNCS, vol. 11214, pp. 614–631. Springer, Cham (2018). https://doi.org/10.1007/978-3-030-01249-6_37
19. Marinoiu, E., Zanfir, M., Olaru, V., Sminchisescu, C.: 3D human sensing, action and emotion recognition in robot assisted therapy of children with autism. In: CVPR (2018)
20. Martinez, J., Hossain, R., Romero, J., Little, J.J.: A simple yet effective baseline for 3D human pose estimation. In: ICCV (2017)
21. McInnes, L., Healy, J., Saul, N., Grossberger, L.: UMAP: uniform manifold approximation and projection. J. Open Sour. Software **3**(29), 861 (2018)
22. Mehta, D., Rhodin, H., Casas, D., Fua, P., Sotnychenko, O., Xu, W., Theobalt, C.: Monocular 3d human pose estimation in the wild using improved CNN supervision. In: 3DV (2017)
23. Mescheder, L., Oechsle, M., Niemeyer, M., Nowozin, S., Geiger, A.: Occupancy networks: Learning 3D reconstruction in function space. In: Proceedings of the IEEE Conference on Computer Vision and Pattern Recognition, pp. 4460–4470 (2019)
24. Moon, G., Chang, J., Lee, K.M.: Camera distance-aware top-down approach for 3D multi-person pose estimation from a single RGB image. In: ICCV (2019)
25. Nikos Kolotouros, Georgios Pavlakos, K.D.: Convolutional mesh regression for single-image human shape reconstruction. In: CVPR (2019)
26. Pavlakos, G., Zhou, X., Derpanis, K.G., Daniilidis, K.: Coarse-to-fine volumetric prediction for single-image 3D human pose. In: CVPR (2017)
27. Pavllo, D., Grangier, D., Auli, M.: Quaternet: a quaternion-based recurrent model for human motion. In: BMVC (2018)
28. Ranjan, R., Patel, V.M., Chellappa, R.: Hyperface: a deep multi-task learning framework for face detection, landmark localization, pose estimation, and gender recognition. In: TPAMI (2016)

29. Richter, S.R., Roth, S.: Matryoshka networks: predicting 3D geometry via nested shape layers. In: Proceedings of the IEEE Conference on Computer Vision and Pattern Recognition, pp. 1936–1944 (2018)

30. Rogez, G., Weinzaepfel, P., Schmid, C.: Lcr-net++: Multi-person 2D and 3D pose detection in natural images. In: PAMI (2019)

31. Shin, D., Fowlkes, C., Hoiem, D.: Pixels, voxels, and views: a study of shape representations for single view 3D object shape prediction. In: IEEE Conference on Computer Vision and Pattern Recognition (CVPR) (2018)

32. Sigal, L., Balan, A.O., Black, M.J.: HumanEva: synchronized video and motion capture dataset and baseline algorithm for evaluation of articulated human motion. In: IJCV (2010)

33. Sun, X., Xiao, B., Wei, F., Liang, S., Wei, Y.: Integral human pose regression. In: Ferrari, V., Hebert, M., Sminchisescu, C., Weiss, Y. (eds.) ECCV 2018. LNCS, vol. 11210, pp. 536–553. Springer, Cham (2018). https://doi.org/10.1007/978-3-030-01231-1_33

34. Tatarchenko, M., Dosovitskiy, A., Brox, T.: Octree generating networks: efficient convolutional architectures for high-resolution 3d outputs. In: Proceedings of the IEEE International Conference on Computer Vision, pp. 2088–2096 (2017)

35. Tatarchenko, M., Richter, S.R., Ranftl, R., Li, Z., Koltun, V., Brox, T.: What do single-view 3D reconstruction networks learn? In: Proceedings of the IEEE Conference on Computer Vision and Pattern Recognition, pp. 3405–3414 (2019)

36. Torralba, A., Efros, A.A.: Unbiased look at dataset bias. In: CVPR (2011)

37. Trumble, M., Gilbert, A., Malleson, C., Hilton, A., Collomosse, J.: Total capture: 3D human pose estimation fusing video and inertial sensors. In: BMVC (2017)

38. Tulsiani, S., Gupta, S., Fouhey, D., Efros, A.A., Malik, J.: Factoring shape, pose, and layout from the 2D image of a 3D scene. In: CVPR (2018)

39. Tulsiani, S., Zhou, T., Efros, A.A., Malik, J.: Multi-view supervision for single-view reconstruction via differentiable ray consistency. In: Computer Vision and Pattern Regognition (CVPR) (2017)

40. Tung, H.Y.F., Tung, H.W., Yumer, E., Fragkiadaki, K.: Self-supervised learning of motion capture. In: CVPR (2009)

41. Iqbal, U., Molchanov, P., Breuel, T., Gall, J., Kautz, J.: Hand pose estimation via latent 2.5D heatmap regression. In: Ferrari, V., Hebert, M., Sminchisescu, C., Weiss, Y. (eds.) ECCV 2018. LNCS, vol. 11215, pp. 125–143. Springer, Cham (2018). https://doi.org/10.1007/978-3-030-01252-6_8

42. Varol, G., Ceylan, D., Bryan Russell, A.J.Y., Yumer, E., Laptev, I., Schmid, C.: Bodynet: volumetric inference of 3D human body shapes. In: CVPR (2019)

43. Varol, G., et al.: Learning from synthetic humans. In: CVPR (2017)

44. Villegas, R., Yang, J., Ceylan, D., Lee, H.: Neural kinematic networks for unsupervised motion retargetting. In: CVPR (2018)

45. Wang, X., Cai, Z., Gao, D., Vasconcelos, N.: Towards universal object detection by domain attention. In: CVPR (2019)

46. Wang, Z., Chen, L., Rathore, S., Shin, D., Fowlkes, C.: Geometric pose affordance: 3D human pose with scene constraints. arxiv (2019)

47. Wang, Z., et al.: Structured triplet learning with pos-tag guided attention for visual question answering. In: WACV (2018)

48. Wang, Z., Wang, L., Wang, Y., Zhang, B., Qiao, Y.: Weakly supervised patchnets: describing and aggregating local patches for scene recognition. In: TIP (2017)

49. Xiao, B., Wu, H., Wei, Y.: Simple baselines for human pose estimation and tracking. In: Ferrari, V., Hebert, M., Sminchisescu, C., Weiss, Y. (eds.) ECCV 2018. LNCS, vol. 11210, pp. 472–487. Springer, Cham (2018). https://doi.org/10.1007/978-3-030-01231-1_29

50. Xie, S., Tu, Z.: Holistically-nested edge detection. In: ICCV (2015)

51. Yan, X., Yang, J., Yumer, E., Guo, Y., Lee, H.: Perspective transformer nets: learning single-view 3D object reconstruction without 3D supervision. In: Advances in Neural Information Processing Systems, pp. 1696–1704 (2016)

52. Yin, X., Liu, X.: Multi-task convolutional neural network for pose-invariant face recognition. IEEE Trans. Image Process. **27**(2), 964–975 (2017)

53. Yu, S., Yun, Y., Wu, L., Wenpeng, G., YiLi, F., Tao, M.: Human mesh recovery from monocular images via a skeleton-disentangled representation. In: ICCV (2019)

54. Zhang, X., Zhang, Z., Zhang, C., Tenenbaum, J., Freeman, B., Wu, J.: Learning to reconstruct shapes from unseen classes. In: Advances in Neural Information Processing Systems, pp. 2257–2268 (2018)

55. Zhou, X., Huang, Q., Sun, X., Xue, X., Wei, Y.: Towards 3D human pose estimation in the wild: a weakly-supervised approach. In: ICCV (2017)

56. Zimmermann, C., Brox, T.: Learning to estimate 3D hand pose from single RGB images (2017)

57. Zimmermann, C., Ceylan, D., Yang, J., Russell, B., Argus, M., Brox, T.: Freihand: a dataset for markerless capture of hand pose and shape from single RGB images. In: ICCV (2019)

Beyond Weak Perspective for Monocular 3D Human Pose Estimation

Imry Kissos, Lior Fritz$^{(\boxtimes)}$, Matan Goldman, Omer Meir, Eduard Oks,
and Mark Kliger

Amazon Lab126, Sunnyvale, USA
{imry,liorf,matang,omermeir,oksed,markklig}@amazon.com

Abstract. We consider the task of 3D joints location and orientation prediction from a monocular video with the skinned multi-person linear (SMPL) model. We first infer 2D joints locations with an off-the-shelf pose estimation algorithm. We use the SPIN algorithm and estimate initial predictions of body pose, shape and camera parameters from a deep regression neural network. We then adhere to the SMPLify algorithm which receives those initial parameters, and optimizes them so that inferred 3D joints from the SMPL model would fit the 2D joints locations. This algorithm involves a projection step of 3D joints to the 2D image plane. The conventional approach is to follow weak perspective assumptions which use ad-hoc focal length. Through experimentation on the 3D poses in the wild (3DPW) dataset, we show that using full perspective projection, with the correct camera center and an approximated focal length, provides favorable results. Our algorithm has resulted in a winning entry for the 3DPW Challenge, reaching first place in joints orientation accuracy.

Keywords: SMPL · Pose estimation · Perspective projection · 3DPW

1 Introduction

Predicting 3D human joints locations from a monocular image is a challenging task. Estimating the correct depth of locations from a single image may present ambiguities which are hard to solve. Moreover, obtaining annotated data for training is a complicated and cost intensive task. In order to account for the ambiguities, prior knowledge of the human body is utilized in many models. Namely, the skinned multi-person linear (SMPL) model [17], obtained by detailed 3D scans of a large number of individuals, provides a strong prior for this task, and has been widely used in the research community [11, 24, 25, 27, 28] (Fig. 1).

The SMPLify algorithm [4], has been shown to achieve compelling results of full 3D human mesh recovery from a single image. The algorithm fits the SMPL model to the image given locations of 2D joints on the image. The optimization is performed by minimizing an objective function that penalizes the error between

---

I. Kissos and L. Fritz—Equal contribution.

© Springer Nature Switzerland AG 2020
A. Bartoli and A. Fusiello (Eds.): ECCV 2020 Workshops, LNCS 12536, pp. 541–554, 2020.
https://doi.org/10.1007/978-3-030-66096-3_37

SPIN   SPIN+SMPLify   Ours

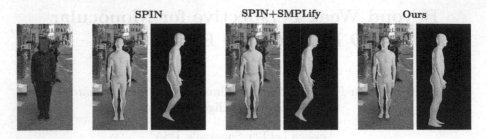

Fig. 1. The weak perspective assumption may create pose inaccuracies due to incorrect projection onto the image plane.

projections of the estimated 3D joints onto image plane and input 2D joints. The recently proposed SPIN (SMPL oPtimization IN the loop) model [14] is a method for regressing SMPL parameters directly from an image. SPIN has introduced a collaboration between an optimization-based SIMPLify algorithm and a deep regression network. A regressed estimate from the network initializes SMPLify with estimated SMPL parameters. The output from SMPLify serves as supervision to train the regression network. This collaboration forms a self-improving loop, so that a better network provides a better SMPLify initialization, which leads to, again, better SMPL parameters supervision.

In both SIMPLify optimization and SPIN deep network training, one of the main losses, so called *reprojection loss*, is derived from the error between input 2D joints locations and the projections of the estimated 3D joints onto the image plane. The projection of a 3D point from the world coordinate frame into the 2D image plane requires knowledge of camera intrinsic and extrinsic parameters. Unfortunately the camera parameters are rarely known. The authors of SPIN have chosen the weak perspective camera model in the projection procedure. Thus, it is assumed that the camera is far from the person. This assumption is realized by using *unrealistically large focal length*. Moreover, the weak perspective assumption facilitates the disregard of the actual location of the input person crop compared to the full resolution image. While this assumption may be reasonable for some data samples, mainly from the COCO dataset [16], it does not hold in some other cases, as in the 3DPW dataset [18]. In fact, the weak perspective assumption may introduce noise into the reprojection loss, and in some degree, undermine its utility as a supervision signal for the estimation of 3D joints.

To this end, we suggest to look beyond the weak perspective assumptions in the SPIN and SMPLify algorithms. We assume a full perspective projection camera model. That is, we assume that the camera is close enough to the person so that changes in depth can result in changes in the projection to the 2D image plane. We perform the projection to the original image, with respect to correct image center and approximated focal length, in contrast to the projection onto the image patch which was cropped for inference. Additionally, we modify SMPLify camera parameters and global body orientation optimization step by leveraging all joints, rather than torso joints alone, to compute re-projection loss which is used in fitting procedure.

At the video level the jitter in results of frame-based 3D joints estimation can be reduced by temporal smoothing. We demonstrate that smoothing using the OneEuro filter [7], which adaptively changes the filter cut-off frequency, produces more accurate results.

Recently, a new dataset for 3D human mesh recovery has been collected, 3D poses in the wild (3DPW) [18]. Using inertial measurement units (IMUs) and 2D joints locations, accurate full 3D human mesh, including 3D joints locations, were obtained for 60 clips in total. We experiment with this dataset, and demonstrate that the SPIN-SMPLify collaborative model with full perspective camera projection procedure achieves state-of-the-art results for joints orientations. Our algorithm was a wining entry for 3DPW Challenge reaching the first place in joints orientation accuracy.

To summarize, the contribution of our paper is the following,

- We demonstrate that using full perspective assumptions, one can achieve state-of-the-arts results for 3D joints predictions from a single image.
- We propose to use all joints within the SMPLify camera translation and global body orientation optimization step, rather than torso joints alone.
- We show that simple smoothing procedure result in better 3D joints location estimation at the video level.

2   Related Work

Human pose in 3D is usually represented with a set of joints positions, or with a parametric representation of a body model. Considering the task of 3D human pose inference from a single image, in the first approach, 3D joints locations are either *lifted* from estimated 2D joints locations on the image [8,19,22,29], or are directly inferred from the image [23,26]. In the second approach, several body models have been proposed, such as the SMPL model [17] and others [2,10]. The popular SMPL model is a skinned vertex-based model that is capable of accurately representing a full mesh of the human body using a compact representation of body pose and shape parameters only.

Recently, it has been shown that SMPL parameters can be directly inferred from an image with a deep neural network [11,24,25,27,28]. Other methods, such as SMPLify [4], consider optimizing these parameters directly given locations of 2D joints on the image. These two paradigms have been recently merged in the SPIN algorithm [15], where the SMPLify algorithm is incorporated in-the-loop of the training procedure of a deep neural network, and possibly during an inference fine-tuning step. The problem of human pose extraction from videos was investigated in [1,3,12,13,21].

Our approach closely follows the SPIN method [15]. To compute reprojection losses of SPIN and SMPLify, authors of [15] use unrealistically large focal length, that is inherently equivalent to weak perspective assumption. Moreover, the reprojection losses are computed with respect to a resized cropped image of the person. In this paper we attempt to correct shortcomings of the original method related to the weak perspective assumption and projection of 3D joints onto the resized cropped image patch. In [20], the authors use corrective rotation to compensate for the perspective distortions from the projection to the cropped patch. However, weak perspective assumption is still used in the projection procedure. In [9] a neural network directly predicts the parameters of the camera projection model, namely a focal length related scaling parameter and principal point. Yet, weak perspective projection is still assumed.

3   Method

SPIN neural network receives as an input a cropped image I of a person, and outputs body pose and shape parameters, θ and β, respectively. The network also estimates 3 camera parameters, (s, t_x, t_y). The translation parameters t_x and t_y represent the shift of the body kinematic tree root (pelvis) relatively to the origin of the cropped image coordinate frame on x and y axes respectively, while the scale parameter s is used to compute translation parameters t_z on z axis. The body pose parameters, θ, represent local rotation transformations of each joint compared to its parent in the kinematic tree. In total, it contains 72 parameters, 3 rotation parameters per each of the 24 joints in the kinematic tree. Additionally, 10 body shape parameters, β, represent linear coefficients of a low-dimensional shape space, learned from a training set of thousands of registered body scans. The SMPL model uses the body pose and shape parameters to compute the locations of 6890 3D mesh vertices. Additionally, a linear joints regressor is used to infer 3D joints locations from the 3D mesh vertices.

The SMPLify algorithm requires an input of 2D joints locations. The popular choice is 25 joints defined by the OpenPose model [6], and we use an off-the-shelf implementation of OpenPose to obtain 2D joints locations for each image. The extracted 3D joints from the SMPL model are projected onto the 2D image plane using perspective projection. The joints re-projection loss together with pose and shape prior losses are minimized to estimate body pose, shape, global body orientation and camera translation parameters. The SMPLify optimization is initialized with the output of SPIN neural network.

3.1   Projection Formulation

We assume a pinhole camera model. In order to perform projection of 3D joints onto the 2D image plane, we first need to define the camera intrinsic matrix,

$$K = \begin{bmatrix} f_x & s_k & o_x \\ 0 & f_y & o_y \\ 0 & 0 & 1 \end{bmatrix}, \tag{1}$$

where f_x, f_y are the camera *focal length* values (in pixels), $[o_x, o_y]$ is the camera principal point (in pixels) and s_k is a skew coefficient. Usually $f_x \equiv f_y \equiv f$,

$[o_x, o_y] \equiv [W/2, H/2]$, where W, H are the image width and height, respectively, and $s_k \equiv 0$. The intrinsic matrix can thus be rewritten as,

$$K = \begin{bmatrix} f & 0 & W/2 \\ 0 & f & H/2 \\ 0 & 0 & 1 \end{bmatrix}. \tag{2}$$

Let us also define $T = [t_x, t_y, t_z] \in \mathbb{R}^3$ as the camera translation in the world coordinate frame. We assume that the camera coordinate frame is aligned with the world frame, i.e., the camera extrinsic matrix is the identity matrix. Moreover, we assume that the camera does not have any radial or tangential distortion. Given a 3D point in the world coordinate system, $p_{3D} = [x, y, z] \in \mathbb{R}^3$, we compute its 2D projection onto the image plane, $p_{2D} \in \mathbb{R}^2$, with the following formulation,

$$[\tilde{x}, \tilde{y}, \tilde{z}]^T = K \cdot ([x, y, z] + T)^T, \tag{3}$$

and,

$$p_{2D} = [\tilde{x}/\tilde{z}, \tilde{y}/\tilde{z}]. \tag{4}$$

In SPIN, the person *square* bounding box is first cropped, and then resized into a fixed resolution of 224×224. The projection of 3D joints onto the image plane, and the computation of re-projection losses are performed directly onto a *resized cropped image* around the person. Since the camera focal length, f, is unknown, the focal length with respect to the resized cropped image patch was defined to be $f = 5000$. The scale parameter s is converted into the camera translation in the z axis, t_z, using the formula,

$$t_z = \frac{2 \cdot f}{Res \cdot s}, \tag{5}$$

where $Res \equiv 224$ is the resized crop resolution. For most images, the resulting t_z is very large comparing to changes in the z coordinate of the 3D joints. The inherent assumption here is of weak perspective projection. It is assumed that the person is very far from the camera, and that the possible changes in the z coordinate of 3D joints are *negligible* compared to the distance from the camera, which is not always true in practice. In fact, this assumption may lead to erroneous projection of the 3D joints onto the image plane, and as a result, a noisy reprojection loss. Moreover, since the parameters (s, t_x, t_y) are estimated with respect to the center of the *resized cropped image*, they do not truly represent the camera translation parameters of the real camera center, which is related to the center of the full resolution image.

We propose to consider a more realistic focal length and to project 3D joints directly onto the original full resolution image plane, rather than to the resized cropped low resolution patch. In case the focal length is known or when the camera can be calibrated, the true focal length should be used. In practice, the focal length is usually unknown and the camera is unavailable for calibration. The focal length cannot be optimized as part of the global optimization process, nor can it be estimated by a neural network, since the problem is too unconstrained to optimize it together with camera translation. To overcome this problem, we suggest to use focal length approximation.

It is known that the focal length can be calculated from the camera *field of view* (FOV),

$$f = \frac{\sqrt{W^2 + H^2}}{2\tan{(\alpha/2)}}, \tag{6}$$

where W, H are the width and height of the original image and α is the diagonal FOV of the camera. Since the FOV of the camera is also unknown, we can simply approximate the focal length by,

$$f \approx \sqrt{W^2 + H^2}. \tag{7}$$

This roughly corresponds to a camera FOV of 55°. In a 1920 × 1080 resolution camera, we get $f \approx 2200$. In Sect. 4.2 we show that the model is insensitive to the exact value of the focal length within a wide range.

We define $r = b/Res$, where b is the size of the detected person square bounding box in native image resolution, as the resizing factor from the cropped image resolution to the actual input image resolution. Down-sampling the image by the factor r changes the focal length of the camera (in pixels) to be f/r. Since the camera scale parameter s is estimated with respect to the resized image patch, in order to convert it into the correct camera translation in the z axis, t_z, we use,

$$t_z = \frac{2 \cdot f}{r \cdot Res \cdot s}. \tag{8}$$

Finally, the estimated translation parameters t_x, t_y, which are obtained from the SPIN neural network output, are related to the center of the resized cropped image and not the actual camera center at the full resolution image center. Thus, we need to perform the adequate correction. Let c_x, c_y be the 2D coordinates of the crop center in the original full resolution image coordinates. We compute the camera center *shift* parameters using,

$$\hat{c}_x = \frac{2(c_x - W/2)}{s \cdot b} \tag{9}$$

$$\hat{c}_y = \frac{2(c_y - H/2)}{s \cdot b},$$

where b is the bounding box size, which is always square in our case, and W and H are the original image width and height. We use the camera center shift parameters, $\hat{c}_x, \hat{c}_y$ to compute the camera translation parameter, $\hat{T}$, with respect to the true camera location,

$$\hat{T} = [t_x - \hat{c}_x, t_y - \hat{c}_y, t_z], \tag{10}$$

which we substitute with T in Eq. 3.

The usage of the modified projection formulation is described in the next subsection.

3.2 SMPLify Camera and Global Orientation Optimization

The SMPLify algorithm works in two separate optimization steps. The first, optimizes the global orientation (first 3 parameters of θ) and camera translation parameters T. In the second steps, only joints orientations θ and body shape parameters β are optimized.

Since the camera translation and global orientation are important when assuming full perspective projection, we propose the following modification to the algorithm. We estimate (s, t_x, t_y) using SPIN deep regression network. We then initialize optimization of camera translation parameter T with $\hat{T}$ obtained from modification of (s, t_x, t_y) using Eqs. 8–10. The fitting loss is obtained by projecting predicted 3D joints to them image plane, and comparing them with given 2D joints. In the projection procedure formulated in Eqs. 2–4 we use the approximated realistic focal length as described in Eq. 7. We also note that in Eq. 2 we use the original image width and height. In SPIN, W and H are set according to the input cropped image size, so that they are both 224.

Finally, while in [14] this reprojection loss is computed only for the torso joints (hips and shoulders), we found it beneficial to use all joints in our case. Similarly to the joints reprojection loss used in the second step of SMPLify optimization, we weight the contribution of each joint by the squared confidence of its estimate provided by the 2D joints estimation algorithm.

4 Experiments on 3DPW

We experiment on the 3D poses in the wild (3DPW) dataset [18]. We do not use the ground truth 2D joints or bounding box locations. Rather, we first predict 25 2D joints locations with the OpenPose algorithm [5,6], using an off-the-shelf implementation[1]. We then use these predicted joints and match them to the provided in 3DPW ground truth joints in each frame in order to track each person in the clip individually. The bounding box at each frame is obtained from the maximal and minimal values of the predicted joints coordinates. We also use the trained SPIN model [14] to obtain an initial prediction of body shape and pose, and camera parameters. We then use SMPLify optimization, following its implementation within SPIN, with 100 iterations with a learning rate of 0.01 to optimize these parameters to match the obtained 2D joints. The SMPLify optimization is modified as was described in Sect. 3.2.

4.1 Results

To evaluate our model, we consider the 24 joints defined in the SMPL kinematic tree (root is used for matching). We measure 6 metrics on the 3DPW dataset to assess our model,

- **MPJPE:** mean per joint position error (in mm). Average distance from prediction to ground truth joint positions (after root matching).

---

[1] https://github.com/CMU-Perceptual-Computing-Lab/openpose.

- **MPJPE_PA:** mean per joint position error (in mm) after Procrustes alignment (rotation, translation and scale are adjusted).
- **PCK:** percentage of correct joints. A joint is considered correct when it is less than 50 mm away from the ground truth. The joints considered here are: shoulders, elbows, wrists, hips, knees and ankles.
- **AUC:** total area under the PCK-threshold curve. Calculated by computing PCKs by varying from 0 to 200 mm the threshold at which a predicted joint is considered correct.
- **MPJAE:** measures the angle in degrees between the predicted part orientation and the ground truth orientation. The orientation difference is measured as the geodesic distance in SO(3). The 9 parts considered are: left/right upper arm, left/right lower arm, left/right upper leg, left/right lower leg and root.
- **MPJAE_PA:** measures the angle in degrees between the predicted part orientation and the ground truth orientation after rotating all predicted orientations by the rotation matrix obtained from the Procrustes alignment step.

We compare ourselves to the results of SPIN [14] and SPIN followed by fine-tuning with its original SMPLify implementation. Table 1 summarizes the consistent improvements over both methods across all metrics. The modifications to the camera optimization listed in Sect. 3.2 lead to improvements in MPJPE and MPJAE from 84.174 to 83.154 and from 20.437 to 19.697, respectively.

Table 1. Results on 3DPW with unknown ground truth person crop. SPIN refers to results obtained from the pretrained network from [14], and SPIN+SMPLify refers to fine-tuning the results with the original SMPLify implementation. Our results depict SPIN fine-tuned with our SMPLify implementation. ***Our MPJAE is a current SOTA on the 3DPW dataset.*

Metric	SPIN [14]	SPIN+SMPLify [14]	Ours
MPJPE (↓)	99.402	95.839	**83.154**
MPJPE_PA (↓)	68.131	66.390	**59.703**
PCK (↑)	30.846	33.264	**42.419**
AUC (↑)	0.534	0.550	**0.623**
MPJAE (↓)	24.380	23.900	**19.697****
MPJAE_PA (↓)	21.198	24.410	**19.149**

4.2 Effect of Focal Length

We experiment with a set of a few focal length values. We note that the camera focal length used in the computation of the camera translation parameters in Eq. 8 is normalized by the resizing factor, r. In the weak perspective implementation of SPIN [14], the focal length of the cropped and *resized* image was assumed to be 5000, which is equivalent to the focal length $5000 \cdot r$ on the full resolution image. As r is usually around 3, the focal length which was effectively assumed in the original SPIN implementation is about 15000.

We present the effect of the focal length in pixels units on the joints distance metrics (MPJPE) and joints orientations distance (MPJAE). As can be observed in Fig. 2, for a large range of focal length values, the results are maintained. However, as the focal length becomes much smaller or larger, the results are deteriorated substantially. We deduce that a close approximation of the focal length is crucial, however the exact value does not have to be known.

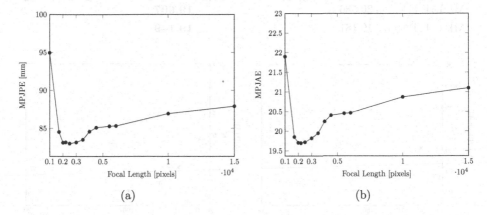

(a)   (b)

Fig. 2. In (a) we show the effect of the focal length on the joints locations metrics, measured in mm. In (b) we show the effect on the orientations metric, MPJAE, which is the geodesic distance measured between predicted and ground truth orientations, in $SO(3)$.

4.3   Effect of Camera Center

In the original SPIN-SMPLify implementation the camera is assumed to be centered at the bounding box center. As detailed in Sect. 3.1, we alter the optimization process so that the camera center is at the actual full resolution image center. In Table 2 we present the effect of altering the camera center on the measured metrics. We observe consistent improvements across all metrics.

4.4   SMPLify Number of Iterations

We experiment with different number of iterations in the SMPLify optimization process. Figure 3 shows the number of SMPLify iterations and the effect on the MPJPE and MPJAE metrics. We observe that as we increase the number of iterations, the metrics improve consistently, while at 200 iterations there is slight degradation of MPJPE.

Table 2. Effect of using different camera center definitions on metrics

Metric	Camera center at bounding box	Camera center at image center
MPJPE ($\downarrow$)	86.103	**83.154**
MPJPE_PA ($\downarrow$)	59.910	**59.703**
PCK ($\uparrow$)	39.208	**42.419**
AUC ($\uparrow$)	0.607	**0.623**
MPJAE ($\downarrow$)	20.586	**19.697**
MPJAE_PA ($\downarrow$)	19.181	**19.149**

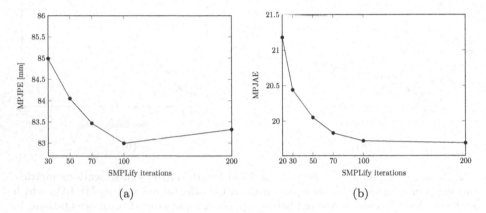

(a)   (b)

Fig. 3. In (a) we show the effect of the number of SMPLify optimization iterations on the joints locations metrics, measured in mm. In (b) we show the effect on the orientations metric, MPJAE, which is the geodesic distance measured between predicted and ground truth orientations, in SO(3).

4.5 Smoothing

At the video clip level, we observe considerable jitter in the predicted results. As a final post processing steps, we perform temporal smoothing on the 3D joints locations and orientations with the OneEuro filter [7]. The advantage of this filter, is that using adaptive cut-off frequency, it maintains small lag in rapid movements, while reducing noise and jitter in slow movements. We summarize the effect of smoothing in Table 3. While the difference is marginal, it is consistent across all metrics. We note that except of joints and orientations temporal smoothing, we do not enforce any other kinematic, skeletal or shape temporal constraints at the video level. Incorporating additional temporal constraints will be a subject for future work.

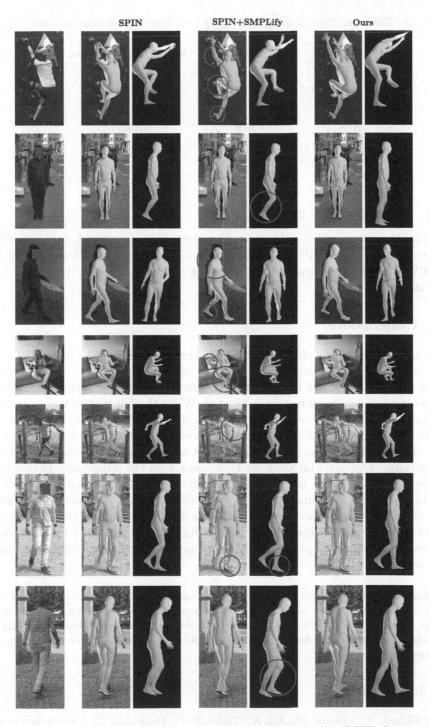

Fig. 4. Examples of some mesh recoveries from frames in the 3DPW dataset. We present results of SPIN, SPIN with the original SMPLify fine-tuning (SPIN+SMPLify) and our results. Points of interest are marked on the images.

Table 3. Effect of using smoothing with OneEuro filter on metrics

Metric	Without smoothing	With smoothing
MPJPE ($\downarrow$)	84.986	**83.154**
MPJPE_PA ($\downarrow$)	60.677	**59.703**
PCK ($\uparrow$)	42.182	**42.419**
AUC ($\uparrow$)	0.619	**0.623**
MPJAE ($\downarrow$)	20.063	**19.697**
MPJAE_PA ($\downarrow$)	19.435	**19.149**

4.6   Examples from 3DPW

In Fig. 4 we show rendered human mesh recovered by our model, and with SPIN (with and without SMPLify fine-tuning) on several extracted frames from the 3DPW dataset. Rendering is done with the same focal length that is used for optimization.

5   Conclusions

We have presented the effect of using full perspective projection instead of weak perspective projection within the SMPLify optimization step of SPIN method. Experiments on the 3DPW dataset show that this method provides considerable improvements across all metrics evaluated. While the full perspective projection requires knowledge of the camera focal length, it can be roughly approximated from the image resolution, and we have shown that the model is insensitive to the exact value of the focal length, and that the results are maintained within a wide range of values. Moreover, we have also shown the importance of using the correct camera center, temporal smoothing and provided some modifications to the SMPLify loss function to accommodate the new optimization scheme. As future work, one can consider removing the weak perspective assumptions from the network training, so that the results can be maintained within a single forward pass and incorporate additional temporal kinematic, skeletal or shape constraints.

Acknowledgements. We thank the anonymous reviewers whose comments and suggestions helped improve and clarify this manuscript. We also thank our colleagues from Amazon Lab 126, Dr. Ilia Vitsnudel, Eli Alshan, Ido Yerushalmi, Liza Potikha, Dr. Ianir Ideses and Dr. Javier Romero from Amazon Body Labs, for multiple useful discussions.

References

1. Alldieck, T., Magnor, M., Xu, W., Theobalt, C., Pons-Moll, G.: Video based reconstruction of 3D people models. In: Proceedings of the IEEE Conference on Computer Vision and Pattern Recognition, pp. 8387–8397 (2018)

2. Anguelov, D., Srinivasan, P., Koller, D., Thrun, S., Rodgers, J., Davis, J.: SCAPE: shape completion and animation of people. In: ACM SIGGRAPH 2005 Papers (2005)

3. Arnab, A., Doersch, C., Zisserman, A.: Exploiting temporal context for 3D human pose estimation in the wild. In: Proceedings of the IEEE Conference on Computer Vision and Pattern Recognition (2019)

4. Bogo, F., Kanazawa, A., Lassner, C., Gehler, P., Romero, J., Black, M.J.: Keep it SMPL: automatic estimation of 3D human pose and shape from a single image. In: Leibe, B., Matas, J., Sebe, N., Welling, M. (eds.) ECCV 2016. LNCS, vol. 9909, pp. 561–578. Springer, Cham (2016). https://doi.org/10.1007/978-3-319-46454-1_34

5. Cao, Z., Hidalgo Martinez, G., Simon, T., Wei, S., Sheikh, Y.A.: OpenPose: real-time multi-person 2D pose estimation using part affinity fields. IEEE Trans. Pattern Anal. Mach. Intell. **43**, 172–186 (2019)

6. Cao, Z., Simon, T., Wei, S.E., Sheikh, Y.: Realtime multi-person 2D pose estimation using part affinity fields. In: CVPR (2017)

7. Casiez, G., Roussel, N., Vogel, D.: 1 filter: a simple speed-based low-pass filter for noisy input in interactive systems. In: Proceedings of the SIGCHI Conference on Human Factors in Computing Systems, pp. 2527–2530 (2012)

8. Chen, C.H., et al.: Unsupervised 3D pose estimation with geometric self-supervision. In: Computer Vision and Pattern Recognition (CVPR) (2019)

9. Habibie, I., Xu, W., Mehta, D., Pons-Moll, G., Theobalt, C.: In the wild human pose estimation using explicit 2D features and intermediate 3D representations. In: Proceedings of the IEEE Conference on Computer Vision and Pattern Recognition (2019)

10. Joo, H., Simon, T., Sheikh, Y.: Total capture: a 3D deformation model for tracking faces, hands, and bodies. In: Proceedings of the IEEE Conference on Computer Vision and Pattern Recognition (2018)

11. Kanazawa, A., Black, M.J., Jacobs, D.W., Malik, J.: End-to-end recovery of human shape and pose. In: Proceedings of the IEEE Conference on Computer Vision and Pattern Recognition (2018)

12. Kanazawa, A., Zhang, J.Y., Felsen, P., Malik, J.: Learning 3D human dynamics from video. In: Computer Vision and Pattern Recognition (CVPR) (2019)

13. Kocabas, M., Athanasiou, N., Black, M.J.: VIBE: video inference for human body pose and shape estimation. In: Proceedings of the IEEE/CVF Conference on Computer Vision and Pattern Recognition (2020)

14. Kolotouros, N., Pavlakos, G., Black, M.J., Daniilidis, K.: Learning to reconstruct 3D human pose and shape via model-fitting in the loop. In: Proceedings of the IEEE International Conference on Computer Vision, pp. 2252–2261 (2019)

15. Kolotouros, N., Pavlakos, G., Daniilidis, K.: Convolutional mesh regression for single-image human shape reconstruction. In: Proceedings of the IEEE Conference on Computer Vision and Pattern Recognition (2019)

16. Lin, T.-Y., et al.: Microsoft COCO: common objects in context. In: Fleet, D., Pajdla, T., Schiele, B., Tuytelaars, T. (eds.) ECCV 2014. LNCS, vol. 8693, pp. 740–755. Springer, Cham (2014). https://doi.org/10.1007/978-3-319-10602-1_48

17. Loper, M., Mahmood, N., Romero, J., Pons-Moll, G., Black, M.J.: SMPL: a skinned multi-person linear model. ACM Trans. Graph. (TOG) **34**, 1–16 (2015)

18. von Marcard, T., Henschel, R., Black, M.J., Rosenhahn, B., Pons-Moll, G.: Recovering accurate 3D human pose in the wild using IMUs and a moving camera. In: Ferrari, V., Hebert, M., Sminchisescu, C., Weiss, Y. (eds.) ECCV 2018. LNCS, vol. 11214, pp. 614–631. Springer, Cham (2018). https://doi.org/10.1007/978-3-030-01249-6_37

19. Martinez, J., Hossain, R., Romero, J., Little, J.J.: A simple yet effective baseline for 3D human pose estimation. In: Proceedings of the IEEE International Conference on Computer Vision (2017)
20. Mehta, D., et al.: Monocular 3D human pose estimation in the wild using improved CNN supervision. In: 2017 Fifth International Conference on 3D Vision (3DV) (2017)
21. Mehta, D., et al.: XNect: real-time multi-person 3d motion capture with a single RGB camera. ACM Trans. Graph. (TOG) 39(4), 82 (2020)
22. Moreno-Noguer, F.: 3D human pose estimation from a single image via distance matrix regression. In: Proceedings of the IEEE Conference on Computer Vision and Pattern Recognition (2017)
23. Nibali, A., He, Z., Morgan, S., Prendergast, L.: 3D human pose estimation with 2D marginal heatmaps. In: 2019 IEEE Winter Conference on Applications of Computer Vision (WACV), IEEE (2019)
24. Omran, M., Lassner, C., Pons-Moll, G., Gehler, P.V., Schiele, B.: Neural body fitting: unifying deep learning and model-based human pose and shape estimation (2018)
25. Pavlakos, G., Zhu, L., Zhou, X., Daniilidis, K.: Learning to estimate 3D human pose and shape from a single color image. In: CVPR (2018)
26. Sárándi, I., Linder, T., Arras, K.O., Leibe, B.: Metric-scale truncation-robust heatmaps for 3D human pose estimation. arXiv preprint arXiv:2003.02953 (2020)
27. Tung, H.Y., Tung, H.W., Yumer, E., Fragkiadaki, K.: Self-supervised learning of motion capture. In: Advances in Neural Information Processing Systems 30 (2017)
28. Varol, G., et al.: BodyNet: volumetric inference of 3D human body shapes. In: Ferrari, V., Hebert, M., Sminchisescu, C., Weiss, Y. (eds.) ECCV 2018. LNCS, vol. 11211, pp. 20–38. Springer, Cham (2018). https://doi.org/10.1007/978-3-030-01234-2_2
29. Zhao, R., Wang, Y., Martinez, A.M.: A simple, fast and highly-accurate algorithm to recover 3D shape from 2D landmarks on a single image. IEEE Trans. Pattern Anal. Mach. Intell. 40(12), 3059–3066 (2017)

W20 - Map-based Localization for Autonomous Driving

W20 - Map-Based Localization for Autonomous Driving

It is with great pleasure that we present the proceedings of the First Workshop on Map-based Localization for Autonomous Driving (MLAD 2020). This workshop was held on August 23, 2020, in conjunction with the 16th European Conference on Computer Vision (ECCV 2020). The focus of this workshop was on state-of-the-art map-based localization for autonomous driving. Part of the workshop was dedicated to the Map-based Visual Re-Localization Challenge, a new challenge that evaluates the long-term performance of visual SLAM systems under changing weather conditions.

The workshop consisted of five invited keynote talks, one tech talk, one talk from submitted work, and two talks from the winner and runner-up of the visual re-localization challenge. The workshop had received five valid submissions. These submissions were reviewed by at least two separate reviewers and discussed to decide on their acceptance. Based on these reviews the Program Committee selected one paper as a short oral presentation (15-minute talk). We would like to thank all the authors who submitted to the workshop. The winner of the visual re-localization challenge received 1,000 USD while the runner-up received 500 USD, which was supported by our sponsors Artisense and Kudan.

The invited talks were presented by Dengxin Dai from ETH Zurich, Switzerland, Andreas Geiger from University of Tübingen, Germany, Germany, and Max Planck Institute for Intelligent Systems, Germany, Stefan Leutenegger from Imperial College London, UK, Raquel Urtasun from Uber ATG and University of Toronto, Canada, and Cyrill Stachniss from University of Bonn, Germany. The tech talk was presented by one of the organizers Niclas Zeller from Artisense, Germany. We would like to thank the ECCV 2020 workshop chairs Adrien Bartoli and Andrea Fusiello, for their support and feedback. We would also like to thank all the invited speakers, authors who presented at the workshop, and the attendees, as well as the participants of the visual re-localization challenge.

We hope you will enjoy the proceedings and we look forward to the next edition!

August 2020

Patrick Wenzel
Niclas Zeller
Nan Yang
Rui Wang
Daniel Cremers

Geographically Local Representation Learning with a Spatial Prior for Visual Localization

Zimin Xia[1], Olaf Booij[2], Marco Manfredi[2], and Julian F. P. Kooij[1]

[1] Intelligent Vehicles Group, Technical University Delft, Delft, The Netherlands
{z.xia,j.f.p.kooij}@tudelft.nl
[2] TomTom, Amsterdam, The Netherlands
{olaf.booij,marco.manfredi}@tomtom.com

Abstract. We revisit end-to-end representation learning for cross-view self-localization, the task of retrieving for a query camera image the closest satellite image in a database by matching them in a shared image representation space. Previous work tackles this task as a global localization problem, i.e. assuming no prior knowledge on the location, thus the learned image representation must distinguish far apart areas of the map. However, in many practical applications such as self-driving vehicles, it is already possible to discard distant locations through well-known localization techniques using temporal filters and GNSS/GPS sensors. We argue that learned features should therefore be optimized to be discriminative within the geographic local neighborhood, instead of globally. We propose a simple but effective adaptation to the common triplet loss used in previous work to consider a prior localization estimate already in the training phase. We evaluate our approach on the existing CVACT dataset, and on a novel localization benchmark based on the Oxford RobotCar dataset which tests generalization across multiple traversals and days in the same area. For the Oxford benchmarks we collected corresponding satellite images. With a localization prior, our approach improves recall@1 by 9% points on CVACT, and reduces the median localization error by 2.45 m on the Oxford benchmark, compared to a state-of-the-art baseline approach. Qualitative results underscore that with our approach the network indeed captures different aspects of the local surroundings compared to the global baseline.

Keywords: Visual localization · Cross-view image matching · Image retrieval · End-to-end representation learning

1 Introduction

Self-localization with respect to a known map is an indispensable part for navigation in mobile robotics and autonomous driving. With the rise of camera-equipped vehicles, visual localization provides an attractive approach to absolute positioning. Many visual localization methods construct a descriptor vector of a query

© Springer Nature Switzerland AG 2020
A. Bartoli and A. Fusiello (Eds.): ECCV 2020 Workshops, LNCS 12536, pp. 557–573, 2020.
https://doi.org/10.1007/978-3-030-66096-3_38

camera image, and match those to a spatial map of descriptors. For instance, image retrieval-based localization simply represents the query image with a single descriptor vector, and the gallery is constructed from exemplar images with known geographic locations. A variant that has recently drawn a lot of attention is cross-view image retrieval-based localization [10,16,17,29,36,40], where the gallery is constructed from aerial or satellite images while a ground-level image is used as the query. Although this requires the construction of a shared feature space for both the ground level and satellite images, the satellite view provides a reliable representation of the local surroundings, plus large databases are nowadays readily available. As in other computer vision tasks, the feature extractors and their descriptor embeddings are nowadays often learned end-to-end [1], e.g. through a triplet loss, surpassing earlier hand-crafted methods [2,11,12,24].

(a) Input image   (b) Geo-global features   (c) Geo-local features (our)

Fig. 1. We reformulate visual localization in order to exploit coarse priors from GNSS/GPS, and thus end-to-end learn feature extractors specialized to discriminate nearby locations (in the order of meters). This is reflected in the visualized attention maps obtained by our approach (c), compared to (b) standard end-to-end learning [29]. Our features capture the location of nearby objects. The baseline focuses on the road, which is globally distinct, but locally ambiguous.

In the robotics domain, localization is traditionally addressed using specialized sensors that provide noisy measurements of the absolute position in a fixed global coordinate frame directly, e.g. through Global Navigation Satellite Systems (GNSS) such as GPS, and through temporal filtering with odometry information. Unfortunately, the localization accuracy of GNSS can vary significantly near obstructions, buildings, trees and tunnels when less satellites are visible. The horizontal positioning error can easily reach tens of meters [3].

We observe however that there are several gaps in how the localization task is addressed in practice in mobile robotics and autonomous driving, and the state-of-the-art visual localization techniques based on deep representation learning.

First, while GNSS alone is not sufficiently accurate, it does provide a coarse estimate of the absolute position. End-to-end image representation learning approaches for visual localization do not consider the presence of such localization priors during training, and often during testing too, which does not reflect practice. We assert that both approaches should be used together, hence we should learn a feature representation that is locally discriminative within the error bounds of the coarse prior, rather than globally discriminative on the entirely mapped area, see Fig. 1.

Second, existing cross-view localization benchmarks, such as the CVACT dataset [17], split the train, validation, and test splits to different geographic regions of the overall map. This means that the standard split intends to demonstrate how well a learned feature representation generalizes to new areas, as neither satellite nor ground images from the validation or test set are available during training. However, in practice we *can* have satellite images of the test region available during training, especially for a navigation task with geolocalized road information, which already presupposes that the target region is known. Mapping companies may even have already collected ground images of the target region at some past date. An alternative but equally relevant question is therefore how well a learned representation generalizes to new observations of the same route, e.g. on a different time, day or even season.

To address the observed gaps, this paper presents the following contributions: (i) We propose a simple but effective adaptation to the commonly used triplet loss to learn an image representation that is specifically discriminative between images from geographically nearby locations, rather than for distant areas. Note that we include the term geographic to avoid potential confusion with image local features, i.e. which represent a local pixel neighborhood. (ii) To demonstrate the effectiveness of the approach compared to a state-of-the-art baseline, we extend the well-known Oxford RobotCar dataset with a map composed of satellite images to serve as a new dense cross-view localization benchmark to test generalization across recording days. We also test on data from the existing CVACT benchmark, for which we propose new splits. (iii) We report quantitative improvements on image retrieval results and qualitatively show that the proposed geographically local representation focuses on different structures in the environment than the baseline.

2 Related Work

Visual localization methods can be roughly divided into three categories. Camera pose regression [4,13,21,37] uses the weights in the convolutional neural network (CNN) to implicitly describe the map by directly learning the complex function that converts the query image to map coordinates, but are in general not that accurate [28]. Structure-based visual localization [26,27,43] relies on extracting local image features from the query image, and matching these to an explicit spatial map of known features. Image retrieval-based localization [1,10,16,25,29–31,36,40] instead formulates the localization problem as simply matching the query image to gallery images and use the location of the matched gallery image as the location of the query image. Our work falls in this third category.

Image retrieval-based localization methods consist of two key steps. The first step is the image descriptor generation. Changes in illumination, appearance and viewing angle create challenges for this task. A good descriptor should be robust against those changes and, in the meantime, should be discriminative enough to allow distinguishing different images. The second key step is the similarity measurement. Similar to the metric learning problem, we need a similarity/distance measurement to measure how similar is the query image to the database image. However, during the image retrieval, the query image needs to be compared to every (in extreme case) image in the gallery. So, a complicated similarity measurement is not desired w.r.t. the fast run time requirement.

Instead of learning a complex matching function [9], many recent image retrieval methods [1,2,11,12,24,25,30,35] aim at the first key step. Those methods usually map the image to Euclidean space and use the L1/L2 distance or dot product as the similarity measurement for distinguishing different images. In the following we describe common approaches to build image/feature descriptors, used in image retrieval methods.

Traditional methods do not require any feature learning process, but usually aggregate hand-crafted local feature descriptors into a global descriptor of the image. For example bag-of-visual-words [25,30], VLAD [2,11] or Fisher vector [12,24]. Recent works employ deep learning to obtain more informative image descriptors. Some works [1,5,10,16–18,27,31,33,36,40] use holistic features to construct the descriptor, and they are often more robust against different illumination and dynamic objects. Other works [6,14,22,23,32,34,38,41] try to let the network learn representative local features. Those learned descriptors are usually more robust against view-point changes comparing to learning on the whole image. PlaNet [39] is an exception since it does not learn a global or local image descriptor for metric learning but treats the image geolocalization problem as a classification problem.

One application of descriptor learning is the ground-to-aerial/satellite image retrieval [10,16,17,29,36,40]. Due to the superior representative capability of learned features, [40] proposes to reuse pre-existing CNNs for extracting ground-level image features, and then learn to predict such features from aerial images of the same location. They successfully used two separate CNNs to encode features from ground query images and aerial images, and matched them in feature space.

Cross-View Matching Network (CVM-Net) [10] has a two-branch CNN architecture to encode features from ground images and satellite images separately. It incorporates two NetVLADs to transform the features into a common space. The final matching score of input pairs is given by the distance measurement of two NetVLAD descriptors.

In [29] the Spatial-Aware Feature Aggregation (SAFA) network was proposed, for cross-view image-based geo-localization. Notably, [29] introduces a polar transformation pre-processing step, that warps satellite images in order to reduce the domain gap with respect to ground images.

Still, all these representation learning approaches focused on the challenge of learning *globally* discriminative localization features, without considering in the training task that in practice a good localization prior can be obtained from GPS and temporal filtering. Our work addresses this gap.

3   Methodology

In this section, we first shortly describe the cross-view matching and feature learning tasks, then summarize the common triplet loss found in the baseline and related work, and then discuss our proposed changes to the loss.

3.1   Cross-View Matching Task

In the image matching approach, the objective is to select for a given query image from the vehicle the closest image from the gallery with known geographic coordinates. We here consider the cross-view matching problem, where the query G_q is a ground-level (possibly panoramic) camera image from the ego-vehicle, and the target dataset $\mathbf{S} = (S_1, S_2, \cdots)$ contains top-down satellite images of the mapped environment. Each satellite image here shows a fixed-sized square area of the Earth's surface with a fixed image resolution. We assume that the 2D geographic position of the center of an image S is known, and given by $\pi(S) \in \mathcal{R}^2$ in meters in the map's coordinate system.

Matching is done by using two learned functions $f(\cdot)$ and $g(\cdot)$ to respectively map the targets and query to an n-dimensional feature space, where the correct target is expected to have the shortest Euclidean distance to the query. In other words, to localize a given ground-based vehicle image G_q, the location $\widehat{p}$ of the best matched target $\widehat{S}$ is returned,

$$\widehat{S} = \mathrm{argmin}_{S \in \mathbf{S}} \, \|f(S) - g(G_q)\|_2, \qquad\qquad \widehat{p} = \pi(\widehat{S}). \qquad (1)$$

In practice, $f(\cdot)$ and $g(\cdot)$ are implemented as deep convolutional neural networks, and trained on training data with known pairs $\mathcal{X} = \{(S_1, G_1), (S_2, G_2), \cdots\}$. This task is typically addressed using the triplet loss.

3.2   Baseline Global Triplet Loss

We define $d_{i,j} = \|f(S_i) - g(G_j)\|_2$ as the Euclidean distance between satellite image S_i and ground image G_j in the embedding space. Ideally, the learned embedding minimizes the *positive* distance term $d_{i,i}$ between a correctly matched satellite (S_i) and ground (G_i) image pair. Meanwhile, it should maximize any *negative* distance term $d_{i,j}$ between a mismatched pair, i.e. where $i \neq j$. This objective is captured by the weighted soft-margin triplet loss, of which we can formulate two versions,

$$l_1(i, j) = \log(1 + e^{\gamma(d_{i,i} - d_{i,j})}), \qquad \text{(satellite-to-ground)} \qquad (2)$$

$$l_2(i, j) = \log(1 + e^{\gamma(d_{i,i} - d_{j,i})}), \qquad \text{(ground-to-satellite)} \qquad (3)$$

where γ is a scalar parameter to adjust the gradient of the loss. The two versions differ in whether we select a mismatched ground image, Eq. (2), or satellite image, Eq. (3), to form the negative term.

For a minibatch $\mathcal{B} = (P_1, P_2, ..., P_N) \subseteq \mathcal{X}$ of N pairs, the baseline implementation [29] computes the final loss as

$$\mathcal{L}(\mathcal{B}) = \frac{1}{2N(N-1)} \sum_{i=1}^{N} \sum_{j=1 \wedge j \neq i}^{N} l_1(i,j) + l_2(i,j). \tag{4}$$

These loss terms can be efficiently computed by performing the forward passes $f(S_i)$ and $g(G_i)$ only once for all samples, and then just computing N^2 Euclidean distances $d_{i,j}$ of all combinations i, j.

An important aspect of the baseline is that it selects minibatches from the training data by randomly shuffling *all* samples in each epoch, thus any two pairs are equally likely to co-occur in the batches, independently if their actual geographic coordinates are close together or far away. This triplet loss thus learns a *globally* discriminative representation.

3.3   Proposed Local Triplet Loss

In many outdoor localization applications, GNSS or temporal filtering can already provide a good estimate of the approximate location. We will assume that the worst-case error in this coarse prior describes a geospatial circle with max. radius of r meters, and more distant locations can be discard a-priori. This leads us to propose two effective but simple to implement adaptations to the original loss, namely *geo-distance weighted loss terms* and *local minibatches*.

Geo-Distance Weighted Loss Terms. We add a weighting term $w(i,j)$ to the triplet losses that adapts their contribution based on the Euclidean distance in meters between the two geographic positions $\pi(S_i)$ and $\pi(S_j)$,

$$l_1(i,j) = w(i,j) \cdot \log(1 + e^{\gamma(d_{i,i} - d_{i,j})}), \qquad \text{(satellite to ground)} \tag{5}$$

$$l_2(i,j) = w(i,j) \cdot \log(1 + e^{\gamma(d_{i,i} - d_{j,i})}). \qquad \text{(ground to satellite)} \tag{6}$$

We define the weighting term using hyperparameters r and σ in meters,

$$w(i,j) = \begin{cases} 0 & \text{iff } ||\pi(S_i) - \pi(S_j)||_2 > r \\ 1 - e^{-||\pi(S_i) - \pi(S_j)||_2^2 / (2\sigma^2)} & \text{otherwise.} \end{cases} \tag{7}$$

The weighting term considers two cases. First, it cancels any triplet term between pairs that are further away than the maximally assumed prior localization error, given by the maximum distance r in meters. Second, if the pairs are within the acceptable distance, a positive weight should be assigned, though we smoothly reduce the weight to zero if the samples are too close together. The smoothness of this reduction is controlled by σ, see Fig. 2a for an example.

We find that down-weighting the loss on geographically nearby samples is crucial to learn a good representation in densely populated data sets. For instance, consider pairs i and j with 1 m interval then without down-weighting the optimization requires both minimizing the embedding distance of positive match S_i and G_i, while maximizing the embedding distance of the almost identical satellite image S_j and ground image G_i leading to severe overfitting.

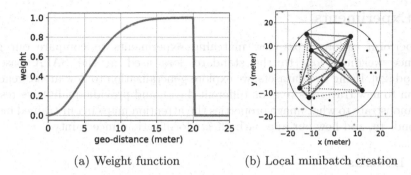

(a) Weight function   (b) Local minibatch creation

Fig. 2. (a) Weight function of Eq. (7), here shown as a function of geo-distance $||\pi(S_i) - \pi(S_j)||_2$ with $r = 20\,\mathrm{m}$ and $\sigma = 5\,\mathrm{m}$. (b) Example of generating a local minibatch of size 8. The black/red dots indicate geographic locations in/outside $\mathcal{N}_r$ of the first picked sample (dot in center). Thick dots mark samples picked for the batch. Edges between picked dots indicate the weight w: red for low weight, blue for high weight, and dashed edges for distances larger than r. (Color figure online)

Local Minibatches. Using the geo-distance weighted loss term, most randomly picked pairs from the training data would have zero weight as they are likely to be at distant geographic locations, especially when the mapped area is large. We therefore construct local minibatches that only contain pairs from nearby geographic locations, maximizing the impact of each sample per epoch:

1. pre-compute before training for each pair $P_i = (S_i, G_i)$ the local neighborhood of pairs within geographic radius of r meters, i.e.

$$\mathcal{N}_r(i) = \{(S_j, G_j) \mid i \neq j \land ||\pi(S_i) - \pi(S_j)||_2 \leq r\} \subset \mathcal{X}. \qquad (8)$$

2. At the start of an epoch, create a fresh set $\tilde{\mathcal{X}}$ containing all training samples, $\tilde{\mathcal{X}} \leftarrow \mathcal{X}$, representing the still unused samples in this epoch.
3. To create a new minibatch $\mathcal{B}$ of size N, first randomly pick a pair P_i from pool $\tilde{\mathcal{X}}$, and then uniformly pick without replacement the remaining $N-1$ samples from the neighborhood set $\mathcal{N}_r(i)$. All picked samples are removed from the epoch's pool, $\tilde{\mathcal{X}} \leftarrow \tilde{\mathcal{X}}/\mathcal{B}$. Once $\tilde{\mathcal{X}}$ is empty, a new epoch is started.

Note that overall each pair occurs in *at most* one minibatch per epoch, and pairs without enough neighbors will not be used. Since all pairs j in the batch are per definition within distance r from the first sampled pair i, two samples j and j' in the minibatch can be *at most* a distance of $2r$ meters geographically apart. Our local minibatch formulation thus maximizes the chance that many pairs in the minibatch are also within each other's r-meter radius, and thus minimizes the chance of near-zero geo-distance weighted loss terms, see Fig. 2b for an example. Contrast this to the standard minibatches, where the maximum distance is bounded by the geographic size of the mapped area, which is potentially several orders of magnitude larger than $2r$ meters.

4   Experiments

We perform various cross-view matching experiments to compare our geo-distance weighted loss to the standard loss used in the SAFA baseline method [29]. Using two datasets, we explore generalization to new areas, generalization to new traversals (e.g. on different days), and provide qualitative results to demonstrate to what image properties the attention maps in our trained model responds to, and how our approach affects localization uncertainty.

4.1   Datasets

We will first review our two adapted and novel localization benchmarks.

CVACT Dataset: CVACT [17] is a large cross-view dataset with GPS footprint for image retrieval. It contains 35532 ground panorama-and-satellite image pairs, denoted as CVACT_train, and 92802 pairs as CVACT_test. Notably, the validation set CVACT_val of 8884 pairs is a subset of CVACT_test, and [29] reported their quantitative results on the CVACT_val rather than CVACT_test. We will not directly follow the data split in [17,29] since CVACT_val is rather sparse and distributed over too large an area, which we found trivialized localization with a prior too much as it discarded all negative samples. Furthermore, we only split the ground images into training, validation and test set, and follow the target use-case where all satellite images are available during training.

The overview of our data split is shown in Fig. 3a. In total, there are 128334 satellite images and the number of ground images is 86469, 21249 and 20616 in training, validation and test set respectively. The data is relatively sparse, using a localization prior of $r = 100$ m most samples having between 25 and 100 other pairs in their local neighborhood.

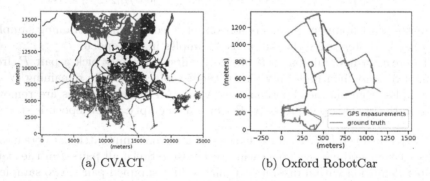

(a) CVACT   (b) Oxford RobotCar

Fig. 3. (a) Our used CVACT train (blue)/validation (green)/test (red) data splits. (b) One traversal from Oxford RobotCar, with raw GPS (red) and ground truth RTK (green). Raw GPS can have large errors over extended periods. (Color figure online)

Oxford RobotCar Dataset: Oxford RobotCar [19,20] is a dataset targeted at autonomous driving which contains images, LiDAR measurements and GPS recordings under different lighting and weather conditions collected over a year over multiple traversals in the Oxford region. The ground truth location is acquired via GPS-RTK. We note that the recordings reveal the limitations of raw GNSS/GPS and the necessity of our research. As shown from a sample traversal in Fig. 3b, the raw GPS error can reach 50 m. This highlights the practical application of our proposed approach as a refining step on the inaccurate GNSS/GPS measurements.

The dataset has not been used for cross-view image matching-based localization, as it does not contain satellite/aerial images. To construct a novel benchmark we collected 600 × 600 pixel satellite images at zoom level 20 (∼0.0924 m per pixel) from Google Maps Static API[1] for each ground front-viewing image. For now, we do not target the most extreme lighting and weather condition and select the traversals recorded in day time with label "sun" or "overcast" and which contain both raw GPS and accurate RTK localization measurements. In the dataset the front-viewing images are taken at 16 Hz. To make sure the consecutive ground images do not look too similar in appearance, we sample the images to make sure there is at least 5 m between two consecutive frames in each traversal. Finally, we acquire the corresponding satellite images centered at the ground truth locations to formulate the ground-to-satellite pairs. In total we acquire 23554 pairs from 13 traversals. We always keep all the satellite images, and use the ground image from 11 traversals as the training set (19707), 1 traversal as the validation set (1953), and 1 traversal as the test set (1894). In this dense dataset, almost all images have more than 200 pairs in a $r = 50$ m neighborhood. Some example ground and satellite pairs are shown in Fig. 4.

4.2 Network Architecture and Implementation Details

In our experiments we apply our new loss to the baseline SAFA method for cross-view matching of ground images to a map of satellite images [29]. We here shortly discuss pre-processing, and the neural network architectures for the functions $g(\cdot)$ and $f(\cdot)$ from Eq. (1).[2]

First, when the ground images are 360° panoramic views, as is the case for the CVACT dataset, [29] proposed to use a polar image transformation as a pre-processing step on the satellite images, as this can make the two image domains more similar, and simplifies the learning task for the network somewhat. In our experiments on CVACT, we will use these pre-processed images too.

Second, the networks $f(\cdot)$ and $g(\cdot)$ are both structured the same. Each network starts with the first 16 layers of a VGG network as feature extractor, and the extracted features are then input into the 8 separate spatial-aware position embedding modules [29], the results of which are concatenated resulting in a 4096-length descriptor in the shared space of $f(\cdot)$ and $g(\cdot)$. During training, both networks are optimized jointly without weight sharing.

---

[1] https://developers.google.com/maps/documentation/maps-static/dev-guide.

[2] Code of our implementation is available at https://github.com/tudelft-iv/Visual-Localization-with-Spatial-Prior.

(a)   (b)   (c)   (d)

Fig. 4. Four sample pairs in the proposed Oxford RobotCar cross-view localization benchmark to highlight some local and global differences. (a) and (b) are 5 m apart, (c) and (d) are 20 m apart. Ground images are from different traversals and recording days in the original dataset, resulting in variations in cars and lighting conditions. Note that the presence of a white road marking would be informative to globally discriminate between locations (a) and (c), but not to locally discriminate between (a) and (b), nor between (c) and (d).

We trained the baseline model on our proposed data split using the code released by the author of [29]. For our method, we do not change the baseline architecture but directly replace the loss with our proposed geo-distance weighted loss. Similar to [29], the VGG model is pre-trained on Imagenet [7]. For the triplet loss, γ is set to 10. Both models are trained with Adam optimizer [15]. On the CVACT dataset, we use a batch size of 16 for the baseline. Since some images do not have more than 15 neighbors, we use batch size of 4 for our model, and the learning rate is set to 10^{-5}. On the Oxford RobotCar dataset, the batch size is set 16. A learning rate of 5×10^{-5} works well for our model, but we find that a learning rate of 10^{-5} works better for the baseline. Due to the dense geospatial distribution of this dataset, many satellite images are very similar. We employ two strategies to combat overfitting. First, we use dropblock [8] with block size of 11 and keep probability of 0.8 for our method. We also tested this on the baseline but did not find that it improved its results. Second, we perform data augmentation by selecting for a query ground image a random satellite image at a small geospatial offsets of maximally 5 m radius for additional robustness.

4.3   Evaluation Metrics

For our main task we assume at test time a known (worst-case) prior localization error of radius r, and thus directly discard for both methods any false negatives beyond r meters of the true location. Still, for reference we also review the case when no such prior would be available (i.e. an *infinite* test radius).

The recall@1 is our main quantitative metric. The reported percentage indicates how often the top-1 retrieved satellite image exactly corresponds to the test query location. On the dense Oxford RobotCar dataset, we also report recall@x-meters, where any satellite image within that radius is counted as correct since these are nearly identical. Our maximal acceptable offset is $x = 5\,\mathrm{m}$, the same distance used to select the camera frames (see Sect. 4.1).

4.4 Experiment on CVACT Dataset

For the CVACT dataset, we use $r = 100\,\mathrm{m}$ as the localization prior for training our model, and testing. Both the baseline and our model are trained for 100 epochs, and we keep the best model for both according to validation split performance. Results are reported on the test split.

The test split is from a region not seen during training, hence the recall@1 is indicative how well the learned feature representation also generalizes to ground images in new areas. With a test radius of 100 m, recall@1 for our method is 74.0%, and for the baseline approach 65.0%, which demonstrates that our representation indeed exploits the availability of a localization prior. For reference, with an infinite test radius (no prior), our recall@1 is 54.5% compared to 58.4% for the baseline. As expected, in this case our model perform indeed somewhat worse than the globally trained baseline. Still, in real world applications where a prior is feasible, this suggests our model outperforms the baseline by 9% points.

To provide a more intuitive view of the difference of the behaviour of the baseline and our model, we visualized the location heat map of a given query using the similarity score provided by the models during inference. As shown in Fig. 5, our model is less certain outside the prior area, but it is capable to localize the image along a road, where the baseline shows high uncertainty.

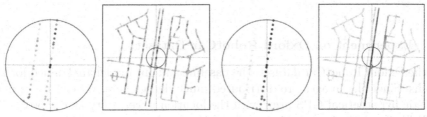

(a) Geo-local representation (ours)   (b) Geo-global representation (baseline)

Fig. 5. Example of localization heat maps on CVACT dataset. Each dot represents a satellite image and the ground truth location is indicated by the cross in the heat map. Darker colors indicate smaller embedding distance between the satellite images at those locations and the ground query taken at the center location. The circle indicates the local neighborhood with 100 m radius, the boxed image the surrounding 1 km² area. Within the local neighborhood, our approach results in a single peak, while the baseline distribution is more spread.

The advantage of our model comes from the geographically local representation it used. We verified this by comparing the encoded features from the baseline and our model. Similar to [29], we follow [42] to back-propagate the spatial embedding maps to the input image to show where the model extracts features from. As shown in Fig. 6, our model pays attention at poles and streetlights. Such objects are repeated at many different places but they are quite useful in distinguishing other images along this road. The baseline model, on the other hand, ignores these objects and pays more attention on the road structure, which is more useful in finding out the global location.

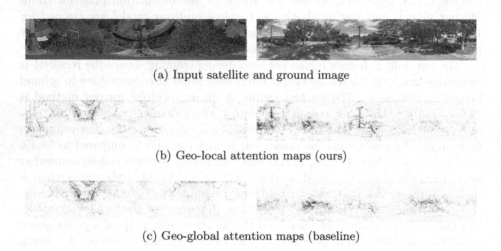

(a) Input satellite and ground image

(b) Geo-local attention maps (ours)

(c) Geo-global attention maps (baseline)

Fig. 6. Visualized back-propagated encoded feature [42] attention maps for two CVACT inputs. Saturated red/blue areas indicate strong positive/negative activation in the maps, bright areas indicate low absolute activation. (Color figure online)

4.5   Experiment on Oxford RobotCar Dataset

On the Oxford RobotCar dataset, the baseline and our model are trained for 200 epochs. Since the images are distributed much denser here, we can use a more realistic hypothetical GPS prior with the location uncertainty at $r = 50\,\mathrm{m}$.

Table 1 summarizes the image matching results. Our model surpasses the baseline by a large margin when tested with location prior of 50 m. The satellite images are densely distributed along the roads, and there are on average 26 satellite images within a 5 m neighborhood. Therefore our model can successfully locate over 99% of query ground images in the test split.

Surprisingly, our model also shows better result in recall@1, 1 m, 2 m, 3 m than the baseline without location prior. A possible reason is that images outside the prior area do not share common local features with the ground truth satellite images. Consequently, our model gains global localization ability with those prominent features. Besides, as seen in Fig. 7c, the localization uncertainty of the baseline approach barely benefits from discarded negatives outside the localization prior. This validates our original hypothesis that exploiting available localization priors during training directly improves the utility of the learnt representations.

Table 1. Recall comparison on Oxford RobotCar (best results in bold).

Test radius	50 m						Infinite (no prior)					
Recall@	1	1 m	2 m	3 m	4 m	5 m	1	1 m	2 m	3 m	4 m	5 m
Our method (%)	**8.9**	**54.7**	**78.0**	**89.3**	**95.1**	**99.2**	5.4	**34.1**	**46.6**	**52.4**	55.6	57.7
Baseline [29] (%)	2.4	22.3	35.9	47.3	56.2	70.2	2.4	22.3	35.9	47.3	**56.2**	**70.2**

Many image retrieval-based localization methods do not report a metric evaluation of their localization capability due to the sparsity of the datasets. We report the distance error of geolocation of the top-1 retrieved satellite image from our model and the baseline on the Oxford RobotCar dataset in Table 2. With 50 m location prior, our model achieved a median localization error of 0.86 m on the test split, which is 2.45 m lower than the baseline.

Table 2. Geo-distance error of top-1 result on Oxford RobotCar (best in bold).

Top1 distance	Median	80% quantile	90% quantile	95% quantile	Mean
Our method (meter)	**0.86**	**2.13**	**3.07**	**3.97**	**1.27**
Baseline [29] (meter)	3.31	5.44	6.74	9.63	3.62

To provide more intuition about how the baseline and our models work on this novel denser dataset, we visualized the localization heat map on the regular grid of satellite images in Fig. 7. In Fig. 7, the cross indicates the center of the circle, which is also the ground truth location. Notice that the ground truth location is always not on the grid point. The color means the probability of the query image located at that grid point. The darker the color the higher the probability. In most of cases, the baseline is quite discriminative globally, but has local uncertainty in around 20 m by 20 m area. For our model, although it has no global localization ability, it is more accurate in local area.

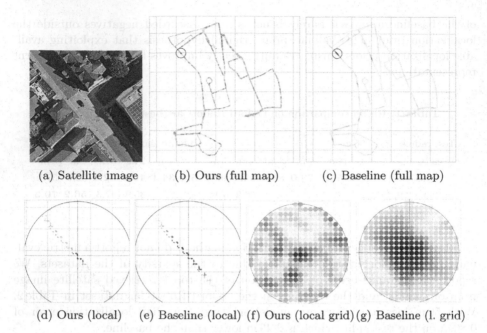

(a) Satellite image   (b) Ours (full map)   (c) Baseline (full map)

(d) Ours (local)   (e) Baseline (local) (f) Ours (local grid) (g) Baseline (l. grid)

Fig. 7. Example localization heat maps comparing our method to the baseline in the Oxford RobotCar benchmark, the circle marks the $r = 50\,\text{m}$ test radius around the query. In the heat maps, darker colors indicate smaller embedding distance between the satellite images at those locations and the ground query. (a) Satellite image of the query. (b), (c) Response to the full map. Our approach also shows matches outside the test radius, since those are ignored during training and testing. The baseline matches the same region as the coarse prior, adding little more information. (d), (e) Within the test radius, our method has less uncertainty. (d), (g) Matching satellite images at regular grid locations reveals the structure of the learned embedding in more detail.

5   Conclusions

Our experiments show that there is a clear quantitative and qualitative difference between learned image representations that must distinguish between either only geographically nearby locations, i.e. a 'geo-local' representation, or that must also distinguish between geographically distant locations, a 'geo-global' representation. While previous work only focused on learning geo-global representations, we have shown that a geo-local representation can already be obtained with easy to implement adjustments to the triplet loss. We find an improvement of 2.45 m and 2.35 m in terms of median and mean localization accuracy given a weak localization prior during inference. Our qualitative visualizations show that the proposed modifications result in different attention patterns. In particular, our method focuses on surrounding trees and lamp posts, which would be at distinct positions when moving only a few meters away. The baseline global approach instead focuses on the road layout that distinguishes distant map regions, but is less discriminative for nearby locations. The proposed geographic localized triplet loss is general, and in future work we will investigate how it affects other learned map representations.

Acknowledgements. This work is part of the research programme Efficient Deep Learning (EDL) with project number P16-25, which is (partly) financed by the Dutch Research Council (NWO).

References

1. Arandjelovic, R., Gronat, P., Torii, A., Pajdla, T., Sivic, J.: NetVLAD: CNN architecture for weakly supervised place recognition. In: Proceedings of the IEEE Conference on Computer Vision and Pattern Recognition, pp. 5297–5307 (2016)
2. Arandjelovic, R., Zisserman, A.: All about VLAD. In: Proceedings of the IEEE Conference on Computer Vision and Pattern Recognition, pp. 1578–1585 (2013)
3. Ben-Moshe, B., Elkin, E., Levi, H., Weissman, A.: Improving accuracy of GNSS devices in urban canyons. In: Proceedings of the Canadian Conference on Computational Geometry (2011)
4. Brahmbhatt, S., Gu, J., Kim, K., Hays, J., Kautz, J.: Geometry-aware learning of maps for camera localization. In: Proceedings of the IEEE Conference on Computer Vision and Pattern Recognition, pp. 2616–2625 (2018)
5. Chen, Z., et al.: Deep learning features at scale for visual place recognition. In: IEEE International Conference on Robotics and Automation, pp. 3223–3230 (2017)
6. Chen, Z., Maffra, F., Sa, I., Chli, M.: Only look once, mining distinctive landmarks from convnet for visual place recognition. In: IEEE/RSJ International Conference on Intelligent Robots and Systems, pp. 9–16 (2017)
7. Deng, J., Dong, W., Socher, R., Li, L.J., Li, K., Fei-Fei, L.: ImageNet: a large-scale hierarchical image database. In: IEEE Conference on Computer Vision and Pattern Recognition, pp. 248–255 (2009)
8. Ghiasi, G., Lin, T.Y., Le, Q.V.: DropBlock: a regularization method for convolutional networks. In: Advances in Neural Information Processing Systems, pp. 10727–10737 (2018)
9. Han, X., Leung, T., Jia, Y., Sukthankar, R., Berg, A.C.: MatchNet: unifying feature and metric learning for patch-based matching. In: Proceedings of the IEEE Conference on Computer Vision and Pattern Recognition, pp. 3279–3286 (2015)
10. Hu, S., Feng, M., Nguyen, R.M., Hee Lee, G.: CVM-Net: cross-view matching network for image-based ground-to-aerial geo-localization. In: Proceedings of the IEEE Conference on Computer Vision and Pattern Recognition, pp. 7258–7267 (2018)
11. Jégou, H., Douze, M., Schmid, C., Pérez, P.: Aggregating local descriptors into a compact image representation. In: IEEE Conference on Computer Vision and Pattern Recognition, pp. 3304–3311 (2010)
12. Jégou, H., Perronnin, F., Douze, M., Sánchez, J., Pérez, P., Schmid, C.: Aggregating local image descriptors into compact codes. IEEE Trans. Pattern Anal. Mach. Intell. **34**(9), 1704–1716 (2011)
13. Kendall, A., Grimes, M., Cipolla, R.: PoseNet: a convolutional network for real-time 6-DOF camera relocalization. In: Proceedings of the IEEE International Conference on Computer Vision, pp. 2938–2946 (2015)

14. Kim, H.J., Dunn, E., Frahm, J.M.: Learned contextual feature reweighting for image geo-localization. In: Proceedings of the IEEE Conference on Computer Vision and Pattern Recognition, pp. 3251–3260 (2017)
15. Kingma, D.P., Ba, J.: Adam: a method for stochastic optimization. In: International Conference on Learning Representations (2014)
16. Lin, T.Y., Cui, Y., Belongie, S., Hays, J.: Learning deep representations for ground-to-aerial geolocalization. In: Proceedings of the IEEE Conference on Computer Vision and Pattern Recognition, pp. 5007–5015 (2015)
17. Liu, L., Li, H.: Lending orientation to neural networks for cross-view geo-localization. In: Proceedings of the IEEE Conference on Computer Vision and Pattern Recognition, pp. 5624–5633 (2019)
18. Lopez-Antequera, M., Gomez-Ojeda, R., Petkov, N., Gonzalez-Jimenez, J.: Appearance-invariant place recognition by discriminatively training a convolutional neural network. Pattern Recogn. Lett. **92**, 89–95 (2017)
19. Maddern, W., Pascoe, G., Gadd, M., Barnes, D., Yeomans, B., Newman, P.: Real-time kinematic ground truth for the Oxford RobotCar dataset. arXiv preprint arXiv: 2002.10152 (2020)
20. Maddern, W., Pascoe, G., Linegar, C., Newman, P.: 1 year, 1000 km: the Oxford RobotCar dataset. Int. J. Robot. Res. **36**(1), 3–15 (2017)
21. Melekhov, I., Ylioinas, J., Kannala, J., Rahtu, E.: Image-based localization using hourglass networks. In: Proceedings of the IEEE International Conference on Computer Vision, pp. 879–886 (2017)
22. Naseer, T., Oliveira, G.L., Brox, T., Burgard, W.: Semantics-aware visual localization under challenging perceptual conditions. In: IEEE International Conference on Robotics and Automation, pp. 2614–2620 (2017)
23. Neubert, P., Protzel, P.: Beyond holistic descriptors, keypoints, and fixed patches: multiscale superpixel grids for place recognition in changing environments. IEEE Robot. Autom. Lett. **1**(1), 484–491 (2016)
24. Perronnin, F., Liu, Y., Sánchez, J., Poirier, H.: Large-scale image retrieval with compressed fisher vectors. In: IEEE Conference on Computer Vision and Pattern Recognition, pp. 3384–3391 (2010)
25. Philbin, J., Chum, O., Isard, M., Sivic, J., Zisserman, A.: Object retrieval with large vocabularies and fast spatial matching. In: IEEE Conference on Computer Vision and Pattern Recognition, pp. 1–8 (2007)
26. Sarlin, P.E., Cadena, C., Siegwart, R., Dymczyk, M.: From coarse to fine: robust hierarchical localization at large scale. In: Proceedings of the IEEE Conference on Computer Vision and Pattern Recognition, pp. 12716–12725 (2019)
27. Sarlin, P.E., Debraine, F., Dymczyk, M., Siegwart, R., Cadena, C.: Leveraging deep visual descriptors for hierarchical efficient localization. In: Conference on Robot Learning (2018)
28. Sattler, T., Zhou, Q., Pollefeys, M., Leal-Taixe, L.: Understanding the limitations of CNN-based absolute camera pose regression. In: Proceedings of the IEEE Conference on Computer Vision and Pattern Recognition, pp. 3302–3312 (2019)
29. Shi, Y., Liu, L., Yu, X., Li, H.: Spatial-aware feature aggregation for image based cross-view geo-localization. In: Advances in Neural Information Processing Systems, pp. 10090–10100. Curran Associates, Inc. (2019)
30. Sivic, J., Zisserman, A.: Video Google: a text retrieval approach to object matching in videos. In: Proceedings of the IEEE International Conference on Computer Vision, vol. 2, pp. 1470–1477 (2003)

31. Sünderhauf, N., Shirazi, S., Dayoub, F., Upcroft, B., Milford, M.: On the performance of convnet features for place recognition. In: IEEE/RSJ International Conference on Intelligent Robots and Systems, pp. 4297–4304 (2015)
32. Sünderhauf, N., et al.: Place recognition with convnet landmarks: viewpoint-robust, condition-robust, training-free. In: Robotics: Science and Systems XI, pp. 1–10 (2015)
33. Taira, H., et al.: InLoc: indoor visual localization with dense matching and view synthesis. In: Proceedings of the IEEE Conference on Computer Vision and Pattern Recognition, pp. 7199–7209 (2018)
34. Tian, Y., Chen, C., Shah, M.: Cross-view image matching for geo-localization in urban environments. In: Proceedings of the IEEE Conference on Computer Vision and Pattern Recognition, pp. 3608–3616 (2017)
35. Torii, A., Arandjelovic, R., Sivic, J., Okutomi, M., Pajdla, T.: 24/7 place recognition by view synthesis. In: Proceedings of the IEEE Conference on Computer Vision and Pattern Recognition, pp. 1808–1817 (2015)
36. Vo, N.N., Hays, J.: Localizing and orienting street views using overhead imagery. In: Leibe, B., Matas, J., Sebe, N., Welling, M. (eds.) ECCV 2016. LNCS, vol. 9905, pp. 494–509. Springer, Cham (2016). https://doi.org/10.1007/978-3-319-46448-0_30
37. Walch, F., Hazirbas, C., Leal-Taixe, L., Sattler, T., Hilsenbeck, S., Cremers, D.: Image-based localization using LSTMs for structured feature correlation. In: Proceedings of the IEEE International Conference on Computer Vision, pp. 627–637 (2017)
38. Weinzaepfel, P., Csurka, G., Cabon, Y., Humenberger, M.: Visual localization by learning objects-of-interest dense match regression. In: Proceedings of the IEEE Conference on Computer Vision and Pattern Recognition, pp. 5634–5643 (2019)
39. Weyand, T., Kostrikov, I., Philbin, J.: PlaNet - photo geolocation with convolutional neural networks. In: Leibe, B., Matas, J., Sebe, N., Welling, M. (eds.) ECCV 2016. LNCS, vol. 9912, pp. 37–55. Springer, Cham (2016). https://doi.org/10.1007/978-3-319-46484-8_3
40. Workman, S., Souvenir, R., Jacobs, N.: Wide-area image geolocalization with aerial reference imagery. In: Proceedings of the IEEE International Conference on Computer Vision, pp. 3961–3969 (2015)
41. Xin, Z., et al.: Localizing discriminative visual landmarks for place recognition. In: IEEE International Conference on Robotics and Automation, pp. 5979–5985 (2019)
42. Zeiler, M.D., Fergus, R.: Visualizing and understanding convolutional networks. In: Fleet, D., Pajdla, T., Schiele, B., Tuytelaars, T. (eds.) ECCV 2014. LNCS, vol. 8689, pp. 818–833. Springer, Cham (2014). https://doi.org/10.1007/978-3-319-10590-1_53
43. Zeisl, B., Sattler, T., Pollefeys, M.: Camera pose voting for large-scale image-based localization. In: Proceedings of the IEEE International Conference on Computer Vision, pp. 2704–2712 (2015)

W22 - Recovering 6D Object Pose

W22 - Recovering 6D Object Pose

The 6th International Workshop on Recovering 6D Object Pose (R6D 2020) was organized in conjunction with the European Conference on Computer Vision (ECCV 2020). The workshop was virtual and featured four invited talks, presentations of accepted workshop papers, and presentation of the BOP Challenge 2020 awards. The talks were given by Leonidas Guibas (Stanford University, USA), Dieter Fox (University of Washington and Nvidia, USA), Shuran Song (Columbia University, USA), and Stephen James (Imperial College London, UK). See the workshop website for details: http://cmp.felk.cvut.cz/sixd/workshop_2020/.

The workshop committee invited submissions of long papers of unpublished work (14 pages excluding references) and short papers documenting methods participating in the BOP Challenge 2020 (6 pages excluding references). Seven out of nine submitted long papers were accepted. Each long paper was reviewed by two to four reviewers, except the paper about the BOP Challenge 2020, which was written after the workshop. Two short papers were submitted, reviewed by the Workshop Committee, and both were accepted (one short paper is by König and Drost, the other by Liu et al.).

We would like to express our gratitude to authors of the submitted papers for moving the field forward, to the reviewers for their rigorous and swift work, and to the invited speakers for their high-quality talks.

August 2020

Tomáš Hodaň
Martin Sundermeyer
Rigas Kouskouridas
Tae-Kyun Kim
Jiří Matas
Carsten Rother
Vincent Lepetit
Ales Leonardis
Krzysztof Walas
Carsten Steger
Eric Brachmann
Bertram Drost
Juil Sock

BOP Challenge 2020 on 6D Object Localization

Tomáš Hodaň[1]($\boxtimes$), Martin Sundermeyer[2], Bertram Drost[3], Yann Labbé[4],
Eric Brachmann[5], Frank Michel[6], Carsten Rother[5], and Jiří Matas[1]

[1] Czech Technical University in Prague, Prague, Czech Republic
hodantom@cmp.felk.cvut.cz
[2] German Aerospace Center, Wessling, Germany
[3] MVTec, Munich, Germany
[4] INRIA Paris, Paris, France
[5] Heidelberg University, Heidelberg, Germany
[6] Technical University Dresden, Dresden, Germany

Abstract. This paper presents the evaluation methodology, datasets, and results of the BOP Challenge 2020, the third in a series of public competitions organized with the goal to capture the status quo in the field of 6D object pose estimation from an RGB-D image. In 2020, to reduce the domain gap between synthetic training and real test RGB images, the participants were 350K photorealistic training images generated by BlenderProc4BOP, a new open-source and light-weight physically-based renderer (PBR) and procedural data generator. Methods based on deep neural networks have finally caught up with methods based on point pair features, which were dominating previous editions of the challenge. Although the top-performing methods rely on RGB-D image channels, strong results were achieved when only RGB channels were used at both training and test time – out of the 26 evaluated methods, the third method was trained on RGB channels of PBR and real images, while the fifth on RGB channels of PBR images only. Strong data augmentation was identified as a key component of the top-performing CosyPose method, and the photorealism of PBR images was demonstrated effective despite the augmentation. The online evaluation system stays open and is available on the project website: bop.felk.cvut.cz.

1 Introduction

Estimating the 6D pose, *i.e.* the 3D translation and 3D rotation, of rigid objects from a single input image is a crucial task for numerous application fields such as robotic manipulation, augmented reality, or autonomous driving. The BOP[1] Challenge 2020 is the third in a series of public challenges that are part of the

---

[1] BOP stands for Benchmark for 6D Object Pose Estimation [25].

Electronic supplementary material The online version of this chapter (https://doi.org/10.1007/978-3-030-66096-3_39) contains supplementary material, which is available to authorized users.

A. Bartoli and A. Fusiello (Eds.): ECCV 2020 Workshops, LNCS 12536, pp. 577–594, 2020.
https://doi.org/10.1007/978-3-030-66096-3_39

BOP project aiming to continuously report the state of the art in 6D object pose estimation. The first challenge was organized in 2017 [26] and the results were published in [25]. The second challenge from 2019 [22] and the third from 2020 share the same evaluation methodology and leaderboard and the results from both are included in this paper.

Participating methods are evaluated on the 6D object localization task [24], where the methods report their predictions on the basis of two sources of information. Firstly, at training time, a method is given 3D object models and training images showing the objects in known 6D poses. Secondly, at test time, the method is provided with a test image and a list of object instances visible in the image, and the goal of the method is to estimate 6D poses of the listed object instances. The training and test images consist of RGB-D (aligned color and depth) channels and the intrinsic camera parameters are known.

The challenge primarily focuses on the practical scenario where no real images are available at training time, only the 3D object models and images synthesized using the models. While capturing real images of objects under various conditions and annotating the images with 6D object poses requires a significant human effort [23], the 3D models are either available before the physical objects, which is often the case for manufactured objects, or can be reconstructed at an admissible cost. Approaches for reconstructing 3D models of opaque, matte and moderately specular objects are well established [39] and promising approaches for transparent and highly specular objects are emerging [14, 42, 52].

In the BOP Challenge 2019, methods using the depth image channel, which were mostly based on the point pair features (PPF's) [10], clearly outperformed methods relying only on the RGB channels, all of which were based on deep neural networks (DNN's). The PPF-based methods match pairs of oriented 3D points between the point cloud[2] of the test scene and the 3D object model, and aggregate the matches via a voting scheme. As each pair is described by only the distance and relative orientation of the two points, PPF-based methods can be effectively trained directly on the 3D object models, without the need to synthesize any training images. In contrast, DNN-based methods require large amounts of annotated training images, which have been typically obtained by OpenGL rendering of the 3D object models on top of random backgrounds [11, 19, 31, 43]. However, as suggested in [29], the evident domain gap between these "render & paste" training images and real test images presumably limits the potential of the DNN-based methods.

To reduce the gap between the synthetic and real domains and thus to bring fresh air to the DNN-based methods, we have created BlenderProc4BOP [6,7], an open-source and light-weight physically-based renderer (PBR). Furthermore, to reduce the entry barrier of the challenge and to standardize the training set, the participants were provided 350K pre-rendered PBR images (Fig. 1).

In 2020, the DNN-based methods have finally caught up with the PPF-based methods – five methods outperformed Vidal-Sensors18 [51], the PPF-based winner from 2017 and 2019. Three of the top five methods, including the top-

---

[2] The point cloud is calculated from the depth channel and known camera parameters.

Commonly used "render & paste" synthetic training images

Photorealistic training images rendered by BlenderProc4BOP [7,6]

Fig. 1. Synthetic training images. DNN-based methods for 6D object pose estimation have been commonly trained on "render & paste" images synthesized by OpenGL rendering of 3D object models randomly positioned on top of random backgrounds. Instead, participants of the BOP Challenge 2020 were 350K photorealistic training images synthesized by ray tracing and showing the 3D object models in physically plausible poses inside a cube with a random PBR material (see Sect. 3.2).

performing one, are single-view variants of CosyPose, a DNN-based method by Labbé *et al.* [33]. Strong data augmentation, similar to [49], was identified as one of the key ingredients of this method. The second is a hybrid DNN+PPF method by König and Drost [32], and the fourth is Pix2Pose, a DNN-based method by Park *et al.* [40]. The first two methods used RGB-D image channels, while the third method achieved strong results with RGB channels only.

Methods achieved noticeably higher accuracy scores when trained on PBR training images than when trained on "render & paste" images. Although adding real training images yielded even higher scores, competitive results were achieved with PBR images only – out of the 26 evaluated methods, the fifth was trained only on PBR images. Interestingly, the increased photorealism from PBR images led to clear improvements of also the CosyPose method, despite the strong data augmentation which this method applies to the training images.

The rest of the paper is organized as follows. Section 2 defines the evaluation methodology, Sect. 3 introduces datasets and the implemented approach to synthesize photorealistic training images, Sect. 4 describes the experimental setup and analyzes the results, Sect. 5 presents the awards of the BOP Challenge 2020, and Sect. 6 concludes the paper. A discussion on the choices made when defining the evaluation methodology is provided in the supplement.

2   Evaluation Methodology

The evaluation methodology detailed in this section defines the challenge task, functions to measure the error of a 6D pose estimate, and calculation of the accuracy score used to compare the evaluated methods. The BOP Challenge 2020 follows the same evaluation methodology as the BOP Challenge 2019 – the scores have not been saturated and following the same methodology allowed using results from 2019 as baselines in 2020.

2.1   Task Definition

Methods are evaluated on the task of 6D localization of a varying number of instances of a varying number of objects from a single RGB-D image. This variant of the 6D object localization task is referred to as ViVo and defined as:

Training Input: For each object with an index $o \in \{1,\ldots,k\}$, a method is given a 3D mesh model of the object (typically with a color texture) and a set of synthetic or real RGB-D images showing instances of the object in known 6D poses. The method may use any of the image channels.

Test Input: The method is provided with an image I and a list $L = [(o_1,n_1),\ldots,(o_m,n_m)]$, where n_i is the number of instances of the object o_i present in I.

Test Output: The method produces a list $E = [E_1,\ldots,E_m]$, where E_i is a list of n_i pose estimates for instances of the object o_i. Each estimate is given by a 3×3 rotation matrix $\mathbf{R}$, a 3×1 translation vector $\mathbf{t}$, and a confidence score s. The matrix $\mathbf{P} = [\mathbf{R}|\mathbf{t}]$ defines a rigid transformation from the 3D coordinate system of the object model to the 3D coordinate system of the camera.

Note that in the first challenge from 2017 [25,26], methods were evaluated on a simpler variant of the 6D object localization task – the goal was to estimate the 6D pose of a single instance of a single object (this variant is referred to as SiSo). If multiple instances of the same object model were visible in the image, then the pose of an arbitrary instance may have been reported. In 2017, the simpler SiSo variant was chosen because it allowed to evaluate all relevant methods out of the box. Since then, the state of the art has advanced and we have moved to the more challenging ViVo variant.

2.2   Pose-Error Functions

The error of an estimated pose $\hat{\mathbf{P}}$ with respect to the ground-truth pose $\bar{\mathbf{P}}$ of an object model M is measured by three pose-error functions. The functions are defined below and discussed in more detail in the supplement.

VSD (Visible Surface Discrepancy):

$$e_{\mathrm{VSD}}(\hat{D},\bar{D},\hat{V},\bar{V},\tau) = \mathrm{avg}_{p\in\hat{V}\cup\bar{V}} \begin{cases} 0 & \text{if } p \in \hat{V}\cap\bar{V} \wedge |\hat{D}(p)-\bar{D}(p)| < \tau \\ 1 & \text{otherwise} \end{cases} \tag{1}$$

The symbols $\hat{D}$ and $\bar{D}$ denote distance maps[3] obtained by rendering the object model M in the estimated pose $\hat{\mathbf{P}}$ and the ground-truth pose $\bar{\mathbf{P}}$ respectively. These distance maps are compared with the distance map D_I of the test image I to obtain the visibility masks $\hat{V}$ and $\bar{V}$, *i.e.* sets of pixels where the model M is visible in the image I. The parameter τ is a misalignment tolerance.

Compared to [24,25], estimation of the visibility masks has been modified – an object is now considered visible at pixels with no depth measurements. This modification allows evaluating poses of glossy objects from the ITODD dataset [9] whose surface is not always captured in the depth image channel.

VSD treats poses that are indistinguishable in shape (color is not considered) as equivalent by measuring the misalignment of only the visible part of the object surface. See Sect. 2.2 of [25] and the supplement of this paper for details.

MSSD (Maximum Symmetry-Aware Surface Distance)

$$e_{\mathrm{MSSD}}(\hat{\mathbf{P}},\bar{\mathbf{P}},S_M,V_M) = \min_{\mathbf{S}\in S_M}\max_{\mathbf{x}\in V_M}\left\|\hat{\mathbf{P}}\mathbf{x} - \bar{\mathbf{P}}\mathbf{S}\mathbf{x}\right\|_2 \qquad (2)$$

The set S_M contains global symmetry transformations of the object model M, identified as described in Sec. 2.3, and V_M is a set of the model vertices.

The maximum distance between the model vertices is relevant for robotic manipulation, where the maximum surface deviation strongly indicates the chance of a successful grasp. Moreover, compared to the average distance used in pose-error functions ADD and ADI [18,24], the maximum distance is less dependent on the geometry of the object model and the sampling density of its surface.

MSPD (Maximum Symmetry-Aware Projection Distance)

$$e_{\mathrm{MSPD}}(\hat{\mathbf{P}},\bar{\mathbf{P}},S_M,V_M) = \min_{\mathbf{S}\in S_M}\max_{\mathbf{x}\in V_M}\left\|\mathrm{proj}(\hat{\mathbf{P}}\mathbf{x}) - \mathrm{proj}(\bar{\mathbf{P}}\mathbf{S}\mathbf{x})\right\|_2 \qquad (3)$$

The function proj(.) is the 2D projection (the result is in pixels) and the meaning of the other symbols is as in MSSD.

Compared to the pose-error function from [3], MSPD considers global object symmetries and replaces the average by the maximum distance to increase robustness against the geometry and sampling of the object model. Since MSPD does not evaluate the alignment along the optical (Z) axis and measures only the perceivable discrepancy, it is relevant for augmented reality applications and suitable for evaluating RGB-only methods, for which estimating the alignment along the optical axis is more challenging.

2.3   Identifying Global Object Symmetries

The set of global symmetry transformations of an object model M, which is used in the calculation of MSSD and MSPD, is identified in two steps. Firstly, a set of

---

[3] A distance map stores at a pixel p the distance from the camera center to a 3D point $\mathbf{x}_p$ that projects to p. It can be readily computed from the depth map which stores at p the Z coordinate of $\mathbf{x}_p$ and which is a typical output of Kinect-like sensors.

candidate symmetry transformations is defined as $S'_M = \{\mathbf{S} : h(V_M, \mathbf{S}V_M) < \varepsilon\}$, where h is the Hausdorff distance calculated between the vertices V_M of the object model M in the canonical and the transformed pose. The allowed deviation is bounded by $\varepsilon = \max(15\,\text{mm}, 0.1d)$, where d is the diameter of the object model M (the largest distance between any pair of vertices) and the truncation at 15 mm avoids breaking the symmetries by too small details. Secondly, the final set of symmetry transformations S_M is defined as a subset of S'_M which consists of those symmetry transformations that cannot be resolved by the model texture (decided subjectively by the organizers of the challenge).

The set S_M covers both discrete and continuous global rotational symmetries. The continuous rotational symmetries are discretized such as the vertex which is the furthest from the axis of symmetry travels not more than 1% of the object diameter between two consecutive rotations.

2.4   Accuracy Score

An estimated pose is considered correct with respect to a pose-error function e, if $e < \theta_e$, where $e \in \{e_{\text{VSD}}, e_{\text{MSSD}}, e_{\text{MSPD}}\}$ and θ_e is a threshold of correctness.

The fraction of annotated object instances for which a correct pose is estimated is referred to as Recall. The Average Recall with respect to a function e, denoted as AR_e, is defined as the average of Recall rates calculated for multiple settings of the threshold θ_e, and also for multiple settings of the misalignment tolerance τ in the case of e_{VSD}. In particular, AR_{VSD} is the average of Recall rates calculated for τ ranging from 5% to 50% of the object diameter with a step of 5%, and for θ_{VSD} ranging from 0.05 to 0.5 with a step of 0.05. AR_{MSSD} is the average of Recall rates calculated for θ_{MSSD} ranging from 5% to 50% of the object diameter with a step of 5%. Finally, AR_{MSPD} is the average of Recall rates calculated for θ_{MSPD} ranging from $5r$ to $50r$ with a step of $5r$, where $r = w/640$ and w is the image width in pixels.

The accuracy of a method on a dataset D is measured by $\text{AR}_D = (\text{AR}_{\text{VSD}} + \text{AR}_{\text{MSSD}} + \text{AR}_{\text{MSPD}})/3$. The overall accuracy on the core datasets is then measured by AR_{Core} defined as the average of the per-dataset AR_D scores. In this way, each dataset is treated as a separate sub-challenge which avoids AR_{Core} being dominated by larger datasets.

3   Datasets

BOP currently includes eleven datasets in a unified format, detailed in Table 1, seven of which were selected as core datasets. A method had to be evaluated on all core datasets to be considered for the main challenge awards (Sect. 5).

3.1   Content of Datasets

Each dataset is provided in a unified format and includes 3D object models and training and test RGB-D images annotated with ground-truth 6D object poses.

Table 1. Parameters of the BOP datasets. Most datasets include also training images obtained by OpenGL rendering of the 3D object models on a black background (not shown in the table). Extra PBR training images can be rendered by Blender-Proc4BOP [6,7]. If a dataset includes both validation and test images, the ground-truth annotations are public only for the validation images. All test images are real. Column "Test inst./All" shows the number of annotated object instances for which at least 10% of the projected surface area is visible in the test images. Columns "Used" show the number of test images and object instances used in the BOP Challenge 2019 & 2020.

Dataset	Core	Objects	Train. im.		Val im.	Test im.		Test inst.	
			Real	PBR	Real	All	Used	All	Used
LM [18]		15	–	50000	–	18273	3000	18273	3000
LM-O [3]	*	8	–	50000	–	1214	200	9038	1445
T-LESS [23]	*	30	37584	50000	–	10080	1000	67308	6423
ITODD [9]	*	28	–	50000	54	721	721	3041	3041
HB [30]	*	33	–	50000	4420	13000	300	67542	1630
YCB-V [53]	*	21	113198	50000	–	20738	900	98547	4123
RU-APC [45]		14	–	–	–	5964	1380	5964	1380
IC-BIN [8]	*	2	–	50000	–	177	150	2176	1786
IC-MI [50]		6	–	–	–	2067	300	5318	800
TUD-L [25]	*	3	38288	50000	–	23914	600	23914	600
TYO-L [25]		21	–	–	–	1670	1670	1670	1670

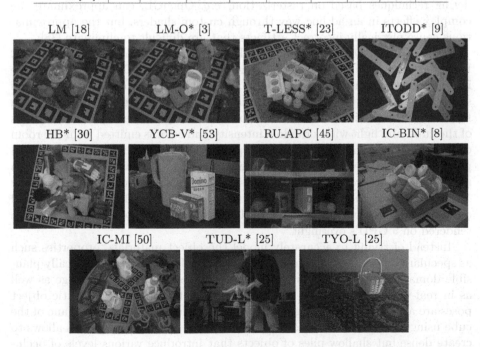

Fig. 2. An overview of the BOP datasets. The core datasets are marked with a star. Shown are RGB channels of sample test images which were darkened and overlaid with colored 3D object models in the ground-truth 6D poses.

The HB and ITODD datasets include also validation images – in this case, the ground-truth poses are publicly available only for the validation images, not for the test images. The object models were created manually or using KinectFusion-like systems for 3D surface reconstruction [39]. The seven core datasets include photorealistic training images described in Sect. 3.2. Datasets T-LESS, TUD-L, and YCB-V include real training images, and most datasets include also training images obtained by OpenGL rendering of the 3D object models on a black background. The test images were captured in scenes with graded complexity, often with clutter and occlusion. The datasets can be downloaded from: bop.felk.cvut.cz/datasets (Fig. 2).

3.2 Photorealistic Training Images

In the BOP Challenge 2020, the participants were provided 50K photorealistic training images for each of the seven core datasets. The images were generated and automatically annotated by BlenderProc4BOP [6,7], an open-source and light-weight physically-based renderer of procedurally generated scenes.

Physically-based rendering (PBR) accurately simulates the flow of light energy in the scene by ray tracing. This naturally accounts for complex illumination effects such as scattering, refraction and reflection, including diffuse and specular interreflection between the scene elements [41]. The rendered images look realistic and are often difficult to differentiate from real photographs. Rendering techniques based on rasterization, *e.g.* OpenGL, can approximate the complex effects in an ad hoc way through custom shaders, but the approximations cause physically incorrect artifacts that are difficult to eliminate [38].

BlenderProc4BOP implements a PBR synthesis approach similar to [29]. However, to improve efficiency, objects are not rendered in 3D models of complete indoor scenes but inside an empty cube, with objects from other BOP datasets serving as distractors. To achieve a rich spectrum of the generated images, a random PBR material from the CC0 Textures library [5] is assigned to the walls of the cube, and light with a random intensity and color is emitted from the room ceiling and from a randomly positioned point source. The number of rays traced per image pixel is set to 50 and the Intel Open Image Denoiser [1] is applied to reduce noise in the rendered image. This setup keeps the computational cost low – the full generation of one 640 × 480 RGB-D image takes **1–3 s** on a standard desktop computer with a modern GPU. A set 50K images can be therefore rendered on 5 GPU's overnight.

Instead of trying to accurately model the object materials, properties such as specularity, roughness and metallicness are randomized. Such physically plausible domain randomization is important since objects in the challenge as well as in real-world scenarios are typically not modeled perfectly. Realistic object poses are achieved by dropping the 3D object models on the ground plane of the cube using the PyBullet physics engine integrated in Blender [4]. This allows to create dense but shallow piles of objects that introduce various levels of occlusion. Since test images from the LM dataset show the objects always standing upright, the objects from LM are not dropped but instead densely placed on the ground plane in upright poses using automated collision checks.

Each object arrangement is rendered from 25 random camera poses. Instead of fitting all objects within the camera frustum, each camera is pointed at a randomly selected object close to the center, which allows generating more diverse camera poses. The azimuth angles, elevation angles, and distances of the cameras are uniformly sampled from ranges determined by the ground-truth 6D object poses from the test images. In-plane rotation angles are generated randomly.

The generated data (object poses, camera intrinsics, RGB and depth) is saved in the BOP format, allowing to interface with utilities from the BOP toolkit [27]. Configuration files to reproduce or modify the generation process are provided[4].

4   Evaluation

This section presents the results of the BOP Challenge 2020, compares them with the results from 2019, and analyzes the effectiveness of PBR training images.

4.1   Experimental Setup

Participants of the BOP Challenge 2020 were submitting the results of their methods to the online evaluation system at bop.felk.cvut.cz from June 5th, 2020, until the deadline on August 19th, 2020. The methods were evaluated on the ViVo variant of the 6D object localization task as described in Sect. 2. The evaluation script is publicly available in the BOP toolkit [27].

A method had to use a fixed set of hyper-parameters across all objects and datasets. For training, a method may have used the provided object models and training images, and rendered extra training images using the object models. However, not a single pixel of test images may have been used for training, nor the individual ground-truth poses or object masks provided for the test images. Ranges of the azimuth and elevation camera angles, and a range of the camera-object distances determined by the ground-truth poses from test images is the only information about the test set that may have been used for training.

Only subsets of test images were used to remove redundancies and speed up the evaluation, and only object instances for which at least 10% of the projected surface area is visible were to be localized in the selected test images.

4.2   Results

In total, 26 methods were evaluated on all seven core datasets. Results of 11 methods were submitted to the BOP Challenge 2019 and results of 15 methods to the BOP Challenge 2020 (column "Year" in Table 2).

In 2020, methods based on deep neural networks (DNN's) have finally caught up with methods based on point pair features (PPF's) [10] – five methods

---

[4] github.com/DLR-RM/BlenderProc/blob/master/README_BlenderProc4BOP.md.

Table 2. Results of the BOP Challenge 2019 and 2020. The methods are ranked by the AR_{Core} score (the third column of the upper table) which is the average of the per-dataset AR_D scores (the following seven columns). The scores are defined in Sect. 2.4. The last column of the upper table shows the average image processing time [s] averaged over the datasets. The lower table shows properties discussed in Sect. 4.

#	Method	Avg.	LM-O	T-LESS	TUD-L	IC-BIN	ITODD	HB	YCB-V	Time
1	CosyPose-ECCV20-Synt+Real-ICP [33]	69.8	71.4	70.1	93.9	64.7	31.3	71.2	86.1	13.74
2	König-Hybrid-DL-PointPairs [32]	63.9	63.1	65.5	92.0	43.0	48.3	65.1	70.1	0.63
3	CosyPose-ECCV20-Synt+Real [33]	63.7	63.3	72.8	82.3	58.3	21.6	65.6	82.1	0.45
4	Pix2Pose-BOP20_w/ICP-ICCV19 [40]	59.1	58.8	51.2	82.0	39.0	35.1	69.5	78.0	4.84
5	CosyPose-ECCV20-PBR [33]	57.0	63.3	64.0	68.5	58.3	21.6	65.6	57.4	0.47
6	Vidal-Sensors18 [51]	56.9	58.2	53.8	87.6	39.3	43.5	70.6	45.0	3.22
7	CDPNv2_BOP20-RGB-ICP [35]	56.8	63.0	46.4	91.3	45.0	18.6	71.2	61.9	1.46
8	Drost-CVPR10-Edges [10]	55.0	51.5	50.0	85.1	36.8	57.0	67.1	37.5	87.57
9	CDPNv2_BOP20-PBR-ICP [35]	53.4	63.0	43.5	79.1	45.0	18.6	71.2	53.2	1.49
10	CDPNv2_BOP20-RGB [35]	52.9	62.4	47.8	77.2	47.3	10.2	72.2	53.2	0.94
11	Drost-CVPR10-3D-Edges [10]	50.0	46.9	40.4	85.2	37.3	46.2	62.3	31.6	80.06
12	Drost-CVPR10-3D-Only [10]	48.7	52.7	44.4	77.5	38.8	31.6	61.5	34.4	7.70
13	CDPN_BOP19-RGB [35]	47.9	56.9	49.0	76.9	32.7	6.7	67.2	45.7	0.48
14	CDPNv2_BOP20-PBR [35]	47.2	62.4	40.7	58.8	47.3	10.2	72.2	39.0	0.98
15	leaping from 2D to 6D [37]	47.1	52.5	40.3	75.1	34.2	7.7	65.8	54.3	0.42
16	EPOS-BOP20-PBR [21]	45.7	54.7	46.7	55.8	36.3	18.6	58.0	49.9	1.87
17	Drost-CVPR10-3D-Only-Faster [10]	45.4	49.2	40.5	69.6	37.7	27.4	60.3	33.0	1.38
18	Félix&Neves-ICRA17-IET19 [46,44]	41.2	39.4	21.2	85.1	32.3	6.9	52.9	51.0	55.78
19	Sundermeyer-IJCV19+ICP [49]	39.8	23.7	48.7	61.4	28.1	15.8	50.6	50.5	0.86
20	Zhigang-CDPN-ICCV19 [35]	35.3	37.4	12.4	75.7	25.7	7.0	47.0	42.2	0.51
21	PointVoteNet2 [15]	35.1	65.3	0.4	67.3	26.4	0.1	55.6	30.8	-
22	Pix2Pose-BOP20-ICCV19 [40]	34.2	36.3	34.4	42.0	22.6	13.4	44.6	45.7	1.22
23	Sundermeyer-IJCV19 [49]	27.0	14.6	30.4	40.1	21.7	10.1	34.6	37.7	0.19
24	SingleMultiPathEncoder-CVPR20 [47]	24.1	21.7	31.0	33.4	17.5	6.7	29.3	28.9	0.19
25	Pix2Pose-BOP19-ICCV19 [40]	20.5	7.7	27.5	34.9	21.5	3.2	20.0	29.0	0.79
26	DPOD (synthetic) [54]	16.1	16.9	8.1	24.2	13.0	0.0	28.6	22.2	0.23

#	Method	Year	PPF	DNN	Train	...type	Test	Refine
1	CosyPose-ECCV20-Synt+Real-ICP [33]	2020	-	3/set	rgb	pbr+real	rgb-d	rgb+icp
2	König-Hybrid-DL-PointPairs [32]	2020	yes	1/set	rgb	syn+real	rgb-d	icp
3	CosyPose-ECCV20-Synt+Real [33]	2020	-	3/set	rgb	pbr+real	rgb	rgb
4	Pix2Pose-BOP20_w/ICP-ICCV19 [40]	2020	-	1/obj	rgb	pbr+real	rgb-d	icp
5	CosyPose-ECCV20-PBR [33]	2020	-	3/set	rgb	pbr	rgb	rgb
6	Vidal-Sensors18 [51]	2019	yes	-	-	-	d	icp
7	CDPNv2_BOP20-RGB-ICP [35]	2020	-	1/obj	rgb	pbr+real	rgb-d	icp
8	Drost-CVPR10-Edges [10]	2019	yes	-	-	-	rgb-d	icp
9	CDPNv2_BOP20-PBR-ICP [35]	2020	-	1/obj	rgb	pbr	rgb-d	icp
10	CDPNv2_BOP20-RGB [35]	2020	-	1/obj	rgb	pbr+real	rgb	-
11	Drost-CVPR10-3D-Edges [10]	2019	yes	-	-	-	d	icp
12	Drost-CVPR10-3D-Only [10]	2019	yes	-	-	-	d	icp
13	CDPN_BOP19-RGB [35]	2020	-	1/obj	rgb	pbr+real	rgb	-
14	CDPNv2_BOP20-PBR [35]	2020	-	1/obj	rgb	pbr	rgb	-
15	leaping from 2D to 6D [37]	2020	-	1/obj	rgb	pbr+real	rgb	-
16	EPOS-BOP20-PBR [21]	2020	-	1/set	rgb	pbr	rgb	-
17	Drost-CVPR10-3D-Only-Faster [10]	2019	yes	-	-	-	d	icp
18	Félix&Neves-ICRA17-IET19 [46,44]	2019	yes	1/set	rgb-d	syn+real	rgb-d	icp
19	Sundermeyer-IJCV19+ICP [49]	2019	-	1/obj	rgb	syn+real	rgb-d	icp
20	Zhigang-CDPN-ICCV19 [35]	2019	-	1/obj	rgb	syn+real	rgb	-
21	PointVoteNet2 [15]	2020	-	1/obj	rgb-d	pbr	rgb-d	icp
22	Pix2Pose-BOP20-ICCV19 [40]	2020	-	1/obj	rgb	pbr+real	rgb	-
23	Sundermeyer-IJCV19 [49]	2019	-	1/obj	rgb	syn+real	rgb	-
24	SingleMultiPathEncoder-CVPR20 [47]	2020	-	1/all	rgb	syn+real	rgb	-
25	Pix2Pose-BOP19-ICCV19 [40]	2019	-	1/obj	rgb	syn+real	rgb	-
26	DPOD (synthetic) [54]	2019	-	1/scene	rgb	syn	rgb	-

from 2020 outperformed Vidal-Sensors18 [51], the PPF-based winner of the first two challenges from 2017 and 2019 (columns "PPF" and "DNN" in Table 2). Almost all participating DNN-based methods applied neural networks only to the RGB image channels and many of these methods used the depth channel for ICP refinement at test time (columns "Train", "Test", and "Refine"). Only PointVoteNet2 [15] applied a neural network also to the depth channel. It is noteworthy that the overall third method does not use the depth channel at all.

Three of the top five methods, including the top-performing one, are single-view variants of the CosyPose method by Labbé *et al.* [33]. This method first predicts 2D bounding boxes of the objects using Mask R-CNN [16], and then applies to each box a DNN model for coarse pose estimation followed by a DNN model for iterative refinement. The top variant of CosyPose, with the AR_{Core} score of 69.8%, additionally applies a depth-based ICP refinement which improves the score by 6.1% (method #1 *vs.* #3 in Table 2). One of the key ingredients of CosyPose is a strong data augmentation technique similar to [48]. As reported in [33], using the augmentation for training the pose estimation models improves the accuracy on T-LESS from 37.0% to 63.8%. Access to a GPU cluster is also crucial as training of a model takes ~10 h on 32 GPU's.

The second is a hybrid method by König and Drost [32] with AR_{Core} of 63.9%. This method first predicts object instance masks by RetinaMask [12] or Mask R-CNN [16], whichever performs better on the validation set. Then, for each mask, the method selects the corresponding part of the 3D point cloud of the test scene, and estimates the object pose using the point pair features [10]. The method is noticeably faster than the top-performing CosyPose variant, mainly thanks to a highly optimized implementation of ICP from HALCON [2].

Another method which outperformed Vidal-Sensors18 is Pix2Pose by Park *et al.* [40] with AR_{Core} of 59.1%. This method predicts 2D-3D correspondences between densely sampled image pixels and the 3D object model, solves for the poses using the PnP-RANSAC algorithm, and refines the poses with a depth-based ICP algorithm. The ICP refinement is crucial for this method as it improves the AR_{Core} score by absolute 24.9% and teleports the method from the 22nd to the 4th place. The importance of a refinement stage has been demonstrated also by other methods – top nine methods applied ICP or an RGB-based refiner, similar to DeepIM [34] (column "Refine" in Table 2).

Training a special DNN model per object has been a common practise in the field, followed also by most participants of the challenge. However, the CosyPose and König-Hybrid-DL-PointPairs methods have shown that a single DNN model can be effectively shared among multiple objects (column "DNN" in Table 2). CosyPose trains three models per dataset – one for detection, one for coarse pose estimation, and one for iterative pose refinement, whereas König-Hybrid-DL-PointPairs trains only one model for instance segmentation.

4.3 The Effectiveness of Photorealistic Training Images

In 2020, most DNN-based methods were trained either only on the photorealistic (PBR) training images, or also on real training images which are available

Table 3. The effect of different training images. The table shows the AR_{Core} scores achieved by the CosyPose method [33] when different types of images were used for training its object detection (*i.e.* Mask R-CNN [16]) and pose estimation stage. The "render & paste v1" images were obtained by OpenGL rendering of the 3D object models on random real photographs. The "render & paste v2" images were obtained similarly, but the CAD models of T-LESS objects were assigned a random surface texture instead of a random gray value, the background of most images was assigned a synthetic texture, and 1M instead 50K images were generated. Interestingly, the increased photorealism brought by the PBR images yields noticeable improvements despite the strong data augmentation applied by CosyPose to the training images.

Detection	Pose estim.	T-LESS	TUD-L	YCB-V
PBR+Real	PBR+Real	72.8	82.3	82.1
PBR	PBR	64.0	68.5	57.4
PBR	Render & paste v1	16.1	60.4	44.9
PBR	Render & paste v2	60.0	58.9	58.5
Render & paste v1	Render & paste v1	6.1	49.5	26.5
Render & paste v2	Render & paste v2	45.3	42.4	25.7

in datasets T-LESS, TUD-L, and YCB-V (column "Train type" in Table 2)[5]. Although adding real training images yields higher scores (compare scores of methods #3 and #5 or #10 and #14 on T-LESS, TUD-L, and YCB-V in Table 2), competitive results can be achieved with PBR images only, as demonstrated by the overall fifth PBR-only variant of the CosyPose method. This is an important result considering that PBR-only training does not require any human effort for capturing and annotating real training images.

The PBR training images yield a noticeable improvement over the "render & paste" synthetic images obtained by OpenGL rendering of the 3D object models on real photographs. For example, the CDPN method with the same hyper-parameter settings improved by absolute 20.2% on HB, by 19.5% on LM-O, and by 7% on IC-BIN when trained on 50K PBR images per dataset *vs.* 10K "render & paste" images per object (compare methods #13 and #20 in Table 2). As shown in Table 3, the CosyPose method improved by a significant 57.9% (from 6.1% to 64.0%) on T-LESS, by 19.0% on TUD-L, and by 30.9% on YCB-V when trained on 50K PBR images per dataset *vs.* 50K "render & paste v1" images per dataset. The "render & paste v1" images used for training CosyPose were

---

[5] Method #2 used also synthetic training images obtained by cropping the objects from real validation images in the case of HB and ITODD and from OpenGL-rendered images in the case of other datasets, and pasting the cropped objects on images from the Microsoft COCO dataset [36]. Method #24 used PBR and real images for training Mask R-CNN [16] and OpenGL images for training a single Multi-path encoder. Two of the CosyPose variants (#1 and #3) also added the "render & paste" synthetic images provided in the original YCB-V dataset, but these images were later found to have no effect on the accuracy score.

obtained by imitating the PBR images, *i.e.* the 3D object models were rendered in the same poses as in the PBR images and pasted on real backgrounds.

As an additional experiment, we have trained the CosyPose method on another variant of the "render & paste" images, generated as in [33] and referred to as "render & paste v2". The main differences compared to the "render & paste v1" variant described in the previous paragraph are: (a) the CAD models of T-LESS objects were assigned a random surface texture instead of a random gray value, (b) the background was assigned a real photograph in 30% images and a synthetic texture in 70% images, and (c) 1M instead 50K images were generated. As shown in Table 3, "render & paste v2" images yield a noticeable improvement of 39.2% over "render & paste v1" on T-LESS, but no improvement on TUD-L (−7.1%) and YCB-V (−0.8%). This may suggest that randomizing the surface texture of the texture-less CAD models of T-LESS objects improves the generalization of the network by forcing the network to focus more on shape than on lower-level patterns, as found in [13]. When generating the PBR images, which yield the highest accuracy on T-LESS, the CAD models were assigned a random gray value, as in "render & paste v1", but the effect of randomizing the surface texture may have been achieved by randomizing the PBR material (Sect. 3.2) – further investigation is needed to clearly answer these questions. The importance of both the objects and the background being synthetic, as suggested in [20], has not been confirmed in this experiment – "render & paste v1" images with only real backgrounds achieved higher scores than "render & paste v2" images on TUD-L and YCB-V. However, the first ten convolutional layers of Mask R-CNN ("conv1" and "conv2_x" of ResNet-50 [17]) used for object detection in CosyPose were pre-trained on Microsoft COCO [36] but not fine-tuned, whereas all layers were fine-tuned in [20]. The benefit of having 1M *vs.* 50K images is indecisive since 50K PBR images were sufficient to achieve high scores.

Both types of "render & paste" images are far inferior compared to the PBR images, which yield an average improvement of 35.9% over "render & paste v1" and 25.5% over "render & paste v2" images (Table 3). Interestingly, the increased photorealism brought by the PBR images is important despite the strong data augmentation that CosyPose applies to the training images. Since object poses in the PBR and "render & paste v1" images are identical, the ray-tracing rendering technique, PBR materials and objects realistically embedded in synthetic environments seem to be the decisive factors for successful "sim2real" transfer [6].

We have also observed that the PBR images are more important for training DNN models for object detection/segmentation (*e.g.* Mask R-CNN [16]) than for training DNN models for pose estimation from the detected regions (Table 3). In the case of CosyPose, if the detection model is trained on PBR images and the later two models for pose estimation are trained on the "render & paste v2" instead of the PBR images, the accuracy drops moderately (64.0% to 60.0% on T-LESS, 68.5% to 58.9% on TUD-L) or does not change much (57.4% *vs.* 58.5% on YCB-V). However, if also the detection model is trained on the "render & paste v1" or "render & paste v2" images, the accuracy drops severely (the low accuracy achieved with "render & paste v1" on T-LESS was discussed earlier).

5   Awards

The following BOP Challenge 2020 awards were presented at the 6th Workshop on Recovering 6D Object Pose [28] organized in conjunction with the ECCV 2020 conference. Results on the core datasets are in Table 2 and results on the other datasets can be found on the project website.

The Overall Best Method (the top-performing method on the core datasets): CosyPose-ECCV20-Synt+Real-ICP by Yann Labbé, Justin Carpentier, Mathieu Aubry, and Josef Sivic [33].

The Best RGB-Only Method (the top-performing RGB-only method on the core datasets): CosyPose-ECCV20-Synt+Real by Yann Labbé, Justin Carpentier, Mathieu Aubry, and Josef Sivic [33].

The Best Fast Method (the top-performing method on the core datasets with the average running time per image below 1 s): König-Hybrid-DL-PointPairs by Rebecca König and Bertram Drost [32].

The Best BlenderProc4BOP-Trained Method (the top-performing method on the core datasets which was trained only with the provided Blender-Proc4BOP images): CosyPose-ECCV20-PBR by Yann Labbé, Justin Carpentier, Mathieu Aubry, and Josef Sivic [33].

The Best Single-Model Method (the top-performing method on the core datasets which uses a single machine learning model, typically a neural network, per dataset): CosyPose-ECCV20-Synt+Real-ICP by Yann Labbé, Justin Carpentier, Mathieu Aubry, and Josef Sivic [33].

The Best Open-Source Method (the top-performing method on the core datasets whose source code is publicly available): CosyPose-ECCV20-Synt+Real-ICP by Yann Labbé, Justin Carpentier, Mathieu Aubry, and Josef Sivic [33].

The Best Method on Datasets LM-O, TUD-L, IC-BIN, and YCB-V: CosyPose-ECCV20-Synt+Real-ICP by Yann Labbé, Justin Carpentier, Mathieu Aubry, and Josef Sivic [33].

The Best Method on Datasets ITODD and TYO-L: Drost-CVPR10-Edges by Bertram Drost, Markus Ulrich, Nassir Navab, and Slobodan Ilic [10].

The Best Method on Dataset LM: DPODv2 (synthetic train data, RGB + D Kabsch) by Sergey Zakharov, Ivan Shugurov, and Slobodan Ilic [54].

The Best Method on Dataset T-LESS: CosyPose-ECCV20-Synt+Real by Yann Labbé, Justin Carpentier, Mathieu Aubry, and Josef Sivic [33].

The Best Method on Dataset HB: CDPNv2_BOP20 (RGB-only) by Zhigang Li, Gu Wang, and Xiangyang Ji [35].

The Best Method on Dataset RU-APC: Pix2Pose-BOP19_w/ICP-ICCV19 by Kiru Park, Timothy Patten, and Markus Vincze [40].

The Best Method on Dataset IC-MI: Drost-CVPR10-3D-Only by Bertram Drost, Markus Ulrich, Nassir Navab, and Slobodan Ilic [10].

6   Conclusions

In 2020, methods based on neural networks have finally caught up with methods based on point pair features, which were dominating previous editions of the challenge. Although the top-performing methods rely on RGB-D image channels, strong results have been achieved with RGB channels only. The challenge results and additional experiments with the top-performing CosyPose method [33] have shown the importance of PBR training images and of strong data augmentation for successful "sim2real" transfer. The scores have not been saturated and we are already looking forward to the insights from the next challenge.

Acknowledgements. This research was supported by CTU student grant (SGS OHK3-019/20), Research Center for Informatics (CZ.02.1.01/0.0/0.0/16_019/0000765 funded by OP VVV), and HPC resources from GENCI-IDRIS (grant 011011181).

References

1. Intel Open Image Denoise (2020). https://www.openimagedenoise.org/
2. MVTec HALCON (2020). https://www.mvtec.com/halcon/
3. Brachmann, E., Krull, A., Michel, F., Gumhold, S., Shotton, J., Rother, C.: Learning 6D object pose estimation using 3D object coordinates. In: Fleet, D., Pajdla, T., Schiele, B., Tuytelaars, T. (eds.) ECCV 2014. LNCS, vol. 8690, pp. 536–551. Springer, Cham (2014). https://doi.org/10.1007/978-3-319-10605-2_35
4. Blender Online Community: Blender - a 3D modelling and rendering package (2018). http://www.blender.org
5. Demes, L.: CC0 textures (2020). https://cc0textures.com/
6. Denninger, M., et al.: BlenderProc: reducing the reality gap with photorealistic rendering. In: Robotics: Science and Systems (RSS) Workshops (2020)
7. Denninger, M., et al.: BlenderProc. arXiv preprint arXiv:1911.01911 (2019)
8. Doumanoglou, A., Kouskouridas, R., Malassiotis, S., Kim, T.K.: Recovering 6D object pose and predicting next-best-view in the crowd. In: CVPR (2016)
9. Drost, B., Ulrich, M., Bergmann, P., Hartinger, P., Steger, C.: Introducing MVTec ITODD - a dataset for 3D object recognition in industry. In: ICCVW (2017)
10. Drost, B., Ulrich, M., Navab, N., Ilic, S.: Model globally, match locally: efficient and robust 3D object recognition. In: CVPR (2010)
11. Dwibedi, D., Misra, I., Hebert, M.: Cut, paste and learn: surprisingly easy synthesis for instance detection. In: ICCV (2017)
12. Fu, C.Y., Shvets, M., Berg, A.C.: RetinaMask: learning to predict masks improves state-of-the-art single-shot detection for free. arXiv preprint arXiv:1901.03353 (2019)
13. Geirhos, R., Rubisch, P., Michaelis, C., Bethge, M., Wichmann, F.A., Brendel, W.: ImageNet-trained CNNs are biased towards texture; increasing shape bias improves accuracy and robustness. arXiv preprint arXiv:1811.12231 (2018)

14. Godard, C., Hedman, P., Li, W., Brostow, G.J.: Multi-view reconstruction of highly specular surfaces in uncontrolled environments. In: 3DV (2015)
15. Hagelskjær, F., Buch, A.G.: PointPoseNet: accurate object detection and 6 DOF pose estimation in point clouds. arXiv preprint arXiv:1912.09057 (2019)
16. He, K., Gkioxari, G., Dollár, P., Girshick, R.: Mask R-CNN. In: ICCV (2017)
17. He, K., Zhang, X., Ren, S., Sun, J.: Deep residual learning for image recognition. In: Proceedings of the IEEE Conference on Computer Vision and Pattern Recognition (2016)
18. Hinterstoisser, S., et al.: Model based training, detection and pose estimation of texture-less 3D objects in heavily cluttered scenes. In: Lee, K.M., Matsushita, Y., Rehg, J.M., Hu, Z. (eds.) ACCV 2012. LNCS, vol. 7724, pp. 548–562. Springer, Heidelberg (2013). https://doi.org/10.1007/978-3-642-37331-2_42
19. Hinterstoisser, S., Lepetit, V., Wohlhart, P., Konolige, K.: On pre-trained image features and synthetic images for deep learning. In: Leal-Taixé, L., Roth, S. (eds.) ECCV 2018. LNCS, vol. 11129, pp. 682–697. Springer, Cham (2019). https://doi.org/10.1007/978-3-030-11009-3_42
20. Hinterstoisser, S., Pauly, O., Heibel, H., Martina, M., Bokeloh, M.: An annotation saved is an annotation earned: using fully synthetic training for object detection. In: ICCVW (2019)
21. Hodaň, T., Baráth, D., Matas, J.: EPOS: estimating 6D pose of objects with symmetries. In: IEEE Conference on Computer Vision and Pattern Recognition (CVPR) (2020)
22. Hodaň, T., et al.: BOP challenge 2019 (2019). https://bop.felk.cvut.cz/media/bop_challenge_2019_results.pdf
23. Hodaň, T., Haluza, P., Obdržálek, Š., Matas, J., Lourakis, M., Zabulis, X.: T-LESS: an RGB-D dataset for 6D pose estimation of texture-less objects. In: IEEE Winter Conference on Applications of Computer Vision (WACV) (2017)
24. Hodaň, T., Matas, J., Obdržálek, Š.: On evaluation of 6D object pose estimation. In: Hua, G., Jégou, H. (eds.) ECCV 2016. LNCS, vol. 9915, pp. 606–619. Springer, Cham (2016). https://doi.org/10.1007/978-3-319-49409-8_52
25. Hodaň, T., et al.: BOP: benchmark for 6D object pose estimation. In: Ferrari, V., Hebert, M., Sminchisescu, C., Weiss, Y. (eds.) ECCV 2018. LNCS, vol. 11214, pp. 19–35. Springer, Cham (2018). https://doi.org/10.1007/978-3-030-01249-6_2
26. Hodaň, T., Michel, F., Sahin, C., Kim, T.K., Matas, J., Rother, C.: SIXD challenge 2017 (2017). http://cmp.felk.cvut.cz/sixd/challenge_2017/
27. Hodaň, T., Sundermeyer, M.: BOP toolkit (2020). https://github.com/thodan/bop_toolkit
28. Hodaň, T., et al.: 6th International Workshop on Recovering 6D Object Pose (2020). http://cmp.felk.cvut.cz/sixd/workshop_2020/
29. Hodaň, T., et al.: Photorealistic image synthesis for object instance detection. In: IEEE International Conference on Image Processing (ICIP) (2019)
30. Kaskman, R., Zakharov, S., Shugurov, I., Ilic, S.: HomebrewedDB: RGB-D dataset for 6D pose estimation of 3D objects. In: ICCVW (2019)
31. Kehl, W., Manhardt, F., Tombari, F., Ilic, S., Navab, N.: SSD-6D: making RGB-based 3D detection and 6D pose estimation great again. In: ICCV (2017)
32. Koenig, R., Drost, B.: A hybrid approach for 6DoF pose estimation. In: Bartoli, A., Fusiello, A. (eds.) ECCV 2020 Workshops. LNCS, vol. 12536, pp. 700–706. Springer, Cham (2020)

33. Labbé, Y., Carpentier, J., Aubry, M., Sivic, J.: CosyPose: consistent multi-view multi-object 6D pose estimation. In: Vedaldi, A., Bischof, H., Brox, T., Frahm, J.M. (eds.) ECCV 2020. LNCS, vol. 12362, pp. 574–591. Springer, Cham (2020). https://doi.org/10.1007/978-3-030-58520-4_34

34. Li, Y., Wang, G., Ji, X., Xiang, Yu., Fox, D.: DeepIM: deep iterative matching for 6D pose estimation. In: Ferrari, V., Hebert, M., Sminchisescu, C., Weiss, Y. (eds.) ECCV 2018. LNCS, vol. 11210, pp. 695–711. Springer, Cham (2018). https://doi.org/10.1007/978-3-030-01231-1_42

35. Li, Z., Wang, G., Ji, X.: CDPN: coordinates-based disentangled pose network for real-time RGB-based 6-DoF object pose estimation. In: ICCV (2019)

36. Lin, T.-Y., et al.: Microsoft COCO: common objects in context. In: Fleet, D., Pajdla, T., Schiele, B., Tuytelaars, T. (eds.) ECCV 2014. LNCS, vol. 8693, pp. 740–755. Springer, Cham (2014). https://doi.org/10.1007/978-3-319-10602-1_48

37. Liu, J., Zou, Z., Ye, X., Tan, X., Ding, E., Xu, F., Yu, X.: Leaping from 2D detection to efficient 6DoF object pose estimation. In: Bartoli, A., Fusiello, A. (eds.) ECCV 2020. LNCS, vol. 12536, pp. 1–11. Springer, Cham (2020)

38. Marschner, S., Shirley, P.: Fundamentals of Computer Graphics. CRC Press, Boca Raton (2015)

39. Newcombe, R.A., et al.: KinectFusion: real-time dense surface mapping and tracking. In: ISMAR (2011)

40. Park, K., Patten, T., Vincze, M.: Pix2Pose: pixel-wise coordinate regression of objects for 6D pose estimation. In: ICCV (2019)

41. Pharr, M., Jakob, W., Humphreys, G.: Physically Based Rendering: From Theory to Implementation. Morgan Kaufmann, Burlington (2016)

42. Qian, Y., Gong, M., Hong Yang, Y.: 3D reconstruction of transparent objects with position-normal consistency. In: CVPR (2016)

43. Rad, M., Lepetit, V.: BB8: a scalable, accurate, robust to partial occlusion method for predicting the 3D poses of challenging objects without using depth. In: ICCV (2017)

44. Raposo, C., Barreto, J.P.: Using 2 point+normal sets for fast registration of point clouds with small overlap. In: ICRA (2017)

45. Rennie, C., Shome, R., Bekris, K.E., De Souza, A.F.: A dataset for improved RGBD-based object detection and pose estimation for warehouse pick-and-place. RA-L 1(2), 1179–1185 (2016)

46. Rodrigues, P., Antunes, M., Raposo, C., Marques, P., Fonseca, F., Barreto, J.: Deep segmentation leverages geometric pose estimation in computer-aided total knee arthroplasty. Healthc. Technol. Lett. 6(6), 226–230 (2019)

47. Sundermeyer, M., et al.: Multi-path learning for object pose estimation across domains. In: CVPR (2020)

48. Sundermeyer, M., Marton, Z.-C., Durner, M., Brucker, M., Triebel, R.: Implicit 3D orientation learning for 6D object detection from RGB images. In: Ferrari, V., Hebert, M., Sminchisescu, C., Weiss, Y. (eds.) ECCV 2018. LNCS, vol. 11210, pp. 712–729. Springer, Cham (2018). https://doi.org/10.1007/978-3-030-01231-1_43

49. Sundermeyer, M., Marton, Z.C., Durner, M., Triebel, R.: Augmented autoencoders: implicit 3D orientation learning for 6D object detection. IJCV 128, 714–729 (2019). https://doi.org/10.1007/s11263-019-01243-8

50. Tejani, A., Tang, D., Kouskouridas, R., Kim, T.-K.: Latent-class hough forests for 3D object detection and pose estimation. In: Fleet, D., Pajdla, T., Schiele, B., Tuytelaars, T. (eds.) ECCV 2014. LNCS, vol. 8694, pp. 462–477. Springer, Cham (2014). https://doi.org/10.1007/978-3-319-10599-4_30

51. Vidal, J., Lin, C.Y., Lladó, X., Martí, R.: A method for 6D pose estimation of free-form rigid objects using point pair features on range data. Sensors **18**, 2678 (2018)
52. Wu, B., Zhou, Y., Qian, Y., Cong, M., Huang, H.: Full 3D reconstruction of transparent objects. ACM TOG **37**, 1–11 (2018)
53. Xiang, Y., Schmidt, T., Narayanan, V., Fox, D.: PoseCNN: a convolutional neural network for 6D object pose estimation in cluttered scenes. In: RSS (2018)
54. Zakharov, S., Shugurov, I., Ilic, S.: DPOD: 6D pose object detector and refiner. In: ICCV (2019)

StructureFromGAN: Single Image 3D Model Reconstruction and Photorealistic Texturing

Vladimir V. Kniaz[1,2]([✉]) [iD], Vladimir A. Knyaz[1,2] [iD], Vladimir Mizginov[1] [iD],
Mark Kozyrev[1] [iD], and Petr Moshkantsev[1] [iD]

[1] State Research Institute of Aviation Systems (GosNIIAS), Moscow, Russia
{vl.kniaz,knyaz,vl.mizginov,mark.kozyrev,moshkantsev}@gosniias.ru
[2] Moscow Institute of Physics and Technology (MIPT), Moscow, Russia

Abstract. We present a generative adversarial model for single photo 3D reconstruction and high resolution texturing. Our framework leverages a neural renderer and a 3D Morphable model of an object. We train our generator on the semantic labelling-to-image translation task. This allows our model to learn rich priors about object appearance and perform all-around texture and shape reconstruction from a single image. Our new generator architecture leverages a power of StyleGAN2 model for image-to-image translation with fine texture detail at the 1024×1024 resolution. We evaluate our framework quantitatively and qualitatively on *Florence Face* and *Appolo Cars* datasets on the tasks of car 3D reconstruction and texturing. Extensive experiments demonstrate that our framework achieves and surpasses the state-of-the-art in single photo 3D object reconstruction and texturing using 3D morphable models. We made our code publicly available (http://www.zefirus.org/StructureFromGAN).

Keywords: 3D object reconstruction · Neural renderer · Conditional GAN

1 Introduction

It is natural for a human to decompose a 3D object into semantic parts. This prior semantic model of an object is consistent with semantic labeling of a 2D image that a human naturally performs.

Such consistency allows us to reason explicitly about a 3D shape of an object using only a single 2D image. The differentiable neural render [1,2] proposed recently improved the quality of single-photo 3D reconstruction significantly. Such neural render-based models as GANFIT [3] provide nearly cinema-grade

Electronic supplementary material The online version of this chapter (https://doi.org/10.1007/978-3-030-66096-3_40) contains supplementary material, which is available to authorized users.

A. Bartoli and A. Fusiello (Eds.): ECCV 2020 Workshops, LNCS 12536, pp. 595–611, 2020.
https://doi.org/10.1007/978-3-030-66096-3_40

Fig. 1. Our `StructureFromGAN` model reconstructs a 3D model and its texture from a single image (or painting). Input color image (left). Example of texture reconstruction (middle). Reconstructed 3D model (right).

quality of the object shape and high resolution textures. Still, training of such models usually requires a large dataset [3] of unmapped textures to train the generator model. The generation of such a dataset is a time-consuming expensive task. On the other hand, all fine details required for training a texture generator are present in real images of objects that were not unwrapped to a certain UV map.

We hypothesize that a consistency between semantic labeling of a color image of an object, its 2D texture and a 3D model can be used to transfer the prior knowledge from the task of the 2D image synthesis to the problem of single-photo 3D reconstruction and texturing. To the best of our knowledge, there is no results in literature regarding single-photo 3D model reconstruction using learned semantics priors. In this paper we present a `StructureFromGAN` framework for inference of a 3D model with high fidelity texture from a single image. We use assumptions of Gecer [3] and Kanazawa [4] as a starting point for our research. Specifically, we use a generative adversarial network (GAN) coupled with a neural renderer to optimize the shape and texture of an object from a single image. We fit a 3D morphable model with a static semantic texture to the input image using a neural renderer. For each iteration of optimization, we perform a translation of a semantic texture to a photorealistic texture.

After that, we render a 3D morphable model (3DMM) with the generated texture and use a combination of an L_1 and adversarial losses to fit the model and texture. We pre-train our GAN model on a large paired dataset of color images of the target object and its semantic labeling. This allows our model to reconstruct detailed shape and textures for parts invisible in the input image. We developed a 3DMM morphable model of a car following the approach of facial 3DMM [5,6].

Inspired by the recent progress in the Style-based GANs [7,8] we developed a conditional style-based GAN. We combine the ResNet-18 encoder with a Style-GANv2 decoder to control the generator's latent vector conditioned by an input image. Furthermore, we add skip connections between the intermediate feature

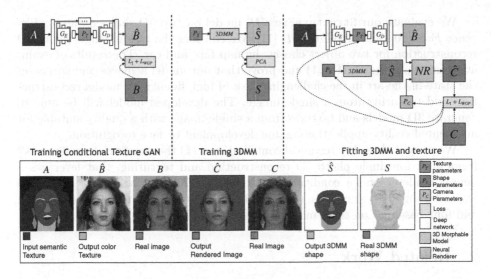

Fig. 2. StructureFromGAN framework overview.

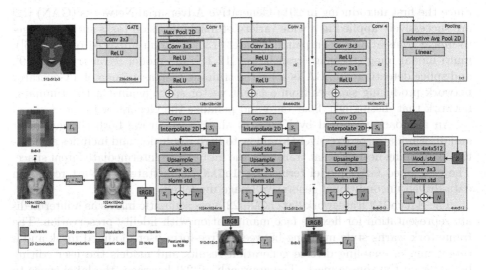

Fig. 3. Our conditional style-based generator: We combine a ResNet-18 [35] encoder with a StyleGAN2 [21] generator. We add an additional skip connections to improve the image-to-image translation.

maps of the ResNet model and 2D noise inputs of the StyleGAN. This allows our texture synthesizing GAN to combine the power of the StyleGAN2 generator with the robustness of the U-Net-like [9] models. The developed framework is a part of a research project that has been recently started by the authors with the aim of developing a fast single-photo 3D reconstruction framework for a mobile augmented reality system.

We evaluate our `StructureFromGAN` model on two 3D shape datasets: *Florence Face* [10], and *ApolloCar3D* [11]. We consider the task of single photo 3D reconstruction for two object classes: human face and car. The results of evaluation are encouraging (Fig. 1) and prove that our model achieves and surpasses the state-of-the-art in the challenging task of high fidelity 3D model reconstruction and texturing from a single image. The developed model will be able to generate 3D models and textures from a single image with a quality suitable for augmented reality applications, game development or face recognition.

We present three key technical contributions: (1) the new `StructureFromGAN` framework for single photo 3D reconstruction and texturing, that leverages a neural renderer and a conditional style-based GAN; (2) a 3DMM car model learned from 1000 car models; (3) an evaluation of our `StructureFromGAN` model and four baselines on three modern 3D shapes datasets.

2 Related Work

2.1 Generative Adversarial Networks

Since the first introducing in 2014 Generative Adversarial Networks (GAN) [12] are successively applied in a wide variety of machine vision tasks such as image-to-image translation (as on paired dataset [13,14], so on unpaired one [15,16]), multi-modal image-to-image translation [17,18], 3D model reconstruction [19], and splice detection [20]. GANs solve the training task as a game of a Generator network producing samples from a latent vector space against a Discriminator network that distinguish 'fake' data and penalize the Generator for it.

An approach proposed by Karras et al. [7,8,21] grows both the generator and discriminator progressively from low to high resolution and includes an additional mapping network that translates the input to an intermediate latent space. The developed GAN model termed `StyleGAN` yields state-of-the-art results in data-driven unconditional generative image modeling.

The `MatchGAN` framework `MatchGAN` [22] uses semantic masks as a intermediate representation for flexible face manipulation with fidelity preservation. The framework learns style mapping between a free-form user modified mask and a target image, enabling diverse generation results and models the user editing behavior on the source mask. The approach of [23] leverages the label space to learn the distribution of the source domain using the few labeled examples available by uniformly sampling source labels and assigning them as target labels. The graph-based convolution neural network of [24] learns expressions of different attributes on human faces, thus allowing to encode the high-order semantic information of target categories and their relative dependencies.

2.2 Neural Renderer

High fidelity 3D face reconstruction based on Generative Adversarial Networks and 3D Morphable Models uses non-linear optimization to find the optimal latent parameters that best reconstruct the test image but under a new perspective [25]. The proposed GANFIT framework demonstrated the state-of-the-art results in photorealistic and identity preserving 3D face reconstructions.

An approximate gradient for rasterization [1] enables the integration of rendering into neural networks. Such neural renderer allows to perform single-image 3D mesh reconstruction with silhouette image supervision. Also it allows gradient-based 3D mesh editing operations such as 2D-to-3D style transfer. Testing applications demonstrated the potential of the integration of a mesh renderer into neural networks. Further developments [26,27] allows reconstructing shapes that look reasonable from any viewpoint even for a single view or a few views per object.

2.3 Pose Estimation and 3D Reconstruction

Object 6DOF pose estimation is essential part of single photo 3D reconstruction and texturing pipeline. Recent progress in 6DOF pose estimation is mostly based on machine learning approaches. Modern neural network models allow estimating the 6D pose of rigid objects with available 3D models from a single RGB input image [28], implicit 3D orienting for 6D object detection by Augmented Autoencoders [29], estimating the camera position and orientation from a single input image relative to a known environment [30], learning robust features for 3D object pose estimation from object poses as guidance [31]. With training dataset being an essential part of data-driven machine vision techniques [32], new powerful methods for dataset creating along with automatic annotation are proposed [33,34].

3 Method

Our aim is 3D reconstructing and texturing of an object of a given class from a single image and a 3DMM of an object textured with a semantic texture. We consider four domains: the semantic texture domain $\mathcal{A} \in \mathbb{R}^{W \times H \times 3}$, the real color texture domain $\mathcal{B} \in \mathbb{R}^{W \times H \times 3}$, the real color image domain $\mathcal{C} \in \mathbb{R}^{W \times H \times 3}$, and the object 3D shape domain $\mathcal{S} \in \mathbb{R}^{N \times 3}$.

We perform the 3D reconstruction and texturing via joint fitting of an object 3D shape $S \in \mathcal{S}$, and its texture $B \in \mathcal{B}$. Specifically, we use an object's 3DMM M and a generator network G, that is pre-trained using generative adversarial setting. The goal of our generator G is to learn a mapping $G : (M, p_T) \to B$, where $p_T \in \mathbb{R}^T$ is the latent vector of texture parameters. We hypothesize, that masked real color images C are similar to color textures $B \in \mathcal{B}$, $B \subset C$. Therefore, we pre-train our generator G on a paired dataset containing masked real images C and their semantic labeling A.

We use assumptions of Gecer er al. [3] as a starting point for our 3DMM fitting pipeline. Unlike the baseline research, our StructureFromGAN framework uses semantic pairs that allows it to reconstruct textures of the objects parts invisible in the input image. We represent the objects 3D shape using a linear model $M : p \to S$ learned from real 3D models using the Principal Component Analysis [5,6], where $p_S \in \mathbb{R}^M$ is the vector of shape parameters.

Inspired by recent advances of the neural render-based losses [1], we construct our objective using a neural render R providing a mapping $R : (S, B, P_S) \rightarrow S$ from the objects shape S, its texture B and camera parameters $P_c \in R^N$ to the rendered image $\hat{C}$. Our contribution to the baseline approach [3] is an adversarial loss function $\mathcal{L}_{adv}(\hat{C}, C)$ facilitating generation of subject specific fine texture details.

The whole fitting process is given in Fig. 2 and consists of four steps. Firstly, given a prior semantic texture A and a render texture parameters $P_T = \mathcal{N}(0,1)$ an initial color texture $\hat{B}$ is generated. After that, we obtain a preliminary random shape $\hat{S} = M(P_S)$ using random shape parameters $P_S = \mathcal{N}(0,1)$. Next, we generate a synthetic image of object $\hat{C} = (\hat{S}, \hat{B}, P_c)$ using random initial camera parameters P_c and generated shape and texture. Finally, we calculate the objective function $\mathcal{L}_{SFG}(C, \hat{C})$ using the input image of object C and the synthesized image $\hat{C}$. After that, the fitting process is repeated until it converges.

The rest of this Section presents details on various components of our StructureFromGAN framework. Section 3.1 presents details on our conditional style-based texture generator. In Sect. 3.2, we discuss the 3DMM details and present our car 3DMM.

3.1 StyleFlow Generator

Recent research [3] demonstrated that GAN models are effective for high resolution texture generation. Still a large dataset of unwrapped textures is a crucial requirement for training models similar to GANFIT. Generation of such dataset is an expensive and time-consuming process.

We propose to use a conditional GAN [14] to overcome this problem. In contrast with a simple GAN model that reconstructs on image B from a latent vector p, a conditional GAN receives an input image A as an additional bit of information. We propose to use a static semantic texture A assigned to 3DMM as an input for the conditional generator that synthesize textures in our StructureFromGAN framework.

To this end, we propose a new conditional generator architecture inspired by the StyleGAN [8,21]. Our aim is to condition the latent vector of the StyleGAN model by a 2D image. We hypothesize, that an additional ResNet-18 encoder could learn a mapping from an input image to the latent code P_T of the style-based decoder. To further increase the convergence of our conditional style-based generator, we add skip connections between intermediate feature maps f_i to noise inputs of the StyleGAN2 generator.

Specifically, we train eight additional point wise convolutional layers with kernel size 1×1 that translate multichannel feature maps $f_i \in \mathbb{R}^{W_i \times H_i \times C_i}$ to a single channel noise inputs $n_i \in \mathbb{R}^{W_j \times M_j}$. We use a nearest neighborhood interpolation to match the size of feature maps. The resulting architecture is show in Fig. 3.

We use a residual discriminator similar to [21] to provide an adversarial loss function $\mathcal{L}_{adv}$. We train our generator G on paired datasets including real color images of objects C and their semantic labelling A. We use a trained generator with fixed weights during the 3DMM fitting process.

Two loss functions govern the training process of our conditional generator G: $\mathcal{L}_{L_1}^G$ and $\mathcal{L}_{adv}^G$. The $\mathcal{L}_{L_1}^G$ loss function penalizes the generator for difference in color between the synthesized image $\hat{B}$ and the real image C.

$$\mathcal{L}_1^G(\hat{B}, C) = \mathbb{E}_{A,\hat{B},C}[||C - G(A)||_1]; \tag{1}$$

The adversarial loss is provided by a modified Wasserstein loss [36] (WGAN-GP) similar to [37,38]

$$\mathcal{L}_{adv}^G(\hat{B}, C) = \mathbb{E}_{\hat{B}\sim p_G}[D(\hat{B})] - \mathbb{E}_{C\sim p_R}\left[D(C)\right]$$
$$+ \lambda \cdot \mathbb{E}_{\hat{B}\sim p_{\hat{B}}}\left[(\left|\left|\boldsymbol{\nabla}_{\hat{B}} D(\hat{B})\right|\right|_2 - 1)^2\big|\big|_1\right], \tag{2}$$

where p_G is the distribution of generated samples, P_R is the distribution of real samples C, and $P_{\hat{B}}$ is the distribution of randomly generated samples. We obtain the final energy to optimize using the weighted sum of two losses

$$\mathcal{L}^G(\hat{B}, C, \boldsymbol{\nabla}_{\hat{B}} D(\hat{B})) = \lambda_{L1} \cdot \mathcal{L}_1^G(\hat{B}, C) + \lambda_{adv} \cdot \mathcal{L}_{adv}^G(\hat{B}, C, \boldsymbol{\nabla}_{\hat{B}} D(\hat{B})); \tag{3}$$

where $\lambda_{L_1}, \lambda_{adv}$ are hyperparameters. We keep $\lambda_{L_1} = \lambda_{adv} = 0.5$ in our experiments.

3.2   3D Morphable Model

The aim of 3D Morphable Model in our pipeline is to match the shape $\hat{S}$ of an object rendered by a neural renderer with its appearance S in real input image C. We use the Basel Face Model (BFM) [5,6] to fit the 3D model of a face to a portrait photo. We develop a new 3D Morphable Car Model to evaluate our StructureFromGAN framework on a car 3D reconstruction.

The widely used approach for generation of 3DMM for a given object class is fitting a linear model to real 3D data using Principle Component Analysis (PCA). Let the model S consists of N vertices $(x_j, y_j, z_j)^T \in \mathbb{R}^3$. Each vertex has an associated texture coordinates $(u_j, v_j)^T \in \mathbb{R}^2$. Then a 3D object is given by two vectors of size $3 \cdot N$ and $2 \cdot M$ [5,6]

$$S = (x_1, y_1, z_1, \ldots, x_n, y_n, z_n)^T, \tag{4}$$
$$T = (u_1, v_1, \ldots, u_n, v_n)^T. \tag{5}$$

We use static texture coordinates for a given object class. The 3D shape is controlled using a linear model.

$$\mathcal{M} : (\mu_s, \sigma_s, U_s, p_s) \to S, \tag{6}$$

where $\mathcal{M} \in \mathbb{R}^{3N}$ is the mean object shape, $\sigma_s \in \mathbb{R}^M$ are the standard deviations, and $U_s = [u_1, \ldots, u_n] \in \mathbb{R}^{3N \cdot M}$ is an orthogonal basis of shape principal components. Therefore, the shape can be parameterized by a vector $p_s \in \mathbb{R}^{3N \cdot M}$.

The new shape is created using the model as a linear combination of the shape vector p_s and the principal components

$$\mathcal{M}(p_s) = \mu_s + U_s \cdot \mathrm{diag}(\sigma_s) \cdot p_s. \tag{7}$$

For the face model, we use the model parameters μ_s, σ_s and U_s provided by [5,6]. To train the car 3DMM we generated a *CarMorph* dataset using 3D shapes from the ShapeNet [39] dataset.

We generated a semantically labeled car mesh S^{car} topology consisting of 1491 vertices and 1336 faces. We selected 1000 car models of different sub-classes from the ShapeNet dataset [39]. We converted the shell voxel models from the ShapeNet dataset to point clouds. After that we manually fitted vertices in our S^{car} mesh to 1000 point clouds. Using such approach we generated 1000 shape vectors $S \in \mathbb{R}^3$ representing shapes of different car models (Fig. 4). Using the collected shape vectors, we found the mean car shape $\mathcal{M}_s^{car}$, the standard deviation σ_s^{car} and the matrix of principal components U_s^{car}.

Fig. 4. Examples of 3D car shapes from our *CarMorph* used to train the car 3DMM.

We use eleven semantic parts classes in our semantic texture: car paint, tires, wheel disc, wind shield, door window, rear window, front lamp, rear lamp, doors, handle, and mirror. We generate a training dataset to pre-train our texture generator using part segmentation masks from the ADE20k dataset [40]. We extracted and cropped all instances of the car from the ADE20k dataset.

For the face semantic texture we use 19 semantic part classes defined in CelebAMask-HQ [41] such as skin, nose, eyes, eyebrows, ears, mouth, lip, hair, hat, eyeglass, earring, neck, necklace and cloth. We pre-train our texture generator on the 30k faces from the CelebAMask-HQ dataset.

We use the 3DMM parameters such as mean shape $\mathcal{M}_s$, the standard deviation σ_s and the matrix of principal components U_s.

3.3   3D Shape and Texture Fitting

The main challenge of the single-photo 3D reconstruction task is definition of a discriminative loss function that can compare the reconstructed 3D shape $\hat{S}$ and texture $\hat{B}$ with a given input 2D image of the same object. The differentiable neural renderer [1,27] provides an elegant solution to this problem.

It allows to optimize model parameters using differences between the real image C and a synthetic image $\hat{C}$ generated using neural renderer. Internally the neural renderer leverages a deferred shading model. Using color and normal attributes at each vertex, the neural renderer generates an image $\hat{C}$ in a forward pass. During the backward pass the neural renderer calculates the gradients using the barycentric coordinates of the corresponding pixels.

Therefore the neural renderer R provides a mapping $R : (S, B, p_c) \rightarrow C$, where p_c is the vector of camera parameters $p_c = \{Q_R, Q_T, f\}$, here $Q_R \in \mathbb{R}^3$ is a rotation matrix, $Q_T = \{x_0, y_0, z_0\}^T \in \mathbb{R}^3$ is the camera pose in the object space, f is the camera's focal length. We assume that object is located at the origin of the object space and its pose and rotation remains static during the fitting process.

Therefore during the fitting process we optimize three vectors: texture parameters p_T, 3D shape parameters p_S and camera parameters p_c. Hence, the space of parameters is extensive and different vectors are correlated. Therefore we perform the fitting sequentially to improve the framework's robustness. Firstly, we generate an initial approximation of the texture latent vector $p_T^0 = G_E(A)$ using the pre-trained ResNet encoder and the model's semantic texture A. After that, we generate an initial texture $\hat{B}^0 = G_D(A, p_T^0)$. During the first part of optimization process our goal is the estimation of the camera's pose and initial parameters p_c. We start the process using the random pose and field of view p_c^0.

After that, we iteratively render the resulting image $\hat{C}^i = R(\hat{S}^0, \hat{B}^0, p_c^i)$, where $\hat{S}^0$ is a random shape $\hat{S}^0 = \mathcal{M}_S(p_S^0)$ generated using initial shape parameters p_S^0. For each image $\hat{C}^i$, we calculate the $\mathcal{L}_{L_1}$ loss and iteratively minimize the energy:

$$\min_{p_c} \mathcal{E}_c(p_c) = \|C - \hat{C}\|_1. \tag{8}$$

The convergence of this process is emphasized be masking the background in the real image C. We assume, that for non-symmetric objects there is a strong correlation between the object's silhouette and the camera pose p_c [1,26]. Hence, the pose estimation is generally robust for non-symmetric objects. The robustness of camera pose estimation process can be further increased using modern pose estimation methods [28,29].

Once an estimating of the camera pose p_c^* is found, we simultaneously iteratively optimize the object's shape $\hat{S}$ and its texture $\hat{B}$. For each iteration, we generate a new shape $\hat{S}^j = \mathcal{M}_S(p_S^j)$ and texture $\hat{B}^j = G_D(A, p_T^j)$ and minimize the energy using a combination of $\mathcal{L}_{L_1}$ and Wasserstein GP losses.

$$\min_{\{S,T\}} \mathcal{E}_{\{S,T\}} = \lambda_1 \cdot \mathcal{L}_{L_1}(C, \hat{C}^j) + \lambda_{WGP} \cdot \mathcal{L}_{WGP}(C, \hat{C}^j). \tag{9}$$

Where λ_1, λ_{WGP} are hyper-parameters. We keep $\lambda_1 = 50$, and $\lambda_{WGP} = 1$ in our experiments. The resulting fitting process is presented in Algorithm 1 in Supplementary Material.

4 Experiments

We evaluate our StructureFromGAN framework and four baselines qualitatively and qualitatively on three modern benchmarks. We consider two object classes: human dace and a car.

4.1 Network Training

Face Fitting. We train out conditional style-based GAN on the 30k samples from the CelebAMask-HQ dataset [22]. We use the Basel Face Model parameters fro 3DMM. We implement all components of our framework using the PyTorch [42] and PyTorch 3D libraries. The models were trained using NVIDIA RTX 2080Ti. The training process took 700k epochs and 480 h. We use an Adam solver with a learning rate dependent in the current image resolution and batch size of one. For image sizes $W \leq 128$ we use the learning rate $l = 1.5 \cdot 10^{-3}$, for $W = 256$, $l = 2 \cdot 10^{-3}$, for $W \geq 512$ $l = 3 \cdot 10^{-3}$. We use momentum parameters $\beta_1 = 0$, $\beta_2 = 0.99$.

Car Fitting. We use color images and semantic parts annotations from the ADE20k dataset [40]. We use all instances of the cars with maximal dimension larger then 256 pixels. We crop each instance to a square limited by maximal dimension and create a paired semantic label $A \in \mathbb{R}^{W \times H \times 3}$. We keep $W = H = 1024$ in our experiments. We use an online dataset augmentation applying random affine transformation and vertical and horizontal flipping to simulate various possible texture maps. We mask the background to focus the model's attention on the details of car texture. We use the pretrained models for all baselines.

Baselines. Category-Specific Mesh Reconstruction (CMR) [46] framework provides single image reconstruction of the objects 3D shape, camera and texture. The model leverages 3D deformable meshes that deform a ball shape to the desired object's shape. The mean category specific mesh is trained using annotated 2D keypoints. The generic shape is reconstructed from 2D keypoints using the Structure-from-Motion approach. The texture is reconstructed using the optical flow from the input image to the texture map. Face Identity Shape Network (FISN) [44] model leverages a ResNet-101 backbone to estimate the 3DMM face model shape and expression parameters. Authors fire-tire the ResNet-101 trained on the face recognition task to estimate 3DMM feature vector $\gamma \in R^{198}$.

PRNet [43] model does not use a 3DMM to reconstruct the 3D model of a face. In contrast, authors propose to use UV position map that provides a mapping $U : (U, V) \rightarrow (X, Y, Z)$, where U, V are the coordinates of a point on a face in texture space, and X, Y, Z are the coordinates of the corresponding point in object space. The model leverages 10 residual blocks in the encoder and 17 transposed convolution blocks in the decoder.

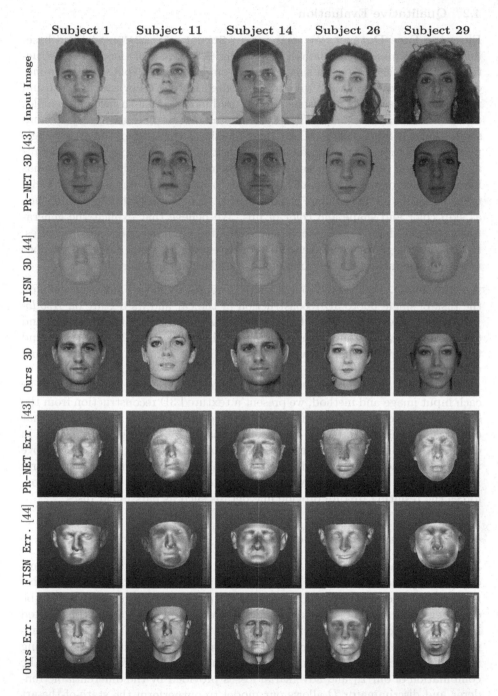

Fig. 5. Examples of car 3D reconstruction on *Florence Face* dataset [45] using our StructureFromGAN and baselines.

4.2   Qualitative Evaluation

Florence Face Dataset. We compare our `StructueFromGAN` model and base-lines on the *Florence Face* dataset [45] on the task of face 3D model reconstruction and texturing. We use a single image from the fronted split of the *Florence* dataset [45]. Experimental results are presented in Fig. 5. For each subject and method, we present the reconstructed textured model and a surface datince plot represented as a heat map. The experimental reconstructions clearly demonstrate that out StructureFromGAN model achieves the state-of-the-art in single photo face 3D reconstruction and surpasses it in terms of textures fine details and perceptual realism. The next best performing model is the `PRNet` that has lowest surface distance error and is capable of generating fine details in facial textures. Still, our `StructureFromGAN` is able to better match fine details such as skin color and shape and color of lips. We believe that explicit the generator with more details and style variety compared to unwrapped facial textures. Hence, our image-to-texture semantic consistency allows our model to produce more realistic facial textures compared to modern state-of-the-art models.

ApolloCar3D. We evaluate our StructureFromGAN model and a baseline on the task of single photo 3D reconstruction of the car and its texture on *Apollo-Car3D* [11]. *ApolloCar3D* is a large scale dataset consisting of 5277 images and 60k annotate car instance. The *ApolloCar3D* dataset doesn't provide ground truth car textures. Therefore, we project the texture from the input image using the annotated camera pose.

We present experimental results for the car 3D reconstruction in Fig. 6. For each input image and method, we present a textured 3D reconstruction from the source and novel view and surface distance plot. Qualitative results prove that out `StructureFromGAN` model outperforms baselines by a large margin both in details of the 3D shape and textures. The texture details in novel view prove that our conditional style-based generator is able to reconstruct the texture parts invisible in the source image. Moreover, our adversarial term in the fitting loss forces the resulting texture provide fine details such as bars in car discs.

4.3   Quantitative Evaluation

Florence Face. We present quantitative results on the Florence dataset in terms of point-to-plane distance [3,47] in Table 1. We perform reconstructions using five frames from 'cooperative', 'indoor', 'outdoor' splits in the Florence dataset to be consistent with [3]. The dense alignment of the ground truth and reconstructed meshes are performed using an iterative closest point method (ICP). Experimental results demonstrate that our `StructureFromGAN` model is the best performing method. The next best results demonstrates the `PRNet` [43]. We believe that, the combination of our L_1 and adversarial losses provided by the differentiable renderer and discriminator D allows our model to outperform the state-of-the-art baselines.

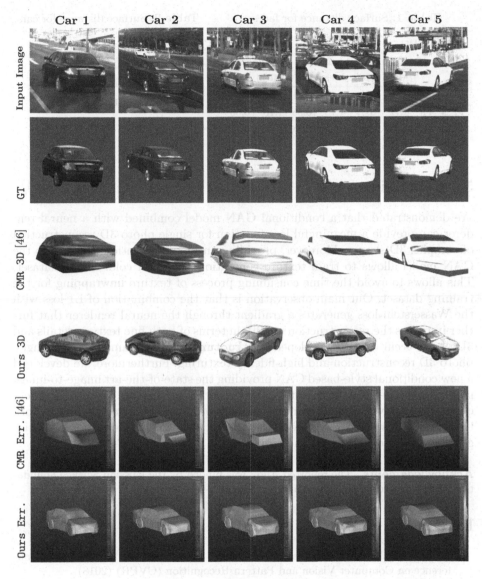

Fig. 6. Examples of 3D reconstruction on *ApolloCar3D* [11] dataset using our StructureFromGAN and CMR [46].

ApolloCar3D. Quantitative results for *ApolloCar3D* dataset [11] are presented in Table 2. Similarly to the face evaluation protocol. We perform an ICP registration of the ground truth car model and the 3D reconstruction results. The evaluation proves that our StructureFromGAN model improves the CMR [46] results by 52%.

Table 1. Surface distance for faces.

Florence [45]

	Cooperative		Indoor		Outdoor	
	Mean	Std	Mean	Std	Mean	Std
PRNet [43]	1.46	0.36	1.49	0.41	1.54	0.44
FISN [44]	1.72	0.32	1.78	0.38	1.78	0.56
Ours	**1.12**	**0.27**	**1.25**	**0.36**	**1.28**	**0.57**

Table 2. Surface distance for cars.

ApolloCar3D [11]

	Mean	Std
CMR [46]	0.111	0.157
Ours	**0.021**	**0.049**

5   Conclusion

We demonstrated that a conditional GAN model combined with a neural renderer can provide a meaningful loss function for single photo 3D reconstruction of complex 3D shapes. Moreover, providing an input semantic label into to the GAN model allows to train texture generation model on color image dataset. This allows to avoid the time consuming process of texture unwrapping for the training dataset. Our main observation is that the combination of L1 loss with the Wasserstein loss generates a gradient through the neural renderer that further improves the reconstruction quality in terms of both fine texture details and 3D shape accuracy. We developed a `StructureFromGAN` framework for single-photo 3D reconstruction and high-fidelity texturing. Furthermore, we developed a new conditional style-based GAN providing the state-of-the-art image-to-image translation. The joint fitting of a 3DMM model and texture using neural renderer and an adversarial discriminator allows our `StructureFromGAN` framework to achieve and surpass the state-of-the-art models in the challenging task of single photo 3D reconstruction and texturing.

Acknowledgments. The reported study was funded by the Russian Science Foundation (RSF) according to the research project N° 19-11-11008.

References

1. Kato, H., Ushiku, Y., Harada, T.: Neural 3D mesh renderer. In: The IEEE Conference on Computer Vision and Pattern Recognition (CVPR) (2018)
2. Nguyen-Phuoc, T.H., Li, C., Balaban, S., Yang, Y.: RenderNet: a deep convolutional network for differentiable rendering from 3D shapes. In: Bengio, S., Wallach, H., Larochelle, H., Grauman, K., Cesa-Bianchi, N., Garnett, R. (eds.) Advances in Neural Information Processing Systems, vol. 31, pp. 7891–7901. Curran Associates, Inc. (2018)
3. Gecer, B., Ploumpis, S., Kotsia, I., Zafeiriou, S.: GANFIT: generative adversarial network fitting for high fidelity 3D face reconstruction. In: 2019 IEEE/CVF Conference on Computer Vision and Pattern Recognition (CVPR), pp. 1155–1164, June 2019
4. Sengupta, S., Kanazawa, A., Castillo, C.D., Jacobs, D.W.: SfSNet: learning shape, reflectance and illuminance of faces 'in the wild'. In: 2018 IEEE/CVF Conference on Computer Vision and Pattern Recognition, pp. 6296–6305, June 2018

5. Paysan, P., et al.: Face reconstruction from skull shapes and physical attributes. In: Denzler, J., Notni, G., Süße, H. (eds.) DAGM 2009. LNCS, vol. 5748, pp. 232–241. Springer, Heidelberg (2009). https://doi.org/10.1007/978-3-642-03798-6_24

6. Gerig, T., et al.: Morphable face models - an open framework. In: 2018 13th IEEE International Conference on Automatic Face Gesture Recognition (FG 2018), pp. 75–82, May 2018

7. Karras, T., Aila, T., Laine, S., Lehtinen, J.: Progressive growing of GANs for improved quality, stability, and variation. In: International Conference on Learning Representations (2018)

8. Karras, T., Laine, S., Aila, T.: A style-based generator architecture for generative adversarial networks. CoRR abs/1812.04948 (2018)

9. Ronneberger, O., Fischer, P., Brox, T.: U-Net: convolutional networks for biomedical image segmentation. In: Navab, N., Hornegger, J., Wells, W.M., Frangi, A.F. (eds.) MICCAI 2015. LNCS, vol. 9351, pp. 234–241. Springer, Cham (2015). https://doi.org/10.1007/978-3-319-24574-4_28

10. Bagdanov, A.D., Del Bimbo, A., Masi, I.: The florence 2D/3D hybrid face dataset. In: Proceedings of the 2011 Joint ACM Workshop on Human Gesture and Behavior Understanding, J-HGBU 2011, pp. 79–80. ACM, New York (2011)

11. Song, X., et al.: ApolloCar3D: a large 3D car instance understanding benchmark for autonomous driving. In: IEEE Conference on Computer Vision and Pattern Recognition, CVPR 2019, Long Beach, CA, USA, 16–20 June 2019, pp. 5452–5462 (2019)

12. Goodfellow, I., et al.: Generative adversarial nets. In: Advances in Neural Information Processing Systems, pp. 2672–2680 (2014)

13. Isola, P., Zhu, J.Y., Zhou, T., Efros, A.A.: Image-to-image translation with conditional adversarial networks. In: 2017 IEEE Conference on Computer Vision and Pattern Recognition (CVPR), pp. 5967–5976. IEEE (2017)

14. Wang, T.C., Liu, M.Y., Zhu, J.Y., Tao, A., Kautz, J., Catanzaro, B.: High-resolution image synthesis and semantic manipulation with conditional GANs. In: Proceedings of the IEEE Conference on Computer Vision and Pattern Recognition (2018)

15. Zhu, J.Y., et al.: Toward multimodal image-to-image translation. In: Advances in Neural Information Processing Systems, vol. 30 (2017)

16. Zhu, J.Y., Park, T., Isola, P., Efros, A.A.: Unpaired image-to-image translation using cycle-consistent adversarial networks. In: 2017 IEEE International Conference on Computer Vision (ICCV), pp. 2242–2251. IEEE (2017)

17. Huang, X., Liu, M.-Y., Belongie, S., Kautz, J.: Multimodal unsupervised image-to-image translation. In: Ferrari, V., Hebert, M., Sminchisescu, C., Weiss, Y. (eds.) ECCV 2018. LNCS, vol. 11207, pp. 179–196. Springer, Cham (2018). https://doi.org/10.1007/978-3-030-01219-9_11

18. Kniaz, V.V., Knyaz, V.A., Hladůvka, J., Kropatsch, W.G., Mizginov, V.: Thermal-GAN: multimodal color-to-thermal image translation for person re-identification in multispectral dataset. In: Leal-Taixé, L., Roth, S. (eds.) ECCV 2018. LNCS, vol. 11134, pp. 606–624. Springer, Cham (2019). https://doi.org/10.1007/978-3-030-11024-6_46

19. Knyaz, V.A., Kniaz, V.V., Remondino, F.: Image-to-voxel model translation with conditional adversarial networks. In: Leal-Taixé, L., Roth, S. (eds.) ECCV 2018. LNCS, vol. 11129, pp. 601–618. Springer, Cham (2019). https://doi.org/10.1007/978-3-030-11009-3_37

20. Kniaz, V.V., Knyaz, V.A., Remondino, F.: The point where reality meets fantasy: mixed adversarial generators for image splice detection. In: Annual Conference on Advances in Neural Information Processing Systems 2019, NeurIPS 2019, Vancouver, BC, Canada, 8–14 December 2019, vol. 32, pp. 215–226 (2019)

21. Karras, T., Laine, S., Aittala, M., Hellsten, J., Lehtinen, J., Aila, T.: Analyzing and improving the image quality of styleGAN (2019)

22. Lee, C.H., Liu, Z., Wu, L., Luo, P.: MaskGAN: towards diverse and interactive facial image manipulation. In: IEEE Conference on Computer Vision and Pattern Recognition (CVPR) (2020)

23. Sun, J.Z., Bhattarai, B., Kim, T.K.: MatchGAN: a self-supervised semi-supervised conditional generative adversarial network. ArXiv abs/2006.06614 (2020)

24. Bhattarai, B., Kim, T.K.: Inducing optimal attribute representations for conditional GANs, March 2020

25. Gecer, B., Ploumpis, S., Kotsia, I., Zafeiriou, S.: GANFIT: generative adversarial network fitting for high fidelity 3D face reconstruction. In: The IEEE Conference on Computer Vision and Pattern Recognition (CVPR), June 2019

26. Kato, H., Harada, T.: Learning view priors for single-view 3D reconstruction. In: The IEEE Conference on Computer Vision and Pattern Recognition (CVPR), pp. 9778–9787. Long Beach, USA, 16-20 June (2019). https://doi.org/10.1109/CVPR. 2019.01001, http://openaccess.thecvf.com/content_CVPR_2019/html/Kato_Learning_View_Priors_for_Single-View_3D_Reconstruction_CVPR_2019_paper.html

27. Kato, H., Harada, T.: Self-supervised learning of 3D objects from natural images. arXiv (2019)

28. Hodan, T., Barath, D., Matas, J.: EPOS: estimating 6d pose of objects with symmetries. In: Proceedings of the IEEE/CVF Conference on Computer Vision and Pattern Recognition (CVPR), June 2020

29. Sundermeyer, M., Marton, Z.C., Durner, M., Triebel, R.: Augmented autoencoders: implicit 3D orientation learning for 6D object detection. Int. J. Comput. Vis. 128(3), 714–729 (2020). https://doi.org/10.1007/s11263-019-01243-8

30. Brachmann, E., Rother, C.: Visual camera re-localization from RGB and RGB-D images using DSAC. ArXiv abs/2002.12324 (2020)

31. Balntas, V., Doumanoglou, A., Sahin, C., Sock, J., Kouskouridas, R., Kim, T.: Pose guided RGBD feature learning for 3D object pose estimation. In: 2017 IEEE International Conference on Computer Vision (ICCV), pp. 3876–3884, October 2017

32. Yuan, S., Stenger, B., Kim, T.: 3D hand pose estimation from RGB using privileged learning with depth data. In: 2019 IEEE/CVF International Conference on Computer Vision Workshop (ICCVW), pp. 2866–2873, October 2019

33. Hodaň, T., et al.: Photorealistic image synthesis for object instance detection. In: 2019 IEEE International Conference on Image Processing (ICIP), pp. 66–70, September 2019

34. Hampali, S., Rad, M., Oberweger, M., Lepetit, V.: HOnnotate: a method for 3D annotation of hand and object poses. In: Proceedings of the IEEE/CVF Conference on Computer Vision and Pattern Recognition (CVPR), June 2020

35. He, K., Zhang, X., Ren, S., Sun, J.: Deep residual learning for image recognition. In: 2016 IEEE Conference on Computer Vision and Pattern Recognition, CVPR 2016, Las Vegas, NV, USA, 27–30 June 2016, pp. 770–778 (2016)

36. Arjovsky, M., Chintala, S., Bottou, L.: Wasserstein generative adversarial networks. In: Precup, D., Teh, Y.W. (eds.) Proceedings of the 34th International Conference on Machine Learning. Volume 70 of Proceedings of Machine Learning Research, PMLR, 06–11 August 2017, pp. 214–223. International Convention Centre, Sydney (2017)

37. Karras, T., Aila, T., Laine, S., Lehtinen, J.: Progressive growing of GANs for improved quality, stability, and variation (2017)

38. Gulrajani, I., Ahmed, F., Arjovsky, M., Dumoulin, V., Courville, A.C.: Improved training of wasserstein GANs. In: Guyon, I., et al. (eds.) Advances in Neural Information Processing Systems, vol. 30, pp. 5767–5777. Curran Associates, Inc. (2017)

39. Chang, A.X., et al.: ShapeNet: an information-rich 3D model repository. CoRR abs/1512.03012 (2015)

40. Zhou, B., Zhao, H., Puig, X., Fidler, S., Barriuso, A., Torralba, A.: Scene parsing through ADE20K dataset. In: Proceedings of the IEEE Conference on Computer Vision and Pattern Recognition (2017)

41. Lee, C.H., Liu, Z., Wu, L., Luo, P.: MaskGAN: towards diverse and interactive facial image manipulation (2019)

42. Paszke, A., et al.: Automatic differentiation in PyTorch (2017)

43. Feng, Y., Wu, F., Shao, X., Wang, Y., Zhou, X.: Joint 3D face reconstruction and dense alignment with position map regression network. In: Ferrari, V., Hebert, M., Sminchisescu, C., Weiss, Y. (eds.) Computer Vision – ECCV 2018. LNCS, vol. 11218, pp. 557–574. Springer, Cham (2018). https://doi.org/10.1007/978-3-030-01264-9_33

44. Tran, A.T., Hassner, T., Masi, I., Medioni, G.G.: Regressing robust and discriminative 3D morphable models with a very deep neural network. In: 2017 IEEE Conference on Computer Vision and Pattern Recognition, CVPR 2017, Honolulu, HI, USA, 21–26 July 2017, pp. 1493–1502 (2017)

45. Bagdanov, A.D., Masi, I., Del Bimbo, A.: The florence 2D/3D hybrid face datset. In: Proceedings of the ACM Multimedia International Workshop on Multimedia Access to 3D Human Objects (MA3HO 2011). ACM Press, December 2011

46. Kanazawa, A., Tulsiani, S., Efros, A.A., Malik, J.: Learning category-specific mesh reconstruction from image collections. In: Ferrari, V., Hebert, M., Sminchisescu, C., Weiss, Y. (eds.) ECCV 2018. LNCS, vol. 11219, pp. 386–402. Springer, Cham (2018). https://doi.org/10.1007/978-3-030-01267-0_23

47. Genova, K., Cole, F., Maschinot, A., Sarna, A., Vlasic, D., Freeman, W.T.: Unsupervised training for 3D morphable model regression. In: 2018 IEEE Conference on Computer Vision and Pattern Recognition, CVPR 2018, Salt Lake City, UT, USA, 18–22 June 2018, pp. 8377–8386 (2018)

6 DoF Pose Estimation of Textureless Objects from Multiple RGB Frames

Roman Kaskman[1,2], Ivan Shugurov[1,2($\boxtimes$)], Sergey Zakharov[1,2], and Slobodan Ilic[1,2]

[1] Technical University of Munich, Munich, Germany
{roman.kaskman,ivan.shugurov,sergey.zakharo}@tum.de
[2] Siemens Corporate Technology, Augsburg, Germany
slobodan.ilic@siemens.com

Abstract. This paper addresses the problems of object detection and 6 DoF pose estimation from a sequence of RGB images. Our deep learning-based approach uses only synthetic non-textured 3D CAD models for training and has no access to the images from the target domain. The image sequence is used to obtain a sparse 3D reconstruction of the scene via Structure from Motion. The domain gap is closed by relying on the intuition that geometric edges are the only prominent features that can be extracted from both the 3D models and the sparse reconstructions. Based on this assumption, we have developed a domain-invariant data preparation scheme and 3DKeypointNet, which is a neural network for detecting of the 3D keypoints in sparse and noisy point clouds. The final pose is estimated with RANSAC and a scale-aware point cloud alignment method. The proposed method has been tested on the T-LESS dataset and compared to methods also trained on synthetic data. The results indicate the potential of our method despite the fact that the entire pipeline is solely trained on synthetic data.

Keywords: Pose estimation · Object detection · Sparse point clouds

1 Introduction

The problem of object detection and pose estimation of 3D objects has been addressed for an infinite number of times in the field of computer vision. As demonstrated in the BOP Challenge [24] for 6 DoF object pose estimation, deep learning dominates if only monocular RGB images are used, while traditional geometry-based methods [14] are still not giving up in depth and RGBD images. On the other hand, deep learning methods operating on unorganized point clouds are massively used in autonomous driving, with one of the task being car detection and pose estimation [9,29,32,45,61,65]. This problem is better posed than

Electronic supplementary material The online version of this chapter (https://doi.org/10.1007/978-3-030-66096-3_41) contains supplementary material, which is available to authorized users.

© Springer Nature Switzerland AG 2020
A. Bartoli and A. Fusiello (Eds.): ECCV 2020 Workshops, LNCS 12536, pp. 612–630, 2020.
https://doi.org/10.1007/978-3-030-66096-3_41

generic object pose estimation due to physical constraints. For instance, cars cannot be in arbitrary poses; sizes and scales do not vary much, while in general cases, an object can be placed completely arbitrarily. Moreover, obtaining labels for 6 DoF pose estimation is extremely difficult. Therefore, training detectors from synthetic renderings of 3D models is desirable. Unfortunately, they still have lower performance than detectors trained on real data. However, [26] showed that detectors trained on synthetic data do not overfit to particular datasets and seem to be more generic when real data from the target domain (labeled and unlabeled) are not available.

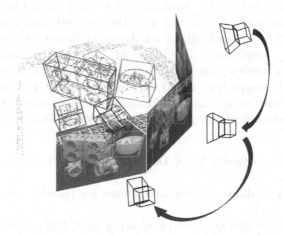

Fig. 1. Illustration of the proposed method. The proposed method uses SfM to obtain a sparse point cloud reconstruction from a frame sequence. Then, object poses are estimated in 3D, after which per-frame poses are computed.

We propose herein a method for 6 DoF pose detection in RGB images, which is trained solely on synthetic data. We address this problem for textureless 3D objects (i.e. objects from the T-LESS dataset [21] as in Fig. 1, which do not have distinctive textures) whose 3D CAD models are available. The CAD models come without any color or texture information associated with them, which is typical in industrial scenarios where non-textured CAD models are available. Renderings of such models appear as grayscale models on arbitrary backgrounds, making training on them more challenging because of the domain gap. As shown in [43,62], classical GAN approaches [5,6,17,30,36,56] depending on the data from the target domain fail in such scenarios. Unlike other related approaches that use a single RGB image for detection, we use an entire sequence of RGB images as illustrated in Fig. 1. Our intuition was to rely on SfM and perform a sparse reconstruction of the scenes. This point cloud reconstruction is then approximated with an edge-like reconstruction by fitting edge segments to the geometric discontinuities in the scene. We designed a neural network that detects the pre-selected keypoints for each object in the sparse reconstruction. Knowing correspondences between these 3D keypoints and their locations on the CAD models, the pose is determined using Umeyama algorithm [57]. We developed an exhaustive data generation scheme that remains easy to use and requires no extra artistic modeling effort, to close the domain gap between Structure from Motion (SfM) reconstructions and CAD models. It starts by generating a large number of 3D scenes using physics-based simulation. Since geometric edges are the only features robust to light changes and present in non-textured CAD models, we represent each CAD model with an edge-like representation obtained by the method of Hofer *et al.* [25]. This representation is then used to replace 3D models in simulated scenes with the corresponding edge-based models. The same method has been applied to SfM reconstructions to obtain "edgy" scene representations. In this way, the synthetic and real domains have a smaller discrepancy, which allows our keypoint detection network to detect object keypoints, which are fed to RANSAC and the Umeyama algorithm to output the object poses. Due to scale ambiguity of SfM reconstructions, we perform pose refinement both in 3D with scale-aware ICP (directly on sparse SfM reconstructions, no real depth information is used) and in the image using multi-view edge-based alignment. Our main contributions are summarized as follows:

1. a pipeline for recovering full 6 DoF object poses from sequences of RGB images;
2. domain-invariant data preparation allowing for training from non-textured CAD models; and
3. a 3D keypoint prediction network allowing for 6 DoF object detection and pose estimation in point clouds.

We evaluated our method on the challenging T-LESS [21] dataset and compared it with the best-performing synthetic methods on the recent BOP 6 DoF pose recovery challenge [23].

2   Related Work

As two of the most classical problems in computer vision with a wide range of applications in different domains, object detection and pose estimation have been extensively studied in the past. In this section, we present a summary of the relevant past works on this topic, ranging from classical methods to modern deep learning approaches. Our method spans between RGB approaches and point cloud based methods; hence, we are going to discuss related methods from both categories.

2.1   DL Methods for RGB Images

Deep learning and convolutional neural networks allow for feature extraction even from surfaces that do not exhibit pronounced textures, thereby making it possible to estimate a pose directly from RGB images.

Training on Synthetic Data. SSD6D [27] paved the way for CNN-based pose estimation approaches that rely solely on synthetic training data. The detector extends the standard SSD detector [34] to predict a discrete approximation of the rotational component of the transformation. The drawback of the approach is that it is slow, and poses estimated without ICP refinement are extremely rough. Moreover, a confidence threshold must be chosen separately for each object to achieve a good recall. The idea of discrete viewpoint approximation was further revisited by the Augmented Autoencoder (AAE) [52,53]. The AAE approach consists of two disconnected stages. The first stage is a 2D object detector trained on real data. At the second stage, each detected object is transformed with a neural network to output a descriptor, which is matched with a dictionary of pre-computed descriptors of all discrete viewpoints. The pre-computed descriptors are obtained using synthetic renderings of available 3D models possessing texture information. The AAE achieves state of the art results on the T-LESS dataset [21]. DPOD [64] estimates dense correspondences between the 3D model and its instance in the scene. This method can be trained both on real and synthetic data, and achieves good results in both cases. When training on synthetic data, we would like to mention methods using GAN networks [1,5,51,54]. These approaches typically start from source domain images (e.g., synthetic renderings of textured objects) and then alter them to resemble the target domain images (e.g., coming from the real camera). For this, the unlabeled images from the target domain must be available. On the contrary, the approaches presented in [43,63] rely on the exhaustive domain randomization applied to synthetic images, which are then fed to a GAN network. The GAN denoises them and makes them look similar to the synthetic images used for training the target classifier and the pose estimation network. DeceptionNet [62] elevates the problem of blind data randomization and performs network-driven domain randomization that generalized well to new domains. However, the domain adaptation methods need object detection to be performed separately as a preprocessing step. Moreover, they are applied separately to the object patches, which is a simpler task than simultaneous detection and pose estimation.

Training on Real Data. The following methods utilize the prediction of 2D-3D correspondences, that are used with PnP [31] to directly compute an object's pose. BB8 [48] proposed the prediction of the location of the projections of the object's 3D bounding box corners. The idea was extended further in YOLO6D [55]. The multi-stage procedure was replaced with a direct one-shot detection with the YOLO detector [49]. YOLO was additionally augmented to simultaneously regress the projection of the 3D bounding box. As a result, YOLO6D has superior performance than BB8 both in terms of runtime and pose quality. Alternatively, CorNet [41] learns to predict generic corners which are then matched to the actual model corners.

Another group of methods relies on semantic segmentation rather than on detection. All methods in this group perform pixel-wise segmentation in order to increase the quantity of 2D-3D correspondences and improve robustness to occlusions. In Pixel-wise Voting Network (PVNet) [40]. each foreground pixel votes for the location of a predefined set of keypoints. This is similar to our approach, but ours is performed on sparse reconstructions represented with a point cloud. Two segmentation-based approaches, that are very similar to each other, are Pix2Pose [38] and DPOD [64]. In contrast to Hough voting for a fixed number of key points in PVNet, both Pix2Pose and DPOD treat each foreground pixel as a key point and predict a 2D-3D correspondence pair for each pixel. CDPN [33] combines a segmentation-based PnP method and direct pose regression. In [59], it is proposed using a two-stage approach. In the first stage, a standard semantic segmentation network is used to localize pixels belonging to the objects of interest. At the second stage, a Pointnet [46,47] is applied to the detected objects to estimate per-pixel pose hypothesis via direct pose regression. An alternative line of research focuses on how to properly deal with the ambiguities caused by symmetries [37,42].

Even though deep learning RGB methods have been extensively studied in the past, as described earlier, they all target pose estimation from a single image. Therefore, they are not directly applicable to the described multi-view scenario.

2.2   Methods for Depth Images and Point Clouds

Hand-crafted features still perform best when it comes to generic pose estimation in depth images. The leading method based on Point Pair Features (PPF) [14] and its numerous extensions [3,20,58] are still among the best-performing methods. However, despite its effectiveness, PPF is not appropriate for our tasks because no reliable normals can be estimated from a sparse point cloud. Another problem is that SfM reconstructions are defined up to a scale, and using them directly will be difficult because PPF are not scale-invariant.

PointNet [46,47] paved the way for feature extraction from raw point clouds for numerous object detection approaches in point clouds [32,44,45]. Even though these approaches are aimed at solving a related task, they are not directly applicable because they are targeted toward the type of challenges found in the KITTI dataset [18]. First, the KITTI dataset has a very limited number of unique object classes. Second, all objects are in the upright position and exhibit rotations only around a single axis. Lastly, all these approaches use real data for training. The most relevant paper to our approach is VoteNet [44]. In [44], it was proposed using semantic segmentation of point clouds and Hough voting for object detection and pose estimation. However, VoteNet does not use Hough votes to directly estimate the pose and does not use geometric constraints. Votes are only used for point cloud clustering and region proposal generation. Our approach differs from [44] in several ways. Our detector votes for multiple key points rather than only for the object's center. Each keypoint has a fixed location on the CAD model. The object pose can then be directly estimated from the votes and the known correspondences using the Umeyama algorithm [57].

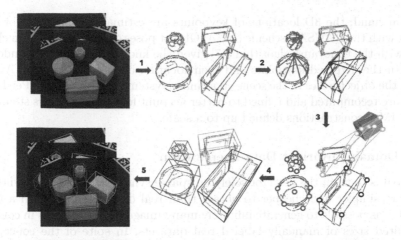

Fig. 2. Illustration of the inference steps of our method. 1) sparse reconstructions are obtained from a sequence of RGB images using COLMAP [50] and Lined3Dpp [25]; 2) seed points belonging to different objects vote for the keypoints. 3) the keypoints are localized, and the correspondences between a CAD model and an object in the scene are established; 4) poses of the objects in the sparse scene are estimated based on model-to-scene correspondences; and 5) poses of the objects in the sparse scene and camera poses from the COLMAP are used to recalculate the object poses in each frame.

3   Method

This section provides an in-depth description of all the components of the proposed method. The section starts with an overview of the pipeline: 1) synthetic data preparation; 2) the proposed network architecture, including the loss functions; 3) the inference stage of the proposed detector; and 4) implementation and training details.

3.1   General Pipeline

We deal herein with the problems of object detection and pose estimation of 3D objects, whose non-textured CAD models are known, in RGB images. In contrast to the other RGB-based deep learning approaches described in Sect. 2, which operate on individual frames, the proposed approach takes advantage of using multiple consecutive frames and jointly estimates poses for all of them. Figure 2 illustrates the overall idea of the presented approach comprising five key steps. 1) A sequence of RGB images (no depth information is used) is fed to the COLMAP SfM algorithm [50]. In this way, a sparse reconstruction of the scene is obtained, which is then approximated with the lines [25]. 2) 3DKeypointNet, which is based on PointNet++, is used to detect the 3D keypoints belonging to the objects. Each point belonging to the object in the scene votes for the locations of a predefined set of 3D keypoints of this particular object. 3) With votes at hand, the 3D locations of keypoints are estimated separately for each object with the RANSAC scheme [16]. 4) Object poses can be computed in closed form with the Umeyama algorithm [57] given the known 3D-3D correspondences between the detected keypoints and their location on the CAD model. At this stage, the object poses in the scene coordinate system are available. 5) Per-frame poses are recomputed and refined to better account for the pose errors stemming from SfM reconstructions defined up to a scale.

3.2   Domain-Invariant Data Preparation

Our goal is to train the detector solely on sparse synthetic data. First, synthetic data are simpler and cheaper to obtain than real data. Second, given a CAD model, it is possible to generate infinitely many images or simulations in contrast to limited sizes of manually labeled real datasets. In spite of the conceptual advantages of synthetic data, special care must be taken to bridge the domain gap. We solve this problem by assuming that 3D geometric edges are invariant to light changes; therefore, they can be reliably extracted from synthetic train and real test data. In both cases, we use the method of Hofer et al. [25] to replace a sparse 3D scene with its line representation.

The data preparation consists of three stages: 1) model preparation to represent the given CAD models with lines; 2) randomized simulation of synthetic 3D scenes and their post-processing; 3) approximation of the generated scenes with lines.

Model Preparation. The first step of the training data preparation is the pre-processing of the provided CAD models. Each CAD model is rendered in 1296 poses sampled from a sphere around the object. They are then used to reconstruct prominent 3D edges of the model, which are visible in RGB images, using [25]. The obtained reconstruction is essentially a sparse representation of a model, with geometric features that can be observed in both the captured RGB images of the object and in its synthetic renderings (see Fig. 3). Subsequently, a set of K keypoints is computed for each sparse model. The first selected keypoint is the object's center. The other points are obtained via the furthest point sampling of the model vertices.

Simulation of Synthetic 3D Scenes. The sparse nature of the test data also affects the training data generation pipeline, which consists of three steps. In the first step, synthetic training sequences are randomly simulated with the Bullet Physics Simulation engine [10]. The library generates scenes by randomly dropping objects on planar surfaces, which are sampled from the ScanNet dataset [11] to introduce more variability and make the scenes more realistic. The original dense CAD models are used in this stage. Each generated scene is saved together with poses of all the objects in the scene coordinate system. Figure 4(a) depicts an example of such a dense scene. These scenes are not yet suitable for training because they are not sparse and contain all the object points, even the invisible ones. The second step of the data preparation pipeline addresses these issues. The view-based model sampling method of Birdal et al. [4] is applied to make the simulated scenes resemble the reconstructions from a frame sequence. A random number of camera poses (i.e., between 2 and 8) located nearby on the upper hemisphere encapsulating the synthetic scene mesh is selected, followed by the removal of the invisible faces of the mesh for each pose. Consequently, this results in a mesh seen from a set of sampled viewpoints with removed invisible faces and respective vertices. However, the mesh is still dense.

Approximation of Synthetic Scenes with Lines. In the third and last step of data preparation, a sparse representation of the scene is computed using the poses obtained during the physical simulation and the sparse CAD models represented with 3D edges. The effect of the view-based sampling is propagated onto the sparse scene. A lookup table is created for each pair of dense and sparse CAD models. It associates the sparse model edges with the nearest vertices on the dense model. The vertices, which were removed during the view-based sampling, are subsequently used to remove the corresponding model edges in the sparse scenes. Finally, the sparse scenes are stored as a set of vertices and 3D edges, with a respective class label assigned for each of the vertices. Figure 4(b) depicts an example of a sparse scene is presented. The keypoints of each model, transformed with their poses in the scene coordinate system, are saved.

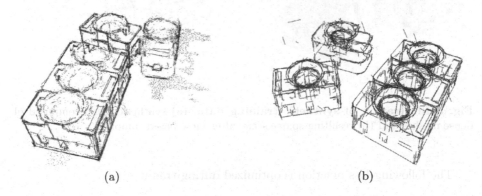

(a)   (b)

Fig. 3. Comparison of the synthetic and real edge reconstructions: (a) synthetic scene composed of edges and (b) real scene composed of edges.

3.3 3DKeypointNet - Keypoint Localization Network

While there are volumetric approaches for object detection and pose estimation [2], it was more natural for the given task to opt for the point cloud-based methods [46,47] because the data are already represented as sparse points and edges between them. This data representation can easily be converted into the point cloud format by sampling points from the existing edges.

The network architecture is based on the PointNet++ [47]. Its backbone architecture has several set abstraction levels followed by upsampling layers utilizing skip connections, which facilitates learning local features with increasing contextual scales. For a set of points $\{\mathbf{p}_i\}_{i=1}^N$, $\mathbf{p}_i \in \mathbb{R}^3$, the backbone module outputs M seed points with corresponding features of dimension D, namely $\{\mathbf{s}_i\}_{i=1}^M$, where $\mathbf{s}_i = [\mathbf{p}_i; \mathbf{f}_i]$, $\mathbf{p}_i \in \mathbb{R}^3$ and $\mathbf{f}_i \in \mathbb{R}^D$. The seed features $\mathbf{f}_i$ are then passed to the voting module composed of a shared multilayer perceptron with the ReLU activation function and batch normalization. For each seed point, the network outputs class confidences $\{\mathbf{c}_i\}_{i=1}^M$, where $\mathbf{c}_i \in \mathbb{R}^C$ and C is a number of classes, and estimated keypoint directions $\{\mathbf{D_i}\}_{i=1}^M$, where $\mathbf{D}_i \in \mathbb{R}^{K \times 3}$ is composed of row-wise normalized vectors $\mathbf{d}_j$ estimating the directions toward keypoints $\mathbf{k}_j \in \mathbb{R}^3$ on an object a seed point belongs to. The approach is aimed at making the network learn to estimate a relative position of a seed point in a more global context based on the information extracted from local neighborhoods of different sizes.

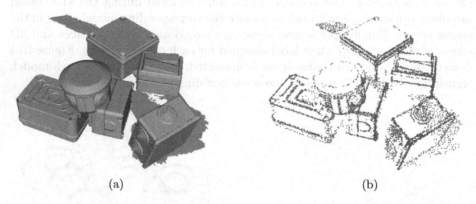

(a)   (b)

Fig. 4. Illustration of synthetic training data: (a) synthetic scene composed of dense meshes and (b) resulting sparse scene after view-based sampling

The following loss function is optimized during training:

$$\mathcal{L} = \mathcal{L}_{cls} + \lambda \mathcal{L}_{dir}, \tag{1}$$

where $\mathcal{L}_{cls}$ is a cross-entropy classification loss and $\mathcal{L}_{dir}$ is a direction regression loss defined as

$$\mathcal{L}_{dir} = \sum_{i=1}^M \sum_{j=1}^K smooth_{L_1}(\mathbf{d}_{ij}, \hat{\mathbf{d}}_{ij}) \mathbb{1}[\mathbf{p}_i \text{ is on object}], \tag{2}$$

where $\hat{\mathbf{d}}_{ij} \in \mathbb{R}^3$ is a ground truth normalized direction vector from a seed point $\mathbf{p}_i$ to a keypoint $\mathbf{k}_j$ of an object, namely $\hat{\mathbf{d}}_{ij} = \frac{\mathbf{p}_i - \mathbf{k}_j}{\|\mathbf{p}_i - \mathbf{k}_j\|_2}$, and $\lambda \in \mathbb{R}$ is a weighting scalar. The smooth L_1 loss is defined as in [34]. The indicator function $\mathbb{1}[\mathbf{p}_i \text{ is on object}]$ is used to eliminate objects on the background.

3.4 Inference

A sequence of RGB images $\{I_1, ..., I_n\}$ is taken as the initial input for inference. Accordingly, sequentially captured images were used in our experiment. The sequence is then processed with the COLMAP SfM method [50] that jointly estimates the camera poses $\Xi_i \in$ SE(3) for each image and sparse 3D points of the scene seen in the image sequence. As in the case of the training data, the method of Hofer et al. [25] is used to obtain a more detailed reconstruction of the edges in 3D.

It needs to be taken into account at the inference time that the reconstruction and the camera poses obtained through the SfM are defined up to a scale because no ground truth depth information or known camera locations are used in our method. The input 3D edges are scaled by a scalar $s = \frac{\mu_{train}}{d}$, where μ_{train} is the mean diameter of the training samples, and d is the diameter of the current test scene. Moreover, PCA whitening is applied to the reconstructed scenes to center and axis-align them, which increases their resemblance to the synthetic scenes used during training. The points are then sampled on the 3D edges with the average density used during the training time. The resulting point cloud is fed as an input to the detector. The network outputs per-seed point classification labels as well as estimation of the keypoint direction vectors, which are further used for the RANSAC-based voting for the object keypoint locations, similar to PVNet [40]. For each object class $c \in \{1, ..., C\}$ and for each object keypoint $\mathbf{k}_j$, $j \in \{1, ..., K\}$, a set of H keypoint location proposals is created by randomly sampling tuples of three seed points with the direction vectors. These seed points and directions define lines in 3D. Accordingly, a potential keypoint candidate $\mathbf{k}^*_{hcj}$ is defined as an approximate intersection of these three lines, which we define herein as an optimization problem that looks for the closest point to all those lines in terms of Euclidean distance

$$\mathbf{k}^*_{hcj} = \arg\min_{\mathbf{k}_{hcj}} \sum_{i \in \mathcal{I}} \|\mathbf{p}_{ij} + \lambda_{ij}\mathbf{d}_{ij} - \mathbf{k}_{hcj}\|^2_2, \tag{3}$$

where $\mathcal{I}$ is an index set of the selected seed points. The solutions to Eq. 3 are computed in closed form. All the other seed points belonging to the object of a particular class then vote for the computed keypoint candidates. If the dot product between the estimated vote vector $\mathbf{d}_j(\mathbf{p})$ of a seed point and the computed direction vector from a seed point $\mathbf{p}$ to a candidate $\mathbf{k}^*_{hcj}$ is above the threshold of θ, then the seed point is counted as an inlier:

$$\sum_{\mathbf{p} \in O_c} \mathbb{1}\left[\frac{(\mathbf{k}^*_{hcj} - \mathbf{p})^T}{\left\|\mathbf{k}^*_{hcj} - \mathbf{p}\right\|_2}\mathbf{d}_j(\mathbf{p}) \geq \theta\right] \tag{4}$$

Finally, all the inlier seed points are used to estimate the keypoints $\mathbf{k}^*_{hcj}$ using Eq. 3. The procedure can be executed several times to generate multiple hypotheses for each keypoint. In practice, the predicted keypoints are relatively unreliable because of data sparsity and the seed points sampling done internally in PointNet. The problem has been circumvented by running PointNet multiple times with random re-sampling, as was also done in [35], to produce more keypoint hypotheses.

Having a set of correspondence hypotheses between the estimated keypoints $\{k_{hcj}^*\}_{j=1}^{K}$ and the keypoints on the canonical model of an object $\{k_{hcj}\}_{j=1}^{K}$ for an object of class c it becomes possible to estimate a similarity transformation $S \in \mathrm{Sim}(3)$,

$$S = \begin{pmatrix} sR & t \\ 0^T & 1 \end{pmatrix} \text{ with } R \in SO(3), t \in \mathbb{R}^3 \text{ and } s \in \mathbb{R}^+, \tag{5}$$

which transforms and scales from the object's coordinate system to the scene point cloud coordinate system. This transformation can be estimated from the point correspondences in closed form using the Umeyama algorithm [57]. A RANSAC-based scheme is employed to choose from the hypotheses and deal with the outliers. Given an object, object pose and a set $\mathcal{PC}_c$ of points classified to belong to this object class, the pose quality is measured as a number of points from $\mathcal{PC}_c$ which lie within a certain threshold from the object's surface. The global scale of the reconstructed sparse scene is also estimated in this step.

However, even a minor scale estimation error may result in a considerable camera translation error in the Z-direction once the poses are reformulated using SE(3) transformations only. Therefore, further pose refinement is necessary. First, a variant of scale-aware point-to-point ICP is used on the reconstructed point cloud, followed by a multi-view edge-based refinement on RGB images inspired by the work of Drummond et al. [15]. The camera poses Ξ_i obtained from COLMAP remain fixed and only the similarity transformation from the model to the scene point cloud coordinate system is optimized. Again, no depth information is used. Multi-view consistency enforces the alignment of the object contours in every image, leading to a better solution, as opposed to the refinement in each RGB image separately, which may suffer from projective ambiguities.

3.5   Training and Implementation Details

We trained our detector on synthetic data generated from non-textured CAD models of the T-LESS dataset [21]. In our experiments, we focused on per-scene training. The detector is trained simultaneously for all the objects present in a particular test scene, as opposed to training one network per object. Training a separate network per each object is commonly done in other object detection and pose estimation pipelines because it tends to improve the results. However, this approach is not scalable and hard to apply in practice. For the training herein, a separate synthetic dataset for each of the scenes was generated. Each dataset 15K training samples. The data were generated completely automatically at random without any artistic modeling effort. With this setup, it took approximately 12 h (with 16 Intel Core i9-9900K) to generate a train set for a particular scene. The points on the edges of the synthetic data samples are randomly sampled online during training. Sampling was done uniformly along the edge. Moreover, a number of samples was determined by $\frac{\|e\|_2}{\nu}$, where $\|e\|_2$ is the length of an edge and $\nu \sim U[3; 10]$. The purpose of the sampling was twofold. It prevented the network from overfitting to exact point locations. Additionally, it enforced the detector to learn how to recognize more global geometric structures. The resulting point cloud was either subsampled or padded to contain 16384 points.

Various augmentations were applied to the input point clouds, including random rotations around the Z-axis and around X and Y axes between $[-20°, 20°]$, scene flipping around the Z-axis. Random scaling by a factor between $[0.5, 2.0]$ is used to make the network more robust to scale changes. In addition, random dropout of points and Gaussian noise are used.

The network has been implemented using PyTorch deep learning framework [39]. Training was done using the Adam optimizer [28] with a learning rate of 0.01, a learning rate decay of 0.5, a and decay step of $2 \cdot 10^5$. On average, convergence was observed within 200 training epochs. The weighting coefficient λ from the loss function in Eq. 1 was set to 5.0 in all the experiments.

4   Experiments

4.1   Dataset and Evaluation Metrics

We evaluate our method on the challenging T-LESS [21] dataset consisting of 30 textureless industrial objects. Two types of 3D models are supplied with the dataset: untextured CAD models and low-quality textured reconstructions. T-LESS features 20 test sequences of various complexities, each of which contains 501 images captured at different camera elevations. We chose the T-LESS dataset because it is still challenging not only for pure RGB detectors but also for RGBD detectors. Several factors contribute to the complexity of the dataset. First, all objects are textureless in a sense that they do not have distinctive colors. All of them are colored in more or less the same shade of gray, except for certain structural parts. As a result, the performance of RGB detectors is automatically hindered because they cannot rely on color information. Second, the T-LESS objects exhibit symmetries leading to pose ambiguity. Mutual and self-occlusions of the objects are extensively present in the test sequences. The presence of similar-looking objects also makes it difficult to distinguish between them in the monocular case. For RGB-based methods, detection becomes even more complicated when only the untextured CAD models with no additional real images are used as an input for training. We aim to demonstrate that by using sequences of RGB images instead of separate frames it is possible to leverage the performance of detection and pose estimation, even when only synthetic CAD models are used as an input for training. Thus, the TLESS dataset is an ideal test set for our approach, since significant performance boosts can be expected for the approaches utilizing multi-frame consistency to overcome the those challenges.

While other popular datasets for pose estimation can be used, such as YCB-Video [60], LINEMOD [19] and OCCLUSION [7], they are not fully suitable for our approach. Evaluation on them is hindered by the fact that they feature RGB images captured with low resolution of 640×480 pixels, which does not allow for reliable 3D reconstruction and approximation with lines. In addition, scenes in LINEMOD and OCCLUSION change too fast. Thus, the existing subsequences of images with a constant scene consist of too few frames with little camera motion, which significantly reduces the amount of extra information that the multi-view setup brings. This is the reason why we have not evaluated our approach on these datasets and fully focused on the T-LESS dataset, which also tends to be more complicated than the aforementioned datasets.

For the evaluation, we followed the BOP challenge [23] protocol for Varying number of Instances of a Varying number of Objects (VIVO) task. The BOP pipeline was chosen because it strives to unify the dataset formats and evaluation methodologies to facilitate a comparison of various methods. We computed the overall performance score as the mean of VSD, MSSD and MSPD recalls, each of which is averaged across several thresholds. Visible Surface Discrepancy (VSD) [22,24] was used as a de-facto standard measure for comparing the results on the T-LESS dataset. VSD compares distance maps of the object rendered in the estimated and ground truth poses. Maximum Symmetry-Aware Surface Distance (MSSD) was defined in [13] as the maximal distance between corresponding model vertices in the ground truth similarly to the symmetric ADD [19]. Maximum Symmetry-Aware Projection Distance (MSPD) extends the idea of the projection error of [8] by taking explicit care of the object symmetries.

Table 1. Per-scene quality on BOP Challenge images. First three methods rely solely on RGB images. Other methods use real depth data for pose refinement.

Modality	Method/scene	1	2	3	4	5	7	8	10	11	15	Average
RGB	DPOD	–	24.22	27.12	31.63	11.53	17.2	7.09	18.78	4.77	20.83	–
	AAE w\o ICP	49.32	64.08	45.2	42.65	38.56	43.81	31.74	26.88	50.57	21.81	41.46
	Ours	72.45	81.45	77.62	75.08	64.23	33.08	53.18	49.46	64.27	49	61.98
Depth	AAE w\ICP	73.78	95.82	77.66	70.29	68.92	58.76	57.83	48.39	88.1	36.99	67.65
	PPF	64.33	68.72	60.88	52	45.05	53.59	56.12	57.44	67.34	42.7	56.82
	PPF with ref.	69.38	73.72	74.37	71.76	73.55	56.52	49.73	62.58	85.25	47	66.39

Table 2. Per scene quality for our method on selected T-LESS sequences

Modality	Method/scene	1	2	3	4	5	7	8	10	11	15	Average
RGB	Ours	71.44	80.77	78.09	74.71	65.15	33.75	55.9	50.25	66.89	48.5	62.60

4.2   Results

We selected a minimal subset of all the scenes such that they cover all objects in the dataset. In the evaluation, subsequences of 72 consecutive frames were used to obtain the sparse reconstructions. Figure 5 demonstrates how the average recall changes depending on the number of frames used for the scene reconstruction. Two type of sequences were used: 1) consecutive frames, 2) frames with interleaving, when only every t-th frame was taken in order to cover as many camera poses around the object as possible. The plot confirms our assumption that a larger number of frames facilitates object detection and pose estimation. Taking frames with interleaving is also more robust when a fewer number of frames is used. The number of keypoints per model K was set to 8, and the inlier threshold θ introduced in Eq. 4 was set to 0.995. We experimented with using from 5 to 20 keypoints, but there was no significant change in performance with the increased number of points.

The evaluation was conducted in two directions: 1) to compare with the other methods utilizing synthetic training data; and 2) to report the recall on all the images in the dataset. In all the experiments only 360 first images of each scene were used. The reason for that is the fact that a significant portions of static background become visible on the lower camera elevations, and motion of the turntable becomes explicit. This violates the static scene requirement which is essential for the SfM, making scene reconstruction impossible.

We ran the evaluation procedure on the BOP subset of the T-LESS data to perform a comparison with the other top-performing methods. Table 1 provides average recall for three different methods: AAE (with and without ICP) [53], DPOD [64], PPF (uses real depth and ICP) [14] and PPF with refinement [12]. The results show that our method clearly outperforms all the other approaches if no depth-based ICP is applied. Even result of AAE, which uses real data for training the detector, fall far behind. The only exception is scene 7, which contains numerous small round-shaped objects exhibiting strong inter-object similarity and no strong geometric features. The sparsity of the reconstructions does not allow for reliable representation of their geometry. This resulted in misdetections and inaccurately predicted poses. Moreover, the network also confuses similarly looking objects. Compared to AAE with ICP and the PPF variants, our approach still shows competitive results even though we do not use any real depth for refinement. With a score of 61.98 it outperforms the classical PPF, which achieves 56.82, by a large margin. In comparison with the PPF and AAE refined with ICP, our detector performs only slightly inferior. Table 2 presents the average per-scene recall of our detector on all the first 360 of images of each scene from the T-LESS dataset. A visual inspection of the predicted poses showed that the

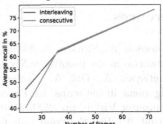

Fig. 5. Ablation study of the necessary number of sequential frames

pose recall is mostly bounded by the object detection performance. If an object is detected, then its estimated pose is almost always nearly perfect.

5   Conclusions

In this work, we have introduced a pipeline for object detection from a sequence of RGB-only images. The presented approach is trained on synthetic simulations and, therefore, does not require any labeled real data. A sequence of images is processed with an SfM algorithm to obtain a sparse reconstruction for the scene to allow for a simultaneous detection for all of the images in one shot. We relied heavily on the intuition that the geometric edges are the only prominent features that can both be extracted from the 3D models as well as from the sequences of real RGB images. The resulting detector was found to work significantly better than DPOD, which was also trained completely on synthetic data, and AAE, which used real data for training the 2D detector and synthetic data for the pose estimation network. Additionally, our detector works better or on par with AAE and the PPF-based approaches even if their poses are refined with depth ICP.

Acknowledgements. We thank the authors of AAE [52,53], DPOD [64] and PPF [12,14] for providing us with the poses estimated with their detectors.

References

1. Antoniou, A., Storkey, A., Edwards, H.: Data augmentation generative adversarial networks. arXiv preprint arXiv:1711.04340 (2017)
2. Avetisyan, A., Dai, A., Nießner, M.: End-to-end cad model retrieval and 9dof alignment in 3D scans. In: Proceedings of the IEEE International Conference on Computer Vision, pp. 2551–2560 (2019)
3. Birdal, T., Ilic, S.: Point pair features based object detection and pose estimation revisited. In: 2015 International Conference on 3D Vision, pp. 527–535. IEEE (2015)
4. Birdal, T., Ilic, S.: A point sampling algorithm for 3D matching of irregular geometries. In: 2017 IEEE/RSJ International Conference on Intelligent Robots and Systems (IROS), pp. 6871–6878. IEEE (2017)
5. Bousmalis, K., Silberman, N., Dohan, D., Erhan, D., Krishnan, D.: Unsupervised pixel-level domain adaptation with generative adversarial networks. In: Proceedings of the IEEE Conference on Computer Vision and Pattern Recognition, pp. 3722–3731 (2017)
6. Bousmalis, K., Trigeorgis, G., Silberman, N., Krishnan, D., Erhan, D.: Domain separation networks. In: Advances in Neural Information Processing Systems, pp. 343–351 (2016)
7. Brachmann, E., Krull, A., Michel, F., Gumhold, S., Shotton, J., Rother, C.: Learning 6D object pose estimation using 3D object coordinates. In: Fleet, D., Pajdla, T., Schiele, B., Tuytelaars, T. (eds.) ECCV 2014. LNCS, vol. 8690, pp. 536–551. Springer, Cham (2014). https://doi.org/10.1007/978-3-319-10605-2_35

8. Brachmann, E., Michel, F., Krull, A., Ying Yang, M., Gumhold, S., et al.: Uncertainty-driven 6D pose estimation of objects and scenes from a single RGB image. In: Proceedings of the IEEE Conference on Computer Vision and Pattern Recognition, pp. 3364–3372 (2016)
9. Chen, X., Ma, H., Wan, J., Li, B., Xia, T.: Multi-view 3D object detection network for autonomous driving. In: Proceedings of the IEEE Conference on Computer Vision and Pattern Recognition, pp. 1907–1915 (2017)
10. Coumans, E.: Bullet physics simulation. In: ACM SIGGRAPH 2015 Courses, p. 7. ACM (2015)
11. Dai, A., Chang, A.X., Savva, M., Halber, M., Funkhouser, T., Nießner, M.: Scan-Net: richly-annotated 3D reconstructions of indoor scenes. In: Proceedings of the IEEE Conference on Computer Vision and Pattern Recognition, pp. 5828–5839 (2017)
12. Drost, B., Ilic, S.: 3D object detection and localization using multimodal point pair features. In: 2012 Second International Conference on 3D Imaging, Modeling, Processing, Visualization & Transmission, pp. 9–16. IEEE (2012)
13. Drost, B., Ulrich, M., Bergmann, P., Hartinger, P., Steger, C.: Introducing MVTec ITODD-a dataset for 3D object recognition in industry. In: Proceedings of the IEEE International Conference on Computer Vision, pp. 2200–2208 (2017)
14. Drost, B., Ulrich, M., Navab, N., Ilic, S.: Model globally, match locally: efficient and robust 3D object recognition. In: 2010 IEEE Computer Society Conference on Computer Vision and Pattern Recognition, pp. 998–1005. IEEE (2010)
15. Drummond, T., Cipolla, R.: Real-time visual tracking of complex structures. IEEE Trans. Pattern Anal. Mach. Intell. 24(7), 932–946 (2002). https://doi.org/10.1109/TPAMI.2002.1017620
16. Fischler, M.A., Bolles, R.C.: Random sample consensus: a paradigm for model fitting with applications to image analysis and automated cartography. Commun. ACM 24(6), 381–395 (1981)
17. Ganin, Y., et al.: Domain-adversarial training of neural networks. J. Mach. Learn. Res. 17(1), 2096-2030 (2016)
18. Geiger, A., Lenz, P., Stiller, C., Urtasun, R.: Vision meets robotics: the KITTI dataset. Int. J. Robot. Res. (IJRR) 32(11), 1231–1237 (2013)
19. Hinterstoisser, S., et al.: Model based training, detection and pose estimation of texture-less 3D objects in heavily cluttered scenes. In: Lee, K.M., Matsushita, Y., Rehg, J.M., Hu, Z. (eds.) ACCV 2012. LNCS, vol. 7724, pp. 548–562. Springer, Heidelberg (2013). https://doi.org/10.1007/978-3-642-37331-2_42
20. Hinterstoisser, S., Lepetit, V., Rajkumar, N., Konolige, K.: Going further with point pair features. In: Leibe, B., Matas, J., Sebe, N., Welling, M. (eds.) ECCV 2016. LNCS, vol. 9907, pp. 834–848. Springer, Cham (2016). https://doi.org/10.1007/978-3-319-46487-9_51
21. Hodaň, T., Haluza, P., Obdržálek, Š., Matas, J., Lourakis, M., Zabulis, X.: T-LESS: an RGB-D dataset for 6D pose estimation of texture-less objects. In: IEEE Winter Conference on Applications of Computer Vision (WACV) (2017)
22. Hodaň, T., Matas, J., Obdržálek, Š.: On evaluation of 6D object pose estimation. In: Hua, G., Jégou, H. (eds.) ECCV 2016. LNCS, vol. 9915, pp. 606–619. Springer, Cham (2016). https://doi.org/10.1007/978-3-319-49409-8_52
23. Hodan, T., Melenovsky, A.: BOP: benchmark for 6D object pose estimation (2019). https://bop.felk.cvut.cz/home/
24. Hodaň, T., et al.: BOP: benchmark for 6D object pose estimation. In: Ferrari, V., Hebert, M., Sminchisescu, C., Weiss, Y. (eds.) ECCV 2018. LNCS, vol. 11214, pp. 19–35. Springer, Cham (2018). https://doi.org/10.1007/978-3-030-01249-6_2

25. Hofer, M., Maurer, M., Bischof, H.: Efficient 3D scene abstraction using line segments. Comput. Vis. Image Underst. **157**, 167–178 (2017)
26. Kaskman, R., Zakharov, S., Shugurov, I., Ilic, S.: HomebrewedDB: RGB-D dataset for 6D pose estimation of 3D objects. In: The IEEE International Conference on Computer Vision (ICCV) Workshops, October 2019
27. Kehl, W., Manhardt, F., Tombari, F., Ilic, S., Navab, N.: SSD-6D: making RGB-based 3D detection and 6D pose estimation great again. In: Proceedings of the IEEE International Conference on Computer Vision, pp. 1521–1529 (2017)
28. Kingma, D.P., Ba, J.: Adam: a method for stochastic optimization. arXiv preprint arXiv:1412.6980 (2014)
29. Ku, J., Mozifian, M., Lee, J., Harakeh, A., Waslander, S.L.: Joint 3D proposal generation and object detection from view aggregation. In: 2018 IEEE/RSJ International Conference on Intelligent Robots and Systems (IROS), pp. 1–8. IEEE (2018)
30. Lee, H.-Y., Tseng, H.-Y., Huang, J.-B., Singh, M., Yang, M.-H.: Diverse image-to-image translation via disentangled representations. In: Ferrari, V., Hebert, M., Sminchisescu, C., Weiss, Y. (eds.) ECCV 2018. LNCS, vol. 11205, pp. 36–52. Springer, Cham (2018). https://doi.org/10.1007/978-3-030-01246-5_3
31. Lepetit, V., Moreno-Noguer, F., Fua, P.: EPnP: an accurate $O(n)$ solution to the PnP problem. Int. J. Comput. Vision **81**(2) (2009). Article number: 155. https://doi.org/10.1007/s11263-008-0152-6
32. Li, Y., Bu, R., Sun, M., Chen, B.: PointCNN. arXiv preprint arXiv:1801.07791 (2018)
33. Li, Z., Wang, G., Ji, X.: CDPN: coordinates-based disentangled pose network for real-time RGB-based 6-DoF object pose estimation. In: The IEEE International Conference on Computer Vision (ICCV), October 2019
34. Liu, W., et al.: SSD: single shot multibox detector. In: Leibe, B., Matas, J., Sebe, N., Welling, M. (eds.) ECCV 2016. LNCS, vol. 9905, pp. 21–37. Springer, Cham (2016). https://doi.org/10.1007/978-3-319-46448-0_2
35. Liu, X., Qi, C.R., Guibas, L.J.: FlowNet3D: learning scene flow in 3D point clouds. In: Proceedings of the IEEE Conference on Computer Vision and Pattern Recognition, pp. 529–537 (2019)
36. Long, M., Cao, Y., Wang, J., Jordan, M.I.: Learning transferable features with deep adaptation networks. arXiv preprint arXiv:1502.02791 (2015)
37. Manhardt, F., et al.: Explaining the ambiguity of object detection and 6D pose from visual data. In: Proceedings of the IEEE International Conference on Computer Vision, pp. 6841–6850 (2019)
38. Park, K., Patten, T., Vincze, M.: Pix2Pose: pixel-wise coordinate regression of objects for 6D pose estimation. In: The IEEE International Conference on Computer Vision (ICCV), October 2019
39. Paszke, A., et al.: Automatic differentiation in PyTorch. In: NIPS Autodiff Workshop (2017)
40. Peng, S., Liu, Y., Huang, Q., Zhou, X., Bao, H.: PVNet: pixel-wise voting network for 6DoF pose estimation. In: Proceedings of the IEEE Conference on Computer Vision and Pattern Recognition, pp. 4561–4570 (2019)
41. Pitteri, G., Ilic, S., Lepetit, V.: CorNet: generic 3D corners for 6D pose estimation of new objects without retraining. In: The IEEE International Conference on Computer Vision (ICCV) Workshops, October 2019
42. Pitteri, G., Ramamonjisoa, M., Ilic, S., Lepetit, V.: On object symmetries and 6D pose estimation from images. In: 2019 International Conference on 3D Vision (3DV), pp. 614–622. IEEE (2019)

43. Planche, B., Zakharov, S., Wu, Z., Hutter, A., Kosch, H., Ilic, S.: Seeing beyond appearance-mapping real images into geometrical domains for unsupervised cad-based recognition. arXiv preprint arXiv:1810.04158 (2018)
44. Qi, C.R., Litany, O., He, K., Guibas, L.J.: Deep hough voting for 3D object detection in point clouds. arXiv preprint arXiv:1904.09664 (2019)
45. Qi, C.R., Liu, W., Wu, C., Su, H., Guibas, L.J.: Frustum PointNets for 3D object detection from RGB-D data. In: Proceedings of the IEEE Conference on Computer Vision and Pattern Recognition, pp. 918–927 (2018)
46. Qi, C.R., Su, H., Mo, K., Guibas, L.J.: PointNet: deep learning on point sets for 3D classification and segmentation. In: Proceedings of the IEEE Conference on Computer Vision and Pattern Recognition, pp. 652–660 (2017)
47. Qi, C.R., Yi, L., Su, H., Guibas, L.J.: PointNet++: deep hierarchical feature learning on point sets in a metric space. In: Advances in Neural Information Processing Systems, pp. 5099–5108 (2017)
48. Rad, M., Lepetit, V.: BB8: a scalable, accurate, robust to partial occlusion method for predicting the 3D poses of challenging objects without using depth. In: Proceedings of the IEEE International Conference on Computer Vision, pp. 3828–3836 (2017)
49. Redmon, J., Divvala, S., Girshick, R., Farhadi, A.: You only look once: unified, real-time object detection. In: Proceedings of the IEEE Conference on Computer Vision and Pattern Recognition, pp. 779–788 (2016)
50. Schonberger, J.L., Frahm, J.M.: Structure-from-motion revisited. In: Proceedings of the IEEE Conference on Computer Vision and Pattern Recognition, pp. 4104–4113 (2016)
51. Shrivastava, A., Pfister, T., Tuzel, O., Susskind, J., Wang, W., Webb, R.: Learning from simulated and unsupervised images through adversarial training. In: Proceedings of the IEEE Conference on Computer Vision and Pattern Recognition, pp. 2107–2116 (2017)
52. Sundermeyer, M., Marton, Z.C., Durner, M., Brucker, M., Triebel, R.: Implicit 3D orientation learning for 6D object detection from RGB images. In: Proceedings of the European Conference on Computer Vision (ECCV), pp. 699–715 (2018)
53. Sundermeyer, M., Marton, Z.C., Durner, M., Triebel, R.: Augmented autoencoders: implicit 3D orientation learning for 6D object detection. Int. J. Comput. Vis. **128**, 714–729 (2020). https://doi.org/10.1007/s11263-019-01243-810.1007/s11263-019-01243-8
54. Taigman, Y., Polyak, A., Wolf, L.: Unsupervised cross-domain image generation. arXiv preprint arXiv:1611.02200 (2016)
55. Tekin, B., Sinha, S.N., Fua, P.: Real-time seamless single shot 6D object pose prediction. In: Proceedings of the IEEE Conference on Computer Vision and Pattern Recognition, pp. 292–301 (2018)
56. Tzeng, E., Hoffman, J., Zhang, N., Saenko, K., Darrell, T.: Deep domain confusion: maximizing for domain invariance. arXiv preprint arXiv:1412.3474 (2014)
57. Umeyama, S.: Least-squares estimation of transformation parameters between two point patterns. IEEE Trans. Pattern Anal. Mach. Intell. **4**, 376–380 (1991)
58. Vidal, J., Lin, C.Y., Lladó, X., Martí, R.: A method for 6D pose estimation of free-form rigid objects using point pair features on range data. Sensors **18**(8), 2678 (2018)
59. Wang, C., et al.: DenseFusion: 6D object pose estimation by iterative dense fusion. In: Proceedings of the IEEE Conference on Computer Vision and Pattern Recognition, pp. 3343–3352 (2019)

60. Xiang, Y., Schmidt, T., Narayanan, V., Fox, D.: PoseCNN: a convolutional neural network for 6D object pose estimation in cluttered scenes. arXiv preprint arXiv:1711.00199 (2017)
61. Yang, B., Luo, W., Urtasun, R.: PIXOR: real-time 3D object detection from point clouds. In: Proceedings of the IEEE Conference on Computer Vision and Pattern Recognition, pp. 7652–7660 (2018)
62. Zakharov, S., Kehl, W., Ilic, S.: DeceptionNet: network-driven domain randomization. In: Proceedings of the IEEE International Conference on Computer Vision, pp. 532–541 (2019)
63. Zakharov, S., Planche, B., Wu, Z., Hutter, A., Kosch, H., Ilic, S.: Keep it unreal: bridging the realism gap for 2.5D recognition with geometry priors only. In: 3DV (2018)
64. Zakharov, S., Shugurov, I., Ilic, S.: DPOD: 6D pose object detector and refiner. In: Proceedings of the IEEE International Conference on Computer Vision, pp. 1941–1950 (2019)
65. Zhou, Y., Tuzel, O.: VoxelNet: end-to-end learning for point cloud based 3D object detection. In: Proceedings of the IEEE Conference on Computer Vision and Pattern Recognition, pp. 4490–4499 (2018)

Semi-supervised Viewpoint Estimation with Geometry-Aware Conditional Generation

Octave Mariotti[(✉)] and Hakan Bilen[iD]

School of Informatics, University of Edinburgh, Edinburgh, UK
o.mariotti@sms.ed.ac.uk

Abstract. There is a growing interest in developing computer vision methods that can learn from limited supervision. In this paper, we consider the problem of learning to predict camera viewpoints, where obtaining ground-truth annotations are expensive and require special equipment, from a limited number of labeled images. We propose a semi-supervised viewpoint estimation method that can learn to infer viewpoint information from unlabeled image pairs, where two images differ by a viewpoint change. In particular our method learns to synthesize the second image by combining the appearance from the first one and viewpoint from the second one. We demonstrate that our method significantly improves the supervised techniques, especially in the low-label regime and outperforms the state-of-the-art semi-supervised methods.

Keywords: 3D viewpoint estimation · Semi-supervised learning · Conditional image generation

1 Introduction

Large-scaled labeled datasets have been an important driving force in the advancement of the state-of-the-art in computer vision tasks. However, annotating data is expensive and is not scalable to a growing body of complex visual concepts. This paper focuses on the problem of viewpoint (azimuth, elevation, and in-plane-rotation) estimation of rigid objects relative to the camera from limited supervision where obtaining annotations typically involves specialized hardware and in controlled environments (*e.g.* [6,11]) or a tedious process of manually aligning 3D CAD models with real-world objects (*e.g.* [43]). State-of-the-art viewpoint estimation methods [8,23,48] have shown to yield excellent results in the presence of large-scale annotated datasets, yet it remains unclear how to leverage unlabeled images.

One way of reducing annotation cost for viewpoint estimation is to produce synthetic datasets by rendering images of 3D CAD models in different views [24]. While it is possible to generate a large amount of labeled synthetic data with rendering and simulator tools and learn viewpoint estimators on them, discrepancies between the synthetic and real world images would make their transfer

© Springer Nature Switzerland AG 2020
A. Bartoli and A. Fusiello (Eds.): ECCV 2020 Workshops, LNCS 12536, pp. 631–647, 2020.
https://doi.org/10.1007/978-3-030-66096-3_42

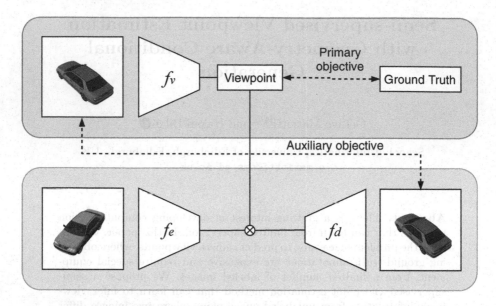

Fig. 1. Overview of the semi-supervised framework. Our primary objective is to learn the camera viewpoint from the picture of an object. Given another picture of the same object, we also reconstruct the first using conditional generation to provide additional supervision.

challenging. Su *et al.* [30] show that overlaying images rendered from large 3D model collections on top of real images results result in realistic training images and boosts the viewpoint performance when they are used in training. Motivated by the fact that accurate 3D models and diverse background scenes are not always available, domain randomization [39] addresses the reality gap by simulating a wide range of environments at training time and assume that the variability of the simulation is significant enough to generalize the real world.

Another line of work [14,29,36,37] learns representations from large sets of unlabeled images by self-supervised training and transfers the knowledge to a supervised down-stream viewpoint and pose estimation. Thewlis *et al.* [36,37] learn sparse and dense facial landmarks based on the principles of equivariance and distinctiveness. Jakab *et al.* [14] learn landmark detectors by factorizing appearance and geometry in a conditional generation framework. However, these techniques are limited to predicting 2D landmarks, small in-plane rotations, insufficient to learn 3D objects in case of significant pose variations and the learned representations (*i.e.* landmarks) are not semantically meaningful. Most related to ours, Rhodin *et al.* [29] propose a geometry aware autoencoder that learns to translate a person image from one viewpoint to another in a multi-camera setup. Unlike [29] that requires the knowledge of the rotation between each camera pairs, our method jointly learns the rotations between *unknown viewpoints* and conditionally generating images. This difference enables learning of our method on images from arbitrary views and extends its use to single camera setups.

In this paper, we follow an orthogonal semi-supervised approach to the previous methods that focus on learning from synthetic data and self-supervision. Semi-supervised learning is one of the standard approaches that learn not only from labeled samples but also unlabeled ones. Many recent semi-supervised methods [1,34,44] employ a regularization techniques that encourages the models to produce consistent output distributions when their inputs are perturbed. However, strong data augmentations (e.g. MixUp [47]) in [1] that are used to perturb images in image classification are not applicable to viewpoint estimation, as mixing up two object images at different views produces an ambiguous input for viewpoint estimation.

Instead, we propose a semi-supervised method that is specifically designed for viewpoint estimation. We pose this as the problem of image synthesis by conditioning on the viewpoint of objects in them. In particular, our method takes in a pair of images that contain an object captured in different viewpoints, encodes the appearance of the object in the first image and estimates the viewpoint of the object in the second image, reconstruct the second image from them. An overview of our method is show on Fig. 1.

While the conditional generation from image pairs forces the network to learn factorized representations for appearance and viewpoint and does not require label supervision, there is a high degree of ambiguity for representing the viewpoint in a deep neural network and no guarantee that the learned representation corresponds to ground-truth viewpoint. Thus we address this challenge by simultaneously training the viewpoint estimator on a small set of labeled images to encourage the inferred viewpoints from unlabeled images to be consistent with the labeled ones. We show that our method can effectively leverage the information in unlabeled images, improves viewpoint estimation with limited supervision and outperforms the state-of-the-art semi-supervised methods in a standard viewpoint estimation benchmark.

2   Related Work

Early Supervised Pose Estimation. The early models proposed in object pose estimation use classical computer vision techniques, rely on matching image features like gradients or surface normals with predefined templates, either recovered from the object itself in a controlled setup, or by using 3D CAD models to obtain rough estimates [9,10]. These methods require pose supervision and have limited applicability due to their lack of generalization.

Recent Supervised Pose Estimation. More recent methods typically split the pose estimation into two subtasks, object localisation and rotation estimation, use a CNN for each. Localisation is most often performed using pretrained models (e.g. r-CNN [7]) while rotation are recovered either by 3D bounding cube regression [8,28,35] or viewpoint classification [20]. As excellent performances have been reported on controlled setups, focus has shifted towards specifications of the task, such as avoiding errors caused by symmetries and lowering the necessary supervision by removing depth maps [28], or targeting real-time performances [20]. Direct regression over the rotation space has also been explored and proved to be on par with other ways of recovering rotations [23,25], while multitask approaches have also been shown to help by adding keypoint detection for instance [41,48]. Viewpoint estimation specific architectures that go beyond generic CNNs are also getting proposed, in a effort to tailor neural network to the characteristics of the task [3–5,16].

Pose Estimation from Synthetic Data. As training labels on real images are expensive to obtain, many works try to reduce the cost of supervision. The most common approach is to use synthetic data obtained from 3D CAD models [30,31, 33], however, these methods tend to have issues generalizing to real data. Other works explore using extremely limited sets of poses [18,29], mainly because of dataset restrictions.

3D Reconstruction. Another line of work focuses on producing a 3D reconstruction of the object from 2D views by geometry-aware deep representations. However, as they are only interested in the 3D-aware representation, they tend to consider pose information as an already-acquired supervision. Nonetheless, several recent works show that pose supervision is not strictly required to produce a 3D model, either voxel-based [40,45,46], point clouds [12], or 3D meshes [19]. The mesh approach was also extended in an unsupervised way [17]. In this case, pose is learned jointly with the reconstruction and supervision is done by projection the 3D shape in camera space. The 2D image obtained is then compared with the ground-truth segmentation mask. These works involve heavy networks to deal with full 3d representations, and a complex differentiable rendering stage. In contrast, we aim for a fully convolutional, more flexible architecture.

Geometry-Aware Representations. Another related line of approaches involves producing lighter weight representations that describe the geometry of the object while being sensitive to pose. Often, these are designed following an equivariance principle, that is, applying a transformation *e.g.* a rotation to the object will have the effect of transforming the representation in similar way. Precursory works specifically targeting equivariance rely on autoencoding architecture and constrain the encoding to respect the structure of the data [22]. A more involved approach consists in entangling a learned embedding with a rotation. This has first been proposed on feature maps and 2D rotations [13], then adapted to general representations [42] and applied on full 3D rotations [29], albeit with a very restricted set of poses. Other rotation-specific equivariant representations were also designed by adapting CNNs to operate on spherical signals [3–5]. These spherical CNNs rely on heavy 3D supervision and typically operate on a coarse scale due to their use of Fourier transform, but their construction guarantees good results on rotation estimation.

Keypoint-Based Methods. Keypoints are a natural equivariant representation: they describe the pose and it is intuitively possible to discover them without supervision. 2D keypoints have been discovered on humans and faces with [14] or without [37] reconstruction. 3D keypoints are used in case of full 3D rotations [32], however, no approach has been shown to reliably estimate them without strong pose supervision. Mapping the image pixels to a sphere has also been explored as a continuous generalization of keypoints, but this technique faces the same issues as its discrete counterpart [36,38].

Generative-Based Methods. Recent advances in generative adversarial networks have allowed frameworks to learn geometry-aware representations, through the generation of images under different viewpoint [26,27]. These methods are still experimental and are still subject to a certain degree of unsuitability, but show a promising and novel angle of attack on viewpoint estimation.

3   Method

3.1   Supervised Viewpoint Estimation

Assume that we are given a set of m labeled images with their ground-truth viewpoints, w.r.t. a fixed camera, $\mathcal{T} = \{(I_i, v_i)\}_{i=1}^{m}$, where $I \in \mathcal{I}$ is an RGB image and $v = (a^1, a^2, a^3) \in \mathcal{V}$ is a 3-dimensional vector represented in azimuth, elevation and in-plane rotations respectively, their values are between 0 and 2π. There exists several ways to represent v, most common methods being the axis-angle representation, a unit quaternion or a rotation matrix. To simplify the learning procedure, we model v simply by a three-dimensional vector interpreted as the camera position in object-centric coordinates. We wish to learn a mapping from an image to its viewpoint $f_v : \mathcal{I} \to \mathcal{V}$ such that $f_v(I; \theta_v) = v$ where θ_v are the parameters of f_v. One can learn such a mapping by minimizing the following empirical loss over the set $\mathcal{T}$ w.r.t. θ_v:

$$\sum_{(I,v)\in\mathcal{T}} ||f_v(I; \theta_v) - v||^2. \tag{1}$$

3.2   Geometry-Aware Representation

We are also given a set of n unlabelled image pairs $\mathcal{U} = \{(I_i, I_i')\}$ where each pair contains two images of an object instance (*e.g.* airplane, car, chair) that are captured at two different viewpoints. We assume that the ground-truth viewpoints of the images are not available and we wish to improve the performance of our viewpoint predictor f by leveraging the information in the unlabeled images.

A commonly used tool for unsupervised learning is autoencoder that encodes its input I into a low dimensional encoding $f_e(I; \theta_e)$ via an encoder network E and maps the encoding to the input space, *i.e.* $f_d(f_e(I; \theta_e); \theta_d)$, via a decoder network f_d to reconstruct the input. The encoder and decoder are parameterized by θ_e and θ_d respectively. Although autoencoders can successfully be utilized to learn informative representations that can reconstruct the original image, there is no guarantee for the embeddings to encode the 3D viewpoints of objects in a disentangled manner.

One solution to relate an embedding of an object in image I to its viewpoint v involves a conditional image generation technique. This was first proposed in [42] for in-plane rotations and extended in [29] for 3D ones, In particular, given an image pair I and I' that contain the same object viewed from two different points and also given the viewpoint of from which the object is seen in the images, this method couples the viewpoint and the appearance of the object in the encoding. To this end, the embedding of image I, $f_e(I)$ is transformed by using the rotation $R(v')$ where v' is the viewpoint in image I' and $R(v') \in SO(3)$ computes the rotation matrix associated to v'. The rotated embedding is then decoded, i.e. $f_d(R(v') \times f_e(I; \theta_e)); \theta_d)$, to reconstruct not the input I but I' by minimizing the following loss w.r.t. the parameters of the encoder and decoder:

$$\sum_{(I,I',v') \in \mathcal{U}} ||f_d(R(v') \times f_e(I; \theta_e)); \theta_d) - I'||^2 \qquad (2)$$

where the output of the encoder $f_e(I; \theta_e)$ is designed to be $3 \times k$ dimensional such that it can be rotated by the rotation matrix $R(v')$.

This presents a slight variation over the framework in [29] as the rotation here is absolute instead of relative. This means that the embedding $f_e(I; \theta_e)$ should represent the object from an canonical viewpoint instead of the one from which it appears in I.

This formulation enables the method to learn a "geometry aware" representation that can relate the viewpoint difference in 3D space to its projection in pixel space. However, it requires the ground-truth viewpoint for each image I', which limits the applicability of the method to supervision-rich setups. To address this limitation and extend learning of the geometry-aware representations to image pairs with unknown viewpoints, we propose an analysis by synthesis method. To this end, we predict the viewpoint as $\hat{v} = f_v(I; \theta_v)$ for I by using the viewpoint estimator f, and substitute it with $R(v')$ in Eq. (2):

$$\sum_{(I,I') \in \mathcal{U}} ||f_d(R(f_v(I'; \theta_v)) \times f_e(I; \theta_e)); \theta_d) - I'||^2 \qquad (3)$$

This formulation models the reconstruction loss as a function of viewpoint predictor f and therefore allows the gradients to flow in the pose regression network without any viewpoint supervision. Furthermore, working with absolute viewpoints not only allows a more straightforward optimization as we only need one viewpoint estimation whereas two would be needed to compute a relative pose, it also makes learning an encoding easier as it factors out the burden of estimating the pose.

3.3   Semi-supervised Viewpoint Prediction

Our hypothesis is that a successful reconstruction of I' requires an accurate viewpoint estimation. However, given high-capacity encoder and decoder architectures, accurate viewpoints enable high-fidelity reconstructions, the converse is not necessarily true as the viewpoints in the encoding can be represented in infinite different ways and there is no guarantee that the learned viewpoints for the images will match with their ground-truth view. For instance, the output of the viewpoint estimator can be distributed between 0 and π for each angle instead of the entire range of $[0, 2\pi)$ or the angles can be mapped to a non-linear and uninterpretable space, while the network preserves its reconstruction performance. Thus, we propose a semi-supervised formulation in which the estimated viewpoints are regularized as below by optimizing the combined loss terms in Eq. (1) and Eq. (3):

$$\min_{\theta_v, \theta_e, \theta_d} \sum_{(I,v) \in \mathcal{T}} \|f_v(I; \theta_v) - v\|^2 + \lambda \sum_{(I,I') \in \mathcal{T} \cup \mathcal{U}} \|f_d(R(f_v(I'; \theta_v)) \times f_e(I; \theta_e)); \theta_d) - I'\|^2$$

(4)

where λ is a tradeoff hyperparameter between the supervised and unsupervised loss terms. In words, the formulation allows gradients for the unsupervised loss to flow in the viewpoint network f_v, and the supervision imposed on the viewpoint space in turn constrains the learned representation to capture the structure of the object.

The supervision provided by the reconstruction task brings the question of unsupervised viewpoint estimation using no pose labels. While theoretically possible, we find that it is likely to fail in complex scenarios, as the supervision signal is too weak to provide good viewpoint supervision. In particular, symmetries in real world objects push the learned pose towards degenerates solutions. This is further demonstrated in Sects. 4.4 and 4.6

4   Experiments

4.1   Dataset

We use the popular Shapenet [2] dataset that consists of a large bank of 3D CAD models, classified in different object categories. This makes obtaining a large number of views spreading various viewpoints fairly straightforward, as well as acquiring several views of the same object, a feature often absent in other 3D datasets like Pascal3D [43]. Because we render the 3D models, we automatically know the ground truth viewpoint as well, making data labeling a triviality. We mainly focus on three object categories, aeroplanes, cars and chairs, as they offer enough models to build a diversified image dataset. For each category, we render each model with 10 randomly selected viewpoints, with azimuth ranging the complete 360° rotation and elevation selected from $-20°$ to 40°. The final datasets contain 40460, 36760 and 67790 images for the aeroplane, car and chair category respectively. We split the data in training, validation and testing sets, accounting for 70, 10 and 20% of the whole dataset respectively. To simulate a semi-supervised setup, we further split the training set by randomly selecting a subset of the data to act as the labeled set, the rest acting as unlabeled. We adjust the ratio of labeled samples in our experiments to show the effect of

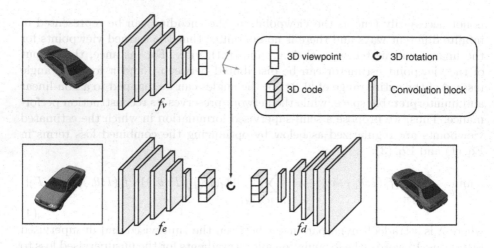

Fig. 2. Detailed architecture of the network. The viewpoint estimator f_v outputs the camera coordinates. This prediction is transformed in a rotation matrix, which is used to rotate the code produced by the encoder f_e. This rotated embedding is given to the decoder f_d to reconstruct the original image.

varying degrees of supervision. The splits are made on a model basis, that is, the different views from the same 3D model are either all labeled or all unlabeled.

To evaluate our framework, we use two popular metrics in viewpoint estimation [12,40,41], the accuracy at 30°, and the median angular error in degrees. The accuracy is computed as the ratio of predictions within 30° of the ground truth viewpoint and gives a rough estimate of the network performances. The aggregator for angular error is chosen to be the median rather than the mean as it is less biased by outliers which are common in pose estimation due to symmetries.

4.2 Implementation Details

We model f_e, f_d and f_v with convolutional neural networks. We use a simple design, stacking several convolutional blocks with batch normalization and ReLU activation function. The encoder network has five blocks each consisting of two convolutions layers, with the second of each block using a stride of 2 in order to reduce the spatial dimension. All layers use 3 by 3 convolutions with channel count starting at 32 and doubling each block. On top of this, we use a fully connected layer to obtain the embedding. In order to interpret it as a geometric representation, we group the embedding values by triplets, effectively creating a collection of points in 3D space. This representation can then be rotated using the viewpoint rotation matrix. The architecture of f_d is simply a mirrored version of that of f_e. A schematic version of our framework is presented in Fig. 2.

For the reconstruction objective, we use perceptual loss [15], as it provides supervision of higher quality, translating in better learning signals for the

Table 1. Viewpoint prediction in terms of accuracy and error rates for varying label supervision. Regression denotes a supervised trained network trained on the corresponding proportion of labeled data.

Method	Labels (%)	Aeroplane		Car		Chair	
		Acc	Err	Acc	Err	Acc	Err
Regression	100	**87.3**	6.9	89.3	6.2	88.9	8.4
Ours	100	**87.3**	**6.1**	**91.4**	**4.6**	**89.7**	**7.8**
Regression	25	80.7	8.9	79.4	9.8	80.8	12.2
Ours	25	**84.9**	**6.4**	**86.6**	**5.8**	**86.2**	**8.5**
Regression	10	75.6	12.1	72.3	13.1	71.8	16.5
Ours	10	**83.2**	**6.5**	**83.7**	**6.4**	**81.0**	**9.4**
Regression	5	70.4	15.1	65.9	17.7	68.4	19.2
Ours	5	**81.4**	**7.4**	**73.8**	**9.0**	**76.3**	**15.1**
Regression	1	54.2	29.5	45.1	36.3	59.1	28.6
Ours	1	**64.9**	**17.1**	**62.4**	**14.5**	**57.9**	**25.1**

viewpoint estimation. All training is done with the ADAM optimizer [21] with default parameters and a batch size of 64. To prevent potential overfitting caused by the reconstruction task, we use early stopping, halting the training when no improvements are observed on the validation set for 30 epochs. We set the hyperparameter λ to be equal to the ratio between labeled and unlabeled samples. This way, when summed over the whole sets, the contributions of both losses are evened out.

4.3 Viewpoint Estimation

We compare the results of our method with a simple regression baseline, as well as Mean Teacher, a state-of-the-art semi-supervised approach. Though it was proposed for classification, it is a generic approach that can therefore be extended to viewpoint regression. Training is done using 10 views per model, with varying degrees of supervision. The baseline is simply set as a viewpoint estimator without any added secondary objective, in order to study the effect adding reconstruction to the framework has.

The quantitative results in Table 1 show that our method outperforms simple regression in all cases. Unsurprisingly, performances are directly correlated with the amount of labeled data for all methods. It is worth noting that even when using 100% of the labels, our method still outperforms simple regression, showing that simply adding a reconstruction task helps refine the network predictions. However, the gap in performances increases more when lowering supervision, as the regression task is losing training samples while ours can still leverage them in a self-supervised way, demonstrating the effectiveness of reconstruction as a proxy for viewpoint estimation. When training with very low supervision, prediction tend to drop sharply, as symmetries in the object make viewpoint estimation

Table 2. Comparison to the Mean Teacher [34] in terms of viewpoint accuracy and error rate.

Method	Labels (%)	Aeroplane		Car		Chair	
		Acc	Err	Acc	Err	Acc	Err
Mean teacher [34]	10	81.4	10.3	72.4	13.8	68.9	19.0
Ours	10	**83.2**	**6.5**	**83.7**	**6.4**	**81.0**	**9.4**
Mean teacher [34]	1	28.9	44.0	8.5	67.7	34.3	39.5
Ours	1	**64.9**	**17.1**	**62.4**	**14.5**	**57.9**	**25.1**

too difficult, and the reconstruction task becomes less effective. Indeed, producing an image from a symmetric viewpoint still provides decent minimization of the reconstruction loss. A significant failure of our system can be observed when using only 1% of the labels on the chair category, which accounts to only 470 labeled images. Further details are discussed in Sect. 4.4.

We are also able to outperform mean teacher [34], demonstrating how building a problem-specific approach can easily lead to better performances (Table 2). Mean teacher relies on prediction consistency over the unlabeled set, using averaged models to predict soft targets. This constrains the learning procedure to be stable during training, making predictions more reliable. However, reliably wrong predictions will not be detected, in which case the unlabeled set is of no help. This is a common pitfall in viewpoint estimation because of the symmetries. In contrast, our method always provides a supervision signal in case of wrong reconstruction, effectively alleviating the issue. Similarly to our approach, mean teacher tends to fail when supervision is scarce, as illustrated by its results with 1% supervision.

4.4 Prediction Analysis

An interesting phenomenon can occur when the supervision is low: the symmetries of the object will cause the emergence of degenerate solutions. If we consider a pair of images from two symmetric viewpoints, not only is it easy to mistake one viewpoint for the other when trying to learn it, reconstructing the wrong image is also not very penalizing. Those effects combined can push the network in a local minimum from which escaping becomes impossible, as the reconstruction objective is likely to push the viewpoint estimation back. Figure 3a shows this behavior with chairs, as 1% supervision sees the predicted azimuth ping back and forth when it should complete a full rotation. Increasing the supervision solves this issue, though we can still spot the occasional mistake (Fig. 3b).

We also compare with predictions of a simple regression. We can see on Fig. 4 that while the global structure of predictions are similar, a simple regression involves more noise in the labels. In contrast, the predictions from our method are much finer, as the additional reconstruction provided gradients to correct small mistakes and give confidence to the viewpoint estimator.

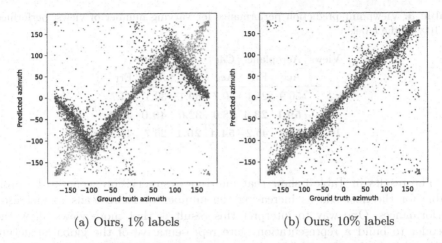

(a) Ours, 1% labels   (b) Ours, 10% labels

Fig. 3. Predicted vs ground truth azimuth for our method on test samples. Each point is colored with ground truth elevation.

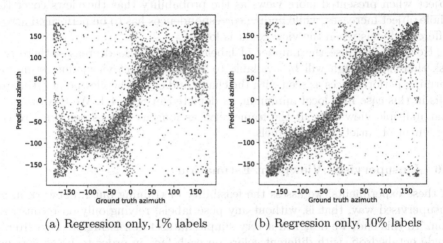

(a) Regression only, 1% labels   (b) Regression only, 10% labels

Fig. 4. Predicted vs ground truth azimuth for simple regression on test samples. Each point is colored with ground truth elevation.

4.5 Multiview Supervision

We conducted experiments with varying number of views per model to assess the importance of multi-view supervision. We compared the performances of a network trained on 2, 5, or 10 views per model. For a fair comparison, we made sure that the training set size was constant throughout the different experiments: we truncated the 5 and 10 views sets in order to match the size of the 2 views for each model. This means that models trained on those sets will see more of each model, but less models in total. Similarly, the viewpoint labels will be concentrated on the less models. Training was conducted with 10% of the labels in all cases.

Table 3. Viewpoint prediction performance for varying number of views, performed at 10% of the labels.

Views	Aeroplane		Car		Chair	
	Acc	Err	Acc	Err	Acc	Err
2	56.9	25.1	40.7	39.1	30.1	44.7
5	**59.1**	**23.4**	48.0	32.6	**49.0**	**30.5**
10	34.4	45.2	**54.4**	**26.1**	26.7	49.2

The results in Table 3 show that multi-view supervision seems to be profitable for the network, as increasing the number of views leads to increased performances. One way to interpret this result is that more views allow the encoder to build a representation more representative of the global structure of the object, therefore making the reconstruction supervision more effective. Indeed, it will be easier for the network to learn global information about the object when presented more views as the probability that the views cover the whole object increases, while finding correspondences has to be performed across different models when the view count is low.

However, because the number of labeled models also decreases, there is a risk that not enough will be available to learn a correct viewpoint estimator, harming performances as seen with the chairs and cars. The viewpoint estimator falls in this case in a local minimum, as depicted in Sect. 4.4. We theorize then that multiple views benefit the framework, as long as it does not come to the detriment of variety in pose labels.

4.6   Unsupervised Viewpoint Estimation

In these experiments, we assess the feasibility of training our framework in an unsupervised way, that is, without any pose labels, relying only on reconstruction. To this end, we designed a very simple dataset consisting of views from a single octahedron, with different colors on each face in order to break symmetries (Fig. 5). The results of the viewpoint prediction shown on Fig. 6a confirm that we can indeed learn the correct structure of the pose in easy cases. Having no reference point, this is learned up to a random rotation, which we recovered using the validation set by minimizing the distance between ground truth and prediction.

However, we found that our model was unable to learn the correct pose when confronted with more complex data, e.g. cars (Fig. 6b). We observe that the learned pose wraps twice around the pose space while the ground truth completes only one rotation. This is easily explainable as cars exhibit a strong symmetry when flipped 180° around the vertical axis. The viewpoint predictor therefore identified these two poses to the same point. We also note that above horizontal views are treated differently from below ones. This is explained by the perceived way the object is rotating depending whether the observer is located above or below the object.

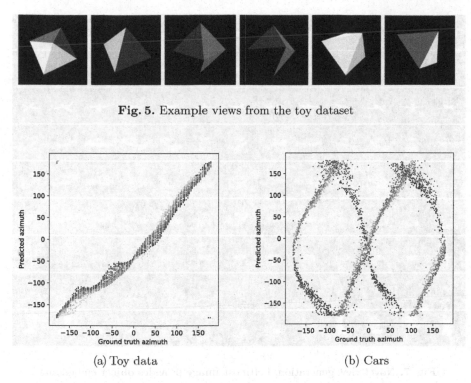

Fig. 5. Example views from the toy dataset

(a) Toy data   (b) Cars

Fig. 6. Predicted vs ground truth azimuth without pose labels. Each point is colored with ground truth elevation.

4.7 Novel View Synthesis

We also demonstrate that our model is able to generate arbitrary views of an unseen object from a single image. To do so, we feed an image to the encoder to obtain an embedding defining the identity of the object we want to generate views from. Then, we rotate it at the desired viewpoint, and decode it. Example results for all three categories are shown on Fig. 7, with viewpoints picked every 30° in azimuth from the origin. We can observe that prominent features defining the identity of the object - *e.g.* global shape, texture - are preserved, and the viewpoints are correctly spaced. Of course, as with any other method doing view synthesis, errors occur as the model has to fill in the parts of the object that are self-occluded. This results on the loss of finer details, like spindles between chair legs. However, the correctness of the viewpoints means those pictures could be used to further refine predictions.

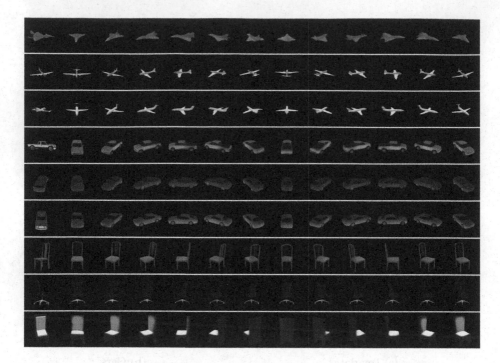

Fig. 7. Novel view generation. Leftmost image provides object embedding

5   Conclusion

We introduced an approach able to leverage unlabeled data in order to efficiently learn viewpoint estimation with minimal supervision. By learning a geometry-aware representation of objects, our framework can use self-supervision as a proxy, retaining reasonable performances when viewpoint supervision is scarce. Our experiments show that we outperform simple supervised approaches at equal supervision, as well as other state of the art semi-supervised methods. Our method can as well produce new views of objects, allowing it to be used as a generative model. While it does show its limitation in cased of extreme supervision, we hope that proper regularization dealing with symmetries can solve the issue and allow for completely unsupervised pose estimation.

Acknowledgements. The authors acknowledge the support of Toyota Motor Europe.

References

1. Berthelot, D., Carlini, N., Goodfellow, I., Papernot, N., Oliver, A., Raffel, C.: Mix-Match: a holistic approach to semi-supervised learning. arXiv:1905.02249 (2019)
2. Chang, A.X., et al.: ShapeNet: an information-rich 3D model repository. arXiv preprint arXiv:1512.03012 (2015)

3. Cohen, T.S., Geiger, M., Köhler, J., Welling, M.: Spherical CNNs. In: Proceedings of the International Conference on Learning Representations (ICLR) (2018)
4. Esteves, C., Allen-Blanchette, C., Makadia, A., Daniilidis, K.: 3D object classification and retrieval with spherical CNNs. arXiv preprint arXiv:1711.06721 (2017)
5. Esteves, C., Sud, A., Luo, Z., Daniilidis, K., Makadia, A.: Cross-domain 3D equivariant image embeddings. arXiv preprint arXiv:1812.02716 (2018)
6. Georgakis, G., Reza, M.A., Mousavian, A., Le, P.H., Košecká, J.: Multiview RGB-D dataset for object instance detection. In: 2016 Fourth International Conference on 3D Vision (3DV), pp. 426–434. IEEE (2016)
7. Girshick, R.: Fast R-CNN. In: Proceedings of the IEEE International Conference on Computer Vision, pp. 1440–1448 (2015)
8. Grabner, A., Roth, P.M., Lepetit, V.: 3D pose estimation and 3D model retrieval for objects in the wild. In: Proceedings of the IEEE Conference on Computer Vision and Pattern Recognition, pp. 3022–3031 (2018)
9. Hinterstoisser, S., et al.: Multimodal templates for real-time detection of texture-less objects in heavily cluttered scenes. In: International Conference on Computer Vision, pp. 858–865. IEEE (2011)
10. Hinterstoisser, S., et al.: Model based training, detection and pose estimation of texture-less 3D objects in heavily cluttered scenes. In: Lee, K.M., Matsushita, Y., Rehg, J.M., Hu, Z. (eds.) ACCV 2012. LNCS, vol. 7724, pp. 548–562. Springer, Heidelberg (2013). https://doi.org/10.1007/978-3-642-37331-2_42
11. Hodan, T., Haluza, P., Obdržálek, Š., Matas, J., Lourakis, M., Zabulis, X.: T-LESS: an RGB-D dataset for 6D pose estimation of texture-less objects. In: 2017 IEEE Winter Conference on Applications of Computer Vision (WACV), pp. 880–888. IEEE (2017)
12. Insafutdinov, E., Dosovitskiy, A.: Unsupervised learning of shape and pose with differentiable point clouds. In: Advances in Neural Information Processing Systems, pp. 2802–2812 (2018)
13. Jaderberg, M., Simonyan, K., Zisserman, A., et al.: Spatial transformer networks. In: Advances in Neural Information Processing Systems, pp. 2017–2025 (2015)
14. Jakab, T., Gupta, A., Bilen, H., Vedaldi, A.: Conditional image generation for learning the structure of visual objects. Methods 43, 44 (2018)
15. Johnson, J., Alahi, A., Fei-Fei, L.: Perceptual losses for real-time style transfer and super-resolution. In: Leibe, B., Matas, J., Sebe, N., Welling, M. (eds.) ECCV 2016. LNCS, vol. 9906, pp. 694–711. Springer, Cham (2016). https://doi.org/10.1007/978-3-319-46475-6_43
16. Joung, S., et al.: Cylindrical convolutional networks for joint object detection and viewpoint estimation. In: Proceedings of the IEEE/CVF Conference on Computer Vision and Pattern Recognition, pp. 14163–14172 (2020)
17. Kanazawa, A., Tulsiani, S., Efros, A.A., Malik, J.: Learning category-specific mesh reconstruction from image collections. In: Proceedings of the European Conference on Computer Vision (ECCV), pp. 371–386 (2018)
18. Kanezaki, A., Matsushita, Y., Nishida, Y.: RotationNet: joint object categorization and pose estimation using multiviews from unsupervised viewpoints. In: Proceedings of the IEEE Conference on Computer Vision and Pattern Recognition, pp. 5010–5019 (2018)
19. Kato, H., Ushiku, Y., Harada, T.: Neural 3D mesh renderer. In: Proceedings of the IEEE Conference on Computer Vision and Pattern Recognition, pp. 3907–3916 (2018)

20. Kehl, W., Manhardt, F., Tombari, F., Ilic, S., Navab, N.: SSD-6D: making RGB-based 3D detection and 6D pose estimation great again. In: Proceedings of the IEEE International Conference on Computer Vision, pp. 1521–1529 (2017)
21. Kingma, D.P., Ba, J.: Adam: a method for stochastic optimization. arXiv preprint arXiv:1412.6980 (2014)
22. Kulkarni, T.D., Whitney, W.F., Kohli, P., Tenenbaum, J.: Deep convolutional inverse graphics network. In: Advances in Neural Information Processing Systems, pp. 2539–2547 (2015)
23. Liao, S., Gavves, E., Snoek, C.G.: Spherical regression: learning viewpoints, surface normals and 3D rotations on n-spheres. In: Proceedings of the IEEE Conference on Computer Vision and Pattern Recognition, pp. 9759–9767 (2019)
24. Liebelt, J., Schmid, C.: Multi-view object class detection with a 3D geometric model. In: 2010 IEEE Computer Society Conference on Computer Vision and Pattern Recognition, pp. 1688–1695. IEEE (2010)
25. Mahendran, S., Ali, H., Vidal, R.: 3D pose regression using convolutional neural networks. In: Proceedings of the IEEE International Conference on Computer Vision, pp. 2174–2182 (2017)
26. Mustikovela, S.K., et al.: Self-supervised viewpoint learning from image collections. In: Proceedings of the IEEE/CVF Conference on Computer Vision and Pattern Recognition, pp. 3971–3981 (2020)
27. Nguyen-Phuoc, T., Li, C., Theis, L., Richardt, C., Yang, Y.L.: HoloGAN: unsupervised learning of 3D representations from natural images. In: Proceedings of the IEEE International Conference on Computer Vision, pp. 7588–7597 (2019)
28. Rad, M., Lepetit, V.: BB8: a scalable, accurate, robust to partial occlusion method for predicting the 3D poses of challenging objects without using depth. In: Proceedings of the IEEE International Conference on Computer Vision, pp. 3828–3836 (2017)
29. Rhodin, H., Salzmann, M., Fua, P.: Unsupervised geometry-aware representation for 3D human pose estimation. In: Proceedings of the European Conference on Computer Vision (ECCV), pp. 750–767 (2018)
30. Su, H., Qi, C.R., Li, Y., Guibas, L.J.: Render for CNN: viewpoint estimation in images using CNNs trained with rendered 3D model views. In: Proceedings of the IEEE International Conference on Computer Vision, pp. 2686–2694 (2015)
31. Sundermeyer, M., Marton, Z.C., Durner, M., Brucker, M., Triebel, R.: Implicit 3D orientation learning for 6D object detection from RGB images. In: Proceedings of the European Conference on Computer Vision (ECCV), pp. 699–715 (2018)
32. Suwajanakorn, S., Snavely, N., Tompson, J.J., Norouzi, M.: Discovery of latent 3D keypoints via end-to-end geometric reasoning. In: Advances in Neural Information Processing Systems, pp. 2059–2070 (2018)
33. Tan, V., Budvytis, I., Cipolla, R.: Indirect deep structured learning for 3D human body shape and pose prediction. In: British Machine Vision Conference (BMVC) (2018)
34. Tarvainen, A., Valpola, H.: Mean teachers are better role models: weight-averaged consistency targets improve semi-supervised deep learning results. In: Advances in Neural Information Processing Systems, pp. 1195–1204 (2017)
35. Tekin, B., Sinha, S.N., Fua, P.: Real-time seamless single shot 6D object pose prediction. In: Proceedings of the IEEE Conference on Computer Vision and Pattern Recognition, pp. 292–301 (2018)
36. Thewlis, J., Bilen, H., Vedaldi, A.: Unsupervised learning of object frames by dense equivariant image labelling. In: Advances in Neural Information Processing Systems, pp. 844–855 (2017)

37. Thewlis, J., Bilen, H., Vedaldi, A.: Unsupervised learning of object landmarks by factorized spatial embeddings. In: Proceedings of the IEEE International Conference on Computer Vision, pp. 5916–5925 (2017)
38. Thewlis, J., Bilen, H., Vedaldi, A.: Modelling and unsupervised learning of symmetric deformable object categories. In: Advances in Neural Information Processing Systems, pp. 8178–8189 (2018)
39. Tobin, J., Fong, R., Ray, A., Schneider, J., Zaremba, W., Abbeel, P.: Domain randomization for transferring deep neural networks from simulation to the real world. In: 2017 IEEE/RSJ International Conference on Intelligent Robots and Systems (IROS), pp. 23–30. IEEE (2017)
40. Tulsiani, S., Efros, A.A., Malik, J.: Multi-view consistency as supervisory signal for learning shape and pose prediction. In: Proceedings of the IEEE Conference on Computer Vision and Pattern Recognition, pp. 2897–2905 (2018)
41. Tulsiani, S., Malik, J.: Viewpoints and keypoints. In: Proceedings of the IEEE Conference on Computer Vision and Pattern Recognition, pp. 1510–1519 (2015)
42. Worrall, D.E., Garbin, S.J., Turmukhambetov, D., Brostow, G.J.: Interpretable transformations with encoder-decoder networks. In: Proceedings of the IEEE International Conference on Computer Vision, pp. 5726–5735 (2017)
43. Xiang, Y., Mottaghi, R., Savarese, S.: Beyond pascal: a benchmark for 3D object detection in the wild. In: IEEE Winter Conference on Applications of Computer Vision, pp. 75–82. IEEE (2014)
44. Xie, Q., Dai, Z., Hovy, E., Luong, M.T., Le, Q.V.: Unsupervised data augmentation for consistency training. arXiv preprint arXiv:1904.12848 (2019)
45. Yan, X., Yang, J., Yumer, E., Guo, Y., Lee, H.: Perspective transformer nets: learning single-view 3D object reconstruction without 3D supervision. In: Advances in Neural Information Processing Systems, pp. 1696–1704 (2016)
46. Yang, G., Cui, Y., Belongie, S., Hariharan, B.: Learning single-view 3D reconstruction with limited pose supervision. In: Proceedings of the European Conference on Computer Vision (ECCV), pp. 86–101 (2018)
47. Zhang, H., Cisse, M., Dauphin, Y.N., Lopez-Paz, D.: mixup: beyond empirical risk minimization. In: International Conference on Machine Learning (2018)
48. Zhou, X., Karpur, A., Luo, L., Huang, Q.: Starmap for category-agnostic keypoint and viewpoint estimation. In: Proceedings of the European Conference on Computer Vision (ECCV), pp. 318–334 (2018)

Physical Plausibility of 6D Pose Estimates in Scenes of Static Rigid Objects

Dominik Bauer$^{(\boxtimes)}$ ⓘ, Timothy Patten ⓘ, and Markus Vincze ⓘ

Vision for Robotics Laboratory, Automation and Control Institute, TU Wien, 1040
Vienna, Austria
{bauer,patten,vincze}@acin.tuwien.ac.at

Abstract. To enable robots to reason about manipulation of objects
and AR applications to present augmented scenes to human users, accurate scene explanations based on objects and their 6D pose are required.
With the pose-error functions commonly used to evaluate 6D object pose
estimation approaches, the accuracy of estimates is measured by surface
alignment of a target object under the estimated and true pose. However, an object floating above the ground may yield the same error as an
object translated on the ground by the same magnitude. We argue that,
to be intelligible for human observers, pose estimates additionally need
to adhere to physical principles. To this end, we provide a definition of
physical plausibility in scenes of static rigid objects, derive novel pose-
error functions and compare them to existing evaluation approaches in
6D object pose estimation. Code to compute the presented pose-error
functions is publicly available at github.com/dornik/plausible-poses.

Keywords: 6D object pose estimation · Evaluation · Physical
plausibility · Static equilibrium

1 Introduction

6D object pose estimates allow to explain and reason about the spatial configuration of a scene of objects. Current approaches aim to determine a pose under
which the estimated object would best align to the observed surface. For evaluation, the surface alignment of a target object under estimated and true pose
is determined. Surface alignment alone, however, cannot disambiguate equally
misaligned but physically implausible object poses. As illustrated in Fig. 1, we
argue that physically more plausible pose estimates should be favored in evaluation as they are more intelligible for human observers. For example, an estimate
of an apple resting on a table will seem more plausible to a human than an apple
floating in thin air, albeit both exhibiting the same translation error.

Two basic assumptions on physical plausibility are that all objects in a scene
are non-intersecting and (indirectly) in contact with a static surface. Violations of
these assumptions are especially noticeable to human observers. More generally,
the static equilibrium of a scene is considered a condition for physical plausibility.

© Springer Nature Switzerland AG 2020
A. Bartoli and A. Fusiello (Eds.): ECCV 2020 Workshops, LNCS 12536, pp. 648–662, 2020.
https://doi.org/10.1007/978-3-030-66096-3_43

But physical plausibility by itself is inherently ambiguous. For example, there is a practically infinite number of plausible poses for an apple to rest on a plane.

Our goal is therefore to extend pose-error functions to jointly consider surface alignment and physical plausibility to overcome the pose ambiguity that occurs when using either evaluation approach in isolation. Under ambiguous surface alignment, the physically more plausible pose should be preferred – under ambiguous physical plausibility, the closer surface alignment should be preferred. We achieve this by

- defining physical plausibility in the context of 6D object pose estimation,
- determining the physically plausible poses of target objects in given scenes and
- deriving two sets of visually and physically coherent pose-error functions.

In the following, we first discuss prior work in Sect. 2. A definition of physical plausibility for evaluation of 6D object pose estimates is given in Sect. 3. In Sect. 4, we derive the *physical plausibility error* e_{PP} and the *observable plausibility error* e_{OP}, both of which extend existing pose-error functions to account for physical plausibility. Section 5 discusses how to determine the set of physically plausible poses of a target object required to evaluate the presented metrics. Finally, we provide extensive evaluation of the proposed approaches and comparison with existing pose-error functions in artificial scenes of varying object-interaction complexity in Sect. 6. We show that our approach favors physically plausible poses where existing pose-error functions suffer from pose ambiguity.

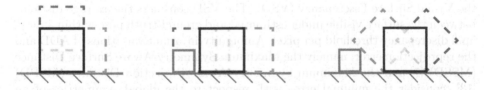

Fig. 1. A scene (gray) with the ground-truth pose (black) and pairs of erroneous pose estimates (dashed) for a target object. Each pair of estimates exhibits the same translation and rotation error, resulting in ambiguous surface alignment. We argue that, instead, the physically plausible estimates (green) should be preferred over floating (left, blue), intersecting (mid, blue) or unstable (right, blue) estimates. (Color figure online)

2   Related Work

Existing pose-error functions in 6D object pose estimation are broadly categorized into model-independent and surface alignment approaches. Model-independent pose-error functions operate on the 6D transformation itself, for example, by determining the Euclidean distance of the estimated translation or the angular distance of the estimated rotation to the ground-truth pose. It is, however, non-trivial to consider both at once. Shotton et al. [19] propose to threshold translation and rotation individually, for example by 5 cm and 5°, to determine whether an estimate is to be considered correct. Kendall et al. [15] combine both components by adding a weighting factor to the rotational error. The authors determine the appropriate weighting factor experimentally, while related work [3] proposes to compute this factor from the object model's covariance matrix for their experiments. Ideally, a model-independent approach considers the structure of the special Euclidean group SE(3) that embeds the space of 3D rotations and translations. Hou et al. [14] use the Riemannian geodesic distance on the manifold to determine the pose error for use in their loss function.

As Hodaň et al. argue [12], approaches based on surface alignment should be favored when evaluating the quality of 6D object pose estimates. Two of the most common pose-error functions from this category are proposed by Hinterstoisser et al. [11]. The Average Distance of Model Points (ADD) considers the average distance between corresponding points of the model under estimated and ground-truth pose, while the Average Distance of Model Points with Indistinguishable Views (ADI; also referred to as ADD-S) averages over the nearest-neighbor distances. As ADI may overestimate the surface alignment, Xiang et al. [21] use ADI only for models that feature indistinguishable views and use ADD otherwise. Similar to ADD, Brachmann et al. [2] compute the average reprojection error resulting from estimated and ground-truth pose. Since these pose-error functions use the full model, the error will vary between two poses even if the misalignment of the visible surface is equal. To overcome this ambiguity, Hodaň et al. [12] propose three ambiguity-invariant pose-error functions, the Average and the Maximum Corresponding Point Distance (ACPD and MCPD) as well as the Visual Surface Discrepancy (VSD). The VSD considers the average distance between the surface visible under estimated and ground-truth pose within a maximal discrepancy threshold per pixel. Ambiguity-invariant variations of ADD and the reprojection error, namely the Maximum Symmetry-Aware Surface Distance (MSSD) [7] and the Maximum Symmetry-Aware Projection Distance (MSPD) [13], consider the minimal error with respect to the global symmetries of an object. Both replace the averaging operation with a maximum over the surface misalignment. For a more in-depth review of the discussed pose-error functions, see [12,13]. In our evaluation, we compare against MSSD, MSPD and VSD.

Recent work in 6D object pose estimation [1,17,20] aims, as this work, to combine the consideration of physical plausibility and surface alignment. Mitash et al. [17] apply physics simulation to improve pose estimates and to generate plausible scenes. In turn, their approach disambiguates scene hypotheses during verification. In addition to hypotheses verification, Bauer et al. [1] integrate physics simulation with iterative refinement to guide the joint process towards physical plausibility and surface alignment. Another approach to integrate plausibility considerations into iterative refinement is presented by Wada et al. [20]. The authors use a volumetric reconstruction of an observed scene to define a collision-aware variant of ICP, called the Iterative Collision Check (ICC). While these methods' goal is to estimate physically consistent and, thereby, accurate object poses from observation, we propose a means to evaluate given estimates.

3   Physical Plausibility of 6D Object Pose Estimates

The predictions of 6D object pose estimators are, in general, error afflicted. To evaluate their accuracy, pose-error functions such as ADD [11] or VSD [12] consider the surface alignment of a target object under estimated and true pose. However, estimates of floating or intersecting objects may yield the same surface alignment as physically plausible estimates of the same error magnitude.

We hypothesize that, for human observers, pose estimates that follow physical principles are more intelligible. In robotic grasping, implausible pose estimates that, e.g., intersect with the scene may result in a collision of the robot with its environment. We thus argue that physically plausible pose estimates should be preferred and that this needs to be reflected in the evaluation of pose estimators. As existing evaluation methods cannot disambiguate (im)plausible estimates, we propose a novel approach that explicitly considers the physical plausibility of object pose estimates and penalizes implausibility.

In the following, we assume that the scene objects are known, rigid (they do not deform under stress) and static (they do not move with respect to a known frame of reference). We further assume that the only external force f_{ext} acting on the scene is due to the gravitational field of the earth, i.e., $f_{ext} = mg$. Friction-afflicted surface contacts are the only type of support that transmits this force. A typical scenario would be objects placed on a piece of furniture, which acts as static support.

3.1   Feasible Object Poses

Let al.l scene objects but a target object be under their ground-truth pose. We describe the interaction of the target object with the scene by how far points on its surface are from the surface of other objects. Let this surface distance be

$$d(x_i, S) = \min_{y_i \in \mathbf{bd}S} \|x_i - y_i\|_2, \tag{1}$$

where $x_i \in \mathbf{bd}O$ is a point on the surface of a target object O and d is its Euclidean distance to the closest point on the surface of scene object S.

Based on the surface distance d, we define the set of contact points of O as

$$\mathcal{C}(O) = \bigcup_{S \in \mathcal{S}} \{x_i \in \mathbf{bd}O | d(x_i, S) < \varepsilon\} \tag{2}$$

and the set of intersecting points of O as

$$\mathcal{I}(O) = \bigcup_{S \in \mathcal{S}} \{x_i \in (\mathbf{bd}O \cap \mathbf{int}S) | d(x_i, S) > \varepsilon\}, \tag{3}$$

where $\mathcal{S}$ is the set of scene objects (excluding target O) and ε is a small constant to account for the finite accuracy of the approximation of the surfaces of O and $S \in \mathcal{S}$, e.g., through a mesh or point cloud. **int** denotes the interior of an object.

We define a pose as *feasible*, if the object is in contact with at least one other object (not *floating*) and does not intersect any other object (not *intersecting*). Thus, for O to be under a feasible pose, the conditions

$$\text{not floating:} \quad |\mathcal{C}(O)| > 0, \tag{4}$$

$$\text{not intersecting:} \quad |\mathcal{I}(O)| = 0 \tag{5}$$

must be satisfied.

3.2 Stable Object Poses

We define the pose of a target object as *stable*, if it is in static equilibrium (SE) when supported at its contact points $\mathcal{C}(O)$. Let m be the mass of the object and $c_m \in \mathbb{R}^3$ its center of mass. Then, in the described scenario, the conditions for an object to be in SE are [6,10]

$$\text{force balance:} \quad \sum_i f_i + f_{ext} = \sum_i f_i + mg = 0, \tag{6}$$

$$\text{torque balance:} \quad \sum_i (c_m - x_i) \times f_i = 0, \tag{7}$$

$$\text{admissible contact force:} \quad f_i \in \mathcal{K}, \tag{8}$$

where $f_i \in \mathbb{R}^3$ is the contact force at contact point $x_i \in \mathcal{C}(O)$ and $\mathcal{K}$ is a friction cone defined [6] as

$$\sqrt{(t_i^\top f_i)^2 + (b_i^\top f_i)^2} \leq \mu_i n_i^\top f_i, \tag{9}$$

using the static friction coefficient μ_i and the tangential plane at x_i spanned by $t_i, b_i, n_i \in \mathbb{R}^3$. Efficient algorithms that find a set of f_i such that (6)–(8) are satisfied, i.e., to test for SE, are proposed in related work [6,10].

3.3 Physically Plausible Object Poses

Note that object pose estimation is, in general, not a physically plausible process and may result in infeasible pose estimates. Such poses are not naturally covered by the notion of stability. Rather, feasibility is a necessary condition for stability. If both feasibility and stability are satisfied, we define this as a physically *plausible* pose.

Using the presented considerations, we can binarily classify whether the respective conditions are satisfied by evaluating the contact and intersecting points of an object under a given pose. On one hand, this can be used to verify pose estimates, e.g., before grasping a related object or when annotating pose estimation datasets. On the other hand, it allows to define a physically plausible pose-error function for evaluation of 6D object pose estimation approaches.

4   Physically Plausible Pose-Error Functions

To enable the evaluation of object pose estimates with regards to their physical plausibility, we want to quantify how far an estimate is from being plausible (*implausibility*). Note that implausibility may be due to violation of any of the conditions (4)–(8). An implausibility metric should consider how these violations are resolved with minimal displacement of the object.

4.1   Implausibility Measure

To quantify this displacement, let $e(T_e, T)$ denote a distance function of a pose estimate T_e with respect to a reference pose T. Realizations of e would be, for example, ADD or a combination of translation and angular distance between T_e and T. We define the implausibility of a pose estimate T_e by

$$e_I(T_e) = \min_{T_p \in \mathcal{T}_p} e(T_e, T_p), \qquad \qquad (10)$$

where $\mathcal{T}_p$ is the set of all physically plausible poses of the target object in the current scene and T_p is the closest plausible pose. For evaluation, a pose estimate is considered *correct* with respect to the scene, if the implausibility is less than a scalar threshold ϕ_e. Note that the choice of ϕ_e depends on e.

4.2   Augmenting Pose-Error Functions

By simply considering the implausibility, we are not able to disambiguate equally plausible but misaligned estimates. For example, if the scene only consists of an object and a supporting plane, any in-plane translation estimate would be considered equally plausible – even-though for most plausible poses, the estimated and true surface would not overlap. Therefore, we want to introduce the notion of plausibility to existing pose-error functions e, combining the disambiguation capabilities of both approaches. For evaluation, a pose estimate is considered *correct* with respect to the ground truth, if the value of e is lower than a scalar threshold θ_e.

We propose two physically plausible variations of existing pose-error functions. For the first variant, the *physical plausibility* error e_{PP}, we want to effectively tighten the correctness threshold θ_e with respect to implausibility and define it as

$$e_{PP} = e(T_e, T_{gt}) + \theta_e \frac{e_I(T_e)}{\phi_e}. \qquad \qquad (11)$$

As a result, for plausible poses ($e_I(T_e) = 0$), the underlying pose-error function is unaffected. Intolerably implausible poses ($e_I(T_e) \geq \phi_e$) are always rejected. Finally, if the pose is tolerably implausible ($0 < e_I(T_e) < \phi_e$), a penalty proportional to the implausibility is added. Note that the search for the closest plausible pose T_p can thus be limited to a range of $(0, \phi_e)$.

For the second variant, we want to limit the consideration of physical plausibility to cases where it is observable with respect to e. We define the *observable plausibility error* e_{OP}, expressing implausibility in terms of e, as

$$e_{OP} = e(T_e, T_{gt}) + e(T_e, T_p), \tag{12}$$

where T_p is determined as in e_I. Note that there is always at least one plausible pose in the scene, the ground-truth pose T_{gt}. Moving away from T_{gt} in a plausible manner $(T_p = T_e)$, the underlying pose-error function is again unaffected. Moving in the most implausible manner $(T_p = T_{gt})$, however, the error is doubled. Moreover, the larger the error of T_e with respect to T_{gt}, the smaller the admissible error with respect to T_p to still be considered a correct pose. The bounds on the admissible implausibility follow from (12) as

$$e(T_e, T_{gt}) \leq e(T_e, T_{gt}) + e(T_e, T_p) < \theta_e \quad \rightarrow \quad 0 \leq e(T_e, T_p) < \theta_e - e(T_e, T_{gt}). \tag{13}$$

Equivalent considerations apply for the bound on the observation error.

5   Determining the Set of Physically Plausible Poses

To allow computation of the proposed pose-error functions, we need to determine the set of plausible poses T_p for a given scene and target object. We propose to generate a set of pose samples T_s, which are tested for physical plausibility to determine the subset $T_p \subseteq T_s$. The sampling should be deterministic to enable reproducible evaluation. As it would be computationally expensive to evaluate every pose within the scene bounds with a reasonable sampling rate, we only consider samples within the ϕ_e bound from T_{gt} and further prune them using the strategies described in this section.

5.1   Isolated Objects

Assume a single object O is resting on a horizontal plane and within the bounds of the scene. Then the object will only interact with the plane and we can simplify the constraints on physically plausible poses to the "support polygon principle" [18]. The convex hull of the xy-projection of the contact points $C(O)$ is called the *support polygon*. The only constraint for SE is that the c_m lies within the support polygon [16, 18]. This can be determined by projecting the c_m in the gravity direction onto the plane.

Consider cases with at least three contact points. These contact points must be on the boundary of the object and must lie within a plane that does not intersect the object. It follows that they must lie on a single face of the convex hull of the object and that the direction of the face normal coincides with the gravity direction. Therefore, if a face of the convex hull is intersected by a ray from c_m in the direction of its face normal, it describes a stable pose up to in-plane translation and in-plane rotation.

In-plane translations are sampled from a regular grid in $\mathbb{R}^2$ with resolution δ_t. Translation samples outside the ϕ_e range are pruned. In-plane rotations are sampled from $[-\pi, \pi)$ at a rate of δ_r. We classify all samples and consider all plausible poses to define $\mathcal{T}_p$.

5.2   Interacting Objects

Assume a scene is constructed by placing one object after the other, i.e, without additional support during construction. Each object can be placed in isolation or is in interaction with other objects in the scene. The first case is handled by the approach discussed in the previous subsection. For the second case of interactions with potentially non-convex objects, we need to consider our general definition of physical plausibility. As discussed before, without further constraints, the set of physically plausible poses of an object is intangibly large. For evaluation purposes, however, it is sufficient to consider plausible poses within the ϕ_e range from the ground-truth pose T_{gt}. In addition, we can delimit the space in which an interaction might occur to further prune samples.

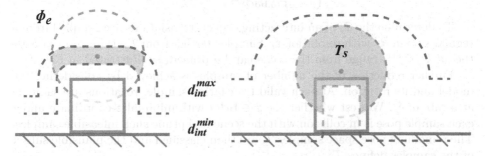

Fig. 2. When the object is in interaction with the scene, the closest and farthest distance of its origin from the scene are given by d_{int}^{min} and d_{int}^{max} (blue). When the object's origin lies outside the objects boundary, d_{int}^{min} is negative (right). To determine the set of physically plausible poses for evaluation, we can further restrict the origin's location to be within the implausibility threshold ϕ_e (green dashed). The remaining sampling region $\mathcal{T}_s$ is shown in green. (Color figure online)

Two objects O and S are interacting if

$$|\{(x_i \in \mathbf{bd}O, y_j \in \mathbf{bd}S)|x_i = y_j\}| > 0, \tag{14}$$

that is, if they are touching at least at one point of their surfaces. We can consider the scene fixed, so only the pose of the target object determines the interaction. To describe the interaction space, we consider the translation of the object's origin $o \in \mathbb{R}^3$ as it is invariant to rotation.

The farthest an object's origin might be from the scene's surface is the farthest distance from o to $x \in \mathbf{bd}O$. If the origin would lie farther from the scene, the object would no longer be in interaction. We call this upper bound the *maximal interaction distance*

$$d_{int}^{max} = \max_{x \in \mathbf{bd}O} \|o - x\|_2. \tag{15}$$

For the closest distance of the object's origin to the scene, we identify two cases. First, if the origin lies inside the object ($x \in \mathbf{int}O$), it cannot get closer to the scene than the closest distance from o to $x \in \mathbf{bd}O$. It would be guaranteed to be in collision if it would lie any closer. Second, if the origin lies outside the object ($x \in \mathbf{ext}O$), it may lie below the contact point with the scene (in gravity direction). Consider, for example, a mug hanging from a hook. The origin may even lie within another object, e.g., if the origin lies outside the convex hull of the object. Let $F(o, \mathbf{bd}O)$ be the set of *front facing* surface points with respect to the origin, that is, the set of points whose surface normals face the origin. The closest distance to the scene is then determined by the farthest $x \in F(o, \mathbf{bd}O)$ and is negative. We define this lower bound as the *minimal interaction distance*

$$d_{int}^{min} = \begin{cases} \displaystyle\min_{x \in \mathbf{bd}O} \|o - x\|_2 & o \in \mathbf{int}O, \\ -\displaystyle\max_{x \in F(o, \mathbf{bd}O)} \|o - x\|_2 & o \in \mathbf{ext}O. \end{cases} \tag{16}$$

To determine the $\mathcal{T}_s$ of an interacting object, translations are sampled from a regular grid in $\mathbb{R}^3$ with resolution δ_t. Samples farther from T_{gt} than ϕ_e or outside the $[d_{int}^{min}, d_{int}^{max}]$ range from the scene can be pruned, as illustrated in Fig. 2.

Further reduction of the number of samples is achieved by considering the model and its rotation. At each valid translation sample, rotations are sampled at a rate of δ_r. We test whether the $x \in \mathbf{bd}O$ with minimal z-coordinate under each sample pose is in collision with the scene and prune such infeasible samples. The remaining pose space samples $\mathcal{T}_s$ are then classified and the plausible subset of the samples defines $\mathcal{T}_p$.

6   Experiments

In the following section, we first validate the sampling of $\mathcal{T}_p$ and the matching of a given estimate T_e to the closest plausible pose T_p. We then evaluate the impact of the proposed pose-error terms on different pose-error functions in the isolated case and in two interaction scenarios. Namely, we compare against MSSD [7], MSPD [13] and VSD [12], all as implemented in the BOP toolkit [13]. Objects from the YCB-video dataset [21] are used to create artificial evaluation scenarios.

We use the Klampt framework [9] to compute the surface distance between the target and scene objects. The target object is represented as `PointCloud` and the scene objects as `VoxelGrid`. To evaluate a given pose, the contact and intersecting points of the object under this pose are determined and we test the conditions (4) and (5) to determine feasibility. For feasible poses, we use the static equilibrium testing implemented in Klampt to test if the contact points satisfy conditions (6)–(8), i.e., if the given pose is stable. If a pose is feasible and stable, it is classified as physically plausible.

6.1   Validation of Sampling and Matching

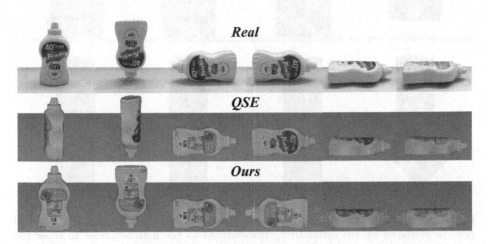

Fig. 3. Stable poses. Top to bottom: The real object, quasi-stable estimation (QSE) [8] and our approach for isolated objects (ours). Multiple representatives of the same stable pose are transparently overlayed for QSE and ours. Both approaches determine the complete set of stable poses, albeit with redundant estimates.

We consider quasi-static pose estimation (QSE) [8] as baseline for stable pose sampling. The implementation in `trimesh` [5] is used. QSE is a probabilistic approach to determine the poses into which an object will settle when dropped onto a planar surface. The results in Fig. 3 show that both, QSE and our approach for isolated objects, are able to determine the complete set of stable poses. Since certain stable poses relate to multiple faces of the convex hull, both estimated sets contain duplicates for a total of 9 poses. In addition to the stable poses, our approach samples the in-plane translations and rotations to cover the set of physically plausible poses.

When matching an estimate T_e to the samples of T_p, the metric used to determine the closest T_p is of importance. As this should be dependent only on the object's pose and not on the viewpoint, we select ADD [11], MSSD [7] and an extended version of the model-invariant metric used for evaluation in [3] (FRO). The latter uses the Euclidean distance on the translation error and the weighted Frobenius norm on the rotation error. The weighting factor is computed using the object's covariance matrix. We extend this metric to consider symmetric poses, analogous to, e.g., MSSD. For a comparison, we sample in-plane rotations at 15deg intervals to generate T_p from the stable poses of the object. We observe slight mismatches using all three metrics, as shown in Fig. 4. ADD mismatches under a translation error, while MSSD and FRO produce a mismatch for an in-plane rotation error. Figure 4 also highlights the importance of a sufficient sampling coverage. In the bottom row, all three compared metrics are unable to find a perfect match due to undersampling of the in-plane rotations. Since the

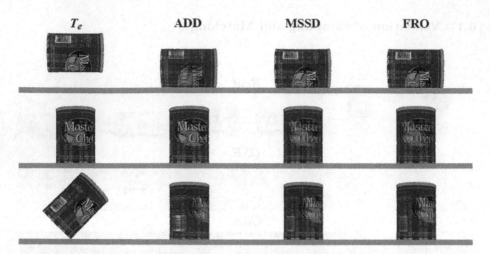

Fig. 4. Comparison of matching functions. For ADD, MSSD and FRO, the matched pose is overlayed by the estimate T_e transformed to the matched pose to show the matching error. There is no perfect match in the bottom row, since in-plane rotations are undersampled in this example. The compared functions thus match to an erroneous closest pose in $\mathcal{T}_p$.

performance of the metrics is comparable in the tested scenarios, we use FRO in the following experiments as it is computationally more efficient.

6.2   Comparison of Pose-Error Functions

To evaluate the impact of the proposed pose-error terms on common pose-error functions, we first consider the case of an isolated object on a plane. This provides a controlled setting for validating the propositions made in Sect. 4.

As shown in Fig. 5, if the estimation error results in an unstable (left) or infeasible pose (right), the proposed terms penalize the respective estimates. Conversely, if the estimation error results in a physically plausible pose, no penalty is added to the pose error. In the example in Fig. 6, in-plane rotation (left) and in-plane translation (right) do not increase implausibility of the estimate. Note that, for VSD, the observable plausibility error is not zero due to mismatched poses of the not perfectly symmetric bowl. The physical plausibility error is not affected as the used metric is symmetry-aware and computes the error with respect to the correct pose. For the same reason, the mismatch does not affect MSSD or MSPD.

In addition, we evaluate the proposed pose-error terms' impact in scenes of interacting objects where one target object per scene is chosen. The results in Fig. 7 and Fig. 8 show the applicability of the presented approach to scenes where convex and non-convex objects interact by stacking, leaning and combinations thereof. In Fig. 7, the rotation error (left) results in collision or floating of the marker, which is penalized by our proposed pose-error terms. The translation

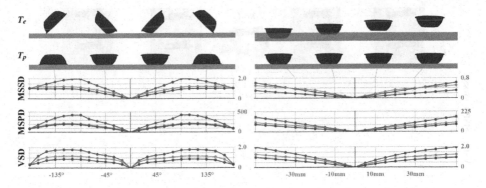

Fig. 5. Comparison of pose-error functions in the isolated scenario. From top to bottom: The erroneous estimates T_e, the closest plausible poses T_p and the pose error using MSSD, MSPD and VSD. Per pose-error function, the baseline (gray), the physical plausibility (green) and observable plausibility error (blue) are shown. Our approaches penalize violation of SE (left) and collision and floating (right). (Color figure online)

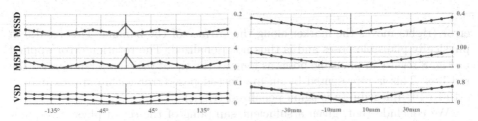

Fig. 6. Comparison of MSSD, MSPD and VSD using our extensions on the *bowl* object (Fig. 5). Per pose-error function, the baseline (gray), the physical plausibility (green) and observable plausibility error (blue) are shown. Our approaches are unaffected by in-plane rotation (left) and in-plane translation (right). (Color figure online)

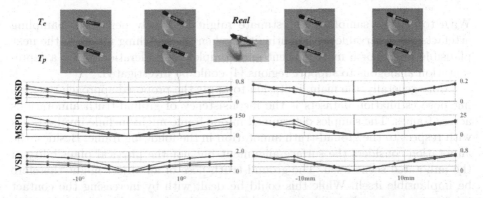

Fig. 7. Comparison of pose-error functions with a leaning target object. From top to bottom: The erroneous estimates T_e, the closest plausible poses T_p and the pose error using MSSD, MSPD and VSD. Per pose-error function, the baseline (gray), the physical plausibility (green) and observable plausibility error (blue) are shown. (Color figure online)

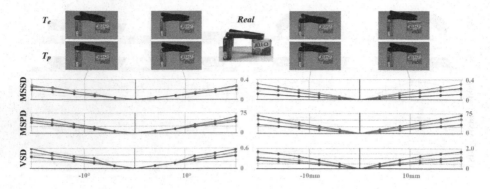

Fig. 8. Comparison of pose-error functions with a stack of objects. From top to bottom: The erroneous estimates T_e, the closest plausible poses T_p and the pose error using MSSD, MSPD and VSD. Per pose-error function, the baseline (gray), the physical plausibility (green) and observable plausibility error (blue) are shown. (Color figure online)

error (right) moves the marker along the surface of the banana. This results in physically plausible poses and is thus not penalized. The rotation error applied in Fig. 8 results in plausible poses as long as the tip of the clamp remains on the red box. This is represented by an unaffected pose error within approximately -10 to $10°$ Infeasibility is again penalized (right).

We conclude that, given a sufficient sampling of the set of physically plausible poses $\mathcal{T}_p$, the proposed pose-error terms are able to detect and penalize implausibility as outlined in Sect. 4.

7   Limitations and Future Work

With too coarse sampling, an estimate might be falsely penalized. Sampling artefacts are observable as discontinuities when the matching moves to the next plausible pose. For a more efficient and complete consideration of $\mathcal{T}_p$, a representation analogous to support regions [4] could be investigated.

More generally, the main limitation to apply the proposed approach to existing pose estimation datasets is the inconsistency of ground-truth annotations across frames. The samples determined in one frame might include invalid poses with respect to the ground-truth annotation in the following frame. Besides, the annotation considers the surface alignment but not the physical plausibility of the annotated scene itself. The ground-truth pose of an object might therefore be implausible itself. While this could be dealt with by increasing the contact tolerance ϵ or the admissible implausibility ϕ_e, the aim should rather be to provide physically plausible ground-truth annotations. Therefore, the use of the presented physical plausibility conditions in object pose annotation should be investigated. We speculate that a physically plausible annotation would exhibit closer surface alignment as well, as it is less reliant on the inherently noisy observation. This would also be beneficial for multi-view or tracking-based approaches. Given a consistent, physically plausible annotation, we would only need to compute samples for each target object only once per scene.

To consider the SE of the whole scene, the presented approach needs to be extended to not only check the SE of the target object but also the objects (indirectly) depending on it for support. Consider the stack in Fig. 8 and let the target object be one of the boxes. Translating it in-plane would not violate SE of the box. The object resting on top, however, would no longer be in SE and thus the SE of the scene would be violated. A straight-forward approach to this would be to integrate this scene-level check into the sampling phase, rejecting poses of the target object that violate SE of the scene.

8   Conclusion

In this work, we propose the evaluation of 6D object pose estimates with regards to their physical plausibility. Our definition of physical plausibility is based on the notion of feasibility and stability. For a pose to be considered feasible, it may not result in floating or intersecting objects. Under a stable pose, the object is in static equilibrium. Based on this definition, we derive a measure for implausibility that quantifies the distance to the closest plausible pose.

Moreover, we present two pose-error terms that allow to jointly consider physical plausibility and surface alignment by extending existing pose-error functions. To enable computation of the proposed pose errors, we discuss sampling of the set of physically plausible poses of a target object in a given scene. Finally, we provide a comparison of our extensions to existing pose-error functions. Our results indicate that the added physical plausibility terms successfully detect and penalize floating, intersecting and unstable pose estimates, while leaving plausible estimates unaffected.

Acknowledgements. This work was supported by the TU Wien Doctoral College TrustRobots and the Austrian Science Fund (FWF) under grant agreements No. I3968-N30 HEAP and No. I3969-N30 InDex.

References

1. Bauer, D., Patten, T., Vincze, M.: VeREFINE: integrating object pose verification with physics-guided iterative refinement. IEEE Robot. Automat. Lett. 5(3), 4289–4296 (2020)
2. Brachmann, E., Michel, F., Krull, A., Ying Yang, M., Gumhold, S., et al.: Uncertainty-driven 6d pose estimation of objects and scenes from a single rgb image. In: Proceedings of the IEEE/CVF Conference on Computer Vision and Pattern Recognition, pp. 3364–3372 (2016)
3. Brégier, R., Devernay, F., Leyrit, L., Crowley, J.L.: Defining the pose of any 3d rigid object and an associated distance. Int. J. Comput. Vision **126**(6), 571–596 (2018)

4. Bretl, T., Lall, S.: Testing static equilibrium for legged robots. IEEE Trans. Robot. **24**(4), 794–807 (2008)
5. Dawson-Haggerty et al.: Trimesh. https://trimsh.org/
6. Del Prete, A., Tonneau, S., Mansard, N.: Fast algorithms to test robust static equilibrium for legged robots. In: Proceedings of the IEEE International Conference on Robotics and Automation, pp. 1601–1607 (2016)
7. Drost, B., Ulrich, M., Bergmann, P., Hartinger, P., Steger, C.: Introducing mvtec itodd: a dataset for 3d object recognition in industry. In: Proceedings of the IEEE International Conference on Computer Vision Workshops, pp. 2200–2208 (2017)
8. Goldberg, K., Mirtich, B.V., Zhuang, Y., Craig, J., Carlisle, B.R., Canny, J.: Part pose statistics: estimators and experiments. IEEE Trans. Robot. Automat. **15**(5), 849–857 (1999)
9. Hauser, K.: Robust contact generation for robot simulation with unstructured meshes. In: Robotics Research, pp. 357–373 (2016)
10. Hauser, K., Wang, S., Cutkosky, M.R.: Efficient equilibrium testing under adhesion and anisotropy using empirical contact force models. IEEE Trans. Robot. **34**(5), 1157–1169 (2018)
11. Hinterstoisser, S., et al.: Model based training, detection and pose estimation of texture-less 3d objects in heavily cluttered scenes. In: Proceedings of the Asian Conference on Computer Vision, pp. 548–562 (2012)
12. Hodaň, T., Matas, J., Obdržálek, Š.: On evaluation of 6d object pose estimation. In: Proceedings of the European Conference on Computer Vision, pp. 606–619 (2016)
13. Hodaň, T., et al.: BOP: Benchmark for 6D object pose estimation. In: Proceedings of the European Conference on Computer Vision (2018)
14. Hou, B., et al.: Computing cnn loss and gradients for pose estimation with riemannian geometry. In: International Conference on Medical Image Computing and Computer-Assisted Intervention, pp. 756–764 (2018)
15. Kendall, A., Grimes, M., Cipolla, R.: Posenet: a convolutional network for real-time 6-dof camera relocalization. In: Proceedings of the IEEE International Conference on Computer Vision, pp. 2938–2946 (2015)
16. McGhee, R.B., Frank, A.A.: On the stability properties of quadruped creeping gaits. Math. Biosci. **3**, 331–351 (1968)
17. Mitash, C., Boularias, A., Bekris, K.E.: Improving 6D pose estimation of objects in clutter via physics-aware Monte Carlo tree search. In: Proceedings of IEEE International Conference on Robotics and Automation, pp. 3331–3338 (2018)
18. Or, Y., Rimon, E.: Analytic characterization of a class of three-contact frictional equilibrium postures in three-dimensional gravitational environments. Int. J. Robot. Res. **29**(1), 3–22 (2010)
19. Shotton, J., Glocker, B., Zach, C., Izadi, S., Criminisi, A., Fitzgibbon, A.: Scene coordinate regression forests for camera relocalization in RGB-D images. In: Proceedings of the IEEE/CVF Conference on Computer Vision and Pattern Recognition, pp. 2930–2937 (2013)
20. Wada, K., Sucar, E., James, S., Lenton, D., Davison, A.J.: Morefusion: multi-object reasoning for 6d pose estimation from volumetric fusion. In: Proceedings of the IEEE/CVF Conference on Computer Vision and Pattern Recognition, pp. 14540–14549 (2020)
21. Xiang, Y., Schmidt, T., Narayanan, V., Fox, D.: PoseCNN: a convolutional neural network for 6D object pose estimation in cluttered scenes. In: Proceedings of Robotics: Science and Systems (2017)

DronePose: Photorealistic UAV-Assistant Dataset Synthesis for 3D Pose Estimation via a Smooth Silhouette Loss

Georgios Albanis(✉) [iD], Nikolaos Zioulis [iD], Anastasios Dimou,
Dimitrios Zarpalas, and Petros Daras

Visual Computing Lab, Information Technologies Institute,
Centre for Research and Technology Hellas, Thessaloniki, Greece
{galbanis,nzioulis,dimou,zarpalas,daras}@iti.gr
http://vcl.iti.gr/

Abstract. In this work we consider UAVs as cooperative agents supporting human users in their operations. In this context, the 3D localisation of the UAV assistant is an important task that can facilitate the exchange of spatial information between the user and the UAV. To address this in a data-driven manner, we design a data synthesis pipeline to create a realistic multimodal dataset that includes both the exocentric user view, and the egocentric UAV view. We then exploit the joint availability of photorealistic and synthesized inputs to train a single-shot monocular pose estimation model. During training we leverage differentiable rendering to supplement a state-of-the-art direct regression objective with a novel smooth silhouette loss. Our results demonstrate its qualitative and quantitative performance gains over traditional silhouette objectives. Our data and code are available at https://vcl3d.github.io/DronePose.

Keywords: 3D pose estimation · Dataset generation · UAV · Differentiable rendering

1 Introduction

Advances in robotics, their autonomy, and computer vision are constituting Unmanned Aerial Vehicles (UAVs) – or otherwise known as drones – an emerging ubiquitous technology. Indeed, the potential that autonomous or piloted UAVs can provide has already been acknowledged in numerous application fields like filming [65], emergency response [31], animal conservation [27], and infrastructure inspection [14]. In addition, a lot of research has focused on the detection of drones in the context of anti-drone systems [55] and their accurate identification [10].

G. Albanis and N. Zioulis—Equal contribution.

Electronic supplementary material The online version of this chapter (https://doi.org/10.1007/978-3-030-66096-3_44) contains supplementary material, which is available to authorized users.

© Springer Nature Switzerland AG 2020
A. Bartoli and A. Fusiello (Eds.): ECCV 2020 Workshops, LNCS 12536, pp. 663–681, 2020.
https://doi.org/10.1007/978-3-030-66096-3_44

Nevertheless, the miniaturization and commoditisation of drones open up new types of applications for mini-UAVs. Moving beyond the role of remote, and/or malicious agents, personal – friendly – drones can operate in tandem with human users, supporting their activities and acting as external assistants [3]. Yet, human operators can also be augmented with modern sensing capabilities (*e.g.* HoloLens), enabling advanced cooperation schemes like XRay vision [13]. Under such conditions, the registration of the human operator and the peer drone is an important task as it facilitates the exchange of spatial information, enabling functionalities like gaze-driven navigation [66].

To address friendly UAV 3D pose estimation in a data-driven manner, we first need to overcome the lack of data. All UAV related datasets either target remote sensing applications, and therefore, offering purely drone egocentric views, or consider drones as malicious agents and offer (multi-modal) sensor exocentric views. However, datasets created for anti-UAV applications cannot be re-used in UAV-Assistant (UAVA) settings mainly because of the very large distance between the sensors and the drones. This is not only out of context, but also suffers from low-resolution modalities (*i.e.* thermal), tiny object image sizes, and a serious lack of finer-grained discriminating information for 3D pose estimation.

The availability of UAV simulators integrated with high-end rendering inside game engines, like AirSim [54] and Sim4CV [39], offers a promising direction for synthesizing UAVA data. This synthetic dataset generation approach has been used for spacecraft pose estimation [47] and generating low-altitude flight data [27]. Still, the synthetic to real domain gap will hinder performance when applied to actual real-world cases. While approaches like FlightGoggles [17] mitigate this gap through photorealistic sensor simulation, actual real-world data are still preferable. Towards that end, we follow a principled approach to create a realistic multimodal UAVA dataset. We employ real-world 3D scanned datasets, physically-based shading, a gamified simulator for realistic drone navigation trajectory collection and randomized sampling, to generate multimodal data both from the user's exocentric view of the drone, as well as the drone's egocentric view. This allows us to train a CNN for single-shot drone 3D pose estimation from monocular (exocentric) input. Given the availability of projected drone silhouettes aligned with the exocentric view, we complement our model with an enhanced smooth silhouette consistency loss. Overall, our contributions are the following:

- We create a realistic multimodal UAVA dataset that offers aligned exocentric (user) and egocentric (drone) data along with the ground-truth poses. We also consider an inter-frame motion for both views, with the ego-motion supported by the scene's optical flow, while the exocentric view provides the drone's optical flow.
- We develop an end-to-end model that combines direct pose regression and differentiable rendering for learning 6DOF pose estimation and train it with complex color images to explore their combined potential.
- We propose a smooth silhouette loss that improves performance compared to traditional alternatives as well as model robustness.

2   Related Work

UAV Datasets: Most existing UAV datasets can be categorized into two main categories, datasets for remote sensing and anti-UAV datasets. The former utilize drones as remote eyes observing remote scenes and aim at either applying real-time computer vision algorithms on live data streams, or recording them for offline analysis. The VisDrone2019 dataset [70] contains diverse data captured from drone-mounted cameras and is annotated with bounding boxes for object detection and tracking tasks, focused on the surveillance aspect of UAVs. Similar data is included in the Stanford Drone Dataset [51] with various bounding box annotations of different classes found in a campus, with the distinct difference being its strict top-down view. The VIRAT video surveillance dataset [40] also contains UAV captured scenes which, apart from object annotations, also includes activity and event annotations. Apart from these close-range egocentric view datasets, typical remote sensing drone datasets involve ground observing aerial images. Examples include the urban settlement dataset of [35], or the Kuzikus dataset used in [27] which contains wildlife detection annotations. Similar aerial top-down view datasets are used for object counting [22] and tracking [38]. Summarizing, datasets that view UAVs as remote sensors, offer the drone's egocentric view, usually with object (*i.e.* bounding box) or image segment (*i.e.* mask) annotations.

The second UAV dataset category, considers UAVs as hostile agents, a topic that is gaining significant traction with the research community lately, mainly because of the challenges it entails. Anti-UAV systems need to operate in-the-wild, in adverse weather conditions, during the whole day-night cycle, and offer timely and accurate information for any neutralizing actions to take place. Towards that end, the available datasets address tiny object detection [52] and adversarial conditions that involve birds [10]. Recent organized challenges like the Anti-UAV challenge [1] include multimodal (*i.e.* color and thermal) inputs to increase detection robustness under different lighting and weather conditions.

All the aforementioned datasets are captured with traditional sensors and are manually annotated. Nonetheless, recent advances in UAV simulators, a prominent one being AirSim [54], enable the generation of data via synthesis, and thus, the availability of information that is traditionally very hard to acquire with traditional means (*i.e* depth, surface orientation, semantics, 3D pose, etc.). This was the case of the AimSim-w dataset [4] which synthesized remote sensing data for wildlife observation, in addition to modelling the thermal imaging process to synthesise infrared data. Similarly, the Mid-Air dataset [15] used AirSim to synthesize low-altitude flight multimodal data and illustrated its efficacy in drone depth estimation.

Still, the domain gap is an important obstacle in using fully synthetic datasets that employ purely computer-generated models and imagery. While domain adaptation itself is another important task, with the reader referred to a survey [62] for more details, we can also find other intermediary approaches in the literature. FlightGoggles [17] is a photorealistic sensor simulator that infuses realism in a data generation pipeline for UAVs. It was used when creating the aggressive drone flights Blackbird dataset [2], which does not fit in the two afore-mentioned categories in the broader sense, as it is used for visual-inertial SLAM benchmarking. Still, the synthesis of realistic data, as encompassed by Flight-Goggles and the Blackbird dataset is highly related to our approach. We also use scanned 3D models like the photogrammetry models used in FlightGoggles and generate external trajectories like those used the Blackbird dataset. Con-trary to those though, we collect UAV flight trajectories with significantly higher variance than the periodic Blackbird ones, and utilize a vastly larger 3D scene corpus than FlightGoggles. Moreover, as it is apparent by the above dataset analysis (with more details available in the supplement), none are suitable for UAVA applications as the exocentric anti-UAV datasets image drones from very far distances, similar to how egocentric remote sensing drone datasets image (very) far scenes. In the UAVA setting, the user and the drone work under a cooperative context that allows for the availability of both the egocentric and exocentric views simultaneously, and will typically be close in close proximity.

Data-Driven 6DOF Pose Estimation: Even before the establishment of deep models, data-driven methods relying on random forests [5,12,57] or deformable part models [45] started producing high-quality results for the task of 3D pose estimation. Early deep models [18,37,53,56] focused on learning rotations (*i.e.* viewpoints) and performed classification after binning them, using either normal maps [18], synthesized [56] or traditional [37] images, or even employed colorized depth inputs [53]. Follow-up works transitioned from binned rotation classification to direct regression of the 6DOF camera pose using varying rotation representations. PoseCNN [64] used a quaternion representation and employed learned segmentation predictions to handle cluttered object scenes, while [36] demonstrated results for an axis-angle representation in addition to the quater-nion one. Currently, the state-of-the-art has been focusing on addressing the discontinuity of rotations by disentangling the rotation manifold [33] or explor-ing continuous rotation representations [69]. Single-shot variants predict the 3D bounding boxes from monocular inputs [58], or formulate multiple pose hypothe-ses from 2D bounding box detections [26], solving either a Perspective-n-Point (PnP) problem or locally optimizing the pose afterwards respectively. A slightly different approach has been introduced in [48] where the image is cropped around the object by first predicting a segmentation mask and then the 2D bound-ing box is predicted. While most works are trained on real-world images, in [49] it was shown that using synthetic images and single channel edge informa-tion can lead to high-quality results, even when directly regressing the 6DOF pose. Even though direct pose regression has demonstrated high-quality results, especially under iterative frameworks [60], most recent research has resorted to correspondence-based pose estimation. Deep keypoint prediction was origi-nally used for 3D pose estimation in [59] and has since spun to a variety of approaches even in drone pose estimation [25]. PVNet [44] votes for keypoints, which are then used to estimate the object's 6DOF pose using PnP. Following a dense correspondence approach, various works directly regress either 2D image to 3D model correspondences [67], normalized object coordinates [61], or leverage deep Hough voting as in the case of PVN3D [20]. Regarding coordinates based regression, separate branches for the translation and rotational components were found to be more robust in predict pose [32], especially for occluded and texture-less objects. More recently, the various advances in differentiable rendering are enabling end-to-end 3D vision, and naturally, their application to 6DOF pose estimation is being explored. A differentiable point cloud projection function was employed [23] that used two simplistic views (*i.e.* white background, silhouette-like images) of an object to jointly estimate its shape and pose, using an MSE silhouette loss. Similarly, a rendering-like occlusion removal operator was added in [63] to handle point cloud viewpoint-based self-occlusions and drive supervision solely from depth images. Given that only the pose needs to be optimized, a lightweight abstract rendering mechanism based on OpenDR [34] was developed in [46] to compare learned feature representations from meshes and the observed images, and then estimate their poses in the observed scenes. LatentFusion [42] learns a reconstructed feature representation that can be rendered in order to optimize for an object's pose as it is observed within an image, and has been shown to also generalize well to unseen objects. Finally, a rendered silhouette error is backpropagated in [41] to refine the CNN estimated pose. However, it was only applied in simplistic CAD renderings and was not trained in an end-to-end fashion. This was also the case for [23] which did not use monocular input and only learned pose estimation using simplistic images. Instead, we leverage end-to-end differentiable rendering using complex imagery for boosting 6DOF pose estimation.

3   Dataset

Our goal is to create a realistic UAVA dataset for applications in which users and drones are considered cooperative agents. To achieve this, we need to overcome a set of challenges associated with the photorealism of the visual data, the plausibility of the drone-to-user spatial relation, the variety/plurality of the generated views, and the drone's trajectories. Contrary to similarly oriented datasets like URSO [47] and Blackbird [2] we are not confined to only a single ego- [2] or exocentric view [47], and thus, we need to consider both viewpoints and synthesize temporally and spatially aligned data. While both [47] and [2] render purely computer-generated scenes, we rely on a recent 3D scanned dataset, Matterport3D [7] that offers us scene photorealism.

The Matterport3D dataset was created after capturing multiple RGB-D panoramas within large buildings. As the poses of each panorama are available, we can leverage them as stationary points (*i.e.* anchors) to drive our UAVA oriented data generation. Aiming to create realistic drone flight trajectories and simultaneously position user viewpoints in a plausible way, we employ a gamified approach. More specifically, we designed and developed a Unity3D game where collectible cube "coins" are placed at each of the known panorama positions (anchors) and use AirSim's drone flight simulator to let players navigate a drone within each building to collect the pre-placed "coins" using a game controller.

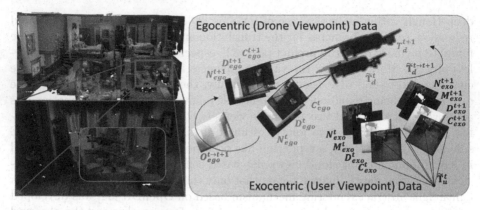

Fig. 1. We use a large-scale photorealistic 3D scene dataset for rendering our UAVA dataset. After sampling a set of drone navigation trajectories created via a gamification process, we raycast data from a drone egocentric view as well as a user's exocentric one. For the former, we generate color (C) images, depth (D) and surface (N) maps, in addition to the optical flow (OF) for two consecutive frames $t, t+1$ sampled from the dense play-through trajectories. Apart from the ego-motion data, the exocentric viewpoints image the drone as posed in the $t, t+1$ frames and offer the same modalities, in addition to the drone's optical flow in the statically observed scene, and its silhouette images (M). Supplementing the images, our dataset offers precise pose annotations for the drone and the user viewpoints.

The players need to collect all "coins" placed inside the building as soon as possible, while at the same time a leaderboard records the quickest runs for boosting engagement among users and adding trajectory diversity. Each run is initialised from a randomized anchor location to further increase trajectory diversity (see Fig. 2). The game controller together with the simulation framework allows for quicker and more intuitive drone navigation. This, combined with expanded colliders for the "coins", the initialization randomness and the timing objective adds the necessary movement pattern variety in our collected trajectories.

The drone's world pose $\mathbf{T}_d^t$ is recorded at each time step t and can be associated with an anchor point a. The drone's pose to anchor's pose association is done on a per nearest Euclidean neighbor basis, thereby providing us with a pair $P := (\mathbf{T}_a, \mathbf{T}_d^t)$ at each time step. As each game run's $60Hz$ trajectories are recorded, we need to sample them to reduce redundancy, filter potentially bad samples due to occlusions and 3D model holes, and also add additional randomness to increase our dataset's variance as follows.

We sample sparse pose samples from the dense trajectories as follows. We first filter all pairs whose Euclidean distance is over $1.5\,\mathrm{m}$ and under $0.8\,\mathrm{m}$, effectively limiting the user-to-drone distance to this range. We then apply ego-motion criteria to the remaining pairs across time, filtering out poses that contain limited positional and angular displacement with respect to their inter-frame poses at $t-1$ and $t+1$. Further, we filter out poses that do not include the entirety of the drone by removing those where the drone's centroid is projected

Fig. 2. Our gamified approach for generating high-quality diversified data. The first column presents the top-view of a Matterport3D building overlayed with the trajectory generated by a single play-through. The second column presents cuboid "coins" placed at the anchor points within the game. These collectible coins ensure that the players will cover all of the building's area and will traverse it near the anchor points. The third column collates two side views of the same building while the last column offers two in-game screenshots.

near the image boundaries, and we also remove samples that contain a lot of invalid pixels (*i.e.* large mesh holes) via percentage-based thresholding. For the remaining pose samples, we introduce a "look at" variance by uniformly sampling an axis-aligned bounding cube around each anchor point $\mathbf{T}_a$ and the drone's pose $\mathbf{T}_d^t$ and setting the exocentric view's origin at the anchor cube sampled point, looking at the drone cube sampled point, generating a randomized user $\mathbf{T}_u^t$.

We then render ego-motion data after pairwise temporally grouping the remaining pairs and using the drone's poses $(\mathbf{T}_d^t, \mathbf{T}_d^{t+1})$. We output color, depth, surface, and the optical flow between them using raytracing. For the exocentric renders we employ a CAD 3D drone model, enhanced with a physically based rendering (PBR) material with a bidirectional scattering distribution function (BSDF) to increase the realism of its renders. We place the drone at each pose pair $(\mathbf{T}_d^t, \mathbf{T}_d^{t+1})$ and then render the scene from each user $\mathbf{T}_u^t$ twice. Essentially, we use the dataset's anchor points as user views, after forcing the drone to run by them in various directions. For the exocentric user views, we output color, depth, surface and the drone's silhouette, in addition to its optical flow between the successive poses $(\mathbf{T}_d^t, \mathbf{T}_d^{t+1})$. An illustration of this process can be found in Fig. 1. Another important factor that should be considered while creating synthetic data is lighting. A recent study has identified the importance of the illumination model, as well as that a proper modelled lighting environment can give the same results as a natural environmental light [68].

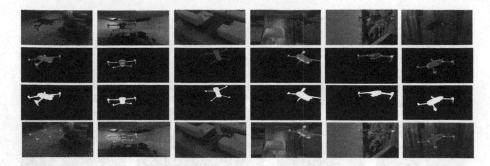

Fig. 3. Our compositing technique for producing realistic results. The top row illustrates the unlit drone model rendered in the already lit scene which produces a consistent appearance across all samples. The second row presents the same model rendered with our randomized lighting, while the third row depicts its anti-aliased silhouette. Finally, the bottom row presents the final composited result where the lit drone has been blended naturally in the environment.

Additionally, given that Matterport3D's scanned models contain pre-baked lighting and the drone model is unlit, a straightforward rendering with no light, or the addition of random lighting would produce unrealistic results as in the former case, the drone's appearance would be very consistent and dark across all renders, while in the latter case the already lit environment would become more saturated.

Therefore, we resort to a compositing approach where the scene is rendered twice, once with no lighting (preserving the emission of the already lit environment) and then, a follow up render which only renders the drone with random lighting as well as its mask. We use an advanced matting technique [16] to perform high-quality compositing of the lit drone to the unlit render with almost no aliasing using the drone mask, as presented in Fig. 3. Taking into account the findings of [68], for the drone lighting, we use a random texture of the rendered scene as an environment map with random light strength drawn from a uniform distribution $l \in \mathcal{U}(0.3, 0.7)$. This offers natural lighting for the 3D model that gets composited into the pre-baked lit environment, while also preserving a certain level of randomness, and thus variety.

Figure 4 presents the final dataset distribution of the train and test splits in terms of the $x - z$ and $y - z$ 3D coordinates density in the user's coordinate system, as well as the drone's yaw, pitch, roll rotations. It can be seen that our gamified and sampling-based approach has led to a smooth distribution of poses around the local exocentric viewpoint, with consistency between the train and test splits. In addition, a large enough variance of plausible drone rotations ensures a high-quality dataset for learning and benchmarking 6DOF pose estimation.

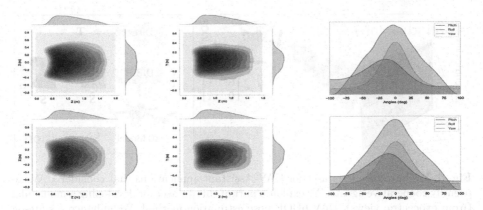

Fig. 4. This figure presents the drone pose distribution on the local coordinate system of the exocentric viewpoint. The top row presents the train split distribution, while the bottom row presents the test split distribution. From left to right: **i)** the x axis 3D coordinate distribution with respect to the depth (z), **ii)** the same for the y axis, and **iii)** the drone's yaw, pitch and roll angle distributions.

4   DronePose

In this section, we describe our single-shot approach in learning to estimate the 6DOF pose of a known UAV using our generated dataset. We address this purely from monocular input from the exocentric view in a supervised manner. Given the user's exocentric pose $\mathbf{T}_u^t$ and the drone's pose $\mathbf{T}_d^t$ in the world coordinate system, we can extract their relative groundtruth pose $\mathbf{T} = \mathbf{T}_u^{-1}\mathbf{T}_d := \begin{bmatrix} \mathbf{R} & \mathbf{t} \\ \mathbf{0} & 1 \end{bmatrix}$, omitting the time index for brevity for the remainder of this document. Inspired by [32] we use a backbone CNN encoder, followed by three fully connected linear units which then disentangle into two prediction heads for the translation and rotation components (see Fig. 5). We employ a state-of-the-art continuous $6d$ rotation parameterisation [69] that is transformed to a $9d$, 3×3 rotation matrix $\tilde{\mathbf{R}}^1$, which when combined with the $3d$ translation head's vector output $\tilde{\mathbf{t}}$, forms a homogeneous 4×4 pose $\tilde{\mathbf{T}} := \begin{bmatrix} \tilde{\mathbf{R}} & \tilde{\mathbf{t}} \\ \mathbf{0} & 1 \end{bmatrix}$. We use a L2 loss for the translation $\mathcal{L}_t = \|\mathbf{t} - \tilde{\mathbf{t}}\|_2^2$, while for the rotation we minimize their inner product on $SO(3)$, or otherwise their angular difference $\mathcal{L}_r = \arccos \frac{trace(\mathbf{R}\tilde{\mathbf{R}}^T)-1}{2}$. The final direct pose regression objective is:

$$\mathcal{L}_{pose} = \lambda_{pose} \mathcal{L}_t + (1 - \lambda_{pose}) \mathcal{L}_r, \tag{1}$$

with the ratio λ_{pose} balancing the errors between the rotation and translation.

Aiming to estimate the pose of a known object whose 3D model is available, and given the availability of high-quality silhouette masks, we support the direct regression loss with a rendered silhouette loss by employing a differentiable renderer. This is also an advantage of our chosen $6d$ representation [69] which in

---

[1] The accent denotes model predicted values.

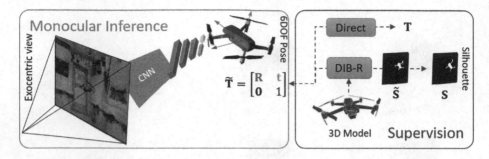

Fig. 5. We introduce a dataset for UAV-Assistant applications that consider UAVs as friendly cooperative agents. We exploit a part of this dataset for developing a monocular (from exocentric views), UAV 6DOF pose estimation method. We enhance a state-of-the-art direct pose regression model with a differentiable rendering (i.e. DIB-R) silhouette consistency objective to improve performance, leveraging our fully differentiable approach.

contrast to other state-of-the-art representations like [26,33,48,58], allows for the end-to-end integration of a rendering module. The approach of [33] splits the quaternion's components sign values into a separate classification branch, a technique that prevents its differentiable reformulation into the actual rotation and can only support pure direct pose regression models. Similarly, for dense keypoint voting or correspondence representations, a soft differentiable approximation would be required to turn this intermediate representation into a rotation matrix.

We transform the drone 3D model's vertices $\mathcal{V} \in \mathbb{R}^3$ using the predicted pose $\tilde{\mathbf{T}}^2$, and then use the recently introduced DIB-R differentiable mesh renderer [8] to render the transformed model's silhouette as observed by the user's viewpoint. Our final loss function supplements direct regression with an exocentric objective

$$\mathcal{L} = (1 - \lambda_{exo}) \mathcal{L}_{pose} + \lambda_{exo} \mathcal{L}_{exo}, \tag{2}$$

with λ_{exo} balancing the contribution of the exocentric loss ($\mathcal{L}_{exo}$). For the latter, a per pixel silhouette consistency loss function, formulated either as an L2 or binary cross entropy loss, would be a sub-optimal choice as it is an asymmetric objective. Indeed, through a differentiable renderer, only the pixels of the predicted silhouette would back-propagate error, neglecting any errors associated with the groundtruth silhouette proximity. This, in combination with the constant error in the non-overlapping cases, contribute to a loss surface that is constant, suffers from local minima, and cannot provide meaningful gradient flows. A typical choice in the literature is the Jaccard [30] loss, or otherwise referred to as the intersection-over-union (IoU) metric, which as a loss is defined as:

$$\mathcal{L}_{iou} = \frac{1}{N} \sum_{\mathbf{p} \in \Omega} 1 - \frac{\mathbf{S} \odot \tilde{\mathbf{S}}}{\mathbf{S} \oplus \tilde{\mathbf{S}} - \mathbf{S} \odot \tilde{\mathbf{S}} + \epsilon}, \tag{3}$$

---

^{2} 4D homogenisation of the 3D coordinates is omitted for brevity.

with $\mathbf{S}$ and $\tilde{\mathbf{S}}$ being the binary groundtruth and rendered predicted silhouette images respectively, $\mathbf{p}$ corresponding to a pixel in the image domain Ω that the silhouettes are defined in, N being the total image domain elements, and ϵ a small numerical stabilization constant.

However, a known weakness of the Jaccard loss (which is a similarity measure metric by mathematical definition) is its plateau when there is no overlap between the silhouettes, offering no notion of proximity to the objective itself. In addition, taking into account that our loss is defined on the projective space, the reduced degrees-of-freedom manifest into loss irregularities, especially due to rotations and the 3D shape variations. Motivated by these shortcomings, we propose to use a smooth silhouette loss defined as:

$$\mathcal{L}_{smooth} = \frac{1}{N} \sum_{\mathbf{p} \in \Omega} \mathbf{S} \odot \mathcal{S}(\tilde{\mathbf{S}}) + \tilde{\mathbf{S}} \odot \mathcal{S}(\mathbf{S}), \tag{4}$$

where the function $\mathcal{S}$ calculates a truncated, continuous silhouette proximity map $\mathcal{S}(\mathbf{S}) = (g \circledast \overline{\mathbf{S}}) - (g \circledast \mathbf{S})$, where $\overline{\mathbf{S}} := 1 - \mathbf{S}$ is the complement of silhouette $\mathbf{S}$ and g is a convolved smoothing kernel. Our smooth silhouette loss exhibits some very important traits, it is quick to evaluate as it is fully parallelizable and it offers a smooth objective function compared to IoU, enhanced with a notion of proximity to the objective. This is controlled by the convolution's kernel size which also adjusts the smoothed silhouette region against the truncated one. Finally, it is a fully symmetric objective that takes into account the groundtruth silhouette as well. More importantly, this is achieved in a fully differentiable manner with respect to the predicted silhouette. Figure 6 illustrates the difference between IoU (Eq. 3) and our introduced smooth loss (Eq. 4) across the silhouettes produced by a dense sampling of poses around a target pose and its silhouette, showcasing the smoothness and advantages of our objective function[3].

5   Results

In this section, we explore the supplementary nature of the exocentric loss for the task of object 3D pose estimation through a set of structured experiments.

Implementation Details: When generating our dataset, we follow the official Matterport3D data scene splits, and thus, our final rendered dataset comprises 38155 pairs (i.e. for t and $t + 1$) of train samples, 5687 of validation samples and 11146 of test samples. We used PyTorch [43] and Kaolin [24] for the implementation of our model. In more detail, we employ a ResNet34 [19] pre-trained on ImageNet [11] as our backbone encoder, followed by fully connected layers for reducing the encoded features progressively by using $1024, 512$ and 128 features respectively, which eventually branch off to the $6d$ and $3d$ rotation and translation heads. We use ELU [9] activation functions for the linear layers, as

---

[3] Additional analysis can be found in our supplement including a loss landscape analysis.

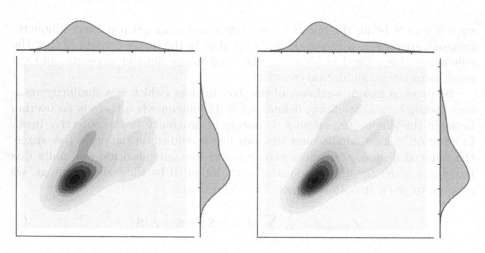

Fig. 6. Distribution of the IoU (left) and our smooth silhouette (right) losses across a dense sampling of poses. Due to the inherent difficulty in plotting 6DOF poses, the presented distributions are generated with the following process. We perform a grid search of 3DOF translational and 3DOF angular displacements, and then bin them according to their Euclidean and angular distances respectively. The binning process accumulates the error of the silhouette rendered by displaced pose against the original pose. Given the different scale of the two loss functions, we first apply min-max normalization before binning and accumulating them. The plots then present the distribution of these bins, with the translational radius distance binned and accumulated errors on the horizontal axis, and the rotational angular distance binned and accumulated errors on the vertical axis. Our smoother loss variant produces a smoother curve for the rotational error as evident in the vertical axis. In addition, the larger number of transitions (*i.e.* color steps) and their smaller steps indicate an overall smoother objective. Further, a smaller convergence region around the groundtruth pose, as well as the smaller constant loss regions indicate that IoU suffers from harder convergence towards the minima.

well as the Adam [28] optimizer with its default momentum parameters. For the smoothing kernel we present results for an efficient 49×49 low-pass box smoothing filter, as well as a 69×69 Gaussian kernel. For the [58] we followed the official implementation. All models were trained for 20 epochs with a batch size of 64 and a learning rate of $1e-4$.

Metrics: We report the following evaluation metrics for all of our experiments, the normalized position error (NPE), the orientation error (OE) and the combined pose error (CPE) as defined in [29], as well as the 6D Pose error [21] and the combined position and orientation accuracy metric ($AccX$). For the latter, a pose is considered as accurate if it lies within an angular error under X degrees and a position error under Xcm. Similarly, the 6D Pose error is reported using the same thresholds as the accuracy metric, and we consider the 3D model's diagonal rather than its diameter.

Experiments: All results reported in Table 1 represent the best performing model across the total epochs. We demonstrate through extensive experiments how differential rendering can be employed for improving pose estimation, and also highlight the weaknesses of common loss functions (i.e. IoU, GIoU [50]). Further, we compare our method with a single-shot variant [58] oriented towards real-time applications, which outperforms prior work [6, 26, 48]. Ablation results with respect to the smoothing kernel size and type can be found in our supplementary material. Our baseline is a *Direct* regression model using a state-of-the-art $6d$ representation [69], *i.e.* setting $\lambda_{exo} = 0.0$. Next, we enhance our model with an IoU-based supervision loss with $\lambda_{exo} = 0.1$ (*I0.1*) and $\lambda_{exo} = 0.2$ (*I0.2*). No apparent performance gain is observable for *I0.1*, while *I0.2* negatively affects the models performance. It should be noted that for higher λ_{exo} the model did not converge, indicating that the exocentric loss is not sufficient to drive optimization alone. Particularly, the IoU loss does not exhibit a smooth learning curve during training, a fact that hurts convergence due to the bigger effect it has while back-propagating gradients. Intuitively though, it should be more effective on a model that produces higher quality predictions as its plateau weakness would be circumvented. Therefore, our next set of experiments focus on increasing the IoU loss during training after a set of epochs. In more details, for the *I0.1-0.4* experiment, we increase the IoU weight λ_{exo} from 0.1 to 0.4 after 15 epochs and train for another 5 epochs. The *I0.1-0.3-0.4* experiment switches at epochs 8 and 12 at the respectively weight values, and the *I0.1-0.3-0.6* experiment accordingly switches at epochs 11 and 15. The results indicate that this is a valid strategy for improving the model's performance. Next, we present results for a GIoU [50] variant that we implemented oriented for silhouettes, using $\lambda_{exo} = 0.1$ (*G0.1*). While GIoU relies on non-differentiable *min* and *max* operations, it has demonstrated better performance than IoU for bounding box regression. In our case though, it does not demonstrate any performance gains even though it aims at reducing IoU's plateaus. The final experiments and results showcase the efficacy of our proposed smooth silhouette consistency loss and similar to the above experiments, are prefixed with an S followed by the λ_{exo} value. The best performing model is *Gauss0.1* that shows the largest gains compared to [58] and our baseline. At the same time, our box-filter implementation *S0.2,S0.2* and *S0.3* offer better performance as then IoU, and *S0.3* managed to converge, in contrast with the higher λ_{exo} experiments for the IoU loss. These results show that the smoother silhouette consistency objective, independently of its implementation (i.e. Guassian or box-filter), behaves better than IoU and can improve the performance of direct pose estimation models when mask annotations are available. They also highlight the sensitivity in tuning the relative importance of the direct and silhouette based losses. Another important trait of the smoother objective is a smoother loss landscape, which is further analysed in the supplementary material, with qualitative results for in-the-wild data and our test-set (Fig. 7) indicating a more robustly trained model as well.

Fig. 7. Qualitative results on our test set. A 3D coordinate axis (X, Y, Z axes) system is overlayed on the image based on the predicted pose. We provide more qualitative results in our supplementary material including results on real-data harvested from YouTube.

Table 1. Results on the generated dataset's test set which contains unseen images.

	NPE ↓	OE ↓	CPE ↓	Acc5 ↑	Acc10 ↑	6D Pose-5 ↑	6D Pose-10 ↑
Singleshotpose [58]	0.025	0.070	0.095	79.418	95.657	47.009	79.669
Direct	0.020	0.059	0.079	89.555	98.661	38.464	88.113
I0.1	0.020	0.059	0.079	88.880	98.661	42.348	87.782
I0.2	0.022	0.058	0.081	89.314	98.759	28.682	84.788
I0.1-0.4	0.020	**0.056**	**0.076**	90.696	98.643	37.098	88.354
I0.1-0.3-0.4	0.020	0.057	0.077	90.071	98.741	39.046	88.259
I0.1-0.3-0.6	0.021	0.057	0.078	89.014	98.571	36.518	88.482
G0.1	0.021	0.057	0.078	89.549	98.702	37.296	86.846
S0.1	0.019	0.057	**0.076**	**91.018**	98.759	46.266	89.652
S0.2	0.020	0.059	0.080	88.871	98.634	41.834	85.563
S0.3	0.019	0.064	0.083	87.523	98.616	42.100	89.086
Gauss0.1	**0.016**	0.059	**0.076**	90.259	**98.795**	**57.371**	**91.607**

6   Conclusions

In this work, we have filled in a data gap for the under-explored UAV-Assistant application context. We introduced a dataset that includes temporally and spatially aligned data, captured by the egocentric view of a cooperative drone, as well as the exocentric view of the user that observes the scene and the drone operating at her/his immediate surroundings. We carefully design a methodology to generate high-quality, multimodal data and then focus on an important aspect of such a cooperative framework, the spatial alignment between the user and the drone. Using data generated via synthesis, albeit realistic, we exploit the availability of drone silhouettes in the exocentric view and explore recent research in differentiable rendering to further improve pose estimation. We also introduce a smoother loss for learning rendered silhouettes and demonstrate its efficacy compared to the typical IoU loss. A parallel can be drawn between losses defined using distance fields with our smooth loss which, nonetheless, is quicker to evaluate and straightforward to implement compared to a symmetric distance field loss evaluation. Still, our works shows that smoother objectives are beneficial for projection based supervision, which warrants further exploration.

Acknowledgements. This research has been supported by the European Commission funded program FASTER, under H2020 Grant Agreement 833507.

References

1. The 1st anti-UAV challenge. In: The IEEE Conference on Computer Vision and Pattern Recognition Workshops (2020). https://anti-uav.github.io/. Accessed 03 Mar 2020
2. Antonini, A., Guerra, W., Murali, V., Sayre-McCord, T., Karaman, S.: The black-bird dataset: a large-scale dataset for UAV perception in aggressive flight. arXiv preprint arXiv:1810.01987 (2018)
3. Belmonte, L.M., Morales, R., Fernández-Caballero, A.: Computer vision in autonomous unmanned aerial vehicles-a systematic mapping study. Appl. Sci. **9**(15), 3196 (2019)
4. Bondi, E., et al.: AirSim-W: a simulation environment for wildlife conservation with UAVs. In: Proceedings of the 1st ACM SIGCAS Conference on Computing and Sustainable Societies, pp. 1–12 (2018)
5. Brachmann, E., Krull, A., Michel, F., Gumhold, S., Shotton, J., Rother, C.: Learning 6D object pose estimation using 3D object coordinates. In: Fleet, D., Pajdla, T., Schiele, B., Tuytelaars, T. (eds.) ECCV 2014. LNCS, vol. 8690, pp. 536–551. Springer, Cham (2014). https://doi.org/10.1007/978-3-319-10605-2_35
6. Brachmann, E., Michel, F., Krull, A., Ying Yang, M., Gumhold, S., et al.: Uncertainty-driven 6D pose estimation of objects and scenes from a single RGB image. In: Proceedings of the IEEE Conference on Computer Vision and Pattern Recognition, pp. 3364–3372 (2016)
7. Chang, A., et al.: Matterport3D: learning from RGB-D data in indoor environments. In: 7th IEEE International Conference on 3D Vision, 3DV 2017, pp. 667–676. Institute of Electrical and Electronics Engineers Inc. (2018)
8. Chen, W., et al.: Learning to predict 3D objects with an interpolation-based differentiable renderer. In: Advances in Neural Information Processing Systems (2019)
9. Clevert, D.A., Unterthiner, T., Hochreiter, S.: Fast and accurate deep network learning by exponential linear units (ELUs). arXiv preprint arXiv:1511.07289 (2015)
10. Coluccia, A., et al.: Drone-vs-bird detection challenge at IEEE AVSS2019. In: 2019 16th IEEE International Conference on Advanced Video and Signal Based Surveillance (AVSS), pp. 1–7. IEEE (2019)
11. Deng, J., Dong, W., Socher, R., Li, L.J., Li, K., Fei-Fei, L.: Imagenet: a large-scale hierarchical image database. In: 2009 IEEE Conference on Computer Vision and Pattern Recognition, pp. 248–255. IEEE (2009)
12. Doumanoglou, A., Kouskouridas, R., Malassiotis, S., Kim, T.K.: Recovering 6D object pose and predicting next-best-view in the crowd. In: Proceedings of the IEEE Conference on Computer Vision and Pattern Recognition, pp. 3583–3592 (2016)
13. Erat, O., Isop, W.A., Kalkofen, D., Schmalstieg, D.: Drone-augmented human vision: exocentric control for drones exploring hidden areas. IEEE Trans. Visual Comput. Graphics **24**(4), 1437–1446 (2018)

14. Fan, R., Jiao, J., Pan, J., Huang, H., Shen, S., Liu, M.: Real-time dense stereo embedded in a UAV for road inspection. In: The IEEE Conference on Computer Vision and Pattern Recognition (CVPR) Workshops, June 2019

15. Fonder, M., Van Droogenbroeck, M.: Mid-air: a multi-modal dataset for extremely low altitude drone flights. In: Proceedings of the IEEE Conference on Computer Vision and Pattern Recognition Workshops (2019)

16. Friedman, J., Jones, A.C.: Fully automatic id mattes with support for motion blur and transparency. In: ACM SIGGRAPH 2015 Posters, p. 1 (2015)

17. Guerra, W., Tal, E., Murali, V., Ryou, G., Karaman, S.: Flightgoggles: photore-alistic sensor simulation for perception-driven robotics using photogrammetry and virtual reality. arXiv preprint arXiv:1905.11377 (2019)

18. Gupta, S., Arbeláez, P., Girshick, R., Malik, J.: Inferring 3D object pose in RGB-D images. arXiv preprint arXiv:1502.04652 (2015)

19. He, K., Zhang, X., Ren, S., Sun, J.: Deep residual learning for image recognition. In: The IEEE Conference on Computer Vision and Pattern Recognition (CVPR), June 2016

20. He, Y., Sun, W., Huang, H., Liu, J., Fan, H., Sun, J.: PVN3D: a deep point-wise 3D keypoints voting network for 6DoF pose estimation. arXiv preprint arXiv:1911.04231 (2019)

21. Hinterstoisser, S., et al.: Model based training, detection and pose estimation of texture-less 3D objects in heavily cluttered scenes. In: Lee, K.M., Matsushita, Y., Rehg, J.M., Hu, Z. (eds.) ACCV 2012. LNCS, vol. 7724, pp. 548–562. Springer, Heidelberg (2013). https://doi.org/10.1007/978-3-642-37331-2_42

22. Hsieh, M.R., Lin, Y.L., Hsu, W.H.: Drone-based object counting by spatially reg-ularized regional proposal networks. In: The IEEE International Conference on Computer Vision (ICCV). IEEE (2017)

23. Insafutdinov, E., Dosovitskiy, A.: Unsupervised learning of shape and pose with differentiable point clouds. In: Advances in Neural Information Processing Systems, pp. 2802–2812 (2018)

24. Jatavallabhula, K.M., et al.: Kaolin: a pytorch library for accelerating 3D deep learning research. arXiv preprint arXiv:1911.05063 (2019)

25. Jin, R., Jiang, J., Qi, Y., Lin, D., Song, T.: Drone detection and pose estimation using relational graph networks. Sensors **19**(6), 1479 (2019)

26. Kehl, W., Manhardt, F., Tombari, F., Ilic, S., Navab, N.: SSD-6D: making RGB-based 3D detection and 6D pose estimation great again. In: Proceedings of the IEEE International Conference on Computer Vision, pp. 1521–1529 (2017)

27. Kellenberger, B., Marcos, D., Tuia, D.: When a few clicks make all the difference: improving weakly-supervised wildlife detection in UAV images. In: Proceedings of the IEEE Conference on Computer Vision and Pattern Recognition Workshops (2019)

28. Kingma, D.P., Ba, J.: Adam: a method for stochastic optimization. arXiv preprint arXiv:1412.6980 (2014)

29. Kisantal, M., Sharma, S., Park, T.H., Izzo, D., Märtens, M., D'Amico, S.: Satellite pose estimation challenge: dataset, competition design and results. arXiv preprint arXiv:1911.02050 (2019)

30. Kosub, S.: A note on the triangle inequality for the Jaccard distance. Pattern Recogn. Lett. **120**, 36–38 (2019)

31. Kyrkou, C., Theocharides, T.: Deep-learning-based aerial image classification for emergency response applications using unmanned aerial vehicles. In: The IEEE Conference on Computer Vision and Pattern Recognition (CVPR) Workshops, June 2019

32. Li, Z., Wang, G., Ji, X.: CDPN: coordinates-based disentangled pose network for real-time RGB-based 6-DOF object pose estimation. In: Proceedings of the IEEE International Conference on Computer Vision, pp. 7678–7687 (2019)

33. Liao, S., Gavves, E., Snoek, C.G.M.: Spherical regression: learning viewpoints, surface normals and 3D rotations on n-spheres. In: The IEEE Conference on Computer Vision and Pattern Recognition (CVPR), June 2019

34. Loper, M.M., Black, M.J.: OpenDR: an approximate differentiable renderer. In: Fleet, D., Pajdla, T., Schiele, B., Tuytelaars, T. (eds.) ECCV 2014. LNCS, vol. 8695, pp. 154–169. Springer, Cham (2014). https://doi.org/10.1007/978-3-319-10584-0_11

35. Maggiori, E., Tarabalka, Y., Charpiat, G., Alliez, P.: Can semantic labeling methods generalize to any city? The inria aerial image labeling benchmark. In: IEEE International Geoscience and Remote Sensing Symposium (IGARSS). IEEE (2017)

36. Mahendran, S., Ali, H., Vidal, R.: 3D pose regression using convolutional neural networks. In: Proceedings of the IEEE International Conference on Computer Vision Workshops, pp. 2174–2182 (2017)

37. Massa, F., Aubry, M., Marlet, R.: Convolutional neural networks for joint object detection and pose estimation: a comparative study. arXiv preprint arXiv:1412.7190 (2014)

38. Mueller, M., Smith, N., Ghanem, B.: A benchmark and simulator for UAV tracking. In: Leibe, B., Matas, J., Sebe, N., Welling, M. (eds.) ECCV 2016. LNCS, vol. 9905, pp. 445–461. Springer, Cham (2016). https://doi.org/10.1007/978-3-319-46448-0_27

39. Müller, M., Casser, V., Lahoud, J., Smith, N., Ghanem, B.: Sim4CV: a photorealistic simulator for computer vision applications. Int. J. Comput. Vision 126(9), 902–919 (2018)

40. Oh, S., et al.: A large-scale benchmark dataset for event recognition in surveillance video. In: CVPR 2011, pp. 3153–3160. IEEE (2011)

41. Palazzi, A., Bergamini, L., Calderara, S., Cucchiara, R.: End-to-end 6-DoF object pose estimation through differentiable rasterization. In: The European Conference on Computer Vision (ECCV) Workshops, September 2018

42. Park, K., Mousavian, A., Xiang, Y., Fox, D.: Latentfusion: end-to-end differentiable reconstruction and rendering for unseen object pose estimation. arXiv preprint arXiv:1912.00416 (2019)

43. Paszke, A., et al.: Automatic differentiation in pytorch (2017)

44. Peng, S., Liu, Y., Huang, Q., Zhou, X., Bao, H.: PVNet: pixel-wise voting network for 6DoF pose estimation. In: Proceedings of the IEEE Conference on Computer Vision and Pattern Recognition, pp. 4561–4570 (2019)

45. Pepik, B., Gehler, P., Stark, M., Schiele, B.: $3D^2PM$ – 3D deformable part models. In: Fitzgibbon, A., Lazebnik, S., Perona, P., Sato, Y., Schmid, C. (eds.) ECCV 2012. LNCS, vol. 7577, pp. 356–370. Springer, Heidelberg (2012). https://doi.org/10.1007/978-3-642-33783-3_26

46. Periyasamy, A.S., Schwarz, M., Behnke, S.: Refining 6D object pose predictions using abstract render-and-compare. arXiv preprint arXiv:1910.03412 (2019)

47. Proenca, P.F., Gao, Y.: Deep learning for spacecraft pose estimation from photorealistic rendering. arXiv preprint arXiv:1907.04298 (2019)

48. Rad, M., Lepetit, V.: BB8: a scalable, accurate, robust to partial occlusion method for predicting the 3D poses of challenging objects without using depth. In: Proceedings of the IEEE International Conference on Computer Vision, pp. 3828–3836 (2017)

49. Rambach, J., Deng, C., Pagani, A., Stricker, D.: Learning 6dof object poses from synthetic single channel images. In: 2018 IEEE International Symposium on Mixed and Augmented Reality Adjunct (ISMAR-Adjunct), pp. 164–169. IEEE (2018)

50. Rezatofighi, H., Tsoi, N., Gwak, J., Sadeghian, A., Reid, I., Savarese, S.: Generalized intersection over union: a metric and a loss for bounding box regression. In: Proceedings of the IEEE Conference on Computer Vision and Pattern Recognition, pp. 658–666 (2019)

51. Robicquet, A., et al.: Forecasting social navigation in crowded complex scenes. arXiv preprint arXiv:1601.00998 (2016)

52. Rozantsev, A., Lepetit, V., Fua, P.: Detecting flying objects using a single moving camera. IEEE Trans. Pattern Anal. Mach. Intell. 39(5), 879–892 (2016)

53. Schwarz, M., Schulz, H., Behnke, S.: RGB-D object recognition and pose estimation based on pre-trained convolutional neural network features. In: 2015 IEEE International Conference on Robotics and Automation (ICRA), pp. 1329–1335. IEEE (2015)

54. Shah, S., Dey, D., Lovett, C., Kapoor, A.: AirSim: high-fidelity visual and physical simulation for autonomous vehicles. In: Hutter, M., Siegwart, R. (eds.) Field and Service Robotics. SPAR, vol. 5, pp. 621–635. Springer, Cham (2018). https://doi.org/10.1007/978-3-319-67361-5_40

55. Shi, X., Yang, C., Xie, W., Liang, C., Shi, Z., Chen, J.: Anti-drone system with multiple surveillance technologies: architecture, implementation, and challenges. IEEE Commun. Mag. 56(4), 68–74 (2018)

56. Su, H., Qi, C.R., Li, Y., Guibas, L.J.: Render for CNN: viewpoint estimation in images using CNNs trained with rendered 3D model views. In: Proceedings of the IEEE International Conference on Computer Vision, pp. 2686–2694 (2015)

57. Tejani, A., Kouskouridas, R., Doumanoglou, A., Tang, D., Kim, T.K.: Latent-class hough forests for 6 DoF object pose estimation. IEEE Trans. Pattern Anal. Mach. Intell. 40(1), 119–132 (2017)

58. Tekin, B., Sinha, S.N., Fua, P.: Real-time seamless single shot 6D object pose prediction. In: Proceedings of the IEEE Conference on Computer Vision and Pattern Recognition, pp. 292–301 (2018)

59. Tulsiani, S., Malik, J.: Viewpoints and keypoints. In: Proceedings of the IEEE Conference on Computer Vision and Pattern Recognition, pp. 1510–1519 (2015)

60. Wang, C., et al.: DenseFusion: 6D object pose estimation by iterative dense fusion. In: Proceedings of the IEEE Conference on Computer Vision and Pattern Recognition, pp. 3343–3352 (2019)

61. Wang, H., Sridhar, S., Huang, J., Valentin, J., Song, S., Guibas, L.J.: Normalized object coordinate space for category-level 6D object pose and size estimation. In: Proceedings of the IEEE Conference on Computer Vision and Pattern Recognition, pp. 2642–2651 (2019)

62. Wang, M., Deng, W.: Deep visual domain adaptation: a survey. Neurocomputing 312, 135–153 (2018)

63. Wu, Y., et al.: Unsupervised joint 3D object model learning and 6d pose estimation for depth-based instance segmentation. In: Proceedings of the IEEE International Conference on Computer Vision Workshops (2019)

64. Xiang, Y., Schmidt, T., Narayanan, V., Fox, D.: Posecnn: a convolutional neural network for 6D object pose estimation in cluttered scenes (2018)

65. Xie, K., et al.: Creating and chaining camera moves for quadrotor videography. ACM Trans. Graph. (TOG) 37(4), 1–13 (2018)

66. Yuan, L., Reardon, C., Warnell, G., Loianno, G.: Human gaze-driven spatial tasking of an autonomous MAV. IEEE Robot. Autom. Lett. 4(2), 1343–1350 (2019). https://doi.org/10.1109/LRA.2019.2895419

67. Zakharov, S., Shugurov, I., Ilic, S.: DPOD: 6D pose object detector and refiner. In: Proceedings of the IEEE International Conference on Computer Vision, pp. 1941–1950 (2019)

68. Zhang, X., Jia, N., Ivrissimtzis, I.: A study of the effect of the illumination model on the generation of synthetic training datasets. arXiv preprint arXiv:2006.08819 (2020)

69. Zhou, Y., Barnes, C., Lu, J., Yang, J., Li, H.: On the continuity of rotation representations in neural networks. In: The IEEE Conference on Computer Vision and Pattern Recognition (CVPR), June 2019

70. Zhu, P., Wen, L., Bian, X., Ling, H., Hu, Q.: Vision meets drones: a challenge. arXiv preprint arXiv:1804.07437 (2018)

How to Track Your Dragon: A Multi-attentional Framework for Real-Time RGB-D 6-DOF Object Pose Tracking

Isidoros Marougkas[1]([⊠])[iD], Petros Koutras[1][iD], Nikos Kardaris[1],
Georgios Retsinas[1][iD], Georgia Chalvatzaki[2][iD], and Petros Maragos[1][iD]

[1] School of E.C.E., National Technical University of Athens, 15773 Athens, Greece
ismarougkas@gmail.com, {pkoutras,maragos}@cs.ntua.gr,
nick.kardaris@gmail.com, gretsinas@central.ntua.gr
[2] Department of Computer Science, TU Darmstadt, 64289 Darmstadt, Germany
georgia@robot-learning.de

Abstract. We present a novel multi-attentional convolutional architecture to tackle the problem of real-time RGB-D 6D object pose tracking of single, known objects. Such a problem poses multiple challenges originating both from the objects' nature and their interaction with their environment, which previous approaches have failed to fully address. The proposed framework encapsulates methods for background clutter and occlusion handling by integrating multiple parallel soft spatial attention modules into a multitask Convolutional Neural Network (CNN) architecture. Moreover, we consider the special geometrical properties of both the object's 3D model and the pose space, and we use a more sophisticated approach for data augmentation during training. The provided experimental results confirm the effectiveness of the proposed multi-attentional architecture, as it improves the State-of-the-Art (SoA) tracking performance by an average score of 34.03% for translation and 40.01% for rotation, when tested on the most complete dataset designed, up to date, for the problem of RGB-D object tracking. Code will be available in: https://github.com/ismarou/How_to_track_your_Dragon.

Keywords: Pose · Tracking · Attention · Geodesic · Multi-task

1 Introduction

Robust, accurate and fast object pose estimation and tracking, i.e. estimation of the object's 3D position and orientation, has been a matter of intense research for many years. The applications of such an estimation problem can be found in Robotics, Autonomous Navigation, Augmented Reality, etc. Although the Computer Vision community has consistently studied the problem of object pose estimation and tracking for decades, the recent spread of affordable and reliable RGB-D sensors like Kinect, along with advances in Deep Learning (DL) and especially the use of CNNs as the new SoA image feature extractors, led to a new

© Springer Nature Switzerland AG 2020
A. Bartoli and A. Fusiello (Eds.): ECCV 2020 Workshops, LNCS 12536, pp. 682–699, 2020.
https://doi.org/10.1007/978-3-030-66096-3_45

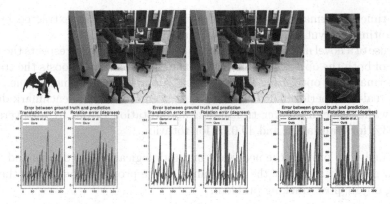

Fig. 1. Top row: *(Left to right)* The "Dragon" model, an estimated pose in the "Hard Interaction" scenario for each of the SoA [8] *(light blue)* and our *(pink)* approaches and an example frame pair of Foreground extraction *(up)* and Occlusion handling *(down)* attention maps which are learned by minimizing the two auxiliary binary cross entropy losses. The following tradeoff occurs: as the occlusion increases, foreground attention, which focuses on the moving parts of the scene (i.e. the hand and the object), gets blurrier, while occlusion attention gets sharper and shifts focus from the object center to its body parts. **Bottom row:** *(Left to right)* Translational and Rotational error plots of the SoA [8] *(blue)* and *(our)* approaches, for the "75% Vert. Occlusion", the "Rotation Only" and the "Hard Interaction" scenario, respectively. Grey regions stand for intervals of high occlusion and green ones for rapid movement. (Color figure online)

era of research and a re-examination of several problems, with central aim the generalization over different tasks. CNNs have achieved ground-breaking results in 2D problems like object classification, object detection and segmentation. Thus, it has been tempting to the research community to increasingly use them in the more challenging 3D tasks, renouncing traditional algorithms.

The innate challenges of object pose estimation from RGB-D streams include background clutter, occlusions (both static, from other objects present in the scene, and dynamic, due to possible interactions with a human user), illumination variation, sensor noise, image blurring (due to fast movement) and appearance changes as the object viewpoint alters. Moreover, one should account for the pose ambiguity, which is a direct consequence of the object's own geometry, in possible symmetries, the challenges of proper parameter representation of rotations and the inevitable difficulties that an effort of forging a model faces, when extracting information about the 3D scene geometry from 2D-projected images.

In this paper, we build upon previous works [7,8], in order to face a series of those challenges that have not been fully resolved, so far. Thus, our main contributions are:

- An explicit background clutter and occlusion handling mechanism that leverages spatial attentions and provides an intuitive understanding of the tracker's region of interest at each frame, while boosting its performance. To the best of our knowledge, this is the first such strategy, that explicitly handles these two challenges, is incorporated into a CNN-based architecture, while achieving

real-time performance. Supervision for this mechanism is extracted by fully exploiting the synthetic nature of our training data.
- The use of a novel multi-task pose tracking loss function, that respects the geometry of both the object's 3D model and the pose space and boosts the tracking performance by optimizing auxiliary tasks along with the principal one.
- SoA real-time performance in the hardest scenarios of the benchmark dataset [8], while achieving lower translation and rotation errors by an average of 34.03% for translation and 40.01% for rotation.

Accordingly, we provide the necessary methodological design details and experimental results that justify the importance of the proposed method in the challenging object pose tracking problem.

2   Related Work

Previous works attempt to tackle the problem using DL, focusing on two different directions: per-frame pose estimation (or, else, "tracking by detection") and temporal tracking.

Tracking-by-Detection. The first family of proposed approaches in literature processes each video frame separately, without any feedback from the estimation of the previous timeframe. In [36], Xiang et al. constructed a CNN architecture that estimates binary object masks and then predicts the object class and its translation and rotation separately, while in [19], Kehl et al. extended the Single Shot Detection (SSD) framework [24] for 2D Object detection by performing discrete viewpoint classification for known objects. Finally, they refine their initial estimations via ICP [32] iterations. In [38], Zakharov et al. proposed a CNN framework that uses RGB images for pixel-wise object semantic segmentation in a mask-level. Following this, UV texture maps are estimated to extract dense correspondences between 2D images and 3D object models minimizing cross entropy losses. Those correspondences are used for pose estimation via P'n'P [22]. This estimation is, ultimately, inserted as a prior to a refinement CNN that outputs the final pose prediction. In PVNet [31], Peng et al. perform per-pixel voting-based regression to match 3D object coordinates with predefined keypoints inside the object surface, in order to handle occlusions. In [30], Pavlakos et al. extract semantic keypoints in single RGB images with a CNN and incorporate them into a deformable shape model. In [35], Wohlhart et al. employed a supervised contrastive convolutional framework to disentangle descriptors of different object instances and impose proportional distances to different poses of the same object. In [33], Sundermeyer et al. built a self-supervised Augmented Auto-Encoder that predicts 3D rotations only from synthetic data. In [29], Park et al. trained an adversarially guided Encoder-Decoder to predict pixel-wise coordinates in a given image and then fed them to a P'n'P algorithm. More recently, iPose [18] is one of the attempts the philosophy of which is the closest to ours. Its authors segment binary masks with a pretrained MaskRCNN [11] to

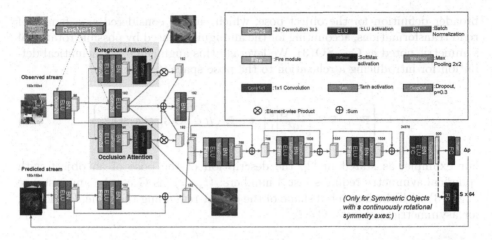

Fig. 2. Overview of the proposed CNN architecture for object pose tracking.

extract background clutter and occluders and they map 2D pixels to dense 3D object coordinates, which, in turn, are used as input to a P'n'P geometric optimization. Our attention modules have the same effect, but are computationally cheaper than MaskRCNN, as they relax the requirement for hard segmentation.

Temporal Tracking. The second category under study is temporal tracking, where feedback is utilized, to allow for skipping steps without prior knowledge of the previous pose. Garon et al. [7,8], formulated the tracking problem exclusively as a learning one, by generating two streams of synthetic RGB-D frame pairs from independent viewpoints and regressing the pose using a CNN. Li et al. [23] initialized a similar CNN architecture using a FlowNet2 [17] backbone and fused its two streams by subtraction. In DeepTAM [39], the training was performed with an Optical flow-based regularization term and the production of multiple heterogenous pose hypotheses was encouraged. Those hypotheses were bootstrapped in the final layer. Last but not least, Deng et al. [4] extended the framework of [33] by combining it with a Rao-Blackwellized Particle Filter [5]. In brief, they randomly sampled 2D bounding boxes to crop RGB images, infer 3D translation probabilities from their dimensions and search for the closest saved rotated sample provided by the Autoencoder of [33]. Then, the particles were weighted according to the orientation probabilities and were prepared for the next sampling iteration.

3 Methodology

3.1 Problem Formulation

Our problem consists in estimating the object pose $\mathbb{P}$, which is usually described as a rigid 3D transformation w.r.t. a fixed coordinate frame, namely an element of the Special Euclidean Lie group in 3D: $SE(3)$. It can be disentangled into two components; a rotation matrix R, which is an element of the Lie Group $SO(3)$ and a translation vector $\mathbf{t} \in \mathbb{R}^3$. However, Brégier et al. [2] proposed a

broader definition for the object pose, which can be considered as a family of
rigid transformations, accounting for the ambiguity caused by possible rotational
symmetry, noted as $G \in SO(3)$. We leverage this augmented mathematical definition for introducing a relaxation to the pose space $\mathscr{C}$ definition:

$$\mathscr{C} = \left\{ \mathbb{P} \mid \mathbb{P} = \left[\frac{R \cdot G | t}{0^T | 1} \right], t \in \mathbb{R}^3, R \in SO(3), G \in SO(3) \right\}. \tag{1}$$

For example, as stated in [2], the description of the pose of an object with
spherical symmetry requires just 3 numbers: $(t_{x,y,z})$, as G can be any instance
of SO(3) with the imprinted shape of the object remaining the same. Obviously,
for asymmetrical objects, $G = \mathbb{I}_3$.

3.2   Architecture Description

The proposed architecture is depicted in Fig. 2. Our CNN inputs two RGB-D
frames of size 150×150: $I(t)$, $\hat{I}(t)$ (with $I(t)$ being the "Observed" and $\hat{I}(t)$ the
"Predicted" one) and regresses an output pose representation $\Delta p \in \mathbb{R}^9$, with 3
parameters for translation ($\hat{t}_{x,y,z} \in [-1, 1]$) and 6 for rotation. The first two layers of the "Observed" stream are initialized with the weights of a ResNet18[13],
pretrained on Imagenet [3], to narrow down the real-synthetic domain adaptation
gap, as proposed in [14]. Since Imagenet contains only RGB images, we initialize
the weights of the Depth input modality with the average of the weights corresponding to each of the three RGB channels. Contrary to [14], we find beneficial
not to freeze those two layers during training. The reason is that we aim to track
the pose of the single objects we train on and not to generalize to unseen ones.
So, overfitting to that object's features helps the tracker to focus only on distinguishing the pose change. The weights that correspond to the Depth stream
are, of course, not frozen in either case. To the output of the second "Observed"
layer, we apply spatial attention for foreground extraction and occlusion handling and we add their corresponding output feature maps with the one of the
second layer, along with a Residual connection [12] from the first layer. As a next
step, we fuse the two streams by concatenating their feature maps and pass this
concatenated output through three sequential Fire modules [16], all connected
with residual connections [13].

Background and Occlusion Handling: After our first "Observed" Fire layer,
our model generates an attention weight map by using a Fire layer dedicated to
occlusion handling and foreground extraction, respectively, followed by a 1×1
convolution that squeezes the feature map channels to a single one (and normalized by softmax). Our goal is to distil the soft foreground and occlusion
segmentation masks from the hard binary ground-truth ones (that we keep from
augmenting the object-centric image with random backgrounds and occluders)
in order to have their estimations available during the tracker's inference. To
this end, we add the two corresponding binary cross entropy losses to our overall
loss function. We argue our design choice of using two attention modules, as

after experimentation, we found that assigning a clear target to each of the two modules is more beneficial, rather than relying on a single attention layer to resolve both challenges (see Sect. 4.3), an observation also reported in [18].

Rotation Representation: From a mathematical standpoint, immediate regression of pose parameters [8] with an Euclidean loss is suboptimal: while the translation component belongs to the Euclidean space, the rotation component lies on a non-linear manifold of SO(3). Thus, it is straightforward to model the rotation loss using a Geodesic metric [10,15] on SO(3), i.e. the length, in radians, of the minimal path that connects two of its elements: $\Delta\hat{R}, \Delta R$:

$$L_{Rot}(\Delta\hat{R}, \Delta R_{GT}) = d_{Rot}^{(Geod)}(\Delta\hat{R}, \Delta R_{GT}) = \arccos\left(\frac{\text{Tr}(\Delta\hat{R}^T \cdot \Delta R_{GT}) - 1}{2}\right). \tag{2}$$

In order to minimize the rotation errors due to ambiguities caused by the parameterization choice, we employ the 6D continuous rotation representation that was introduced in [40]: $\Delta\mathbf{r} = (\Delta\mathbf{r_x}^T, \Delta\mathbf{r_y}^T)$, where $\Delta\mathbf{r_{x/y}} \in \mathbb{R}^3$. Given $\Delta\mathbf{r}$, the matrix $\Delta R = (\Delta\mathbf{R_x}, \Delta\mathbf{R_y}, \Delta\mathbf{R_z})^T$ is obtained by:

$$\Delta\mathbf{R_x} = N(\Delta\mathbf{r_x})$$
$$\Delta\mathbf{R_y} = N[\Delta\mathbf{r_y} - (\Delta\mathbf{R_x^T} \cdot \mathbf{r_y}) \cdot \Delta\mathbf{R_x})] \tag{3}$$
$$\Delta\mathbf{R_z} = \Delta\mathbf{R_x} \times \Delta\mathbf{R_y}$$

where $\Delta\mathbf{R_{x/y/z}} \in \mathbb{R}^3$, $N(\cdot) = \frac{(\cdot)}{\|(\cdot)\|}$ is the normalization function. Furthermore, as it has already been discussed in [2], each 3D rotation angle has a different visual imprint regarding each rotation axis. So, we multiply both rotation matrices with an approximately diagonal Inertial Tensor Λ, calculated on the object model's weighted surface and with respect to its center mass, in order to assign a different weight to each rotational component. We note here that since we want that matrix product to still lie in SO(3), we perform a Gramm-Schmidt orthonormalization on the Inertial Tensor Λ before right-multiplying it with each rotation matrix. Finally, we weigh the translation and rotation losses using a pair of learnable weights $\mathbf{v} = [v_1, v_2]^T$ that are trained along with the rest of the network's parameters using Gradient Descent-based optimization, as proposed in [20].

Symmetric Object Handling. In the special case of symmetric objects, we disentangle the ambiguities inserted due to this property from the core of rotation estimation. We classify such ambiguities to two distinctive categories: a continuous set of rotational ambiguities (the unweaving of which we incorporate into our loss function) and a discrete set of reflective ambiguities that appear due to our rotation representation choice and are handled heuristically.

Normally, the presence of the RGB input cue would break any symmetry ambiguities as their origin is its Depth counterpart that depicts the object's 3D shape. However, our preliminary experiments have shown that this is only partially true since the tracker places more emphasis to the Depth cue, in general,

Fig. 3. Comparison of the Rotational Estimation for the 127th frame of the "Hard Interaction Scenario" without/with our proposed reflective symmetry handling algorithm. (a) The ground-truth prediction for frame 127. (b) The rotation estimation of the 126th frame. Rotational error between the prediction and ground truth is small. (c) An erroneous rotational estimation of the tracker for frame 127. The prediction is discarded and replaced by the one of the previous timeframe. The error is kept small and (although larger than in the 126th frame) reflective ambiguity is not propagated to the next timestep via the previous pose feedback rendering.

in its effort to estimate the object's pose. This inclination keeps the ambiguities present during inference and incurs the need to explicitly model this disentanglement in the loss function formulation.

Symmetric Object Handling: Discrete Reflective Symmetry. By replacing the 3D Euler rotational parameter regression of Garon et al. [8], with its 6D continuous counterpart, we face the extra problem of being unable to constrain the network's rotational output. This has a severely negative effect to objects with reflective symmetry, as there are configurations in which the tracker predicts unacceptable values for one or more rotational components. For example, in Fig. 3 we observe that the "Cookie Jar" symmetric object has been turned upside down with respect to both the prediction of the previous timeframe and the ground truth pose. As a result, we end up with adding significant extra errors during the mean rotational error calculation over the total motion length, since that discrepancy is not limited to a single frame, but is accumulated as we proceed to the following frames, due to the temporal nature of the tracker, until it is reset. In order to handle this challenge, we employ the following heuristic algorithm: for each Euler rotational component we calculate the angular distance $d_A^{(o)}(\hat{r}_i(t), \hat{r}_i(t-1))$ (in degrees), between the current and the previous timestep. If a $d_A^{(o)}$ exceeds a certain threshold (here, it is set to $100°$), then the value of this particular Euler angle is set to $\hat{r}_i(t-1)$. Then, we may choose to perform a second (or more) iterative forward CNN pass(es), if the time constraints of our broader application allow so.

Symmetric Object Handling: Continuously Rotational Symmetry. In order to form G, we train a batch (of size B_2) of separate Euler angle triplets $\hat{g} \in \mathbb{R}^3$. At each timestep, one of them is selected and it is converted to a rotation matrix $\hat{G}^*$, which gets right-multiplied with $\Delta\hat{R}$ before being weighted by the parameters of $\Lambda_{(G.S.)}$ (see Eq. 4). Aiming to select the appropriate parameter from the batch, we train a linear classification layer on top of the first fully connected layer of the tracker. Moreover, we encourage the symmetry triplets to be as uniform as possible by incorporating an appropriate penalty to the overall loss function. To test our approach for the symmetric object case, we used the cylindrical "Cookie Jar" model of [8], the shape of which has only one axis of continuous symmetry. Consequently, we estimate a single rotational symmetry parameter, that of the object-centric z-axis (and keep the rest to 0). On the other hand, in the previous case, we define all three of its axes as axes of reflective symmetry. Before the conversion, that parameter is passed through a tanh function and multiplied by π to constrain its values.

Overall Loss. As a result, our overall tracking loss function is formulated as:

$$L_{Track}(\Delta\hat{\mathbb{P}}, \Delta\mathbb{P}) = e^{(-v_1)} \cdot MSE[(\Delta\hat{\mathbf{t}}, \Delta\mathbf{t})] + v_1 + v_2$$
$$+ e^{(-v_2)} \cdot arcos\left(\frac{\mathrm{Tr}\left((\Delta\hat{R} \cdot \hat{G}^* \cdot \Lambda_{(G.S.)})^T \cdot (\Delta R \cdot \Lambda_{(G.S.)})\right) - 1}{2}\right) \quad (4)$$

Using a similar external multi-task learnable weighting scheme ($\mathbf{s} = [s_1, s_2, s_3]^T$) as in Eq. (4), we combine our primary learning task, pose tracking, with the two auxiliary ones: clutter and occlusion handling. Both $\mathbf{s}$ and $\mathbf{v}$ are initialized to $\mathbf{0}$.

$$Loss = e^{(-s_1)} \cdot L_{Track} + e^{(-s_2)} \cdot L_{Unoccl} + e^{(-s_3)} \cdot L_{Foregr} + s_1 + s_2 + s_3 \quad (5)$$

For objects with continuously rotational symmetry the loss becomes:

$$Loss^{(Symm)} = Loss + e^{(-s_4)}\left(\frac{1}{B}\sum_{b=1}^{B}\frac{1}{\xi_b}\right) + s_4, \text{ with} \quad (6)$$

$$\xi_b = \frac{1}{B_2(B_2 - 1)}\sum_{j=1}^{B_2}\sum_{k\neq j}d_{Rot}^{(Geod)}(\hat{G}_k, \hat{G}_j), \quad (7)$$

The extra term added to the multi-task loss is a penalty that guides the classification layer(s) to select the proper rotational symmetry parameter(s) at each timestep. It encourages the geodesic rotational distances between all pairs of parameters in the batch to be maximum and, thus, ultimately converge to as a uniform distribution as possible. Here, we train $B_2 = 64$ such parameters for each continuous rotational component.

3.3 Data Generation and Augmentation

Following [7], for our network (Fig. 2), we generate two synthetic RGB-D pairs I(t),Î(t), but we alter their sampling strategy using the "Golden Spiral" approach [21], and we modify the augmentation procedure of [7,8] as follows: Firstly, we blend the object image with a background image, sampled from a subset of

Table 1. Characteristics of the five objects we test our approach on. The fact that there are no two identical items validates the generalization capabilities of our tracker.

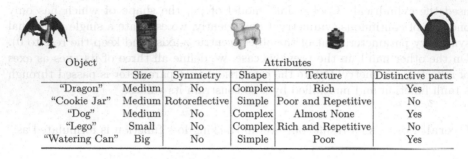

Object	Attributes				
	Size	Symmetry	Shape	Texture	Distinctive parts
"Dragon"	Medium	No	Complex	Rich	Yes
"Cookie Jar"	Medium	Rotoreflective	Simple	Poor and Repetitive	No
"Dog"	Medium	No	Complex	Almost None	Yes
"Lego"	Small	No	Complex	Rich and Repetitive	No
"Watering Can"	Big	No	Simple	Poor	Yes

the SUN3D dataset [37]. We also mimic the procedure of [7,8] in rendering a 3D hand model-occluder on the object frame with probability 60%. A twist we added, is preparing our network for cases of 100% occlusion, by completely covering the object by the occluder for 15% of the occluded subset. Note that both the foreground and unoccluded object binary masks are kept during both of these augmentation procedures. Hence, we can use them as ground truth segmentation signals for clutter extraction and occlusion handling in our auxiliary losses to supervise the corresponding spatial attention maps. We add to the "Observed" frame pair I(t): (i) Gaussian RGB noise, (ii) HSV noise, (iii) blurring (to simulate rapid object movement), (iv) depth downsampling and (v) probabilistic dropout of one of the modalities, all with same parameters as in [8]. With a probability of 50%, we change the image contrast, using parameters $\alpha \sim U(0,3)$, $\beta \sim U(-50,50)$ (where U($\cdot$) is a uniform distribution) and gamma correction $\gamma \sim U(0,2)$ with probability 50%, to help generalize over cases of illumination differences between rendered and sensor generated images. Instead of modelling the noise added to the "Observed" Depth modality with an ad-hoc Gaussian distribution as in [8], we consider the specific properties of Kinect noise [28] and model it with a 3D Gaussian noise (depending on depth and the ground truth object pose), used for simulating the reality gap between synthetic and real images. Its distribution consists of a product of an z-Axial: $n_A \sim \mathcal{N}(0, \sigma_A)$ and two z-Lateral: $n_{L_x} \sim \mathcal{N}(0, \sigma_{L_x})$, $n_{L_y} \sim \mathcal{N}(0, \sigma_{L_y})$ 1D distributions that vary with the object depth z and its angle around the y-axis, θ_y: with standard deviations σ_A, σ_{L_x}, σ_{L_y} respectively. The rest of the preprocessing follows [7].

4   Evaluation and Results

4.1   Implementation Details

We use ELU activation functions, a minibatch size of 128, Dropout with probability 0.3, Adam optimizer with decoupled weight decay [26] by a factor $1e^{-5}$, learning rate $1e^{-3}$ and a scheduler with warm restarts [25] every 10 epochs. All network weights with ELU activation function (except those transferred from

ResNet18 [13]) are initialized via a uniform K.He [12] scheme, while for all those with a symmetric one we use a corresponding Xavier [9] distribution. Since the Geodesic distance suffers from multiple local minima [6], following [27], we first warm-up the weights, aiming first to minimize the LogCosh [1] loss function for 25 epochs. Then, we train until convergence, minimizing the loss (5). The average training time is 12 h in a single GeForce 1080 Ti GPU.

4.2 Dataset and Metrics

We test our approach on all the "Interaction" scenarios and the highest percentage "Occlusion" scenarios of [8], which are considered the most challenging. As in [8], we initialize our tracker every 15 frames, and use the same evaluation metrics.

Due to limited computational resources, we produced only 20,000 samples, whose variability covers the pose space adequately enough to verify the validity of our experiments, both for the ablation study and the final experimentation. In the following tables, similarly to [8], we report the mean and standard deviation of our error metrics, as well, as the overall tracking failures (only in the final experimentation section).

Table 2. Comparison of different attentional foreground/occlusion handling configurations added to the baseline architecture of Garon et al. [8].

	Translational error (mm)	Rotational error (degrees)
Garon et al. [8]	34.38 ± 24.65	36.38 ± 36.31
Only occlusion	17.60 ± 10.74	37.10 ± 35.08
Hierarchical clutter & occlusion	$14.99 \pm \mathbf{9.89}$	39.07 ± 33.22
Parallel clutter & occlusion	$\mathbf{14.35} \pm 10.21$	$\mathbf{34.28 \pm 29.81}$

Table 3. The evolution of the proposed rotation loss, on the baseline architecture of Garon et al. [8] (without our proposed attention modules).

	Rotational error (degrees)
Garon et al. [8]	36.38 ± 36.31
Rotational MSE	46.55 ± 40.88
Geod.	37.69 ± 35.39
Geod. + [40]	14.90 ± 21.76
Geod. + [40] + $\Lambda_{(G.S.)}$	$\mathbf{9.99 \pm 13.76}$

Table 4. Comparison of different multi-task weighting schemes.

	Translational error (mm)	Rotational error (degrees)
Garon et al. [8]	48.58 ± 38.23	36.38 ± 36.31
Steady weights	11.83 ± 8.94	10.98 ± 16.74
Recursive batch standarization [34]	13.97 ± 10.23	14.76 ± 19.24
Learnable weights [20]	**11.63 ± 8.79**	**8.31 ± 6.76**

4.3 Ablation Study

In this section, we discuss our main design choices and we demonstrate quantitative results that led to their selection.

Hierarchy Choices for the Attention Modules. Here, we justify the need for both attention modules of our architecture (Fig. 2). We build upon the network proposed by [8] and we firstly introduce a single convolutional attention map just for occlusion handling . Then, we explore the possibility for a seperate attentional weighting of the "Observed" feature map for foreground extraction, prior to the occlusion one, and we, finally, leverage both in parallel and add their resulting maps altogether.

The comparison of Table 2 establishes not only the need for both attentional modules in our design, but also that the parallel layout is the optimal one. We can observe the effect of parallel connection in Fig. 1 as both attentions present sharp peaks. We can, also, observe a visual tradeoff between the parallel attentions: while the object is not occluded (either in steady state or when moving), the module responsible for foreground extraction is highlighted more intensely than the occlusion one. As the object gets more and more covered by the user's hand, the focus gradually shifts to the module responsible for occlusion handling. Note that this is not an ability we explicitly train our network to obtain, but rather a side effect of our approach, which fits our intuitive understanding of cognitive visual tracking. Moreover, although our supervising signals are uniform, both attentional modules learn to highlight specific keypoints of interest during the tracker's inference.

We, also, observe another interesting property: the tracker learns to handle self-occlusion patterns as well. For example, for the "Dragon" object of Fig. 1, it learns to ignore the one wing when it is in front and focuses on the other one, at the back, if its appearance is more distinctive of the pose. The same can be said for the legs of the "Dog" model of Fig. 6. This is a clue that this module has, indeed, learned the concept of occlusions and has not overfitted to the shape of the user's hand, the occluder model that was used for training.

Contributions of the Rotation Loss Components. We demonstrate the value of every component included in our rotation loss (leaving symmetries temporarily out of study), by: (i) regressing only the rotational parameters with the

Table 5. Comparison of different selection methods for the continuously rotational symmetry parameter.

	Translational error (mm)	Rotational error (*degrees*)	$d_A^{(o)}(\hat{r}_z, r_z^{GT})$
Garon et al. [8]	10.75 ± 6.89	23.53 ± 18.85	10.60 ± 38.90
Ours	10.87 ± 8.14	20.55 ± 18.06	4.60 ± 35.42
Ours+Unique, frozen learnable symmetry parameter	11.38 ± 8.94	10.98 ± 16.74	2.98 ± 25.07
Ours+Regression of learnable symmetry parameter	13.03 ± 6.88	17.25 ± 12.40	2.84 ± 24.95
Ours+Mean of a batch of frozen, learnable symmetry parameters	11.98 ± 9.23	13.84 ± 11.87	2.16 ± 29.25
Ours+Optimal selection out of a batch of frozen, learnable symmetry parameters	$\mathbf{10.43 \pm 6.63}$	$\mathbf{9.57 \pm 10.01}$	$\mathbf{2.07 \pm 24.52}$

baseline architecture of [8], (ii), replacing the MSE loss with the Geodesic one, (iii), replacing the rotation parameterization of [8] with the continuous one of (3), and, (iv) including the Inertial Tensor weighting of each rotational component.

Table 3 indicates the value that translation estimation brings to rotation estimation, as when the former's regression is excluded, the latter's performance decreases. Moreover, Table 3 justifies our progressive design selections in formulating our rotation loss, as with the addition of each ambiguity modelling, the 3D rotation error decreases, starting from $46.55° \pm 40.88°$ and reaching $9.99° \pm 13.76°$.

Weighting the Multi-task Loss. Here, we explore various weighting schemes of the multiple loss functions of our approach, both the main and the auxiliary ones. Our first approach is the crude addition of the tracking and the two Binary Cross Entropy losses . A second one is standarizing the three losses by subtracting their batchwise means and dividing by their batchwise standard deviations, that we calculate using the Welford algorithm [34]. Lastly, we consider the learnable weighting strategy that we, ultimately, utilize. In quantitative comparison of Table 4 the scheme of [20] emerges as the clear favourite.

Comparison of Continuously Rotational Symmetry Regression Methods ("Cookie Jar" Model). In our effort to disentangle the rotation estimation and the continuously rotational symmetries, we try different configurations for optimally choosing the appropriate parameter(s): (i) learning a unique symmetry parameter over all possible pose changes in the training set and keeping

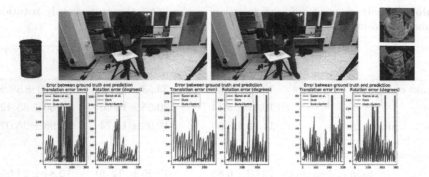

Fig. 4. Comparison of the SoA [8] *(light blue)* and our *(pink)* approaches for the "Cookie Jar" in 3 scenarios: "Translation Only", "Rotation Only" and "Full Interaction". (Color figure online)

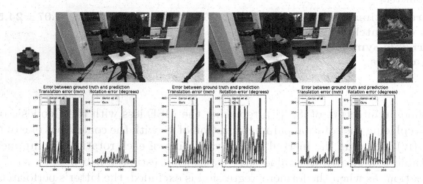

Fig. 5. Comparison of the SoA [8] *(light blue)* and our *(pink)* approaches for the "Lego" in 3 scenarios: "Translation Only",'Full' and "Hard Interaction". (Color figure online)

it frozen during inference, (ii) regressing a different one per pose pair, (iii) learning a batch of them and taking their average during inference and, ultimately, (iv) selecting the optimal from the aforementioned batch using an appropriate classification layer while encouraging the values of this batch to be as uniform as possible, at the same time. This freedom of ours resides from the fact that the minimization of the tracking loss w.r.t. the symmetry matrix $\hat{G}^*$ (see [2]) does not explicitly impose a global-solution constraint. This time, the comparison is done w.r.t. the full approach of Sect. 3 that does not account for symmetries and, apart from the classic 3D translational and rotational errors, we, also, report the Euler angle error for the z-component. As we can see in Table 5, our proposed approach is the "golden medium" between accuracy and robustness since both its mean and standard deviation are the lowest across all metrics.

4.4   Experimental Results

According to our ablation study, we proceed to merge our parallel attention modules with the Geodesic rotation loss of Eq. (4), along with the remaining elements of Sect. 3. We evaluate our method on five objects of dataset [8]: the "Dragon", the "Cookie Jar", the "Dog", the "Lego" block and the "Watering Can", aiming for maximum variability (see Table 1). In Fig. 1, 2, 3, 4, 5, 6 and 7, we plot the 3D translational and rotational errors in three randomly selected scenarios for each object both for the SoA and our tracker.

Evidently, the object most benefited by our methodological improvements is the "Dragon". Since its geometry is the most complex, its texture is rich and it has several distinctive parts that stand out of the user's grip, both our geometric modelling and the parallel attention modules find their best application in this case. When the user's hand occludes parts of the "Dragon", the attention shifts to its body parts of interest that stand out of the grip, like its neck, wings or tail (Fig. 1). For the symmetric "Cookie Jar", the differences between our method and the baseline are lower. The attentions' effect is less prominent here since this model is of simpler, symmetric shape and poorer texture. This replaces the distinctive clues of the dragon case with ambiguities, denying the corresponding modules of the ability to easily identify the pose. Alongside the "Lego" model, they make the most out of the reflective symmetry handling algorithm as they avoid large abrupt errors that propagate to future frames. Although our CNN primarily focuses on the object's shape, appearance seems to play a significant role in its predictions, as well, since the errors of the "Dog" and the "Watering Can" models, the less textured ones, decrease more mildly. The foreground attention map aids disentangling the "Dog" model from its background, a table of the same color, in the "75% Occlusion" scenarios. On the other hand, for the "Watering Can", the most ambiguities are presented when viewpoint-induced symmetries appear, with the effects of our modelling declining in this case.

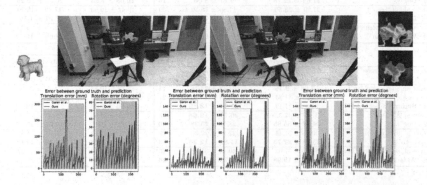

Fig. 6. Comparison of the SoA [8] *(light blue)* and our *(pink)* approaches for the "Dog" in 3 scenarios: "75% Vertical Occlusion", "Rotation Only" and "Hard Interaction". (Color figure online)

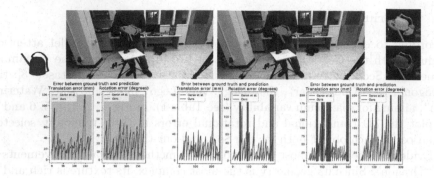

Fig. 7. Comparison of the SoA [8] *(light blue)* and our *(pink)* approaches for the "Watering Can" in 3 scenarios: "75% Horizontal Occlusion", "Rotation Only" and "Full Interaction". (Color figure online)

Table 6. 3D Translational and Rotational errors and overall tracking failures in six different scenarios for five employed objects.

Approach	75% Horizontal Occlusion			75% Vertical Occlusion		
	Translational Error(mm)	Rotational Error(degrees)	Fails	Translational Error(mm)	Rotational(degrees)	Fails
Garon et al.[8] ('Dragon')	16.02 ± 8.42	18.35 ± 11.71	13	18.20 ± 11.81	14.66 ± 12.98	13
Ours("Dragon")	**12.68 ± 11.49**	**13.00 ± 9.14**	10	**12.87 ± 10.49**	**13.14 ± 8.85**	8
Garon et al.[8]("Cookie Jar")	21.27 ± 9.74	21.90 ± 13.97	17	20.77 ± 6.88	24.86 ± 13.64	20
Ours("Cookie Jar")	9.51 ± 4.17	15.48 ± 9.50	15	20.97 ± 7.32	16.14 ± 10.06	15
Ours+Symm.("Cookie Jar")	**6.37 ± 2.14**	**7.22 ± 3.97**	11	**19.01 ± 7.53**	**13.00 ± 7.49**	14
Garon et al.[8]("Dog")	37.96 ± 23.39	47.94 ± 31.55	21	32.84 ± 34.07	22.44 ± 13.60	21
Ours("Dog")	**24.43 ± 18.92**	**17.24 ± 12.41**	25	36.53 ± 22.39	**12.67 ± 7.95**	20
Garon et al.[8]("Lego")	**68.25 ± 46.97**	40.04 ± 47.37	28	40.04 ± 47.37	35.30 ± 31.32	20
Ours("Lego")	72.04 ± 34.10	**18.41 ± 13.84**	28	**12.92 ± 5.73**	**12.92 ± 9.02**	20
Garon et al.[8]("Watering Can")	21.59 ± 11.32	23.99 ± 16.95	14	32.76 ± 24.12	26.74 ± 19.05	18
Ours("Watering Can")	**20.71 ± 10.24**	**17.00 ± 18.99**	13	**17.66 ± 17.95**	**13.46 ± 10.43**	12

Approach	Translation Interaction			Rotation Interaction		
	Translational Error(mm)	Rotational Error(degrees)	Fails	Translational Error(mm)	Rotational(degrees)	Fails
Garon et al.[8] ("Dragon")	41.60 ± 39.92	11.55 ± 15.58	15	23.86 ± 17.44	27.21 ± 22.40	15
Ours("Dragon")	**11.05 ± 8.20**	**3.55 ± 2.27**	1	**9.37 ± 6.07**	**7.86 ± 6.69**	2
Garon et al.[8]("Cookie Jar")	20.43 ± 25.44	17.19 ± 12.99	16	10.75 ± 5.89	23.53 ± 18.85	19
Ours("Cookie Jar")	8.64 ± 8.23	8.31 ± 5.97	5	10.87 ± 8.14	20.55 ± 18.06	16
Ours+Symm.("Cookie Jar")	**8.09 ± 7.67**	**5.83 ± 5.50**	3	**9.98 ± 10.63**	**13.84 ± 11.87**	16
Garon et al.[8]("Dog")	58.87 ± 71.86	16.42 ± 13.51	20	11.16 ± 10.28	**20.00 ± 21.31**	17
Ours("Dog")	**21.64 ± 22.78**	**9.27 ± 8.03**	14	**10.68 ± 7.53**	20.07 ± 19.29	17
Garon et al.[8]("Lego")	27.90 ± 23.53	11.89 ± 18.50	29	16.42 ± 10.90	17.83 ± 15.90	32
Ours("Lego")	**22.66 ± 24.58**	**9.08 ± 7.60**	12	**10.13 ± 6.79**	**7.22 ± 4.55**	4
Garon et al.[8]("Watering Can")	24.95 ± 42.91	13.26 ± 11.34	16	13.14 ± 8.99	22.19 ± 25.93	15
Ours("Watering Can")	**24.30 ± 21.51**	**8.79 ± 6.35**	16	**12.22 ± 9.46**	**18.66 ± 15.51**	15

Apporach	Full Interaction			Hard Interaction		
	Translational Error(mm)	Rotational Error(degrees)	Fails	Translational Error(mm)	Rotational(degrees)	Fails
Garon et al.[8] ("Dragon")	35.23 ± 31.97	34.98 ± 29.46	18	34.38 ± 24.65	36.38 ± 36.31	17
Ours("Dragon")	**10.31 ± 8.66**	**6.40 ± 4.52**	1	**11.63 ± 8.79**	**8.31 ± 6.76**	2
Garon et al.[8]("Cookie Jar")	**13.06 ± 9.35**	31.78 ± 23.78	24	15.78 ± 10.43	24.29 ± 20.84	15
Ours("Cookie Jar")	17.03 ± 11.94	22.24 ± 20.86	21	15.29 ± 16.06	16.73 ± 14.79	11
Ours+Symm.("Cookie Jar")	14.63 ± 11.19	**15.71 ± 13.80**	21	**14.96 ± 9.06**	**15.00 ± 13.20**	8
Garon et al.[8]("Dog")	37.73 ± 42.32	**20.77 ± 19.66**	23	23.95 ± 38.86	24.38 ± 26.39	20
Ours("Dog")	**24.88 ± 35.85**	28.52 ± 25.38	20	**19.32 ± 15.97**	**19.72 ± 20.17**	19
Garon et al.[8]("Lego")	30.96 ± 31.44	22.10 ± 20.20	20	30.71 ± 42.62	36.38 ± 34.99	20
Ours("Lego")	**23.58 ± 27.73**	**11.80 ± 12.28**	13	**16.47 ± 12.95**	**14.29 ± 11.68**	11
Garon et al.[8]("Watering Can")	33.76 ± 37.62	40.16 ± 35.90	26	28.31 ± 19.49	23.04 ± 24.27	28
Ours("Watering Can")	**19.82 ± 19.98**	**28.76 ± 30.27**	26	**18.03 ± 14.99**	**19.57 ± 17.47**	23

The accuracy of our approach exceeds that of the SoA [8], across all objects and in almost all scenarios, especially for 3D rotations. According to Table 6, both errors are generally lower (in terms of both mean and standard deviation) and our tracker fails equally or less often. It presents aggravated errors in fast object motions more rarely than [8] and handles both static and dynamic high-percentage occlusion patterns better. Also, it not only keeps track of the object's 3D position under severe occlusions, but extends this property to 3D rotations, as well. Although more computationally intense than [8], it runs in 40 fps.

5   Conclusion

In this work, we propose a CNN for fast and accurate single object pose tracking. We perform explicitly modular design of clutter and occlusion handling and we account for the geometrical properties of both the pose space and the object model during training. As a result, we reduce both SoA pose errors by an average of 34.03% for translation and 40.01% for rotation for a variety of objects with different properties. Our tracker exceeds the SoA performance in challenging scenarios with high percentage occlusion patterns and rapid movement and we gain an intuitive understanding of our artificial tracking mechanism.

Acknowledgements. This research has been co-financed by the European Union and Greek national funds through the Operational Program Competitiveness, Entrepreneurship and Innovation, under the call RESEARCH CREATE INNOVATE (project code: T1EDK-01248, acronym: i-Walk).

References

1. Belagiannis, V., Rupprecht, C., Carneiro, G., Navab, N.: Robust optimization for deep regression. In: Proceedings of the IEEE International Conference on Computer Vision, pp. 2830–2838 (2015)
2. Brégier, R., Devernay, F., Leyrit, L., Crowley, J.L.: Defining the pose of any 3D rigid object and an associated distance. Int. J. Comput. Vision (IJCV) **126**(6), 571–596 (2018)
3. Deng, J., Dong, W., Socher, R., Li, L.J., Li, K., Fei-Fei, L.: Imagenet: a large-scale hierarchical image database. In: Proceedings of IEEE Conference on Computer Vision and Pattern Recognition (CVPR), pp. 248–255. IEEE (2009)
4. Deng, X., Mousavian, A., Xiang, Y., Xia, F., Bretl, T., Fox, D.: Poserbpf: a rao-blackwellized particle filter for 6d object pose tracking. arXiv preprint arXiv:1905.09304 (2019)
5. Doucet, A., De Freitas, N., Murphy, K., Russell, S.: Rao-blackwellised particle filtering for dynamic Bayesian networks. arXiv preprint arXiv:1301.3853 (2013)
6. Fletcher, T.: Terse notes on riemannian geometry (2010)
7. Garon, M., Lalonde, J.F.: Deep 6-DOF tracking. IEEE Trans. Visual Comput. Graphics **23**(11), 2410–2418 (2017)
8. Garon, M., Laurendeau, D., Lalonde, J.F.: A framework for evaluating 6-DOF object trackers. In: Proceedings of European Conference on Computer Vision (ECCV), pp. 582–597 (2018)
9. Glorot, X., Bengio, Y.: Understanding the difficulty of training deep feedforward neural networks. In: Proceedings of the Thirteenth International Conference on Artificial Intelligence and Statistics, pp. 249–256 (2010)

10. Hartley, R., Trumpf, J., Dai, Y., Li, H.: Rotation averaging. Int. J. of Comp. Vision (IJCV) **103**(3), 267–305 (2013)
11. He, K., Gkioxari, G., Dollár, P., Girshick, R.: Mask R-CNN. In: Proceedings of IEEE International Conference on Computer Vision (ICCV), pp. 2961–2969 (2017)
12. He, K., Zhang, X., Ren, S., Sun, J.: Delving deep into rectifiers: surpassing human-level performance on imagenet classification. In: Proceedings of IEEE International Conference on Computer Vision (ICCV), pp. 1026–1034 (2015)
13. He, K., Zhang, X., Ren, S., Sun, J.: Deep residual learning for image recognition. In: Proceedings of IEEE Conference on Computer Vision and Pattern Recognition (CVPR), pp. 770–778 (2016)
14. Hinterstoisser, S., Lepetit, V., Wohlhart, P., Konolige, K.: On pre-trained image features and synthetic images for deep learning. In: Proceedings of European Conference on Computer Vision (ECCV) (2018)
15. Huynh, D.Q.: Metrics for 3D rotations: comparison and analysis. J. Math. Imaging Vision **35**(2), 155–164 (2009)
16. Iandola, F.N., Han, S., Moskewicz, M.W., Ashraf, K., Dally, W.J., Keutzer, K.: Squeezenet: alexnet-level accuracy with 50x fewer parameters and <0.5mb model size. arXiv:1602.07360 (2016)
17. Ilg, E., Mayer, N., Saikia, T., Keuper, M., Dosovitskiy, A., Brox, T.: Flownet 2.0: evolution of optical flow estimation with deep networks. In: Proceedings of IEEE Conference on Computer Vision and Pattern Recognition (CVPR), pp. 2462–2470 (2017)
18. Jafari, O.H., Mustikovela, S.K., Pertsch, K., Brachmann, E., Rother, C.: iPose: instance-aware 6D pose estimation of partly occluded objects. In: Jawahar, C.V., Li, H., Mori, G., Schindler, K. (eds.) ACCV 2018. LNCS, vol. 11363, pp. 477–492. Springer, Cham (2019). https://doi.org/10.1007/978-3-030-20893-6_30
19. Kehl, W., Manhardt, F., Tombari, F., Ilic, S., Navab, N.: SSD-6D: making RGB-based 3D detection and 6D pose estimation great again. In: Proceedings of IEEE International Conference on Computer Vision (ICCV), pp. 1521–1529 (2017)
20. Kendall, A., Gal, Y., Cipolla, R.: Multi-task learning using uncertainty to weigh losses for scene geometry and semantics. In: Proceedings of IEEE Conference on Computer Vision and Pattern Recognition (CVPR), pp. 7482–7491 (2018)
21. Leopardi, P.C.: Distributing points on the sphere: partitions, separation, quadrature and energy. Ph.D. thesis, University of New South Wales, Sydney, Australia (2007)
22. Lepetit, V., Moreno-Noguer, F., Fua, P.: EPnP: an accurate O(n) solution to the PnP problem. Int. J. Comput. Vision (IJCV) **81**, 155 (2009). https://doi.org/10.1007/s11263-008-0152-6
23. Li, Y., Wang, G., Ji, X., Xiang, Y., Fox, D.: Deepim: deep iterative matching for 6D pose estimation. In: Proceedings of European Conference on Computer Vision (ECCV), pp. 683–698 (2018)
24. Liu, W., et al.: SSD: single shot MultiBox detector. In: Leibe, B., Matas, J., Sebe, N., Welling, M. (eds.) ECCV 2016. LNCS, vol. 9905, pp. 21–37. Springer, Cham (2016). https://doi.org/10.1007/978-3-319-46448-0_2
25. Loshchilov, I., Hutter, F.: SGDR: stochastic gradient descent with warm restarts. arXiv preprint arXiv:1608.03983 (2016)
26. Loshchilov, I., Hutter, F.: Fixing weight decay regularization in adam. arXiv preprint arXiv:1711.05101 (2017)
27. Mahendran, S., Ali, H., Vidal, R.: 3D pose regression using convolutional neural networks. In: Proceedings of the IEEE International Conference on Computer Vision Workshops, pp. 2174–2182 (2017)

28. Nguyen, C.V., Izadi, S., Lovell, D.: Modeling kinect sensor noise for improved 3D reconstruction and tracking. In: 2012 Second International Conference on 3D Imaging, Modeling, Processing, Visualization & Transmission, pp. 524–530. IEEE (2012)

29. Park, K., Patten, T., Vincze, M.: Pix2pose: pixel-wise coordinate regression of objects for 6D pose estimation. In: Proceedings of the IEEE International Conference on Computer Vision, pp. 7668–7677 (2019)

30. Pavlakos, G., Zhou, X., Chan, A., Derpanis, K.G., Daniilidis, K.: 6-DOF object pose from semantic keypoints. In: 2017 IEEE International Conference on Robotics and Automation (ICRA), pp. 2011–2018. IEEE (2017)

31. Peng, S., Liu, Y., Huang, Q., Zhou, X., Bao, H.: PVNet: pixel-wise voting network for 6DOF pose estimation. In: Proceedings of the IEEE Conference on Computer Vision and Pattern Recognition, pp. 4561–4570 (2019)

32. Segal, A., Haehnel, D., Thrun, S.: Generalized-ICP. In: Robotics: Science and Systems, Seattle, WA, vol. 2, p. 435 (2009)

33. Sundermeyer, M., Marton, Z.C., Durner, M., Brucker, M., Triebel, R.: Implicit 3D orientation learning for 6D object detection from RGB images. In: Proceedings of the European Conference on Computer Vision (ECCV), pp. 699–715 (2018)

34. Welford, B.: Note on a method for calculating corrected sums of squares and products. Technometrics 4(3), 419–420 (1962)

35. Wohlhart, P., Lepetit, V.: Learning descriptors for object recognition and 3D pose estimation. In: Proceedings of the IEEE Conference on Computer Vision and Pattern Recognition, pp. 3109–3118 (2015)

36. Xiang, Y., Schmidt, T., Narayanan, V., Fox, D.: PoseCNN: a convolutional neural network for 6D object pose estimation in cluttered scenes. arXiv preprint arXiv:1711.00199 (2017)

37. Xiao, J., Owens, A., Torralba, A.: SUN3D: a database of big spaces reconstructed using SFM and object labels. In: Proceedings of IEEE International Conference on Computer Vision (ICCV), pp. 1625–1632 (2013)

38. Zakharov, S., Shugurov, I., Ilic, S.: DPOD: dense 6D pose object detector in RGB images. arXiv preprint arXiv:1902.11020 (2019)

39. Zhou, H., Ummenhofer, B., Brox, T.: DeepTAM: deep tracking and mapping. In: Proceedings of European Conference on Computer Vision (ECCV), pp. 822–838 (2018)

40. Zhou, Y., Barnes, C., Lu, J., Yang, J., Li, H.: On the continuity of rotation representations in neural networks. In: Proceedings of IEEE Conference on Computer Vision and Pattern Recognition (CVPR), pp. 5745–5753 (2019)

A Hybrid Approach for 6DoF Pose Estimation

Rebecca König[✉][iD] and Bertram Drost[iD]

MVTec Software GmbH, Munich, Germany
{koenig,drost}@mvtec.com

Abstract. We propose a method for 6DoF pose estimation of rigid objects that uses a state-of-the-art deep learning based instance detector to segment object instances in an RGB image, followed by a point-pair based voting method to recover the object's pose. We additionally use an automatic method selection that chooses the instance detector and the training set as that with the highest performance on the validation set. This hybrid approach leverages the best of learning and classic approaches, using CNNs to filter highly unstructured data and cut through the clutter, and a local geometric approach with proven convergence for robust pose estimation. The method is evaluated on the BOP core datasets where it significantly exceeds the baseline method and is the best fast method in the BOP 2020 Challenge.

1 Introduction

Many of the recently published approaches for 6DoF object detection, especially on the BOP benchmark [9], follow a two-stage pipeline. The first stage is a state of the art deep learning object detector that outputs the potential locations of object instances, often as bounding boxes or instance masks. The second stage iterates over those instances and, for each, estimates the instance's pose.

The main technical differences in the approaches are in the second, pose estimation stage. The deep-learning based approaches can roughly be categorized by the type of data representation they use (mostly image-based convolutions [12,17–19] vs. Graph-based networks [5]), and the kind of pose estimation they employ (direct regression of pose parameters [5], regression of 3D model coordinates of the scene points usually followed by PnP [8,12,17,21], or employing a codebook for estimating the rotation of an object [18,19]).

A key observation from the BOP 2019 challenge was that while point-pair voting based methods [2,20], which are not learning based, overall had the highest recognition rates, they were also among the slowest methods. One reason is the large search space, as the voting is performed on the complete scene without pre-segmentation or pre-detection of instances. Well-trained deep-learning based instance segmentation methods, on the other hand, estimate the locations of the objects in a scene rather fast.

We therefore combine the two approaches and perform the point-pair voting of [2] only on locations returned by an instance segmentation network. This

© Springer Nature Switzerland AG 2020
A. Bartoli and A. Fusiello (Eds.): ECCV 2020 Workshops, LNCS 12536, pp. 700–706, 2020.
https://doi.org/10.1007/978-3-030-66096-3_46

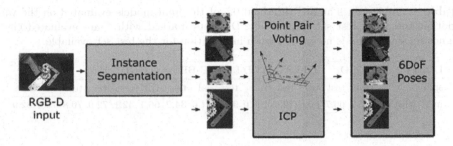

Fig. 1. Overview of the method, which follows a classical two-stage approach. First, a state-of-the-art network is used to find object instances (masks and object IDs) in the RGB image. Second, the point-pair voting is used to recover an object pose for each instance, using the depth image.

combines the advantages of both methods: the deep network's ability to quickly filter through complex real-world data and to narrow down the search space, and the provable robustness of the point-pair voting for recovering the pose (Fig. 1).

2   Method

We use a detection pipeline that uses a Deep-Learning based instance segmentation method as first stage, which returns regions and class IDs, followed by a point-pair voting in the regions of the detected instances as second stage. To account for the large domain differences in the BOP datasets, we automatically select the best instance segmentation method and training dataset based on the performance on the validation set.

Instance Segmentation. The datasets in the BOP benchmark cover a variety of different object types and object placements. The objects have different geometric features and textures, while the placements range from isolated single objects to cluttered, unordered heaps of objects of the same instance. We found that a single object detector does not always cover all those cases properly. Instead, we train for each dataset a Mask-RCNN [6] and a RetinaMask [4] network and automatically select the detector with the highest mean average precision (mAP) with an Intersection over Union (IoU) threshold at 0.5 [3] on the validation set. We use Mask-RCNN for the datasets YCB-V, T-LESS and ITODD, and RetinaMask for LM-O, HB, TUD-L and IC-BIN. We assume that Mask-RCNN performs better on these datasets since they have many classes of which some are very similar to each other. The two-stage approach of Mask-RCNN is probably better suited for these kind of datasets whereas RetinaMask directly classifies the anchor-boxes.

Training Set. For successfully training a deep learning model, the choice of the training data is crucial. In the best case, the training and test data come from the same distribution. Then, it should be relatively easy for the model to

Table 1. mAP values at IoU threshold 0.5 of the final models evaluated on the validation and BOP test set respectively. Datasets marked with * are evaluated class agnostic, since there is no ground truth information for the test set available.

Dataset	LM-O		T-LESS		TUD-L		IC-BIN		ITODD*		HB*		YCB-V	
split	val	test	val	test	val	test	val	test	val	test	val	test	val	test
mAP@IoU0.5	87.7	66.7	69.0	72.6	100.0	94.6	84.6	34.2	66.1	42.1	72.9	70.8	73.4	82.9

generalize from the training to the test images. Unfortunately, not all datasets in the BOP challenge have real labeled training images available. To train the instance segmentation methods we use real training images whenever provided for a dataset, i.e. TUD-L and YCB-V. For all other datasets we generate synthetic training images. Since we a priori do not know the distribution of test images, we apply the same augmentation strategy for all datasets. The augmentation is done by cropping the objects from either validation images (e.g. HB) or synthetic training images (e.g. IC-BIN) and pasting them randomly on images from the COCO dataset [14]. Thereby we vary the objects' rotation, translation and scale. At most 20 objects are pasted into one image. For each dataset we generate 10000 such images. We use 10% of them as validation images and 90% as training images. Some example images are shown in Fig. 2. Comparing these synthetic images to the real test data, it is obvious that the domain gap is large. Therefore, it is important to avoid overfitting on the training data as much as possible. During training we additionally apply online augmentation to 70% of the samples by either flipping them horizontally or applying color variations. This further increases the variance in the training data and increases the generalization capability of the instance segmentation method.

For each dataset, we also evaluated if including the provided PBR images [1] further close the domain gap. We choose the final training set based on the mAP on the validation set. Based on this metric, the PBR images are additionally used in training for the datasets LM-O, YCB-V, ITODD and T-LESS. We report the mAP values of the final models on both the validation and the BOP test set in Table 1. For most datasets the gap between validation and test set is significant. It can additionally be seen that the augmentation method is not suited equally for each dataset.

Fig. 2. Examples of our synthetic training images.

Training Details. For both Mask-RCNN and RetinaMask we use a ResNet-50 [7] as backbone with input dimensions $512 \times 384 \times 3$ ($512 \times 384 \times 1$ for ITODD). We also include a Feature Pyramid Network (FPN) [13] in the model. The models were pre-trained on the COCO dataset [14]. As anchor parameters we always use the default setting of three aspect ratios (0.5, 1.0 and 2.0) and three subscales. The minimum and maximum levels of the FPN are automatically determined by the object sizes in the training set. We train the models with Stochastic Gradient Descent (SGD) using an initial learning rate of 0.0001 and a momentum of 0.9 for 20 epochs. For regularization we add a L2-loss on the weights with factor 10^{-5}. We apply early stopping, i.e. we evaluate at every epoch and choose the model with the best mAP. Results on some example images are shown in Fig. 3.

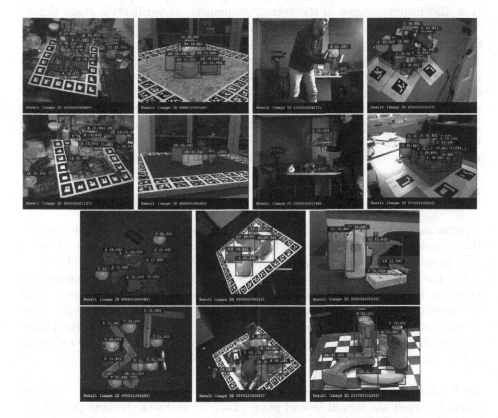

Fig. 3. Qualtitative results of instance segmentation on some example images for all datasets.

Pose Estimation. Given a set of instance masks and their corresponding object ID, we apply the point-pair voting of [2] to recover the pose of the object instances, using the implementation in HALCON 20.05 progress [15]. Note that this method uses depth only and performs the alignment using only the 3D

Table 2. Comparison of the proposed approach with its baseline method, which performs point pair voting only, on the BOP core datasets

Dataset	LM-O	T-LESS	TUD-L	IC-BIN	ITODD	HB	YCB-V	avg	time
Voting only [2]	0.527	0.444	0.775	0.388	0.316	0.615	0.344	0.487	7.704 s
Ours	0.631	0.655	0.920	0.430	0.483	0.651	0.701	0.639	0.633 s

points and their normal vectors. We experimented with variants of the method that also include edges in the depth or RGB images, but found those to be significantly slower while only marginally improving the results. This is in contrast to the results of the BOP 2019 challenge, where point-pair based methods that also included edges in the voting, refinement, or verification stage significantly exceeded the baseline method. We believe that this is due to the good segmentation from the instance segmentation network.

For datasets where textured objects are available and where the texture is relevant to find the correct pose from a set of symmetric poses (YCB-V), we use a feature-point based approach [11,15,16] to select the symmetry pose that best matches the instance segmented in the RGB image. After recovering an object pose, the object is rendered at the found location in all symmetric positions and the feature points are extracted. The symmetry with the most matching feature points between rendered object and scene is used as final pose.

3   Results

Comparison to Baseline. Compared to the baseline approach [2], which searches the complete scene, the proposed approach is over 12 times faster and has a 15% higher average recognition rate on the BOP core datasets (see Table 2). While the speedup is due to the reduced search space, the increased recognition rate can be explained by using the RGB images as additional modalities. Since the baseline method uses geometry only, it often finds false positives if clutter is similarly shaped as an object. This is common for objects with large planar sides (such as boxes), which are then found in background planes. The reduction of the search space based on the RGB images effectively avoids this.

BOP Challenge 2020. The method was submitted to the BOP 2020 challenge where it scored the overall second place (Table 3) and was the best performing method with an average runtime of less than 1 second per image. Notably, the introduced method has 7% higher average recognition rate than the winner of the BOP 2019 challenge, while being around 5 times faster.

4   Conclusion

We introduced a method that recovers the rigid 3D pose of an object in an RGB-D scene, using a two-stage detector. The first stage is a state of the art, off the

Table 3. Leaderboard of the BOP 2020 Challenge. The methods are sorted by the average recognition rate over all seven core datasets. The proposed method has the overall rank 2 and is the best method with a runtime faster than 1 s. The baseline method without instance segmentation pre-processing has rank 12. Time is the average runtime per image.

Rank	Method	Test Modality	AR_{Core}	Time (s)
1	CosyPose SYNT+REAL-ICP [10]	RGB-D	0.698	13.74
2	Koenig-Hybrid-DL-PointPairs (ours)	RGB-D	0.639	0.63
3	CosyPose SYNT+REAL	RGB	0.637	0.44
4	Pix2Pose-BOP20_w/ICP-ICCV19 [17]	RGB-D	0.591	4.84
5	CosyPose PBR	RGB	0.570	0.47
6	Vidal-Sensors18 [20]	D	0.569	3.22
7	CDPNv2 (RGB-only & ICP) [12]	RGB-D	0.568	1.46
8	Drost-CVPR10-Edges	RGB-D	0.550	87.56
9	CDPNv2 (PBR-only & ICP)	RGB-D	0.534	1.49
10	CDPNv2 (RGB-only)	RGB	0.529	0.93
11	Drost-CVPR10-3D-Edges	D	0.500	80.05
12	Drost-CVPR10-3D-Only [2] (baseline)	D	0.487	7.70
13	CDPN_BOP19 (RGB-only)	RGB	0.479	0.48
14	CDPNv2 (PBR-only & RGB-only)	RGB	0.472	0.97

shelf instance segmentation network that detects, segments and identifies object instances in the RGB image. The second stage is a vanilla point pair voting scheme that recovers the locally optimal rigid pose. Additionally, we automatically select the best instance segmentation network and training set using the validation error.

The proposed method is fast and robust, and significantly outperforms the baseline method in both runtime and detection performance and is the second best method in the BOP 2020 challenge, and the best with a runtime of less than one second.

References

1. Denninger, M., et al.: Blenderproc. arXiv preprint arXiv:1911.01911 (2019)
2. Drost, B., Ulrich, M., Navab, N., Ilic, S.: Model globally, match locally: efficient and robust 3D object recognition. In: CVPR (2010)
3. Everingham, M., Van Gool, L., Williams, C.K., Winn, J., Zisserman, A.: The pascal visual object classes (VOC) challenge. IJCV **88**(2), 303–338 (2010)
4. Fu, C.Y., Shvets, M., Berg, A.C.: Retinamask: learning to predict masks improves state-of-the-art single-shot detection for free. arXiv:1901.03353 (2019)
5. Gao, G., Lauri, M., Zhang, J., Frintrop, S.: Occlusion resistant object rotation regression from point cloud segments. In: ECCV (2018)
6. He, K., Gkioxari, G., Dollár, P., Girshick, R.: Mask R-CNN. In: ICCV (2017)
7. He, K., Zhang, X., Ren, S., Sun, J.: Deep residual learning for image recognition. In: CVPR (2016)

8. Hodan, T., Barath, D., Matas, J.: EPOS: estimating 6D pose of objects with symmetries. In: CVPR (2020)
9. Hodan, T., et al.: BOP: benchmark for 6D object pose estimation. In: ECCV (2018)
10. Labbe, Y., Carpentier, J., Aubry, M., Sivic, J.: Cosypose: consistent multi-view multi-object 6D pose estimation. In: ECCV (2020)
11. Lepetit, V., Fua, P.: Keypoint recognition using randomized trees. IEEE Trans. Pattern Anal. Mach. Intell. **28**(9), 1465–1479 (2006)
12. Li, Z., Wang, G., Ji, X.: CDPN: coordinates-based disentangled pose network for real-time RGB-based 6-DOF object pose estimation. In: ICCV (2019)
13. Lin, T.Y., Dollár, P., Girshick, R., He, K., Hariharan, B., Belongie, S.: Feature pyramid networks for object detection. In: Proceedings of the IEEE Conference on Computer Vision and Pattern Recognition, pp. 2117–2125 (2017)
14. Lin, T.Y., et al.: Microsoft coco: common objects in context. In: ECCV (2014)
15. MVTec Software GmbH: HALCON 20.05 progress. MVTec (2020). https://www.mvtec.com
16. Ozuysal, M., Fua, P., Lepetit, V.: Fast keypoint recognition in ten lines of code. In: CVPR (2007)
17. Park, K., Patten, T., Vincze, M.: Pix2pose: pixel-wise coordinate regression of objects for 6d pose estimation. In: ICCV (2019)
18. Sundermeyer, M., et al.: Multi-path learning for object pose estimation across domains. In: CVPR (2020)
19. Sundermeyer, M., Marton, Z.C., Durner, M., Triebel, R.: Augmented autoencoders: implicit 3D orientation learning for 6D object detection. Int. J. Comput. Vision **128**(3), 714–729 (2020)
20. Vidal, J., Lin, C.Y., Lladó, X., Martí, R.: A method for 6D pose estimation of free-form rigid objects using point pair features on range data. Sensors **18**(8), 2678 (2018)
21. Zakharov, S., Shugurov, I., Ilic, S.: DPOD: dense 6D pose object detector in RGB images. CoRR abs/1902.11020 (2019). http://arxiv.org/abs/1902.11020

Leaping from 2D Detection to Efficient 6DoF Object Pose Estimation

Jinhui Liu[1,2], Zhikang Zou[1], Xiaoqing Ye[1], Xiao Tan[1], Errui Ding[1], Feng Xu[2], and Xin Yu[3(✉)]

[1] Baidu Inc., Beijing, China
[2] Tsinghua University, Beijing, China
[3] University of Technology Sydney, Ultimo, Australia
xin.yu@uts.edu.au

Abstract. Estimating 6DoF object poses from single RGB images is very challenging due to severe occlusions and large search space of camera poses. Keypoint voting based methods have demonstrated its effectiveness and superiority on predicting object poses. However, those approaches are often affected by inaccurate semantic segmentation in computing the keypoint locations. To enable our model to focus on local regions without being distracted by backgrounds, we first localize object regions by a 2D object detector. In doing so, we not only reduce the search space of keypoints but also improve the robustness of the pose estimation. Moreover, since symmetric objects may suffer ambiguity along the symmetric dimension, we propose to select keypoints on the geometrically symmetric locations to resolve the ambiguity. The extensive experimental results on seven different datasets of the BOP challenge benchmark demonstrate that our method outperforms the state-of-the-art and achieves the 3-rd place in the BOP challenge.

Keywords: Detection · Keypoint localization · 6DoF pose estimation

1 Introduction

The goal of object pose estimation is to obtain 3D orientations and 3D translations of an object relative to a camera. Considering that an object may undergo occlusions and various positions, estimating 6 degrees of freedom (6DoF) pose is very difficult. Moreover, symmetric objects along the symmetric axis will cause ambiguity, which further leads to large errors when adopting keypoints to estimate object poses.

To address the above issues, we propose a 6DoF object pose estimation framework. Directly regressing object poses in 6d dimension is difficult due to the large search space [22,29]. Instead, we employ a 2D object detector [2] to firstly localize objects in the 2D image plane, similar to [30], and then predict poses within local regions. Moreover, the detected bounding boxes can be used to filter out

---

The first three authors contributed equally to this work.

© Springer Nature Switzerland AG 2020
A. Bartoli and A. Fusiello (Eds.): ECCV 2020 Workshops, LNCS 12536, pp. 707–714, 2020.
https://doi.org/10.1007/978-3-030-66096-3_47

some inaccurate object segmentation or reduce the regions to be segmented. Thus, the bounding boxes can either facilitate object keypoint localization or reduce computational cost of following pose estimation network since poses are now estimated in local regions.

Once objects have been localized in an image plane, we estimate keypoints as well as foreground object segmentation similar to PVNet [16]. Note that there are two factors limiting the performance of PVNet: (i) the backbone is not powerful enough; (ii) the selected keypoints do not guarantee the symmetry with respect to symmetric objects; Original PVNet employs a shallow backbone ResNet18 [3] in order to achieve the trade-off of performance and GPU memory, since it takes entire images as inputs and thus requires larger GPU memory for training. Since our detector has cropped object regions out, the resolutions of inputs are significantly reduced. Therefore, we are able to replace ResNet18 with a more discriminative backbone (i.e., ResNet50) to predict keypoints and object masks.

As reported in [7, 28], the symmetry ambiguity will lead to large estimation errors. For instance, when the selected keypoints are not symmetric along the symmetric axis, the ground-truth locations and estimated ones might be different due to the symmetry. Taking the symmetric factor into account, we select keypoints symmetrically on 3D models to mitigate this problem. Furthermore, the removal of the symmetric ambiguity eases the network training. By tackling the above issues successfully, we improve the performance of 6DoF pose estimation significantly and achieve the 3-rd place in the BOP challenge.

The main contributions of our work are summarized as follows:

– Leveraging 2D objection explicitly for localizing the potential instances on 2D images both for efficiency and robustness.
– Solve the Asymmetry problem of 3D models and perform dense vector voting within the disturbed patches.
– Apply the framework on the BOP Challenge and improve the performance significantly.

2   Related Works

In this section, we mainly review single RGB image based 6DoF pose estimation approaches.

Traditional Methods: Conventional object pose estimation methods mainly leverage on the local feature/keypoint matching. The extracted local feature descriptors from 2D images, such as SIFT [15] and deep local image descriptors [23, 27], need to be robust to viewpoint, illumination, rotation and scale variations. After associating the extracted local features with points on a 3D model, the object poses are solved via a Perspective-n-Point (PnP) problem [12]. However, these methods can only tackle textured objects, where local features are detectable. Other than local features, image templates [1, 5, 19, 31], and image edges [4, 13] are also exploited for pose estimation.

Deep Model Based Methods: Due to the powerful feature representation ability of deep neural networks, deep learning based methods have demonstrated impressive results on object pose estimation [10,16,26].

Some methods, such as Viewpoints and Keypoints [24] and Render for CNN [20], formulate the 3D pose estimation as a classification task by discretizing the pose space and then assigning objects with discrete pose labels. Motivated by the state-of-the-art image detection methods [14,18], pose estimation approaches are designed to localize objects while predicting their viewpoints based on the estimation of 3D bounding-boxes [10,17,22], features of interest [16,26] or coordinate maps [11,25,29]. SSD6D [10] extends the ideas of 2D object detection and classifies localized objects with discrete poses while YOLO6D [22] regresses 3D bounding-boxes of objects. BB8 [17] firstly generates 2D segmentation masks for objects and predicts 3D bounding-boxes from the 2D masks. CPDN [30], DPOD [29] and Pix2Pose [11] regress the 2D/3D coordinates of 3D object models from images. Object poses are estimated by PnP after obtaining 2D-3D correspondences.

Since directly regressing 2D projections of 3D points is not reliable, PoseCNN [26] firstly estimates a vector-field pointing to an object center from object pixels and then employs Hough voting to determine the center. The translations and rotations of the object are regressed subsequently by a sub-network. Rather than only estimating a centroid, PVNet [16] votes several features of interest, while the work [9] votes the corners of a 3D bounding-box from each segmentation grid. Due to the voting strategy, the locations of estimated 2D projections are more robust to occlusions. However, small errors in a direction vector field may lead to large deviations of hypotheses.

3 Methodology

3.1 2D Detection for Localization

As illustrated in Fig. 1, 2D detection is the first step of the framework, which is responsible for reducing the distraction from backgrounds and filtering out potentially inaccurate object segmentation. The performance of detectors directly affects the accuracy of pose estimation results. To achieve precise localization, we adopt Mask R-CNN [2] to train separate detectors for each single object.

Since most datasets only contain synthetic training data, we employ data augmentations (*i.e.*, saturation, contrast, brightness, Gaussian blur) to reduce the domain gap between synthetic and real data. Different datasets have different characteristics (*i.e.*, object sizes and the number of real images). Thus, we adjust the hyperparameters of our detector, such as anchor sizes and learning rate decay steps, accordingly.

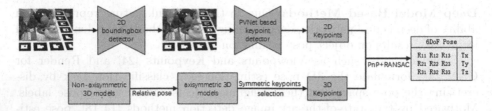

Fig. 1. An overview of our pipeline. Given an input RGB image, we first crop the regions of interest, and then apply a voting based keypoint detector to estimate 2D keypoints. Meanwhile, we select 3D keypoints on 3D models after aligning their principal directions to axes. Finally, we estimate 6DoF poses by RANSAC PnP algorithm.

3.2 Solving Symmetry Ambiguity of 3D Models

Symmetry ambiguity leads to large pose estimation errors if the selected keypoints are not symmetric along the symmetric axis. This may confuse the keypoint detector.

To avoid ambiguity caused by symmetry and reducing estimation errors, we propose to select keypoints symmetrically on 3D models. For instance, in regard to one symmetric object, we first check which axis causes symmetry ambiguity. We adjust the object w.r.t. this axis to reduce ambiguity by rigid transformation, as shown in Fig. 2. Then we sample keypoints along the symmetric axis, and the selected keypoints will be symmetric on a model.

Fig. 2. 3D model symmetry adjustment

3.3 Keypoint Vector-Field Estimation

Since the sizes of objects vary significantly, we opt to estimate a vector-field for each keypoint instead of predicting their keypoint positions from images. The vector-field is composed of unit direction vectors pointing from a pixel to a certain keypoint. Our direction vectors are estimated by a deep neural network with a larger receptive field covering a large portion of objects. In this manner, even though a keypoint is not visible, it is able to be deduced from the visible parts of an object. Our network simultaneously outputs a segmentation mask for an object and keypoint vector-fields.

4   Experiment

4.1   Experimental Settings

Datasets. The proposed approach is evaluated on the public BOP challenge benchmark that are designed to evaluate 6DoF pose estimation methods [8]. The challenge mainly involves seven datasets, namely Linemod-Occluded, T-LESS, MVTec ITODD, HomebrewedDB, YCB-Video, IC-BIN and TUD-Light. Each dataset contains 3D object models, training and test RGB/RGBD images annotated with ground-truth 6D object poses and intrinsic camera parameters. Note that since our method estimates object poses from a single RGB images, the depth images in those datasets are not used. Furthermore, in the BOP challenge, the training data include real and synthetic data. To clarify the training data, we list the used data in different datasets in Table 1.

Table 1. Training data used in 7 datasets

	LMO	TLESS	ITODD	HB	YCB-V	IC-BIN	TUD-L
Real		√		√			√
Synthetic	√	√	√	√	√	√	√

Evaluation Metric. We evaluate the performance of 6D pose estimation by Average Recall (AR) of three error functions, as follows:

$$AR = (AR_{VSD} + AR_{MSSD} + AR_{MSPD})/3 \qquad (1)$$

The VSD, MSSD and MSPD error functions represent Visible Surface Discrepancy, Maximum Symmetry-Aware Surface Distance and Maximum Symmetry-Aware Projection Distance, respectively. Due to the space limit, we omit the details of those functions and refer the readers to [8]. Compared to the traditional 2D projection error and ADD score [6], the newly proposed evaluation metrics are less dependent on the surface sampling density.

Implementation Details. In the 2D boundingbox detection phase, we resize an image to 640 × 480 pixels. We use ResNet101 as our backbone and train the maskrcnn detector for 40 epochs on the seven datasets with a batchsize of 16. The learning rate is set to 0.01 with a decay rate of 0.1. In the 2D Keypoint detection phase, we crop images according to the detected boundingbox, and then resize the cropped images to 128 × 128 pixels. We use ResNet50 as our backbone in this phase and train for 200 epochs with a batchsize of 128. The learning rate in this model is set to 0.001 and decays 50% every 20 epochs.

Fig. 3. Visualization results on the T-LESS and TUD-L datasets. Green bounding boxes represent the ground-truth poses and Blue ones represent our predictions. (Color figure online)

4.2   Comparisons with the State-of-the-Art

Since we predict object poses from a single RGB image, we also compare with RGB based methods (Fig. 3). The hyberparameters are fixed in training and testing the pose estimation network for all the datasets and we do not adopt any pose refinement methods. The SoTA RGB-based approaches, including CDPN [30], Augmented Autoencoders [21], Pix2Pose [11], and DPOD (Synethetic) [29], are compared on the 7 core datasets. As indicated in Table 2, our method outperforms the state-of-the-art on the overall AR.

Table 2. Comparison results on all 7 core BOP datasets.

Method	AR_{core}	LMO	TLESS	TUD-L	ICBIN	ITODD	HB	YCB-V	Time(s)
CDPN [30]	**0.529**	**0.624**	**0.478**	**0.772**	**0.473**	0.102	**0.722**	0.532	0.935
Sundermeyer [21]	0.270	0.146	0.304	0.401	0.217	0.101	0.346	0.377	0.186
Pixel2Pose [11]	0.342	0.363	0.344	0.420	0.226	0.134	0.446	0.457	1.215
DPOD (Syn.) [29]	0.161	0.169	0.081	0.242	0.130	0.000	0.286	0.222	0.231
Ours	0.471	0.525	0.403	0.751	0.342	0.077	0.658	**0.543**	0.425

5   Conclusions

In this paper, we proposed an efficient 6DoF pose estimation approach by leveraging 2D detection explicitly. 2D detection not only reduce the distraction from backgrounds and filtering out potentially inaccurate object segmentation but also allow us to adopt a much deeper backbone to learn more discriminative vector-field keypoints while keeping efficiency. By sampling the symmetric points on 3D models, we significantly mitigate the symmetry ambiguity of 3D models. Extensive experiments demonstrate the superiority and robustness of our proposed method.

Acknowledgement. This work was supported by Baidu Inc., China, the National Key R&D Program of China 2018YFA0704000, the NSFC (No. 61822111, 61727808, 61671268) and Beijing Natural Science Foundation (JQ19015, L182052).

References

1. Gu, C., Ren, X.: Discriminative mixture-of-templates for viewpoint classification. In: Daniilidis, K., Maragos, P., Paragios, N. (eds.) ECCV 2010. LNCS, vol. 6315, pp. 408–421. Springer, Heidelberg (2010). https://doi.org/10.1007/978-3-642-15555-0_30
2. He, K., Gkioxari, G., Dollár, P., Girshick, R.: Mask R-CNN. In: ICCV (2017)
3. He, K., Zhang, X., Ren, S., Sun, J.: Deep residual learning for image recognition. In: CVPR (2016)
4. Hinterstoisser, S., et al.: Gradient response maps for real-time detection of textureless objects. IEEE Trans. Pattern Anal. Mach. Intell. **34**(5), 876–888 (2011)
5. Hinterstoisser, S., et al.: Multimodal templates for real-time detection of textureless objects in heavily cluttered scenes. In: Proceedings of the IEEE International Conference on Computer Vision (ICCV), pp. 858–865. IEEE (2011)
6. Hinterstoisser, S., et al.: Model based training, detection and pose estimation of texture-less 3D objects in heavily cluttered scenes. In: ACCV (2012)
7. Hodan, T., Barath, D., Matas, J.: EPOS: estimating 6D pose of objects with symmetries. In: CVPR (2020)
8. Hodaň, T., et al.: BOP: benchmark for 6D object pose estimation. In: ECCV (2018)
9. Hu, Y., Hugonot, J., Fua, P., Salzmann, M.: Segmentation-driven 6D object pose estimation. In: Proceedings of the IEEE Conference on Computer Vision and Pattern Recognition (CVPR), pp. 3385–3394 (2019)
10. Kehl, W., Manhardt, F., Tombari, F., Ilic, S., Navab, N.: SSD-6D: making RGB-based 3D detection and 6D pose estimation great again. In: Proceedings of the IEEE International Conference on Computer Vision (ICCV), pp. 1521–1529 (2017)
11. Kiru, P., Timothy, P., Markus, V.: Pix2pose: pixel-wise coordinate regression of objects for 6D pose estimation. In: ICCV (2019)
12. Lepetit, V., Moreno-Noguer, F., Fua, P.: EPNP: an accurate O(n) solution to the PnP problem. Int. J. Comput. Vis. **81**(2), 155 (2009)
13. Liu, M.Y., Tuzel, O., Veeraraghavan, A., Chellappa, R.: Fast directional chamfer matching. In: Proceedings of the IEEE Conference on Computer Vision and Pattern Recognition (CVPR), pp. 1696–1703. IEEE (2010)
14. Liu, W., et al.: SSD: single shot MultiBox detector. In: Leibe, B., Matas, J., Sebe, N., Welling, M. (eds.) ECCV 2016. LNCS, vol. 9905, pp. 21–37. Springer, Cham (2016). https://doi.org/10.1007/978-3-319-46448-0_2
15. Lowe, D.G.: Distinctive image features from scale-invariant keypoints. Int. J. Comput. Vis. **60**(2), 91–110 (2004)
16. Peng, S., Liu, Y., Huang, Q., Zhou, X., Bao, H.: PVNet: pixel-wise voting network for 6DoF pose estimation. In: Proceedings of the IEEE Conference on Computer Vision and Pattern Recognition (CVPR), pp. 4561–4570 (2019)

17. Rad, M., Lepetit, V.: BB8: a scalable, accurate, robust to partial occlusion method for predicting the 3D poses of challenging objects without using depth. In: Proceedings of the IEEE International Conference on Computer Vision (CVPR), pp. 3828–3836 (2017)
18. Ren, S., He, K., Girshick, R., Sun, J.: Faster R-CNN: towards real-time object detection with region proposal networks. In: Advances in Neural Information Processing Systems, pp. 91–99 (2015)
19. Rios-Cabrera, R., Tuytelaars, T.: Discriminatively trained templates for 3D object detection: a real time scalable approach. In: Proceedings of the IEEE International Conference on Computer Vision (ICCV), pp. 2048–2055 (2013)
20. Su, H., Qi, C.R., Li, Y., Guibas, L.J.: Render for CNN: viewpoint estimation in images using CNNs trained with rendered 3D model views. In: Proceedings of the IEEE International Conference on Computer Vision (ICCV), pp. 2686–2694 (2015)
21. Sundermeyer, M., Marton, Z.C., Durner, M., Triebel, R.: Augmented autoencoders: implicit 3D orientation learning for 6D object detection. IJCV **128**(3), 714–729 (2020)
22. Tekin, B., Sinha, S.N., Fua, P.: Real-time seamless single shot 6d object pose prediction. In: CVPR (2018)
23. Tian, Y., Yu, X., Fan, B., Wu, F., Heijnen, H., Balntas, V.: Sosnet: second order similarity regularization for local descriptor learning. In: Proceedings of the IEEE Conference on Computer Vision and Pattern Recognition, pp. 11016–11025 (2019)
24. Tulsiani, S., Malik, J.: Viewpoints and keypoints. In: Proceedings of the IEEE Conference on Computer Vision and Pattern Recognition (CVPR), pp. 1510–1519 (2015)
25. Wang, H., Sridhar, S., Huang, J., Valentin, J., Song, S., Guibas, L.J.: Normalized object coordinate space for category-level 6D object pose and size estimation. In: Proceedings of the IEEE Conference on Computer Vision and Pattern Recognition (CVPR), pp. 2642–2651 (2019)
26. Xiang, Y., Schmidt, T., Narayanan, V., Fox, D.: Posecnn: a convolutional neural network for 6D object pose estimation in cluttered scenes. Robotics: Science and Systems (2017)
27. Yu, X., et al.: Unsupervised extraction of local image descriptors via relative distance ranking loss. In: Proceedings of the IEEE International Conference on Computer Vision Workshops, pp. 1–8 (2019)
28. Yu, X., Zhuang, Z., Koniusz, P., Li, H.: 6DoF object pose estimation via differentiable proxy voting loss. In: BMVC (2020)
29. Zakharov, S., Shugurov, I., Ilic, S.: DPOD: 6D pose object detector and refiner. In: ICCV (2019)
30. Zhigang, L., Gu, W., Xiangyang, J.: CDPN: coordinates-based disentangled pose network for real-time RGB-based 6-DoF object pose estimation. In: ICCV (2019)
31. Zhu, M., et al.: Single image 3D object detection and pose estimation for grasping. In: IEEE International Conference on Robotics and Automation (ICRA), pp. 3936–3943. IEEE (2014)

W23 - SHApe Recovery from Partial Textured 3D Scans

W23 - SHApe Recovery from Partial Textured 3D Scans

The First Workshop and Challenge on SHApe Recovery from Partial Textured 3D Scans (SHARP 2020) is the 1st event around data collected during multiple campaigns starting from 2017. It was sponsored by Artec 3D, a global leader in 3D handheld scanners. The goal of this workshop was to promote concepts that exploit both shape and texture in the processing of 3D scans and specifically in the task of recovery from incomplete data. Indeed, recently, many successful learning-based approaches have been developed for 3D shape reconstruction. However, very little has been proposed for reconstructing full 3D objects with shape and texture at the same time.

This workshop articulated around two challenges on the reconstruction of full 3D textured meshes from partial 3D scans. The first challenge involved the recovery of textured 3D human body scans. The dataset used in this scope is the 3DBodyTex.v2 dataset. Two tracks were included in this challenge: (a) recovery of large body regions and (b) recovery of fine body details. The second challenge involved the recovery of generic object scans from the new 3DObjectTex dataset, which is a subset from the ViewShape online repository of 3D scans. This first edition attracted 32 participants with 9 validated registrations for Challenge 1 and 6 for Challenge 2, and 3 teams reaching to the final evaluation phase. Only participants in the challenge were eligible to submit a paper. With that, the number of final full paper submissions to the workshop was three with two solid contributions accepted in these proceedings. Artec 3D awarded a prize of four thousand euros to the winners, Julian Chibane and Gerard Pons-Moll from the Max Planck Institute for Informatics, Germany, and donated two thousand euro to UNICEF on behalf of the runner-up, a mixed team from SnT, University of Luxembourg, Luxembourg, and Artec 3D, Luxembourg, composed of Alexandre Saint, Anis Kacem, Kseniya Cherenkova, and Djamila Aouada.

The workshop featured: (1) two exciting plenary talks by Didier Stricker, Director of DFKI, Germany, and by Hao Li, CEO and co-founder of Pinscreen, USA, (2) talks by challenge finalists, (3) a review of challenge results, and finally (4) a panel discussion. Perspectives from industry and academia were shared by the guest panelists Hao Li and David Fofi, Director of the Robotics Department at the University of Burgundy, France, and brainstormed with the SHARP team.

August 2020

Djamila Aouada
Kseniya Cherenkova
Alexandre Saint
David Fofi
Gleb Gusev
Björn Ottersten

Implicit Feature Networks for Texture Completion from Partial 3D Data

Julian Chibane$^{(\boxtimes)}$ and Gerard Pons-Moll

Max Planck Institute for Informatics, Saarbrücken, Germany
{jchibane,gpons}@mpi-inf.mpg.de

Abstract. Prior work to infer 3D texture use either texture atlases, which require uv-mappings and hence have discontinuities, or colored voxels, which are memory inefficient and limited in resolution. Recent work, predicts RGB color at every XYZ coordinate forming a texture field, but focus on completing texture given a single 2D image. Instead, we focus on 3D *texture* and geometry completion from partial and incomplete *3D scans*. IF-Nets [2] have recently achieved state-of-the-art results on 3D geometry completion using a multi-scale deep feature encoding, but the outputs lack texture. In this work, we generalize IF-Nets to texture completion from partial textured scans of humans and arbitrary objects. Our key insight is that 3D texture completion benefits from incorporating local and global deep features extracted from *both* the 3D partial texture and completed geometry. Specifically, given the partial 3D texture and the 3D geometry completed with IF-Nets, our model successfully in-paints the missing texture parts in consistence with the completed geometry. Our model won the SHARP ECCV'20 challenge, achieving highest performance on all challenges.

Keywords: Implicit representation · Implicit function learning · Texture field · Implicit feature networks · Texture completion · 3D reconstruction · Human reconstruction

1 Introduction

Motivated by difficulties in the 3D capturing process of complete scans the ECCV 2020 SHApe Recovery from Partial textured 3D scans (SHARP) Workshop[1] initialized a challenge on reconstructing full 3D textured meshes from partial 3D scan acquisitions. Complete 3D scanning, amongst other challenges, need to capture varying levels of details from the scene, need to handle occlusions, transparency, movement and require bulky studio setups. On the other hand, mobile hand-held scanners[2] allow an adaptive usage. Longer acquisition times, can result in partial scans with inaccuracies which we target to complete in this work.

---

[1] https://cvi2.uni.lu/sharp2020/.
[2] Artec3D, https://www.artec3d.com.

© Springer Nature Switzerland AG 2020
A. Bartoli and A. Fusiello (Eds.): ECCV 2020 Workshops, LNCS 12536, pp. 717–725, 2020.
https://doi.org/10.1007/978-3-030-66096-3_48

For the geometry reconstruction we rely on the state-of-the-art Implicit Feature Networks [2] (IF-Nets) neural 3D processing architecture. We find exciting results for reconstruction of humans: even in the absence of whole body parts, as arms or feet, in the corrupted input, the fully learned IF-Nets are generating plausible human shape completions, we expected to require a human body model.

However, the reconstructions are missing texture - an integral part of a human scan, consumers are interested in. There are two common texture representation which both have limitations: 1) texture can be represented as 2D texture atlases stored as images, which need geometry templates to find uv-mappings from 3D to 2D and have hard to handle discontinuities and 2) colorized voxel grids, which are memory inefficient and restrict to low-frequency texture. A novel texture representation, learned texture fields, predict rgb color at a specific xyz coordinate. However, prior work do inference only based on 2D image evidence [8–10,15]. In this work we extend the IF-Net architecture for use of texture completion from colored, partial 3D data: humans and arbitrary objects. As input to our texture field prediction we use the partial textured input surface and an IF-Net untextured geometry completion, and feed both as voxelized grids into our network. For every point on the input full geometry we predict the rgb color. We find our model successfully inpaints the missing texture parts in consistence with the completed geometry.

2   Related Work

Implicit Function Leaning (IFL). IFL methods use either binary occupancies [2,3,6,15] or signed distance functions [1,4,7,11] as shape representation for learning. These methods incorporate a simple but very powerful trick: a network predicts occupancy or the SDF valuea at continuous point locations (x-y-z).

IF-Nets[2] showed state-of-the-art performance on reconstruction from partial 3D. However, the reconstructions are missing texture. We therefor, in this work, extend IF-Nets to reconstruction of complete, textured reconstructions.

Another application of IFL methods is novel view synthesis, that is, generating novel view-points given one or multiple images [8,16], however, this is not the focus of our work.

Texture Fields. Recent work, predicts RGB color at every XYZ coordinate forming a texture field, but focus on completing texture given a single 2D image [10,15] or multiple 2D images [8,9]. Instead, we focus on 3D *texture* and geometry completion from partial and incomplete *3D scans*, which is required for the given challenge.

3 Method

Our goal is to reconstruct a completed textured surface of humans and objects given only a textured partial observation. To predict the full, textured reconstruction we extend IF-Nets [2] to inference of texture fields. (Sect. 3.1) To obtain geometry reconstructions we train a regular IF-Net (Sect. 3.2).

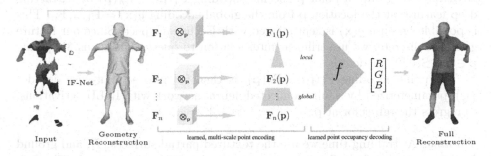

Fig. 1. Overview of inference-time prediction of textured, complete surfaces from corrupted, partial input. We train a standard IF-Net to reconstruct untextured geometry given the corrupted, partial input. An rgb value at point **p** is predicted by explicitly extracting local and global deep features computed from *both* the 3D partial texture and completed geometry. Our key insight is that this enables our model to generate texture in consistence with the completed geometry.

3.1 Texture Inference

We learn to complete the texture of a given partial 3D surface, $\mathcal{T}_i$. For this, we learn a texture field, that is, a mapping of points **p**, on a complete but untextured surface, to a color at that point. As input **x** to the texture field prediction, we additionally use a complete untextured surface geometry of the object. During training the complete surface geometry is provided by the ground truth surfaces, $\mathcal{S}_i$, during inference it is predicted as described in Sect. 3.2.

Encoding. We construct an input encoding *aligned* with the input data. That is, using a 3D CNN we neurally process the input to feature grids, that lie in the same Euclidean space as the input. By recursively applying n times, 3D convolutions followed by down scaling through max pooling, we create *multi-scale deep feature grids* $\mathbf{F}_1, .., \mathbf{F}_n$. The feature grids at the early stages capture texture and shape details, whereas feature grids at the late stages have large receptive fields and capture global structure, for example to segment garments for giving them a coherent texture. See [2] for details.

To adapt the procedure for texture inference, we feed 4 channels of input data into the encoder, 3 channels for the textured partial observation - one channel per rgb - and the fourth channel encodes the complete surface geometry. For usage with a 3D CNN we need to voxelize the surfaces, we do this by densely sampling surface points and marking their nearest neighbor in an enclosing voxel grid. For the partial textured input, we mark the nearest neighbour voxels by the rgb intensities in $\{0, \ldots, 255\}$ and all other with -1. For the complete surface geometry, we mark voxels selected as nearest neighbours with 1 and all other with 0. We denote the encoder as $g(\mathbf{x}) := \mathbf{F}_1, .., \mathbf{F}_n$, where our input is denoted as $\mathbf{x}$.

Decoding. We create a point $\mathbf{p}$ specific encoding $\mathbf{F}_1(\mathbf{p}), .., \mathbf{F}_n(\mathbf{p})$ by extracting deep features at the location $\mathbf{p}$ from the global encoding $g(\mathbf{x}) = \mathbf{F}_1, .., \mathbf{F}_n$. This is possible because $g(\mathbf{x})$ is kept aligned with Euclidean space. Since our feature grids are discrete, we use trilinear interpolation to query continuous 3D points $\mathbf{p} \in \mathbb{R}^3$. See [2] for details.

The point encoding $\mathbf{F}_1(\mathbf{p}), .., \mathbf{F}_n(\mathbf{p})$, is then fed into a point-wise decoder $f(\cdot)$, parameterized by a fully connected neural network with ReLU activations, to regress the rgb color at $\mathbf{p}$.

Training. At training time we use the textured partial surfaces, $\mathcal{T}_i$. and ground truth complete surface, $\mathcal{S}_i$, without texture, as inputs for the network. The task of the network is then, to learn to regress the correct color $\mathrm{rgb}(\mathbf{p}, \mathcal{S}_i)$ at a surface point $\mathbf{p} \in \mathcal{S}_i$ of the ground truth surface. We construct training data by sampling points $\mathbf{p}$ uniform at random on the surface $\mathcal{S}_i$ and find their ground truth $\mathrm{rgb}(\mathbf{p}, \mathcal{S}_i)$ values. More specifically, we have $\mathcal{S}_i$ available as mesh .obj-files with attached texture atlases. Therefore, to find $\mathrm{rgb}(\mathbf{p}, \mathcal{S}_i)$, we check for the triangle $\mathbf{p}$ is on, find the uv-coordinates of $\mathbf{p}$ by Barycentric interpolation of the uv-coordinates of the triangle vertices and extract the rgb value from the texture atlas at the found uv location. We use an L1 mini-batch loss:

$$\mathcal{L}_{\mathcal{B}}(\mathbf{w}) := \sum_{\mathbf{x} \in \mathcal{B}} \sum_{\mathbf{p} \in \mathcal{P}} ||f^{\mathbf{w}}(g_{\mathbf{w}}(\mathbf{x}, \mathbf{p})) - \mathrm{rgb}(\mathbf{p}, \mathcal{S}_{\mathbf{x}})||_1 \tag{1}$$

where $\mathcal{B}$ is a input mini-batch, $\mathcal{P}$ is a sub-sample of points, $\mathbf{w}$ are the neural parameters of encoder and decoder, and $g_{\mathbf{w}}(\mathbf{x}, \mathbf{p}) := \mathbf{F}_1^{\mathbf{w}}(\mathbf{p}), \ldots, \mathbf{F}_n^{\mathbf{w}}(\mathbf{p})$.

Inference. At inference time we feed the partial textured surface, $\mathcal{T}_i$, and its surface reconstruction (untextured) (Sect. 3.2) as input into the texture inference. The surface reconstruction is a mesh and for all its vertices we regress the rgb value and attach it to the mesh. This yields our final colored surface reconstruction. See Fig. 1 for an overview of our method.

3.2 Geometry Reconstruction

During inference, we predict the geometry using an IF-Net and condition the texture generation (Sect. 3.1) on this geometry. For learning the geometry reconstruction, we use a standard IF-Net [2]. Our training data consists of pairs $(\mathcal{T}_i, \mathcal{S}_i)_i$, of partial surfaces, $\mathcal{T}_i$, and complete ground truth surfaces, $\mathcal{S}_i$. The shape prediction given $\mathcal{T}_i$, of IF-Nets is done implicitly, by predicting for any point $\mathbf{p}$ in the continuous space $\mathbb{R}^3$, if $\mathbf{p}$ is inside (classification as 1) or outside (classification as 0) of the ground truth $\mathcal{S}_i$. For inference of surfaces, these predictions are evaluated on a dense gird in $\mathbb{R}^3$ and converted to a mesh using marching cubes [5].

Encoding & decoding is done with the same architecture described above. However, the input to the encoder consists *only* of one (untextured) channel, created from the partial surface. To encode the surface we again, sample points on it and create a voxel grid. We mark a voxel with 1, if it is a nearest neighbour of a point, and 0 else. We use a grid resolution of 256^3. Instead of 3 values for rgb we decode into one value for the above mentioned occupancy classification.

Training. For each ground truth surface, $\mathcal{S}_i$, we sample 100.000 points and compute their occupancy. Samples are created in the surface vicinity to concentrate the model capacity on details. To this end, we first uniformly at random sample surface points $\mathbf{p}_{\mathcal{S}}$ and apply Gaussian distributed displacements $\mathbf{n} \sim \mathcal{N}(0, \boldsymbol{\Sigma})$, i.e. $\mathbf{p} := \mathbf{p}_{\mathcal{S}} + \mathbf{n}$. We use a diagonal co-variance matrix $\boldsymbol{\Sigma} \in \mathbb{R}^{3 \times 3}$ with entries $\boldsymbol{\Sigma}_{i,i} = \sigma$. To capture detail we sample 50% of the point samples very near the surface with a small $\sigma_1 = 0.015$, and to learn about the global, more homogeneously filled space, we sample 50% with a larger $\sigma_2 = 0.2$. During training 50.000 points are sub-sampled and learning is unaltered from [2].

4   SHARP ECCV 2020 Challenge

In this section we present the challenges and the qualitative results of our method. For a quantitative result analysis, including other participants and baselines, we refer to the SHARP summary paper corresponding to this workshop.

4.1   Challenge 1

Track 1. For track 1 we were kindly given access to the 3DBodyTex.v2 dataset, similar in quality to 3DBodyTex [12][3]. It consists of about 2500 of human scans with high diversity in poses. Some humans wear minimal fitness clothing others are fully clothed in varying clothing. We train our algorithm solely on the officially provided training set. The task is to reconstruct a completed textured 3D surface from a 3D human scan with large missing areas. The ground truth surfaces, $\mathcal{S}_i$, are the raw scans. The textured partial surfaces, $\mathcal{T}_i$, are generated synthetically from the ground truth shapes, using the provided script with default values[4]. For each ground truth mesh we generate 4 partial scans with different incompleteness patterns. The partial data should simulate an acquisition produced by a hand-held 3D scanner. For all scans we found the bounding box with

$$(min_x, max_x, min_y, max_y, min_z, max_z) = (-0.8, 0.8, -0.15, 2.1, -0.8, 0.8)$$

---

[3] https://cvi2.uni.lu/datasets/.

[4] https://gitlab.uni.lu/cvi2/eccv2020-sharp-workshop/-/tree/master.

to be sufficient and use it to place our voxel grid encoding (see Sect. 3.1). In Fig. 2 we show the results obtained with our method from Sect. 3.

Fig. 2. Six testing results a)–f) from our method (unseen during training), left to right: textured, partial input, textured reconstruction, ground truth. Our geometry reconstructions notably show generated body parts in correct positions even for largely missing body parts, see right arm of person e). Our texture generation is visibly coherent with the reconstructed geometry, through the geometry conditioning, see transition from shirt to leggings of b). The texture generation learned can rely on symmetry for generation, see the right foot of person in c).

Track 2. In Track 2, the task is to reconstruct fine geometry details of the body such as ears, fingers, feet or a nose, without texture. For this we are given around 1000 detailed ground truth meshes, $\mathcal{S}_i$, obtained by fitting a human body model to human data in minimal clothing from 3DBodyTex.v2. See [13,14] for methods on automatic and robust model fitting proposed by the dataset authors. On these ground truth meshes a scanning process of the Shapify booth is simulated in software. Additionally, we again shoot holes into the mesh using the provided script in its default setting, shooting holes also at other body parts. Again, we generate 4 partial scans with different incompleteness patterns. Only when the evaluation data was released, we found, that holes only occur at ears, fingers, feet or noses. Therefore, an obvious enhancement for our training would be to concentrate model capacity to those regions by only shooting holes there. We reuse the bounding box found for Track 1. In Fig. 3 we show qualiatative results obtained with our method, IF-Nets.

4.2   Challenge 2

In this challenge we are given a dataset (3DObjectTex.v1) of 2000, high quality, textured 3D ground truth scans, $\mathcal{S}_i$, of very diverse objects (real and stuffed animals, statues, technology, furniture,...). When scanning with a hand-held 3D scanner, technical infeasibility of reaching some parts of an object can lead to

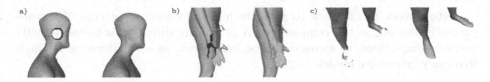

Fig. 3. Results on evaluation data (GT disclosed), for reconstruction of the ear region a), hand b) and feet c) regions. Although trained for geometry reconstruction of holes at arbitrary regions, plausible shape completion for these regions is achieved.

partial textured scans. Therefore, the task of this challenge is to reconstruct a textured, complete mesh from such partial data. In contrast to challenge 1, the diversity of objects makes it infeasible to build object specify shape priors. As before, we create 4 partial scans per ground truth. Due to huge size variations, we rescale all objects to lie in [-0.5,0.5] in each dimension, by subtracting each vertex with the object center and multiplying by the inverse of its longest bounding box edge. In Fig. 4 we show qualitative results obtained with our IF-Nets.

Fig. 4. Results on challenge evaluation data (GT disclosed), for reconstruction of textured, arbitrary objects. This is a highly challenging dataset and problem: objects come from no common class. Thus, no shape prior of objects can be learned - the textured reconstruction can solely rely on surface statistics common in any object. Our network performs reasonable textured reconstruction of what we believe to be a head, orange juice, a shoe and an Egyptian statue.

5   Discussion and Conclusions

We proposed an extension of IF-Nets for *textured*, complete 3D reconstruction from textured, highly incomplete 3D scans. For this we predict a continuous texture field, that is, we predict the rgb color at any given point in 3D. Our model won the SHARP ECCV'20 challenge, achieving highest performance on all challenges.

We found that 3D texture completion benefits from incorporating local and global deep features extracted from *both* the 3D partial texture and completed geometry. Specifically, given the partial 3D texture and the 3D geometry completed with IF-Nets, our model successfully in-paints plausible texture in consistence with the completed geometry. We hypothesize, this is because areas of homogeneous texture are often strongly correlated with the geometry: a uni-colored t-shirt or dress can be well textured given a geometry segmentation.

Future work can address to generate higher frequency patterns of texture currently missing in the completions. A promising direction is to use our 3D texture completions, in a coarse to fine framework, as a conditioning for high frequency generative models in 2D.

References

1. Chen, Z., Zhang, H.: Learning implicit fields for generative shape modeling. In: IEEE Conference on Computer Vision and Pattern Recognition, CVPR 2019, Long Beach, CA, USA, 16–20 June 2019, pp. 5939–5948 (2019)
2. Chibane, J., Alldieck, T., Pons-Moll, G.: Implicit functions in feature space for 3D shape reconstruction and completion. In: IEEE Conference on Computer Vision and Pattern Recognition (CVPR). IEEE, June 2020
3. Genova, K., Cole, F., Sud, A., Sarna, A., Funkhouser, T.: Deep structured implicit functions. In: 2020 IEEE Conference on Computer Vision and Pattern Recognition (2019)
4. Jiang, C.M., Sud, A., Makadia, A., Huang, J., Nießner, M., Funkhouser, T.: Local implicit grid representations for 3D scenes. In: 2020 IEEE Conference on Computer Vision and Pattern Recognition (2020)
5. Lorensen, W.E., Cline, H.E.: Marching cubes: a high resolution 3D surface construction algorithm. In: Computer Graphics and Interactive Techniques, pp. 163–169 (1987). https://doi.org/10.1145/37401.37422
6. Mescheder, L.M., Oechsle, M., Niemeyer, M., Nowozin, S., Geiger, A.: Occupancy networks: learning 3D reconstruction in function space. In: IEEE Conference on Computer Vision and Pattern Recognition, CVPR 2019, Long Beach, CA, USA, 16–20 June 2019, pp. 4460–4470 (2019)
7. Michalkiewicz, M., Pontes, J.K., Jack, D., Baktashmotlagh, M., Eriksson, A.P.: Deep level sets: implicit surface representations for 3D shape inference. CoRR abs/1901.06802 (2019). http://arxiv.org/abs/1901.06802
8. Mildenhall, B., Srinivasan, P.P., Tancik, M., Barron, J.T., Ramamoorthi, R., Ng, R.: Nerf: representing scenes as neural radiance fields for view synthesis. arXiv preprint arXiv:2003.08934 (2020)
9. Niemeyer, M., Mescheder, L., Oechsle, M., Geiger, A.: Differentiable volumetric rendering: learning implicit 3D representations without 3D supervision. In: Proceedings IEEE Conference on Computer Vision and Pattern Recognition (CVPR) (2020)
10. Oechsle, M., Mescheder, L., Niemeyer, M., Strauss, T., Geiger, A.: Texture fields: learning texture representations in function space. In: International Conference on Computer Vision, October 2019
11. Park, J.J., Florence, P., Straub, J., Newcombe, R.A., Lovegrove, S.: DeepSDF: learning continuous signed distance functions for shape representation. In: IEEE Conference on Computer Vision and Pattern Recognition, CVPR 2019, Long Beach, CA, USA, 16–20 June 2019, pp. 165–174 (2019)
12. Saint, A., et al.: 3DBodyTex: textured 3D body dataset. In: 2018 International Conference on 3D Vision (3DV), pp. 495–504 (2018)
13. Saint, A., Rahman Shabayek, A.E., Cherenkova, K., Gusev, G., Aouada, D., Ottersten, B.: Bodyfitr: robust automatic 3D human body fitting. In: 2019 IEEE International Conference on Image Processing (ICIP), pp. 484–488 (2019)

14. Saint, A., Shabayek, A., Aouada, D., Ottersten, B., Cherenkova, K., Gusev, G.: Towards automatic human body model fitting to a 3D scan. In: 8th International Conference and Exhibition on 3D Body Scanning and Processing Technologies, Montreal QC, Canada, pp. 274–280 (2017). https://doi.org/10.15221/17.274
15. Saito, S., Huang, Z., Natsume, R., Morishima, S., Kanazawa, A., Li, H.: PIFU: pixel-aligned implicit function for high-resolution clothed human digitization. arXiv preprint arXiv:1905.05172 (2019)
16. Sitzmann, V., Zollhöfer, M., Wetzstein, G.: Scene representation networks: continuous 3D-structure-aware neural scene representations. In: Advances in Neural Information Processing Systems, pp. 1119–1130 (2019)

3DBooSTeR: 3D Body Shape and Texture Recovery

Alexandre Saint[1(✉)], Anis Kacem[1], Kseniya Cherenkova[1,2], and Djamila Aouada[1]

[1] SnT, University of Luxembourg, Luxembourg City, Luxembourg
{alexandre.saint,anis.kacem,djamila.aouada}@uni.lu
[2] Artec3D, Luxembourg City, Luxembourg
kcherenkova@artec-group.com

Abstract. We propose 3DBooSTeR, a novel method to recover a textured 3D body mesh from a textured partial 3D scan. With the advent of virtual and augmented reality, there is a demand for creating realistic and high-fidelity digital 3D human representations. However, 3D scanning systems can only capture the 3D human body shape up to some level of defects due to its complexity, including occlusion between body parts, varying levels of details, shape deformations and the articulated skeleton. Textured 3D mesh completion is thus important to enhance 3D acquisitions. The proposed approach decouples the shape and texture completion into two sequential tasks. The shape is recovered by an encoder-decoder network deforming a template body mesh. The texture is subsequently obtained by projecting the partial texture onto the template mesh before inpainting the corresponding texture map with a novel approach. The approach is validated on the 3DBodyTex.v2 dataset.

Keywords: 3D shape completion · Human body shape · Point cloud · Texture · Inpainting

1 Introduction

The completion of a partial textured 3D body shape is key to enable the digital representation of 3D body shape with realistic details, in a reasonable time and in an automated way. This is required in applications such as virtual reality. Capturing the 3D human shape and texture of the human body is complex due to the occlusion of body parts, the complex shape of the clothing wrinkles, the variation of the pose in time, etc. Some photogrammetric scanner systems, on the one hand, use a large array of cameras to cover the body shape from all possible angles. These systems are able to capture textured 3D shape sequences at high frame rates (120 kHz). However, they still suffer from occlusion and cannot represent fine details, such as the fingers and the ears. Hand-held scanners, on the other hand, can be brought to resolve fine details and cover all view angles, but they require a static target. For an unconstrained usage, it is then more desirable to acquire a partial shape and come with an effective completion solution

© Springer Nature Switzerland AG 2020
A. Bartoli and A. Fusiello (Eds.): ECCV 2020 Workshops, LNCS 12536, pp. 726–740, 2020.
https://doi.org/10.1007/978-3-030-66096-3_49

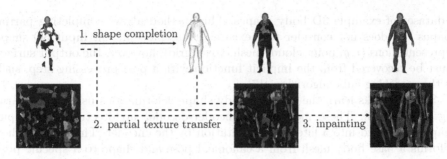

Fig. 1. Overview of the proposed approach for completing a partial textured 3D body mesh. 1) The complete shape is estimated. 2) The partial texture is transferred onto the estimated shape. 3) The corresponding texture image is inpainted.

that recovers the missing data. Aware of this emergent need, some state-of-art works have tried to recover the missing information provided by the scanning devices. Most of them consider the problems of shape and texture completion independently. Accordingly, the relevant literature is presented separately below.

Shape Completion. A simple approach to shape completion is the hole-filling algorithm (*e.g.* Davis et al. [4]), in which the missing shape regions are filled with a surface patch joining the boundaries of the available surface. This approach is limited to relatively small holes with respect to the surrounding surface and to relatively smooth regions.

An approach to regularise the shape completion is to rely on a template shape that is deformed to match the input partial shape. Szeliski et al. [26] deform a simple convex shape to represent anatomical body parts such as the head. Anguelov et al. [1] learn a parametric model of the human body pose and shape to regularise the completion of a full 3D body shape while handling the large deformations caused by variation in pose. This sort of methods usually requires manual initialisation, as shown by Saint et al. [22–24], who propose fully-automatic body model fitting approaches by exploiting the colour or texture information in human scans, as available in 3DBodyTex [22]. This allows recovering shapes with relatively large proportions of missing data. The body models based on SMPL provide a reasonable trade-off between computational efficiency and expressiveness [16,19]. However, body models smooth out the shape details and are limited to the body shape without clothing. In these works, the completion of the texture is not considered, even though the texture might be used to regularise the shape completion [22,23].

Some works use volumetric convolutions to complete partial 3D shapes [3, 10,28]. The achievable resolution is limited due to the high computational complexity of 3D convolutions. Moreover, this category of approaches works well on relatively rigid shapes [3,28] (*e.g.* objects of the same class) but less well on deformable shapes [14] (*e.g.* shape of the human body or of animals). Chibane et al. [2] represent the 3D body shape with an implicit function. The implicit function is approximated by a deep neural network and learned from a dataset of example 3D body shapes. This method allows completing partial shapes but does not consider the texture. It accepts different input 3D shape representations (*e.g.* point cloud, mesh, voxel grid), however, the output surface must be recovered from the implicit function with a post-processing step, such as the marching cube algorithm [17].

Several works learn the space of body shape deformations using deep learning [9,13,14,18]. These models use encoder-decoder architectures. An input shape is encoded into a latent representation by the encoder. The decoder then deforms a base body mesh from a canonical pose and shape to a specific pose and identity, using the intermediate representation as input. The deformations are performed with mesh convolutions (*e.g.* PointNet [20] or FeaStNet [27]). The parameters of the network are learned from a dataset of example 3D body shapes. Some works target only the body shape with minimal close-fitting clothing [9,13,14], which is locally smooth and regular. Other works target the body shape with casual clothing [18], which contains irregular local variations, such as wrinkles, due to factors including the cut and the fabric. The completion of texture information is not tackled in these works.

Texture Completion. Deng et al. [6] recover the 3D shape and the colour information of a face from a non-frontal 2D view. Shape and texture completion are decoupled. A 3D morphable model (3DMM) is first fitted to the image. Then, the available colour information is projected onto the UV map of the template mesh. Finally, the UV map is inpainted to recover the missing colour information. The fitting of a body is more complex due to the pose variation, larger and more non-linear than the variation in the expression. The UV map for the face is a single chart. For a body model, it is a set of multiple charts representing different body regions.

In the context of partial shape and texture completion, we present our approach to solve the SHARP challenge [25] on recovering large regions of partial textured body meshes. This challenge provides 3DBodyTex.v2, a dataset with thousands of textured body meshes. The training set and the validation set contain the ground-truth textured body meshes. The evaluation set contains only partial meshes. The goal is to estimate the complete shapes in the evaluation set.

Our contribution, sketched in Fig. 1, is a method, named 3DBooSTeR, to recover a 3D body mesh with a corresponding high-resolution texture from a textured partial 3D body scan. The tasks of shape and texture completion are decoupled into a sequential pipeline. The shape completion method is a data-driven mesh deformation deep learning network (based on Groueix et al. [9]) that produces an output mesh of fixed topology. The texture completion is reduced to an inpainting task of the texture image of the reconstructed mesh. An novel inpainting method (based on Liu et al. [15]) is proposed. It is specifically designed to handle the inpainting of a texture image with robustness to irregularly-shaped incomplete regions and irregularly-shaped background regions that must be ignored.

The rest of the paper is organised as follows: Section 2 introduces the problem and the notations used in the paper. Section 3 presents the proposed approach for shape and texture completion. Experimental results are reported in Sect. 4. In Sect. 5, we conclude the paper.

2   Problem Statement

A textured body shape is denoted $\mathcal{X} = (\mathcal{S}, T)$, where $\mathcal{S} = (\mathbf{V}, \mathbf{F}, \pi)$ is a body mesh with n_v vertices stacked in a matrix $\mathbf{V} \in \mathbb{R}^{n_v \times 3}$, n_f triangular faces encoded in $\mathbf{F} \in \mathbb{N}^{n_f \times 3}$ as triplets of vertex indices, and a 2D parametrisation, π, defining a mapping of the faces between the 3D shape, $\mathcal{S}$, and the 2D texture image, T.

Given a partial textured body shape $\mathcal{X}_p = (\mathcal{S}_p, T_p)$, with, $\mathcal{S}_p$, the partial mesh, and, T_p, the partial texture, we aim to predict a complete textured body mesh $\hat{\mathcal{X}} = (\hat{\mathcal{S}}, \hat{T})$ that approximates well the ground truth $\mathcal{X} = (\mathcal{S}, T)$. Moreover, the estimation $\hat{\mathcal{X}}$ should preserve the partially provided texture and shape information as much as possible.

Texture Atlas. A texture image T has a texture atlas structure [12] consisting of a set of charts (*i.e.* small pieces of the body texture) gathered together in a single image. Each of these charts is mapped onto a different region of the 3D mesh $\mathcal{S}$ using the 2D parametrisation π. This allows for densely colouring a 3D mesh from a 2D image. Figure 2a shows an example texture atlas corresponding to a complete body mesh. Figure 2b shows its corresponding background mask. The background corresponds to the regions outside of the charts. They do not contain any texture information and are coloured black by convention. The background is defined in a *background mask* M_b where $M_b(i, j) = 0$ if (i, j) is a background pixel, and $M_b(i, j) = 1$ otherwise (foreground). Figure 2c and 2d, show the partial texture atlas and background mask of a corresponding partial mesh (generated synthetically).

A complete texture atlas.   Background mask of complete texture.   A partial texture atlas.   Background mask of partial texture.

Fig. 2. Example of complete and partial texture atlases with their corresponding background masks M_b. Sample from the 3DBodyTex.v2 dataset.

3   Proposed Approach

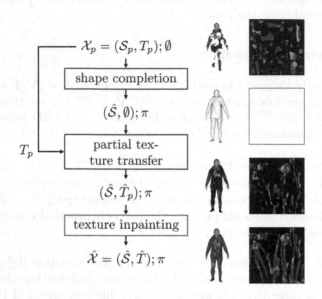

$$\mathcal{X}_p = (\mathcal{S}_p, T_p); \emptyset$$

shape completion

$$(\hat{\mathcal{S}}, \emptyset); \pi$$

T_p → partial texture transfer

$$(\hat{\mathcal{S}}, \hat{T}_p); \pi$$

texture inpainting

$$\hat{\mathcal{X}} = (\hat{\mathcal{S}}, \hat{T}); \pi$$

Fig. 3. Overview of the proposed approach for 3D body shape and texture completion.

We propose to solve the problem of textured 3D body shape completion with two sequential tasks: shape completion, followed by texture completion (Fig. 3). First, a complete 3D shape $\hat{\mathcal{S}}$ is predicted from the partial shape $\mathcal{S}_p$ by an encoder-decoder model. The encoder-decoder completes the input partial shape by deforming a template mesh of a full 3D body into the corresponding pose and shape of the input. The texture information of the partial input mesh is then projected onto the estimated shape, $\hat{\mathcal{S}}$, to obtain a completed shape with partial texture, $\hat{T}_p$. The regions with missing texture information are then identified on the texture image, $\hat{T}_p$. Given the partial texture and the missing regions, the task of texture completion on a 3D shape is turned into an image inpainting task with additional constraints to handle the specific image representation of texture atlas. Indeed, the texture image contains irregularly-shape background regions that must be correctly ignored to avoid their propagation and unrealistic inpainting results. The different stages of the approach are detailed below.

3.1   3D Body Shape Completion

The 3D body shape completion is performed in two steps, as illustrated in Fig. 4. First, an encoder-decoder network predicts a rough estimation of the pose and shape of the partial input shape. Second, the estimation is refined to better match the clothing shape.

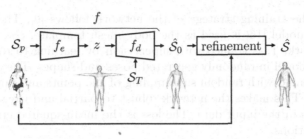

Fig. 4. Pipeline for 3D shape completion: 1) An encoder-decoder network produces a first estimate of a complete shape. 3) The estimate is refined to better fit the clothing.

The *encoder-decoder*, f, maps a partial 3D shape, $\mathcal{S}_p$, onto a completed shape, $\hat{\mathcal{S}}$. This model is based on [9]. The encoder, f_e, transforms the input partial shape into a latent representation, $z \in \mathbb{R}^{n_z}$, of the body pose and human shape. The decoder, f_d, uses this latent code to deform a template body mesh, $\mathcal{S}_T$, into the pose and shape of the input. The result is a first estimation, $\hat{\mathcal{S}}_0$, of the ground-truth complete shape, $\mathcal{S}$.

To refine the first shape estimate, $\hat{\mathcal{S}}_0$, the corresponding latent code $\hat{z}_0$ is adjusted such that the decoded shape better fits the input partial shape. This is cast as the optimisation problem

$$\hat{\mathcal{S}} = \arg\min_{z} d_{\mathrm{Chamfer}}(\mathcal{S}_p, f_d(z)). \tag{1}$$

The decoder, f_d, is taken as a black-box function. The objective function is the directed Chamfer distance [7] from the partial shape, $\mathcal{S}_p$, to the estimation, $\hat{\mathcal{S}}$. The directed Chamfer distance is important to only fit the partial shape where there is information and prevent uncontrolled deformations in holes (as reported in the experiments in Sect. 4.1). Additionally, the fitting makes use a higher-resolution shape than the one used in the encoder-decoder to fit clothing shape details more precisely.

Architecture. The encoder-decoder is parametrised by a deep neural network with 3D convolutions. The encoder, f_e, follows a PointNet [20] architecture. It takes as input the set of mesh vertices, $\mathbf{V} \in \mathbb{R}^{n_v \times 3}$, and applies successive point convolutions. A point convolution consists in a shared multi-layer perceptron (MLP) applied on the features of a set of points, to produce transformed features of a possibly different size. The feature size of the successive layers are $(3, 64, 128, 1024)$. The last layer is max-pooled across the points into a vector, z_0, of size $n_z = 1024$. This vector is then refined using two densely connected layers of size 1024 to produce the latent vector z of size n_z as well. The decoder, f_d, concatenates the latent code, z, to each vertex of the template mesh and then applies a series of point convolutions, as above. The feature size of the layers in the decoder are $(3 + 1024, 513, 256, 128, 3)$.

Training. The training strategy of the network follows [9]. The mesh of the SMPL body model [16] is used as the body mesh template, $\mathcal{S}_T$. The encoder-decoder network, f, is trained with supervision by learning to reconstruct the SMPL body model in randomly generated poses and shapes. The input training data is augmented with random subsampling of the points and random shifts in the positions. This makes the network robust to partial and irregular sampling and variations in the input data. The loss is the mean-squared error (MSE) on the point positions.

3.2   Body Texture Completion

After estimating the complete 3D shape (Sect. 3.1), a corresponding complete texture image is estimated with the following steps. First, the input partial texture is transferred onto the texture image of the estimated shape. Then, the regions to be inpainted are identified. Finally, the completion of the texture is performed by inpainting the partial texture image with specific constraints for handling the topology of the texture atlas. These steps are detailed below.

Partial Texture Transfer. The method of Sect. 3.1 estimates a complete mesh $\hat{S}$ aligned with the input partial shape $\hat{S}_p$. The partial texture T_p of the input mesh is transferred onto $\hat{S}$ by a ray-casting algorithm that propagates the texture information along the normal directions. The result is a mesh with a complete shape and a partial texture, $\hat{\mathcal{X}}_{T_p} = (\hat{S}, \hat{T}_p)$. This is illustrated by the mesh in Fig. 5a, where the regions without mapped colour are rendered in black (default background colour). These regions must be identified on the corresponding texture image prior to inpainting.

Identification of the Regions with Missing Texture. If no texture information is transferred in a particular region of the mesh $\hat{\mathcal{X}}_{T_p}$, the corresponding region in the texture image is left unmodified with the default black background colour. Thus, the black pixels inside the charts of the texture atlas indicate missing texture information. This is illustrated in Fig. 5b where the identified regions without texture are highlighted in white. A binary mask M with the same dimension as the partial texture image is derived such that $M(i,j) = 0$ if the pixel (i,j) corresponds to a missing texture information due to partial data, and $M(i,j) = 1$ otherwise. An example of the computed mask is shown in Fig. 5c. The corresponding background mask M_b is shown in Fig. 5d.

Texture Inpainting. To the transferred partial texture image $\hat{T}_p$ is associated the mask M indicating the regions with missing information. Additionally, the background mask M_b of the texture is known from the definition of the charts in the texture atlas (Sect. 2). Given this information, the problem of texture completion is turned into an image inpainting task. However, the inpainting should only occur in the foreground regions, *i.e.* on the charts of the texture

Partial texture transferred on a complete mesh.

Identified regions with missing texture (white).

Binary mask of the partial texture.

Binary background mask.

Fig. 5. Identification of missing regions on a partial texture and binary masks calculation.

atlas. Moreover, the non-informative background of the image must be explicitly ignored to prevent irrelevant background colour (*e.g.* black) to propagate onto the charts. The proposed adapted inpainting algorithm is detailed below.

Image inpainting is extensively studied in the literature [15,29–31]. While some works focus on image inpainting with regular masking shapes (*e.g.* rectangular masks) [29,30], more recent works try to address the inpainting problem in case of irregular masking shapes [15,31]. In our case, the masks of the missing texture are derived from partial 3D shapes. This makes the masks irregular and not restricted to specific shapes as it can be observed in Fig. 5c. Consequently, the selected image inpainting approach should take into account these irregularities. Accordingly, we build on the method proposed in [15] handling irregular masks. In [15], the authors use partial convolutional layers instead of conventional convolutional layers. These layers consist of mask-aware convolutions and a mask update step.

Given a binary mask M, partial convolutions extend standard convolutions to focus the computations on the information from unmasked regions (*i.e.* pixels (i, j) such that $M(i, j) = 1$) and discard the information from masked regions. With the goal of inpainting, the masks are updated after every partial convolutional operation by removing the masking (*i.e.* changing the mask value from 0 to 1) for each location that was involved in the convolution. The mask update forces the masked regions to disappear after a sufficient number of updates. More formally, let W be the weights for a specific convolution filter and b its corresponding bias. T_w are the feature values for the current sliding window and M is the corresponding binary mask. The partial convolution at at every location, similarly defined in [15], is expressed as:

$$
t_c = \begin{cases} W^T(T_w \odot M) \cdot \frac{\text{sum}(\mathbf{1})}{\text{sum}(M)} + b & \text{if sum}(M) > 0 \\ 0 & \text{otherwise} \end{cases}
\tag{2}
$$

where $\odot$ denotes element-wise multiplication, and $\mathbf{1}$ has same shape as M but with all elements being 1. After every partial convolution, a masked value in M ($M(i, j) = 0$) is updated to unmasked ($M(i, j) = 1$) if the convolution was able to condition its output on at least one valid input value. In practice this is achieved by applying fixed convolutions, with the same kernel size as the partial convolution operation, but with weights identically set to 1 and no bias.

One important observation in the two texture atlases provided in Fig. 2, is that they contain some non-informative black regions used as background to gather the body charts in a single image. The inpainting of the missing texture information (white regions in Fig. 5b) could be impacted by the non-informative background (*i.e.* black) using the original form of partial convolutions introduced in [15]. This is confirmed and visualised by experiments in Sect. 4.3. As a solution, we propose to ignore these regions during the partial convolutions as done with the masked values of the missing texture to be recovered. However, these regions should not be updated during the mask update as the background mask should stay fixed through all the partial convolution layers. This is achieved by including the *background mask* M_b of the texture image in the partial convolution as follows,

$$t_c = \begin{cases} W^T(T_w \odot M \odot M_b) \cdot \frac{\text{sum}(1)}{\text{sum}(M \odot M_b)} + b & \text{if sum}(M \odot M_b) > 0 \\ 0 & \text{otherwise} \end{cases} \quad (3)$$

The background mask M_b is passed to all partial convolutions layers without being updated by applying *do-nothing* convolution kernels with the same shape as the ones used for the masks M. A *do-nothing* kernel consists of a kernel with zeros values everywhere except for the central location which is set to 1. Moreover, before updating the original mask M we apply on it this background mask M_b by element-wise multiplication so that we guarantee that the mask M will not be updated using the background regions.

The aforementioned partial convolutional layers are employed in a UNet-like architecture [21] instead of standard convolutions. Several loss functions are used to optimise the network. Two pixel-wise reconstruction losses are defined separately on the masked and unmasked regions with a focus on masked regions. Style transfer losses are also considered by constraining the feature maps of the predictions and their auto-correlations to be close those of the ground truth [8]. Finally a Total-Variation (TV) loss [11] is employed on the masked regions to enforce their smoothness. For more details about the aforementioned inpainting method are presented in [15].

The inpainting task is facilitated by the fact that the texture atlas images to inpaint have a fixed arrangement of the charts. This is because they are all defined on the same template mesh $\mathcal{X}_T$ of used for the shape completion in Sect. 3.1. This means that semantic body regions are placed consistently on the texture images, regularising the inpainting problem.

In the experiments (Sect. 4.3), two training strategies are investigated for this inpainting method. First, the network is trained from scratch on the 3DBody-Tex.v2 dataset [25]. Second, the network, pretrained on the ImageNet dataset [5], is fine-tuned on the 3DBodyTex.v2 dataset [25].

4   Experiments

This work focuses on the completion of textured 3D human shapes using the 3DBodyTex.v2 dataset introduced in the SHARP challenge [25].

The *SHApe Recovery from Partial Textured 3D Scans* (SHARP) [25] challenge aims at advancing the research on the completion of partial textured 3D shape. Two challenges are proposed with two corresponding datasets of 3D scans: 3DBodyTex.v2, a dataset of human scans, and 3DObjectTex, a dataset of generic objects. 3DBodyTex.v2 contains about 2500 humans scans of a few hundred people in varied poses and clothing types. It is an extension of 3DBodyTex [22].

4.1   Shape Completion

Fig. 6. Results of shape completion for 6 examples of the test set. From left to right: input partial shape (white), initial shape estimate (orange), refined shape estimate (green), ground truth (white). In the input partial shapes, the visible interior surface is rendered in black. (Color figure online)

Figure 6 shows the results of the shape completion (Sect. 3.1). It can be seen that initial shape estimate (orange) captures the pose of the partial input but not the loose-fitting clothing. The refined shape (green) represents the clothing more accurately. This shows the validity of the approach in recovering clothed body shapes.

However, several limitations are observed. A topology significantly different from the template body mesh is difficulty recovered. This happens for example with hair and clenched fists. Moreover, in the example in row 1 column 3 of Fig. 6, the left foot is not recovered because it is completely cropped from the partial input. This suggests that the shape estimation can fail locally on an extremity of the body when no information is available in the partial shape. This could be improved by retraining the encoder-decoder model on a dataset of partial shapes. Furthermore, the pose of the human skeleton is not always sufficiently accurate in the first shape estimate produced by the encoder-decoder network. As a consequence, the refinement fails and the final shape estimate is not correctly aligned. This is due in part to the variety in clothing shapes for which the network has not been trained. Similarly, in row 1 column 2 of Fig. 6, the refined shape (green) does not capture the shape of the skirt realistically. This is also due to the network being trained on body shapes only. The encoder-decoder, f, could thus profit from a training or fine-tuning on a dataset of clothed shapes and also possibly from adaptations of the architecture to handle the more complex deformations of the clothing.

Fig. 7. Shape refinement with symmetric versus directed (one-way) Chamfer distance for three examples of the test set. The one-way Chamfer distance (green) is the one retained in the proposed approach. From left to right: input partial shape (white), refined shape with symmetric Chamfer distance (orange), refined shape with directed (one-way) Chamfer distance (green), ground truth (white). In the input partial shapes, the visible interior surface is rendered in black. (Color figure online)

Figure 7 illustrates the importance of the chosen objective function in the optimisation problem (1) to refine the initial shape estimate. With a symmetric Chamfer distance (from partial input to estimated shape and conversely), the shape refinement fails (orange shape in Fig. 7). With a directed Chamfer distance (from partial input to estimated shape only), the shape refinement is sound. This is due to the holes in the input partial shape. With the symmetric distance, the measure from the estimated shape to the partial input has the effect of dragging the estimated shape into regions of the partial input without holes. This creates unrealistic distortions in the estimated shape.

4.2   Texture Transfer

Figure 8 illustrates the texture transfer from the partial shape onto the refined shape estimate. Overall, the texture is mapped correctly when the shape estimate is close the partial shape. When the estimated shape is incorrect (e.g. foot in third column), the transferred texture is directly impacted.

4.3   Texture Inpainting

Visual results on the validation set for texture completion are presented in Fig. 9. The completed textures are displayed on the completed shapes obtained with the method from Sect. 4.1. The first column (a) shows the input partial texture while the last column (f) depicts the ground-truth complete texture. The intermediate columns show the inpainting results and training strategies: (b) the original inpainting model, pretrained on ImageNet; (c) the improved inpainting model

 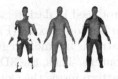

Fig. 8. Illustration of the texture transfer (right) from the partial shape (left) onto the refined shape estimate (orange, middle) for three examples of the test set. (Color figure online)

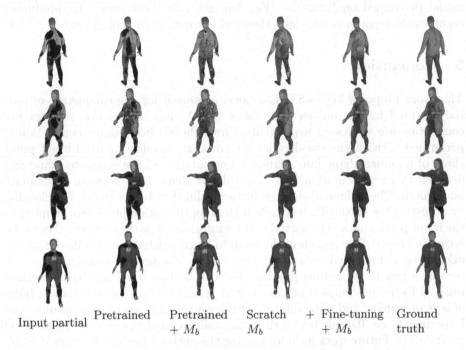

| Input partial | Pretrained | Pretrained + M_b | Scratch M_b | + Fine-tuning + M_b | Ground truth |

Fig. 9. Results for texture inpainting using different strategies.

with the proposed background masks (Sect. 3.2), pretrained on ImageNet; (d) the improved inpainting model with background masks, trained from scratch on 3DBodyTex.v2 and (e) the improved inpainting model with background masks, pretrained on ImageNet and fine-tuned on 3DBodyTex.v2.

As seen in Fig. 9b, the original inpainting model pretrained on ImageNet is able to complete some of the missing regions with colour matching the local context. However, the holes are not completed fully. This is due to the black background of a texture atlas which is used as a local context for inpainting, as explained in Sect. 3.2. With the addition of the proposed background masks to the inpainting model (Fig. 9c), the holes are fully completed. This validates the proposed approach tailored to the data at hand. However, the completed colour does not match the local context accurately and contains artefacts. For example, some holes are filled in with random colour patterns and some white patches are produced in dark regions. Training the improved inpainting model from scratch on 3DBodyTex.v2 (Fig. 9d) reduces the colour artefacts. The completed colour patterns are more regular but the colour does not follow closely the surrounding context. Thus, the 3DBodyTex.v2 dataset seems enough to regularise the colour pattern inside the clothing but not rich and varied enough for the model to learn what colour to complete with. Indeed, 3DBodyTex.v2 is relatively small (a few thousands samples) in comparison to ImageNet (millions of examples). Finally, the proposed method of fine-tuning on 3DBodyTex.v2 the improved inpainting model pretrained on ImageNet (Fig. 9e) gives the best results by producing regular colour patterns matching the local surrounding regions closely.

5   Conclusion

This work proposes 3DBooSTeR, a novel approach for the completion of partial textured human meshes. The tasks of 3D shape completion and texture completion are addressed sequentially. First, the 3D body shape completion is performed with an encoder-decoder system that encodes a partial input point cloud of a human shape into a latent representation of the complete shape and decodes this representation into a completed shape by deforming a template body mesh. The estimated shape is further refined to better match the clothing by adjusting the encoded latent code with an optimisation procedure adapted to the input partial data. The partial texture information is then projected onto the estimated shape. The regions of the mesh to be completed are identified from the 3D shapes and mapped onto the texture image. The texture completion is then seen as a texture inpainting problem. For this task, a novel inpainting method tailored to texture maps is proposed. It is specifically designed to handle holes of irregular shape and to be robust to irrelevant background image information. Experiments on 3DBodyTex.v2 show the validity of the proposed approach on partial data. Future work includes making the encoder-decoder network capture the clothing shape better, by training on a dataset of clothing shape and/or adapting the architecture. The texture transfer could be made more robust to bad shape estimates by enforcing a continuity in the mapping from partial shape to estimated shape. Overall, the pipeline might profit from a coupling between the shape and texture completion, for example in an end-to-end neural network architecture. This involves at least designing differentiable alternatives to the two intermediate manual steps of shape refinement and texture transfer.

Acknowledgements. This work was supported by the Luxembourg National Research Fund (FNR), projects BODYFIT (11806282) and IDFORM (11643091), and Artec3D.

References

1. Anguelov, D., Srinivasan, P., Koller, D., Thrun, S., Rodgers, J., Davis, J.: Scape: shape completion and animation of people. In: ACM SIGGRAPH 2005 Papers, pp. 408–416 (2005)
2. Chibane, J., Alldieck, T., Pons-Moll, G.: Implicit functions in feature space for 3D shape reconstruction and completion. In: Proceedings of the IEEE/CVF Conference on Computer Vision and Pattern Recognition, pp. 6970–6981 (2020)
3. Dai, A., Ruizhongtai Qi, C., Nießner, M.: Shape completion using 3D-encoder-predictor CNNs and shape synthesis. In: Proceedings of the IEEE Conference on Computer Vision and Pattern Recognition, pp. 5868–5877 (2017)
4. Davis, J., Marschner, S.R., Garr, M., Levoy, M.: Filling holes in complex surfaces using volumetric diffusion. In: Proceedings. First International Symposium on 3D Data Processing Visualization and Transmission, pp. 428–441. IEEE (2002)
5. Deng, J., Dong, W., Socher, R., Li, L.J., Li, K., Fei-Fei, L.: Imagenet: a large-scale hierarchical image database. In: 2009 IEEE Conference on Computer Vision and Pattern Recognition, pp. 248–255. IEEE (2009)
6. Deng, J., Cheng, S., Xue, N., Zhou, Y., Zafeiriou, S.: UV-GAN: adversarial facial UV map completion for pose-invariant face recognition. In: Proceedings of the IEEE Conference on Computer Vision and Pattern Recognition, pp. 7093–7102 (2018)
7. Fan, H., Su, H., Guibas, L.J.: A point set generation network for 3D object reconstruction from a single image. In: Proceedings of the IEEE Conference on Computer Vision and Pattern Recognition, pp. 605–613 (2017)
8. Gatys, L.A., Ecker, A.S., Bethge, M.: A neural algorithm of artistic style. arXiv preprint arXiv:1508.06576 (2015)
9. Groueix, T., Fisher, M., Kim, V.G., Russell, B.C., Aubry, M.: 3D-coded: 3D correspondences by deep deformation. In: Proceedings of the European Conference on Computer Vision (ECCV), pp. 230–246 (2018)
10. Han, X., Li, Z., Huang, H., Kalogerakis, E., Yu, Y.: High-resolution shape completion using deep neural networks for global structure and local geometry inference. In: Proceedings of the IEEE International Conference on Computer Vision, pp. 85–93 (2017)
11. Johnson, J., Alahi, A., Fei-Fei, L.: Perceptual losses for real-time style transfer and super-resolution. In: Leibe, B., Matas, J., Sebe, N., Welling, M. (eds.) ECCV 2016. LNCS, vol. 9906, pp. 694–711. Springer, Cham (2016). https://doi.org/10.1007/978-3-319-46475-6_43
12. Lévy, B., Petitjean, S., Ray, N., Maillot, J.: Least squares conformal maps for automatic texture atlas generation. ACM Trans. Graph. (TOG) **21**(3), 362–371 (2002)
13. Li, C.L., Simon, T., Saragih, J., Póczos, B., Sheikh, Y.: LBS autoencoder: self-supervised fitting of articulated meshes to point clouds. In: Proceedings of the IEEE Conference on Computer Vision and Pattern Recognition, pp. 11967–11976 (2019)
14. Litany, O., Bronstein, A., Bronstein, M., Makadia, A.: Deformable shape completion with graph convolutional autoencoders. In: Proceedings of the IEEE Conference on Computer Vision and Pattern Recognition, pp. 1886–1895 (2018)
15. Liu, G., Reda, F.A., Shih, K.J., Wang, T.C., Tao, A., Catanzaro, B.: Image inpainting for irregular holes using partial convolutions. In: The European Conference on Computer Vision (ECCV) (2018)

16. Loper, M., Mahmood, N., Romero, J., Pons-Moll, G., Black, M.J.: SMPL: a skinned multi-person linear model. ACM Trans. Graph. (TOG) **34**(6), 1–16 (2015)

17. Lorensen, W.E., Cline, H.E.: Marching cubes: a high resolution 3D surface construction algorithm. ACM Siggraph Comput. Graph. **21**(4), 163–169 (1987)

18. Ma, Q., et al.: Learning to dress 3D people in generative clothing. In: Proceedings of the IEEE/CVF Conference on Computer Vision and Pattern Recognition, pp. 6469–6478 (2020)

19. Pavlakos, G., et al.: Expressive body capture: 3D hands, face, and body from a single image. In: Proceedings IEEE Conference on Computer Vision and Pattern Recognition (CVPR) (2019)

20. Qi, C.R., Su, H., Mo, K., Guibas, L.J.: Pointnet: deep learning on point sets for 3D classification and segmentation. In: Proceedings of the IEEE Conference on Computer Vision and Pattern Recognition, pp. 652–660 (2017)

21. Ronneberger, O., Fischer, P., Brox, T.: U-Net: convolutional networks for biomedical image segmentation. In: Navab, N., Hornegger, J., Wells, W.M., Frangi, A.F. (eds.) MICCAI 2015. LNCS, vol. 9351, pp. 234–241. Springer, Cham (2015). https://doi.org/10.1007/978-3-319-24574-4_28

22. Saint, A., Ahmed, E., Cherenkova, K., Gusev, G., Aouada, D., Ottersten, B., et al.: 3dbodytex: textured 3D body dataset. In: 2018 International Conference on 3D Vision (3DV), pp. 495–504. IEEE (2018)

23. Saint, A., Cherenkova, K., Gusev, G., Aouada, D., Ottersten, B., et al.: Bodyfitr: robust automatic 3D human body fitting. In: 2019 IEEE International Conference on Image Processing (ICIP), pp. 484–488. IEEE (2019)

24. Saint, A., Shabayek, A.E.R., Aouada, D., Ottersten, B., Cherenkova, K., Gusev, G.: Towards automatic human body model fitting to a 3D scan. In: Proceedings of 3DBODY. TECH 2017–8th International Conference and Exhibition on 3D Body Scanning and Processing Technologies, Montreal QC, Canada, 11–12 October 2017, pp. 274–280. Hometrica Consulting (2017)

25. SHARP team: SHARP Challenge ECCV 2020 (2020). http://gitlab.uni.lu/cvi2/eccv2020-sharp-workshop. Accessed 02 Aug 2020

26. Szeliski, R., Lavallée, S.: Matching 3-D anatomical surfaces with non-rigid deformations using octree-splines. Int. J. Comput. Vision **18**(2), 171–186 (1996)

27. Verma, N., Boyer, E., Verbeek, J.: Feastnet: feature-steered graph convolutions for 3D shape analysis. In: Proceedings of the IEEE Conference on Computer Vision and Pattern Recognition, pp. 2598–2606 (2018)

28. Wu, Z., et al.: 3D shapenets: a deep representation for volumetric shapes. In: Proceedings of the IEEE Conference on Computer Vision and Pattern Recognition, pp. 1912–1920 (2015)

29. Yeh, R.A., Chen, C., Yian Lim, T., Schwing, A.G., Hasegawa-Johnson, M., Do, M.N.: Semantic image inpainting with deep generative models. In: Proceedings of the IEEE Conference on Computer Vision and Pattern Recognition, pp. 5485–5493 (2017)

30. Yu, J., Lin, Z., Yang, J., Shen, X., Lu, X., Huang, T.S.: Generative image inpainting with contextual attention. In: Proceedings of the IEEE Conference on Computer Vision and Pattern Recognition, pp. 5505–5514 (2018)

31. Yu, J., Lin, Z., Yang, J., Shen, X., Lu, X., Huang, T.S.: Free-form image inpainting with gated convolution. In: Proceedings of the IEEE International Conference on Computer Vision, pp. 4471–4480 (2019)

SHARP 2020: The 1st Shape Recovery from Partial Textured 3D Scans Challenge Results

Alexandre Saint[1]([✉]), Anis Kacem[1], Kseniya Cherenkova[1,2],
Konstantinos Papadopoulos[1], Julian Chibane[3], Gerard Pons-Moll[3],
Gleb Gusev[2], David Fofi[4], Djamila Aouada[1], and Björn Ottersten[1]

[1] SnT, University of Luxembourg, Luxembourg City, Luxembourg
{alexandre.saint,anis.kacem,konstantinos.papadopoulos,
djamila.aouada,bjorn.ottersten}@uni.lu, kseniya.cherenkova@ext.uni.lu
[2] Artec 3D, Luxembourg City, Luxembourg
{kcherenkova,gleb}@artec-group.com
[3] Max Planck Institute for Informatics, Saarbrücken, Germany
{jchibane,gpons}@mpi-inf.mpg.de
[4] University of Burgundy, Dijon, France
david.fofi@u-bourgogne.fr

Abstract. The *SHApe Recovery from Partial textured 3D scans* challenge, SHARP 2020, is the first edition of a challenge fostering and benchmarking methods for recovering complete textured 3D scans from raw incomplete data. SHARP 2020 is organised as a workshop in conjunction with ECCV 2020. There are two complementary challenges, the first one on 3D human scans, and the second one on generic objects. Challenge 1 is further split into two tracks, focusing, first, on large body and clothing regions, and, second, on fine body details. A novel evaluation metric is proposed to quantify jointly the shape reconstruction, the texture reconstruction and the amount of completed data. Additionally, two unique datasets of 3D scans are proposed, to provide raw ground-truth data for the benchmarks. The datasets are released to the scientific community. Moreover, an accompanying custom library of software routines is also released to the scientific community. It allows for processing 3D scans, generating partial data and performing the evaluation. Results of the competition, analysed in comparison to baselines, show the validity of the proposed evaluation metrics, and highlight the challenging aspects of the task and of the datasets. Details on the SHARP 2020 challenge can be found at https://cvi2.uni.lu/sharp2020/.

1 Introduction

Representing the physical world in 3D, including shape and colour, is key for industrial and research purposes [1,3,4,7,10,11,16,17]. It includes, for example, areas from virtual reality to heritage conservation, or from medical treatment to fitness, entertainment and fashion. 3D scanning allows to digitise the physical

© Springer Nature Switzerland AG 2020
A. Bartoli and A. Fusiello (Eds.): ECCV 2020 Workshops, LNCS 12536, pp. 741–755, 2020.
https://doi.org/10.1007/978-3-030-66096-3_50

world, *e.g.* objects and humans. Acquired 3D scans vary in quality depending on the scanning system used, the properties of the target and the environment. For example, a high-end photogrammetric scanning system with a fixed camera array might capture high-quality data at a high frame rate but might be bulky, have a fixed structure, suffer from occlusion and limited in scanning volume. Other high-end systems such as hand-held devices might produce accurate results, while easily transported and easily oriented to limit occlusion, but cannot handle movable targets and are time-consuming. On the other hand, low-end scanning systems might be flexible and easy to manipulate but produce low-quality scans. Limiting factors due to the target or the environment include varying levels of details (*e.g.* finer anatomical parts), occlusion, non-rigidity, movement, and optical properties (*e.g.* fabric, material, hair and reflection). Moreover, for time-consuming acquisition systems or moving targets, it might be desirable or only possible to capture partial data. In this work, defective and/or partial acquisitions, are both viewed as data with missing information that must be completed.

The SHARP 2020 challenge for *SHApe Recovery from Partial textured 3D scans* is proposed to foster research and provide a benchmark on 3D shape and texture completion from partial 3D scan data. First, two new unique datasets of 3D textured scans are proposed to serve as reference data. These datasets contain thousands of scans of humans and generic objects with varied identities, clothing, colours, shapes and categories. One challenge is proposed per dataset, challenge 1 focusing on human scans and challenge 2 on object scans. Second, partial scans are generated synthetically, but randomly, to simulate a general pattern of partial data acquisition while still having access to ground truth data. Third, specific evaluation metrics are proposed to quantitatively measure the quality of the shape and texture reconstructions, and the amount of completed data. Fourth, reusable software libraries developed for the challenge are also made available. These contain routines to process 3D scans, to generate partial data, and to evaluate and analyse the submissions on the proposed benchmark. This paper summaries the SHARP challenge with a presentation of the proposed datasets, benchmark and evaluation method, as well as the results of the submitted methods and an analysis of the results. SHARP 2020 is the first edition of the challenge, held in conjunction with the 16th European Conference on Computer Vision (ECCV).

In the following, Sect. 2 describes the challenge and the proposed datasets. Section 3 describes the proposed evaluation protocol and, in Sect. 4, an extensive analysis on the results is presented. To conclude, the results and outcomes of the challenge are discussed in Sect. 5.

2   Challenges and Datasets

The SHARP challenge is split into two separate challenges: challenge 1 focuses on human scans, and challenge 2 focuses on generic object scans. Two corresponding datasets are introduced, 3DBodyTex.v2 for human scans, and 3DObjectTex for generic object scans. Table 1 describes the datasets with figures on the number of samples for different subsets, including the splits used in the challenges and categories of body pose and clothing type for 3DBodyTex.v2.

3DBodyTex.v2 is an extension of 3DBodyTex proposed by Saint et al. [12]. See sample scans in Fig. 1. It contains about 3000 static 3D human scans with high-resolution texture. It features a large variety of poses and clothing types, with about 500 different subjects. Each subject is captured in about 3 poses. Most subjects perform the corresponding poses in both standard close-fitting clothing and arbitrary casual clothing. The faces are anonymised, for privacy reasons, by blurring the shape and the texture.

3DObjectTex is a subset of the *viewshape* [2] repository. See sample scans in Fig. 2. It consists of about 1200 textured 3D scans of generic objects with a large variation in categories and in physical dimensions.

Both datasets encode the scans as 3D triangle meshes. The colour is encoded in a texture atlas with an independent and arbitrary UV mapping [18] for each mesh.

Table 1. Contents of the datasets and categorical subsets, along with associated challenge and track. The *standard poses* are the *A* and *U* rest poses. The *other poses* are varied, from a predefined list or arbitrary. The *casual* and *fitness* clothing types are shown in Fig. 1.

Dataset	Subset		Samples				Challenge	Track
			Train	Val	Test	Total		
	Full		2094	454	451	2999	1	1
3DBodyTex.v2	Clothing	Fitness	844	178	182	1204	1	2
		Casual	1250	276	269	1795	–	–
	Poses	Standard	977	219	224	1420	–	–
		Other	1117	235	227	1579	–	–
3DObjectTex	–		799	205	205	1209	2	–

2.1 Challenge 1: Recovery of Human Body Scans

Challenge 1 covers the reconstruction of human scans, both with loose casual clothing and minimal close-fitting clothing.

Track 1: Recovery of Large Regions. Track 1 focuses on the reconstruction of large regions of human scans, excluding hands and head. Figure 1 shows samples of the data, with ground-truth and partial scans. Both shape and texture are considered. These large regions are of relatively high quality in the raw reference data. The fine details (hands and head) are of unreliable quality and thus ignored in this track. The full 3DBodyTex.v2 dataset is used (see Table 1).

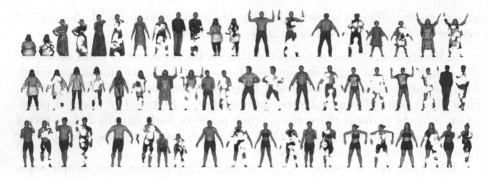

Fig. 1. Samples of 3DBodyTex.v2 in casual (top rows) and fitness (bottom row) clothing. For each person, ground truth scan (left), sample synthetic partial scan (right).

Track 2: Recovery of Fine Details. Track 2 focuses on fine body details not considered in Track 1, *i.e.*, hands, fingers, and nose. The raw scans are not of reliable quality for these details and the faces are not released due to privacy concerns. Thus, the reference data is generated synthetically from a body model [9] and the scans of 3DBodyTex.v2 in *fitness* clothing (see Table 1), where the fine body details are not occluded, to capture to the real distribution of rough poses and shapes. The reference data is generated in two steps: (1) fit a parametric body model to the scans to obtain the ground-truth data; (2) simulate the scanning process in software to obtain a synthetic scan (with simulated artefacts in the regions of interest, *i.e.* hands, ears...) from which the partial data is generated. The fitting is performed with the approach of Saint et al. [12,13,15]. The texture is not considered in this setting as the raw data does not contain texture of reliable quality (and the parametric body model represents only the shape).

2.2   Challenge 2: Recovery of Generic Object Scans

Challenge 2 focuses on the shape and texture completion of generic objects. Figure 2 shows some example objects.

2.3   Partial Data

In all challenges, the partial data is generated synthetically by removing surface regions randomly, as shown in Fig. 1 and Fig. 2. This is done with a hole cutting operation following the steps below:

(1) take as input a central vertex v_c and the number of vertices to remove k;
(2) select the k vertices closest to v_c in Euclidean distance;
(3) remove the selected vertices and adjacent triangles from the mesh.

Fig. 2. Samples of the 3DObjectTex dataset (normalised in scale for visualisation). The objects vary widely in scale and categories. For each object, ground-truth scan (left), sample synthetic partial scan (right).

The process is repeated 40 times, with k set to 2% of the points of the mesh. Most meshes in the datasets being regularly sampled, this is equivalent to defining a nearest-neighbour radius proportional to the size of the mesh. For challenge 1, the partial data is generated only in the considered regions (everywhere except hands and head for Track 1, and only on the hands, ear and nose in Track 2). The partial data is generated by the participants themselves. Additional methods for partial data generation were allowed if reported. Routines to generate the partial data were distributed in the provided software library.

2.4   Evaluation Data

For evaluation, the partial data was generated by the organisers and shared with the participants. The reference data was held secret.

3   Evaluation Metrics and Scores

Entries to the challenge were ranked with an overall score, S, that considers jointly the quality of the shape and texture reconstructions, and the amount of completeness. It is based on the metrics proposed by Jensen et al. [8], with modifications and extensions for the task of shape and texture completion. The main terms in computing the scores are a surface-to-surface distance accounting for missing data in determining correspondences, a measure of the texture distance (on top of the shape distance), surface area and hit-rate measures reflecting the degree of completion, and a mapping function to convert distances to scores, empirically adjusted from baseline data. Below, the ground-truth mesh is denoted, Y, and the estimated reconstruction, X.

Overall Score. A single reconstruction is scored with,

$$S = S_\alpha \frac{S_s + S_t}{2} \in [0,1], \tag{1}$$

where S_a, S_s and S_t are independent scores for the surface area, shape and texture, respectively. All scores take as input the reconstructed and the ground-truth meshes, $S = S(X, Y)$, and map to the interval $[0, 1]$. A perfect reconstruction has a score of 1 and a poor reconstruction has a score tending towards 0. A submission to the challenge contains reconstructions for all the samples of the test set. The submission is ranked by averaging the individual scores into a final global score.

Surface Area Score. The surface area score,

$$S_\alpha = 1 - |\bar{A}_X - \bar{A}_Y| \in [0, 1], \tag{2}$$

penalises a reconstruction proportionally to the deviation of its surface area with respect to the ground truth. $\bar{A}_X = \frac{A_X}{A_X + A_Y}$ is the normalised surface area of X with respect to Y. With a surface area lower or greater than the ground truth, S_a decreases proportionally the overall score (1). As the surface area approaches the ground truth, S_a approaches 1, less affecting the overall score. The surface area of a mesh is computed in practice by adding the surface areas of all the individual triangles.

Surface-to-Surface Distance. Both shape and texture scores, S_s and S_t, are determined by estimating the directed distances, d^{XY} and d^{YX}, between the ground truth mesh Y and the estimated reconstruction X.

The directed distance between mesh A and mesh B, d^{AB}, is computed by sampling N points uniformly on the surface of A, finding the corresponding closest points on the surface of B, and averaging the associated distances.

For a point $p^A \in \mathbb{R}^3$ on A, the corresponding closest point on B is determined by computing the smallest point-to-triangle distance between p^A and all triangles of B. The point-to-triangle distance, $d = d_0 + d_1$, is made of two components. For a specific triangle in B, d_0 is the Euclidean distance from p^A to the closest point p_0 on the plane of the triangle. d_1 is then the Euclidean distance from p_0 to the nearest point p_1 of the triangle (in the plane of the triangle). If the intersection p_0 is inside the triangle, it is denoted as a *hit*, otherwise it is a *miss*. In case of a hit, $p_0 = p_1$, thus $d_1 = 0$ and $d = d_0$.

Hit Rate. When computing the surface-to-surface distance from mesh A to mesh B, the hit rate,

$$h^{AB} = \frac{H^{AB}}{N} \in [0, 1], \tag{3}$$

is the proportion of the N points sampled on A *hitting* B (see previous paragraph).

Shape Score. The shape score,

$$S_s = \frac{S_s^{XY} + S_s^{YX}}{2} = \frac{h^{XY}\phi_s(d_s^{XY}) + h^{YX}\phi_s(d_s^{YX})}{2} \tag{4}$$

is a measure of the similarity of the shape of two meshes. The measure is symmetric by averaging the directed measures. The hit rates, h^{XY} and h^{YX}, penalise overcomplete and incomplete reconstructions, respectively. In the directed shape score,

$$S_s^{XY} = h^{XY} \phi_s(d_s^{XY}), \tag{5}$$

the mapping function $\phi_s : [0, \infty] \mapsto [0, 1]$ converts the computed distance to a score in $[0, 1]$. It is defined by a normal distribution function with zero mean,

$$\phi_s(d) = \frac{1}{\sigma_s \sqrt{2\pi}} e^{-\frac{1}{2}\left(\frac{d}{\sigma_s}\right)^2}, \tag{6}$$

where the standard deviation σ_s is estimated from baselines, including the ground-truth data, the input partial data, additional perturbations thereof with local and/or global white Gaussian noise on the shape, and a baseline of shape reconstruction based on a hole-filling algorithm.

Texture Score. The texture score,

$$S_t = \frac{S_t^{XY} + S_t^{YX}}{2} = \frac{h^{XY} \phi_t(d_t^{XY}) + h^{YX} \phi_t(d_t^{YX})}{2} \tag{7}$$

is similar in principle to the shape score, S_s, except that the distance d_t is computed in texture space for all point correspondences obtained by the surface-to-surface distance. Additionally, the parameter σ_t for the mapping function ϕ_t specific to the texture is estimated from the ground-truth data, the input partial data, and additional perturbations with local and/or global white Gaussian noise, in both shape and texture. Below, the texture score is also interchangeably denoted colour score.

4   Results and Analysis

This section presents and analyses the submissions to both challenges. The challenge has attracted 32 participants with 9 validated registrations for Challenge 1 and 6 for Challenge 2. Table 2 gives the number of valid submissions, received and accepted, and the number of submitted solutions.

Table 2. Figures on validated registrations and entries for the challenges of SHARP 2020.

Challenge	Track	Registrations	Submissions/Participants	
			Received	Accepted
1	1	9	4/3	3/2
1	2	9	2/2	2/2
2	–	6	4/1	4/1

The accepted entries are *Implicit Feature Networks for Texture Completion of 3D Data* [5,6], from RVH (Real Virtual Humans group at Max Planck Institute for Informatics), submitted in several variants to both Challenge 1 and Challenge 2, and *3DBooSTeR: 3D Body Shape and Texture Recovery* [14], from SnT (Interdisciplinary Centre for Security, Reliability and Trust at the University of Luxembourg), submitted to Challenge 1. In the following, the entries are interchangeably abbreviated RVH-IF and SnT-3DB, respectively. Table 3 shows the quantitative results of the submissions for both challenges. The scores are reported in percent in an equivalent way to the scores mapping to [0, 1] in Sect. 3. The methods are compared to a baseline consisting of the unmodified partial data (UPD). The rest of this section presents and analyses the results.

Table 3. Reconstruction scores (%) of the proposed methods for both challenges. UPD: unmodified partial data (baseline).

Challenge	Track	Method	Score (%)		
			Shape	Texture	Overall
1	1	UPD	38.95 ± 4.67	40.29 ± 4.24	39.62 ± 4.41
		SnT-3DB	54.21 ± 14.28	70.55 ± 7.26	62.38 ± 9.61
		RVH-IF-1	85.24 ± 5.72	87.69 ± 5.96	86.47 ± 5.38
		RVH-IF-2	**85.24 ± 5.72**	**88.26 ± 5.46**	**86.75 ± 5.19**
1	2	UPD	41.1 ± 3.31	–	–
		SnT-3DB	60.7 ± 10.98	–	–
		RVH-IF	**83.0 ± 4.87**	–	–
2	–	UPD	42.09 ± 4.99	41.64 ± 5.24	41.87 ± 4.74
		RVH-IF-1	72.68 ± 23.47	76.44 ± 14.33	74.56 ± 16.89
		RVH-IF-2	**73.91 ± 22.85**	**76.93 ± 14.31**	**75.42 ± 16.68**
		RVH-IF-3	72.68 ± 23.47	53.13 ± 18.21	62.91 ± 16.09
		RVH-IF-4	73.91 ± 22.85	53.73 ± 18.33	63.82 ± 16.01

4.1 Challenge 1 - Track 1

In challenge 1, track 1, the RVH-IF [5,6] approach ranks first with an overall reconstruction score of 86.75% (see Table 3). SnT-3DB comes second with 62%. RVH-IF surpasses the baseline unmodified partial data with an overall score of 46% higher and performs significantly better than SnT-3DB [14] with a score increment of 24%. RVH-IF-2 has similar shape and texture scores with differences of 2-3%, while SnT-3DB has a much higher texture score, 16% above the shape score. The RVH-IF-2 variant slightly improves the texture score over RVH-IF-1, with 88.26% instead of 87.69%, but the shape scores are identical.

Figure 3 shows the frequency distribution of the scores. RVH-IF appears relatively tightly located around the mean score 85% with a slight tail expanding

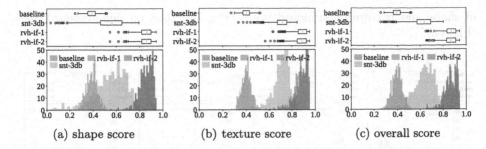

(a) shape score   (b) texture score   (c) overall score

Fig. 3. Challenge 1 - track 1: Boxplots and frequency distributions of the reconstruction scores of the samples of the test set, for the baseline unmodified partial data, and all submissions, SnT-3DB and RVH-IF-{1,2}.

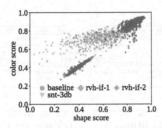

Fig. 4. Challenge 1 - track 1: Correlation between shape and texture scores, for the baseline unmodified partial data, and all submissions, SnT-3DB and RVH-IF-{1,2}.

in the lower scores down to 60%. SnT-3DB appears more spread for the shape score and with a tail reaching very low scores down to 10% below the baseline.

Figure 4 highlights the correlation of the shape and texture scores. The baseline unmodified partial data is highly correlated, which is expected because the partial data available is exact. RVH-IF methods display a high correlation, with overall a tendency towards better texture scores than shape scores, except for a small proportion of grouped outlier samples with higher shape and lower texture scores. The SnT-3DB method displays the same tendency towards better texture than shape but with more dispersed results. Not a significant group of outliers is observed. The weaker correlation in SnT-3DB could be due to at least two factors: the sequential nature of the method, making the shape and texture reconstructions somewhat independent of each other; the mostly uniform colour of most clothing and of the body shape, resulting in good texture recovery even if the spatial regions are not matched correctly.

Figure 5 and 6 show the distribution of scores and the correlation between shape and texture scores for subsets of the 3DBodyTex.v2 dataset. The casual clothing subset (Fig. 5a) shows lower and more dispersed scores than the fitness clothing (Fig. 5b). This reflects the diversity in texture and shape in the casual clothing, which is challenging for all proposed methods. Moreover, to a small but noticeable extent, the reconstruction scores are higher and more correlated in shape and texture on standard poses (Fig. 6d) than on non-standard ones (Fig. 6c).

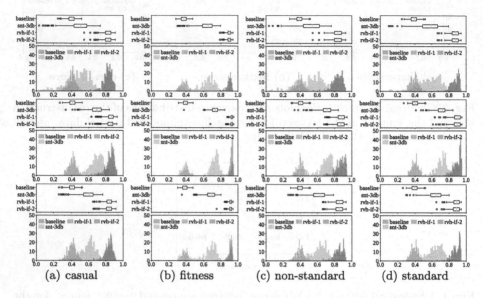

(a) casual   (b) fitness   (c) non-standard   (d) standard

Fig. 5. Challenge 1 - track 1: Boxplots and frequency distributions of the shape (top), texture (middle) and overall (bottom) scores on the test set, for subsets of 3DBody-Tex.v2, and for the baseline unmodified partial data and all submissions, SnT-3DB and RVH-IF-{1,2}. Subsets (columns): casual and fitness clothing, non-standard and standard (A and U) poses.

As a qualitative assessment, the best and worst reconstructions are shown in Fig. 7 for both approaches SnT-3DB and the RVH-IF. The best reconstructions are for scans in fitness clothing and standard pose, as also observed quantitatively above. The worst reconstructions are for scans in casual clothing and non-standard sitting/crouching poses, containing more shape and texture variation. It could also be that the ground truth for this data is less reliable, biasing the results towards lower scores.

4.2   Challenge 1 - Track 2

Challenge 1 - Track 2 targets the reconstruction of fine details on the hands, ears and nose, with only a shape ground truth. The only score evaluated is thus the shape score. As in Track 1, and as visible in Fig. 8, RVH-IF is the highest-performing approach with a score of 83% compared to 60.7% for SnT-3DB and 41.1% for the baseline. The distribution of scores is also more concentrated around higher values for RVH-IF.

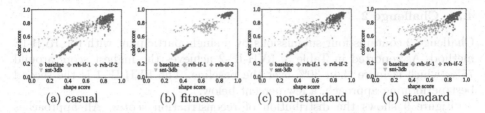

| (a) casual | (b) fitness | (c) non-standard | (d) standard |

Fig. 6. Challenge 1 - track 1: Correlation of shape and texture scores on the test set, for subsets of 3DBodyTex.v2, and for the baseline unmodified partial data and all submissions, SnT-3DB and RVH-IF-{1,2}. Subsets (columns): casual and fitness clothing, non-standard and standard (A and U) poses.

SnT-3DB RVH-IF-1   SnT-3DB RVH-IF-1

best   worst

Fig. 7. Challenge 1 - track 1: Best and worst reconstructions for submissions SnT-3DB and RVH-IF-1. From top to bottom: partial scan, reconstruction, ground truth.

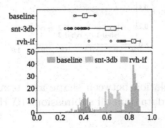

Fig. 8. Challenge 1 - track 2: Boxplots and frequency distributions of shape scores on the test set, for the baseline unmodified partial data and all submissions, SnT-3DB and RVH-IF.

4.3   Challenge 2

Challenge 2 contains four submissions by a single participant with the RVH-IF method. As reported in Table 3, RVH-IF-2 achieves the highest score around 75%, which is more than 30% over the baseline. The RVH-IF-1 is the second best-performing approach, a few percent below.

Figure 9 shows the distribution of reconstruction scores. All approaches achieve high shape scores. For the texture, RVH-IF-{3,4} perform less well and overlap the baseline, not improving much on the unmodified partial data. Overall, the scores are widely spread, even for the baseline. This reflects the diversity of object classes in 3DObjectTex, making both the reconstruction and the evaluation tasks challenging. This is confirmed in the shape-texture correlation in Fig. 10 where the correlation is less than in Challenge 1.

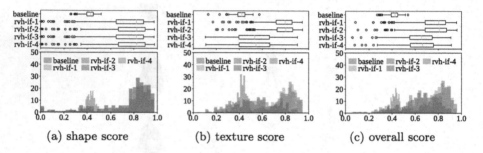

(a) shape score   (b) texture score   (c) overall score

Fig. 9. Challenge 2: Boxplots and frequency distributions of scores on the test set for the baseline unmodified partial data, and all submissions RVH-IF-{1,4}.

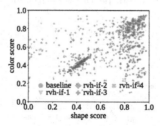

Fig. 10. Challenge 2: Correlation between shape and texture on the test set, for the baseline unmodified partial data, and all submissions RVH-IF-{1,4}.

As Fig. 11 shows, the best reconstructions are of meshes with a closed surface, and with both a smooth shape and a relatively uniform texture. The worst reconstructions are of meshes with complex shapes, *i.e.* non-convex and with holes, creases, sharp edges, steps, etc.

RVH-IF-1	RVH-IF-2	RVH-IF-3	RVH-IF-4	RVH-IF-1	RVH-IF-2	RVH-IF-3	RVH-IF-4
		best				worst	

Fig. 11. Challenge 2: Best and worst reconstruction results for all submissions (RVH-IF-{1,4}). From top to bottom: partial scan, reconstruction, ground truth.

5   Conclusion

This paper presented the SHARP 2020 challenge for *SHApe Recovery from Partial textured 3D scans* held in its first edition in conjunction with the 16th European Conference on Computer Vision. The SHARP challenge proposes to foster research and provide a benchmark on 3D shape and texture completion from partial 3D scan data. With two aspects, the recovery of human scans and of object scans, two unique datasets of reference high-quality textured 3D scans were proposed and released to the scientific community. Moreover, new specific evaluation metrics were proposed to measure simultaneously the quality of shape and texture reconstruction, and the amount of completion. The results of the participants show the validity of the proposed metrics, the challenging nature of the datasets and highlight the difficulties of the task. The RVH-IF submission obtained the highest scores in both challenges with the *Implicit Feature Networks for Texture Completion of 3D Data*. The variation in clothing seems a major difficulty in Challenge 1, and to a lesser extent, the pose. The texture seems more easily reconstructed than the shape, probably due to it being mostly uniform on clothing. The reconstruction of fine details was more demanding than the reconstruction of the full body. Challenge 2 shows that the proposed dataset of generic objects contains a lot of variation that makes both the shape and the texture challenging to recover. As in Challenge 1, smooth objects were better reconstructed.

The SHARP 2020 challenge has thus promoted the development of new methods for 3D shape and texture completion. The addition of the texture aspect on top of the shape aspect makes the contributions stand out from the current scientific literature. As the proposed metrics show, there is still room for improvement. This will be the object of the next editions of SHARP challenges.

Acknowledgements. We thank Artec3D for sponsoring this challenge with cash prizes and releasing the data for the 3DObjectTex dataset. This work and the data collection of 3D human scans for 3DBodyTex.v2 were partly supported by the Luxembourg National Research Fund (FNR) (11806282 and 11643091). We also gratefully acknowledge the participation, at different times, of all members of the Computer Vision, Imaging and Machine Intelligence (CVI^2) Research Group at the SnT, University of Luxembourg, including the moderation of the workshop event by Renato Baptista and the support of Pavel Chernakov in the development of the evaluation software. Finally, we express our appreciation to all the reviewers of the workshop submissions.

References

1. Anguelov, D., Srinivasan, P., Koller, D., Thrun, S., Rodgers, J., Davis, J.: Scape: shape completion and animation of people. In: ACM SIGGRAPH 2005 Papers, pp. 408–416 (2005)
2. Artec3D: viewshape: online repository of 3D scans (2020). https://viewshape.com/. Accessed 10 Sept 2020
3. Bogo, F., Romero, J., Loper, M., Black, M.J.: Faust: dataset and evaluation for 3D mesh registration. In: Proceedings of the IEEE Conference on Computer Vision and Pattern Recognition, pp. 3794–3801 (2014)
4. Bronstein, A.M., Bronstein, M.M., Kimmel, R.: Numerical Geometry of Non-Rigid Shapes. MCS. Springer, New York (2009). https://doi.org/10.1007/978-0-387-73301-2
5. Chibane, J., Alldieck, T., Pons-Moll, G.: Implicit feature networks for texture completion of 3D data. In: SHARP Workshop, ECCV (2020)
6. Chibane, J., Alldieck, T., Pons-Moll, G.: Implicit functions in feature space for 3D shape reconstruction and completion. In: Proceedings of the IEEE/CVF Conference on Computer Vision and Pattern Recognition, pp. 6970–6981 (2020)
7. Hasler, N., Stoll, C., Sunkel, M., Rosenhahn, B., Seidel, H.P.: A statistical model of human pose and body shape. In: Computer Graphics Forum, vol. 28, pp. 337–346. Wiley Online Library (2009)
8. Jensen, R., Dahl, A., Vogiatzis, G., Tola, E., Aanæs, H.: Large scale multi-view stereopsis evaluation. In: Proceedings of the IEEE Conference on Computer Vision and Pattern Recognition, pp. 406–413 (2014)
9. Pavlakos, G., et al.: Expressive body capture: 3D hands, face, and body from a single image. In: Proceedings of the IEEE Conference on Computer Vision and Pattern Recognition, pp. 10975–10985 (2019)
10. Pishchulin, L., Wuhrer, S., Helten, T., Theobalt, C., Schiele, B.: Building statistical shape spaces for 3D human modeling. Pattern Recogn. **67**, 276–286 (2017)
11. Robinette, K.M., Daanen, H., Paquet, E.: The caesar project: a 3-D surface anthropometry survey. In: Second International Conference on 3-D Digital Imaging and Modeling (Cat. No. PR00062), pp. 380–386. IEEE (1999)
12. Saint, A., Ahmed, E., Cherenkova, K., Gusev, G., Aouada, D., Ottersten, B., et al.: 3dbodytex: textured 3D body dataset. In: 2018 International Conference on 3D Vision (3DV), pp. 495–504. IEEE (2018)
13. Saint, A., Cherenkova, K., Gusev, G., Aouada, D., Ottersten, B., et al.: Bodyfitr: robust automatic 3D human body fitting. In: 2019 IEEE International Conference on Image Processing (ICIP), pp. 484–488. IEEE (2019)

14. Saint, A., Kacem, A., Cherenkova, K., Aouada, D.: 3dbooster: 3D body shape and texture recovery. In: SHARP Workshop, ECCV (2020)
15. Saint, A., Shabayek, A.E.R., Aouada, D., Ottersten, B., Cherenkova, K., Gusev, G.: Towards automatic human body model fitting to a 3D scan. In: Proceedings of 3DBODY. TECH 2017–8th International Conference and Exhibition on 3D Body Scanning and Processing Technologies, Montreal QC, Canada, 11–12 October 2017, pp. 274–280. Hometrica Consulting (2017)
16. Xu, Z., Zhang, Q., Cheng, S.: Multilevel active registration for kinect human body scans: from low quality to high quality. Multimedia Syst. **24**(3), 257–270 (2018)
17. Yang, Y., Yu, Y., Zhou, Y., Du, S., Davis, J., Yang, R.: Semantic parametric reshaping of human body models. In: 2014 2nd International Conference on 3D Vision, vol. 2, pp. 41–48. IEEE (2014)
18. Zayer, R., Lévy, B., Seidel, H.P.: Linear angle based parameterization (2007)

Author Index

Printed in the United States
By Bookmasters